STEVENS' HANDBOOK OF EXPERIMENTAL PSYCHOLOGY

THIRD EDITION

Volume 4:   Methodology in Experimental Psychology

STEVENS' HANDBOOK OF EXPERIMENTAL PSYCHOLOGY

THIRD EDITION

Volume 4:   Methodology in Experimental Psychology

Editor-in-Chief

HAL PASHLER

Volume Editor

JOHN WIXTED

John Wiley & Sons, Inc.

This book is printed on acid-free paper.

This publication is designed to provide accurate and authoritative information in
regard to the subject matter covered. It is sold with the understanding that the
publisher is not engaged in rendering professional services. If legal, accounting,
medical, psychological or any other expert assistance is required, the services of a
competent professional person should be sought.

Designations used by companies to distinguish their products are often claimed as
trademarks. In all instances where John Wiley & Sons, Inc. is aware of a claim, the
product names appear in initial capital or all capital letters. Readers, however,
should contact the appropriate companies for more complete information
regarding trademarks and registration.

Library of Congress Cataloging-in-Publication Data

Stevens' handbook of experimental psychology / Hal Pashler, editor-in-chief — 3rd ed.
   p. cm.
Includes bibliographical references and index.
Contents: v. 1. Sensation and perception — v. 2. Memory and cognitive processes — v.
3. Learning, motivation, and emotion — v. 4. Methodology in experimental psychology.
ISBN 0-471-44333-6 (set) — ISBN 0-471-37777-5 (v. 1 : cloth : alk. paper) — ISBN
0-471-38030-X (v. 2 : cloth : alk. paper) — ISBN 0-471-38047-4 (v. 3 : cloth : alk. paper)
— ISBN 0-471-37888-7 (v. 4 : cloth : alk. paper) — ISBN 0-471-44333-6 (set)
   1. Psychology, Experimental. I. Pashler, Harold E.

BF181 H336 2001
150—dc21

                                          2001046809

Contributors

Kimmo Alho, PhD
University of Helsinki, Finland

Norman H. Anderson, PhD
University of California, San Diego

F. Gregory Ashby, PhD
University of California,
Santa Barbara

Rachel Barr, PhD
Rutgers University

Nathan Brody, PhD
Wesleyan University

Max Coltheart, DSc
Macquarie University, Australia

M. Robin DiMatteo, PhD
University of California, Riverside

Shawn W. Ell, MA
University of California,
Santa Barbara

George A. Gescheider, PhD
Hamilton College

Ronald K. Hambleton, PhD
University of Massachusetts

Luis Hernandez-García, PhD
University of Michigan

John Jonides, PhD
University of Michigan

Daniel S. Levine, PhD
University of Texas at Arlington

Geoffrey R. Loftus, PhD
University of Washington

Gordon D. Logan, PhD
Vanderbilt University

R. Duncan Luce, PhD
University of California, Irvine

Neil A. Macmillan, PhD
Brooklyn College, City University
of New York

Lawrence E. Marks, PhD
John B. Pierce Laboratory,
Yale University

In Jae Myung, PhD
Ohio State University

Risto Näätänen, PhD
University of Helsinki, Finland

Stephen A. Petrill, PhD
Pennsylvania State University

Mary J. Pitoniak, MA
University of Massachusetts

Mark A. Pitt, PhD
Ohio State University

Patrick Rabbitt, PhD
The Victoria University of Manchester

Robert Rosenthal, PhD
University of California, Riverside

Carolyn Rovee-Collier, PhD
Rutgers University

Erich Schröger, PhD
University Leipzig, Germany

Patrick Suppes, PhD
Stanford University

Trisha Van Zandt, PhD
Ohio State University

Tor Wager, MA
University of Michigan

Contents

Preface

The precise origins of experimental psychology can be debated, but by any count the field is more than a hundred years old. The past 10 years have been marked by tremendous progress: a honing of experimental strategies and clearer theoretical conceptualizations in many areas combined with a more vigorous cross-fertilization across neighboring fields.

Despite the undeniable progress, vigorous debate continues on many of the most fundamental questions. From the nature of learning to the psychophysical functions relating sensory stimuli to sensory experiences and from the underpinnings of emotion to the nature of attention, a good many of the questions posed in the late 19th century remain alive and in some cases highly controversial.

Although some have viewed this fact as discouraging, it should scarcely be surprising. As in the biological sciences generally, early hopes that a few simple laws and principles would explain everything that needed to be explained have gradually given way to a recognition of the vast complexity of human (and nonhuman) organisms in general, and of their mental faculties in particular. There is no contradiction between recognizing the magnitude of the progress that has been made and appreciating the gap between current understanding and the fuller understanding that we hope to achieve in the future.

Stanley Smith ("Smitty") Stevens' *Handbook of Experimental Psychology,* of which this is the third edition, has made notable contributions to the progress of the field. At the same time, from one edition to the next, the *Handbook* has changed in ways that reflect growing recognition of the complexity of its subject matter. The first edition was published in 1951 under the editorship of the great psychophysical pioneer himself. This single volume (described by some reviewers as the last successful single-volume handbook of psychology) contained a number of very influential contributions in the theory of learning, as well as important contributions to psychophysics for which Stevens was justly famous. The volume had a remarkably wide influence in the heyday of a period in which many researchers believed that principles of learning theory would provide the basic theoretical underpinning for psychology as a whole.

Published in 1988, the second edition was edited by a team comprised of Richard Atkinson, Richard J. Herrnstein, Gardner Lindzey, and Duncan Luce. The editors of the second edition adopted a narrower definition of the field, paring down material that overlapped with physics or physiology and reducing the role of applied psychology. The result was a set of two volumes, each of which was substantially smaller than the single volume in the first edition.

Discussions of a third edition of the Stevens' *Handbook* began in 1998. My fellow editors and I agreed that experimental psychology had broadened and deepened to such a point that two volumes could no longer reasonably encompass the major accomplishments that have occurred in the field since 1988. We also felt that a greatly enlarged treatment of methodology would make the *Handbook* particularly valuable to those seeking to undertake research in new areas, whether graduate students in training or researchers venturing into subfields that are new to them.

The past 10 years have seen a marked increase in efforts to link psychological phenomena to neurophysiological foundations. Rather than eschewing this approach, we have embraced it without whittling down the core content of traditional experimental psychology, which has been the primary focus of the *Handbook* since its inception.

The most notable change from the previous edition to this one is the addition of a new volume on methodology. This volume provides rigorous but comprehensible tuto-

rials on the key methodological concepts of experimental psychology, and it should serve as a useful adjunct to graduate education in psychology.

I am most grateful to Wiley for its strong support of the project from the beginning. The development of the new *Handbook* was initially guided by Kelly Franklin, now Vice President and Director of Business Development at Wiley. Jennifer Simon, Associate Publisher, took over the project for Wiley in 1999. Jennifer combined a great measure of good sense, good humor, and the firmness essential for bringing the project to a timely completion. Although the project took somewhat longer than we initially envisioned, progress has been much faster than it was in the second edition, making for an up-to-date presentation of fast-moving fields. Both Isabel Pratt at Wiley and Noriko Coburn at University of California at San Diego made essential contributions to the smooth operation of the project. Finally, I am very grateful to the four distinguished volume editors, Randy Gallistel, Doug Medin, John Wixted, and Steve Yantis, for their enormous contributions to this project.

Hal Pashler

CHAPTER 1

Representational Measurement Theory

R. DUNCAN LUCE AND PATRICK SUPPES

CONCEPT OF REPRESENTATIONAL MEASUREMENT

Representational measurement is, on the one hand, an attempt to understand the nature of empirical observations that can be usefully recoded, in some reasonably unique fashion, in terms of familiar mathematical structures. The most common of these representing structures are the ordinary real numbers ordered in the usual way and with the operations of addition, $+$, and/or multiplication, $\cdot$. Intuitively, such representations seems a possibility when dealing with variables for which people have a clear sense of "greater than." When data can be summarized numerically, our knowledge of how to calculate and to relate numbers can usefully come into play. However, as we will see, caution must be exerted not to go beyond the information actually coded numerically. In addition, more complex mathematical structures such as geometries are often used, for example, in multidimensional scaling.

On the other hand, representational measurement goes well beyond the mere construction of numerical representations to a careful examination of how such representations relate to one another in substantive scientific

theories, such as in physics, psychophysics, and utility theory. These may be thought of as applications of measurement concepts for representing various kinds of empirical relations among variables.

In the 75 or so years beginning in 1870, some psychologists (often physicists or physicians turned psychologists) attempted to import measurement ideas from physics, but gradually it became clear that doing this successfully was a good deal trickier than was initially thought. Indeed, by the 1940s a number of physicists and philosophers of physics concluded that psychologists really did not and could not have an adequate basis for measurement. They concluded, correctly, that the classical measurement models were for the most part unsuited to psychological phenomena. But they also concluded, incorrectly, that no scientifically sound psychological measurement is possible at all. In part, the theory of representational measurement was the response of some psychologists and other social scientists who were fairly well trained in the necessary physics and mathematics to understand how to modify in substantial ways the classical models of physical measurement to be better suited to psychological issues. The purpose of this chapter is to outline the high points of the 50-year effort from 1950 to the present to develop a deeper understanding of such measurement.

The authors thank János Aczél, Ehtibar Dzhafarov, Jean-Claude Falmagne, and A.A.J. Marley for helpful comments and criticisms of an earlier draft.

Empirical Structures

Performing any experiment, in particular a psychological one, is a complex activity that we never analyze or report completely. The part that we analyze systematically and report on is sometimes called *a model of the data* or, in terms that are useful in the theory of measurement, *an empirical structure.* Such an empirical structure of an experiment is a drastic reduction of the entire experimental activity. In the simplest, purely psychological cases, we represent the empirical model as a set of stimuli, a set of responses, and some relations observed to hold between the stimuli and responses. (Such an empirical restriction to stimuli and responses does not mean that the theoretical considerations are so restricted; unobservable concepts may well play a role in theory.) In many psychological measurement experiments such an empirical structure consists of a set of stimuli that vary along a single dimension, for example, a set of sounds varying only in intensity. We might then record the pairwise judgments of loudness by a binary relation on the set of stimuli, where the first member of a pair represents the subject's judgment of which of two sounds was louder.

The use of such empirical structures in psychology is widespread because they come close to the way data are organized for subsequent statistical analysis or for testing a theory or hypothesis.

An important cluster of objections to the concept of empirical structures or models of data exists. One is that the formal analysis of empirical structures includes only a small portion of the many problems of experimental design. Among these are issues such as the randomization of responses between left and right hands and symmetry conditions in the lighting of visual stimuli. For example, in most experiments that study aspects of vision, having considerably more intense light on the left side of the subject than on the right would be considered a mistake. Such considerations do not ordinarily enter into any formal description of the experiment. This is just the beginning. There are understood conditions that are assumed to hold but are not enumerated: Sudden loud noises did not interfere with the concentration of the subjects, and neither the experimenter talked to the subject nor the subject to the experimenter during the collection of the data—although exceptions to this rule can certainly be found, especially in linguistically oriented experiments.

The concept of empirical structures is just meant to isolate the part of the experimental activity and the form of the data relevant to the hypothesis or theory being tested or to the measurements being made.

Isomorphic Structures

The prehistory of mathematics, before Babylonian, Chinese, or Egyptian civilizations began, left no written record but nonetheless had as a major development the concept of number. In particular, counting of small collections of objects was present. Oral terms for some sort of counting seem to exist in every language. The next big step was the introduction, no doubt independently in several places, of a written notation for numbers. It was a feat of great abstraction to develop the general theory of the constructive operations of counting, adding, subtracting, multiplying, and dividing numbers. The first problem for a theory of measurement was to show how this arithmetic of numbers could be constructed and applied to a variety of empirical structures.

To investigate this problem, as we do in the next section, we need the general notion of isomorphism between two structures. The intuitive idea is straightforward: Two structures are isomorphic when they exhibit the same structure from the standpoint of their basic concepts. The point of the formal definition of isomorphism is to make this notion of *same structure* precise.

As an elementary example, consider a *binary relational structure* consisting of a nonempty set A and a binary relation R defined on this set. We will be considering pairs of such structures in which both may be empirical structures, both may be numerical structures, or one may be empirical and the other numerical. The definition of isomorphism is unaffected by which combination is being considered.

The way we make the concept of having the same structure precise is to require the existence of a function mapping the one structure onto the other that preserves the binary relation. Formally, a binary relation structure (A, R) is *isomorphic* to a binary relation structure (A', R') if and only if there is a function f such that

 (i) the domain of f is A and the codomain of f is A', i.e., A' is the image of A under f,
 (ii) f is a one-one function,[1] and
 (iii) for a and b in A, aRb iff[2] $f(a)R'f(b)$.

To illustrate this definition of isomorphism, consider the question: Are any two finite binary relation structures with the same number of elements isomorphic? Intuitively, it seems clear that the answer should be negative, because in one of the structures all the objects could stand in the relation R to each other and not so in the other. This is indeed the case and shows at once, as intended, that isomorphism depends not just on a one-one function from one set to another, but also on the structure as represented in the binary relation.

---

[1] In recent years, conditions (i) and (ii) together have come to be called *bijective*.
[2] This is a standard abbreviation for "if and only if."

Ordered Relational Structures

Weak Order

An idea basic to measurement is that the objects being measured exhibit a qualitative attribute for which it makes sense to ask the question: Which of two objects exhibits more of the attribute, or do they exhibit it to the same degree? For example, the attribute of having greater mass is reflected by placing the two objects on the pans of an equal-arm pan balance and observing which deflects downward. The attribute of loudness is reflected by which of two sounds a subject deems as louder or equally loud. Thus, the focus of measurement is not just on the numerical representation of any relational structures, but of ordered ones, that is, ones for which one of the relations is a *weak order,* denoted $\gtrsim$, which has two defining properties for all elements a, b, c in the domain A:

 (i) *Transitive:* if $a \gtrsim b$ and $b \gtrsim c$, then $a \gtrsim c$.
 (ii) *Connected:* either $a \gtrsim b$ or $b \gtrsim a$ or both.

The intuitive idea is that $\gtrsim$ captures the ordering of the attribute that we are attempting to measure.

Two distinct relations can be defined in terms of $\gtrsim$:

$$a \succ b \text{ iff } a \gtrsim b \text{ and not } (b \gtrsim a);$$
$$a \sim b \text{ iff both } a \gtrsim b \text{ and } b \gtrsim a.$$

It is an easy exercise to show that $\succ$ is transitive and irreflexive (i.e., $a \succ a$ cannot hold), and that $\sim$ is an equivalence relation (i.e., transitive, symmetric in the sense that $a \sim b$ iff $b \sim a$, and reflexive in the sense that $a \sim a$). The latter means that $\sim$ partitions A into equivalence classes.

Homomorphism

For most measurement situations one really is working with weak orders—after all, two entities having the same weight are not in general identical. But often it is mathematically easier to work with isomorphisms to the ordered real numbers, in which case one must deal with the following concept of simple orders. We do this by inducing the preference order over the equivalence classes defined by $\sim$. When $\sim$ is $=$, each element is an equivalence class, and the weak order $\succeq$ is called a *simple order*. The mapping from the weakly ordered structure via the isomorphisms of the (mutually disjoint) equivalences classes to the ordered real numbers is called a *homomorphism*. Unlike an isomorphism, which is one to one, an homomorphism is many to one. In some cases, such as additive conjoint measurement, discussed later, it is somewhat difficult, although possible, to formulate the theory using the equivalence classes.

Two Fundamental Problems of Representational Measurement

Existence

The most fundamental problem for a theory of representational measurement is to construct the following representation: Given an empirical structure satisfying certain properties, to which numerical structures, if any, is it isomorphic? These numerical structures, thus, represent the empirical one. It is the existence of such isomorphisms that constitutes the representational claim that measurement of a fundamental kind has taken place.

Quantification or measurement, in the sense just characterized, is important in some way in all empirical sciences. The primary significance of this fact is that given the isomorphism of structures, we may pass from the particular empirical structure to the numerical one and then use all our familiar computational methods, as applied to the isomorphic arithmetical structure, to infer facts about the isomorphic empirical structure. Such passage from simple qualitative observations to quantitative ones—the isomorphism of structures

passing from the empirical to the numerical—is necessary for precise prediction or control of phenomena. Of course, such a representation is useful only to the extent of the precision of the observations on which it is based. A variety of numerical representations for various empirical psychological phenomena is given in the sections that follow.

Uniqueness

The second fundamental problem of representational measurement is to discover the uniqueness of the representations. Solving the representation problem for a theory of measurement is not enough. There is usually a formal difference between the kind of assignment of numbers arising from different procedures of measurement, as may be seen in three intuitive examples:

1. The population of California is greater than that of New York.
2. Mary is 10 years older than John.
3. The temperature in New York City this afternoon will be 92 °F.

Here we may easily distinguish three kinds of measurements. The first is an example of counting, which is an absolute scale. The number of members of a given collection that is counted is determined uniquely in the ideal case, although that can be difficult in practice (witness the 2000 presidential election in Florida). In contrast, the second example, the measurement of difference in age, is a ratio scale. Empirical procedures for measuring age do not determine the unit of age—chosen in the example to be the year rather than, for example, the month or the week. Although the choice of the unit of a person's age is arbitrary—that is, not empirically prescribed—that of the zero, birth, is not. Thus, the ratio of the ages of any two people is independent of its choice, and the age of people is an example of a ratio scale. The measurement of distance is another example of such a ratio scale. The third example, that of temperature, is an example of an interval scale. The empirical procedure of measuring temperature by use of a standard thermometer or other device determines neither a unit nor an origin.

We may thus also describe the second fundamental problem for representational measurement as that of determining the scale type of the measurements resulting from a given procedure.

A BRIEF HISTORY OF MEASUREMENT

Pre-19th-Century Measurement

Already by the fifth century B.C., if not before, Greek geometers were investigating problems central to the nature of measurement. The Greek achievements in mathematics are all of relevance to measurement. First, the theory of number, meaning for them the theory of the positive integers, was closely connected with counting; second, the geometric theory of proportion was central to magnitudes that we now represent by rational numbers (= ratios of integers); and, finally, the theory of incommensurable geometric magnitudes for those magnitudes that could not be represented by ratios. The famous proof of the irrationality of the square root of two seems arithmetic in spirit to us, but almost certainly the Greek discovery of incommensurability was geometric in character, namely, that the length of the diagonal of a square, or the hypotenuse of an isosceles right-angled triangle, was not commensurable with the sides. The Greeks well understood that the various kinds of results just described applied in general to magnitudes and not in any sense only to numbers or even only to the length of line segments. The spirit of this may be seen in the first definition of *Book 10* of Euclid, the one dealing

with incommensurables: "Those magnitudes are said to be commensurable which are measured by the same measure, and those incommensurable which cannot have any common measure" (trans. 1956, p. 10).

It does not take much investigation to determine that theories and practices relevant to measurement occur throughout the centuries in many different contexts. It is impossible to give details here, but we mention a few salient examples. The first is the discussion of the measurement of pleasure and pain in Plato's dialogue *Protagoras*. The second is the set of partial qualitative axioms, characterizing in our terms empirical structures, given by Archimedes for measuring on unequal balances (Suppes, 1980). Here the two qualitative concepts are the distance from the focal point of the balance and the weights of the objects placed in the two pans of the balance. This is perhaps the first partial qualitative axiomatization of conjoint measurement, which is discussed in more detail later. The third example is the large medieval literature giving a variety of qualitative axioms for the measurement of weight (Moody and Claggett, 1952). (Psychologists concerned about the difficulty of clarifying the measurement of fundamental psychological quantities should be encouraged by reading O'Brien's 1981 detailed exposition of the confused theories of weight in the ancient world.) The fourth example is the detailed discussion of intensive quantities by Nicole Oresme in the 14th century A.D. The fifth is Galileo's successful geometrization in the 17th century of the motion of heavenly bodies, done in the context of stating essentially qualitative axioms for what, in the earlier tradition, would be called the quantity of motion. The final example is also perhaps the last great, magnificent, original treatise of natural science written wholly in the geometrical tradition—Newton's *Principia* of 1687. Even in his famous three laws of motion, concepts were formulated in a qualitative, geometrical way, characteristic of the later formulation of qualitative axioms of measurement.

19th- and Early 20th-Century Physical Measurement

The most important early 19th-century work on measurement was the abstract theory of extensive quantities published in 1844 by H. Grassmann, *Die Wissenschaft der Extensiven Grösse oder die Ausdehnungslehre*. This abstract and forbidding treatise, not properly appreciated by mathematicians at the time of its appearance, contained at this early date the important generalization of the concept of geometric extensive quantities to n-dimensional vector spaces and, thus, to the addition, for example, of n-dimensional vectors. Grassmann also developed for the first time a theory of barycentric coordinates in n dimensions. It is now recognized that this was the first general and abstract theory of extensive quantities to be treated in a comprehensive manner.

Extensive Measurement

Despite the precedent of the massive work of Grassmann, it is fair to say that the modern theory of one-dimensional, extensive measurement originated much later in the century with the fundamental work of Helmholtz (1887) and Hölder (1901). The two fundamental concepts of these first modern attempts, and later ones as well, is a binary operation ∘ of combination and an ordering relation ≿, each of which has different interpretations in different empirical structures. For example, mass ordering ≿ is determined by an equal-arm pan balance (in a vacuum) with $a \circ b$ denoting objects a and b both placed on one pan. Lengths of rods are ordered by placing them side-by-side, adjusting one end to agree, and determining which rod extends beyond the other at the opposite end, and ∘ means abutting two rods along a straight line.

The ways in which the basic axioms can be stated to describe the intertwining of these two concepts has a long history of later development. In every case, however, the fundamental isomorphism condition is the following: For a, b in the empirical domain,

$$f(a) \geq f(b) \Leftrightarrow a \succsim b, \tag{1}$$

$$f(a \circ b) = f(a) + f(b), \tag{2}$$

where f is the mapping function from the empirical structure to the numerical structure of the additive, positive real numbers, that is, for all entities a, $f(a) > 0$.

Certain necessary empirical (testable) properties must be satisfied for such a representation to hold. Among them are for all entities a, b, and c,

Commutativity: $a \circ b \sim b \circ a$.
Associativity: $(a \circ b) \circ c \sim a \circ (b \circ c)$.
Monotonicity: $a \succsim b \Leftrightarrow a \circ c \succsim b \circ c$.
Positivity: $a \circ a \succ a$.

Let a be any element. Define a *standard sequence based on a* to be a sequence $a(n)$, where n is an integer, such that $a(1) = a$, and for $i > 1$, $a(i) \sim a(i-1) \circ a$. An example of such a standard sequence is the centimeter marks on a meter ruler. The idea is that the elements of a standard sequence are equally spaced. The following (not directly testable) condition ensures that the stimuli are commensurable:

Archimedean: For any entities a, b,
 there is an integer n such that $a(n) \succ b$.

These, together with the following structural condition that ensures very small elements,

Solvability: if $a \succ b$,
 then for some c, $a \succ b \circ c$,

were shown to imply the existence of the representation given by Equations (1) and (2). By formulating the Archimedean axiom differently, Roberts and Luce (1968) showed that the solvability axiom could be eliminated.

Such empirical structures are called *extensive*. The uniqueness of their representations is discussed shortly.

Probability and Partial Operations

It is well known that probability P is an additive measure in the sense that it maps events into [0, 1] such that, for events A and B that are disjoint,

$$P(A \cup B) = P(A) + P(B).$$

Thus, probability is close to extensive measurement—but not quite, because the operation is limited to only disjoint events. However, the theory of extensive measurement can be generalized to partial operations having the property that if a and b are such that $a \circ b$ is defined and if $a \gtrsim c$ and $b \gtrsim d$, then $c \circ d$ is also defined. With some adaptation, this can be applied to probability; the details can be found in Chapter 3 of Krantz, Luce, Suppes, and Tversky (1971). (This reference is subsequently cited as FM I for Volume I of *Foundations of Measurement*. The other volumes are Suppes, Krantz, Luce, & Tversky, 1990, cited as FM II, and Luce, Krantz, Suppes, & Tversky, 1990, cited as FM III.)

Finite Partial Extensive Structures

Continuing with the theme of partial operation, we describe a recent treatment of a finite extensive structure that also has ratio scale representation and that is fully in the spirit of the earlier work involving continuous models. Suppose X is a finite set of physical objects, any two of which balance on an equal-arm balance; that is, if $a_1, \ldots, a_n$ are the objects, for any i and j, $i \neq j$, then $a_i \sim a_j$. Thus, they weigh the same. Moreover, if A and B are two sets of these objects, then on the balance we have $A \sim B$ if and only if A and B have the same number of objects. We also have a concatenation operation, union of disjoint sets. If $A \cap B = \emptyset$, then $A \cup B \sim C$ if and only if the objects in C balance the objects in A

together with the objects in B. The qualitative strict ordering $A \succ B$ has an obvious operational meaning, which is that the objects in A, taken together, weigh more on the balance than the objects in B, taken together.

This simple setup is adequate to establish, by fundamental measurement, a scheme for numerically weighing other objects not in X. First, our homomorphism f on X is really simple. Since for all a_i and a_j and X, $a_i \sim a_j$, we have

$$f(a_i) = f(a_j),$$

with the restriction that $f(a_i) > 0$. We extend f to A, a subset of X, by setting $f(A) = |A| =$ the cardinality of (number of objects in) A. The extensive structure is thus transparent: For A and B subsets of X, if $A \cap B = \emptyset$ then

$$f(A \cup B) = |A \cup B| = |A| + |B|$$
$$= f(A) + f(B).$$

If we multiply f by any $\alpha > 0$ the equation still holds, as does the ordering. Moreover, in simple finite cases of extensive measurement such as the present, it is easy to prove directly that no transformations other than ratio transformations are possible. Let f^* denote another representation. For some object a, set $\alpha = f(a)/f^*(a)$. Observe that if $|A| = n$, then by a finite induction

$$\frac{f(A)}{f^*(A)} = \frac{nf(a)}{nf^*(a)} = \alpha,$$

so the representation forms a ratio scale.

Finite Probability

The "objects" $a_1, \ldots, a_n$ are now interpreted as possible outcomes of a probabilistic measurement experiment, so the a_is are the possible atomic events whose qualitative probability is to be judged.

The ordering $A \gtrsim B$ is interpreted as meaning that event A is at least as probable as event B; $A \sim B$ as A and B are equally probable; $A \succ B$ as A is strictly more probable than B.

Then we would like to interpret $f(A)$ as the numerical probability of event A, but if f is unique up to only a ratio scale, this will not work since $f(A)$ could be 50.1, not exactly a probability.

By adding another concept, that of the probabilistic independence of two events, we can strengthen the uniqueness result to that of an absolute scale. This is written $A \perp B$. Given a probability measure, the definition of independence is familiar: $A \perp B$ if and only if $P(A \cap B) = P(A)P(B)$. Independence cannot be defined in terms of the qualitative concepts introduced for arbitrary finite qualitative probability structures, but can be defined by extending the structure to elementary random variables (Suppes and Alechina, 1994). However, a definition can be given for the special case in which all atoms are equiprobable; it again uses the cardinality of the sets: $A \perp B$ if and only if $|X| \cdot |A \cap B| = |A| \cdot |B|$. It immediately follows from this definition that $X \perp X$, whence in the interpretation of $\perp$ we must have

$$P(X) = P(X \cap X) = P(X)P(X),$$

but this equation is satisfied only if $P(X) = 0$, which is impossible since $P(\emptyset) = 0$ and $X \succ \emptyset$, or $P(X) = 1$, which means that the scale type is an absolute—not a ratio—scale, as it should be for probability.

Units and Dimensions

An important aspect of 19th century physics was the development, starting with Fourier's work (1822/1955), of an explicit theory of units and dimensions. This is so commonplace now in physics that it is hard to believe that it only really began at such a late date. In Fourier's famous work, devoted to the theory of heat, he announced that in order to measure physical quantities and express them numerically, five different kinds of units of measurement were needed, namely, those of length, time, mass, temperature, and heat.

Of even greater importance is the specific table he gave, for perhaps the first time in history of physics, of the dimensions of various physical quantities. A modern version of such a table appears at the end of FM I.

The importance of this tradition of units and dimensions in the 19th century is to be seen in Maxwell's famous treatise on electricity and magnetism (1873). As a preliminary, he began with 26 numbered paragraphs on the measurement of quantities because of the importance he attached to problems of measurement in electricity and magnetism, a topic that was virtually unknown before the 19th century. Maxwell emphasized the fundamental character of the three fundamental units of length, time, and mass. He then went on to derive units, and by this he meant quantities whose dimensions may be expressed in terms of fundamental units (e.g., kinetic energy, whose dimension in the usual notation is ML^2T^{-2}). Dimensional analysis, first put in systematic form by Fourier, is very useful in analyzing the consistency of the use of quantities in equations and can also be used for wider purposes, which are discussed in some detail in FM I.

Derived Measurement

In the Fourier and Maxwell analyses, the question of how a derived quantity is actually to be measured does not enter into the discussion. What is important is its dimensions in terms of fundamental units. Early in the 20th century the physicist Norman Campbell (1920/1957) used the distinction between fundamental and derived measurement in a sense more intrinsic to the theory of measurement itself. The distinction is the following: Fundamental measurement starts with qualitative statements (axioms) about empirical structures, such as those given earlier for an extensive structure, and then proves the existence of a representational theorem in terms of numbers, whence the phrase "representational measurement."

In contrast, a derived quantity is measured in terms of other fundamental measurements. A classical example is density, measured as the ratio of separate measurements of mass and volume. It is to be emphasized, of course, that calling density a derived measure with respect to mass and volume does not make a fundamental scientific claim. For example, it does not allege that fundamental measurement of density is impossible. Nevertheless, in understanding the foundations of measurement, it is always important to distinguish whether fundamental or derived measurement, in Campbell's sense, is being analyzed or used.

Axiomatic Geometry

From the standpoint of representational measurement theory, another development of great importance in the 19th century was the perfection of the axiomatic method in geometry, which grew out of the intense scrutiny of the foundations of geometry at the beginning of that century. The driving force behind this effort was undoubtedly the discovery and development of non-Euclidean geometries at the beginning of the century by Bolyai, Lobachevski, and Gauss. An important and intuitive example, later in the century, was Pasch's (1882) discovery of the axiom named in his honor. He found a gap in Euclid that required a new axiom, namely, the assertion that if a line intersects one side of a triangle, it must intersect also a second side. More generally, it was the high level of rigor and abstraction of Pasch's 1882 book that was the most important step leading to the modern formal axiomatic conception of geometry, which has been so much a model for representational measurement theory in the 20th century. The most influential work in this line of development was Hilbert's *Grundlagen der Geometrie,* first edition in 1899, much of its prominence resulting from Hilbert's position as one of the outstanding mathematicians of this period.

It should be added that even in one-dimensional geometry numerical representations arise even though there is no order relation. Indeed, for dimensions ≥ 2, no standard geometry has a weak order. Moreover, in geometry the continuum is not important for the fundamental Galilean and Lorentz groups. An underlying denumerable field of algebraic numbers is quite adequate.

Invariance

Another important development at the end of the 19th century was the creation of the explicit theory of invariance for spatial properties. The intuitive idea is that the spatial properties in analytical representations are invariant under the transformations that carry one model of the axioms into another model of the axioms. Thus, for example, the ordinary Cartesian representation of Euclidean geometry is such that the geometrical properties of the Euclidean space are invariant under the Euclidean group of transformations of the Cartesian representation. These are the transformations that are composed from translations (in any direction), rotations, and reflections. These ideas were made particularly prominent by the mathematician Felix Klein in his Erlangen address of 1872 (see Klein, 1893). These important concepts of invariance had a major impact in the development of the theory of special relativity by Einstein at the beginning of the 20th century. Here the invariance is that under the Lorentz transformations, which are those that leave invariant geometrical and kinematic properties of the spacetime of special relativity. Without giving the full details of the Lorentz transformations, it is still possible to give a clear physical sense of the change from classical Newtonian physics to that of special relativity.

In the case of classical Newtonian mechanics, the invariance that characterizes the Galilean transformations is just the invariance of the distance between any two simultaneous points together with the invariance of any temporal interval, under any permissible change of coordinates. Note that this characterization requires that the units of measurement for both spatial distance and time be held constant. In the case of special relativity, the single invariant is what is called the *proper time* τ_{12} between two space-time points (x_1, y_1, z_1, t_1) and (x_2, y_2, z_2, t_2), which is defined as

$$\tau_{12} = \sqrt{(t_1 - t_2)^2 - \frac{1}{c^2}\left[(x_1 - x_2)^2 + (y_1 - y_2)^2 + (z_1 - z_2)^2\right]},$$

where c is the velocity of light in the given units of measurement. It is easy to see the conceptual nature of the change. In the case of classical mechanics, the invariance of spatial distance between simultaneous points is separate from the invariance of temporal intervals. In the case of special relativity, they are intertwined. Thus, we properly speak of space-time invariance in the case of special relativity. As will be seen in what follows, the concepts of invariance developed so thoroughly in the 19th and early 20th century in geometry and physics have carried over and are an important part of the representational theory of measurement.

Quantum Theory and the Problem of Measurement

Still another important development in the first half of the 20th century, of special relevance to the topic of this chapter, was the creation of quantum mechanics and, in particular, the extended analysis of the problem of measurement in that theory. In contrast with the long tradition of measurement in classical physics, at least three new problems arose that generated what in the literature is termed the *problem of measurement* in quantum mechanics. The first difficulty arises in measuring microscopic objects, that is, objects as small as atoms or electrons or other particles of a similar nature. The very attempt to measure a property of these particles creates a disturbance in the state of the particle, a disturbance that is not small relative to the particle itself. Classical physics assumed that, in principle, such minor disturbances of a measured object as did occur could either be eliminated or taken into account in a relatively simple way.

The second aspect is the precise limitation on such measurement, which was formulated by Heisenberg's uncertainty principle. For example, it is not possible to measure both position and momentum exactly. Indeed, it is not possible, in general, to have a joint probability distribution of the measurements of the two. This applies not just to position and momentum, but also to other pairs of properties of a particle. The best that can be hoped for is the Heisenberg uncertainty relation. It expresses an inequality that bounds away from zero the product of the variances of the two properties measured, for example, the product of the variance of the measurement of position and the variance of the measurement of velocity or momentum. This inequality appeared really for the first time in quantum mechanics and is one of the principles that separates quantum mechanics drastically from classical physics. An accessible and clear exposition of these ideas is Heisenberg (1930), a work that few others have excelled for the quality of its exposition.

The third aspect of measurement in quantum mechanics is the disparity between the object being measured and the relatively large, macroscopic object used for the measurement. Here, a long and elaborate story can be told, as it is, for example, in von Neumann's classical book on the foundations of quantum mechanics, which includes a detailed treatment of the measurement problem (von Neumann, 1932/1955). The critical aspect of this problem is deciding when a measurement has taken place. Von Neumann was inclined to the view that a measurement had taken place only when a relevant event had occurred in the consciousness of some observer. More moderate subsequent views are satisfied with the position that an observation takes place when a suitable recording has been made by a calibrated instrument.

Although we shall not discuss further the problem of measurement in quantum mechanics, nor even the application of the ideas to measurement in psychology, it is apparent that there is some resonance between the difficulties mentioned and the difficulties of measuring many psychological properties.

19th- and Early 20th-Century Psychology

Fechner's Psychophysics

Psychology was not a separate discipline until the late 19th century. Its roots were largely in philosophy with significant additions by medical and physical scientists. The latter brought a background of successful physical measurement, which they sought to re-create in sensory psychology at the least. The most prominent of these were H. Helmholtz, whose work among other things set the stage for extensive measurement, and G. T. Fechner, whose *Elemente der Psychophysik* (*Elements of Psychophysics*; 1860/1966) set the stage for subsequent developments in psychological measurement. We outline the problem faced in trying to transplant physical measurement and the nature of the proposed solution.

Recall that the main measurement device used in 19th-century physics was concatenation: Given two entities that exhibit the attribute to be measured, it was essential to find a method of concatenating them to form a third entity also exhibiting the attribute. Then one showed empirically that the structure satisfies the axioms of extensive measurement, as discussed earlier. When no empirical concatenation operation can be found, as for example with density, one could not do fundamental measurement. Rather, one sought an invariant property stated in terms of fundamentally

measured quantities called derived measurement. Density is an example.

When dealing with sensory intensity, physical concatenation is available but just recovers the physical measure, which does not at all well correspond with subjective judgments such as the half loudness of a tone. A new approach was required. Fechner continued to accept the idea of building up a measurement scale by adding small increments, as in the standard sequences of extensive measurement, and then counting the number of such increments needed to fill a sensory interval. The question was: What are the small equal increments to be added? His idea was that they correspond to "just noticeable differences" (JND); when one first encounters the idea of a JND it seems to suggest a fixed threshold, but it gradually was interpreted to be defined statistically. To be specific, suppose x_0 and $x_1 = x_0 + \xi(x_0, \lambda)$ are stimulus intensities such that the probability of identifying x_1 as larger than x_0 is a constant λ, that is, $\Pr(x_0, x_1) = \lambda$. His idea was to fix λ and to measure the distance from x to y, $x < y$, in terms of the number of successive JNDs between them. Defining $x_0 = x$ and assuming that x_i has been defined, then define x_{i+1} as

$$x_{i+1} = x_i + \xi(x_i, \lambda).$$

The sequence ends with $x_n \leq y < x_{n+1}$. Fechner postulated the number of JNDs from x to y as his definition of distance without, however, establishing any empirical properties of justify that definition. Put another way, he treated without proof that a sequence of JNDs forms a standard sequence.

His next step was to draw on an empirical result of E. H. Weber to the effect that

$$\xi(x, \lambda) = \delta(\lambda)x, \quad \delta(\lambda) > 0,$$

which is called *Weber's law*. This is sometimes approximately true (e.g., for loudness of white noise well above absolute threshold), but more often it is not (e.g., for pure tones).

His final step was to introduce, much as in extensive measurement, a limiting process as λ approaches $\frac{1}{2}$ and δ approaches 0. He called this an auxiliary mathematical principle, which amounts to supposing without proof that a limit below exists. If we denote by ψ the counting function, then his assumption that, for fixed λ, the JNDs are equally distant can be interpreted to mean that for some function η of λ

$$\eta(\lambda) = \psi[x + \xi(x, \lambda)] - \psi(x)$$
$$= \psi([\delta(\lambda) + 1]x) - \psi(x).$$

Therefore, dividing by $\delta(\lambda)x$

$$\frac{\psi([\delta(\lambda) + 1]x) - \psi(x)}{\delta(\lambda)x} = \frac{\eta(\lambda)}{\delta(\lambda)x} = \frac{\alpha(\lambda)}{x},$$

$$\text{where } \alpha(\lambda) = \frac{\eta(\lambda)}{\delta(\lambda)}.$$

Assuming that the limit of $\alpha(\lambda)$ exists, one has the simple ordinary differential equation

$$\frac{d\psi(x)}{dx} = \frac{k}{x}, \quad k = \lim_{\lambda \to \frac{1}{2}} \alpha(\lambda),$$

whose solution is well known to be

$$\psi(x) = r \ln x + s, \quad r > 0.$$

This conclusion, known as *Fechner's law,* was soon questioned by J. A. F. Plateau (1872), among others, although the emprical evidence was not conclusive. Later, Wiener (1915, 1921) was highly critical, and much later Luce and Edwards (1958) pointed out that, in fact, Fechner's mathematical auxiliary principle, although leading to the correct solution of the functional equation $\eta(\lambda) = \psi[x + \xi(x, \lambda)] - \psi(x)$ when Weber's law holds, fails to discover the correct solution in any other case—which empirically really is the norm. The mathematics is simply more subtle than he assumed.

In any event, note that Fechner's approach is not an example of representational measurement, because no empirical justification was provided for the definition of standard sequence used.

Reinterpreting Fechner Geometrically

Because Fechner's JND approach using infinitesimals seemed to be flawed, little was done for nearly half a century to construct psychophysical functions based on JNDs— that is, until Dzhafarov and Colonius (1999, 2001) reexamined what Fechner might have meant. They did this from a viewpoint of distances in a possible representation called a Finsler geometry, of which ordinary Riemannian geometry is a special case. Thus, their theory concerns stimuli of any finite dimension, not just one. The stimuli are vectors, for which we use bold-faced notation. The key idea, in our notation, is that for each person there is a universal function Φ such that, for λ sufficiently close to $\frac{1}{2}$, $\Phi(\psi[\mathbf{x} + \xi(\mathbf{x}, \lambda)] - \psi(\mathbf{x}))$ is comeasurable[3] with $\mathbf{x}$. This assumption means that this transformed differential can be integrated along any sufficiently smooth path between any two points. The minimum path length is defined to be the Fechnerian distance between them. This theory, which is mathematically quite elaborate, is testable in principle. But doing so certainly will not be easy because its assumptions, which are about the behavior of infinitesimals, are inherently difficult to check with fallible data. It remains to be seen how far this can be taken.

Ability and Achievement Testing

The vast majority of what is commonly called "psychological measurement" consists of various elaborations of ability and achievement testing that are usually grouped under the label "psychometrics." We do not cover any of this material because it definitely is neither a branch of nor a precursor to the representational measurement of an attribute. To be sure, a form of counting is employed, namely, the

---

[3]For the precise definition, see the reference.

items on a test that are correctly answered, and this number is statistically normed over a particular age or other feature so that the count is transformed into a normal distribution. Again, no axioms were or are provided. Of the psychometric approaches, we speak only of a portion of Thurstone's work that is closely related to sensory measurement. Recently, Doignon and Falmagne (1999) have developed an approach to ability measurement, called knowledge spaces, that is influenced by representational measurement considerations.

Thurstone's Discriminal Dispersions

In a series of three 1927 papers, L. L. Thurstone began a reinterpretation of Fechner's approach in terms of the then newly developed statistical concept of a random variable (see also Thurstone, 1959). In particular, he assumed that there was an underlying psychological continuum on which signal presentations are represented, but with variability. Thus, he interpreted the representation of stimulus x as a random variable $\Psi(x)$ with some distribution that he cautiously assumed (see Thurstone, 1927b, p. 373) to be normal with mean ψ_x and standard deviation (which he called a "discriminal dispersion") σ_x and possibly covariances with other stimulus representations. Later work gave reasons to consider extreme value distributions rather than the normal. His basic model for the probability of stimulus y being judged larger than x was

$$P(x, y) = \Pr[\Psi(y) - \Psi(x) > 0], \quad x \leq y. \tag{3}$$

The relation to Fechner's ideas is really quite close in that the mean subjective differences are equal for fixed $\lambda = P(x, y)$.

Given that the representations are assumed to be normal, the difference is also normal with mean $\psi_y - \psi_x$ and standard deviation

$$\sigma_{x,y} = \left(\sigma_x^2 + \sigma_y^2 - 2\rho_{x,y}\sigma_x\sigma_y\right)^{1/2}$$

so if $z_{x,y}$ is the normal deviate corresponding to $P(x, y)$, Equation (3) can be expressed as

$$\psi_y - \psi_x = z_{x,y}\sigma_{x,y}.$$

Thurstone dubbed this "a law of comparative judgment." Many papers before circa 1975 considered various modifications of the assumptions or focused on solving this equation for various special cases. We do not go into this here in part because the power of modern computers reduces the need for specialization.

Thurstone's approach had a natural one-dimensional generalization to the absolute identification of one of $n > 2$ possible stimuli. The theory assumes that each stimulus has a distribution on the sensory continuum and that the subject establishes $n - 1$ cut points to define the intervals of the range of the random variable that are identified with the stimuli. The basic data are conditional probabilities $P(x_j | x_i, n)$ of responding x_j when x_i, i, $j = 1, 2, \ldots, n$, is presented. Perhaps the most striking feature of such data is the following: Suppose a series of signals are selected such that adjacent pairs are equally detectable. Using a sequence of n adjacent ones, absolute identification data are processed through a Thurstone model in which $\psi_{x,n}$ and $\sigma_{x,n}$ are both estimated. Accepting that $\psi_{x,n}$ are independent of n, then the $\sigma_{x,n}$ definitely are not independent of n. In fact, once n reaches about 7, the value is independent of size, but $\sigma_{x,7} \approx 3\sigma_{x,2}$. This is a challenging finding and certainly casts doubt on any simple invariant meaning of the random variable $\Psi(x)$—apparently its distribution depends not only on x but on what might have been presented as well. Various authors have proposed alternative solutions (for a summary, see Iverson & Luce, 1998).

A sophisticated treatment of Fechner, Thurstone, and the subsequent literature is provided by Falmagne (1985).

Theory of Signal Detectability

Perhaps the most important generalization of Thurstone's idea is that of the theory of signal detectability, in which the basic change is to assume that the experimental subject can establish a response criterion β, in general different from 0, so that

$$P(x, y) = \Pr[\Psi(y) - \Psi(x) > \beta], \quad x \leq y.$$

Engineers first developed this model. It was adoped and elaborated in various psychological sources, including Green and Swets (1974) and Macmillan and Creelman (1991), and it has been widely applied throughout psychology.

Mid-20th-Century Psychological Measurement

Campbell's Objection to Psychological Measurement

N. R. Campbell, a physicist turned philosopher of physics who was especially concerned with physical measurement, took the very strong position that psychologists, in particular, and social scientists, in general, had not come up with anything deserving the name of measurement and probably never could. He was supported by a number of other British physicists. His argument, though somewhat elaborate, actually boiled down to asserting the truth of three simple propositions:

(i) A prerequisite of measurement is some form of empirical quantification that can be accepted or rejected experimentally.

(ii) The only known form of such quantification arises from binary operations of concatenation that can be shown empirically to satisfy the axioms of extensive measurement.

(iii) And psychology has no such extensive operations of its own.

Some appropriate references are Campbell (1920/1957, 1928) and Ferguson et al. (1940).

Stevens's Response

In a prolonged debate conducted before a subcommittee of the British Association for the Advancement of Sciences, the physicists agreed on these propositions and the psychologists did not, at least not fully. They accepted (iii) but in some measure denied (i) and (ii), although, of course, they admitted that both held for physics. The psychophysicist S. S. Stevens became the primary spokesperson for the psychological community. He first formulated his views in 1946, but his 1951 chapter in the first version of the *Handbook of Experimental Psychology,* of which he was editor, made his views widely known to the psychological community. They were complex, and at the moment we focus only on the part relevant to the issue of whether measurement can be justified outside physics.

Stevens' contention was that Proposition (i) is too narrow a concept of measurement, so (ii) and therefore (iii) are irrelevant. Rather, he argued for the claim that "Measurement is the assignment of numbers to objects or events according to rule. . . . The rule of assignment can be any consistent rule" (Stevens, 1975, pp. 46–47). The issue was whether the rule was sufficient to lead to one of several *scale types* that he dubbed nominal, ordinal, interval, ratio, and absolute. These are sufficiently well known to psychologists that we need not describe them in much detail. They concern the uniqueness of numerical representations. In the *nominal* case, of which the assignment of numbers to football players was his example, any permutation is permitted. This is not generally treated as measurement because no ordering by an attribute is involved. An *ordinal* scale is an assignment that can be subjected to any strictly increasing transformation, which of course preserves the order and nothing else. It is a representation with infinite degrees of freedom. An *interval* scale is one in which there is an arbitrary zero and unit; but once picked, no degrees of freedom are left. Therefore, the admissible transformation is $\psi \longmapsto r\psi + s, (r > 0)$. As stated, such a representation has to be on all of the real numbers. If, as is often the case, especially in physics, one wants to place the representation on the positive real numbers, then the transformation becomes $\psi_+ \longmapsto s'\psi_+^r, (r > 0, s' > 0)$. Stevens (1959, pp. 31–34) called a representation unique up to power transformations a *log-interval* scale but did not seem to recognize that it is merely a different way of writing an interval scale representation ψ in which $\psi = \ln \psi_+$ and $s = \ln s'$. Whichever one uses, it has two degrees of freedom. The *ratio* case is the interval one with $r = 1$. Again, this has two forms depending on the range of ψ. For the case of a representation on the reals, the admissible transformations are the translations $\psi \longmapsto \psi + s$. There is a different version of ratio measurement that is inherently on the reals in the sense that it cannot be placed on the positive reals. In this case, 0 is a true zero that divides the representation into inherently positive and negative portions, and the admissible transformations are $\psi \longmapsto r\psi, r > 0$.

Stevens took the stance that what was important in measurement was its uniqueness properties and that they *could* come about in ways different from that of physics. The remaining part of his career, which is summarized in Stevens (1975), entailed the development of new methods of measurement that can all be encompassed as a form of sensory matching. The basic instruction to subjects was to require the match of a stimulus in one modality to that in another so that the subjective ratio between a pair of stimuli in the one dimension is maintained in the subjective ratio of the matched signals. This is called *cross-modal matching*. When one of the modalities is the real numbers, it is

one of two forms of magnitude matching—*magnitude estimation* when numbers are to be matched to a sensory stimuli and *magnitude production* when numbers are the stimuli to be matched by some physical stimuli. Using geometric means over subjects, he found the data to be quite orderly—power functions of the usual physical measures of intensity. Much of this work is covered in Stevens (1975).

His argument that this constituted a form of ratio scale measurement can be viewed in two distinct ways. The least charitable is that of Michell (1999), who treats it as little more than a play on the word "ratio" in the scale type and in the instructions to the subjects. He feels that Stevens failed to understand the need for empirical conditions to justify numerical representations. Narens (1996) took the view that Stevens' idea is worth trying to formalize and in the process making it empirically testable. Work along these lines continues, as discussed later.

REPRESENTATIONAL APPROACH AFTER 1950

Aside from extensive measurement, the representational theory of measurement is largely a creation by behavioral scientists and mathematicians during the second half of the 20th century. The basic thrust of this school of thought can be summarized as accepting Campbell's conditions (i), quantification based on empirical properties, and (iii), the social sciences do not have concatenation operations (although even that was never strictly correct, as is shown later, because of probability based on a partial operation), and rejecting the claim (ii) that the only form of quantification is an empirical concatenation operation. This school disagreed with Stevens' broadening of (i) to any rule, holding with the physicists that the rules had to be established on firm empirical grounds.

To do this, one had to establish the existence of schemes of empirically based measurement that were different from extensive measurement. Examples are provided here. For greater detail, see FM I, II, III, Narens (1985), or for an earlier perspective Pfanzagl (1968).

Several Alternatives to Extensive Measurement

Utility Theory

The first evidence of something different from extensive measurement was the construction by von Neumann and Morgenstern (1947) of an axiomatization of *expected utility theory*. Here, the stimuli were gambles of the form $(x, p; y)$ where consequence x occurs with probability p and y with probability $1 - p$. The basic primitive of the system was a weak preference order $\gtrsim$ over the binary gambles. They stated properties that seemed to be at least rational, if not necessarily descriptive; from them one was able to show the existence of a numerical utility function U over the consequences and gambles such that for two binary gambles g, h

$$g \gtrsim h \Leftrightarrow U(g) \geq U(h),$$
$$U(g, p; h) = U(g)p + U(h)(1 - p).$$

Note that this is an averaging representation, called *expected utility*, which is quite distinct from the adding of extensive measurement (see the subsection on averaging).

Actually, their theory has to be viewed as a form of derived measurement in Campbell's sense because the construction of the U function was in terms of the numerical probabilities built into the stimuli themselves. That limitation was overcome by Savage (1954), who modeled decision making under uncertainty as acts that are treated as an assignment of consequences to chance states of nature.[4] Savage assumed that each act had a finite number of consequences, but subsequent generalizations permitted infinitely many. Without building any numbers into the domain and using assumptions defended by arguments of rationality, he showed that one can construct both a utility function U and a subjective probability function S such that acts are evaluated by calculating the expectation of U with respect to the measure S. This representation is called *subjective expected utility* (SEU). It is a case of fundamental measurement in Campbell's sense. Indirectly, it involved a partial concatenation operation of disjoint unions, which was used to construct a subjective probability function.

These developments led to a very active research program involving psychologists, economists, and statisticians. The basic thrust has been of psychologists devising experiments that cast doubt on either a representation or some of its axioms, and of theorists of all stripes modifying the theory of accommodate the data. Among the key summary references are Edwards (1992), Fishburn (1970, 1988), Luce (2000), Quiggin (1993), and Wakker (1989).

Difference Measurement

The simplest example of difference measurement is location along a line. Here, some point is arbitrarily set to be 0, and other points are defined in terms of distance (length) from it, with those on one side defined to be positive and those on the other side negative. It is clear in this case that location measurement forms an example of interval scale measurement

---

[4] Some aspects of Savage's approach were anticipated by Ramsey (1931), but that paper was not widely known to psychologists and economists. Almost simultaneously with the appearance of Savage's work, Davidson, McKinsey, and Suppes (1955) drew on Ramsey's approach, and Davidson, Suppes, and Segal (1957) tested it experimentally.

that is readily reduced to length measurement. Indeed, all forms of difference measurement are very closely related to extensive measurement, but with the stimuli being pairs of elements (x, y) that define "intervals." Axioms can be given for this form of measurement where the stimuli are pairs (x, y) with both x, y in the same set X. The goal is a numerical representation φ of the form

$$(x, y) \gtrsim (u, v)$$
$$\Leftrightarrow \varphi(x) - \varphi(y) \geq \varphi(u) - \varphi(v).$$

One key axiom that makes clear how a concatenation operation arises is that if $(x, y) \gtrsim (x', y')$ and $(y, z) \gtrsim (y', z')$, then $(x, z) \gtrsim (x', z')$.

An important modification is called *absolute difference measurement,* in which the goal is changed to

$$(x, y) \gtrsim (u, v)$$
$$\Leftrightarrow |\varphi(x) - \varphi(y)| \geq |\varphi(u) - \varphi(v)|.$$

This form of measurement is a precursor to various ideas of similarity measurement important in multidimensional scaling. Here the behavioral axioms become considerably more complex. Both systems can be found in FM I, Chap. 4.

An important generalization of absolute difference measurement is to stimuli with n factors; it underlies developments of geometric measurement based on stimulus proximity. This can be found in FM II, Chap. 14.

Additive Conjoint Measurement

Perhaps the single development that most persuaded psychologists that fundamental measurement really could be different from extensive measurement consisted of two versions of what is called additive conjoint measurement. The first, by Debreu (1960), was aimed at showing economists how indifference curves could be used to construct cardinal (interval scale) utility functions. It was,

therefore, naturally cast in topological terms. The second (and independent) one by Luce and Tukey (1964) was cast in algebraic terms, which seems more natural to psychologists and has been shown to include the topological approach as a special case. Again, it was an explanation of the conditions under which equal-attribute curves can give rise to measurement. Michell (1990) provides a careful treatment aimed at psychologists.

The basic idea is this: Suppose that an attribute is affected by two independent stimulus variables. For example, preference for a reward is affected by its size and the delay in receiving it; mass of an object is affected by both its volume and the (homogeneous) material of which it is composed; loudness of pure tones is affected by intensity and frequency; and so on. Formally, one can think of the two factors as distinct sets A and X, so an entity is of the form (a, x) where $a \in A$ and $x \in X$. The ordering attribute is $\gtrsim$ over such entities, that is, over the Cartesian product $A \times X$. Thus, $(a, x) \gtrsim (b, y)$ means that (a, x) exhibits more of the attribute in question than does (b, y). Again, the ordering is assumed to be a weak order: transitive and connected. Monotonicity (called independence in this literature) is also assumed: For $a, b \in A, x, y \in X$

$$(a, x) \gtrsim (b, x) \Leftrightarrow (a, y) \gtrsim (b, y).$$
$$(a, x) \gtrsim (a, y) \Leftrightarrow (b, x) \gtrsim (b, y). \tag{4}$$

This familiar property is often examined in psychological research in which a dependent variable is plotted against, say, a measure of the first component with the second component shown as a parameter of the curves. The property holds if and only if the curves do not cross.

It is easy to show that this condition is not sufficient to get an additive representation of the two factors. If it were, then any set of nonintersecting curves in the plane could be rendered parallel straight lines by suitable nonlinear transformations of the axes. More is required, namely, the Thomsen condition, which arose in a mathematically closely related area called the theory of webs. Letting $\sim$ denote the indifference relation of $\succsim$, the *Thomsen condition* states

$$\left.\begin{array}{l}(a, z) \sim (c, y) \\ (c, x) \sim (b, z)\end{array}\right\} \Rightarrow (a, x) \sim (b, y).$$

Note that it is a form of cancellation—of c in the first factor and z in the second.

These, together with an Archimedean property establishing commensurability and some form of density of the factors, are enough to establish the following additive representation: There exist numerical functions ψ_A on A and ψ_X on X such that

$$(a, x) \succsim (b, y)$$
$$\Leftrightarrow \psi_A(a) + \psi_X(x) \geq \psi_A(b) + \psi_X(y).$$

This representation is on all of the real numbers. A multiplicative version on the positive real numbers exists by setting $\xi_i = \exp \psi_i$. The additive representation forms an interval scale in the sense that ψ_A', ψ_X' forms another equally good representation if and only if there are constants $r > 0, s_A, s_X$ such that

$$\psi_A' = r\psi_A + s_A,$$
$$\psi_X' = r\psi_X + s_X \Leftrightarrow \xi_A' = s_A'\xi_A^r, \quad \xi_X' = s_X'\xi_X^r,$$
$$s_i' = \exp s_i > 0.$$

Additive conjoint measurement can be generalized to finitely many factors, and it is simpler in the sense that if monotonicity is generalized suitably and if there are at least three factors, then the Thomsen condition can be derived rather than assumed.

Although no concatenation operation is in sight, a family of them can be defined in terms of $\sim$, and they can be shown to satisfy the axioms of extensive measurement. This is the nature of the mathematical proof of the representation usually given.

Averaging

Some structures with a concatenation operation do not have an additive representation, but rather a weighted averaging representation of the form

$$\varphi(x \circ y) = \varphi(x)w + \varphi(y)(1 - w), \quad (5)$$

where the weight w is fixed. We have already encountered this form in the utility system if we think of the gamble $(x, p; y)$ as defining operations $\circ_p$ with $x \circ_p y \equiv (x, p; y)$, in which case $w = w(p)$. A general theory of such operations was first given by Pfanzagl (1959). It is much like extensive measurement but with associativity replaced by *bisymmetry:* For all stimuli x, y, u, v,

$$(x \circ y) \circ (u \circ v) \sim (x \circ u) \circ (y \circ v). \quad (6)$$

It is easy to verify that the weighted-average representation of Equation (5) implies bisymmetry, Equation (6), and $x \circ x \sim x$. The easiest way to show the converse is to show that defining $\succsim'$ over $X \times X$ by

$$(a, x) \succsim' (b, y) \Leftrightarrow a \circ x \succsim b \circ y$$

yields an additive conjoint structure, from which the result follows rather easily.

Nonadditive Representations

A natural question is: When does a concatenation operation have a numerical representation that is inherently nonadditive? By this, one means a representation for which no strictly increasing transformation renders it additive. Before exploring that, we cite an example of nonadditive representations that can in fact be transformed into additive ones. This is helpful in understanding the subtlety of the question.

One example that has arisen in utility theory is the representation

$$U(x \oplus y) = U(x) + U(y) - \delta U(x)U(y), \quad (7)$$

where δ is a real constant and U is the SEU or rank-dependent utility generalization (see

Luce, 2000, Chap. 4) with an intrinsic zero—no change from the status quo. Because Equation (7) can be rewritten

$$1 - \delta U(x \oplus y) = [1 - \delta U(x)][1 - \delta U(y)],$$

the transformation $V = -\kappa \ln(1 - \delta U)$, $\delta \kappa > 0$, is additive, that is, $V(x \oplus y) = V(x) + V(y)$, and order-preserving. The measure V is called a *value function*. The form in Equation (7) is called *p-additive* because it is the only polynomial with a fixed zero that can be put in additive form. The source of this representation is examined in the next major section. It is easy to verify that both the additive and the nonadditive representations are ratio scales in Stevens' sense. We know from extensive measurement that the change of unit in the additive representation is somehow reflecting something important about the underlying structure. Is that also true of the changes of units in the nonadditive representation? We will return to this point, which can be a source of confusion.

It should be noted that in probability theory for independent events, the p-additive form with $\delta = 1$ arises since

$$P(A \cup B) = P(A) + P(B) - P(A)P(B).$$

An earlier, similar example concerning velocity concatenation arose in Einstein's theory of special relativity. Like the psychological one, it entails a representation in the standard measure of velocity that forms a ratio scale and a nonlinear transformation to an additive one that also forms a ratio scale. We do not detail it here.

Nonadditive Concatenation

What characterizes an inherently nonadditive structure is the failure of the empirical property of associativity; that is, for some elements x, y, z in the domain,

$$x \circ (y \circ z) \not\sim (x \circ y) \circ z.$$

Cohen and Narens (1979) made the then-unexpected discovery that if one simply drops associativity from any standard axiomatization of extensive measurement, not only can one still continue to construct numerical representations that are onto the positive reals but, quite surprisingly, they continue to form a ratio scale as well; that is, the representation is unique up to similarity transformations. They called this important class of nonadditive representations *unit structures*. For a full discussion, see Chaps. 19 and 20 of FM III.

A Fundamental Account of Some Derived Measurement

Distribution Laws

The development of additive conjoint measurement allows one to give a systematic and fundamental account of what to that point had been treated as derived measurement. For classical physics, a typical situation in which derived measurement arises takes the form $\langle A \times X, \gtrsim, \circ_A \rangle$. For example, let A denote a set of volumes and X a set of homogeneous substances; the ordering is that of mass as established by an equal-arm pan balance in a vacuum. The operation $\circ_A$ is the simple union of volumes. For this case we know that $m = V\rho$, where m is the usual mass measure, V is the usual volume measure, and ρ is an inferred measure of density.

Observe that $\langle A \times X, \gtrsim \rangle$ forms an additive conjoint structure. By the monotonicity assumption of conjoint measurement, Equation (4), $\gtrsim$ induces the weak order $\gtrsim_A$ on A. It is assumed that $\langle A, \gtrsim_A, \circ_A \rangle$ forms an extensive structure. Thus we have the extensive representation φ_A of $\langle A, \gtrsim_A, \circ_A \rangle$ onto the positive real numbers and a multiplicative conjoint one $\xi_A \xi_X$ of $\langle A \times X, \gtrsim \rangle$ onto the positive real numbers.

The question is how φ_A and ξ_A relate. Because both preserve the order $\gtrsim_A$, there must be a strictly increasing function F such that $\xi_A = F(\varphi_A)$. Beyond that, we can say nothing without some assumption describing how the two structures interlock. One that holds for many physical cases, including the motivating mass example, is a qualitative *distribution law* of the form: For all a, b, c, d in A and x, y in X,

$$\left.\begin{array}{l}(a, x) \sim (c, y) \\ (b, x) \sim (d, y)\end{array}\right\} \Rightarrow (a \circ_A b, x) \sim (c \circ_A d, y).$$

Using this, one is able to prove that, for some $r > 0, s > 0, F(z) = rz^s$. Because the conjoint representation is unique up to power transformations, we may select $s = 1$, that is, choose $\xi_A = \varphi_A$.

Note that distribution is a substantive, empirical property that in each specific case requires verification. In fact, it holds for many of the classical physical attributes. From that fact one is able to construct the basic structure of (classical) physical quantities that underlies the technique called *dimensional analysis,* which is widely used in physical applications in engineering. It also accounts for the fact that physical units are all expressed as products of powers of a relatively small set of units. This is discussed in some detail in Chap. 10 of FM I and in a more satisfactory way in Section 22.7 of FM III.

Segregation Law

Within the behavioral sciences we have a situation that is somewhat similar to distribution. Suppose we return to the gambling structure, where some chance "experiment" is performed, such as drawing a ball from an urn with 100 red and yellow balls of which the respondent knows that the number of red is between 50 and 80. A typical binary gamble is of the form $(x, C; y)$, where C denotes a chance event such as drawing a red ball, and the consequence x is received if C occurs and y otherwise, that is, x if a red ball and y if a yellow ball. A weak preference order $\succsim$ over

gambles is postulated. Let us distinguish gains from losses by supposing that there is a special consequence, denoted e, that means no change from the status quo. Things preferred to e are called gains, and those not preferred to it are called losses. Assume that for gains (and separately for losses) the axioms leading to a subjective expected utility representation are satisfied. Thus, there is a utility function U over gains and subjective probability function S such that

$$U(x, C; y) = U(x)S(C) + U(y)[1 - S(C)] \tag{8}$$

$$U(e) = 0. \tag{9}$$

Let $\oplus$ denote the operation of receiving two things, called *joint receipt*. Therefore, $g \oplus h$ denotes receiving both of the gambles g and h. Assume that $\oplus$ is a commutative[5] and monotonic operation with e the identity element; that is, for all gambles g perceived as a gain, $g \oplus e \sim g$. Again, some law must link $\oplus$ to the gambles. The one proposed by Luce and Fishburn (1991) is *segregation:* For all gains x, y,

$$(x, C; e) \oplus y \sim (x \oplus y, C; y). \tag{10}$$

Observe that this is highly rational in the sense that both sides yield $x \oplus y$ when C occurs and y otherwise, so they should be seen as representing the same gamble. Moreover, there is some empirical evidence in support of it (Luce, 2000, Chap. 4). Despite its apparent innocence, it is powerful enough to show that $U(x \oplus y)$ is given by Equation (7). Thus, in fact, the operation $\oplus$ forms an extensive structure with additive representation $V = -\kappa \ln(1 - \delta U), \delta\kappa > 0$. Clearly, the sign of δ greatly affects the relation between U and V: it is a negative exponential for $\delta > 0$, proportional for $\delta = 0$, and an exponential for $\delta < 0$.

---

[5]Later we examine what happens when we drop this assumption.

Applications of these ideas are given in Luce (2000). Perhaps the most interesting occurs when dealing with $x \oplus y$ where x is a gain and y a loss. If we assume that V is additive throughout the entire domain, then with $x \succsim e \succsim y$, $U(x \oplus y)$ is not additive. This carries through to mixed gambles that no longer have the simple bilinear form of binary SEU, Equation (8).

Invariance and Meaningfulness

Meaningful Statistics

Stevens (1951) raised the following issues in connection with the use of statistics on measurements. Some statistical assertions do not seem to make sense in some measurement schemes. Consider a case of ordinal measurement in which one set of three observations has ordinal measures 1, 4, and 5, with a mean of 10/3, and another set has measures 2, 3, and 6, with a mean of 11/3. One would say the former set is, on average, smaller than the second one. But since these are ordinal data, an equally satisfactory representation is 1, 5, and 6 for the first set and 2, 2.1, and 6.1 for the latter, with means respectively 12/3 and 10.2/3, reversing the conclusion. Thus, there is no invariant conclusion about means. Put another way, comparing means is meaningless in this context. By contrast, the median is invariant under monotonic transformations. It is easy to verify that the mean exhibits suitable invariance in the case of ratio scales.

These observations were immediately challenged and led to what can best be described as a tortured discussion that lasted many years. It was only clarified when the problem was recognized to be a special case of invariance principles that were well developed in both geometry and dimensional analysis.

The main reason why the discussion was confused is that it was conducted at the level of numerical representations, where two kinds of transformations are readily confused, rather than in terms of the underlying structure itself. Consider a cubical volume that is 4 yards on a side. An appropriate change of units is from yards to feet, so it is also 12 feet on a side. This is obviously different from the transformation that enlarges each side by a factor of 3, producing a cube that is 12 yards on a side. At the level of numerical representations, however, these two factor-of-3 changes are all too easily confused. This fact was not recognized when Stevens wrote, but it clearly makes very uncertain just what is meant by saying that a structure has a ratio or other type of representation and that certain invariances should hold.

Automorphisms

These observations lead one to take a deeper look into questions of uniqueness and invariance. Mapping empirical structures onto numerical ones is not the most general or fundamental way to approach invariance. The key to avoiding confusion is to understand what it is about a structure that corresponds to correct admissible transformations of the representation. This turns out to be isomorphisms that map an empirical structure onto itself. Such isomorphisms are called *automorphisms* by mathematicians and *symmetries* by physicists. Their importance is easily seen, as follows. Suppose α is an automorphism and f is a homomorphism of the structure into a numerical one, then it is not difficult to show that $f * \alpha$, where $*$ denotes function composition, is another equally good homomorphism into the same numerical structure. In the case of a ratio scale, this means that there is a positive numerical constant r_α such that $f * \alpha = r_\alpha f$. The automorphism captures something about the structure itself, and that is just what is needed.

Consider the utility example, Equation (7), where there are two nonlinearly related representations, both of which are ratio scales in Stevens' sense. Thus, calculations of the mean utility are invariant in any one representation, but they certainly are not across representations. Which should be used, if either? It turns out on careful examination that the one set of transformations corresponds to the automorphisms of the underlying extensive structure. The second set of transformations corresponds to the automorphisms of the SEU structure, not $\oplus$. Both changes are important, but different. Which one should be used depends on the question being asked.

Invariance

An important use of automorphisms, first emphasized for geometry by Klein (1872/1893) and heavily used by physicists and engineers in the method of dimensional analysis, is the idea that meaningful statements should be invariant under automorphisms. Consider a structure with various primitive relations. It is clear that these are invariant under the automorphisms of the structure, and it is natural to suppose that anything that can be meaningfully defined in terms of these primitives should also be invariant. Therefore, in particular, given the structure of physical attributes, any physical law is defined in terms of the attributes and thus must be invariant. This definitely does not mean that something that is invariant is necessarily a physical law. In the case of statistical analyses of measurements, we want the result to exhibit invariance appropriate to the structure underlying the measurements.

To answer Stevens' original question about statistics then entails asking whether the hypothesis being tested is meaningful (invariant) when translated back into assertions about the underlying structure. Doing this correctly is sometimes subtle, as is discussed in Chap. 22 of FM III and much more fully by Narens (2001).

Trivial Automorphisms and Invariance

Sometimes structures have but one automorphism, namely the function that maps each

element of the structure into itself—the identity function. For example, in the additive structure of the natural numbers with the standard ordering, the only automorphism is the one that simply matches each number to itself: 0 to 0, 1 to 1, and so on.

Within the weak ordering $\succsim$ of a structure, there are trivial automorphisms beyond the identity mapping, namely, those that just map an element a to an equivalent element b; that is, the relation $a \sim b$ holds.

Consider invariance in such structures. We quickly see that the approach cannot yield any significant results because everything is invariant. This remark applies to all finite structures that are provided with a weak ordering. Thus, the only possibility is to examine the invariant properties of the structure of the set of numerical representations.

Let a finite empirical structure be given with a homomorphism f mapping the structure into a numerical structure. We have already introduced the concept of an admissible numerical transformation φ of f, namely, a one-one transformation of the range of f onto a possibly different set of real numbers, such that $\varphi * f$ is a homomorphism of the empirical structure. In order to fix the scale type and thus the nature of the invariance of the empirical structure, we investigate the set of all such homomorphisms for a given empirical structure. In the case of weight, any two homomorphisms f_1 and f_2 are related by a positive similarity transformation; that is, there is a positive real number $r > 0$ such that $r f_1 = f_2$. In the qualitative probability case with independence, $r = 1$, so the set of all homomorphisms has only one element. With $r \neq 1$ in the general similarity case, invariance is then characterized with respect to the multiplicative group of positive real numbers, each number in the group constituting a change of unit. A numerical statement about a set of numerical quantities is then *invariant* if and only if its truth value is constant under any changes of unit of any of the quantities. This definition is easily generalized to other groups of numerical transformations such as linear transformations for interval scales.

In contrast, consider a finite difference structure with a numerical representation as characterized earlier. In general, the set of all homomorphisms from the given finite structure to numerical representations has no natural and simple mathematical characterization. For this reason, much of the general theory of representational measurement is concerned with empirical structures that map onto the full domain of real numbers. It remains true, however, that special finite empirical structures remain important in practice in setting up standard measurement procedures using well-defined units.

Covariants

In practice, physicists hold on to invariance by introducing and using the concept of co-variants. Typical examples of such covariants are velocity and acceleration, neither of which is invariant from one coordinate frame to another under either Galilean or Lorentzian transformations, because, among other things, the direction of the velocity or acceleration vector of a particle will in general change from one frame to another. (The scalar magnitude of acceleration is invariant.)

The laws of physics are written in terms of such covariants. The fundamental idea is conveyed by the following. Let $Q_1, \ldots, Q_n$ be quantities that are functions of the space-time coordinates, with some Q_is possibly being derivatives of others, for example. Then, in general, as we go from one coordinate system to another (note that $'$ does not mean derivative) $Q'_1, \ldots, Q'_n$ will be covariant, rather than invariant, so their mathematical form is different in the new coordinate system. But any physical law involving them, say,

$$F(Q_1, \ldots, Q_n) = 0, \qquad (11)$$

must have the same form

$$F(Q'_1, \ldots, Q'_n) = 0$$

in the new coordinate frame. This same form is the important invariant requirement.

A simple example from classical mechanics is the conservation of momentum of two particles before and after a collision. Let v_i denote the velocity before and w_i the velocity after the collision, and m_i the mass, $i = 1, 2$, of each particle. Then the law, in the form of Equation (11), looks like this:

$$v_1 m_1 + v_2 m_2 - (w_1 m_1 + w_2 m_2) = 0,$$

and its transformed form will be, of course,

$$v'_1 m_1 + v'_2 m_2 - (w'_1 m_1 + w'_2 m_2) = 0,$$

but the forms of v_i and w_i will be, in general, covariant rather than invariant.

An Account of Stevens' Scale-Type Classification

Narens (1981a, 1981b) raised and partially answered the question of why the Stevens' classification into ratio, interval, and ordinal scales makes as much sense as it seems to. His result was generalized by Alper (1987), as described later. The question may be cast as follows: These familiar scale types have, respectively, one, two, and infinitely many degrees of freedom in the representation; are there not any others, such as ones having three or 10 degrees of freedom? To a first approximation, the answer is "no," but the precise answer is somewhat more complex than that.

To arrive at a suitable formulation, a special case may be suggestive. Consider a structure that has representations onto the reals—*continuous representations*—that form an interval scale. Then the representation has the following two properties. First, given numbers $x < y$ and $u < v$, there is a positive affine transformation that takes the pair (x, y) into

(u, v). It is found by setting $u = rx + s$, $v = ry + s$, whence $r = \frac{v-u}{y-x}$ and $s = \frac{yu-xv}{y-x}$. Thus, in terms of automorphisms we have the property that there exists one that maps any ordered pair of the structure into any other ordered pair. This is called *two-point homogeneity*. Equally well, if two affine transformations map a pair into the same pair, then they are identical. This follows from the fact that two equations uniquely determine r and s. In terms of automorphisms, this is called 2-*point uniqueness*. The latter can be recast by saying that any automorphism having two fixed points must be the identity automorphism.

In like manner, the ratio scale case is 1-point homogeneous and 1-point unique. The generalizations of these concepts to M—point homogeneity and N—point uniqueness are obvious. Moreover, in the continuous case it is easy to show that $M \leq N$. The question addressed by Narens was: Given that the structure is at least 1-point homogeneous and N—point unique for some finite N, what are the possibilities for (M, N)? Assuming $M = N$ and a continuous structure, he showed that the only possibilities are $(1, 1)$ and $(2, 2)$, that is, the ratio and interval scales. Alper (1987) dropped the condition that $M = N$ and showed that $(1, 2)$ can also occur, but that is the only added possibility. In terms of numerical representations on all of the real numbers, the $(1, 2)$ transformations are of the form $x \longmapsto rx + s$ where s is any real and r is in some proper, nontrivial subgroup of the multiplicative, positive real group. One example is when r is of the form k^n, where $k > 0$ is fixed and n ranges over the positive and negative integers.

This result makes clear two things. First, we see that there can be no continuous scales between interval and ordinal, which of course is not finitely unique. Second, there are scales between ratio and interval. None of these has yet played a role in actual scientific measurement. Thus, for continuous structures

Stevens' classification was almost complete, but not quite.

The result also raises some questions. First, how critical is the continuum assumption? The answer is "very": Cameron (1989) showed that nothing remotely like the Alper-Narens result holds for representations on the rational numbers. Second, what can be said about nonhomogeneous structures? Alper (1987) classified the $M = 0$ case, but the results are quite complex and apparently not terribly useful. Luce (1992) explored empirically important cases in which homogeneity fails very selectively. It does whenever there are *singular points,* which are defined to be points of the structure that remain fixed under all automorphisms. Familiar examples are 0 in the nonnegative, multiplicative real numbers and infinity if, as in relativistic velocity, it is adjoined to the system. For a broad class of systems, he showed that if a system has finitely many singular points and is homogeneous between adjacent ones, then there are at most three singular points—a minimum, an interior, and a maximum one. The detailed nature of these fixed points is somewhat complicated and is not discussed here. One specific utility structure with an interior singular point—an inherent zero—is explored in depth in Luce (2000).

Models of Stevens' Magnitude Methods

Stevens' (1975) empirical findings, which were known in the 1950s, were a challenge to measurement theorists. What underlies the network of (approximate) power function relations among subjective measures? Luce (1959) attempted to argue in terms of representations that if, for example, two attributes are each continuous ratio scales,[6] with typical physical representations φ_1 and φ_2, then

---

[6] Scale types other than ratio were also studied by Luce and subsequent authors.

a matching relation M between them should exhibit an invariance involving an admissible ratio-scale change of the one attribute corresponding under the match to a ratio-scale change of the other attribute, that is, $M[r\varphi_1(x)] = \alpha(r)\varphi_2(x)$. From this it is not difficult to prove that M is a power function of its argument. A major problem with this argument is its failure to distinguish two types of ratio scale transformations—changes of unit, such as centimeters to meters—and changes of scale, such as increasing the linear dimensions of a volume by a factor of three. Rozeboom (1962) was very critical of this failure. Luce (1990) reexamined the issue from the perspective of automorphisms. Suppose M is an empirical matching relation between two measurement structures, and suppose that for each translation (i.e., an automorphism with no fixed point) τ of the first structure there corresponds to a translation σ_τ of the second structure such that for any stimulus x of the first structure and any s of the second, then xMs holds if and only if for each automorphism τ of the first structure $\tau(x)M\sigma_\tau(s)$ also holds. This assumption, called *translation consistency,* is an empirically testable property, not a mere change of units. Assuming that the two structures have ratio scale representations, this property is equivalent to a power function relation between the representations.

Based on some ideas of R. N. Shepard, circulated privately and later modified and published in 1981, Krantz (1972) developed a theory that is based on three primitives: magnitude estimates, ratio estimates, and cross-modal matches. Various fairly simple, testable axioms were assumed that one would expect to hold if the psychophysical functions were power functions of the corresponding physical intensity and the ratios of the instructions were treated as mathematical ratios. These postulates were shown to yield the expected power function repre-

sentations except for an arbitrary increasing function. This unknown function was eliminated by assuming, without a strong rationale, that the judgments for one continuum, such as length judgments, are veridical, thereby forcing the function to be a simple multiplicative factor. This model is summarized in Falmagne (1985, pp. 309–313). A somewhat related approach was offered by Falmagne and Narens (1983), also summarized in Falmagne (1985, pp. 329–339). It is based not on behavioral axioms, but on two invariance principles that they call meaningfulness and dimensional invariance. Like the Krantz theory, it too leads to the form $G(\varphi_i^{r_i}\varphi_j^{r_j})$, where G is unspecified beyond being strictly increasing.

Perhaps the deepest published analysis of the problem so far is Narens (1996). Unlike Stevens, he carefully distinguished numbers from numerals, noting that the experimental structure involved numerals whereas the scientists' representations of the phenomena involved numbers. He took seriously the idea that internally people are carrying out the ratio-preservation calculations embodied in Stevens' instructions. The upshot of Narens' axioms, which he carefully partitioned into those that are physical, those that are behavioral, and those that link the physical and the behavioral, was to derive two empirical predictions from the theory. Let $(x, \mathbf{p}, y)$ mean that the experimenter presents stimulus x and the numeral $\mathbf{p}$ to which the subject produces stimulus y as holding the p relation to x. So if $\mathbf{2}$ is given, then y is whatever the subject feels is twice x. The results are, first, a commutativity property: Suppose that the subject yields $(x, \mathbf{p}, y)$ and $(y, \mathbf{q}, z)$ when done in that order and $(x, \mathbf{q}, u)$ and $(u, \mathbf{p}, v)$ when the numerals are given in the opposite order. The prediction is $z = v$. A second result is a multiplicative one: Suppose $(x, \mathbf{pq}, w)$, then the prediction is $w = z$. It is clear that the latter property implies the former, but not conversely. Empirical data reported by Ellemeirer and Faulhammer

(2000) sustain the former prediction and un-ambiguously reject the latter.

Luce (2001) provides a variant axiomatic theory, based on a modification of some mathematical results summarized in Luce (2000) for utility theory. The axioms are formulated in terms of three primitives: a sensory ordering $\succsim$ over physical stimuli varying in intensity, the joint presentation $x \oplus y$ of signals x and y (e.g., the presentation of pure tones of the same frequency and phase to the two ears), and for signals $x > y$ and positive number p denote by $z = (x, p, y)$ the signal that the subject judges makes interval $[y, z]$ stand in proportion p to interval $[y, x]$. The axioms, such as segregation, Equation (10), are behavioral and structural, and they are sufficient to ensure the existence of a continuous psychophysical measure ψ from stimuli to the positive real numbers and a continuous function W from the positive reals onto the positive reals and a constant $\delta > 0$ such that for $\oplus$ commutative

$$x \succsim y \Leftrightarrow \psi(x) \geq \psi(y), \qquad (12)$$
$$\psi(x \oplus y) = \psi(x) + \psi(y) + \delta \psi(x)\psi(y)$$
$$(\delta > 0), \quad (13)$$
$$\psi(x, p, y) - \psi(y) = W(p)[\psi(x) - \psi(y)]. \qquad (14)$$

We have written Equation (14) in this fashion rather than in a form comparable to the SEU equation for two reasons: It corresponds to the instructions given the respondents, and $W(p)$ is not restricted to [0, 1]. Recent, currently unpublished, psychophysical data of R. Steingrimsson showed an important case of $\oplus$ (two-ear loudness summation) that is rarely, if ever, commutative. This finding motivated Aczél, Luce, and Ng (2001) to explore the noncommutative, nonassociative cases on the assumption $\oplus$ has a unit representation (mentioned earlier) and assuming Equations (12) and (14) and that certain unknown functions are differentiable. To everyone's surprise, the only new representations replacing (13) are

either

$$\psi(x \oplus y) = \alpha \psi(x) + \psi(y), \qquad (\alpha > 1)$$

when $x \oplus 0 \succ 0 \oplus x$, or

$$\psi(x \oplus y) = \psi(x) + \alpha' \psi(y), \qquad (\alpha' > 1)$$

when $x \oplus 0 \prec 0 \oplus x$. These are called *left-* and *right-weighted additive* forms, respectively. These representations imply that some fixed dB correction can compensate the noncommutativity. Empirical studies evaluating this are underway.

One invariance condition limits the form of ψ to the exponential of a power function of deviations from absolute threshold, and another one limits the form of W to two parameters for $p \geq 1$ and two more for $p < 1$.

The theory not only is able to accommodate the Ellemeier and Faulhammer data but also predicts that the psychophysical function is a power function when $\oplus$ is not commutative and only approximately a power function for $\oplus$ commutative. Over eight or more orders of magnitude, it is extremely close to a power function except near threshold and for very intense signals. Despite its not being a pure power function, the predictions for cross-modal matches are pure power functions.

Errors and Thresholds

To describe the general sources of errors and why they are inevitable in scientific work, we can do no better than quote the opening passage in Gauss's famous work on the theory of least squares, which is from the first part presented to the Royal Society of Göttingen in 1821:

> However much care is taken with observations of the magnitude of physical quantities, they are necessarily subject to more or less considerable errors. These errors, in the majority of cases, are not simple, but arise simultaneously from several distinct sources which it is convenient to distinguish into two classes.

Certain causes of errors depend, for each observation, on circumstances which are variable and independent of the result which one obtains: the errors arising from such sources are called *irregular* or *random*, and like the circumstances which produce them, their value is not susceptible of calculation. Such are the errors which arise from the imperfection of our senses and all those which are due to irregular exterior causes, such as, for example, the vibrations of the air which make vision less clear; some of the errors due to the inevitable imperfection of the best instruments belong to the same category. We may mention, for example, the roughness of the inside of a level, the lack of absolute rigidity, etc.

On the other hand, there exist causes which in all observations of the same nature produce an identical error, or depend on circumstances essentially connected with the result of the observation. We shall call the errors of this category *constant* or *regular*.

It is evident that this distinction is relative up to a certain point and depends on how broad a sense one wishes to attach to the idea of observations of the same nature. For instance, if one repeats indefinitely the measurement of a single angle, the errors arising from an imperfect division of the circular scale will belong to the class of constant errors. If, on the other hand, one measures successively several different angles, the errors due to the imperfection of the division will be regarded as random as long as one has not formed the table of errors pertaining to each division. (Gauss, 1821/1957, pp. 1–2)

Although Gauss had in mind problems of errors in physical measurement, it is quite obvious that his conceptual remarks apply as well to psychological measurement and, in fact, in the second paragraph refer directly to the "imperfection of our senses." It was really only in the 19th century that, even in physics, systematic and sustained attention was paid to quantitative problems of errors. For a historical overview of the work preceding Gauss, see Todhunter (1865/1949). As can be seen from the references in the section on 19th- and early 20th-century psychology,

quantitative attention to errors in psychological measurement began at least with Fechner in the second half of the 19th century. Also, as already noted, the analysis of thresholds in probabilistic terms really began in psychology with the cited work of Thurstone. However, the quantitative and mathematical theory of thresholds was discussed earlier by Norbert Wiener (1915, 1921). Wiener's treatment was, however, purely algebraic, whereas in terms of providing relatively direct methods of application, Thurstone's approach was entirely probabilistic in character. Already, Wiener (1915) stated very clearly and explicitly how to deal with the fact that with thresholds in perception, the relation of indistinguishability—whether we are talking about brightness of light, loudness of sound, or something similar—is not transitive.

The detailed theory was then given in the 1921 paper for constructing a measure up to an interval scale for such sensation-intensities. This is, without doubt, the first time that these important psychological matters were dealt with in rigorous detail from the standpoint of passing from qualitative judgments to a measurement representation. Here is the passage with which Wiener ends the 1921 paper:

In conclusion, let us consider what bearing all this work of ours can have on experimental psychology. One of the great defects under which the latter science at present labours is its propensity to try to answer questions without first trying to find out just what they ask. The experimental investigation of Weber's law[7] is a case in point: what most experimenters do take for granted before they begin their experiments is infinitely more important and interesting than any results to which their experiments lead. One of these unconscious assumptions is that sensations or sensation-intervals can be measured,

---

[7]Wiener means what is now called Fechner's logarithmic law.

and that this process of measurement can be carried out in one way only. As a result, each new experimenter would seem to have devoted his whole energies to the invention of a method of procedure logically irrelevant to everything that had gone before: one man asks his subject to state when two intervals between sensations of a given kind appear different; another bases his whole work on an experiment where the observer's only problem is to divide a given colour-interval into two equal parts, and so on indefinitely, while even where the experiments are exactly alike, no two people choose quite the same method for working up their results. Now, if we make a large number of comparisons of sensation-intervals of a given sort with reference merely to whether one seems larger than another, the methods of measurement given in this paper indicate perfectly unambiguous ways of working up the results so as to obtain some quantitative law such as that of Weber without introducing such bits of mathematical stupidity as treating a "just noticeable difference" as an "infinitesimal," and have the further merit of always indicating *some* tangible mathematical conclusion, no matter what the outcome of the comparisons may be. (pp. 204–205)

The later and much more empirical work of Thurstone, already referred to, did not, however, give a representational theory of measurement as Wiener, in fact, in his own way did.

The work over the last few decades on errors and thresholds from the standpoint of representation theory of measurement naturally falls into two parts. The first part is the algebraic theory, and the second is the probabilistic theory. We first survey the algebraic results.

Algebraic Theory of Thresholds

The work following Wiener on algebraic thresholds was only revived in the 1950s and may be found in Goodman (1951), Halphen (1955), Luce (1956), and Scott and Suppes (1958). The subsequent literature is reviewed

in some detail in FM II, Chap. 16. We follow the exposition of the algebraic ordinal theory there. We restrict ourselves here to finite semiorders, the concept first introduced axiomatically by Luce and in a modified axiomatization by Scott and Suppes.

Let A be a nonempty set, and let $\succ$ be a binary irreflexive relation on A. Then, $(A \succ)$ is a *semiorder* if for every a, b, c, and d in A

(i) If $a \succ c$ and $b \succ d$, then either $a \succ d$ or $b \succ c$.

(ii) If $a \succ b$ and $b \succ c$, then either $a \succ d$ or $d \succ c$.

For finite semiorders $(A, \succ)$ we can prove the following numerical representational theorem with constant threshold, which in the present case we will fix at 1, so the theorem asserts that there is a mapping f of A into the positive real numbers such that for any a and b in A,

$$a \succ b \quad \text{iff} \quad f(a) > f(b) + 1.$$

A wealth of more detailed and more delicate results on semiorders is to be found in Section 2 of Chap. 16 of FM II, and research continues on semiorders and various generalizations of them, such as interval orders.

Axioms extending the ordinal theory of semiorders to the kind of thing analyzed by Wiener (1921) are in Gerlach (1957); unfortunately, to obtain a full interval-scale representation with thresholds involves very complicated axioms. This is true to a lesser extent of the axioms for semiordered qualitative probability structures given in Section 16.6.3 of FM II. The axioms are complicated when stated strictly in terms of the relation $\succ$ of semiorders.

Probabilistic Theory of Thresholds

For applications in experimental work, it is certainly the case that the probabilistic theory of thresholds is more natural and easier to apply. From various directions, there are extensive developments in this area, many but not all of which are presented in FM II and III. We discuss here results that are simple to formulate and relevant to various kinds of experimental work. We begin with the ordinal theory.

A real-valued function P on $A \times A$ is called a *binary probability function* if it satisfies both

$$P(a, b) \geq 0,$$
$$P(a, b) + P(b, a) = 1.$$

The intended interpretation of $P(a, b)$ is as the probability of a being chosen over b. We use the probability measure P to define two natural binary relations.

$$aWb \quad \text{iff} \quad P(a, b) \geq \frac{1}{2},$$
$$aSb \quad \text{iff} \quad P(a, c) \geq P(b, c), \text{ for all } c.$$

In the spirit of semiorders we now define how the relations W and S are related to various versions of what is called *stochastic transitivity,* where stochastic means that the individual instances may not be transitive, but the probabilities are in some sense transitive. Here are the definitions. Let P be a binary probability function on $A \times A$. We define the following for all a, b, c, d in A:

Weak stochastic transitivity: If $P(a, b) \geq \frac{1}{2}$ and $P(b, c) \geq \frac{1}{2}$, then $P(a, c) \geq \frac{1}{2}$.

Weak independence: If $P(a, c) > P(b, c)$, then $P(a, d) \geq P(b, d)$.

Strong stochastic transitivity: If $P(a, b) \geq \frac{1}{2}$ and $P(b, c) \geq \frac{1}{2}$, then $P(a, c) \geq \max[P(a, b), P(b, c)]$.

The basic results for these concepts are taken from Block and Marschak (1960) and Fishburn (1973). Let P be a binary probability function on $A \times A$, and let W and S be defined as in the previous equations. Then

1. Weak stochastic transitivity holds if W is transitive.

2. Weak independence holds if S is connected.

3. Strong stochastic transitivity holds if $W = S$. Therefore strong stochastic transitivity implies weak independence; the two are equivalent if $P(a, b) \neq \frac{1}{2}$ for $a \neq b$.

Random Variable Representations

We turn next to random variable representations for measurement. In the first type, an essentially deterministic theory of measurement (e.g., additive conjoint measurement) is assumed in the background. But it is recognized that, for various reasons, variability in response occurs even in what are apparently constant circumstances. We describe here the approach developed and used by Falmagne (1976, 1985). Consider the conjoint indifference $(a, p) \sim (b, q)$ with a, p, and q given and b to be determined so that the indifference holds. Suppose that, in fact, b is a random variable which we may denote $\mathbf{B}(a, p; q)$. We suppose that such random variables are independently distributed. Since realizations of the random variables occur in repeated trials of a given experiment, we can define the equivalents we started with as holding when the value b is the Pth percentile of the distribution of the random variable $\mathbf{B}(a, p; q)$. Falmagne's proposal was to use the median, $P = \frac{1}{2}$, and he proceeded as follows. Let ϕ_1 and ϕ_2 be two numerical representations for the conjoint measurement in the usual deterministic sense. If we suppose that such an additive representation is approximately correct but has an additive error, then we have the following representation:

$$\varphi_1[\mathbf{B}(a, p; q)] = \varphi_1(a) + \varphi_2(q) - \varphi_2(p) + \epsilon(a, p; q),$$

where the ϵs are random variables. It is obvious enough how this equation provides a natural approximation of standard conjoint measurement. If we strengthen the assumptions a bit, we get an even more natural theory by assuming that the random variable

$\epsilon(a, p; q)$ has its median equal to zero. Using this stronger assumption about all the errors being distributed with a median of zero, Falmagne summarizes assumptions that must be made to have a measurement structure.

Let A and P be two intervals of real numbers, and let $\mathcal{U} = \{\mathbf{U}_{pq}(a) \mid p, q \in P, a \in A\}$ be a collection of random variables, each with a uniquely defined median. Then $\mathcal{U}$ is a structure for *random additive conjoint measurement* if for all p, q, r in P and a in A, the medians $m_{pq}(a)$ satisfy the following axioms:

(i) They are continuous in all variables p, q, and a.

(ii) They are strictly increasing in a and p, and strictly decreasing in q.

(iii) They map A into A.

(iv) They satisfy the cancellation rule with respect to function composition $*$, i.e.,

$$(m_{pq} * m_{qr})(a) = m_{pr}(a),$$

whenever both sides are defined.

For such random additive conjoint measurement structures, Falmagne (1985, p. 273) proved that there exist real-valued continuous strictly increasing functions ϕ_1 and ϕ_2, defined on A and P respectively, such that for any $\mathbf{U}_{pq}(a)$ in $\mathcal{U}$,

$$\varphi_1[\mathbf{U}_{pq}(a)]$$
$$= \varphi_2(p) + \varphi_2(q) - \varphi_1(a) + \epsilon_{pq}(a),$$

where $\epsilon_{pq}(a)$ is a random variable with a unique median equal to zero. Moreover, if φ_1' and φ_2' are two other such functions, then

$$\varphi_1'(a) = \alpha\varphi_1(a) + \beta$$

and

$$\varphi_2'(p) = \alpha\varphi_2(p) + \gamma,$$

where $\alpha > 0$.

Statistical tests of these ideas are not a simple matter but have been studied in order to make the applications practical. Major references are Falmagne (1978); Falmagne and Iverson (1979); Falmagne, Iverson, and Marcovici (1979); and Iverson and Falmagne (1985). Recent important work on probability models includes Doignon and Regenwetter (1997); Falmagne and Regenwetter (1996); Falmagne, Regenwetter, and Grofman (1997); Marley (1993); Niederée and Heyer (1997); Regenwetter (1997); and Regenwetter and Marley (in press).

Qualitative Moments

Another approach to measuring, in a representational sense, the distribution of a random variable for given psychological phenomena is to assume that we have a qualitative method for measuring the moments of the distribution of the random variable. The experimental procedures for measuring such raw moments will vary drastically from one domain of experimentation to another. Theoretically, we need only to assume that we can judge qualitative relations of one moment relative to another and that we have a standard weak ordering of these qualitatively measured moments. The full formal discussion of these matters is rather intricate. The details can be found in Section 16.8 of FM II.

Qualitative Density Functions

As is familiar in all sorts of elementary probability examples, when a distribution has a given form, it is often much easier to characterize it by a density distribution of a random variable than by a probability measure on events or by the method of moments as just mentioned. In the discrete case, the situation is formally quite simple. Each atom (i.e., each atomic event) in the discrete density has a qualitative probability, and we need judge only relations between these qualitative probabilities. We require of a representing discrete density function p on $\{a_1, \ldots, a_n\}$ the following three properties:

(i) $p(a_i) \geq 0$.

(ii) $\sum_{i=1}^{n} p(a_i) = 1$.

(iii) $p(a_i) \geq p(a_j)$ iff $a_i \succsim a_j$.

Note that the a_i are *not* objects or stimuli in an experiment, but qualitative atomic events, exhaustive and mutually exclusive. Also note that in this discrete case it follows that $p(a_i) \leq 1$, whereas in the continuous case this is not true of densities.

We also need conditional discrete densities. For this purpose we assume that the underlying probability space X is finite or denumerable, with probability measures P on the given family $\mathcal{F}$ of events. The relation of the density p to the measure P is, for a_i an atom of X,

$$p(a_i) = P(\{a_i\})$$

Then if A is any event such that $P(A) > 0$,

$$p(a_i \mid A) = P(\{a_i\} \mid A),$$

and, of course, $p(a_i \mid A)$ is now a discrete density itself, satisfying (i) through (iii).

Here are two simple, but useful, examples of this approach. Let X be a finite set. Then the uniform density on X is characterized by all atoms being equivalent in the qualitative ordering $\succsim$, that is,

$$a_i \sim a_j.$$

We may then easily show that the unique density satisfying the equivalence and (i), (ii), and (iii) is

$$p(a_i) = \frac{1}{n},$$

where n is the number of atoms in X.

Among the many possible discrete distributions, we consider just one further example, which has application in experiments in which the model being tested assumes a probability of change of state independent of the time spent in the current state. In the case of discrete trials, such a memoryless process has

a geometric distribution that can be tested or derived from some simple properties of the discrete but denumerable set of atomic events $\{a_1, \ldots, a_n, \ldots\}$, on each of which is a positive qualitative probability of the occurrence of the change of state. The numbering of the atoms intuitively corresponds to the trials of an experiment. The atoms are ordered in qualitative probability by the relation $\succsim$. We also introduce a restricted conditional probability. If $i > j$ then $a_i \mid A_j$ is the conditional event that the change of state will occur on trial i given that it has *not* occurred on or before trial j. (Note that here A_j means no change of state from trial 1 through j.) The qualitative probability ordering relation is extended to include these special conditional events as well.

The two postulated properties, in addition to (i), (ii), and (iii) given above, are these:

(iv) Order property: $a_i \succsim a_j$ iff $j \geq i$;

(v) Memoryless property: $a_{i+1} \mid A_i \sim a_1$.

It is easy to prove that (iv) implies a weak ordering of $\succsim$. We can then prove that $p(a_n)$ has the form

$$p(a_n) = c(1 - c)^{n-1} \quad (0 < c < 1).$$

Properties (i) through (v) are satisfied, but they are also satisfied by any other c', $0 < c' < 1$. For experiments testing only the memoryless property, no estimation of c is required. If it is desired to estimate c, the standard estimate is the sample mean m of the trial numbers on which the change of state was observed, since the mean μ of the density $p(a_n) = c(1-c)^{n-1}$ satisfies the following equation:

$$\mu = \frac{1 - c}{c}.$$

For a formal characterization of the full qualitative probability for the algebra of events—not just atomic events—in the case of the geometric distribution, see Suppes (1987). For the closely related but mathematically more complicated continuous analogue (i.e., the exponential distribution), see Suck (1998).

GENERAL FEATURES
OF THE AXIOMATIC APPROACH

Background

History

The story of the axiomatic method begins with the ancient Greeks, probably in the fifth century B.C. The evidence seems pretty convincing that it developed in response to the early crisis in the foundations of geometry mentioned earlier, namely, the problem of incommensurable magnitudes. It is surprising and important that the axiomatic method as we think of it was largely crystallized in Euclid's *Elements,* whose author flourished and taught in Alexandria around 300 B.C. From a modern standpoint, Euclid's schematic approach is flawed, but compared to any other standard to be found anywhere else for over two millennia, it is a remarkable achievement. The next great phase of axiomatic development occurred, as already mentioned, in the 19th century in connection with the crisis generated in the foundations of geometry itself. The third phase was the formalization within logic of the entire language used and the realization that results that could not be proved otherwise can be achieved by such complete logical formalization. In view of the historical review presented earlier in this article, we will concentrate on only this third phase in this section.

What Comes before the Axioms

Three main ingredients need to be fixed in an axiomatization before the axioms are formulated. First, there must be agreement on the general framework used. Is it going to be an informal, set-theoretical framework or one formalized within logic? These two alternatives are analyzed in more detail later.

The second ingredient is to fix the primitive concepts of the theory being axiomatized. For example, in almost all theories of choice we need an ordering relation as a primitive concept, which means, formally, a binary relation. We also often need, as mentioned earlier, a binary operation as, for example, in the cases of extensive measurement and averaging. In any case, whatever the primitives may be, they should be stated at the beginning. The third ingredient, at least as important, is clarity and explicitness about what other theories are being assumed. It is a characteristic feature of empirical axiomatizations that some additional mathematics is usually assumed, often without explicit notice. This is not true, however, of many qualitative axiomatizations of representational measurement and often is not true in the foundations of geometry. In contrast, many varieties of probabilistic modeling in psychology do assume some prior mathematics in formulating the axioms. A simple example of this was Falmagne's axioms for random additive conjoint measurement, presented earlier. There, such statistical notions as the median and such elementary mathematical notions as that of continuity were assumed without further explanation or definition.

Another ingredient, less important from a formal standpoint but of considerable importance in practice, are the questions of whether notions defined in terms of the primitive concepts should be introduced when formulating the axioms and whether auxiliary mathematical notions are assumed in stating the axioms. The contrasting alternative is to state the axioms strictly in terms of the primitive notions. From the standpoint of logical purity, the latter course seems desirable, but in actual fact it is often awkward and intuitively unappealing to state all of the axioms in terms of the primitive concepts only. A completely elementary but good example of this is the introduction of a strict ordering and an equivalence relation defined in terms of a weak ordering, a move that is often used as a way of simplifying and making more perspicuous the formulation of axioms in choice or preference theory within psychology.

Theories with Standard Logical Formalization

Explicit and formally precise axiomatic versions of theories are those that are formalized within first-order logic. Such a logic can be easily characterized in an informal way. This logic assumes

- **(i)** one kind of variable;
- **(ii)** logical constants, mainly the sentential connectives such as *and;*
- **(iii)** a notation for the universal and existential quantifiers; and
- **(iv)** the identity symbol $=$.

A theory formulated within such a logical framework is called a *theory with standard formalization*. Ordinarily, three kinds of nonlogical constants occur in axiomatizing a theory within such a framework: the relation symbols (also called predicates), the operation symbols, and the individual constants.

The grammatical expressions of the theory are divided into terms and formulas, and recursive definitions of each are given. The simplest terms are variables or individual constants. New terms are built up by combining simpler terms with operation symbols in the manner spelled out recursively in the formulation of the language of the theory. Atomic formulas consist of a single predicate and the appropriate number of terms. Compound formulas are built up from atomic formulas by means of sentential connectives and quantifiers.

Theories with standard formalization are not often used in any of the empirical sciences, including psychology. On the other hand, they can play a useful conceptual role in answering

some empirically important questions, as we illustrate later.

There are practical difficulties in casting ordinary scientific theories into the framework of first-order logic. The main source of the difficulty, which has already been mentioned, is that almost all systematic scientific theories assume a certain amount of mathematics a priori. Inclusion of such mathematics is not possible in any elegant and reasonable way in a theory beginning only with logic and with no other mathematical assumptions or apparatus. Moreover, a theory that requires for its formulation an Archimedean-type axiom, much needed in representational theories of measurement when the domain of objects considered is infinite, cannot even in principle be formulated within first-order logic. We say more about this well-known result later. For these and other reasons, standard axiomatic formulations of most mathematical theories, as well as scientific theories, follows the methodology to which we now turn.

Theories Defined as Set-Theoretical Predicates

A widely used alternative approach to formulating representational theories of measurement and other scientific theories is to axiomatize them within a set-theoretical framework. Moreover, this is close to the practice of much mathematics. In such an approach, axiomatizing a theory simply amounts to defining a certain set-theoretical predicate. The axioms, as we ordinarily think of them, are a part of the definition—its most important part from a scientific standpoint. Such definitions were (partially) presented earlier in a more or less formal way (e.g., weak orderings, extensive structures, and other examples of qualitative characterizations of empirical measurement structures). Note that the concept of isomorphism, or the closely related notion of homomorphism, is defined for structures satisfying some set-theoretical predicate. The language of set-theoretical predicates is not ordinarily used except in foundational talk; it is just a way of clarifying the status of the axioms. It means that the axioms are given within a framework that assumes set theory as the general framework for all, or almost all, mathematical concepts. It provides a seamless way of linking systematic scientific theories that use various kinds of mathematics with mathematics itself. An elementary but explicit discussion of the set-theoretical approach to axiomatization is found in Suppes (1957/1999, chap. 12).

Formal Results about Axiomatization

We sketch here some of the results that we think are of significance for quantitative work in experimental psychology. A detailed treatment is given in FM III, Chap. 21. We should emphasize that all the systematic results we state here hold only for theories formalized in first-order logic.

Elementary Languages

First, we need to introduce, informally, some general notions to be used in stating the results. We say that a language $\mathcal{L}$ of a theory is *elementary* if it is formulated in first-order logic. This means that, in addition to the apparatus of first-order logic, the theory only contains nonlogical relation symbols, operation symbols, and individual constants. Intuitively, a *model* of such a language $\mathcal{L}$ is simply an empirical structure, in the sense already discussed; in particular, it has a nonempty domain, a relation corresponding to each primitive relation symbol, an operation corresponding to each primitive operation symbol, and individuals in the domain corresponding to each individual constant.

Using such logical concepts, one major result is that there are infinite weak orders that cannot be represented by numerical order. A

specific example is the lexicographic order of points in the plane, that is $(x, y) \gtrsim (x', y')$ if and only if either $x > x'$ or $x = x'$ and $y \geq y'$.

In examining the kinds of axioms given earlier (e.g., those for extensive measurement), it is clear that some form of an Archimedean axiom is needed to get a numerical representation, and such an axiom cannot be formulated in an elementary language $\mathcal{L}$, a point to which we return a little later.

A second, but positive, result arises when the domains of the measurement structures are finite. A class of such structures closed under isomorphism is called a *finitary* class of measurement structures. To that end, we need the concept of a language being recursively axiomatizable; namely, there is an algorithm for deciding whether a formula of $\mathcal{L}$ is an axiom of the given theory. It can be shown that any finitary class of measurement structures with respect to an elementary language $\mathcal{L}$ is axiomatizable but not necessarily recursively axiomatizable in $\mathcal{L}$.

The importance of this result is in showing that the expressive power of elementary languages is adequate for finitary classes but not necessarily for the stating of a set of recursive axioms. We come now to another positive result guaranteeing that recursive axioms are possible for a theory. When the relations, operations, and constants of an empirical structure are definable in elementary form when interpreted as numerical relations, functions, and constants, then the theory is recursively axiomatizable.

Nonaxiomatizability Results

Now we turn to a class of results of direct psychological interest. As early as the work of Wiener (1921), the nontransitive equivalence relation generated by semiorders was defined (see the earlier quotation); namely, if we think of a semiorder, then the indistinguishability or indifference relation that complements it will have the following numerical representation.

For two elements a and b that are indistinguishable or indifferent with respect to the semiorder, the following equivalence holds:

$$|f(a) - f(b)| \leq 1 \quad \text{iff} \quad a \sim b.$$

Now we have already seen that finite semiorders have a very simple axiomatization. Given how close the indistinguishability relation is to the semiorder itself, it seems plausible that this relation, too, should have a simple axiomatization. Surprisingly, Roberts (1968, 1969) proved that this is not the case. More precisely, let $\mathcal{L}$ be the elementary language whose only nonlogical symbol is the binary relational symbol $\sim$. Then the finitary class $\mathcal{J}$ of measurement structures for the binary relation of indistinguishability is not axiomatizable in $\mathcal{L}$ by a universal sentence.

Note that there is a restriction in the result. It states that $\sim$ is not axiomatizable by a universal sentence. This means that existential statements are excluded. The simple axiomatization of semiorders, given earlier, is such a universal axiomatization because no quantifiers were required. But that is not true of indistinguishability. A little later, we discuss the more general question of axioms with existential quantifiers for elementary languages.

This result about $\sim$ is typical of a group of theorems concerning familiar representations for which it is impossible to axiomatize the class of finite structures by adjoining a universal sentence to an elementary language $\mathcal{L}$. Scott and Suppes (1958) first proved this to be true for a quaternary relation symbol corresponding to a difference representation. Titiev (1972) obtained the result for additive conjoint measurement; he also showed that it holds for the n-dimensional metric structure using the Euclidean metric; and in 1980 he showed that it is true for the city-block metric when the number of dimensions $n \leq 3$. It is worth mentioning that the proof for $n = 3$ given by Titiev required computer assistance to examine 21,780 cases, each of which

involved 10 equations and 12 unknowns in a related set of inequalities. To our knowledge, nothing is known about $n > 3$.

This last remark is worth emphasizing to bring out a certain point about the results mentioned here. For any particular case (e.g., an experiment using a set of 10 stimuli), a constructive approach, rather than the negative results given here, can be found for each particular case. One can simply write down the set of elementary linear inequalities that must be satisfied and ask a computer program to decide whether this finite set of inequalities in a fixed number of variables has a solution. If the answer is positive, then a numerical representation can be found, and the very restricted class of measurement structures built up around this fixed number of variables and fixed set of inequalities is indeed a measurement structure. What the theorems show is that the general elementary theory of such inequalities cannot be given in any reasonable axiomatic form. We cannot state for the various kinds of cases that are considered an elementary set of axioms that will guarantee a numerical solution for any finite model (i.e., a model with a finite domain) satisfying the axioms.

Finally, in this line of development, we mention a theorem requiring more sophisticated logical apparatus that was proved by Per Lindstrom (stated as Theorem 17, p. 243, FM III), namely, that even if existential quantifiers are permitted, the usual class of finite measurement structures for algebraic difference cannot be characterized by a finite set of elementary axioms.

Archimedean and Least-Upper-Bound Axioms

We have mentioned more than once that Archimedean axioms play a special role in formulating representational theories of measurement when the domain of the empirical structures is infinite. Recall that the Archimedean axiom for extensive measurement of weight or mass asserts that for any objects a and b, there exists some integer n such that n replicas of object a, written as $a(n)$, exceeds b, that is, $a(n) \succsim b$. This axiom, as well as other versions of it, cannot be directly formulated in an elementary language because of the existential quantification in terms of the natural numbers. In that sense, the fact that an elementary theory cannot include an Archimedean axiom has an immediate proof. Fortunately, however, a good deal more can be proved: For such elementary theories, of the kind we have considered in this chapter, there can be no elementary formulas of the elementary language $\mathcal{L}$ that are equivalent to an Archimedean axiom. After all, we might hope that one could simply replace the Archimedean axiom by a conjunction of elementary formulas, but this is not the case. For a proof, and references to the literature, see FM III, Section 21.7.

It might still be thought that by avoiding the explicit introduction of the natural numbers, we might be able to give an elementary formulation using one of the other axioms invoked in real analysis. Among these are Dedekind's (1872/1902) axiom of completeness, Cantor's (1895) formulation of completeness in terms of Cauchy sequences, and the more standard modern approach of assuming that a bounded nonempty set has a least-upper-bound in terms of the given ordering. We consider only the last example because its elementary form allows us to see easily what the problem is. To invoke this concept, we need to be able to talk in our elementary language not only about individuals in the given domain of an empirical structure, but also about sets of these individuals. But the move from individuals to sets of individuals is a mathematically powerful one, and it is not permitted in standard formulations of elementary languages. As in the case of the Archimedean axiom, then,

we have an immediate argument for rejecting such an axiom. Moreover, as in the case of the Archimedean axiom, we can prove that no set of elementary formulas of an elementary language $\mathcal{L}$ is equivalent to the least-upper-bound axiom. The proof of this follows naturally from the Archimedean axiom, since in a general setting the least-upper-bound axiom implies an Archimedean axiom.

Proofs of Independence of Axioms and Primitive Concepts

All the theorems just discussed can be formulated only within the framework of elementary languages. Fortunately, important questions that often arise in discussions of axioms in various scientific domains can be answered within the purely set-theoretic framework and do not require logical formalization. The first of these is proving that the axioms are independent in the sense that none can be deduced from the others. The standard method for doing this is as follows. For each axiom, a model is given in which the remaining axioms are satisfied and the one in question is not satisfied. Doing this establishes that the axiom is independent of the others. The argument is simple. If the axiom in question could be derived from the remaining axioms, we would then have a violation of the intuitive concept of logical consequence. An example of lack of independence among axioms given for extensive measurement is the commutativity axiom, $a \circ b \sim b \circ c$. It follows from the other axioms with the Archimedean axiom playing a very important role.

The case of the independence of primitive symbols requires a method that is a little more subtle. What we want is an argument that will prove that it is not possible to define one of the primitive symbols in terms of the others. Padoa (1902) formulated a principle that can be applied to such situations. To prove that a given primitive concept is independent of the other primitive concepts of a theory, find two models of the axioms of the theory such that the primitive concept in question is essentially different in the two models and the remaining primitive symbols are the same in the two models.

As a very informal description of a trivial example, consider the theory of preference based on two primitive relations, one a strict preference and the other an indifference relation. Assume both are transitive. We want to show what is obvious—that strict preference cannot be defined in terms of indifference. We need only take a domain of two objects, for example, the numbers 1 and 2. Then for the indifference relation we just take identity: $1 = 1$ and $2 = 2$. But in one model the strict preference relation has 1 preferred to 2, and in the second preference model the preference relation has 2 preferred to 1. This shows that strict preference cannot be defined in terms of indifference because indifference is the same in both models whereas preference is different.

CONCLUSIONS

The second half of the 20th century saw a number of developments in our understanding of numerical measurement. Among these are the following: (a) examples of fundamental measurement different from extensive structures; (b) an increased understanding of how measurement structures interlock to yield substantive theories; (c) a classification of scale types for continuous measurement in terms of properties of automorphism groups; (d) an analysis of invariance principles in limiting the mathematical forms of various measures; (e) a logical analysis of what sorts of theories can and cannot be formulated using purely first-order logic without existential or Archimedean statements; and (f) a number of psychological applications especially in psychophysics and utility theory.

A major incompleteness remains in the socially important area of ability and achievement testing. Except for the work of Doignon and Falmange (1999), no representational results of significance exist for understanding how individuals differ in their grasp of certain concepts. This is not to deny the extensive development of statistical models, but only to remark that fundamental axiomatizations are rarely found. This is changing gradually, but as yet it is a small part of representational measurement theory.

REFERENCES

Aczél, J., Luce, R. D., & Ng, C. T. (2001). Functional equations arising in a theory of rank dependence and homogeneous joint receipts. Submitted.

Alper, T. M. (1987). A classification of all order-preserving homeomorphism groups of the real that satisfy finite uniqueness. *Journal of Mathematical Psychology, 31,* 135–154.

Block, H. D., & Marschak, J. (1960). Random orderings and stochastic theories of responses. In I. Olkin, S. Ghurye, W. Hoeffding, W. Madow, & H. Mann (Eds.), *Contributions to probability and statistics* (pp. 97–132). Stanford, CA: Stanford University Press.

Cameron, P. J. (1989). Groups of order-automorphisms of the rationals with prescribed scale type. *Journal of Mathematical Psychology, 33,* 163–171.

Campbell, N. R. (1920/1957). *Physics: The elements.* Cambridge: Cambridge University Press. [Reprinted under the title *Foundations of science: The philosophy of theory and experiment,* New York: Dover.] (Original work published 1920)

Campbell, N. R. (1928). *An account of the principles of theory and experiment.* London: Longmans, Green.

Cantor, G. (1895). Beiträge zur Begründung der transfiniten Mengenlehre. *Mathematische Annalen, 46,* 481–512.

Cohen, M. A., & Narens, L. (1979). Fundamental unit structures: A theory of ratio scalability. *Journal of Mathematical Psychology, 20,* 192–232.

Davidson, D., McKinsey, J. C. C., & Suppes, P. (1955). Outlines of a formal theory of value: I. *Philosophy of Science, 22,* 140–160.

Davidson, D., Suppes, P., & Segal, S. (1957). *Decision-making: An experimental approach.* Stanford, CA: Stanford University Press. [Reprinted as Midway Reprint, 1977, Chicago: University of Chicago Press.]

Debreu, G. (1960). Topological methods in cardinal utility theory. In K. J. Arrow, S. Karlin, & P. Suppes (Eds.), *Mathematical methods in the social sciences, 1959.* Stanford, CA: Stanford University Press (pp. 16–26).

Dedekind, R. (1872/1902). Stetigkeit und Irrationale Zahlen. Brunswick, 1872. [*Essays on the theory of numbers.* New York: Dover, 1963 (reprint of the English translation).]

Doignon, J.-P., & Falmagne, J.-C. (1999). *Knowledge spaces.* Berlin: Springer.

Doignon, J.-P., & Regenwetter, M. (1997). An approval-voting polytope for linear orders. *Journal of Mathematical Psychology, 41,* 171–188.

Dzhafarov, E. N., & Colonius, H. (1999). Fechnerian metrics in unidimensional and multidimensional spaces. *Psychonomic Bulletin and Review, 6,* 239–268.

Dzhafarov, E. N., & Colonius, H. (2001). Multidimensional Fechnerian scaling: Basics. *Journal of Mathematical Psychology, 45,* 670–719.

Edwards, W. (Ed.). (1992). *Utility theories: Measurements and applications.* Boston: Kluwer.

Ellemeirer, W., & Faulhammer, G. (2000). Empirical evaluation of axioms fundamental to Stevens' ratio-scaling approach: I. Loudness production. *Perception & Psychophysics, 62,* 1505–1511.

Euclid. (1956). *Elements, Book 10* (Vol. 3, T. L. Heath, Trans.) New York: Dover.

Falmagne, J.-C. (1976). Random conjoint measurement and loudness summation. *Psychological Review, 83,* 65–79.

Falmagne, J.-C. (1978). A representation theorem for finite random scale systems. *Journal of Mathematical Psychology, 18,* 52–72.

Falmagne, J.-C. (1985). *Elements of psychophysical theory.* New York: Oxford University Press.

Falmagne, J.-C., & Iverson, G. (1979). Conjoint Weber laws and additivity. *Journal of Mathematical Psychology, 20,* 164–183.

Falmagne, J.-C., Iverson, G., & Marcovici, S. (1979). Binaural "loudness" summation: Probabilistic theory and data. *Psychological Review, 86,* 25–43.

Falmagne, J.-C., & Narens, L. (1983). Scales and meaningfulness of quantitative laws. *Synthese, 55,* 287–325.

Falmagne, J.-C., & Regenwetter, M. (1996). A random utility model for approval voting. *Journal of Mathematical Psychology, 40,* 152–159.

Falmagne, J.-C., Regenwetter, M., Grofman, B. (1997). A stochastic model for the evolution of preferences. In A. A. J. Marley (Ed.), *Choice, decision, and measurement: Essays in honor of R. Duncan Luce* (pp. 111–129). Mahwah, NJ: Erlbaum.

Fechner, G. T. (1966). *Elements of psychophysics* (H. E. Adler, Trans.). New York: Holt, Rinehart & Winston. (Original work published 1860)

Ferguson, A., Meyers, C. S. (Vice Chairman), Bartlett, R. J. (Secretary), Banister, H., Bartlett, F. C., Brown, W., Campbell, N. R., Craik, K. J. W., Drever, J., Guild, J., Houstoun, R. A., Irwin, J. O., Kaye, G. W. C., Philpott, S. J. F., Richardson, L. F., Shaxby, J. H., Smith, T., Thouless, R. H., & Tucker, W. S. (1940). Quantitative estimates of sensory events. The advancement of science. *Report of the British Association for the Advancement of Science, 2,* 331–349.

Fishburn, P. C. (1970). *Utility theory for decision making.* New York: Wiley.

Fishburn, P. C. (1973). Binary choice probabilities: On the varieties of stochastic transitivity. *Journal of Mathematical Psychology, 10,* 327–352.

Fishburn, P. C. (1988). *Nonlinear preference and utility theory.* Baltimore, MD: Johns Hopkins Press.

Fourier, J. (1955). *The analytical theory of heat* (A. Freeman, Trans.). New York: Stechert. (Original work published 1822)

Gauss, K. F. (1821/1957). *Theory of least squares* (H. F. Trotter, Trans.). Princeton, NJ: Princeton University Press.

Gerlach, M. W. (1957). *Interval measurement of subjective magnitudes with subliminal differences* (Tech. Rep. No. 7). Stanford, CA: Stanford University, Behavioral Sciences Division, Applied Mathematics and Statistics Laboratory.

Goodman, N. (1951). *Structure of appearance.* Cambridge: Harvard University Press.

Grassmann, H. G. (1895). *Die Wissenschaft der Extensiven Grösse oder die Ausdehnungslehre,* republished in *Gesammelte Mathematische und Physikalische Werke.* Leipzig. (Original work published 1844)

Green, D. M., & Swets, J. A. (1974). *Signal detection theory and psychophysics.* Huntington, NY: Krieger. (Original work published 1966)

Halphen, E. (1955). La notion de vraisemblance. *Publication de l'Institut de Statistique de l'Université de Paris, 4,* 41–92.

Heisenberg, W. (1930). *Quantum theory.* Chicago: University of Chicago Press.

Helmholtz, H. V. (1887). Zählen und Messen erkenntnis-theoretisch betrachet. *Philosophische Aufsätze Eduard Zeller gewidmet,* Leipzig. Reprinted in *Gesammelte Abhandl.,* Vol. 3, 1895, 356–391. [English translation by C. L. Bryan, *Counting and Measuring.* Princeton, New Jersey: van Nostrand, 1930.]

Hilbert, D. (1899). *Grundlagen der Geometrie* (8th edition, with revisions and supplements by P. Bernays, 1956). Stuttgart: Teubner.

Hölder, O. (1901). Die Axiome der Quantität und die Lehre vom Mass. *Berichte über die Verhandlungen der Königlich Sächsischen Gesellschaft der Wissenschaften zu Leipzig, Mathematische-Physische Klasse, 53,* 1–64.

Iverson, G., & Falmagne, J.-C. (1985). Statistical issues in measurement. *Mathematical Social Sciences, 10,* 131–153.

Iverson, G., & Luce, R. D. (1998). The representational measurement approach to psychophysical and judgment problems. In M. H. Birnbaum (Ed.), *Measurement, judgment, and decision making* (pp. 1–79). San Diego: Academic Press.

Klein, F. (1872/1893). A comparative review of recent researches in geometry. *Bulletin of the New York Mathematical Society, 2,* 215–249.

Krantz, D. H. (1972). A theory of magnitude estimation and cross-modality matching. *Journal of Mathematical Psychology, 9,* 168–199.

Krantz, D. H., Luce, R. D., Suppes, P., & Tversky, A. (1971). *Foundations of measurement, Vol. I.* New York: Academic Press.

Luce, R. D. (1956). Semiorders and a theory of utility discrimination. *Econometrica, 24,* 178–191.

Luce, R. D. (1959). On the possible psychophysical laws. *Psychological Review, 66,* 81–95.

Luce, R. D. (1990). "On the possible psychophysical laws" revisited: Remarks on cross-modal matching. *Psychological Review, 97,* 66–77.

Luce, R. D. (1992). Singular points in generalized concatenation structures that otherwise are homogeneous. *Mathematical Social Sciences, 24,* 79–103.

Luce, R. D. (2000). *Utility of gains and losses: Measurement-theoretical and experimental approaches.* Mahwah, NJ: Erlbaum. [Errata: see Luce's Web page at http://socsci.uci.edu.]

Luce, R. D. (2001). A psychophysical theory of intensity proportions, joint presentations, and matches. *Psychological Review,* in press.

Luce, R. D., & Edwards, W. (1958). The derivation of subjective scales from just-noticeable differences. *Psychological Review, 65,* 227–237.

Luce, R. D., & Fishburn, P. C. (1991). Rank- and sign-dependent linear utility models for finite first-order gambles. *Journal of Risk and Uncertainty, 4,* 29–59.

Luce, R. D., Krantz, D. H., Suppes, P., & Tversky, A. (1990). *Foundations of measurement, Vol. III.* San Diego: Academic Press.

Luce, R. D., & Tukey, J. (1964). Simultaneous conjoint measurement: A new type of fundamental measurement. *Journal of Mathematical Psychology, 1,* 1–27.

Macmillan, N. A., & Creelman, C. D. (1991). *Detection theory: A user's guide.* Cambridge: Cambridge University Press.

Marley, A. A. J. (1993). Aggregation theorems and the combination of probabilistic rank orders. In D. E. Critchlow, M. A. Fligner, & J. S. Verducci (Eds.), *Probability models and statistical analyses for ranking data* (pp. 216–240). New York: Springer.

Maxwell, J. C. (1873). *A Treatise on electricity and magnetism.* London: Oxford University Press.

Michell, J. (1990). *An introduction to the logic of psychological measurement.* Hillsdale, NJ: Erlbaum.

Michell, J. (1999). *Measurement in psychology: A critical history of a methodological concept.* Cambridge: Cambridge University Press.

Moody, E., and Claggett, M. (Eds.). (1952). *The medieval science of weights (scientia de ponderibus): Treatises ascribed to Euclid, Archimedes, Thabit ibn Qurra, Jordanus de Nemore, and Blasius of Parma.* Madison: University of Wisconsin Press.

Narens, L. (1981a). A general theory of ratio scablity with remarks about the measurement-theoretic concept of meaningfulness. *Theory and Decision, 13,* 1–70.

Narens, L. (1981b). On the scales of measurement. *Journal of Mathematical Psychology, 24,* 249–275.

Narens, L. (1985). *Abstract measurement theory.* Cambridge: MIT Press.

Narens, L. (1996). A theory of magnitude estimation. *Journal of Mathematical Psychology, 40,* 109–129.

Narens, L. (2001). *Theories of meaningfulness.* Mahwah, NJ: Erlbaum, in press.

Niederée, R., & Heyer, D. (1997). Generalized random utility models and the representational theory of measurement: A conceptual link, In A. A. J. Marley (Ed.), *Choice, decision, and measurement: Essays in honor of R. Duncan Luce* (pp. 153–187). Mahwah, NJ: Erlbaum.

O'Brien, D. (1981). *Theories of weight in the ancient world.* Paris: Les Belles Lettres.

Padoa, A. (1902). Un nouveau système irreductible de postulats pour l'algèbre. *Compte Rendu du deuxième Congres International de Mathématiciens,* 249–256.

Pasch, M. (1882). *Vorlesungen über Neuere Geometrie.* Leipzig: Springer.

Pfanzagl, J. (1959). A general theory of measurement-applications to utility. *Naval Research Logistics Quarterly, 6,* 283–294.

Pfanzagl, J. (1968). *Theory of measurement.* New York: Wiley.

Plateau, J. A. F. (1872). Sur la measure des sensations physiques, et sur loi qui lie l'intensité de ces sensation à l'intensité de la cause excitante. *Bulletin de l'Academie Royale de Belgique, 33,* 376–388.

Quiggin, J. (1993). *Generalized expected utility theory: The rank-dependent model.* Boston: Kluwer.

Ramsey, F. P. (1931). Truth and probability. In F. P. Ramsey (Ed.), *The foundations of mathematics and other logical essays* (pp. 156–198). New York: Harcourt, Brace.

Regenwetter, M. (1997). Random utility representations of finite n-ary relations. *Journal of Mathematical Psychology, 40,* 219–234.

Regenwetter, M., & Marley, A. A. J. (in press). Random relations, random utilities, and random functions. *Journal of Mathematical Psychology.*

Roberts, F. S. (1968). *Representations of indifference relations.* Unpublished doctoral dissertation, Stanford University, Stanford, CA.

Roberts, F. S. (1969). Indifference graphs. In F. Harary (Ed.), *Proof techniques in graph theory* (pp. 139–146). New York: Academic Press.

Roberts, F. S., & Luce, R. D. (1968). Axiomatic thermodynamics and extensive measurement. *Synthese, 18,* 311–326.

Rozeboom, W. E. (1962). The untenability of Luce's principle. *Psychological Review, 69,* 542–547. [With a reply by Luce, 548–551, and an additional comment by Rozeboom, 552].

Savage, L. J. (1954). *The foundations of statistics.* New York: Wiley.

Scott, D., & Suppes, P. (1958). Foundational aspects of theories of measurement. *Journal of Symbolic Logic, 23,* 113–128.

Shepard, R. N. (1981). Psychophysical relations and psychophysical scales: On the status of "direct" psychophysical measurement. *Journal of Mathematical Psychology, 24,* 21–57.

Stevens, S. S. (1951). Mathematics, measurement and psychophysics. In S. S. Stevens (Ed.), *Handbook of experimental psychology* (pp. 1–49). New York: Wiley.

Stevens, S. S. (1959). Measurement, psychophysics and utility. In C. W. Churchman & P. Ratoosh (Eds.), *Measurement: Definitions and theories* (pp. 18–64). New York: Wiley.

Stevens, S. S. (1975). *Psychophysics: Introduction to its perceptual, neural, and social prospects.* New York: Wiley.

Suck, R. (1998). A qualitative characterization of the exponential distribution, *Journal of Mathematical Psychology, 42,* 418–431.

Suppes, P. (1999). *Introduction to logic.* New York: Dover. (Original work published 1957)

Suppes, P. (1980). Limitations of the axiomatic method in ancient Greek mathematical sciences. In P. Suppes (Ed.), *Models and methods in the philosophy of science: Selected essays* (pp. 25–40). Dordrecht, Netherlands: Kluwer.

Suppes, P. (1987), Propensity representations of probability. *Erkenntnis, 26,* 335–358.

Suppes, P., & Alechina, N. (1994). The definability of the qualitative independence of events in terms of extended indicator functions. *Journal of Mathematical Psychology, 38,* 366–376.

Suppes, P., Krantz, D. H., Luce, R. D., & Tversky, A. (1990). *Foundations of measurement, Vol. II.* San Diego: Academic Press.

Thurstone, L. L. (1927a). A law of comparative judgement. *Psychological Review, 34,* 273–287.

Thurstone, L. L. (1927b). Psychophysical analysis. *American Journal of Psychology, 38,* 368–389.

Thurstone, L. L. (1927c). Three psychophysical laws. *Psychological Review, 34,* 424–432.

Thurstone, L. L. (1959). *The measurement of values.* Chicago: University of Chicago Press.

Titiev, R. J. (1972). Measurement structures in classes that are not universally axiomatizable. *Journal of Mathematical Psychology, 9,* 200–205.

Titiev, R. J. (1980). Computer-assisted results about universal axiomatizability and the three-dimensional city-block metric. *Journal of Mathematical Psychology, 22,* 209–217.

Todhunter, I. (1949). *A history of the mathematical theory of probability.* New York: Chelsea. (Original work published 1865)

von Neumann, J. (1932/1955). *Mathematical foundations of quantum mechanics* (R. T. Byer, Trans.). Princeton: Princeton University Press.

von Neumann, J., & Morgenstern, O. (1947). *The theory of games and economic behavior.* Princeton, NJ: Princeton University Press.

Wakker, P. P. (1989). *Additive representations of preferences: A new foundation of decision analysis.* Dordrecht, Netherlands: Kluwer Academic Publishers.

Wiener, N. (1915). Studies in synthetic logic. *Procedings of the Cambridge Philosophical Society, 18,* 14–28.

Wiener, N. (1921). A new theory of measurement: A study in the logic of mathematics. *Proceedings of the London Mathematical Society, 17,* 181–205.

CHAPTER 2

Signal Detection Theory

NEIL A. MACMILLAN

To err is human, and psychologists routinely take advantage of this inconsistency: Accuracy is one of the two primary dependent variables in behavioral research (response time being the other). If errors cannot be eliminated, an understanding of how they arise is valuable for interpreting psychological phenomena and their application to fields such as medicine and law, where the consequences of errors can be grave.

Many situations allow a choice between *kinds* of errors. In diagnosing cancer with imperfect methods, is it better to fail to detect a tumor or to detect one that is not present? Which way should an eyewitness lean—toward failing to report recognizing someone who has perpetrated a crime, or toward accusing someone who was not the criminal? Error tradeoffs are also evident in the laboratory; in cases of doubt, should an experimental participant report seeing an ambiguously dim light flash or remembering a vaguely familiar face? That such choices are possible makes clear the importance of decision processes in perception.

Signal detection theory (SDT) is a framework for understanding accuracy that makes the role of decision processes explicit. To do so, the theory also takes a stand on the way in which the relevant information is represented by the observer, identifying some aspects of the representation with *sensitivity,* or inherent accuracy, and others with response factors. The key assumption is that the strength of sensory and cognitive events is continuously variable. An observer who is trying to distinguish two stimulus types, for example Signal and Noise[1], is faced over trials with *distributions* of values for each possibility, as sketched in Figure 2.1. Errors arise because the Signal and Noise distributions overlap, and the degree of overlap is an inverse measure of accuracy, or sensitivity. Improvements in sensitivity can only occur if this overlap is reduced, and such reductions are often not under the immediate control of the observer.

The overlap of the distributions shown in Figure 2.1 presents the observer with a problem in choosing a response. The solution—the decision component of SDT—is to divide the strength axis into two regions with a *criterion,* so that high values lead to "yes" responses (e.g., there was a signal; I have seen this word before; there is a tumor), and low values lead to "no" responses. The observer can change the location of the criterion and thus the way in which values of the internal dimension are mapped onto responses. The theory therefore provides a conceptual distinction between sensitivity and response bias.

---

[1] Names of stimuli or stimulus sets used in experiments are capitalized.

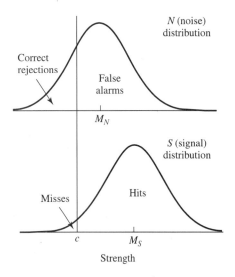

Figure 2.1   Distributions of strength for Noise and Signal.

NOTE: The upper curve is the distribution due to Noise trials; values above the criterion c lead to false alarms, and those below to correct rejections. The lower curve is the distribution due to Signal trials; values above the criterion lead to hits, those below to misses. The means of the distributions are M_N and M_S, and the variances are equal.

A central strategy in SDT research is to manipulate the presumed decision criterion through instructions or other aspects of experimental procedure in order to expose the sensitivity factors that remain unchanged. The success of this technique implies that decisional aspects can be available to conscious manipulation, but the theory itself is more general, assuming that decisions are being made whether observers know it or not.

SCOPE OF THE THEORY AND ORGANIZATION OF THE CHAPTER

This material in this chapter falls roughly into two parts, and the distinction between the parts can be viewed as one of history, methodology, or theory. The first half covers material that, for the most part, was developed earliest. Methodologically, the experimental situation is the one-interval design: On each of a succession of trials, a single stimulus is presented. In variants of this procedure, the stimulus can be one of two or drawn from a larger set, and the response can be binary or drawn from a larger set. Table 2.1 summarizes some useful terminology.

If the stimulus is one of two, the design is called *discrimination;* for example, pattern discrimination may be assessed by displaying a vertical grating on some trials and a horizontal one on others. If one of the stimulus possibilities is a "null" stimulus, the experiment is *detection,* as when the vertical grating is discriminated from an unvarying gray stimulus. Discrimination experiments are sometimes called *recognition:* in recognition memory experiments participants study a list of items and are then tested with items that may be Old (from the study list) or New (distractors, or lures). In all of these cases, the observer may be allowed just two responses, with the goal of assigning one to each stimulus, but may also be asked to express confidence that one or the other stimulus was presented using a rating scale.

Table 2.1   Terminology for One-Interval Experiments

Number of stimuli (N)	Task	Number of responses (M)	
		$M = 2$	$M > 2$
$N = 2$	Discrimination, Recognition, Detection	Yes-No	Rating, Confidence
$N > 2$	Classification, Identification	Classification	Classification ($M < N$), Identification ($M = N$)

Discrimination experiments, with and without ratings, were the grist for the early SDT program of doing away with older methods and advancing a new solution to the question of sensitivity versus bias. At the time SDT was introduced, two measures of accuracy were used commonly in attempts to take account of such contamination. In one, observed success was corrected for the degree to which it might have been inflated by guessing, which was estimated from performance on catch trials that contained no signals. The second measure, proportion correct $[p(c)]$, incorporates a similar adjustment. The latter index is of course still very popular, and most users believe it to be innocent of theory. This chapter shows that it, like the correction for guessing, implies a discrete representation in which stimuli are seen or not, remembered or not—with no possible gradations.

Many one-interval tasks employ a larger number of stimuli, to be sorted into a number of categories, M, that ranges from 2 up to N, the number of stimuli. When $M < N$, the design is called *classification,* and the $M = N$ case is called *identification,* or *absolute identification.* An important example of two-response classification is the *method of constant stimuli:* On each trial of an auditory experiment, the observer is presented with a sound having one of N intensities, and the weakest stimulus is Noise. The task is to assign one response to the Noise stimulus, the other to all the rest. In another example a continuum of speech sounds is constructed to range from /ga/ to /ka/, and the listener decides for each presentation which syllable is more likely. Either experiment can be transformed into identification (as has often been done for the auditory example and rarely for this speech example) by asking the observer to assign a distinct response to each stimulus. I consider several experiments of this type, in which all stimuli are apparently represented as differing on a single subjective characteristic, such as loudness or memory strength.

The second half of the chapter examines problems for which the representation can be thought of as multidimensional. Such representations allow for the analysis of experiments that use more than one stimulus per trial, namely, two-alternative forced-choice (2AFC), the same-different task, and the multiple-look design.

Consideration of different experimental designs raises the question of how they should be related to each other. That paradigms vary in inherent difficulty has long been recognized, and until the development of SDT this led to the conclusion that some tasks were therefore to be preferred over others. Detection theory allows the estimation of a single sensitivity index from any discrimination paradigm, and one of its most important contributions is to permit comparison of data across tasks. More broadly, discrimination tasks can be compared with classification and absolute identification. Again, SDT provides comparable sensitivity measures across tasks, but here the conclusions are discrepant: Discrimination is easier for the observer than are other resolution problems. Theories that attempt to account for this important discrepancy typically use SDT as a framework and postulate changes in representation for different tasks.

Multidimensional representations are also useful in two complementary content areas: attention and perceptual interaction. In attention, the multiple sources among which the observer must allocate resources are naturally considered as dimensions in a psychological space. The question in studies of interaction is how multiple dimensions combine. In both domains, concepts of independence are crucial.

The chapter ends with a brief discussion of statistical methods.

THE BASIC EXPERIMENT: ONE STIMULUS INTERVAL PER TRIAL

The Yes-No Design

In the simplest task that can be posed, and the one with historical precedence (Tanner & Swets, 1954), a series of trials is presented in which the Signal sometimes, but not always, appears in the Noise. The observer tries to say "yes" when a signal is present and "no" when it is not, leading to the four possible outcomes on any trial shown in Table 2.2. The total number of presentations of each stimulus type is not of interest, so the data can be reduced to proportions. As there are only two choices for the observer, the proportions of "yes" and "no" responses must add to 1, and the matrix can be summarized by two values:

$$H = \text{hit rate} = P(\text{"yes"} \mid S)$$
$$F = \text{false-alarm rate} = P(\text{"yes"} \mid N). \quad (1)$$

Normal-Distribution, Equal-Variance Representation

The most common detection-theory model assumes that repeated presentations of either stimulus give rise to equal-variance Gaussian distributions along a dimension. The addition of a Signal to the Noise increases the mean of the S distribution (M_S) compared to that of the N distribution (M_N), as shown in Figure 2.1, but in general not so much as to eliminate the region of uncertainty in which events could arise from either distribution. The observer does best (Green & Swets, 1966, chap. 2) by

Table 2.2   Possible Outcomes on a Trial of a Yes-No Experiment

Stimulus	Response	
	"yes"	"no"
S (Signal)	hit	miss
N (Noise)	false alarm	correct rejection

setting a criterion value c on the strength axis and responding "yes" for events above it and "no" for events below.

Figure 2.1 shows that the observed hit rate and false-alarm rate correspond to areas under the S and N distributions, respectively. Choosing a low, liberal location for the criterion (as in Figure 2.1) leads to high values of H and F, whereas choosing a high, conservative value leads to low ones. To express these proportions in terms of the representation, the variances of the distributions can be set equal to 1, so that the distributions are unit-normal. Letting $z(p)$ represent the z-score corresponding to a proportion p,

$$z(H) = M_S - c$$
$$z(F) = M_N - c. \quad (2)$$

The theory thus expresses the two observable pieces of data in terms of the parameters of the underlying distributions. But what aspects of the representation provide the best summary of the observer's performance?

Measures of Sensitivity and Response Bias

The true sensitivity of the observer is unaffected by criterion location and is reflected instead by the difference between the means of the two distributions, which is denoted by d' and can be derived easily from Equation (2):

$$d' = M_S - M_N = z(H) - z(F). \quad (3)$$

An important characteristic of this definition is that it expresses accuracy as the difference between the hit rate and false-alarm rate, each subjected to a transformation. In this case, the transformation, z, is the same for both proportions.

The location of the criterion is an obvious measure of response bias, the tendency to say "yes" (or "no"). To define this measure, it is necessary to decide what point on the decision axis represents 0, or no bias; a natural choice is the halfway point between the distribution means. Negative values of c thus correspond to liberal biases (as in Figure 2.1) with many "yes" responses, whereas positive values correspond to conservative biases with many "no" responses. A midpoint of 0 implies that $M_S = -M_N$, and c can be found from Equation (2) to equal

$$c = -\frac{1}{2}[z(H) + z(F)]. \qquad (4)$$

Early SDT theorists focused on an apparently separate aspect of the representation: The *likelihood ratio* is the ratio of the heights of the S and N distribution functions. As shown in Figure 2.1, this ratio increases toward the upper end of the strength axis and decreases toward the lower end. In fact, one could say that the axis that I have been calling "strength" *is* the likelihood ratio, which suggests that c and the likelihood ratio, β, should be monotonically related. The exact relation (Macmillan & Creelman, 1991, p. 40) is

$$\ln(\beta) = cd', \qquad (5)$$

where ln is the natural logarithm. Criterion location and likelihood ratio are indeed monotonic as long as d' is constant (though far from it otherwise).

How to Calculate d', c, and β

Equations (3), (4), and (5) prescribe more complex operations than those needed to compute such performance measures as proportion correct; in particular, they cannot be evaluated on most hand calculators. Tables of the normal distribution suffice, but there is another problem: If $H = 1$ or $F = 0$, as can certainly happen in experiments with small numbers of trials, z cannot be calculated. The difficulty of perfect proportions (0 or 1) discourages some potential users of SDT but need not: Some recent calculations (Kadlec, 1999b) show that a good approximation can be obtained by adding and subtracting 0.5 to

the frequency matrix when necessary. (An alternative correction is to add 0.5 to all cells, as is done in log-linear statistical analysis [see also Snodgrass and Corwin, 1988].) Examples of this adjustment for two sample data matrices follow:

	"yes"	"no"		"yes"	"no"
S	10	0	$\rightarrow$	9.5	0.5
N	2	8		2	8

	"yes"	"no"		"yes"	"no"
S	9	1	$\rightarrow$	9	1
N	0	10		0.5	9.5

A simple way to compute SDT statistics is with a spreadsheet; this is especially appealing for the many laboratories in which the data themselves are collected or stored in spreadsheets. Basic calculations are illustrated in Table 2.3 for QuattroPro, but are very similar in Excel and other programs. The function z is written @NORMSINV, and the height of the distribution is @NORMSDIST. The indexes to be entered or computed are listed in column A, and formulas are given that can be inserted in rows 5 through 11 of column B, then copied to subsequent columns. Sorkin (1999) has explored the use of spreadsheets for SDT calculations in greater detail.

Evaluating Sensitivity Measures: Receiver Operating Characteristic Curves

What justifies the use of d' as a measure of accuracy? As the criterion moves from right to left along the decision axis of Figure 2.2, both H and F increase. The relation between them is called a *receiver operating characteristic* (ROC), examples of which are shown in Figure 2.2a. The form of this curve that is predicted by SDT can be found from Equation (2) and is easier to evaluate if the coordinates are

Table 2.3 Formulas for Spreadsheet Calculation of SDT Statistics, with Examples

	A (labels only)	Formula (for column B; then copy to C and other columns)	B (Set 1)	C (Set 2)
1	#hits		10	9
2	#misses		0	1
3	# false alarms		2	0
4	#correct rejections		8	10
5	H (hit rate)	@IF(B2 > 0, B1/(B1 + B2), (B1 − 0.5)/(B1 + B2))	0.950	.900
6	F (false-alarm rate)	@IF(B3 > 0, B3/(B3 + B4), 0.5/(B3 + B4))	0.200	.050
7	$z(H)$	@NORMSINV(B5)	1.645	1.282
8	$z(F)$	@NORMSINV(B6)	−0.842	−1.645
9	d'	(B7 − B8)	2.486	2.926
10	c	(−0.5)*(B7 + B8)	−0.220	0.182
11	β	@EXP(B9*B10)	0.579	1.703

transformed to z scores. Equation (3) can be rewritten as

$$z(H) = d' + z(F), \qquad (6)$$

which is a straight line with unit slope and intercept d' (Figure 2.2b). Early ROC data in auditory and visual detection experiments often conformed to this shape, or at least were far better described in this way than by the predictions of competing theories.

Predicting Sensitivity and Bias Measures from Experimental Variables

Having decided on appropriate statistics for sensitivity and response bias, can one predict their *values* from aspects of the experiment? Predicting sensitivity requires development of an ideal-observer model that calculates optimal d' from stimulus characteristics. This approach has been most successful in sensory experiments, with either stimulus

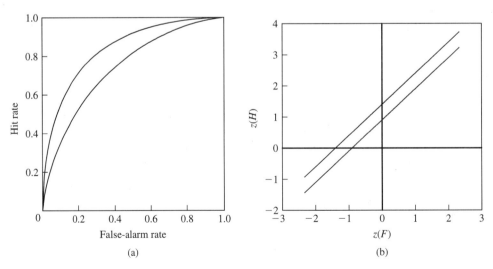

(a)   (b)

Figure 2.2 Receiver operating characteristics (ROCs) for two normal distributions with the same variance. (a) Probability coordinates. (b) z coordinates.

NOTE: In both panels, the two curves are for $d' = 0.9$ (lower curve) and 1.4 (higher curve).

characteristics or neural modeling as the presumed basis for the observer's decision. Detection of a tone signal in a noise background is well predicted by an energy-detector model, according to which the energy in the observation interval is the only information used in a decision (Green, McKey, & Licklider, 1959). The approach can be extended beyond the stimulus to multiple levels of processing: Geisler and Chou (1995) were able to predict performance in complex visual search tasks involving stimuli that differed in color and orientation from discrimination accuracy for these attributes. Thus, "low-level" tasks were enough to construct an ideal observer for "high-level" ones.

To predict response bias, one must know the goal of the observer, whose strategies will depend on how the possible experimental outcomes are understood. For example, minimizing false alarms requires a high criterion, whereas minimizing misses requires a low one. A quantitative prediction can be derived by assigning numerical values to the outcomes; concretely, the observer can be rewarded with "payoffs," financial incentives and disincentives. A payoff matrix designed to inhibit false alarms is shown in Table 2.4.

The optimal value of likelihood ratio depends on these payoffs, and also on the relative probability with which the signal is presented: It is reasonable to respond "yes" more often if there are a lot of signals. Green and Swets (1966) showed that the optimal value is

$$\beta = \{[V(\text{correct rejection}) - V(\text{false alarm})] \times P(N)\}/\{[V(\text{hit}) - V(\text{miss})]P(S)\}, \quad (7)$$

where V is the financial value associated with an outcome. For example, if three quarters of the trials contain a signal and the payoff matrix in Table 2.4 is in effect, the optimal value of β is $(0.15)(.25)/[(0.06)(.75)] = 0.833$. This is slightly liberal (below the equal-bias point, where $\beta = 1$), indicating that the asymmetric presentation probabilities favoring "yes" outweigh the asymmetric payoffs favoring "no." For a given d', the exact hit rate and false-alarm rate can be predicted: For example, if $d' = 1$, then c is found from Equation (5) to be $-.182$, and Equation (2) leads to $H = .75$ and $F = .38$.

Most subjects are conservative in responding to payoffs; that is, they do not adopt criteria that are as extreme as would be optimal (Green & Swets, 1966). Altering presentation probabilities can also help to control response bias; criteria are lower when Signals are more likely. However, this manipulation appears to have multiple effects, affecting sensitivity as well as response bias (Dusoir, 1983; Markowitz & Swets, 1967; Van Zandt, 2000).

The Rating Design

Being able to examine complete ROC curves is advantageous for many reasons. First, the results are not restricted to a single, possibly unusual, hit, false-alarm pair. Second, a full ROC allows calculation of what is in many applications the best single measure of accuracy, the area under the curve (Swets, 1986; Swets, Dawes, & Monahan, 2000). Third, in some content areas the exact shape of the ROC is predicted from one or more theories, as in recognition memory (Ratcliff, Sheu, & Gronlund, 1992; Yonelinas, 1994). To generate an ROC, it is necessary for response bias to be manipulated, and a straightforward but expensive way to accomplish this is to conduct separate experimental conditions for several different payoffs or instructions. But if observers can adopt multiple criteria in separate conditions, they may be able to use several

Table 2.4   Possible Outcomes on a Trial of a Yes-No Experiment

	Response	
Stimulus	"yes"	"no"
S	$0.05	−$0.01
N	−$0.10	$0.05

criteria simultaneously, a possibility that motivates the rating experiment.

Experimental Design

In the one-interval rating experiment, the observer is still presented with a sample of Noise or Signal, but the response set varies from great confidence in one alternative to great confidence in the other. A set of numerals ("1" to "6" is common) or phrases ("sure it was signal," "might have been Signal,"...,"sure it was Noise") may be used. Alternatively, the observer may make two responses on each trial, first "yes" or "no", and then a level of confidence in that response, for example "1" for high, "2" for medium, and "3" for low confidence. No matter what the experimental realization, the data can be represented as a stimulus-response matrix, with successive responses corresponding to decreasing levels of confidence that a signal was presented, as shown in Table 2.5. The entries $f(S, i)$ and $f(N, i)$ are the frequencies of response i when S and N are presented, and $T(S)$ and $T(N)$ are the total numbers of S and N trials.

To generate an ROC curve, these data are treated as though they arose from a series of yes-no experiments. The lowest point arises if response "1" is treated as a "yes" and the other responses as "no." To obtain the next point, responses "1" and "2" correspond to "yes," and so forth. In general, for the kth point,

$$H = \sum_{i=1}^{k} f(S, i)/T(S)$$

$$F = \sum_{i=1}^{k} f(N, i)/T(N)$$

(8)

For computational examples of rating experiments, see Macmillan and Creelman (1991, in press).

It is, of course, an empirical question whether an ROC generated in this way is the same as one generated from a series of yes-no experiments. Early experiments (Egan, Schulman, & Greenberg, 1959) showed good equivalence of rating data to yes-no data obtained with different instructions or payoffs. The rating experiment is far more efficient than the other methods, in that a single experimental run can produce an entire ROC curve, and is the favorite in practice.

Normal-Distribution Unequal-Variance Representation

The ROC shape found with almost all methods and in almost all areas of application is a straight line on z-coordinates, as is expected if the underlying distributions are normal. The equal-variance model (Equation [6]) also implies that the slope of the zROC should equal 1, however, and this prediction is often not confirmed. If the slope of the line is s, then a change of one z-unit on the F axis leads to a change of s units on the H axis. Moving along the zROC corresponds to moving the criterion along the decision axis, so a change of one unit on this axis relative to the N distribution equals a change of s units relative to the S distribution. The inferred representation still has two normal distributions, but with unequal variances $[\sigma^2(S) \neq \sigma^2(N)]$, and the slope of the ROC, s, is the ratio of the standard deviations, $\sigma(N)/\sigma(S)$. Figure 2.3 shows an unequal-variance representation and its ROC.

How can the accuracy of the observer in Figure 2.3 be summarized? In the

Table 2.5   A Stimulus-Response Matrix for Two Versions of the Rating Experiment

Response	Numerals	"1"	"2"	"3"	"4"	"5"	"6"	Total
	Dual	"yes, 1"	"yes, 2"	"yes, 3"	"no, 3"	"no, 2"	"no, 1"	
Stimulus	S	$f(S, 1)$	$f(S, 2)$	$f(S, 3)$	$f(S, 4)$	$f(S, 5)$	$f(S, 6)$	$T(S) = \Sigma f(S, i)$
	N	$f(N, 1)$	$f(N, 2)$	$f(N, 3)$	$f(N, 4)$	$f(N, 5)$	$f(N, 6)$	$T(N) = \Sigma f(N, i)$

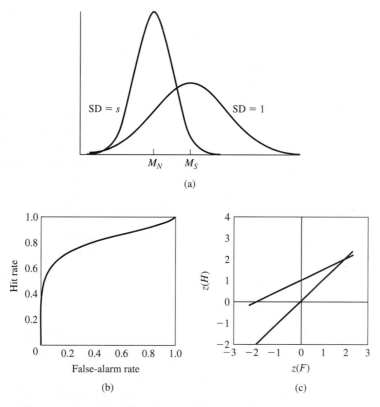

Figure 2.3 (a) Two normal distributions with unequal variance. (b) The corresponding ROC on probability coordinates. (c) The ROC on z coordinates.
NOTE: The ratio of the standard deviations $s = .5$, and sensitivity $d_a = 1.26$.

equal-variance case, sensitivity is the difference between the zROC $[z(H) = z(F) + d']$ and the chance line $[z(H) = z(F)]$, and it always equals d' (see Figure 2.2b). In the unequal-variance case, however, this difference is a function of location on the curve (Figure 2.3c) and thus is not bias-free. In terms of the representation, the difference between the means of the S and N distributions, ΔM, is still appropriate as a sensitivity parameter because it is not affected by criterion location. This difference must be divided by a standard deviation; a common statistic, d_a, uses the root-mean-square average of the standard deviations of S and N:

Computationally, d_a can be estimated using a maximum-likelihood procedure first developed by Dorfman and Alf (1969). Current programs are available at http://www.radiology.arizona.edu/~eye-mo/rocprog.htm.

The rationale for d_a is not just heuristic. Green (1964) showed that the area under the yes-no (or rating) ROC equals the proportion correct in a two-interval forced-choice experiment (discussed later in this chapter) by an unbiased observer, a plausible nonparametric measure of sensitivity. If the representation is as shown in Figure 2.3a, this area A_z is monotonically related to d_a (Swets & Pickett, 1982):

$$d_a = \Delta M/(1 + s^2)^{1/2} \qquad (9)$$

$$d_a = \sqrt{2}\, z(A_z). \qquad (10)$$

The area A_z is, like the other accuracy indexes discussed so far, based on the assumption of normal distributions; I consider some area measures that either are or claim to be nonparametric shortly. The monotonic relation between the statistics A_z and d_a, one an area and the other a distance, means that (for a given value of s) they have the same implied ROC. Measures with this characteristic are said to be *equivalent:* If one is a bias-free measure of accuracy, so is the other.

In general, three aspects of sensitivity measures are interrelated: the statistic itself, the ROC that it implies, and the representation that it assumes. In the present example, the statistic d_a implies normal distributions and a linear zROC, and the use of d' is a further commitment to equal-variance distributions and unit-slope ROCs. To decide between these measures requires collecting an ROC curve; without information about how performance changes with bias, an appropriate measure of accuracy cannot be determined.

The rating experiment does allow, however, for accuracy statistics that are not model-dependent. We have seen that the true area under the ROC is a nonparametric index of accuracy, and if there are enough data points, this can be estimated without fitting a theoretical model. Balakrishnan (1998) developed a related measure for the dual-response version of the rating paradigm. The separate distributions of confidence ratings for Signal and Noise take over the role of the hypothetical distributions in SDT. The difference between the cumulative distributions of these ratings measures the discrepancy between the hit rate and false-alarm rate at each level of confidence. The sum of these differences is S', an estimate of the difference between the two confidence distributions under the assumption that the criteria used by the observer are equally spaced. In simulations, Balakrishnan showed that S' did a better job than d' of rank ordering conditions that differed slightly in sensitivity. A similar strategy, applied to the two-response rating design ("yes" or "no" followed by a confidence judgment), leads to a nonparametric measure of response bias.

MODELS WITH SIMPLER ASSUMPTIONS (OR NONE AT ALL?)

Although this chapter is largely restricted to SDT itself, two alternative approaches are treated briefly here. The first is *threshold theory,* in which the continuous representation of SDT is replaced by a small set of discrete states. The theory is important both because it is usually wrong (most ROC data contradict this representation) and because it is sometimes right (some ROC data are consistent with it). The second approach is not a theory, but an attempt to find measures of accuracy that are not at all dependent on theory. "Nonparametric" measures for the yes-no design have turned out, on examination, to be equivalent to threshold theory, SDT variants, or a combination of the two.

Thresholds, High and Low

High-Threshold Theory

The idea of a threshold, a fixed level dividing sensation from its absence, received its most explicit treatment from Blackwell (1963). In Blackwell's version, a signal presentation sometimes leads to an above-threshold event, but noise alone never does; in this sense, the threshold is high. False alarms occur because of guessing, a strategy that also inflates the hit rate. This theory captured the contemporary intuitions about detection experiments and was easy to test.

Because threshold-theory representations have only a small number of internal events, it is convenient to express them as flow charts, or state diagrams, as in Table 2.6. In high-threshold theory, there are two internal states,

Table 2.6   State Diagram for High-Threshold Theory

Stimulus	Internal event	$P(\text{event})$	$P(\text{"yes"} \mid \text{event})$	$P(\text{"yes"})$
S	Detect	q_s	1	q_s
	Nondetect	$1 - q_s$	u	$u(1 - q_s)$
N	Detect	0	1	0
	Nondetect	·1	u	u

Detect and Nondetect. Signals are detected with probability q_s; noise is never detected. Detections always lead to the "yes" response, but the observer also responds "yes" to a proportion u of nondetections, whether these events arise from Signal or Noise. The hit rate and false-alarm rate are

$$H = q_s + u(1 - q_s)$$
$$F = u. \tag{11}$$

Equation (11) is easily transformed into the predicted ROC:

$$H = q_s + (1 - q_s)F, \tag{12}$$

which is a straight line from the point $(0, q_s)$ to $(1, 1)$ in ROC space (Figure 2.4). One of SDT's early successes was the demonstration that empirical ROCs did not have this form, but were well described instead by the normal-normal shape of Figures 2.2 and 2.3.

Equation (12), solved for q_s, is sometimes used to correct observed hit rates for guessing. The method can be extended to multiple-choice examinations, in which the guess rate is 1 over the number of alternative answers. Many who use this correction for guessing view it as atheoretical, but it makes a strong assumption that is rarely honored in practice: that the test taker is truly guessing (i.e., has no partial information) when a Nondetection occurs. In an early auditory detection experiment, Swets, Tanner, and Birdsall (1961) showed that, contrary to this assumption, listeners' second-choice responses in a four-alternative paradigm were more accurate than chance. Together with the failure of ROC experiments to follow the form of Equation (12), this result is strong evidence that the correction for guessing should not be used.

A Three-State, Double-Threshold Model

The idea of a small number of internal states can be used to generate theories that are not so easily rejected. Luce (1963b) introduced the idea of a low threshold that allowed Noise trials to lead sometimes to the Detect state. One way in which a low threshold can be added to the high-threshold model is to suppose that the observer has three states: Detect, Uncertain, and Nondetect. Signals never fall below threshold into the Nondetect state (a high-threshold assumption), but may lead to either a Detect or an Uncertain state (low-threshold). Noise never exceeds threshold (high) but may lead to either Nondetect or Uncertain (low). Table 2.7 gives the state diagram, which leads to the hit rate and

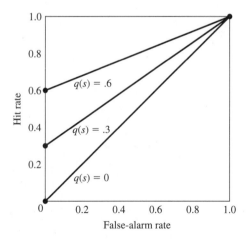

Figure 2.4   Predicted ROCs for high-threshold theory, for three values of the sensitivity parameter q_s.

Table 2.7   State Diagram for Double-Threshold Theory

Stimulus	Internal Event	P(event)	P("yes" | event)	P("yes")
S	Detect	q_s	1	q_s
	Uncertain	$1 - q_s$	u	$u(1 - q_s)$
	Nondetect	0	0	0
N	Detect	0	1	0
	Uncertain	q_n	u	uq_n
	Nondetect	$1 - q_n$	0	0

false-alarm rate:

$$H = q_s + u(1 - q_s)$$
$$F = uq_n. \qquad (13)$$

The most conservative response strategy, setting u to 0, leads to the point $(0, q_s)$; the most liberal, $u = 1$, leads to the point $(q_n, 1)$; and other values of u track a line segment between these two points. ROCs of this form have (to my knowledge) never been reported in perception experiments but *are* found in certain studies of recognition memory. Figure 2.5 displays both curvilinear (left panel) and linear (right panel) ROCs reported for different recognition tasks by Yonelinas (1997). In a conventional task in which single words were presented, the data are well-described by a normal-distribution model, but in associative recognition, in which pairs of words were to be remembered, a double-threshold model provides a better fit. This finding means that when word pairs are recollected with highest confidence as having been in the study list, or when they are recollected with highest confidence as *not* having been in the list, no errors are made. Thus, there must be very high-fidelity Detect and Nondetect states, as in the double-threshold model. Single words, on the other hand, display a continuous ROC, consistent with a graded strength axis. Other recognition-memory ROCs with threshold features have been reported by Yonelinas (1994) and Rotello, Macmillan, and Van Tassel (2000).

The double-threshold model is most often employed implicitly, without collecting ROCs. Suppose sensitivity is the same for both

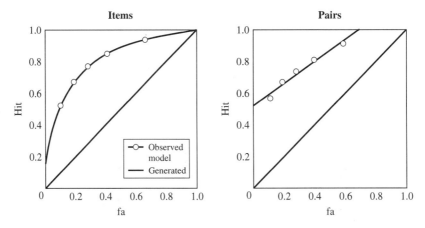

Figure 2.5   ROCs obtained by Yonelinas (1997) for recognition memory of single words (left panel) and word pairs (right panel). Reprinted by permission.

stimulus alternatives, so that $q_s = 1 - q_n = q$. Assuming equal presentation probabilities, the proportion correct equals the average of the hit rate and correct-rejection rate; using Equation (13), this equals

$$p(c) = \frac{1}{2}[H + (1 - F)] = \frac{1}{2}[q + 1]. \quad (14)$$

Equation (14) shows $p(c)$ and q to be equivalent, so the use of $p(c)$ as a measure of accuracy implies an ROC like that in Figure 2.5b, but parallel to the chance line. Except in rare cases, such ROCs are not found, and $p(c)$ is thus not a pure measure of accuracy. It is least problematic when the observer is unbiased, so that performance is near the minor diagonal in ROC space. Note that $p(c)$, like d', equals the difference between the transformed hit rate and false-alarm rate; in this case, however, the transformation is the identity function, and $p(c)$ depends simply on $H - F$.

Measures Based on ROC-Space Areas for Single ROC Points

The area under the ROC is an appealing measure of sensitivity in the rating experiment and can be assumption-free with a large number of ROC points. This section considers ROC area measures of sensitivity and bias for *single* hit/false-alarm pairs that were developed without recourse to psychophysical theory. For the most part, these "nonparametric" indexes turn out to be equivalent to parameters of a standard SDT model with underlying distributions that are close to normal in shape.

If only one point in ROC space is obtained in an experiment, there are many possible ROCs on which it could lie, and some assumptions must be made to estimate the area under the ROC. One possibility is to find the smallest possible area consistent with that point. As shown in Figure 2.6, this is equivalent to finding the area under the two-limbed ROC for which the obtained point forms the

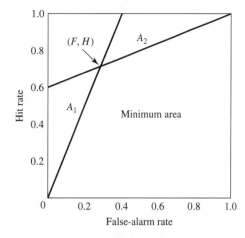

Figure 2.6 Calculation of the area under the ROC containing the single point (F, H).
NOTE: The minimum is the area under the quadrilateral below and to the right of (F, H); the statistic A' is the minimum area plus one-half the sum of areas A_1 and A_2.

corner. When presentation probabilities are equal, this area turns out to equal proportion correct, a measure already shown to imply a threshold model.

A better estimate, proposed by Pollack and Norman (1964), is also diagrammed in Figure 2.6. Their measure A' is a kind of average between minimum and maximum performance. Macmillan and Creelman (1996) have shown that A' (for above-chance performance) can be written as a function of two other sensitivity measures. One is $p(c)$, and the other is the parameter α of choice theory (Luce, 1959, 1963a), which is the analog of d' if the underlying distributions are logistic in form rather than normal. The relation is

$$A' = \frac{1}{2} + \frac{1}{2} p(c)(1 - \alpha^{-2}). \quad (15)$$

At low sensitivity, this expression is dominated by α, whereas at high sensitivities $p(c)$ is more important. The shift is illustrated in Figure 2.7, which shows the implied ROCs for A' on the same plot as those for α (panel a)

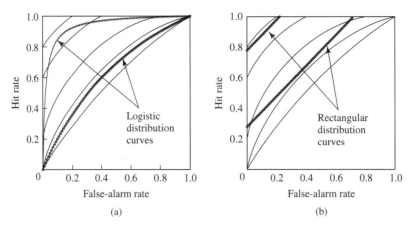

Figure 2.7   Families of ROC curves implied by A'.

NOTE: In panel (a), ROCs for two values of α (logistic sensitivity) are also shown; in panel (b), ROCs for two levels of $p(c)$ are shown. The comparison shows that A' is approximately consistent with an SDT model at low levels, and with a threshold model at high levels.

and $p(c)$ (panel b). At low levels, a constant-A' ROC is very similar to a constant-α curve, which is in turn very similar to a constant-d' curve. At high levels, it is quite similar to a constant-$p(c)$ curve.

One appeal of the area measure is that, unlike d', it can be calculated directly even when the observed hit or correct-rejection rate is 1.0. Unfortunately, perfect performance on one of the two stimulus classes tends to mean high performance overall, and it is for high values that A' has undesirable, threshold-like characteristics. At low performance levels, A' is much like α (and thus much like d'). In neither case is it assumption-free.

Several bias measures have been proposed as companion statistics to A'. The most popular is B'' (Grier, 1971), which is equivalent to B'_H, suggested by Hodos (1970). In fact, B'' is only superficially related to A', but is equivalent to the logistic likelihood ratio (Macmillan & Creelman, 1990, 1996). A different measure based on ROC geometry, proposed by Donaldson (1992), is equivalent to the logistic criterion b.

Two conclusions appear justified: First, there are no "nonparametric" measures of sensitivity or bias in the yes-no experiment, because any candidate index is consistent with some representations and not others. Second, there *is* such a measure in the rating experiment—area under the multipoint ROC—and the collection of rating data in discrimination experiments is therefore well worth the slight additional effort.

One-Dimensional Identification and Classification

In a classification experiment, observers use M responses to sort N stimuli into categories, and in an identification experiment, $M = N$. We first consider classification experiments with one-dimensional stimulus sets, that is, stimuli that differ for the participant in only one characteristic. Detection theory allows a theoretical meaning to be assigned to the term "one-dimensional," as Figure 2.8 illustrates. The sensitivity statistic d' is a distance measure, and distances along a single dimension add up. Thus if $S_1, S_2,$ and S_3 give rise to distributions along a continuum, with their means in the order $\mu_1 < \mu_2 < \mu_3$, then

$$d'(1, 3) = d'(1, 2) + d'(2, 3). \qquad (16)$$

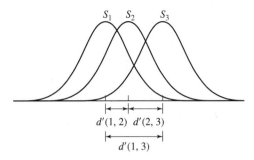

Figure 2.8 Three normal distributions on a single dimension display additivity: $d'(1, 3) = d'(1, 2) + d'(2, 3)$.

Equation (16) can be viewed as a prediction about the result of three different two-stimulus experiments, or an assumption about a single classification experiment in which all three stimuli occur. The sensitivity distance between any stimulus and the endpoint stimulus is a useful measure, *cumulative d',* that can be computed by adding up adjacent d' values. The value of cumulative d' obtained between both endpoint stimuli represents the total sensitivity of the observer to the stimulus set and is called *total d'.* Total d' is the basic measure of observer performance on the entire stimulus ensemble. If there is reason to believe that a stimulus set will lead to a one-dimensional representation, Equation (16) can be used to infer sensitivity between remote stimulus pairs (like S_1 and S_3) from sensitivities to adjacent pairs (S_1 versus S_2 and S_2 versus S_3). This is especially useful if the extreme stimuli are perfectly discriminable and cannot be directly compared.

Bias and Sensitivity in Two-Response Classification

Distinguishing bias and sensitivity is as valuable in classification and identification as it is in discrimination, but the presence of more stimuli complicates the analysis. We first con-sider the important special case in which the observer must partition the N stimuli into only two categories; according to SDT, this is accomplished by using a single criterion to divide the decision axis. Whereas the two-stimulus experiment can be summarized by just two independent proportions, the hit rate and the false-alarm rate, classification yields N values, $P(\text{"yes"} \mid S_i)$ for $S_1, S_2, \ldots, S_N$. Multiple bias and sensitivity measures can be defined.

A single proportion is enough to locate the criterion relative to the mean of a single distribution. Consider Figure 2.9a, in which the criterion is located so that $P(\text{"yes"} \mid S_1) = .31$. Because the distribution is normal, the criterion is 0.5 standard deviations above the S_1 mean. Criterion location is clearly a bias measure, and it can be calculated relative to any of the three distributions.

Sensitivity indexes require two proportions: the d' distance between stimuli S_i and S_j is the difference in the corresponding z scores, $z[P(\text{"yes"} \mid S_i)] - z[P(\text{"yes"} \mid S_j)]$. There are $N(N-1)/2$ such values, although only $N-1$ of them are independent. In Figure 2.9a, any of the three d' values can be found using the same criterion location; for example, $d'(2, 3) = z(.84) - z(.69) = 0.99 - 0.50 = 0.49$. This computation does not require that S_2 and S_3 be associated with different correct responses, or even that correct responses be defined. Dosher (1984) proposed the term *pseudo-d'* for a sensory distance estimated from two response rates identified with the same correct response.

As in discrimination, the important question in classification often concerns *changes* in bias and sensitivity across conditions. A change in bias requires only two proportions: the corresponding "yes" rates to the same stimulus in each of two conditions. In Figure 2.9b all "yes" rates, and thus all criterion locations, are different from those in Figure 2.9a, but the d' values are the same.

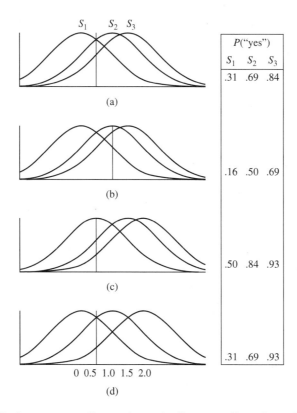

Figure 2.9 Distributions corresponding to three stimuli on one dimension, with a single criterion defining the regions leading to the two responses.

NOTE: Compared to panel (a), panel (b) shows a criterion shift, panel (c) a shift in all the distributions, and panel (d) a change in the spacing of the distributions.

In Figure 2.9c all distributions have shifted upward compared to Figure 2.9a by the same amount, but the criterion has remained the same. The data are exactly the same as if the reverse had occurred (i.e., the criterion shifted downward and the distributions remained the same). Which situation has occurred cannot be diagnosed with SDT tools.

Finally, to infer a change in sensitivity requires two d' values and thus two z-score differences. In Figure 2.9d, the S_3 distribution has moved relative to the others, and a comparison of $z[P(\text{"yes"} \mid S_3)] - z[P(\text{"yes"} \mid S_2)]$ for Figures 2.9d and 2.9a reveals the discrepancy.

Next I consider four examples of two-response classification and evaluate them according to whether they measure bias, sensitivity, or changes therein. Table 2.8 gives a prospective summary of the conclusions, which do not always agree with claims made by experimenters about such data. Throughout, the analyses use the simplest one-dimensional representation that is consistent with the results.

Psychometric Functions

Detection experiments often use N stimuli, the "weakest" of which is noise alone. The possible responses are "yes" and "no," and the data can be plotted as $P(\text{"yes"})$ against stimulus level. An example is shown in Figure 2.10a. Historically, the importance of

Table 2.8   Evaluation of Sensitivity and Bias in Two-Response Classification

Task	Measure	Number of Proportions	Conclusion
Psychometric function—detection	Absolute threshold	1	Bias
Psychometric function—discrimination	PSE	1	Bias
	JND	2	Sensitivity
Speech classification	Boundary location	1	Bias
	Trading relation	2	Change in bias? Sensitivity?
False memory	Difference between "yes" rates for two types of lures	2	Sensitivity

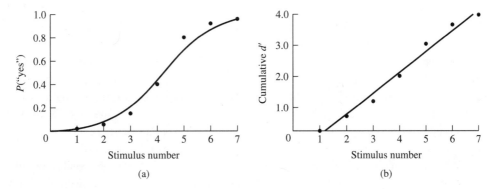

Figure 2.10   A psychometric function for detection.
NOTE: Stimulus 1 is Noise, and the other stimuli are increasing nonzero levels of intensity. In panel (a), $P(\text{"yes"})$ is plotted, in panel (b), the z score of this value is plotted. The plot in panel (b) can also be interpreted as portraying values of cumulative d'.

the noise-alone stimulus was not immediately appreciated, but from an SDT perspective it is obviously necessary to distinguish sensitivity from response bias. The observer sets a criterion along the decision axis, responding "yes" to points above and "no" to points below it. Traditionally, the datum most often abstracted from a psychometric function (*frequency-of-seeing curve,* in vision) is the (absolute) threshold, the stimulus value corresponding to some fixed performance level such as 50% "yes." This is just a bias measure, as it depends on a single proportion.

In a discrimination context, a null stimulus is not used, and it is the *difference threshold* whose value is sought.[2] Historical precedence (Fechner is responsible, according to Jones, 1974) and lasting influence belong to the *method of constant stimuli:* A standard stimulus (usually drawn from the middle of the stimulus range) is presented on each trial, and the observer labels each comparison

---

[2]Two meanings of *threshold* must be distinguished. Earlier I presented examples of threshold theories that assumed discrete representations, but here the term is used to refer to the weakest stimulus that can be detected, or discriminated, and has no theoretical implications.

stimulus as "larger" or "smaller" than the standard. The presence of standards makes no difference to SDT analysis because it gives no information regarding which response is appropriate. The 50% point is now interpreted as the point of subjective equality (PSE), the stimulus value that appears equal to the standard, another measure of bias. The difference threshold itself, the just noticeable difference (JND), is a measure of how rapidly the psychometric function increases; traditionally, it is half the difference between the 75% and 25% points. Because two proportions are involved, the JND indexes sensitivity.

A useful modification to both experiments is to change the dependent variable from a "yes" rate to d'. In the case of absolute threshold, response rates for each stimulus are compared with the false-alarm rate (that is, the "yes" rate for S_1); in the difference threshold situation, the rate corresponding to the standard stimulus is used. The resulting plot gives information about sensitivity and is also often a straight line, as in Figure 2.10b. In detection, the threshold is defined by a value of d', often 1.0. In discrimination, the PSE can also be defined this way; the JND, which is usually of more interest, is replaced by the slope of the function.

The threshold estimation methods just described are classical and are included here because they serve to illustrate one-dimensional classification. Current techniques for analyzing psychometric functions, and for finding thresholds, are more sophisticated in two ways: first, "adaptive" procedures are often used so that stimulus presentations can cluster in the region of interest, rather than being spread across a range of predetermined values. Second, psychometric functions can be fit with a curve from a known family (normal or logistic, for example), and the parameters of the best-fitting curve are used to summarize the outcome. For a sampler of current methods, see Klein and Macmillan (2001).

Two-Response Classification in Nonsensory Contexts

Two-response experiments with one-dimensional stimulus sets are common in more cognitive areas as well. This section briefly considers two examples, one from speech perception and one from recognition memory.

Trading Relations in Speech

In a common type of speech perception experiment, a set of synthetic stimuli is constructed along a continuum between two waveforms that correspond to different speech sounds. For example, a stimulus waveform perceived as /ga/ can be gradually converted into one perceived as /ka/ by lengthening voice-onset time (VOT), the amount of time between the beginning of the consonant and the onset of voicing. An apparently straightforward way to find out what a listener hears is to present a series of randomly chosen stimuli from this set and to ask whether each sounds more like /ka/ or /ga/. The result is that the proportion of trials on which "ka" is the response increases as VOT increases (Lisker, 1975).

Two features distinguish this experiment from the sensory detection example given earlier. First, there are no correct answers; the point of the experiment is to find out how each sound is perceived. Second, the psychological interest is largely in the criterion location, whereas the detection experiment measures a sensory distance (if the dependent measure is d'). The most popular dependent measure in speech classification studies of this type, sometimes called the *category boundary,* is the point at which each response is used on 50% of trials.

The perception of voicing is influenced not only by VOT but also by the frequency at which F_1, the first formant (or frequency band) begins. When Lisker (1975) redid the experiment with a higher value of F_1 onset, the percentage of "ka" responses increased across the board. Results like these are called *trading relations* (Repp, 1982) and reflect a kind of perceptual interaction between cues. If the rate of responding "yes" is increasing by the same amount (in z-score units) for all stimuli on the new continuum, then the inferred representation will be the same except for the location of the criterion (as in the comparison between Figures 2.9a and 2.9c). Whether this should be considered a criterion or sensitivity effect is unclear: It is not possible to tell whether the criterion or the distributions has moved, because only their relative location can be inferred from the data. A later section introduces approaches to measuring such interactions that are clearly sensitivity-based.

"False-Memory" Experiments

Roediger and McDermott (1995) conducted a recognition memory experiment in which the study items on each list were thematically related, for example, *bed, night, dream, blanket.* At test, one of the lures (New items) was *sleep,* the core concept to which the study items were related. (Of course, there were many such sets of critical lures and related study items.) Participants tended to recognize (incorrectly) the critical lures, such as *sleep,* at a higher rate than other lures, and sometimes at a higher rate than Old items. The experiment is of interest because it demonstrates, in a controlled situation, the phenomenon of false memory.

A natural question about false memory is whether it is a sensitivity or a response-bias effect: Do participants really remember the critical lures as having been presented, or is the finding somehow due to a bias (that could, in principle, be manipulated)? To answer this question, M. B. Miller and Wolford (1999) conducted a variant of the Roediger and McDermott (1995) experiment in which participants were presented at test with six kinds of items: Unrelated, Related, and Critical

words, each category including some words that were Old and some that were New. They then measured statistics closely related to d' and c for each type of word and found that criterion changed while sensitivity did not. Thus, the false-memory finding was attributed to response bias.

Considering the implications of assuming that a single underlying dimension is judged will help in understanding these data. In memory models, *familiarity* is often considered to be the relevant decision axis, and the familiarity of a word can be influenced by two factors: how frequently the item has occurred and the number of associated words that have recently been presented (Wixted & Stretch, 2000). Thus, New words that are Unrelated, Related, or Critical might lead to distributions like those in Figure 2.9a, whereas Old words would be shifted upwards, as in Figure 2.9c. A single criterion is of course used at test, leading to a pattern of "yes" rates that is similar to that observed by M. B. Miller and Wolford (1999).

How then did M. B. Miller and Wolford (1999) conclude that response bias was responsible? In calculating c, they found the locations of the criterion relative to the midpoint of two distributions (see Equation [4]) for each of the three distribution pairs. In Figure 2.9, this statistic decreases from .25 for S_1 to -0.75 for S_2 to -1.25 for S_3. The pattern reflects the different average locations of the Unrelated, Related, and Critical distributions on a common axis, not a change in response strategy.

The methodological importance of the example is this: Estimates of sensitivity and bias for designs using multiple stimuli must be made with reference to a representation. A representation like that in Figure 2.9, which is consistent with past work on memory for words, leads to an analysis and conclusion that are different from those of a representation that treats each of several pairs of distributions in isolation. Wixted and Stretch (2000) provide more detailed discussion.

Experiments with More than Two Responses

The assignment of many stimuli to just two responses in the examples so far seems natural; all waveforms in the speech experiment, for example, resemble either /ga/ or /ka/, not a third utterance. However, there are at least two reasons why an experimenter might prefer a number of responses closer to the size of stimulus set. First, as in two-stimulus experiment, a graded response provides more information—specifically, information from which the variances of the underlying distributions can be estimated. Second, the range of stimulus values in one-dimensional classification experiments is often large. In such cases, sensitivity to differences between stimuli that are close together in the set may be found, but not for far-apart stimuli that are never confused.

For example, Braida and Durlach (1972) conducted a series of auditory identification experiments. The largest range was 54 dB. On each trial, one stimulus was presented, and listeners tried to select the corresponding response. The number of responses varied across conditions; if it was 10, for example, then the data filled a 10×10 matrix, and although many cells contained frequencies of 0, adjacent stimuli were always confusable. ROCs generated from those pairs were described well by an equal-variance representation. Experiments of this sort permit calculation of the global sensitivity parameter, total d', the sum of values for adjacent stimuli, by repeated application of Equation (16). Braida and Durlach estimated total d' for their auditory intensity continuum to be about 13.

Note that this method of analyzing the data does not require that the number of responses M equal the number of stimuli N, only that there be enough responses so that confusions exist between each adjacent pair. Advantages of the $M = N$ case are that there are correct answers, that the proportion correct can be calculated, and that it is possible to attempt to train observers by using trial-by-trial feedback. On the other hand, detection-theory analysis puts no great stake in proportion correct, which in identification, as in discrimination, is not a true measure of accuracy.

Relation of Classification to Discrimination

Although classification and discrimination data both lead to estimates of sensitivity, they need not converge on the same truth. In detection theory, comparing classification and discrimination in detection-theoretic terms is uncomplicated: One measures d' in one experiment of each type and examines the result to see if sensitivity is constant.

In a few special cases, classification and discrimination d' are (theoretically or empirically) very nearly equivalent. Empirically, Pynn, Braida, and Durlach (1972) compared identification and discrimination of pure-tone intensity on a very small range (2.25 dB) and found close agreement. Theoretically, an influential proposal about speech perception experiments, the *categorical perception hypothesis,* says, in part, that discrimination is exactly as good as classification for some speech continua. This hypothesis has been presented in SDT language by Macmillan, Kaplan, and Creelman (1977); its original statement (Liberman, Harris, Hoffman, & Griffith, 1957) was in threshold terms.

Almost always, though, there is a large discrepancy between classification and discrimination accuracy. G. A. Miller (1956) summarized experiments showing that increases in the number of stimuli to classify led to corresponding increases in total sensitivity only up to a total of about seven stimuli. When the range of stimuli was increased beyond that point, there were no further increases in classification performance, but discrimination performance continued to improve.

Durlach and Braida (1969) offered a model that relates classification and discrimination. Although originally presented as a theory of intensity perception, the model also applies to domains as disparate as localization (Searle, Colburn, Davis, & Braida, 1976) and speech perception (Macmillan, Goldberg, & Braida, 1988). According to Durlach and Braida, fixed discrimination tasks (those using only two stimuli) measure sensory resolution, whereas classification depends on both sensory and context-coding, or labeling processes. Both sensory and context-coding processes contribute to the variance of the internal distributions, so if ΔM is the distance between the two means, B^2 is the sensory variance and C^2 is the context-coding variance, then

$$d'_{discriminate} = \Delta M / B \tag{17}$$
$$d'_{classify} = \Delta M / (B^2 + C^2)^{1/2} \tag{18}$$

Clearly, the discrepancy between fixed discrimination and identification depends on the relative magnitude of the sensory and context variance components. The *relative context variance*—the size of the context variance in units of the sensory variance—can be estimated as follows:

$$C^2 / B^2 = \left(d'_{discriminate}/d'_{classify}\right)^2 - 1. \tag{19}$$

Equation (19) can be applied to total d' values as well as d' for particular stimulus pairs, and relative context variance provides a measure of the importance of context memory for a stimulus pair or continuum. As stimulus range increases, the precision of context coding drops: Berliner and Durlach (1973) estimated relative context variance to be 47.6 when the range was 54 dB, but only 1.62 when it was 10 dB.

This descriptive approach to identification leaves open the question of mechanism. In a later version of their theory, Braida and Durlach (1988) proposed that the memory limitation arises because observers use a "noisy ruler" to locate stimuli with respect to perceptual anchors near the edges of the range. The unreliability of the measuring instrument accounts for the increase in context variance with range, and the use of anchors explains the edge effect, the common finding of better performance for extreme stimuli. An alternative theory (Luce, Green, & Weber, 1976) postulates an adjustable "attention band" that allows for high performance within a narrow range (about 10–20 dB in auditory intensity) and degraded performance elsewhere. As the range increases, the proportion that can be included in the band decreases, and so does performance. The attention-band model does not account directly for the edge advantage, but the assumption of gradual shifts in the location of the band does explain the presence of sequential effects, which are substantial in identification data. One way in which such dependencies might arise is through criterion shifts—it is plausible that more variance is associated with the many criteria in classification than with the single criterion in discrimination. Criterion variance adds to sensory variance and provides another possible mechanism for context memory effects. Treisman and Williams (1984) have proposed a criterion-setting theory that accounts directly for sequential effects and indirectly for other aspects of identification findings. The shape of a fully-integrated account of identification experiments is dimly visible in these related proposals but is not yet completely defined.

OTHER DISCRIMINATION DESIGNS

The one-interval experiment, with or without ratings, is a natural way to measure discrimination in detection, recognition memory, and some other applications. In other situations, experimenters have preferred paradigms in which each trial contains two or more stimuli separated in time or location. The three paradigms discussed here, two alternative forced choice (2AFC) same-different, and multiple-look, have played different roles in the development of SDT. The ability to predict 2AFC performance from yes-no was one of detection theory's first accomplishments, whereas a thorough understanding of same-different arose later. The multiple-look experiment provided an early test of SDT but has more recently been important in describing the performance of groups of observers.

The common approach is to interpret each interval's output as a separate dimension in a multidimensional space. The multidimensional analysis generalizes conveniently to the problems treated in the final sections of this chapter.

Two-Alternative Forced-Choice

In 2AFC a sample of both S and N is presented on each trial and the observer must choose the interval that contains the signal. The two possible sequences are $<S, N>$ and $<N, S>$, the corresponding correct responses "1" and "2." In auditory work, the intervals

are almost always presented sequentially, but in other senses and especially in cognitive applications, simultaneous presentation is more common.

Representation and Analysis

Figure 2.11 displays a representation of the 2AFC problem in which each of the axes measures the effect of one of the intervals. On $<S, N>$ trials the mean value is $(d', 0)$, whereas on $<N, S>$ trials it is $(0, d')$, and the variability in both intervals is assumed equal. Figure 2.11a shows bivariate normal distributions whose height at each point is the likelihood of the corresponding pair of values; in Figure 2.11b, the same distributions are schematically represented by circles 1 standard deviation from the mean.

The best strategy for the observer is to base a decision on the difference between the effects of the two intervals. The decision axis is the diagonal line connecting the means of the two distributions, and it follows from the Pythagorean theorem that the distance between these means is $\sqrt{2}\,d'$. As with

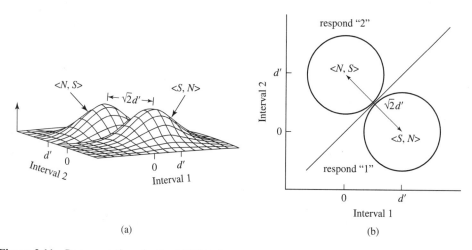

(a)   (b)

Figure 2.11   Representations for the 2AFC task.

NOTE: Panel (a): In three dimensions. On the x-axis are values of strength for interval 1, and on the y-axis are values for interval 2. The heights of the bivariate distributions give the likelihoods of $<x, y>$ points for the two possible stimulus sequences. Panel (b): In two dimensions. The decision axes are still x and y, but the distributions are represented by the means and circles at a fixed distance from them. The criterion line separates the space into regions for which the response is "1" (below the line) and "2" (above it). The distance between the means is $\sqrt{2}\,d'$.

yes-no, this sensitivity statistic can be esti-mated as the difference between the hit rate $H = P(\text{"1"} \mid <S, N>)$ and the false-alarm rate $F = P(\text{"1"} \mid <N, S>)$, so

$$z(H) - z(F) = \sqrt{2}\,d'. \qquad (20)$$

Thus, having two samples instead of one leads to a $\sqrt{2}$ improvement in performance; this is an example of the general $\sqrt{n}$ effect that is well known in statistics.

Response bias is, empirically, less likely to be extreme in 2AFC than in yes-no, but can occur. Performance as measured by $p(c)$ is greatest when there is no bias, and unbi-ased $p(c)$ is therefore often denoted $p(c)_{max}$. In Green's (1964) area theorem, already men-tioned, it is $p(c)_{max}$ that equals the area under the yes-no ROC.

Effects of Interstimulus Interval and Stimulus Range in 2AFC

Having two intervals allows for the manipu-lation of two basic experimental parameters that cannot be varied in yes-no discrimi-nation: the time between the two intervals and the stimulus range. An increase in either of these variables leads to a decline in perfor-mance.

In 2AFC experiments with stimuli differ-ing in intensity, the second interval is com-monly called "larger" more often than the first, an effect called *time order error*. The sequence <Small, Large> is, accordingly, correctly re-ported more often than <Large, Small>, a response-bias effect that increases with inter-stimulus interval (ISI). These data have been interpreted to show decay of a central repre-sentation of the stimulus over time (Kohler, 1923). This explanation suggests that there should also be an overall sensitivity drop, and there is: Berliner and Durlach (1973), Kinchla and Smyzer (1967, in a same-different task), and Tanner (1961) systematically varied ISI, and all found sensitivity to be a decreasing function of time. In Tanner's auditory exper-

iment, a very short ISI (less than 0.8 s) also led to decreased discrimination, a result that Tanner interpreted as evidence for short-term auditory interference.

Berliner and Durlach (1973) noted that the one-interval task has, in effect, a very long ISI, so that d' values obtained from that task should be lower than those from 2AFC. This is in fact a typical result for discrimination data (Jesteadt & Bilger, 1974; Creelman & Macmillan, 1979), though not for detection (for summaries, see Green and Swets, 1966, chap. 4; Luce, 1963a).

The 2AFC design also permits manipu-lation of the range of stimulus values, with stimulus pairs from different parts of a wide range being presented on successive trials. Al-though this *roving discrimination* task is more difficult than the corresponding *fixed discrim-ination* experiment, the decision strategy of subtracting the effects of the two intervals is optimal for both.

Roving and fixed 2AFC discrimination have been compared for auditory amplitude and frequency by Jesteadt and Bilger (1974). The fixed task used one pair of tones, differ-ing in (say) amplitude; the roving design used a constant amplitude difference, but the two stimuli ranged together over many amplitudes from trial to trial. A 40-dB range of ampli-tudes yielded a 27% drop in intensity discrim-ination d', and a 465-Hz range in frequency led to a 37% drop in frequency discrimina-tion. Berliner and Durlach (1973) found that the decline in intensity discrimination perfor-mance depended systematically on the inten-sity range, reaching 58% for the largest range (60 dB).

The range and ISI effects have both been interpreted as reflecting a limitation of per-ceptual memory and need to be incorpo-rated into the model for 2AFC: After all, the same $\sqrt{2}$ relation between 2AFC and yes-no clearly cannot hold for all ISIs, or for both roving and fixed discrimination. Durlach and Braida's (1969) trace-context theory addresses this problem and unifies the perceptual phenomena discussed so far. As in their model for one-dimensional classification, discussed earlier, both sensory variance (B^2) and range-dependent context variance (C^2) limit performance in roving 2AFC. In identification, context coding allows the observer to locate the stimulus within the stimulus set, and an observer who uses context coding for each of the two stimuli on a 2AFC trial is said to be in context mode. Alternatively, the trace mode allows direct comparison of the two intervals. Context coding is best when the range is small, and trace coding is best when the ISI is short. Durlach and Braida suggested that these limitations combine optimally, so that whichever memory process has smaller variance dominates. Trace-context theory has been tested extensively for sets of tones differing in intensity, and it describes many regularities of the data (Berliner & Durlach, 1973).

The Same-Different Design

In 2AFC the observer chooses the interval that has a particular characteristic, and for some kinds of stimuli it can be difficult to explain what that characteristic is. The same-different design has the appeal of simplicity from the point of view of the experimental participant: On each trial the decision is merely whether the two stimuli are the same or different. Any one of the four pairs constructed from $\{S, N\}$ may be presented: <S, S> and <N, N> are to be called "same," <S, N> and <N, S> "different." Figure 2.12 shows a representation for this task, following the same approach as with 2AFC. There are four distributions arranged in the space, and d' is the distance between the means of any two distributions that differ on only one axis.

Two decision strategies based on this representation have been developed, an independent-observation and a differencing rule. The independent-observation rule is optimal, but differencing is the best available in some experimental designs.

Independent-Observation Decision Rule

The optimal decision rule (Noreen, 1981) is to decide separately whether each interval is

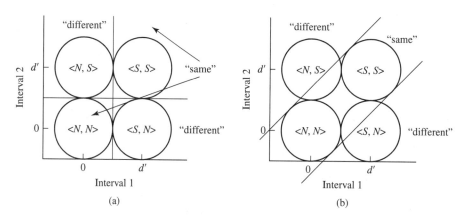

Figure 2.12   Decision spaces for the same-different task.
NOTE: Either S or N can occur in either interval, leading to four bivariate distributions, displayed as in the lower panel of Figure 2.11. In panel (a), the effects of the two observations are combined independently; in (b), the effects of the two intervals are subtracted.

S or *N*, then report whether these subdecisions are the same or different. In the decision space, the observer establishes a pair of criterion lines that divides the space into four quadrants. To start, consider the symmetric case, in which these lines bisect the distribution means, as in Figure 2.12a. When <*S*, *N*> is presented, a "different" response (a hit) occurs if the observation falls either to the right of the vertical criterion line and below the horizontal one, or to the left and above. The likelihood of this happening (the hit rate) can be expressed using the normal distribution function $\Phi(z)$, which gives the area up to the point z. The area to the right of the vertical boundary is $\Phi(d'/2)$, and the proportion below the horizontal criterion is the same value, so the probability of falling in the lower right corner is the product of these, $[\Phi(d'/2)]^2$. Similarly, the probability of being in the upper left corner is $[\Phi(-d'/2)]^2$. The sum of these is the hit rate for <*S*, *N*> trials; because the decision rule is symmetric, this is also the proportion correct for all other trials, and for the task as a whole. Therefore,

$$p(c) = [\Phi(d'/2)]^2 + [\Phi(-d'/2)]^2. \quad (21)$$

The same-different task is more difficult than the corresponding yes-no task. An unbiased participant in yes-no obtains a proportion correct of $\Phi(d'/2)$, so the relation between the two paradigms is

$$p(c)_{\text{SDindependent-observation}} = p(c)_{\text{YN}}^2 + [1 - p(c)_{\text{YN}}]^2. \quad (22)$$

If $d' = 1$, $p(c)$ will be .69 in yes-no but only .57 in same-different; for $d' = 2$, the values are .84 and .73.

Equation (22) contains no explicit reference to d', and the relation does not in fact depend on any assumption about the shape of the distributions. The requirement is that the distributions display no correlation between the two intervals, and that the mean on one axis does not depend on the stimulus value on the other axis (e.g., that the <*S*, *N*> and <*N*, *N*> distributions have the same projections on the interval-2 axis). These assumptions seem quite plausible when the two axes are intervals in an experiment.

ROCs for the independent-observation model can be constructed by assuming that the observer divides the space into regions in which the likelihood ratio of same versus different is greater than or less than some fixed value (this value is 1 in the symmetric case). Systematically varying this critical value of likelihood ratio and calculating H and F for each value traces out the same-different ROC. Such curves are approximately straight lines, with slope 1.0 on normal coordinates.

Differencing Rule

An alternative to the independent-observation rule is a differencing strategy like that used in 2AFC: The two observations on a trial are subtracted, and the result is compared to a criterion. This strategy, first described by Sorkin (1962), is illustrated in Figure 2.12b. The criterion lines for a constant difference resemble the line for 2AFC, but the decision space is more complicated. The differencing rule is greatly at odds with the independent-observation rule in certain regions of the space.

Because the differencing rule depends on a single variable (the difference between two observations) the decision space can be represented in one dimension. When both trials contain the same stimulus, either <*S*, *S*> or <*N*, *N*>, the mean difference is zero. There are, however, two types of different pairs: those that, when subtracted, yield a mean difference of d', and those yielding a mean of $-d'$. The decision problem in one dimension thus involves three difference distributions on one axis. The hit rate and false-alarm rate result from combining areas under these distributions:

$$H = P(\text{"different"} \mid \text{Different})$$
$$= \Phi[(-k + d')/\sqrt{2}] + \Phi[(-k - d')/\sqrt{2}]$$
$$F = P(\text{"different"} \mid \text{Same}) = 2\Phi(-k/\sqrt{2}).$$
$$(23)$$

If k is varied, Equations (23) can be used to trace out an ROC. Unlike the ROCs for the independent-observation rule, these have less than unit slope, so two points with equal values of $z(H) - z(F)$ do not necessarily have the same d'.

Although not optimal, the differencing model may be the only one practical in roving designs: Calculation of likelihood ratios for large stimulus sets requires more knowledge of the situation than observers typically have, whereas subtraction has minimal requirements. Roving and fixed discrimination thus differ in the appropriate decision strategy, as well as the memory limitations discussed earlier. The only paradigm in which the appropriate decision rule is the same for both, apparently, is 2AFC.

Because it is nonoptimal, the differencing strategy leads to performance levels that are poorer than those with independent observations. The decline in $p(c)$ is small at low levels (.02 when $d' = 1$) but equals .08 for $d' = 3$. Turning the comparison around, a value of $p(c) = .90$ implies a d' of 4.14 with the differencing model, 3.24 for independent observations, and just 2.56 in yes-no. Perversely, the inherent difficulty of the same-different task recommends its use when d' is high: An experimenter who wishes to avoid ceiling effects of, say, $p(c) > .95$, can estimate a d' of 5.10 with same-different, assuming the differencing model, but is limited (for unbiased observers) to $d' = 3.29$ in yes-no and $d' = 2.33$ in 2AFC.

Relation between the Two Strategies

The independent-observation and differencing strategies are special cases of a general situation (Dai, Versfeld, & Green, 1996). Consider what would happen if the correlation ρ between the intervals (which is zero in the diagrams so far) were substantial, and the same for all four stimulus sequences. The left panel of Figure 2.13 shows ellipses with correlation $\rho > 0$. Because the correlations (and variances) are the same in all distributions, this representation is equivalent to one in which the distributions are uncorrelated but the axes intersect at an angle of $\cos^{-1}(-\rho)$ (Ashby & Townsend, 1986). The right panel shows that when ρ is not 0 (and the angle between the

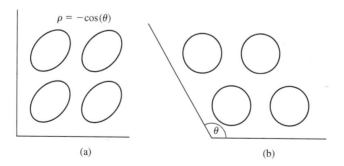

(a)   (b)

Figure 2.13   Two equivalent forms of the representation for the same-different paradigm in which there is a correlation between the two intervals.
NOTE: In panel (a) the bivariate distributions themselves include the correlation parameter ρ, whereas in (b) the distributions are uncorrelated but the two axes intersect at an angle $\theta = \cos^{-1}(-\rho)$.

axes is not 90°), spacing between the distributions is wider along the negative diagonal than along the positive one, an effect that results from the smaller standard deviation in that direction. The optimal rule for this case is not straight lines intersecting at a right angle; in fact, the larger ρ is, the closer the rule is to two parallel lines perpendicular to the negative diagonal, as in the differencing model.

Some Experimental Results

Irwin and Francis (1995a) explored the perception of line drawings of objects that were either *natural* (e.g., alligator, leaf) or *manu-*

factured (e.g., various tools). Pairs of such objects were briefly presented, and the observers had to say whether they belonged to the same or different categories. Thus, the correct response for the pair (hammer, leaf) was "different," whereas it was "same" for the pair (leaf, alligator).

The observers in this experiment produced ROCs supporting the independent-observation model, as shown in Figure 2.14 (first row). Irwin and Francis (1995a, 1995b; Francis & Irwin, 1995) have shown, however, that participants may adopt either strategy spontaneously, depending on the stimulus set.

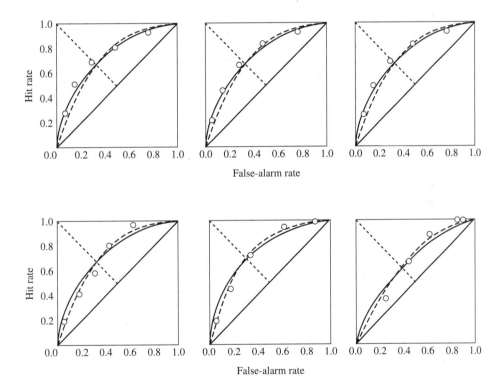

Figure 2.14   ROC curves for same-different experiments.
NOTE: In all panels, the solid lines are for the independent-observation model, and the dashed lines are for the differencing model. The first row shows data from an experiment in which pictures in natural and manufactured categories were discriminated, and the three panels are for presentation to the left visual field, right visual field, and both visual fields. The independent-observation model provides a better fit. The second row shows data from an experiment in which colored patches were discriminated, and the three panels are for three observers. The differencing model provides a better fit.
SOURCE: Irwin and Francis (1995a, Figures 1 and 3). Reprinted with permission.

The independent-observation model applied when observers compared letters varying in orientation (correct vs. reversed); whereas the differencing model was supported by data using color patches that could vary in any direction in color space (a type of roving design), as can be seen in Figure 2.14 (second row).

Multiple-Look Experiments

In the multiple-look experiment, either S or N is presented in each of n intervals, so the observer has n pieces of information to make a decision. When $n = 2$, the representation is as shown in Figure 2.15. It is immediately clear that having two chances to detect the stimulus produces a $\sqrt{2}$ increase in the mean separation of the distributions. The situation is parallel to 2AFC, as is evident when the figure is compared with Figure 2.11, and predicted performance is exactly the same as for that paradigm (Equation [20]). The design can easily be extended to larger values of n, the predicted improvement being $\sqrt{n}$. Early studies (Swets, Shipley, McKee, & Green, 1959) showed that the rate of improvement was slightly less, presumably because of inefficiency in integrating the observations.

This same relation can be derived in a different way, with reference to a single decision axis. Assume that the decision variable is the sum of observations (on a single dimension). The n stimuli will produce a mean difference of nd' and a variance of n (because the variance for one observation is 1), so the effective normalized mean difference is $nd'/\sqrt{n} = \sqrt{n}d'$. This one-dimensional perspective has the advantage that it allows one to go easily beyond two samples, whereas visualizing six-dimensional spaces is hard.

Sorkin and colleagues (Sorkin & Dai, 1994; Sorkin, Hays, & West, 2001) have studied analogous designs in which different individuals, rather than different observations by the same individual, contribute to a single decision. Each member of a team of observers makes yes-no decisions in a visual discrimination task, and their votes are combined into a group response using rules ranging from simple majority to unanimity. The group performs better than the individuals, and better for a simple majority rule than for stricter rules. Group accuracy is poorer than would be predicted by analogy to multiple-look experiments, but this is not surprising because subdecisions, rather than d' values, are being combined: In fact, group data are well-predicted from the individual sensitivities when this is taken into account.

Other Tasks

Other tasks have been subjected to detection-theory analysis: (a) matching-to-sample (ABX), in which the first two intervals or each trial contain S and N, in either order, and the observer must decide which of them matches the stimulus in the third interval (Pierce & Gilbert, 1958; Macmillan et al., 1977); (b) mAFC, an extension of 2AFC in which one m interval contains S, the others N (to be discussed later); and (c) oddity, in which all the possibilities in mAFC are included, as well as sequences in which one interval contains N, the others S (Versfeld, Dai, & Green, 1996). By considering only cases of unbiased responding, it is possible to compare $p(c)$

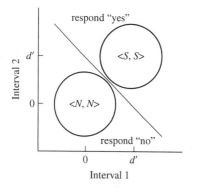

Figure 2.15   Decision space for the two-interval multiple-look experiment.

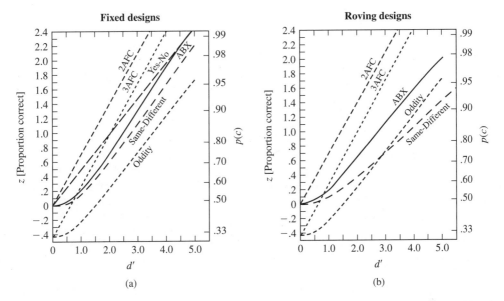

Figure 2.16   Proportion correct as a function of d' for several discrimination paradigms (unbiased responding).

NOTE: (a) Fixed designs, assuming independent-observation models for all paradigms except oddity, which has only a differencing model. (b) Roving designs, assuming differencing models for all paradigms.

SOURCE: Macmillan and Creelman (1991).

for these paradigms, as a function of d', as shown in Figure 2.16. Most designs offer both an independent-observation and a differencing strategy, and the two panels correspond to these two cases.

The figure permits several interesting conclusions. There are large differences in performance across paradigms, and the magnitudes (and in some cases even the direction) of the discrepancies depend on d'. Clearly, the shape of the psychometric function depends on the paradigm if $p(c)$ is the dependent variable, supporting the recommendation made in discussing psychometric functions to plot such functions in terms of d' instead.

MULTIDIMENSIONAL CLASSIFICATION: INDEPENDENCE AND ATTENTION

The multidimensional representations with which same-different and other discrimination designs are analyzed can be generalized to handle more substantive issues. Multidimensional representations provide good descriptions of many cognitive and perceptual problems. For stimulus sets whose members are completely discriminable, multidimensional scaling has proved an invaluable tool (see Chap. 3). An extended version of detection theory is called for when discriminabilities are imperfect.

The representation of multiple stimuli can be estimated from the pattern of discriminabilities in a number of ways. The simplest, conceptually, is to find d' or another distance measure for each pair and then to infer a geometrical pattern of the means of the distributions in euclidean space. One interesting result of such calculations is that distinct physical dimensions may interact, that is, may not be independent in the perceptual space. The independence question was the first, historically, to which multidimensional detection theory models were applied (by Tanner, in 1956); this section considers both Tanner's findings and more recent applications of the same strategy.

Classification experiments (N stimuli) are commonly used, sometimes in combination with discrimination ($N = 2$) tests, to infer multidimensional representations. Because classification experiments require grouping multiple stimuli together (i.e., assigning them the same response), they are the natural tools for the study of attention. If several distinct stimuli may occur that require the same response, it is natural to refer to the design as one of uncertainty about which of these stimuli will occur. If the response partition is such that some aspects of the stimulus set must be appreciated and other ignored, attention is selective; if all aspects are relevant, attention must be divided.

Attention is often studied with response time and other measures not strictly within the bounds of detection theory; see Pashler (1998) for an integrative survey. The SDT approach is particularly valuable in providing baselines for attention "deficits." The critical distinction is between extrinsic and intrinsic results (Graham, 1989): Extrinsic uncertainty is inherent in the situation, whereas intrinsic uncertainty is internal to the observer. It is essential to find the extrinsic difficulty of a classification design so that poor performance that is in fact inevitable is not blamed on the experimental participant's inefficiency.

Introduction to Multidimensional Decision Spaces

In a 1956 article, Tanner measured the discriminability of each pair in a set of three stimuli: Noise alone and tones of two different frequencies (S_1 and S_2). From the three possible two-stimulus discrimination experiments, he could determine whether the S_1 and S_2 dimensions were orthogonal. Nonorthogonality implies (for normal distributions) a correlation between the dimensions, as in Figure 2.17; if the dimensions intersect at an angle θ, the

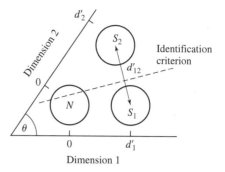

Figure 2.17 Decision space showing distributions due to Noise and two Signals that differ from it, each along a different dimension.
NOTE: The angle between the axes measures the dependence between the two dimensions.

correlation equals $\cos(\theta)$. The results of the three experiments can be used to estimate θ from the geometry of Figure 2.17:

$$(d'_{1,2})^2 = {d'_1}^2 + {d'_2}^2 - 2d'_1 d'_2 \cos(\theta) \quad (24)$$

Equation (24) covers all possible relations between pairs of imperfectly detectable stimuli. In one important special case, the alternative stimuli produce independent effects, which are said to require independent sensory channels, a metaphor introduced by Broadbent (1958). In that case the axes are orthogonal, so that $\theta = 90°$, $\cos(\theta) = 0$, and

$$(d'_{1,2})^2 = {d'_1}^2 + {d'_2}^2. \quad (25)$$

This same equation will be useful in describing capacity models of attention later in this chapter. It also characterizes the euclidean metric used in similarity scaling.

Values of θ less than 90° arise from overlap between the channels' regions of sensitivity: A Signal that activates one maximally also activates the other to some extent. Angles of θ greater than 90° might arise from inhibition between the separate perceptual or sensory channels (Graham, Kramer, & Haber, 1985; Klein, 1985). When $\theta = 0°$, the representation is one-dimensional, and pairwise d' values are subtracted: $\cos(\theta) = 1.0$, so

$d'_{1,2} = d'_1 - d'_2$. When $\theta = 180°$, another one-dimensional case, the distance between the two Signals in the recognition task is the sum of the individual detectability values. This is the well-known city-block metric, first described by Shepard (1964) for the scaling of similarity judgments.

In his experiments, Tanner found that dimensional orthogonality held when tones were sufficiently different in frequency, but that θ was less than 90° when they were similar. The result is consistent with the critical-band hypothesis, according to which auditory inputs are divided into channels according to frequency. Tanner's approach offers a convenient summary of the data in geometric terms, but it has a shortcoming: The three experiments result in three values of d'. These data are just enough to determine the internal angles of the triangle in Figure 2.17, but they do not provide any internal test of validity (Ashby & Townsend, 1986). The addition of even one more stimulus can give more confidence in the representations inferred from data like these.

Concepts of Independence

The idea of perceptual independence is a crucial one in many psychological applications, but there are many varieties of this construct. Ashby and Townsend (1986) distinguished these in the context of a generalized version of detection theory they called generalized recognition theory (GRT). The three most important are perceptual independence, perceptual separability, and decisional separability.

Perceptual independence is a characteristic of a single distribution in which the component dimensions are statistically independent. For normal distributions, this is equivalent to the lack of correlation between them, as in the left-hand distribution in Figure 2.18. The opposite, perceptual dependence, is illustrated by the right-hand distribution, for which increasing values of X tend to go with increasing values of Y. The figure displays the marginal

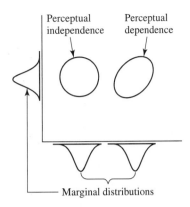

Figure 2.18   Perceptual independence and dependence in bivariate distributions.
NOTE: Perceptually independent distributions can be obtained by multiplying marginal distributions together; perceptually dependent distributions cannot.

as well as the joint distributions, and one way to see that the elliptical distribution is not perceptually independent is to compare it with the circular (and therefore perceptually independent) distribution to its left. This circular distribution is the product of the marginals, and therefore the elliptical one is not.

Perceptual separability, the characteristic in which Tanner (1956) was interested, is defined by a rectangular arrangement of distribution means, as in Figure 2.19a: A change on one dimension has no effect on the value of the other. In perceptually integral cases (Figure 2.19b), the two dimensions are perceptually correlated, so a change on one is at least partly confusable with a change on the other. Such representations display mean-shift integrality (or just mean integrality; Kingston & Macmillan, 1995; Maddox, 1992) because the means of the distributions are shifted compared to the perceptually separable case. In Figure 2.19b, lines connecting the means are drawn, and the angle θ is a measure of integrality. The presence of a fourth stimulus—rather than the three used by Tanner—allows the experimenter to test the fit of the representation.

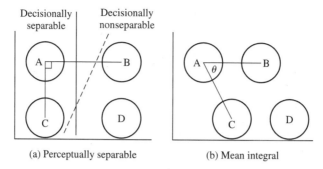

(a) Perceptually separable   (b) Mean integral

Figure 2.19 Perceptual separability and mean-integrality.
NOTE: (a) In perceptually separable sets, the marginal distribution for one value of X is the same for all values of Y, and vice versa. (b) In mean-integral sets, the means are shifted so that this is not true. The two decision bounds in (a) illustrate decisional separability and nonseparability.

The third important variety of independence concerns the decision rule rather than the distributions. Figure 2.19a shows two ways in which an observer might divide the space for a classification task in which stimuli A and C are to be assigned to one response, B and D to the other. The solid line describes a decisionally separable rule in which the decision depends only on X, whereas the dashed line indicates a rule in which both variables contribute to a decision.

Extrinsic Attention: Classification of Multidimensional Stimuli

Performance is typically poorer in classification designs than in a simple two-stimulus discrimination experiment, and it is important to determine the locus of this effect. This section describes several experiments that can be used to distinguish extrinsic (ideal observer) explanations from intrinsic (limited attention) ones.

Detection under Conditions of Uncertainty

In an uncertain detection experiment, each trial may or may not contain a signal; if present, the signal may be one of several possibilities. The observer reports only whether a signal is present, not its identity. In many applications, it is reasonable to suppose that the signals are carried by independent channels: They may arise in vision from far-apart spatial regions or different spatial frequencies (Graham & Nachmias, 1971), or in audition from frequencies falling into different critical bands (Creelman, 1960; Green, 1961).

The decision space for an uncertain detection experiment with two possible signals is shown in Figure 2.20a. Presentation of the null signal N leads to a bivariate distribution centered at (0, 0); the S_1 distribution produces an increase on dimension 1 and the S_2 distribution produces an increase on dimension 2. The uncertainty task requires observers to establish a decision boundary in the space of Figure 2.20a that accurately assigns stimuli S_1 and S_2 to one response and N to the other. The optimal decision boundaries follow lines of constant likelihood ratio, and varying the critical value of this statistic allows the calculation of ROC curves for the uncertain detection experiment. Nolte and Jaarsma (1967) showed that these curves have two interesting characteristics, as shown in Figure 2.20b. First, performance levels are lower under uncertainty and are increasingly poor as the number of possible signals increases; this is true even though the various signals are carried by independent channels. Second, the slope of the ROC decreases with the number of channels.

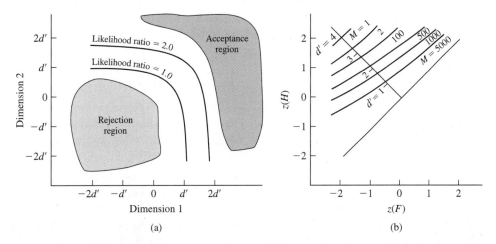

Figure 2.20   Optimal model for uncertain detection.

NOTE: (a) Decision space showing likelihood-ratio criterion curves for the two-signal case. The noise distribution is centered at (0, 0), the signal distributions at $(d', 0)$ and $(0, d')$. (b) ROCs for uncertain detection of M orthogonal signals, on z coordinates. Values of d' are given along the minor diagonal.

SOURCE: (a) Adapted from Figure 4 of Green and Birdsall (1978), by permission of the publisher. Copyright 1978 by the American Psychological Association. (b) Adapted from Nolte and Jaarsma (1967), by permission of the Acoustical Society of America.

Consider, as an example, an experiment by Bonnel and Miller (1994), who asked observers to detect a change in background that, on different trials, was unpredictably an increment in either the luminance of a spot or the intensity of a tone. The research question was whether uncertainty would lower performance compared to control conditions in which the modality to be attended to was known in advance. Bonnel and Miller assumed that there was no interaction between their visual and auditory stimuli, and that the representation was thus perceptually separable, as illustrated in Figure 2.21. The

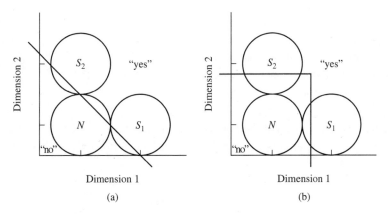

Figure 2.21   Decision spaces for uncertain detection, in which the observer must say whether either of two signals was presented.

NOTE: (a) Channel integration rule. (b) Independent-observation rule.

locations of the distribution means for visual (S_1) and auditory (S_2) distributions are the d' values found in the control conditions in which each increment was discriminated from no change (N).

A simple nonoptimal rule is available in this experiment. If the observer bases a decision on total subjective intensity, the effective decision axis is the line $y = x$. A possible decision boundary consistent with this rule is shown in Figure 2.21a. When the S_1 and S_2 distributions are projected onto the decision axis, the means are closer together than along the x-axis or y-axis, and the model predicts a drop in accuracy due to uncertainty. This summation rule is natural and is the best available strategy that uses a straight-line decision boundary; it resembles the optimal strategy for detecting compound "multiple looks" (Figure 2.15). It is clear, however, that Bonnel and Miller's (1994) observers did not use this rule, because their performance was better than the rule predicts.

Bonnel and Miller's (1994) data are better described assuming a different rule: Compare the observation to criteria on each dimension independently, and say "yes" if either criterion is exceeded. This "minimum" rule leads to the two-segment rectilinear decision boundary shown in Figure 2.21b and predicts a smaller deficit due to uncertainty than does the summation rule. It is almost identical to the optimal boundary, and for more than two dimensions the discrepancy between the minimum and optimal rules is even smaller.

Shaw (1982) explored an interesting extension of uncertain bisensory detection. In her task, an auditory signal, a visual one, or both together could occur, and the observer still had only to respond "yes" to these stimuli and "no" to the null stimulus. The presence of the compound stimulus allowed her to derive nonparametric constraints on the data for both the summation and the independent-

observation rule, and the data supported independent decisions.

Selective and Divided Attention

It is useful to distinguish between selective attention, in which the observer's goal is to attend to one dimension and ignore others, and divided attention, in which attention to both dimensions is necessary. The uncertain-detection task can be viewed either way, depending on the model assumed: The summation model treats attention as selective, in that the observer must attend to subjective intensity and ignore characteristics, such as modality, that distinguish stimuli S_1 and S_2. The minimum and optimal models, however, appear to be strategies for dividing attention.

Selective and divided attention are easier to distinguish operationally with four-stimulus sets. There are three ways in which four elements can be partitioned into two equal parts, two of these being examples of selective attention and one of divided. These are considered here in turn.

Figure 2.22a displays a perceptually separable representation. In one selective-attention task, observers are instructed to respond strictly on the basis of the x variable, assigning one response to A and C, the other to B and D. A decisionally separable boundary—the vertical line in the figure—is optimal. Performance is just as good as if only the two distributions A and B were being discriminated, so the model predicts that for separable dimensions there is no performance deficit due to filtering, as the selective task is sometimes called. An analogous task for selective attention to the vertical dimension is analyzed in the same way.

A mean-integral arrangement requires a different boundary. Figure 2.22b shows the optimal curve, for which the likelihood of either A or C is the same as the likelihood of either B or D, that is, for which the likelihood

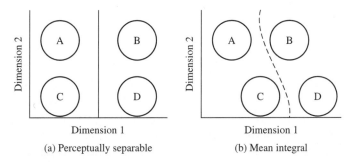

Figure 2.22   Decision spaces, with optimal decision bounds, for a selective attention task in which *A* and *C* are assigned to one response and *B* and *D* to another.
NOTE: (a) Perceptually separable stimulus set. (b) Mean-integral set.

ratio is 1. The attention question is how performance in the task sketched in Figure 2.22b compares to performance with only stimuli *A* and *B*. Performance is lower than for the baseline task, and by an amount that increases as θ (defined as in Figure 2.19b) nears 0° or 180°. The predicted (extrinsic) drop in proportion correct when $d' = 2$ can be as large as .11.

To force attention to both dimensions, the observer is required to assign stimuli *A* and *D* to one response, *B* and *C* to the other. An optimal strategy for doing this in a perceptually separable representation resembles that for the same-different task shown in Figure 2.12a: The observer divides the decision space into four quadrants and gives one response for the upper right and lower left regions, the other for upper left and lower right. The problem is a generalization of the independent-observation model for the same-different paradigm discussed earlier. The proportion correct is the same for all four stimuli, so one needs to consider only one of them, say stimulus *A*. Denoting the discriminability of *A* and *B* by d'_x and that of *A* and *C* by d'_y, the observer makes a correct response to this stimulus if the observation falls in either the upper-left or lower-right quadrant, and the total $p(c)$ is the sum of these components:

$$p(c) = \Phi(d'_x/2)\Phi(d'_y/2)]$$
$$+ \Phi(-d'_x/2)\Phi(-d'_y/2)]. \quad (26)$$

It was shown in considering the same-different task that this is a low level of performance compared to two-stimulus discrimination. If $d' = 2$ on both dimensions, so that baseline $p(c) = 0.84$, these terms are $(0.84)^2 = 0.706$ and $(0.16)^2 = 0.026$, for a sum of 0.732. For $d' = 1$, the decline is from 0.69 to 0.572. Clearly, the divided attention task is, extrinsically, quite difficult.

This section does not discuss the mean-integral case in detail. The optimal decision boundary is constructed by combining two curves like the one in Figure 2.22b, and the interesting result is that performance is relatively unaffected by θ over its entire range.

Kingston and Macmillan (1995) have measured baseline discrimination, selective attention, and divided attention for vowel sounds varying in two dimensions, vowel height and nasalization. They used the baseline d' values to construct mean-integral representations like those in Figure 2.22b and predicted optimal selective and divided performance. Selective and divided attention were always lower than baseline, but the extrinsic model predicted most of the drop (e.g., for vowels in consonantal context, the model accounted for 75% of the decline in selective attention and 66% of the decline in divided attention). Kingston and Macmillan concluded that listeners suffered little loss due to allocating attention to the two dimensions; rather, these dimensions were to a large degree integrated into a single perceptual property.

The Garner Paradigm

Many stimulus sets can be constructed by varying two or more dimensions: height and width to make rectangles, the first and second formants to make vowels, contrast and spatial frequency to make gratings, and so on. Such sets have been studied extensively by Garner (1974) and his colleagues, with the intent of distinguishing "integral" pairs of dimensions (which interact) from "separable" ones (which do not), and it is from this line of research that GRT takes its terminology. Garner proposed a series of classification tests to distinguish these possibilities operationally, and his terms, applied mostly in speeded tasks with completely discriminable stimuli, do not exactly map onto the GRT concepts.

Garner (1974) argued that determining whether two dimensions interact should not rely on a single test, but on converging operations. Separability is defined by no filtering loss (i.e., selective attention equal to baseline performance) and no redundancy gain (e.g., ability to distinguish A and D being the same as the ability to distinguish A and B in Figure 2.22). Integrality is the opposite pattern, both a filtering loss and a redundancy gain. Divided attention is not always included and is not considered diagnostic in distinguishing integrality and separability.

Does the perceptual-space model agree with Garner's (1974) definitions? Both approaches agree that integrality is associated with filtering loss and that separability is associated with no loss. As for redundancy gain, the parallelogram model predicts this effect for *all* arrangements if optimal decision rules are used, but can predict no gain in the separable case if decisional separability is assumed. In many experiments using the Garner paradigm, participants are instructed to attend to one dimension even in the redundant case,

so it is perhaps not surprising that redundancy gains are not found.

A multidimensional detection-theory analysis provides a theoretical convergence of operations that allows for quantitative predictions of the relations among these tasks, but there are two important limitations: Predicted performance depends on the particular decision strategy used by the observer, and detection theory applies to imperfectly discriminable stimulus sets and the measurement of accuracy. Most Garner-paradigm (1974) studies have used response time, which requires explicit modeling if quantitative predictions are to be made.

Intrinsic Attention: Capacity Models and Attention Operating Characteristics

The models thus far are not very explicit about "paying attention," or about the connection between attentional instructions and performance. To model these important constructs, it helps to return to the multiple-look discrimination designs discussed earlier. The optimal model led to the prediction that an observer who had n "looks" at the same stimulus would improve detectability by $\sqrt{n}$.

The application to attention is this: Suppose that a person has a fixed "capacity" T to allocate among whatever (controlled) tasks are at hand. As in the previous discussion of multiple looks, assume that as each unit is allocated, it adds a fixed amount to both the mean and variance. Consider now the uncertain detection experiment. If all attention is allocated to dimension x, performance will be $\sqrt{T}d'$ on that dimension, but 0 on dimension y. The reverse is true if all attention is allocated to y. In general, if P of the T units are allocated to x and $T - P$ to y, then performance on x, d'_x, will be $\sqrt{P}d'$ and d'_y will be $\sqrt{(T - P)}d'$.

The model says that capacity can be allocated to one dimension only at the cost of the other and thus describes a tradeoff between accuracy on the two tasks. When P is large, the observer will do well on dimension x and poorly on dimension y, and when P is small (so that $T - P$ is large) the opposite will be true. The relation between x and y performance is an attention operating characteristic (AOC), analogous to the receiver operating characteristic (ROC), which describes a tradeoff between hits and correct rejections.

The form of the AOC between d'_x and d'_y can be derived from these assumptions. In terms of the squares of the sensitivities,

$$d'^2_y = (T - P)d'^2 = Td'^2 - Pd'^2$$
$$= Td'^2 - d'^2_x. \tag{27}$$

This is a circle—the usual equation is $y^2 = r^2 - x^2$—as shown in Figure 2.23. Rearranging the terms provides another perspective:

$$d'^2_x + d'^2_y = Td'^2 = \text{constant.} \tag{28}$$

The idea that squared sensitivities are added to estimate overall capacity was first proposed by Lindsay, Taylor, and Forbes (1968).

What would happen if participants were instructed to give, say, 80% attention to x and 20% to y? They should allocate 80% of their capacity to x and operate at the point labeled (80, 20) on the diagram. Experiments of this type have often shown that participants not only follow a circular tradeoff function but also are accurate at assigning the requested percentage of capacity (Bonnel & Hafter, 1998). For some pairs of stimuli, however, no tradeoff is found, and the AOC consists of two straight line segments, as shown by the dashed lines in Figure 2.23. For example, Graham and Nachmias (1971) found that attention could be paid simultaneously to superimposed gratings of two different frequencies, thus providing strong quantitative evidence that separate perceptual channels are used in processing the two gratings.

MULTIDIMENSIONAL IDENTIFICATION

This chapter has already presented one version of the identification experiment: A single stimulus from a known set is presented on each trial, and it is the observer's job to say which it was, that is, to identify it. The purposes of such experiments vary but usually include obtaining an overall index of performance, as well as a measure of sensitivity for each stimulus pair and bias for each response.

If there are only two stimuli, identification is simply the yes-no task, and performance can be summarized by one sensitivity parameter and one bias parameter. The nature of the stimuli is unimportant; it does not even matter if they differ along one physical dimension (lights of different luminance) or many (X-rays of normal and diseased tissue). With more than two stimuli, the task is easily described: One stimulus from a set of M is

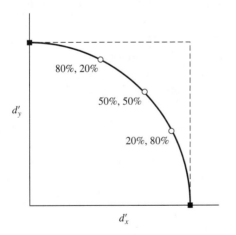

Figure 2.23 An attention operating characteristic showing joint performance in the dual-task paradigm.
NOTE: Solid points are single-task performance; the circle segment is the prediction of a fixed-capacity model (Equation [28]); and the dashed line is the prediction of an independent-channel model.

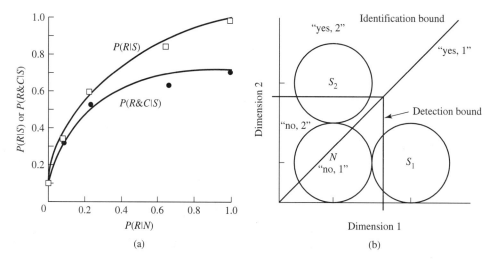

Figure 2.24 Analysis of simultaneous detection and identification.
NOTE: (a) ROC [$P(R \mid S)$] and IOC [$P(R\&C \mid S)$] for an X-ray detection and spatial identification task. The IOC plots the proportion of trials on which identification and detection responses were both correct. (b) Decision space with possible criteria. The observer gives both a detection response ("yes" or "no") and an identification response ("1" or "2" was presented). The space is therefore divided into four regions, one for each compound response.
SOURCE: (a) Adapted from Figure 2 of Starr et al. (1975). Reprinted by permission of the Radiological Society of North America.

presented on each trial, and the observer must say which it was. From the participant's point of view there is nothing more to say, but in order to extend the analysis to M (more than two) stimuli, the dimensionality of the representation must be known. If all stimuli differ perceptually on a single dimension, then $M - 1$ sensitivity distances between adjacent stimuli and $M - 1$ criterion locations can be found along it, as we saw earlier. Perceptual distances for all other pairs of stimuli are easily calculated as the sum of the stepwise distances between them. To characterize overall performance, it is natural to add sensitivity distances across the range.

The assumption of unidimensionality is a restrictive one, and this section considers some other cases, beginning with stimulus sets in which all members are independent of each other. Such stimuli may be thought of as being processed by different channels. In perceptual-space models, each stimulus produces a mean shift along a different dimension, and the discriminability of each pair of stimuli yields $M(M - 1)/2$ independent distances in a multidimensional space. This section describes two models that use simplifying assumptions to reduce the complexity of this problem, and one that provides a more complete analysis. Analysis of arbitrary situations with perceptual or cognitive objects is discussed first and then is applied to the special case in which identification is of intervals in discrimination experiments.

Models for Identification

Pollack and Ficks (1954) systematically studied how performance in absolute identification depends on the number of stimuli and the number of dimensions on which they varied. They analyzed their data using information theory (G. A. Miller, 1956; Shannon & Weaver, 1949) and found that although information transmitted along one dimension was limited to 2 or 3 bits (equivalent to perfectly distinguishing 4 to 8 stimuli), performance reached 7 or 8 bits (128 to 256 stimuli) when stimuli differed on 7 or 8 dimensions.

Information theory does not allow for independent assessment of sensitivity and bias, but a variety of SDT models can be applied. First, assume that all stimuli are processed by independent channels. The decision space contains M distributions, each removed from a common origin in a different dimension. The simplest (and most optimistic) calculations assume that there is no bias, so $p(c)$ can be used to summarize accuracy. An SDT analysis that relates the proportion correct to d' for equally detectable stimuli was developed by Elliott (1964) and improved by Hacker and Ratcliff (1979). The decision rule is simply to choose the dimension on which the maximum value is produced.

An implication of Luce's (1959) choice axiom is that the ratios of response frequencies in a confusion matrix do not depend on the number stimuli in the experiment. This *constant ratio rule* (Clarke, 1957) can be used to extract a 2×2 matrix from a larger one, and thus to calculate sensitivity to any stimulus pair. Hodge (1967; Hodge & Pollack, 1962) concluded that the constant ratio rule was more successful when applied to multidimensional than to one-dimensional stimulus domains.

Multi-Interval Forced-Choice

It is easy to translate to the identification of one *interval* in which a stimulus might be presented. The analogous task is one in which there are m spatial or temporal intervals, one containing S_2 and the others S_1. The analytic problem is formally the same as for identification of objects, just as the same-different discrimination task was formally the same as

divided attention. In the initial statement of the 2AFC problem (Figure 2.11), each interval corresponded to a separate dimension in the decision space, and this representation is also appropriate for $m > 2$ intervals. As in object identification, there are as many dimensions in the representation as there are intervals in the task. The optimal unbiased strategy is to choose the interval with largest observation.

The general models for multidimensional identification apply directly to the multi-interval forced-choice (mAFC) problem, and the assumptions of equal sensitivity and of independent effects for all alternatives are apparently quite reasonable. If one is still willing to assume unbiased responding, the Hacker and Ratcliff (1979) tables can be used to find d' values.

Simultaneous Detection and Identification

In some situations, detection and identification are both interesting. (Obviously, the detection must be under uncertainty; otherwise there is nothing to identify.) In the laboratory, participants may try to detect a grating that has one of several frequencies, and also to identify which grating was seen. In eyewitness testimony, the witness must both "detect" whether a perpetrator is present (in the lineup, or in court) and also identify which person that is. In recognition memory, the participant must decide whether the stimulus was presented earlier in the experiment and, if so, from which of two sources.

When a rating response is included in the simultaneous detection-identification experiment, two types of ROCs can be constructed. The first is the usual detection curve, plotting the cumulative probability of a hit versus that of a false alarm at each confidence level. The second is the probability of both detecting and correctly identifying a stimulus, again at each level of confidence. There is only one set of false-alarm probabilities; it makes no sense to ask the likelihood of being right in identification when no signal is present. Figure 2.24a shows the two performance curves: the familiar ROC and (below it) the new identification operating characteristic (IOC).

The independent-observation model can be used to predict the identification operating curve of Figure 2.24 from the uncertain-detection ROC (Green, Weber, & Duncan, 1977; Starr, Metz, Lusted, & Goodenough, 1975). Within this model there is a natural decision rule: The channel with the maximum output determines the identification response and is compared to a criterion to determine the detection response. Integration models are not so easily adapted to identification.

To understand the relation between the two operating characteristics, consider the decision space. Figure 2.24b shows a single detection boundary of the independent-observation type used in uncertain detection (as in Figure 2.21b). The identification criterion line is symmetric, because the observer is simply choosing the dimension (channel) with the larger output. The two criteria divide the space into four regions, those in which the observer responds "yes-1" (there was a signal, and it was S_1), "yes-2," "no-1," and "no-2."

The probability of both detecting and correctly identifying S_1—the height of the IOC—is that part of the S_1 distribution in the "yes-1" area. The probability of just detecting it—the height of the ROC—includes both the "yes-1" and the "yes-2" areas and must therefore be larger. To trace out the IOC and ROC by increasing the false-alarm rate, the detection criterion curve is moved down and to the left. When the curve has been moved as far as possible in this direction, both the false-alarm rate and the detection (ROC) hit rate equal 1. The identification (IOC) success rate equals the proportion correct by an unbiased observer in mAFC, as can be seen by comparing Figure 2.24b with Figure 2.11. For $m = 2$, the area theorem implies that the asymptote of the

IOC equals the area under the ROC. Green et al. (1977) have generalized the area theorem to the case of m signals.

An interesting extension of the simultaneous detection-identification experiment requires the observer to make an identification response even if the detection response is "no." Traditionally, the ability to identify stimuli without detecting them has been considered a hallmark of "subliminal perception," so it is interesting to ask whether a detection-theory analysis predicts this result. Clearly the answer is yes: In Figure 2.24b, points in the "no" region are likely to be on the correct side of the identification criterion. The surprise would be *not* to get subliminal perception.

Testing Independence with Identification Data

Identification experiments are a valuable tool for testing whether perceptual dimensions interact, or are perceived independently. The advent of GRT has clarified various type of independence (Ashby & Townsend, 1986) and has provided two general approaches to testing it with identification designs. One such method is considered next.[3]

The basic stimulus set for testing independence is the *feature-complete identification design,* in which each value of one dimension is factorially combined with each value of the others. In two dimensions, choosing two values on each dimension leads to four stimuli, two on one and three on the other leads to six, and so forth. As in all identification

---

[3]The method not discussed, hierarchical model-fitting (Ashby & Lee, 1991), is more computationally intensive. A set of models is constructed in which more complex models are "nested" within and tested against simpler ones. For example, a model that includes decisional separability might be compared with one that does not; failure to find a statistically-significant improvement in fit for the latter model is considered evidence for decisional separability.

experiments, the task is to assign a unique label to each stimulus.

Earlier, three meanings of independence were distinguished (see Figures 2.18 and 2.19). Perceptual independence is the independence of two variables and can be observed for a single stimulus. If X and Y are perceptually independent, then their joint distribution is the product of the marginal distributions,

$$f(x, y) = g(x)g(y), \qquad (29)$$

and has circular equal-likelihood contours, that is, no correlation. Perceptual separability refers to sets of stimuli and is present if the marginal distributions on one dimension, say X, are the same for different values of Y, that is,

$$g(x)_{y=1} = g(x)_{y=2} \qquad (30)$$

and so forth for other values of Y. Decisional separability also refers to sets of stimuli and means that the decision criterion on one variable does not depend on the value of the other. When decisional separability occurs, decision bounds are straight lines perpendicular to a perceptual axis.

These independence qualities, or their opposites, are theoretical characteristics of the perceptual representation, and certain statistics calculated from the data provide information about each type of independence. An approach called multidimensional signal detection analysis (MSDA), devised by Kadlec and Townsend (1992a, 1992b), can be implemented using a straightforward computer program (Kadlec, 1995, 1999a). The MSDA technique includes several distinct analyses.

Consider an experiment reported by Kadlec (1995), in which observers made judgments of both the curvature and orientation of visual stimuli. In a macroanalysis of perceptual and decisional separability, the question to be asked is whether judgments of curvature are perceptually or decisionally independent of orientation. Three aspects of the data are important:

1. *Marginal response rates.* Does the probability of reporting a particular curvature response depend on the orientation?
2. *Marginal d' values.* The hit rate and false-alarm rate can be used to find curvature d' for both values of orientation.
3. *Marginal criterion values.* The hit rate and false-alarm rate can be used to find curvature criterion values for both values of orientation.

In MSDA, differences of these three kinds are tested for statistical significance. Conclusions and perceptual and decisional separability can then be made by consulting Table 2.9 (from Kadlec, 1995; Kadlec & Townsend,

Table 2.9   Inferences about Perceptual and Decisional Separability from Identification Data

Observed results			Conclusions	
Marginal response invariance?	Marginal d' equal?	Marginal criteria equal?	Perceptual separability	Decisional separability
T	T	T	yes	yes
T	T	F	yes	no
T	F	T	no	yes
T	F	F	no	no
F	T	T	yes	possibly no
F	T	F	yes	no
F	F	T	no	unknown
F	F	F	no	unknown

1992b). The left-hand columns give possible outcomes of the three statistical comparisons, in which the marginal statistics can be equal (T, or true, in the table) or not (F, or false). Conclusions about separability are in the right-hand columns. Notice that if the marginal responses are invariant, then perceptual separability is associated with equal marginal d' and decisional separability is associated with equal criteria. In the absence of marginal response invariance, as in the example, conclusions are less firm.

A different MSDA analysis can be used to evaluate perceptual independence. Identification tasks build on a detailed theoretical analysis (Ashby & Townsend, 1986; Kadlec & Townsend, 1992b) and are a powerful tool for analyzing interaction and independence.

STATISTICAL ISSUES

Signal detection analysis of data leads to estimates of sensitivity and bias, and standard statistical questions can be asked about these estimates. This section first considers single-subject designs (or those in which a small number of observers are each analyzed separately), in which the special characteristics of SDT measures are most salient; then situations in which the performance of groups of participants is evaluated. The focus will be on sensitivity, with pointers to treatments of bias.

The first question is the distribution of d'. For single participants, Gourevitch and Galanter (1967) showed that this distribution is approximately normal and provided a formula for estimating the variance of d'. In recent studies (Kadlec, 1999b; J. O. Miller, 1996) the accuracy of the approximation has been tested and largely confirmed for a range of sensitivity and bias values (using the adjustments for false-alarm rates of 0, discussed earlier). Variance estimates can be used to construct confidence intervals and to test hy-

potheses about differences between two experimental conditions; Marascuilo (1970) has extended the analysis to multiple conditions.

The accuracy or precision of the estimates improves, of course, as the number of trials on which they are based increases. In some applications (e.g., in studies of infants or of people with impairments of some kind) a large number of trials is not practical, and it is necessary to pool data across observers to avoid overuse of the correction for perfect scores. Two questions are raised by this procedure. First, what is the effect on the accuracy and precision of SDT parameter estimates, and second, how can hypothesis testing be done? Macmillan and Kaplan (1985) provide reassurance on the first matter, showing that only in cases of widely varying individual response biases do estimates suffer. The hypothesis-testing problem is that if all observers in a group are combined to estimate d', then variability across participants is no longer available to provide an error term for ANOVAs and related procedures. One possibility is to apply the Gourevitch and Galanter (1967) and Marascuilo (1970) single-observer methods to the pooled data. Another approach (adopted, e.g., by Maddox and Estes, 1997) is to estimate d' from pooled data but conduct hypothesis tests on the simpler (albeit threshold-theoretic) statistic $H - F$.

If the number of trials is sufficient to estimate a value of d' for each participant in each condition, then standard parametric hypothesis testing procedures can be used (and the knowledge that d' is normally distributed is reassuring). An approach that unifies hypothesis-testing and detection theory has recently been set forth by DeCarlo (1998). If an SDT model with underlying logistic rather than normal distributions is assumed, then hypotheses about signal detection parameters (e.g., ROC slope) correspond to tests conducted by standard logistic regression software. This approach can be extended to other distributions (including the normal) by the use of generalized linear models, in which a "link function" scales the data in accordance with the assumed underlying distributions.

DETECTION THEORY AND ALTERNATIVE APPROACHES

In this chapter, I have presented SDT as a framework in which to analyze discrimination and classification data. The theory allows sensitivity to be separated from bias, accuracy to be compared across paradigms, and the extrinsic limitations of an experimental design to be distinguished from intrinsic ones. Without pretending to offer equal time, let me acknowledge two lines of dissent.

One reason for hesitation in using SDT is a reluctance to adopt its assumptions, but the alternative of truly assumption-free methods is rarely available and measures in common use such as proportion correct entail alternative assumptions about underlying distributions that are almost always found wanting when tested. Explicit threshold ("multinomial") models have been proposed for complex experimental problems such as source memory (Batchelder & Riefer, 1990). Like all models, they are useful to the degree that they capture the phenomena of interest, but they also bear the burden of proving that the threshold assumptions do not distort the picture that they draw. For an instructive exchange on the multinomial source monitoring model, see Kinchla (1994) and Batchelder, Riefer, and Hu (1994).

Detection theory's power derives from its explicitness about the representation on which observer performance is based. The essential claim of SDT is that aspects of this representation reflecting sensitivity remain the same across experimental paradigms or when response bias changes, and a substantial body of data supports this assertion. All of it can be reinterpreted, however, and Balakrishnan (1999) has offered just such a tour de force, arguing that response biases affect the representation itself rather than decision processes. So far, supporting data come from the dual-response rating paradigm, and it will take time to establish the broad usefulness of this revisionist perspective. Arising just after the first edition of this handbook was published, SDT has needed a half-century to reach its present standing. As a data-analysis framework and rather general psychological model, it is not the kind of intellectual structure that is easily defeated by isolated experiments, but its virtues and failings are sure to look different in another 50 years—or even in the fourth edition.

REFERENCES

Ashby, F. G., & Lee, W. W. (1991). Predicting similarity and categorization from identification. *Journal of Experimental Psychology: General, 120,* 150–172.

Ashby, F. G., & Townsend, J. T. (1986). Varieties of perceptual independence. *Psychological Review, 93,* 154–179.

Balakrishnan, J. D. (1998). Some more sensitive measures of sensitivity and response bias. *Psychological Methods, 3,* 68–90.

Balakrishnan, J. D. (1999). Decision processes in discrimination: Fundamental misconceptions of signal detection theory. *Journal of Experimental Psychology: Human Perception and Performance, 25,* 1189–1206.

Batchelder, W. H., & Riefer, D. M. (1990). Multinomial processing models of source monitoring. *Psychological Review, 97,* 548–564.

Batchelder, W. H., Riefer, D. M., & Hu, X. (1994). Measuring memory factors in source monitoring: Reply to Kinchla. *Psychological Review, 101,* 172–176.

Berliner, J. E., & Durlach, N. I. (1973). Intensity perception: IV. Resolution in roving-level discrimination. *Journal of the Acoustical Society of America, 53,* 1270–1287.

Blackwell, H. R. (1963). Neural theories of simple visual discriminations. *Journal of the Optical Society of America, 53,* 129–160.

Bonnel, A.-M., & Hafter, E. R. (1998). Divided attention between simultaneous auditory and visual signals. *Perception & Psychophysics, 60,* 179–190.

Bonnel, A.-M., & Miller, J. (1994). Attentional effects on concurrent psychophysical discriminations: Investigations of a sample-size model. *Perception & Psychophysics, 55,* 162–179.

Braida, L. D., & Durlach, N. I. (1972). Intensity perception: II. Resolution in one-interval paradigms. *Journal of the Acoustical Society of America, 51,* 483–502.

Braida, L. D., & Durlach, N. I. (1988). Peripheral and central factors in intensity perception. In G. M. Edelman, W. E. Gall, & W. M. Cowan (Eds.), *Auditory function* (pp. 559–583). New York: Wiley.

Broadbent, D. (1958). *Perception and communication.* London: Pergamon.

Clarke, F. R. (1957). Constant-ratio rule for confusion matrices in speech communication. *Journal of the Acoustical Society of America, 29,* 515–520.

Creelman, C. D. (1960). Detection of signals of uncertain frequency. *Journal of the Acoustical Society of America, 32,* 805–810.

Creelman, C. D., & Macmillan, N. A. (1979). Auditory phase and frequency discrimination: A comparison of nine paradigms. *Journal of Experimental Psychology: Human Perception and Performance, 5,* 146–156.

Dai, H., Versfeld, N. J., & Green, D. M. (1996). The optimum decision rules in the *same-different* paradigm. *Perception & Psychophysics, 58,* 1–9.

DeCarlo, L. T. (1998). Signal detection theory and generalized linear models. *Psychological Methods, 3,* 186–205.

Donaldson, W. (1992). Measuring recognition memory. *Journal of Experimental Psychology: General, 121,* 275–277.

Dorfman, D. D., & Alf, E., Jr. (1969). Maximum likelihood estimation of parameters of signal detection theory and determination of confidence intervals: Rating method data. *Journal of Mathematical Psychology, 6,* 487–496.

Dosher, B. A. (1984). Discriminating preexperimental (semantic) from learned (episodic) associations: A speed-accuracy study. *Cognitive Psychology, 16,* 519–584.

Durlach, N. I., & Braida, L. D. (1969). Intensity perception: I. Preliminary theory of intensity resolution. *Journal of the Acoustical Society of America, 46,* 372–383.

Dusoir, T. (1983). Isobias curves in some detection tasks. *Perception & Psychophysics, 33,* 403–412.

Egan, J. P., Schulman, A. I., & Greenberg, G. Z. (1959). Operating characteristics determined by binary decisions and by ratings. *Journal of the Acoustical Society of America, 31,* 768–773.

Elliott, P. B. (1964). Tables of d'. In J. A. Swets (Ed.), *Signal detection and recognition by human observers* (pp. 651–684). New York: Wiley.

Francis, M. A., & Irwin, R. J. (1995). Decision strategies and visual-field asymmetries in *same-different* judgments of word meaning. *Memory & Cognition, 23,* 301–312.

Garner, W. R. (1974). *The processing of information and structure.* Potomac, MD: Erlbaum.

Geisler, W. S., & Chou, K. L. (1995). Separation of low-level and high-level factors in complex tasks: Visual search. *Psychological Review, 102,* 356–378.

Gourevitch, V., & Galanter, E. (1967). A significance test for one-parameter isosensitivity functions. *Psychometrika, 32,* 25–33.

Graham, N. V. (1989). *Visual pattern analyzers.* New York: Oxford University Press.

Graham, N. V., Kramer, P., & Haber, N. (1985). Attending to the spatial frequency and spatial position of near-threshold visual patterns. In M. I. Posner & O. S. M. Marin (Eds.), *Attention and performance: Vol. 11* (pp. 269–284). Hillsdale, NJ: Erlbaum.

Graham, N. V., & Nachmias, J. (1971). Detection of grating patterns containing two spatial frequencies: A test of single-channel and multiple-channel models. *Vision Research, 11,* 251–259.

Green, D. M. (1961). Detection of auditory sinusoids of uncertain frequency. *Journal of the Acoustical Society of America, 33,* 897–903.

Green, D. M. (1964). General prediction relating yes-no and forced-choice results [Abstract]. *Journal of the Acoustical Society of America, 36,* 1042.

Green, D. M., & Birdsall, T. G. (1978). Detection and recognition. *Psychological Review, 85,* 192–206.

Green, D. M., McKey, M. J., & Licklider, J. C. R. (1959). Detection of a pulsed sinusoid in noise as a function of frequency. *Journal of the Acoustical Society of America, 31,* 1446–1452.

Green, D. M., & Swets, J. A. (1966). *Signal detection theory and psychophysics.* New York: Wiley.

Green, D. M., Weber, D. L., & Duncan, J. E. (1977). Detection and recognition of pure tones in noise. *Journal of the Acoustical Society of America, 62,* 948–954.

Grier, J. B. (1971). Nonparametric indexes for sensitivity and bias: Computing formulas. *Psychological Bulletin, 75,* 424–429.

Hacker, M. J., & Ratcliff, R. (1979). A revised table of d' for M-alternative forced-choice. *Perception & Psychophysics, 26,* 168–170.

Hodge, M. H. (1967). Some further tests of the constant-ratio rule. *Perception & Psychophysics, 2,* 429–437.

Hodge, M. H., & Pollack, I. (1962). Confusion matrix analysis of single and multidimensional auditory displays. *Journal of Experimental Psychology, 63,* 129–142.

Hodos, W. (1970). Nonparametric index of response bias for use in detection and recognition experiments. *Psychological Bulletin, 74,* 351–354.

Irwin, R. J., & Francis, M. A. (1995a). Perception of simple and complex visual stimuli: Decision strategies and hemispheric differences in same-different judgments. *Perception, 24,* 787–809.

Irwin, R. J., & Francis, M. A. (1995b). *Psychophysical analysis of same-different judgments of letter parity.* Paper presented at the Fechner Day 95, Cassis, France.

Jesteadt, W., & Bilger, R. C. (1974). Intensity and frequency discrimination in one- and two-interval paradigms. *Journal of the Acoustical Society of America, 55,* 1266–1276.

Jones, F. N. (1974). History of psychophysics and judgment. In E. C. Carterette & M. P. Friedman (Eds.), *Handbook of perception: Vol. 2. Psychophysical judgment and measurement* (pp. 1–22). New York: Academic Press.

Kadlec, H. (1995). Multidimensional signal detection analyses (MSDA) for testing separability and independence: A Pascal program. *Behavior Research Methods, Instruments, & Computers, 27,* 442–458.

Kadlec, H. (1999a). MSDA2: Updated version of software for multidimensional signal detection analyses. *Behavior Research Methods, Instruments, & Computers, 31,* 384–385.

Kadlec, H. (1999b). Statistical properties of d' and β estimates of signal detection theory. *Psychological Methods, 4,* 22–43.

Kadlec, H., & Townsend, J. T. (1992a). Implications of marginal and conditional detection parameters for the separabilities and independence of perceptual dimensions. *Journal of Mathematical Psychology, 36,* 325–374.

Kadlec, H., & Townsend, J. T. (1992b). Signal detection analyses of dimensional interactions. In F. G. Ashby (Ed.), *Multidimensional probabilistic models of perception and cognition.* Hillsdale, NJ: Erlbaum.

Kinchla, R. A. (1994). Comments on Batchelder and Riefer's multinomial model for source monitoring. *Psychological Review, 101,* 166–171.

Kinchla, R. A., & Smyzer, F. (1967). A diffusion model of perceptual memory. *Perception & Psychophysics, 2,* 219–229.

Kingston, J., & Macmillan, N. A. (1995). Integrality of nasalization and F1 in vowels in isolation and before oral and nasal consonants:

A detection-theoretic application of the Garner paradigm. *Journal of the Acoustical Society of America, 97,* 1261–1285.

Klein, S. A. (1985). Double-judgment psychophysics: Problems and solutions. *Journal of the Optical Society of America, A, 2,* 1560–1585.

Klein, S. A., & Macmillan, N. A. (2001). Symposium on psychometric functions and adaptive methods [Special issue]. *Perception & Psychophysics, 63*(8).

Kohler, W. (1923). Zur Theorie des Sukzessivvergleichs und der Zeitfehler. *Psychologische Forschung, 4,* 115–175.

Liberman, A. M., Harris, K. S., Hoffman, H. S., & Griffith, B. C. (1957). The discrimination of speech sounds within and across phoneme boundaries. *Journal of Experimental Psychology, 54,* 358–368.

Lindsay, P. H., Taylor, M. M., & Forbes, S. S. (1968). Attention and multidimensional discrimination. *Perception & Psychophysics, 4,* 113–117.

Lisker, L. (1975). Is it VOT or a first-formant transition detector? *Journal of the Acoustical Society of America, 57,* 1547–1551.

Luce, R. D. (1959). *Individual choice behavior.* New York: Wiley.

Luce, R. D. (1963a). Detection and recognition. In R. D. Luce, R. R. Bush, & E. Galanter (Eds.), *Handbook of mathematical psychology* (Vol. 1, pp. 103–189). New York: Wiley.

Luce, R. D. (1963b). A threshold theory for simple detection experiments. *Psychological Review, 70,* 61–79.

Luce, R. D., Green, D. M., & Weber, D. L. (1976). Attention bands in absolute identification. *Perception & Psychophysics, 20,* 49–54.

Macmillan, N. A., & Creelman, C. D. (1990). Response bias: Characteristics of detection theory, threshold theory, and "nonparametric" measures. *Psychological Bulletin, 107,* 401–413.

Macmillan, N. A., & Creelman, C. D. (1991). *Detection theory: A user's guide.* New York: Cambridge University Press.

Macmillan, N. A., & Creelman, C. D. (1996). Triangles in ROC space: History and theory of "nonparametric" measures of sensitivity and response bias. *Psychonomic Bulletin & Review, 3,* 164–170.

Macmillan, N. A., & Creelman, C. D. (in press). *Detection theory: A user's guide* (2nd ed.). Mahwah, NJ: Erlbaum.

Macmillan, N. A., Goldberg, R. F., & Braida, L. D. (1988). Resolution for speech sounds: Basic sensitivity and context memory on vowel and consonant continua. *Journal of the Acoustical Society of America, 84,* 1262–1280.

Macmillan, N. A., & Kaplan, H. L. (1985). Detection theory analysis of group data: Estimating sensitivity from average hit and false-alarm rates. *Psychological Bulletin, 98,* 185–199.

Macmillan, N. A., Kaplan, H. L., & Creelman, C. D. (1977). The psychophysics of categorical perception. *Psychological Review, 84,* 452–471.

Maddox, W. T. (1992). Perceptual and decisional separability. In F. G. Ashby (Ed.), *Multidimensional models of perception and cognition* (pp. 147–180). Hillsdale, NJ: Erlbaum.

Maddox, W. T., & Estes, W. K. (1997). Direct and indirect stimulus-frequency effects in recognition. *Journal of Experimental Psychology: Learning, Memory, and Cognition, 23,* 539–559.

Marascuilo, L. A. (1970). Extensions of the significance test for one-parameter signal detection hypotheses. *Psychometrika, 35,* 237–243.

Markowitz, J., & Swets, J. A. (1967). Factors affecting the slope of empirical ROC curves: Comparison of binary and rating responses. *Perception & Psychophysics, 2,* 91–100.

Miller, G. A. (1956). The magical number seven, plus or minus two: Some limits on our capacity for processing information. *Psychological Review, 63,* 81–96.

Miller, J. O. (1996). The sampling distribution of d'. *Perception & Psychophysics, 58,* 65–72.

Miller, M. B., & Wolford, G. L. (1999). Theoretical commentary: The role of criterion shift in false memory. *Psychological Review, 106,* 398–405.

Nolte, L. W., & Jaarsma, D. (1967). More on the detection of one of M orthogonal signals.

Journal of the Acoustical Society of America, 41, 497–505.

Noreen, D. L. (1981). Optimal decision rules for some common psychophysical paradigms. In S. Grossberg (Ed.), *Mathematical psychology and psychophysiology* (pp. 237–280). Providence, RI: American Mathematical Society.

Pashler, H. (Ed.). (1998). *Attention*. Hove, England: Psychology Press.

Pierce, J. R., & Gilbert, E. N. (1958). On AX and ABX limens. *Journal of the Acoustical Society of America, 30,* 593–595.

Pollack, I., & Ficks, L. (1954). Information of elementary multidimensional auditory displays. *Journal of the Acoustical Society of America, 26,* 155–158.

Pollack, I., & Norman, D. A. (1964). A nonparametric analysis of recognition experiments. *Psychonomic Science, 1,* 125–126.

Pynn, C. T., Braida, L. D., & Durlach, N. I. (1972). Intensity perception: III. Resolution in small-range identification. *Journal of the Acoustical Society of America, 51,* 559–566.

Ratcliff, R., Sheu, C.-F., & Gronlund, S. D. (1992). Testing global memory models using ROC curves. *Psychological Review, 99,* 518–535.

Repp, B. H. (1982). Phonetic trading relations and context effects: New experimental evidence for a speech mode of perception. *Psychological Bulletin, 92,* 81–110.

Roediger, H. L., III, & McDermott, K. B. (1995). Creating false memories: Remembering words not presented in lists. *Journal of Experimental Psychology: Learning, Memory, and Cognition, 21,* 803–814.

Rotello, C. M., Macmillan, N. A., & Van Tassel, G. (2000). Recall-to-reject in recognition: Evidence from ROC curves. *Journal of Memory and Language, 43,* 67–88.

Searle, C., Colburn, H. S., Davis, M., & Braida, L. D. (1976). Model for auditory localization. *Journal of the Acoustical Society of America, 60,* 1164–1175.

Shannon, C. E., & Weaver, W. (1949). *The mathematical theory of communication*. Urbana: University of Illinois Press.

Shaw, M. L. (1982). Attending to multiple sources of information: I. The integration of information in decision-making. *Cognitive Psychology, 14,* 353–409.

Shepard, R. N. (1964). Attention and the metric structure of the stimulus space. *Journal of Mathematical Psychology, 1,* 54–87.

Snodgrass, J. G., & Corwin, J. (1988). Pragmatics of measuring recognition memory: Applications to dementia and amnesia. *Journal of Experimental Psychology: General, 117,* 34–50.

Sorkin, R. D. (1962). Extensions of the theory of signal detectability to matching procedures in psychoacoustics. *Journal of the Acoustical Society of America, 34,* 1745–1751.

Sorkin, R. D. (1999). Spreadsheet signal detection. *Behavior Research Methods, Instruments, & Computers, 31,* 46–54.

Sorkin, R. D., & Dai, H. (1994). Signal detection analysis of the ideal group. *Organizational Behavior and Human Decision Processes, 60,* 1–13.

Sorkin, R. D., Hays, C. J., & West, R. (2001). Signal detection analysis of group decision making. *Psychological Review, 108,* 183–203.

Sorkin, R. D., West, R., & Robinson, D. E. (1998). Group performance depends on the majority rule. *Psychological Science, 9,* 456–463.

Starr, S. J., Metz, C. E., Lusted, L. B., & Goodenough, D. J. (1975). Visual detection and localization of radiographic images. *Radiology, 116,* 533–538.

Swets, J. A. (1986). Indices of discrimination or diagnostic accuracy: Their ROCs and implied models. *Psychological Bulletin, 99,* 100–117.

Swets, J. A., Dawes, R. M., & Monahan, J. (2000). Psychological science can improve diagnostic decisions. *Psychological Science in the Public Interest, 1,* 1–26.

Swets, J. A., & Pickett, R. M. (1982). *Evaluation of diagnostic systems: Methods from signal detection theory*. New York: Academic Press.

Swets, J. A., Shipley, E. F., McKee, J. M., & Green, D. M. (1959). Multiple observations of signals in noise. *Journal of the Acoustical Society of America, 31,* 514–521.

Swets, J. A., Tanner, W. P., Jr., & Birdsall, T. G. (1961). Decision processes in perception. *Psychological Review, 68,* 301–340.

Tanner, W. P., Jr. (1956). Theory of recognition. *Journal of the Acoustical Society of America, 28,* 882–888.

Tanner, W. P., Jr. (1961). Physiological implications of psychophysical data. *Annals of the New York Academy of Sciences, 89,* 752–765.

Tanner, W. P., Jr., & Swets, J. A. (1954). A decision-making theory of visual detection. *Psychological Review, 61,* 401–409.

Treisman, M., & Williams, T. C. (1984). A theory of criterion setting with an application to sequential dependencies. *Psychological Review, 91,* 68–111.

Van Zandt, T. (2000). ROC curves and confidence judgments in recognition memory. *Journal of Experimental Psychology: Learning, Memory, and Cognition, 26,* 582–600.

Versfeld, N. J., Dai, H., & Green, D. M. (1996). The optimum decision rules for the oddity task. *Perception & Psychophysics, 58,* 10–21.

Wixted, J. T., & Stretch, V. (2000). The case against a criterion-shift account of false memory. *Psychological Review, 107,* 368–376.

Yonelinas, A. P. (1994). Receiver-operating characteristics in recognition memory: Evidence for a dual-process model. *Journal of Experimental Psychology: Learning, Memory, & Cognition, 20,* 1341–1354.

Yonelinas, A. P. (1997). Recognition memory ROCs for items and associative information: The contribution of recollection and familiarity. *Memory & Cognition, 25,* 747–763.

CHAPTER 3

Psychophysical Scaling

LAWRENCE E. MARKS AND GEORGE A. GESCHEIDER

INTRODUCTION: DEFINITIONS AND GOALS

The term *psychophysics* was coined nearly a century and a half ago by Gustav Fechner (1860), who defined it as "an exact theory of the functionally dependent relations of body and [mind] or, more generally, of the material and the mental, of the physical and the psychological worlds" (p. 7). Although he was interested in a wide range of mental phenomena, including dreams and imagination, Fechner is best known for his research and writings on sensory psychophysics. In Fechner's scheme, physical stimuli impinge on the sense organs, thereby evoking responses that ultimately lead to patterns of neural activity in the brain that are themselves, of course, physical in nature. For the neural-physical activity in the brain, there is corresponding sensory, or mental, activity. It follows, Fechner argued, that there are actually two domains of psychophysics: an *inner psychophysics,* which treats the relation between neural events and mental events, and an *outer psychophysics,* which treats the relation between external stimuli and mental events.

In modern parlance the domain of psychophysics corresponds to Fechner's (1860) outer psychophysics; in particular, psychophysics refers to the relation between external physical stimuli and the resulting sensations and perceptions. *Psychophysical scaling* refers to the process of quantifying mental events, especially sensations and perceptions, after which it is possible to determine how these quantitative measures of mental life are related to quantitative measures of the physical stimuli. Finally, *psychophysical functions* refer, in turn, to mathematical relations between scales of sensation, perception, or any other mental event and the corresponding physical stimuli.

Consider as an example the perception of loudness. As the physical intensity of a tone increases, its loudness increases. Further, the tone will appear louder when presented simultaneously to both ears (binaurally) rather than to just one ear (monaurally). How much does loudness increase when sound intensity increases? And how much louder is a tone heard binaurally compared to the same tone heard monaurally? These are psychophysical questions, and the answers to them require psychophysical scaling, that is, a way to quantify the perception of loudness. Determining psychophysical functions for loudness provides a means to measure the degree to which loudness increases when, for instance, a tone increases in intensity by 10 dB. Furthermore, determining loudness functions for both binaural and monaural listening, under

Preparation of this chapter was supported in part by grants DC02752 to Lawrence E. Marks and DC00380 to George A. Gescheider from the National Institutes of Health.

conditions that measure binaural and monaural loudness on a unitary scale, makes it possible to say whether a tone heard with two ears is twice as loud as the same tone heard with just one, and whether the ratio of binaural loudness to monaural loudness is constant across all levels of sound intensity.

What makes psychophysical functions important, and interesting, is the fact that they are rarely linear. It was clear to Fechner, as to others, that our sensory experiences do not simply mirror the physical world in a quantitative manner. To paraphrase Fechner, a chorus of 100 male voices does not sound 10 times as loud as an ensemble of 10, although the acoustic energy presumably is about 10 times as great. Awakening one morning with what he believed to be a great insight, Fechner proposed that the magnitudes of our sensations are not proportional to the intensities of the stimuli that arouse them, but instead grow with the logarithm of intensity, a rule that has come to be called Fechner's law. This rule is one of diminishing returns. It implies that uniform increases in the physical intensity of a stimulus will lead to successively smaller and smaller increments in the resulting sensation magnitude.

Why is psychophysical scaling necessary, and why is it important? Modern psychology arose from the framework and traditions of Western culture in general, and from Western philosophy and science in particular. Within these broad traditions, psychophysical scaling can be traced to two crucial developments: the dichotomy between physical and mental quantities and qualities, and the rise of quantification. The emphasis on quantification was a crucial factor not only in the rise of modern science but also in the rise of Western economies (see Crosby, 1997). Little wonder that when scientific psychology emerged in the second half of the 19th century, under the aegis of Gustav Fechner, Wilhelm Wundt, and others, it put such great stock in quantification. And little wonder that modern scientific psychology is rooted to a large extent in psychophysics, which for decades was the most estimably quantifiable branch of experimental psychology. In psychophysical scaling, quantification came to be applied to internal psychological events, to sensations in particular but in principle also to feelings and thoughts—at least to the extent that these vary in some kind of magnitude. Perhaps it is not surprising that Ebbinghaus (1885), for instance, was inspired by Fechner's psychophysics to apply quantitative methods to the study of human memory.

To conceive of scaling sensory or other mental magnitudes, or to consider what data to use and what theoretical frameworks to deploy in using those data in order to quantify sensory states, is ipso facto to acknowledge that the quantification of mental events may differ in important ways from the quantification of overt physical stimuli. This is to say that psychophysical scaling requires a broad conception of what it is that can be measured or quantified. Measurements can be made not only of denumerable items that can be counted such as the fingers on a hand, of extensive quantities such as the area of a football field, and of intensive quantities such as the radiant intensity of a fire, but also of our perception of number, of our perception of size, and of our perception of heat intensity. When a person stands by a fire, a physicist might measure the thermal energy, or irradiance, that is incident on the person's face, in physical units such as watts per square meter, whereas a psychophysicist might endeavor to measure how warm the radiation feels.

A primitive psychophysics can be found in Locke's (1690) account of primary and secondary ideas, and in Galileo's (1623/1960) anticipation of this account: "I do not believe that for exciting in us tastes, odors, and sounds there are required in external bodies anything but sizes, shapes, numbers, and slow or rapid movements; and I think that if ears, tongues, and noses were taken away, shapes, numbers, and motions would remain, but not odors or tastes or sounds" (p. 311). One might construe Galileo's statement as an answer to the question, "If a tree falls in the forest and no one hears it, is there a sound?" To distinguish the physical world from the perceptual world is also to distinguish the domain of physical science from the domain of mental science, or what would eventually become psychology.

Locke (1690) distinguished between two kinds of physical properties or qualities, between what we might call macroscopic and microscopic properties, or, in his terms, between primary and secondary qualities. Primary qualities, such as the number of items and their sizes and shapes, are macroscopic features of objects in the physical world, and these qualities pertain mainly to the objects' extension in space and in time. Further, Locke claimed that we perceive these primary qualities much as they really are. When, in modern terms, two acoustic events occur in succession, then as long as the time interval between them is not too brief, we experience their temporal succession, hearing two sounds as distinct. When we see a sphere, we perceive its roundness. Primary qualities, according to Locke, are experienced more or less veridically, pretty much as they are. In the case of extensive qualities such as linear extent, it seems fair to infer that Locke believed in what would now be called linear psychophysical functions, for example, that the perception of the length of an object is more or less proportional to its physical length.

Secondary qualities, by way of contrast, are those microscopic features of objects that, according to Locke (1690), we do not experience as they are. Light waves differ in their refractiveness, as Locke's contemporary Sir Isaac Newton showed, but we perceive this physical property of light not in terms of variations in wavelengths but in terms of variations in colors. Whereas some psychological attributes of experience may resemble the physical qualities that produce them—by and large the primary qualities of shape, size, and number of objects look and feel as they really are—other psychological attributes do not resemble their qualities or causes and must be distinguished from them. We would say that an object that is 20 cm long looks longer—in fact, probably about once again longer—than an object that is 10 cm long, and we believe that our perceptions of the sizes of objects more or less resemble or match the objects themselves. But light of 440 nm (billionths of 1 m) does not look shorter than light of 540 nm. The one looks blue and the other green. Color does not resemble wavelength.

If perception does not faithfully reflect the qualitative and quantitative properties of the physical world around us, then the scientific analysis of the world is not complete if one treats the world of physics alone. There is also a world of sensation, perception, cognition, and emotion—a world of mental events. The qualitative and quantitative psychophysics implicit in Locke's doctrine of primary and secondary qualities helped set the stage for philosophical discourse over the next two centuries on the sources and validity of knowledge—the domain known as epistemology—in which a psychology of perception would implicitly play a major role. This line of inquiry culminated in the 19th century psychophysics of Fechner and those who followed, a psychophysics that asks how sensory and other psychological magnitudes might be quantified (the problem of psychophysical scaling proper) and how these psychological magnitudes relate to the corresponding physical events in the world that produce them (the problem of the psychophysical function).

BRIEF HISTORY OF SCALING

In proposing his psychophysical rule, Fechner (1860) was anticipated by the mathematician Daniel Bernoulli, who a century earlier had suggested that a similar psychophysical formula characterizes the psychological value of economic goods, or what is called utility (see S. S. Stevens, 1975). As in Fechner's law, Bernoulli's equation is one of decreasing marginal gain: Each additional $1,000 provides much greater marginal happiness to a poor person than to a rich one. But for a law to show diminishing returns, it need not be logarithmic. Many mathematical formulas show decreasing marginal gains, one example being a square-root formula. In fact, just such a formula was proposed by Bernoulli's contemporary, Gabriel Cramer, as an alternative to the logarithmic rule (S. S. Stevens, 1975). Unfortunately, in the 18th century there was little in the way of evidence with which one could critically test the two proposals. Fechner's postulate would lead generations of researchers to seek evidence supporting or disconfirming the logarithmic rule.

As discussed later in this chapter, Fechner sought to bolster his logarithmic law through measures of sensory discrimination. Soon after conceiving his law, Fechner became aware of Weber's work, which showed the relativity of intensity discrimination. Weber found that the difference in stimulus intensity needed to be just noticeable was proportional to stimulus intensity. Once aware of this work, Fechner saw how Weber's findings could be enlisted to support Fechner's own logarithmic psychophysical equation. Fechner simply made the assumption that every just noticeable difference (JND) in stimulation constitutes a constant increment in sensation magnitude. By doing so, the magnitude of a sensation elicited by a particular stimulus could then be specified as the number of JNDs that the stimulus stood above the absolute threshold of detection. The logarithmic law follows from Weber's finding that the physical size of the JND ($\Delta\phi$) increases with stimulus intensity (ϕ), whereas, according to Fechner, its psychological size ($\Delta\psi$) does not.

This approach to psychophysical scaling came to be characterized as *indirect* in that the measures of sensation must be derived from the data through the application of a particular theoretical model. To note that a pair of stimuli is just barely discriminable is by itself to say nothing about the magnitudes of the evoked sensations, until a theory specifies how discrimination depends on sensory magnitudes. On the other hand, certain kinds of psychophysical judgment seem prima facie to quantify sensations, to yield scales in a fashion that is more *direct*. Indeed, by the second half of the 19th century sensory scientists were already developing such methods. Plateau (1872) and Delboeuf (1873), for example, used what came later to be called *partition methods* to assess sensation, asking observers to judge when two sensory intervals or differences appeared equal. If three stimuli are ordered in increasing physical intensity as A, B, and C, such that the ratio B/A of physical intensities equals the ratio C/B, then, according to Fechner's law, it follows that the perceived difference between B and A should equal the perceived difference between C and B. This can be put to an empirical test by asking observers to set a stimulus B to appear midway between A and C, a method known as *bisection*. Fechner's law predicts that $B = \sqrt{A \times C}$.

The 19th century also saw the first suggestions that observers may be able to judge directly, even quantitatively, the ratios as well as the differences between sensations. Merkel (1888) proposed a method that he called "doubled stimuli," actually a method of doubled sensations, in that an observer had to set one stimulus so that its magnitude appeared to be twice that of another. Fechner doubted such an approach, questioning whether sensations can even be said to have magnitudes per se. Although it may be possible to speak of the size of a difference between two sensations, it was far from evident that one could speak of the magnitude of a sensation. This doubt was expressed by James (1892) when he wrote, with his usual rhetorical flourish, "Surely, our feeling of scarlet is not a feeling of pink with a lot more pink added; it is something quite other than pink. Similarly with our sensations of an electric arc-light: it does not contain that many smoky tallow candles in itself" (pp. 23–24).

James's *quantity objection* may have persuaded many of his contemporaries, but it eventually gave way to the view that sensations can indeed be considered to have magnitudes: Surely we can match lights with regard to their brightness or decide whether one light is brighter than another, and surely we can match sounds with regard to their loudness or decide whether one sound is louder than another. The quantification of sensation requires more than this, to be sure, and even if one obtains direct estimates of sensation magnitudes, the assignment of numerical representations to sensations requires an appropriate underlying theory, making the scaling ultimately indirect. It is probably fair to say that most contemporary psychophysicists view sensation magnitude as a psychological variable that is never measured directly but that is inferred from some kind of empirically based operation or judgment, given an explicit or implicit model or theory. Thus, the terms *direct scaling* and *indirect scaling* ultimately turn out to be convenient labels that distinguish psychophysical methods that do or do not ask subjects to assess sensory differences or magnitudes per se. This should not be taken, however, to mean that the use of a direct scaling method automatically gives rise to a particular numerical scale of sensation.

Psychophysical scaling requires both a set of empirical operations and a theoretical framework through which one derives and characterizes the numerical values or representations. The latter is the domain of measurement theory. For example, conjoint measurement theory (Luce & Tukey, 1964) provides an axiomatic framework from which it is possible to determine numerical representations for stimuli in ordered pairs if these meet certain criteria. That is, in certain instances, one can derive scales that define sensory intervals from rank-order information. On the other hand, the rank-order information might arise from so-called direct judgments, and the representations derived through conjoint scaling need not be identical to the overt judgments themselves (for a discussion of measurement theory and scaling, see Luce & Krumhansl, 1988).

Most attempts at psychophysical scaling aim at either *interval scale* or *ratio scale* measurement, although it is not always clear which (if either) has been achieved in any particular study. Interval scales and ratio scales are characterized by the uniqueness of the numerical representations (see Suppes & Zinnes, 1963). Ratio scales permit multiplication by a positive integer, whereas interval scales permit multiplication by a positive integer and addition of a constant (see Stevens, 1946, 1951). Ratio-scale measurement of length allows transformation between metric scales and English scales, between feet or yards and centimeters or meters. Ratio scales are limited by a fixed lower bound of zero. Interval scales, by way of contrast, do not have a fixed zero, as witnessed by the measurement of temperature in degrees Fahrenheit and Celsius, both of which have arbitrary zero points. It may be tempting to classify the scale characterizing a particular set of results solely on the basis of the empirical operations that produce those measurements—tempting to assume, for example, that when an observer adjusts the lightness of a color to fall midway between two others, the resulting stimuli mark off equal steps of sensation, and thus provide measures on an interval scale of lightness, or that when an observer judges the loudness of one sound to be twice another, the outcome is a ratio scale of loudness. This temptation should be resisted, however, for the determination of the type of scale requires, in addition to the basic empirical measurements, a theoretical basis for representing the scale values numerically.

Implicit in this discussion is a distinction between *metric* and *nonmetric* scaling methods. Metric methods are typically direct in that they rely on judgments that have some prima facie metric properties. Observers may be asked, for example, to estimate numerically the differences in loudness between various pairs of sounds that vary in intensity. One form of metric analysis takes the numerical estimates at face value, defining each difference in loudness as proportional to the average numerical estimate. It is possible, however, if not likely, that such an approach would turn up inconsistencies within the data. An observer might judge the difference between stimulus i and stimulus j as 10 units, and the difference between j and k as 12.6 units, but the difference between i and k as 45 units. But the predicted difference between i and k would be 22.6 units, assuming a unidimensional representation of loudness. Given such a result, it would not be possible to assign a single numerical scale value to each stimulus and still predict the estimates accurately, as the judged difference between i and k is much too great. Although it is possible that loudness simply does not have the requisite properties to derive a scale, it is more likely that the inconsistency reflects the operation of some kind of nonlinear numerical response process. That is, a nonlinear rule might relate the underlying loudness differences to the overt judgments. If so, then it should be possible to derive a set of scale values for the stimuli that would accurately reflect the underlying sensation magnitude if it were possible to uncover and undo the nonlinear response transformation.

Such rescaling may be accomplished in two ways. The first is to find an appropriate equation to transform the estimates in order to make them consistent with a uniform numerical representation. In the example just given, one might simply take the square root of the observer's estimates, in which case the rescaled difference between A and B becomes 3.16, the rescaled difference between B and C becomes 3.55, and the rescaled difference between A and C becomes 6.71, this last value being equal to the sum of the first two. This approach is also metric in that one starts with the numerical responses, then transforms them according to a rule that seeks to maximize the consistency of the rescaled values with a single representation for each stimulus.

Another approach is to jettison the numerical values altogether and simply rank the judged differences from the smallest to the greatest. As it turns out, if certain conditions are met—if the underlying sensations have a unidimensional representation and if there is a sufficient number of appropriately spaced stimuli—then the rank-order information alone is sufficient to constrain the possible numerical representations to values on an interval scale (Shepard, 1966). A procedure to define such a set of scale values would be nonmetric in that it relies on only nonmetric (ordinal) properties of the data (it could, of course, be applied to data that had no overt metric properties, for instance, to ordinal comparisons of sensory differences). The nonmetric approach has been used successfully on many occasions to scale sensory magnitudes (e.g., Birnbaum & Elmasian, 1977; Parker & Schneider, 1974; Schneider, 1980; Schneider, Parker, Valenti, Farrell, & Kanow, 1978).

VALIDATION OF PSYCHOPHYSICAL SCALES

As the last section implies, and as will be evident in the sections that follow, different scaling methods frequently produce different psychophysical scales. Assuming that the

underlying perceptual scales themselves remain unchanged when methods vary, the
question arises, if different methods produce
different scales, then which method (if any)
gives the right answer? One approach to validation is to require methods to give consistent
and coherent results—for example, to require
internal consistency in ratings of perceptual
intervals, as described in the last section. In
a similar vein, as described later, Fechner's
assumptions have been challenged by evidence that augmenting two stimuli matched
for perceived intensity by adding equal numbers of JNDs to both can produce new stimuli
that no longer match. Further, variants of the
very same scaling method can produce different scales—for example, both category-rating
scales and magnitude-estimation scales depend on a variety of methodological and contextual factors—making it necessary to determine which variant produces a valid result.

Beyond measures of consistency, one can
try to embed the process of scaling within a
theoretical framework that makes empirically
testable predictions. In Anderson's (1970,
1982) model, scaling data are analyzed in
terms of compatibility with simple cognitive rules such as addition and subtraction,
which provide a functional theoretical framework, much like that of conjoint measurement
theory (Luce & Tukey, 1964). Marks and
Algom (1998) have set forth a challenge:
that psychophysical scales both inform and
be informed by substantive theories of sensory, perceptual, and cognitive processes. As
the remainder of the chapter shows, at least
some tentative steps have been taken in this
direction.

SCALING BY DISCRIMINATION
METHODS

The approach established by Fechner and later
elaborated by others such as Thurstone (1927)

"reflects the belief that differences between
sensations can be detected, but that their absolute magnitudes are less well apprehended"
(Luce & Krumhansl, 1988, p. 39). If magnitudes are poorly apprehended, then it will
be necessary to infer sensation magnitudes
not from judgments of magnitude per se but
from the proportion of times that one stimulus is reported to be greater than another,
coupling these measures of discrimination
with assumptions about the relation between
sensation magnitudes or differences and the
measures of discriminability. Generally, results using this approach are consistent with
Fechner's logarithmic law when a fixed range
of stimuli is used and it is assumed that sensation changes by a constant unit whenever two
stimuli are equally discriminable. Given a different set of assumptions, however, the very
same measures of stimulus discrimination can
lead to different numerical representations of
sensation and, consequently, to different psychophysical relations.

Fechnerian Discrimination Scales

Discrimination-scaling methods are designed
to construct scales of psychological attributes
from the discriminative or comparative responses of observers. These methods are
based on the Fechnerian principle that an observer's ability to discriminate two stimuli
grows as the difference between their psychological magnitudes grows. Fechner (1860)
applied this principle in the use of the difference limen (DL) or JND to construct scales
of sensation magnitude. Because the DL or
JND is the physical difference between two
stimuli that can be discriminated on a specific proportion of trials (e.g., a proportion of
0.75), all JNDs define pairs of stimuli that are
equally discriminable. Recognizing this fact,
Fechner went on to derive a psychological
scale, ψ, by then assuming that every (equally
noticed) difference between stimuli separated

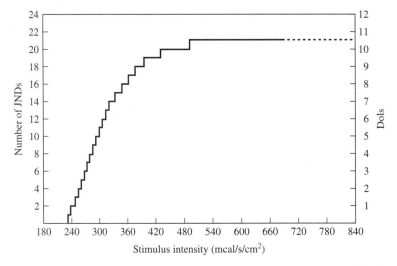

Figure 3.1   The dol scale of pain. One dol of pain intensity is equal to two successive JNDs.
SOURCE: From Hardy, Wolff, & Goodell, 1947. Copyright © 1947 by the *Journal of Clinical Investigation*.
Reproduced by permission of the Copyright Clearance Center, Inc.

by a JND, $\Delta\phi$, corresponds to an equal psychological difference. By making this assumption that JNDs represent equal increments in sensation magnitude ($\Delta\psi$), Fechner established a unit of measurement for sensation. Subsequently, using Weber's law, which says that the physical size of the JND ($\Delta\phi$) is proportional to stimulus intensity, ϕ, he derived his eponymous law, which states that sensation magnitude is proportional to the logarithm of stimulus intensity:

$$\psi = k \log \phi.$$

It is well established that the Weber fraction ($\Delta\phi/\phi$) is never constant over the entire range of stimulus intensities as dictated by Weber's law. The possibility remains, however, that a valid psychophysical scale may nevertheless be established from JNDs; one can accomplish this by measuring JNDs as a function of stimulus intensity instead of calculating them from Weber's law. If one assumes that every JND corresponds to an equal increment in sensation magnitude, then one can derive a scale by adding the subjective JNDs and plotting them as a function of their stimulus values (see Falmagne, 1971, 1974, 1985; Luce & Galanter, 1963).

An example is the *dol scale* for the perception of pain derived by Hardy, Wolff, and Goodell (1947). Hardy et al. focused radiant heat onto the forehead of an observer for a period of 3 s at various levels from the absolute threshold for pain to the most intense stimulus that could be tolerated without tissue damage. Between these limits, Hardy et al. measured 21 JNDs of pain. The dol scale, illustrated in Figure 3.1, is based on the cumulative number of subjective (pain) JNDs as a function of stimulus intensity. The dol, a Fechnerian unit of measurement of pain, is equal to two JNDs.

JNDs and the Form of the Psychophysical Function

If one makes the Fechnerian assumption that all JNDs represent equal changes in sensation magnitude, then it follows that the physical size of the JND ($\Delta\phi$) must be inversely related to the slope of the psychophysical function relating sensation magnitude to stimulus intensity. Unfortunately, the empirical evidence suggests otherwise. When psychophysical functions are measured by techniques other than the integration of JNDs, experimental results fail to demonstrate that $\Delta\phi$ is inversely related to the rate of growth of sensation magnitude (Gescheider, Bolanowski, Zwislocki, Hall, & Mascia, 1994; Hellman, Scharf, Teghtsoonian, & Teghtsoonian, 1987; Stillman, Zwislocki, Zhang, & Cefaratti, 1993; Zwislocki & Jordan, 1986).

Take the study of Hellman et al. (1987) as an example. These investigators measured loudness functions by asking observers to adjust the intensity of a 1000-Hz tone presented in quiet to be as loud as the same tone presented with a background of either narrow-band or wide-band noise. When this was done at various intensity levels of the tone, the rate of growth of the tone's loudness was found to be greater when heard in a background of narrow-band noise. As seen in Figure 3.2,

there is a point where the two functions cross, that is, a point at which the loudness of the tones is the same but the slopes of the functions differ. The insert of the figure shows that at the crossing point, the Weber fraction ($\Delta\phi/\phi$) for discriminating a change in the tone's intensity was essentially the same when the tone was presented in narrow-band and wide-band noise. Because the values of ϕ are, by definition, constant at the crossing point, a constant Weber fraction at the crossing point entails a constant JND ($\Delta\phi$). Contrary to Fechner's hypothesis, this was true even though the slopes of the loudness functions differed substantially.

These findings support an alternate hypothesis, set forth by Zwislocki and Jordan (1986), that the physical size of the JND is independent of the slope of the psychophysical function. Zwislocki and Jordan's hypothesis contradicts Fechner's assumption that JNDs are subjectively equal. The alternate hypothesis arose from the observation in patients with unilateral hearing impairment that JNDs for intensity are the same when sounds are presented to the normal ear and to the ear with cochlear impairment, even though the growth of loudness with increasing intensity is abnormally rapid in the impaired ear. Evidence that the physical size of the JND is independent of the slope of the psychophysical function has been reported in other sensory modalities as well. For example, although the slopes of vibrotactile functions are affected greatly by the presence of a background masking stimulus, the JND at a fixed level of sensation magnitude is not (Gescheider et al., 1994).

The finding that the physical size of the JND is independent of the slope of the psychophysical function is compatible with findings of earlier studies demonstrating that JNDs are not subjectively equal; these findings suggest that JNDs do not always provide an internally consistent set of psychophysical scales. For example, Durup and Piéron (1933)

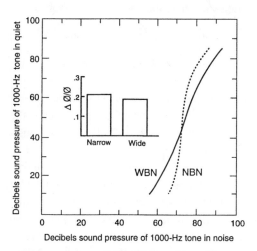

Figure 3.2 Growth of loudness of a 1000-Hz tone presented against a background of narrow-band noise (NBN) or wide-band noise (WBN). At the point where the curves cross, the difference limens (DLs) do not differ significantly.
SOURCE: From Hellman, Scharf, Teghtsoonian, & Teghtsoonian, 1987. Copyright © 1987 by the *Journal of the Acoustical Society of America.* Reproduced by permission.

had observers adjust the intensities of blue and red lights to appear equal in brightness and found that the two stimuli no longer had the same brightness when their intensities were increased by the same number of JNDs. It follows that JNDs did not provide equal increments in sensation and, as a result, cannot be used universally as a basic unit for measuring sensation magnitude (for overviews, see Krueger, 1989; Marks, 1974b; Piéron, 1952).

Ekman's Law

Ekman (1956, 1959) proposed that the subjective size of the JND, rather than being constant as Fechner presumed, increases in proportion to sensation magnitude. This principle, which became known as *Ekman's law,* states that

$$\Delta \psi = b \psi$$

where $\Delta \psi$ is the subjective size of the JND at sensation magnitude ψ. This equation, which applies to the psychological continuum, is exactly analogous to Weber's law, $\Delta \phi = c \phi$, in the physical continuum. The value of c in Weber's law refers to the constant fraction by which the stimulus, ϕ, must change in order for the change to be just noticeable. The value of b in Ekman's law refers to the constant fraction by which all values of sensation magnitude, ψ, change when the stimulus changes by one JND.

It is interesting that Stevens's power law, which was derived mainly from the results of magnitude-scaling procedures, implies that Ekman's law must also be valid if Weber's law is valid. Given that sensation magnitude ψ increases as stimulus intensity ϕ increases, Weber's law means that the physical size of the JND increases, whereas Ekman's law means that the corresponding subjective size of the JND increases. It follows mathematically that sensation magnitude will grow as a power function of stimulus intensity, with the exponent of the power function determined by

the values of c and b. Had Fechner assumed, as did Brentano (1874), that Weber's law applies to the sensation continuum as well as to the stimulus continuum, he might have derived a psychophysical power law instead of a logarithmic law (see Gescheider, 1997). In mathematical terms, Fechner assumed that Weber's law held at the differential level, $\delta \phi / \phi = c$. Given Fechner's assumption that JNDs are subjectively equal, $\delta \psi = b$, integrating the equation

$$\delta \psi / b = \delta \phi / c \phi$$

yields Fechner's logarithmic law

$$\psi = k \log \phi + \text{constant.}$$

On the other hand, given Brentano's assumption that JNDs are proportional to sensation magnitude, $\delta \psi / \psi = b$, integration of the equation

$$\delta \psi / b \psi = \delta \phi / c \phi$$

yields the equation

$$\log \psi = (c/b) \log \phi + \text{constant}$$

which is the logarithmic form of a power law.

According to R. Teghtsoonian (1971), the ratio of the weakest to the most intense sensation magnitude that can be experienced is the same in all sensory modalities, even though the stimulus ranges are very different. Thus, a single value of b may apply to all modalities. Using power functions and values of c gleaned from discrimination data in nine different modalities, Teghtsoonian found b to be nearly constant at about .03. To the extent that this is correct, Ekman's law can be stated more precisely as

$$\Delta \psi = .03 \psi$$

Note, however, that Ekman's and Teghtsoonian's hypothesis that JNDs reflect constant sensory ratios, like Fechner's hypothesis that JNDs are subjectively equal, is challenged by empirical evidence at the end of the last section (see Marks, 1974b).

Thurstonian Scaling

Law of Comparative Judgment

In 1927 Thurstone published a paper on the law of comparative judgment as applied to paired comparison judgments. The law of comparative judgment consists of a theoretical model describing internal processes that enable the observer to make paired comparison judgments of two stimuli with regard to some psychological attribute. From the proportion of times that one stimulus is judged to be greater on the attribute than another stimulus, it is possible to use the law of comparative judgment to calculate the average psychophysical scale values for each of the two stimuli (see Dawes, 1994; Luce, 1994).

Consider a hypothetical situation in which an observer compares the loudness of two sounds. If one sound is very much louder than the other, then it should be judged louder on most or all trials. As the intensity of the louder sound decreases, the proportion of times it is judged louder will decrease, until the proportion reaches 0.50, indicating equal loudness. If stimulus B is judged to be louder than stimulus A on only 0.55 of the trials, then the average loudness of B must be only slightly greater than that of A. But if stimulus C is judged louder than stimulus A on 0.95 of the trials, then the average loudness of C presumably is considerably greater than that of A. That is, if the average sensation magnitudes produced by two stimuli differ by only a small amount, then the stimuli will be confused often and the probability that one will be judged greater than the other will be close to 0.50. But if the average sensation magnitudes are very different, then they will be confused much less often, and the probability that the stronger will be judged greater than

the weaker will approach 1.0. Working on the relative excellence of handwriting samples, Thorndike (1910) recognized that such a principle might serve as a basis for psychophysical scaling. He determined the proportion of times one sample of handwriting was judged better than another, then took the z score associated with this proportion to represent the number of units on a psychological scale separating the perception of excellence elicited by the two samples.

In his law of comparative judgment, Thurstone (1927) clarified the reason for using z scores rather than proportions as units of the psychological scale. In Thurstone's terms, presenting a stimulus to the observer results in a *discriminal process* (sensory process) that has some value on a *psychological continuum*. Because of random fluctuations in the nervous system, repeated presentations of the same stimulus do not produce exactly the same perceptual effect every time but instead result in a variable discriminal process. This variability can be described by a Gaussian distribution, the standard deviation of which is called the *discriminal dispersion*. The psychological scale value of the stimulus is designated as the mean of the distribution of discriminal processes.

But how can one measure this distribution on the psychological continuum in order to find the average discriminal process for a particular stimulus? Thurstone decided that the characteristics of the distribution of discriminal processes can be obtained only indirectly, by considering the proportions associated with the observer's comparative judgments of pairs of stimuli. When stimulus i and stimulus j are presented for comparative judgment, each generates a discriminal process. The difference between the two discriminal processes on a single presentation of the stimuli is called a *discriminal difference*. Because the discriminal processes resulting from repeated presentations of stimuli i and j

are variable, the size of the discriminal difference also varies randomly from trial to trial. The distribution of discriminal differences is also Gaussian, with a mean equal to the difference between the means of the distributions of discriminal processes for stimuli i and j. The standard deviation of the distributions of discriminal differences is given by

$$S_{i-j} = \left(s_i^2 + s_j^2 - 2r_{ij}s_is_j\right)^{1/2}$$

where s_i and s_j represent the discriminal dispersions resulting from repeated presentation of stimuli i and j, and r is the correlation between momentary values of the discriminal processes.

On each presentation of the stimulus pair, the observer chooses the discriminal process that is stronger. As seen in Figure 3.3, the shaded area of the distribution of discriminal differences corresponds to the proportion of times that experience i is greater than j, whereas the unshaded area corresponds to the reverse. These areas can be expressed as z

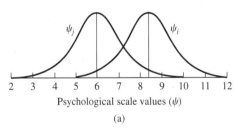

Psychological scale values (ψ)

(a)

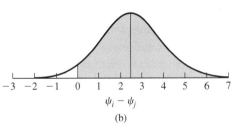

$\psi_i - \psi_j$

(b)

Figure 3.3   Two overlapping distributions of discriminal processes on the psychological continuum resulting from the repeated presentation of stimulus i and stimulus j and the distribution of discriminal differences.

scores that designate distance in standard deviation units. Therefore, Thurstone's law of comparative judgment is

$$U_i - U_j = z_{ij}\left(s_i^2 + s_j^2 - 2r_{ij}s_is_j\right)^{1/2}$$

where U_i and U_j are the means of the distributions of discriminal processes corresponding to the presentation of stimuli i and j, respectively. Thurstone outlined five versions or cases for applying the law of comparative judgment, with Case V being the easiest to solve because of its simplifying assumptions (for ways to evaluate simplifying assumptions, see Guilford, 1954; Torgerson, 1958). In Case V the discriminal dispersions of the two distributions are assumed to be equal, and the discriminal processes sampled from them during comparative judgments are assumed to be uncorrelated. With a common discriminal dispersion serving as a unit of measurement, the law of comparative judgment becomes

$$U_i - U_j = (z_{ij}\,s)\sqrt{2}.$$

Because s_i and s_j have the same value, the value assigned to s is arbitrary and affects only the size of the unit of measurement. Thus, if we set $s = 1/\sqrt{2}$, Case V implies that the difference between two scale values, $U_i - U_j$, is equal to the proportion of times that stimulus j is judged greater than stimulus i, expressed as a normal deviate; for example, a proportion of 0.84 would correspond to a difference of one scale unit.

When the law of comparative judgment is applied to an actual scaling problem, scale values are determined for several, not just two, stimulus values. For example, one might be interested in finding the psychological scale values of stimuli S_i, S_j, S_k, and S_l. The simplest procedure is to use one of the stimuli, such as S_i, as a standard stimulus to compare to the other three. The proportions of times that the psychological attribute is judged greater for S_j, S_k, and S_l than for S_i is determined. These proportions are then converted to z scores by referring to a table of the cumulate Gaussian distribution. The differences in the psychological scale values of S_i and each of the other three stimuli can then be computed.

A similar logic appears in the theory of signal detection (TSD), as developed by Tanner and Swets (1954) to apply to problems of stimulus detection and discrimination. The theory assumes that the observer's task in a discrimination experiment is to decide which of two signals is more intense, and that, over repeated trials, the effects in the nervous system of these signals are noisy and therefore produce overlapping distributions. The observer acts like a statistical hypothesis tester (Gigerenzer & Murray, 1987), deciding on each trial the likelihood that one stimulus is stronger than the other, or that a given stimulus was the stronger or the weaker of the two. Various measures of discriminability can be determined from the results. One of these is d', which is interpreted to represent the distance between the means of the two distributions along the psychological continuum. Formally, d' is equivalent to the difference in scale values derived from Thurstone's law of comparative judgment, so the principles underlying TSD are inherent in Thurstonian scaling (Gigerenzer & Murray, 1987; Luce, 1977), making it possible to use TSD methods to derive psychophysical scales (for examples, see Braida & Durlach, 1972; Durlach & Braida, 1969; Luce, Green, & Weber, 1976; see also Macmillan & Creelman, 1991). For a thorough account of TSD, see Chapter 2 in this volume.

Method of Paired Comparison

The method of paired comparison is most often used to collect data for constructing scales based on comparative judgments. It is an elaboration of the method just described, but in this case the observer is required to compare all possible pairs of stimuli. Given stimuli S_i, S_j, S_l, and S_m, an observer compares

Table 3.1 Scale Value Differences and Mean Scale Values Obtained Using the Method of Paired Comparison

	S_i	S_j	S_k	S_l	Mean
S_i	—	$U_i - U_j$	$U_i - U_k$	$U_i - U_l$	U_i
S_j	$U_j - U_i$	—	$U_j - U_k$	$U_j - U_l$	U_j
S_k	$U_k - U_i$	$U_k - U_j$	—	$U_k - U_m$	U_k
S_l	$U_l - U_i$	$U_l - U_j$	$U_l - U_k$	—	U_l

stimulus pairs $S_i - S_j$, $S_i - S_k$, $S_i - S_l$, $S_j - S_k$, $S_j - S_l$, and $S_k - S_l$. The number of comparative judgments for each pair must be sufficiently great—at least 100 if the scale is to be constructed for a single observer. The number may be reduced proportionally when the final scale is to be constructed from the judgments of several observers. Because every stimulus is compared to every other stimulus in paired comparison, a matrix can be constructed like that in Table 3.1, which gives the differences between scale values for all possible nonidentical pairs of stimuli. The final scale value assigned to each stimulus is the average of the scale distances between that stimulus and other stimuli.

Because the law of comparative judgment provides a model for converting observed proportions of paired comparisons into scale values, it is possible to reverse the procedure and calculate proportions from scale values. In the example of Case V given in the last section, a difference in scale value of one unit would correspond to a proportion of 0.84. The proportions calculated from the final scale values obtained by paired comparison can be compared with those obtained in the experiment. If the proportions predicted from the model agree closely with those obtained experimentally, then the results support the application of the model with its particular assumptions (see Torgerson, 1958).

When measurable physical stimuli such as sounds and weights are judged by paired comparison and Thurstone's Case V is applied, the results are consistent with Fechner's law provided that Weber's law holds. This result is expected because the assumption that the variability of discriminal processes is constant for different stimuli in Case V amounts to the Fechnerian assumption that the subjective size of the JND is constant. If Thurstone had proposed a Case VI in which the discriminal dispersions increase in proportion to sensation magnitude, then a power function relating sensation magnitude to stimulus intensity might have resulted (Stevens, 1959b, 1975).

Thurstone's model requires that paired comparisons be *transitive*. If stimulus A is preferred over stimulus B and stimulus B is preferred over C, then stimulus A should be preferred over stimulus C. Some results, however, fail to exhibit transitivity. Coombs (1950, 1964) developed a model to explain intransitivity as resulting from the observer's having a preferred value at an intermediate point on the psychological dimension, a point that does not correspond to one of the extremes. In paired comparison, the observer may tend to choose the stimulus that is closer to the preferred value; as a consequence, the scale is folded around this value. Using Coombs's unfolding model, scale values on the psychological continuum are recovered by unfolding the continuum using the observer's preference data.

There is another possible explanation for lack of transitivity. Transitivity may fail if the psychological experiences vary in several dimensions rather than just one. This leads to the topic of multidimensional scaling.

Multidimensional Scaling

Much of psychophysical scaling consists of attempts to measure an observer's experience on a single psychological dimension. For example, magnitude-estimation, category-scaling, and discrimination-scaling procedures have often been used to measure the loudness of sounds, the brightness of lights, and the intensity of pain. The success of these procedures depends on the ability of the observer to make appropriate judgments of magnitudes or differences on a single psychological dimension while ignoring concomitant changes along other dimensions. For example, in judging loudness an observer must ignore any change in the pitch of tones that may occur as the intensity of the stimulus changes (S. S. Stevens, 1935; see also Gulick, Gescheider, & Frisina, 1989). The problem is compounded if the dimension of interest cannot be clearly defined, especially if the sensations vary substantially along more than one dimension. Fortunately, methods of *multidimensional scaling* (Schiffman, Reynolds, & Young, 1981) make it possible both to identify the underlying subjective dimensions associated with the perception of differences among stimuli and to assign to each stimulus a psychological scale value on each of these dimensions.

Multidimensional scaling provides methods to derive a unit of measurement that is common to all of the underlying psychological dimensions. Measuring the overall psychological distance between two colored stimuli that differ in hue (which color), saturation (how much color), and brightness (how intense) is meaningful only if hue, saturation, and brightness are measured with a common unit. In multidimensional scaling, observers typically judge the overall similarity or dissimilarity of all possible stimulus pairs in an ensemble, and it is assumed that the judgments depend on some kind of integration of commensurable differences along all of the constituent dimensions. From these measures it is then possible to derive the underlying psychological dimensions mathematically and, for each stimulus, to determine scale values on each dimension. To do this, one often needs to know nothing more than the rank orders of the overall similarities, that is, which two stimuli are most similar, which are next, and so forth. Given a sufficiently large set of stimuli, the rank-order information suffices to determine a metric structure (Shepard, 1966).

The dimensions revealed by multidimensional scaling can often be represented in a multidimensional space. A common assumption is that the multidimensional space is euclidean. Euclidean space is the space of everyday experience, where any point in space can be defined in terms of a set of coordinates and the shortest distance between two points is a straight line. For example, in the two-dimensional space of Figure 3.4, each point is specified in terms of values of X and Y. If one knows the coordinate values for any two points within the euclidean space, it is possible to compute the distance between points from the Pythagorean theorem. The principle is illustrated for points A and B, where the distance between i and j (D_{ij}) is determined by

$$D_{ij} = [(X_i - X_j)^2 + (Y_i - Y_j)^2]^{1/2}.$$

In traditional nonmetric multidimensional scaling, the distances between stimuli are estimated from experimental observations, and a quantitative model is used to compute the coordinate values for each stimulus. On successive iterations, the distances between the stimuli are adjusted and then compared to the rank order of the data. Iterations end when any improvement in goodness of fit falls below a predetermined threshold. The number of dimensions is fixed for a given computation, but it is possible to iterate the computation assuming different numbers of dimensions. A solution is accepted when adding dimensions no longer substantially improves the fit to the data, or the additional dimensions are not readily interpretable. An example appears in Figure 3.5, in which a model called ALSCAL was used to recreate a map of the positions of cities in the United States from a rank ordering of their distances (Schiffman et al., 1981).

Euclidean space is easily understood when depicted graphically. Another type of space, also easy to understand graphically, is a city block, in which the distance between stimuli is given as the sum of the individual component distances along the individual dimensions,

$$D_{ij} = (X_i - X_j) + (Y_i - Y_j).$$

In New York City, to go from 41st Street and 1st Avenue to 42nd and 2nd Avenue, one must either walk from 41st to 42nd, then from 1st

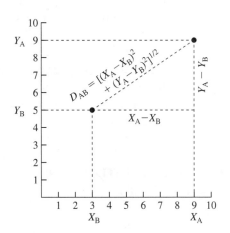

Figure 3.4 Two-dimensional space illustrating euclidean distance and city-block distance.

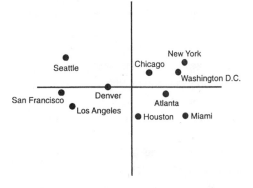

Figure 3.5 ALSCAL analysis of intensity of flying distances.
SOURCE: From Schiffman, Reynolds, & Young, 1981. Copyright © 1981 by Academic Press, Inc. Reproduced by permission.

to 2nd, or vice versa—a city-block path. In euclidean space, one traverses the diagonal (presumably by passing through the intermediate buildings). Torgerson (1958) pointed out that city-block representations of distances seem to fit the data better when the psychological dimensions are obvious to the observer. This conjecture is supported by results of Attneave (1950), in which a city-block space provided the best representation of similarity judgments of visual stimuli that varied along such clearly distinguishable dimensions as form, size, and hue. Euclidean space may represent the data better when the observer does not easily separate the dimensions such as pitch and loudness or hue and saturation. Note, however, that it is not always easy to distinguish the fit of city-block and euclidean models (see Schneider & Bissett, 1981).

The generalized formula that describes the distance, D, between two points in euclidean or city-block space is

$$D = \left(\sum d^n \right)^{1/n}$$

where d is the distance along one of the component dimensions and n is equal to or greater than 1. In city-block space, $n = 1$, and in Euclidean space, $n = 2$. Both of these multidimensional spaces are examples of Minkowski n metrics. Minkowski metrics with values of n other than 1 or 2 are more difficult to conceptualize but sometimes provide superior fits (e.g., Gregson, 1965, 1966).

The attractiveness of multidimensional scaling derives from the presumed properties of the space formed by the dimensions extracted. According to Melara (1992), there are two fundamental characteristics associated with this space: First, it serves as a psychological model, and second, it provides a metric. As a model, the spatial relations among stimuli, defined by the values of the coordinates of the space, provide a representation of the psychological similarities among stimuli.

Psychologically similar stimuli fall close to one another in multidimensional space, and psychologically dissimilar stimuli fall far apart. For the distances between pairs of points to satisfy the requirements of a metric, three conditions must be satisfied (Beals, Krantz, & Tversky, 1968). First, symmetry is demonstrated when the distance from X to Y equals that from Y to X. Second, positivity dictates that distances can never be negative. And third, the *triangle* inequality requires that the sum of distances X to Y plus Y to Z can never be smaller than the distance between any two of them (e.g., X to Z). These three conditions, called metric axioms, must be satisfied in order to measure the observers' experiences as they vary along multiple psychological dimensions (see also Luce & Krumhansl, 1988).

Several analytic strategies are available for multidimensional scaling (see Schiffman et al., 1981). Typically, one seeks to establish the minimal number of dimensions needed to represent the data adequately and, for each stimulus, to establish scale values on each dimension. Because measures of goodness of fit improve as the number of dimensions increases, one must decide when the fit of the model to the proximities (similarities or differences) no longer substantially improves with additional dimensions. Detailed information regarding empirical methods and analytic strategies can be found in sources specifically devoted to the topic (e.g., Davison, 1983; Schiffman et al., 1981).

SCALING BY PARTITION AND MAGNITUDE METHODS

Partition methods and magnitude methods of psychophysical scaling require observers to estimate or compare directly the subjective magnitudes of stimuli or the differences between stimuli. These methods developed largely as doubts grew about the validity of scales derived indirectly by applying the logic of Fechner and Thurstone to measures of sensory discrimination. Whereas scaling methods grounded in discrimination data call on observers to make ordinal judgments about sensations, partition-scaling and magnitude-scaling methods call on observers to make more sophisticated judgments of the relationships among the subjective magnitudes, such as their subjective difference or ratio.

Partition Scaling

Methods of partition scaling are designed to construct interval scales of psychological attributes directly from the judgments of observers. In these methods, observers try to partition the psychological continuum into equal perceptual intervals. Two main methods, equisection scaling and category scaling, have been developed to accomplish this objective. In equisection scaling, observers adjust the values of stimuli to set off equal-appearing intervals of sensations, and in category scaling, observers label various stimuli so that successive labels represent uniform subjective steps.

Equisection Scaling

As the name implies, equisection scaling requires observers to section the psychological continuum into distances that are judged equal. For instance, an observer may be told that stimulus A represents the lowest value and stimulus D the highest value of the range, and then may be asked to set the levels of stimuli B and C so that the distances between A and B, B and C, and C and D are all equal. Because observers are instructed to adjust stimuli so that successive intervals or differences are equal, it is commonly assumed that the results provide interval-scale measurement of the psychological attribute. But the interval

properties of the scale need to be validated independently. Unfortunately, validation procedures are often not used even when the psychological attribute has never before been scaled by the method.

The bisection method, originally used by Plateau (1872), was the earliest version of equisection. In bisection, two stimuli, A and C, are presented for inspection, and the observer is asked to choose a third stimulus, B, that falls exactly between, so that the distance from A to B equals that from B to C. Thus, Plateau had artists paint a gray that was midway between black and white. Generally, in equisection scaling experiments, the observer sections more than two intervals on the psychological continuum. Munsell, Sloan, and Godlove (1933) used equisection to construct a psychophysical scale of the lightness of grays. Beginning with black and ending with white, observers chose a series of gray surfaces to divide the psychological continuum into eight psychologically equal steps.

There are two techniques for determining a series of equal sense distances from equisection. In the simultaneous solution, the observer is presented with two stimuli and asked to choose $n - 1$ intermediate stimuli to create n equal psychological distances. In constructing the psychophysical scale, subjective magnitudes on the psychological continuum are represented by any arbitrary series of numbers separated by equal numerical intervals (e.g., 1, 2, 3, 4, 5), and the relevant physical characteristic of the stimuli corresponding to these equally spaced subjective magnitudes are determined by physical measurement. The results of the experiment are generally presented as a psychophysical function, which shows the scale values of subjective magnitude as a function of the relevant physical dimension of the stimulus. In this way, for example, one can determine how the brightness of lights or the pain of

noxious stimuli depends on the intensities of
the stimuli that elicit the experiences.

An alternative approach is the progressive
solution, in which the observer on a given trial
chooses only a single stimulus to bisect a single sensory distance. Each of the two smaller
intervals may then be subsequently bisected,
and the procedure continued until one obtains
the desired number of equal psychological intervals. If four equal intervals are desired, for
example, then the interval between the two
end stimuli would be bisected first, and the
two resulting equal intervals would be subsequently bisected, first one and then the other.
The simultaneous solution and the progressive solution are illustrated schematically in
Figure 3.6.

A good example of the simultaneous solution is provided by Stevens and Volkmann
(1940), who used the method of equisection to scale the pitch of pure tones over a
wide range of stimulus frequencies. On different occasions, observers sectioned into four
psychologically equal intervals each of three
overlapping frequency ranges (40–1000 Hz,
200–6500 Hz, and 3000–12000 Hz). For each
of these frequency ranges, the end tones were

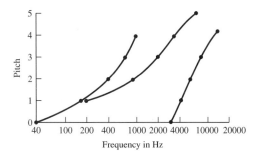

Figure 3.7   Three equisection scales of the pitch
of pure tones for three overlapping frequency
ranges.
NOTE: Data of S. S. Stevens and Volkmann (1940).
SOURCE: From Gescheider, 1997. Copyright ©
1997 by Lawrence Erlbaum, Inc. Reproduced by
permission.

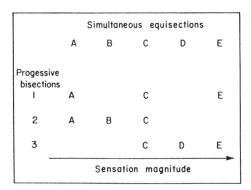

Figure 3.6   Sensations that are separated by equal
sense differences as determined by simultaneous
and progressive solutions.
SOURCE: From Gescheider, 1997. Copyright ©
1997 by Lawrence Erlbaum, Inc. Reproduced by
permission.

fixed in frequency, and the observer adjusted
the frequency of three variable tones to create four psychologically equal steps in pitch.
Stevens and Volkmann then assigned numerals increasing by unit steps to the five successive frequencies in each of three frequency
ranges. This procedure resulted in the three
psychophysical functions seen in Figure 3.7.

Because the objective of the experiment
was to construct a single psychophysical function for pitch, the three component functions
had to be combined into one function extending over the entire frequency range from
40 to 12000 Hz. To accomplish this, S. S.
Stevens and Volkmann (1940) used a graphic
procedure to construct a single function that
maximized overlap of the three component
functions while at the same time accurately
representing the steps measured within each.
Torgerson (1958) suggested a more systematic procedure. For the overlapping portions
of the frequency ranges, he simply plotted the
values in the midrange as a function of the
values in both the lower range and the upper range. From the linear functions fitted to
the points, he was able to convert the units of
the lower and upper ranges into the units of the
middle scale, thereby creating a single pitch

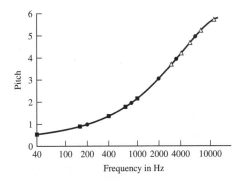

Figure 3.8   Pitch scale for frequencies from 40 to 12000 Hz.

NOTE: The squares, circles, and triangles represent data obtained from the lower, middle, and upper frequency ranges, respectively. Data of Stevens and Volkmann (1940).

SOURCE: From Torgerson, 1958. Copyright © 1958 by John Wiley & Sons, Inc. Reproduced by permission of the Social Science Research Council.

scale covering the entire frequency range. The resulting pitch scale appears in Figure 3.8.

Torgerson (1958) made the important point that although a scale can always be constructed using equisection procedures, the procedures themselves usually have no built-in criterion for accepting or rejecting the hypothesis that the observer is in fact capable of making equal-interval judgments. To demonstrate that the intervals are indeed mathematically equal, validating procedures should be built into the experiment, or additional experiments should be conducted. If, for example, stimulus B is found in a bisection experiment to lie halfway between A and C, then B should also lie halfway between A and C in an equisection experiment in which the observers create four intervals by setting three stimuli between A and C. The equality of sensory intervals means that the intervals or differences themselves have ratio properties. In this example, the psychological distance between A and C is twice that between A and B or that between B and C.

The pitch scale of S. S. Stevens and Volkmann (1940) satisfied one criterion for validity, namely internal consistency, in that the scale values obtained for the lower and upper ranges of stimulus frequency were linearly related to the scale values obtained for the overlapping portion of the middle range. Indeed, it was this finding that made it possible to combine scale values from the three frequency ranges into a single psychophysical function for pitch.

Category Scaling

Methods of category scaling, like those of equisection scaling, are designed to measure psychological attributes on an interval scale. Category techniques and equisection techniques, however, require the observer to perform somewhat different tasks. In equisection scaling observers must adjust or choose from a large set those stimuli that serve to mark off equal distances on the psychological continuum. In category scaling observers assign a category label to each of several stimuli in such a way that the categories are equidistant on the psychological continuum. For example, with a five-point category scale, observers should assign categories to stimuli so that the distances on the psychological continuum between categories 1 and 2, between categories 2 and 3, between categories 3 and 4, and between categories 4 and 5 are all equal. The method of equal-appearing intervals is the simplest version of category scaling, in which it is assumed that observers are able to keep the intervals between category boundaries psychologically equal as they assign stimuli to the various categories. Under this assumption, the category values assigned to stimuli are treated as interval scale measures on the psychological continuum.

Accurate estimation of scale values requires that a fairly large number of judgments be given to each stimulus. This can be achieved by having many observers judge each stimulus once, or by having one observer, or a few observers, judge each stimulus many times. For a particular stimulus, the psychological scale value of the psychological attribute under investigation is taken as the average (mean or median) value assigned. A plot of the average category against the value of the stimulus reveals the form of the psychophysical function.

Several kinds of response bias can affect category scales constructed by the method of equal-appearing intervals. The judgments of an observer, if determined solely by the perceived magnitude on the psychological continuum of the stimulus, should be independent of the values of other stimuli presented on other trials. The scale values for a particular stimulus, however, are often found to depend on the values of other stimuli used in the experiment. This contaminating effect results from a strong tendency for observers to use the categories about equally often. When an observer is biased to respond in this way, the particular spacing of the stimuli on the physical continuum can greatly influence the form of the psychophysical function. If, for example, the function relating the mean ratings to stimulus intensity is negatively accelerated, then the curvature will tend to be exaggerated if the observers are presented a cluster of low-intensity stimuli and only a few high-intensity stimuli. In this case, observers tend to assign all but a few of the highest categories to the weak stimuli, leaving the remaining one or two categories for the strong ones. The result is an exaggeration of the distances among the low-intensity stimuli. The same tendency can reduce the curvature if the observers are presented many stimuli near the high end of the stimulus continuum and only a few at the low end. The effects of stimulus spacing are illustrated in Figure 3.9. In this hypothetical example, when the stimuli cluster near the low end of the stimulus range, the curvature of the function is very negatively accelerated, whereas the function is almost linear when the stimuli cluster near the high end.

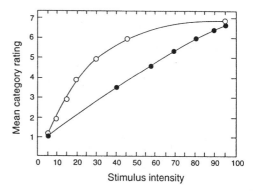

Figure 3.9   Hypothetical example of the effects of stimulus spacing on the form of the category scale.
SOURCE: From Gescheider, 1997. Copyright © 1997 by Lawrence Erlbaum, Inc. Reproduced by permission.

Parducci (1965, 1974) developed a range-frequency model for category scaling. According to this model, the observer's distribution of categorical responses depends on both the range of the stimuli and the frequency with which various stimuli are presented. Specifically, Parducci proposes that observers tend to divide the stimulus range into equal intervals over which they distribute their response categories. According to the first part of the model, observers use all of the categories regardless of whether the stimulus range is narrow or wide, so the slope of the resulting function is inversely related to the range of the stimuli. According to the second part of the model, observers assign categories equally often independent of the frequency with which various stimuli are presented, so the curvature of the resulting function depends on the stimulus distribution.

Skewing the frequency distribution of stimulus presentations positively, so that weak stimuli are presented more often than strong ones, causes observers to distribute their responses widely over the range of weak stimuli, leaving only a few high categories for the strong stimulus levels. The resulting category scale, when plotted against stimulus intensity, becomes more negatively accelerated than it is when the distribution is uniform. On the other hand, skewing the frequency distribution of stimulus presentations negatively, so that the strong stimuli are presented most often, causes observers to distribute their responses widely over the strong stimuli, leaving relatively few categories for the weak stimulus levels. In this case, the resulting psychophysical function is less negatively accelerated than one obtained with a uniform stimulus distribution, and may even become positively accelerated.

The problems that arise in category scaling as a result of the tendency to use categories equally often can be minimized, according to S. S. Stevens and Galanter (1957), through the use of an iterative procedure requiring observers to scale the stimuli successively several times. In the first scaling, the spacing of the stimuli is arbitrary, and a scale is constructed from the category judgments. This scale gives a first approximation to the uncontaminated scale. A new series of stimuli is then chosen with these stimuli separated by equal distances as defined by the first scale. Using a new group of observers, a second scale is determined. The second scale is then used to define yet another set of stimuli, spaced to give equal distances on that scale, and a third set of ratings is obtained. The procedure continues until successive scales no longer differ, indicating that an uncontaminated scale has been achieved by neutralizing the effects of the observers' expectation that the stimulus series is arranged so that categories appear equally often (see also Pollack, 1965a, 1965b).

Another approach to minimizing these response tendencies is to provide the observers with a verbal label for each category. Under appropriate conditions, the verbal labels may provide landmarks or anchors that help the observers to resist tendencies to assign categories equally often (e.g., Borg & Borg,

1994). An example is Borg's (1972) rating of perceived effort (RPE) scale, in which verbal labels are applied to perceived exertion experienced in exercise, such as riding a stationary bicycle under various work loads. In its earliest version, the highest number on the RPE scale is 20 and has the verbal label of "maximal exertion," and the lowest number on the scale is 6 and has a label of "no exertion at all"—these values being chosen to equal about 10% of the corresponding heart rate (200 to 60 beats/min) induced in young observers. Between the values of 6 and 20 are seven descriptive labels, uniformly distributed along with the numerical scale values; experimental results showed that RPE judgments are linearly related to the work loads during exercise as measured by the bicycle ergometer. A major advantage of the RPE scale compared to unlabeled category scales lies in the use of the label "maximal exertion," which presumably represents an experience common to all observers. Men and women, for example, presumably experience a similar level of exertion at maximum, even though the levels of physical work differ, as in Figure 3.10. Borg has

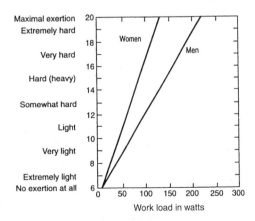

Figure 3.10 Borg's (1972) scale of perceived exertion.
SOURCE: From Gescheider, 1997. Copyright © 1997 by Lawrence Erlbaum, Inc. Reproduced by permission.

argued that this method makes it possible to compare individuals and groups directly.

In addition to producing consistent results, the use of verbally labeled category scales seems to reduce the susceptibility of category scales to some of the potentially biasing effects of stimulus spacing. Ellermeier, Westphal, and Heidenfelder (1991) had observers rate the pain produced by pressure applied to the finger. Observers were instructed to rate pain by first determining into which of the following categories each stimulus fell: very slight pain, slight pain, medium pain, severe pain, or very severe pain. After choosing a verbal category, the observers then had to fine-tune the rating by giving a numerical rating on a 10-point scale within each category. Thus, the number ranges within categories were very slight pain (1–10), slight pain (11–20), medium pain (21–30), severe pain (31–40), and very severe pain (41–50). As seen in Figure 3.11, when observers rated pain produced by stimulus sets containing relatively low or high intensities, they showed only a small tendency to give the same range

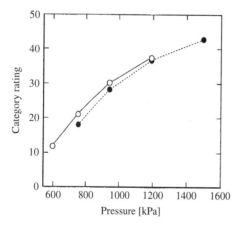

Figure 3.11 Category ratings of pain as a function of pressure applied to the fingertip for stimuli in a low range and stimuli in an overlapping higher range of intensities.
SOURCE: From Ellermeier, Westphal, & Heidenfelder, 1991. Reproduced by permission.

of category judgments to both stimulus sets. Instead, the category judgments tended to reflect more closely the absolute levels of the stimuli presented. Ellermeier et al. concluded that the verbal labels provided a *Bezugssystem* (reference frame), derived from an accumulation of everyday experiences, for making category ratings that are independent of the context of the particular stimuli presented in the testing session (Heller, 1985). When the observers are given only numerical labels as categories, with no verbal descriptors, then the observers tend to use the numbers to categorize any given set of stimuli relative to one another instead of categorizing them within the broader frame of reference of experiences obtained outside, as well as inside, the laboratory.

Although verbally labeled category-scaling procedures may encourage observers to categorize stimuli according to an external frame of reference and thus may help minimize certain response biases, they may introduce others. For example, the form of the psychophysical function may be influenced by the experimenter's arbitrary choice of the numbers assigned to the various labels (Gescheider, 1997). Therefore, when using verbally labeled category scales, it is important that the assignment of numbers to verbal categories not be arbitrary but have a well-developed rationale.

Category scaling, like equisection, purports to provide measurements on an interval scale; as mentioned earlier, however, deciding whether it does depends on deeper theoretical considerations. If we assume that the psychological representation of a set of stimuli, the values of sensation magnitude, are independent of the particular psychophysical task or method used to measure them, then what does it mean when two different versions of category scaling produce ratings that are nonlinearly related to each other, or when category ratings are nonlinearly related to magnitude estimations? How is it possible to decide which scale, if either, is valid?

Functional Measurement

One approach to validation has emerged from the work of Anderson (1970, 1974, 1976, 1982, 1992) on integration psychophysics, which focuses on measuring how separate perceptual components combine, as when the taste and smell of a fine wine merge to produce the perceptual experience that we might describe as its exquisite flavor. To see how psychological values combine, Anderson has developed an approach called functional measurement. In functional measurement, two or more stimuli produce separate subjective impressions. When the stimuli are combined, these impressions are integrated by some rule, often referred to as cognitive algebra, and the observer is asked to rate the overall impressions. The cognitive algebra is revealed by examining how the observer's ratings change when the combination of stimuli changes. Typically, an experimenter presents stimuli in all possible combinations to an observer, who rates the combinations on some psychological dimension. If the effects of the stimulus components combine according to a simple rule, such as linear addition, and if responses are linearly related to the underlying psychological values, then the scale values will reveal the algebraic rule directly.

Within this framework, Anderson (e.g., 1974) has advocated the use of category scales that have at least 20 values, or continuous rating lines (sometimes called visual-analog scales), because results obtained with these scales, but often not with other scales, reveal that the integration of perceptions obeys simple, theoretically interesting algebraic rules of combination. If the scale is not linearly related to the underlying psychological values but a simple rule such as linear addition does underlie them, then it may nevertheless be possible to retrieve the underlying algebraic structure,

and thus the underlying scale values, by appropriately rescaling the results (see the section titled "Examples of Partition Scaling and Magnitude Scaling").

Closely related to functional measurement is the axiomatic approach called conjoint measurement (Luce & Tukey, 1964). If the rank-order properties of the data are consistent with axioms of transitivity and cancellation, then there is an underlying additive structure, and analytic methods of conjoint scaling make it possible to retrieve scale values that are consistent with additivity. Conjoint scaling may be applied to rating-scale data, but it may be applied just as readily to paired comparisons, as the method is nonmetric.

Anderson (1982) reported, for example, that children as young as three years of age are able to integrate cognitive information by adding effects together. It has been found, for example, that the judged naughtiness of an act depends on the linear sum of the perceived harm or damage of the act and the perceived intention of the offender (Leon, 1980). The results seem to validate simultaneously the psychological principle of additivity of psychological impressions and the category-scaling procedure. Because categorical judgments often indicate simple algebraic rules for the interaction of impressions, Anderson and his associates have taken the results to support the validity of the category scales themselves. Note, however, that this approach presumes that when category scaling reveals simple algebraic rules but other methods reveal more complex ones, the latter are invalid. Though perhaps parsimonious, the conclusions need not be correct.

Consider the example of loudness summation. It has long been known that the loudness of two acoustic signals that lie very close in frequency (within a critical band) depends on the total sound energy; that is, sound energies sum linearly within a critical band (e.g., Scharf, 1959). In a functional measurement paradigm using tones falling within a critical band, if judgments of loudness were linearly related to sound energy, then the judgments would reveal an additive structure. This outcome might lead one to infer that the judgments are necessarily valid and that loudness is a linear function of sound energy. But other considerations indicate that loudness is nonlinearly related to sound energy, and that the rule describing the combination of loudnesses within a critical band is not additive, in that the components mask each other (see Marks, 1979). As Gescheider (1997) noted, functional measurement may be verified if there is an independent way to test the assumed cognitive algebra. If not, then the claim that category scales are valid because the results suggest simple a cognitive algebra is insufficient.

Estimating Perceptual Differences

Another approach to partition scaling is to have observers judge sensory differences between stimuli. In one version of the method, observers are asked to give numerical ratings to perceptual intervals defined by pairs of stimuli. For example, an observer could use a category scale (or magnitude estimation) to judge the perceived differences between stimulus i and stimulus j, between stimulus j and stimulus k, between stimulus i and stimulus k, and so forth. If the sensations corresponding to stimuli i, j, and k lie on a single psychological dimension and if the judgments are linearly related to the underlying psychological differences, then the results should be numerically consistent; that is, the judged difference between i and k should equal the sum of the judged difference between i and j and the judged difference between j and k.

A simpler version of the method asks observers to make only ordinal judgments of the intervals, for example, to decide whether the perceptual interval defined by stimuli i and j is greater or smaller than the interval defined

by stimuli k and l. Here, the objective is to rank the perceptual differences from the smallest to the greatest. Because the set of rank orders constrains the metric properties of the scale (given a sufficient number of stimulus values), from the ranking of perceptual differences it is possible, by using a mathematical procedure of nonmetric scaling (akin to the methods used in multidimensional scaling), to construct an interval scale of perceptual magnitude. That is, simply by knowing the rank order of perceptual differences and the corresponding stimulus pairs, it is possible to establish a psychophysical function describing the relationship between the magnitude of a perceptual attribute and the corresponding physical values of the stimulus (Shepard, 1966). Even if the data are collected with a numerical procedure, such as category rating or magnitude estimation, there may be reasons to use only the rank order information. To perform the nonmetric scaling, the rank ordering of the intervals must exhibit two properties. One is weak transitivity

$$\text{if } S_i S_j > S_j S_k \quad \text{and} \quad S_j S_k > S_k S_l,$$
$$\text{then } S_i S_j > S_k S_l$$

and the other is monotonicity

$$\text{if } S_i S_j > S_k S_l \quad \text{and} \quad S_j S_k > S_m S_n,$$
$$\text{then } S_i S_k > S_l S_n$$

(for review, see Marks & Algom, 1998).

The results obtained with this method, as with some category-rating methods and many magnitude-scaling methods, commonly indicate that sensation magnitude increases as a power function of stimulus intensity, although the exponents are consistently smaller than those obtained with methods such as magnitude estimation. Much of the work using this method has focused on the problem of constructing scales of loudness (Algom & Marks, 1984; Parker & Schneider, 1974; Popper, Parker, & Galanter, 1986; Schneider,

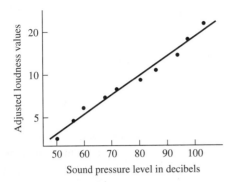

Figure 3.12   Loudness scale constructed from a nonmetric scaling procedure.
SOURCE: From Schneider, Parker, & Stein, 1971. Copyright © 1974 by Academic Press, Inc. Reproduced by permission.

Parker, & Stein, 1974). The results plotted in Figure 3.12, from a study by Schneider et al. (1974), illustrate a typical loudness scale obtained with the method of nonmetric scaling of perceptual differences.

Magnitude Scaling

Measurement of physical properties on ratio scales is highly desirable because ratio scales contain characteristics of order, distance, and origin while retaining maximal correspondence with the number system. That the virtues of ratio scales are equally applicable to psychophysical measurement was recognized as far back as 1888, when Merkel conducted experiments to determine the change in a stimulus that doubled the magnitude of a sensation. A similar procedure was used by Fullerton and Cattell (1892), who asked observers to adjust a stimulus to produce a sensation that was some fraction or multiple of the sensations produced by a standard stimulus of fixed intensity. The procedure, called ratio production, results in ratio scales of sensation if the stimuli do in fact define a sensory ratio and if it is possible to specify the ratio's numerical value. It was not until the 1930s, however, when acoustical engineers became

concerned with the problem of numerically specifying psychological values of loudness, that techniques for ratio scaling of sensations began to be used widely.

The practical problem of constructing scales for loudness arose out of an obvious failure of Fechner's law. The law had been accepted by those acoustical engineers who, when they converted sound intensity to the logarithmic decibel scale, thought they had thereby also quantified the loudness of sound. It soon became apparent, however, that the decibel scale conflicted with direct experience of loudness; an 80-dB sound appears to most people to be much more than twice as loud as a 40-dB sound. Consequently, numerous studies were conducted in the 1930s in an attempt to construct ratio scales of loudness (e.g., Fletcher & Munson, 1933, Geiger & Firestone, 1933; Ham & Parkinson, 1932; Richardson & Ross, 1930; Rschevkin & Rabinovich, 1936).

This endeavor started with the work of Richardson and Ross (1930), who were the first to use the method that S. S. Stevens (1953) later called magnitude estimation. In Richardson and Ross's study, observers listened to a standard tone and were told that its loudness should be represented by the numeric response "1." The observers were then asked to give other numbers to test tones that varied in intensity in proportion to the number "1" associated with the standard. When the numerical judgments were plotted against sound intensity, the result was a power function, rather than the Fechnerian logarithmic function. The observers' loudness judgments were proportional to the sound pressure raised to the power of 0.44 or, equivalently, proportional to sound energy raised to the power of 0.22.

A procedure for measuring loudness on a ratio scale that did not require the observers to assign numbers was developed by Fletcher and Munson (1933). They began with the assumption that listening to a tone with two ears instead of only one doubles the tone's loudness. By determining the intensity of a sound presented to two ears ($\phi*$) that sounds as loud as a given sound presented to one ear (ϕ), Fletcher and Munson could calculate the sound intensities that corresponded to a 2:1 ratio of loudness—in this case ϕ should have twice the loudness of $\phi*$ when both are heard with just one ear. Fletcher and Munson obtained confirming evidence first by making the parallel assumption that the loudness of tones widely separated in sound frequency (falling in separate and non-overlapping critical bands) sums linearly and then by collecting comparable loudness matches.

From monaural and binaural loudness matches and from matches of single tones to complex tones, Fletcher and Munson (1933) constructed the loudness scale seen in Figure 3.13. When loudness is plotted on a logarithmic axis as a function of the logarithmic decibel scale, the linear function reveals that between 40 and 100 dB SPL loudness is a power function of sound intensity (exponent of 0.30 in terms of sound energy or 0.60 in terms of sound pressure). The log-log slope of the loudness function becomes steeper at lower sound intensities and is approximately proportional to sound energy (the square of pressure) near threshold.

Magnitude Estimation

One of the most popular scaling methods used in current investigations is magnitude estimation, the method first used by Richardson and Ross (1930) and then elaborated by S. S. Stevens (1953, 1955, 1975). In magnitude estimation, observers are asked to make direct numerical estimates of the perceptual magnitudes produced by various stimuli. Stevens, whose name is most closely associated with the early use of this method, conducted numerous experiments using magnitude estimation to study brightness, loudness, and other sensory continua. Experiments on loudness typically produced a power function with an exponent of 0.3, in excellent agreement with the scale derived by Fletcher and Munson (1933) from the loudness-matching procedure just described. Since the publication of Stevens's original papers on the topic, the results of hundreds of experiments, conducted on many perceptual dimensions and under many stimulus conditions, have revealed that the numeric responses R of observers in magnitude estimation as stimulus intensity ϕ is varied can be described by a power function with exponent β and constant k in the equation

$$R = k\phi^{\beta}.$$

Based on such findings, Stevens (1957, 1975) proposed a power function as the psychophysical law to replace Fechner's logarithmic formulation. This hypothesis, which has become widely known as Stevens's power law, is

$$\psi = k\phi^{\beta}$$

where ψ is sensation magnitude. Implicit in Stevens's hypothesis was his assumption that the average observer's responses are proportional to the magnitude of the sensory experience ($R \propto \psi$).

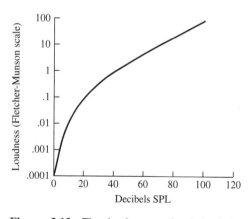

Figure 3.13 The loudness scale derived by Fletcher and Munson (1933), plotted against sound intensity in decibels.

S. S. Stevens (1957, 1958) described two main versions of magnitude estimation. In one, the observer is presented with a standard stimulus and is told that the sensation it produces has a certain numerical value called the modulus. On subsequent trials, the observer tries to assign numbers to the sensations produced by other stimuli relative to the assigned value of the modulus. The observer is instructed to make judgments, on a particular sensory dimension, that reflect how many times one sensation is greater than another sensation (the ratio between the sensation of the modulus and that of the test stimulus). Generally, approximately 8 to 12 stimulus values are used, and each is presented two or three times in random order to several observers. The data are combined by calculating the median or geometric mean response given to each stimulus by each observer, then by calculating overall averages (median or geometric mean) across all observers. Geometric means are commonly used because the logarithms of magnitude estimates tend to be normally distributed, and because the standard deviation tends to increase linearly with the mean. Arithmetic means are seldom used because their values may be greatly affected by a few unrepresentative high judgments. Further, geometric averaging can preserve characteristics of psychophysical functions that are lost in arithmetic averaging. If different observers give power functions with different exponents, then geometric averaging yields a power function whose exponent is the arithmetic average of the individual exponents, whereas arithmetic averaging may yield a result that is inconsistent with a power function.

In the other version of magnitude estimation, the standard stimulus with its experimenter-defined modulus is omitted. Instead, the various stimuli are randomly presented to the observer, who assigns numbers to sensations in proportion to their magnitudes. Instructions to the observer may be modeled after the following example, provided by S. S. Stevens (1975, p. 30):

> You will be presented with a series of stimuli in irregular order. Your task is to tell how intense they seem by assigning numbers to them. Call the first stimulus any number that seems appropriate to you. Then assign successive numbers in such a way that they reflect your subjective impression. There is no limit to the range of numbers that you may use. You may use whole numbers, decimals, or fractions. Try to make each number match the intensity, as you perceive it.

Because observers have a strong tendency to use numbers that appear to match naturally the magnitudes of perceived stimuli, biases may arise when observers are given a standard stimulus and modulus chosen by the experimenter (Hellman & Zwislocki, 1961). Therefore, it is generally considered better to allow the observer to choose the modulus rather than to designate one. In either method, the average of the numbers assigned to a particular stimulus defines the psychological scale value for that stimulus, and a plot of the scale values as a function of some property of the stimulus constitutes the psychophysical function. Because extensive practice is not necessary and because it often suffices to present each stimulus only a few times to each observer, magnitude estimation can be used in experiments that vary several parameters of the stimulus.

An experiment by J. C. Stevens and Marks (1971) illustrates how the method of magnitude estimation has been used to investigate sensory information processing. The problem under investigation was spatial summation in the perception of warmth. At the detection threshold, spatial summation is expressed as the inverse relationship between the intensity of a stimulus required to detect a stimulus and the size (areal extent) of the stimulus (Kenshalo, Decker, & Hamilton, 1967). As the area of the stimulus applied to the skin is made larger, the increase in temperature needed to detect a sensation of warmth decreases. Indeed, to elicit a threshold sensation, it is roughly the total heat applied to the skin—the product of the intensity (energy per unit area) and area—that is critical.

J. C. Stevens and Marks (1971) were interested in how the intensity and area of a stimulus combine to produce warmth sensations above the detection threshold. In their experiment, observers gave magnitude estimates of the warmth produced by radiant heat emitted from a lamp positioned near the back or the forehead. The data in Figure 3.14 are geometric means of the magnitude estimates, plotted as a function of stimulus intensity for stimuli of different sizes applied to the forehead. Spatial summation is indicated by the greater estimates given to larger areas of stimulation for any particular stimulus intensity. It is clear, however, that the area of the stimulus has a diminishing effect on the judgments of warmth as stimulus intensity increases. In fact, extrapolating the functions for different areas of stimulation indicates that spatial summation should disappear at an intensity of

about 800 mW/cm^2, a level corresponding to the threshold for pain. Because body heating (thermal load) is determined by the total energy integrated over large body areas, it is advantageous to sense warmth in this way. On the other hand, because tissue damage due to burning depends more on the absolute temperature of the skin than on total energy absorbed, it is biologically advantageous to feel pain once the temperature of any portion of the skin reaches a critical level (Marks, 1974a).

The description of this experiment on warmth perception illustrates how magnitude estimation has been used to investigate the complex problem of sensory function. The method has become a valuable tool for the study of sensory processes, but it has not been restricted to the research on the senses. The simplicity of magnitude estimation makes it easily applicable to the scaling of any psychological attribute. For example, attributes as different as the brightness of lights (J. C. Stevens & Stevens, 1963), the psychological worth of money (Galanter, 1962), the judged severity of crimes (Sellin & Wolfgang, 1964), the perception of emotional stress (Holmes & Rahe, 1967), and the pain of labor contractions (Algom & Lubel, 1994) have all yielded to magnitude estimation.

Magnitude Production

Magnitude production, often used in conjunction with magnitude estimation, is the inverse procedure. In magnitude production, an observer is given numerical values of sensation and is asked to adjust stimuli to produce the corresponding sensory magnitudes. The psychophysical function is constructed by plotting the prescribed values of sensation magnitude against the average settings of the stimulus.

The use of magnitude-production and magnitude-estimation procedures in the same scaling experiment has been proposed as a way to offset systematic errors inherent in

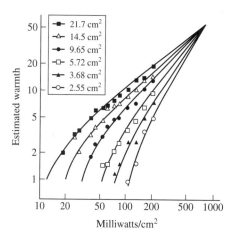

Figure 3.14 Magnitude estimation of warmth as a function of stimulus intensity on the forehead for several different areas of stimulation.
SOURCE: From J. C. Stevens & Marks, 1971. Reprinted by permission.

either method (S. S. Stevens, 1958). For example, many observers tend to exhibit what has been termed a regression effect, where they appear reluctant to make extremely low or extremely high responses. Thus, magnitude estimates given to very weak stimuli may be "too large," and those given to strong stimuli may be "too small." Analogously, stimuli in magnitude production may be set too high when observers are given small numbers and too low when given high numbers. The so-called regression effect is typically seen as a reduction in the log-log slope of a psychophysical function obtained with magnitude estimation but as an increase in the slope of a function obtained with magnitude production.

The regression effect is illustrated in Figure 3.15, which shows the results of experiments on loudness reported by Stevens and Guirao (1962). Each data point is the geometric mean of two magnitude estimations or two magnitude productions given by each of 10 observers. Because of the regression effect, the sensation-magnitude functions are steeper in magnitude production than in magnitude estimation (although the direction may

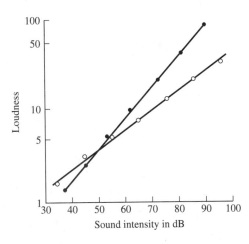

Figure 3.15   Loudness of a 1000-Hz tone as determined by magnitude estimation (open circles) and magnitude production (filled circles). Data of S. S. Stevens and Guirao (1962).

reverse when the range of stimuli or numbers is very small; see R. Teghtsoonian & Teghtsoonian, 1978). When the functions differ in this way, it is generally assumed (albeit not proven) that the unbiased function lies somewhere between the two, and thus it is advisable to combine the results by some procedure. Hellman and Zwislocki (1963) have recommended using a method of numerical magnitude balance, in which the functions obtained by magnitude estimation and magnitude production are geometrically averaged.

Absolute Magnitude Estimation

The method of absolute magnitude estimation derives from the notion that for an individual observer, at any moment in time, there is an absolute connection between the observer's conception of the magnitude of a number and the observer's perception of sensory magnitudes. If so, then observers behave as though scale values defined by these numbers are absolute and, unlike ratio scales, cannot be transformed even by multiplication by a positive constant. Operationally, the implication is that the assignment of a "deviant" numerical modulus to a stimulus will distort the resulting magnitude estimation scale.

Hellman and Zwislocki (1961) argued that observers tend to use absolute values rather than ratio relations when giving magnitude estimates of sensation. In their experiment, they found that the ratio of magnitude estimations given to a fixed pair of stimuli depended strongly on the value of the modulus assigned to the standard stimulus. By this time, S. S. Stevens (1956) had already recognized the distortions that may arise from the use of a standard stimulus and an arbitrary modulus. Consequently, he recommended dropping the use of the standard stimulus so that observers could choose their own modulus when assigning a number to the stimulus presented on the first trial. As evidence that the modulus chosen by observers on the first trial is not arbitrary, there is a fairly high correlation between the numbers chosen on the first trial by different observers and the intensity of the stimulus presented.

These findings and others eventually led to the development of a method called absolute magnitude estimation (AME; Zwislocki, 1983; Zwislocki & Goodman, 1980), in which the observers are instructed to assign a number to each stimulus so that the subjective magnitude of the number matches that of the stimulus and to ignore numbers assigned to preceding stimuli. The following instructions arc a generalized version of those used by Zwislocki and Goodman (1980).

> In this experiment, we would like to find out how intense various stimuli appear to you. For this purpose, I am going to present a series of stimuli to you one at a time. Your task will be to assign a number to every stimulus in such a way that your impression of how large the number is matches your impression of how intense the stimulus is. You may use any positive numbers that appear appropriate to you—whole numbers, decimals, or fractions. Do not worry about running out of numbers—there will always be a smaller number than the smallest you use and a larger one than the largest you use. Do not worry about numbers you assigned to preceding stimuli. Do you have any questions?

These instructions contrast most directly with those of ratio magnitude estimation (RME), in which observers are instructed to make the ratio of successive numbers equal to the ratio of successive sensations (e.g., Luce & Green, 1974). In many instances, as in the experiment of J. C. Stevens and Marks (1971) described earlier, magnitude-estimation instructions fall somewhere between AME and RME in that observers are asked to make their judgments proportional to sensation magnitudes but are not explicitly asked to estimate each sensation relative to the previous one.

Proponents of AME have argued that observers are capable of judging sensation magnitudes not on the basis of the ratios of their sensations but by a matching operation (Gescheider, 1993; Zwislocki, 1991), whereby numbers are assigned according to perceived magnitudes—according to the magnitudes of their sensations. This operation of matching, which occurs on an ordinal scale, is claimed to be the basis of all physical and psychophysical measurement.

The method of AME has been used successfully with young children as well as adults (Collins & Gescheider, 1989; Zwislocki & Goodman, 1980). This finding supports the hypothesis that matching the perceived magnitudes of numbers and stimuli is a natural and relatively simple process, which may develop at an early age when children begin to learn cardinal properties of numbers. Indeed, Collins and Gescheider (1989) found that lines and tones assigned the same number in AME were also judged to be equal in a cross-modality matching task. The AME method may even reduce contextual effects associated with response bias found in RME (e.g., Gescheider, 1993; Gescheider & Hughson, 1991), although AME probably does not completely eliminate contextual effects (Gescheider & Hughson, 1991; Ward, 1987).

Individual Differences

Magnitude-estimation functions of individual observers vary substantially. When power functions are fitted to individual results, the largest exponent is commonly two or even three times as great as the smallest (e.g., Algom & Marks, 1984; Hellman, 1981; Logue, 1976, Ramsay, 1979; J. C. Stevens & Guirao, 1964), and sometimes even greater (Collins & Gescheider, 1989; M. Teghtsoonian & Teghtsoonian, 1983). An important problem in psychophysical scaling has been to determine how much of this variability reflects real interindividual variation in the relation between stimulus and sensation.

It is generally agreed that the variability seen in individual magnitude judgments far exceeds the variability of the underlying sensory processes (Gescheider, 1988; Gescheider & Bolanowski, 1991). For example, interobserver variability in magnitude-estimation scales of loudness is thought to be much greater than the variability in the underlying loudness functions (Algom & Marks, 1984; Collins & Gescheider, 1989; Zwislocki, 1983). If two observers gave loudness exponents of 0.4 and 0.8, and if these exponents accurately reflected differences in their underlying loudness perceptions, then the ratio of loudnesses of a near-threshold tone (say, 10 dB SPL) and an extremely loud tone (say, 100 dB) would be more than 60 times greater in the observer with the larger exponent. People undoubtedly differ far more in their overt judgments than they do in their actual perceptions. Judgments of sensory magnitude reflect both sensory and judgmental processes, and both kinds of processes contribute to the total variability across individual observers. This contention has been supported by the finding that correcting magnitude estimation functions of individual observers for the idiosyncratic ways that they assign numbers to sensations can substantially reduce the variability seen in individual results (Algom & Marks, 1984; Collins & Gescheider, 1989; Zwislocki, 1983).

It is clear that judgmental processes, which govern how numeric responses are mapped onto sensations, account for much of the variability found in the results of individual observers (see Baird, 1997; Gescheider, 1997; Marks & Algom, 1998; Poulton, 1989). One component of the processes of judgment has been characterized by Baird (1975) and his colleagues (Baird & Noma, 1975; Noma & Baird, 1975; Weissmann, Hollingsworth, & Baird, 1975) as numeric response preference (e.g., preference for particular numbers, for multiples of "5" and "10," etc.). Individual differences in numeric response preference likely account for some of the interindividual variability seen in magnitude estimation. For example, numeric response preferences could influence the absolute size of numbers chosen, the range of numbers, and whether the numbers are linearly applied to sensation magnitudes. Although the nature of such judgmental processes is not yet entirely understood, it is clear that in order for numerical estimates to be of value in measuring psychological magnitude, one should use experimental controls to minimize potential biases. The use of experimental controls can be understood best in the context of stimulus transformations and response transformations.

Stimulus Transformations and Response Transformations

Of fundamental importance in psychophysics is the stimulus-transformation function (also known as the psychophysical law), represented as the quantitative relation between stimulus and sensation. Although measurement of physical stimuli has improved markedly in the last century as physics and engineering have provided increasingly better methods for measuring environmental energies, measurement of sensation has remained problematic. Because they are subjective events, sensations cannot be directly observed in others. Instead, we must infer their existence and magnitude from observable behavior such as magnitude estimations. Consequently, to produce a valid stimulus-transformation function, it is necessary to derive a valid measurement of sensation magnitude from observable sensory responses. When the responses of observers accurately reflect the underlying sensation magnitudes, formulating a valid stimulus-transformation function consists of describing mathematically how the responses are related to the stimuli that evoke them. Unfortunately, it is

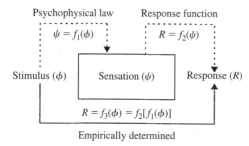

Figure 3.16   Relations among the stimulus transformations function, the response transformations function, and the empirically determined stimulus-response function.
SOURCE: From Gescheider, 1997. Copyright © 1997 by Lawrence Erlbaum, Inc. Reproduced by permission.

often unknown whether observers' sensory responses accurately reflect the underlying sensations.

For this reason the assumption that magnitude estimates are proportional to sensation magnitudes has been challenged (e.g., Anderson, 1970; Birnbaum, 1982; Shepard, 1981). The problem is illustrated in Figure 3.16. The limitations of the method of magnitude estimation, or other "direct" measures, become apparent when an investigator treats the experimentally determined function (f_3) relating stimulus (ϕ) and numeric response (R)

$$R = f_3(\phi)$$

as equivalent to the (unknown) stimulus-transformation function (f_1) that describes the relation between the intervening variable, sensation (ψ), and the stimulus (ϕ)

$$\psi = f_1(\phi).$$

Shepard (1981) pointed out that one must consider the characteristics of a second transformation, a response transformation, which mediates between sensation and response. This second transformation (f_2) defines the relation between the numeric response and the intervening variable of sensation magni-

tude (ψ)

$$R = f_2(\psi).$$

The experimentally observed relationship, $R = f_3(\phi)$, between stimulus and response results from a concatenation of the stimulus transformation and the response transformation.

Shepard noted that ψ is not observable and, consequently, the equation for R must be written as

$$R = f_3(\phi) = f_2[f_1(\phi)].$$

Knowing f_3 does not make it possible to determine either of the component functions (i.e., f_1 or f_2) unless one of these is also known. Therefore, the conclusion drawn by S. S. Stevens (1957) from magnitude estimation that f_1 is a power function relies on the implicit assumption that instructions to the observer have ensured that f_2 is a simple power function. Further, for the exponent of the underlying function f_1 to be identical to the exponent of the overt function f_3, f_2 must be linear, that is, must have an exponent equal to 1. Shepard argued that Stevens never adequately grounded his assumption that instructions would have exactly this effect, and therefore questioned the validity of the power law as an account of the stimulus-transformation function.

These considerations lead to a two-stage theory of magnitude estimation. In the two-stage theory, the first stage is sensory, involving the neural transformation of stimuli to sensations, whereas the second stage is more cognitive, involving processes of judgment. The theory originated in the early work of Attneave (1962) and Curtis, Attneave, and Harrington (1968), according to which an observer's responses result from two processes: First, the stimulus produces a sensation, and second, the sensation leads to an overt response. To the extent that the first of these two stages is of primary interest, the second stage must be taken into account when making inferences from observed relations between the stimulus and response.

Category-Ratio Scales

Both RME and AME leave unresolved the matter of how to measure individual differences in underlying sensory magnitudes. As Borg (1982) wrote, "if one subject calls the loudness of a certain sound '8' and another '20,' this does not necessarily mean that the person who says '20' perceives the sound to be louder than the one who says '8.' If, on the other hand, one says 'weak' and the other says 'loud' or 'strong,' we can be fairly sure that the first person perceived the sound to be weaker than the second one" (p. 28). According to Borg, numeric procedures such as magnitude estimation yield information about the relative differences in the subjective impressions of stimuli but provide little information about the absolute levels of these impressions. Consequently, magnitude estimates given by individual observers cannot be meaningfully compared in any simple or direct manner. This is true in AME as well as in RME because the natural number systems used in AME can differ among observers by as much as two orders of magnitude (Collins & Gescheider, 1989).

Borg's (1982) solution was to create a scaling procedure with properties of both verbally labeled category scales and magnitude scales—which he calls a category-ratio scale. Borg initially designed the category-ratio scale to measure perceived exertion during exercise, such as pedaling a stationary bicycle. A critical assumption is that different individuals experience the same subjective value at maximal perceived exertion, even though they vary in their physical capacity. Borg also assumes that the psychological range from "minimal" to "maximal" perceived exertion is roughly the same in different individuals. Given these assumptions, all observers should have a common scale

of perceived exertion, with a common anchor at the point of maximal exertion. The theory also assumes that through association of descriptive adjectives (e.g., "extremely strong," "strong," "moderate," "weak," "very weak") with various everyday experiences of exertion, different observers learn to associate verbal descriptors with comparable levels of perceived exertion. So, for example, if one person is able to exercise at a maximal level of 250 W, another at only 150 W, the first person may report "moderate exertion" at 75 W, the second at 50 W; and when they do, they have comparable perceptual experiences. In constructing his category-ratio scale, Borg assigned numbers to the descriptive adjectives in such a way as to make the results obtained with his scale agree well with those obtained with magnitude scaling (see Marks, Borg, & Ljunggren, 1983). A related method, called labeled-magnitude scaling, developed by Green, Shaffer, and Gilmore (1993), has seen increasing use in recent years, especially in studies of oral sensations, such as taste and oral irritation.

Line-Length Calibration

Zwislocki (1983) developed a technique to estimate the response transformations of individual observers from magnitude estimates of the perceived length of lines. Perceived length is assumed to be linearly related to physical length. If this assumption is correct, then the function relating magnitude estimates to physical length reveals the response transformation for perceived length. By assuming further that a given observer uses the same response transformation when judging loudness as well as line length, Zwislocki was able to correct the loudness judgments of individual observers. When he did this, the results showed that all observers exhibited perfect linear summation of the loudness of tones of widely different frequencies (i.e., tones presented in different critical bands).

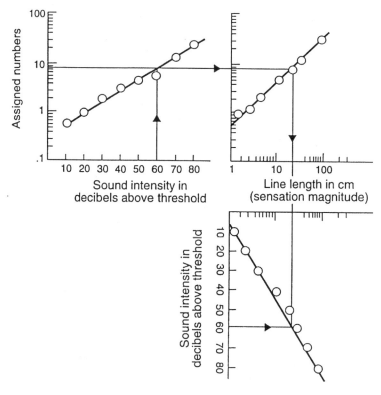

Figure 3.17 Magnitude estimates of loudness corrected by the response transformations functions estimated from magnitude estimates of apparent length of lines.
NOTE: Data of Collins and Gescheider (1989).

The technique of line-length calibration is illustrated in Figure 3.17 for one observer who gave magnitude estimates of the loudness of tones and the perceived lengths of lines (Collins & Gescheider, 1989). At each tone intensity, the magnitude estimate of loudness is converted to a line length that was given the same magnitude estimate as the tone. Assuming that the sensation magnitude of line length is proportional to actual line length, line length becomes the measure of sensation magnitude (in this case, loudness). The function in the lower right quadrant of the figure is the corrected loudness function. The procedure is simplified when magnitude estimates of both the continuum of interest and line length are power functions. For example, the corrected

power function exponent (θ) for loudness is

$$\theta = \alpha/\beta$$

where α is the exponent for magnitude estimation of loudness and β is the exponent for magnitude estimation of perceived length (see Collins & Gescheider, 1989; Zwislocki, 1983).

A related method, cross-modality matching, avoids the necessity of having observers use numbers at all. In cross-modality matching, observers adjust the intensities of stimuli in different modalities to make them appear equally intense (J. C. Stevens, Mack, & Stevens, 1960; J. C. Stevens & Marks, 1965; S. S. Stevens, 1959a). When Collins and Gescheider (1989) had observers match line length to loudness, the resulting loudness scales were essentially the same as those measured by the line-length calibration procedure just described. The calibrated loudness function in Figure 3.17, for example, agrees closely with the results obtained by directly matching perceived length to loudness. Because scales obtained by length matching are essentially the same as those determined from the calibration method, both methods may be used with confidence, so practical considerations govern which approach to take in a given situation. The variability across observers, presumably due largely to variation in response transformations, is much smaller than that in magnitude estimation when one of these cross-modality methods is used (Collins & Gescheider, 1989).

Magnitude Matching

A closely related way to deal with individual differences in the use of numbers in magnitude estimation is through a method called magnitude matching that was developed by J. C. Stevens and Marks (1980). Here, the objective is to have observers judge the sensory magnitudes of stimuli from two different modalities, A and B, on a single common scale. To this end, stimuli from the two modalities are presented within the same session, sometimes alternating between modalities from trial to trial. One of the two modalities serves as the standard and the other as the test modality. If the individuals or groups can be assumed alike in their perception of stimuli presented to the standard modality, then judgments in the standard modality can serve as a basis for correcting judgments made of stimuli presented to the test modality.

To illustrate the method, we turn to an experiment by Marks, Stevens, Bartoshuk, Gent, Rifkin, and Stone (1988) on the perception of taste in two groups of observers: "nontasters" and "tasters." Nontasters, about 30% of the population, have genetically determined high thresholds, relative to tasters, for detecting a particular class of bitter compounds such as PTC (phenylthiourea) and PROP (6-*n*-propylthiouracil). The standard continuum, within which the sensory experiences of tasters and nontasters were assumed to be the same, was the loudness of 1000-Hz tones, and the test continua were the taste intensities of PROP and NaCl (salt).

Converting the judgments of each observer to a common scale involved the following steps: (a) for each observer, computing the average of all loudness judgments (pooled over trials and intensities); (b) determining the multiplicative factor F_i needed to bring the average loudness judgment of each observer i to a common value, such as 10 ($F_i = 10$/average judgment for observer i); and (c) then multiplying all of the taste judgments of each observer by the value of F_i. After this computation, the corrected results were averaged and plotted as shown in Figure 3.18. It is clear that PROP but not NaCl was less intense to the nontasters than to the tasters. In addition to determining whether groups of observers differ, the method may be useful in

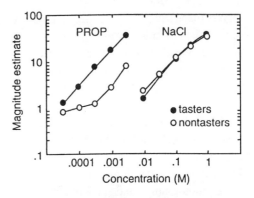

Figure 3.18 Magnitude estimates of PROP and NaCl by tasters and nontasters after correction by magnitude matching.
SOURCE: From Marks et al., 1988. Copyright © 1998 by Oxford University Press. Reproduced by permission.

determining whether the sensory magnitudes experienced by an individual differ from the norm or from those of another individual. Furthermore, magnitude matching is reliable in that results obtained from individual observers are consistent over repeated testing (Marks, 1991).

Master Scaling

Another procedure for dealing with individual differences was developed by Berglund (1991) and is called master scaling. In this case, the main goal has been primarily to compare perceptions of different sets of environmental stimuli. Because practical considerations may require these stimuli to be judged by different groups of subjects (for instance, one might want to compare traffic noises in large cities of different countries), the problem ipso facto requires calibrating the scaling behavior of different groups of subjects. In a study of traffic noise, for example, a master scale would first be constructed by having a group of observers make magnitude estimations of the loudness of a fixed set of noises of varied intensity. Once the master scale is established, it becomes possible to examine the perception of traffic noises by having observers judge sample stimuli from the master set as well as the traffic noises. In this way, it is possible to rescale the judgments of the stimuli of interest into values on the master scale.

EXAMPLES OF PARTITION SCALING AND MAGNITUDE SCALING

This section provides more detailed examples of partition-scaling and magnitude-scaling experiments. As is typical in experimental science, the starting point was a substantive question about perception: in this case, how the two ears sum loudness when sounds are presented binaurally. Various decisions of experimental design and analysis followed both from the question being asked and from research on psychophysical methodology.

Choosing a Psychophysical Question

As discussed earlier, Fletcher and Munson (1933) were able to construct a scale for loudness by assuming that a tone presented to two ears is exactly twice as loud as the same tone presented to one ear. But is this assumption correct? Two studies by Marks (1978, 1979) sought to shed some light on the question by testing the additivity of loudnesses more directly. Not only did Fletcher and Munson assume simple linear summation of loudness, but their experimental measurements were taken on only a limited class of stimuli, namely, tones presented to one ear (monaural tones) and tones presented at equal intensity levels to the two ears (binaural tones). A more thorough test of the additivity of loudness is possible if both unequal and equal sound levels are presented to the two ears (dichotic tones). In particular, Marks based his experiments on the logic of Anderson's (1970, 1974) functional measurement theory. Functional measurement proposes that perceptual (or cognitive) systems may combine stimulus inputs linearly. In the present case, Marks proposed that individual loudnesses at the two ears add linearly. If this is true, then a sound presented to either ear will contribute to the overall impression of loudness an amount that is independent of any sound presented to the other ear.

Assume for simplicity that the two ears are equally sensitive, and arbitrarily say that a 40-dB tone presented to either ear produces one unit of loudness. If loudnesses sum linearly in the two ears, then a 40-dB tone presented to an ear will always contribute one unit of loudness, regardless of the sound level presented to the other ear; if both ears receive 40 dB, the total loudness will equal two units. Assume that one ear receives 40 dB and the

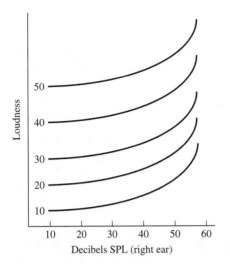

Loudness

Decibels SPL (right ear)

Figure 3.19 Theoretical family of functions showing linear binaural loudness summation.
NOTE: Regardless of the SPL presented to the right ear, a fixed SPL presented to the left ear adds a constant amount of loudness, so each successive loudness function is displaced up from the previous function by a constant distance.

other ear receives 60 dB, and assume further that the 60-dB sound produces four loudness units at that ear. Given additivity, it follows that the total loudness would be five units. Finally, if both ears receive 60-dB sounds, the total loudness will be eight units.

A graphical display of the additive functional measurement model appears in Figure 3.19. The stimuli used in the experiment are chosen according to a factorial design in which each of a fixed number of stimulus intensities presented to the left ear is presented in combination with each of a fixed number of stimulus intensities presented to the right ear. If the loudnesses produced at the two ears combine linearly, and if the response measure is linearly related to loudness, then the resulting factorial plot will look like Figure 3.19. In this figure, it is assumed that there are five stimulus levels presented to each ear, making 25 different stimulus combinations in all. The abscissa represents the intensity level in dB

SPL of the component presented to the right ear, and each curve gives the overall loudness (shown on the ordinate) for a particular SPL of the component presented to the left ear. Given linear addition of loudness, the amount of loudness evoked by a fixed SPL at the left ear will be the same regardless of the SPL at the right ear, and curves will all be parallel, displaced uniformly up and down.

Choosing a Method

Many factors enter into the choice of a psychophysical method, as every method has its virtues and its limitations. Under ideal circumstances, magnitude methods may produce ratio scales of sensory or perceptual magnitudes, making it possible to say that a given stimulus produces a psychological magnitude that is two or three or seven times that of another stimulus. Under ideal circumstances, categorical methods with verbal labels may make it possible to know that a particular stimulus level is perceived as very weak, or as moderately strong, a kind of information not provided by magnitude methods. But all methods are susceptible to various contextual effects and response biases. For example, ratings and magnitude estimates alike generally show sequential effects. The response to a given stimulus depends not only on the physical characteristics of that stimulus such as its intensity, but also on the stimulus presented on previous trials and on the responses made to those stimuli (e.g., DeCarlo, 1992; Jesteadt, Luce, & Green, 1977; Luce & Green, 1974; Staddon, King, & Lockhead, 1980; Ward, 1973; see Marks & Algom, 1998, for a review).

Categorical methods are especially sensitive to the range and distribution of the stimuli (e.g., Marks, 1978; Parducci & Perrett, 1971), reflecting a tendency for observers to use categories equally often (Parducci, 1965, 1974). But magnitude estimation is also sensitive to the range of stimulation. Thus, it has often been reported that exponents of power functions fitted to magnitude estimates decrease when the range of stimulation increases (R. Teghtsoonian, 1973; R. Teghtsoonian & Teghtsoonian, 1978). Categorical methods generally have fixed upper and lower response boundaries; consequently, these methods may also show end effects. What should observers do if, for example, they have already assigned the highest category to a previous stimulus and now encounter one that is even stronger?

Categorical methods are also sensitive to the number of response categories made available to the observer (Marks, 1968; Parducci & Wedell, 1986), an issue that does not arise with methods that use continuous scales, such as visual-analog scaling and magnitude estimation. On the other hand, magnitude estimates are sensitive to the level of the stimulus used as a standard and to the number assigned to the standard—the numerical modulus—when a standard and modulus are used (Hellman & Zwislocki, 1961). Given all of these considerations, Marks (1978, 1979) attacked the question of binaural loudness summation by using both a rating method and a magnitude method.

Graphic Rating

For this study, Marks (1979) chose a graphic (visual-analog) scale, a device that has seen increasing use in many domains, notably in studies of pain perception (see Collins, Moore, & McQuay, 1997; Huskisson, 1983). A virtue of the graphic-rating method is that it avoids potential problems that are associated with categorical methods, such as deciding on the number of response categories to make available to the observers. With the graphic-rating method, on each trial the observer is presented a line, about 150 mm long, and is instructed to denote the perceived magnitude of the stimulus by marking the appropriate location on the line.

Graphic-rating scales behave much like categorical scales in cases in which the number of categories is very large (e.g., around 100), which makes graphic rating an especially good option given the evidence suggesting that categorical scales should provide at least 15 to 20 response categories (e.g., Anderson, 1981). To minimize the potential problems associated with end effects, Marks (1979) took two precautions. First, the observers had available throughout the test session a sample line on which two marks appeared, 10 mm from each end of the line. At the beginning of the test session, the observers were presented two sample stimuli representing the softest and loudest sounds they would hear. The softest sound was a 15-dB tone presented to just one ear, and the observers were informed that the left-hand mark on the sample indicated its loudness. The loudest sound was a 50-dB tone presented to both ears, and the observers were informed that the right-hand mark on the sample indicated its loudness. By anchoring the weakest and softest sounds to points medial to the ends of the line, the observers were provided extra room on the scale to help minimize end effects. As a second precaution, the observers were told that, if necessary, they could extend the line in either direction, where an additional 30 mm were available (6 of the 15 observers did this). These precautions provide the graphic-rating scale with positive features of magnitude estimation.

Magnitude Estimation

For magnitude scaling, Marks (1978) used a common form of the method of magnitude estimation described earlier, one that has no designated standard stimulus or modulus. The particular version of magnitude estimation used in the experiment may be thought of as a hybrid of ratio magnitude estimation and absolute magnitude estimation: Observers were instructed to assign to the first sound whatever number seemed to them most appropriate to represent its loudness. This aspect of the instructions is much like the instruction in absolute magnitude estimation. To each subsequent sound, observers were instructed to assign other numbers in proportion to their relative loudness. In this respect, the instructions more closely resembled the instructions of RME. In RME, however, observers are explicitly told to judge each stimulus relative to the previous stimulus, an instruction that Marks did not use. Although there is probably no formal way to decide whether the instructions used in this experiment were more similar to AME or RME, it is our view that these instructions fall closer to AME than to RME.

Designing the Graphic-Rating and Magnitude-Estimation Experiments

Aside from the scaling methods themselves and the associated instructions to the observers, the graphic-rating experiment (Marks, 1979) and the magnitude-estimation experiment (Marks, 1978) were virtually identical in their design. It should be noted that both studies reported results from several experiments, but the present exposition focuses on two experiments that used different scaling methods but comparable experimental designs to study binaural summation. For example, the experiments used the same set of stimuli. In any given experiment, the choice of stimuli is dictated primarily by the goals of the study and by constraints that may be imposed by the sensory or perceptual system.

In the present case, the stimulus levels were relatively low, a decision based on the desire to avoid any potentially confounding effects that might arise from conduction of sound through bone from one ear to the other. Bone conduction might become significant at high sound levels, especially if the sound level at one ear were high and the level at the other ear were low. For this reason, the maximal

SPL of the 1000-Hz tone was held to 50 dB. At the lower end, younger observers' absolute thresholds for detecting these tones typically lie in the vicinity of 5 dB SPL; consequently, to preclude the possibility that some observers might fail to hear the weakest tones, the lowest SPL in the two experiments was set to a value of 15 dB. Within the range of 15 to 50 dB SPL, the sound levels were spaced, as a matter of convenience, in steps of 5 dB. This entailed a stimulus ensemble in which each of 8 SPLs at the left ear was combined with each of the same 8 SPLs at the right ear, making 64 different stimulus combinations in all. Furthermore, to provide additional comparisons, each of the 8 SPLs was also presented monaurally to each ear, that is, with no stimulation to the contralateral ear. Thus the stimulus set contained 80 different stimuli in all. This set of 80 stimuli was used in both the graphic-rating experiment and the magnitude-estimation experiment, but the latter also included a null stimulus, that is, a stimulus of zero intensity to both ears, making a total set of 81.

In both experiments, the entire stimulus ensemble (80 stimuli for graphic rating, 81 for magnitude estimation) was presented in two replicates to each observer, with 15 observers tested in graphic rating and 14 observers tested in magnitude estimation. This meant that each stimulus received a total of 28 or 30 ratings in all, probably about the smallest number necessary to provide stable results. With only two judgments made of each stimulus by each observer, it was not feasible to examine results of individual subjects; to obtain reasonably reliable data from individual observers it would have been necessary to present each stimulus at least 8 to 10 times to each observer.

Analyzing the Data

As just mentioned, the experiments under consideration did not lend themselves to analysis of data on individual observers. Instead, data were pooled over observers to assess the characteristics of the resulting psychophysical relations. It should be noted that ratings and magnitude estimates typically have rather different statistical characteristics. With various kinds of ratings, including graphic rating, the distributions of responses made to a given stimulus tend to be reasonably symmetrical, and measures of variability tend to be more or less uniform across the range of stimulus values. By contrast, distributions of magnitude estimates tend to be highly skewed, and the variability tends to increase as the level of the stimulus increases. These properties have led to the use of different measures of central tendency, with ratings typically being averaged arithmetically and magnitude estimates typically being averaged geometrically.

The use of geometric averaging with magnitude estimates serves to preserve the ratio relations among the numbers given by each observer to the various stimuli, while at the same time weighting each observer's ratios equivalently. Were one simply to pool magnitude estimates linearly across observers, the resulting means would be dominated by the data of any observers who used very large numbers. Arithmetic averaging may be necessary, however, if there are many estimates of zero. In such cases, before the data are averaged, it is necessary to normalize them in order to bring observers to a common scale. One way to accomplish this is to calculate, for each observer, the geometric or arithmetic average of the estimates given by that observer to all stimuli, and then divide this average into all of the observer's magnitude estimates. This procedure serves to make the overall geometric or arithmetic mean of the transformed judgments of every observer identical, thereby eliminating differences in absolute size of numbers, and making subsequent arithmetic averaging more appropriate.

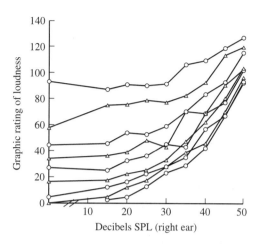

Figure 3.20 Graphic ratings of loudness of 1000-Hz tone in a binaural-summation paradigm, like that of Figure 3.19.
SOURCE: From Marks, 1979. Copyright © 1979 by the American Psychological Association. Reproduced by permission.

Figure 3.20 shows the results obtained by averaging arithmetically the graphic ratings of loudness, and Figure 3.21 shows the comparable results obtained by averaging

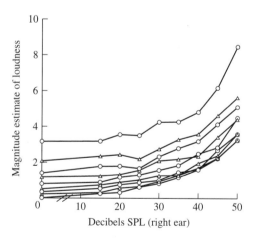

Figure 3.21 Magnitude estimates of loudness of 1000-Hz tone in a binaural-summation paradigm, like that of Figure 3.19.
SOURCE: From Marks, 1978. Copyright © 1978 by the *Journal the Acoustical Society of America*. Reproduced by permission.

geometrically the magnitude estimates of
loudness. Following the paradigm of Figure 3.19, each figure shows the judgment of
loudness plotted against the SPL of the component presented to the right ear, with each
curve representing a different but constant
SPL of the component presented to the left ear.
In both Figures 3.20 and 3.21, the lowermost
curve shows the results obtained with monaural presentation to the right ear (zero intensity
to the left ear); each successively higher-lying
curve represents constant SPLs of 15, 20, 25,
30, 35, 40, 45, and 50 dB.

At first glance, the two sets of curves appear strikingly different. Graphic rating produced a family of psychophysical functions
that tend to converge at the upper right,
whereas magnitude estimation produced a
family of functions that appear to be spaced
more or less uniformly in the vertical plane—
as they should be if (a) component loudnesses
evoked by stimulating the left and right ears
add linearly, and (b) the magnitude-estimation
scale is linearly related to loudness. It is notable, however, that the two sets of data are
closely related ordinally. That is, for any given
pair of stimuli, whichever was judged louder
by graphic rating was also judged louder by
magnitude estimation. This is shown in Figure 3.22, in which the graphic ratings are plotted against the corresponding magnitude estimates. That most of the data points collapse
onto a single function implies that the ordinal
relation between the two scales is very close,
and the nonlinear form of the function—its
downward concavity—is typical of comparisons between ratings and magnitude estimates (e.g., S. S. Stevens & Galanter, 1957).
Given the reasonable assumption that different scaling methods tap the same underlying perceptions, this outcome should not
be surprising; the only important difference
between scaling methods is the way that
observers map their response scale onto these
perceptions. That is, different scaling methods

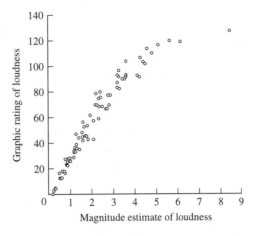

Figure 3.22 Magnitude estimates of Fig-
ure 3.21 plotted against magnitude estimates of
Figure 3.20.
SOURCE: From Marks, 1979. Copyright © 1979
by the American Psychological Association.
Reproduced by permission.

induce observers to apply different response
transformations, as discussed earlier (see
Figure 3.17). If different scaling methods do
nothing more than induce different response
transformations, however, then there will be
for every method a single function relating
loudness to the overt response. If this is so,
then if any two stimuli are equal in loudness, it should not matter whether observers
judge loudness by graphic rating or by magnitude estimation. Certain invariant characteristics of perception are revealed by all scaling
methods.

It follows from these considerations that
it should be possible to apply a nonlinear
but monotonic response transformation to either set of data in order to make them resemble the other set. Thus, if a function that fits
the data of Figure 3.22 is used to transform
the graphic ratings, the outcome is a new
family of loudness functions that resembles
the magnitude estimates, showing a rough
parallelism consistent with linear additivity
(Figure 3.23). One simple interpretation of

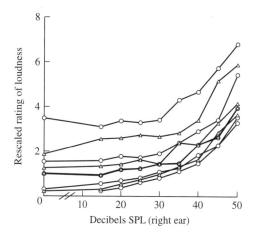

Figure 3.23 Graphic ratings of Figure 3.20, rescaled through the function in Figure 3.22 relating magnitude estimates to graphic ratings.
SOURCE: From Marks, 1979. Copyright © 1979 by the American Psychological Association. Reproduced by permission.

these results is that loudness is binaurally additive, at least to a first approximation, and that magnitude estimates are linearly related to loudness. As discussed earlier, however, there remains nonetheless a degree of theoretical indeterminacy. It is conceivable that the parallelism obtained through magnitude estimation is fortuitous, that loudness is not binaurally additive (see Gigerenzer & Strube, 1983), and that some other, still unknown transformation of the data would be necessary to reveal the "true" underlying values of loudness.

CONCLUSION

As Marks and Algom (1998) pointed out, psychophysical scaling can serve two broad purposes. The traditional purpose, which originated with Fechner (1860), is to elucidate the relation between the mental realm and the physical, as characterized by the psychophysical law. Now, nearly a century and a half later, psychophysicists have a warehouse of methods, yet questions remain as to what method produces valid measures of sensory and perceptual experiences. In this epistemic role, as Marks and Algom called it, psychophysical scaling still lacks a widely accepted theoretical framework, although there have been several notable attempts along these lines (see, for example, Baird, 1997).

On the other hand, psychophysical scaling methods have continued to play a major role, a more pragmatic role, in the study of sensory and perceptual processes. This is especially true when scaling methods are used to examine how sensory or perceptual experiences vary under multivariate stimulation. Category scaling and magnitude scaling alike can reveal how the perception of loudness or brightness or taste or smell intensity depends not only on the intensity of a stimulus but on its duration, its spatial distribution over the receptor surface, the presence of other stimuli that may serve as maskers, the age of the observer, the state of adaptation of the sensory system, and countless other variables. For thorough accounts, see Marks (1974b) and Marks and Algom (1998).

REFERENCES

Algom, D., & Lubel, S. (1994). Psychophysics in the field: Perception and memory for labor pain. *Perception & Psychophysics, 55,* 133–141.

Algom, D., & Marks, L. E. (1984). Individual differences in loudness processing and loudness scales. *Journal of Experimental Psychology: General, 113,* 571–593.

Anderson, N. H. (1970). Functional measurement and psychophysical judgment. *Psychological Review, 77,* 153–170.

Anderson, N. H. (1974). Algebraic models in perception. In E. C. Carterette & M. P. Friedman (Eds.), *Handbook of perception: Volume 2. Psychophysical judgment and measurement* (pp. 215–298). New York: Academic Press.

Anderson, N. H. (1976). Integration theory, functional measurement, and the psychological law. In H.-G. Geissler & Y. M. Zabrodin (Eds.), *Advances in psychophysics* (pp. 93–130). Berlin: VEB Deutscher Verlag der Wissenschaften.

Anderson, N. H. (1981). *Foundations of information integration theory.* New York: Academic Press.

Anderson, N. H. (1982). Cognitive algebra and social psychophysics. In B. Wegener (Ed.), *Social attitudes and psychophysical measurement* (pp. 123–148). Hillsdale, NJ: Erlbaum.

Anderson, N. H. (1992). Integration psychophysics and cognition. In D. Algom (Ed.), *Psychophysical approaches to cognition* (pp. 13–113). Amsterdam: North-Holland.

Attneave, F. (1950). Dimensions of similarity. *American Journal of Psychology, 63,* 516–556.

Attneave, F. (1962). Perception and related areas. In S. Koch (Ed.), *Psychology: A study of a science* (Vol. 4, pp. 619–659). New York: McGraw Hill.

Baird, J. C. (1975). Psychophysical study of numbers: Generalized preferred state theory. *Psychological Research, 38,* 175–187.

Baird, J. C. (1997). *Sensation and judgment: Complementarity theory of psychophysics.* Mahwah, NJ: Erlbaum.

Baird, J. C., & Noma, E. (1975). Psychological studies of numbers: I. Generation of numerical responses. *Psychological Research, 37,* 291–297.

Beals, R., Krantz, D. H., & Tversky, A. (1968). Foundations of multidimensional scaling. *Psychological Review, 75,* 127–142.

Berglund, B. (1991). Quality assurance in environmental psychophysics. In S. J. Bolanowski & G. A. Gescheider (Eds.), *Ratio scaling of psychological magnitude: In honor of the memory of S. S. Stevens* (pp. 140–162). Hillsdale, NJ: Erlbaum.

Birnbaum, M. H. (1982). Controversies in psychophysical measurement. In B. Wegener (Ed.), *Social attitudes and psychophysical measurement* (pp. 401–485). Hillsdale, NJ: Erlbaum.

Birnbaum, M. H., & Elmasian, R. (1977). Loudness "ratios" and "differences" involve the same psychophysical operation. *Perception & Psychophysics, 22,* 383–391.

Borg, G. A. (1972). A ratio scaling method of interindividual comparisons. *Reports from the Institute of Applied Psychology,* No. 27, University of Stockholm.

Borg, G. A. (1982). A category scale with ratio properties for intermodal and interindividual comparisons. In H.-G. Geissler & P. Petzold (Eds.), *Psychophysical judgment and the process of perception* (pp. 25–34). Berlin: Deutscher Verlag der Wissenschaften.

Borg, G. A., & Borg, E. (1994). Principles and experiments in category-ratio scaling. *Reports from the Department of Psychology,* No. 789, Stockholm University.

Braida, L. D., & Durlach, N. I. (1972). Intensity perception: II. Resolution in one-interval paradigms. *Journal of the Acoustical Society of America, 51,* 483–502.

Brentano, F. (1874). *Psychologie vom empirischen Standpunkte.* Leipzig: Duncker und Humblot.

Collins, A. A., & Gescheider, G. A. (1989). The measurement of loudness in children and adults by absolute magnitude estimation and cross-modality matching. *Journal of the Acoustical Society of America, 85,* 2012–2021.

Collins, S. L., Moore, R. A., & McQuay, H. J. (1997). The visual analogue pain intensity scale: What is moderate pain in millimetres? *Pain, 72,* 95–97.

Coombs, C. H. (1950). Psychological scaling without a unit of measurement. *Psychological Review, 57,* 145–158.

Coombs, C. H. (1964). *A theory of data.* New York: Wiley.

Crosby, A. W. (1997). *The measure of reality: Quantification and Western society, 1250–1600.* Cambridge: Cambridge University Press.

Curtis, D. W., Attneave, F., & Harrington, T. L. (1968). A test of a two-stage model of magnitude estimation. *Perception & Psychophysics, 3,* 25–31.

Davison, M. L. (1983). *Multidimensional scaling.* New York: Wiley.

Dawes, R. M. (1994). Psychological measurement. *Psychological Review, 101,* 278–281.

DeCarlo, L. T. (1992). Intertrial interval and sequential effects in magnitude scaling. *Journal of Experimental Psychology: Human Perception and Performance, 18,* 1080–1088.

Delboeuf, J. R. L. (1873). Étude psychophysique: Recherches théoretiques et expérimentales sur la mesure des sensations, et spécialement des sensations de lumière et de fatigue. *Mémoires de l'Académie Royale de Belgique, 23,* No. 5.

Durlach, N. I., & Braida, L. D. (1969). Intensity perception: I. A theory of intensity resolution. *Journal of the Acoustical Society of America, 46,* 372–383.

Durup, G., & Piéron, H. (1933). Recherches au sujet de l'interpretation du phénomène de Purkinje par des différences dans les courbes de sensation des recepteurs chromatiques. *L'Année Psychologique, 33,* 57–83.

Ebbinghaus, H. (1885). *Über das Gedachtnis. Untersuchungen zur experimentellen Psychologie.* Leipzig: Duncker & Humblot.

Ekman, G. (1956). Discriminal sensitivity on the subjective continuum. *Acta Psychologica, 12,* 233–243.

Ekman, G. (1959). Weber's law and related functions. *Journal of Psychology, 47,* 343–352.

Ellermeier, W., Westphal, W., & Heidenfelder, M. (1991). On the "absoluteness" of category and magnitude scales of pain. *Perception & Psychophysics, 49,* 159–166.

Falmagne, J.-C. (1971). The generalized Fechner problem and discrimination. *Journal of Mathematical Psychology, 8,* 22–43.

Falmagne, J.-C. (1974). Foundation of Fechnerian psychophysics. In D. H. Krantz, R. C. Atkinson, R. D. Luce, & P. Suppes (Eds.), *Contemporary developments in mathematical psychology: Measurement, psychophysics, and neural information processing* (Vol. 2, pp. 129–159). San Francisco: Freeman.

Falmagne, J.-C. (1985). *Elements of psychophysical theory.* Oxford: Oxford University Press.

Fechner, G. T. (1860). *Elemente der Psychophysik.* Leipzig: Breitkopf & Härtel.

Fletcher, H., & Munson, W. A. (1933). Loudness, its definition, measurement and calculation. *Journal of the Acoustical Society of America, 5,* 82–108.

Fullerton, G. S., & Cattell, J. M. (1892). *On the perception of small differences.* Philadelphia: University of Pennsylvania Press.

Galanter, E. (1962). The direct measurement of utility and subjective probability. *American Journal of Psychology, 75,* 208–220.

Galileo Galilei (1960). The assayer. In *The controversy on the comets of 1618* (S. Drake & C. D. O'Malley, Trans.; pp. 151–336). Philadelphia: University of Pennsylvania Press. (Original work published 1623)

Geiger, P. H., & Firestone, F. A. (1933). The estimation of fractional loudness. *Journal of the Acoustical Society of America, 5,* 25–30.

Gescheider, G. A. (1988). Psychophysical scaling. *Annual Review of Psychology, 39,* 169–200.

Gescheider, G. A. (1993). What is absolute about absolute magnitude estimation? In R. T. Verrillo (Ed.), *Sensory research: Multimodal perspectives* (pp. 211–231). Hillsdale, NJ: Erlbaum.

Gescheider, G. A. (1997). *Psychophysics: The fundamentals* (3rd ed.). Mahwah, NJ: Erlbaum.

Gescheider, G. A., & Bolanowski, S. J., Jr. (1991). Final comments on ratio scaling of psychological magnitude. In S. J. Bolanowski Jr. & G. A. Gescheider (Eds.), *Ratio scaling of psychological magnitude: In honor of the memory of S. S. Stevens* (pp. 295–311). Hillsdale, NJ: Erlbaum.

Gescheider, G. A., Bolanowksi, S. J., Jr., Zwislocki, J. J., Hall, K. L., & Mascia, C. (1994). The effects of masking on the growth of vibrotactile sensation magnitude and on the intensity DL: A test of the equal sensation magnitude-equal DL hypothesis. *Journal of the Acoustical Society of America, 96,* 1479–1488.

Gescheider, G. A., & Hughson, B. A. (1991). Stimulus context and absolute magnitude estimation: A study of individual differences. *Perception & Psychophysics, 50,* 45–57.

Gigerenzer, G., & Murray, D. J. (1987). *Cognition as intuitive statistics.* Hillsdale, NJ: Erlbaum.

Gigerenzer, G., & Strube, G. (1983). Are there limits to binaural additivity of loudness? *Journal of Experimental Psychology: Human Perception and Performance, 9,* 126–136.

Green, B. G., Shaffer, G. S., & Gilmore, M. M. (1993). Derivation and evaluation of a semantic scale of oral sensation magnitude with apparent ratio properties. *Chemical Senses, 18,* 683–702.

Gregson, R. A. M. (1965). Representation of taste mixture cross-modality matching on a Minkowski-R metric. *Australian Journal of Psychology, 17,* 195–204.

Gregson, R. A. M. (1966). Theoretical and empirical multidimensional scalings of taste mixture matchings. *British Journal of Mathematical and Statistical Psychology, 19,* 59–75.

Guilford, J. P. (1954). *Psychometric methods* (2nd ed.). New York: McGraw-Hill.

Gulick, W. L., Gescheider, G. A., & Frisina, R. D. (1989). *Hearing: Physiological acoustics, neural coding, and psychoacoustics.* New York: Oxford University Press.

Ham, L. B., & Parkinson, J. S. (1932). Loudness and intensity relations. *Journal of the Acoustical Society of America, 3,* 511–534.

Hardy, J. D., Wolff, H. G., & Goodell, H. (1947). Studies on pain: Discrimination of differences in pain as a basis of a scale of pain intensity. *Journal of Clinical Investigation, 26,* 1152–1158.

Heller, O. (1985). Hörfeldaudiometrie mit dem Verfahren der Kategorienunterteilung (KU). *Psychologische Beiträge, 27,* 478–493.

Hellman, R. P. (1981). Stability of individual loudness functions obtained by magnitude estimation and production. *Perception & Psychophysics, 29,* 63–70.

Hellman, R. P., Scharf, B., Teghtsoonian, M., & Teghtsoonian, R. (1987). On the relation between the growth of loudness and the discrimination of intensity for pure tones. *Journal of the Acoustical Society of America, 82,* 448–452.

Hellman, R. P., & Zwislocki, J. J. (1961). Some factors affecting the estimation of loudness. *Journal of the Acoustical Society of America, 33,* 687–694.

Hellman, R. P., & Zwislocki, J. J. (1963). Monaural loudness function of a 1000-cps tone and internal summation. *Journal of the Acoustical Society of America, 35,* 856–865.

Holmes, T. H., & Rahe, R. H. (1967). The social readjustment rating scale. *Journal of Psychosomatic Research, 11,* 213–218.

Huskisson, E. C. (1983). Visual analog scales. In R. Melzack (Ed.), *Pain measurement and assessment* (pp. 33–37). New York: Raven.

James, W. (1892). *Psychology: Briefer course.* New York: Holt.

Jesteadt, W., Luce, R. D., & Green, D. M. (1977). Sequential effects in judgments of loudness. *Journal of Experimental Psychology: Human Perception and Performance, 3,* 92–104.

Kenshalo, D. R., Decker, T., & Hamilton, A. (1967). Spatial summation on the forehead, forearm, and back produced by radiant and conducted heat. *Journal of Comparative and Physiological Psychology, 63,* 510–515.

Krueger, L. E. (1989). Reconciling Fechner and Stevens: Toward a unified psychophysical law. *The Behavioral and Brain Sciences, 12,* 251–320.

Leon, M. (1980). Integration of intent and consequence information in children's moral judgment. In F. Wilkening, J. Becker, & T. Trabasso (Eds.), *Information integration by children* (pp. 71–97). Hillsdale, NJ: Erlbaum.

Locke, J. (1690). *An essay concerning humane understanding.* London: Basset.

Logue, A. W. (1976). Individual differences in magnitude estimation of loudness. *Perception & Psychophysics, 19,* 279–280.

Luce, R. D. (1977). Thurstone discriminal processes fifty years later. *Psychometrika, 42,* 461–498.

Luce, R. D. (1994). Thurstone and sensory scaling: Then and now. *Psychological Review, 101,* 271–277.

Luce, R. D., & Galanter, E. (1963). Discrimination. In R. D. Luce, R. R. Bush, & E. Galanter (Eds.), *Handbook of mathematical psychology* (Vol. 1, pp. 191–243). New York: Wiley.

Luce, R. D., & Green, D. M. (1974). The response ratio hypothesis for magnitude estimation. *Journal of Mathematical Psychology, 11,* 1–14.

Luce, R. D., Green, D. M., & Weber, D. L. (1976). Attention bands in absolute identification. *Perception & Psychophysics, 20,* 49–54.

Luce, R. D., & Krumhansl, C. L. (1988). Measurement, scaling, and psychophysics. In R. C. Atkinson, R. J. Herrnstein, G. Lindzay, & R. D. Luce (Eds.), *Stevens' handbook of experimental psychology* (2nd ed.; Vol. 1, pp. 3–74). New York: Wiley.

Luce, R. D., & Tukey, J. (1964). Simultaneous conjoint measurement: A new type of fundamental measurement. *Journal of Mathematical Psychology, 1,* 1–27.

Macmillan, N. A., & Creelman, C. D. (1991). *Detection theory: A user's guide.* Cambridge: Cambridge University Press.

Marks, L. E. (1968). Stimulus-range, number of categories, and form of the category-scale. *American Journal of Psychology, 81,* 467–479.

Marks, L. E. (1974a). Spatial summation in the warmth sense. In H. R. Moskowitz, B. Scharf, & J. C. Stevens (Eds.), *Sensation and measurement: Papers in honor of S. S. Stevens* (pp. 369–378). Dordrecht, Netherlands: Reidel.

Marks, L. E. (1974b). *Sensory processes: The new psychophysics.* New York: Academic Press.

Marks, L. E. (1978). Binaural summation of the loudness of pure tones. *Journal of the Acoustical Society of America, 64,* 107–113.

Marks, L. E. (1979). Sensory and cognitive factors in judgments of loudness. *Journal of Experimental Psychology: Human Perception and Performance, 5,* 426–443.

Marks, L. E. (1991). Reliability of magnitude matching. *Perception & Psychophysics, 49,* 31–37.

Marks, L. E., & Algom, D. (1998). Psychophysical scaling. In M. H. Birnbaum (Ed.), *Measurement, judgment, and decision making* (pp. 81–178). San Diego: Academic Press.

Marks, L. E., Borg, G., & Ljunggren, G. (1983). Individual differences in perceived exertion assessed by two new methods. *Perception & Psychophysics, 34,* 280–288.

Marks, L. E., Stevens, J. C., Bartoshuk, L. M., Gent, J. F., Rifkin, B., & Stone, V. K. (1988). Magnitude-matching: The measurement of taste and smell. *Chemical Senses, 13,* 63–87.

Melara, R. D. (1992). The concept of perceptual similarity: From psychophysics to cognitive psychology. In D. Algom (Ed.), *Psychophysical approaches to cognition* (pp. 303–388). Amsterdam: North Holland Elsevier.

Merkel, J. (1888). Die Abhängigkeit zwischen Reiz und Empfindung. *Philosophische Studien, 4,* 541–594.

Munsell, A. E. O., Sloan, L. L., & Godlove, I. H. (1933). Neutral value scales: I. Munsell neutral value scale. *Journal of the Optical Society of America, 23,* 394–411.

Noma, E., & Baird, J. C. (1975). Psychophysical study of numbers: II. Theoretical models of number generation. *Psychological Research, 38,* 81–95.

Parducci, A. (1965). Category judgment: A range-frequency model. *Psychological Review, 75,* 407–418.

Parducci, A. (1974). Contextual effects: A range-frequency analysis. In E. C. Carterette & M. P. Friedman (Eds.), *Handbook of perception: Vol. 2. Psychophysical judgment and measurement* (pp. 127–141). New York: Academic Press.

Parducci, A., & Perrett, L. F. (1971). Category rating scales: Effects of relative spacing and frequency of stimulus values. *Journal of Experimental Psychology Monographs, 89,* 427–452.

Parducci, A., & Wedell, D. H. (1986). The category effect with rating scales: Number of categories, number of stimuli, and method of presentation. *Journal of Experimental Psychology: Human Perception and Performance, 12,* 496–516.

Parker, S., & Schneider, B. (1974). Non-metric scaling of loudness and pitch using similarity and difference estimates. *Perception & Psychophysics, 15,* 238–242.

Piéron, H. (1952). *The sensations: Their functions, processes and mechanisms.* New Haven, CT: Yale University Press.

Plateau, J. A. F. (1872). Sur la mesure des sensations physiques, et sur la loi qui lie l'intensité de ces sensations à l'intensité de la cause excitante. *Bulletins de l' Academie Royale des Sciences, des Lettres, et des Beaux-Arts de Belgique, 33,* 376–388.

Pollack, I. (1965a). Iterative techniques for unbiased rating scales. *Quarterly Journal of Experimental Psychology, 17,* 139–148.

Pollack, I. (1965b). Neutralization of stimulus bias in the rating of grays. *Journal of Experimental Psychology, 69,* 564–578.

Popper, R. D., Parker, S., & Galanter, E. (1986). Dual loudness scales in individual subjects. *Journal of Experimental Psychology: Human Perception and Performance, 12,* 61–69.

Poulton, E. C. (1989). *Bias in quantifying judgments.* Hove, England: Erlbaum.

Ramsay, J. O. (1979). Intra- and interindividual variation in the power law exponent for area summation. *Perception & Psychophysics, 26,* 495–500.

Richardson, L. F., & Ross, J. S. (1930). Loudness and telephone current. *Journal of General Psychology, 3,* 288–306.

Rschevkin, S. N., & Rabinovich, A. V. (1936). Sur le problème de l'estimation quantitative de la force d'un son. *Revue d'Acoustique, 5,* 183–200.

Scharf, B. (1959). Critical bands and the loudness of complex sounds near threshold. *Journal of the Acoustical Society of America, 31,* 365–370.

Schiffman, S. S., Reynolds, M. L., & Young, F. W. (1981). *Introduction to multidimensional scaling: Theory, methods and applications.* New York: Academic Press.

Schneider, B. (1980). Individual loudness functions determined from direct comparisons of loudness intervals. *Perception & Psychophysics, 27,* 493–503.

Schneider, B., & Bissett, R. J. (1981). The dimensions of tonal experience: A nonmetric multidimensional scaling approach. *Perception & Psychophysics, 30,* 39–48.

Schneider, B., Parker, S., & Stein, D. (1974). The measurement of loudness using direct comparisons of sensory intervals. *Journal of Mathematical Psychology, 11,* 259–273.

Schneider, B., Parker, S., Valenti, M., Farrell, G., & Kanow, G. (1978). Response bias in category and magnitude estimation of difference and similarity for loudness and pitch. *Journal of Experimental Psychology: Human Perception and Performance, 4,* 483–496.

Sellin, T., & Wolfgang, M. E. (1964). *The measurement of delinquency.* New York: Wiley.

Shepard, R. N. (1966). Metric structures in ordinal data. *Journal of Mathematical Psychology, 3,* 287–315.

Shepard, R. N. (1981). Psychological relations and psychological scales: On the status of "direct" psychophysical measurement. *Journal of Mathematical Psychology, 24,* 21–57.

Staddon, J. E., King, M., & Lockhead, G. R. (1980). On sequential effects in absolute judgment experiments. *Journal of Experimental Psychology: Human Perception and Performance, 6,* 290–301.

Stevens, J. C., & Guirao, M. (1964). Individual loudness functions. *Journal of the Acoustical Society of America, 36,* 2210–2213.

Stevens, J. C., Mack, J. D., & Stevens, S. S. (1960). Growth of sensation on seven continua as measured by force of handgrip. *Journal of Experimental Psychology, 59,* 60–67.

Stevens, J. C., & Marks, L. E. (1965). Cross-modality matching of brightness and loudness. *Proceedings of the National Academy of Sciences, 54,* 407–411.

Stevens, J. C., & Marks, L. E. (1971). Spatial summation and the dynamics of warmth sensation. *Perception & Psychophysics, 9,* 291–298.

Stevens, J. C., & Marks, L. E. (1980). Cross-modality matching functions generated by magnitude estimation. *Perception & Psychophysics, 27,* 379–389.

Stevens, J. C., & Stevens, S. S. (1963). Brightness function: Effects of adaptation. *Journal of the Optical Society of America, 53,* 375–385.

Stevens, S. S. (1935). The relation of pitch to intensity. *Journal of the Acoustical Society of America, 6,* 150–154.

Stevens, S. S. (1946). On the theory of scales of measurement. *Science, 103,* 677–680.

Stevens, S. S. (1951). Mathematics, measurement, and psychophysics. In S. S. Stevens (Ed.), *Handbook of experimental psychology* (pp. 1–49). New York: Wiley.

Stevens, S. S. (1953). On the brightness of lights and loudness of sounds. *Science, 118,* 576.

Stevens, S. S. (1955). The measurement of loudness. *Journal of the Acoustical Society of America, 27,* 815–820.

Stevens, S. S. (1956). The direct estimation of sensory magnitude—loudness. *American Journal of Psychology, 69,* 1–25.

Stevens, S. S. (1957). On the psychophysical law. *Psychological Review, 64,* 153–181.

Stevens, S. S. (1958). Problems and methods of psychophysics. *Psychological Bulletin, 55,* 177–196.

Stevens, S. S. (1959a). Cross-modality validation of subjective scales for loudness, vibration, and electric shock. *Journal of Experimental Psychology, 57,* 201–209.

Stevens, S. S. (1959b). L. L. Thurstone's *The measurement of values* [Review]. *Contemporary Psychology, 4,* 388–389.

Stevens, S. S. (1975). *Psychophysics: Introduction to its perceptual, neural and social prospects.* New York: Wiley.

Stevens, S. S., & Galanter, E. H. (1957). Ratio scales and category scales for a dozen perceptual continua. *Journal of Experimental Psychology, 54,* 377–411.

Stevens, S. S., & Guirao, M. (1962). Loudness, reciprocality, and partition scales. *Journal of the Acoustical Society of America, 34,* 1466–1471.

Stevens, S. S., & Volkmann, J. (1940). The relation of pitch to frequency: A revised scale. *American Journal of Psychology, 53,* 329–353.

Stillman, J. A., Zwislocki, J. J., Zhang, M., & Cefaratti, L. K. (1993). Intensity just-noticeable differences at equal-loudness levels in normal and pathological ears. *Journal of the Acoustical Society of America, 93,* 425–434.

Suppes, P., & Zinnes, J. L. (1963). Basic measurement theory. In R. D. Luce, R. R. Bush, & E. Galanter (Eds.), *Handbook of mathematical psychology* (Vol. 1, pp. 1–76). New York: Wiley.

Tanner, W. P., Jr., & Swets, J. A. (1954). A decision-making theory of visual detection. *Psychological Review, 61,* 401–409.

Teghtsoonian, M., and Teghtsoonian, R. (1983). Consistency of individual exponents in cross-modal matching. *Perception & Psychophysics, 33,* 203–214.

Teghtsoonian, R. (1971). On the exponents in Stevens' law and the constant in Ekman's law. *Psychological Review, 78,* 71–80.

Teghtsoonian, R. (1973). Range effects of psychophysical scaling and a revision of Stevens' law. *American Journal Psychology, 86,* 3–27.

Teghtsoonian, R., & Teghtsoonian, M. (1978). Range and regression effects in magnitude scaling. *Perception & Psychophysics, 24,* 305–314.

Thorndike, E. L. (1910). Handwriting. *Teachers College Record, 11,* No. 2.

Thurstone, L. L. (1927). A law of comparative judgment. *Psychological Review, 34,* 273–286.

Torgerson, W. S. (1958). *Theory and methods of scaling.* New York: Wiley.

Ward, L. M. (1973). Repeated magnitude estimation with a variable standard: Sequential effects and other properties. *Perception & Psychophysics, 13,* 193–200.

Ward, L. M. (1987). Remembrance of sounds past: Memory and psychophysical scaling. *Journal of Experimental Psychology: Human Perception and Performance, 13,* 216–227.

Weissmann, S. M., Hollingsworth, S. R., & Baird, J. C. (1975). Psychological study of numbers: III. Methodological applications. *Psychological Research, 38,* 97–115.

Zwislocki, J. J. (1983). Group and individual relations between sensation magnitudes and their numerical estimates. *Perception & Psychophysics, 33,* 460–468.

Zwislocki, J. J. (1991). Natural measurement. In S. J. Bolanowski Jr. & G. A. Gescheider (Eds.), *Ratio scaling of psychological magnitude: In honor of the memory of S. S. Stevens* (pp. 18–26). Hillsdale, NJ: Erlbaum.

Zwislocki, J. J., & Goodman, D. A. (1980). Absolute scaling of sensory magnitudes: A validation. *Perception & Psychophysics, 28,* 28–38.

Zwislocki, J. J., & Jordan, H. N. (1986). On the relations of intensity jnd's to loudness and neural noise. *Journal of the Acoustical Society of America, 79,* 772–780.

CHAPTER 4

Cognitive Neuropsychology

MAX COLTHEART

The aim of cognitive psychology is to learn more about the mental information-processing systems that people use when engaged in such cognitive activities as producing or understanding language, recognizing objects or faces, acting skillfully, retrieving information from memory, doing mental calculations, and so on. There are two ways of carrying out such research. One is to study people who have acquired skill in these cognitive activities and who perform them well. The other is to study people who perform such activities abnormally.

Such abnormality has two possible forms. An investigator might be studying an individual who had attained a normal degree of skill in some cognitive activity but who then suffered some form of brain damage that impaired performance of that activity; here the investigator is studying an acquired disorder of cognition. Alternatively, an investigator might be studying an individual who had never attained a normal degree of skill with respect to the cognitive activity in question; here such an investigator is studying a developmental disorder of cognition.

Cognitive neuropsychology is the investigation of disordered cognition with the aim of learning more about normal cognition. Therefore, it is a branch of cognitive psychology. When an acquired disorder of cognition is studied, the aim is to learn about the normal processes of cognition by studying how they can break down after brain damage. When a developmental disorder of cognition is studied (the area of investigation known as developmental cognitive neuropsychology), the aim is to learn how cognitive abilities are normally acquired by studying ways in which such acquisition fails or proceeds abnormally.

Even though most cognitive neuropsychologists study people with brain damage, and despite the impression that might be given by the prefix "neuro" in the term "cognitive neuropsychology," cognitive neuropsychology is not about the brain; it is about the mind. Many scientists, of course, are interested in the neural structures subserving cognition, and investigation of the brain in people with acquired disorders of cognition is one obvious way to pursue such an interest. But this is not cognitive neuropsychology; it is cognitive neuroscience. Just as cognitive neuropsychology is a branch of cognitive psychology, cognitive neuroscience is a branch of neuroscience. One is about the mind; the other is about the brain (and the rest of the nervous system).

Contemporary cognitive psychology treats cognition as mental information processing, that is, as involving the formation and

The author thanks Colin Davis, Phil Gold, Elaine and Graham Funnell, John Marshall, Genevieve McArthur, Niels Schiller, and John Wixted for helpful comments and criticisms.

transformation of mental representations. Therefore, any theory about how a particular cognitive activity is achieved will take the general form of a description of information flow. Such descriptions require statements about what specific information-processing mechanisms are the components of the hypothesized mental information-processing system as well as statements about the flow of information between these components.

Quite often, these descriptions are expressed as box-and-arrow flow charts, such as the diagram shown in Figure 4.1. This way of notating theories has the advantage of making them explicit and complete. Each box represents a particular component of the postulated information-processing system; each of the pathways of information flow between these components is represented by an arrow.

This, by the way, is not a novel notation for expressing theories about cognition; on the contrary, it was widely used by the cognitive neuropsychologists of the 19th century (see Coltheart, Rastle, Perry, Langdon, & Ziegler, 2001, for some examples).

MODULARITY

We need some term to refer to the components of a system such as that shown in Figure 4.1, and the term I use here is *module;* thus the system in Figure 4.1 has eleven modules, and the system itself is said to have the property of modularity.

Fodor (1983) provided a valuable explication of the concept of modularity, and I use the term essentially as he did. Although it is quite often suggested that Fodor's book proposed a definition of modularity, and that the book contains proposals about necessary conditions for the application of this term, neither of these suggestions is correct. Fodor emphasized that he was not intending to provide a definition of the term, nor any necessary characteristics; instead, he was suggesting a list of features that were *characteristic of* modules. The features he listed included (a) domain specificity, (b) innateness, (c) informational encapsulation, (d) fast operation, (e) neural specificity, and (f) automaticity. According to Fodor, each of these features is typical of modules, although none is necessary. I use the term *module* in essentially this sense, except that I follow Coltheart (1999) in believing that one feature of modules *is* necessary for the term to be applicable. This necessary feature is domain specificity: "A cognitive system is domain-specific if it only responds to stimuli of a particular class: thus, to say that there is a domain-specific face-recognition module is to say that there is a cognitive system that responds when its input is a face, but does not respond when its input is, say, a written word, or a visually-presented object, or someone's

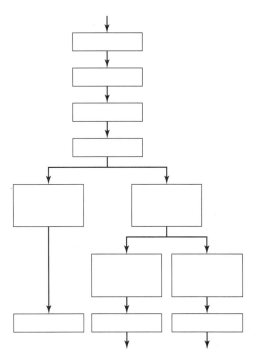

Figure 4.1   An information-processing system.

voice" (Coltheart, 1999, p. 118). I take the other five Fodorian features as commonly, but not invariably, true of modules; thus, for example, some modules may not be innate, even if many modules are innate.

To be more specific, the focus here is on functional modularity because modules are being described in terms of their particular mental information-processing functions. One can distinguish functional modularity from anatomical modularity (an anatomical module is a specific delimited region of the brain that carries out some specific form of information-processing; for example, area V5 is a specific brain region responsible for the processing of motion and thus can be referred to as an anatomical module for motion-detection). Perhaps one can also distinguish functional modularity from neurochemical modularity (a neurochemical module is a system in the brain that uses a particular specific neurotransmitter). These are logically independent concepts; for example, the mind could be functionally modular even if the brain were neither anatomically nor neurochemically modular. If that were so, cognitive neuropsychology would be impossible because anatomical or neurochemical brain damage could never impair some functional modules while sparing others, and it is such selective patterns of cognitive impairment and sparing that are the basic data of cognitive neuropsychology. Because cognitive neuropsychology *is* possible, it would seem that both the mind and the brain are modular in structure. That is presumably what Fodor (1983) had in mind with the term *neurally specific:* to say that a functional module is neurally specific is to say that it is also an anatomical module.

It needs to be emphasized here that if what we mean by "module" is "a domain-specific information-processing system," then we have to be willing to call the *entire* system

depicted later in Figure 4.3 a module because that system is an information-processing system and because it is domain-specific (it does not respond to auditory input or olfactory input, just to visual input). But we also have to be willing to call the individual components of the system in Figure 4.3 modules too, because those components are also domain-specific information-processing systems: for example, the component labeled "visual word recognition" responds only to input that is letters. Even an individual component in Figure 4.3 may have an internal modular structure. For example, in patients with semantic impairments, some patients have impairment in the understanding only of words referring to animate objects, and others only of words referring to inanimate objects (for a review of this literature, see Caramazza & Shelton, 1998). This suggests that within the semantic system there are at least two modules, one whose domain is inanimate objects and another whose domain is animate objects. In general, then, the conception of modularity used here commits one to the view that modules can be within modules that are within modules, and hence to an abandonment of the view, proposed in Fodor (1983) but not in Fodor (2000), that an important property of modules is that they are "not assembled"—not composed of smaller processing components. Block (1995) discusses where the nesting of modules within modules might stop, and this issue is considered later in this chapter.

One can distinguish two types of functional modules: knowledge modules and processing modules. A knowledge module is a body of knowledge that is autonomous (i.e., independent) of other bodies of knowledge (e.g., the on-line catalog of a library, which is independent of other bodies of knowledge about the library, such as its floor plan, its wiring diagram, or the layout of its sewage disposal system). A processing module is an autonomous system for processing information (e.g., the search engine used to retrieve information from the library's on-line catalog, or the library's fire-protection mechanism that detects smoke and dispenses water). One way to make diagrams such as that of Figure 4.1 even more precise is to replace the rectangular boxes with symbols that distinguish the two types of functional module: ellipses for knowledge modules, say, and rectangles for processing modules (Funnell, 1983; Gane & Sarsen, 1977). This is probably a useful notational discipline, although it will not be adopted here: Both types of functional modules will be represented just by rectangles.

Although the diagram in Figure 4.1 is explicit about how many modules and how many pathways of communication the depicted processing system has, it is nevertheless utterly opaque: What is it supposed to *do?* What sort of input does it accept, what sort of output does it produce, and what processing procedures does it apply to the input in order to create the output? This opacity can only be eliminated if the nature of the input and output is stated and if each module in the system is labeled according to what processing procedure it carries out. That is done in Figure 4.2, which makes clear the fact that Figure 4.1 is a diagram of a system that makes chocolate and cocoa.

As shown in Figure 4.3, however, there is a very different way of labeling the modules and the inputs and outputs of (a minor variant of) Figure 4.1. This second way of labeling makes clear the fact that Figure 4.1 is a diagram of a system for naming pictures, printed words, and printed nonwords, as well as a diagram of a system that makes chocolate and cocoa.

The example represented by Figures 4.1 through 4.3 is meant to illustrate several points. First, although Figure 4.1 is an explicit description of the structure of a modular processing system, this description is

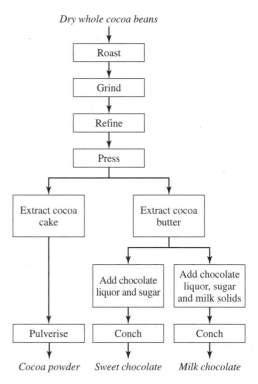

Figure 4.2   A system for manufacturing chocolate.
SOURCE: Adapted from McGee (1984, p. 405).

at such an abstract level that it can apply equally well to a chocolate factory as to a mind; its input can be cocoa beans or reflected light, and its output can be chocolate, cocoa, or speech.

Labeling the modules eliminates this level of abstraction: Figure 4.2 cannot be about the mind, and Figure 4.3 cannot be about a chocolate factory. However, a crucial level of abstraction remains: Neither of these two diagrams specifies anything at all about hardware. Figure 4.2 says nothing about any physical properties of the machinery within the factory, and Figure 4.3 says nothing about any neural systems in the brain. For example, *conching* is the process by which chocolate is heated to between 130 and 200 degrees Fahrenheit and then slowly kneaded and folded for hours or days; this reduces bitter

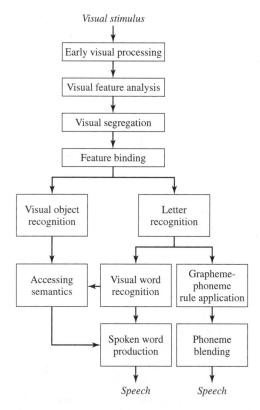

Figure 4.3   A system for naming pictures, words, and nonwords.

Figure 4.4   A conching machine.

flavors and makes the chocolate smoother in texture. This functional description of the conching process says nothing about the actual machine that does the conching. Furthermore, even if people were allowed full access to the factory and could thoroughly inspect all the machines in it, they would not be able to work out what the conching machine does just from scrutinizing it unless they were already armed with the functional description of the conching process. Close inspection of the machine shown in Figure 4.4 would not tell anyone that what it does is conching. In just the same way, if people were able to obtain a complete description of the neural structure of the part of the brain that does letter recognition during reading, they would not be able to work out what function that part of the brain actually serves.

Similarly, imagine someone who was interested in determining whether a particular desktop computer could do word processing. Taking the lid off and looking at the hardware inside could not provide an answer to this question. In contrast, imagine that someone who is a programmer were given the code for a program and asked whether this program could do word processing. That question *could* be answered by scrutiny of the program. Considerations like this led Block (1995, p. 376) to the doctrine that "the mind is the software of the brain," a corollary of which is that cognitive psychology is the study of that software.

This same perspective on cognitive science was also offered by Marr (1982, p. 24). He distinguished "three levels at which any machine carrying out an information-processing task must be understood"; these were the levels of computational theory, representation and algorithm, and hardware implementation and emphasized the independence of understanding at the representation-and-algorithm level from understanding at the hardware-implementation level: "Trying to understand perception by studying only neurons is like trying to understand bird flight by studying only feathers. It just cannot be done" (p. 27).

COGNITIVE-
NEUROPSYCHOLOGICAL
INFERENCE AND
THE CHOCOLATE FACTORY

Imagine now that a person were interested in discovering exactly how the chocolate factory functions—in learning exactly what procedures the factory uses to turn cocoa beans into milk chocolate, sweet chocolate, or cocoa powder—but the only data available from which one might infer anything about this are data about what goes into the factory and what comes out. Looking inside the factory is not allowed.

Careful chronometry might reveal that after a consignment of cocoa beans is delivered, packages of cocoa powder begin to emerge from the factory sooner than packages of sweet chocolate or milk chocolate, whereas the latter two products begin emerging at about the same time. From that difference in latency of response one might deduce that the production of cocoa powder requires fewer processing stages than the production of sweet chocolate or milk chocolate, with these two requiring the same number of processing stages. One might even begin to sketch out a theory of the factory's operations according to which all the stages needed to make cocoa powder are also needed to make sweet chocolate or milk chocolate, and on top of this there is one extra stage, or several extra stages, required for making sweet chocolate or milk chocolate but not for making cocoa powder. That would be a wild extrapolation, however. It could be that the three products depend on three completely different processing procedures that have nothing at all in common; it just so happens that one of these procedures works quickly, and the other two relatively slowly.

Then one day it appears that there is something wrong with both the cocoa powder and the chocolate that are produced; their forms and textures are appropriate, but they taste raw rather than roasted, though they have the right sweetness. What might be deduced from these data concerning the processing system inside the factory? It seems reasonable to conclude that the control of the form, texture, and sweetness of the product must depend on a system or systems that are separate from the system that roasts the beans; in other words, there is a single Roasting Module that is used for producing all three products. If so, that provides a simple explanation for why all three products show the same defect: the Roasting Module is down, so unroasted beans are being passed on to the rest of the system. The rest of the system is still functioning normally, so the products still have normal form, texture, and sweetness.

An alternative possibility, though—an alternative possible functional architecture for the factory—is that there are three separate Roasting Modules, one for each of the three products, and all three of these happen to have gone down simultaneously. Would that be rather a coincidence? Not necessarily. If there were three separate Roasting Modules, it would make sense for them to be physically located very close together, because the cocoa beans they need could then be delivered to only one location in the factory rather than three. If these three modules were physically adjacent, then any trauma to the factory that affected one of them (e.g., a fire in one part of the factory, or the collapse of part of the factory roof) would be likely to affect all three. Thus, the association seen here among three deficits (unroasted cocoa powder, unroasted sweet chocolate, and unroasted milk chocolate) might be an uninteresting consequence of some physical fact about the factory, rather than an interesting consequence of some functional fact.

Suppose that on another day one notices that something is wrong with the cocoa powder that is produced. It tastes as it should, but it isn't powdered; instead, it is emerging from the factory in the form of solid cakes. Yet the sweet chocolate and milk chocolate are absolutely normal. This immediately suggests that there is a processor in the factory whose job is specifically to turn solid cakes into powder—called, for example, the Pulverizer—and that this processor does not play any part in the production of sweet chocolate or milk chocolate. If there is such a Pulverizer, and if it is not working just now, the outcome would be that sweet chocolate and milk chocolate would still be produced normally, but cocoa powder would not. Specifically, the cocoa would still be coming out, but abnormally—as cakes rather than as powder.

This inference seems entirely reasonable, but again an alternative explanation comes fairly readily to mind. Perhaps there is no Pulverizer Module; perhaps instead there's a single machine that both presses and (when required) pulverizes, and so is needed in the making of all three products. Suppose, as might seem natural, that this machine needs more electrical power to pulverize than to press, and the electricity supply to the factory has weakened. In that case, pressing will still happen but pulverizing will not—but not because the two functions are functionally distinct. Here the dissociation (cocoa powder defective yet chocolate intact) can be plausibly explained without postulating the existence of a distinct Pulverizer Module.

Finally, suppose that on yet another day a different defect emerges: Both the sweet chocolate and the milk chocolate begin to taste bitter and to be coarse in texture. The cocoa powder is just fine, however. One possible explanation for these data is that there is a processor in the factory whose job is specifically to reduce the bitterness and smooth the texture of the two types of chocolate—called the Concher—and that this does not play any part in the production of cocoa powder.

Data suggesting that the factory contains a Pulverizer Module and a Concher Module cannot instead be explained in terms of possible effects of a weakened electricity supply, because on that hypothesis one could never see bad pulverizing and good conching on one occasion, and good pulverizing but bad conching on another. A single dissociation could be explained on the electricity-supply hypothesis; but a double dissociation between the two defects cannot. Thus, the hypothesis that the system in the factory contains a Pulverizer Module and a Concher Module looks strong, and until someone devises an alternative hypothesis that is also compatible with the data on the two different patterns of breakdown that have been observed, it is reasonable to conclude that the functional architecture of the factory includes a Pulverizer Module and a Concher Module.

ASSOCIATIONS, DISSOCIATIONS, AND DOUBLE DISSOCIATIONS

The discussion of these studies of breakdowns of the chocolate factory introduced three concepts that loom large in discussions of the methodology of cognitive neuropsychology: associated deficits, dissociated deficits, and doubly dissociated deficits.

Association

Two deficits X and Y are referred to as associated when both are present (for the chocolate factory example, cocoa powder not roasted and chocolate not roasted; or, with a brain-damaged patient, faces not recognized and printed words not recognized). The cause of these associations might be damage to a single module on which two tasks depend: There might be a single roasting module used both in the production of cocoa powder and in the production of chocolate, and there might be a single visual recognition system used both in the recognition of faces and in the recognition of printed words.

The one-module conclusions could in fact be correct, but cognitive neuropsychologists are wary of drawing such conclusions from associations because there is always a plausible alternative explanation of an association of deficits, an alternative according to which there are two modules in the relevant system, rather than one. On this alternative, whatever causes damage to a particular physical part of the system might be likely to cause damage to physically adjacent parts of the system as well. That point was illustrated earlier in relation to the chocolate factory; in relation to humans, there could be two visual recognition modules, one for faces and another for words, located in adjacent regions of the brain. Brain injury due to a blow to the head or to a bullet wound that damaged one module would often damage physically adjacent modules; or if two modules shared a common blood supply, a stroke that interfered with that supply would generate two deficits. Nevertheless, there are two modules here, not one. Arguments like these weaken conclusions about modular organization that are based upon the observation of associated deficits.

Module used in the production of cocoa powder but not in the production of chocolate; a Face Recognition Module used for recognizing faces but not for recognizing printed words).

Such conclusions about the existence of modules dedicated to one task but not another, reached because of observations of dissociated deficits, could in fact be correct; but once again cognitive neuropsychologists are wary of drawing such conclusions from dissociations because there is always a plausible alternative explanation of a dissociation of deficits, an alternative according to which the system does not in fact contain these inferred modules. In the case of the chocolate factory, that point has already been made: Perhaps the factory just needs more electrical power to carry out pulverization than to carry out other functions. In the case of humans, there could be a single Visual Recognition Module used for recognizing both faces and printed words, and partial damage to this single system could impair face recognition without impairing visual word recognition because faces are visually more complex, so stress this system more, so are more affected than are printed words when the module is partially damaged. Arguments like these weaken conclusions about modular organization that are based on the observation of dissociated deficits.

Dissociation

Two deficits X and Y are referred to as dissociated when one is present and the other is absent (for the chocolate factory example, the cocoa powder is abnormal but the chocolate is normal; or, with a brain-damaged patient, faces are not recognized but printed words are). These dissociations might arise because there is a module in each system that is used for one task but not for the other (a Pulverizer

Double Dissociation

Two deficits X and Y are referred to as "doubly dissociated" when there is a case where deficit X is present and deficit Y is absent, and another case where the reverse is true, i.e., deficit X is absent and deficit Y is present (for the chocolate factory example, on one occasion the cocoa powder is abnormal but the chocolate is normal, whereas on another occasion the cocoa powder is normal but the chocolate is abnormal; or, with brain-damaged patients, in one patient faces are not recognized but printed words are, whereas in another patient face recognition is intact but word recognition is impaired).

One way in which double dissociations can be interpreted is in terms of the existence of a module that is used for task A but not for task B, and the existence of another module that is used for task B but not for task A. For the chocolate factory, these two modules are the Pulverizer and the Concher. For the human, they are the face recognition system and the visual word recognition system.

As indicated earlier, the problem with associations and with single dissociations is that they are inherently ambiguous; in both cases, both a one-module interpretation and a two-module interpretation are plausibly available. Double dissociations are different: A plausible alternative interpretation is not inevitably present. An interpretation in terms of differential difficulty is untenable if in one case performance of task A is worse and in another case performance of Task B is worse, and an interpretation in terms of neuroanatomical proximity is irrelevant because that only applies to associations. For this reason, cognitive neuropsychologists regard double dissociation evidence as, on the whole, superior to evidence based on associations or single dissociations.

That is not to say that an alternative (one-module) interpretation can *never* be offered when a double dissociation has been used to draw a two-module conclusion. The point is that alternatives are not *automatically* present, as they are in the case of associations and single dissociations. Thus, in any situation in which a double dissociation has been observed, it is incumbent upon any theorist wishing to dispute the two-module theory (for which the double dissociation has been used as evidence) to demonstrate that there is a different plausible theory that is also consistent with the double dissociation data. Whenever this has not been demonstrated it is reasonable for one to propose, at least for the time being, that the two-module theory is correct.[1]

Challenging a two-module theory by demonstrating that there is an alternative theory that is also consistent with the double dissociation data is quite different from challenging the two-module theory by arguing that there *could be* a different theory also consistent with the data. It is true for every theory in every science that there *could be* an alternative theory also consistent with the relevant data, so this kind of challenge is a feeble one that requires no answer. To put this point another way: No cognitive neuropsychologist ever argues that because there is a double dissociation there *must be* two modules. To argue like that is to claim that a theory can be logically required by data; and surely no scientists, including cognitive neuropsychologists, believe that.

It was explained earlier why in cognitive neuropsychology double dissociation data

---

[1] Plaut (1995) provided some simulation data in which various forms of lesioning of a small-scale neural network model of reading via meaning produced a double dissociation between the network's ability to read abstract words and its ability to read concrete words, even though the network contained nothing that could be construed as a module for concrete words and a separate module for abstract words; he therefore challenged the utility of double dissociations as evidence of modularity. Bullinaria and Chater (1995, p. 227) argued that Plaut's results were an artifact of using only a very small network, and their studies of lesioning of larger neural networks led them to this conclusion: "Investigation on the effects of damage on a range of small artificial neural networks that have been trained to perform two distinct mappings suggest that a double dissociation is possible without modularity. When these studies are repeated using sufficiently larger and more distributed networks, double dissociations are not observed. Further analysis suggests that double dissociation between performance on rule-governed and exceptional items is only found when the contribution of individual units to the overall network performance is significant, suggesting that such double dissociations are artifacts of scale."

tend to be accorded stronger weight than association or single dissociation data. But it would be quite wrong to conclude from this that association data and single dissociation data are worthless for theoretical purposes. The reason this would be wrong is as follows: When two alternative plausible hypotheses are consistent with the data (one arguing for the existence of a particular module, the other not), the theorist is not compelled to stop there. Instead, what can be done is to acknowledge that there are two alternative theories both consistent with the existing empirical data, and then to seek to adjudicatc between them on the basis of new empirical data.

To illustrate this point, let us return to the example of associated deficits in the chocolate factory: the case where the cocoa powder, sweet chocolate, and milk chocolate do not taste roasted. That association of deficits might have occurred because there is a single Roasting Module that is needed for roasting all three products; but there is an alternative theory, which is that there are three Roasting Modules, that they are located close together in the factory (to allow beans to be delivered to one location), and that a collapse of the roof above them has damaged all three of them.

Now suppose that we measure just how underroasted the cocoa powder is, how underroasted the sweet chocolate is, and how underroasted the milk chocolate is, and we obtain exactly the same answer for each: All three products are roasted to exactly 19% of the correct level.

How is that to be explained by the theory of three Roasting Modules? Why should the three Roasting Modules have been damaged to exactly the same degree by the physical insult from the roof? That would be sheer coincidence. In contrast, the theory of one Roasting Module predicts that the degree of underroasting must be the same for all three products; if this degree were different for the different products, that would be evidence directly falsifying this theory.

Here, then, is an example of how, with adequate further investigation, soundly based theoretical conclusions can be drawn starting off from an observation of an association of deficits. The same is true in human cognitive neuropsychology, as the following example shows.

Suppose that after brain damage a patient shows both a reading impairment and a spelling impairment. The patient misreads many irregular words by giving rule-based responses to them (regularization errors such as reading *have* to rhyme with "cave"). The patient also misspells many irregular words, again by giving rule-based responses to them (such as spelling "tomb" as *toom*). One might reach an exciting theoretical conclusion here. This conclusion says that there is a body of whole-word orthographic knowledge that must be accessed from print if irregular words are to be read correctly; that there is a body of whole-word orthographic knowledge from which information must be retrieved if irregular words are to be spelled correctly; and that the reason this patient both misreads and misspells irregular words is that the same body of orthographic knowledge is used both for recognizing and for spelling words. Thus Patterson and Shewell (1987) were wrong in proposing that there is an orthographic input lexicon and a separate orthographic output lexicon, whereas Allport and Funnell (1981) were right in proposing that there is only a single orthographic lexicon used both for reading and for spelling.

This view is a major claim about functional architecture; but it derives from the observation of an association of deficits, so the alternative two-lexicon view can be defended in the standard way. It could be that an orthographic input lexicon is used for reading and a separate orthographic output lexicon is used for spelling, that these are located very close together in the brain, and that the patient's lesion is extensive enough that both of these adjacent brain regions are affected. Thus, there are two alternative explanations of the association: a one-module explanation and a two-module explanation.

Instead of giving up in the face of this ambiguity, the investigator can do further work to try to resolve it. Suppose that the patient were given exactly the same irregular words to read and to spell, and it was found that the patient could spell all the irregular words that he or she could read, and that the patient could not spell all the irregular words that he or she could not read. For example, the patient reads *tomb* as "tom" and spells it as *toom,* and the patient reads *have* to rhyme with "cave" and spells it as *hav.* The patient both reads and spells correctly "yacht" and "aunt."

Why is it exactly the same words that the patient misreads and misspells? The two-module theory can only ascribe this to sheer coincidence. In contrast, the one-module theory can offer an explanation: that a single orthographic lexicon is used for both reading and spelling, that the brain damage has caused some of its entries to be deleted or to have become inaccessible while others can still be used, and that accordingly some words will be both read and spelled correctly and all other words will be both misread and misspelled.

Thus, as argued also by McCloskey (2001), the difference between double dissociation data on the one hand and association or single dissociation data on the other is not that the former are worthy and the latter worthless; association or single dissociation data can be just as compelling theoretically, provided one has the patience to acknowledge the alternative interpretations and to seek to adjudicate between them by carrying out the right kinds of further studies. Hence, all three types of data can be of value in cognitive neuropsychology.

A WORKED COGNITIVE-NEUROPSYCHOLOGICAL EXAMPLE: HOW ARE VISUAL STIMULI RECOGNIZED?

Three important classes of visual stimuli for the human being are faces, objects, and printed words. The literate person can recognize stimuli from all three classes. By *recognize* I mean that such people can correctly say, "I have seen this face before but never that one; I have seen this object before but never that one; I have seen this printed letter string before but never that one." When people can perform these tasks, they must possess knowledge representing those visual stimuli that they can recognize and also a means of accessing this knowledge.

A typical cognitive-neuropsychological question here is: How many distinct bodies of knowledge and access procedures are involved here? Is a single visual recognition module used for all three types of input, or are there two modules (one for linguistic input, the other for nonlinguistic input, say), or are there three (one for each of the three categories of stimuli)?

If there is just one module, then faces, objects, and printed words are recognized by the same procedures and with reference to the same single body of stored knowledge. In that case, a difficulty in recognizing seen objects (*visual agnosia*) should always be accompanied by a difficulty in recognizing faces (*prosopagnosia*) and in recognizing printed words (*alexia without agraphia,* also known as *pure alexia*); dissociations between any of these three deficits should never be observed.

However, such dissociations have been reported. Profoundly impaired face recognition accompanied by no detectable defect of object recognition has been reported by De Renzi (1986); patient 4 in this paper could no longer recognize the faces of his own relatives and close friends but performed flawlessly on tests of recognition of household objects, samples of writing (his own versus those of others), cats, coins, and his car among many other cars in a parking lot. This is consistent with the view that there are separate modules for face, object, and word recognition, with only the first of these three modules damaged in this patient.

Of course, because this result is a single dissociation, the standard alternative interpretation of single dissociations could be offered: Perhaps faces, objects, and printed words are recognized by a common visual-recognition module, but faces might be more difficult stimuli than objects or printed words, so partial impairment of that module might affect faces without affecting objects or printed words.

The standard reply to this standard alternative explanation is to consider whether there is a relevant double dissociation: Are there reports of impaired object recognition with intact face recognition, for example? The answer is yes, as reported by Feinberg, Gonzalez-Rothi, and Heilman (1986); Hecaen and Ajuriaguerra (1956); McCarthy and Warrington (1986); Pillon, Signoret, and Lhermitte (1981); and others. Hence, one cannot propose that there is a single module for recognizing faces and objects where mild damage will result only in prosopagnosia while more extensive damage will result in prosopagnosia plus visual agnosia, because on that hypothesis one will never see cases of visual agnosia without prosopagnosia.

It is therefore reasonable to conclude from these neuropsychological data that faces and objects are recognized by different modules. Note, however, what "different modules" means here. The face recognition module is itself likely to have an internal modular structure: One of its modules might be, for example, a visual feature processing system. Similarly, the object recognition module is also likely to have an internal modular structure:

One of its modules might be, for example, a visual feature processing system. Thus the two recognition modules might share common, smaller, modular subcomponents; it would not seem reasonable to suggest that there is both a visual feature processing system that is dedicated to face recognition and a second and separate visual feature processing system that is dedicated to object recognition. The claim that faces and objects are recognized by different modules simply says that there is at least one such smaller modular subcomponent that is part of the face recognition module but not part of the object recognition module, and at least one other such smaller modular subcomponent that is part of the object recognition module but not part of the face recognition module.

This is an important point, so I will offer another example. In the form of acquired reading impairment known as *surface dyslexia* (Patterson, Marshall, & Coltheart, 1985), patients can read aloud nonwords much better than they can exception words; in the form of reading impairment known as *phonological dyslexia* (Coltheart, 1996), patients can read aloud exception words much better than they can nonwords. This is often taken (e.g., by Coltheart et al., 2001) as evidence for the existence of separate lexical-reading and nonlexical-reading modules. But few people would deny that letter recognition is needed both for the reading of exception words and for the reading of nonwords. Therefore, the lexical-reading module contains a letter recognition submodule, and the nonlexical-reading module contains the same submodule. Figure 4.3 makes the same point: It contains an Object Recognition Module and a Word Recognition Module, and these two modules share their first four submodules.

If the two recognition modules, one for faces and one for objects, share many modular subcomponents, damage to any one of those components will affect both face and object recognition; this offers an account of why the two abilities so rarely dissociate. Most patients with prosopagnosia have visual agnosia, and vice versa. Association is common here, but as documented earlier, dissociations in both directions have been found.

Note also that although there are numerous reports of visual agnosia without prosopagnosia, case 4 of De Renzi (1986) is, as far as I know, the only really clear report of prosopagnosia without visual agnosia. One might therefore ask whether we should be drawing major theoretical conclusions about how faces and objects are normally recognized by everybody on the basis of data from only a single brain-damaged individual. Later I discuss the assumption of uniformity of cognitive architecture, which licenses such use of single-patient data.

If we conclude that there are separate recognition modules for faces and objects (using "separate" in the sense described earlier), what about printed words? Do they have their own separate recognition module? The way to investigate that is to look for dissociations between word and face recognition impairments and between word and object recognition impairments. The form of acquired impairment of reading in which it is specifically the rapid visual recognition of the printed word that is impaired is, as mentioned earlier, known as pure alexia. Thus the topic of study here is the pattern of associations and dissociations one sees among prosopagnosia, visual agnosia, and pure alexia. This has been comprehensively discussed by Farah (1990, 1991).

Consider first visual word recognition and face recognition. These doubly dissociate. Pure alexia can occur when face recognition is normal (Larrabee, Levin, Huff, Kay, & Guinto, 1985), and prosopagnosia can occur when visual word recognition is normal (Gomori & Hawyrluk, 1984).

Next consider visual word recognition and object recognition. These also doubly dissociate. Pure alexia can occur when object recognition is normal (Chialant & Caramazza, 1998), and visual agnosia can occur when visual word recognition is normal (Albert, Reches, & Silverberg, 1975).

Because each of the three abilities doubly dissociate from the other two, one might be led to the conclusion that there are three separate visual recognition modules. However, Farah (1990, 1991) has proposed an alternative theory: that there are not three distinct visual recognition modules, but only two.

Farah (1990, 1991) developed this proposal from the argument that the recognition of certain kinds of visual stimuli (e.g., tools) is based on a decomposition of the stimulus into many parts and on recognition via these parts; other kinds of visual stimuli (e.g., faces) are recognized much more holistically. Imagine, therefore, that there is one module that is responsible for the ability to represent parts themselves, including parts for objects that undergo little or no decomposition (and faces might be "parts" that are not decomposed at all); call this module P (for Parts). Further imagine that there is a second module whose task is the rapid encoding of multiple parts, and call this module E (for Encoding). Given this hypothesis about the cognitive architecture for visual recognition, Farah was able to develop a plausible account of the patterns of associations and dissociations evident in her literature review. This account was based on two premises:

(a) that decomposition into multiple parts is most crucial for visual word recognition (the parts being letters in this case), less crucial for object recognition, and least crucial for face recognition (because it is done so holistically); and

(b) that the parts themselves are least complex in the case of words (the parts being letters), more complex in the case of objects, and most complex in the case of faces (a face being represented as just one very complex part, the whole face).

Suppose now that module P is impaired. Objects whose parts are especially complex will suffer most here because the more complex a part is the more difficult it will be to represent, so the more stress it will put on module P. A mild impairment of module P will only harm faces; here we will have prosopagnosia without object agnosia. In another patient where module P is somewhat more severely impaired, only those stimuli with the simplest parts will survive; these are printed words, so this patient will exhibit prosopagnosia and visual agnosia without pure alexia. All three disorders will be present in a patient with a very severe impairment of module P (or sufficiently severe impairments of both modules). But there is no kind of impairment of module P that could result in pure alexia without prosopagnosia, nor any that could result in pure alexia without visual agnosia.

Next consider the consequences of impairment of module E. This will have the most serious consequence for stimuli with many different parts, all or most of which must be recognized for the stimulus to be recognized (i.e., printed words). Here, then, if there is a mild impairment of module E, one would see pure alexia in the absence of visual agnosia and prosopagnosia. A more severe impairment of module E would impair object recognition as well, producing pure alexia and visual agnosia in the absence of prosopagnosia. All three disorders will be present in a patient with a very severe impairment of module E. But there is no kind of impairment of module P that could result in prosopagnosia without pure alexia, nor any that could result in prosopagnosia without visual object agnosia.

These ideas about the cognitive architecture of the visual recognition system are important for at least two reasons. The first is that a major theoretical claim is being made about how people recognize visual stimuli. The second is that implicit here is a second claim (which Farah makes explicitly elsewhere): that only abilities that are old in evolutionary terms can be cognitively modular (Farah & Wallace, 1991). Reading is an ability that has been attained by humankind so recently that it cannot have evolved; and on Farah's view about the cognitive architecture of visual recognition, there is no reading module. Instead, reading is accomplished by piggybacking on two modules that are arguably evolutionarily old (module P and module E).

Farah has applied this view more generally to other kinds of acquired impairment of reading. For example, in phonological dyslexia (see Coltheart, 1996, for review) patients are specifically impaired at reading nonwords aloud. If there is a reading module, one might expect it to contain a submodule that uses knowledge about correspondences between graphemes and phonemes to read aloud, and one could then interpret phonological dyslexia as a specific impairment of this submodule. But if one denies that there is a reading module, then some other interpretation of phonological dyslexia is needed. Hence Farah, Stowe, and Levinson (1996) raised the possibility that this form of reading disorder is caused not by an orthographic impairment but by an impairment of phonological abilities (which are evolutionarily old). Patterson and Lambon Ralph (1999) have discussed whether it might in general be the case that all acquired impairments of reading might be explicable as arising from impairments of some nonorthographic cognitive system, thus envisaging the possibility that there is no reading module (and, of course, no spelling module).

It remains to be seen whether this fascinating view that the only cognitive modules that can exist are those that reflect evolutionarily old abilities could turn out to be true in general. As far as the specific claim made by Farah about pure alexia is concerned, however, empirical evaluation of this claim is possible, because the claim is falsifiable because there is one pattern of impairment of visual recognition that, according to this claim, cannot ever be observed (Farah, 1991, p. 8), namely, visual object agnosia without prosopagnosia or pure alexia. This pattern cannot occur on her theory, because if the object agnosia is due to a sufficiently severe impairment of module E, then visual word recognition, for which module E is particularly vital, must be affected too, so pure alexia must be present. If, on the other hand, the object agnosia is due to a sufficiently severe impairment of module P, then face recognition, for which module P is particularly vital, must be affected too, so prosopagnosia must be present. Hence the prediction is that visual agnosia will never be seen in isolation from the other two visual disorders.

Two Competing Theories of Visual Recognition

This chapter has presented two different theories about how visually presented stimuli are recognized: the three-module theory (a Faces module, an Objects module, and a Words module) and Farah's two-module theory (a P module and an E module).

The three-module theory predicts the occurrence of all possible patterns of preservation and impairment of the three abilities. The two-module theory predicts that one of these patterns will never be seen: isolated visual object agnosia with neither prosopagnosia nor pure alexia.

Humphreys and Rumiati (1998) described a patient MH who had a profound visual object agnosia: She could name fewer than 50% of line drawings of objects; she performed similarly when asked to name visually presented miniature models of animals; and she was very poor at tests of picture comprehension. This was not due to some low-level visual impairment, as she was good at copying pictures. In contrast, she was within the normal range in a test of naming familiar faces and in a test of reading aloud single words. Thus, MH exhibited object agnosia without prosopagnosia and pure alexia—the pattern that, according to the two-module theory of visual recognition, will never be observed, but that is expected on the three-module theory. This result therefore supports the three-module theory and is inconsistent with the two-module theory.

THE ASSUMPTION OF UNIFORMITY OF COGNITIVE ARCHITECTURE

The literature review by Farah (1990) covered 99 cases; 97 of these were consistent with the two-module account of visual recognition, and the two that were not were sufficiently unclear as to be plausibly discounted. Thus, if one adds patient MH (just described) to these 99 cases, there are 100 relevant patients, and only a single one of these is inconsistent with the two-module account. Might the enormous preponderance of cases consistent with the two-module account be taken as strong evidence for this account?

Not on the cognitive-neuropsychological approach, according to which a single inconsistent case is enough to falsify a model, no matter how many consistent cases have been observed. This methodological tenet of cognitive neuropsychology is justified by the assumption of uniformity of cognitive architecture.

According to this assumption, in all people who do not have acquired or developmental disorders of cognition, the architectures of cognitive systems are identical. A particular module might vary quantitatively from person to person—some people may have larger auditory vocabularies than others, for example—but what modules there are and what modules there are not are the same from person to person. It follows that if one concludes from just one case study that the person studied had three different visual recognition modules prior to brain injury, one may then conclude that this is true for everyone. That is why just one case can be sufficient to falsify a theory, no matter how many other cases are consistent with that theory.

This is, of course, a strong assumption, but it is not an assumption peculiar to cognitive neuropsychology. It is an assumption generally made in cognitive psychology, because cognitive-psychological theorists want to make statements about the cognitive architectures of everyone on the basis of data about the cognitive architectures of a relative few. If the assumption of uniformity of cognitive architecture is completely false, then cognitive neuropsychology cannot be done; but nor can the rest of cognitive psychology.

It is sometimes argued that sampling error is a problem here. If only one patient in a hundred shows a particular effect, might not that just be a statistical artifact? This objection is misguided. If just one task is administered to a hundred patients, and just one patient shows a statistically significant difference between two conditions with that task, taking that result seriously could indeed be capitalizing on sampling error. But that is not how cognitive neuropsychologists do their work. To show, for example, that a certain patient has visual object agnosia but no prosopagnosia or pure alexia, cognitive neuropsychologists would typically administer many tests of object recognition, many tests of face recognition, and many tests of reading. If the patient is impaired on all of the object recognition tests and normal on all the tests of face processing and all the tests of reading, it is reasonable to claim that this is a case of an isolated visual object agnosia, even if all other patients in the literature who had visual object agnosia have also had either prosopagnosia or pure alexia. Here the multiple testing and its consistent results render untenable an objection based on sampling error.

WHY THE EMPHASIS ON SINGLE-CASE STUDIES IN COGNITIVE NEUROPSYCHOLOGY?

Research in cognitive neuropsychology characteristically takes the form of extremely detailed case studies of individual people with disorders of cognition. Whole doctoral theses (e.g., Haywood, 1996)—even whole books (e.g., Howard & Franklin, 1988)—have been written about single patients. One reason for this has already been mentioned: If the assumption of uniformity of cognitive architecture is made, data from just one case are sufficient to falsify a theory.

There is a more general reason, however, for this emphasis on single-case studies (see Coltheart, 1984; Howard & Franklin, 1988; Marshall, 1984). Any modular model of any system used for carrying out any interesting cognitive activity will consist of a substantial number of submodules and pathways of communication between them. For example, the model depicted in Figure 4.3 has 11 boxes and 14 arrows for a total of 25 components. If there is anatomical modularity as well as functional modularity, then there are 25 different loci that are independently damageable by brain injury. This means that the number of different possible patterns of impairments and preservations to the functional components of that model is 2^{25}. All but one of those patterns corresponds to a different brain-damaged patient (the one pattern that does not is where all boxes and arrows are intact). Because $2^{25} - 1$ is an unimaginably large number, the probability of coming across two patients with exactly the same cognitive impairment is unimaginably small. Therefore, every patient the cognitive neuropsychologist sees will be effectively unique, so averaging across groups of patients cannot be justified. Instead, every patient must be investigated, and his or her data reported, individually.

Take surface dyslexia, for example. The defining symptom of this syndrome is the regularization error in reading aloud: An exception word is read as if it conformed to English spelling-sound rules, so that *broad* is read as if it rhymed with "road," and *have* as if it rhymed with "cave." Coltheart and Funnell (1987) demonstrated that on any plausible model of the reading system, there are numerous different loci in the system at which damage would lead to the occurrence of regularization errors; given the particular model of the reading system they proposed, there were seven such different loci. Some of these are quite remote from each other; for example, the orthographic input lexicon and the phonological output lexicon are both loci at which damage would lead to the reading of *broad* to rhyme with "road."

If each member of a group of patients classified as exhibiting the same syndrome (all classified as surface dyslexics, for example, or all classified as Broca's aphasics) can have a unique pattern of impairment of the relevant cognitive system, then the syndrome is not an appropriate object of scientific study. If, as is the case, there is no specific impairment of the language-processing system that all Broca's aphasics have in common, then there is no coherent scientific entity to be called Broca's aphasia, so there's nothing to study here.

This does not mean that there is no place at all in cognitive neuropsychology for syndrome-oriented research. The history of the subject shows that when one is beginning cognitive-neuropsychological investigation of a cognitive domain that has not been investigated at all from that approach, identifying subgroups of patients with similar impairments is a good way to start off—a valuable ground-clearing exercise. For example, the cognitive neuropsychological investigation of reading was launched by Marshall and Newcombe (1973), who distinguished between three different syndromes of acquired reading disorder (surface dyslexia, deep dyslexia, and visual dyslexia), and described

for each syndrome two characteristic patients. This seminal paper has been the stimulus for an enormous amount of work on acquired dyslexia over the past quarter of a century; but in subsequent work the syndrome approach was soon abandoned by cognitive neuropsychologists as it became clear that within any one of these syndromes of acquired dyslexia patients differed in important ways from each other.

GENERALIZATION IN COGNITIVE NEUROPSYCHOLOGY

If, from the cognitive-neuropsychological point of view, one does not study patients in order to learn more about the characteristics of some neuropsychological syndrome, and if every patient is unique, how can one seek to generalize one's research findings here? The answer is that one studies particular patients with the aim of learning something about some general theory of the cognitive architecture of the relevant cognitive system; data from the patient are used to develop or extend or test such a general theory. It is no problem that each patient in such a study has a unique pattern of impairments of that cognitive system; indeed, it may be a benefit. What matters is that all the patients had the same architecture of the system prior to damage— the assumption of uniformity of cognitive architecture.

DEVELOPMENTAL COGNITIVE NEUROPSYCHOLOGY

Figure 4.3 could be a correct account of the system that adults use for naming pictures and reading aloud words and nonwords; that is, it could be a correct description of the cognitive architecture of people aged, say, 40. But it could not be a correct description of the cognitive architecture of people aged 4.

As a rule, people of that age know nothing about reading, so their cognitive architectures will not contain modules that carry out orthographic tasks such as letter or word recognition (though they will contain modules for visual object recognition, semantic processing, and speech production, all of which 4-year-olds can do).

But what about people aged 8? Most of them have learned something about reading but have not attained maximum skill at that task. What can cognitive neuropsychology say about the cognitive architecture of these people's juvenile reading systems, and about how this relates to the cognitive architecture of the skilled reading system? Some developmental psychologists have been extremely dubious about whether cognitive neuropsychology can contribute anything useful to the study of cognitive development.

Initially this concern was expressed specifically in relation to reading: "The already existing structural model, useful as it is in describing the skilled reading process, needs to be complemented by a developmental model in order to make sense of the varieties of developmental dyslexia" (Frith, 1985, p. 326); "A far greater problem arises when researchers [on children's reading] fail to adopt a developmental perspective when analyzing their data" (Snowling, 1987, p. 83); "A static model of adult performance, such as dual route theory, is inadequate for understanding how children learn to read and why some children learn to read easily while others have difficulties" (Snowling, Bryant, & Hulme, 1996, p. 444).

It was difficult to evaluate such concerns because the people expressing them had not explained what errors might ensue when static models of adult performance were applied. Fortunately, Bishop (1997) has recently not only spelled out these concerns but also discussed them in relation to other forms of developmental cognitive impairment. This is clearest in her discussion of specific language impairment (SLI), a developmental disorder in which a child's language acquisition lags far behind other aspects of the child's cognitive development for no apparent reason. Bishop (1997) mentions three competing explanations of the occurrence of SLI:

1. Language difficulties are caused by impairment in discriminating rapid brief auditory stimuli (Tallal & Katz, 1989).

2. Language difficulties are caused by limitations in phonological short-term memory (Gathercole & Baddeley, 1990).

3. Specialized mechanisms for grammar acquisition are impaired (Crago & Gopnik, 1994).

She then says: "The traditional logic of cognitive neuropsychology is inadequate to discriminate these possibilities" (p. 903).

This is a valuable challenge. The way to meet it is by invoking a distinction between the proximal and distal causes of cognitive impairments, a distinction that is central in developmental cognitive neuropsychology.

Proximal versus Distal Cause

Returning just for a moment to the example of the chocolate factory, one can imagine the following conversation between a chocolate consumer and a person familiar with the functional architecture of the factory:

> "Why does the chocolate taste bitter and have a coarse texture today?"
> "Because the Concher isn't working properly."
> "Why not?"
> "Beats me. You'll have to ask a hardware guy about that."
> [Asks hardware guy] "It's because the Concher's splinges are worn out and need to be replaced."

What is the cause of the chocolate defect here? Is it that the Concher is not working properly, or is it that the splinges are worn out? Obviously, both are causes: The chocolate is poor because the Concher is not working properly, and the Concher is not working properly because of its defective splinges. Notice that these are not the same cause, because "The Concher is not working properly" could be true even if "The splinges are worn out" is not true (because the Concher problem could have been due to its cron being clogged up, rather than to its splinges being worn out). In the chocolate factory as in the mind, the same functional defect can be caused by various different physical defects.

When a system's operation is defective, there is not just one cause, but a chain of causes. The cause that is closest to the defective behavior is the proximal cause; the other (more remote) causes are distal causes (Jackson & Coltheart, 2001).

This distinction applies to Bishop's (1997) SLI example as follows. Part of the human language-processing system is a system that handles grammatical inflections—a system that people use for creating past tenses when we need to, for example. In some cases of SLI, there is a specific difficulty in dealing with inflections, even if some other aspects of the language system (e.g., phonology) have been acquired appropriately. In such children there is presumably a defect of a syntactic part of the language-processing system that is responsible for processing grammatical inflections.[2] What might cause such a defect? There are many possibilities; one is that specialized innate mechanisms for acquiring this part

of grammar are genetically impaired in this particular child.

Here the proximal cause of the child's abnormal speech is a particular defect of the language system, and the distal cause of the child's abnormal speech is a genetic deficit in mechanisms for acquisition of grammar.

Or instead the distal cause could be a limitation of phonological working memory that affected the child's ability to acquire grammar from exposure to spoken language; or it could be that the child has a difficulty in speech discrimination for brief and rapidly changing auditory stimuli that affects the perception of very brief and unstressed segments of speech (such as inflections).

Here there are three different possible distal causes of the proximal cause of the child's abnormal spoken language.

Bishop's claim was that the methods of cognitive neuropsychology are not suitable for discriminating between these alternative possible distal causes. Whether this is true is not important because the central aim of cognitive neuropsychology is to discover the proximal cause of abnormal behavior in any cognitive domain.

This is easily demonstrated by considering any acquired disorder of cognition, for example, prosopagnosia. The proximal cause of this disorder is an abnormality of one or more of the components of the cognitive system used for recognizing faces; it is cognitive neuropsychology's job to propose theories about what these components might be, and then to see whether any such theory can explain details of the patient's face-processing performance. The distal cause of this disorder is damage to mechanisms of the brain that are involved in face processing, and that is the province of cognitive neuroscience, not of cognitive neuropsychology.

Although this point is most easily demonstrated with respect to acquired disorders of

---

[2]This seems circular but is not. If a child responds when asked "What's your mother doing with the peas?" by saying "shell" rather than "shelling," that could be due to some problem with syntactic processing, but that is not the only possibility. Another possibility is that the defect is phonological (specifically, a difficulty in producing unstressed syllables). These alternatives could be distinguished by asking the child, at least in predecimal times, "What's the name of the coin that twelve pennies make?" Can the child respond "shilling"?

cognition, it applies equally to developmental disorders. The job of developmental cognitive neuropsychology is to propose theories about the functional architecture of the mental information-processing system that children of a certain age use to perform some particular cognitive activity (e.g., sentence production) and to investigate whether the performance of children of that age who have an abnormality in this cognitive domain can be understood with reference to that theory. The system abnormality is the hypothesized proximal cause of the performance abnormality. The system abnormality itself will have some cause or causes, and these are distal causes of the performance abnormality. These distal causes might, like the proximal cause, be at the cognitive level (e.g., the proximal cause of inflectional errors in sentence production might be an impairment of syntactic knowledge, and the cause of that impairment, a distal cause of the performance abnormality, might be impaired phonological short-term memory, which is also at the cognitive level). However, distal cause can also be at the biological level (such as genetic causes, or anoxic brain damage that occurred perinatally), or at the environmental level (such as high concentrations of lead in the environment).

Suppose, then, that one is studying an 8-year-old boy whose reading ability is much worse than that of the other 8-year-olds in his class. It is conceivable that his reading system is no worse than theirs, and that his poor performance when his reading is being assessed is due to inattentiveness or contrariness rather than to an abnormality of his reading system. That possibility can be discounted if the boy is performing normally in assessments of all other school subjects except for reading. If that can be demonstrated, then there must be some difference between this boy's reading system and the reading systems of all the other children in the class; that will be the proximal cause of his reading disorder.

Furthermore, there must be some reason why his reading system is different from the others; that will be the distal cause of his reading disorder.

The cognitive neuropsychologist's job is to discover what this proximal cause is. Because this proximal cause is an abnormality of the reading system, this job can only be accomplished if it is known what the reading system is normally like in 8-year-old children. How big is the sight vocabulary of a typical 8-year-old normal reader? What kinds of nonwords can 8-year-old normal readers read aloud correctly, and what kinds typically cause them problems?

In general, then, the way developmental cognitive neuropsychology works is as follows. A child is found who is strikingly less capable of performing some cognitive task than are other children of the same age. A developmental cognitive neuropsychologist would be interested in studying such a child because such an investigation might reveal more about how the relevant cognitive system is normally acquired, and about what that cognitive system is typically like for children of that age. A functional architecture for that cognitive system at that age might then be hypothesized, followed by an investigation of whether the pattern of normal and abnormal performance of that child on a battery of relevant tests could be understood as being due to a pattern of normally and abnormally acquired components of that functional architecture. If such an understanding is achieved, then a hypothesis about the proximal cause of the child's relative incapability in this cognitive domain will have been generated.

After that, an investigation of possible distal causes of this proximal cause can be pursued. But analysis of proximal cause—the developmental cognitive neuropsychological work—must come first. Consider, for example, the question of whether SLI has a genetic cause. That is asking about a distal cause of a particular developmental performance pattern without first considering proximal cause, and it lays such an investigation open to a problem. Children can earn the diagnosis of SLI because they perform poorly on tests of language comprehension or because the sentences that they produce are abnormally syntactically simple for their age. Here there are two different proximal causes of the child's language impairment. It could be that one of these has a genetic basis and that the other does not. A genetic investigation that did not treat these two groups of children separately would be unlikely to yield anything useful. This specific example illustrates a general point: Hypotheses about distal causes of developmental disorders of cognition need to be hypotheses about the distal cause of a proximal cause. Hence, to pursue any research on distal (e.g., genetic) causes of developmental disorders, one needs first to identify the proximal cause—the particular abnormality of the relevant cognitive system. Identifying proximal causes of developmental cognitive disorders is what developmental cognitive neuropsychology does.

Yet another way in which the perspective of developmental cognitive neuropsychology can assist attempts to understand developmental disorders of cognition is to make the point that it is likely to be a mistake to think of the three explanations of SLI just listed as competing theories among which there must be adjudication. SLI is a syndrome and, as such, is an ultimately inappropriate object of study even though the syndrome approach may be a useful way to begin investigation of some cognitive disorder. Children classified as SLI are not a homogenous group all having a single, identical impairment of the language system. Because this is a heterogeneous group of children with a variety of forms of impaired language, it is perfectly possible that each of these three accounts of

SLI apply to some of the children in any such group. Some of the children may have impaired abilities to discriminate rapid brief auditory stimuli, and this may have impaired some other aspects of their language learning; others may have deficient phonological short-term memory, and this may have impaired some other aspects of their language learning. Still others may have a genetic impairment of innate mechanisms, and this may have impaired yet other aspects of their language learning.

Finally, in any case, the claim that "the traditional logic of cognitive neuropsychology is inadequate to discriminate between these possibilities" (Bishop, 1997, p. 903) is not even true. It was once argued that the distal cause of visual agnosia was some combination of a low-level visual impairment plus some impairment of frontal lobe function. The traditional logic of cognitive neuropsychology in this circumstance is to investigate whether there are any people who possess low-level visual impairments and frontal lobe damage but do not possess visual agnosia. Such cases were found, so this particular theory about the distal cause of visual agnosia was refuted. Applying this logic to SLI would involve identifying children with impaired ability to discriminate rapid brief auditory stimuli and determining whether any of them showed no evidence of SLI; the discovery of one such child would refute this theory of the distal cause of SLI. Similarly, one could investigate children with deficient phonological short-term memory to see whether any such child shows no evidence of SLI. Investigations like these represent the application of the traditional logic of cognitive neuropsychology for the purpose of discriminating between these possible accounts of SLI.[3]

---

[3] I thank John Marshall for providing me with this example.

SOME PRACTICALITIES PECULIAR TO COGNITIVE NEUROPSYCHOLOGY

Suppose there is a researcher in cognitive psychology who has so far carried out laboratory research exclusively involving cognitively normal college students. The researcher can see, however, that a particular question of interest could be addressed by appropriate investigations of a person suffering from a cognitive impairment caused by brain damage.

For example, the question of interest might be the following. People know various facts about inanimate objects, including facts about the correct way in which to interact physically with the object (for those objects that actually have a correct way) and facts about the functions that these objects serve (for those objects that actually have a function). Is there a single body of knowledge about objects that contains both types of information? Or is information about how to interact physically with a key stored quite separately from the fact that keys are for opening locked things and for locking open things?

The researcher has read this chapter attentively up to this point, so he or she can already see how an investigation of people whose brain damage has affected their knowledge of objects in some way might provide an answer to this question. Suppose, for example, that when such a person was shown a key and asked what it was for, the person could say, "It's for locking and unlocking things"; but that when given the instruction "Show me how you would use it," the person was quite unable to do so. This person can accurately imitate key-turning behavior when the investigator performs this action (so there's no question of paralysis), but nevertheless cannot produce this behavior in response to the stimulus of a key.

The researcher has read this chapter very attentively, however, so he or she knows that a

dissociation is not really what is needed. The data that the researcher has observed might be evidence for distinct knowledge systems for object function and object use; but there is an alternative explanation, which is that there is a single object knowledge system, but for some reason information about object use in that system is more vulnerable to brain damage than is information about object function. The researcher knows, of course, the answer to this problem: a double dissociation is necessary. The researcher needs to find a second brain-damaged person who can pick up a key and put it in a lock and turn it, and mime the use of a key when shown one, but who when shown a key and asked what it is for will say, "I don't know. What is that thing?"

As it happens, both kinds of patients have been reported in the cognitive-neuropsychological literature. The condition in which patients can normally use objects and mime their use but are poor at providing verbal information about what an object is used for when shown it is known as optic aphasia (Beauvois, 1982). The opposite pattern—impaired object use and miming with intact verbal knowledge—also occurs (Leiguarda & Marsden, 2000).

I believe that anyone interested in how object knowledge is represented, even someone who has so far only studied this via experiments with cognitively normal college students, would be fascinated by such observations and would consider them directly relevant to the development of a theory about how object knowledge is represented in people's cognitive systems. So the researcher in this example decides to do research with people in whom brain damage has affected such knowledge in various different ways. What is the researcher's next step?

The researcher will need to develop a relationship with a neuropsychology clinic or a neurology ward, a relationship in which it is clear to all parties, and accepted by them, that the researcher's interest is in research and not in treatment. After this, the researcher is ready to study patients with interesting disorders of object knowledge.

Unfortunately, experiments in cognitive neuropsychology are experiments of nature. The researcher has no control at all over the neuroanatomical location and the functional consequences of the brain injuries suffered by the patients admitted to the ward or clinic with which the researcher has established a relationship. Hence, it is quite possible that the researcher will never have access to a patient who has an interesting disorder of object knowledge, because it could happen that none of the admitted patients have suffered the appropriate kind of brain injury.

There are at least three ways for the fledgling cognitive neuropsychologist to maneuver a solution to this problem. The first is to establish relationships with a large number of neuropsychology clinics and neurology wards, and to ensure that the clinicians in those centers not only are willing to draw attention to any relevant patients who come along but also are sufficiently well briefed that they are able to identify which patients might be of interest because they have disorders of object knowledge and which patients—no matter how fascinating their cognitive deficits might be—are not relevant. Then the researcher must simply be patient.

The second is to find some way of developing a collaboration with a cognitive neuropsychology laboratory where such connections are already well established and where work on patients with disorders of object knowledge is already under way. Examples of relevant laboratories include the Cognitive Science Research Centre at the University of Birmingham, the Center for Cognitive Neuroscience at the University of Pennsylvania, and the Moss Rehabilitation Research Institute in Philadelphia.

The third, and much more common, maneuver is to recognize that very many brain-injured patients are capable of informing cognitive neuropsychologists about *some* domain of cognition. Thus, even if a cognitive neuropsychologist has access only to patients admitted to one clinical center, that will guarantee access to a variety of patients who would richly repay cognitive-neuropsychological investigation. The problem here is that the investigator has no control over which domain of cognition could profitably be studied with each patient. Thus, an investigator whose field of expertise is, say, high-level vision in particular and object knowledge in general might be confronted first with a patient with an interesting acquired disorder of speech production, and next with a patient with an interesting acquired disorder of calculation, and then with a patient with an interesting acquired disorder of auditory recognition of environmental sounds. All three patients might have uninterestingly intact high-level vision and object knowledge. The only recourse that cognitive neuropsychologists have here is to be willing to become jacks-of-all-trades: to be prepared to educate themselves in new areas of cognitive psychology as a function of the kinds of patients who turn up in the clinical center. That is what most cognitive neuropsychologists do.

John Marshall, for example, began his cognitive-neuropsychological career by working on impairments of word retrieval and of reading but subsequently has studied spelling, spoken language comprehension, global and local processing, visual attention, and hallucinations, all from a cognitive-neuropsychological perspective. Tim Shallice's first cognitive-neuropsychological work was on impairments of short-term memory, but he has subsequently studied reading, spelling, semantic memory, executive function, and consciousness, all from a cognitive-neuropsychological perspective. Alfonso Caramazza's first cognitive-neuropsychological work was on impairments in the production and comprehension of spoken language, but he has subsequently investigated reading, spelling, morphology, semantic memory, visual attention, and bilingualism, all from a cognitive-neuropsychological perspective. Such extreme diversity of interests is rarely seen in cognitive psychologists who work solely with cognitively normal individuals. It is common amongst cognitive neuropsychologists, however, because they need to work with whatever kinds of cognitive disorders nature provides to them.

How one can develop access to appropriate brain-damaged patients is one purely practical consideration for the cognitive neuropsychologist; there are others. A patient being studied may not be in a stable condition: Cognitive abilities can worsen as a study progresses (the patient may suffer a second stroke, or may be suffering from a progressive disorder such as Alzheimer's disease) or can improve as a study progresses (e.g., because the patient is receiving rehabilitation, or because in the weeks or months after insult to the brain the condition of the brain itself can improve because of such factors as reduction in swelling and intracranial pressure as fluid produced by the insult drains away). Whenever such worsening or improvement over time might be happening, the investigator has to be particularly careful in drawing conclusions from comparisons between tests administered at different points in time.

Finally, there is the issue of statistical methods appropriate to data from single case studies. It might be thought that when $N = 1$, many forms of statistical analysis common in areas of cognitive psychology that use group data cannot be applied. However, this is not really so. Imagine, for example, that you were investigating the effects of word frequency and word imageability on a patient's ability to repeat words. This would be done by selecting a sufficiently large set of words in which these two variables were orthogonally varied, administering these in random order to the patient, and for each word measuring, say, latency of repetition. This would result in a 2×2 table of data, each cell of the table containing a set of latencies for one combination of the word frequency and word imageability categories. A two-factor independent-groups analysis of variance is entirely appropriate here. Why is it an independent-groups analysis? Because the set of words in any one cell is independent of the set in each other cell; no word belongs to more than one cell (just as, in an independent-groups analysis of group data, the set of subjects in any one cell is independent of the set in each other cell; no subject belongs to more than one cell). In general, then, the emphasis on single case studies in cognitive neuropsychology does not lead to any particular statistical difficulties in selecting appropriate statistical techniques for analysis of cognitive-neuropsychological data. There might be occasions when the fact that data are drawn from only one subject leads to violation of some assumption of a parametric test (e.g., the data might be highly skewed), but that is easily dealt with by using randomization tests (Edgington, 1995) that do not rely on these assumptions and yet are of equal power to parametric tests.

FUTURE DIRECTIONS IN COGNITIVE NEUROPSYCHOLOGY

Cognitive Neuroimaging and Cognitive Neuropsychology

A great deal of recent work in cognitive neuroscience has been devoted to imaging the brains of people as they perform cognitive tasks online. One can imagine two kinds of motivation for such work. The first is the hope that investigations of this kind could tell us more about the nature of cognition itself—about the functional architecture of some cognitive system. The second and different motivation is to seek to localize in the brain the individual components, the modules, of the proposed functional architecture of some cognitive system.

I know of no neuroimaging work so far reported that has clearly achieved the first of these aims—that is, to reveal something new about the organization of the functional architecture of any cognitive system. Indeed, it is not absolutely clear how this aim might ever be achieved. Suppose one were serious in proposing Figure 4.3 as a correct description of the functional architecture of the cognitive system that people use to understand and name pictures and to read aloud words and nonwords. What is an example of a possible outcome of a cognitive neuroimaging experiment that would be regarded as falsifying this claim about cognitive architecture? Suppose, for example, one has in mind the double dissociation between surface dyslexia (interpreted as selective impairment of the reading route that proceeds via visual word recognition) and phonological dyslexia (interpreted as selective impairment of the reading route that proceeds via the application of grapheme-phoneme rules). This might motivate one to carry out a neuroimaging study in which brain activation occurring while people were reading aloud exception words was compared with brain activation occurring while people were reading aloud nonwords. Suppose one could detect absolutely no difference between these two conditions. Would that be evidence falsifying the Figure 4.3 model? No, because the Figure 4.3 model makes no claims about anatomical modularity; it is a claim about the mind and not about the brain. Figure 4.3 could be a correct description of a human functional architecture even if the system it describes is represented in the brain in a completely nonmodular way (which would prevent activation patterns from differing as a function of which reading routes were being used).

Perhaps I am revealing a failure of imagination here; perhaps there are ways of showing that, at least in principle, data from cognitive neuroimaging studies are capable of constraining theories about functional architectures of cognition. However, I am not alone in being dubious about this: see Van Orden & Paap (1997) for an even more skeptical view concerning whether cognitive neuroimaging could ever inform theorizing about the functional architecture of cognition. Only the future will tell; but it does seem that at least up to the present time no cognitive neuroimaging work has made any serious difference to ideas about the functional architecture of cognition.

In response to the above, Marshall (personal communication, March 2001) said, "You claim that imaging cannot tell you anything much about the functional architecture. I kind of agree, but consider this example: A woman cannot move (or at best doesn't move) the left side of her body, although there is no discoverable structural lesion. You think up a few "functional" (?) explanations. (i) Her relevant motor centers have nonetheless been put out of action; (ii) Her relevant motor centers have been disconnected from her "volition" centers; (iii) Her relevant motor centers are OK, but get inhibited by some other center, etc., etc., etc. Marshall, Halligan, Fink, Wade, and Frackowiack (1997) in *Cognition* is an attempt (not too unsuccessful I would argue) to distinguish between these hypotheses using PET. Note that this is not quite the same as using functional neuroimaging to test the right hemisphere hypothesis for deep dyslexia. I was, I think, testing a functional, not anatomical, hypothesis." The imaging data in this study of a hysterical paralysis revealed that when the patient tried to move her left leg, motor and/or premotor areas of the right hemisphere associated with movement preparation and execution were activated, but the right motor primary cortex was not; the right orbitofrontal and right anterior cingulated cortex were also activated. The authors concluded that the latter two areas "inhibit prefrontal (willed) effects on the right primary motor cortex when the patient tries to move her left leg" (Marshall et al., 1997, p. B1). These are fascinating results, but they still do not, *pace* Marshall, constitute an example in which functional neuroimaging has told us something new about the functional architecture of cognition. The functional architecture described by Marshall earlier in this paragraph (a motor center system; a "volition" center; a center for inhibiting motor activity) was not proposed as a consequence of the imaging data. Quite the contrary: It was proposed as a framework that then allowed the design of the imaging study.

Perhaps one can be a little more sanguine about the second of the two possible aims of cognitive neuroscience, the aim of localizing cognitive modules. But this is very different from the first aim because this kind of work presupposes, rather than attempts to discover, what the functional architecture of a particular cognitive system is like; the question "Where is module X located in the brain?" presupposes that there is a module X. Because one of the most fertile sources of information about what the modules of some cognitive system might be is cognitive neuropsychology, the assertion here is a dependence of cognitive neuroscience upon cognitive neuropsychology.

To illustrate this with an example, imagine that someone with an interest in the brain mechanisms used for reading decides to investigate this by imaging the brains of people who had suffered brain damage that had impaired their reading, in order to discover which particular part of the brain was damaged in such people. That part of the brain could then be claimed to be the brain site for reading. One reason why this would be pointless is that the cognitive system we use for reading is functionally modular in nature, and damage to any one of these modules would impair reading in some way; if the reading system is also anatomically modular, then a group of people selected just because brain damage had affected their reading in some way or other will have various different loci of brain damage. There will be no single brain site for reading. Obviously the problem here is that reading is a process with many modules, and questions about localization can only be posed with respect to single modules; thus, that question needs to be posed separately in relation to each of the modules of the reading system.

Instead of imaging the brains of patients with various different kinds of reading difficulties, then, it is necessary to focus on only one kind of reading difficulty, for example, a difficulty in reading aloud nonwords accompanied by good reading of words (i.e., phonological dyslexia). Imaging the brains of a group of people with this highly specific reading difficulty should provide us with information about where in the brain the nonword reading module is.

One problem that would need to be faced here is that typical causes of brain damage such as stroke or head injury produce damage to various parts of the brain. There might be various separate small lesions, or there might be one lesion that is large and covers several brain regions, only one of which has to do with nonword reading. Therefore, imaging the brain of one person with phonological dyslexia might reveal several small lesion sites, in which case one would not know which of these should be blamed for the phonological dyslexia; or it might reveal one large lesion, in which case one would not know which particular region within this large lesioned area should be blamed for the phonological dyslexia.

A typical solution to this problem is to image the brains of a series of patients with phonological dyslexia and to superimpose the successively determined lesion sites on a diagram of the brain, the idea being that only overlapping areas—sites lesioned in every brain—could possibly be related to phonological dyslexia. If, as brains are added in, the regions of complete overlap get fewer and fewer until there is only one very small region left that is abnormal, that region could be the anatomical module for nonword reading (or at least could contain that module).

In practice, however, what is very likely to happen in such an investigation is either

(a) that as brains are added in, the regions of complete overlap get fewer and fewer until there are none left, or

(b) that as brains are added in, an originally large single region of complete overlap shrinks and shrinks until it vanishes completely.

Either result would suggest that there is no brain region that is damaged in all cases of phonological dyslexia. Yet brain damage can selectively impair nonword reading. What is going on here?

These hypothetical researchers arrived at this puzzling state of affairs by initially recognizing that because the reading system has a modular organization, it makes no sense to seek the location of the reading center in the brain by imaging the brains of patients with some or other form of impaired reading. What the researchers did instead was to specify just one particular module of the reading system— the nonword reading module—and to image the brains of patients all of whom had selectively impaired nonword reading. Why did they still end up with a result that makes no sense? It is because they failed to solve the original problem. They saw that it makes no sense to use imaging to search for the reading center in the brain because the reading system is modular in structure—but for the same reason it makes no sense to use imaging to search

for the nonword reading center in the brain, because the nonword reading system is itself modular in structure.

It is known that this is so because research on patients with a specific impairment in the ability to read nonwords has shown that such patients are heterogeneous; that is, the same symptom (many nonwords read wrongly, or not at all) can arise from impairments at different loci in the functional architecture of the nonword reading system. For example, in the first study of phonological dyslexia, by Beauvois and Derouesné (1979), four such patients were studied. Two showed better reading for pseudomophonic nonwords (English examples would be *brane* or *yot*) than for nonpseudomophonic nonwords (*brone* or *yut*), but were unaffected by whether in nonwords there were many-to-one mappings of letters to phonemes (*choof, thish*) or only one-to-one mappings (*clisk, trint*). The other two patients showed the reverse result. Thus, although all four patients had the same reading symptom (all four read nonwords far less well than they read words), they did not have the same impairment in the reading system; two different loci of impairment of the nonword reading component of the reading system were present here. One could propose that two of these patients had an impairment of a graphemic parsing module of the nonword reading component of the reading system (and thus could not cope when graphemes consisted of more than one letter) and that the other two had a difficulty in activating the level of phonemic representation in the nonword reading module (a difficulty that could be partly ameliorated by feedback to that level from a phonological lexicon, feedback which would only be available if the set of phonemes being activated was a word, as is the case when the printed stimulus is a pseudohomophone).

Hence, the move from imaging any kind of patient with a reading disorder to imaging only patients with a specific reading disorder—phonological dyslexia—was insufficient: The original problem, heterogeneity of damage to functional architecture, is still there. How is that problem to be solved?

This is not easy, but a plausible answer is offered by Block (1995). In his terms, what has been going on in the preceding paragraphs is "functional decomposition." The reading system has been decomposed into smaller components, such as the nonword reading system, and the nonword reading system has been decomposed into still smaller components, such as the grapheme parsing system. Decomposition stops when all the components are primitive processors—because the operation of a primitive processor cannot be further decomposed into suboperations. For example an AND-gate: it is just defined in terms of its input-output function, and that function is not decomposable. "Primitive processors are the only computational devices for which behaviorism is true . . . the largest components of the system whose operation must be explained, not in terms of cognitive science, but rather in terms of electronics or mechanics or some other realization science. . . . If the mind is the software of the brain, then we must take seriously the idea that the functional analysis of human intelligence will bottom out in primitive processors in the brain" (Block, 1995, p. 389).

Thus, perhaps the solution to the problem for cognitive neuroimaging here is that it makes sense to use that technique to localize cognitive modules only when these modules are Blockian primitive processors—cognitive subsystems that are, in the term used by Fodor (1983), "not assembled."

Be that as it may, my aim in this section of the chapter is to make the case that cognitive neuroimaging studies whose aims are to determine the neuroanatomical localization of cognitive modules have to be predicated on some prior and explicit conception of what the constituent modules of the relevant cognitive system are. Because the richest source of such conceptions is cognitive neuropsychology, then cognitive neuroscience, if it is to progress, needs to develop a much closer dependence on cognitive neuropsychology.

Computational Cognitive Neuropsychology

An important recent advance in cognitive psychology is the development of computational modeling as an aid to theory evaluation. A computational model of some theory in cognitive psychology is achieved by representing that theory in the form of a computer program that is capable of carrying out the cognitive task in question, and which does so using exactly the procedures that, according to the cognitive theory, are used by human beings when they are carrying out that cognitive task. Making a theory into a computational model helps theorizing in a variety of ways. For example, it reveals hitherto unsuspected ways in which the theory is underspecified or implicit: One cannot make a running program from a theory unless that theory is fully specified and explicit. Furthermore, if the program does run and is able to perform the cognitive task in question, and if the speed or accuracy of its performance is affected by the same stimulus variables that affect the speed or accuracy of human performance, that shows that the theory is a sufficient one.

This way of doing cognitive psychology is called computational cognitive psychology, and its virtues are sufficiently extensive that one might argue that all theorizing in cognitive psychology should be accompanied by computational modeling—that is, that it should be standard practice for theorists in cognitive psychology to express their theories in the form of executable computer programs.

Here it is important to distinguish between the terms *computational model, connectionist model,* and *neural-net model.* Figure 4.3

is helpful here. An ambitious project in theoretical cognitive psychology would be to seek to make the cognitive theory represented by Figure 4.3 into a computer program that actually performed the tasks of naming pictures and reading aloud words and nonwords; this would provide a way of rigorously testing the theory depicted by Figure 4.3. This program's structure would have to be isomorphic to the structure of Figure 4.3 if the program were to be a computational realization of the theory. Thus, for example, the program would have to contain program modules for each of the processing models of Figure 4.3. Such a program would be a computational model in the sense in which I am using that term.

Would it be a connectionist model as well? Not necessarily. For a model to be properly termed connectionist, communication between adjacent modules of the model would need to be conceptualized in terms of connections between elements of one module and elements of the other. For example, communication between the letter recognition and visual word recognition components would be effected via actual connections between letter units and word units: The letter unit for P-in-the-first-position would be literally connected to all the word units for words that begin with P. Because this connectionist conception of the nature of intermodule communication is only one of various possible ways in which such communication could be conceptualized in computational models, not all computational models are connectionist models. For example, the models of reading aloud offered by Coltheart et al. (2001); Plaut, McClelland, Seidenberg, and Patterson (1996); Seidenberg and McClelland (1989); and Zorzi, Houghton, and Butterworth (1998) are all computational models (because all are expressed as working computer programs), but only three are connectionist models; the model of Coltheart et al. (2001) is not a connectionist model.

A major motivation for connectionist computational modeling is the hope that the connections by which adjacent modules communicate could be given an actual physical interpretation—as neurons or neuronal tracts. Connectionist modelers with particularly strong hopes of this kind refer to their connectionist models as neural-net models. In Chapter 6 of this volume, Levine considers just how justified such modelers are in asserting that their connectionist models are "neurally plausible." Here I merely note that the arrows in a diagram like that of Figure 4.3 denote pathways of communication between modules, that Figure 4.3 does not assert anything at all about how such pathways are physically realized in the brain, and that a computational realization of Figure 4.3—a computational model of the relevant cognitive processes—may be neither a connectionist model nor a neural-net model.

Computational models can be used to simulate not only normal behavior but abnormal behavior as well. Researchers can interfere with the programs in various ways in order to see whether they then produce patterns of impaired cognitive performance that correspond in detail to the patterns of impaired performance seen in people with acquired or developmental disorders of cognition. This is computational cognitive neuropsychology.

Computational cognitive psychology is only now beginning to develop, so computational cognitive neuropsychology is still very underdeveloped. Nevertheless, a certain amount has already been done on the computational cognitive neuropsychology of acquired dyslexia. This work has focused largely on the simulation of the two types of acquired dyslexia discussed at several points in this chapter—surface dyslexia and phonological dyslexia. The work on computational modeling of reading by Seidenberg and McClelland (1989), Plaut et al. (1996), and Zorzi et al. (1998) has included some attempts to simulate acquired dyslexia, but not one of these implemented models was able to simulate successfully both phonological dyslexia and surface dyslexia. In contrast, the dual-route cascaded (DRC) model of visual word recognition and reading aloud (Coltheart et al., 2001)— a computational realization of the dual-route theory of reading—has been successful in simulating both of these acquired dyslexias (Coltheart, Langdon & Haller, 1996; Coltheart et al., 2001).

Figure 4.3 includes, in somewhat simplified form, the two routes of the DRC model and is therefore convenient for illustrating the DRC work on simulating acquired dyslexia. Suppose Figure 4.3 were turned into a computational model. It would have a computational route that can read all words aloud correctly (the route via visual word recognition) but cannot read nonwords, and another computational route that can read all nonwords and regular words aloud correctly (the route via application of grapheme-phoneme rules) but misreads exception words.

Now, it would be merely trivial to interfere with such a model so as to make it able to read all words aloud correctly but no nonwords— to make it severely phonologically dyslexic. One would only have to delete the grapheme-phoneme rule application subroutine from the program. It would be equally trivial to interfere with the model so as to make it able to read all nonwords and regular words aloud correctly, but misread all exception words. One would only have to delete all the units in the visual word recognition database of the program. Thus, the computational cognitive neuropsychologist must be more ambitious here and seek to simulate much more detailed aspects of the reading performances seen in phonological and surface dyslexia.

No person with surface dyslexia has ever been reported who could read no exception words at all. These patients can correctly read some exception words, and there is a frequency effect here: The more frequent an exception word is, the more likely the surface dyslexic will be able to read it correctly. That is a more subtle effect that one might seek to simulate. Coltheart et al. (2001) succeeded in making the DRC model misread some exception words while correctly reading others by altering the sensitivity to frequency of the visual word recognition component of the model in such a way that this component no longer responded adequately to low-frequency words. The model now read some exception words correctly, reading all the others by regularizing them (reading them as if they obeyed the rules); the more frequent an exception word was, the more likely the model was to read it correctly. Thus, this simulation produced quite a detailed match between the behavior of the lesioned model and the behavior of patients with surface dyslexia.

As discussed, some phonological dyslexics read pseudohomophonic nonwords with a higher accuracy rate than they read nonpseudohomophonic nonwords (Beauvois and Derouesné, 1979); furthermore, these authors reported that this pseudohomophone advantage was found to be greater when the pseudohomophone was orthographically very close to its parent word (an English example would be "koat") than when it was not (an English example would be "kote"). When the nonlexical route of the DRC model is interfered with by slowing down the rate at which the grapheme-phoneme rules are applied, the model now begins to misread some nonwords. Also, its performance shows a pseudohomophone advantage as well as an interaction of this advantage with visual similarity to parent word (Coltheart et al., 2001), just as reported for human phonological dyslexics by Beauvois and Derouesné. Thus, again this simulation produced quite a detailed match between the behavior of the lesioned model and the behavior of phonological dyslexic patients.

As mentioned, this kind of work is still in its infancy. Prospects do seem good, however, that as computational modeling becomes more widespread in cognitive psychology, one of the important ways of using a computational model to test the theory from which it was derived will be to lesion the model in various ways and then to investigate the success with which the lesioned model's behavior reproduces detailed aspects of the performance of people with impairments of the relevant cognitive system. That is computational cognitive neuropsychology.

Cognitive Neuropsychiatry

When cognitive neuropsychology was reborn 45 or 50 years ago,[4] it initially focused largely on just one cognitive ability, namely, reading aloud. Its scope, however, widened rapidly, and the cognitive abilities mentioned so far in this chapter that have been thoroughly investigated from the cognitive-neuropsychological perspective include, in addition to reading aloud, visual word recognition, spelling, face recognition, object recognition, object knowledge, language comprehension, spoken language production, attention, skilled action, and short-term memory.

Visual scientists would regard visual object recognition as an example of high-level vision, but for cognitive scientists it is an example of low-level cognition, as is every other cognitive ability listed in the previous paragraph. All of these are classified as low-level cognitive abilities so as to contrast them with such high-level cognitive abilities as belief formation, belief evaluation, and reasoning.

It is therefore interesting to note that so far cognitive neuropsychology has confined itself almost entirely to the study of low-level cognitive abilities. Why might that be? Could it be because Fodor's "first law of the nonexistence of cognitive science" (Fodor, 1983) is true? This law avers that the scientific study of such high-level cognitive abilities as belief formation, belief evaluation, and reasoning will never be possible. According to this law, then, cognitive science can only make discoveries about relatively low-level (i.e., modular) cognitive abilities, a view reiterated by Fodor (2000).

It is even more interesting to note, therefore, that the cognitive-neuropsychological approach, in the past few years, has begun to be applied to the investigation of belief formation and belief evaluation. Let me remind the reader of the definition of cognitive neuropsychology with which this chapter began: it is the investigation of disordered cognition with the aim of learning more about normal cognition. Thus, the investigation of belief formation and belief evaluation from the cognitive-neuropsychological perspective necessarily involves the study of people with disorders of belief formation and belief evaluation (e.g., people with delusions).

This domain of cognitive neuropsychology is known as cognitive neuropsychiatry (David & Halligan, 1996) because it typically involves the investigation of people with disorders that might be seen as the province of the psychiatrist. Just as cognitive neuropsychology began by focusing on just one disorder of low-level cognition (impaired reading), so cognitive neuropsychiatry has begun by focusing on just one disorder of high-level cognition (delusion), though it is already beginning to branch out to other high-level disorders, such as hallucination.

I will conclude this chapter, then, with an illustration of the nature of cognitive

---

[4]Cognitive neuropsychology had flourished in the last 40 years of the 19th century but disappeared in the first part of the 20th century as behaviorism came to the fore in psychology and antilocalizationist tendencies came to the fore in neurology.

neuropsychiatry that uses current work on delusional belief as an example.

Many delusions are monothematic or encapsulated: The deluded person has only a single delusory belief, or at most a small collection of closely related delusory beliefs. Outside the domain of the delusory belief, the person is, or at least appears to be, entirely rational; for example, the person accepts that the belief he or she holds is an improbable one and is not surprised when others challenge it, though the person nevertheless clings to it. Table 4.1 lists some examples of monothematic delusional beliefs that are currently being studied by cognitive neuropsychiatrists.

A key discovery in the cognitive neuropsychiatry of delusion was that of Ellis, Young, Quayle, and de Pauw (1997). When normal subjects are shown pictures of faces, they exhibit an arousal response indexed by, for example, substantially increased skin conductance; and the skin conductance response (SCR) is larger when the face is familiar than when it is unfamiliar. Ellis et al. found that this was not so for patients with Capgras delusion: Only very weak SCRs were observed in response to faces, and familiarity of the face did not increase the SCR. These authors suggested that this was a key factor in the delu-

Table 4.1   Eight Monothematic Delusions

- Capgras delusion: My closest relatives have been replaced by impostors.
- Cotard delusion: I am dead.
- Fregoli delusion: I am being followed around by people who are known to me but who are unrecognizable because they are in disguise.
- Mirrored-self misdentification: The person I see in the mirror is not really me.
- Reduplicative paramnesia: A person I knew who died is nevertheless in the hospital ward today.
- This arm [the speaker's left arm] is not mine, it is yours; you have three arms.
- Alien control: Someone else is able to control my actions.
- Thought insertion: Someone else's thoughts are being inserted into my mind.

sion: Capgras sufferers are confronted with the curious situation that they do not experience any emotional response when they encounter a person who should evoke such a response, such as a spouse. How could the person account for this? Perhaps it is because the encountered person is not the spouse, despite his or her claims to be; in that case, the encountered person is an impostor.

However, although this impairment in emotional responsiveness may be necessary for the occurrence of the Capgras delusion, Davies and Coltheart (2000) have argued that it is not sufficient because of the work of Tranel, Damasio, and Damasio (1995), who described cases of patients in whom brain damage had also eliminated the SCR to faces, but who were not delusional. This led Davies and Coltheart (see also Langdon & Coltheart, 2000) to the view that in patients with Capgras syndrome a second deficit must also be present. One deficit (affecting emotional responsiveness to faces) is responsible for the initial entertainment of the false, bizarre, and implausible belief; the second deficit (an impairment of the belief formation system) prevents the patient from being able to evaluate and so reject this belief. Davies and Coltheart then went on to explore the possibility that this two-deficit theory might offer an account of all forms of monothematic delusion—all the forms of delusion listed in Table 4.1, for example.

The general idea here is that in all cases of monothematic delusion, there is

(a) a neuropsychological impairment that produces an abnormality of a perceptual or affective response to the environment that leads the patient to some false belief about the environment (this impairment will vary from patient to patient), and

(b) a second impairment affecting belief. This is an impairment of the system we use to evaluate beliefs that occur to us and to decide whether to accept or reject these beliefs (this impairment is of the same nature for all people with delusions, and there is evidence that it is associated with damage to the right hemisphere of the brain, which is commonly present in patients with monothematic delusions).

To illustrate this theory, consider two patients described by Breen, Caine, Coltheart, Hendy, and Roberts (2000), both of whom had the condition known as mirrored-self misidentification—each man expressed the belief that the person he saw whenever he looked in a mirror was not himself, but some stranger who happened to look like him. For both men, this was the only abnormal belief they expressed; they knew that it was implausible; and they were not surprised at the attempts of their families to dissuade them. Nevertheless, they retained the belief steadfastly.

Breen et al. (2000) sought to establish whether in both men there were two deficits of the kind proposed in the theory of delusion just outlined. They were able to show that one man was suffering from an impairment of face-processing, so his face in the mirror might well look rather different now from the face he had been used to seeing in the mirror. The other man had intact face processing but was suffering from mirror agnosia, which is a loss of the ability to understand how mirrors work. When he was looking into a mirror and an investigator held an object above his shoulder (so that he could only see it in the mirror) and asked him to touch the object, the patient invariably reached for or behind the mirror, just as if the mirror were an open window and the object was on the other side of it. If this were the true nature of mirrors, then anyone seen in a mirror must be in a different position in space from the viewer—from which it follows that anyone seen in a mirror cannot be oneself. Hence, both patients had perceptual deficits of a kind that could suggest the implausible belief that they held.

Did they also have the second deficit? This belief formation deficit is currently so poorly characterized that it is quite unclear how one would go about investigating such a question. However, on neuropsychological testing both men showed normal left-hemisphere functioning and impaired right-hemisphere functioning, which is at least consistent with the presence of this second deficit.

It seems, then, that this cognitive-neuropsychological account of monothematic delusion has some promise. Its major problem at present is that far too little is said about the nature of the second deficit, and many important questions regarding this deficit are left unanswered—for example, if these patients have a defective belief evaluation system, why are they not deluded about many different things, rather than just about the one thing?

This kind of attempt to explain delusions in cognitive-neuropsychological terms is particularly challenging precisely because cognitive psychology does not currently offer an adequate theory of the normal processes of belief formation and evaluation; perhaps Fodor's first law is correct, which means that such a theory will never be found, in which case cognitive neuropsychiatry will never flourish.

But let us not despair. When Marshall and Newcombe (1973) published their seminal paper on acquired dyslexia almost 30 years ago, theorizing about the nature of the normal reading system was quite primitive; now it is so sophisticated (thanks in considerable part to cognitive-neuropsychological work on acquired dyslexia) that interpreting acquired reading disorders in the context of a theory of the normal reading system is often comfortably achieved. Perhaps after 30 more years theorizing about the nature of the normal system responsible for belief formation and evaluation will be so sophisticated (thanks in considerable part to cognitive-neuropsychiatric work on delusion) that interpreting cognitive-neuropsychiatric disorders in the context of a theory of the normal processes of belief formation and evaluation will also often be comfortably achieved.

REFERENCES

Albert, M. L., Reches, A., & Silverberg, R. (1975). Associative visual agnosia without alexia. *Neurology, 29,* 876–879.

Allport, D. A., & Funnell, E. (1981). Components of the mental lexicon. *Philosophical Transactions of the Royal Society of London B, 295,* 397–410.

Beauvois, M.-F. (1982). Optic aphasia: A process of interaction between vision and language. *Philosophical Transactions of the Royal Society of London B, 298,* 35–47.

Beauvois, M.-F., & Derouesné, J. (1979). Phonological alexia: Three dissociations. *Journal of Neurology, Neurosurgery, and Psychiatry, 42,* 115–124.

Bishop, D. V. M. (1997). Cognitive neuropsychology and developmental disorders: Uncomfortable bedfellows. *Quarterly Journal of Experimental Psychology, 50A,* 899–923.

Block, N. (1995). The mind as the software of the brain. In D. Osherson, L. Gleitman, S. Kosslyn, E. Smith, & S. Sternberg (Eds.), *An invitation to cognitive science* (pp. 377–425). Cambridge: MIT Press.

Breen, N., Caine, D., Coltheart, M., Hendy, J., & Roberts, C. (2000). Delusional misidentification. *Mind & Language, 15,* 74–110.

Bullinaria, J. A., & Chater, N. (1995). Connectionist modelling: Implications for cognitive neuropsychology. *Language & Cognitive Processes, 10,* 227–264.

Caramazza, A., & Shelton, J. (1998). Domain-specific knowledge systems in the brain: The animate-inanimate distinction. *Journal of Cognitive Neuroscience, 10,* 1–34.

Chialant, D., & Caramazza, A. (1998). Perceptual and lexical factors in a case of letter-by-letter reading. *Cognitive Neuropsychology, 15,* 167–202.

Coltheart, M. (1984). Acquired dyslexias and normal reading. In R. N. Malatesha & H. A. Whitaker (Eds.), *Dyslexia: A global issue* (pp. 357–474). Hague, Netherlands: Nijhoff.

Coltheart, M. (Ed.). (1996). *Phonological dyslexia.* Hove, England: Erlbaum.

Coltheart, M. (1999). Modularity and cognition. *Trends in Cognitive Sciences, 3,* 115–120.

Coltheart, M., & Davies, M. (Eds.). (2000). *Pathologies of belief.* Oxford: Blackwell.

Coltheart, M., & Funnell, E. (1987). Reading and writing: One lexicon or *two*? In A. Allport, D. G. MacKay, W. Prinz, & E. Scheerer (Eds.), *Language perception and production: Relationships between listening, speaking, reading and writing* (pp. 313–339). London: Academic Press.

Coltheart, M., Langdon, R., & Haller, M. (1996). Computational cognitive neuropsychology. In B. Dodd, L. Worrall, & R. Campbell (Eds.), *Models of language: Illuminations from impairment* (pp. 9–36). London: Whurr.

Coltheart, M., Rastle, K., Perry, C., Langdon, R. J., & Ziegler, J. C. (2001). DRC: A dual route cascaded model of visual word recognition and reading aloud. *Psychological Review, 108,* 204–256.

Crago, M. B., & Gopnik, M. (1994). From families to phenotypes: Theoretical and clinical implications of research into the genetic basis of specific language impairment. In R. Watkins & M. Rice (Eds.), *Specific language impairments in children* (pp. 35–51). Baltimore, MD: Brookes.

David, A. S., & Halligan, P. W. (1996). [Editorial]. *Cognitive Neuropsychiatry, 1,* 1–3.

Davies, M., & Coltheart, M. (2000). Introduction: Pathologies of belief. In M. Coltheart & M. Davies (Eds.), *Pathologies of belief.* Oxford: Blackwell.

De Renzi, E. (1986). Prosopagnosia in two patients with CT-scan evidence of damage confined to the right hemisphere. *Neuropsychologia, 24,* 385–389.

Edgington, E. S. (1995). *Randomization tests* (3rd ed.). New York: Dekker.

Ellis, H. D., Young, A. W., Quayle, A. H., & de Pauw, K. W. (1997). Reduced autonomic responses to faces in Capgras delusion.

Proceedings of the Royal Society: Biological Sciences, B264, 1085–92.

Farah, M. J. (1990). *Visual agnosia: Disorders of object recognition and what they tell us about normal vision.* Cambridge: MIT Press.

Farah, M. J. (1991). Patterns of co-occurrence among the associative agnosias: Implications for visual object recognition. *Cognitive Neuropsychology, 8,* 1–20.

Farah, M. J., Stowe, R. M., & Levinson, K. L. (1996). Phonological dyslexia: Loss of a reading-specific component of the cognitive architecture. *Cognitive Neuropsychology, 13,* 849–868.

Farah, M. J., & Wallace, M. A. (1991). Pure alexia as a visual impairment: A reconsideration. *Cognitive Neuropsychology, 8,* 313–334.

Feinberg, T. E., Gonzalez-Rothi, L. J., & Heilman, K. M. (1986). Multimodal agnosia after unilateral left hemisphere lesion. *Neurology, 36,* 864–867.

Fodor, J. A. (1983). *The modularity of mind.* Cambridge: MIT Press.

Fodor, J. A. (2000). *The mind doesn't work that way.* Cambridge: MIT Press.

Frith, U. (1985). Beneath the surface of developmental dyslexia. In K. E. Patterson, J. C. Marshall, & M. Coltheart (Eds.), *Surface dyslexia: Neuropsychological and cognitive studies of phonological reading.* London: Erlbaum.

Funnell, E. (1983). *Ideographic communication in aphasia.* Unpublished doctoral thesis, University of Reading, England.

Gane, C., & Sarsen, T. (1977). *Structured systems analysis: tools and techniques.* New York: Improved System Technologies.

Gathercole, S. E., & Baddeley, A. D. (1990). Phonological memory deficits in language disordered children: Is there a causal connection? *Journal of Memory and Language, 29,* 336–360.

Gomori, A. J., & Hawyrluk, G. A. (1984). Visual agnosia without alexia. *Neurologica, 34,* 947–950.

Haywood, M. (1996). Unpublished doctoral thesis, Macquarie University, Sydney, Australia.

Hecaen, H., & Ajuriaguerra, J. (1956). Agnosie visuelle pour les objets inanimés. *Revue Neurologique, 94,* 222–233.

Howard, D., & Franklin, S. (1988). *Missing the meaning? A cognitive neuropsychological study of the processing of words by an aphasic patient.* Cambridge: MIT Press.

Humphreys, G. W., & Rumiati, R. (1998). Agnosia without prosopagnosia or alexia: Evidence for stored visual memories specific to objects. *Cognitive Neuropsychology, 15,* 243–277.

Jackson, N., & Coltheart, M. (2001). *Routes to reading success and failure: Towards an integrated cognitive psychology of atypical reading.* Hove, England: Psychology Press.

Langdon, R., & Coltheart, M. (2000). The cognitive neuropsychology of delusions. *Mind & Language, 15,* 184–218.

Larrabee, G. J., Levin, H. S., Huff, F. J., Kay, M. C., & Guinto, F. C. (1985). Visual agnosia contrasted with visual-verbal disconnection. *Neuropsychologia, 23,* 1–12.

Leiguarda, R. C., & Marsden, C. D. (2000). Limb apraxias: Higher-order disorders of sensorimotor integration. *Brain, 123,* 860–879.

Marr, D. (1982). *Vision.* San Francisco: Freeman.

Marshall, J. C. (1984). Towards a rational taxonomy of the acquired dyslexias. In R. N. Malatesha & H. A. Whitaker (Eds.), *Dyslexia: A global issue* (pp. 211–232). Hague, Netherlands: Nijhoff.

Marshall, J. C., Halligan, P. W., Fink, G. R., Wade, D. T., & Frackowiack, R. S. J. (1997). The functional anatomy of a hysterical paralysis. *Cognition, 64,* B1–B8.

Marshall, J. C., & Newcombe, F. (1973). Patterns of paralexia: A psycholinguistic approach. *Journal of Psycholinguistic Research, 2,* 175–199.

McCarthy, R. A., & Warrington, E. K. (1986). Phonological reading: Phenomena and paradoxes. *Cortex, 22,* 359–380.

McCloskey, M. (2001). The future of cognitive neuropsychology. In B. Rapp (Ed.), *Handbook of cognitive neuropsychology* (pp. 593–610). Hove, England: Psychology Press.

McGee, H. (1984). *On food and cooking*. London: Hyman.

Patterson, K. E., & Lambon Ralph, M. A. (1999). Selective disorders of reading? *Current Opinion in Neurobiology, 9,* 235–239.

Patterson, K. E., & Shewell, C. (1987). Speak and spell: Dissociations and word-class effects. In M. Coltheart, R. Job, & G. Sartori (Eds.), *The cognitive neuropsychology of language* (pp. 273–294). London: Erlbaum.

Patterson, K. E., Marshall, J. C., & Coltheart, M. (Eds.). (1985). *Surface dyslexia: Neuropsychological and cognitive studies of phonological reading*. London: Erlbaum.

Pillon, B., Signoret, J. L., & Lhermitte, F. (1981). Agnosie visuelle associative: Role de l'hemisphere gauche dans la perception visuelle. *Revue Neurologique, 137,* 831–842.

Plaut, D. C. (1995). Double dissociation without modularity: Evidence from connectionist neuropsychology. *Journal of Clinical & Experimental Neuropsychology, 17*(2), 291–321.

Plaut, D. C., McClelland, J. L., Seidenberg, M. S., & Patterson, K. (1996). Understanding normal and impaired word reading: Computational principles in quasi-regular domains. *Psychological Review, 103,* 56–115.

Seidenberg, M. S., & McClelland, J. L. (1989). A distributed, developmental model of word recognition and naming. *Psychological Review, 96,* 523–568.

Snowling, M. (1987). *Dyslexia: A cognitive developmental perspective*. Oxford, England: Blackwell.

Snowling, M., Bryant, P. B., & Hulme, C. (1996). Theoretical and methodological pitfalls in making comparisons between developmental and acquired dyslexia: Some comments on A. Castles and M. Coltheart (1993). *Reading and Writing, 8,* 443–451.

Tallal, P., & Katz, W. (1989). Neuropsychological and neuroanatomical studies of developmental language/reading disorders: Recent advances. In C. Von Euler, I. Lundberg, & G. Lennerstrand (Eds.), *Brain and reading* (pp. 183–196). New York: Stockton Press.

Tranel, D., Damasio, H., & Damasio, A. R. (1995). Double dissociation between overt and covert recognition. *Journal of Cognitive Neuroscience, 7,* 425–32.

Van Orden, G. C., & Paap, K. R. (1997). Functional neuroimages fail to discover pieces of mind in the parts of the brain. *Philosophy of Science, 64* (4 Suppl. S): S85–S94.

Zorzi, M., Houghton, G., & Butterworth, B. (1998). Two routes or one in reading aloud? A connectionist dual-process model. *Journal of Experimental Psychology: Human Perception and Performance, 24,* 1131–1161.

CHAPTER 5

Functional Brain Imaging

LUIS HERNANDEZ-GARCÍA, TOR WAGER, AND JOHN JONIDES

In recent years there has been explosive interest in the use of brain imaging to study cognitive and affective processes. For example, Figure 5.1 shows the dramatic rise in the number of publications from 1992 to 1999 in which the term functional magnetic resonance imaging (fMRI) appears in the title. Because of the surge of empirical work that now relies on a combination of behavioral and neuroimaging data, it is critical that students of the mind be students of the brain as well because data about each inform the other. Our goal in this chapter is to provide an introduction to the growing field of neuroimaging research for those not expert in it. The chapter provides general coverage of the various steps involved in conducting a neuroimaging experiment, from the design of tasks to the interpretation of results. We begin by detailing several reasons that one might want to use neuroimaging data to understand cognitive and other processes. Having provided this motivation, we then trace out several techniques that are used in the design and execution of imaging experiments. Finally, in the last section of the chapter we provide a detailed overview of positron-emission tomography (PET) and functional magnetic resonance imaging (fMRI): a review of the physics underlying each technique and of the analytical tools that can be used to work with the resulting data. With these three sections we hope to illustrate to the reader the why, the what, and the how of functional neuroimaging.

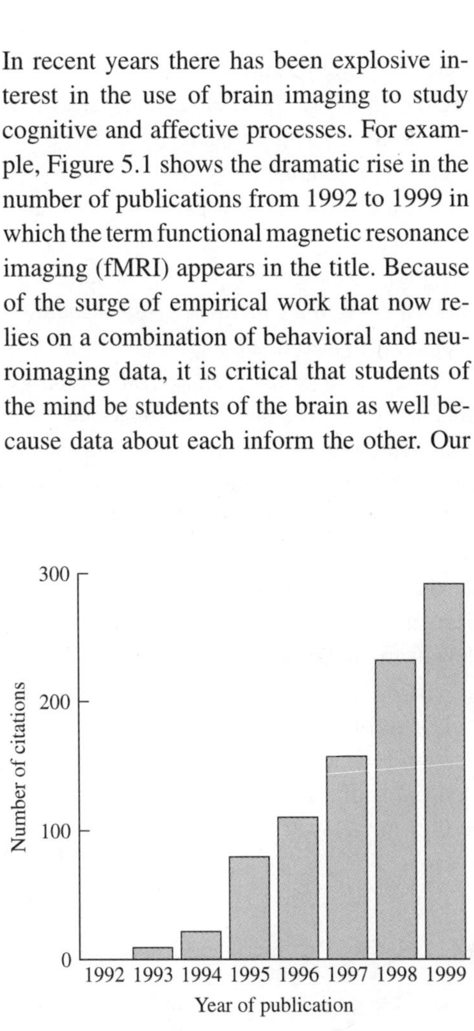

Figure 5.1 A graph showing the results of a search of the Medline database for articles with the words "functional magnetic resonance imaging (fMRI)" in the title.

THE WHY: USES OF DATA FROM FUNCTIONAL NEUROIMAGING

Brain Mapping

Perhaps the most obvious rationale for conducting functional neuroimaging experiments is to correlate structure with function. Although some psychologists in the last century argued that the brain operated by the principle of mass action (Lashley, 1950), we now know that many functions are substantially localized in the neural tissue of the brain. Knowing this, many investigators have sought to map out the primitive processes that are engaged when various brain structures are active. In a certain gross sense, modern neuroimaging is similar to the 18th-century practice of phrenology, whose practitioners read patients' personality traits from bumps on their skulls. To be sure, both modern functional imaging and phrenology are attempts to map out the localization of functions in the brain. But the similarity ends there. Modern neuroimaging measures processes within the brain that are replicable and have been extensively cross-validated with other neuroscientific methodologies. Phrenology, of course, turned out to be wrong. However, it is instructive to compare the assumptions of phrenology with those of modern neuroimaging. Phrenologists believed that a lump at a certain place on the head corresponded with a particular personality trait; the larger the lump, the larger that trait. So, for example, a larger bump might indicate more agreeableness, or a better memory. In neuroimaging, by contrast, it is assumed that complex psychological processes are best described in terms of combinations of constituent elementary operations. The elementary processes may not be localized in single locations in the brain. Rather, they are often the result of networks of neurons (often spatially distributed) acting together. Unlike phrenologists, moreover, most modern researchers do not assume that skill at one mental operation is a function of the sheer size of the underlying neural tissue involved. The assumptions of neuroimaging lead naturally to a search for the brain activations that accompany elementary psychological processes. Mapping these elementary processes onto regions and functional networks

in the brain is a major goal of modern research on brain imaging.

We should note that once certain regions of the brain have been identified with certain psychological processes, researchers may go beyond simple assignment of structure to function. Instead, they can examine circuits of activation that might be involved in a complex psychological task by using statistical techniques such as interregional correlations, factor analysis, and structural equation modeling, which we review below. These techniques add value because they permit us to go beyond the functions of any single region or small set of regions involved in an elementary cognitive operation. These tools can be used to help analyze what combinations of elementary processes are involved in a psychological task. Thus, we can go from the elementary to the complex by examining patterns of activation and knowing the functions of the structures that are activated in a pattern.

Overall, the sort of behavioral neurology that is provided by studies of functional neuroimaging is quite helpful on several fronts. A detailed mapping of the functions of various brain structures will give us solid evidence about the primitive psychological processes of the brain. It will also provide detailed information for neurosurgical planning and allow us to predict which functions will be lost on the occasion of brain injury, whether focal or diffuse. Thus, if there were no other reason to conduct studies that use functional neuroimaging, mapping the brain would be sufficient. However, there *are* additional reasons.

Dissociating Psychological Processes

One of the great benefits of having data on the patterns of activation caused by two different psychological tasks is that it permits one to examine whether the two tasks doubly dissociate (Smith and Jonides, 1995). The logic is this: Suppose there is some brain region A that mediates some cognitive process a. Suppose, similarly, that there is some other brain region B that mediates some other cognitive process b. Now imagine that we can devise two psychological tasks, 1 and 2, such that Task 1 requires cognitive process a but not b and Task 2 requires cognitive process b but not a. If we have subjects perform these two tasks while we image the activations in their brains, we should find activation of region A during performance of Task 1 but not during performance of Task 2, and vice versa for region B. This pattern of evidence would permit one to argue that there are two separable psychological processes involved in the tasks, as there are two brain regions that are activated (within the spatial limitations of the neuroimaging technique, of course). This logic applies, by the way, whether regions A and B are single sites in the brain or networks of sites, thus generalizing the method to a wide variety of circumstances.

Now consider a similar but more complex case. Suppose that both Task 1 and Task 2 require several psychological processes. By the assumptions outlined above, we should find activations in various regions of the brain when subjects engage in Task 1 and Task 2. If Task 1 activates some group of sites that is wholly different from that activated while subjects engage in Task 2, we would have evidence of differing processes in the two tasks. However, the two tasks may activate some quite different sites as well as some similar sites. In this case, we get leverage in accounting for the processes involved in the two tasks by noting the sites whose activations are shared by or unique to each task. If we knew the functions of each site from other research, we would then have a more complete understanding of the processes involved in these tasks, both those that they share in common and those that differ between the tasks.

The use of imaging data to evaluate double dissociations has become quite widespread. These data go beyond previous demonstrations of double dissociations that have involved behavioral data on subjects with and without brain injury. In the case of behavioral data on normal subjects, double dissociations can be established by finding two experimental variables, one of which affects performance on Task 1 but not on Task 2, and another of which affects performance on Task 2 but not on Task 1. This pattern permits one to argue that the two tasks differ in their engagement of some set of psychological processes, although it is not very specific about the particular processes that are engaged. In the case of behavioral data on brain-injured subjects, a researcher seeks two patients: one who can perform Task 1 but not Task 2, and one who can perform Task 2 but not Task 1. This pattern again allows one to argue that the tasks differ in the underlying processes that they recruit, but there are weaknesses to this approach: Often, damage in patients is not tightly localized; sometimes patients develop compensatory mechanisms for their deficits; and studies of this sort require one to make conclusions about normal performance from patients who have selective deficits, perhaps compromising the generality of the conclusions one can reach. Because double dissociations in neuroimaging have a different set of weaknesses (most prominently, they are limited by the spatial resolution of the techniques), they complement neuropsychological dissociations, making neuroimaging another important point of leverage in distinguishing psychological processes.

To see how successful this double-dissociation technique can be, consider an example. For some time, researchers have suspected that working memory may consist of at least two subsystems, one concerned with spatial information and one concerned with verbal information. This was originally proposed by Baddeley (e.g., 1986, 1992), and the proposal has received support from behavioral studies of normal and brain-injured adults (see Jonides et al., 1996, for a review). A critical finding that helps seal the case for two subsystems of working memory comes from a pair of experiments that compared the brain regions activated by parallel spatial and verbal working memory tasks (for details, see Awh et al., 1996; Jonides et al., 1993; Smith, Jonides, & Koeppe, 1996). A schematic that illustrates the two tasks is shown in Figure 5.2. In the spatial case, subjects had to encode three locations marked by dots on a screen and to retain these in memory for 3 s. Following the retention interval, a single location was marked, and subjects had to indicate whether this location matched one of the three in memory. The verbal task was similar in that subjects had to encode 4 letters and to retain these in memory for 3 s, after which a single

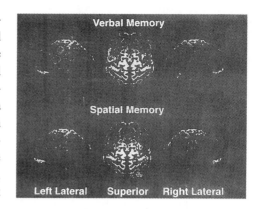

Figure 5.3 Lateral and superior images revealing activations in spatial and verbal working memory tasks.

NOTE: In each row, three views of the brain in grey-scale renderings of a composite MRI have superimposed on them activations from a PET experiment, where the activations are shown in a color scale with blue the least active and red the most active.

Spatial and verbal item recognition

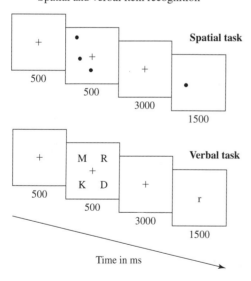

Figure 5.2 A spatial and a verbal task used to study item-recognition performance in working memory.

NOTE: The two tasks are similar in structure except for the material that must be retained and retrieved.

letter was presented and subjects had to decide whether it matched one of the three in memory.

As shown in Figure 5.3 (see insert), PET scans of subjects engaged in these two tasks revealed a striking dissociation in the circuitry that underlies them. The figure includes left and right lateral as well as superior views of the brain; the activations for each of the memory tasks are superimposed on these. The spatial task recruited mechanisms of neocortex predominantly of the right hemisphere, whereas the verbal task recruited mechanisms predominantly of the left hemisphere. The details of which regions were activated and what these activations might signal for the processes in each task are reported elsewhere (Smith et al., 1996). For the present, it is sufficient to note that this pattern of results provides sufficient support for the claim that working memory is composed of separable systems for different sorts of information, a claim that relies on the sort of double dissociation shown in the figure.

Convergence of Neuroimaging and Behavioral Data in Normal Adults

One of the great strides forward that the advent of neuroimaging will make possible arises because of the opportunity for convergence between behavioral data and neuroimaging data drawn from normal experimental participants. The leverage that is gained from this convergence is large. If we have data from behavioral studies that suggest a dissociation between two different psychological processes, we have the opportunity to study whether these processes are represented in separable neural tissue. If so, this greatly strengthens the case for separable processing systems.

Consider the following example from work in our laboratory (Badre et al., 2000). This work has been concerned with identifying executive processes and their neural implementations. One such executive process is task management, the ability to manage multiple tasks simultaneously. We have constructed a situation that requires task management of two sorts, illustrated in Figure 5.4. Subjects see a series of computer displays that have two panels, one on the left and one on the right. Each display contains a single arrow that points up or down. Subjects begin each series of trials with two counters set at "20" each, and each time an arrow appears on one side or the other, they are to change that count up or down, depending on whether the arrow points up or down. At the end of a run of trials, subjects are queried about each of the counter values to be sure that they have kept the counts accurately. Notice that in this task there are two counters that must be managed. On successive trials, subjects may have to access the same counter, or they may have to switch counters from one to the other. Notice also that the task requires two types of counting operations: incrementing and decrementing. Again, on successive trials, subjects may use the same operation or may have to switch from one operation to the other. Behavioral data about the time it takes subjects to complete each trial (measured by subjects' depressing a response button when they are ready to accept the next stimulus display) show a clear effect: There is a cost in switching between counters, and there is a cost in switching between

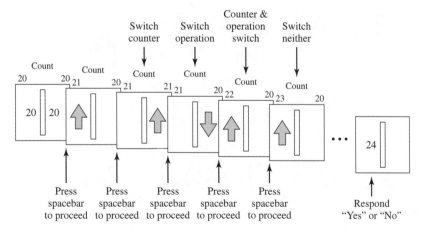

Figure 5.4   A schematic of a task used to study processes required to switch between two tasks.
NOTE: The figure shows that the task entails two types of switches: between different internal counters or between different operations on the contents of those counters.

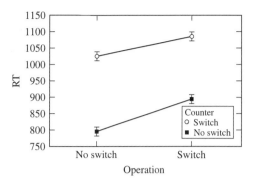

Figure 5.5 Behavioral data from the dual-switching task.
NOTE: There are main effects of both types of switch, and there is no interaction between these two separate effects.

operations. Importantly, these two costs are independent of one another, as shown in Figure 5.5. The time cost of each type of switch does not reliably influence the time cost of the other. This result leads to the implication that there may be two mechanisms involved in the two types of switches (two dissociable executive processes); if so, we may be able to find neural evidence of the two mechanisms.

In fact, a follow-up experiment that studied subjects performing this task in an fMRI environment found just this evidence. Some data from this experiment are shown in Figure 5.6. The figure shows that there is a region of lateral frontal cortex that is activated by the switch in counters but not by the switch in operations; similarly, there is another region of medial frontal cortex, anterior to the first, that is activated by a switch in operations but not by a switch in counters. This sort of double dissociation follows the behavioral data well in suggesting two (at least partially) independent mechanisms for the two executive processes. So, here is a case in which the behavioral data about a task led to an imaging experiment whose data converged with the behavior in normal adults.

Convergence of Neuroimaging and Behavioral Data in Patients

It is possible to extend this hunt for convergence beyond the study of normal adults as well. An excellent example comes from the study of memory processes. It is by now well

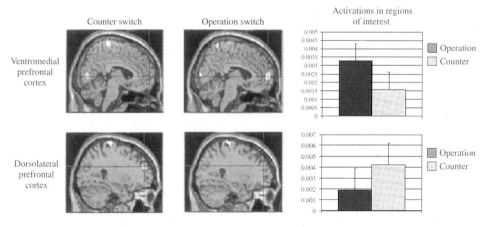

Figure 5.6 One contrast in brain activations between the two types of switches in the dual-switching task.
NOTE: The top panel shows activation in a ventromedial prefrontal site, and the bottom panel shows activation in a lateral prefrontal site for each type of switch. Note the double dissociation in patterns of activations in these two sites for the two types of switch.

documented that two memory systems subserve long-term memory in adults. The distinction between the two types is often called a distinction between explicit and implicit memory. Take the concept of a bicycle, for example. You may be able to remember where you parked your bicycle this morning or yesterday, or where you bought that bike. These would be examples of explicit memory because you are explicitly retrieving a piece of information that you have previously stored. By contrast, most adults can ride a bicycle with little trouble, but any young child will tell you that it is quite difficult. The skill to ride a bicycle reflects that adults have stored some information that translates into motor movements that make possible balancing, pedaling, turning, and so forth. This is a kind of implicit memory because while riding a bike, a person has no sense of explicitly retrieving information from memory; rather, information is retrieved in the course of executing the required behavior.

As it happens, the distinction between explicit and implicit memory is well supported by studies that reveal a double dissociation between these two types of memory in patients with brain lesions. Some patients with medial temporal lobe lesions, including extensively studied patients such as H.M. (Milner, Corkin, & Teuber, 1968), have an inability to acquire new information and retrieve that information explicitly, but they have intact implicit memory for motor skills and other procedural knowledge. By contrast, Gabrieli, Fleishman, Keane, Reminger, and Morell (1995) reported the result of a patient with damage to the right occipital lobe, M.S., who has an intact and functioning explicit memory system but impaired implicit memory (although probably not of bicycle riding, as in the earlier example). Taken together, pairs of patients such as these suggest the existence of two memory systems that dissociate in their functions and in the neural tissue that

subserves them. This claim leads naturally to the prediction that testing normal adults on explicit and implicit memory tasks ought to find different patterns of brain activation as the signatures of these two memory systems. By now, various reports that support this contention have surfaced (see, e.g., Schacter and Buckner, 1998). In general, explicit memory tasks (compared to a control condition) cause increased activation of medial temporal lobe structures, and implicit memory tasks cause decreased activation in association cortex of posterior regions of the brain. Why these two particular patterns of increase and decrease of activation should occur in response to explicit and implicit tasks respectively is a question beyond our scope here; but the result illustrates how imaging evidence and evidence from patient populations can be used in tandem to converge on a view of cognitive processing.

Convergence of Neuroimaging Data in Humans with Behavioral Data in Animals

Invasive and recording studies on animals other than humans have raised important hypotheses about the layout of various cognitive systems residing in sensory, motor, or association cortex. Neuroimaging studies with humans now permit tests of these hypotheses. One caveat regarding this convergence between animal and human studies that researchers must heed has to do with homology. It is often difficult to determine just what structure in the brain of some animal (e.g., a monkey) is homologous to a structure in a human brain. Sometimes this homology can be approached cytoarchitectonically by examining the morphology of cells in brain regions of the two species in question; sometimes functional data from other studies give good leads about which areas in the brains of two species are performing related functions. Regardless of the approach one takes to the problem of homology, one must carefully ensure that a case can be made for a structural or functional similarity.

However, sometimes the homology is reasonably straightforward, as it appears to be for a leading case that has exploited the opportunity to relate data from monkeys and humans concerning visual function. Since the pioneering work of Ungerleider and Mishkin (1982), it has become increasingly clear that early visual processing proceeds along two streams. A ventral stream of information flows from primary visual cortex to temporal cortex; this stream contains increasingly complex computations performed on the information in the service of revealing the forms, colors, and identities of objects in the environment. A dorsal stream also flows from primary visual cortex to structures of the parietal lobe and is responsible for processing information about the spatial locations and movements of objects. The data from which this view of the visual system derives come from studies of lesioned monkeys performing tasks of object recognition or spatial localization as well as from single-cell recording studies of the functions of temporal and parietal systems. Both sorts of studies have provided quite strong support for the duality of the visual processing stream.

Much more recently, evidence from human neuroimaging studies has provided convergence with the data from monkeys. Perhaps the seminal study was that by Haxby et al. (1994), in which human volunteers performed a matching-to-sample task under two conditions. In one, subjects compared a sample face to two alternatives and picked the alternative that matched the sample. In the other, subjects compared the position of a dot in a frame to the positions of two other dots in frames to see which of the two was identical to the first. The first task required the processing of information about shape and form, whereas the second required the processing of information

about spatial position. As predicted by the data from monkeys, the two tasks resulted in activation of separable regions in cortex: The task involving form caused activation of occipital and temporal cortex, whereas the task involving location caused activation of occipital and parietal cortex. Here, then, is an illustration of how data from cognitive studies with animals can motivate researchers to use neuroimaging techniques to examine cortical function in humans.

Let us summarize. We have devoted significant space at the opening of this chapter to a detailed examination of why one would want to conduct research using neuroimaging techniques, especially PET and fMRI. The motivations for these techniques are numerous, as we have elaborated. Overall, there is good reason to believe that neuroimaging methods will become centerpieces in the array of tools available to cognitive psychology (and to other fields in psychology as well). Therefore, it is well worth the effort for the student of cognition to learn what techniques are available and how they can be applied to the study of psychological tasks. We turn now to these issues.

THE WHAT: NEUROIMAGING TECHNIQUES AND TASK DESIGN

Neuroimaging Techniques

Imaging methods for human studies include a number of alternatives: fMRI, PET, single positron emission computerized tomography (SPECT), event-related potentials (ERP), electroencephalography (EEG), magnetoencephalography (MEG), and near-infrared spectroscopy. A number of other brain imaging techniques are available for use in animals using radiolabeling, histological, or optical imaging techniques.

Although all these techniques are in frequent use and provide important insights into

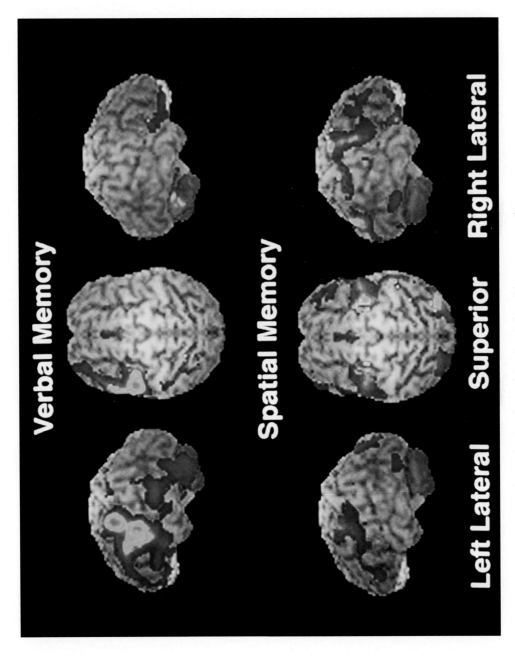

Figure 5.3 Lateral and superior images revealing activations in spatial and verbal working memory tasks.

Table 5.1 Summary of PET and fMRI Methods

What Is Imaged	PET	fMRI
Brain structure		Structural T_1 and T_2 scans
Regional brain activation	Blood flow (^{15}O)	BOLD (T_2^*)
	Glucose metabolism (^{18}FDG)	Arterial spin tagging (AST)
	Oxygen consumption	FAIR
Anatomical connectivity		Diffusion tensor imaging
Receptor binding and regional chemical distribution	Benzodiazapines, dopamine, acetylcholine, many others	MR spectroscopy
	Kinetic modeling	
Gene expression	Various radiolabeling compounds	MR spectroscopy with kinetic modeling

brain function, we focus on the two techniques most commonly used in current human research concerned with localization of function: PET and fMRI. The main advantages of these techniques are that they can be used on humans, that they offer a useful balance between spatial resolution and temporal resolution, and that they can be used to create images of the whole brain. This last feature offers a great potential for synergy with animal research. Single-cell recording in animals, for example, offers not only spatial resolution down to a single neuron but also millisecond temporal resolution. Its main weakness is that testing usually occurs within single, isolated brain regions, and thus other regions important to performance of some task may be missed. Neuroimaging using PET and fMRI is well suited to exploratory analyses of brain processes and allows new hypotheses about specific brain areas to be developed and tested in animal models. In addition, neuroimaging with PET and fMRI offers a broad view of how remote brain regions interact in particular psychological functions, complementing the detailed analysis of individual cell behavior that is possible using animal models.

What PET and fMRI Can Measure

The number of techniques for imaging brain processes with PET and fMRI is growing. Although a thorough discussion of all of these is far beyond the scope of this chapter, it is important to realize what sorts of processes can be imaged using these techniques. Some of the alternatives are described here briefly; our subsequent discussions of task design will focus on measures of regional brain activation because these are the ones used most often to study human cognition and affect. Table 5.1 shows a summary of the various methods available using PET and fMRI as measurement tools. Following is a brief description of each method.

Structural Scans. Functional magnetic resonance imaging can provide detailed anatomical scans of gray and white matter with resolution well below 1 mm^3. This can be useful if one expects either structural differences between two populations, such as between individuals with and without schizophrenia (Andreasen et al., 1994), or changes in gross brain structure with practice or some other variable. An example is a recent study that reported larger posterior hippocampi in London taxi drivers who had extensive training in spatial navigation (Maguire et al., 2000). Another structural scanning technique is diffusion tensor imaging, described later. This technique allows one to identify white matter tracts in the human brain, which is useful for studying not only structures such as the corpus callosum but also changes in these structures as a function of some variable, such as age.

Regional Brain Activation. Perhaps the most frequent use of both PET and fMRI, and the one that is the focus of this chapter, is the study of changes in some property of metabolism or of the vasculature that accompany changes in neural activity. With PET, one may separately measure glucose metabolism, oxygen consumption, and regional cerebral blood flow (rCBF). Each of these techniques allows one to make inferences about the localization of neural activity based on the assumption that neural activity is accompanied by a change in metabolism, oxygen consumption, or blood flow. Functional MRI using the blood oxygen level dependent method (BOLD) is sensitive to changes in blood volume and in the concentration of deoxygenated hemoglobin in the blood across regions of the brain. The rationale is that (a) more deoxygenated blood in an area causes a decrease in BOLD signal and (b) neural activity is accompanied by increased blood flow, which dilutes the concentration of deoxygenated hemoglobin and produces a relative increase in signal (Hoge et al., 1999). Since both BOLD fMRI and PET measurements of rCBF take advantage of changes in blood flow with changed neural activation, there should be good correspondence between these two measures for the same tasks, and this is generally the case (Joliot et al., 1999; Kinahan & Noll, 1999; Ramsey et al., 1996). One difference appears to be that fMRI activations are usually located several millimeters dorsal to those of PET, consistent with the idea that fMRI is sensitive to deoxygenated hemoglobin in the capillaries and draining venules surrounding synapses.

Anatomical Connectivity. Diffusion tensor imaging is the name of a new methodology being developed to map the white matter tracts that connect regions of the brain. Several current methods use standard MRI scanners configured to be sensitive to the diffusion of water in order to estimate water diffusion tensors in each area of the brain (Peled, Gudbjartsson, Westin, Kikinis, & Jolesz, 1998). We explore this technique in greater detail later, but for now thinking of a tensor as a measure of motion in the x, y, and z dimensions (a vector is a special kind of tensor) should suffice. Researchers are interested in the shapes of the tensors in different brain locations. Water diffuses with equal ease in all directions in the ventricles and other fluid spaces, producing a spherical tensor. At the edges of the brain and in other areas, water may be restricted from diffusing in one direction, producing a planar tensor. Near a white matter tract, however, water diffuses most easily along the tract, producing a diffusion tensor that is large along the axis of the tract and small in the other dimensions. These linear tensors mark the existence and direction of a white matter tract in the brain. Factors that affect the shape of a tensor are the density of axon fibers in the tract, the degree of myelination, the fiber diameter, and the similarity in the directions of the fiber projections. Diffusion tensors can be measured on a time scale of a minute or less.

In the published literature, diffusion tensor images are usually labeled with different colors for the x, y, and z components of motion; a solid block of one color indicates fiber tracts running along the x-, y-, or z-axis of the image. Although most studies of diffusion tensor imaging have so far focused on the methodology itself, there are many potential applications to the study of brain function, including combined studies of structure and brain activation to help define functional networks.

Receptor Binding. The affinity of particular chemicals for specific types of neurotransmitter receptors offers researchers a leverage point for investigating the functional neurochemistry of the human brain. Radioactive labels are attached to carefully chosen compounds, which are then injected into the arteries of a subject either by a single injection (called a bolus) or by a continuous infusion of the substance until the brain concentrations reach a steady state. This method can be used to image the density of a specific type of receptor throughout the brain. It can also be used to image the amount of binding to a particular type of receptor that accompanies performance of a task, as it was used in one study of dopamine binding during video game playing (Koepp, 1998).

The most common radioligands and transmitter systems studied are dopamine (particularly D2 receptors) using [^{11}C]raclopride or [^{123}I]iodobenzamide, muscarinic cholinergic receptors using [^{11}C]scopolamine, and benzodiazepines using [^{11}C]flumazenil. In addition, researchers have developed radioactive compounds that bind to serotonin, opioids, and a number of other receptors. Because the dynamics of radioligands are complex, researchers have developed a special class of mathematical models, called kinetic models, to describe their distribution. Kinetic modeling allows researchers to estimate how much of the radiolabeled compound is in the vasculature, how much is freely circulating in brain tissue, how much is bound to the specific receptor type under investigation, and how much is bound at nonspecific sites in the brain. Estimation of all these parameters requires a detailed knowledge of the properties of the specific substances used and of the way in which they act in the brain over time.

Gene Expression.   Very recently, new methods of both PET and fMRI have allowed researchers to investigate local gene expression within the living brain. Researchers can use PET to image the distribution of an enzyme in the brain by radiolabeling one of its substrate compounds. When the labeled substrate is converted into the enzyme, the label becomes trapped in tissue and emits a persistent signal that can be detected by the PET camera. One recent study used this method to label a substrate of an adenoviral enzyme that directs the expression of a particular gene in mice, thereby indirectly indexing gene expression (Gambhir et al., 1999).

Magnetic resonance spectroscopy provides a different way to image enzymes and biochemicals related to gene expression. The arrangement of atoms in their constituent molecules gives rise to very small inhomogeneities in the scanner's magnetic field. These magnetic variations alter the spectrum of energy that the atoms will absorb, giving rise to a characteristic frequency signature for various types of atoms. One research group used magnetic resonance spectroscopy to quantify the amount of fluorine-containing compounds related to expression of a particular gene (Stegman et al., 1999). A combination of creativity and specific knowledge of the relevant physics and biochemistry can lead to imaging solutions for a very large number of experimental questions.

Having provided a brief summary of these various techniques, we shall concentrate on PET and fMRI as they are used to measure changes in blood flow and oxygenation.

Limitations of PET and fMRI

Spatial Limitations.   Certain limitations restrict what both PET and fMRI can measure. Neither technique is good for imaging small subcortical structures or for doing fine-grained analysis of cortical activations. The spatial resolution of PET, on the order of 1 cm^3 to 1.5 cm^3, precludes experiments testing for neural activity in focused areas of the brain (e.g., mapping receptive fields of cells in visual cortex). The spatial resolution of fMRI is much greater: as low as 1 mm^3 but often on the order of 3 mm^3 for functional studies. The impact of this limitation in spatial resolution is that activation in some structures may be mislocated or missed entirely, although recent fMRI studies have reported activity in structures as small as the nucleus accumbens (Breiter et al., 1997). Also, fMRI techniques often cause distortions of the images in areas that are close to interfaces between tissue and air (e.g., the basal ganglia or areas of the frontal lobe that are adjacent to the sinuses).

Artifacts. Artifactual activations (i.e., patterns that appear to be activations but arise from nonneural sources) may come from a number of sources, some unexpected. One study, for example, found a prominent PET activation related to anticipation of a painful electric shock in the temporal pole (Reiman, Fusselman, Fox, & Raichle, 1989). However, it was discovered some time later that this temporal activation was actually located in the jaw; the subjects were clenching their teeth in anticipation of the shock!

As mentioned, fMRI signals are especially susceptible to artifacts near air and fluid sinuses and at the edges of the brain. Testing of hypotheses related to activity in brain regions near these sinuses, particularly orbitofrontal cortex and inferior temporal cortex among neocortical regions, is problematic using fMRI. Functional MRI also contains more sources of signal variation due to noise than does PET, including a substantial slow drift of the signal in time and higher frequency changes in the signal due to physiological processes accompanying heart rate and respiration (the high-frequency noise is especially troublesome for imaging the brainstem). The low-frequency noise component can obscure results related to a psychological process of interest and can produce false positive results, so it is usually removed statistically prior to

analysis. The low-frequency source of noise also makes it difficult to test hypotheses of slow changes during a session (e.g., effects of practice during scanning), although careful design still allows such issues to be tested (Frith & Friston, 1997).

Temporal Resolution and Trial Structure. Another important limitation of scanning with PET and fMRI is the temporal resolution of data acquisition. The details of this are discussed in later sections, but it is important to note here that PET and fMRI measure very different things over different time scales. Because PET computes the amount of radioactivity emitted from a brain region, at least 30 s of scanning must pass before a sufficient sample of radioactive counts is collected. This limits the temporal resolution to blocks of time of at least 30 s, well longer than the temporal resolution of most cognitive processes. Functional MRI has its own temporal limitation due largely to the latency and duration of the hemodynamic response to a neural event. Typically, changes in blood flow do not reach their peak until several seconds after a neural event, so the locking of neural events to the vascular response is not very tight.

Duty Cycle. A final limitation for both PET and fMRI has to do with what is often called the duty cycle of a task. To create a measurable hemodynamic response, the neural event must take up a substantial proportion of the time taken in any measurement period. For example, if only a small number of nerve cells fire for some process or if the duration of firing is small with respect to the temporal resolution of the measurement technique, then the signal-to-noise ratio for that event is low and may be difficult to detect. Although processes that elicit very brief neural activity, such as brief flashes of light, can be detected using neuroimaging, experiments need to be designed so that the process of interest occupies a substantial proportion of the measurement window of time.

As an example of how differences in duty cycle may cause problems, consider a hypothetical neuroimaging study of the Stroop task. In the task participants see a series of color words printed in colored ink, and they must name the color of the ink in which each word is printed. Words in a study may be congruent, in which case the color and the word match (e.g., "blue" printed in blue ink), or they may be incongruent, in which case the color and word are different (e.g., "blue" printed in red ink). In the PET scanner, participants alternate every 2 min between performing the task on blocks of congruent words and blocks of incongruent words. Suppose, for the sake of this example, that we present each word 500 ms after the participant responds to the previous word and allow participants to complete as many words as they can in a 2-min block.

By allowing the participants to perform at their own pace, we have created a duty-cycle problem. Participants are faster in the congruent condition, and they perform more congruent than incongruent trials during each 2-min scan. Accordingly, visual, motor, and other cognitive processes are becoming activated more frequently during the congruent scans than during the incongruent scans. As a result, participants spend more time planning and making vocal responses in the congruent conditions. Researchers comparing the incongruent to the congruent control blocks in an analysis of these data would likely find relative decreases in activation in Broca's area, motor cortex, and premotor cortex—all of which are related to response planning and execution. They might erroneously attribute these deactivations (which are really activations in the congruent condition) to the at-

tentive processes required to resolve conflict between mismatching ink colors and words. Alternatively, areas that *are* more heavily recruited in the incongruent than in the congruent condition might be missed: Even though the incongruent words produce higher peaks of activation in such areas, the congruent trials activate them more *frequently,* and the mean level of activation during the scanning block may be the same.

Duty cycle can be an insidious problem because it is often hard to know if participants are really spending the same amount of time on each task, which in turn makes it difficult to compare the tasks in a meaningful way. Consider a neuroimaging experiment that aims to study affect-related brain responses to viewing emotionally positive versus negative pictures. This study might show increases in extrastriate visual cortex activity for positive pictures relative to negative ones. Rather than being a brain area that participates in affect, however, the activation might be due only to the fact that participants fail to look at or attend as long to negative pictures because of their unpleasant content. The difference in the duty cycle of attention is a hidden confound that might make interpretation of this activation difficult without converging evidence from other sources.

Summary of Advantages of PET and fMRI

We have commented on the limitations of PET and fMRI, but we also need to point out their advantages when used as tools to measure the vascular response to neural events. Each has some unique features that makes it apt for certain types of experiment. Table 5.2 summarizes these advantages.

An inspection of the table shows that PET and fMRI have different characteristics that make each particularly suited to certain types of imaging questions.

Table 5.2   Relative Advantages of PET and fMRI

PET	fMRI
• Mapping of receptors and other neuroactive agents • Direct measurement of glucose metabolism • No magnetic susceptibility artifacts • Quiet environment for auditory tasks • Imaging near fluid spaces • Easily combined with ERP and other measurements because there is no magnetic field	• Repeated scanning • Single-subject analyses possible • Higher spatial resolution • Higher temporal resolution • Single trial designs • Estimation of hemodynamic response and separation of stimulus and task set related variables • Lower cost

A Road Map of a Neuroimaging Experiment

Before starting a neuroimaging experiment, several important decisions must be made. First, a specific hypothesis must be chosen, much as we described several hypotheses in the introduction to this chapter and how these led to imaging experiments. Second, appropriate methods must be selected; these choices will be constrained by the nature of the task chosen, the available imaging technology and its limitations, and the types of inferences one wishes to draw from the study. Third, an experiment must be conducted, analyzed, and interpreted. Here is an overview of some of the highlights in each of these steps, with details to follow.

The design of a task limits the ultimate interpretability of the data. Tasks must be chosen that yield theoretical insight into the neural and psychological processes under investigation, and they must avoid the influence of nuisance variables. Nuisance variables may be neural processes unrelated to the question of interest (either prescribed by the task or unrelated to it); they may be technological artifacts such as slow drift in the signal from an fMRI scanner; or they may be artifacts due to heart rate, respiration, eye movements, or other physiological processes. To the extent that nuisance variables influence the brain activations in a task, they will mitigate the uniqueness of an interpretation that one may

place on the data. That is, one would like to claim that neuroimaging activations are related to psychological process X, not that activations are related to process X or process Y or some physiological artifact such as irrelevant eye movements during a task. Constructing adequate tasks can be quite challenging, and it may not be possible in some situations.

Once a task is designed and data are collected, analysis of those data is composed of two important substages: preprocessing of the images and statistical analysis of the resulting activations. Preprocessing consists of several steps. Before statistical tests are performed, the various images in a set of data must be aligned to correct for head motion that may have occurred from one image acquisition to the next. Following alignment, images are often normalized to a standard template brain so that results from several subjects can be combined into averages and plotted in standard coordinates for comparison with other studies. Many researchers also smooth images, averaging activity levels among neighboring voxels to achieve smooth regions of activation. Although smoothing decreases the spatial resolution of the images, it helps to estimate and control for statistical noise.

Following these preprocessing stages, statistical tests are performed on the data. Most analyses are essentially variants of the general linear model. Studies are often analyzed using t tests that compare one or more experimental conditions of interest with a control condition. Slightly more complicated designs may use analysis of variance (ANOVA) with one or more factors. An increasingly popular technique uses multiple regression both to model the processes of interest and to take into account the influence of nuisance covariates. This kind of analysis constructs a covariate that contrasts periods when activity of interest is supposed to occur (i.e., the experimental condition in a blocked study or a neural response-evoking event in an event-related study) with control periods. Nuisance covariates are constructed in order to model the activity related to processes of no interest, such as heartbeat or processes included in the task that are of no theoretical relevance. The effects of the nuisance covariates are statistically removed from the data during the analysis, decreasing the statistical error and increasing the power of the analysis. With fMRI, signals at low spatial frequencies—essentially slow, random drift due to variations in the magnetic field—may produce artifacts in the data, so these are usually either modeled as nuisance covariates as well or filtered out before beginning the analysis.

With this brief summary, we are ready to launch into a more thorough treatment of experimental design. We do this by reviewing the various designs that have become popular in experiments using PET and fMRI measurement techniques. Following our description of these designs, we review techniques that can be used with these designs to contrast different experimental conditions.

Types of Experimental Designs

Blocked Designs

Because PET experiments demand long intervals of time (30 s or more) for collecting data sufficient to yield a good image, the standard experimental design used in PET activations studies is the blocked design. A blocked design is one in which different conditions in the experiment are presented as separate blocks of trials, with each block representing one scan during an experiment. Thus, the activations of interest in a PET experiment are ones that accumulate over the entire recording interval of a scan. If one is interested in observing the neural effect of some briefly occurring psychological process (e.g., the activation due to a briefly flashed light stimulus), in a PET experiment one would have to iterate the event repeatedly during a block of trials so that activations due to it accumulate over the recording interval of a scan. One could then compare the activations in this scan to an appropriate baseline control scan in which the event did not occur. Given the temporal limitation of this technique, PET is not well suited to examining the fine time course of brain activity that may change within seconds or fractions of a second.

The blocked structure of PET designs is a major factor in the interpretability of results. Activations related to slowly changing factors such as task set or general motivation are captured in the imaging study. This is an advantage if one wishes to image such effects. However, PET is not suited to imaging neural responses to individual stimuli. Even if such slowly changing processes are of interest, one must take care to elevate their duty cycle within a scan so that their neural signatures form a significant portion of the entire scan's processes.

Some researchers have made good use of differences in duty cycle as a way to circumvent some limitations of blocked designs (e.g., Garavan, Ross, Li, & Stein, 2000). These studies have used trial blocks with different percentages of certain trial types to capture a process of interest. For example, one might conduct a blocked study of a particular process of interest but parametrically vary the number of trials within the block that recruit that process. Rather than comparing blocks of the active task with rest, one might compare blocks in which the task of interest was performed, for example, on 80% of the trials with blocks in which the task of interest was performed on 20% of the trials.

Many studies using fMRI have also made good use of blocked designs. One advantage of a blocked design is that it offers more statistical power to detect a change—one estimate is that it offers four times the power of a single-trial design (authors, unpublished observations). As with PET, the ability to examine brain activations due to single trials is lost. Because the time to acquire a stable image is substantially less with fMRI than with PET, fMRI does allow one to conduct experiments in which activations due to single trials can be collected in a stable way. A sample of the MRI signal in the whole brain can be obtained in 2 to 3 s on average, depending on the way in which data are acquired and depending on the required spatial resolution of the voxels that are imaged. For studies that do not sample the whole brain, acquisition can be much more rapid: as low as 100 ms for single-slice fMRI. In fact, the limiting factor in the temporal resolution of fMRI is not the speed of data acquisition, but the speed of the underlying hemodynamic response to a neural event, which peaks 5 to 8 s after that neural activity has peaked.

Individual-Trial, Event-Related fMRI

To take advantage of the rapid data-acquisition capabilities of fMRI, researchers developed an event-related fMRI technique to create images of the neural activity related to specific stimuli or to cognitive events within a trial. The technique involves spacing stimuli far enough apart in time that the hemodynamic response to a stimulus or cognitive event is permitted to return to baseline before the onset of the next stimulus or event. Most researchers consider 14 to 16 s enough time for this to occur (Aguirre, Zarahn, & D'Esposito,

1998; Dale & Buckner, 1997), although some data have revealed that the hemodynamic response can persist somewhat longer (Boynton, Engel, Glover, & Heeger, 1996). Using this technique, signals from individual trials of the same task can be averaged together, and the time course of the hemodynamic response within a trial can be determined. This technique permits the randomization of trials from different conditions, which is essential for certain tasks. It also allows researchers to analyze only selected types of trials in a mixed trial block, enabling the study of error monitoring (to name one example) and a number of other processes that occur only on some trials.

Selective averaging provides one way around the temporal limitations imposed by the hemodynamic response function. By averaging across trials of the same type and by comparing these averages across different conditions, researchers can distinguish the time course of fMRI signals differing by as little as 100 ms. An example comes from the work of Aguirre, Singh, and D'Esposito (1999), who studied activation in the fusiform gyrus in response to upright and inverted faces. When they compared trials from the two conditions, they found that the BOLD response was shifted 100 ms later for inverted faces, paralleling increased reaction times to recognize inverted faces.

Another creative example of the added hypothesis-testing power of event-related fMRI comes from studies of episodic memory. Buckner et al. (Buckner et al., 1998) studied people encoding lists of words, and they subsequently tested the participants to see which words they remembered correctly. Functional MRI scanning during the learning of each word allowed the researchers to compare activity during the encoding of words that were successfully retrieved with the encoding of words that were later forgotten, revealing important differences.

Rapid Event-Related fMRI

More recent developments in event-related fMRI designs have made experimental trials more similar to those found in standard behavioral experiments (Zarahn, Aguirre, & D'Esposito, 1997). The main problem with the event-related design discussed earlier is that trials are very slow in pacing (12–16 s required between successive trials). It is possible to accelerate this pace substantially by making use of knowledge of the precise shape of the hemodynamic response function to a pulse of neural event. Various investigators have measured the nature of this response, and good models of it now are used routinely. Using prior knowledge of the typical hemodynamic response function, or measuring it individually for each subject, one can now perform experiments in which successive stimuli or cognitive events can be presented with as little as 750 ms intervening (Burock, Buckner, Woldorff, Rosen, & Dale, 1998; Dale & Buckner, 1997). Closely packed trials of a number of experimental conditions can then be presented in random order in a scanning interval. One then creates a model function that includes the timing of critical stimuli or cognitive events convolved with a model of the known or hypothesized hemodynamic response function. This convolved predictor function can then be used as a regressor in a multiple regression analysis, and the fit of the actual data to the expected pattern of BOLD signal can be measured. Of course, one would have several regressors to fit to the data, each one designed to predict the effect of one type of cognitive event (i.e., one condition). In this way, one can compare different regressors to examine which fit the data best, thereby accounting for the pattern of obtained activations. We describe this technique in more detail later.

This method has led to several important advances. One is the ability to space trials closely in time, resulting in a pacing that is more in line with the large body of literature in experimental psychology. Another is that the design minimizes the effects of fatigue, boredom, and systematic patterns of thought unrelated to the task during long intertrial intervals. In addition, the ability to obtain images of more trials per unit time, compared with individual event-related designs, counters the loss of power that occurs when using a single-trial design instead of a blocked design. This makes designs with closely packed trials more efficient than those with long intertrial intervals. Of course, if trials are spaced too closely, the ability to tell which part of the signal came from which type of trial is decreased, so there is a trade-off between the number of trials one can include and how much resolving power is lost. Some researchers have estimated that a 4-s intertrial interval is optimal for detecting task-related activations (Postle & D'Esposito, 1999), although much more research needs to be done on the specifications and limitations of this new technique.

An important element of these rapid event-related designs is that the intertrial interval must be varied from trial to trial. The ability to separate signals coming from different trial types when the hemodynamic responses to each trial overlap in time depends on jittering the time between trials and on either randomly intermixing trials of different experimental conditions or carefully counterbalancing their order. To get an intuition about how rapid designs allow one to discriminate the effects of different conditions, consider that with a randomized and jittered design, sometimes several trials of a single type will follow one another and that because the hemodynamic response to closely spaced events sums in a roughly additive fashion (although there are minor nonlinearities; e.g., Boynton et al., 1996; Dale & Buckner, 1997), the expected response to that trial type will build to a high peak. Introducing longer delays between some trials and shorter ones between others allows for the development of peaks and valleys in activation that are specific to particular experimental conditions. A regression model will be more sensitive to a design with such peaks and valleys than it will be to a design that has a uniform spacing of trials because one with peaks and valleys will create a unique signature for that type of trial. The effect of jittering is essentially to lower the effective temporal frequency of the design, so it is particularly appropriate for rapidly presented trials. Without jittering the intertrial interval, the neural events would occur too rapidly to be sampled effectively.

One problem with the hemodynamic response-convolution technique used in rapid event-related designs is that it is based on a predicted shape of the hemodynamic response. Therefore, if one misspecifies this response function, one will lose significant power in this experimental technique. This problem is especially acute when comparing different subject populations (e.g., older versus younger adults, or patients and normal controls) because their hemodynamic response functions may differ from one another (D'Esposito, Zarahn, Aguirre, & Rypma, 1999). One approach that researchers have used to avoid this problem is the measurement of hemodynamic responses in each individual subject, often by presenting brief flashes of light and measuring the BOLD response over the seconds following the stimulation in the primary visual cortex or by measuring the hemodynamic response in motor cortex to simple finger movements (Aguirre et al., 1998). Of course, this technique is best used when the region of interest in an experiment corresponds to the region in which the hemodynamic response is measured. If it does not, one must assume that the measured hemodynamic response in one region of the brain is equivalent to that in another region.

Techniques for Contrasting Experimental Conditions

For a psychologist, the main value of neuroimaging data is that they provide new tools for understanding psychological processes. For example, finding that premotor cortex is activated during the identification of tool-like objects opens up a new set of hypotheses about the nature of object recognition (Martin, Haxby, Lalonde, Wiggs, & Ungerleider, 1995). Likewise, finding that visual cortex is activated in blind individuals who perform tactile tasks suggests a set of hypotheses about the extent of plasticity in the sensory nervous system (Sadato et al., 1996).

Of course, the value of neuroimaging data to psychological inference depends on an accurate assessment of which brain regions are activated in any task. The problem with making inferences about cognitive processes from neuroimaging data is that nearly any task, performed alone, produces changes in most of the brain. To associate changes in brain activation with a particular cognitive process requires that we isolate changes related to that process from changes related to other processes. In short, it requires that we have contrasting experimental conditions that isolate the processes that interest us. One can understand how these contrasts can be designed without understanding details of data acquisition and analysis, topics that we treat in the final section of this chapter. However, one fact about data acquisition is particularly useful: Data in neuroimaging experiments are in the form of a matrix of signal intensity values in each region of the brain. The brain is divided up into voxels, typically 60,000 to 100,000 small volumes of brain tissue, whose size and number vary from study to study depending on the acquisition methods used to gather the data. These voxels are the elementary units of data; we assume that the signal in a voxel represents the neural activation in that region of the brain (more on the biophysics of that assumption later). The behavior of these voxels is the focus of an imaging experiment. Four techniques are most frequently used to study the behavior of brain voxels: subtraction, parametric variation, factorial designs, and correlational studies.

Subtraction

The first method devised for making inferences about psychological processes from neuroimaging data involves statistically comparing activations derived from an experimental condition with activations from a control condition that is putatively identical except that it does not recruit the process of interest. This is the subtraction method, the logic of which dates back to Donders (1868). The technique was first used by Posner and colleagues (Petersen, Fox, Posner, Mintun, & Raichle, 1988; Posner, Petersen, Fox, & Raichle, 1988) in a study of reading processes. The logic of subtraction is this: If one tests two experimental conditions that differ by only one process, then a subtraction of the activations of one condition from those of the other should reveal the brain regions associated with the target process. This subtraction is accomplished one voxel at a time. Together, the results of the voxel-wise subtractions yield a three-dimensional matrix of the difference in activation between the two conditions throughout the scanned regions of the brain. T tests can be performed for each voxel to discover which of the subtractions is reliable (of course, one needs to correct for the fact that multiple comparisons are being conducted—more about this later). The resulting parametric map of the t values for each voxel shows the reliability of the difference between the two conditions throughout the brain, and images of t maps or comparable statistics (z or F maps) are what generally appear in published reports of neuroimaging studies.

As an example of the implementation of subtraction logic, consider an experiment from our laboratory (Reuter-Lorenz et al., 2000) that was similar to the task shown in Figure 5.2. In the experiment of Reuter-Lorenz et al., subjects had to encode the locations of three target dots on a screen and store these in memory for 3 s, following which a single probe dot appeared and subjects had to decide whether the probe dot was in the same spatial position as one of the previous three target dots. In order to isolate processes of spatial storage, we constructed a control condition that was identical to this experimental condition, but with one difference: In the experimental condition, the retention interval was 3 s, whereas in the control condition it was 200 ms. We reasoned that a subtraction of the activations from the control condition from those of the experimental condition would then reveal the brain regions responsible for the extra storage required in the experimental condition.

In our experiment the logic of the subtraction method was fairly safe. In general, however, subtraction logic rests on a critical assumption that has been called the assumption of pure insertion (Sternberg, 1969). According to this assumption, changing one process does not change the way other processes are performed. Thus, by this assumption the process of interest may be *purely* inserted into the sequence of operations without altering any other processes. Although violations of subtraction logic have been demonstrated experimentally (Zarahn et al., 1997), the logic is still widely used because it greatly simplifies the inference-making process. If this assumption is violated, a difference in the observed neuroimaging signal between an experimental and a control condition may be due to one of these other altered processes rather than the process of interest.

To appreciate the difficulty of implementing subtraction logic in an experimental setting, consider a hypothetical study. In the experimental condition subjects must press a button every time they see a red stimulus; in the control condition they passively view the same stimulus sequence as in the experimental condition. The experimenter might assume that activity related to visual processing is the same in both conditions and that the two tasks differ only in that the first requires the execution of a response. Thus, when activations from the control condition are subtracted from those of the experimental condition, the experimenter may attribute the significantly activated areas to response-execution processes.

This conclusion has a number of flaws, and these provide some insight into the assumptions of subtraction logic. First, several processes vary at once, because the experimental condition includes an overt manual response as well as a cognitive decision to execute a response. We cannot know whether activated areas are related to the decision, to response preparation, to response execution, or to an interaction between two or more of those processes. In addition, the experiment may violate the assumption of pure insertion. When we assume pure insertion in this case, we assume that adding decision and response processes will not change the nature of the perceptual processing of the stimuli. However, making a stimulus relevant and causing attention to be directed to the stimulus alter perceptual processing in very early areas of visual cortex (Hopfinger, Buonocore, & Mangun, 2000; Hopfinger and Mangun, in press). Our naive experimenter may assume that activations in the occipital lobe revealed by the subtraction are related to the response process, when in fact those areas may be involved in processing the color of the stimuli, modulated by changes in attentional focus.

This example illustrates the difficulty in selecting experimental and control conditions appropriately. It also illustrates another point about subtraction logic. Several researchers have argued that pure insertion can be tested within the experiment, and that violations of pure insertion will appear as significant *decreases* in signal when the control task is subtracted from the experimental task (Petersen, van Mier, Fiez, & Raichle, 1998). Although this may be true in many cases, there are two problems with assuming that pure insertion is only violated in cases in which deactivations occur. First, it is difficult to tell whether decreases in signal are due to a violation of pure insertion (i.e., the control task includes a process that the experimental task does not) or to an actual inhibition of a certain brain area related to the process of interest. Second, our hypothetical example illustrates a case in which pure insertion may be violated, but the violation would produce no decreases in activity, just an increase unrelated to the process under investigation. Clearly, inferences about cognitive processes that rely on subtraction of activation in two conditions must be interpreted with caution.

Parametric Variation

Several approaches have been used to improve upon subtraction logic and to strengthen the credibility of inferences drawn from differences between conditions. One of these is parametric variation over several levels of a particular process of interest. Examples of experimental parameters that can be varied incrementally include the number of words to remember in a memory experiment, the percentage of a certain type of trial, or the time on task.

An example of this is the studies of working memory by Jonides et al. (1997) using the n-back task in a PET experiment. In the n-back task, participants see a string of letters appearing one at a time and must match each letter to the one that appeared n items back in the series. In separate conditions, the values of n varied from 1 to 2 to 3. A 0-back control condition required participants to indicate a match each time a fixed letter (e.g., "G") appeared. Encoding and response processes are common to all tasks, but the working memory load and the requirement to update information stored in working memory differ. Jonides et al. found that several regions varied in their activations systematically with variations in working memory load, as compared to other regions that showed no systematic variation. In a later experiment by Cohen et al. (1997) using fMRI, a finer dissociation was documented among the regions showing variation with working memory load. Some regions, such as posterior parietal cortex, showed monotonic increases in activity with increases in load, whereas dorsolateral prefrontal cortex (DLPFC) showed a step-function increase in activation from 1-back to 2-back, with no other differences in activation. Thus, the parametric technique permitted a fine discrimination of areas involved in working memory from other brain regions, and it permitted an examination of the details of activation differences even among the regions involved in working memory.

Another example of parametric variation is a study of the Tower of London task by Dagher, Owen, Boecker, and Brooks (1999). This task requires participants to make a sequence of moves to transfer a stack of colored balls from one post to another in the correct order. Participants must plan out a number of moves, devising them and storing them in memory in advance of completing the task. The experimenters varied the number of moves incrementally from 1 to 6. As shown in Figure 5.7, their results showed linear increases in activity in DLPFC across the six levels of the variable, suggesting that this area served the planning operations critical for Tower of London performance.

The power of parametric variation lies in two features. First, the reliance on pure insertion is weakened. Rather than assuming that insertion of a process does not change other processes, the logic assumes that altering the load on one process does not change other component processes in the task. Second, the results are more highly constrained because unlike a subtraction study, parametric variation permits one to make multiple comparisons among multiple levels of a variable (e.g., 1- vs. 2- vs. 3-back in the n-back task). This feature permits researchers to search for a pattern of change in activation across all

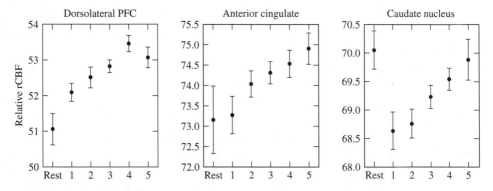

Figure 5.7   Measured rCBF responses in three areas across six conditions (one rest condition and five levels of increasing difficulty) in the Tower of London task.
NOTE: These areas showed linear increases in rCBF with increasing difficulty, whereas other areas (such as visual cortex) showed a response to task vs. rest but no changes among the five difficulty levels.
SOURCE: Reproduced from Dagher et al. (1999).

levels of a variable, such as a monotonic increase. Such a pattern renders more unlikely false positives and spurious activations due to improperly controlled variables.

Factorial Designs

Factorial designs are an extension of subtraction logic. Whereas the foundation of subtraction studies is the *t* test, factorial studies rely on factorial analysis of variance. Consider a simple factorial design from our studies of task switching presented in the introduction of this chapter. Our studies contained two types of switching, each varied independently: switching which of two mental counters was to be updated, and switching which of two operations (add or subtract) should be applied. This design is a simple 2×2 factorial, with two levels of counter switching and two levels of operation switching. The neuroimaging data from this experiment can be analyzed with a factorial ANOVA on a voxel-by-voxel basis and subsequently corrected for multiple comparisons. By testing for main effects, we would then be asking if each voxel is sensitive to switching counters, to switching operations, or to both. By testing for the interaction, we would be asking whether activity in the voxel was affected by both kinds of switch in a nonadditive fashion. For example, a voxel might be activated only when both counter-switch and operation-switch are required, signaling that this brain area might be involved in the coordination of two kinds of executive processes.

In principle, factorial designs suffer from the same problems as subtraction designs, but pooling activity across different levels of a factor may make the estimation of main effects more interpretable. Because main effects are estimated by collapsing across several conditions that share a common cognitive process of interest, activations due to cognitive components that vary among the conditions (e.g., idiosyncrasies of particular task conditions) will tend to wash out.

Another advantage of factorial designs is that they allow one to investigate the effects of several variables on brain activations. They also permit a more detailed characterization of the range of processes that activate a particular brain region (e.g., counter-switch only, operation-switch only, either, or both). Factorial designs also permit one to discover double dissociations of functions within a single experiment. To restate, a double dissociation occurs when one variable affects one brain region but not another, and when a second variable affects a second region but not the first. A factorial design is required in order to infer that a manipulation (e.g., counter switching) affected DLPFC but that a second manipulation (e.g., operation switching) did not.

Factors whose measurements and statistical comparisons are made within subjects, as are those just described, are within-subjects factors. When researchers examine differences between older and younger subjects, between normal individuals and members of a patient population, or between other groups, the subject group becomes a between-subjects factor because different levels of the factor are represented by different subjects. Because there are many reasons that two groups of subjects might differ in brain activation, researchers typically compare between-subjects differences in activation related to a specific task. This comparison involves first subtracting a control task from a task of interest within subjects and then comparing the different images between subjects. As an example, consider the fact that older and younger subjects differ in the amount of atrophy present in their brains, with older subjects typically showing some 15% more atrophy than younger subjects. To mitigate this difference in comparing activations between old and young, Reuter-Lorenz et al. (2000) tested older and younger subjects in a working memory task and a control condition. They then subtracted the activations of the control from the memory task and compared older and younger subjects on their differences in these subtracted activations. This technique allows one to remove statistically any effects of the differences in brain atrophy between the groups.

Correlational Studies

Correlational designs are often considered a weaker type of design from the perspective of making inferences because a correlation between two variables does not carry any information about the causal relationship between them. However, correlations have been used effectively in neuroimaging studies in several ways.

The most straightforward way is to examine the correlation of regional activation with behavioral performance variables. For example, Casey et al. (1997) found correlations between anterior cingulate activation and errors in a go/no-go task in children, suggesting that the anterior cingulate plays a role in response selection or inhibition. As another example, Lane et al. (1998) found that a region of anterior cingulate correlated with self-ratings of emotional awareness in women.

Another important way that researchers use correlations is by examining the interregional correlations among brain areas. A high correlation between two voxels is taken to be a measure of functional or effective connectivity—the tendency for two brain areas to be coactive (Frith & Friston, 1997). One recent trend is to examine the effects of different tasks on functional connectivity. For example, a study by Coull, Buchel, Friston, and Frith (1999) found that connectivity patterns were different between an attention-demanding task and rest, suggesting that attention changes the functional connectivity of the brain.

Although functional connectivity is often taken to mean the degree to which one brain area activates another, caution must be taken in the interpretation of such data, as with all correlational data. The data do not indicate which of two functionally connected areas sends output to the other, or if both are influenced by a third area as the cause of the correlations between the two.

Although functional neuroimaging data are often analyzed in terms of separate regions that are differentially active among conditions, most psychological processes that researchers may want to study do not map one to one onto unique brain regions. They are often served by processing in distributed networks of interconnected areas, some of which overlap and some of which do not. The mapping of regional correlations in conjunction with principal components analysis, described later, can be used to identify separate distributed networks that are related to different processes. Intuitively, voxels whose signals are correlated are grouped together to define a functional network in the brain, or spatial mode, which then becomes the unit of analysis for task-related effects. For example, Frith and Friston (1997) described a study in which they identified three distributed networks of brain areas that tended to be coactivated. One area was related to task performance; a second was related to the effects of practice within a session; and a third was related to magnetic artifact during the initial scans. The inference about which mode corresponds to which part of the task can be made by examining the pattern of activation that voxels in each spatial mode displayed. If the activity of most voxels in a spatial mode varies with the frequency of the task, one can infer that the mode is related to task performance. If the activity of the voxels varies in a linear fashion across the entire session, the spatial mode is likely to be related to practice or fatigue effects.

Another technique for examining networks of connectivity using correlational data is structural equation modeling. To use this technique, one creates an a priori model of expected patterns of connectivity and determines how well the data fit the prespecified theoretical model. This approach can be very useful for testing hypotheses about networks of activations that may be involved in a task. Marshuetz et al. (1999), for example, investigated the ability of a tripartite model of working memory to account for imaging data in working memory tasks, and they were able to compare this model to several others to determine which provided the best fit.

Kanwisher, McDermott, and Chun (1997) employed one particularly useful generalization of factorial designs to study face recognition. They identified an area on the fusiform gyrus that responded to pictures of faces and drawings of faces, but not to houses, scrambled faces, partial faces, facial features, animal faces, and other control stimuli. By presenting a large number of control stimuli of various types, Kanwisher et al. were able to infer that the brain area they studied was specific to the perception of faces. In general terms, they presented a number of different kinds of stimuli (each one a sort of factor, but without clearly defined levels) in an attempt to define which stimuli do and do not elicit a response from a region. In the case of face recognition, it was very important to use a wide variety of control stimuli, as it could be argued that face-specific activations are really related to the color, general shape, or spatial frequency of the stimuli. This technique is particularly powerful for ruling out alternative explanations based on variables of no interest (e.g., spatial frequency of visual stimuli) that are confounded with processes of interest (e.g., face perception).

We have now provided broad coverage of the motivation for using neuroimaging data and of the various techniques that can be used with PET and fMRI as the imaging tools. Having covered this ground, we are now prepared to examine the details of these two imaging modalities.

THE HOW: DATA ACQUISITION AND ANALYSIS

The Physics of PET and fMRI

Currently, functional neuroimaging techniques are based on the assumption that neuronal activity will cause changes in regional blood flow and metabolism that can be detected by the imaging technique of choice. If one discovers a regional change in blood flow or metabolism, then one infers that the neural activity in that region has changed. These changes in blood flow and metabolism are usually elusive and require sophisticated statistical analyses to distinguish a real signal from the surrounding statistical noise. Very often, the statistical analysis of functional imaging data requires corrections for different effects that are specific to the acquisition technique, so it is quite important that the investigator understand the physics and the details of the experiment. An array of methods for functional neuroimaging exists, each method constituting an area of research in itself. Unfortunately, an in-depth review of all the available techniques is beyond the scope of this chapter, so we focus on PET and fMRI. Our aim is to provide the reader with the background necessary for understanding the data acquisition process and the relationship between the acquisition and the analysis of functional data.

A Brief Summary of the Physics of PET

Positron-emission tomography is based on the detection of positrons emitted by a radioactive tracer that is injected into the subject. Some man-made isotopes decay by emitting positrons (subatomic particles having the same mass as an electron but the opposite charge—they are "antimatter electrons"). Some isotopes that emit positrons include ^{75}Br, ^{18}F, ^{11}C, ^{15}O, ^{13}N, ^{68}Ga, and ^{82}Rb, and they are usually made by bombarding the atoms with accelerated particles. The decay rate of such isotopes is quite fast, and their half-lives are on the order of a few hours or less. Oxygen-15, for example, is the isotope used most frequently in studies of blood flow using PET, and its half-life is approximately 2 min. This makes PET scans quite expensive because a cyclotron must be nearby in order to obtain a fresh supply of isotopes for the tracer.

When an emitted positron encounters an electron (from either the same isotope or from a neighboring atom), they collide. The result of this collision is that the positron and the electron are annihilated, and two photons get ejected in opposite directions from one another. Thus, the scanner does not directly detect the positrons themselves; rather, it detects the energy released by their annihilation. The laws of conservation of energy and mass dictate that the energy of the emitted photons be equal to the added masses of the electron

and the positron. The law of conservation of momentum predicts that the momenta of the emitted photons be equal, but in exactly opposite directions. The implications are that each emitted photon can be detected at around 511 keV (the equivalent mass of an electron), and that they must be detected *simultaneously* and *in pairs* by two detectors situated opposite one another. These two facts are important because they allow us to differentiate photons that arise from a positron annihilation from other sources of radiation, and they allow us to localize the annihilation.

Thus, in order to establish the location of an annihilation event as well as to make sure that the detected photons indeed came from an annihilation event, one needs a set of detector pairs placed around the source, the subject's head. Additionally, each pair of detectors must be wired to a coincidence detector circuit, as illustrated in Figure 5.8. The coincidence detector counts only the photons that are detected pairwise within a few nanoseconds of each other, and it dismisses other photons as background radiation. Ideally, the only photons detected are those that emerge from

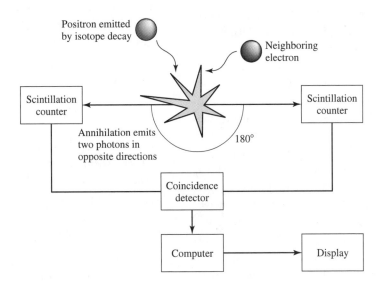

Figure 5.8   A schematic diagram of the main components of a PET scanner.

the annihilation of positrons in the tissue directly between the detectors in the pair. Unfortunately, photons from other locations can also be counted if they arrive simultaneously at the pair of detectors by sheer chance. To avoid detecting events that happen outside of the column of tissue between a given pair of detectors, small tubes (called septa or collimators) are usually placed around the detectors to shield them from radiation from the sides, while letting in the radiation from the front. Depending on the design, most PET scanners are made up of an array of detectors that are arranged in a circle around the subject's head, or in two separate flat arrays that are rotated around the subject's head by a gantry.

Using PET for Neuroimaging

When researchers inject a tracer into a subject, the tracer distributes itself through the brain and accumulates in some locations more than others, depending on the tissue and the nature of the tracer. Let's use a two-dimensional function $D(\mathbf{r})$ to describe the density of the tracer in a given slice of brain, where $\mathbf{r}$ is a vector that indicates a location in space. The coincidence detectors simply count the number of coincidences (and therefore the number of emitted positrons) detected by a pair of detectors during the scan time. Thus, the number of positrons that are counted by each pair of detectors around the subject is proportional to the amount of tracer in a column of tissue running between the two detectors, as shown in Figure 5.9. In essence, the raw data from a PET scanner are a set of projections of the function $D(\mathbf{r})$ onto the detector array at different angles, and the objective is to reconstruct the function $D(\mathbf{r})$ from the projections.

An intuitive way to think about the image formation process is to start with a blank image in which all the pixels have a value of 0. Next, one takes the individual intensities (number of counts) in one of the projections along a given angle and adds these values to

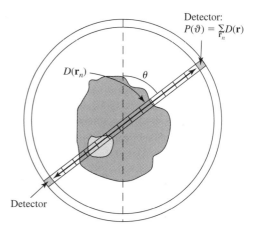

Figure 5.9 The PET scanner.
NOTE: Each detector counts the number of annihilation events that take place in a column of tissue. The column can be subdivided into smaller units that represent the image pixels. The detector counts the sum of the events in each of the elements in the column.

the image pixels along a line perpendicular to the projection, as illustrated in Figure 5.10a. We then move on to the next projection angle and repeat the procedure, adding the counts from the detectors along the new projection, and so on. The result is that different areas of the image will accumulate different numbers of counts from the projections, depending on the original distribution of the tracer in the plane, as shown in Figures 5.10b and 5.10c. This distribution of tracer density constitutes the image. Now, because neither the number of projections nor the number of pixels in the image is infinite, some severe artifacts will occur in the image, and one must compensate for them by applying different filters to the data. This method is referred to as *filtered backprojection*.

In practice, this procedure is usually implemented by using a Fourier transform. More rigorously, the projections can be described by

$$P(\theta) = \sum_{r} D(r) \cdot \Delta r$$

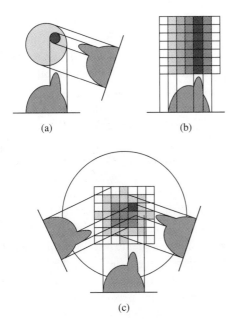

(a)   (b)

(c)

Figure 5.10   PET image reconstruction.
NOTE: The raw data are a set of projections (sums) at different angles as shown in *A*. "Backprojecting" the raw data onto the image means adding the numbers of counts in the projection to the pixels that are aligned with each point in the projection, as shown in *B*. An image can be obtained after the data from all the projections has been added, as shown in *C*.

where $P(\theta)$ is the projection, or sum of the counts through the columns at the angle θ. Each Δr constitutes a portion of the object along the projection, as shown in Figure 5.9. The function $D(\mathbf{r})$ can be reconstructed from all the projections, $P(\theta)$ by computing the inverse Fourier transform of the data. Thus, the two-dimensional function describing the density of the tracers in a slice of tissue being imaged is given by

$$D(r) = FT^{-1}\{r \cdot P(\theta)\}.$$

The reader should be aware that there are a number of other methods to reconstruct PET images, as well as corrections for scattering and other nuisances, that are beyond the scope of this chapter. We refer the user to the texts by Macovski (1983), Sandler (1995), and Bendriem and Townsend (1998) for greater details.

Thus, PET allows the investigator to determine a map of the density of a radioactive tracer by reconstructing an image from the projections of the different angles. The tracers are usually physiologically relevant molecules that are labeled radioactively. One can label tracers that flow through the tissue, such as water, or specific radioligands that will bind to specific sites. This is where the strength of PET resides: it allows the researcher to measure a number of parameters with spatial specificity depending on the choice of tracer. There are three classes of techniques in which PET is used, as summarized earlier. One is tracking regional cerebral blood flow; a second is tracking regional metabolism; and the third is tracking the binding of neurotransmitters to their receptors.

In most blood flow studies, radioactive water (H_2O^{15}) is injected intravenously, permitting measurement of blood flow by monitoring the passage of the labeled water through the tissue and measuring the uptake rate of the water into the tissue. Metabolism is measured using 18-fluorodeoxyglucose (FDG), a deoxyglucose molecule labeled with a radioactive 18-Fluorine atom. Just like glucose, it is taken up by tissue for energy production; one can identify regions of activity by monitoring its uptake rate. For studies of receptor binding, radioactive labels have been developed for several hundred compounds related to specific neurochemical systems in the brain. The major neurotransmitter systems are most commonly studied, and this is accomplished by attaching radioactive labels such as ^{11}C, ^{13}C (carbon), or ^{123}I (iodine) to a receptor agonist or antagonist. The researcher must exercise great care in selecting and imaging radiolabeled compounds because the observed signal level depends on the concentration of the radiolabeled substance in the blood, on the blood flow and volume, on the binding affinity of the substance to receptors, on the presence of other endogenous chemicals that compete with the labeled substance, on the rate of dissociation of the substance from receptors, and on the rate at which the substance is broken down by endogenous chemicals.

A Brief Summary of the Physics of fMRI

Functional MRI evolved from nuclear magnetic resonance (NMR), a technique employed by chemists and physicists since the 1940s to study quantum mechanics and to identify or characterize the structure of molecules (Bloch 1946; Hahn 1950; Purcell, Torrey, & Pound 1946). The raw signals in both NMR and fMRI are produced the same way. As we explain in more detail later, a sample is placed in a strong magnetic field and is radiated with a radiofrequency (RF) electromagnetic field pulse. The nuclei absorb the energy only at a particular frequency, which is dependent on their electromagnetic environment, and then return it at the same frequency. The energy is in turn detected by the same antenna that produced the RF field. In NMR experiments, the types of nuclei present in a molecule can then be identified and quantified by analyzing the frequency characteristics of the returned signal. In the 1970s researchers discovered that one could obtain spatial information about the nuclei emitting the radiation by manipulating the magnetic fields around the sample (Lauterbur, 1973; Mansfield & Pykett, 1978).

Let us now examine more closely the production of a signal in an NMR experiment and then proceed to how one can obtain spatial information from that signal to obtain an image. As most people know, the human body consists mostly of water, and the brain is no exception. Let us then consider the hydrogen atoms that are present in a water molecule. A hydrogen atom consists of a single pro-

ton and a single electron. Every proton has its own magnetic dipole moment represented by a vector. A magnetic moment is the amount of magnetization of an object, and it determines how strongly it interacts with magnetic or electric fields (a bar magnet is a dipole, and a very strong one would have a very large dipole moment).

When they are placed in a magnetic field, such as that of a magnetic resonance (MR) scanner, a portion of the protons (or spins, as they are often referred to in the literature) will align with or against the magnetic field. A couple of things should be kept in mind about this alignment. First, the larger the magnetic field, the greater the proportion of spins that are aligned, which makes the alignment easier to detect. Second, whether the spins are aligned with or against the field is determined by their spin quantum number, which can have values of $+1/2$ and $-1/2$. Being aligned with the magnetic field takes less energy than being aligned against it, so a greater number of spins will be aligned in the direction of the field.

Magnetic dipoles are represented by vectors. The interaction between the main magnetic field (usually labeled $\mathbf{B}_0$) with the proton dipole produces a set of forces that result in the *precession* of the dipole. Precession of a vector is a movement that takes place such that the origin of the vector stays fixed, whereas the tip spins and describes a circle around a vertical axis, as shown in Figure 5.11. The vectors representing the magnetic moment of the $+1/2$ spins will precess about the magnetic field, and the $-1/2$ spins will precess about the opposite direction of the magnetic field. The rate of precession, ω_0 (i.e., the angular velocity of the spins' precession) is proportional to the magnetic field $\mathbf{B}_0$, as described by

$$\omega_0 = \gamma \cdot B_0$$

where γ is a constant called the gyromagnetic ratio. This nicely linear relationship between

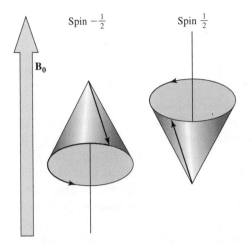

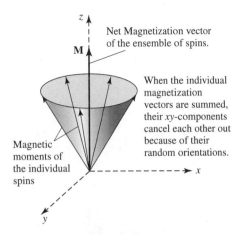

Figure 5.12 The spin ensemble.

The magnetic moment of the spins precesses around the axis of the main magnetic field ($\mathbf{B_0}$). Its orientation is determined by their quantum state.

Figure 5.11 Representation of the proton's magnetization.

the precession frequency and the magnetic field is a key factor that, as we will see, enables us to obtain spatial information about the sample by simple manipulations of the magnetic field. The gyromagnetic ratio is specific for the nucleus in question (a hydrogen nucleus's γ is 42.58 MHz/T), which can allow us to obtain NMR signals from specific nuclei without interference from other nuclei. The molecular environment around the nuclei (the number of electrons present, the proximity of other nuclei, etc.) can change the $\mathbf{B_0}$ field around the nuclei and thus alter their precession rate, as predicted by the previous equation (which is how one can make inferences about the molecular structure of a molecule that contains protons).

Let us now consider the *net* magnetization vector of a population of spins. Together, the spins' magnetization vectors add up to a single magnetization vector that is aligned with the magnetic field (see Figure 5.12). Because the x and y components of the magnetic moments are randomly oriented at any given time, they cancel each other when all the

vectors in a large population are added together. Thus, all that remains is the component that is parallel to the magnetic field along the z-axis (remember that more spins align with the field than against it).

Now that we have a picture of the behavior of the magnetic moments of water protons in a large magnetic field ($\mathbf{B_0}$), let us consider what happens when a second magnetic field ($\mathbf{B_1}$) is applied in a direction perpendicular to the main magnetic field. This $\mathbf{B_1}$ field is generated by the transmitter coil in magnetic resonance experiments, and it rotates at a particular frequency. If the $\mathbf{B_1}$ field rotates at the precession frequency of the spins, it looks to them like a stationary magnetic field because they are both rotating at the same rate. In fact, to simplify things, one can look at the whole system from a rotating frame of reference. Consider how things look when one rides a carousel. The other children do not seem to be moving, but their parents and anything outside the carousel do. In this rotating frame of reference, we now have a magnetization vector, $\mathbf{M}$, which is aligned with the main magnetic field, $\mathbf{B_0}$, and a second magnetic field $\mathbf{B_1}$, which is rotating in the laboratory frame of reference but is stationary in our new rotating frame of reference. According to classical physics, the

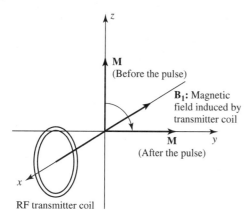

Figure 5.13 Tipping the magnetization vector from the z-axis onto the xy-plane.
NOTE: The duration and strength of the B_1 field determine how far the vector is tipped (i.e., the "flip angle").

B_1 field will exert a torque on the magnetization vector such that it is rotated onto the x-y plane at an angular velocity determined by the magnitude of $\mathbf{B}_1$. This is illustrated in Figure 5.13.

In our rotating frame of reference, after we turn the $\mathbf{B}_1$ field off, the magnetization vector is stationary on the x-y plane, but relative to the real world, the magnetization vector is rotating about the z-axis on the x-y plane at an angular velocity ω_0. A property of classical electromagnetism is that changes in a magnetic field will induce electrical currents in a wire coil. The antenna used for transmission of the RF pulse is such a coil, and when the magnetization vector rotates through it, it induces a current. This current induced in the coil is the NMR signal that we observe. The induced current oscillates at the frequency of the angular rotation of the magnetization vector (this is the same frequency that is used to transmit the RF pulse, also called the resonance frequency).

When the transmitter is turned off after the application of a pulse, the magnetization vector will relax back to its equilibrium posi-

tion. This relaxation happens through several mechanisms: Spin-lattice relaxation occurs as the spins give away their energy and return to their original quantum state. This translates into the longitudinal (i.e., along the z-axis) component returning to its equilibrium value at a rate T_1. Spin-spin relaxation happens along the transverse (i.e., on the x-y plane) component of the magnetization vector and is due to the ensemble of spins falling out of phase with each other and thus adding destructively to the net magnetization vector, as illustrated in Figure 5.14. These two mechanisms are often referred to as T_1 and T_2 relaxation, respectively.

Another kind of relaxation is caused by inhomogeneities in the magnetic field at the microscopic level. If there are variations in the magnetic field, there will also be variations

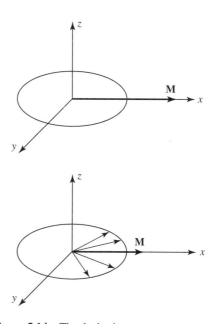

Figure 5.14 The dephasing process.
NOTE: This process occurs because all the spins in the ensemble do not precess at the exact same rate. Some of them get ahead, and some of them lag behind. The net effect is that they start canceling each other out, shortening the length of the magnetization vector.

in the individual protons' precession frequencies, which cause the ensemble to lose phase coherence faster than expected due to simple T_2. This change is referred to as T_2^* (pronounced "T-2-star"). The relaxation rate constants T_1, T_2, and T_2^* are dependent on a number of properties of the nuclei themselves and of their environment at the molecular level. This is quite useful in several ways. The relaxation constants can be used to identify the nuclei in an NMR spectroscopy experiment, or they can provide a mechanism for image contrast between different tissues, such as white and gray mater, or lesions, when performing an imaging experiment. For example, T_1-weighted images are acquired with parameters such that the image contrast between tissues is mostly determined by their T_1 relaxation rate. An example of the same slice of tissue imaged with T_1 and T_2 weighting can be seen in Figure 5.15; as one can see, the images look strikingly different. Changing the contrast mechanism can be very useful in differentiating brain structures or lesions because some structures will be apparent in some kind of images but not in others. For example, multiple sclerosis lesions are virtually invisible in T_1-weighted images but appear very bright in T_2-weighted ones.

From the NMR Signal to Neuroimaging

Now that we have an idea of how a signal is produced, let us take a look at how we can extract spatial information from it to form an image. We mentioned earlier that the precession frequency of the spins (and thus their resonance frequency) was proportional to the strength of the magnetic field. Now, consider what happens when we apply another magnetic field in the direction of $\mathbf{B}_0$, but one that varies linearly with location along the x-axis (This is referred to as a magnetic field gradient in the x direction). What we have now is a magnetic field whose intensity changes in direct proportion to the location in space along the x-axis. Because the magnetic field strength varies with the position in space, the resonance frequencies of the spins also vary with their position in space (recall the equation $\omega_0 = \gamma \, \mathbf{B}_0$).

Thus, if we tip the spins onto the x-y plane with a $\mathbf{B}_1$ pulse and then turn on a magnetic field gradient, the signal that we get back from

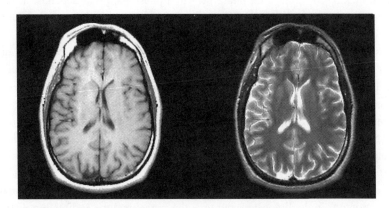

Figure 5.15   The same slice of brain tissue can appear very different, depending on which relaxation mechanism is emphasized as the source of the contrast in the pulse sequence.
NOTE: Using long echo times emphasizes T_2 differences between tissues, and shortening the repetition time emphasizes T_1 differences in tissue. Left: one slice of a T_1 image. Right: the same slice acquired as a T_2 image.

the sample will not simply oscillate at the resonant frequency, as we described earlier. It will be a more complex signal made up of the sum of the signals generated by the tissue at different locations along the x-axis, and thus oscillating at different frequencies. This technique is usually called frequency encoding.

The contribution of each frequency component of the signal is proportional to the magnitude of the magnetization vector at the corresponding location. Therefore, if we can separate the different frequency components of the signal, we will get the distribution of magnetization across the x-axis in space. Luckily, there is a mathematical technique designed to do exactly that: The Fourier transform separates a function into its frequency components, providing a distribution of how much each component contributes to the original function.

In reality, things are a bit more complex. Because the spins at different locations along the x-axis are precessing at different rates in the presence of the gradient, their magnetization vectors get out of phase with each other, causing the net x-y magnetization to decay quickly. The spins can be brought back into phase in two different ways. One could reverse the gradient, making the spins gain phase in the opposite direction, but at the same rate as during the dephasing period. At some point, the spins will regain their phase coherence, inducing a signal on the receiver coil. This signal is called a gradient-echo. Alternatively, one could also apply another RF pulse to rotate the magnetization 180 degrees, then reapply the original gradient, such that the spins regain their phase coherence, as shown in Figure 5.16.

We have seen how we can obtain spatial information along a single dimension, but to form an image we need to extract the distribution of proton densities along at least two dimensions. We need to devise a method to encode the spatial information along both the

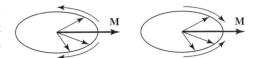

Gradient echo technique: A gradient in the magnetic field causes the spins to lose phase coherence. Reversal of the gradient causes them to regain it.

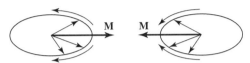

Spin echo technique: Spins are dephased by the gradient. After application of a 180° pulse, all the spins are rotated about the y-axis, and the application of the same gradient causes the spins to regain coherence along the negative x-axis.

Figure 5.16   Refocusing of the spins by gradient echoes and spin echoes.

x- and y-axes. The way to do that is to perform frequency encoding along the x-axis, as before, with an additional brief gradient field applied in the y-direction. This second gradient causes the precession of the spins to get a little bit ahead (or gain phase) depending on where they are along the y-axis. Recall that applying a gradient causes the spins to precess faster or slower depending on their location, so a short gradient pulse causes them to change their precession rate briefly, resulting in a phase gain that depends on the location of the spins along the y-axis and the duration of the gradient pulse.

The sequence is repeated a number of times, increasing the magnitude of the phase encoding gradient, so that we can get a whole distribution of phase gains along the y-axis. The end result is a set of echoes acquired with a distribution of phase gains along the y-direction. This forms a two-dimensional data set that contains the x-direction distribution of densities encoded in frequency along the x-axis and the y-direction distribution of densities encoded in phase along the y-axis. The Fourier transform of this raw data image along both the horizontal and vertical dimensions produces an image of the magnetization vector across the imaging plane. Before the Fourier transform, the data are said to be in K space, and the objective of most MR imaging techniques is to sample this K space. Once we have an image of K space, forming an image of the brain is as simple as applying the Fourier transform to the data.

It is very useful to have such an image of the magnetization vector across tissue because a number of tissue-specific properties affect the magnetization and thus provide a contrast between different kinds of tissues. These include the water content as well as the T_1, T_2, and T_2^* relaxation rates. As mentioned, the pulse sequence parameters can be manipulated to emphasize the contrast due to any of those properties individually.

There are many different ways to form an image using MR, and we have discussed only one of them in order to give the reader an idea of the principles underlying the formation of an MR image. Acquiring individual gradient or spin echoes in the traditional way, with their many individual phase encoding repetitions, simply takes too long for functional imaging. Thus, we must resort to alternative techniques that will acquire the raw K space data faster. Most commonly, one tries to acquire each plane of K space with a single excitation of the tissue. Such techniques are referred to as echo planar, and the most commonly used ones are called echo planar imaging (EPI) and spiral imaging. The specifics of these are beyond the scope of this chapter; for a more rigorous treatment of the subject of MR imaging techniques, we refer the reader to excellent texts such as Nishimura (1996) or Elster (1994).

Functional MRI Using the BOLD Effect

Let us now explore how we can use MR imaging to obtain functional images by taking advantage of the BOLD effect. Functional studies can be made because the intensity of the water signal depends on many parameters, as mentioned earlier. Among those parameters are the water density and the T_2^* relaxation rate of the tissue. Hemoglobin in blood can take two different conformations, depending on whether it is oxygenated. In the deoxygenated state, iron atoms are more exposed to the surrounding water, creating small distortions in the $\mathbf{B}_0$ field. The magnetic susceptibility of a substance is its ability to distort a magnetic field, and it affects the relaxation constant T_2^*. Thus, the magnetic susceptibility of hemoglobin is higher when it is in its deoxygenated state, and this change in susceptibility translates into a shortening of the T_2^* of the deoxygenated blood (Ogawa, Lee, Kay, & Tank, 1990).

When brain tissue becomes active, it requires more oxygen than when it is at rest. In order to accommodate this need, a blood flow increase raises the amount of oxygenated blood to the tissue. During periods of activation, the increase in blood flow brings in more oxygenated blood, decreasing the concentration of deoxyhemoglobin. Thus, the increases in blood flow and blood volume contribute to an increase in signal, and the increase in magnetic susceptibility increases the amplitude of the water signal. The net result is an increase in signal following activation. It is important to realize that the degree to which the blood flow and the deoxyhemoglobin content are coupled can vary, and modeling the exact properties of the BOLD response is currently a topic of intense research (Buxton, Wong, & Frank, 1998; Frahm, Merboldt, Hanicke, Kleinschmidt, & Boecker, 1994; Vazquez & Noll, 1998).

An alternative technique is to measure changes in blood flow alone using arterial spin labeling (ASL) techniques (Detre, Leigh, Williams, & Koretsky, 1992; Kim, 1995; Williams, Detre, Leigh, & Koretsky, 1992), which are based in magnetic resonance imaging techniques and mimic PET blood flow techniques by tracking the passage of a tracer through the tissue. In the case of PET, the tracer is a radioactive substance that is injected intravenously. In the case of ASL, the tracer is simply the water in the arterial blood, which is magnetically labeled by an RF pulse. The label consists of tipping the arterial water's magnetization vector all the way to the negative z-axis by a $\mathbf{B}_1$ pulse that is applied somewhere upstream from the tissue of interest. As those inverted spins flow through the tissue, they can be detected by changes in the signal intensity of the image. A number of limitations render the technique impractical for many applications, but overcoming these limitations is a growing area of research (Kim 1995; Gonzalez, Alsop, & Detre, 2000; Wong, Buxton, & Frank, 1997), and the technique will likely soon become a powerful tool for functional studies.

Diffusion Tensor Imaging

Diffusion tensor imaging can be used to explore questions about connectivity among brain regions by identifying the orientation of white matter tracts. The technique produces images whose intensity is dependent on the diffusion of the tissue water, and this can yield information about the orientation of the tissue fibers. For example, in the case of a pot of water, the water molecules are equally likely to diffuse in all directions, except near the walls, which restrict the movement of the water molecules. If we were to put some lasagna noodles into the pot of water such that they lay flat on top of each other, the water would be more likely to move horizontally than vertically because the water molecules would be more likely to bump against the lasagna noodles when they try to move vertically than when they try to move horizontally. Similarly, the geometry of the white matter tracts in the brain running parallel between two different structures restricts the diffusion of water molecules along all directions *perpendic-*

ular to the direction of the tracts. As we soon discuss, the diffusion of the spins can affect the MR signal. We can take advantage of this phenomenon to obtain images that are sensitive to the microscopic geometry of the tissue, even though MR images do not afford the resolution to see the actual microscopic structures.

In an imaging experiment, when a spin moves in the presence of a magnetic field gradient, its precession frequency varies depending on its location along that gradient, as we saw earlier. That means that it acquires a phase difference in its rotation relative to the rest of the ensemble of stationary spins (recall that *acquiring phase* means that the magnetization vector for that spin gets ahead of the rest). If all spins move together in the same direction and at the same speed, then they all acquire the same amount of phase coherently, and the magnitude of the net magnetization vector is altered. However, in the diffusion process movement occurs randomly and incoherently among the spins in the ensemble, so the net effect is a signal loss because some of the moving spins will gain and some will lose phase, depending on which direction they move. The degree of attenuation seen in the signal is related to the freedom of movement of the water molecules in the direction of the applied gradient, as well as to the duration and magnitude of that gradient.

This has found a number of applications for clinical imaging, such as providing information about membrane integrity in brain tissue cells. It can also give information about the orientation of the tissue through acquiring diffusion tensor images. Diffusion tensor images are produced by applying diffusion gradients during the imaging process in different combinations of the x, y, and z gradients. The result is a set of images that are weighted according to the restriction of water movement along the direction of the applied gradient combination. (Le Bihan, 1995; Moseley et al., 1990).

Consider again the shape of white matter tracts. If two areas are functionally connected, then one can expect that there are a large number of tracts running between the two areas. If in a region of tissue there is a large number of tracts running parallel, then the diffusion of water is less restricted along that direction because the water molecules are more likely to collide against fibers when they move in directions other than those of the fibers. Thus, by obtaining images whose intensity is proportional to the diffusion coefficient of water in a particular direction in space, one can obtain information about how the tissue is structurally laid out, giving information about what regions of the brain are structurally interconnected.

The Biophysics of PET and fMRI

We have described several ways that changes in blood flow and oxygenation can be detected by neuroimaging scanners. Critical to the undertaking is the assumption that these changes reliably result in a signal that can be detected by a scanner. However, before this signal change can be interpreted as neural activation, another critical assumption must be justified: the assumption that changes in blood flow and oxygenation reflect changes in neural activity.

Roy and Sherrington (1890) were the first to hypothesize a connection between blood flow and neural activity. Since then, researchers have investigated at length the mechanism behind the relationship between blood flow and neural activity. For example, Shulman and Rothman (1998) have proposed that increased glucose uptake is controlled by astrocytes, whose end-feet contact the endothelial cells lining the walls of blood vessels. Glutamate, the primary excitatory neurotransmitter in the brain, is released by some 60% to 90% of the brain's neurons. When glutamate is released into synapses, astro-cytes absorb it and transform it into glutamine. When glutamate activates the uptake transporters in an astrocyte, it may signal the astrocyte to increase glucose uptake from the blood vessels. Vasodilation, resulting in increased blood flow and increased oxygen consumption, may be coupled to neural activity through similar mechanisms. If it is only glutamate release that triggers the vascular, oxygen, and glucose uptake effects, then activation is excitatory. However, release of GABA (gamma amino butiric acid) or other inhibitory neurotransmitters could trigger these responses as well. Further research is needed before firm conclusions are reached about what specific changes produce the observed changes in blood flow or BOLD signal.

Also, importantly, the relationship between neural activity and glucose uptake indicates that the neuroimaging signal reflects activity in the neuropil, at the synapses where neurotransmitters are released, and not in the brain regions containing cell bodies. A neuroimaging signal may therefore be related to increased *input* in an area, which may lead to increased output from that area to other local or remote brain regions. If a task activates DLPFC, for example, it means that DLPFC is receiving substantial input from other areas. That input could be excitatory or inhibitory.

Although there is still uncertainty about the exact mechanism by which a neuroimaging signal is produced, sufficient evidence has been collected that we may proceed forward with reasonable confidence. In the end, all the available indices of neural activation—rCBF, oxygen uptake, or glucose utilization—may be suitable for most studies of psychological function.

Statistical Analysis of Neuroimaging Data

Armed with a general understanding of the physical information contained in PET and fMRI images, we are now in a position to extract information about brain function from our imaging studies. In the case of PET, images will be acquired under different experimental conditions, and their signal intensity will be dependent on the amount of tracer present in each voxel. In the case of fMRI, the signal intensity will be dependent on the BOLD response (based on oxygenation and blood flow). The task at hand for analysis of the signal is primarily to identify those voxels whose activity matches a predicted model, be it a model due to subtraction logic, parametric variation, factorial manipulation, or correlation. Because fMRI has become the dominant modality for the collection of data about rCBF, we focus our discussion on the analysis of data from an fMRI experiment. However, most of the principles apply to PET as well.

The General Linear Model

Consider an ideal experiment in which a subject's brain is inactive when there is no task to perform and is activated only by an experimental task of interest. Each time the task is performed, a set of physiological events takes place in a functional region resulting in a BOLD response, as described earlier. To simplify the statistical analysis, we approximate the behavior of brain tissue as a linear, time-invariant system, whose input is the task and whose output is the BOLD response. Thus, for our ideal experiment the input function can be considered as a train of spikes corresponding to the psychological events involved in the task (e.g., encoding stimuli, making decisions, executing responses). Each of these events may cause neural tissue somewhere in the brain to become activated, which in turn causes hemodynamic changes. As with any linear, time-invariant system, the output (change in signal intensity in any voxel of the brain) is described by the convolution of the input (a function describing the train of

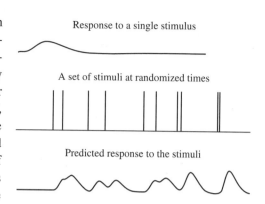

Response to a single stimulus

A set of stimuli at randomized times

Predicted response to the stimuli

Figure 5.17 The BOLD response to a single event is shown in the top portion of the figure. NOTE: This is commonly referred to as the hemodynamic response function (HRF). A train of events, like the one shown in the middle figure, would produce a BOLD response like the one shown in the bottom part of the figure.

events) with the system's transfer function (a function that describes the hemodynamic response to a single stimulus). Figure 5.17 shows the response to a single stimulus, as well as the response to a train of stimuli occurring at random times.

By design, psychological events from different conditions of an experiment may be intermingled, as in an event-related design, or they may be grouped into epochs, as in a blocked design. Under the assumptions of a general linear model, different tasks constitute different input functions that give rise to their own BOLD responses. So, if one constructed an experiment with different conditions (i.e., different tasks) intermingled in an event-related design, one could construct different input functions to model the output function. In order to create a more realistic model for the observed signal, one must also include other input functions for such variables as drift in the scanner signal, effects due to motion of the subject, effects of respiration and heart rate, and other nuisance variables. Thus, the observed signal from a voxel can be thought of as a sum of weighted functions corresponding to the different predicted effects. Some of these effects are of interest, some are not, and the weights of those functions are a set of scalar parameters that determine the amplitude of those functions. For example, if our model is made up of effects that are represented by functions $x_1(t)$, $x_2(t)$, $x_3(t) \ldots$, and each of these is weighted by a coefficients β_1, β_2, $\beta_3 \ldots$, then the *predicted* signal is given by

$$y(t) = \beta_1 \cdot x_1(t) + \beta_2 \cdot x_2(t) + \beta_3 \cdot x_3(t)$$
$$+ \cdots + \varepsilon_1 + \varepsilon_2 + \varepsilon_3 + \cdots$$

where the ε germs represent the error. All of this can be expressed in matrix form as

$$Y = \beta X + E$$

where Y is the observed signal in a given voxel expressed as a vector whose elements are the individual time observations, X is a matrix whose columns contain the individual functions that make up the model, β is a vector containing the weights of the individual component functions, and E is the residual noise in the measurement. The matrix X is often referred to as the design matrix and displayed as an image whose intensities correspond to the values of the elements, as shown in Figure 5.18. Our tasks in the analysis are to obtain an estimate for β and to identify the voxels that fit the estimated model.

It can be shown that β can be estimated by

$$\hat{\beta} = (X^T X)^{-1} X^T Y.$$

Note that $\hat{\beta}$ is used to represent the estimated value of β. Now, what remains is to test each individual voxel in the image to see which ones fit the model described by Y and $\hat{\beta}$. This can be accomplished by computing the significance of the estimate of the coefficient. Depending on the statistical approach taken, one can obtain a T or F score for the correlation. In the simplest case, when there is only a single coefficient and a baseline intensity, this

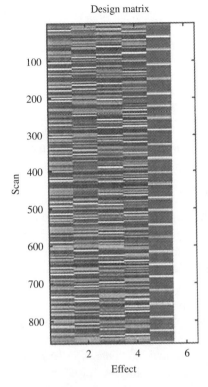

Design matrix

Scan

Effect

Figure 5.18   The design matrix.
NOTE: The design matrix should include all the significant effects that are present in the experiment. Each effect is represented by a column of data containing the expected time series that one would see if that were the only effect present.

is identical to performing a linear regression analysis of the data and the model.

One could ask many questions using the same model; in fact, one can test for the presence of any given linear combination of the covariates contained in the design matrix's columns by multiplying the parameter estimates by a *contrast* vector **c**. This vector contains additional weights to be multiplied by the parameter estimates in the vector β. In the design matrix shown in Figure 5.18, for example, we could test for the voxels in which the activity in the first condition minus the activity in the second condition is significant, while disregarding all other effects as nuisance covariates, by using a contrast [1 −1 0 0 0 0].

If the difference is significant, this would imply that the first covariate's intensity is greater than the second's.

Statistical Inference from the General Linear Model

As usual with all statistical procedures, we must calculate the significance of the correlation between the model and the data in each voxel (whether it is a correlation coefficient or a T, F, or Z score). This is usually done by calculating the probability of obtaining that value by sheer chance, given the probability distribution of the statistic. In neuroimaging, however, we must be aware of the fact that there are hundreds of thousands of voxels in an image, so a number of them are bound by chance to be correlated to the design matrix. If the voxels' signals were independent of each other, we could compute a Bonferroni correction of the significance level, but that is not usually the case because the voxels tend to be correlated with their neighbors. Additionally, the Bonferroni correction tends to be very conservative. Instead, we must come up with a method for examining the statistical image (made up of T values or such) and calculating the likelihood of having a *cluster* of voxels above a given threshold. Random fields theory does exactly that. Based on the assumption of Gaussian-distributed background noise in an image, we can measure the spatial characteristics of the distribution in three dimensions, and from those measurements we can make predictions about the number of clusters expected to appear significant in the statistical image just by chance.

The Euler characteristic of a solid geometric figure is a measure of how many of its elements are connected together and how many holes exist within it. As it turns out, the expected Euler characteristic of a thresholded statistical image is a good approximation of the likelihood that a cluster of voxels above a certain threshold will occur by chance in a random image. The calculation of the expected Euler characteristic is based on a calculation of the smoothness of the image, and is beyond our scope. The smoothness of an image is a measure of how many independent measurements exist within the image. These independent measurements are referred to as resels (short for resolution elements). This sort of technique has great applications in the analysis of noisy imaging data, when the objective is to identify significant clusters (not just in functional neuroimaging, but in astronomy as well). For greater detail on the calculation of the smoothness of the image and the Euler characteristic, see Worsley and colleagues (Worsley, Evans, Marrett, & Neelin, 1992; Poline et al., 1995; Worsley et al., 1996); Petersson, Nichols, Poline, and Holmes (1999); and Friston, Holmes, Price, Buchel, and Worsley (1999).

Assumptions

The main assumption underlying the general linear model is that the BOLD response to a set of neuronal processes is a time-invariant, linear combination of those processes. A time-invariant system is one whose response to a given input is always the same, regardless of the previous events. Linearity means that if two separate inputs are applied to the system, its response will equal the sum of the individual responses to those inputs. It is becoming increasingly clear that the BOLD response is neither linear nor time-invariant (Boynton et al., 1996; Buxton & Frank, 1998; Vazquez & Noll, 1998), but these violations are not severe within reasonable boundary conditions.

Because of the necessity of evaluating significance for the computed statistics, the general linear model is also heavily dependent on the theory of Gaussian random fields, whose main underlying assumption is that the residual variance in the images after applying a model is distributed normally, and that each voxel's signal is independent of the signal in other voxels. Unfortunately, for both PET and fMRI, the signal intensity in one voxel is always contaminated by the signal of other voxels. In the case of PET, the correlation is due to scattering of the positrons and to smoothing of images during data preprocessing. In the case of fMRI, it is largely a function of limitations in resolution and of any smoothing that is done during preprocessing. Thus, one must take care that these correlations are not serious contaminants of the data, and the data must be spatially smoothed, as described later.

Pitfalls

A major concern in the analysis of fMRI data is that the BOLD effect is a vascular one, not an electrochemical one. It is a response to the underlying neuronal activity, and it distorts that neuronal activity to the extent that it does not mimic it directly. The limitations here are ones of time and space. In time, the hemodynamic response lags behind the neuronal response by as long as several seconds, and it is stretched out longer than the neuronal response as well. In space, the blood flow changes that are measured may or may not be in the immediate neighborhood of the underlying neuronal response that caused them because the vasculature is not tuned precisely to the spatial location of the neural tissue to which it is responding. Thus, to have a good idea of when and where a neural response occurred, one needs to have a good idea of the nature of the hemodynamic response in that part of the brain; this is currently a matter of extensive study.

Using the general linear model also poses a number of limitations on the analysis of neuroimaging data. The general linear model is used to ask whether the data fit a set of predictions. Thus, one must have a set of predictions. If these are wrong, then one might repeat an analysis with a different model, looking for a better fit. There are other approaches to data analysis (discussed briefly below), such as principal components analysis and independent components analysis. These extract the underlying functions from the response without an a priori guess. At the same time, though, these approaches yield no information about which component corresponds to which process.

When building a design matrix for the general linear model, one must be very careful to include all the effects present in the data, including confounds. At the same time, one must also be careful not to include too many effects in a single experiment. If one underparameterizes the analysis, the variance of the confounds can overwhelm the signal, making the effects of interest insignificant. If one overparameterizes, one expands the search space for the β coefficients, making erroneous results more likely.

As discussed earlier, the BOLD response is not always linear, and at the present time experiments must be designed such that the BOLD responses will be in the near-linear range. Otherwise, the regressors in the model will not fit the data well enough to yield accurate results. To approximate linearity, one must ensure that the intervals between trials are within 1 to 15 s long. In addition, longer stimulus durations tend to produce more linear responses (Vazquez, 1998).

Preprocessing Requirements

Several conditions about the fMRI images must be met in order to carry out a successful data analysis. Most analyses are based on the assumption that all voxels in any given image from the series of images taken over time were acquired at the same time. They also assume that each data point in the time series from a given voxel was collected from that voxel only. Another assumption is that the residual variance (i.e., variance remaining after removing all the effects of interest) will have a

Gaussian distribution. Additionally, when carrying out analyses across different subjects, the researcher assumes that any given voxel will correspond to the same brain structure in all subjects in the study. Without any preprocessing, not one of these assumptions holds entirely true, and they will introduce errors in the results. Therefore, the researcher must carry out several steps before diving into an analysis so that the data will meet (or at least approximate) the assumptions.

Slice Timing. Because most image-acquisition sequences acquire brain images slice by slice, there can be a difference of 1 to 3 s between the acquisition of the first slice and the acquisition of the last slice. The problem is that an analysis assumes that all voxels in an image acquired at a given time point of the time series are acquired at the same time. In reality, the data from different slices are shifted in time relative to each other. Thus, the researcher must calculate the signal intensity of all slices at the same moment in the acquisition period. This is done by interpolating the signal intensity at the chosen time point from the same voxel in previous and subsequent acquisitions. A number of interpolation techniques exist, from bilinear to sinc interpolations, with varying degrees of accuracy and speed. Event-related experiments require more precise control over the onset time of the stimulus than do blocked-design experiments, so the interpolation is often not necessary in blocked designs, in which the epochs can last many seconds (e.g., more than 30 s). Because of the long length of epochs, not much sensitivity will be lost if the slices are not collected at the same time.

Realignment. A major problem in most time-series experiments is movement of the subject's head during acquisition of the time series. When this happens, the voxels' signal intensity gets contaminated by the signals from its neighbors. Thus, one must rotate and translate each individual image to undo the subject's movements.

The coordinates of a point in three-dimensional space (x, y, z) can be expressed as a vector. It can be shown that the coordinates of a given point in space after any given translation, rotation, or combination of both can be calculated by multiplying a matrix by the original vector. Such a matrix is called an affine transformation matrix. Thus, in order to undo the rotation and translation of the head, one must calculate the elements in this affine transformation matrix and apply the matrix to all voxels in the image. Usually, this is done by a least squares approximation that will minimize the difference between the image to be corrected and the first image in the time series.

Smoothing. Random field theory assumes that each voxel is independent of the other voxels, and that the images have normally distributed noise. This is not the case in most experiments, because the signal is often correlated among different voxels, especially in fMRI experiments. To make the noise in the images meet the assumption, the images are convolved with a Gaussian kernel, which gives the noise a more Gaussian distribution. This smoothing of images also effectively produces a weighted average of the signal across neighboring voxels, which gives the smoothed images a blurry appearance. A side effect of smoothing is a reduction of the amount of high-frequency spatial noise present in the data. This can be an advantage by increasing the overall signal-to-noise ratio of the individual images in the time series, making the tests more sensitive at the expense of spatial resolution.

Normalization. In order to make quantitative comparisons across subjects, the corresponding brain structures must have the same spatial coordinates. Of course, this is usually not the case, because people's brains are different. We can, however, stretch and compress the images (not the actual brains, of course!) in different directions so that the brain structures are in approximately the same locations. Usually we normalize all the brain images so that they will match a standard brain (e.g., the Talairach or Montreal Neurological Institute brain templates).

The normalization process includes an initial realignment of a set of images so that they approximate the template in orientation. Additionally, the images are transformed by multiplying them by a series of cosine basis functions, whose coefficients are estimated by a least squares error-minimization approach. This is analogous to searching for some function that will give the right transformation of the image. Because we do not know what the function is, we search for coefficients in the lower-order terms that would make up the unknown function. For more information on techniques for estimating the parameters, see Frackowiak (1997).

Random Effects

One approach to analyzing multisubject data is to normalize all images from all subjects and concatenate them into the design matrix, while including additional regressors for each subject. The result is a massive analysis including all trials from all subjects, which is quite expensive from a computational point of view. This is referred to as a fixed-effects analysis. Such an analysis would answer the question: If we repeat this experiment many times on the same subjects, what is the likelihood that we will get the same significant voxels?

If, on the other hand, one is interested in making a statistical inference about the *population* from which those subjects were taken, one would need first to analyze each subject separately, then look for commonalities across the statistical maps obtained in this first level of analysis. It has been shown that one can make statistical inferences across subjects by simple statistical tests performed on the statistical parameter maps (Friston et al., 1999; Holmes and Friston, 1998). The tests (usually t tests) can be carried out on the maps of β estimates calculated in the general linear model to search for those voxels that give the same magnitude of response to the condition. Those tests can also be carried out across the T-statistic maps obtained from the analysis of individual subjects, in order to search for voxels with the same level of significance.

Thus, one can perform a multisubject analysis in two stages: first, the estimation of parameters at the individual-subject level, and then another test of the individuals' statistical maps across subjects to see which voxels show the same level of activation across subjects. In doing this, one assumes that (a) the images have been spatially normalized such that the tests are conducted on corresponding structures from subject to subject, (b) the global intensity of the images has been scaled to a common level, and (c) all brains have similar BOLD responses to the same activity. These assumptions are not always met perfectly, and they introduce some errors into across-subjects analyses.

Other Approaches: Principal Components and Independent Components Analysis

An analysis based on the general linear model allows researchers to identify the voxels whose brain activity matches their model, but it does not reveal any additional information about the activations. Additionally, in the presence of unknown or nonlinear confounds, analyses based on the general linear model are not effective in removing the variance due to those confounds. A few methods based on the temporal signal have been designed to identify the major task-related patterns of activation in the brain without any a priori knowledge of the stimulation paradigm. Principal components analysis and independent components analysis are among these.

Principal components analysis calculates spatial patterns that account for the greatest amount of variability in a time series of images. This is done by obtaining the eigenvectors of a matrix containing the covariance among all voxels of the time series images. The eigenvectors, $\mathbf{x}$, of a matrix, $\mathbf{A}$, are those that satisfy the condition

$$\mathbf{Ax} = \lambda\mathbf{x}$$

where λ is a scalar value called the eigenvalue. Eigenvectors of a matrix are useful because they provide a set of basis functions for the original matrix.

There are a number of techniques for calculating the eigenvectors of an image. In neuroimaging, the eigenvectors are usually calculated through single value decomposition (SVD) of a covariance matrix. The result of SVD of a matrix is a set of three matrices whose columns are orthogonal vectors, $\mathbf{U}$, $\mathbf{S}$, and $\mathbf{V}$. In the framework of neuroimaging, $\mathbf{U}$ is interpreted as the temporal patterns present in the time series, $\mathbf{V}$ as the spatial patterns of covariant voxels, and $\mathbf{S}$ is a diagonal matrix whose elements are a measure of how much variance is accounted for by a particular spatial pattern. The columns of the matrix $\mathbf{V}$ can be shown to be the eigenvectors of the original data matrix. For details on eigenvectors, eigenvalues, and SVD, see a linear algebra text such as Strang (1988).

Independent components analysis is akin to principal components analysis in that the independent components algorithm also produces a set of components of the signal. However, in independent components analysis, there is an additional constraint that the components be statistically independent, and not necessarily orthogonal. Orthogonality, which characterizes principal components analysis, implies that the voxel values are uncorrelated between all pairs of components. Statistical

independence, which characterizes independent components analysis, implies that the joint probability of all the components is the same as the product of the individual probabilities, and that higher-order correlations between the components are also zero. Thus, independent components analysis involves a different criterion (McKewon et al., 1998a). The algorithm for extracting the independent components is an iterative procedure based on information theory and is beyond the scope of this chapter; suffice it to say that the algorithm searches for a solution that will maximize the entropy (or minimize the mutual information) between the components. For more details, see McKewon et al. (1998a, 1998b), Bell and Sejnowski (1995), and Petersson et al. (1999).

SUMMARY

We have completed our tour of the why, the what, and the how of neuroimaging. There are many reasons one might delve into neuroimaging, both for an understanding of brain mechanisms and for an understanding of psychological mechanisms. Having recognized this, cognitive neuroscientists have developed a number of techniques that allow one to implement neuroimaging techniques in experimental contexts of interest to psychology. Understanding the physics of how these techniques work is crucial to understanding what they offer and what constrains them. Equally important is understanding how experiments are designed to maximize their inference-making power as well as what analysis methods are available. Having surveyed these issues, we have proffered a tour of the highlights. The interested student of cognitive neuroscience will benefit from deeper analyses of all the topics we have surveyed, which are available from several sources. Other excellent introductory papers include those by Frith and Friston (1997), Aguirre and D'Esposito (1999), and Buckner and Braver (1999). Some useful texts include Elster (1994) for a clear explanation of magnetic resonance imaging principles, Strang's (1988) linear algebra text, and Frackowiak et al.'s (1997) *Human Brain Function*. There is also a vast amount of information on functional imaging on the Internet, at sites such as the Cambridge University's (http://www.mrc-cbu.cam.ac.uk/Imaging/) or the FIL's (Functional Imaging Laboratory) (http://www.fil.ion.ucl.ac.uk/spm/) among many others.

REFERENCES

Aguirre, G. K., & D'Esposito, M. (1999). Experimental design for brain fMRI. In C. T. W. Moonen & P. A. Bandettini (Eds.), *Functional MRI*. New York: Springer.

Aguirre, G. K., Singh, R., & D'Esposito, M. (1999). Stimulus inversion and the responses of face and object-sensitive cortical areas. *Neuroreport, 10,* 189–194.

Aguirre, G. K., Zarahn, E., & D'Esposito, M. (1998). The variability of human, BOLD hemodynamic responses. *Neuroimage, 8,* 360–369.

Andreasen, N. C., Arndt, S., Swayze, V., II, Cizadlo, T., Flaum, M., O'Leary, D., Ehrhardt, J. C., & Yuh, W. T. (1994). Thalamic abnormalities in schizophrenia visualized through magnetic resonance image averaging. *Science, 266,* 294–298.

Awh, E., Jonides, J., Smith, E. E., Schumacher, E. H., Koeppe, R. A., and Katz, S. (1996). Dissociation of storage and rehearsal in verbal working memory: Evidence from PET. *Psychological Science, 7,* 25–31.

Baddeley, A. D. (1986). *Working memory*. Oxford: Oxford University Press.

Baddeley, A. D. (1992). Working memory. *Science, 225,* 556–559.

Badre, D. T., Jonides, J., Hernandez, L., Noll, D. C., Smith, E. E., & Chenevert, T. L. (2000). *Behavioral and neuroimaging evidence of dissociable switching mechanisms in executive functioning* [Poster]. Presented at the Annual Meeting of the Cognitive Neuroscience Society, San Francisco.

Bell, A. J., & Sejnowski, T. J. (1995). An information-maximization approach to blind separation and blind deconvolution. *Neural Computation, 7,* 1129–1159.

Bendriem, B., & Townsend, D. (1998). *The theory and practice of 3D PET*. Dordrecht, Netherlands: Kluwer.

Bloch, F. (1946). Nuclear induction. *Physics Review, 70,* 460–473.

Boynton, G. M., Engel, S. A., Glover, G. H., & Heeger, D. J. (1996). Linear systems analysis of functional magnetic resonance imaging in human V1. *Journal of Neuroscience, 16,* 4207–4221.

Breiter, H. C., Gollub, R. L., Weisskoff, R. M., Kennedy, D. N., Makris, N., Berke, J. D., Goodman, J. M., Kantor, H. L., Gastfriend, D. R., Riorden, J. P., Mathew, R. T., Rosen, B. R., & Hyman, S. E. (1997). Acute effects of cocaine on human brain activity and emotion. *Neuron, 19,* 591–611.

Buckner, R. L., & Braver, T. S. (1999). Event-related functional MRI. In C. T. W. Moonen & P. A. Bandettini (Eds.), *Functional MRI*. New York: Springer.

Buckner, R. L., Koutstaal, W., Schacter, D. L., Dale, A. M., Rotte, M., & Rosen, B. R. (1998). Functional-anatomic study of episodic retrieval: II. Selective averaging of event-related fMRI trials to test the retrieval success hypothesis. *Neuroimage, 7,* 163–175.

Burock, M. A., Buckner, R. L., Woldorff, M. G., Rosen, B. R., & Dale, A. M. (1998). Randomized event-related experimental designs allow for extremely rapid presentation rates using functional MRI. *Neuroreport, 9,* 3735–3739.

Buxton, R. B., & Frank, L. R. (1998). A model for coupling between cerebral blood flow and oxygen metabolism during neural stimulation. *Journal of Cerebral Blood Flow and Metabolism, 17,* 64–72.

Buxton, R. B., Wong, E. C., & Frank, L. R. (1998). Dynamics of blood flow and oxygenation changes during brain activation: The balloon model. *Magnetic Resonance in Medicine 39,* 855–864.

Casey, B. J., Trainor, R. J., Orendi, J. L., Schubert, A. B., Nystrom, L. E., Giedd, J. N., Castellanos, F. X., Haxby, J. V., Noll, D. C., Cohen, J. D., Forman, S. D., Dahl, R. E., & Rapoport, J. L. (1997). A developmental functional MRI study of prefrontal activation during performance of a go-no-go task. *Journal of Cognitive Neuroscience, 9,* 835–847.

Cohen, J. D., Perlstein, W. M., Braver, T. S., Nystrom, L. E., Noll, D. C., Jonides, J., and Smith, E. E. (1997). Temporal dynamics of brain activation during a working memory task. *Nature, 386,* 604–608.

Coull, J. T., Buchel, C., Friston, K. J., & Frith, C. D. (1999). Noradrenergically mediated plasticity in a human attentional neuronal network. *Neuroimage, 10,* 705–715.

Dagher, A., Owen, A. M., Boecker, H., & Brooks, D. J. (1999). Mapping the network for planning: A correlational PET activation study with the Tower of London task. *Brain, 122,* 1973–1987.

Dale, A. M., & Buckner, R. L. (1997). Selective averaging of rapidly presented individual trials using fMRI. *Human Brain Mapping, 5,* 329–340.

D'Esposito, M., Zarahn, E., Aguirre, G. K., & Rypma, B. (1999). The effect of normal aging on the coupling of neural activity to the bold hemodynamic response. *Neuroimage, 10,* 6–14.

Detre, J. A., Leigh, J. S., Williams, D. S., & Koretsky, A. P. (1992). Perfusion imaging. *Magnetic Resonance in Medicine, 23,* 37–45.

Donders, F. C. Ouer de snelheid van psychische processen. (On the speed of mental processes.) Onderzoekingen degaan in net physiologisch Laboratorion der Ugtrechtsche Hoogeschool, 1868–69, Tureede Reeks, 11, 92–130. In W. G. Koster (ed.), Attention and Performance II, Acta Psychologica, 1969, 30, 412–431.

Elster, A. D. (1994). *Questions and answers in MRI.* St. Louis, MO: Mosby Yearbook.

Frackowiack, R. S. J., Friston, K. J., Frith, C. D., Dolan, R. J., & Mazziotta, J. C. (1997). *Human Brain Function.* London: Academic Press.

Frahm, J., Merboldt, K. D., Hanicke, W., Kleinschmidt, A., & Boecker, H. (1994). Brain or vein—oxygenation or flow? On signal physiology in functional MRI of human brain activation. *NMR in Biomedicine, 7,* 45–53.

Friston, K. J., Holmes, A. P., Price, C. J., Buchel, C., & Worsley, K. J. (1999). Multisubject fMRI studies and conjunction analyses. *Neuroimage, 10,* 385–396.

Frith, C. D., & Friston, K. (1997). Studying the brain with neuroimaging. In M. D. Rugg (Ed.), *Cognitive neuroscience* (pp. 169–195). Cambridge: MIT Press.

Gabrieli, J., Fleischman, D., Keane, M., Reminger, S., & Morell, F. (1995). Double dissociation between memory systems underlying explicit and implicit memory in the human brain. *Psychological Science, 6,* 76–82.

Gambhir, S. S., Barrio, J. R., Phelps, M. E., Iyer, M., Namavari, M., Satyamurthy, N., Wu, L., Green, L. A., Bauer, E., MacLaren, D. C., Nguyen, K., Berk, A. J., Cherry, S. R., & Herschman, H. R. (1999). Imaging adenoviral-directed reporter gene expression in living animals with positron emission tomography. *Proceedings of the National Academy of Sciences of the United States of America, 96,* 2333–2338.

Garavan, H., Ross, T. J., Li, S., & Stein, E. A. (2000). A parametric manipulation of central executive functioning. *Cereb Cortex, 10,* 585–592.

Gonzalez, J. B., Alsop, D. C., & Detre, J. A. (2000). Cerebral perfusion and arterial transit time changes during task activation determined with continuous arterial spin labeling. *Magnetic Resonance in Medicine, 43,* 739.

Hahn, E. L. (1950). Spin echoes. *Physics Review, 80,* 580–594.

Haxby, J. V., Horwitz, B., Ungerleider, L. G., Maisog, J. M., Pietrini, P., & Grady, C. L. (1994). The functional organization of human extrastriate cortex: A PET-rCBF study of selective attention to faces and locations. *Journal of Neuroscience, 14,* 6336–6353.

Hoge, R. D., Atkinson, J., Gill, B., Crelier, G. R., Marrett, S., & Pike, G. B. (1999). Investigation of BOLD signal dependence on cerebral blood flow and oxygen consumption: The deoxyhemoglobin dilution model. *Magnetic Resonance in Medicine, 42,* 849–863.

Holmes, A. P., & Friston, K. J. (1998). Generalisability, random effects and population inference. *Neuroimage, 7,* S754.

Hopfinger, J. B., Buonocore, M. H., & Mangun, G. R. (2000). The neural mechanisms of top-down attentional control. *Nature Neuroscience,* 284–291.

Hopfinger, J. B., & Mangun, G. R. (in press). Tracking the influence of reflexive attention on sensory and cognitive processing. *Cognitive, Affective, and Behavioral Neuroscience.*

Joliot, M., Papathanassiou, D., Mellet, E., Quinton, O., Mazoyer, N., Courtheoux, P., & Mazoyer, B. (1999). FMRI and PET of self-paced finger movement: comparison of intersubject stereotaxic averaged data. *Neuroimage, 10,* 430–447.

Jonides, J., Reuter-Lorenz, P., Smith, E. E., Awh, E., Barnes, L., Drain, M., Glass, J., Lauber, E., Patalano, A., & Schumacher, E. H. (1996). Verbal and spatial working memory. In D. Medin (Ed.), *The psychology of learning and motivation* (pp. 43–88).

Jonides, J., Schumacher, E. H., Smith, E. E., Lauber, E. J., Awh, E., Minoshima, S., & Koeppe, R. A. (1997). Verbal-working-memory load affects regional brain activation as measured by PET. *Journal of Cognitive Neuroscience, 9,* 462–475.

Jonides, J., Smith, E. E., Koeppe, R. A., Awh, E. Minoshima, S., & Mintun, M. A. (1993). Spatial working memory in humans as revealed by PET. *Nature, 363,* 623–625.

Kanwisher, N., McDermott, J., & Chun, M. M. (1997). The fusiform face area: A module in human extrastriate cortex specialized for face perception. *Journal of Neuroscience, 17,* 4302–4311.

Kim, S. G. (1995). Quantification of relative cerebral blood flow change by flow sensitive alternating inversion recovery (FAIR) technique: Application to functional mapping. *Magnetic Resonance in Medicine, 34,* 293–301.

Kinahan, P. E., & Noll, D. C. (1999). A direct comparison between whole-brain PET and BOLD fMRI measurements of single-subject activation response. *Neuroimage, 9,* 430–438.

Koepp, M. J. (1998). Evidence for striatal dopamine release during a video game. *Nature, 393,* 266–268.

Lane, R. D., Reiman, E. M., Axelrod, B., Yun, L. S., Holmes, A., & Schwartz, G. E. (1998). Neural correlates of levels of emotional awareness: Evidence of an interaction between emotion and attention in the anterior cingulate cortex. *Journal of Cognitive Neuroscience, 10,* 525–535.

Lashley, K. S. (1950). In search of the engram. In *Symposium of the Society of Experimental Biology, 4,* 454–482. New York: Cambridge University Press.

Lauterbur P. C. (1973). Image formation by induced local interactions: Examples employing nuclear magnetic resonance. *Journal of Magnetic Resonance, 81,* 43–56.

Le Bihan, D. (1995). Molecular diffusion, tissue microdynamics and microstructure. *NMR in Biomedicine, 8,* 375–386.

Macovski, A. (1983). *Medical imaging systems.* Englewood Cliffs, NJ: Prentice-Hall.

Maguire, E. A., Gadian, D. G., Johnsrude, I. S., Good, C. D., Ashburner, J., Frackowiak, R. S., & Frith, C. D. (2000). Navigation-related structural change in the hippocampi of taxi drivers. *Proceedings of the National Academt of Sciences of the United States of America, 97,* 4398–4403.

Mansfield, P., & Pykett, I. L. (1978). Biological and medical imaging by NMR. *Journal of Magnetic Resonance, 29,* 355–373.

Marshuetz, C., Salthouse, T. A., Ombao, H., Smith, E. E., Jonides, J., Diego, L. R., Bates, J. E., Chenevert, T. L., Krishnan, S., & Betley, A. T. (1999). *A single subject statistical approach to modeling the componenets of verbal working memory.* Paper presented at the Annual Meeting of the Society for Neuroscience, Miami Beach, FL.

Martin, A., Haxby, J. V., Lalonde, F. M., Wiggs, C. L., & Ungerleider, L. G. (1995). Discrete cortical regions associated with knowledge of color and knowledge of action. *Science, 270,* 102–105.

McKewon, M. J., Jung, T. P., Makeig, S., Brown, G., Kindermann, S. S., Lee, T. W., & Sejnowski, T. J. (1998a). Spatially independent activity patterns in functional MRI data during the stroop color-naming task. *Proceedings of the National Academy of Sciences of the United States of America, 95*(3): 803–810.

McKewon, M. J., Makeig, S., Brown, G. B., Jung, T. P., Kindermann, S. S., Bell, A. J., & Sejnowski, T. J. (1998b). Analysis of fMRI data by blind separation into independent spatial components. *Human Brain Mapping, 6,* 160–188.

Milner, B., Corkin, S., & Teuber, H. (1968). Further analysis of the hippocampal amnesic syndrome: 14-year follow-up study of H.M. *Neuropsychologia, 6,* 215–234.

Moseley, M. E., Cohen, Y., Mintorovitch, J., Chileuitt, L., Shimizu, H., Kucharczyck, J., Wendland, M. F., & Weinstein, P. R. (1990). Early detection of regional cerebral ischemia in cats: Comparison of diffusion- and T2-weighted MRI and spectroscopy. *Magnetic Resonance in Medicine, 14,* 330–346.

Nishimura, D. G. (1996). *Principles of magnetic resonance imaging.* Stanford University.

Ogawa, S., Lee, T. M., Kay, A. R., & Tank, D. W. (1990). Brain magnetic resonance imaging with contrast dependent on blood oxygenation. *Proceedings of the National Academy of Sciences of the United States of America, 87,* 9868–9872.

Peled, S., Gudbjartsson, H., Westin, C. F., Kikinis, R., & Jolesz, F. A. (1998). Magnetic resonance imaging shows orientation and asymmetry of white matter fiber tracts. *Brain Resonance, 780,* 27–33.

Petersen, S. E., Fox, P. T., Posner, M. I., Mintun, M., & Raichle, M. E. (1988). Positron emission tomographic studies of the cortical anatomy of single-word processing. *Nature, 331,* 585–589.

Petersen, S. E., van Mier, H., Fiez, J. A., & Raichle, M. E. (1998). The effects of practice on the functional anatomy of task performance. *Proceedings of the National Academy of Sciences of the United States of America, 95,* 853–860.

Petersson, K. M., Nichols, T. E., Poline, J. B., & Holmes, A. P. (1999). Statistical limitations in functional neuroimaging (I and II): Philosophical Transactions of the Royal Society of London—Series B. *Biological Sciences, 354,* 1239–1281.

Poline, J. B., Worsley, K. J., Holmes, A. P., Frackowiak, R. S. J., & Friston, K. J. (1995). Estimating smoothness in statistical parameter maps: Variability of *p* values. *Journal of Computer Assisted Tomography, 19,* 788–796.

Posner, M. I., Petersen, S. E., Fox, P. T., & Raichle, M. E. (1988). Localization of cognitive operations in the human brain. *Science, 240,* 1627–1631.

Postle, B. R., & D'Esposito, M. (1999). "What"-then-"where" in visual working memory: An event-related fMRI study. *Journal of Cognitive Neuroscience, 11,* 585–597.

Purcell, E. M., Torrey, H. C., & Pound, R. V. (1946). Resonance absorption by nuclear magnetic moments in a solid. *Physics Review, 69,* 37–38.

Ramsey, N. F., Kirkby, B. S., Van Gelderen, P., Berman, K. F., Duyn, J. H., Frank, J. A., Mattay, V. S., Van Horn, J. D., Esposito, G., Moonen, C. T., & Weinberger, D. R. (1996). Functional mapping of human sensorimotor cortex with 3D BOLD fMRI correlates highly with H2(15)O PET rCBF. *Journal of Cerebral Blood Flow and Metabolism, 16,* 755–764.

Raz, N. (2000). Aging of the brain in its impact on cognitive performance: Integration of structural and functional findings. In F. I. M. Craik & T. A. Salthouse (Eds.), *Handbook of aging and cognition* 2nd Ed. (Vol. 2) (pp. 1–90). Mahwah, NJ: Erlbaum.

Reiman, E. M., Fusselman, M. J., Fox, P. T., & Raichle, M. E. (1989). Neuroanatomical correlates of anticipatory anxiety [published erratum appears in *Science, 256,* 1696]. *Science, 243,* 1071–1074.

Reuter-Lorenz, P. A., Jonides, J., Smith, E., Hartley, A., Miller, A., Marshuetz, C., & Koeppe, R. (2000). Age differences in the frontal lateralization of verbal and spatial working memory revealed by PET. *Journal of Cognitive Neuroscience, 12,* 174–187.

Roy, C. S., & Sherrington, C. S. (1890). On the regulation of the blood supply of the brain. *Journal of Physiology, 11,* 85–108.

Sadato, N., Pascual-Leone, A., Grafman, J., Ibanez, V., Deiber, M. P., Dold, G., & Hallett, M. (1996). Activation of the primary visual cortex by Braille reading in blind subjects [see comments]. *Nature, 380*, 526–528.

Sandler, M. P. (1995). *Diagnostic nuclear medicine.* Baltimore, MD: Williams and Wilkins.

Schacter, D. L., & Buckner, R. L. (1998). Priming and the brain. *Neuron, 20*, 185–195.

Shulman, R. G., & Rothman, D. L. (1998). Interpreting functional imaging studies in terms of neurotransmitter cycling. *Proceedings of the National Academy of Sciences of the United States of America, 95*, 11993–11998.

Smith, E. E., & Jonides, J. (1995). Working memory in humans: Neuropsychological evidence. In M. Gazzaniga (Ed.), *The cognitive neurosciences* (pp. 1009–1020). Cambridge: MIT Press.

Smith, E. E., Jonides, J., & Koeppe, R. A. (1996). Dissociating verbal and spatial working memory using PET. *Cerebral Cortex, 6*, 11–20.

Strang G. (1998). *Linear algebra and its applications* (3rd ed.). San Diego: Harcourt Brace Jovanovich.

Stegman, L. D., Rehemtulla, A., Beattie, B., Kievit, E., Lawrence, T. S., Blasberg, R. G., Tjuvajev, J. G., & Ross, B. D. (1999). Noninvasive quantitation of cytosine deaminase transgene expression in human tumor xenografts with in vivo magnetic resonance spectroscopy. *Proceedings of the National Academy of Sciences of the United States of America, 96*, 9821–9826.

Sternberg, S. (1969). Memory-scanning: Mental processes revealed by reaction-time experiments. *American Science, 57*, 421–57.

Ungerleider, L. G., & Mishkin, M. (1982). Two cortical visual systems. In D. J. Engle, M. A. Goodale, and R. J. Mansfield (Eds.), *Analysis of visual behavior* (pp. 549–586). Cambridge: MIT Press.

Vazquez, A. L., & Noll, D. C. (1998). Non-linear aspects of the blood oxygenation response in functional MRI. *NeuroImage, 8,*108–118.

Williams, D. S., Detre, J. A., Leigh, J. S., & Koretsky, A. P. (1992). Magnetic resonance imaging of perfusion using spin inversion of arterial water. *Proceedings of the National Academy of Sciences of the United States of America, 89*, 212–216.

Wong, E. C., Buxton, R. B., & Frank, L. R. (1997). Implementation of quantitative perfusion imaging techniques for functional brain mapping using pulsed arterial labeling. *NMR in Biomedicine, 10*, 237–249.

Worsley, K. J., Evans, A. C., Marrett, S., & Neelin, P. (1992). A three-dimensional statistical analysis for CBF activation studies in human brain. *Journal of Cerebral Blood Flow and Metabolism, 12*, 900–918.

Worsley, K. J., Marret, S., Neelin, P., Vandal, A. C., Friston, K. J., & Evans, A. C. (1996). A unified statistical approach for determining significant signals in images of cerebral activation. *Human Brain Mapping, 4*, 58–73.

Zarahn, E., Aguirre, G., & D'Esposito, M. (1997). A trial-based experimental design for fMRI. *Neuroimage, 6*, 122–138.

CHAPTER 6

Neural Network Modeling

DANIEL S. LEVINE

WHAT IS NEURAL NETWORK MODELING?

The use of neural networks studied through computer simulations or mathematical theorems in modeling psychological data dates back to the late 1960s and early 1970s. Yet it took until the late 1980s for this methodology to become widely accepted by experimental psychologists. The reasons for the acceptance were mainly the greater availability of powerful personal computers and the wide distribution of a few influential multidisciplinary publications in cognitive science, notably the two-volume collection by Rumelhart and McClelland (1986).

Of all the neural network methods, the three-layer back-propagation technique (Rumelhart, Hinton, & Williams, 1986; Werbos, 1974, 1993; also sometimes called the multilayer perceptron) has been the most widely used—in psychological modeling as well as in engineering applications—because of the method's relative simplicity and universality. In fact, I have often heard psychologists and other researchers say the words "neural network" when they mean a back-propagation network. There are even commentaries with titles such as "Are neural networks like the brain?" which is absurd because the brain *is* of course a network of neurons and neural structures!

A better question is "*What* neural networks are like the brain?" Back-propagation networks have a very specific structure: feedforward and reliance on an external "teacher" to set their weights, with feedback in the form of weight transport between synapses. There is debate over whether structures of this sort exist in the brain at all (see Levine, 2000, Section 6.2, for a partial discussion), but it is certain that they are hardly representative of actual brain networks. Feedback, at the level of neurons and not of synapses, is the norm for connections between different brain regions.[1] Furthermore, the tight supervision of back-propagation learning, the constraints that move it in the direction of specific input-output responses, are uncharacteristic of learning as it takes place in the brain. Thus, the field of neural networks encompasses much more than that one type of network structure.

If the neural networks used in models are not necessarily back-propagation networks, what do they have in common? They consist of

---

[1] Some neuroscientists follow Edelman (1987) in replacing the term "feedback" by "reentry." This is because his definition of "feedback" is a narrow one based on engineering control structures. I do not mean feedback in that sense, but simply in the sense of reciprocal connections, such as the cortex sending out axons that synapse on the thalamus and the thalamus sending out axons that synapse on the cortex.

nodes, which may or may not be interpreted as single neurons, but have activities that are idealized action potential frequencies. The connections between nodes have weights that are idealized synaptic strengths. The ultimate aim is to make these networks as biologically realistic as possible. Sometimes nodes correspond to brain areas or specific cell types in those brain areas. At other times, when not enough is known about brain processes or when one desires modeling at a functional level, nodes correspond to cognitive entities such as the memory of a specific word, the tendency to approach a specific object, or the intensity of a specific drive or emotion.

Neural networks are also, of course, used by computer scientists and engineers for "intelligent" applications (pattern recognition, signal processing, robotics, medical and financial data analysis, etc.). The diverse range of researchers who study them have not agreed on one definition for the concept. The closest to a widely recognized definition is probably the following from the 1988 Defense Advanced Research Projects Agency (DARPA) study:

> A neural network is a system composed of many simple processing elements operating in parallel whose function is determined by network structure, connection strengths, and the processing performed at computing elements or nodes.... Neural network architectures are inspired by the architecture of biological nervous systems. (p. 60)

More recently, the notion that biological neurons are "simple processing elements" has been challenged as researchers have discovered the complexity of subthreshold electrical interactions among the thousands of dendrites of a single neuron and of biochemical interactions among transmitters and receptors involving various messenger compounds (see, e.g., Aparicio & Levine, 1994; Pribram, 1993). Neural networks encompass neurons

with realistic dendritic interactions as well as those with formal, simpler neurons.

As neural networks have evolved, two trends have emerged. The first trend is that more detail about simulated brain areas has appeared in network models. This means that as more behaviorally relevant biological data has been available, due to such advances as positron-emission tomography and magnetic resonance imaging, different schools of neural network modeling (such as back propagation and adaptive resonance) have converged somewhat. The modeling architectures of major neural network research groups are increasingly driven as much by the data as by their own characteristic network structures.

The second trend is that models have covered an expanded range of psychological data. In the 1970s network modeling was most advanced in the area of visual perception, and second most advanced in serial learning and short-term memory. The early and middle 1980s saw the growth of models of animal learning and conditioning data. The late 1980s and early 1990s, buoyed by the interdisciplinary cognitive science revolution, saw early models of high-level cognition, including language acquisition, and its breakdown in various mental disorders. All these areas are still active, and now a few models have appeared in social psychology. By now, although there is little agreement on the "right" model for any of these phenomena, the network tools available, as well as the knowledge of cognitive neuroscience, are sophisticated enough that all areas of psychology—cognitive, behavioral, physiological, social, developmental, and clinical—are amenable to neural network modeling.

The next section gives a historical overview of major trends in psychologically relevant neural network modeling over about 50 years. It ends with a short description of the mathematical processes of building one simple network model. The succeeding sections discuss current modeling trends, organized into specific (interacting yet partially dissociable) areas of application: sensory processes, motor control, cognitive-emotional interactions, and high-level cognition. The goal is to describe the modeling process by communicating the intuitive flavor of networks used to model different phenomena. A concluding section discusses possible future trends and provides suggestions for experimental psychologists interested in learning more about neural networks.

HISTORY OF NEURAL NETWORK MODELING

The Cybernetic Revolution

The history herein is partly adapted from more technical accounts in Levine (1983, Sections 1–4; 2000, chap. 2). It begins with the work of McCulloch and Pitts (1943), which was also connected with the early development of digital computers. Perceived similarities between computers and brains spurred an interdisciplinary group to develop a new science they called cybernetics, the science of control systems (Wiener, 1948). The computer-brain analogy was based on the fact that neurons are all-or-none, either firing or not firing, just as binary switches in a digital computer are either on or off. All-or-none neurons are oversimplified because graded electrical potentials in neurons are important, not just action potentials. Also, functional units in current neural network models tend to be neuron populations rather than single neurons. Nevertheless, current approaches still owe many of their formulations to cybernetic pioneers from the 1940s.

McCulloch and Pitts (1943) demonstrated that a neuron can be embedded into a network of all-or-none neurons so as to fire selectively in response to any given pattern of network activity representing a class of stimuli impinging on the network. McCulloch-Pitts networks include abstract neurons[2] connected by excitation and inhibition with computations done in discrete time intervals. Each neuron obeys a simple linear threshold law: It fires whenever at least a given (threshold) number of excitatory pathways, and no inhibitory pathways, impinging on it are active from the previous time. The connections do not change with experience; thus the network deals with performance but not with learning.

Despite its simplifications, the McCulloch-Pitts (1943) model presages important issues in current models. For example, many McCulloch-Pitts networks have neurons analogous to the three types of nodes in back propagation networks: input units, output units, and hidden units. Input units react to data features from the environment, whereas output units generate organismic responses. Hidden units, via network connections, influence output units to respond to prescribed patterns of input-unit activities. These three classes are analogous to sensory neurons, motor neurons, and all other neurons (interneurons) in the brain. The output, however, may not be a motor output but an internal state (e.g., a categorization or an emotion) that could influence a present or future motor response.

Also, McCulloch and Pitts (1943) dealt with how to create output-unit responses to given inputs that depend on previous inputs. For example, one of their networks modeled a sensation of heat obtained from holding a cold object to the skin and then removing it. Hence, this network responds to the difference between a present input and a previous one. Response to change has been used in neural network models of conditioning

---

[2]In most neural network models, network elements are called "nodes" or "units" rather than "cells" or "neurons," because they might represent more or less than a single neuron. In the McCulloch-Pitts (1943) network, however, the term "neurons" is used because the network is inspired by the all-or-none firing properties of neurons.

data (Grossberg, 1972a, 1972b; Grossberg & Schmajuk, 1987; Klopf, 1988). These data include results showing that a motor act is reinforced when it turns off an unpleasant stimulus (relief); that withholding an expected reward is unpleasant (frustration); and that the reward value of food is enhanced if the food is unexpected (partial reinforcement).

McCulloch and Pitts (1943) encoded memory by reverberatory neural circuits. Other investigators, starting with Hebb (1949), added the distinction between short-term memory (STM), due to reverberation, and long-term memory (LTM), due to changes at synapses.

Modeling Learning

Hull (1943) proposed that the two memory processes involved the storage of two sets of traces, as in classical conditioning experiments. He distinguished between *stimulus traces* subject to rapid decay and *associative strengths* (habit strengths) able to persist longer. Although Hull's model did not include neural connections, his stimulus traces can be considered as the amounts of activity of particular nodes in a neural network, and his associative strengths are the strengths of connections between nodes. This suggests that such connection strengths should change with experience.

Hebb (1949) declared that reverberatory feedback loops, which McCulloch and Pitts (1943) had suggested as a memory mechanism, could be a useful mechanism for STM but not for LTM, because they would be too sensitive to external interruptions. He recognized that a stable LTM depended on some structural change. His hypothesis was, "When the axon of cell *A* is near enough to excite a cell *B* and repeatedly or persistently takes part in firing it, some growth process or metabolic change takes place in one or both cells such that *A*'s efficiency, as one of the cells firing *B*, is increased" (p. 62). Later investigators inter-

preted Hebb's rule mathematically in various ways, most often that the strength of a connection between two nodes changed by an amount proportional to the product of the activities of those two nodes.

Hebb's (1949) rule for learning was incorporated into networks of all-or-none McCulloch-Pitts (1943) neurons by many early modelers, particularly Rosenblatt (1962) in the perceptron. In this network, the McCulloch-Pitts linear threshold law was generalized to laws whereby activities of all pathways impinging on a neuron are computed, and the neuron fires whenever some weighted sum of those activities is above a given threshold.

Rosenblatt's (1962) work anticipated many themes of modern adaptive networks such as those of the parallel distributed processing (PDP) research group (cf. Rumelhart & McClelland, 1986); in fact, the latter type of network is often called multilayer perceptrons. The main function he proposed for his perceptrons was to make and learn choices between different patterns of sensory stimuli. Rosenblatt set out to study the pattern-classification capabilities of networks of sensory (*S*), associative (*A*), and response units (*R*) with various connection structures— mostly feedforward but some including feedback from *R* to *A* units—and various learning rules, which he called the reinforcement system.

Rosenblatt (1962) found that the perceptrons that learned fastest were those using an error-correcting reinforcement system, whereby the connection strength changes upward or downward if the response is determined elsewhere to be incorrect. Reinforcement rules of the error-correcting type were concurrently developed by Widrow and Hoff (1960) and are still used widely (e.g., Abdi, Valentin, & O'Toole, 1997; Anderson & Murphy, 1986; J. D. Cohen & Servan-Schreiber, 1992).

In one of Rosenblatt's (1962) experiments, the S units are arranged in a rectangular grid. Connections from S units to A units are random, whereas all A units connect to the single R unit. The perceptron was taught to discriminate vertical from horizontal bars. Rosenblatt found that if *all* possible vertical and horizontal bars are presented to the perceptron, and the perceptron is reinforced positively for responding to the vertical bars and negatively for responding to the horizontal,[3] eventually the network gives the desired response reliably to each one. However, if only some vertical and horizontal bars are presented and reinforced, the perceptron cannot generalize its behavior to other bars that have not been presented. In models of visual pattern discrimination, issues such as translation invariance (ability to recognize a given pattern regardless of where it is in the visual field) remain difficult. This property is exhibited by the Neocognitron of Fukushima (1980) and the What-and-Where filter inspired by visual cortex architecture (Carpenter, Grossberg, & Lesher, 1998).

Because these were computational experiments that did not include much brain structure, they attracted researchers (the term "computer scientist" was not yet widely used) who were interested in building machines with "intelligent" functions, regardless of whether the mechanisms for those functions were similar to brain mechanisms. This was the birth of the field now known as artificial intelligence. In particular, Minsky and Papert (1969) studied mathematically a class of abstract perceptrons that were inspired by Rosenblatt's previous work, with parts that corresponded loosely to sensory, associative, and response areas. Minsky and Papert proved that their abstract perceptrons can learn any

classification of patterns, but that the perceptrons needed to make some geometrically important classifications had to get arbitrarily large as the pattern size increased. Theorems of this sort were widely interpreted as discrediting perceptron-like devices as learning machines, even though some of the visual discriminations that are difficult for perceptrons are also difficult for humans.

The discrediting of perceptrons was related to the growth of mainstream artificial intelligence and its emphasis on design of devices based on heuristic computer programs and not involving networks and connections at all. This type of work is still very active, but around the mid-1980s heuristic programs were found inadequate for many programming problems involving imprecise data (e.g., signal processing and face recognition). This led to a rebirth of interest among computer scientists in brain-like networks, a development known as connectionism.

As part of the connectionist revival, the PDP research group's models, which originated about 1981 and are summarized in Rumelhart and McClelland (1986), recaptured some threads from Rosenblatt's work. They showed that some distinctions difficult for Minsky and Papert's perceptrons can be made by perceptrons with additional hidden unit layers *and* nonlinear functions representing intelayer transmission. I return to the PDP models later, after reviewing the controversy over discrete (digital) versus continuous (analog) models.

Continuous and Nonlinear Dynamics

While the cybernetic revolution was stimulating discrete (digital) models of intelligent behavior, a concurrent proliferation of results from both neurophysiology and psychology stimulated the development of continuous (analog) neural models. In most applications of mathematics to physical phenomena,

[3]Rosenblatt (1962) used the term "negative reinforcement" to mean what psychologists now call "punishment."

including the biophysics of current flow in single neurons, there are variables that are not all-or-none but may take on any of a range of values. Hence, such processes are typically modeled using differential equations, which are equations describing continuous changes over time in an interacting collection of variables (cf. Levine, 2000, Appendix 2). For this reason, Rashevsky (1960) used differential equations to model perceptual data such as relations of reaction times to stimulus intensities and just noticeable differences among intensities. It was difficult to reconcile this approach with the all-or-none McCulloch-Pitts (1943) framework. This paradox was resolved with the observation that behavioral data reflect the combined activity of large numbers of neurons. Hence "the discontinuous laws of interaction of individual neurons lead to a sort of average continuous effect which is described by . . . differential equations" (Rashevsky, 1960, p. 3).

Rashevsky's reconciliation between continuous and discrete models is still in common use. The description in terms of average activity is in line with modeling based on nodes that may represent large numbers of neurons. This idea dates back to Hebb (1949), who proposed

that percepts or concepts are coded by groups of neurons called cell assemblies. Researchers have yet to define precisely the boundaries of cell assemblies in actual mammalian brains. Edelman (1987) speculated that groups on the order of several thousand neurons in size encode significant stimulus categories. Burnod (1988) stressed the functional importance of cell columns in the cerebral cortex. Other theorists speculated that concepts or percepts could be coded by synchronized electrical activity of large distributed groups of neurons (see, e.g., Gray & Singer, 1989).

Neural models often average random single-neuron effects across the functional groups of neurons that constitute network nodes, making the interactions between nodes deterministic. In addition, many models average random effects over short time intervals so that the node activity variable is interpreted as representing a firing frequency rather than a voltage. Rashevsky assumed that the average frequency of impulses transmitted by a neuron is a linear function of the cell's suprathreshold activity (see Figure 6.1a), a useful assumption for some neural models of sensory transduction (e.g., Hartline & Ratliff, 1957). Yet averaging can also lead to nonlinear, notably

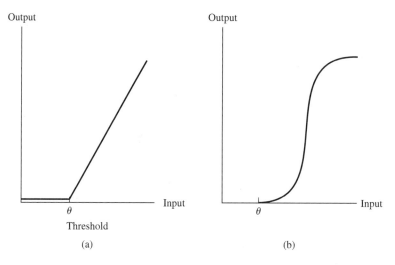

Figure 6.1   Schematic of linear (a) and sigmoid (b) functions of suprathreshold activity.

sigmoid, functions (Figure 6.1b). If the firing threshold of an all-or-none neuron is a random variable with a normal distribution, the mean value of its output signal is a sigmoid function of activity. For this reason, and because they have been observed in real neurons (Kernell, 1965), sigmoids are popular in neural models (e.g., Grossberg, 1973; Rumelhart et al., 1986).

Some data have indicated that brain connections may be random *within* certain neural populations and specific *between* these populations. Lashley (1929) showed that memories for specific events are retained after extensive brain lesions, inspiring the idea that representations of events are distributed throughout the brain rather than localized. Other experiments showed, however, that specific connections are important for other functions. Mountcastle (1957) found that the somatosensory cortex includes a well-organized topographic encoding of the body. Hubel and Wiesel (1962, 1965) found that cells in the visual cortex are organized into columns that code specific retinal positions or line orientations.[4] The paradox between the Lashley data and the Hubel-Wiesel or Mountcastle data is resolved by means of a principle of "randomness in the small and structure in the large" (Anninos, Beek, Csermely, Harth, & Pertile, 1970, p. 121). This principle is implicit in the bulk of commonly used neural network models of psychological phenomena. Most of these models use purely deterministic equations at the level of nodes (interpreted as neuron populations) that could be interpreted as the averaging over large ensembles of probabilistic effects at the single-cell level.

Now we turn to the history of classes of models that are in common use today, such as back-propagation, autoassociative, and adaptive resonance models.

Perceptrons and Back Propagation

The descent of the three-layer back-propagation network from Rosenblatt's (1962) perceptrons has been noted. Like the original perceptrons, back-propagation networks have typically been used for supervised learning, that is, teaching a network to perform a desired response to specific stimuli by adjustment of its connection weights via error-correcting "reinforcement" procedures. This has been applied extensively both in psychology, to cause a network to behave in accordance with some set of data, and in engineering, to make a device learn a particular function.

The back-propagation algorithm was developed by Werbos (1974, 1993) as a procedure for optimizing the predictive ability of mathematical models and was placed in a widely studied connectionist framework by Rumelhart et al. (1986). It is often applied to discrimination or classification of sensory input patterns. The network is feedforward with three layers, composed of input units, hidden units, and output units (Figure 6.2; see also the second section of this chapter). A particular pattern of output responses to particular input patterns is desired. If the actual response to the current input deviates from the desired response, the weights of connections from hidden to output units are changed. Then those weight changes propagate backward to cause changes in weights from input to hidden units that will reduce future error. The hidden units thereby come to encode specific patterns of input activities.

In the back-propagation algorithm, an expression is found for the total network error (based on the desired response), and the weight changes that cause the sharpest possible decrease in error are computed. The rate

---

[4]It is important to note, however, that visual and somatosensory maps are modifiable; the somatosensory maps, at least, can be altered even in adult life (see Edelman, 1987, for a summary).

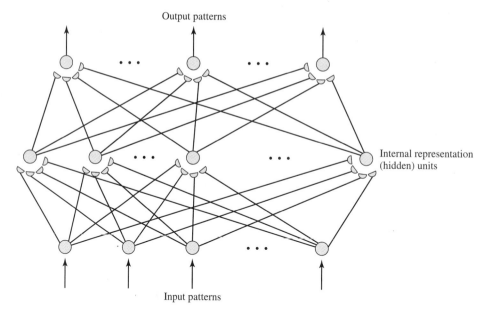

Output patterns

Internal representation
(hidden) units

Input patterns

Figure 6.2   Generic three-layer back-propagation network. Error signals from output nodes propagate backward from hidden-to-output weights to input-to-hidden weights. In the process, hidden units learn to encode certain input pattern classes. Semicircles represent modifiable synapses.
SOURCE: Adapted from Rumelhart et al. (1986), with permission of MIT Press.

of error correction (at both hidden-to-output and input-to-hidden synapses) is proportional to the derivative (rate of change) of a sigmoid function of presynaptic node activity. Because this rate of change is fastest over the middle range of the sigmoid, this means heuristically that weights are changed fastest from nodes that have not "made up their minds" to be active or inactive (Terence Sejnowski, personal communication, April 1987). This scheme allows for credit assignment, that is, deciding which connections at an earlier level in the network to alter if the responses of later stages are inappropriate (see also Barto & Anandan, 1985).

Back-propagation networks essentially can learn arbitrary nonlinear input-output relationships. Instead of converging to the desired response, however, the system sometimes gets trapped in a response that is not desired. Also, the network varies enormously in how many steps it requires to converge to the response

it is supposed to learn. The convergence rate depends on the number of hidden units, and that number must be decided separately for each application.

Back propagation is widely considered biologically unrealistic because it uses feedback of synaptic weights, not of neuronal signals, and no brain mechanism for weight transport is known. Nonetheless, several researchers have noted the utility of such an error-correcting mechanism[5] and have suggested possible neuronal bases for it. These have included (a) backward flows in microtubules, a part of the structural support system of neurons and all other living cells (Dayhoff, Hameroff, Swenberg, & Lahoz-Beltra, 1993); (b) neurons responsive to combined activities of other neurons (Levine, 1996); and

---

[5]There are many other error-correcting mechanisms used in neural network models of motor control that do not employ back propagation (see Section 4).

(c) backward-flowing signals at some synapses or dendritic trees (Stuart, Spruston, Sakmann, & Hauser, 1997). Later backpropagation networks added recurrent (feedback) connections, which are useful for modeling sequence learning and make the networks somewhat more brain-like (Elman, 1990; Hinton, 1993; Jordan, 1986).

Autoassociation and Heteroassociation

A set of fairly abstract models representing aspects of associative learning and memory was developed in the late 1960s and early 1970s independently by two groups, one led by James Anderson and the other by Teuvo Kohonen. This work is still finding applications in recognizing and classifying patterns and also in modeling memory storage areas of the brain, such as the hippocampus.

Anderson (1968, 1970, 1972) described a memory trace as a vector or array of numbers, each of whose components is the activity of a single network node. Anderson's emphasis was on developing a simple model that would capture some basic properties of memory, such as recognition, retrieval, and association, without resorting to much physiological detail. Association was related to a theory of synaptic connection weights in Anderson (1972). In these articles, Anderson proposed a model for association that involved two sets of nodes, each encoding a stimulus pattern. Anderson found mathematically that the optimal set of weights for associating these patterns was one based on the Hebb (1949) rule for connection weights, in which activities of presynaptic and postsynaptic nodes were multiplied.

If the association is between two distinct patterns, such as occurs in classical conditioning, it is called heteroassociative. If it is between a pattern and itself (i.e., recovering a pattern from a slight distortion of it or all of a pattern from part of it), it is called autoasso-

ciative. Those two terms come from Kohonen (1977). As Kohonen et al. (1977, p. 1065) said, "Consequently, for instance, both the recall of a visual image from its fraction, and a paired association in the classical conditioning, can be regarded as different aspects in the functioning of the associative memory."

In one version of the autoassociative model, a mathematical transformation (matrix) encoding connection weights is repeatedly applied to a stimulus pattern, and then boundaries are imposed on node activities. Anderson, Silverstein, Ritz, and Jones (1977) and Anderson and Murphy (1986) called this brain state in a box (BSB) and applied it to pattern categorization, with the repeated application of this transformation leading ultimately to what is interpreted as a category prototype. Other autoassociative networks, with selective attention added, have been applied to categorization of faces, such as by gender (Abdi et al., 1997). Finally, autoassociative networks have been used to model the memory processes of the hippocampus (e.g., Levy, 1996).

The heteroassociative version of the model is somewhat similar to other models that are more biologically inspired, such as the early work of Grossberg and his colleagues, to be discussed next.

Biologically Inspired Models and Modeling Principles

In the late 1960s several modelers began to develop principles for fitting biologically relevant neural network architectures to specific cognitive and behavioral functions. This led to models requiring partial verification on both the physiological and the behavioral levels, and to a toolkit of modeling techniques and modules that is still in wide use.

The work of Grossberg and his group is particularly important for this development. Grossberg's first major architecture was the outstar, developed to model associative learning of a pattern along lines suggested by Hull (1943) and Hebb (1949). Grossberg (1969) posed the question of how an organism learns to produce one sound (say B) in response to another (say A) after repeatedly hearing them in sequence. He devised a network to do this using differential equations. The variables defining these equations were based on Hull's notions of stimulus trace and associative strength. For each stimulus A, the stimulus trace $x_A(t)$ measures how active the memory for A is at any given time t. For each pair of stimuli A and B, the associational strength $w_{AB}(t)$ measures how strong the sequential association AB is in the network's memory at time t.

Table 6.1 summarizes the effects Grossberg incorporated into his equations. B should be produced if, and only if, A has been presented *and* AB is strong in memory. AB should become stronger if A is presented and followed by B. Replacing A and B by the ith and jth stimuli in general, the variable x_j should increase if both x_i and w_{ij} are high. Likewise, w_{ij} should increase if both x_i and x_j are high.

In the outstar (Figure 6.3) one node, called a source, projects to other nodes, called sinks. Long-term storage is interpreted as residing in the proportions between the weights

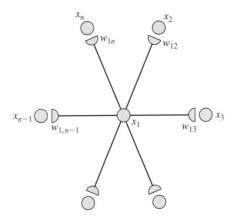

Figure 6.3 Outstar architecture.
SOURCE: Adapted from *Mathematical Biosciences*, *66*, D. S. Levine, Neural population modeling and psychology: A review, 1-86, Copyright 1983, with permission from Elsevier Science.

$w_{12}, \ldots, w_{1n}$ of source-to-sink connections. The outstar is affected by an input to the source node x_1, and a pattern (vector) of inputs to the sink nodes $x_2, \ldots, x_n$. (Grossberg sometimes interpreted the source input as a conditioned stimulus, or CS, and the sink inputs as an unconditioned stimulus, or US.) The activity of x_1 tends to increase if its input is present and to decay toward a baseline otherwise. The activity of each x_i increases if both x_1 and w_{1i} (associative strength between x_1 and x_i) are significant, and w_{1i} increases if x_1 and x_i are significant. The next section describes the resulting equations.

Stimulus traces are analogous to STM, and associative strengths are analogous to LTM. The decay rate for LTM traces is set much smaller than the decay rates for STM traces. If the inputs to the sink nodes form what Grossberg (1974) called a spatial pattern, that is, where the relative proportions of inputs to the different sink nodes are unchanged over time (Figure 6.4), the input pattern weights were shown to be stored in LTM at the relative associative weights from source to sink.

Table 6.1 Effects Incorporated into Grossberg's Differential Equations

A is presented	AB has been learned	B is expected
Yes	Yes	Yes
Yes	No	No
No	Yes	No
No	No	No

A is presented at a given time	B is presented a short time later	AB is learned
Yes	Yes	Yes
Yes	No	No
No	Yes	No
No	No	No

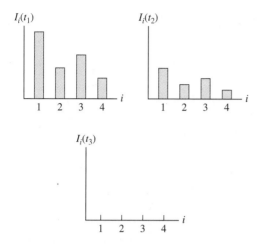

Figure 6.4 Example of a spatial pattern input, in which inputs may change over time but always remain in the same proportions.
SOURCE: Adapted from Levine (2000), with the permission of Lawrence Erlbaum Associates.

Concurrently, STM models were developed by Grossberg (1973), Wilson and Cowan (1973), Amari (1971), and others. These models were mathematical representations of the concept of reverberatory storage previously considered by McCulloch, Pitts, and Hebb. Yet what was stored in STM was not a faithful representation of the original input pattern, but a pattern transformed by means of lateral interactions, such as the lateral inhibition that Hartline and Ratliff (1957) found to be important in vision.

These STM models ultimately led to many models of sensory pattern processing, particularly of the preattentive stages of vision (see the third section of this chapter). The models reproduced a range of data in visual illusions and in the interaction of different visual features such as form, color, depth, and lightness. They also dealt with abstract theories about the large-time behavior of dynamical systems and their approach to attractors (M. A. Cohen & Grossberg, 1983; Hopfield, 1982).

Associative learning and lateral inhibition are two major organizing principles in the toolkit for making models of more complex cognitive phenomena. Some of the other principles are shown in Table 6.2. An example of a network that combines several principles is the adaptive resonance network for categorization, originated in Carpenter and Grossberg (1987) with many later variations. Adaptive resonance networks have two layers of nodes that code individual features and categories, with bidirectional connections and outstar-like associative learning in both directions, and lateral inhibition between competing categories. Combining categorization with other effects (e.g., selective attention and reinforcement learning) uses still more complex combinations of principles.

Principles such as those shown in Table 6.2 reflect general neural operations that are likely to occur, with variations, in different parts of the brain (e.g., there can be lateral inhibition between representations of different retinal locations, different categories, different emotions, different action plans, or different movements). Since the mid-1990s, network architectures have combined general toolkit principles with more direct physiological knowledge about specific brain areas and specific modulatory transmitter systems. Some of these will appear in later sections of

Table 6.2 Summary of Some Important Principles in Neural Network Organization

Associative learning, to enable strengthening or weakening of connections by contiguity or probable causality.
Lateral inhibition, to enable choices between competing percepts, drives, categorizations, plans, or behaviors.
Opponent processing, to enable selective enhancement of events that change over time.
Neuromodulation, to enable contextual refinement of attention.
Interlevel resonant feedback, to enable reality testing of tentative classifications.

SOURCE: Adapted from Hestenes (1992), with the permission of Lawrence Erlbaum Associates.

this chapter under the psychological functions they are designed to simulate.

Some Examples of Neural Network Methodology

There is such a diversity of neural network methods that it would be incorrect to label anything as a generic neural network. But let me illustrate the process of model making by showing how equations have been developed and solved for the outstar network of Figure 6.3, one of the simplest networks that embodies a key principle (associative learning) and is a building block for psychologically interesting networks.

Like most models described by Grossberg and his colleagues, the outstar is based on differential equations. Differential equations represent rates of change of interacting variables in continuous time, and it is possible to understand them and solve them computationally without having taken a standard course in differential equation theory. Such equations say that the rate of change of each node activity or connection weight is some (possibly time-dependent) function of that activity or weight and all the other activities or weights. This means that a differential equation can be thought of as a continuous-time update rule.

Let us represent the activity of the outstar source node (at the center of Figure 6.3) by x_1, and the activities of the other nodes, called sinks, by $x_2, x_3, \ldots, x_n$, called sinks. (The ellipsis after x_3 are a generally accepted notation for an indeterminate number of values or variables that fit into a general form.) Let us call the connection weights between the source node and each of the sink nodes by $w_2, w_3, \ldots, w_n$.

The source node activity x_1 is affected positively by the source node input I_i and negatively by decay back to a baseline rate (interpreted as 0). The notation for the rate of change (derivative) of x_1 as a function of time

is dx_1/dt. This leads to a differential equation of the form

$$\frac{dx_1}{dt} = -ax_1 + I_1 \qquad (1a)$$

where a is a positive constant (the decay rate). The sink node activities $x_i, i = 2, \ldots, n$ obey an equation similar to (1a) with the addition of an effect of the source node activity weighted by source-to-sink connection strength. Hence

$$\frac{dx_i}{dt} = -ax_i + bx_1w_i + I_i, \quad i = 2, \ldots, n \qquad (1b)$$

where b is another positive constant (coupling coefficient). The source-to-sink synaptic weights, or LTM traces w_i, in one version of the theory, decay only when x_1 is active; this represents what happens in conditioning when a CS is presented and not followed by a US. This decay is counteracted by US (i.e., x_i) activity. Thus

$$\frac{dw_i}{dt} = x_1(-cw_i + ex_i), \quad i = 2, \ldots, n \qquad (1c)$$

where c and e are still other positive constants (c typically smaller than a, representing the slow decay of LTM as compared to STM).

How does one solve a system of differential equations such as (1a), (1b), and (1c) on a computer? There are many software packages for solving differential equations, some of them attached to high-level languages such as Mathematica and MATLAB. One needs to write a routine that specifies the right-hand sides of the differential equations and then feed that into the differential equation solver, usually called an ordinary differential equation (ODE) solver. Or with relatively simple equations such as these, one obtains a good approximation by taking very small time steps, of size .1 or less, multiplying the time steps by the right-hand sides, and then adding to the current value of the variable whose derivative is being calculated to get the value of the same variable at the next time step. For example, if the time step is .1, the equation (1a) for the source node activity x_1, can be approximated by an updating rule of the form

$$x_1 (\text{at time } t+1)$$
$$= x_1 (\text{at time } t) + .1(-ax_1 (\text{at time } t)$$
$$+ I_1 (\text{at time } t)).$$

The high-level languages also typically include packages for graphing the resulting variables as functions of time. Exact closed-form mathematical solutions, such as are traditionally emphasized in differential equations classes, are not necessary; in fact, closed-form solutions are almost never obtainable in neural network equations.

Another fairly simple set of equations I have used in introductory graduate courses is the network for a set of nodes connected by lateral inhibition (discussed further in the third section). These nodes (arbitrarily many of them) typically interact by means of shunting excitation proportional to the difference of activity from a maximum value, and shunting inhibition proportional to the difference of activity from a minimum value (such as 0). This leads to a set of (arbitrarily many) equations of a form such as

$$\frac{dx_i}{dt} = -Ax_i + (B-x_i)f(x_i) - x_i \sum_{k \neq i} f(x_k)$$

where A and B are constants and f is typically either a sigmoid function or the square function (Grossberg, 1973). The "Σ" represents summed inhibition from all other nodes.

Another well-known network that I have found to be fairly user-friendly for introductory students is the conditioning model from Sutton and Barto (1981). This model does not use differential equations but instead uses separated time steps and direct updating rules for all the node activities, eligibilities, and weights. Levine (2000, Appendix 2) gives a detailed description of their dynamics.

MODELS OF SENSORY PROCESSES

Sensory perception, particularly visual, was the first area of psychology to be modeled successfully using neural networks. It is also perhaps the easiest area to quantify because of the direct connection between system processes and events in the external world.

Short-Term Memory and Preattentive Vision

In the middle to late 19th century, the noted physicists Helmholtz and Mach both observed that edges or contours between light and dark portions of a scene tend to be enhanced relative to the light or dark interiors of the scene. They explained this phenomenon by means of networks of retinal cells, each excited by light within a central area and inhibited by light within a surrounding area. Receptive fields with that structure were later found experimentally, in the compound eye of the horseshoe crab *Limulus* (Hartline & Ratliff, 1957) and in the vertebrate retina (Kuffler, 1953). This kind of structure is variously referred to as lateral inhibition or on-center off-surround.

The earliest STM models, as well as models in current use, reflect the fact that lateral inhibition and similar operations transform the "raw" sensory data well before they reach the cortex, even in the preattentive stages. In the case of vision, such transformations serve the function of compensating for imperfections in the process of perception, such as occur because of blind spots on the retina. Yet it is well established that this compensation mechanism creates some distortions of its own, such as illusions in every aspect of vision (for a network analysis see, e.g., Grossberg & Mingolla, 1985a).

There is controversy among both psychologists and neuroscientists about how widespread the principle of lateral inhibition is and whether it operates not just in the retina but in the cortex and other central brain areas as well. Yet McGuire, Gilbert, Rivlin, and Wiesel (1991) and others have found that the largest neurons in the cerebral cortex, which are called pyramidal cells, typically excite smaller neurons called stellate cells, which in turn project to and inhibit other, nearby pyramidal cells. Similar kinds of interactions between large and small cells occur in subcortical areas such as the hippocampus (Andersen, Gross, Lømo, & Sveen, 1969) and cerebellum (Eccles, Ito, & Szentagothai, 1967). Longer-range lateral inhibition in the cortex may be mediated by pathways connecting cortex to thalamus and basal ganglia (Taylor & Alavi, 1993).

Hartline and Ratliff (1957) modeled inhibition in the horseshoe crab eye by means of simultaneous linear equations for two mutually inhibiting receptors. However, other effects, many of them nonlinear, have been added by other modelers to explain mammalian visual data. For example, Sperling and Sondhi (1968) developed a lateral inhibitory model of the retina, including feedback, in order to explain certain data on luminance and flicker detection. The inhibition exerted by the feedback in their model is shunting rather than subtractive (see the section titled "Some Examples of Neural Network Methodology"). In subtractive inhibition, the incoming signal is linearly weighted, and an amount proportional to that signal is subtracted from the activity of the receiving node. In shunting inhibition, the amount subtracted is also proportional to the activity of the receiving node. Thus the inhibiting node acts as if it *divides* the receiving node's activity by a given amount, that is, shunts a given fraction of the node's activity onto another, parallel pathway.

In addition to shunting (multiplicative) inhibition, lateral inhibitory models often include shunting excitation, whose strength is proportional to the difference of a node's activity from its maximum possible level. This contrasts with additive excitation, which simply adds an amount proportional to the excitatory signal to the activity of a receiving node. Shunting interactions in neural networks have been suggested by experimental results on the effects of a presynaptic neuron on conductances of various ions across the postsynaptic membrane (cf. Freeman, 1983; Grossberg, 1973).

Sperling and Sondhi (1968) described the effect of shunting inhibition as reducing dynamic range. This means that although sensory inputs can be arbitrarily intense, the response of network nodes to these inputs has an upper limit. But while lateral inhibition can reduce distinctions between input intensities at extreme ranges, it can enhance such distinctions at intermediate ranges, an effect called contrast enhancement (Ellias & Grossberg, 1975; Grossberg & Levine, 1975).

Contrast enhancement is an outgrowth of decision or competition between inputs. Competition can be biased in favor of either more intense or less intense inputs by nonlinear interactions. Also, competition can be biased in favor of motivationally significant inputs; we return to that point in a later section on attention.

In early models involving lateral inhibition, nonrecurrent (feedforward) and recurrent (feedback) inhibition were preferred for different purposes and used to model different processes. The retina is designed to encode a fairly accurate representation of ongoing visual events, so nonrecurrent lateral inhibition is often preferred in retinal models in order to shorten the duration of pattern representations. The visual cortex, by contrast, is designed to encode both present events and memories of recent past ones; thus in cortical modeling, patterns should remain active in memory for longer periods, and recurrent lateral inhibition tends to be preferred in cortical models (e.g., Grossberg, 1973; Wilson & Cowan, 1973). Differences between actual network architecture in the retina and in the cortex generally reflect this functional difference.

In typical lateral inhibition models, an input pattern is regarded as the initial state of a mathematical *dynamical system,* which can be defined roughly as the movement through time of the solutions of a system of differential equations for interacting variables. This solution is described by a vector composed of the values of all the variables in the system at any given time. The equations describe the transformation of this pattern and its storage in STM; the stored pattern is then regarded as a limiting vector to which the system converges as time increases.

Lateral inhibitory architectures tend to enhance contrasts between pattern intensities. Inhibitory connections mean that larger activities tend to suppress smaller ones, so after a while some subcollection of nodes becomes, and remains, dominant. As a consequence, dynamical systems defined by such networks often, but not always, converge to an attractor as time increases. An attractor is a state in which the system interactions are in balance, so that once the system reaches that state, it will not be perturbed from it (M. A. Cohen & Grossberg, 1983; Hopfield, 1982).

Wilson and Cowan (1973) described a lateral inhibitory network for representing an area of cerebral cortex or thalamus. This network includes distance-dependent interactions whereby excitation falls off more sharply with distance than does inhibition. Different positions in the visual field, or different line orientations, can be represented at different cortical or thalamic locations. Their distance-dependent networks sometimes approach attractors, but also include the possibility of hysteresis, whereby if the amount of external stimulation is changed, the dynamics are dependent on the past history of stimula-

tion. For some parameters they also can exhibit oscillations in their long-term behavior, which were interpreted as possible analogs of the reverberatory loops between the cerebral cortex and the thalamus. The network reproduced such visual phenomena as metacontrast, responses to different spatial frequencies, and a hysteresis phenomenon found in stereopsis. Ermentrout and Cowan (1980), studying a more abstract version of Wilson and Cowan's network, proved the existence of oscillatory solutions that had properties in common with some simple visual hallucinations.

Grossberg (1973) studied on-center off-surround networks with both shunting excitation and shunting inhibition. He found that the attractor approached by the system was heavily influenced by what activation function was used for transformations at the node level (see the section titled "Perceptrons and Back Propagation"). Linear activation functions led to faithful representation of the input pattern, and therefore to an inability to suppress insignificant noise appearing on the retina. Sigmoid activation functions, by contrast, led to proportional representation of the pattern values above a certain activity level and suppression of those below (contrast enhancement plus noise suppression).

Such lateral inhibitory (on-center off-surround) modules have since been modified and embedded in larger networks to capture more realistic properties of preattentive vision and visual system structure. In particular, several network models (Grossberg & Mingolla, 1985a, 1985b; Levine & Grossberg, 1976; Wilson & Cowan, 1973) incorporate the notion that such illusions are by-products of a lateral inhibitory network designed to correct for irregularities in the luminance data that reaches the retina. Models of visual illusions typically involve both competition (from shunting lateral inhibition) and cooperation (from shunting lateral excitation),

Figure 6.5   Illusory white square induced by four black "pac-man" figures.

SOURCE: Kanizsa, Gaetano, Subjective contours. Copyright by Jerome Kuhl. All rights reserved.

sometimes along different dimensions and sometimes within the same dimension.

Orientation and visual field position are coded by cell populations in the visual cortex, along with spatial frequency, disparity of the right and left retinal images (a measure of depth), color, ocularity (cells may have a preference for one or another eye or else respond equally to inputs from either eye), and motion. Some neural networks used to simulate

visual data combine two or more of these variables. For example, the networks of Grossberg and Mingolla (1985a), which simulate some illusory percepts of visual contours, use both orientation and position information. In Figure 6.5, from Kanizsa (1976), two white line segments that are present and of the same orientation are perceptually joined together by an illusory longer line segment. In their network, boundaries are perceived as signals "sensitive to the orientation and amount of contrast at a scenic edge, but not to its direction of contrast" (Grossberg & Mingolla, 1985a, p. 176).

Figure 6.6a illustrates insensitivity to contrast direction. Each node responds to lines of a particular orientation at a particular position. There is competition between receptors for like orientations at nearby positions (Figure 6.6b) and between receptors for widely different orientations at the same location (Figure 6.6c). Short-range competition is supplemented by long-range cooperation (Figure 6.6d). Such long-range cooperation enables continuous contours to form by linking together separated lines of the same orientation. One of the benefits to the organism of this linkage of contours is compensation for discontinuities (caused by blind spots) in the image on the retina.

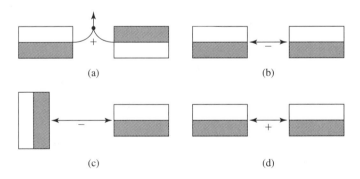

Figure 6.6   (a) Boundary signals sensitive to orientation and amount of contrast, but not to direction of contrast. (b) Like orientations compete at nearby perceptual locations. (c) Different orientations compete at each perceptual location. (d) Once activated, aligned orientations cooperate across a larger visual domain to form contours.

SOURCE: Grossberg & Mingolla, *Psychological Review, 92,* 173–211, 1985. Copyright 1985 by the American Psychological Association. Reprinted by permission.

Some models of vision are based on the importance of boundaries for detecting objects. For example, Marr (1982) described boundaries between light and dark areas of a scene as points of zero curvature (or inflection points) of the curve for luminance as a function of distance, as shown in Figure 6.7. Mathematically, this represents the point of sharpest transition in the luminance value.

However, the mechanism for perceiving boundaries must be supplemented by another mechanism for perceiving the form of what is *inside* those boundaries. The feature-detecting mechanism, unlike the boundary-detecting mechanism, should be sensitive to direction of contrast. Grossberg (1983) discusses one possible combination of boundary and feature contour mechanisms (Figure 6.8). A linear nonrecurrent mechanism that can only generate boundaries (Figure 6.8b) is contrasted with a nonlinear recurrent mechanism that can generate both boundaries and interiors (Figure 6.8c). Initially, all nodes excited by the rectangular input of Figure 6.8a receive equal inputs. Because the inhibitory interaction coefficients are distance-dependent, nodes excited by the part of the rectangle near its boundary receive less inhibition than do those nodes nearer the rectangle's center. As

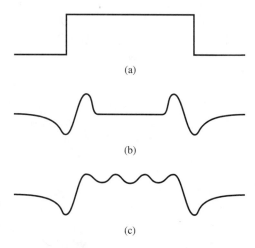

Figure 6.8   (a) Input pattern whereby a region is activated uniformly. (b) Response of feedforward competitive network to pattern (a); edges of the activated region are enhanced and its interior is suppressed. (c) Response of a feedback competitive network to pattern (a); interior is activated in a spatially periodic fashion.
SOURCE: Grossberg (1983), with permission of Cambridge University Press.

time goes on, those enhanced boundary nodes inhibit other nodes whose preferred positions are contiguous to those boundaries but closer to the center. This in turn disinhibits some nodes still nearer to the center, leading to a wave-like pattern (Figure 6.8c). The distance between peaks of the wave is dependent nonlinearly on excitatory and inhibitory interaction coefficients.

Figure 6.8 provides a possible explanation for the experimental result that many visual cortical neurons fire preferentially to some specific spatial frequency (Robson, 1975). From this result, many theorists have concluded that spatial frequency is one of the primitives of the visual system, or, more speculatively, that the visual system performs Fourier analysis of patterns into frequency components (e.g., Pribram, 1991).

The interacting feature and boundary contour systems provided the basis for a theory of visual object recognition. In contrast to Marr's (1982) view that people see mainly

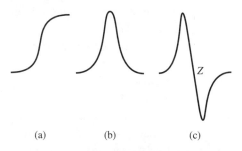

(a)   (b)   (c)

Figure 6.7   Zero-crossing. (a) Transition (edge) between dark and light regions is shown by a sharp rise in the graph of luminance as a function of distance. (b) First derivative of this function has a peak. (c) Second derivative has a zero-crossing (transition from positive to negative) at Z.
SOURCE: Adapted from Marr (1982), with permission of W. H. Freeman and Company.

boundaries, Grossberg (1987a) advanced the "radical claim that *all* boundaries are invisible until they can support different filled-in featural contrasts within the FC [feature contour] System" (p. 108). Within the feature contour system in this theory, the apparently separate modules that neurophysiologists have discovered in the cerebral cortex for processing form, color, and depth are seen as part of a unified whole.

Recall that one function suggested for recurrent lateral interactions is to compensate for imperfections in the retina's uptake of visual stimuli. Some of these imperfections result from blind spots or blood vessels in the eye. Others result from possible distortions of relative brightness or color relationships in the scene by the ambient light; hence, one of the functions of the cortical networks is to discount the illuminant, that is, calculate color or brightness of the actual scene rather than what impinges directly on the retina. The proposed brain mechanisms for all this involve several different parts of the visual cortex and lateral geniculate body.

Competitive-cooperative neural networks have also been fruitful in modeling the construction of a three-dimensional image from the disparate images received by the left and right retinas. Many binocular vision theorists (e.g., Dev, 1975) have explained the formation of depth percepts using networks whose nodes detect specific disparities between the two retinal images. The basic computational problem involved in stereo vision was described in Marr and Poggio (1979) as the elimination of false targets. That is, given a point in the left-eye image, the eyes and brain first calculate its disparity with respect to many points on the right-eye image. Hence, several depth measurements are possible, and one must choose (using a competitive mechanism) the correct corresponding point in the right-eye image.

Marr and Poggio (1979) also noted that retinal image disparity measures are insuffi-

cient to compute perceived depth but must be integrated with orientation and spatial frequency information. In Marr and Poggio's (1979) model, a three-dimensional scene is filtered through channels (masks) that select particular orientations. Boundaries can be located by taking the image through given orientation masks and locating the edges at zeros of the second derivative of perceived luminance (see Figure 6.7). Similar filtering is done through spatial frequency channels. Marr and Poggio showed how to integrate disparity, orientation, and spatial frequency information into a coherent three-dimensional approximation of a given three-dimensional scene preceding binocular integration, which they called a $2\frac{1}{2}$-D sketch.

Another approach to binocular vision has been developed by M. A. Cohen and Grossberg (1984) and Grossberg (1987b). Their networks include feedback between monocular and binocular representation areas, each with its own separate on-center off-surround network and including opponent processing. In contrast to Marr and Poggio's idea of the pre-binocular $2\frac{1}{2}$-D sketch, Grossberg and Cohen developed a theory in which binocular integration is nearly inseparable from the processing of other visual information such as color and form.

As for visual motion perception, this visual phenomenon, like others, has an illusory as well as a veridical component; for example, apparent motion can be generated by two separate flashes of light in different locations at particular time intervals. Marr and Ullman (1981) explained this using a neural network that combines different nodes with sustained and transient responses to stimuli. The sustained units respond to particular contrast and orientation patterns that persist even if their location in the visual field shifts slightly. The transient units respond to changes in light intensity, color, and the like at particular locations. Marr and Ullman based the visual responses in their network on zero crossings that represent transition points or boundaries (see Figure 6.7). Grossberg and Rudd (1992) combined the Marr-Ullman idea of sustained and transient detectors with the feature and boundary contour systems (Grossberg & Mingolla, 1985a, 1985b) achieved by shunting on-center off-surround interactions. Grossberg and Rudd saw "a complex interdependency between such stimulus variables as contrast, size, duration, color, and figural organization in determining the perceived motion" (p. 82). They described how this approach leads to a system including nodes combining signals from both sustained and transient units, and with properties analogies to the visual motion area of the cortex (V4 or medial temporal).

Sensory Coding

Building on models of sensory STM, several researchers starting in the 1970s modeled how a node in a neural network can learn to respond to particular patterns of activity at other groups of nodes. These patterns of activity, in turn, could represent combinations of sensory features. This section deals with coding in that sense, not in the sense of how the primary representation of a sensory stimulus is actually formed in the nervous system. Network mechanisms for this kind of coding have possible implications for biological organisms during development.

Current models of coding and categorization are often based on ideas introduced by Malsburg (1973). Malsburg's model is based on recurrent excitation and inhibition between simulated cortical nodes, combined with modifiable (by associative or Hebbian learning) synapses to the "cortex" from an input ("retinal") layer of nodes. His motivation for developing this model was a body of experimental results on the mammalian visual system. These results suggested that

the "task of the cortex for the processing of visual information is different from that of the peripheral optical system. Whereas eye, retina and lateral geniculate body (LGB) transform the images in a 'photographic' way, i.e., preserving essentially the spatial arrangement of the retinal image, the cortex transforms this geometry into a space of concepts" (p. 85).

In particular, Malsburg's (1973) model and subsequent ones discussed in this section drew their inspiration from physiological results on single-cell responses to line orientations. These models can explain findings that neurons in the cat or monkey visual cortex respond preferentially to lines of a particular orientation, and that cells responding to similar orientations are grouped close together anatomically, in columns (Hubel & Wiesel, 1962, 1965, 1968). These models also explain findings that preferred orientations of neurons are influenced by early visual experience (e.g., Blakemore & Cooper, 1970; Hirsch & Spinelli, 1970).

Some models (e.g., Bienenstock, Cooper, & Munro, 1982, p. 32; Grossberg, 1976a, p. 131) also address evidence that there is a critical period in the development of orientation detectors. That is, for a short period of time (in cats, age 23 days to 4 months; in humans, 6 months to 2 years), cortical orientation tuning is much more modifiable than it is either earlier or later.

Malsburg's (1973) simulated cortex is organized into two separate populations, excitatory and inhibitory nodes. The variation of connection strengths with distance endows the simulated cortex with a crude form of the lateral inhibitory architecture of narrow-range excitation and broad-range inhibition. In the terminology of the last section, Malsburg's laws for lateral interaction between nodes are additive rather than shunting. Excitatory and inhibitory nodes are organized into two parallel planes, each with a hexagonal

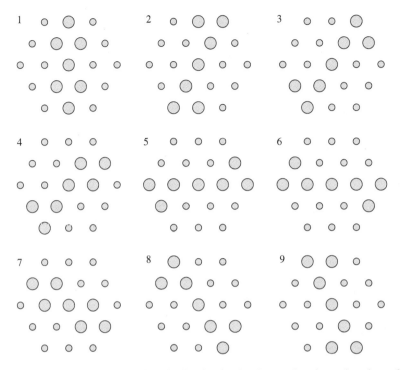

Figure 6.9   Standard set of stimuli used on the simulated retina. Larger dots denote locations of activated nodes.
SOURCE: Reprinted from Malsburg (1973) with permission of Springer-Verlag.

arrangement of nodes. Excitatory nodes excite neighboring nodes, both excitatory and inhibitory ones, whereas inhibitory nodes inhibit excitatory nodes that are a distance of two away.

Of the connections in Malsburg's (1973) model, only those from retinal afferents to cortical nodes have modifiable weights. The rule for changing these weights combines an associative learning law with a synaptic conservation rule that makes inactive connections decay as active ones grow with learning. Synaptic conservation was imposed to prevent the unbounded growth of synaptic strengths that would otherwise result from associative learning.

Figure 6.9 shows the standard set of stimuli used on Malsburg's (1973) model retina. These stimuli correspond to bars of light at different orientations. As shown in Figure 6.10, orientation detectors, such as were found by

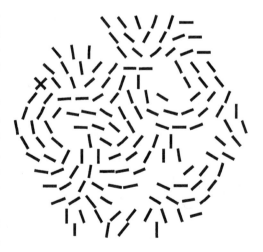

Figure 6.10   Simulated cortex after 100 time steps of learning. Each bar indicates the orientation to which the excitatory node at that location is most responsive. Blank spaces represent locations of nodes that never learn to react to any of the standard stimuli.
SOURCE: Adapted from Malsburg (1973) with permission of Springer-Verlag.

Hubel and Wiesel (1962, 1968), develop spontaneously among Malsburg's simulated cortical cells. After 100 learning steps, the lateral excitatory and inhibitory interactions lead to self-organization of cortical nodes, whereby most nodes have preferred orientations and nodes of similar preferred orientations tend to be grouped together.

The idea of synaptic conservation is intuitively based on the notion that some chemical substance, whether a transmitter or second messenger, is present in a fixed amount at postsynaptic sites and is distributed in variable fashion across impinging synapses. This mechanism is necessary for the effects in Malsburg (1973) and in a related model of the visual cortex by Wilson (1975). Some categorization models (e.g., Carpenter & Grossberg, 1987; Rumelhart & Zipser, 1985) also use learning laws whereby strengthening of some synapses weakens other synapses. Such laws are reminiscent of Rescorla and Wagner's (1972) learning scheme, which includes an upper bound on the total associative strength of all stimuli with a given reinforcer.

Grossberg (1976a) developed a model that has many principles in common with Malsburg's (1973) but does not use a synaptic conservation law for learning. He argued mathematically that such a conservation law is incompatible with secondary classical conditioning. Moreover, although Malsburg used this law to keep synaptic strengths— and therefore total network activity—from growing too large, one can also achieve this by replacing additive lateral interactions with shunting interactions. His model for development and tuning of feature detectors, combining lateral inhibition for STM with associative synaptic modification for LTM, is discussed in Grossberg (1976a). Figure 6.11 shows the minimal network of that article. This network, like that of Malsburg, includes unidirectional modifiable synapses from an input layer F_1 to a "cortical" layer F_2, leading to coding of input patterns by cortical nodes. Grossberg (1976b) extended this model to include modifiable feedback from F_2 to F_1. To describe the mutually excitatory dynamics that emerge in a modifiable network with top-down feedback, he coined the term *adaptive resonance*. This work ultimately led to the well-known adaptive resonance theory (ART) of Carpenter and Grossberg (1987).

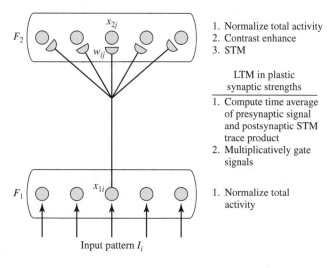

Figure 6.11 Minimal model of development and tuning of feature detectors using STM and LTM mechanisms.
SOURCE: Adapted from Grossberg (1976a) with permission of Springer-Verlag.

The network of Figure 6.11 has nonrecurrent (feedforward) on-center off-surround connections between the input-receiving nodes x_{1i} and recurrent on-center off-surround connections between the pattern-coding nodes x_{2i}. F_1 and F_2 represent successive layers in a hierarchical network. Grossberg suggested that variations on the same hierarchy could be repeated in different brain regions. In Malsburg (1973), F_1 was interpreted as either retina or thalamus, and F_2 as visual cortex. But F_1 might also be identified with a composite of early processing areas in the retina and F_2 with retinal areas closer to the optic nerve (Grossberg, 1976a). Also, because the visual cortex itself contains several processing stages, identified with cell groups known as simple, complex, and hypercomplex cells (Hubel & Wiesel, 1962, 1965, 1968), F_1 and F_2 might be interpreted as different parts of cortex. Nor are these architectures restricted to vision: Grossberg (1976a) described yet another interpretation, whereby F_1 is the olfactory bulb and F_2 is olfactory cortex.

Malsburg's and Grossberg's coding architectures follow a similar generic plan: two layers hierarchically arranged, with associative learning in bottom-up synapses and the second-level nodes coding patterns of activities in the first level. Other neural networks with similar designs include Bienenstock et al. (1982) and Edelman and Reeke (1982). In addition to modeling the development of visual feature (especially orientation) detectors, these networks provide a basis for the more complex process of modeling categorization (see the sixth section). The set of patterns that preferentially excites each of the high-level nodes in a coding model forms a category. In order to stabilize the code representations under the barrage of possible new input patterns, Grossberg (1976b) also included associative learning in top-down as well as bottom-up connections. This provides in his model the basis for learning prototypes (which change with experience) and is the heart of the adaptive resonance model that he and Carpenter developed. Yet even without top-down feedback, models of coding lead naturally into models of categorization.

MODELS OF MOTOR CONTROL

Neural network modeling of brain processes has basically proceeded from the outside in, so that sensory and motor processes began to be modeled before more central ones. First came models of planned individual movements, then sequences of movements.

Individual Movements

Kuperstein (1988, p. 1308) discussed some issues involved in modeling motor control: "The human brain develops accurate sensorimotor coordination despite many unforeseen changes in the dimensions of the body, strength of the muscles, and placements of the organs. This is accomplished for the most part without a teacher." Two other issues are the ability to learn an invariant movement regardless of velocity and the synchronization of different muscles into a coordinated movement.

Modelers disagree about whether motor control has requirements similar to or different from those for sensory pattern processing. Discussing their arm movement control model, Wada and Kawato (1993, p. 932) state, "It is expected that this trajectory formation model can be used as a pattern recognition network because a kind of duality exists between pattern formation and recognition in this framework." Yet Gaudiano and Grossberg (1991, pp. 180–181) suggest that the two sets of tasks require fundamentally different architectures, because sensory pattern processing needs to be based on *match* learning (such as adaptive resonance; see the sixth section), whereas motor control needs to be based on *mismatch* learning (i.e., some form of error correction).

Because of space limitations this chapter will only cover models of arm movement control, except to note that some of the principles used in arm movement modeling have also been applied to eye movements (Grossberg & Kuperstein, 1989) and speech production (Guenther, 1995). Bullock and Grossberg (1988) modeled a variety of data on the invariances of planned arm movements. This includes, for example, the bell-shaped velocity profile based on data of Atkeson and Hollerbach (1985): The velocity of movement as a function of time has the same qualitative shape over a wide range of movement sizes and speeds. Such invariances can be modeled using a network that includes high-level nodes that explicitly calculate the trajectory optimizing some physical function (e.g., Flash & Hogan, 1985; Wada & Kawato, 1993). However, the variable-speed and synchronization issues mentioned at the start of this section led Bullock and Grossberg toward a network in which globally invariant properties are not explicitly programmed but emerge from events distributed across many interacting sensory, neural, and muscular loci. Such models include error correction (of a type reminiscent of the circular reaction of Piaget, 1952) but no explicit optimization.

In Bullock and Grossberg's (1988) vector integration to endpoint (VITE) model, a given movement is performed at variable velocities depending on the activity of a "GO" signal (see Figure 6.12). The GO activity is multiplied by the computed vector of muscle activities. Such factorization of a neural activity vector into a product of energy (total intensity) and pattern (relative strengths) has been a theme of Grossberg's work, in perceptual as well as motor contexts. For example, this theme appears in the studies of relative weights in an outstar (discussed in the

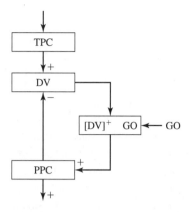

Figure 6.12   VITE motor control circuit. TPC = target position command; PPC = present position command; DV = difference vector (error); GO = GO signal, which is multiplied by the difference vector. The full circuit includes interactions between DV and PPC stages of agonist and antagonist muscle commands.
SOURCE: Adapted by permission of the publisher from Bullock & Grossberg, in W. A. Hershberger (ed.), *Volitional Action*, pp. 253–298. Copyright 1989 by Elsevier Science Publishing Co., Inc.

second section) and of discounting the illuminant (discussed in the third section). The present position command (PPC) is compared with a target position command (TPC) to form a difference vector (DV). The GO command (identified with output from the globus pallidus of the basal ganglia) interacts with the DV. The PPC is gradually updated by integrating the multiplied vector, that is, summing it over (continuous) time. The effect of the PPC on motoneurons is organized through agonist-antagonist pairs of muscles. Cells analogous to DV nodes have been located in arm zones of the premotor, motor, and parietal areas of the cerebral cortex (e.g., Georgopoulos, Kalaska, Caminiti, & Massey, 1984).

Gaudiano and Grossberg (1991) developed an adaptive extension of the VITE model called the vector associative map (VAM) to enable the corrective DV calculations to be influenced by visual feedback. This involves learning that depends on random generation of potential arm positions at the PPC by motor "babbling," which is again reminiscent of Piaget's circular reaction. This class of models was also extended to multiple arm joints in Bullock, Grossberg, and Guenther (1993). Still further extensions of this class of models involve specific roles for the cerebellum, motor cortex, and other brain motor control regions (Bullock, Cisek, & Grossberg, 1998; Cisek, Grossberg, & Bullock, 1998). Hence a network theory previously developed to model task-imposed constraints was extended in order to map closely onto cortical neuroanatomy and neurophysiology.

Kawato, Furukawa, and Suzuki (1987) and Kawato, Isobe, Maeda, and Suzuki (1988) simulated a control circuit driven by sensory signals and inspired by known anatomy and physiology of several brain areas. Like the Bullock-Grossberg (1988) network, the networks of Kawato et al. can learn a movement at one speed and then perform the same movement at a different speed. These models combine solution of the inverse problem (calculating movements from a desired position) with that of the forward problem (calculating possible consequences of particular movements). Unlike the models of Grossberg's group, those of Kawato's group are based on explicit minimization of a motor-related variable: rate of change of torque. Interleaved learning of forward and inverse mappings is found in some other models (e.g., Jordan & Rumelhart, 1992, which is based on back propagation with additional units, and Bullock et al., 1993).

Models of Motor Sequence Learning

Several investigators have added recurrent interactions to the basic supervised backpropagation network in order to train a network to produce a specified time sequence of outputs. The first of these was Jordan (1986), who added to a standard back-propagation network some feedback and some plan units

activated by external stimuli. The net effect is to have a decaying memory of past events blended with current plans. The sequential network has been applied to controlling arm motor trajectories (Massone & Bizzi, 1989) and also to learning linguistic sequences (Elman, 1990).

Other sequence models have been based on the ART model (Carpenter & Grossberg, 1987), which is based on high-level nodes classifying patterns of low-level node activity. Bapi and Levine (1994, 1997) combined ART with a mechanism for storing multiple copies of list items combined with learnable long-term transition weights between items. They applied their network to simulating monkey data showing that prefrontal lesions do not disrupt learning simple motor sequences but disrupt learning of sequences classes.

Bapi and Levine's networks can learn many sequences composed of rearrangements of the same elements by encoding them at sequence detector nodes. Sequence nodes also appear in the models of Dominey and Arbib (1992) and Dominey, Arbib, and Joseph (1995) for learning a sequence of eye movements based on associations between visual cues and target positions. These models include basal ganglia, along with parietal and frontal cortex and various parts of thalamus and midbrain, in generating eye movements. This includes learnable signals from the cortex to basal ganglia pathways involved in selective disinhibition of generations of saccades in particular directions. In one set of simulations, learnable signals to basal ganglia from inferotemporal cortex were used to simulate data on conditioned discrimination of associations between visual cues and target eye movement responses in monkeys. A variant of the model, using prefrontal instead of inferotemporal cortex, learns to produce a sequence of saccades in response to a sequence of spatial targets. These networks also use reward and punishment signals to change weights between context elements and sequence generators.

Modeling motor sequence learning relates to modeling temporal sequence perception. Some models of temporal sequence perception incorporate specific neurophysiological interactions, such as those in the hippocampus. Levy (1996) developed a sequence-discriminating network based on autoassociation (see the section titled "Autoassociation and Heteroassociation")—inspired by long-term potentiation at hippocampal synapses—that solved disambiguation problems in temporal sequence learning. Denham and McCabe (1996) emphasized the role of the hippocampal CA3 region in comparing inputs from two other regions, one representing a predicted next element of a sequence and the other representing the actual element.

MODELS OF COGNITIVE-EMOTIONAL INTERACTIONS

Neural network models considered the effects of reward and punishment fairly early in their development (Grossberg, 1972a, 1972b; Klopf, 1982; Werbos, 1974). Some of them also considered the interplay of positive and negative affect via opponent processing (Grossberg, 1972a, 1972b). The interactions of cognitive and emotional variables have played a major role in models of conditioning and, more recently, of interactions among brain areas such as the cortex, limbic system, and basal ganglia.

Models of Conditioning

Klopf (1982) proposed that a synapse is increased in efficacy if its activity is followed by a net increase in the depolarization (positive stimulation) received by the postsynaptic cell. In other words, he proposed that depolarization acts as positive reinforcement for neurons. Klopf's theory was based on an analogy between single neurons and whole brains, both treated as goal-seeking devices. This is the reason why he titled his book *The Hedonistic Neuron*.

The importance of activity change, as opposed to activity itself, was also highlighted in Rescorla and Wagner's (1972) theory, which is not neurally based but has influenced the work of many neural modelers. Their theory is based on the results of classical conditioning experiments indicating that associative learning of a CS can be greatly influenced by the background stimuli present during both training and recall trials. The main tenet of their theory was that "organisms only learn when events violate expectations. Certain expectations are built up about the events following a stimulus complex: expectations initiated by the complex and its component stimuli are then only modified when consequent events disagree with the composite expectation" (p. 75).

Sutton and Barto (1981) set out to explain classical conditioning with a theory that included elements of both the Rescorla-Wagner (1972) and Klopf (1982) theories. Their conditioning model includes n stimulus traces $x_i(t)$, an output signal $y(t)$, and n synaptic weights $w_i(t)$, as shown in Figure 6.13. These weights are considered to denote associations between CSs and a primary reinforcer or US.

Sutton and Barto (1981) proposed that in addition to the stimulus traces that denote the duration and intensity of given CSs, additional traces are separate from the stimuli and last longer. These are the actual memory traces, but Sutton and Barto termed them *eligibility traces* because they indicate when a particular synapse is eligible for modification. Possible cellular mechanisms involving calcium ions and cyclic nucleotides were suggested for eligibility traces. Finally, the current amount of reinforcement, $y(t)$, was compared with the

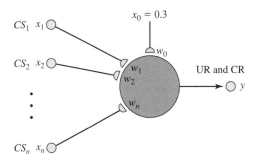

Figure 6.13 Network with n learnable conditioned stimulus (CS) pathways, and a pathway with fixed weight w_0 for the unconditioned stimulus (US). The node y represents unconditioned and conditioned responses (UR and CR).
SOURCE: From Sutton & Barto, *Psychological Review, 88,* 135–170, 1981. Copyright 1981 by the American Psychological Association. Adapted by permission.

weighted average of values of y over some time interval preceding t.

The two innovations in Sutton and Barto's (1981) model—eligibility traces and learning dependent on change in postsynaptic activity—were motivated by results on timing in classical conditioning. In particular, the model can explain the fact that in many conditioning paradigms, the optimal interstimulus interval is greater than 0. Sutton and Barto's network can also simulate other contextual effects in classical conditioning, such as blocking the formation of associations to a new stimulus if another stimulus that has already been conditioned is simultaneously present.

Sutton and Barto's (1981) work was elaborated by Klopf (1988) and others into the differential Hebbian learning rule (also called the drive-reinforcement rule), whereby synapses change in strength as a function of changes over time in both presynaptic and postsynaptic activities. Klopf was led to such a rule by his earlier hedonistic neuron theory, in which neurons themselves were goal-seeking.

Klopf's (1988) network simulated a wide variety of classical conditioning data. These data included blocking, secondary conditioning, extinction and reacquisition of an extinguished response, conditioned inhibition, effects of interval between CS and US occurrences, and effects of stimulus durations and amplitudes. (However, the simulations of CS and US interval effects depend on some weighting factors for time delays, and these factors were chosen specifically to match those data. Klopf did not suggest an underlying mechanism for generating those weighting factors.) A summary of classical conditioning data reproduced by the Klopf model and its comparison with other conditioning models appear in Chance, Cheung, Lykins, and Lawton (1997).

The synaptic learning law involving change in postsynaptic activity is not the only possible way to simulate timing effects or blocking in classical conditioning. The same data were simulated by Grossberg and Levine (1987) using a network that combines associative learning with attentional effects due to lateral inhibition. Also, the Grossberg school has incorporated into conditioning models a mechanism for affective opponent processing, which is the basis for an architecture called the gated dipole. The gated dipole theory was motivated by an effort to compare current values of stimulus or reinforcement variables with recent past values of the same variables.

Gated dipoles were introduced by Grossberg (1972a, 1972b) to answer the following question about reinforcement. Suppose an animal receiving steady electric shock presses a lever that turns off the shock. Later, in the same context, the animal's tendency to press the lever is increased. How can a motor response associated with the *absence* of a punishing stimulus (shock) become itself positively reinforcing?

Figure 6.14 shows a schematic gated dipole. The synapses w_1 and w_2, marked with squares, have a chemical transmitter that tends to be depleted with activity, as indicated by

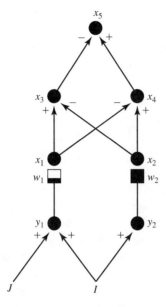

Figure 6.14   Schematic gated dipole network. J is a significant input (electric shock in the example of Grossberg, 1972b), and I is nonspecific arousal. Synapses w_1 and w_2 can undergo depletion (as w_1 has in this diagram), as indicated by partial lightening of square boxes. After J is shut off, $w_1 < w_2$ (transiently), so $x_1 < x_2$. By competition, x_4 is activated, enhancing a motor output suppressed by J.

the $-y_i w_i$ terms in the differential equations for those w_i values. This could be called an anti-Hebbian law because the direction of change with use is opposite to the one Hebb and others use for associative learning. Other terms in those equations denote new trans-

mitter production, which is greatest when the transmitter is much less than its maximum. In Figure 6.14, the input J represents shock, for example. The input I is a nonspecific arousal to both channels y_1-to-x_1-to-x_3 and y_2-to-x_2-to-x_4, which compete for activation. While shock is on, the left channel receives more input than the right channel; hence transmitter is more depleted at w_1 than at w_2. But the greater input overcomes the more depleted transmitter, so left channel activity x_1 exceeds right channel activity x_2. This leads, by feedforward competition between channels, to net positive activity from the left channel output node x_3. For a short time after shock is removed, both channels receive equal inputs I, but the right channel is less depleted of transmitter than the left channel. Hence, right channel activity x_2 now exceeds x_1 until the depleted transmitter recovers. Again, competition leads to net positive activity from the right channel output node x_4. Whichever channel has greater activity either excites or inhibits x_5, thereby enhancing or suppressing a particular motor response.

The network is called a gated dipole because it has two channels that are opposite (negative and positive) and that gate signals based on the amount of available transmitter. Characteristic output of one gated dipole is graphed in Figure 6.15. This graph illustrates the rebound in x_4 activity after the cessation of

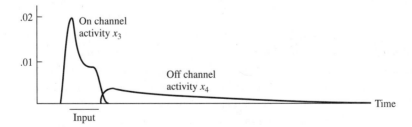

Figure 6.15   Typical time course of the channel outputs of a gated dipole.
SOURCE: Adapted from *Neural Networks, 2,* D. S. Levine & P. S. Prueitt, Modeling some effects of frontal lobe damage: Novelty and perseveration, 103–116, with permission from Elsevier Science.

x_3 activity. Grossberg's work was concurrent with Solomon and Corbit's (1974) opponent-processing theory of motivation, whereby significant events elicit both an initial reaction and a subsequent counterreaction. Indeed, Grossberg (1987b) hinted that a gated dipole can exhibit switching back and forth between opposite responses.

Grossberg (1987b) used this transmitter-depletion mechanism instead of a simple time-difference mechanism to model the effects of stimulus changes in order to capture two effects in conditioning. One is that the positive reinforcement value of escape from shock is sensitive to both its intensity and its duration. The other is that the amount of reinforcement depends on the overall arousal level of the network (or organism).

If the two channels in Figure 6.14 are reversed in sign so that the channel receiving input is the positive one, the network provides an explanation for frustration when a positively reinforcing event either is terminated or does not arrive when expected. The rebounds between positive and negative also explain the partial reinforcement acquisition effect. According to the gated dipole theory, a reward's attractiveness is enhanced by comparison with an expected lack of reward.

The idea of opponent processing can be generalized to many other neural processes. It is an old idea in vision; for example, the retina contains pairs of receptors for opponent colors (e.g., green and red), and one of the two colors is transiently perceived after removal of the other one. The dipole in the sensory domain includes nodes responding to presence or absence of specific sensory stimuli. Grossberg (1980) used transient rebounds in such dipoles to model visual phenomena such as color-dependent tilt aftereffects. Also, gated dipoles have been applied to modeling motor systems. In those models, dipoles simulate the actions of neuron populations innervating agonist-antagonist muscle pairs (Bullock &

Grossberg, 1988; Grossberg & Kuperstein, 1989; see the fourth section).

Involvement of Different Brain Areas

Many of the conditioning models discussed in the last section were inspired by data on the rabbit's nictitating membrane response (NMR), that is, the conditioned eye blink in response to a clicking sound paired with a tap to the forehead. Since the early 1990s, more data has appeared on brain areas involved in the NMR, and these data have influenced the development of neural network models. Thompson (1990) mapped the detailed circuitry of the NMR involving connections between the cerebellum and areas of the brainstem controlling facial sensation and eye movement. Perrett, Ruiz, and Mauk (1993) found that lesions to the cerebellar cortex disrupt timing of conditioned NMRs.

The role of the cerebellum in mediating timing of the conditioned response is complemented by a role of the hippocampus in encoding the timing of stimulus arrivals. In particular, Berger, Berry, and Thompson (1986) found that during the NMR and conditioned jaw movement paradigms, the pattern of neuron responses in hippocampal pyramidal neurons mimics the time course of the conditioned response. This time course fits the learned timing of US arrival.

These adaptively timed cell responses are from the CA3 subregion of hippocampus, which receives inputs from different types of cells in another region of hippocampus, the dentate gyrus. These dentate cells are time-locked to the CS; that is, each cell exhibits an increase in firing rate starting at a fixed time interval after the CS. Hence, the hippocampal network has to convert an array of fixed time delays into adaptive timing.

Grossberg and Schmajuk (1989) designed a neural network, an extension of their 1987 model (see the previous subsection), whereby a collection of neurons with a range of time delays is involved in timing a conditioned response. Subsequent models related their insights to cerebellar and hippocampal data (Bullock, Fiala, & Grossberg, 1994; Fiala, Grossberg, & Bullock, 1996; Grossberg & Merrill, 1996; see also Gluck & Myers, 1993, and Myers & Gluck, 1994, for related models). Their technique for accomplishing this timing function consists of a network with a large number (80 in their first simulation) of gated dipoles (the opponent processing model of Figure 6.14), each becoming activated and habituated at a different rate. The authors called this device spectral timing because it includes a spectrum of possible activation rates, thereby enabling the network to learn to expect stimuli or perform responses at specific time delays after the CS.

Grossberg and Merrill (1996) proposed that the spectral timing architecture appears in both the cerebellum and the hippocampus and performs different functions in each. In the cerebellum it controls the timing of the conditioned motor response. In the hippocampus it controls the relationship between timing of sensory stimuli and learning of their appetitive or aversive significance; for example, if an animal expects to receive food at a given time after a bell is rung, it should not have a frustration response to the nondelivery of food before that time. Bullock et al. (1994) modeled the neurophysiology of cerebellar aspects of timing on the NMR. Fiala et al. (1996) elaborated that model by incorporating detailed biochemistry of transmitters, receptors, and second messengers that affect both climbing fiber and parallel fiber input to Purkinje cells.

In addition to these animal learning models, there have been many neural network studies of brain involvement in human cognitive-emotional interactions. Many of these studies relate to the prefrontal cortex, a region long implicated as playing a special role in coordinating and integrating plans of

action based on combining sensory signals from the environment and visceral and motivational signals from the organism.

Most efforts at neural network modeling of frontal lobe function have focused on specific cognitive tasks that illustrate certain common themes in effects of prefrontal lesions in human patients or monkeys. These themes include, for example, reduced ability to learn and perform planned sequences of behaviors, disruption of cognitive-motivational interactions, and disturbance in the processing of context. The models of sequence learning were discussed in the fourth section, so we now discuss models of the other two types of disruption.

Disruption of Cognitive-Motivational Interactions

The frontal lobes are the part of cortex with the strongest reciprocal connections with subcortical parts of the brain involved in processing internal drive levels (the hypothalamus) and positive or negative valences of stimuli (the limbic system). For this reason, frontal lobe damage leads to diminished influence of reinforcement on behavioral performance. An aspect of this syndrome is perseveration in behaviors that were formerly, but are no longer, rewarding.

An example of perseveration occurs in the Wisconsin Card Sorting Test (WCST), whereby the participant is given a sequence of 128 cards, each displaying a number, color, and shape, and is asked to match each card to one of four template cards. The experimenter then says whether the match is right or wrong, without saying why. After 10 correct color matches, the experimenter switches the criterion to shape, without warning. After 10 correct shape matches, the criterion is switched to number, then back to color, and so on. Milner (1963, 1964) showed that most patients with damage to a certain region of frontal cortex (the dorsolateral region) can learn the color

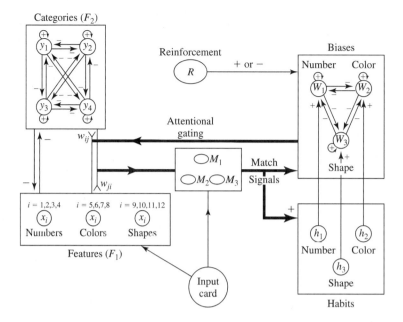

Figure 6.16   Network used to simulate card-sorting data. Frontal damage is modeled by reduced gain of signals from the reinforcement node to bias nodes W_i ($i = 1$ for number, 2 for color, 3 for shape). Bias nodes gate signals from feature to category nodes. Each bias node is influenced by the corresponding habit node, which encodes past decisions that used the given matching criterion. The match signal generators M_i send positive signals to habit nodes, and signals (of the same sign as the reinforcement) to bias nodes. Dark lines signify the positive feedback loop between habits and decisions, which can be broken only by strong penalty signals.
SOURCE: Adapted from Leven & Levine, 1987, copyright © 1987 IEEE; reprinted by permission of the publishers.

criterion as rapidly as normals, but then cannot switch to shape.[6]

Leven and Levine (1987) simulated the card-sorting data using the network of Figure 6.16. In this network, based on adaptive resonance theory (see the next section), nodes in F_1 code features (numbers, colors, and shapes), whereas nodes in F_2 code template cards. Corresponding to each feature class (number, color, or shape) is a "habit node" and a "bias node." Habit nodes code how often classifications have been made, rightly or wrongly, on the basis of each feature. Bias nodes add habit node activities to reinforcement signals (the experimenter's "Right" or "Wrong"), then gate the excitatory signals from F_1 to F_2. A network parameter measuring the strength of reinforcement signals to bias nodes was varied. The network with high reinforcement acted like Milner's normal subjects, whereas the network with low reinforcement acted like Milner's frontal patients.

But perseveration due to frontal damage can be overridden by attraction to novelty, as in the monkey data of Pribram (1961). Pribram placed a peanut under a junk object several times, unobserved by a monkey. Each time this was done, he added a new object to the scene and waited for the monkey to choose which object to lift for food. On the first trial with a novel object present, normal monkeys

---

[6]Since Milner's (1963, 1964) work, other clinicians have found that the WCST may not be the most sensitive test of dorsolateral prefrontal damage, so use other tests such as verbal fluency (for left prefrontal damage) and design fluency (for right prefrontal damage).

tended to choose another object that had previously been rewarded, whereas monkeys with lesions of the ventral frontal cortex chose the novel object immediately. Levine and Prueitt (1989) simulated the novelty data using a network based on the gated dipole (see the last section). In their network, each sensory stimulus has an on and off channel structured like the two competing channels of a gated dipole (cf. Figure 6.14). With weak reward signals, as in frontally lesioned animals, the on channel for the old object is more depleted than the on channel for the new object, because

the old cue channel has been active longer. Hence, the new object is approached. With strong reward signals, as in normal animals, associative learning at synapses between the output node corresponding to the previously rewarded object and the node related to the food reward enhances approach to that object enough to counteract transmitter depletion, and the old object is approached.

Another network model of the WCST was developed by Dehaene and Changeux (1991). Dehaene and Changeux's model (Figure 6.17) was intended to represent somewhat more

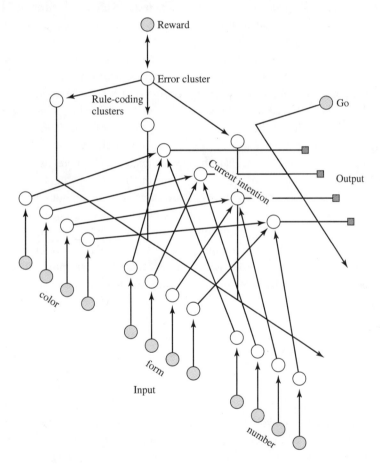

Figure 6.17   Schematic architecture of Dehaene and Changeux's model of the Wisconsin Card Sorting Test. Cards are coded along the dimensions of color, shape, and number, and their features are stored at memory clusters. Memory clusters activate the clusters defining current intention (about which card to sort with). Rule-coding clusters modulate the transmission between memory and intention clusters, thus deciding the sorting rule. Positive or negative reward strengthens or weakens the rule currently in force. SOURCE: Adapted from Dehaene and Changeux (1991) with the permission of Oxford University Press.

general cognitive and inferential capabilities than those manifested by the WCST. Despite different underlying foundations, most parts of Dehaene and Changeux's network can be mapped fairly closely either into Levine and Prueitt's (1989) WCST model or into their novelty preference model. For example, Dehaene and Changeux's "memory" and "intention" nodes are closely analogous to Levine and Prueitt's (ART-based) "feature" and "category" fields. Also, the "rule-coding clusters" of Figure 6.17 are similar structurally and functionally to the "bias nodes" of Figure 6.16. Dehaene and Changeux added to their model a feature that they called episodic memory, though it differs somewhat from the common psychological usage of that term (Tulving, 1972). Their version of episodic memory kept track of rules that had been previously tried and did not lead to reinforcement, and selectively reduced the activation of nodes representing such rules. This is analogous to the opponent processing mechanism (via the gated dipole network) used by Levine and Prueitt to enhance selectively representations of novel inputs.

Recently, several authors have simulated the WCST using models that are formally similar to the Levine et al. or Dehaene-Changeux models but incorporate more details of known neuroanatomy, such as the interconnections among frontal cortex, basal ganglia, and thalamus. The most detailed of these models is that of Monchi and Taylor (1999).

Disruption of Context Processing

J. D. Cohen and Servan-Schreiber (1992) used a back propagation network to simulate three cognitive tasks that require the participant to perform a nondominant but contextually appropriate response. One of these was the Stroop test, whereby the participant sees the word for a color printed in ink of either the same or a different color and must state the color of the ink. Reaction time is slower if the ink color and word do not match (e.g., if the word "red" is written in green ink). People with dorsolateral frontal damage, as well as many schizophrenics, have an even slower reaction time under these incongruent conditions. Cohen and Servan-Schreiber also simulated a continuous performance task, whereby subjects were instructed to respond to a target pattern while receiving a steady stream of other stimuli, and a lexical disambiguation task.

J. D. Cohen and Servan-Schreiber (1992) reproduced deficits of schizophrenics on all three tasks, which they attributed to a deficit of dopamine inputs to the dorsolateral prefrontal cortex. Their network includes a node that selectively influences signals along two competing neural pathways (e.g., pathways coding words and colors in the Stroop test) and that is assumed to be decreased in activity in the case of dorsolateral frontal damage or schizophrenia. Although their network appears anatomically unrealistic, they captured some qualitative functional relationships that are important for a wide class of tasks that involve prefrontal executive function.

Context is also involved in the frontal task of discriminating which of two items in a sequence occurred more recently (Milner, 1982). Simulation results on that task were presented in Monchi and Taylor (1998) using a network called ACTION, which was based on mimicking interactions between the prefrontal cortex, thalamus, and basal ganglia combined with back-propagation learning.

There has been much recent work wherein lesions in particular parts of a neural network cause the network to perform a cognitive function deficiently in a manner reminiscent of some mental or neurological disorder. There are four edited books (Parks, Levine, & Long, 1998; Reggia, Ruppin, & Berndt, 1996; Reggia, Ruppin, & Glanzman, 1999; Stein & Ludik, 1998) about models of mental and cognitive disorders. The models conform in varying degrees to known neuroanatomy and physiology. Even those models that are less biologically realistic illustrate principles that will be required for a more refined theory of the dynamic processes involved in such mental disorders.

Perhaps the first article of this type was Grossberg (1984), which discusses network analogs of Parkinson's disease, some forms of schizophrenia, some forms of depression, and juvenile hyperactivity. Grossberg showed mathematically that in the gated dipole (Figure 6.14), if the nonspecific arousal is within a certain range, the network behaves in a fashion that is usually considered normal. Above or below that range, the network exhibits pathologies that suggest symptoms of certain common mental disorders. When the network is underaroused, its threshold of response to limited-duration (phasic) inputs is raised. Paradoxically, once this threshold is exceeded, the on-reaction is hypersensitive to input increments. Giving the network a "drug" that increases nonspecific arousal (analogous to an upper) reduces these symptoms of hypersensitivity. But if too much of the upper is administered, the network can develop the opposite syndrome associated with overarousal. Grossberg compared underarousal effects in his network to observed symptoms of both juvenile hyperactivity and Parkinsonism. These illnesses are frequently treated by drugs that enhance the efficacy of the neural transmitter dopamine: Ritalin (at the time Grossberg wrote, amphetamine) for hyperactive children and L-DOPA for Parkinson patients. The side effects of overdoses of those drugs can include schizophrenic-like symptoms. Conversely, some drugs used to treat schizophrenics by suppressing dopamine have Parkinson-like side effects.

Based on these analogies, Grossberg (1984) made two experimental predictions about sufferers from these two disorders that, to my knowledge, have still not been tested.

First, he suggested that hyperactive and Parkinson patients should exhibit a weak affective rebound. For example, they should have an abnormally small reaction to halving a reward or punishment and an abnormally small aftereffect to halving the brightness of a visual cue. Second, he suggested that the same sudden increments in nonspecific arousal that would cause an off-rebound in normals would cause increased on-channel activity in hyperactive and Parkinson patients. This could lead to dishabituation, thence distractibility, by irrelevant yet unexpected events.

The effects of overarousal in this network are opposites of some underarousal effects. The threshold for response to a phasic input is reduced. But once the threshold is achieved, the network is abnormally *insensitive* to increments in input intensity. This is analogous to the flatness of affect characteristic of some kinds of schizophrenia.

Grossberg (1984) discussed neurochemical analogs for some of his network variables. He compared overarousal to excessive activity in the diffuse synapses from the substantia nigra (an area of the midbrain) to the cortex, limbic system, and corpus striatum. The input to the striatum plays an important role in Parkinson's disease. The synapses from the substantia nigra use the neurotransmitter dopamine. Contreras-Vidal and Stelmach (1995) developed a network model, based on Grossberg's principles, of the effects of Parkinsonism on both the motor and cognitive functions of the basal ganglia and of remediation with L-DOPA.

MODELS OF HIGH-LEVEL COGNITION

Neural networks have been applied to modeling many high-level cognitive processes: categorization, decision making, language understanding, and reasoning and analogy. We consider these in turn and then discuss the fledgling applications of neural networks to social psychology. Pattern categorization and classification has engaged three of the best known neural network architectures: back propagation, ART, and BSB.

Categorization and Classification

Categorization models have been divided into supervised and unsupervised models. Supervised means that there is a training set and that the network is told to which categories each training stimulus belongs and then adjusts its weights so as to categorize a more general class of stimuli. Unsupervised means that the system is self-organizing and picks out the regularity in the stimuli it receives, a process often called clustering. The back-propagation model is entirely supervised. The ART and BSB models were originally unsupervised but added supervision later on. The brain probably uses a mixture of unsupervised architectures, which enable it to detect regularity in the environment, and supervised architectures, which enable it to learn similar responses to dissimilar stimuli based on feedback from the environment (e.g., which mushrooms are poisonous or edible and which phonetic distinctions one should not make in a given language).

Neural networks for supervised learning of predetermined classifications date back to Rosenblatt (1962; cf. the second section of this chapter) and were developed further by Rumelhart et al. (1986) in the back-propagation architecture. To illustrate use of back propagation in a specific problem domain, they taught the network to discriminate between a "T" and a "C" regardless of position or orientation in the visual field. Figure 6.18 illustrates the different rotations of the T and C. Translation invariance is achieved by adding an additional transformation to the rule for learning input-to-hidden-unit connec-

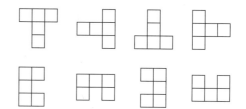

Figure 6.18 Stimulus set for the T-versus-C problem. The set consists of a block T and a block C in each of four orientations. One of the eight patterns is presented on each trial.
SOURCE: Reprinted from Rumelhart et al. (1986) with permission of MIT Press.

tions. To make the learning of a pattern independent of its location in the visual field, all hidden units are constrained to learn exactly the same pattern of weights. This is accomplished by adding together the weight changes dictated by the error correction rule for each unit and then changing all weights by averages of those amounts.

The unsupervised version of ART is best introduced in Carpenter and Grossberg (1987a), which describes the ART 1 model for classifying binary (0 or 1 to each node) inputs. Modifications of this algorithm for classifying analog (running over a range, e.g., between 0 and 1) inputs are ART 2 (Carpenter & Grossberg, 1987b) and fuzzy ART (Carpenter, Grossberg, & Rosen, 1991). The architectures of all these networks were based on the idea of adaptive resonant feedback between two layers of nodes (Grossberg, 1976b; see Section 3.2).

Figure 6.19 illustrates the structures of ART 1. The F_1 layer consists of nodes responding to input features, analogous to cell groups in a sensory area of cortex. The F_2 layer consists of nodes responding to categories of F_1 node activity patterns. Connection weights between the two layers are learnable in both directions. The F_1 nodes do not directly interact with each other, but the F_2 nodes are connected via recurrent lateral

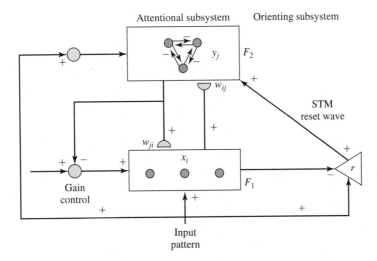

Figure 6.19   ART 1 architecture. Short-term memory at the feature level F_1 and category level F_2, and bottom-up and top-down interlevel long-term memory traces, are modulated by other nodes. The orienting system generates a reset wave at F_2 when bottom-up and top-down patterns mismatch at F_1, that is, when the ratio of F_1 activity to input activity is less than *vigilance r*. This wave tends to inhibit recently active F_2 nodes. (Adapted from Carpenter & Grossberg, 1987, with permission of Academic Press.)

inhibition (cf. the third section of this chapter). Recall that lateral inhibition is a common device in neural networks for making choices in STM. In this version, the simplest form of choice (winner-take-all) is made: Only the F_2 node receiving the largest signal from F_1 becomes active. Inhibition from F_2 to F_1 (via "gain control" nodes) prevents F_2 activity from always exciting F_1, thereby preventing "hallucinations" from occurring when a category node is active. Also, it shuts off most neural activity at F_1 if there is mismatch between the input pattern and the active category's prototype. Only with a sufficient match are enough of the same F_1 nodes excited by both the input and the active F_2 category node, which is needed to overcome nonspecific inhibition from F_2. The criterion for match uses an adjustable parameter, called vigilance, that determines category size.

If match occurs, enhanced F_1 activity inhibits the activity of the node r representing the orienting subsystem. This stabilizes the categorization of the given input pattern in the given F_2 node. By contrast, if mismatch occurs, F_1 activity is not sufficient to inhibit r, which thereby becomes active. The orienting system node activity leads to F_2 reset, which shuts off the active category node as long as the current input is present. The F_2 node receiving the next largest F_1 signal is then tested, and the process is repeated.

Supervision was added to the ART structure in the ARTMAP network of Carpenter, Grossberg, and Reynolds (1991). ARTMAP is an autonomous learning network that learns the association between two sets of categories based on predictive success. This supervised learning system consists of a pair of ART modules (ART$_a$ and ART$_b$). These ART modules learn stable recognition categories in response to the inputs at their feature layers. They are joined by an internal controller that enables an association to be formed between the categories learned in each ART module. During training, the ART$_a$ module receives a set of input vectors, and ART$_b$ receives a set of input patterns, each of which is the correct prediction given one of the ART$_a$ vectors. If there is a predictive error at ART$_b$, then the map field orienting subsystem adjusts the vigilance parameter of ART$_a$ so that the category size of the ART$_a$ input is adjusted to minimize this error. For example, if ART$_a$ and ART$_b$ categorize bananas based on visual and taste features respectively, then green and yellow bananas can share the common features of the banana category in ART$_a$ and still can predict different taste categories in ART$_b$. This can be achieved in training by feeding back the taste information from ART$_b$ to enable ART$_a$ to form different categories for these two kinds.

The BSB model (Anderson et al., 1977; Anderson & Murphy, 1986) associates vector patterns of activities at a set of nodes with other patterns at the same nodes. The matrix consisting of the connection weights between nodes provides feedback that transforms the pattern. The network then converges to one of the characteristic system states corresponding to corners of a box in n-dimensional space (n being the number of nodes). Categorization of the original input pattern is based on whichever of these corners is reached. The BSB model is applicable to both autoassociative and heteroassociative encoding (see the section titled "Autoassociation and Heteroassociation").

This algorithm represents positive feedback as it might occur in the brain, due to the past operation of a Hebbian associative learning law. This feedback has the desirable property of enhancing significant activities or stimuli, but often has an additional property that is undesirable. Repeated application to a pattern vector will drive the state of the system outside the box, that is, cause values of some or all of the x_i to get outside the bounds of the system. To prevent activities from becoming unbounded, Anderson et al. (1977) imposed

an additional rule whereby if any one of the activities becomes greater or less than the limits imposed by the box, it is reset to the closest limiting value. Hence, the BSB model, like all neural network models, includes a method for keeping activities within bounds, corresponding to the limits on possible neuron firing frequencies.

Anderson and Murphy (1986) combined BSB with an error-correction learning rule (cf. Rumelhart & McClelland, 1986). This was applied to processing linguistic inputs that are converted to vectors of 1s and −1s by means of ASCII codes. This model has reproduced the disambiguation by context of words with more than one meaning. Other applications of this categorization system have included prototype learning in random-dot patterns, retrieving medical information, classifying radar signals, learning how to do arithmetic, and perceptually disambiguating the Necker cube. In addition, Abdi et al. (1997) applied an autoassociative network based not on BSB but on a variant of Anderson (1972) to classifying human faces by gender. The face classification employs a modified autoassociator designed to allow for selective attention to different parts of the feature space.

Decision Making

Most psychologists by now are very familiar with Tversky and Kahneman's (e.g., 1974, 1981) results indicating that human decision processes violate rational utility-maximizing norms in some systematic and repeatable ways. The influence of nonrational factors in cognitive tasks poses a challenge for quantitative modeling but has been approached using the type of models previously used for cognitive-emotional interactions (see the fifth section of this chapter).

Grossberg and Gutowski (1987) applied opponent processing (the gated dipole of Figure 6.14) to explaining some Tversky-

Kahneman data on decision making under risk. Previously, Kahneman and Tversky (1979) themselves had proposed a variant of utility theory, called prospect theory, whereby preferences are a nonlinear function of both gain (or loss) and its probability of occurrence. But prospect theory excludes the context of statements and the past experience of decision makers. Grossberg and Gutowski's theory considers such dynamic variables. Recall from the last section that gated dipoles provide a means to compare current values of motivational or sensory variables with expected values of those same variables. Such expectation could be based either on recent past events or on verbally induced anticipation. The latter possibility explains Tversky and Kahneman's data on effects of linguistic framing on decisions, for example, that preferences among possible public health measures are different if framed in terms of people dying versus people saved.

Grossberg and Gutowski's (1987) explanation of Tversky and Kahneman's choice data is a significant but incomplete advance. Their network still optimizes a single variable, even if its optimization is not analogous to rational calculation in humans. In this case, the variable is net activity of the positive channel in a gated dipole, the dipole interpreted as relating to affect or motivation. More realistic explanations of decision processes are likely to depend on multiple decision criteria, including affect, habit, and novelty, and on multiple attributes or features of the data to be decided about. *Which* criterion is used depends both on the cognitive task involved and on the current state of the organism (or network). Thus far, researchers have not modeled extensive psychological data on mood and memory.

Leven and Levine (1996) developed an extension of this gated dipole model of choice to multiattribute decision making. These authors modeled soft drink consumer preferences during the New Coke fiasco of the mid-1980s. New Coke had outscored Coke in blind taste tests because of its sweetness but was a failure in the market because it lacked the familiarity of the earlier Coke. This suggests that the mood change due to changed context altered selective attention to different features of soft drinks. This was modeled using a network connecting gated dipoles for features, drives, and drink categories, with a categorization mechanism similar to ART (Figure 6.19) but with feature vectors attentionally weighted as well as associative learning of connections between drives and features. More work needs to done on applying this model to simulation of other multiattribute decision data and on relating the decision modules to specific brain regions. One other application of a similar model has been to animal foraging under predation risk (Coleman, Brown, Levine, & Mellgren, 1998).

Neural network answers to questions about decision processes are beginning to emerge from physiological and biochemical data on complex circuits, including such brain regions as the association (particularly prefrontal) cortex, limbic system, basal ganglia, and parts of the midbrain. Some articles edited by Damasio, Damasio, and Christen (1995) discuss tentative connections between brain regions and decision making that still need to be incorporated into neural network models.

Models of Language Understanding

The cognitive science revolution of the mid-1980s had a strong component of linguists as well as computer scientists and psychologists (such as Rumelhart and McClelland) interested in language. Thus, it was not surprising that many early applications of back propagation and other PDP networks dealt with language understanding. For example, Rumelhart and McClelland (1986, Chap. 18) dealt with learning past tenses of English verbs. Words were treated as binary patterns, and the network learned transformations (such as from a word to the same word followed by "-ed") that it saw repeatedly in the training set. This network reproduced characteristic development of children's past tense learning. In its early stages, the network learned a few common past tenses such as *go* → *went* and *look* → *looked*. As the network developed, it learned the "-ed" rule and regularized irregular forms, producing either *go* → *goed* or *go* → *wented*. Eventually it could know the "-ed" rule and also remember exceptions, but it would tend to regularize any new verbs it learned.

Cognitive connectionist modeling of language has been carried out ever since then, with back propagation networks (some non-recurrent and some recurrent) for different linguistic tasks, including both phonological and lexical information. This has been applied particularly to mental and cognitive disorders that impair verbal abilities. For example, Plaut and Shallice (1994) modeled the condition called deep dyslexia. This condition involves varying types of word errors in reading text aloud, with a preponderance in each patient either of semantic errors (e.g., substituting "wind" for "blowing") or visual errors (e.g., substituting "white" for "while"). They simulated this form of dyslexia by selectively "lesioning" different parts of a network that first mapped from writing units to meaning units and from there to sound units, with recurrent interactions at meaning and sound levels via "cleanup units."

These language models illustrate important distinctions and properties, and therefore account for a range of experimental and clinical data. They have not yet tapped the extensive knowledge of cognitive neuroscience and how such linguistic interactions are embodied in the brain; this should be a major growth area of neural networks as more such knowledge emerges.

Models of Analogical Reasoning

A few neural network models of different types of analogy making have appeared recently. Some of them are hybrids of traditional artificial intelligence with connectionism, and thus are of limited interest for understanding human reasoning processes. Of the fully connectionist models, the most ambitious is Hummel and Holyoak's (1997) Learning and Inference with Schemas and Analogies (LISA) model, which deals with complex semantic analogies. LISA relied on previous models of binding particular entities to particular roles in a sentence. It was designed to account for the two analogical processes of "access" (i.e., how potential analogs in both source and target domains are retrieved from memory) and "mapping" (i.e., the working memory process that discerns relationships between source and target elements). Hummel and Holyoak's model can account for various psychological data on differential factors influencing access and mapping. Hence, it reproduced characteristic human patterns of analogical inference, such as learning close and natural analogies better than logically consistent but contrived analogies. The limitations of this model are that it relies heavily on the assumed previous learning of very high-level abstract concepts and that its structure does not appear to be based in any way on biologically realistic models of simpler mental processes.

Jani and Levine (2000) worked with simpler proportional analogies (e.g., apple : red :: banana : ?) in an attempt to understand the basics of a process that begins at a young age (typically about 2 to 3) in humans. Their model was based on adaptive resonance (Carpenter & Grossberg, 1987) with the addition of modules that represented characteristic transformations such as adding, deleting, keeping, or changing an item and a form of "weight transport" that allows generalizing from "keep red" to "keep color." It reproduced several simple proportional analogies and allowed for queries such as "What is the color of an apple?" However, this network fell short of a theory of how analogies might be encoded in the brain. Such neurally realistic models probably depend on more detailed brain imaging data: Some results indicate parietal, prefrontal, and cingulate cortices as being involved in reasoning tasks, but the details of what area is involved in what stage of the task have yet to be discovered.

Applications to Social Psychology

A few neural network models of social-psychological phenomena are reviewed in the collection edited by Read and Miller (1998). These models cover person perception and impression formation, stereotyping and social categorization, causal attribution, personality and behavior, attitudes and beliefs (including cognitive dissonance), and social influence and group interaction. These are mostly based on the recurrent form of the back-propagation network. The nodes in these networks represent neither brain regions nor all-purpose cognitive modules but rather interrelated cognitive entities; for example, in a model of a cognitive dissonance paradigm involving children being punished for playing with an attractive toy, the nodes included evaluation, play, and threat. Other models in this same general vein include the work of Westen (1999) on judgment of President Clinton's sexual conduct by people with different political opinions, and of Brown, Tumeo, Larey, and Paulus (1998) on creativity in group brainstorming.

As with many models of language and mental disorders, these social-psychology models do not yet incorporate principles (cf. Table 6.2) that govern the processes by which the brain achieves effective interactions with a complex environment. However, these recurrent connectionist models capture some relationships among social cognitions that need to be included in models that are more brain-like and therefore more likely to be predictive of human behavior. Predictive models may be derived from extending models of other cognitive phenomena: For example, a model of stereotyping might be based on the work of Furl (1999), who extended the ART categorization model (Carpenter & Grossberg, 1987) to include property inheritance and exception learning.

CONCLUSIONS

The work reviewed herein indicates that neural network modeling is extremely diverse and that there is no standard way to construct models. My own recommendation to the psychologist wishing to become involved in modeling is to become as familiar as possible with the principles outlined in Table 6.2. That is, he or she should learn how researchers have employed associative learning, lateral inhibition (shunting and additive, recurrent and nonrecurrent), opponent processing, neuromodulation, resonant feedback, error correction, and other network constructs in models of different phenomena as well as what types of cognitive constraints each of these principles enables the network to satisfy (the table briefly summarizes those constraints). Other sources on the use of these principles include Grossberg (1980), Hestenes (1992), Levine (2000), and—for relationships with cognitive psychology—Martindale (1991). Also, familiarity with brain regions relevant to the process being modeled, as suggested by human imaging and EEG and animal neurophysiological studies, helps to constrain network designs.

In much of cognitive and social psychology, the brain mechanisms involved in generating the behavior are only dimly known, and qualitative models based on PDP mechanisms (Rumelhart & McClelland, 1986) are useful. For that type of modeling, a great deal of software is available on the Internet and commercially. However, enough is known about interrelationships among psychological processes that even in these areas of psychology one can venture to construct more brain-like models. For this purpose, again, what is most important is a knowledge of principles such as those of Table 6.2 and of the cognitive neuroscience of relevant brain regions. This type of modeling requires flexibility: For example, someone modeling a process that includes categorization (of personalities, percepts, or whatever) might build on the adaptive resonance model (Carpenter & Grossberg, 1987) but adapt the details of control of interlevel connections in that model to fit the constraints of the data set one is trying to model. Similarly, someone modeling a process that involves opponent processing or enhancement of novel percepts might adapt the gated dipole (Grossberg, 1972a, 1972b) to fit the constraints of the data set.

Because flexibility is desired for this richer type of modeling, my opinion is that almost any commercially available neural network software is too restrictive. Several research groups have worked on developing object-oriented software so that particular structures might be taken as adaptable submodules, but I have found this approach difficult to master. A better course is to use a high-level programming language such as C++, Mathematica, or Matlab (the latter two are particularly good for graphing), to write equations for network interactions, and to use the ordinary differential equation or difference equation solving program within that language. The ability to translate network interactions into equations does *not* require advanced mathematical knowledge (e.g., a course in differential equations). It does require some familiarity with the calculus notion of a derivative as a rate of change and with a few mathematical

rules such as using a minus sign for inhibition, a plus sign for multiplication, and particular types of multiplication for shunting interactions or for transmitter modulation; these rules are discussed, with fragments of simulation code, in Levine (2000, Appendix 2).

This type of neural network modeling (which is also called, by some biological purists, computational neuroscience) plays a major role in providing bridges between psychology and neuroscience. It is also bridging some gaps between different specialties and schools within psychology (Staats, 1999; Tryon, 1995) and thereby contributing to the conceptual foundations of psychology itself.

REFERENCES

Abdi, H., Valentin, D., & O'Toole, A. J. (1997). A generalized autoassociator model for face processing and sex categorization: From principal components to multivariate analysis. In D. S. Levine & W. R. Elsberry (Eds.), *Optimality in biological and artificial networks?* (pp. 317–337). Mahwah, NJ: Erlbaum.

Amari, S.-I. (1971). Characteristics of randomly connected threshold element networks and network systems. *Proceedings of the IEEE, 59,* 35–47.

Andersen, P., Gross, G. N., Lømo, T., & Sveen, O. (1969). Participation of inhibitory and excitatory interneurones in the control of hippocampal cortical output. In M. Brazier (Ed.), *The Interneuron* (pp. 415–465). Los Angeles: University of California Press.

Anderson, J. A. (1968). A memory storage model utilizing spatial correlation functions. *Kybernetik, 5,* 113–119.

Anderson, J. A. (1970). Two models for memory organization using interacting traces. *Mathematical Biosciences, 8,* 137–160.

Anderson, J. A. (1972). A simple neural network generating an interactive memory. *Mathematical Biosciences, 14,* 197–220.

Anderson, J. A., & Murphy, G. L. (1986). Psychological concepts in a parallel system. *Physica D, 22*, 318–336.

Anderson, J. A., Silverstein, J. W., Ritz, S. A., & Jones, R. S. (1977). Distinctive features, categorical perception, and probability learning: Some applications of a neural model. *Psychological Review, 84*, 413–451.

Anninos, P. A., Beek, B., Csermely, T. J., Harth, E. M., & Pertile, G. (1970). Dynamics of neural structures. *Journal of Theoretical Biology, 26*, 121–148.

Aparicio, M., IV, & Levine, D. S. (1994). Why are neural networks relevant to higher cognitive function? In D. S. Levine & M. Aparicio IV (Eds.), *Neural networks for knowledge representation and inference* (pp. 1–26). Hillsdale, NJ: Erlbaum.

Atkeson, C. G., & Hollerbach, J. M. (1985). Kinematic features of unrestrained vertical arm movements. *Journal of Neuroscience, 5*, 2318–2330.

Bapi, R. S., & Levine, D. S. (1994). Modeling the role of the frontal lobes in performing sequential tasks: I. Basic structure and primacy effects. *Neural Networks, 7*, 1167–1180.

Bapi, R. S., & Levine, D. S. (1997). Modeling the role of the frontal lobes in sequential task performance: II. Classification of sequences. *Neural Network World, 1/97*, 3–28.

Barto, A. G., & Anandan, P. (1985). Pattern recognizing stochastic learning automata. *IEEE Transactions on Systems, Man, and Cybernetics, 15*, 360–375.

Berger, T. W., Berry, S. D., & Thompson, R. F. (1986). Role of the hippocampus in classical conditioning of aversive and appetitive behaviors. In R. L. Isaacson & K. H. Pribram (Eds.), *The hippocampus* (Vol. 4, pp. 203–239). New York: Plenum.

Bienenstock, E. L., Cooper, L. N., & Munro, P. W. (1982). Theory for the development of neuron selectivity: Orientation specificity and binocular interaction in visual cortex. *Journal of Neuroscience, 2*, 32–48.

Blakemore, C., & Cooper, G. F. (1970). Development of the brain depends on the visual environment. *Nature, 228*, 477–478.

Brown, V., Tumeo, M., Larey, T., & Paulus P. (1998). Modeling cognitive interactions during group brainstorming. *Small Group Research, 29*, 495–526.

Bullock, D., Cisek, P. E., & Grossberg, S. (1998). Cortical networks for control of voluntary arm movements under variable force conditions. *Cerebral Cortex, 8*, 48–62.

Bullock, D., Fiala, J. C., & Grossberg, S. (1994). A neural model of timed response learning in the cerebellum. *Neural Networks, 7*, 1101–1114.

Bullock, D., & Grossberg, S. (1988). Neural dynamics of planned arm movements: Emergent invariants and speed-accuracy properties during trajectory formation. *Psychological Review, 95*, 49–90.

Bullock, D., Grossberg, S., & Guenther, F. H. (1993). A self-organizing neural model of motor equivalent reaching and tool use by a multijoint arm. *Journal of Cognitive Neuroscience, 5*, 408–435.

Burnod, Y. (1988). *An adaptive neural network: The cerebral cortex.* Paris: Masson.

Carpenter, G. A., & Grossberg, S. (1987). A massively parallel architecture for a self-organizing neural pattern recognition machine. *Computer Vision, Graphics, and Image Processing, 37*, 54–115.

Carpenter, G. A., & Grossberg, S. (1987b). ART2: Self-organization of stable category recognition codes for analog input patterns. *Applied Optics, 26*, 4919–4930.

Carpenter, G. A., Grossberg, S., & Lesher, G. W. (1998). The what-and-where filter: A spatial mapping neural network for object recognition and image understanding. *Computer Vision and Image Understanding, 69*, 1–22.

Carpenter, G. A., Grossberg, S., & Reynolds, J. H. (1991). ARTMAP: Supervised real-time learning and classification of nonstationary data by a self-organizing neural network. *Neural Networks, 4*, 759–771.

Carpenter, G. A., Grossberg, S., & Rosen, D. B. (1991). Fuzzy ART: Fast stable learning and categorization of analog patterns by an adaptive resonance system. *Neural Networks, 4*, 759–771.

Chance, D. C., Cheung, J. Y., Lykins, S., & Lawton, A. W. (1997). An examination of mathematical models of learning in a single neuron. In D. S. Levine & W. R. Elsberry (Eds.), *Optimality in biological and artificial networks?* (pp. 229–264). Mahwah, NJ: Erlbaum.

Cisek, P., Grossberg, S., & Bullock, D. (1998). A cortico-spinal model of reaching and proprioception under multiple task constraints. *Journal of Cognitive Neuroscience, 10,* 425–444.

Cohen, J. D., & Servan-Schreiber, D. (1992). Context, cortex and dopamine: A connectionist approach to behavior and biology in schizophrenia. *Psychological Review, 99,* 45–77.

Cohen, M. A., & Grossberg, S. (1983). Absolute stability of global pattern formation and parallel memory storage by competitive neural networks. *IEEE Transactions on Systems, Man, and Cybernetics, SMC-13,* 815–826.

Cohen, M. A., & Grossberg, S. (1984). Some global properties of binocular resonances: Disparity matching, filling-in, and figure-ground synthesis. In P. Dodwell & T. Caelli (Eds.), *Figural synthesis* (pp. 117–152). Hillsdale, NJ: Erlbaum.

Coleman, S., Brown, V. R., Levine, D. S., & Mellgren, R. L. (1998). A cognitive-emotional network model of foraging under predation risk. *Proceedings of WCCI98/IJCNN'98,* pp. 625–629.

Contreras-Vidal, J. L., & Stelmach, G. E. (1995). A neural model of basal ganglia-thalamocortical relations in normal and Parkinsonian movement. *Biological Cybernetics, 73,* 467–476.

Damasio, A. R., Damasio, H., & Christen, Y. (1995). *Neurobiology of decision-making.* Berlin: Springer. *DARPA Neural Network Study.* (1988). Alexandria, VA: AFCEA International Press.

Dayhoff, J., Hameroff, S., Swenberg, C. E., & Lahoz-Beltra, R. (1993). The neuronal cytoskeleton: A complex system that subserves neural learning. In K. H. Pribram (Ed.), *Rethinking neural networks: Quantum fields and biological data* (pp. 389–442). Hillsdale, NJ: Erlbaum.

Dehaene, S., & Changeux, J.-P. (1991). The Wisconsin card sorting test: Theoretical analysis and modeling in a neural network. *Cerebral Cortex, 1,* 62–79.

Denham, M. J., & McCabe, S. L. (1996). Biological basis for a neural model of learning and recall of goal-directed sensory-motor behaviours. In *World congress on neural networks* (pp. 1283–1286). Mahwah, NJ: Erlbaum.

Dev, P. (1975). Perception of depth surfaces in random-dot stereograms: A neural model. *International Journal of Man-Machine Studies, 7,* 511–528.

Dominey, P., & Arbib, M. A. (1992). A cortico-subcortical model for generation of spatially accurate sequential saccades. *Cerebral Cortex, 2,* 153–175.

Dominey, P., Arbib, M. A., & Joseph, J.-P. (1995). A model of corticostriatal plasticity for learning oculomotor associations and sequences. *Journal of Cognitive Neuroscience, 7,* 311–336.

Eccles, J. C., Ito, M., & Szentagothai, J. (1967). *The cerebellum as a neuronal machine.* New York: Springer.

Edelman, G. M. (1987). *Neural Darwinism.* New York: Basic Books.

Edelman, G. M., & Reeke, G. N., Jr. (1982). Selective networks capable of representative transformation, limited generalizations, and associative memory. *Proceedings of the National Academy of Sciences, 79,* 2091–2095.

Ellias, S. A., & Grossberg, S. (1975). Pattern formation, contrast control, and oscillations in the short-term memory of shunting on-center off-surround networks. *Biological Cybernetics, 20,* 69–98.

Elman, J. L. (1990). Finding structure in time. *Cognitive Science, 14,* 179–211.

Ermentrout, G. B., & Cowan, J. D. (1980). Large scale spatially organized activity in neural nets. *SIAM Journal on Applied Mathematics, 38,* 1–21.

Fiala, J. C., Grossberg, S., & Bullock, D. (1996). Metabotropic glutamate receptor activation in cerebellar Purkinje cells as substrate for adaptive timing of the classically conditioned eye-blink response. *Journal of Neuroscience, 16,* 3760–3774.

Flash, T., & Hogan, N. (1985). The coordination of arm movements: An experimentally confirmed mathematical model. *Journal of Neuroscience, 5,* 1688–1703.

Freeman, W. J. (1983). Experimental demonstration of "shunting networks," the "sigmoid function," and "adaptive resonance" in the olfactory system. *The Behavioral and Brain Sciences, 6,* 665–666.

Fukushima, K. (1980). Neocognitron: A self-organizing neural network model for a mechanism of pattern recognition unaffected by shift in position. *Biological Cybernetics, 36,* 193–204.

Furl, N. O. (1999). *Category induction and exception learning.* Unpublished master's thesis, University of Texas at Arlington.

Gaudiano, P., & Grossberg, S. (1991). Vector associative maps: Unsupervised real time error-based learning and control of movement trajectories. *Neural Networks, 4,* 147–183.

Georgopoulos, A. P., Kalaska, J. F., Caminiti, R., & Massey, J. T. (1984). The representation of movement direction in the motor cortex: Single cell and population studies. In G. M. Edelman, W. E. Gall, & W. M. Cowan (Eds.), *Dynamic aspects of neocortical function* (pp. 501–524). New York: Wiley.

Gluck, M. A., & Myers, C. E. (1993). Hippocampal mediation of stimulus representation: A computational theory. *Hippocampus, 3,* 491–516.

Gray, C. M., & Singer, W. (1989). Stimulus-specific neuronal oscillations in orientation columns of cat visual cortex. *Proceedings of the National Academy of Sciences, 86,* 1698–1702.

Grossberg, S. (1969). Embedding fields: A theory of learning with physiological implications. *Journal of Mathematical Psychology, 6,* 209–239.

Grossberg, S. (1972a). A neural theory of punishment and avoidance: I. Qualitative theory. *Mathematical Biosciences, 15,* 39–67.

Grossberg, S. (1972b). A neural theory of punishment and avoidance: II. Quantitative theory. *Mathematical Biosciences, 15,* 253–285.

Grossberg, S. (1973). Contour enhancement, short-term memory, and constancies in reverberating neural networks. *Studies in Applied Mathematics, 52,* 213–257.

Grossberg, S. (1974). Classical and instrumental learning in neural networks. In R. Rosen & F. Snell (Eds.), *Progress in theoretical biology* (Vol. 3). New York: Academic Press.

Grossberg, S. (1976a). Adaptive pattern classification and universal recoding: Parallel development and coding of neural feature detectors. *Biological Cybernetics, 23,* 121–134.

Grossberg, S. (1976b). Adaptive pattern classification and universal recoding: Feedback, expectation, olfaction, and illusions. *Biological Cybernetics, 23,* 187–202.

Grossberg, S. (1980). How does a brain build a cognitive code? *Psychological Review, 87,* 1–51.

Grossberg, S. (1983). The quantized geometry of visual space: The coherent computation of depth, form, and lightness. *The Behavioral and Brain Sciences, 4,* 625–692.

Grossberg, S. (1984). Some normal and abnormal behavioral syndromes due to transmitter gating of opponent processes. *Biological Psychiatry, 19,* 1075–1117.

Grossberg, S. (1987a). Cortical dynamics of three-dimensional form, color, and brightness perception: I. Monocular theory. *Perception and Psychophysics, 41,* 87–116.

Grossberg, S. (1987b). Cortical dynamics of three-dimensional form, color, and brightness perception: II. Binocular theory. *Perception and Psychophysics, 41,* 117–158.

Grossberg, S., & Gutowski, W. (1987). Neural dynamics of decision making under risk: Affective balance and cognitive-emotional interactions. *Psychological Review, 94,* 300–318.

Grossberg, S., & Kuperstein, M. (1989). *Neural dynamics of adaptive sensory-motor control: Ballistic eye movements.* Elmsford, NY: Pergamon.

Grossberg, S., & Levine, D. S. (1975). Some developmental and attentional biases in the contrast enhancement and short-term memory of recurrent neural networks. *Journal of Theoretical Biology, 53,* 341–380.

Grossberg, S., & Levine, D. S. (1987). Neural dynamics of attentionally modulated Pavlovian conditioning: Blocking, interstimulus interval, and secondary reinforcement. *Applied Optics, 26,* 5015–5030.

Grossberg, S., & Merrill, J. W. L. (1996). The hippocampus and cerebellum in adaptively timed learning, recognition, and movement. *Journal of Cognitive Neuroscience, 8,* 257–277.

Grossberg, S., & Mingolla, E. (1985a). Neural dynamics of form perception: Boundary completion, illusory figures, and neon color spreading. *Psychological Review, 92,* 173–211.

Grossberg, S., & Mingolla, E. (1985b). Neural dynamics of perceptual grouping: Textures, boundaries, and emergent segmentations. *Perception and Psychophysics, 38,* 141–171.

Grossberg, S., & Rudd, M. E. (1992). Cortical dynamics of visual motion perception: Short-range and long-range apparent motion. *Psychological Review, 99,* 78–121.

Grossberg, S., & Schmajuk, N. A. (1987). Neural dynamics of attentionally-modulated Pavlovian conditioning: Conditioned reinforcement, inhibition, and opponent processing. *Psychobiology, 15,* 195–240.

Grossberg, S., & Schmajuk, N. A. (1989). Neural dynamics of adaptive timing and temporal discrimination during associative learning. *Neural Networks, 2,* 79–102.

Guenther, F. H. (1995). Speech sound acquisition, coarticulation, and rate effects in a neural network model of speech production. *Psychological Review, 102,* 594–621.

Hartline, H. K., & Ratliff, F. (1957). Inhibitory interactions of receptor units in the eye of *Limulus. Journal of General Physiology, 40,* 351–376.

Hebb, D. O. (1949). *The organization of behavior.* New York: Wiley.

Hestenes, D. O. (1992). A neural network theory of manic-depressive illness. In D. S. Levine & S. J. Leven (Eds.), *Motivation, emotion, and goal direction in neural networks* (pp. 209–257). Hillsdale, NJ: Erlbaum.

Hinton, G. E. (1993). How neural networks learn from experience. In *Mind and brain: Readings from Scientific American magazine* (pp. 113–124). New York: Freeman.

Hirsch, H. V. B., & Spinelli, D. N. (1970). Visual experience modifies distribution of horizontally and vertically oriented receptive fields in cats. *Science, 168,* 869–871.

Hopfield, J. J. (1982). Neural networks and physical systems with emergent collective computational abilities. *Proceedings of the National Academy of Sciences, 79,* 2554–2558.

Hubel, D. H., & Wiesel, T. N. (1962). Receptive fields, binocular interaction, and functional architecture in the cat's visual cortex. *Journal of Physiology, 160,* 106–154.

Hubel, D. H., & Wiesel, T. N. (1965). Receptive fields and functional architecture in two nonstriate visual areas (18 and 19) of the cat. *Journal of Neurophysiology, 28,* 229–298.

Hubel, D. H., & Wiesel, T. N. (1968). Receptive fields and functional architecture of monkey striate cortex. *Journal of Physiology (London), 195,* 215–243.

Hull, C. L. (1943). *Principles of behavior.* New York: Appleton.

Hummel, J. E., & Holyoak, K. J. (1997). Distributed representations of structure: A theory of analogical access and mapping. *Psychological Review, 104,* 427–466.

Jani, N. G., & Levine, D. S. (2000). A neural network theory of proportional analogy-making. *Neural Networks, 13,* 149–183.

Jordan, M. I. (1986). Attractor dynamics and parallelism in a connectionist sequential machine. *Proceedings of the Eighth Annual Conference of the Cognitive Science Society* (pp. 531–546). Hillsdale, NJ: Erlbaum.

Jordan, M. I., & Rumelhart, D. E. (1992). Forward models: Supervised learning with a distal teacher. *Cognitive Science, 16,* 307–354.

Kahneman, D., & Tversky, A. (1979). Prospect Theory: An analysis of decision under risk. *Econometrica, 47,* 263–291.

Kanizsa, G. (1976). Subjective contours. *Scientific American, 234,* 48–64.

Kawato, M., Furukawa, K., & Suzuki, R. (1987). A hierarchical neural-network model for control and learning of voluntary movement. *Biological Cybernetics, 57,* 169–185.

Kawato, M., Isobe, M., Maeda, Y., & Suzuki, R. (1988). Coordinates transformation and learning control for visually-guided voluntary movement with iteration: A Newton-like method in function space. *Biological Cybernetics, 59,* 161–177.

Kernell, D. (1965). The adaptation and the relation between discharge frequency and current strength of cat lumbosacral motoneurones stimulated by long-lasting injected currents. *Acta Physiologica Scandinavica, 65,* 65–73.

Klopf, A. H. (1982). *The hedonistic neuron.* Washington, DC: Hemisphere.

Klopf, A. H. (1988). A neuronal model of classical conditioning. *Psychobiology, 16,* 85–125.

Kohonen, T. (1977). *Associative memory: A system-theoretical approach.* New York: Springer.

Kohonen, T., Lehtio, P., Rovamo, J., Hyvarinen, J., Bry, K., & Vainio, L. (1977). A principle of neural associative memory. *Neuroscience, 2,* 1065–1076.

Kuffler, S. (1953). Discharge patterns and functional organization of mammalian retina. *Journal of Neurophysiology, 16,* 37–68.

Kuperstein, M. (1988). Neural model of adaptive hand-eye coordination for single postures. *Science, 239,* 1308–1311.

Lashley, K. (1929). *Brain Mechanisms and Intelligence.* Chicago: University of Chicago Press.

Leven, S. J., & Levine, D. S. (1987). Effects of reinforcement on knowledge retrieval and evaluation. *IEEE First International Conference on Neural Networks* (Vol. 2, pp. 269–279). San Diego: IEEE/ICNN.

Leven, S. J., & Levine, D. S. (1996). Multiattribute decision making in context: A dynamic neural network methodology. *Cognitive Science, 20,* 271–299.

Levine, D. S. (1983). Neural population modeling and psychology: A review. *Mathematical Biosciences, 66,* 1–86.

Levine, D. S. (1996). Modeling dysfunction of the prefrontal executive system. In J. A. Reggia, E. Ruppin, & R. Berndt (Eds.), *Neural modeling of brain and cognitive disorders* (pp. 413–439). Singapore: World Scientific.

Levine, D. S. (2000). *Introduction to neural and cognitive modeling* (2nd ed.). Mahwah, NJ: Erlbaum.

Levine, D. S., & Grossberg, S. (1976). Visual illusions in neural networks: Line neutralization, tilt after-effect, and angle expansion. *Journal of Theoretical Biology, 61,* 477–504.

Levine, D. S., & Prueitt, P. S. (1989). Modeling some effects of frontal lobe damage: Novelty and perseveration. *Neural Networks, 2,* 103–116.

Levy, W. B. (1996). A sequence predicting CA3 is a flexible associator that learns and uses context to solve hippocampal-like tasks. *Hippocampus, 6,* 579–590.

Malsburg, C. von der (1973). Self-organization of orientation sensitive cells in the striate cortex. *Kybernetik, 14,* 85–100.

Marr, D. (1982). *Vision: A computational investigation into the human representation and processing of visual information.* San Francisco: Freeman.

Marr, D., & Poggio, T. (1979). A computational theory of human stereo vision. *Proceedings of the Royal Society of London, Series B, 204,* 301–328.

Marr, D., & Ullman, S. (1981). Directional selectivity and its use in early visual processing. *Proceedings of the Royal Society of London, Series B, 211,* 151–180.

Martindale, C. (1991). *Cognitive psychology: A neural network approach.* Pacific Grove, CA: Brooks/Cole.

Massone, L., & Bizzi, E. (1989). Generation of limb trajectories with a sequential network. *International Joint Conference on Neural Networks* (Vol. II, pp. 345–349). Piscataway, NJ: IEEE.

McCulloch, W. S., & Pitts, W. (1943). A logical calculus of the ideas immanent in nervous activity. *Bulletin of Mathematical Biophysics, 5,* 115–133.

McGuire, B. A., Gilbert, C. D., Rivlin, P. K., & Wiesel, T. N. (1991). Targets of horizontal connections in macaque primary visual cortex. *Journal of Comparative Neurology, 305,* 370–392.

Milner, B. (1963). Effects of different brain lesions on card sorting. *Archives of Neurology, 9,* 90–100.

Milner, B. (1964). Some effects of frontal lobectomy in man. In J. M. Warren & K. Akert (Eds.), *The Frontal Granular Cortex and Behavior* (pp. 313–334). New York: McGraw-Hill.

Milner, B. (1982). Some cognitive effects of frontal-lobe lesions in man. *Philosophical Transactions of the Royal Society of London, Series B, 298,* 211–226.

Minsky, M. L., & Papert, S. (1969). *Perceptrons: An introduction to computational geometry.* Cambridge: MIT Press.

Monchi, O., & Taylor, J. G. (1999). A hard wired model of coupled frontal working memories for various tasks. *Information Sciences Journal, 113,* 221–243.

Mountcastle, V. B. (1957). Modality and topographic properties of single neurons of cat's somatic sensory cortex. *Journal of Neurophysiology, 20,* 408–434.

Myers, C. E., & Gluck, M. A. (1994). Context, conditioning, and hippocampal re-representation. *Behavioral Neuroscience, 108,* 835–847.

Parks, R. W., Levine, D. S., & Long, D. L. (Eds.). (1998). *Fundamentals of neural network modeling: Neuropsychology and cognitive neuroscience.* Cambridge: MIT Press.

Perrett, S. P., Ruiz, B. P., & Mauk, M. D. (1993). Cerebellar cortex lesions disrupt learning-dependent timing of conditioned eyelid responses. *Journal of Neuroscience, 13,* 1708–1718.

Piaget, J. (1952). *The origin of intelligence in children* (M. Cook, Trans.). New York: International University Press.

Plaut, D. C., & Shallice, T. (1994). *Connectionist modeling in cognitive neuropsychology: A case study.* Hillsdale, NJ: Erlbaum.

Pribram, K. H. (1961). A further experimental analysis of the behavioral deficit that follows injury to the primate frontal cortex. *Journal of Experimental Neurology, 3,* 432–466.

Pribram, K. H. (1991). *Brain and perception: Holonomy and structure in figural processing.* Hillsdale, NJ: Erlbaum.

Pribram, K. H. (Ed.). (1993). *Rethinking neural networks: Quantum fields and biological data.* Hillsdale, NJ: Erlbaum.

Rashevsky, N. (1960). *Mathematical biophysics* (Vol. 2). New York: Dover.

Read, S. J., & Miller, L. C. (Eds.). (1998). *Connectionist models of social reasoning and social behavior.* Mahwah, NJ: Erlbaum.

Reggia, J. A., Ruppin, E., & Berndt, R. (Eds.). (1996). *Neural network modeling of brain disorders.* Singapore: World Scientific.

Reggia, J. A., Ruppin, E., & Glanzman, D. L. (Eds.). (1999). *Disorders of brain, behavior, and cognition: The neurocomputational perspective.* Amsterdam: Elsevier.

Rescorla, R. A., & Wagner, A. B. (1972). A theory of Pavlovian conditioning: Variations in the effectiveness of reinforcement and non-reinforcement. In A. H. Black & W. F. Prokasy (Eds.), *Classical conditioning II: Current research and theory* (pp. 64–99). New York: Appleton-Century-Crofts.

Robson, J. G. (1975). Receptive fields: Neural representation of the spatial and intensive attributes of the visual image. In E. C. Carterette & M. P. Friedman (Eds.), *Handbook of perception* (Vol. 5, pp. 82–116). New York: Academic Press.

Rosenblatt, F. (1962). *Principles of neurodynamics.* Washington, DC: Spartan Books.

Rumelhart, D. E., Hinton, G. E., & Williams, R. J. (1986). Learning internal representations by error propagation. In D. E. Rumelhart & J. L. McClelland (Eds.), *Parallel distributed processing* (Vol. 1, pp. 318–362). Cambridge: MIT Press.

Rumelhart, D. E., & McClelland, J. L. (Eds.). (1986). *Parallel distributed processing* (Vols. 1–2). Cambridge: MIT Press.

Rumelhart, D. E., & Zipser, D. (1985). Feature discovery by competitive learning. *Cognitive Science, 9,* 75–112.

Solomon, R. L., & Corbit, J. D. (1974). An opponent-process theory of motivation: I. Temporal dynamics of affect. *Psychological Review, 81,* 119–145.

Sperling, G., & Sondhi, M. M. (1968). Model for visual luminance detection and flicker detection. *Journal of the Optical Society of America, 58,* 1133–1145.

Staats, A. W. (1999). Unifying psychology requires new infrastructure, theory, method, and a research agenda. *Review of General Psychology, 3,* 3–13.

Stein, D., & Ludik, D. (Eds.). (1998). *Neural Networks and Psychopathology.* Cambridge, UK: Cambridge University Press.

Stuart, G., Spruston, N., Sakmann, B., & Hauser, M. (1997). Action potential initiation and backpropagation in neurons of the mammalian central nervous system. *Trends in Neurosciences, 20,* 125–131.

Sutton, R. S., & Barto, A. G. (1981). Toward a modern theory of adaptive networks: Expectation and prediction. *Psychological Review, 88,* 135–170.

Taylor, J. G., & Alavi, F. N. (1993). A global competitive network for attention. *Neural Network World, 5,* 477–502.

Thompson, R. F. (1990). Neural mechanisms of classical conditioning in mammals. *Philosophical Transactions of the Royal Society of London (Biology), 329,* 161–170.

Tryon, W. W. (1995). Synthesizing animal and human behavior research via neural network learning theory. *Journal of Behavior Therapy and Experimental Psychiatry, 26,* 303–312.

Tulving, E. (1972). Episodic and semantic memory. In E. Tulving & W. Donaldson (Eds.), *Organization of memory* (pp. 382–403). New York: Academic Press.

Tversky, A., & Kahneman, D. (1974). Judgment under uncertainty: Heuristics and biases. *Science, 185,* 1124–1131.

Tversky, A., & Kahneman, D. (1981). The framing of decisions and the rationality of choice. *Science, 211,* 453–458.

Wada, Y., & Kawato, M. (1993). A neural network model for arm trajectory formation using forward and inverse dynamics models. *Neural Networks, 6,* 919–932.

Werbos, P. J. (1974). *Beyond regression: New tools for prediction and analysis in the behavioral sciences.* Unpublished doctoral dissertation, Harvard University.

Werbos, P. J. (1993). *The roots of backpropagation: From ordered derivatives to neural networks and political forecasting.* New York: Wiley.

Westen, D. (1999). All the President's women. Paper presented at Department of Psychology, University of Texas at Arlington, April.

Widrow, B., & Hoff, M. E. (1960). *Adaptive switching circuits* (Stanford Electronics Laboratories Tech. Rep. 1553–1). Stanford University, Stanford, CA.

Wiener, N. (1948). *Cybernetics.* New York: Wiley.

Wilson, H. R. (1975). A synaptic model for spatial frequency adaptation. *Journal of Theoretical Biology, 50,* 327–352.

Wilson, H. R., & Cowan, J. D. (1973). A mathematical theory of the functional dynamics of cortical and thalamic nervous tissue. *Kybernetik, 13,* 55–80.

CHAPTER 7

Parallel and Serial Processing

GORDON D. LOGAN

INTRODUCTION

I remember myself as a preschooler asking my mother whether a person could do two things at once. I remember where we stood in the hallway when I asked the question, and I remember her answer: "Sometimes you can and sometimes you can't. It depends." I remember not being very satisfied with that answer. Too many years later, I find myself an expert on the question. I earned my doctorate asking it, and I spent a good part of my career asking it. After all this experience, my expert answer is this: Sometimes you can process things in parallel, and sometimes you process things in series. It depends. My mother was right all along, and my expert answer is no more satisfying than hers. In my expert opinion, the problem lies in the question, not in the answer. The question of parallel versus serial processing can be answered meaningfully only in the context of other issues and other concepts—the things on which "it depends."

A major difficulty in answering the question lies in knowing what the answer means. How could one tell if processing were parallel or serial? In many ways, serial processes behave like parallel ones. They are affected similarly by experimental manipulations. One can trace the logic from the assumption of parallel versus serial processing to prediction of reaction time (RT) and accuracy, and the predictions are often very similar. This makes it hard, if not impossible, to argue from the data back to the theory. There are two routes to the same end, and given the end point, one cannot tell which route was taken. When parallel and serial processing predict the same results, the results do not distinguish the theories. This is the problem of mimicry. I was also into mimicry at an early age—it was a good way to annoy my brother Jack—but those experiences are more relevant to abnormal than to experimental psychology.

My purpose in writing this chapter is to discuss the methods that people use to ask whether processing is parallel or serial. In the years since I first asked my mother the question, researchers have been asking Mother Nature the same thing. They learned a lot about the things on which "it depends." Much of the progress involved understanding the mimicry problem and finding ways to solve it. At the same time, researchers investigating attention and memory found themselves having to ask questions about serial versus parallel processing. They, too, made a lot of progress, though their conclusions were usually more specific. My goal is to explain the ways in which people ask the question and the issues that they confront in doing so. This chapter is intended more as a guidebook to orient people to the issues than as a user's manual to teach specific methods (for reviews of the various issues, see J. Miller, 1988; Townsend, 1990; Van Zandt & Townsend, 1993).

BASIC DEFINITION

Put most simply, the question of parallel versus serial processing is about *simultaneity* and *precedence* in processing. Imagine two processes, A and B. If A and B go on simultaneously, then processing is parallel. If A precedes B or B precedes A, then processing is serial. Parallel and serial processing are illustrated in the top two panels of Figure 7.1. The

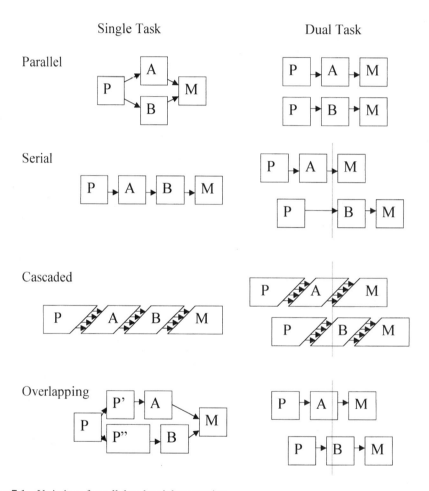

Figure 7.1   Varieties of parallel and serial processing.
NOTE: The boxes represent stages of processing, and the arrows represent information flow between the boxes. The letters on the boxes represent different processes. *P* represents perceptual processes, *M* represents motor processes, and *A* and *B* represent central processes. The left column represents single-task situations, and the right column represents dual-task situations. The top row represents parallel processes; *A* and *B* are simultaneous, and neither precedes the other. The second row represents serial processes. *A* and *B* are never simultaneous. *A* begins and ends before *B* begins. The third row represents cascaded processes. *B* begins before *A* finishes, and *A* begins to transmit information to *B* before *A* finishes. *A* and *B* are simultaneous, but *A* precedes *B*. The bottom row represents overlapping processes. *A* and *B* begin at different times but run simultaneously for some period.

left column represents the processes underlying performance of a single task (i.e., producing a single response to a single stimulus), and the right column represents the processes underlying performance in a dual task (i.e., producing two responses to two stimuli). In the parallel processing examples, A and B begin at the same time and end at the same time. In the serial processing examples, A begins and ends before B.

The simple question of whether processing is parallel or serial has intrigued every generation of cognitive psychologists. In the 1950s Broadbent (1957, 1958) argued that sensory processes were parallel and that cognitive ("perceptual") processes were serial. In the 1960s Sternberg (1966, 1969) argued that short-term memory scanning was serial rather than parallel. In the 1970s Shiffrin and Schneider (1977) argued that automatic processes were parallel and that controlled processes were serial. In the 1980s Treisman and colleagues (Treisman & Gelade, 1980; Treisman & Schmidt, 1982) argued that feature search was parallel and that conjunction search was serial. In the 1990s Meyer and Kieras (1997) argued that dual tasks could be performed in parallel, contradicting conventional wisdom, which says that dual tasks are carried out strictly in series (e.g., Pashler & Johnston, 1989; Welford, 1952). Also in the 1990s Rickard (1997) and I (Logan, 1988) argued over the serial nature of memory retrieval (see also Delaney, Reder, Straszewski, & Ritter, 1998). Many of these issues are not resolved, and the arguments will continue throughout the new century.

The zeitgeist has changed considerably over the generations, and the relative plausibility of serial and parallel processing has changed with it. In the early years, when the idea that mind is computation first took hold, people took the serial nature of computation quite seriously. Computers were serial, and people took the mind-as-serial-computer analogy quite literally. They were more likely to think of processing as serial than parallel. In recent years, at the end of the "decade of the brain," people have been impressed with the massive parallel nature of the brain and seem more likely to think that processing is parallel because that seems more brain-like than does serial processing. How serial behavior can emerge from a parallel brain has become an important question once again (see Lashley, 1951). I presume that the brain and the way it implements thinking have not changed with the zeitgeist.

COMPLICATIONS

The simple question of whether processing is parallel or serial is seductive because it seems so easy to answer. One need only be able to detect process A and process B and measure the times at which they occur. This turns out to be harder than it seems. There is no direct way to observe the occurrence of mental processes. One must infer their existence from changes in behavior that result from experimental manipulations. Most investigations of serial and parallel processing focus on accuracy and RT in relatively simple tasks. Accuracy and RT are final outcome measures that reflect the combined effects of all processes that go into producing a response. Most often, the question of serial or parallel processing concerns only some of the processes that contribute to a response, and separating the interesting processes from the uninteresting ones makes the inference from behavior to theoretical processes more complicated. In order to have a theory of the processes of interest, one must have also some kind of theory of the other processes and of how they combine to perform the whole task. The other processes may interact with the process of interest, and clever experiments may have to be done to tease them apart. Even with the cleverest experiment, the chain of inference from observation to conclusion grows more complex.

Researchers have responded to these complications in two ways. One, which might be called the *general class* approach, is to create general classes of theory by combining binary (or ternary) distinctions among theories and then deriving in-principle predictions that distinguish the classes. To use a familiar example, visual search may be either parallel or serial and either exhaustive or self-terminating. The factorial combination yields four general classes of models from which predictions can be derived and tested (and these will be considered in the next section). Perhaps the most important results from this approach concern mimicry, showing that some models make the same predictions as other models so that observation of the predicted effects cannot distinguish the models.

The alternative approach, which might be called the *specific theory* approach, is to propose theories that account for specific sets of experimental data (e.g., Bundesen, 1990; Cave & Wolfe, 1990; Humphreys & Müller, 1993; Logan, 1996; Meyer & Kieras, 1997; Wolfe, 1994). Creating these theories requires making decisions about the binary distinctions studied in the other approach, so the general theories may fit into some category in the general class approach. The focus is different, however. The theories are often interpreted as models of the computations that underlie performance in the tasks they address, and the focus is on the nature of the computation and the way it is executed rather than on general properties of the computation, such as serial versus parallel processing. The most important results from this approach may be an increased understanding of the computational problems that underlie cognition and the discovery of some ways to solve them.

This chapter is organized around these two approaches to the problem of complexity. The main topics are organized around the general class approach, introducing the complexities one by one. The different complexities highlight different empirical situations and, consequently, illustrate different specific theories. Thus, the specific theory approach is embedded in the general class approach.

FOUR BASIC DISTINCTIONS

The general class approach involves making broad distinctions between classes of models and combining distinctions factorially to produce subclasses of models that differ from each other in fundamental ways. Most of the work has focused on four binary distinctions that combine to produce 16 classes of theory: parallel versus serial processing, discrete versus continuous processing, limited versus unlimited capacity, and self-terminating versus exhaustive search. From the perspective of this chapter, parallel versus serial processing is the focal distinction, and the others are complications. I begin with discrete versus continuous processing because it is the most general complication.

Discrete versus Continuous Processing

The first broad distinction is between discrete and continuous processes. *Discrete* processes transmit the information that they produce in a single step at a discrete point in time. Discrete transmission implies that processes begin and end at discrete points in time; they begin when they receive input (a transmission from a logically precedent process), and they end when they give output (a transmission to a logically subsequent process). The idea of discrete processing has been with us since the beginning of experimental psychology (e.g., Donders,

1868). It prevailed throughout history (e.g., Sternberg, 1969), and it prevails today (e.g., Meyer & Kieras, 1997; Pashler & Johnston, 1989). The assumption of discrete processing makes formal modeling easier. It allows the modeler to derive predictions that are clear and intuitively compelling. Consequently, it has been popular among theorists. Indeed, much of the formal work on serial versus parallel processing that was done in the general class approach assumes discrete processing. Discrete processes fit the simple definitions of parallel and serial processing nicely. If A and B are discrete processes that are part of the same task, then they are serial if one precedes the other and parallel if they are simultaneous. The most commonly used techniques for analyzing RT assume discrete processing, including Donders' (1868) *subtractive method,* Sternberg's (1969) *additive factors method,* and the various analyses derived from them (e.g., Fisher & Goldstein, 1983; Goldstein & Fisher, 1991; Pashler & Johnston, 1989; Schweickert, 1978; Schweickert & Townsend, 1989; Townsend & Schweickert, 1989).

Donders' (1868) subtractive method assumes that RT is the sum of the durations of a series of stages that extend from stimulus to response. Different tasks require different stages and different numbers of stages. The subtractive method considers special cases in which two tasks differ in exactly one stage; the remaining stages are the same in both tasks. In these special cases, the duration of the extra stage can be estimated by subtracting RT for the simpler task from RT for the more complex task. Sternberg's (1969) additive factors method also assumes that RT is the sum of the durations of a series of stages, but the goal is to identify processing stages rather than to estimate their durations. Stages are identified with experimental variables that affect them. Variables that affect different stages will have

additive effects because the durations of different stages add together to produce RT. Variables that affect the same stage will interact in a superadditive manner. Both methods assume discrete stages.

The alternative *continuous* processes transmit the information they produce gradually in an infinite number of infinitesimally small steps. Their beginning points and end points are not so clear, nor is the point at which they begin transmitting information to logically subsequent processes. It is clear, however, that logically subsequent processes can begin well before logically prior processes end. Continuous processes constantly report their current state to subsequent processes. Small changes in the current state propagate rapidly to the next stage and begin to affect its processing well before either stage has accumulated enough change to finish processing. Precedent processes are active simultaneously. Thus, continuous processes do not fit nicely into the simple definition of parallel and serial processes. The logical and temporal precedence suggest that processing is serial, but the simultaneous processing suggests that processing is parallel. To escape this quandary, some researchers refer to processes like this as *cascaded,* which reflects the mixture of precedence and simultaneity (e.g., McClelland, 1979). Other researchers think of continuous processes as parallel. Cascaded processes are illustrated in the third row of Figure 7.1. Single-task processing is on the left, and dual task processing is on the right.

Processes that are not continuous may be precedent and simultaneous if the precedence is only temporal and not logical (i.e., if the stage that begins second does not require information from the stage that begins first). In these cases, the processes may be discrete and parallel. Consider a single-task situation in which A and B are discrete parallel processes preceded by processes P' and P'', respectively. If P'' takes longer than P', A will start before B. At some later point, they both operate simultaneously. This is illustrated in the left side of the bottom row in Figure 7.1. In this case, the simultaneity and precedence of A and B do not require one to assume that they are continuous stages.

In dual-task situations, process A may be part of one task, and process B may be part of the other. Process A may begin before B, and thus be precedent, but A may end after B begins, and thus be simultaneous. In this case, the precedence is due to stimulus conditions (e.g., stimulus onset asynchrony) or to differences in the durations of processes prior to A and B. There is no logical contingency between A and B because they are parts of different tasks. Processes A and B are parallel and could be discrete. Their simultaneity and precedence do not require one to assume that they are continuous. Overlapping dual-task processes are illustrated in the bottom-right row of Figure 7.1.

A second case of precedent but simultaneous processing can occur in continuous tasks, such as typing, in which there is a chain of precedent processes and each process is active all the time. The discrete processing assumption can be salvaged if the different processes operate on different parts of the input. In typing "red ball," for example, perceptual processes may be working on "ball" while motor processes are busy with "red" (see, e.g., Butsch, 1932; Inhoff, Briihl, Bohemier, & Wang, 1992). An individual input would still be processed discretely, activating only one process at a time and jumping from one process to the next in a single discrete step. Jolicoeur, Tombu, Oriet, and Stevanovsky (in press) call this sort of processing *pipelining*. Pipelining speeds performance by allowing the system as a whole to process several inputs concurrently (in parallel) while each component of the system processes its input discretely (in series). For example, a three-stage model could process three inputs concurrently if each stage took the next input as soon as it was finished with the current one. By analogy, it takes four hours to build a single car in an assembly line, but the different stations on the line work on different cars at the same time, so the lag between successive cars is very short. The four-hours-per-car pipeline produces several cars in a single hour. Pipelining may save the discrete stage assumption, but it does not require it. Continuous processes may also be pipelined. It is interesting that the major formal theory of typewriting assumes continuous processing (Rumelhart & Norman, 1982).

Continuous processing has had a much shorter history than has discrete processing. It was proposed first around 1980 (e.g., C. W. Eriksen & Schultz, 1979; McClelland, 1979) as an alternative to discrete stage analyses of RT. Shortly afterward, the connectionist revolution began and adopted continuous processing as a fundamental assumption. Continuous processing is the "parallel" part of "parallel distributed processing" (e.g., McClelland, Rumelhart, & the PDP Research Group, 1986). Many connectionist models address response probability rather than RT and so do not address the issue of parallel versus serial processing in the usual sense. Connectionist approaches to RT are often very complicated and require simulation instead of mathematical analysis, and that makes it hard to produce general predictions (but see McClelland, 1993).

As J. Miller (1988, 1993) pointed out, discrete and continuous processes are at opposite ends of a continuum. Miller argued that information passes from one stage to another in chunks that can vary in size. The continuum that links discrete and continuous processes is defined by the chunk-size variable, which Miller called *grain size*. Grain size is determined by the number of chunks that must accumulate before processing terminates.

Discrete processes have the largest grain; processing terminates when one chunk is produced. Continuous processes have the smallest grain; processing terminates when an infinite number of infinitesimally small chunks are produced. Processes in the middle of the continuum have intermediate grain. Several chunks must be accumulated before processing terminates.

The issue of discrete versus continuous processing was a central focus of the empirical literature in the 1980s and 1990s, and the bulk of the evidence appears to contradict strictly discrete processes. Behavioral experiments by J. Miller showed evidence of continuous processing (e.g., 1982a, 1983, 1987). Meyer, Irwin, Osman, and Kounois (1988) found evidence of partial information with a response signal method that required subjects to respond on signal even if they had not finished processing. Psychophysiological experiments by Coles and colleagues showed evidence of concurrent, subthreshold activation of competing responses in electromyographic (EMG; Coles, Gratton, Bashore, Eriksen, & Donchin, 1985) and electroencephalographic (EEG; Gratton, Coles, Sirevaag, Eriksen, & Donchin, 1988) data in the B. A. Eriksen and Eriksen (1974) flanker task. J. Miller and Hackley (1992) and Osman, Bashore, Coles, and Donchin (1992) showed evidence of subthreshold activation of responses on no-go trials in go/no-go tasks. These data may rule out pure discrete processes, in which one chunk is enough to terminate processing, but they do not distinguish between continuous and intermediate grain-size partial-information discrete processes (see J. Miller, 1988; see also Meyer et al., 1988, vs. Ratcliff, 1988).

Limited versus Unlimited Capacity

The idea that the capacity for processing information is limited has been an essential part of cognitive psychology since the 1950s, particularly in research on attention (e.g., Broadbent, 1958) and memory (e.g., G. A. Miller, 1956). The idea that capacity may not always be limited has been a part of cognitive psychology for just as long (e.g., Sperling, 1960). Many careers have been made in deciding whether particular processes are limited or unlimited in capacity. The capacity issue intersects the parallel versus serial processing issue because limited capacity processes are often thought of as serial whereas unlimited capacity processes are often thought of as parallel (e.g., Treisman & Gelade, 1980; Van der Heijden, 1992). Parallel processes need not be unlimited in capacity. Indeed, *resource* or *general capacity* theories often assume parallel allocation of a limited pool of "mental energy" (e.g., Kahneman, 1973; Navon & Gopher, 1979; Norman & Bobrow, 1975), so processing is parallel but limited in capacity.

In the modern attention literature, the idea that serial processing is limited in capacity and parallel processing is unlimited in capacity plays out in two lines of investigation. One is the visual search literature that distinguishes between *preattentive processes* that are parallel and unlimited in capacity and *focal attentive processes* that are serial and limited in capacity (Cave & Wolfe, 1990; Duncan & Humphreys, 1989; Humphreys & Müller, 1993; Treisman & Gelade, 1980; Wolfe, 1994). The other is the memory and skill acquisition literature that distinguishes between *automatic processing* that is parallel and unlimited in capacity and *controlled, strategic, effortful,* or *attentional processing* that is serial and limited in capacity (Jacoby, 1991; Logan, 1988; Shiffrin & Schneider, 1977).

Processing capacity can be defined as the rate at which information is processed, expressed in units of information per unit time (Townsend & Ashby, 1983; Wenger & Townsend, 2000). From this perspective, capacity limitations are defined in terms of changes in the processing rate for a particular element when another element is added to the task. Capacity is *unlimited* if the processing rate does not change when another element is added to the task. That is,

$$v(x, i)_N = v(x, i)_{N-1} \qquad (1)$$

where $v(x, i)_N$ is the rate at which object x is compared to category i when there are N elements in the task, and $v(x, i)_{N-1}$ is the rate at which object x is compared to category i when there are $N - 1$ elements in the task. Capacity is *limited* if the processing rate slows down when another element is added to the task. That is,

$$v(x, i)_N < v(x, i)_{N-1}. \qquad (2)$$

Capacity is *fixed* if, when another element is added, the processing rate decreases in a manner in which the sum of the processing rates over all elements in the task remains constant. If capacity is allocated equally to all N elements, then

$$v(x, i)_N = v(x, i)_{N-1} \frac{N-1}{N}. \qquad (3)$$

If capacity is fixed and capacity allocation is not equal, then there is little constraint on a particular processing rate. The sum of rates is constrained to add to a constant C, but the amount allocated to a particular process can vary between 0 and C. The rate of processing for a particular process may even increase (e.g., if the person shifted from dividing attention among elements to focusing primarily on one element). Limited and fixed capacity are very hard to distinguish from each other.

Capacity and Resources

The idea of capacity is often confused with the idea of processing resources. Sometimes researchers use the terms interchangeably. In my view, however, "capacity" and "resources" have distinctly different meanings and one does not necessarily imply the other. The term

"capacity" is relatively neutral theoretically; capacity is simply a rate measure, the amount of information processed per unit time. The term "resource" embeds the idea of capacity in complex theories of attention and performance that make many more assumptions than the simple assertion that performance can be measured in terms of processing rate (e.g., Kahneman, 1973; Navon & Gopher, 1979; Norman & Bobrow, 1975). Resource theories assume that capacity is fixed or severely limited, that capacity is a kind of mental energy that can be allocated selectively to activate mental processes, that capacity can be allocated in parallel, and that performance changes smoothly as capacity is added and withdrawn (Logan, 1997; Navon, 1984). Each of these additional assumptions is controversial, and not one of them is implied by the idea of capacity as a measure of processing rate. Resource theory may imply limited or fixed capacity, but limited or fixed capacity does not imply resource theory. Researchers should only say "resource" if they mean it. They should not say "resource" when they mean "capacity."

Capacity Limitations and Load Effects

Many investigations of search tasks and dual tasks manipulate processing load. In search tasks, load depends on the number of items to be processed (i.e., the number of items in a search display, the number of items in a set of targets to be compared with the display, or both). In dual tasks, load depends on the difficulty of one or both tasks. Many people interpret load effects as evidence for capacity limitation. However, load effects can occur for several reasons other than capacity limitations (see, e.g., Duncan, 1980; Navon, 1984). The occurrence of load effects depends in part on the assumptions one makes about the cognitive architecture in which processing occurs. Load effects occur regardless of capacity limitations in certain *independent race models* (e.g., Bundesen, 1990) and in equivalent *Luce choice models* (e.g., Luce, 1963). Consider an independent race model in which N objects in the display race to be categorized as members of category i. If the distributions of finishing times are exponential in form, then the probability that object x wins the race is given by

$$P(\text{``}x\text{ is }i\text{''}) = \frac{v(x, i)}{\sum_{z=1}^{N} v(z, i)}. \qquad (4)$$

Marley and Colonius (1992) and Bundesen (1993) showed that independent race models such as this one are equivalent to Luce choice models in the sense that one can construct an independent race model that mimics the choice probabilities of any given Luce choice model. Consequently, Equation (4) describes response probabilities in Luce choice models as well as in independent race models.

Now consider what happens when another item is added to the display, so that N increases by 1. If processing capacity is fixed, $P(\text{``}x\text{ is }i\text{''})$ will decrease because $v(x, i)$ in the numerator of Equation (4) must decrease so that the sum of processing rates over the display—that is, $\sum v(z, i)$ in the denominator of Equation (1)—remains constant. If processing capacity is limited but not fixed, $P(\text{``}x\text{ is }i\text{''})$ will also decrease because $v(x, i)$ decreases in the numerator and because the processing rate for the Nth item, $v(N, i)$, is added to the denominator, and the denominator increases. If processing capacity is unlimited, $v(x, i)$ will remain the same in the numerator, but $P(\text{``}x\text{ is }i\text{''})$ will decrease because the processing rate for the Nth item, $v(N, i)$, will be added to the denominator. Thus, for independent exponentially distributed race models and Luce choice models, load affects response probability whether capacity is fixed, limited, or unlimited. Therefore, contrary to popular opinion, the observation of load effects does not indicate fixed or limited capacity (see also Duncan, 1980; Navon, 1984).

Functional and Stochastic Independence

Fixed or limited capacity suggests a kind of dependence among concurrent processes in that the rate of processing one element depends on the number of concurrently processed elements. However, formal models of fixed and limited capacity processes often assume independence. These ideas may seem contradictory, but they are not. They reflect different kinds of independence: functional independence and stochastic independence, respectively. Processes A and B are *stochastically independent* if the probability that A and B occur together is the product of the probabilities that each occurs separately. That is,

$$P(A \cap B) = P(A)P(B). \qquad (5)$$

One tests stochastic independence by manipulating $P(A)$ and $P(B)$ and observing changes in $P(A \cap B)$. If it remains predictable through the relationship in Equation (5), then A and B are stochastically independent. If it departs significantly from the relationship in Equation (5), then A and B are not stochastically independent. Stochastic independence is a very important assumption in mathematical modeling of parallel and serial processing. It simplifies the mathematics tremendously (see, e.g., Townsend & Ashby, 1983).

Processes A and B are *functionally independent* if the probability that A occurs is not correlated with the probability that B occurs. One tests functional independence by manipulating $P(A)$ and observing changes in $P(B)$. If $P(B)$ does not change when $P(A)$ changes, then A and B are functionally independent. If $P(B)$ changes when $P(A)$ changes, then A and B are functionally dependent. Functional independence has been important in studies in cognitive psychology and neuropsychology that rely on the logic of *dissociations* (e.g., Kelley & Lindsay, 1996). A dissociation occurs when a factor affects two processes differently—when processes are functionally independent or negatively correlated. Functional independence represents *a single dissociation;* negative correlation represents a *double dissociation.*

Researchers often confuse stochastic and functional independence even though they are quite distinct conceptually. The two kinds of independence are tested by manipulating the same probability—$P(A)$—but conclusions about them are based on different probabilities. Stochastic independence rests on changes in $P(A \cap B)$ when $P(A)$ is manipulated; functional independence rests on changes in $P(B)$ when $P(A)$ is manipulated. Relationships between $P(A \cap B)$ and $P(A)$ are separate from relationships between $P(B)$ and $P(A)$, so the two kinds of independence address different aspects of the data. In particular, the functional dependence seen in fixed capacity and limited capacity models does not imply stochastic dependence. In a fixed or limited capacity system, taking capacity from A and giving it to B would increase $P(A)$ and decrease $P(B)$, signaling a violation of functional independence. However, stochastic independence rests on what happens to $P(A \cap B)$, not to $P(B)$. If $P(A \cap B)$ changes in accord with the relationship in Equation (5), then A and B are stochastically independent even though they are functionally dependent.

Capacity Limitations in Search

Capacity limitations were central issues in the memory search literature of the 1970s and the visual search literature of the 1980s, where they were bound together with the issue of parallel versus serial processing. Sternberg (1966) contrasted serial processing with parallel processing in his classic paper on memory search, arguing that serial processing predicted the observed linear increase in RT with the number of items in the memory set to which the probe was compared (*memory set size,* or N), whereas parallel processing predicted a negatively accelerated increase (see

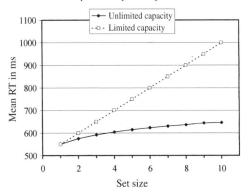

Exponential parallel processes

Figure 7.2 Predicted mean reaction times (RTs) for limited-capacity (broken lines and open squares) and unlimited-capacity (solid lines and filled diamonds) parallel models with exponentially distributed processing times.
NOTE: The rate parameter was 0.04 in both cases.

Figure 7.2). The predictions for serial processing are clear: There is one comparison for each item in the memory set, and the mean time for successive comparisons is constant, so RT increases linearly with N. Sternberg modeled parallel processing by assuming that memory search involves N independent parallel comparisons between the probe and the memory set. The probe is compared against all the items in the memory set before a decision is made (i.e., processing is exhaustive, as discussed later), so RT is the maximum of N independent samples from the distribution of comparison times. The maximum of N independent samples increases as a negatively accelerated function of N (see Gumbel, 1958), so RT should increase in that fashion if processing is parallel. The data contradicted that prediction, so Sternberg rejected parallel models.

Townsend and Ashby (1983) presented a derivation of Sternberg's (1966) prediction with independently and identically distributed (i.i.d.) exponential comparison processes. There is one such process for each of the N items in the memory set, and the comparisons continue until all have finished (i.e., processing is exhaustive). The time for the last one to finish can be broken down into a sum of *intercompletion times* that represents the intervals between the finishing times of successive processes. The N processes begin together but finish at different times, and they can be ranked in the order in which they finish. Intercompletion time is the time between successive ranks. The processes race against each other, each at the same rate, v. The first completion occurs when the fastest of the N processes finishes. The distribution of finishing times for the fastest runner in a race between exponential distributions is an exponential distribution itself with a rate parameter equal to the sum of the rate parameters of all the runners in the race.[1] Because there are N runners with the same rate parameter, the rate parameter for the first comparison to finish is Nv, and the mean finishing time for the first comparison is $1/Nv$. Because the distributions are exponential, the interval between the first completion and the second is also exponentially distributed. This intercompletion time can be thought of as a race between the $N - 1$ remaining comparisons. The winner of that race is exponentially distributed with a rate parameter of $(N - 1)v$ and a mean finishing time of $1/(N - 1)v$. The interval between the second and third comparison is also exponentially distributed with a rate parameter of $(N - 2)v$ and a mean finishing time of $1/(N - 2)v$, and so on. Continuing this process, mean finishing time for all N comparisons is

$$E(T)$$
$$= \frac{1}{Nv} + \frac{1}{(N-1)v} + \frac{1}{(N-2)v} + \cdots + \frac{1}{v}$$
$$= \frac{1}{v} \sum_{i=1}^{N} \frac{1}{i}. \tag{6}$$

It is instructive to reverse the series to see what happens as items are added to the memory set:

$$E(T) = \frac{1}{v} + \frac{1}{2v} + \frac{1}{3v} + \cdots + \frac{1}{Nv}.$$

Each successive item that is added to the memory set increases comparison time, but the amount by which it increases gets progressively smaller as N increases. This produces negative acceleration in the function relating mean RT to set size. This effect can be seen in the predicted mean RTs from the i.i.d. exponential parallel (exhaustive) model plotted in Figure 7.2.

Atkinson, Holmgren, and Juola (1969) and Townsend (1974) noticed that Sternberg's (1966) parallel model assumed unlimited capacity. The rate at which individual comparisons were executed was the same for each value of N; for example, in Equation (6) it is always v. This assumption was central to the derivation of the prediction (Gumbel, 1958), so changing the assumption may change the prediction. Atkinson et al. and Townsend discovered that parallel processing could predict the observed linear increase in RT with N if capacity was fixed and it could be reallocated as soon as a comparison was finished and the distribution of comparison times was exponential. This was an important discovery

---

[1] The probability density function for the minimum of two samples' probability density functions $f(x)$ and $g(x)$ is

$$f_1(x) = f(x)[1 - G(x)] + g(x)[1 - F(x)]$$

where $F(x)$ and $G(x)$ are cumulative distribution functions (Townsend & Ashby, 1983). If $f(x)$ and $g(x)$ are both exponential with rate parameters v_1 and v_2, respectively, then the distribution of the minima of two samples drawn from them is

$$f_1(x) = v_1 \exp[-v_1 x]\exp[-v_2 x]$$
$$+ v_2 \exp[-v_2 x]\exp[-v_1 x]$$
$$= (v_1 + v_2)\exp[-(v_1 + v_2)x]$$

which is an exponential distribution itself with a rate parameter that is the sum of the rate parameters for the two runners in the race. This derivation can be generalized by recursion to a race between N exponential distributions. If the rate parameters for the different runners are all the same, then the expected finishing time for a race between N processes is $1/Nv$.

because it was one of the first formal demonstrations of mimicry.

The argument is similar to the argument for unlimited capacity processing. The time that the last comparison finishes can be broken down into a sum of the first finishing time and $N - 1$ intercompletion times. If capacity is fixed at C and allocated equally among all simultaneous comparisons during the first period before any of the comparisons finish, then the rate of processing for each individual comparison is C/N. When the first comparison finishes, capacity is immediately reallocated, and the rate for the first intercompletion time is $C/(N - 1)$. The rate for the second intercompletion time is $C/(N - 2)$, and so on. The expected finishing time for all N processes can be computed by substituting these processing rates for the vs in Equation (6):

$$E(T) = \frac{N}{NC} + \frac{N-1}{(N-1)C}$$
$$+ \frac{N-2}{(N-2)C} + \cdots + \frac{1}{C}$$
$$= \frac{1}{C} + \frac{1}{C} + \frac{1}{C} + \cdots + \frac{1}{C}$$
$$= \frac{N}{C}. \tag{7}$$

Equation (7) shows that the mean finishing time for a parallel fixed-capacity exponential process with immediate reallocation increases linearly with set size (with a slope of $1/C$), just as mean finishing time increases in serial models. Predicted RTs from the parallel fixed-capacity model are plotted along with the predictions of the parallel unlimited-capacity model in Figure 7.2.

The contrast between Equations (6) and (7) shows why fixed capacity produces a linear increase in RT with set size. When capacity is unlimited, as in Equation (6), each additional comparison takes progressively less time. The new comparison adds another runner to a race that is already fast; the more runners in the race, the smaller the new runner's impact on the expected finishing time. When capacity is fixed and allocated equally among runners, adding a new runner reduces the amount of capacity that each runner gets, and the race slows down. The slowdown from the reduction in capacity per item compensates for the statistical speedup that results from having more runners in the race, so each new runner adds about the same amount of time to the race (see Equation [7]).[2]

---

[2] The argument depends on the idea that the finishing time for all N parallel processes can be broken down into the sum of the first finishing time and $N - 1$ intercompletion times. The focus on intercompletion times suggests that the race begins anew with one less runner when each comparison finishes, and this idea often runs counter to people's intuitions about parallel processing. The runners that continue to run after the first one finishes were supposed to have begun running at the same time as the first runner, and all that time spent running ought to count for something. It seems that the interval between the first runner and the second should be a lot shorter than the time it took for the first runner to finish. The counterintuitive idea that the race begins anew and takes the same time to run each time, on average, stems from the "memoryless" property of exponential distributions. Because of that property, the probability that an event occurs before time $t_1 + t_2$ given that it has not occurred before time t_1 is equal to the probability that the event occurs in the first t_2 time units. The relationship goes as follows:

$$P(T < t_1 + t_2 \mid T > t_1)$$
$$= \frac{P(T < t_1 + t_2 \cap T > t_1)}{P(T > t_1)}$$
$$= \frac{F(t_1 + t_2) - F(t_1)}{1 - F(t_1)}$$
$$= \frac{(1 - \exp[-v(t_1 + t_2)]) - (1 - \exp[-vt_1])}{1 - (1 - \exp[-vt_1])}$$
$$= \frac{\exp[-vt_1] - \exp[-v(t_1 + t_2)]}{\exp[-vt_1]}$$
$$= \frac{\exp[-vt_1] - \exp[-vt_1]\exp[-vt_2]}{\exp[-vt_1]}$$
$$= \frac{\exp[-vt_1](1 - \exp[-vt_2])}{\exp[-vt_1]}$$
$$= 1 - \exp[-vt_2] = F(t_2) = P(T < t_2).$$

In other words, the distribution of finishing times for events in the race that continues after the first event finishes at time t_1 is the same as the distribution of finishing times for a race with the same number of runners that begins at time 0.

In my view, Townsend's (1974) demonstrations of mimicry between serial and parallel processes signaled the beginning of the end of a period of intense interest in memory search. Models that could account for the linear increase in mean RT with set size proliferated, and the empirical arena shifted to other aspects of the data, such as sequential effects and RT distributions, and mimicry issues appeared in these other aspects as well (for reviews, see Luce, 1986; Townsend & Ashby, 1983). By the early 1980s, research on parallel versus serial processing in memory search seemed to have reached a stalemate, and interest shifted elsewhere.

Around 1980, inspired by Treisman and Gelade's (1980) elegant experiments, attention researchers embraced the issue of parallel versus serial processing in visual search. Treisman and Gelade showed that search RT for simple targets such as a red item among green items or an X among Os (i.e., *feature search*) was independent of the number of items in the display (i.e., display size), whereas search RT for conjunctive targets such as a red X among red Os and green Xs (i.e., *conjunction search*) increased linearly with N. Their *feature integration theory* interpreted their data as indicating that feature search was parallel and that conjunction search was serial. Citing Townsend (1971), they acknowledged the possibility that the linear functions in conjunction search could be produced by parallel processes, but they preferred to interpret them as evidence for serial processing. The burgeoning literature on feature and conjunction search followed their lead, mostly ignoring the mimicry issue. The functions relating RT to display size were markedly different in feature search and conjunction search, and that difference was enough to sustain the idea that the tasks were performed by different processes, regardless of the possible mimicry.

Wolfe and colleagues proposed *guided search* theory as an improvement on feature integration theory (Cave & Wolfe, 1990; Wolfe, 1994; Wolfe, Cave, & Franzel, 1989) but still interpreted the linear functions in conjunction search as evidence for serial processing. Duncan and Humphreys (1989) were more neutral on the issue, interpreting the slopes of RT × display size functions as measures of search efficiency. Humphreys and Müller (1993) made the mimicry problem concrete by proposing *search by recursive rejection* that accounted for flat RT × display size functions in feature search and for steep, linear RT × display size functions in conjunction search with the same parallel model. Researchers pitting their model against feature integration theory or guided search theory must grapple with the issue of parallel versus serial processing.

Several researchers proposed compromise models that sample regions of the display in series but process items within regions in parallel (Duncan & Humphreys, 1989; Grossberg, Mingolla, & Ross, 1994; Logan, 1996; Treisman & Gormican, 1988). It seems to me that these models are on the right track if theories of visual search are to be generalized to real-world behavior. Although we do spend more and more time staring at computer screens like in visual search experiments, even the most sedentary among us spends a lot of time each day searching large-scale environments such as refrigerators, rooms, shopping malls, streets, and freeways. The gradient of retinal acuity forces us to move our eyes to search these large-scale environments, imposing serial processing on our search behavior. Search may be parallel within fixations, processing all items in the fovea and parafovea.

Capacity Limitations in Dual-Task Situations

Capacity limitations may be most apparent in dual-task situations, in which the ability to do one task is strongly affected by the requirement to do another (for a review, see Pashler, 1994a). The contrast between serial and parallel processing has played out in this literature since the beginning of the modern era of cognitive psychology. The first modern theory of dual-task performance was Welford's (1952) single channel theory, which assumed that people dealt with dual tasks in series. Welford's idea was adopted and extended by Broadbent (1957, 1958), who made serial processing a core property of attention within and beyond dual-task situations.

Serial processing was the favored explanation of dual-task performance until the end of the 1960s, when resource theory arose (e.g., Kahneman, 1973; Moray, 1967; Posner & Boies, 1971). Resource theories argued that people perform dual tasks in parallel but with less efficiency than in single-task conditions because capacity is severely limited. Kahneman proposed the broadest theory. He applied a single-resource theory to all problems in attention but focused especially on dual-task performance. In his theory, resources were allocated in parallel whenever it was beneficial to do so. By the end of the 1970s, single-resource theory was replaced by multiple-resource theory (e.g., Navon & Gopher, 1979), but dual-task performance was still thought to be parallel. Multiple-resource theory agreed with single-resource theory in suggesting that a single resource could be allocated in parallel, but it went beyond single-resource theory in arguing that different resources could also be allocated in parallel. This added a new wrinkle: Two tasks that demanded different resources could go on in parallel without interference.

In the middle of the 1980s, Pashler (1984; Pashler & Johnston, 1989) resurrected single-channel theory and derived new predictions from it that confirmed the idea of serial processing in dual-task situations. Predictions derived from resource theory, on the hypothesis

that dual-task processing is parallel, fared less well (e.g., Pashler, 1994b).

In the 1990s the parallel versus serial issues played in two areas, one empirical and one theoretical. The empirical arena contrasted dual-task effects seen in speeded tasks, such as the *psychological refractory period* (PRP) procedure championed by Welford (1952) and Pashler (1984), with effects seen in unspeeded tasks with brief exposures, such as the *attentional blink* procedure introduced by Raymond, Shapiro, and Arnell (1992) and Chun and Potter (1995). The speeded tasks seemed to tax a central bottleneck that selected one response at a time (i.e., serial processing), whereas the unspeeded tasks seemed to tax central resources involved in forming perceptual representations (i.e., parallel processing). In the theoretical arena, Meyer and Kieras (1997) challenged the fundamental idea underlying both central bottleneck and resource theories of dual-task interference, arguing that dual-task effects were often artifacts of the strategies that subjects adopted to deal with dual-task experiments rather than central capacity limitations (see also Logan & Gordon, 2001). They focused primarily on the PRP situation, explaining PRP effects in a model that had no central bottlenecks or central capacity limitations, but their argument generalizes to many dual-task situations.

Researchers noted the potential for mimicry between serial and parallel explanations of dual-task interference early on. A serial process that alternated rapidly enough would seem like a parallel process. This idea was exploited in early multiuser operating systems for serial computers: If the computer switched back and forth between users rapidly enough, the users could think they were operating the computer at the same time. In the empirical arena, subjects could seem to be performing two tasks in parallel even though they were switching rapidly between them (see, e.g., Broadbent, 1982). This kind of mimicry seems amenable to empirical testing. One can measure the time required to switch attention in order to see if it switches rapidly enough. Unfortunately, there is no consensus on methods for estimating the time required to shift attention, and estimated switching time varies across methods by two orders of magnitude. Estimated switching time is fastest in search tasks, where it may be on the order of 20 ms to 40 ms, and slowest in cuing tasks, where it may be on the order of 1,000 ms to 2,000 ms. Duncan, Ward, and Shapiro (1994; see also Ward, Duncan, & Shapiro, 1996) estimated the time required to switch attention in an attentional blink task and argued that it was too slow to support serial processing in search tasks. Moore, Egeth, Berglan, and Luck (1996) contested that conclusion, arguing that their procedure substantially overestimated switching time.

Recent studies of the PRP procedure have used the parallel versus serial issue to localize a hypothesized bottleneck in processing (e.g., Pashler, 1984; Pashler & Johnston, 1989). By hypothesis, stages prior to the bottleneck can go on in parallel within and between tasks, whereas the bottleneck stage is strictly serial. Task 1 and Task 2 can be processed in parallel up to the stage at which they require the bottleneck. At that point, one task gets the bottleneck (usually Task 1) and the other task has to wait for it (usually Task 2). The period during which Task 2 has to wait for the bottleneck is called *slack,* and the bottleneck can be located by finding the locus of the slack in the processing chain. Processes prior to the bottleneck are parallel and so can begin as soon as they receive input. There is no slack before them. The slack period appears just before the bottleneck begins, so localizing the slack also localizes the bottleneck.

The method, often called the *locus of slack* method, is illustrated in Figure 7.3. It involves a factorial experiment with at least two factors: the stimulus onset asynchrony (SOA)

between the stimulus for Task 1 (S1) and the stimulus for Task 2 (S2) and a manipulation of Task 2 difficulty. SOA usually produces a strong main effect on RT to S2 (RT2), and the difficulty manipulation is chosen so that it also produces a strong main effect on RT2. The key datum is the interaction between SOA and the Task 2 difficulty variable. Task 2 difficulty variables that affect stages prior to the bottleneck will produce *underadditive* interactions with SOA; Task 2 difficulty variables that affect stages at or after the bottleneck will produce null or *additive* interactions with SOA (see Pashler & Johnston, 1989; see also Fisher & Goldstein, 1983; Goldstein & Fisher, 1991; Schweickert, 1978; Schweickert & Townsend, 1989; Townsend, 1984; Townsend & Schweickert, 1989).

Figure 7.3A shows why variables that affect prebottleneck stages produce underadditive interactions with SOA. The top part shows flow charts for Task 1 and easy and hard versions of Task 2 with a short SOA. Because SOA is short, Task 2 has to wait for the bottleneck stage, and there is slack in the easy version of Task 2. The hard version of Task 2 has time to catch up to the easy version during the slack period, and it is almost finished when the slack period ends. The effects of the Task 2 difficulty manipulation are absorbed into the slack, so the Task 2 difficulty manipulation has only a small effect on RT2. The bottom part shows the same Task 1 and Task 2 conditions when SOA is long and Task 2 does not have to wait for the bottleneck. There is no slack period to absorb the Task 2 difficulty effect, so it appears full-blown in RT2. When RT2 is plotted against SOA, as in the right side of Figure 7.3A, Task 2 difficulty effects are smaller when the SOA effects are larger. Consequently, Task 2 difficulty interacts underadditively with SOA.

Figure 7.3B shows why variables that affect bottleneck stages produce additive or null interactions with SOA. The top part shows

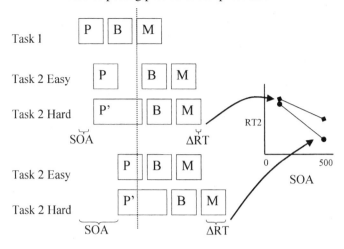

A: Postponing prebottleneck processes

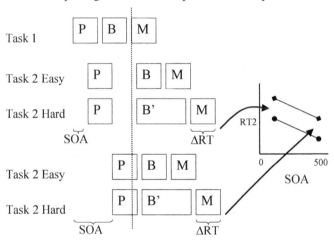

B: Postponing bottleneck and postbottleneck processes

Figure 7.3 Postponing prebottleneck processes vs. postponing bottleneck and postbottleneck processes.

NOTE: Panel A: The effects of postponing prebottleneck processes. The left side presents flow diagrams of processes underlying Task 1 and Task 2. *P* represents prebottleneck perceptual processes, *B* represents bottleneck processes, and *M* represents motor processes. The top part represents short stimulus onset asynchrony (SOA). Stage *P'* is a prolonged version of stage *P*. The short SOA causes Task 2 to wait for the bottleneck stage *B*, and both *P* and *P'* have time to finish during the "slack" period while Task 2 waits for the bottleneck. The effect of *P* versus *P'* on RT2 is given by ΔRT and is plotted on the RT2 × SOA graph beside the flow diagram. The bottom part represents long SOA. Task 2 does not have to wait for the bottleneck, so the effect of *P* versus *P'* propagates to RT2. The ΔRT value is much larger and results in an underadditive interaction between SOA and *P* versus *P'* when plotted on the RT2 × SOA graph beside the flow diagram. Thus, prolonging prebottleneck Task 2 processes produces underadditive interactions between Task 2 difficulty variables and SOA.

Panel B: The effects of postponing bottleneck or postbottleneck processes. The left side presents flow diagrams of processes underlying Task 1 and Task 2. In this panel, the bottleneck stage *B* is prolonged in Task 2. The effects of prolongation appear undiminished in RT2 because the Task 2 bottleneck processing does not begin until Task 1 is finished with the bottleneck, regardless of SOA. The right side plots the effects in a graph of RT2 × SOA. The effect of *B* versus *B'* is clearly additive with SOA. Thus, prolonging bottleneck or postbottleneck Task 2 processes produces additive (null) interactions between Task 2 difficulty variables and SOA.

flow charts for Task 1 and easy and hard versions of Task 2, but now difficulty affects the bottleneck stage. Because SOA is short, Task 2 has to wait for the bottleneck. Because the Task 2 difficulty manipulation affects the bottleneck stage, which has to wait, the easy and hard versions start at the same time, and the difficulty effect appears full-blown in RT2. The bottom part shows the same conditions with a long SOA. Task 2 does not have to wait, and the difficulty manipulation appears full-blown in RT2 once again. Its magnitude is the same as in the short SOA condition, so the joint effects of SOA and Task 2 difficulty, plotted on the right side of the panel, are additive; the interaction is null.

The locus of slack logic is a generalization of Sternberg's (1969) *additive factors method* for decomposing single tasks into component stages. The locus of slack logic is also a special case of a much broader and more formal generalization of the additive factors logic by Schweickert, Townsend, and Fisher (e.g., Fisher & Goldstein, 1983; Goldstein & Fisher, 1991; Schweickert, 1978; Schweickert & Townsend, 1989; Townsend, 1984; Townsend & Schweickert, 1989). In the general logic, underadditive interactions between difficulty variables are often diagnostic of parallel processes, whereas additive or null interactions are often diagnostic of serial processes (Townsend, 1984). These principles cannot be applied universally, however. The issue of parallel versus serial processing remains complicated; interested readers should refer to the original sources.

Like many other tests of parallel versus serial processing, the locus of slack method assumes that processing in the bottleneck stage is discrete, not continuous. Task 1 finishes with the bottleneck at a distinct point in time, and Task 2 starts using the bottleneck at another distinct point in time. The latter never precedes the former. However, some recent data from the PRP procedure suggest that

response selection—a favorite candidate for bottleneck processing—may not be discrete. Hommel (1998) and Logan and Schulkind (2000) showed that RT to the first PRP stimulus was influenced by the response category of the second PRP stimulus, speeding up if that response category was congruent with its own and slowing down if it was incongruent. This suggests that Task 2 response selection began before Task 1 response selection finished, arguing against the hypothesis that response selection is discrete and serial.

The seriousness of the consequences of violating the assumption of discrete processing remains to be seen. Although it is clear that the logic of the locus of slack model and the generalizations of it were developed on the assumption of discrete processing, it is not clear whether a continuous model would make different predictions. As yet, no one has worked out the predictions, although several investigators are working on applications of a single-resource theory to the SOA × difficulty manipulation factorial experiments, and the theory appears to be able to predict the same kinds of underadditive and additive features as can a serial discrete model. That would be a most interesting result.

Self-Terminating versus Exhaustive Search

One of the most important complications of the issue of parallel versus serial processing in the search literature is how processing stops. Search tasks require several comparisons between items in the display and items in memory. At some point, the comparisons stop, and the results are passed on to the next stage so that, ultimately, they can be reported. The key question is, how the comparison processes stop? Traditionally, there have been two alternatives: Search is self-terminating or exhaustive. Search is *self-terminating* if it stops as soon as a target is found or *exhaustive* if it continues until all of the comparisons are finished, regardless of whether or when a target is found.

The issue of self-terminating versus exhaustive search interacts with the issue of parallel versus serial processing in search tasks. The way that search terminates determines the number of items that need to be compared (i.e., N if search is exhaustive; less than N if search is self-terminating), and parallel versus serial processes are distinguished in terms of the effects of the number of items in the display or in the memory set. If search is self-terminating, the number compared may not equal the number displayed or memorized. Indeed, the predictions of unlimited capacity parallel models and the mimicry of fixed capacity parallel models and serial models described earlier requires the assumption that search is exhaustive. If search is self-terminating, parallel unlimited capacity models can predict a null effect of set size (i.e., no increase in RT with set size). In an unlimited capacity model, the rate at which the target comparison is executed is the same regardless of the number of concurrent nontarget comparisons, so the time required to find the target should be independent of display size. (Display size is usually manipulated by varying the number of nontargets.)

Intuition suggests that search should always be self-terminating, because that seems most efficient. Perhaps the most remarkable aspect of Sternberg's (1966) data is that they suggested that search is exhaustive. Sternberg noted that self-terminating search requires the system to decide whether to terminate search after each comparison, whereas exhaustive search requires only one decision after all the comparisons are finished. Sternberg argued that if the decision to terminate was costly, then exhaustive search may be more efficient than self-terminating search. The cost of extra comparisons that finish after the target has been found may be small compared to the accumulated cost of deciding whether to terminate search after each comparison, particularly if the number of items to be compared is small. Search may become self-terminating with larger numbers of items. Indeed, Sternberg studied memory sets of one to five items. Visual search experiments show evidence of exhaustive search when the number of items in the display (display size) varies between one and five (e.g., Atkinson et al., 1969) and evidence of self-terminating search when display size varies over a larger range (e.g., 4–40; Treisman & Gelade, 1980).

The issue of self-terminating versus exhaustive search focuses primarily on the interaction between display size or memory set size and target presence or absence. In general, self-terminating search predicts superadditive interactions between set size and target presence, whereas exhaustive search predicts additive or null interactions. Often, RT increases linearly with set size, and the predictions are expressed in terms of ratios of the slopes of the functions relating RT to set size. Self-terminating search is often said to predict that the ratio of the target-absent slope to the target-present slope is 2:1, whereas exhaustive search predicts a ratio of 1:1. Sternberg's (1966) data showed the 1:1 ratio, so he rejected self-terminating search in favor of exhaustive search. Treisman and Gelade's (1980) data showed the 2:1 ratio, so they rejected exhaustive search in favor of self-terminating search.

The predicted slope ratios follow from the expected number of comparisons when the target is present versus absent. With exhaustive search, subjects perform all comparisons whether the target is present or absent, so the expected number of comparisons for set size N is N for both target-present and target-absent trials. With self-terminating search, subjects perform all comparisons only if there is no target; self-terminating search is exhaustive on target-absent trials. Target-absent trials require N comparisons if set size is N. On target-present trials, however, processing can terminate whenever a target is found. If search is random, the target could be found after the first, second, third, or later comparison but on average would be found after $(N+1)/2$ comparisons. For the same set size, self-terminating search requires about twice as many comparisons for target-absent trials as for target-present trials. If the slope of the function relating RT to the number of comparisons is the same for target-absent and target-present trials (i.e., if each comparison takes the same amount of time), then the slope of the function relating RT to set size will be twice as large for target-absent trials.

Van Zandt and Townsend (1993) showed that self-terminating search does not always predict a 2:1 slope ratio and that in some cases it predicts a 1:1 slope ratio (see also Townsend & Colonius, 1997). That suggests a potentially paralyzing mimicry. However, they showed that exhaustive models almost always predict a 1:1 slope ratio, so finding a ratio other than 1:1 allows us to reject exhaustive models in favor of self-terminating models.

The issue of self-terminating versus exhaustive search usually focuses on target-present trials, asking whether subjects stop when they find a target. Chun and Wolfe (1996) focused on target-absent trials and asked how subjects decide to stop searching when they do not find a target. Environments are usually cluttered with many things, but people ignore most of them when they search for something. When I search for my car in a parking lot, I look at the cars, not the trees and buildings and people. Chun and Wolfe argued that subjects set some criterion for similarity to the target object and restrict their search to items that are similar to the target. They argued that the criterion is set dynamically, decreasing if the distractors are dissimilar to the target and increasing if the distractors are

similar to the target. This adjustment process can reduce the number of items examined on target-absent trials to a value that is substantially smaller than N, and that may affect the ratio of target-absent to target-present slopes. In their view, self-terminating search does not necessarily predict a 2:1 slope ratio.

Data beyond mean RT can be used to distinguish between self-terminating and exhaustive search. Townsend and Ashby (1983) noted that the models make different predictions about the variance of RT. For serial exhaustive search, the variance of the comparison times is simply the sum of the variances in the processing times for each comparison. If the variances are all equal, then

$$Var_{\text{exhaustive}} = N Var(T) \qquad (8)$$

where $Var(T)$ is the variance in a single comparison time. The same prediction can be derived for parallel exhaustive search, where T is intercompletion time (Townsend & Ashby, 1983).

Equation (8) also describes the relation between variance and set size for target-absent trials in serial self-terminating search. For target-present trials, however, serial self-terminating search predicts a stronger increase in variance with set size:

$$Var_{\text{self-terminating}}$$
$$= \frac{N+1}{2} Var(T) + \frac{(N-1)(N+1)}{12} E(T)^2. \qquad (9)$$

The variance on target-present trials depends on the variance in time required for each comparison, as it did on target-absent trials, but it also depends on variation in the number of items compared before the target is found. This additional source of variation makes the overall variance increase faster with N on target-present than on target-absent trials. Again, similar arguments can be made for parallel self-terminating processes (see Townsend & Ashby, 1983).

ALTERNATIVES TO PARALLEL PROCESSING

The four basic distinctions that drove the general class approach were discovered in the 1950s and 1960s. Since then, two new alternatives to parallel processing have come on the scene, one in the attention literature that deals with the effects of redundant signals and one in the skill acquisition literature that addresses the development of automaticity.

Statistical Facilitation versus Coactivation

Parallel processing is an important issue in divided attention. When participants look (or listen) for a target in two channels (two display locations or two acoustic sources), they respond faster if a target appears in both channels than if it appears in only one of them (Miller, 1978, 1982b). This *redundant signals effect* is interesting because it rules out most of the parallel and serial models considered so far in this chapter. Serial and parallel exhaustive models can be ruled out by the effect itself. If targets and distractors take the same amount of time to process, they predict no advantage of redundant targets (but see Townsend & Nozawa, 1997). Parallel and serial self-terminating models can predict the occurrence of the effect—processing can stop as soon as one target is found, and that will be faster when there are two targets—but they can be ruled out in many cases because their quantitative predictions underestimate the observed effect.

Serial self-terminating models predict an advantage of redundant targets when each channel contains either a target or a distractor. If search is random and targets are assigned randomly to channels, then the first object examined will always be a target on redundant trials, but it will only be a target half of the time on single-target trials. On the other half of single-target trials, the distractor will be

examined first, so RT will increase. Averaging the two kinds of single-target trials produces a mean RT that is slower than the mean RT for redundant target trials, thus predicting a redundant signals effect. The observed effects are often larger than these models predict, however (see Miller, 1982b). Moreover, serial self-terminating models predict no advantage when no distractors are presented (i.e., targets appear alone or in tandem), because the first object examined will always be a target, and redundant signals effects are often found under those circumstances (Miller, 1978, 1982b).

The strongest candidate among the models discussed so far is the class of independent unlimited-capacity parallel self-terminating models. They predict *statistical facilitation* with redundant signals. The time to find a target when two are present is the minimum of the times required to find each target alone, and the minimum is generally faster than the mean of the parent distributions from which it is sampled (Gumbel, 1958). This argument extends to distributions as well as means, and Miller (1978, 1982b) developed it into a general test for cumulative distribution functions. The distribution of minima sampled from two parent distributions can be constructed from the parent distributions themselves. If the samples are independent, then

$$P(\min(T_1, T_2) < t) = P(T_1 < t) + P(T_2 < t) \\ - P(T_1 < t \cap T_2 < t)$$

$$(10)$$

where $P(\min(T_1, T_2) < t)$ is the observed cumulative RT distribution with redundant signals and $P(T_1 < t)$ and $P(T_2 < t)$ are the observed cumulative distributions with targets in channels 1 and 2, respectively. The final term is not easy to observe directly, so Miller (1978, 1982b) suggested rearranging the equation to produce an inequality called the *race model inequality* that investigators could use to test the predictions of independent unlimited-capacity parallel self-terminating models:

$$P(\min(T_1, T_2) \le P(T_1 < t) + P(T_2 < t). \quad (11)$$

The race model inequality has the advantage over Equation (10) in that all the terms in it are observable, so it can be used to test empirical data.

Miller (1978, 1982b) and others tested the race model inequality in several data sets. Amazingly, the data violated the predicted inequality. Performance with redundant signals was better than what was predicted from the most efficient parallel model. In order to explain the redundant signals effect, something more than unlimited-capacity parallel processing had to be proposed. Miller (1978, 1982b) proposed *coactivation,* which he viewed as resulting from interactions and cross talk between concurrent channels. Mordkoff and Yantis (1991; see also Mordkoff & Egeth, 1993) suggested an *interactive race model,* which they simulated and applied to their data. Townsend and Nozawa (1997) suggested the idea of *supercapacity,* an alternative to fixed, limited, and unlimited capacity in which the processing rate actually increases as load increases.

Races versus Mixtures

Parallel processing is an important issue in skill acquisition. Logan's (1988) instance theory of automaticity seems salient in this context. Instance theory explains automatization as a transition from a *general algorithm* that is used to solve novel problems and *memory retrieval* of past solutions to familiar problems. The theory assumes that people store memory traces, or *instances,* of each encounter with each stimulus, so a task-relevant knowledge base builds up with practice. The theory assumes that people

retrieve memory traces when familiar stimuli are encountered and that retrieval is a self-terminating unlimited-capacity parallel process, also known as an *independent race model.* Instance theory explains the learning curve—the ubiquitous speedup in RT with practice—as statistical facilitation from a race between the instances in memory, whose number grows with each encounter with the stimulus.

Newell and Rosenbloom (1981) reviewed 50 years of research on skill acquisition and declared the power law; RT decreased as a power function of practice:

$$RT = a + b\,N^{-c} \quad (12)$$

where a is an irreducible asymptote, b is the amount by which RT can change over learning, and c is the learning rate. Logan (1992) reviewed studies published in the 10 years after Newell and Rosenbloom's paper and found power function learning in each of them. A typical power function with $a = 500$, $b = 500$, and $c = 0.5$ is plotted in Figure 7.4.

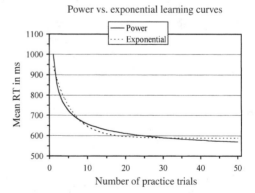

Power vs. exponential learning curves

Figure 7.4   Mean reaction time (RT) as a function of the number of practice trials for a power function learning curve (solid line) and an exponential function learning curve (dotted line).
NOTE: The power function was generated from the equation $RT = 500 + 500N^{-0.5}$. The exponential function $RT = 589 + 429e^{-0.2N}$ was generated by fitting an exponential function to the power function data. The similarity in the learning curves reflects the potential for one to mimic the other.

Logan (1988, 1992) showed that the independent race model predicted a power function speedup on the assumption that the distribution of retrieval times was *Weibull*. The Weibull is a generalization of the exponential in which the exponent is raised to a power. Its distribution function is

$$F(x) = 1 - \exp[-wx^c]. \quad (13)$$

Per Gumbel (1958), the distribution function of minima from N i.i.d. distributions is

$$F_{\min}(x) = 1 - [1 - F(x)]^N. \quad (14)$$

Substituting Equation (13) into Equation (14) yields

$$
\begin{aligned}
F_{\min}(x) &= 1 - \{1 - (1 - \exp[-wx^c])\}^N \\
&= 1 - \exp[-wx^c]^N \\
&= 1 - \exp[-Nwx^c] \\
&= 1 - \exp[-w(N^{1/c}x)^c] \\
&= F(N^{1/c}x). \quad (15)
\end{aligned}
$$

Thus, the distribution of minima of N samples from i.i.d. Weibull distributions is itself a Weibull distribution with its scale reduced by a power function of N. This implies that the entire distribution of retrieval times decreases as a power function of practice—the mean, the standard deviation, and all of the quantiles of the distribution should all decrease as power functions of practice[3] with a common exponent, $1/c$. Logan (1988) tested the prediction for means and standard deviations, and Logan (1992) tested the prediction for distribution. The predictions were mostly confirmed.

---

[3]The Weibull is a special case of the exponential distribution with the variable x raised to a power (i.e., c). If the exponential distribution function, $F(x) = 1 - \exp[-wx]$, is substituted into Equation (14) instead of the Weibull, then the distribution of minima becomes $F_1(x) = 1 - \exp[-Nwx]$, which is an exponential distribution with rate parameter Nw and mean $1/Nw$, which is consistent with previous results in this chapter (see, e.g., n. 1). Note that the mean of the exponential decreases as a power function of N with an exponent of -1.

Instance theory assumes two races. One, just described, is between the various traces in memory. It determines the speedup in memory retrieval over practice. The other is between the algorithm and memory retrieval. The algorithm is necessary early in practice before instances are available in memory, so subjects are prepared to use it on each trial. If the stimulus is novel, they have no other choice but to execute the algorithm. If the stimulus is familiar, the algorithm and memory retrieval start at the same time, and the faster of the two determines performance. The theory assumes that the time for the algorithm does not change over practice whereas the time for memory retrieval speeds up. This allows memory retrieval to win the race more and more often, until the subject relies on it entirely and abandons the algorithm.

The assumption that the algorithm does not change with practice was made for convenience. With that assumption, the finishing time for the algorithm can be thought of as just another Weibull distribution in the race whose effects will be dominated by other runners as practice continues. Instance theory assumes also that the time to retrieve an individual memory trace does not change over practice. This assumption was made for convenience and for rhetorical force. The "parent" distributions of algorithm finishing time and memory retrieval time do not change with practice. All that changes is the number of traces, and that produces the statistical facilitation that predicts the power law of learning.

Compton and Logan (1991) pitted the independent race model against a probability mixture model in which subjects choose to use the algorithm with probability p and memory retrieval with probability $1 - p$. The parent distributions do not change with practice. Memory retrieval is faster than the algorithm at the outset and remains so throughout practice. Instead, p changes in a manner that produces the power function speedup required by the power law. This model predicted the same change in mean RT as instance theory but a different change in the standard deviation of RT. Whereas instance theory predicts a power function reduction in the standard deviation over practice, the probability mixture model predicts that the standard deviation will first increase and then decrease over practice. The variance of a probability mixture of memory retrieval and algorithm finishing times is

$$Var(T)_{mix}$$
$$= p \, Var(T)_a + (1 - p)Var(T)_m$$
$$+ p(1 - p)[E(T)_a - E(T)_m]^2 \quad (16)$$

where $Var(T)$ is the variance of RT, $E(T)$ is mean RT, and the subscripts a and m refer to the algorithm and memory retrieval, respectively. The rightmost term in Equation (16) produces a "bubble" in the variance as p goes from 1 to 0, reaching a maximum when $p = .5$. The observed standard deviations disconfirmed this prediction and confirmed the prediction of instance theory.

Nosofsky and Palmeri (1997; see also Palmeri, 1997) extended instance theory, combining it with Nosofsky's (1984, 1986, 1988) *generalized context model* of classification to form the *exemplar-based random walk* model. It accounted for a great deal of data in categorization and skill acquisition, expanding the scope of the theory substantially (see also Logan, in press). The sun shone brightly on the instance theory empire. Then two clouds rose on the horizon.

The first was Rickard's (1997) *component power law* model. Like instance theory, it assumed that automatization was a transition from algorithm to memory retrieval. Unlike instance theory, a probability mixture, rather than a race, made the choice between algorithm and memory retrieval. Rickard solved the problem with mixture models raised by Compton and Logan (1991) by assuming that both the algorithm and memory retrieval improved with practice. He assumed that each improved as a power function of practice

(hence, "component power law") and that the choice between them depended on their relative strengths. Equation (16) still described the change in RT variance with choice probability, but the means and variances of the parents decreased over practice, changing the predicted learning curve. Rickard pointed out a bubble in data that Logan (1988) reported in favor of instance theory, and he produced bubbles in several data sets of his own. He convinced me that under some circumstances, the algorithm and memory retrieval do not race; the subject chooses to do one or the other (for further discussion of parallel and serial processing in memory retrieval, see Rohrer, Pashler, & Etchegaray, 1998; Rohrer & Wixted, 1994).

The other cloud on the horizon is an attack on the generality of the power law. Delaney et al. (1998) proposed a model in which performance was a mixture of different strategies, each of which improved as a power function of practice. They had subjects report the strategies they used on individual trials. When they aggregated data over strategy reports (i.e., over blocks of trials, as researchers typically do), the power function did not fit the data very well. However, when they sorted the data by strategy report, power functions fit the data from each strategy very well. They argued for a mixture model like Rickard's (1997). Moreover, Van Zandt and Ratcliff (1995) analyzed probability mixtures of gamma distributions with stochastic rate parameters and found that they produced the same power-function reduction in the RT distribution as did the instance theory.

The most serious challenge may be empirical. Heathcote, Brown, and Mewhort (2000) argued that the ubiquity of the power law is an artifact of averaging over exponential learning curves for individual items (but see Myung, Kim, & Pitt, 2000). They showed that an exponential learning curve

$$RT = a + b \exp[-cN] \quad (17)$$

fit the data at the level of individual items better than the power function in several data sets. Rickard and I confirmed their findings in our own laboratories. This is a serious threat to instance theory and to all theories of skill acquisition that predict a power-function learning curve (i.e., most theories). If the data do not conform to the predicted power law, the prediction—as well as the theories from which it was derived—is falsified.

A typical exponential learning curve is plotted along with the power function in Figure 7.4. The exponential learning curve is very similar to the power function learning curve. They can be hard to discriminate, particularly when the data are noisy (e.g., data from individual items). However, averaging over items or subjects (or both) tends to distort the function, and averages of exponential functions are often better fit by power functions than by exponential functions (Anderson, & Tweney, 1997; Heathcote et al., 2000). This bias toward the power function can be minimized by averaging geometrically instead of arithmetically (Myung et al., 2000; Wixted & Ebbesen, 1997), but analysis of averaged data remains problematic.

DISCUSSION

So that is how people ask whether processing is parallel or serial. There are many different methods and many different situations to which they may be applied. In terms of research publications, the question of parallel versus serial processing must be one of the most productive questions ever asked in experimental psychology. But what do all these publications amount to? What kind of cumulative progress have we made in the last 50 years?

The question of parallel versus serial processing epitomizes the difference between two general approaches to psychology. One,

endorsed by Broadbent (e.g., 1971), might be called the *general principle* approach or "*20 questions*" approach. It suggests that the right theory can be found by conducting a series of experiments that addresses a succession of general principles (like parallel versus serial processing), ruling out alternatives until only one remains. The experimenter plays 20 questions with Mother Nature, trying to choose questions that divide the remaining alternatives in half (Platt, 1964). The other approach, endorsed by Newell (1973), might be called the *general theory* approach. Newell argued that "you can't play 20 questions with nature and win," claiming that investigations of general dichotomies such as parallel versus serial processing were doomed to failure. Processes interact with each other and therefore cannot be studied separately. One needs a theory of the whole system to understand a single process. Newell's own work (e.g., 1990) exemplified the promise of the general theory approach.

The issue of parallel versus serial processing figures prominently in the contrasts between these approaches. Nearly 30 years later we can examine the progress in the field and count up the score. It seems to me that Newell (1973, 1990) was right about parallel and serial processing. After all this research, we still cannot say definitively whether search is parallel or serial or whether two tasks are done in parallel or serially. As my mother said, it depends. To decide whether search is parallel or serial, one must decide also whether it is limited or unlimited in capacity and whether it is exhaustive or self-terminating. To predict performance, one must model the whole task, a tactic that Newell would have endorsed. On the other hand, we have made a lot of progress in answering more specific versions of the question, and lots of methods are available for asking them. In my view, learning to ask better questions is an important kind of cumulative progress.

Newell (1973, 1990) appears to have been right also about the capacity issue. The nature of capacity limitations remains unclear. It may seem clear in specific cases, but there is little generality across procedures and paradigms, so the big picture may be even sketchier than it was in 1973. It is hard enough to tell *whether* capacity is limited. We are only beginning to address the question *why* capacity is limited. Theories seem to have internalized my mother's observation that sometimes you can do two things at once and sometimes you cannot, proposing that one part of the mind can do two things at once and another can do only one thing at a time. This internalization generated a lot of research aimed at localizing one part relative to the other. However, it does not explain why the part that can do only one thing at a time *must* do one thing at a time or why the part that can do two things at once *can* do so. The selection-for-action view (Allport, 1987; Neumann, 1987; Van der Heijden, 1992) and the selection-for-cognition view (Logan & Zbrodoff, 1999) provide alternatives to the standard view, and the contrast between them may shed new light on the capacity issue.

Broadbent was right about the issue of continuous versus discrete processing. Behavioral and psychophysiological data clearly rule out strict discrete processing (for a review, see Miller, 1988). Nevertheless, many theorists continue to propose discrete models, and popular empirical tests of parallel versus serial processing assume discrete processing. Discrete processing makes the mathematics easier, and that makes the reasoning clearer. A comprehensible discrete theory that approximates continuous reality may be better than an incomprehensible but more realistic continuous theory (McCloskey, 1991).

Broadbent was also right about the issue of self-terminating versus exhaustive search. It is pretty clear that search is self-terminating, at least with large displays (more than 6 items;

Chun & Wolfe, 1996; Van Zandt & Townsend, 1993). Broadbent may be right about the parallel versus coactivation issue in divided attention, and it remains to be seen whether Newell (1973, 1990) or Broadbent is right about the race versus mixture issue in skill acquisition.

At this point, the 20 questions approach is ahead of the general theory approach 3 to 2 with 1 issue still playing itself out. It looks like a tie. Perhaps the game of pitting one general approach against another cannot be won either. From one perspective, sitting in the empirical trenches, it may not matter much which approach we take. How we got there may matter less than what we do while we are there. The best experiments fit neatly into a tight web of logic, as the general theory approach recommends, and they pit crucial alternatives against each other, as the 20 questions approach recommends. A person in the trenches had better do something that works, regardless of the approach that recommends it. There are plenty of things to choose from. I hope that this chapter helps those who are in the trenches to find the tools that they need. My mother would like that.

REFERENCES

Allport, D. A. (1987). Selection for action: Some behavioural and neurophysiological considerations of attention and action. In H. Heuer & A. F. Sanders (Eds.), *Perspectives on perception and action* (pp. 395–419). Hillsdale, NJ: Erlbaum.

Anderson, R. B., & Tweney, R. D. (1997). Artifactual power curves in forgetting. *Memory & Cognition, 25,* 724–730.

Atkinson, R. C., Holmgren, J. E., & Juola, J. F. (1969). Processing time as influenced by the number of elements in a visual display. *Perception & Psychophysics, 6,* 321–326.

Broadbent, D. E. (1957). A mechanical model for human attention and immediate memory. *Psychological Review, 64,* 205–215.

Broadbent, D. E. (1958). *Perception and communication.* Elmsford, NY: Pergamon.

Broadbent, D. E. (1971). *Decision and stress.* London: Academic Press.

Broadbent, D. E. (1982). Task combination and the selective intake of information. *Acta Psychologica, 50,* 253–290.

Bundesen, C. (1990). A theory of visual attention. *Psychological Review, 97,* 523–547.

Bundesen, C. (1993). The relationship between independent race models and Luce's choice axiom. *Journal of Mathematical Psychology, 37,* 446–471.

Butsch, R. L. C. (1932). Eye movements and the eye-hand span in typewriting. *Journal of Educational Psychology, 23,* 104–121.

Cave, K. R., & Wolfe, J. M. (1990). Modeling the role of parallel processing in visual search. *Cognitive Psychology, 22,* 225–271.

Chun, M., & Potter, M. C. (1995). A two-stage model for multiple target detection in rapid serial visual presentation. *Journal of Experimental Psychology: Human Perception and Performance, 21,* 109–127.

Chun, M., & Wolfe, J. M. (1996). Just say no: How are visual searches terminated when there is no target present? *Cognitive Psychology, 30,* 39–78.

Coles, M. G. H., Gratton, G., Bashore, T. R., Eriksen, C. W., & Donchin, E. (1985). A psychophysiological investigation of the continuous flow model of human information processing. *Journal of Experimental Psychology: Human Perception and Performance, 11,* 529–553.

Compton, B. J., & Logan, G. D. (1991). The transition from algorithm to retrieval in memory based theories of automaticity. *Memory and Cognition, 19,* 151–158.

Delaney, P. F., Reder, L. M., Straszewski, J. J., & Ritter, F. E. (1998). The strategy-specific nature of improvement: The power law applies by strategy within task. *Psychological Science, 9,* 1–7.

Donders, F. C. (1868). Die schnelligkeit psychischer processe. *Archiv der Anatomie and Physiologie,* 652–681.

Duncan, J. (1980). The demonstration of capacity limitation. *Cognitive Psychology, 12,* 75–96.

Duncan, J., & Humphreys, G. W. (1989). Visual search and stimulus similarity. *Psychological Review, 96,* 433–458.

Duncan, J., Ward, R., & Shapiro, K. L. (1994). Direct measurement of attentional dwell time in human vision. *Nature, 369,* 313–315.

Eriksen, B. A., & Eriksen, C. W. (1974). Effects of noise letters upon the identification of a target letter in a nonsearch task. *Perception & Psychophysics, 16,* 143–149.

Eriksen, C. W., & Schultz, D. W. (1979). Information processing in visual search: A continuous flow conception and experimental results. *Perception & Psychophysics, 25,* 249–263.

Fisher, D. L., & Goldstein, W. M. (1983). Stochastic PERT networks as models of cognition: Derivation of mean, variance, and distribution of reaction time using order-of-processing diagrams. *Journal of Mathematical Psychology, 27,* 121–151.

Goldstein, W. M., & Fisher, D. L. (1991). Stochastic networks as models of cognition: Derivation of response time distributions using the order-of-processing method. *Journal of Mathematical Psychology, 35,* 214–241.

Gratton, G., Coles, M. G. H., Sirevaag, E., Eriksen, C. W., & Donchin, E. (1988). Pre- and post-stimulus activation of response channels: A psychophysiological analysis. *Journal of Experimental Psychology: Human Perception and Performance, 14,* 331–344.

Grossberg, S., Mingolla, E., & Ross, W. D. (1994). A neural theory of attentive visual search: Interactions of boundary, surface, spatial, and object representations. *Psychological Review, 101,* 470–489.

Gumbel, E. J. (1958). Statistics of extremes. New York: Columbia University Press.

Heathcote, A., Brown, S., & Mewhort, D. J. K. (2000). The power law repealed: The case for an exponential law of practice. *Psychonomic Bulletin & Review, 7,* 185–207.

Hommel, B. (1998). Automatic stimulus-response translation in dual-task performance. *Journal of Experimental Psychology: Human Perception and Performance, 24,* 1368–1384.

Humphreys, G. W., & Müller, H. J. (1993). SEarch via Recursive Rejection (SERR): A connectionist model of visual search. *Cognitive Psychology, 25,* 43–110.

Inhoff, A. W., Briihl, D., Bohemier, G., & Wang, J. (1992). Eyehand span and coding of text during copytyping. *Journal of Experimental Psychology: Learning, Memory and Cognition, 18,* 298–306.

Jacoby, L. L. (1991). A process dissociation framework: Separating automatic from intentional uses of memory. *Journal of Memory and Language, 30,* 513–541.

Jolicoeur, P., Tombu, M., Oriet, C., & Stevanovsky, B. (in press). From perception to action: Making the connection. In W. Prinz & B. Hommel (Eds.), *Attention and performance* (Vol. 19). Oxford: Oxford University Press.

Kahneman, D. (1973). *Attention and effort.* Englewood Cliffs, NJ: Prentice-Hall.

Kelley, C. M., & Lindsay, D. S. (1996). Conscious and unconscious forms of memory. In E. L. Bjork & R. S. Bjork (Eds.), *Memory* (pp. 31–63). San Diego: Academic Press.

Lashley, K. S. (1951). The problem of serial order in behavior. In L. A. Jeffress (Ed.), *Cerebral mechanisms in behavior* (pp. 112–136). New York: Wiley.

Logan, G. D. (1988). Toward an instance theory of automatization. *Psychological Review, 95,* 492–527.

Logan, G. D. (1992). Shapes of reaction time distributions and shapes of learning curves: A test of the instance theory of automaticity. *Journal of Experimental Psychology: Learning, Memory and Cognition, 18,* 883–914.

Logan, G. D. (1996). The CODE theory of visual attention: An integration of space-based and object-based attention. *Psychological Review, 103,* 603–649.

Logan, G. D. (1997). The automaticity of academic life: Unconscious applications of an implicit theory. In R. S. Wyer (Ed.), *Advances in social*

cognition (Vol. 10, pp. 157–179). Mahwah, NJ: Erlbaum.

Logan, G. D. (in press). An instance theory of attention and memory. *Psychological Review.*

Logan, G. D., & Gordon, R. D. (2001). Executive control of visual attention in dual task situations. *Psychological Review, 108,* 393–434.

Logan, G. D., & Schulkind, M. D. (2000). Parallel memory retrieval in dual-task situations: I. Semantic memory. *Journal of Experimental Psychology: Human Perception and Performance, 26,* 1072–1090.

Logan, G. D., & Zbrodoff, N. J. (1999). Selection for cognition: Cognitive constraints on visual spatial attention. *Visual Cognition, 6,* 55–81.

Luce, R. D. (1963). Detection and recognition. In R. D. Luce, R. R. Bush, & E. Galanter, (Eds.), *Handbook of mathematical psychology* (pp. 103–189). New York: Wiley.

Luce, R. D. (1986). *Response times: Their role in inferring elementary mental organization.* New York: Oxford University Press.

Marley, A. A. J., & Colonius, H. (1992). The "horse race" random utility model for choice probabilities and reaction times, and its competing risks interpretation. *Journal of Mathematical Psychology, 36,* 1–20.

McClelland, J. L. (1979). On the time relations of mental processes: An examination of systems of processes in cascade. *Psychological Review, 86,* 287–330.

McClelland, J. L. (1993). Toward a theory of information processing in graded, random, and interactive networks. In D. E. Meyer & S. Kornblum (Eds.), *Attention and Performance* (Vol. 14, pp. 655–688). Cambridge: MIT Press.

McClelland, J. L., Rumelhart, D. E., & the PDP Research Group. (1986). *Parallel distributed processing: Explorations in the microstructures of cognition: Vol. 1. Foundations.* Cambridge: MIT Press.

McCloskey, M. (1991). Networks and theories: The place of connectionism in cognitive science. *Psychological Science, 2,* 387–395.

Meyer, D. E., Irwin, D. E., Osman, A. M., & Kounois, J. (1988). The dynamics of cognition and action: Mental processes inferred from speed-accuracy decomposition. *Psychological Review, 95*, 183–237.

Meyer, D. E., & Kieras, D. E. (1997). A computational theory of executive cognitive processes and multiple-task performance: Part 1. Basic mechanisms. *Psychological Review, 104*, 3–65.

Miller, G. A. (1956). The magical number seven, plus or minus two: Some limits on our capacity for processing information. *Psychological Review, 63*, 81–97.

Miller, J. (1978). Multidimensional same-different judgments: Evidence against independent comparisons of dimensions. *Journal of Experimental Psychology: Human Perception and Performance, 4*, 411–422.

Miller, J. (1982a). Discrete versus continuous stage models of human information processing: In search of partial output. *Journal of Experimental Psychology: Human Perception & Performance, 8*, 273–296.

Miller, J. (1982b). Divided attention: Evidence for coactivation with redundant signals. *Cognitive Psychology, 14*, 247–279.

Miller, J. (1983). Can response preparation begin before stimulus recognition finishes? *Journal of Experimental Psychology: Human Perception & Performance, 9*, 161–182.

Miller, J. (1987). Evidence of preliminary response preparation from a divided attention task. *Journal of Experimental Psychology: Human Perception & Performance, 13*, 425–434.

Miller, J. (1988). Discrete and continuous models of human information processing: Theoretical distinctions and empirical results. *Acta Psychologica, 67*, 191–257.

Miller, J. (1993). A queue-series model for reaction time, with discrete-stage and continuous-flow models as special cases. *Psychological Review, 100*, 702–715.

Miller, J., & Hackley, S. A. (1992). Electrophysiological evidence for temporal overlap among contingent mental processes. *Journal of Experimental Psychology: General, 121*, 195–209.

Moore, C. M., Egeth, H., Berglan, L. R., & Luck, S. J. (1996). Are attentional dwell times inconsistent with serial visual search? *Psychonomic Bulletin & Review, 3*, 360–365.

Moray, N. (1967). Where is capacity limited? A survey and a model. *Acta Psychologica, 27*, 84–92.

Mordkoff, J. T., & Egeth, H. E. (1993). Response time and accuracy revisited: Converging support for the interactive race model. *Journal of Experimental Psychology: Human Perception and Performance, 19*, 981–991.

Mordkoff, J. T., & Yantis, S. (1991). An interactive race model of divided attention. *Journal of Experimental Psychology: Human Perception and Performance, 17*, 520–538.

Myung, I. J., Kim, C., & Pitt, M. A. (2000). Toward an explanation of the power law artifact: Insights from response surface analysis. *Memory & Cognition, 28*, 832–840.

Navon, D. (1984). Resources: A theoretical soup stone? *Psychological Review, 91*, 216–234.

Navon, D., & Gopher, D. (1979). On the economy of the human processing system. *Psychological Review, 86*, 214–255.

Neumann, O. (1987). Beyond capacity: A functional view of attention. In H. Heuer & A. F. Sanders (Eds.), *Perspectives on perception and action* (pp. 361–394). Hillsdale, NJ: Erlbaum.

Newell, A. (1973). You can't play 20 questions with nature and win: Projective comments on the papers of this symposium. In W. G. Chase (Ed.), *Visual information processing* (pp. 283–308). New York: Academic Press.

Newell, A. (1990). *Unified theories of cognition.* Cambridge: Harvard University Press.

Newell, A., & Rosenbloom, P. S. (1981). Mechanisms of skill acquisition and the law of practice. In J. R. Anderson (Ed.), *Cognitive skills and their acquisition* (pp. 1–55). Hillsdale, NJ: Erlbaum.

Norman, D. A., & Bobrow, D. G. (1975). On data-limited and resource-limited processes. *Cognitive Psychology, 7*, 44–64.

Nosofsky, R. M. (1984). Choice, similarity, and the context theory of classification. *Journal of Experimental Psychology: Learning, Memory and Cognition, 10*, 104–114.

Nosofsky, R. M. (1986). Attention, similarity, and the identification-categorization relationship. *Journal of Experimental Psychology: General, 115,* 39–57.

Nosofsky, R. M. (1988). Exemplar-based accounts of relations between classification, recognition, and typicality. *Journal of Experimental Psychology: Learning, Memory and Cognition, 14,* 700–708.

Nosofsky, R. M., & Palmeri, T. J. (1997). An exemplar-based random walk model of speeded classification. *Psychological Review, 104,* 266–300.

Osman, A., Bashore, T. R., Coles, M. G. H., & Donchin, E. (1992). On the transmission of partial information: Inferences from movement-related brain potentials. *Journal of Experimental Psychology: Human Perception and Performance, 18,* 217–232.

Palmeri, T. J. (1997). Exemplar similarity and the development of automaticity. *Journal of Experimental Psychology: Learning, Memory and Cognition, 23,* 324–354.

Pashler, H. (1984). Processing stages in overlapping tasks: Evidence for a central bottleneck. *Journal of Experimental Psychology: Human Perception and Performance, 10,* 358–377.

Pashler, H. (1994a). Dual-task interference in simple tasks: Data and theory. *Psychological Bulletin, 116,* 220–244.

Pashler, H. (1994b). Graded capacity sharing in dual-task interference? *Journal of Experimental Psychology: Human Perception and Performance, 20,* 330–342.

Pashler, H., & Johnston, J. C. (1989). Chronometric evidence for central postponement in temporally overlapping tasks. *Quarterly Journal of Experimental Psychology, 41A,* 19–45.

Platt, J. R. (1964). Strong inference. *Science, 146,* 347–353.

Posner, M. I., & Boies, S. J. (1971). Components of attention. *Psychological Review, 78,* 391–408.

Raymond, J. E., Shapiro, K. S., & Arnell, K. M. (1992). Temporary suppression of visual processing an RSVP task: An attentional blink? *Journal of Experimental Psychology: Human Perception and Performance, 18,* 849–860.

Ratcliff, R. (1988). Continuous versus discrete information processing: Modeling the accumulation of partial information. *Psychological Review, 95,* 238–255.

Rickard, T. C. (1997). Bending the power law: A CMPL theory of strategy shifts and the automatization of cognitive skills. *Journal of Experimental Psychology: General, 126,* 288–311.

Rohrer, D., Pashler, H., & Etchegaray, J. (1998). When two memories can and cannot be retrieved concurrently. *Memory & Cognition, 26,* 731–739.

Rohrer, D., & Wixted, J. T. (1994). An analysis of latency and interresponse time in free recall. *Memory & Cognition, 22,* 511–524.

Rumelhart, D. E., & Norman, D. A. (1982). Simulating a skilled typist: A study of skilled cognitive motor performance. *Cognitive Science, 6,* 1–36.

Schweickert, R. (1978). A critical path generalization of the additive factor method. *Journal of Mathematical Psychology, 18,* 105–139.

Schweickert, R., & Townsend, J. T. (1989). A trichotomy: Interactions of factors prolonging sequential and concurrent processes in stochastic discrete (PERT) networks. *Journal of Mathematical Psychology, 33,* 328–347.

Shiffrin, R. M., & Schneider, W. (1977). Controlled and automatic human information processing: II. Perceptual learning, automatic attending, and a general theory. *Psychological Review, 84,* 127–190.

Sperling, G. (1960). The information available in brief visual presentations. *Psychological Monographs, 74*(whole no. 498).

Sternberg, S. (1966). High-speed scanning in human memory. *Science, 153,* 652–654.

Sternberg, S. (1969). The discovery of processing stages: Extensions of Donders' method. In W. G. Koster (Ed.), *Attention and Performance* (Vol. 2, pp. 276–315). Amsterdam: North Holland.

Townsend, J. T. (1971). A note on the identifiability of parallel and serial processes. *Perception & Psychophysics, 10,* 161–163.

Townsend, J. T. (1974). Issues and models concerning the processing of a finite number of inputs. In B. H. Kantowitz (Ed.), *Human information processing: Tutorials in performance and cognition* (pp. 133–168). Hillsdale, NJ: Erlbaum.

Townsend, J. T. (1984). Uncovering mental processes with factorial experiments. *Journal of Mathematical Psychology, 28,* 363–400.

Townsend, J. T. (1990). Serial versus parallel processing: Sometimes they look like Tweedledum and Tweedledee but they can (and should) be distinguished. *Psychological Science, 1,* 46–54.

Townsend, J. T., & Ashby, F. G. (1983). *Stochastic modeling of elementary psychological processes.* Cambridge: Cambridge University Press.

Townsend, J. T., & Colonius, H. (1997). Parallel processing response times and experimental determination of the stopping rule. *Journal of Mathematical Psychology, 41,* 392–397.

Townsend, J. T., & Nozawa, G. (1997). Serial exhaustive models can violate the race model inequality: Implications for architecture and capacity. *Psychological Review, 104,* 595–602.

Townsend, J. T., & Schweickert, R. (1989). Toward the trichotomy method of reaction times: Laying the foundation of stochastic mental networks. *Journal of Mathematical Psychology, 33,* 309–327.

Treisman, A., & Gelade, G. (1980). A feature integration theory of attention. *Cognitive Psychology, 12,* 97–136.

Treisman, A., & Gormican, S. (1988). Feature analysis in early vision: Evidence from search asymmetries. *Psychological Review, 95,* 14–48.

Treisman, A., & Schmidt, H. (1982). Illusory conjunctions in the perception of objects. *Cognitive Psychology, 14,* 107–141.

Van der Heijden, A. H. C. (1992). *Selective attention in vision.* New York: Routledge

Van Zandt, T., & Ratcliff, R. (1995). Statistical mimicking of reaction time data: Single-process models, parameter variability, and mixtures. *Psychonomic Bulletin & Review, 2,* 20–54.

Van Zandt, T., & Townsend, J. T. (1993). Self-terminating versus exhaustive processes in rapid visual and memory search: An evaluative review. *Perception & Psychophysics, 53,* 563–580.

Ward, R., Duncan, J., & Shapiro, K. (1996). The slow time-course of visual attention. *Cognitive Psychology, 30,* 79–109.

Welford, A. T. (1952). The "psychological refractory period" and the timing of high speed performance: A review and a theory. *British Journal of Psychology, 43,* 2–19.

Wenger, M. J., & Townsend, J. T. (2000). Basic response time tools for studying general processing capacity in attention, perception, and cognition. *Journal of General Psychology, 127,* 67–99.

Wixted, J. T., & Ebbesen, E. B. (1997). Genuine power curves in forgetting: A quantitative analysis of individual subject forgetting functions. *Memory & Cognition, 25,* 731–739.

Wolfe, J. M. (1994). Guided search 2.0: A revised model of visual search. *Psychonomic Bulletin & Review, 1,* 202–238.

Wolfe, J. M., Cave, K. R., & Franzel, S. L. (1989). Guided search: An alternative to the feature integration model for visual search. *Journal of Experimental Psychology: Human Perception and Performance, 15,* 419–433.

CHAPTER 8

Methodology and Statistics in Single-Subject Experiments

NORMAN H. ANDERSON

Single-subject design and analysis is an experimental ideal. An individual is studied under a number of conditions, and the analysis is performed on the data of this individual. The prime advantage is substantive: maximal congruence with psychological phenomena. A collateral substantive advantage is that longer-term investigations may be practicable, unfolding phenomena barely present in the common one-session experiment. There is the further advantage that error variability will be even less than it is in repeated-measures design.

Single-subject design has always been a mainstay in perception. One reason is that many perceptual phenomena can be embodied in stable-state tasks. One subject can thus provide a complete pattern of data across all experimental conditions. Many studies use just two or three subjects and present results separately for each. Generalization is often possible on the basis of extrastatistical background knowledge about similarity of sensory-perceptual process across individuals.

Single-subject design has been useful also in diverse other areas. Among these are classical and operant conditioning, judgment-decision theory, physiological psychology, behavior modification, and medical science. Also notable are studies of unusual individuals.

A pall hangs over single-subject design and analysis. This topic goes virtually unmentioned in current graduate statistics texts. Whole areas of experimental analysis that could benefit from this approach make little use of it. The reader may check how very few single-subject studies appear in any issue of any journal published by the American Psychological Association.

On the other hand, areas that have emphasized single-subject research have mostly been averse to formal statistics. As a consequence, the potential of single-subject design has been markedly underutilized.

SINGLE-SUBJECT DATA

Analysis of single-subject data faces special difficulties that arise because the data are a temporal (or spatial) sequence of observations. Successive observations may thus be

For helpful comments on drafts of this chapter, the author is indebted to Ted Carr, Joe Farley, Etienne Mullet, Laura Schreibman, Saul Sternberg, Ben Williams, Wendy Williams, and John Wixted. This chapter is adapted from Chapter 11 of *Empirical Direction in Design and Analysis* (Anderson, 2001) with permission of the publishers, Lawrence Erlbaum Associates.

intercorrelated, which complicates the relia-bility analysis. Furthermore, position and carryover effects may occur, which compli-cates the validity analysis. These two difficul-ties are considered in the following sections.

Reliability

Reliability is a basic problem in empirical analysis, no less important with studies of single subjects than with studies of multiple subjects. With a single subject, however, the issue of reliability faces a special difficulty because typical data constitute an interrelated temporal sequence. To illustrate, consider a subject who receives a sequence of trials under treatment A followed by a sequence of trials under treatment B.

The reliability question is whether the mean response differs reliably between the two treatments. Some difference must be expected simply from chance, that is, from natural variability among responses to each separate treatment. Any argument that the observed mean difference is reliable should show at least that it is larger than could rea-sonably be expected by chance. Common sense points to the answer: Compare the dif-ference *between* the means with the differ-ences among the separate responses *within* each treatment condition.

This commonsense comparison may sometimes be done by visual inspection, as illustrated later in the behavior modification experiment of Figure 8.4. This commonsense answer, not surprisingly, is the foundation for statistical theory; the cited comparison is quantified by the *F* ratio of ANOVA.

But this reliability comparison faces a crit-ical problem because of the likelihood of *serial correlation,* that is, correlation between successive responses. One source of serial correlation is assimilation or contrast across successive trials. Trial-to-trial assimilation appears in various tasks of psychophysics and judgment-decision, for example, even though subjects are otherwise in a stable state. Thus, the response on one trial is positively correlated with the response on the previous trial.

A rather different source of serial corre-lation may be called local drift. This refers to organismic changes in response level that extend over two or more successive obser-vations but fluctuate unsystematically over longer periods. The subject's attention may drift away and snap back; mood and moti-vation may wax and wane. The state of the subject is thus more similar across successive trials than across nonsuccessive trials. This in-duces serial correlation in the observed behav-ior even though there is no systematic trend.

Serial correlation means that successive observations are not *independent;* each new observation is partly implicit in the pre-ceding observation, so it carries only partial information. To see the consequence, sup-pose that the response is plotted as a function of successive trials. With a high positive se-rial correlation, responses on successive trials will be highly similar. The data will look less variable, so to speak, than the behavior they represent.

Visual inspection has no way to allow for the serial correlation. Instead, visual inspec-tion tends to treat successive responses as independent. With positive serial correlation, visual inspection sees the data falsely as too reliable. The usual formula for variance does the same, of course, thereby producing confi-dence intervals that are falsely too short and *F* ratios that are falsely too large. Statistical method, however, can assess the magnitude of the serial correlation, estimate the likely bias, and perhaps even correct for it, which visual inspection cannot do.

At the same time, any happenstance in-fluence on one trial may carry over partly to successive trials. To visual inspection, a one-trial external influence may seem to be a systematic effect lasting several trials. A visually convincing trend in the graph of the data may thus be an artifact of serial correlation, not a real effect of treatment.

Serial correlation can be controlled in two main ways. One way is with treatment randomization, which can break up the serial correlation to obtain independence. The other way is to minimize serial correlation through experimental procedure, as by allowing ample time between observations or by interpolating a baseline treatment between successive experimental treatments.

Validity

Confounding from position and carryover effects is a universal concern for single-subject design. Any two treatments differ in time and order of presentation; external and internal temporal effects are thus both confounded with treatment effects. Such confounding affects the meaning and validity of the results.

External temporal factors include events in the environment that influence the behavior. If treatment B follows treatment A, any difference in response may be due to some environmental factor: drift or shift in experimental procedure, happenstance events in the environment, and so forth. Any and all such external factors, known and unknown, confound the A-B comparison. External factors can, in principle, be handled with replication over successive time periods. Consistency of the A-B difference over successive time periods argues against external influences.

Internal temporal factors include *position* and *carryover* effects. Position effects refer to temporal changes due to practice, fatigue, adaptation, and so forth, that occur as a function of position, independently of particular treatments. Carryover effects include treatment-specific transfer from one treatment to following treatments, as well as to local drift in organism or environment.

Position and carryover effects are usually undesirable. Unless learning or transfer are under study, position and carryover effects generally need to be controlled through procedure and design. One common control is to adapt the subject to the task before collecting the main data. Other forms of control are noted later.

DESIGN AND ANALYSIS

Extrastatistical Generalization

Scientific inference depends largely on extrastatistical considerations. Appropriate use of statistical methods requires appreciation of their limitations that is at least as good as appreciation of their capabilities. This basic matter deserves preliminary discussion (see Anderson, 2001, chap. 1).

Virtually all scientific inference rests on evidence from samples. The investigator seeks to generalize the results from one particular sample to some larger population. If the sample was chosen randomly from that population, then such generalization is obtainable with standard statistical techniques.

Most samples, however, are *handy samples*. Rarely are the observations a random sample from some larger population. This basic fact is manifestly true of most experiments with groups of subjects; it applies no less to behavior samples from a single subject.

This limitation of handy samples can be ameliorated by *random assignment*. Group experiments, accordingly, routinely assign subjects at random across experimental conditions. Statistical inference can then be applied to assess whether the observed group differences are reliable by comparing differences *between* groups to response variability *within* groups. Statistically, of course, this inference does not extend beyond the given handy sample, but it is nonetheless a remarkable accomplishment. It can show that the observed treatment differences are reliable for the handy sample, which is prerequisite to extrastatistical generalization beyond this handy sample.

The same approach may be applied to one class of single-subject experiments by assigning treatment conditions at random across serial positions in the sequence of treatments. Statistical inference then becomes feasible in the same way as it does for group experiments. This approach is discussed in the later section titled "Randomized Treatment Design."

Generalization beyond the handy sample, however, depends on extrastatistical considerations. Standard statistical techniques have an essential role with single subject experiments, exactly as with group experiments. In either case, however, this role is a minor part in the overall chain of scientific inference.

Data Analysis

Two points of terminology need mention. First, *statsig* is employed as short for *statistically significant* to avoid unjustified meanings of "significant" from everyday language. Second, *ANOVA* (analysis of variance) is used as an convenient umbrella term for standard statistical techniques, virtually all of which rely on some measure of variance.

Visual Inspection

The first rule of data analysis is to look at the data. Sometimes no more is needed. In fact, nearly all the experiments reported in the 11 figures of this chapter are clear from visual inspection. Even in such cases, however, a confidence interval or other statistical index of prevailing variability may help the reader.

Visual inspection is also sensitive to pattern or trend, which may well be obscured in standard statistical techniques. Above all, the data should be scrutinized for extreme

scores, which have disproportionate effects on the likely error of the mean. Statistics texts and courses should place heavy emphasis on developing skills of visual inspection.

Confidence Interval

The confidence interval is an ideal statistic. It represents the mean, or difference between two means, not as a single number, but in its proper form: a range of likely location. The confidence interval is thus more informative than a significance test, for the latter may be derived from the former. At the same time, the confidence interval provides visual indications of the response variability and of the size of the effect.

Unfortunately, confidence intervals have limited usefulness. One limitation is that there is no confidence interval for three or more groups. The obvious tack of constructing confidence intervals for each pair of means markedly increases the false-alarm (type I error) parameter. To appreciate the severity of this problem, consider the usual 95% confidence interval between the largest and smallest sample means from three populations with equal true means. The false-alarm parameter for this confidence interval is not .05, but almost .13. The true confidence is thus not .95 but little more than .87. This loss of confidence increases with additional conditions. The overall F test, however, maintains the false-alarm parameter at its assigned value regardless of the number of treatment conditions.

Significance Test

A brief comment on the significance test may ameliorate the opprobrium under which this concept suffers. One standard class of experiments seeks to compare mean response under two treatment conditions, as in the classic experimental-versus-control paradigm. The essential question is whether the difference between the two conditions is reliable. Evidence that the observed difference is not a likely outcome of chance, that is, of prevailing variability, is surely prerequisite to asking others to pay attention to the results. The function of a significance test is to provide such evidence.

In this view, visual inspection may suffice as a test of significance. In the experiment on behavior modification of Figure 8.4, for example, the reliability of the difference is clear to visual inspection. To include a formal significance test not only is unnecessary clutter but also would betray a weak understanding of the nature of science.

Often, of course, more formal statistical analysis is needed. Nevertheless, the main problems of scientific inference are extrastatistical and should receive primary attention. The rule that less is more is as applicable with formal statistics as so often elsewhere in life.

Reducing Variability

Statistical theory emphasizes the importance of reducing variability, which determines the likely error of the observed means. This is one reason, already noted, for preferring single-subject design to repeated-measures design, and for preferring repeated-measures design to independent-groups design. Within each of these classes of designs, however, *extreme scores* are sometimes a major headache, as in studies of various patient classes.

The first line of defense against extreme scores is good experimental procedure. Good procedure, however, may not be enough. Statistical theory has given extensive attention to various supplementary aids, including response transformation, rank-order statistics, and outlier rejection techniques. Of these aids, *trimming* seems to have high potential but is surprisingly little used (see Anderson, 2001, chap. 12).

Experimental Design

The most important functions of statistics appear before the data are collected, when planning the experimental design. Most statistical inference, however, applies after the data have been collected. Then it is too late to remedy deficiencies of the design, too late to apply procedural precautions to minimize extreme scores, and too late to use a Latin square to balance and measure position effects.

Power

Before doing an experiment, it seems prudent to determine that it has a reasonable chance of demonstrating a desired result. In statistics, this is called *power*—the probability that the result will be statsig. Everyone makes some intuitive estimate of power in any experiment, but usually by guess and by God. Statistics provides simple formulas that can make such intuitive estimates more precise.

This issue of power is illustrated later in the behavior modification experiment of Figure 8.5. These data give little sign of reliable differences between placebo and any level of drug. The differences *between* different treatment means are comparable to the differences *within* each treatment condition. This could have been foreseen with a preliminary power calculation, and steps could have been taken to increase power.

Confounding

The big problem in any investigation is not reliability, the province of ANOVA, but *validity*. Granted a real effect, what does it mean?

Confounds are the big threat to meaningful interpretation. That some medicine improves a patient's condition may mean little if a placebo control has been neglected. A placebo control may be less than useless unless it is blind. The experiment of Figure 8.5 was well designed in these and related respects.

Problems of confounding are mainly extrastatistical. A complete chapter is devoted to this issue in Anderson (2001, chap. 8). Statistical theory can help. One such aid is the Latin square design for control of position and carryover effects.

Latin Square Design

The main defense against position and carryover effects is with experimental procedure, as already noted. But these effects can hardly be eliminated completely; some will remain. The experimental design should guard against confounding them with treatments. Even when these effects are expected to be negligible, moreover, showing that they are may still be desirable.

Latin square design can help deal with position and carryover effects. The following table shows a balanced Latin square for four treatment conditions, A_1 to A_4, which are listed in different order in each row of the square. The subject would receive these 16 treatment conditions in the given lexicographic order.

Balanced Latin Square

A_1	A_2	A_3	A_4
A_4	A_3	A_2	A_1
A_2	A_4	A_1	A_3
A_3	A_1	A_4	A_2

Two forms of balance appear in this square. First, each treatment occurs once in each row and once in each column. The row and column means of the corresponding 4×4 data table are thus measures of whatever position effects may be present. Because of the balance, the treatment means themselves are deconfounded from these position effects.

In addition, each treatment follows each other treatment exactly once. This balance provides partial control of possible carryover effects, as well as some information about their magnitude.

This balanced Latin square design could have been useful in the behavior modification study of Figure 8.5. Treatment conditions would be the four drug levels. Each row of the square would represent four days of one week. Position effects, which may show a within-week pattern, are thus balanced across treatments, and their magnitudes are given by the column means of the 4×4 data table. Adaptation across weeks would appear similarly in the row means. These position effects may well be negligible, of course, but demonstrating that they are has advantages over assuming that they are.

The drug in this experiment (Ritalin) is thought to be completely eliminated from the body in 24 hours. If so, carryover effects might well be expected to be negligible. Their magnitude can be assessed because of the balance in this design. The calculations are simpler if the last column is replicated so that each treatment follows itself once as well as each other treatment. Statistical details together with a numerical example are given by Cochran and Cox (1957, Section 4.6a).

Stimulus Integration

Every behavior is an integrated outcome of multiple coacting variables. Understanding and predicting behavior accordingly depend on understanding the rules that govern such integration. Two aspects of this integration problem are considered here.

Psychological Measurement Theory

A fundamental difficulty with analysis of stimulus integration appears in the simplest integration rule, namely, addition of two determinants. Such an addition rule occurs in standard factorial ANOVA, in which the statistical interaction term represents deviations from additivity. Statsig interaction, accordingly, is commonly interpreted to mean that the effect of one variable depends on the level of the other.

But this interpretation of Anova interactions rests on a critical assumption, namely, that the observed response is a linear (equal-interval) scale. There is ample reason to doubt this in psychology, as many writers have emphasized. Strength of response, for example, may be measured either with time or speed (rate) in certain tasks, yet both cannot be linear scales. Hence, a statistical interaction obtained with one measure may disappear with the other, or even reverse direction (Anderson, 1961). This measurement problem, it may be reemphasized, does not afflict main effects in randomized designs.[1]

The problem of psychological measurement has been controversial ever since Fechner's claim that just noticeable differences are equal psychologically and hence may be considered additive units. Fechner's approach was amplified by Thurstone (see Link, 1994), but nearly all applications of Thurstonian techniques deal with proportions of groups of people and thus are sociological rather than psychological scales. The conjoint measurement approach of axiomatic measurement theory (e.g., Krantz, Luce, Suppes, & Tversky, 1971) has been devoid of empirical applications and therefore has been called the "revolution that never happened" by Cliff (1992, p. 186; see similarly, Anderson, 1981, pp. 347–356; 2001, pp. 734–736). But without

---

[1] The importance of psychological measurement for interpreting interactions is clear in the following example revised slightly from Anderson (1961). Consider an organism performing a certain task under two incentives, each of which may be Low or High, in a 2×2 design. The left 2×2 data table shows the times taken to perform the task under the four pairs of incentive conditions. Raising either incentive from low to high reduces response time by 0.5 s; but raising the other incentive as well yields an additional decrease of only 0.25 s. An interaction is present, as shown by the nonparallelism, and its direction seems meaningful.

	Low	High	Low	High
Low:	1.0	.50	1.0	2.0
High:	.50	.25	2.0	4.0

But we could just as well have measured speed (rate). Indeed, speed may be preferable as a direct measure of action dynamics. The speed data, obtainable as the reciprocals of the time data, are shown in the right 2×2 data table. Raising one incentive from low to high raises speed from 1 to 2; but if the other incentive is also raised, speed jumps from 2 to 4, an apparent synergy. An interaction is present, but it is in the opposite direction.

This example illustrates the general truth that unless we know the true linear scale, interpretation of this—and any other—factorial-type data pattern is hazardous. This serious problem is almost completely neglected in current texts for graduate courses on design and analysis.

This issue is a general problem for analysis of stimulus integration, which depends heavily on meaning of response patterns. Joint manipulation of two or more stimulus variables leads naturally to factorial-type designs and to factorial-type data patterns. With a true linear response scale, the pattern in such graphs is a direct reflection of the integration process, as shown in Figures 8.2 and 8.3. But without a true linear response scale, the observable pattern may be totally misleading.

(To avoid confusion, it should be emphasized that main effects in randomized designs do not suffer this affliction of interactions. There is a qualitative difference between main effects and interactions. In the 2×2 design, each main effect makes a direct comparison between two means, that is, between two points on the response scale. The direction of this difference cannot generally be changed by a monotone transformation of the response. In contrast, interactions compare differences between two pairs of means, that is, between two intervals at different locations on the response scale. Barring crossover, the direction of this difference can readily be changed, as the given example shows.)

Psychological measurement theory, as this example shows, needs to shift away from its traditional focus on stimulus measurement. Response measurement has far greater importance. The linearity of the rating method established in the work on functional measurement theory means that ratings can be interpreted with some confidence in other situations, at least if standard precautions are adopted (see, e.g., Anderson, 1996, pp. 92–98). With a linear response, pattern in the observed data is a veridical reflection of pattern in the underlying process. Linear response methodology thus provides a priceless foothold on analysis of stimulus integration that follows configural or nonalgebraic rules.

a measurement theory that can yield linear scales, analysis of stimulus integration cannot get very far, as illustrated with the time-speed example of note 1.

Functional Measurement Theory

A solution to the integration-measurement problem was obtained with functional measurement theory, which employs algebraic integration rules as the base and frame for psychological measurement. The simplest version of this approach involves the *parallelism theorem*. Two premises are employed in this theorem: that the integration is additive, and that the response scale is linear (equal interval). Two conclusions follow directly: The factorial graph will be parallel, showing no statistical interaction; and the row and column means will be linear (equal-interval) scales of the functional psychological values of the row and column variables.

Observed parallelism thus provides joint support for both premises, including the linearity of the response measure. If additive rules exist, accordingly, they can be used to obtain true psychological measurement, both for the response and for the stimulus variables (see Anderson, 1996, chap. 2 and chap. 3). The conceptual validity of this functional measurement logic has been acknowledged by Krantz et al. (1971, p. 445).

What is important, of course, is empirical validity. Unless additive integration rules hold empirically, the parallelism theorem will not be worth much. As it happened, adding/averaging rules have been found in almost every area of psychology, even with young children (e.g., Figures 8.2, 8.6, and 8.9). An analogous linear fan theorem applies to multiplication models, and an application is shown in the operant experiment of Figure 11.

Of the three indicated benefits of the parallelism theorem, that of support for *response linearity* deserves special emphasis. Linear response measures are invaluable because pattern in the observed data is then a veridical picture of pattern in the underlying process. Response linearity thus provides a unique tool for analysis of configural integration. Reponse linearity is also invaluable for analysis of situations in which factorial-type design cannot be used (e.g., Figure 8.10).

RANDOMIZED TREATMENT DESIGN

In randomized treatment design, treatment conditions are given in randomized order. The line-box illusion of Figure 8.1 is an example from visual perception. Although two line-box figures are shown here to dramatize the illusion, only one was presented in the experimental task, in which the subject drew a line equal in length to the apparent length of the centerline. A three-factor design was used to vary the sizes of the two flanking boxes and the length of the centerline. All stimulus combinations from this design could be presented in random order within each replication. For

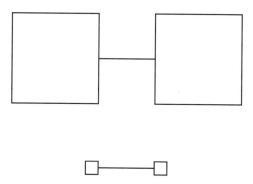

Figure 8.1   Line-box illusion.
NOTE: Apparent length of centerline is affected by flanking boxes. For experimental analysis, just one of the two line-box figures is presented; the subject draws a line equal to the apparent length of the centerline. Contrary to century-long belief, the illusion involves assimilation, not contrast. The boxes make the line look longer, not shorter.

a given subject, factorial graphs would show how the apparent length of the centerline depends on the separate and integrated effects of the two boxes. These graphs revealed the perceptual structure of the comparison processes involved in this illusion.

Similar treatment randomization is used in many other perceptual tasks as well as in tasks of judgment-decision in diverse fields (e.g., Figures 8.2, 8.3, 8.9, and 8.10). Although such investigations often use repeated-measures design with multiple subjects, single-subject design and analysis may sometimes be preferable.

Two Benefits of Treatment Randomization

Treatment randomization has two important potential benefits. It can deconfound treatments from position effects and from some carryover effects, markedly easing questions about validity. Also, it can make treatment responses independent, markedly easing questions about reliability.

Position and Carryover Effects

The first potential benefit of treatment randomization is to nullify confounding from position effects. If one presents treatments to the subject in the same lexicographic order as one lists data for the computer, then one embraces temporal confounding. Response to early and late levels of a variable could differ because of learning, fatigue, and other internal factors. External happenstance could cause similar confounding.

Such confounding tends to be nullified with treatment randomization. Temporal effects are randomized across treatments, thereby reducing or eliminating the confounding from the treatment means. Of course, the position effects do not disappear. Instead, they are randomized into the variability of the treat-

ment means. The logic is identical to that for random assignment of subjects to conditions in group experiments.

This logic also applies to some carryover effects. Among these are local drift in the organism or environment and carryover effects from one treatment to the following response that do not depend on the treatment on the following trial. With numerous treatment conditions, moreover, as with many experiments in perception and judgment-decision, carryover that depends on the specific treatments on successive trials tends to be diluted.

Independent Observations

Treatment randomization also helps ensure independence of different responses to the same treatment. Suppose instead that all replications of a given treatment were presented in one consecutive block. Independence could then be violated by trial-to-trial assimilation, for example, which would induce positive serial correlation in the sequence of responses to each treatment. Something similar would occur if the treatments were given in any systematic order, say, from low to high.

To appreciate how randomization produces independence, consider the responses to two replications of a given treatment. Because their location is randomized in the sequence of trials, knowing the response to one tells us nothing about the component of momentary variability in the response to the other; the two responses are statistically independent. With independence, differences between responses to the same treatment provide a valid estimate of error variability and valid confidence intervals. An early experimental application of randomized treatment design to single subjects is shown later in Figure 8.2.

Limitation of Treatment Randomization

Treatment randomization may not be effective with small numbers of treatments or trials. To illustrate, consider two treatments, A and B, each presented twice. The random sequence, A-A-B-B, which has probability 1/6, confounds treatments with temporal change. With this sequence, practice or adaptation can make B appear more (or less) different from A than it really is. Serial position effects are randomized out over all six possible sequences, it is true, but the investigator is stuck with whatever confounding may accompany the one particular sequence selected. Such treatment-independent temporal effects can, however, be randomized out over a long sequence.

Treatment-specific carryover effects are more serious, as when one treatment affects response to some specific other treatment. Treatment randomization may dilute the confounding but does not nullify it.

When the number of treatment conditions or number of trials is small, systematic order is usually needed. Thus, a better alternative to A-A-B-B would seem to be A-B-B-A. Systematic design can help balance and measure position and carryover effects, as was discussed with the Latin square.

Analysis of Randomized Treatment Designs

Independence of observations is the main requirement for applying concepts and methods of statistics. The central limit theorem (which states that the sampling distribution of the mean becomes more normal for larger samples) is usually even more efficacious with independent observations from a single subject than from a group of subjects. This central limit theorem provides a foundation of confidence intervals and other techniques of ANOVA. With independence, these ANOVA techniques have identical formulas and implications for single-subject data as for data from independent groups.[2]

Besides independence, the equinormality (normal distribution and equal variance) assumption also needs consideration. Normality, on the whole, may be better satisfied with single-subject data than with group data. The same holds for the equal variance assumption. Equinormality is not usually an empirical problem, although it may be badly violated in some situations. Aversive tasks may yield extreme scores, for example, and time scores may be skewed. Alternative analyses such as trimming may then be needed. Personal experience and pilot work with the task at hand are, as always, the foundation for prudent choice of analysis.

Restricted randomization may generally be advisable. When treatments are replicated, each successive replication could be randomized separately in consecutive blocks of trials. In the experiment of Figure 8.2, for example, the 27 treatments were randomized sep-

---

[2]Randomization tests, extensively developed by Edgington (1987), provide an alternative to ANOVA that do not assume normality and are less sensitive to unequal variance. However, randomization tests rely on massive computation, which may need hand-tailoring to each new experiment. Some writers have advocated randomization tests instead of ANOVA, without realizing that the independence assumption is equally essential, as Edgington makes clear.

ANOVA is far more general and far more flexible than randomization tests. Edgington's (1987) book is focused entirely on significance tests; confidence intervals seem to go unmentioned despite their value as descriptive statistics. Other advantages of ANOVA include simple formulas for power, trimming, multiple comparison range tests, Latin square designs, and so forth.

These advantages of ANOVA rest of an empirical base—variance as a key empirical entity. The variability *within* a set of data obtained under each separate treatment condition is no less important that the differences *between* conditions. The latter is only meaningful relative to the former, as the confidence interval makes clear. In randomization tests, however, this variability is lost to sight, a loss of contact with an important aspect of the behavior. Randomization tests can be useful with badly distributed data, but they are not a general purpose tool.

arately for each of the five days of the experiment. In some situations, as with studies of motivation or emotion, it may be advisable to include blocks as a factor in the analysis, perhaps treating blocks as a random factor so that block × treatment interactions are used for error, exactly as with subject × treatment interactions in repeated-measures design.

SERIAL OBSERVATION DESIGN

Treatment randomization is not always appropriate or even possible. In some operant studies, a single treatment may last a month and may hardly be repeatable. Some studies in behavior modification and medical science have only two treatments, one of which represents the normal, pretreatment situation. Validity and reliability both present difficulties.

A-B-Type Design

A-B refers to designs that present a sequence of trials under treatment A followed by a sequence of trials under treatment B. *A-B-type* includes the simple A-B design as well as A-B-A, A-B-B-A, and other such designs. This section comments briefly on the validity problem.

Temporal Confounding in A-B-Type Design

In the simple A-B design, a single treatment B is initiated at some time point subsequent to a sequence of trials under some comparison treatment A. In a prototypical application, A represents the normal situational condition before the experimental treatment. In general, however, A and B may be experimental treatments of equal importance. A sequence of observations is assumed to be available under both A and B conditions. The researcher's task is to scrutinize the pattern of these two sets of data to assess reliability and validity of the observed difference in the A and B effects.

The validity question, whether B does better than A, might seem unanswerable; B is completely confounded with any and all temporal factors. Suppose, however, that a graph of the behavior as a function of time shows a flat trend over a longish sequence of A observations, followed by a sharp change when B is introduced. This is prima facie evidence for a B effect. Given a long, flat trend under A, it seems unlikely that the behavior would change just when B was introduced unless B had a real effect.

In practical affairs, the simple A-B design is sometimes all that is available. If one's child's health/behavior problem is improving under some treatment, one would hardly insist on inclusion of a control treatment. A-B design is thus common in medicine and behavior modification, as well as in everyday life. A-B design also occurs naturally with laws or regulations intended to improve some undesirable state of affairs, such as environmental pollution or teaching in the universities.

One difficulty with simple A-B design is that real effects are often not clear-cut. Temporal confounding is thus a serious threat, a threat that can be reduced with stronger designs. The next strongest is the A-B-A design, obtained by terminating B and reverting to A. If the behavior also reverts, the case for a B effect is strengthened. The A-B-A design also gives some protection against temporal trend. Additional periods of A and B provide further protection.

Baseline Procedure

Baseline procedure is a form of control intended to produce a standard state between successive experimental treatments. Baseline conditions are common for minimizing carryover effects in perception. In olfactory studies, for example, one baseline condition requires subjects to smell their own elbows between trials with the experimental stimuli. Each of us has a personal odor, as any bloodhound can tell, and smelling our own elbow appears to be an effective way to readapt to a standard state. Analogous procedure may be useful with the choice and rating responses widely employed in cognitive domains. In judgment-decision tasks, interspersing a standard stimulus between successive experimental stimuli may absorb carryover effects and also firm up the frame of reference for the judgment-decision. Baseline conditions are also common in medical science, where they are called washout conditions.

Many operant studies use treatment schedules that produce systematic, cumulative changes in behavior. Accordingly, a standard baseline schedule may be introduced after each experimental schedule, hoping to return the subject to a standard state before proceeding. If A and B_j denote the baseline and experimental treatments, the design would be A-B_1-A-B_2-A-B_3, and so on. Effectiveness of baseline procedure cannot be taken for granted, of course, but needs situation-specific justification.

Serial Independence

With serial observation data, reliability must usually be estimated from trial-to-trial variability in response. This estimate is biased when serial correlation is present. In experimental analysis, the best hope is usually to avoid or minimize serial correlation.

Serial Independence Assumption

Standard ANOVA is directly applicable if successive responses are statistically independent. To illustrate, consider an A-B design with n independent responses in each treatment condition. To assess reliability of the mean difference between treatments, construct a confidence interval. To estimate power of a proposed experiment, apply standard ANOVA power analysis.

The reasonableness of the independence assumption depends on situational specifics.

With only a single observation in each session, as in some of the later experimental examples, serial correlation may well be small enough to cause no problem. If multiple A observations are taken in a single session, on the other hand, serial correlation is a real possibility. Even in this case, however, interpolation of a standard treatment between successive experimental treatments, as in the cited example of elbow smelling, may reduce any serial correlation to an acceptably small size.

Zero Serial Correlation in Behavior Modification?

Serial correlation may not be too serious in many behavior modification studies. Single-subject A-B-type design is common in this area, as in the two later examples of behavior modification with children. On the face of it, of course, serial correlation seems likely. In part because of this expectation, standard statistical methods have been shunned.

Little empirical evidence was available, however, because the number of observations per period has typically been no more than 10, far too few for adequate power to assess possible serial correlation. Instead, the problem was considered serious on the plausible feeling that behavior should be more similar on successive than on nonsuccessive observations. Positive serial correlation was thus considered normal, and proposals to use ANOVA were harshly criticized.

Huitema (1985) cogently proposed that the question of serial correlation should be studied empirically. Accordingly, he considered all articles from the first 10 years of the *Journal of Applied Behavior Analysis,* the premier journal in this field. Of these, 441 studies reported data that could be used to calculate a serial correlation. On the expectation of positive serial correlation in even a good fraction of these studies, the mean of all 441 serial correlations should be positive. This mean should have a narrow confidence interval, moreover, based on such a large N.

Contrary to expectation, the actual mean was slightly negative for the data of the initial baseline phase. This absence of serial correlation was supported by similar results from subsequent treatment phases. Huitema did find indirect evidence for a small proportion of positive serial correlations, and a somewhat larger proportion was found similarly by Matyas and Greenwood (1996) for the subsequent seven-year period in the same journal.[3]

These analyses suggest that serial correlation is not a problem in many studies

---

[3] Although Huitema's (1985) Herculean effort should have been welcomed, the reaction was remarkably negative (see critiques cited in Huitema, 1988). In every critique the central objection was that the small number of observations in each separate study yielded very low power. The objection was mistaken; this power problem had been addressed by Huitema, who saw how to resolve it by considering the aggregate of studies. If the true correlation was generally positive in the 441 studies, the mean of the 441 serial correlations would have been positive. That was why he went to the great labor of reading and analyzing the data from all 441 studies; had each separate study had adequate power, a small random sample would have sufficed. More recently, Matyas and Greenwood (1996) have given a sensible discussion of the issue, together with additional data that suggest more serial correlation than was obtained by Huitema, although markedly less than had generally been expected.

Two complications with Huitema's analysis should be noted. First, under the null hypothesis, a serial correlation based on N observations has an expected value of $-1/(N - 1)$, not 0 (Huitema & McKean, 1991). Under the total null hypothesis of zero true serial correlation in all 441 studies, the expected mean of the observed values would be about $-.10$, whereas the actual value was $-.01$.

Second, Huitema sought more detailed information by standardizing each serial correlation on the assumption that this would yield a unit normal distribution under the total null hypothesis. A statsig overplus of data in either tail of the distribution would then suggest that some cases had nonzero serial correlation. This procedure was also followed by Matyas and Greenwood (1996), who discussed some problematic aspects of the standardization formula. It was on this uneasy, indirect basis that the excess of positive serial correlations noted in the text was obtained.

A more informative alternative would correlate the observed serial correlations with likely determinants, such as intertrial interval. This approach makes direct, empirical use of all the data, not just extreme cases, and is potentially more revealing.

of behavior modification and that standard ANOVA techniques will often be applicable. Regrettably, little information on the empirical conditions that do and do not produce serial correlation is available. Serial correlation seems likely with short intertrial intervals and has been explicitly studied in psychophysics. More generally, when drift in the subject's state has a longer period than the interval between trials, it will induce serial correlation. With one observation per day, however, negligible serial correlation seems a good hope.

Obtaining a solid data base on serial correlation is an urgent need for methodology of serial observation design. This need is no less for visual inspection than for confidence intervals and power estimates. Unfortunately, criticisms of Huitema's (1985) efforts have obscured the importance of obtaining longer sequences of observations to allow reliable estimates of serial correlation in different kinds of experimental situations. Such data could be collected in some empirical situations without too much trouble if their importance was recognized. Likely determinants of serial correlation are of special concern, such as intertrial interval, type of task, and interspersed baseline treatment.

Serial Correlation as Substantive Phenomenon

Serial correlation embodies behavioral processes. It tells us something about the organization and dynamics of behavior. From this standpoint, serial correlation is not a statistical complication, but a phenomenon of potential importance.

Huitema's (1985) evidence on serial correlation thus has deeper importance. It indicates that the prevailing expectation about serial correlation rested on a misconception about the organization of behavior. Lack of knowledge about serial correlation reflects lack of knowledge about what controls behavior.

ILLUSTRATIVE SINGLE-SUBJECT EXPERIMENTS

Illustrative single-subject investigations from seven areas are presented in the following sections. These include randomized treatment design and serial observation design, as well as one time series of field data. These diverse investigations point up the potential of single-subject design across the whole of psychology.

Person Cognition

When Thales, the ancient Greek philosopher, was asked "What is the hardest thing?" he replied, "To know thyself," a view well supported throughout modern psychology. If self-cognition is hard, cognition about other persons would seem still harder.

Meaning Invariance

One perennially attractive hypothesis holds that person cognition is configural. One's cognition of another person—one's spouse, for example—is developed by integrating multiple informers over the course of time. This cognition seems clearly unified, not a reproductive memory list, but an organized, functional system of knowledge. Such organization suggests that each new informer is interpreted in relation to what is already known. Its effective meaning is not fixed, it would seem, but is configurally dependent on other informers. With concrete examples of experimental stimuli, such meaning change becomes overwhelmingly convincing to common sense. Self-reports of thought processes by expert judges in every field are replete with similar expressions of configural integration.

This configural view appeared in numerous approaches that postulated one or another principle of cognitive consistency. The guiding idea was that the mind shuns inconsistency and strives for consistency. Cognitive consistency promised to be a sovereign principle, a foundation for a unified theory of cognition.

This principle of cognitive consistency implies *meaning change:* The informer stimuli interact and change one another's meanings in order to make a more consistent, unified whole. Similar hypotheses of meaning change appear in psycholinguistics. Quite different is the hypothesis of *meaning invariance:* The informers are integrated with no change of meaning.

ANOVA provides an easy, cogent test of the hypothesis of meaning change. Single-subject ANOVA allows for individual differences in meaning of the stimulus informers; idiosyncratic changes in meaning are not averaged away, as could happen with group analysis.

In the initial experiment, each of 12 subjects received sets of three personality trait adjectives that described a hypothetical person. They judged how much they would like the person on a scale of 1 to 20. The 27 person descriptions were constructed from a 3^3 design, with Lo, Med, and Hi adjectives as the levels of each factor. To assess stimulus generality, six different stimulus designs were used, each with a different selection of adjectives, with two subjects in each stimulus design. Subjects were run individually for five successive days. Each day began with eight warm-up descriptions, followed by the 27 experimental descriptions in random order. Treatment randomization made the responses statistically independent, thereby allowing single-subject ANOVAs, which were performed on the data of the last three days, the first two being treated as practice to bring the subject into a stable state.

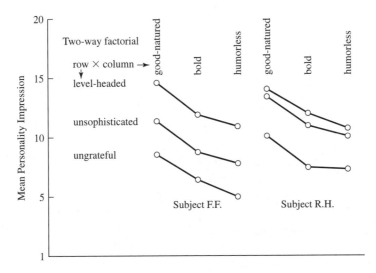

Figure 8.2   Parallelism pattern supports nonconfigural, adding-type rule in person cognition.
NOTE: Subjects judged likableness of hypothetical persons described by two trait adjectives listed in the
row × column design: row adjectives of *level-headed, unsophisticated,* and *ungrateful;* column adjectives
of *good-natured, bold,* and *humorless.* Each of these $3 \times 3 = 9$ person descriptions corresponds to one
data point. Data averaged over third trait for simplicity; see Figure 1.4 of Anderson, 1982.
SOURCE: After Anderson (1962).

Visual inspection and ANOVA provide
simple, direct tests of the hypothesis of meaning change. Suppose that the meaning of
each adjective does change depending on
which other adjectives it is combined with.
Then its effect on the response will differ
from one cell to another in the design. Being thus variable, the effect of a given adjective can hardly be an additive constant. Instead, systematic deviations from parallelism
will be obtained. This nonparallelism will appear in ANOVA as nonadditive interaction
residuals.

On the other hand, suppose each adjective
has a fixed, invariant meaning. Suppose also
that the adjectives in each person description
are added or averaged to determine the likableness of the person. Then the interaction
residuals are zero in principle, and the factorial graphs should exhibit parallelism.

Two-factor graphs for the first two subjects
in this experiment are shown in Figure 8.2,
together with illustrative trait adjectives. Both

subjects show parallelism. Parallelism dis-
confirms the cognitive consistency theories
en bloc because they imply nonparallelism.
Parallelism supports the averaging model
together with the hypothesis of meaning
invariance.

Most subjects showed similar parallelism,
and this visual inspection was supported by
the single-subject ANOVAs. The pooled interaction residuals, with $20/54 \, df$, have high
power to detect deviations from the prediction of the averaging model. This initial application of functional measurement
thus disconfirmed an entire class of cognitive
consistency theories in a simple, effective
way. This disconfirmation was constructive,
for it revealed unexpected organization of
cognition—perhaps the first established algebraic law of thought—together with meaning
invariance. No less important, this result implied distinct modules for the *valuation* of the
separate informers and for their *integration*
into a unified response.

Blame Schema

Blaming and avoiding blame are prominent in social-personal dynamics but have received little scientific study. Pioneering work by Piaget (1932/1965) led him to conclude that young children cannot integrate the two main determinants of blame, namely, the intent behind a harmful act and the amount of harm. Instead, they center on one or the other determinant and judge solely on that. This doctrine of *centration* was later extended to Piaget's main field of commonsense physics and became a central concept in his theory. Centration, however, has been found to be an artifact of confounding in Piaget's standard methodology.

These confoundings were avoided by Leon (1976, 1980), who asked children to judge the amount of deserved punishment for a story child who had interfered with workmen painting a house. Each story presented one of three levels of the intention that the story child had to cause harm, and one of four levels of physical damage. Children at five age levels, from first to seventh grade, judged each of the 12 stories on a graphic rating scale. Each child thus provided a factorial graph, which allowed diagnosis of individual integration schemas.

Piaget's (1932/1965) centration hypothesis was disproved at once with this factorial design, for centration implies only one main effect in the ANOVA. Leon's functional measurement analysis showed that the majority of children followed the algebraic blame schema:

Deserved punishment = Intent + Damage.

This algebraic schema goes further to show that children have cognitive abilities qualitatively different from those recognized in Piagetian theory.

Some children showed certain other integration schemas. Spontaneous verbalizations had indicated that some children thought no punishment should be given when the dam-

age was accidental. Being clumsy, young children have a personal interest in this schema. Accordingly, all children were selected who showed at most a one-point difference in their judgments of the two stories with least and most damage, both accidental.

Visual inspection of the individual factorial graphs of these 43 children revealed three distinct response patterns, corresponding to three distinct integration schemas. Six children followed an intent-only schema, shown in the right panel of Figure 8.3. The large separation between these curves indicates a large effect of intent; their flatness indicates a very small effect of damage. Another eight children had a similar pattern (not shown), but with a little larger effect of damage.

An accident-configural schema was exhibited by the other 29 children, shown in the left panel of Figure 8.3. The flatness of the

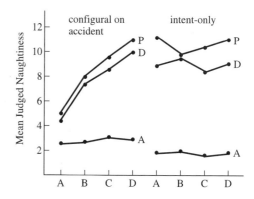

Figure 8.3   Schema diagnosis for single subjects in moral judgment.

NOTE: Two forms of the blame schema: intent-only schema in right panel, accident-configural schema in left panel. Children judged deserved punishment for harmful action by a story child, given the *intent* behind the action and the *damage* it caused. Curve parameter indicates level of intent: A = accident; D = displaced aggression; P = purposive damage. Increasing levels of damage on horizontal axis, A, B, C, D. Schemas diagnosed from pattern in individual factorial graphs, here pooled over subgroups of subjects.

SOURCE: After Leon (1976, 1980).

bottom curve shows that these children disregarded damage when it was accidental. However, the near-parallelism of the two top curves shows that these same children averaged Intent + Damage when the act had some deliberate intent behind it. This accident-configural schema appeared at all ages, even with a few adults.

Leon's (1980) seminal study illustrates the importance of individual analyses. It also illustrates a cognitive methodology with notable advantages over the choice methodology popularized by Piaget.

Behavior Modification

Operant conditioning techniques have been applied to a wide spectrum of behavior problems, especially with children. Among the advantages of operant techniques are their flexibility and the power of reinforcement over behavior. Two examples of single-subject analysis are cited here.

Aggression in Retarded Children

Sam was a mentally retarded, nonverbal 9-year-old who understood only simple commands. He was referred by his teacher because he met all attempts at instruction with aggression (pinching, hair pulling, and scratching). Drugs and a special diet had been ineffective.

The rationale for this study began with the hypothesis that Sam's aggressive behavior functioned as a means to escape aversive demand situations. A further hypothesis was that the aggression could be controlled with positive reinforcers (Carr, Newsom, & Binkoff, 1980).

This study is instructive because, among other reasons, it illustrates the development of an effective task—the foundation of experimental analysis. Some behavioral task must be found that will elicit Sam's aggression but also elicit correct responses that can be rein-

forced. In addition, personal reinforcers must be found to suit Sam's idiosyncracies.

The behavioral task was a buttoning board that had been used in Sam's classroom. At the beginning of each daily 10-min session, Sam was handed a buttoning board and was told every 10 s to do one button. Although this demand typically elicited aggression, it was nearly always performed.

In addition, pretesting was needed to establish effective reinforcers for Sam. One potato chip and a music box turned on for 4 s by the experimenter were two that were selected. These reinforcers have the advantage of not interfering unduly with the opportunity to emit aggressive behavior.

Sam and the experimenter sat in two facing chairs, 40 cm apart, so Sam had easy opportunity to aggress against the experimenter. One or two observers, seated separately, recorded frequency of aggression.

Two conditions were used in the A-B-A-B design of Figure 8.4. The control A condition consisted of demands to fasten a button, which received brief verbal praise just as in Sam's classroom instruction. The experimental B condition consisted of the same treatment plus one of the cited reinforcers. Successive data points represent successive days.

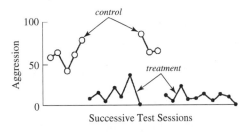

Figure 8.4 Positive reinforcement decreases aggression.

NOTE: Aggressive responses by Sam in 10-min daily sessions in aversive task. Open circles represent performance of simple aversive motor task under classroom task situation; filled circles represent same situation plus positive reinforcers.

SOURCE: After Carr, Newsom, & Binkoff (1980).

The data of Figure 8.4 speak for themselves: Aggression is high during the control condition and drops immediately when the personal reinforcers are used. The serial independence assumption seems reasonable in this situation, so a formal ANOVA could be applied to supplement the visual inspection. Of course a formal test is obviously not needed here.

Figure 8.4 presents one of two experiments with Sam. The published paper also included two experiments with Bob, a 14-year-old who was so aggressive that the experimenter had to wear protective clothing and could only tolerate a 5-min session. This case was further complicated by the lack of positive reinforcers; Bob had an eating problem and no interest in music. To see how the investigators succeeded in extinguishing Bob's aggressive behavior and shaping him into an instructable person, see Carr et al. (1980, Experiment 4).

Attention-Deficit Disorder

About 1.5 million children in the United States suffer from attention-deficit disorder. These children often have poor literary skills and may have trouble following teacher instructions. Special education services are often required.

About half of these children are treated with stimulant medication, most commonly with methylphenidate (Ritalin). Evidence for positive effects of methylphenidate comes from a careful, intensive study by Rapport et al. (1987), who presented both group and individual data for 42 children. These individual data were thought to indicate that drug effects are somewhat idiosyncratic across children as well as across tasks. This pattern, however, may simply reflect marginal power. Marginal power may also explain why the optimal dose level does not seem predictable. In practice, the operative dose is usually determined by reports of parents or teachers, which is not too satisfactory. Parents and teachers are likely to

judge on docility, not on what the children learn, as noted long ago by Binet in his pioneering studies of intelligence.

An experimental approach to the problem of determining optimal dosage was presented by Stoner, Carey, Ikeda, and Shinn (1994). One response measure was the number of words read aloud in the classroom situation from a passage of a school text. Such curriculum-based assessment, as it is called, has been extensively developed and has many attractive properties. Among these are simplicity, reliability, suitability for repeated administration, and face ecological validity.

Both subjects were rural children who had been referred to a university clinic by their family physician. A double-blind procedure was used. Following a coded schedule, each morning's dose was administered by the parents, who had been involved in the decision to perform the experiment. Performance was measured 1 to 2 hr later in school, at which time the drug effects were thought to be maximal. Besides the reading measure, an analogous arithmetic measure was also used. Many careful, thoughtful details of procedure are passed over here.

The outcome of this experiment is illustrated in Figure 8.5, which presents reading scores for 32 school days for Bill, a 13-year-old eighth-grader. The article presents a similar graph for Bill's arithmetic performance as well as graphs for the other subject, who received a different sequence of dosage levels.

Visual inspection of Figure 8.5, in my opinion, shows no evidence for treatment effects. The response is about as high for the placebo as for the 10-mg and 15-mg doses. Response to the 5-mg dose is considerably higher, but it also shows high variability, and the difference is visibly unreliable. Indeed, the later follow-up under 5 mg actually shows lower performance than the placebo.

The authors took a more positive view, presenting their data to the parents and physician

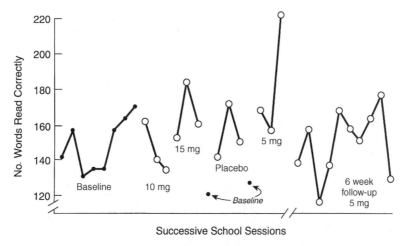

Figure 8.5 Methylphenidate medication evidently fails to help attention-deficit child.
NOTE: Each data point represents number of words read aloud from standardized text in classroom situation. No medication in baseline treatment (filled circles); 5, 10, and 15 mg indicate daily dosage of medication; placebo is a comparable dose with 0 mg medication.
SOURCE: After Stoner, Carey, Ikeda, & Shinn (1994).

as a basis for selecting a dosage level for continued treatment. Their published paper includes cautionary comments about the threat of temporal confounding and about high variability, it is true, but the other three graphs in this article were about equally negative.

This study illustrates the need for standard statistics in the field of behavior modification—especially at the design stage. In this study, a power calculation would surely have shown that the given design had little chance of success. Moreover, a Latin square design would have been markedly more effective, as indicated in the earlier discussion. And because the literature had shown inconsistent results, visual inspection could not have been expected to be adequate.

Standard statistics seems applicable in this case. With one trial per day, serial correlation could be expected to be near zero. Positive serial correlation would yield an effective false-alarm parameter somewhat larger than its nominal value, which might be tolerable in this situation. Taking advantage of standard statistics, to paraquote the authors on the need

for replication of their study "holds promise for contributing to improved outcomes for the hundreds of thousands of children who are prescribed stimulant medication annually" (Stoner et al., 1994, p. 111).

Personality and Clinical Psychology

Single-subject design, especially randomized treatment design, should be central in personality-clinical psychology. However, "these designs are rarely taught in research training in clinical psychology despite their potential for widespread use" (Kazdin, 1992, p. 470). The one chapter in Kazdin's edited book that focuses on this issue is a light overview of serial observation design (Hayes, 1992). Little more is found in Hersen, Kazdin, and Bellack (1991).

The work on behavior modification constitutes a resource for clinical applications which also aim at behavior modification. Much is there to be learned, both dos and don'ts, as from the two foregoing studies. Indeed, the discussions cited in the previous paragraph rest largely on methods developed in behavior modification, which is much neglected in personality-clinical psychology.

Another resource comes from judgment-decision theory, illustrated with the studies of person cognition in Figures 8.2 and 8.3. Such randomized treatment design with single subjects seems almost totally neglected in personality-clinical psychology, yet it offers unique advantages.[4]

The lack of progress in personality-clinical psychology has been repeatedly bewailed by Mcehl (e.g., 1990, pp. 229–230, Meehl's italics):

> Null hypothesis testing of correlational predictions from weak substantive theories in soft psychology is subject to the influence of ten obfuscating factors whose effects are usually (1) sizeable, (2) opposed, (3) variable, and (4) unknown. The net epistemic effect of these ten obfuscating influences is that the usual literature research review is well-nigh uninterpretable.

Meehl explicitly considers only "soft psychology," dealing with "nonmanipulated factors" and relying on correlational analysis. His main "obfuscating factor" is the "crud factor," essentially that "everything correlates to some extent with everything else" (p. 204), which makes analysis of causal process almost impossible. This lack of progress contrasts sharply, it may be added, with impressive recent progress in developmental psychology, psycholinguistics, perception, behavior genetics, neuroscience, and some other fields that employ experimental analysis.

A new way of thinking is needed in personality-clinical psychology. The root of the problem lies in a conceptual framework that leads to the *"bunch of nothing"* that Meehl (1990, p. 230) decries. Single-subject methodology provides one potentially useful approach discussed in the later section titled "Personal Design."

Perception

Single-subject design is natural and appropriate in many tasks of perception and judgment–decision. Surprisingly few, however, utilize single-subject ANOVA.[5]

Color Contrast

In color contrast, one hue induces its complementary hue. A gray field adjacent to a red field appears tinged with green, the hue complementary to red. Even more striking, a green

---

[4]My concern about the conceptual framework that guides research in clinical psychology coalesced when I did some studies of judgment-decision in marriage in the late 1970s. Despite the overwhelming social importance of marriage and family life, despite the great opportunities for clinical research, and despite the importance of family therapy, clinical branches of psychology departments showed near-zero interest in marriage at that time. This concern was sharpened by one participant at an American Psychological Association symposium who declared that to go into marital therapy, the first thing to do was to throw away everything you had learned about clinical psychology. Working through the problem, the classical approach, was sure to aggravate the trouble. Instead, the goal should be to forget the past and move forward.

The paucity of single-subject experiments in personality-clinical psychology contrasts dramatically with the idiographic emphasis on the uniqueness of the individual. Meehl's (1990) criticisms of significance tests and hypothesis testing miss the main problem. The main problem is that the hypotheses being tested stem from an ineffectual conceptual framework, symptomatized in his "crud factor," based on correlation analysis of groups of people. A shift to a conceptual framework oriented toward experimental analysis with single persons is needed.

A few comments relevant to single-subject design in personality-clinical psychology are given for emotion in Anderson (1989) and for ego defense in Anderson (1991b). Marriage and family life are considered in Anderson and Armstrong (1989) and Anderson (1991a). Of special interest and high potential are the studies of self-experimentation reported by Roberts and Neuringer (1998).

[5]I am surprised by the paucity of single-subject ANOVAs in perception. In fact, I had trouble finding experimental illustrations. I should appreciate information about other applications in this area, and in other areas as well.

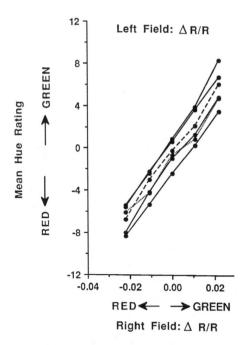

Figure 8.6   Additivity of red-green contrast.
NOTE: Hue judgments plotted as a function of hue of judged test field (horizontal axis) and hue of contrast-inducing field (curve parameter). Parallelism of solid curves implies that the apparent hue of the test field is the sum of its own proper hue and the contrast hue from the inducing field. (Dotted curve represents baseline response to test field by itself; its greater slope provides evidence for secondary induction. Scale on horizontal is relative activation of red cones, with the total [red + green] luminance held constant.)
SOURCE: After Stefurak (1987); see Anderson (1996, pp. 290*ff*).

field adjacent to a red field appears greener. Such *contrast effects* misrepresent physical reality but provide important information on the operation of the visual system. Contrast is also found with affective senses and seems to be a general adaptive process.

A single-subject study of red-green contrast is shown in Figure 8.6. The subject saw two small, adjacent color fields, *test field* and *inducing field,* each varied independently from red to green in five steps. The subject rated the test field (horizontal axis) on a scale from "red 9" to "green 9." Each curve represents one inducing field, which produced contrast. Each point is the mean of 10 judgments for subject K.F.P.

The main conclusion is that color contrast follows an exact additive model. It might seem that a red inducing field would have less effect on a red test field than on a gray or green test field. Instead, the effect is constant, as shown by the parallelism of the solid curves.

Also of interest are the implications for psychophysical measurement. The parallelism of the solid curves indicates that the rating response is a true linear scale of subjective hue. Furthermore, because the solid curves are straight lines, it follows that the physiological hue scale for the test field on the horizontal is also a true linear scale of subjective hue. This physiological hue scale was defined in terms of activation of red and green cones, but whether it was a true linear scale of subjective sensation was not known. This application of functional measurement theory illustrates a novel link between objective physical measures and subjective psychological measures.

Our Knowledge of the External World

A primary goal of psychological science is to understand how an organism develops knowledge of the external world. As noted elsewhere (Anderson, 1996, pp. 281*f*),

> We live in two worlds together. One is the external physical world, in which our bodies move and function. Within our bodies is a very different world, a world of everyday sights, sounds, and other sensory-perceptual experience. We take it for granted that this internal psychological world mirrors the physical world. . . .
>
> Everyday theory of perception assumes we have direct contact with the external world. We think, without really thinking, that the eye somehow transmits little images of the external world to our conscious apprehension. The reason we see objects and motions is simple: That's what's there. . . .

This naive theory of direct perception has persuasive arguments in its favor. Perception seems effortless and immediate. Simple arithmetic and memory tasks often give us trouble, but perceiving complex scenes does not. . . .

Of course, this commonsense theory of direct perception is not correct. This became clear when systematic study of the sensory systems was begun. The sensory nerves do not transmit little images. Instead, they transmit neuroelectrical impulses, a biological computer code. Everyday consciousness is totally unaware of nature's engineering marvels by which our sensory systems convert physical energy, such as light, into neuroelectrical impulses—and from this computer code of the nerves construct this fantastic internal world of three-dimensional shapes, motions, and chromatic magnificence.

What are nature's engineering marvels? One is neurons sensitive to specific physical features, such as orientation of the contour lines of an object. Certain single neurons will fire in response to a vertical line, for example, but not to a horizontal line. Indeed, orientation assessment is one of the most important components of vision. Detection of such visual features is thought to occur very early in the chain of visual processing, at a preattentive stage that does not require focusing of attention.

A curious result is at issue in the following study (Shiu & Pashler, 1992). Subjects improved on a difficult task of discriminating angular orientation of a line—without feedback about correctness. However, this improvement occurred only if the subjects attended to orientation; it did not occur if subjects were trained to judge these same lines in terms of brightness. Over the first two experiments, moreover, there was little transfer to a new, equivalent position in the retinal field. The learning thus appeared to occur locally in the retina and in topographically connected regions of the brain.

Data from one subject in Experiment 2 are used here to illustrate aspects of single-subject design in perception. The main purpose was to verify the suggestion of Experiment 1 that accuracy improved even when subjects received no accuracy feedback. Subject P. P. received 12 blocks of 40 trials each day, under instructions to identify which of two lines with slightly different tilt had been presented on each trial. No feedback about correctness was given.

The results are shown in Figure 8.7, which plots percentage correct on successive days. A linear trend test over days 1 through 5 yielded a comfortably statsig result. This

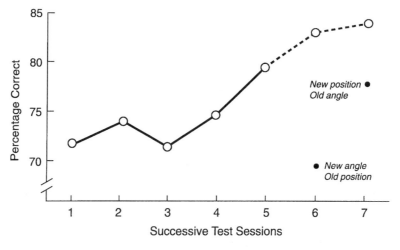

Figure 8.7 Visual discrimination learning under no feedback.
Source: After Shiu & Pashler (1992).

verified the previous experiment's suggestion that learning occurred without feedback. This learning is not some initial adjustment to the task, for it occurred mainly on later days.

Transfer tests were given on alternating trial blocks on days 6 and 7. The two open circles at the top right of Figure 8.7 show mild continued improvement on the training task itself. The most notable transfer is the large decrement shown by the lower filled circle, for trials on which the line angle was changed by 90°, a curious result that seems to have remained unexplored. In addition, the statsig difference between the two data points for day 7 shows substantial decrement from merely changing the position in the visual field at which the test line occurs. Together, these two results imply that the learning did not represent a focusing of attention.

Three subjects were run, of which P. P. showed the slowest improvement over days. This slowest subject was chosen here to reemphasize limitations of the common one-session experiment.

To buttress the visual inspection, some measure of error variability is needed to assess the reliability of the visible trends. The base for analysis was the unit score, namely, percentage correct in each block of 40 trials. This yielded 12 scores per day. A days × blocks ANOVA yielded a statsig linear trend over days.

Additive-Factor Method in Perception/Cognition

Sternberg's (1969) additive-factor method is an ingenious application of factorial design to dissect the sequence of processes that lead from a given stimulus to a response. Further, it illustrates a class of perceptual/cognitive tasks that may require joint use of individual and group analysis.

Donders's subtraction method, published just one century before Sternberg, was a historic attempt to dissect components of stimulus-response processing. Donders measured reaction time to a given stimulus with and without insertion of an additional component of the task. The difference in reaction time, he argued, measured the time required for the inserted component.

The critical assumption of Donders' subtraction method is that the inserted component does not alter the times for processes that precede or follow it. This assumption is uncertain, and there is no way to test it. As a consequence, Donders' method has seen only sporadic use.

This difficulty is resolved with Sternberg's (1969) additive-factor method. In one experiment, the subject saw a numeral either intact or degraded with visual noise (Stimulus Quality) and was to respond either with the numeral itself or with the numeral plus 1 (Stimulus-Response Mapping). Stimulus Quality and Stimulus-Response Mapping may be expected to influence independent stages of the overall response process, the former at the stimulus encoding stage, the latter at the response output stage. If so, their times should be additive, and this additivity will be revealed in the ANOVA. Observed parallelism in this 2 × 2 design would thus support stage independence of the two manipulated factors.

Data for two of the five subjects are shown in Figure 8.8. The two dashed curves for each subject represent the case in which the numeral on each trial could be 1, 2, . . . , 8. Visual inspection indicates little deviation from parallelism. The two solid curves for the condition in which the numeral was either 1 or 8 show a little nonparallelism, but hardly enough to cause worry.[6]

---

[6]The logic of Sternberg's additive-factor method seems compelling. As with all theories, however, some alternative may hold instead. In fact, it appears that reasonable alternatives very different in nature can also yield additive results (Miller, van der Ham, & Sanders, 1995).

Additive models can also produce linear fan patterns in some tasks, as illustrated in Shanteau's (1991) application of functional measurement to a list-search task.

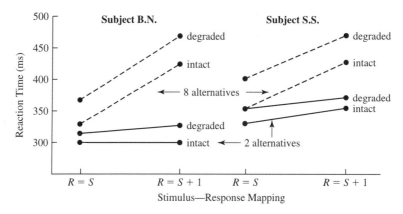

Figure 8.8   Test of additive-factor method.

NOTE: Parallelism of paired dashed lines and paired solid lines for each subject supports additivity of processing times for stimulus quality and stimulus-response mapping.

SOURCE: After Sternberg (1969).

It is instructive to compare advantages of single-subject ANOVA with the repeated-measures ANOVA that Sternberg used. Sternberg gave extensive preliminary training to bring subjects to a near-stable state and collected ample data that would have allowed individual ANOVA. Many studies in perception/cognition present similar opportunities.

Advantages of the group analysis are that only one ANOVA is required and that the error term for each ANOVA source is composed of the corresponding interactions with subjects. If subjects were a random sample from some population, this error term would warrant statistical generalization of the sample results to the population. Subjects are virtually always handy samples, of course, but this same error term is appropriate for extrastatistical generalization to other subjects.

Single-subject ANOVA has advantages of greater sensitivity. The error term contains only response unreliability of each individual; the repeated-measures error is larger because it includes also the subject interaction residuals. Group analysis may thus obscure pertinent aspects of the individual behavior, especially an occasional deviant individual. In this regard, single-subject analysis may

actually be more appropriate for extrastatistical generalization.

Judgment-Decision

The field of judgment-decision seems ideal for single-subject design because most investigators aim to employ stable-state tasks. Instead, repeated-measures analysis is generally used. Even so, it seems advisable to collect enough data from each subject to allow supplementary single-subject analysis, as in the following study.

Fundamental Violation of Classical Utility Theory

"More is better" is a basic principle of utility theory, widely used in economic theory and in judgment-decision theory. Some form of this principle appears in the sure-thing axiom and in the dominance axiom, both of which have been central in attempts to develop general theory.

The ubiquitous averaging process of cognitive algebra, however, implies that more may be worse. If a positive object is added to another positive object, the overall value may actually decrease. A well-planned study by

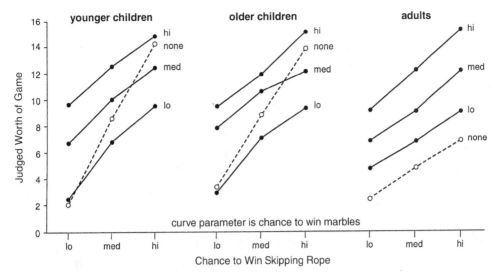

Figure 8.9   More may be worse, contrary to classical utility theory.
NOTE: Crossover of dashed and solid curves for both ages of children shows that adding one positive object to another may actually decrease the value of the two together.
SOURCE: After Schlottmann (2000).

Schlottmann (2000) showed that this averaging process held for children at two age levels.

Schlottmann's (2000) results are in Figure 8.9. The near-parallelism of the three solid curves in each panel of Figure 8.9 supports an exact cognitive integration rule, by virtue of the parallelism theorem. These solid curves come from the two-factor design that combined each of three chances to win the skipping rope with each of three chances to win the marbles. The near-parallelism thus suggests an exact algebra of subjective utility at all age levels.

Parallelism, however, can result from either of two rules: averaging or adding. To get a critical test between these two rules, compare the dashed curve (the judged value of the low, medium, or high chance to win the skipping rope alone) with the solid curve labeled *medium* (for the same chance to win the skipping rope together with a medium chance to win the marbles).

Utility theory requires the dashed curve to lie below all the solid curves; even a low chance of winning the marbles is worth something and so should raise the dashed curve at every point. Utility theory is disordinally violated by the crossover of the dashed and solid curves for both ages of children.

Instead, the crossover of the dashed and solid curves implies that children averaged: The medium chance to win the marbles averages down the high chance and averages up the low chance to win the skipping rope. Adults, in contrast, integrate by adding in this task, as shown by the location of the dashed curve below and parallel to all the solid curves.

Schlottmann's (2000) application of functional measurement is cited here to illustrate a common class of situations in which a few subjects are not enough, unlike most previous examples, yet individual analyses are important. The double difficulty is that children's judgments are more variable than adults' judgments and that relatively few judgments can be obtained before they lose interest. Schlottmann obtained two replications for each child, but even two replications requires experimenter skill to maintain children's interest and motivation. Because many subjects were used, an overall repeated-measures ANOVA was used to summarize the main trends. This was supplemented with visual inspection of the factorial graph for each subject, together with single-subject ANOVAs that were reported in verbal summaries. At each age level, all individuals exhibited similar patterns. In fact, the dashed curve lay below the solid curves for all 16 adults, but for none of the 32 children at each age group. Such agreement across children is notable in this hard task and should not be expected in general (e.g., Figure 8.3).

Personal Design with Self-Estimated Parameters

Values of the stimulus informers may need to be measured beforehand to account for an integrated response. This problem of stimulus measurement was neatly finessed with the parallelism theorem, which requires measurement only of the response. But parallelism analysis requires factorial-type design, which is often not possible.

The problem of stimulus measurement arises when a stimulus object has attributes that cannot be manipulated as independent factors. In the following experiment, for example, female subjects judged photographs of males on desirability as dates. Preliminary work had suggested that the judgment of each photograph was the product of two attributes: physical attractiveness of the male and the probability that he would go out with the subject. This probability may well depend on the attractiveness. Hence, the two variables could not well be manipulated independently in factorial design.

In this experiment (Shanteau & Nagy, 1979), accordingly, the subject was asked to judge each photograph on each separate attribute as well as on desirability as a date. To test the cited multiplication hypothesis, these two attribute judgments were multiplied and compared with the judged desirability.

The integration hypothesis is well supported in Figure 8.10. The predicted judgments (dotted lines) are close to the observed judgments (solid lines). The seven males are located on the horizontal axis according to their physical attractiveness, which differs across subjects. The dashed curves at the top give the corresponding probability judgments. Note the low desirability judgments of the two most attractive males by Subject B. W. This low desirability presumably stems from fear of rejection, as reflected in the low probability judgments for these two males.

Analysis of many situations, perhaps most, faces the same difficulty: that the separate stimulus attributes cannot be manipulated independently. This important integration issue seems largely buried under the general concern with one-variable experiments and factorial manipulation. As this experiment shows, methodology for linear response measures can be useful for attacking this difficult class of problems (see further Anderson & Zalinski, 1991).

Operant Matching Law

In matching behavior, subjects adjust their response rates to match relative rates of reinforcement. Matching behavior has been extensively demonstrated with two-choice tasks, both in probability learning with humans and in concurrent operant schedules with pigeons.

In operant theory, this matching law is usually expressed in terms of observable quantities as

$$\frac{R_1}{R_2} = \frac{S_1}{S_2}, \quad \text{(observable matching law)}$$

where R_1 and R_2 denote response rates on the two alternatives, and S_1 and S_2 denote corresponding rates of reinforcement. Tests of this

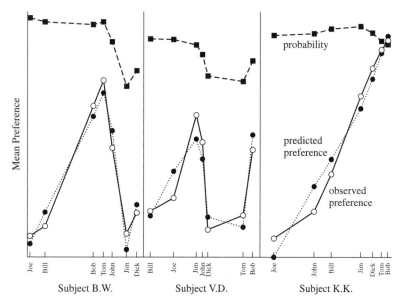

Figure 8.10   Females judge date desirability of photographs of males.

NOTE: Functional measurement prediction supported by closeness of observed and predicted preferences (solid and dotted lines, respectively). Female subjects judged photographs of males on (a) physical attractiveness (horizontal axis), (b) probability of acceptance (upper dashed curve), and (c) desirability as a date (solid curve). Dotted curve gives theoretical predictions from theoretical model. Note that the three females give different rank orders for physical attractiveness of the seven males on the horizontal axis.

SOURCE: After Shanteau & Nagy (1979); see Anderson (1981, p. 76).

matching law are straightforward because all four terms are directly observable.

However, this matching law rests on a strong implicit assumption that the two choices yield equivalent reinforcements. This will not generally be true. Reinforcements on the two choices may differ in amount, for example, or in quality. It is desirable, accordingly, to allow different values for each reinforcer. Because these values will in general be unknown, they are denoted by ψ instead of S. This psychological version of the matching law may be written

$$\frac{R_1}{R_2} = \frac{\psi_1}{\psi_2}. \quad \text{(psychological matching law)}$$

This psychological matching law has been declared tautological on the argument that values of ψ_1 and ψ_2 could always be found to make the data fit the law.

In fact, functional measurement provides a strong test of the psychological matching law. With $R = R_1/R_2$, the equation may be written as a multiplication rule, $R = \psi_1 \times \psi_2^{-1}$. By the linear fan theorem of functional measurement theory, varying the two reinforcers in a factorial design should yield a linear fan (Anderson, 1978).

Just such linear fans appear for the two pigeons of Figure 8.11, based on the careful, arduous experiment by Farley and Fantino (1978). Joint food-shock reinforcement was used for each choice alternative. The ψ value of each was varied across three schedules to yield the 3×3 design indicated in the figure. Functional measurement theory goes beyond

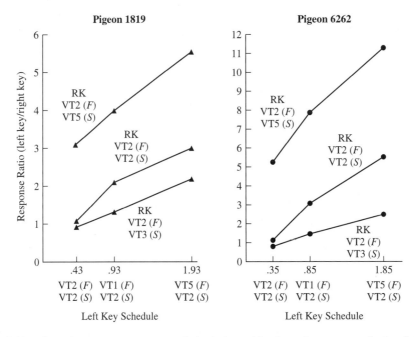

Figure 8.11   Linear fan pattern supports psychological matching law; also measures food and shock in common units.

NOTE: Factorial design presents conjoint, response-independent, variable-time (VT) schedules for food (F) and shock (S), as listed in figure. Three schedules for left key listed on horizontal axis; three schedules for the right key (R. K.) listed as curve parameter.

SOURCE: After Farley & Fantino (1978).

verifying the psychological matching law to provide validated scales of the ψ values. In this tour de force, Farley and Fantino were thus able to express food and shock in equivalent units, a milestone in attempts to unify positive and negative reinforcement.[7]

Time Series

Most experimental analysis of single-subject data uses one of the two foregoing approaches of treatment randomization or serial observation design to deal with serial correlation. A third approach rests on diagnosing the nature of the operative serial correlation and incorporating it in a mathematical model. The model is intended to control the serial correlation by factoring it out of the data, thereby satisfying the independence assumption. This approach, which goes under the name of *time series analysis,* is used frequently with temporal sequences of economic data, as in forecasts of the economy.

A behavioral application of time series analysis to study effectiveness of wearing seat belts is included here to emphasize the importance of nonexperimental field research. In this time series, which is typical of data on many social issues, the subject was the entire population of North Carolina.

---

[7]The operant study by Farley and Fantino (1978) cited in Figure 8.11 was the first application with animal subjects of the linear fan analysis for multiplication models introduced by Anderson and Shanteau (1970). Other applications of linear fan analysis to animal experiments are given by Hawkins, Roll, Puerto, and Yeomans (1983), Roberts (1987), and Gibbon and Fairhurst (1994). This work gives substantial support to the hypothesis that response rate is a true psychological scale.

This example has multiple purposes. First, it illustrates a large class of social issues that lie outside the scope of traditional experimental analysis. These issues require a different perspective. Second, this example illustrates an enlightened state legislature that recognized the need to evaluate the effects of their laws. Third, it illustrates the value of forethought to broaden the database, as with the preliminary program of observations on actual seat belt usage. Fourth, it underscores the need to develop and verify statistical theory for time series within specific empirical contexts.

Foresighted provision for an evaluation of effectiveness was included in the 1985 law passed by the state of North Carolina that required wearing seat belts for front seat occupants of passenger cars and light-duty trucks and vans. A well-designed probability sampling study began assessing frequency of seat belt wearing three months before the law took effect. Beginning 1 October 1985, violators were issued warning tickets for 15 months. Beginning 1 January 1987, violators were subject to fines of $25 (Reinfurt, Campbell, Stewart, & Stutts, 1990).

A time series graph showing seat belt usage at successive monthly times, was dramatically clear: 25% in the prelaw baseline period; an immediate jump to a stable 45% in the warning period; and an instant jump to near 80% at the beginning of the fine period, with a slow decline to about 65%.

But was this increase in belt usage effective in reducing accidents? Accident data were available from police records, which provided a baseline period back to 1981. Visual inspection of this times series showed perhaps a mild decline in vehicle accidents from baseline in the warning period, with a more definite mild decline in the fine period. Although this time series was quite irregular and complicated by a pronounced seasonal decline at year-end, visual inspection seems fairly persuasive.

Visual inspection was supplemented by a statistical time series analysis, which was used to forecast what would have happened without the law. Comparing these forecasts to the observed data yielded an inferred reduction of 5.4% for the warning period and 14.6% for the fine period. Both inferred reductions were statsig, suggesting that the law had substantial social benefits.

But these two values, 5.4% and 14.6%, are not real data. They come from forecasts, obtained from the time series, about what would have happened had no law been passed. These forecasts rest on the empirical validity of the model employed in the time series, which could hardly be considered solidly established. How far the time series statistics can be trusted is thus uncertain. This exemplifies a common difficulty with observational data.

In the present investigation, however, a comparison time series was at hand. This gave corresponding percentages for rear seat occupants, who were not required to wear seat belts. The corresponding analysis of this time series showed a 10.2% decrease, nearly as large as the 14.6% for the front seat occupants. This comparison clouds the main analysis and leaves the results less convincing. At the same time, it emphasizes the value of forethought in obtaining such comparison time series.

The need to deal with time series is clear; behavior is normally a continuous temporal evolution. The discrete trials that characterize so many experiments miss a dynamic of perception, thought, and action. Unfortunately, analysis of time series depends on empirical validity of some assumed statistical model, which is not often well established. In learning theory and psychophysics, time series have been studied in terms of sequential dependencies. This work, however, has had mixed success, even with the inestimable advantages of experimental control. It is surprising that books on time series have not paid more attention to the mass of data available from these two fields.

METHODOLOGY IN SINGLE-SUBJECT DESIGN

Much methodology is area- and task-specific. Methods and procedures differ in many ways across person cognition, behavior modification, visual perception, judgment-decision, and field studies, as illustrated in the foregoing eleven studies. Each area needs its own single-subject methodology.

Some issues of method, however, are common across areas. Foremost is independence, already discussed. A few additional issues of single-subject methodology are taken up in the following sections.

Generalizing within Subjects

Generality for a single subject has both external and internal aspects. External generality refers to other situations and other times for the same subject. Present behavior may not generalize to other situations because they differ from the present situation in some pertinent way. Present behavior may not generalize to future times because the organism changes over time, whether in fluctuations of health and motivation or in systematic changes of maturation and experience.

Assessment of external generality can be assisted with experimental design. Stimulus generality can be studied by including stimulus materials as a factor in the design, as in the study of person cognition of Figure 8.2. Some information on temporal generality can be obtained with designs that can assess position and carryover effects, especially through replication of the experiment over time. For the most part, though, external generality depends on extrastatistical judgment about stability of the behavior and about similarity of the experimental situation to other situations.

Internal outcome generality refers to the reliability of the present behavior. In one sense, the present behavior is a fact, so no question of reliability arises. In a more useful sense, each present response is considered to include variability from causes specific to the moment of response. The pertinent question, accordingly, is whether treatment differences are larger than could be expected from this momentary variability.

This question of internal outcome generality is illustrated in the two foregoing studies of behavior modification. In one of these, the treatment difference is clearly reliable. In the other, it is clearly not. Internal outcome generality is prima facie a statistical question: mean differences relative to variability. Although this comparison can sometimes be made by visual inspection, as in the two cited studies, it is essentially statistical in nature.

Generalizing across Subjects

Most studies of single subjects seek to generalize to a population of subjects. Even the cited studies of behavior modification, concerned with treatment of particular children, were expected to be relevant to treatment for other children.

Response pattern thus becomes a primary concern. Individuals will surely differ in magnitude of response but may still show similar patterns. Individual analysis is often necessary to assess individual patterns, which can be obscured by averaging over individuals.

Commonality of response patterns across individuals, however, differs between substantive tasks. In some tasks, virtually all subjects are expected to show similar response patterns, with individual differences appearing merely as amount or magnitude parameters. Two or three subjects may then suffice, with data presented separately for each. This approach is common in perception, as illustrated in three of the foregoing studies, and in some operant tasks.

In other areas, individuals may be expected to differ in response pattern. The study of person cognition in Figure 8.2, for example, used 12 subjects for this reason. As it happened, most subjects in this experiment showed the parallelism pattern. With judgments of blame, however, several different response patterns are found (Figure 8.3), and the same may happen even in intuitive physics (Karpp & Anderson, 1997).[8]

Diagnosis of individual differences in response pattern presents two practical problems. The first is to get enough data to obtain adequately firm pattern diagnosis for each individual. The second is that a fairly large number of subjects may be required to get even two or three instances of less common patterns. In the blame example, the intent-only pattern occurs in perhaps 1 subject in 10. If only one subject showed this pattern, its reliability and validity would seem uncertain. A total of 30 subjects would not seem too many to be reasonably sure of getting two or three in

this subgroup. This, however, yields an overplus in the modal subgroup. In such situations it could be helpful to develop a procedure to screen out subjects likely to exhibit common patterns.

Single-Subject or Repeated-Measures Analysis of Variance

Many investigations replicate a single-subject design for each of a substantial number of subjects. Two modes of ANOVA are then possible: a number of single-subject ANOVAs or a single repeated-measures ANOVA. The repeated-measures ANOVA is simpler and more compact. It also bears on the question of generality because the error term includes individual differences in the form of subject-treatment interaction residuals.

An ideal approach is to design the experiment so that both modes of analysis are possible and to do both. Apposite illustrations of this combined approach appeared in the foregoing discussion of Figure 8.3, which required breakdown into subgroups characterized by different response patterns, and in Figure 8.9, in which the group means gave an adequate picture of the individual response patterns.

This ideal approach requires that each single subject provide enough data to yield an adequately reliable response pattern. In particular, replication of the experiment for each single subject is usually necessary. At least two observations are then available under each treatment, thereby allowing a proper measure of response variability for each individual. This point is not always realized in planning the experiment.

Too many experiments in perception and cognition that could be treated in single-subject manner are instead studied with repeated-measures design. The line-box illusion of Figure 8.1 is a typical example. Many workers in these areas adopt repeated-measures design without considering the

---

[8]Other examples of individual analysis of response pattern include Anderson and Butzin (1978), Carterette and Anderson (1979), Cuneo (1982), Falk and Wilkening (1998), Karpp and Anderson (1997), Léoni and Mullet (1993), Lopes (1976), Shanteau and Anderson (1969, 1972), Surber (1985), and Wilkening and Anderson (1991). Assessing the generality of these individual patterns across time and task, as in Dozier and Butzin (1988), is a prime need.

The importance of visual inspection of individual data with group experiments is nicely illustrated in Farkas (1991, p. 89, n. 2). By looking at the individual data, Farkas uncovered an unclarity in stimulus materials that he rectified in his subsequent thesis experiments.

Schlottmann's ingenious analysis of individual behavior patterns in Michotte's task of phenomenal causality deserves special mention (see Schlottmann & Anderson, 1993). Schlottmann established a solid base of single-subject data and used the averaging model to estimate the weight that each individual placed on different informers. These measured weights, leveraged with a prescient instructional manipulation, revealed five response strategies that could never be seen in the data themselves.

potential of single-subject design. If different individuals exhibit the same response pattern, this deserves to be shown. If they exhibit different response patterns, this deserves even more to be shown.

Personal Design

Single-subject design culminates in *personal design,* in which the task or stimuli are personalized to the individual subject and the analysis allows for personal values. Personal design thus aims to embed the experimental task within experiential knowledge systems of the individual. Such embedding has a twofold advantage: It maximizes the meaning and relevance of the experimental task and it can tap into well-established psychological processes. Both advantages increase the meaningfulness of the results.

The study of Figure 8.4 on aggressive behavior is a fine example of personal design, for it was personalized through choice of task and reinforcers for each child. The studies of person cognition of Figures 8.2 and 8.3 were partly personalized in that functional measurement analysis took full account of personal meanings of the stimuli.

Individual differences are prominent in human affairs. Affective differences are substantial even in so biological an activity as eating. Individual differences in attitudes underlie virtually all social thought and action: marital roles of wife and husband, parent-child interaction, work, friendship, and so on.

This basic fact of individual differences lies as a quagmire in the path of psychological science. Three main strategies for navigating this quagmire have been tried. The experimental strategy sought to capitalize on the power of experimental method for causal analysis. The dominant experimental approach, however, was predicated on an assumption about general laws of behavior that would hold across individuals and even across species. Too often, this experimental strategy relied on standard group design that consigned individual differences to the statistical error term, thus burying much that needed study.

The strategy of differential psychology did focus squarely on individual differences, but with methods of correlation and personality tests that have little power for cognitive analysis. Strategies of phenomenology, ranging from the historical school of introspection to case histories in the psychoanalytic tradition and to contemporary action theories, have given primary attention to the person. These strategies are severely limited, however, because much of everyday cognition is not accessible to phenomenological scrutiny. Whereas the dominant experimental approach failed to take adequate account of the individual, phenomenological approaches generally lack the analytical power needed for theory of social cognition.

What is needed is a strategy that can combine experimental control with phenomenology. This is the aim of *personal design,* which uses experimental method to study the individual at the individual level. (Anderson, 1990, pp. 243–244)

The experimental and phenomenological approaches cited in this quotation are often called *nomothetic* and *idiographic,* respectively. Personal design unifies nomothetic search for general laws with idiographic recognition of individual differences in values. Such unification is illustrated in the study of person cognition of Figure 8.2, which demonstrated generality of the integration rule across subjects at the same time that it measured and used the personal values of the stimuli. The nomothetic conclusion rested squarely on the idiographic capability.

Personal design usually requires a considerable number of responses from each individual, often assumed to be in a stable state, which limits its applicability. Within its limits, however, personal design may be useful in bringing experimental analysis to areas not ordinarily considered experimental, such as marriage and family life. Personal designs constructed around focal incidents or emotions in an individual's life may provide new methods for personality-clinical psychology.

Functions of Statistics

Visual inspection is always necessary and sometimes sufficient. It is unscientific, not to say unseemly, to muddle one's results with statistical busywork. But more objective methods are sometimes essential to assess reliability of data patterns. Visual inspection and ANOVA are complementary tools. Both help one to understand the data.

Statistics is most important in planning stages of an investigation, before the main data have been collected. The standard stereotype of statistics as significance tests obscures these more basic functions.

One function of statistics concerns independence, important for both classes of single-subject design. Thus, treatment randomization is important regardless of whether the data are analyzed by visual inspection or formal test. With serial observation design, assessment of variability perforce relies on some conceptual model of the behavior, although this model is often left implicit and uncertain. Visual inspection generally makes an implicit assumption of independence and lacks capability to allow for serial correlation. Formal statistics is essential for understanding and helping to deal with serial correlation. Indeed, the problems of serial correlation can hardly be understood without formal statistics.

A second function of statistics concerns description. Thus, the confidence interval for a sample mean rightly conceptualizes the mean not as a single number, but as an interval of likely location. As another example, the after-minus-before difference score seems the obvious measure of change, but this hides surprising and sometimes fatal shortcomings that

are revealed only through statistical analysis. Statistical theory has many such uses: understanding selection-regression artifacts, avoiding inappropriate measures of effect size and importance, using trimmed means to reduce effective variability, and so on.

Another function of statistics concerns power. All experiments rest on some assumption that they have adequate power; statistics can help decide how far this assumption is justified. The need for power calculation has been illustrated in the foregoing study of attention-deficit children (Figure 8.5).

Perhaps the most important functions of statistics appear in experimental design. One example is the Latin square, especially squares balanced for carryover effects. With this design, formal statistical analysis is essential to estimate means for treatment and carryover effects and to get confidence intervals. Statistical understanding of these and other designs is especially important for single-subject studies.

A major hindrance is that single-subject research has often originated with phenomenological approaches or with experimental tasks for which visual inspection was enough. Negative attitudes toward more formal statistics often developed that hindered later work as better methods became increasingly needed. A prime example is psychophysics, which still suffers from certain methods that were once at the forefront but now are largely obsolete. One sign of this backwardness may be seen in the paucity of single-subject ANOVA in the psychophysical literature.

Behavior modification, although the most articulately averse to formal statistics, is the main area that has given concerted attention to single-subject methodology. Several books have been written, all of which can be read with profit, as they attack real problems that are important also in other areas. These books, like the present book, represent an empirical direction in design and analysis.

Methodology consists of cumulative experimental procedure—not static precepts, but evolving knowledge systems.[9]

Each area faces its own special problems and needs to develop its own single-subject methodology. Methodology is a continual concern of active investigators, and beginners

---

[9]Reference books on single-subject design include Barlow and Hersen (1984); Franklin, Allison, and Gorman (1996); Kratochwill and Levin (1992); and Lattal and Perone (1988). Many chapters in these books can be helpful. But these books are almost entirely limited to serial observation design, mainly in operant tasks. Typical studies have only two treatment conditions, moreover, which limits the effectiveness of treatment randomization. In many areas, however, randomized treatment design with single subjects is feasible, as in perception, cognition, psycholinguistics, and personality/social. Systematic methodology is largely undeveloped in these areas, although modest progress has been made in information integration theory (Anderson, 1982).

Contributors to Franklin, Allison, and Gorman (1996) give useful coverage of statistical topics, including power and serial correlation. Chapters in other books, however, not infrequently show shortcomings in statistical understanding that compromise some of their conclusions. It is common to read, for example, that standard statistics is only applicable to group data; in fact, single-subject ANOVA has been around for decades (e.g., Figure 8.2).

One consequence of this negative attitude toward statistics has been neglect of needed groundwork for single-subject methodology, most notably with the problem of serial correlation. A vital first step would be to obtain longer sequences of observations, which would be feasible in some situations but is rarely done, partly because the need for doing so has not been appreciated. Finding determinants of serial correlation, which is essential to get the problem under control, has hardly begun.

The total absence of single-subject design in graduate statistics texts may be due partly to narrowness in previous presentations of single-subject methodology. Although these presentations have made important contributions to serial observation design, treatment randomization is largely ignored. Some identify single-subject design with the rise of operant psychology in the 1930s, seemingly unaware that single-subject design had been common for well over a century in the fields of perception and learning. Some argue that group design and single-subject design have an "intractable divergence" or are even "fundamentally incompatible" (see Baron & Perone, 1998).

There are important differences between single-subject and group design. But the principles of design and analysis are the same in both.

in a field can profit from attention to issues of design and procedure in published articles. Much methodology, however, remains task- and area-specific lore. Efforts to crystallize such lore and make it useful to workers in other areas would be helpful.

> *Methodology* is a bad word to many. Most investigators are truly concerned with methods, of course, but the term *methodology* suggests a dogmatic stance on standardization of procedure and correct data analysis. It connotes involvement in niceties and complexities of apparatus and especially statistics that are generally barren, often useless digressions, sometimes active hindrances to productive inquiry.
>
> Properly considered, however, methodology is an organic part of substantive inquiry. Necessarily so, for the validity of methods derives from the empirical results that they bring in. . . . Knowledge is not divorced from the methods by which it was acquired; those methods themselves constitute an integral part of knowledge. (Anderson, 1982, p. 349)

REFERENCES

Anderson, N. H. (1961). Scales and statistics: Parametric and nonparametric. *Psychological Bulletin, 58,* 305–316.

Anderson, N. H. (1962). Application of an additive model to impression formation. *Science, 138,* 817–818.

Anderson, N. H. (1978). Measurement of motivation and incentive. *Behavior Research Methods & Instrumentation, 10,* 360–375.

Anderson, N. H. (1981). *Foundations of information integration theory.* New York: Academic Press.

Anderson, N. H. (1982). *Methods of information integration theory.* New York: Academic Press.

Anderson, N. H. (1989). Information integration approach to emotions and their measurement. In R. Plutchik & H. Kellerman (Eds.), *Emotion: Theory, research, and experience* (Vol. 4, pp. 133–186). New York: Academic Press.

Anderson, N. H. (1990). Personal design in social cognition. In C. Hendrick & M. S. Clark (Eds.), *Research methods in personality and social psychology: Review of personality and social psychology* (Vol. 11, pp. 243–278). Beverly Hills, CA: Sage.

Anderson, N. H. (1991a). Family life and personal design. In N. H. Anderson (Ed.), *Contributions to information integration theory: Vol. 3. Developmental* (pp. 189–242). Hillsdale, NJ: Erlbaum.

Anderson, N. H. (1991b). Psychodynamics of everyday life: Blaming and avoiding blame. In N. H. Anderson (Ed.), *Contributions to information integration theory: Vol. 2. Social* (pp. 243–275). Hillsdale, NJ: Erlbaum.

Anderson, N. H. (1996). *A functional theory of cognition.* Mahwah, NJ: Erlbaum.

Anderson, N. H. (2001). *Empirical direction in design and analysis.* Mahwah, NJ: Erlbaum.

Anderson, N. H., & Armstrong, M. A. (1989). Cognitive theory and methodology for studying marital interaction. In D. Brinberg & J. Jaccard (Eds.), *Dyadic decision making* (pp. 3–50). New York: Springer.

Anderson, N. H., & Butzin, C. A. (1978). Integration theory applied to children's judgments of equity. *Developmental Psychology, 14,* 593–606.

Anderson, N. H., & Shanteau, J. C. (1970). Information integration in risky decision making. *Journal of Experimental Psychology, 84,* 441–451.

Anderson, N. H., & Zalinski, J. (1991). Functional measurement approach to self-estimation in multiattribute evaluation. In N. H. Anderson (Ed.), *Contributions to information integration theory: Vol. 1. Cognition* (pp. 145–185). Hillsdale, NJ: Erlbaum.

Barlow, D. H., & Hersen, M. (1984). *Single case experimental designs* (2nd ed.). New York: Pergamon.

Baron, A., & Perone, M. (1998). Experimental design and analysis in the laboratory study of human operant behavior. In K. A. Lattal & M. Perone (Eds.), *Handbook of research meth-* ods in human operant behavior (pp. 45–91). New York: Plenum.

Carr, E. G., Newsom, C. D., & Binkoff, J. A. (1980). Escape as a factor in the aggressive behavior of two retarded children. *Journal of Applied Behavior Analysis, 13,* 101–117.

Carterette, E. C., & Anderson, N. H. (1979). Bisection of loudness. *Perception & Psychophysics, 26,* 265–280.

Cliff, N. (1992). Abstract measurement theory and the revolution that never happened. *Psychological Science, 3,* 186–190.

Cochran, W. G., & Cox, G. M. (1957). *Experimental designs* (2nd ed.). New York: Wiley.

Cuneo, D. O. (1982). Children's judgments of numerical quantity: A new view of early quantification. *Cognitive Psychology, 14,* 13–44.

Dozier, M., & Butzin, C. (1988). Cognitive requirements of ulterior motive information usage: Individual child analyses. *Journal of Experimental Child Psychology, 46,* 88–99.

Edgington, E. S. (1987). *Randomization tests* (2nd ed.). New York: Marcel Dekker.

Falk, R., & Wilkening, F. (1998). Children's construction of fair chances: Adjusting probabilities. *Developmental Psychology, 34,* 1340–1357.

Farkas, A. J. (1991). Cognitive algebra of interpersonal unfairness. In N. H. Anderson (Ed.), *Contributions to information integration theory: Vol. 2. Social* (pp. 43–99). Hillsdale, NJ: Erlbaum.

Farley, J., & Fantino, E. (1978). The symmetrical law of effect and the matching relation in choice behavior. *Journal of the Experimental Analysis of Behavior, 29,* 37–60.

Franklin, R. D., Allison, D. B., & Gorman, B. S. (Eds.). (1996). *Design and analysis of single-case research.* Mahwah, NJ: Erlbaum.

Gibbon, J., & Fairhurst, S. (1994). Ratio versus difference comparators in choice. *Journal of the Experimental Analysis of Behavior, 62,* 409–434.

Hawkins, R. D., Roll, P. L., Puerto, A., & Yeomans, J. S. (1983). Refractory periods of neurons mediating stimulation-elicited eating and brain stimulation reward: Interval scale measurement and tests of a model of neural integration. *Behavioral Neuroscience, 97,* 416–432.

Hayes, S. C. (1992). Single case experimental design and empirical clinical practice. In A. E. Kazdin (Ed.), *Methodological issues and strategies in clinical research* (pp. 491–521). Washington, DC: American Psychological Association.

Hersen, M., Kazdin, A. E., & Bellack, A. S. (Eds.). (1991). *The clinical psychology handbook* (2nd ed.). New York: Pergamon Press.

Huitema, B. E. (1985). Autocorrelation in applied behavior analysis: A myth. *Behavioral Assessment, 7,* 107–118.

Huitema, B. E. (1988). Autocorrelation: 10 years of confusion. *Behavioral Assessment, 10,* 253–294.

Huitema, B. E., & McKean, J. W. (1991). Autocorrelation estimation and inference with small samples. *Psychological Bulletin, 110,* 291–304.

Karpp, E. R., & Anderson, N. H. (1997). Cognitive assessment of function knowledge. *Journal of Research in Science Teaching, 34,* 359–376.

Kazdin, A. E. (Ed.). (1992). *Methodological issues & strategies in clinical research.* Washington, DC: American Psychological Association.

Krantz, D. H., Luce, R. D., Suppes, P., & Tversky, A. (1971). *Foundations of measurement* (Vol. 1). New York: Academic Press.

Kratochwill, T. R., & Levin, J. R. (1992). *Single-case research design and analysis.* Hillsdale, NJ: Erlbaum.

Lattal, K. A., & Perone, M. (Eds.). (1998). *Handbook of research methods in human operant behavior.* New York: Plenum.

Leon, M. (1976). *Coordination of intent and consequence information in children's moral judgments.* Unpublished doctoral dissertation, University of California, San Diego.

Leon, M. (1980). Integration of intent and consequence information in children's moral judgments. In F. Wilkening, J. Becker, & T. Trabasso (Eds.), *Information integration by children* (pp. 71–97). Hillsdale, NJ: Erlbaum.

Léoni, V., & Mullet, E. (1993). Evolution in the intuitive mastery of the relationship between mass, volume, and density from nursery school to college. *Genetic, Social, and General Psychology Monographs, 119,* 389–412.

Link, S. W. (1994). Rediscovering the past: Gustav Fechner and signal detection theory. *Psychological Science, 5,* 335–340.

Lopes, L. L. (1976). Individual strategies in goal setting. *Organizational Behavior and Human Performance, 15,* 268–277.

Matyas, T. A., & Greenwood, K. M. (1996). Serial dependency in single-case times series. In R. D. Franklin, D. B. Allison, & B. S. Gorman (Eds.), *Design and analysis of single-case research* (pp. 215–243). Mahwah, NJ: Erlbaum.

Meehl, P. E. (1990). Why summaries of research on psychological theories are often uninterpretable. *Psychological Reports,* Monog. Suppl. 1-V66, 195–244.

Miller, J., van der Ham, F., & Sanders, A. F. (1995). Overlapping stage models and reaction time additivity: Effects of the activation equation. *Acta Psychologica, 90,* 11–28.

Piaget, J. (1965). *The moral judgment of the child* (M. Gabain, Trans.). New York: Free Press. (Originally published 1932)

Rapport, M. D., Jones, J. T., DuPaul, G. J., Kelly, K. L., Gardner, M. J., Tucker, S. B., & Shea, M. S. (1987). Attention deficit disorder and methylphenidate: Group and single-subject analyses of dose effects on attention in clinic and classroom settings. *Journal of Clinical Child Psychology, 16,* 329–338.

Reinfurt, D. W., Campbell, B. J., Stewart, J. R., & Stutts, J. C. (1990). Evaluating the North Carolina safety belt wearing law. *Accident Analysis & Prevention, 22,* 197–210.

Roberts, S. (1987). Evidence for distinct serial processes in animals: The multiplicative-factors method. *Animal Learning & Behavior, 15,* 135–173.

Roberts, S., & Neuringer, A. (1998). Self-experimentation. In K. A. Lattal & M. Perone (Eds.), *Handbook of research methods in human operant behavior* (pp. 619–655). New York: Plenum.

Schlottmann, A. (2000). Children's judgments of gambles: A disordinal violation of utility. *Journal of Behavioral Decision Making, 13,* 77–89.

Schlottmann, A., & Anderson, N. H. (1993). An information integration approach to phenomenal causality. *Memory & Cognition, 21,* 785–801.

Shanteau, J. (1991). Functional measurement analysis of response times in problem solving. In N. H. Anderson (Ed.), *Contributions to information integration theory: Vol. 1. Cognition* (pp. 321–350). Hillsdale, NJ: Erlbaum.

Shanteau, J., & Anderson, N. H. (1969). Test of a conflict model for preference judgment. *Journal of Mathematical Psychology, 6,* 312–325.

Shanteau, J., & Anderson, N. H. (1972). Integration theory applied to judgments of the value of information. *Journal of Experimental Psychology, 92,* 266–275.

Shanteau, J., & Nagy, G. F. (1979). Probability of acceptance in dating choice. *Journal of Personality and Social Psychology, 37,* 522–533.

Shiu, L.-P., & Pashler, H. (1992). Improvement in line orientation discrimination is retinally local but dependent on cognitive set. *Perception & Psychophysics, 52,* 582–588.

Stefurak, D. L. (1987). *Studies in chromatic induction.* Unpublished doctoral dissertation, University of California, San Diego.

Sternberg, S. (1969). The discovery of processing stages: Extensions of Donders' method. *Acta Psychologica, 30,* 276–315.

Stoner, G., Carey, S. P., Ikeda, M. J., & Shinn, M. R. (1994). The utility of curriculum-based measurement for evaluating the effects of methylphenidate on academic performance. *Journal of Behavior Analysis, 27,* 101–113.

Surber, C. F. (1985). Measuring the importance of information in judgment: Individual differences in weighting ability and effort. *Organizational Behavior and Human Decision Processes, 35,* 156–178.

Wilkening, F., & Anderson, N. H. (1991). Representation and diagnosis of knowledge structures in developmental psychology. In N. H. Anderson (Ed.), *Contributions to information integration theory: Vol. 3. Developmental* (pp. 45–80). Hillsdale, NJ: Erlbaum.

CHAPTER 9

Analysis, Interpretation, and Visual Presentation of Experimental Data

GEOFFREY R. LOFTUS

Following data collection from some experiment, two goals arise that should guide subsequent data analysis and data presentation. The first goal is for the data collector to understand the data as thoroughly as possible in terms of (a) how they may bear on the specific question that the experiment was designed to address, (b) what surprises the data may have produced, and (c) what such surprises may imply about the original questions, related questions, or anything else. The second goal is to determine how to present the data to the scientific community in a manner that is as clear, complete, and intuitively compelling as possible. This second goal is intimately entwined with the first: Whatever data-analysis and data-presentation techniques best instill understanding in the investigator to begin with are generally also optimal for conveying the data's meaning to the data's eventual consumers.

So what *are* these data-analysis and data-presentation techniques? It is not possible in

The writing of this chapter was supported by NIMH grant MH41637. The author thanks the late Merrill Carlsmith for introducing him to many of the techniques described in this chapter and David Krantz for a great deal of more recent conceptual enlightenment about some of the subtler aspects of hypothesis testing, confidence intervals, and planned comparisons.

a single chapter or even in a very long book to describe them all, because there are an infinite number of them. Although most practicing scientists are equipped with a conceptual foundation with respect to the basic tools of data analysis and data presentation, such a foundation is far from sufficient: It is akin to an artist's foundation in the tools of color mixing, setting up an easel, understanding perspective, and the like. To build on this analogy, a scientist analyzing any given experiment is like an artist rendering a work of art: Ideally, the tools comprising the practitioner's foundation should be used creatively rather than dogmatically to produce a final result that is beautiful, elegant, and interesting, instead of ugly, convoluted, and prosaic.

My goal in this chapter is to try to demonstrate how a number of data-analysis techniques may be used creatively in an effort to understand and convey to others the meaning and relevance of a data set. It is not my intent to go over territory that is traditionally covered in statistics texts. Rather, I have chosen to focus on a limited, but powerful, arsenal of techniques and associated issues that are related to, but are not typically part of, a standard statistics curriculum. I begin this chapter with an overview of data analysis as generically carried out in psychology, accompanied by a critique of some standard procedures and assumptions, with particular emphasis on a critique of null hypothesis significance testing (NHST). Next, I discuss a collection of topics representing some supplements and alternatives to the kinds of standard analysis procedures about which I will have just complained. These discussions include (a) a description of various types of pictorial representations of data, (b) an overview of the use of confidence intervals that, I believe, constitutes an attractive alternative to NHST, (c) a review of the benefits of planned comparisons that entail an analysis of percent between-conditions variance accounted for, (d) a description of techniques involving percent *total* variance accounted for, (e) a brief set of suggestions about presentation of results based on mathematical models (meant to complement the material in Chapter 11 of this volume), and, finally, (f) a somewhat evangelical description of what I have termed *equivalence techniques.*

My main expositional strategy is to illustrate through example. In most instances, I have invented experiments and associated data to use in the examples. This strategy has the disadvantage that it is somewhat divorced from the real world of psychological data, but it has the dominating advantage that the examples can be tailored specifically to the illustration of particular points.

The logic and mathematical analysis in this chapter is not meant to be formal or complete. For proofs of various mathematical assertions that I make, it is necessary to consult a mathematically oriented statistics text. There are a number of such texts; my personal favorite is Hays (1973), and where appropriate, I supply references to Hays along with specific page numbers.

My choice of material and the recommendations that I selected to include in this chapter have been strongly influenced by 35 years of experience in reviewing and editing journals. In the course of these endeavors I have noticed

an enormous number of data-analysis and data-presentation techniques that have been sadly inimical to insight and clarity—and conversely, I have noticed enormous numbers of missed opportunities to analyze and present data in such a way that the relevance and importance of the findings are underscored and clearly conveyed to the intended recipients. Somewhere in this chapter is an answer to approximately 70% of these complaints. It is my hope that, among other things, this chapter will provide a reference to which I can guide authors whose future work passes across my desk—as an alternative, that is, to trying to solve what I believe to be the world's data-analysis and data-presentation problems one manuscript at a time.

FOUNDATIONS: THE LINEAR MODEL AND NULL HYPOTHESIS SIGNIFICANCE TESTING

Suppose that a memory researcher were interested in how stimulus presentation time affects memory for a list of words as measured in a free-recall paradigm. In a hypothetical experiment to answer this question, the investigator might select $J = 5$ presentation times consisting of 0.5, 1.0, 2.0, 4.0, and 8.0 s/word and carry out an experiment using a between-subjects design in which $n = 20$ subjects are assigned to each of the 5 word-duration conditions—hence, $N = 100$ subjects in all. Each subject sees 20 words, randomly selected from a very large pool of words. For each subject, the words are presented sequentially on a computer screen, each word presented for its appropriate duration. Immediately following presentation of the last word, the subject attempts to write down as many of the words as possible. The investigator then calculates the proportion correct number of words (out of the 20 possible) for each subject.

Table 9.1   Types of Models

Model	Model Name
$R = \alpha + \beta X + \gamma Y$	Multiple regression (additive)
$R = \alpha + \beta X + \gamma Y + \delta XY$	Multiple regression (bilinear)
$R = \alpha + \beta X + \gamma Y + \delta Y^2$	Multiple regression (quadratic in Y)
$R = \alpha + \beta_i + \gamma_j$	Two-way ANOVA (additive)
$R = \alpha + \beta_i + \gamma_j + \delta_{ij}$	Two-way ANOVA with interaction
$R = \alpha + \beta X + \gamma_j$	One-way ANCOVA (additive)
$R = \alpha + \beta_i + \gamma_j + \delta\beta_i\gamma_j$	Tukey's one-degree-of-freedom interaction model

NOTE: The response measure is R, and the values of independent variables are labeled X and Y. The model parameters are indicated by Greek letters α, β, γ, and δ. All models listed are linear models except for the last, which is not linear because it includes the product of three parameters, $\delta\beta_i\gamma_j$.

The results of this experiment therefore consist of 100 numbers: one for each of the 100 subjects. How are these 100 numbers to be treated in order to address the original question of how memory performance is affected by presentation time? There are two steps to this data-interpretation process. The first is the specification of a mathematical model[1], within the context of which each subject's experimentally observed number results from assumed events occurring within the subject. There are an infinite number of ways to formulate such a mathematical model. The most widely used formulation, on which I focus in this chapter, is referred to as the *linear model* (LM).

The second step in data interpretation is to carry out a process by which the mathematical model, once specified, is used to answer the question at hand. Note that there are numerous possibilities for how this can be done. The process that is the most widely used is NHST.

Most readers of this chapter are probably familiar with both the LM and the process of NHST. Nonetheless, to ensure a common conceptual and notational foundation, I describe both of them briefly in the next two sections.

---

[1] I have sometimes observed that the term *mathematical model* casts fear into the hearts of many researchers. However, if it is numbers from an experiment that are to be accounted for, then the necessity of some kind of mathematical model is logically inevitable.

The Linear Model

Although central to most statistical analysis, the LM is described by surprisingly few introductory statistics books (Hays, 1973—my statistics reference of choice in this chapter—is one of them). The LM includes a variety of assumptions, the exact configuration of which depends on the nature of the experimental design. At its most general level, within the context of the LM, some response variable, R, is modeled as a linear function of various parameters, labeled α, β, γ, δ, and so on. Table 9.1 provides some examples of common LMs along with the names of these models. For comparison purposes, the last entry in Table 9.1 is an example of a nonlinear model in which one term is a product of several of the parameters. It is noteworthy, incidentally, that (unlike many social science statistics texts and statistics courses) the LM does not make a sharp distinction between ANOVA and regression. Instead, both are simply viewed as instances of the same general model.

In the simple free-recall example just described, the LM is formulated as follows.

1. The subjects in the experiment are assumed to constitute a random sample from some population to which conclusions are to apply.

2. Similarly, the words provided to each subject are assumed to be a random

sample drawn from a large population of words.

3. Across the subjects × words population there is a "grand mean," denoted μ, of the dependent variable measured in the experiment. The grand mean is a theoretical entity but can be construed roughly as the number that would result if all individuals in the target population were run in the experiment for an infinite number of times in all conditions, using in the course of this lengthy process the entire population of words, and the mean of all the resulting scores were computed.

4. Each condition j in the experiment has associated with it an effect that is referred to as α_j. Any score obtained by a subject in condition j is increased by α_j compared to the grand mean, μ. Over the population, the mean score for condition j, which is referred to as μ_j, is $\mu_j = \mu + \alpha_j$. The model defines these effects such that

$$\sum_{j=1}^{J} \alpha_j = 0$$

which means, of course, that either all the α_js are zero, or that some are positive while others are negative.

5. Associated with each subject participating in the experiment is an error term that is specific to that subject. This error term is independent of condition, and the error term for subject i in condition j is labeled e_{ij}. It is assumed that the e_{ij}s are randomly drawn from a normal distribution whose mean is zero and whose variance is σ^2, a value that is constant over conditions.[2]

---

[2]A technical point is in order here. The error term for this experiment has two components. The first is a subject component reflecting the fact that proportion correct varies among subjects. The second is a binomial component reflecting variation over the 20 words. Because the binomial variance component changes with the mean, the overall error variance cannot be assumed to be fully constant. Nonetheless, the LM formulated would still be a very useful approximation.

These assumptions imply that the X_{ij}, the score of subject i in condition j, is equal to

$$X_{ij} = \mu + \alpha_j + e_{ij}$$

which in turn implies that X_{ij}s within each condition j are distributed with a variance of σ^2.

Null Hypothesis Significance Testing

Equipped with a mathematical model, the investigator's next step in the data-analysis process is to use the model to arrive at answers to the question at hand. As noted, the most pervasive means by which this is done is via NHST, which works as follows.

1. A null hypothesis (H_0) is established. Technically, a null hypothesis is any hypothesis that specifies quantitative values for all the α_js. In practice, however, a null hypothesis almost always specifies that the independent variable has no effect on the dependent variable, which means that

$$H_0 : \alpha_1 = \alpha_2 = \cdots = \alpha_J = 0$$

or, equivalently, that,

$$H_0 : \mu_1 = \mu_2 = \cdots = \mu_J.$$

Mathematically, the null hypothesis may be viewed a single-dimensional hypothesis: The only variation permissible is the single value of the J population means.

2. An alternative hypothesis (H_1) is established that in its most general sense is "Not H_0." That is, the general alternative hypothesis states that one way or another, at least one of the J population means must differ from at least one of the others. Mathematically, such an alternative hypothesis may be viewed as a composite hypothesis, representable in J dimensions corresponding to the values of the J population means.

3. The investigator computes a single summary score, which constitutes evidence

that the null versus the alternative hypothesis is correct. Generally, the greater the value of the summary score is, the greater is the evidence that the alternative hypothesis is true. In the present example—a one-way ANOVA design—the summary score is an F-ratio that is proportional to the variance among the sample means. A small F constitutes evidence for H_0, whereas the larger F is, the greater is the evidence for H_1.

4. The sampling distribution of the summary score is determined under the assumption that H_0 is true.

5. A criterion summary score is determined such that if H_0 is correct, the obtained value of the summary score will be achieved or exceeded with some small probability referred to as α (traditionally, $\alpha = .05$).

6. The obtained value of the summary score is computed from the data.

7. If the obtained summary score equals or exceeds the criterion summary score, a decision is made to reject the null hypothesis, which is equivalent to accepting the alternative hypothesis. If the obtained summary score is less than the criterion summary score, a decision is made to fail to reject the null hypothesis.

8. By this logic, the probability of rejecting the null hypothesis given that the null hypothesis is actually true (thereby making what is known as a type I error) is equal to α. As indicated, α is set by the investigator via the investigator's choice of a suitable criterion summary score. Given that the alternative hypothesis is true, the probability of failing to reject H_0 is known as a type II error. The probability of a type II error is referred to as β. Closely related to β is $(1 - \beta)$ or *power*, which is the probability of correctly rejecting the null hypothesis given that H_1 is true. Typically, β and power cannot be easily measured, because to do so requires a specific alternative hypothesis, which typically is not available.[3]

Problems with the LM and with NHST

The LM can be used without proceeding on to NHST, and NHST can be used with models other than the LM. However, a conjunction of the LM and NHST is used in the vast majority of experiments within the social sciences as well as in other sciences, notably the medical sciences. Both the LM and NHST have shortcomings with respect to the insight into a data set that they provide. However, it is my opinion that the shortcomings of NHST are more serious than the shortcomings of the LM. In the next two subsections, I briefly describe the problems with the LM, and I then provide a somewhat lengthier discussion of the problems with NHST.

Problems with the LM

The LM is what might be termed an off-the-shelf model: That is, the LM is a plausible model that probably bears at least some approximation to reality in many situations. However, its pervasiveness often tends to blind investigators to alternative ways of representing the psychological processes that underlie the data in some experiment.

More specifically, although there are different LM equations corresponding to different experimental designs, all of them are additive with respect to the dependent variable; that is, the dependent variable is assumed to be the sum of a set of theoretical parameters (see, e.g., Table 9.1 and Equation [1]). The simplicity of this arrangement is elegant, but it deemphasizes other kinds of equations that might better elucidate the underlying psychological processes.

---

[3]More precisely, power can be represented as a function over the J-dimensional space, mentioned earlier, that corresponds to the J-dimensional alternative hypothesis.

I will illustrate this point in the context of the classic question: What is the effect of degree of original learning on subsequent forgetting, and more particularly, does forgetting *rate* depend on degree of original learning? My goal is to show how the LM leads investigators astray in their attempts to answer this question and how an alternative to the LM provides considerably more insight.

Slamecka and McElree (1983) reported a series of experiments with the goal of determining the relation between degree of original learning and forgetting rate. In their experiments, subjects studied word lists to one of two degrees of proficiency. Subjects' memory performances then were measured following forgetting intervals of 0, 1, or 5 days. Within the context of the LM, the relevant equation relating mean performance μ_{jk} to delay interval j and initial learning level k is

$$\mu_{jk} = \mu + \alpha_j + \beta_k + \gamma_{jk} \qquad (1)$$

where α_j is the effect of delay interval j (presumably, α_j monotonically decreases with increasing j), β_k is the effect of degree of learning k (presumably, β_k monotonically increases with increasing k) and γ_{jk}, a term applied to each combination of delay interval and learning level, represents the interaction between delay interval and learning level.

Within the context of the LM, two theoretical components are construed as independent if there is no interaction between them. In terms of Equation (1), degree of learning and forgetting are independent if all the γ_{ij}s are equal to zero. The critical null hypothesis tested by Slamecka and McElree (1983) was therefore that $\gamma_{ij} = 0$ for all i, j. They used their resulting failure to reject this null hypothesis as evidence for the proposition that forgetting rate is independent of degree of original learning.

This conclusion is dubious for a variety of reasons. For present purposes, I want to emphasize that Slamecka and McElree's (1983)

analysis technique (which Slamecka, 1985, vigorously defended) emerged quite naturally from the LM-based Equation (1). Because the LM is so simple and so ingrained as a basis for data analysis, it seemed, and still seems, unnatural for workers in the field to consider alternatives to the LM.

What would such an alternative look like? In the final section of this chapter, I provide some illustrations of alternatives to the LM. In the present context, I briefly discuss an alternative model within which the learning-forgetting independence issue can be investigated. This model, described by Loftus (1985a, 1985b; see also Loftus & Bamber, 1990) rests on an analogy to forgetting of radioactive decay. Consider two pieces of radioactive material, a large piece (say 9 g) and a small piece (say 5 g). Suppose that the decay rates are the same in the sense that both can be described by the equation

$$M = M_0 e^{-kd} \qquad (2)$$

where M is the remaining mass after an interval of d days, M_0 is the original mass, and k is the decay constant.[4]

Decay curves generated by Equation (2) corresponding to the two different chunks are shown in Figure 9.1, with the same decay constant, $k = 0.5$, describing the two curves. These curves could, of course, be described by the LM (Equation [1]). The γ_{jk} terms would be decidedly nonzero, reflecting the interaction that is represented in Figure 9.1 by the decreasing vertical distance between the two decay curves with increasing decay time. Thus, using the LM, and Slamecka and McElree's (1983) logic, one concludes that large-chunk decay is faster than small-chunk decay.

---

[4]This is not a technically correct description of radioactive decay, as radioactive material actually decays to some inert substance instead of to nothing, as implied by Equation (2). For the purposes of this discussion, the decaying material may be thought of as that portion of the material that actually does decay, and the logic is unaffected.

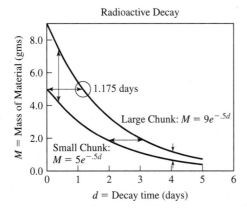

Radioactive Decay

Figure 9.1 Radioactive decay curves.
NOTE: The decay rate is the same ($k = 5$) for both the large chunk (9 units) and small chunk (5 units). Note that the vertical distance between the curves decreases over decay time, whereas the horizontal distance between the two curves is independent of amount of decay time.

This conclusion would, in a very powerful sense, be incorrect: As noted earlier, the decay curves in Figure 9.1 were generated by equations having identical decay rates ($k = 0.5$). The key to understanding this error is that independence of radioactive decay rates is not associated with lack of interaction within the context of the LM. Instead, it is associated with another kind of lack of interaction that can be intuitively understood as follows. Consider the large chunk. After some time period (which is approximately 1.175 days, as indicated in Figure 9.1), the large chunk has decayed to the point at which only 5 g remain; that is, it is physically identical to what the small chunk had been at time zero. Therefore, the large-chunk decay curve following time 1.175 days must be identical to the small-chunk decay curve following time zero; that is, the two decay curves are *horizontally parallel,* separated by a constant delay of 1.175 days. This corresponds to "no interaction" in the horizontal rather than the LM-oriented vertical sense.

The original question, "What is the effect of learning rate on memory?" can now be

addressed using the same logic and: forgetting curves resulting from different degrees of original learning must be compared horizontally rather than vertically. The finding of horizontally parallel curves implies that forgetting rate is independent of degree of original learning, whereas horizontally nonparallel curves imply that forgetting rate depends on degree of original learning.[5]

The general model to be tested, given this logic, is

$$\mu(L_1, d_j) = \mu[L_2, f(d_j)] \qquad (3)$$

where $\mu(X, d_j)$ refers to mean performance at learning level X following delay interval d_j, and $f(d_j)$ is some function of d_j. Of interest is the nature of the function f on the right side of Equation (3). Various possibilities can be considered. A finding of $f(d_j) = d_j$ would imply no effect at all of original learning on performance. A finding of $f(d_j) = d_j + c, c \neq 0$, would imply that forgetting rate is independent of degree of original learning: The curves are parallel, separated by some interval c. Finally, a finding of $f(d_j) = d_j + c + \alpha_j$, where α_j is an amount that varies with d_j, would imply that forgetting rate depends on degree of original learning: The curves are not horizontally parallel.

To summarize, the LM is widely used and probably an approximately correct description of many experimental situations. However, it is not always the best model within which an experimental situation can be described, and it is sometimes seriously misleading. It is imperative to realize that one is not bound by the LM just because it is pervasive.

---

[5] For ease of exposition, I have assumed exponential decay in this description. However, as proved by Loftus (1985b, Appendix 2), the implication of independence from horizontally parallel curves does not require the assumption of exponential decay.

Problems with Null Hypothesis Significance Testing

Upon stepping down as editor of the *Journal of Experimental Psychology,* Arthur Melton published a highly influential editorial (Melton, 1962). In this editorial Melton emphasized that the criteria used by his journal for accepting manuscripts revolved heavily around NHST, pointing out that (a) articles in which the null hypothesis was not rejected were almost never published and (b) rejection at the .05 significance level was rarely adequate for acceptance; rather, rejection at the .01 level was typically required.

This is a remarkable position. Essentially, it places the process of NHST at the heart not only of data analysis but also of personal scientific advancement: If you do not reject null hypotheses, you do not publish. It is little wonder that NHST is so pervasive in psychology.

Over the past half-century, periodic articles have questioned the value of NHST.[6] Until recently, these articles seem to have had little effect on the means by which data analysis has been carried out. Over the past 10 years, however, there has at least been some recognition of the issues raised by these articles; this recognition has resulted in APA and APS task forces and symposia on the topic, editorials explicitly questioning the use of NHST (e.g., Loftus, 1993b), and occasional calls for the banning of NHST (with which I do not agree), along with a small but still dimly perceptible shift away from exclusive reliance on NHST

---

[6]A sample of these writings is, in chronological order, Tyler (1935); Jones (1955); Nunnally (1960); Rozebloom (1960); Grant (1962); Bakan (1966); Meehl (1967); Lykken (1968); Carver (1978); Meehl (1978); Berger and Berry (1988); Hunter and Schmidt (1990); Gigerenzer et al. (1989); Rosnow and Rosenthal (1989); Cohen (1990); Meehl (1990); Loftus (1991, 1993b); Carver (1993); Cohen (1994); Loftus and Masson (1994); Maltz (1994); Loftus (1995, 1996); Schmidt (1996); and Harlow, Mulaik, and Steiger (1997).

as a means of interpreting and understanding data.

As I suggested earlier in this chapter, problems with the LM pale in comparison to problems with NHST. These problems have been reviewed in the books and articles cited in note 3, and it is not my goal here to provide a detailed rehash of them. Instead, I sketch them here briefly; the reader is referred to the cited articles for more detailed information. I should note, in the interests of full disclosure, that a number of well-reasoned arguments have been made in favor at assigning NHST at least a minor supporting role in the data-comprehension drama. The reader is directed to Abelson (1995) and Krantz (1999) for the best of such arguments.

The major difficulties with NHST are the following.

Information Loss as a Result of Binary Decision Processes. A data set is often quite rich. As a typical example, a 3×5 factorial design contains 15 conditions and hence 15 sample means to be accounted for (ignoring per the LM, of course, the raw data from within each condition along with less favored statistics such as the variance, the kurtosis, etc.). However, a standard ANOVA reduces this data set to three bits of information: Rejection or failure to reject the null hypotheses corresponding to the effects of Factor 1, Factor 2, and the interaction. Granted, one can carry out additional post hoc tests or simple-effects tests, but the end result is still that the complex data set is understood, via the NHST process, only in terms of a series of binary decisions rather than as a unified pattern. This is a poor basis for acquiring the kind of gestalt that is necessary for insight and gut-level understanding of a data set.

The Implausibility of the Null Hypothesis. Consider the hypothetical experiment described at the beginning of this chapter.

There were five conditions, involving five exposure durations in a free-recall experiment. In a standard ANOVA, the null hypothesis would be

$$\mu_1 = \mu_2 = \mu_3 = \mu_4 = \mu_5 \qquad (4)$$

where the μ_js refer to the population means of the five conditions. Note here that =s in Equation (4) must be taken seriously: Equal means *equal* to an infinite number of decimal places. If the null hypothesis is fudged to specify that "the population means are about equal" then the logic of NHST collapses, or at least must be supplemented to include a precise definition of what "about equal" means.

As has been argued by many, a null hypothesis of the sort described by Equation (4) cannot literally be true. Meehl (1967) makes the argument most eloquently, stating,

> Considering ... that everything in the brain is connected with everything else, and that there exist several "general state-variables" (such as arousal, attention, anxiety and the like) which are known to be at least *slightly* influenceable by practically any kind of stimulus input, it is highly unlikely that *any* psychologically discriminable situation which we apply to an experimental subject would exert literally *zero* effect on any aspect of performance. Alternatively, the μ_js can be viewed as measurable values on the real-number line. Any two of them being identical implies that their difference (also a measurable value on the real-number line) is exactly zero—which has a probability of zero.[7] (p. 104)

---

[7] A caveat is in order here. Most null hypotheses are of the sort described by Equation (4); that is, they are *quantitative,* specifying a particular set of relations among a set of population parameters. It is possible, in contrast, for a null hypothesis to be *qualitative* (see, e.g., Frick, 1995, for a discussion of this topic). An example of such a hypothesis, described by Greenwald et al., 1996, is that the defendant in a murder case is actually the murderer. This null hypothesis could certainly be true; however, the kind of qualitative null hypothesis that it illustrates constitutes the exception rather than the rule.

And therein lies a serious problem: It is meaningless to reject a null hypothesis that is impossible to begin with. An analogy makes this clear: Suppose an astronomer were to announce, "Given our data, we have rejected the null hypothesis that Saturn is made of green cheese." Although it is unlikely that this conclusion would be challenged, a consensus would doubtless emerge that the astronomer must have been off his rocker for even considering such a null hypothesis to begin with. Strangely, psychologists who make equally meaningless statements on a routine basis continue to be regarded as entirely sane. (Even stranger is the common belief that an α-level of .05 implies that an error is made in 5% of all experiments in which the null hypothesis is rejected. This is analogous to saying that, of all planets reported not to be made of green cheese, 5% of them actually *are* made of green cheese.)

Decision Asymmetry.   Putting aside for the moment the usual impossibility of the null hypothesis, there is a decided imbalance between the two types of errors that can be made in a hypothesis-testing situation. The probability of a type I error, α, can be, and is, set by appropriate selection of a summary-score criterion. However, the probability of a type II error, β, is, as noted earlier, generally unknowable because of the lack of a quantitative alternative hypothesis. The consequence of this situation is that rejecting the null hypothesis is a "real" decision, whereas failing to reject the null hypothesis is, as the phrase suggests, a nondecision: It is simply an admission that the data do not provide sufficient information to support a clear decision.

Accepting H_0.   The teaching of statistics generally emphasizes that "we fail to reject the null hypothesis" does not mean the same thing as "we accept the null hypothesis." Nonetheless, the temptation to accept the null hypothesis (usually implicitly so as not to disobey the rules brazenly) often seems to be overwhelming, particularly when an investigator has an investment in such acceptance. As I noted in the previous section, accepting a typical null hypothesis involves faulty reasoning anyway because a typical null hypothesis is impossible. However, particularly in practically oriented situations, an investigator is justified in accepting the null hypothesis "for all intents and purposes" if the investigator has convincingly shown that there is adequate statistical power (see Cohen, 1990, 1994). Such a power analysis is most easily carried out by computing some kind of confidence interval (described in detail later) that would allow a meaningful conclusion such as "the population mean difference between Conditions 1 and 2 is, with 95% confidence, between $\pm\varepsilon$," where ε is a sufficiently small number that the actual difference between Conditions 1 and 2 is inconsequential from a practical perspective.

The Misleading Dichotomization of "$p < .05$" vs. "$p > .05$" Results.   As indicated in his 1962 editorial, summarized earlier, Melton considered an observed p value of .05 to be maximal for acceptance of an article. Almost four decades later, more or less this same convention holds sway: Who among us researchers has not observed the heartrending spectacle of a student or colleague struggling to somehow transform a vexing 0.051 into an acceptable 0.050?

This is bizarre. The actual difference between a data set that produces a p value of 0.051 versus one that produces a p value of 0.050 is, of course, miniscule. Logically, very similar conclusions should issue from both data sets, yet they do not: The .050 data set produces a "reject the null hypothesis" conclusion, whereas the .051 data set produces a "fail to reject the null hypothesis" conclusion. This is akin to a chaotic situation in which small initial differences distinguishing

two situations lead to vast and unpredictable eventual differences between the situations.

The most obvious consequence of this situation is that the lucky recipient of the .050 data set gets to publish, whereas his unlucky .051 colleague does not. There is another consequence, however, which is more subtle but probably more insidious: The reject/fail-to-reject dichotomy keeps the field awash in confusion and artificial controversy. This is because investigators, like most humans, are loath to make and stick to conclusions that are both weak and complicated (e.g., "we fail to reject the null hypothesis"). Instead, investigators are prone to (often unwittingly) transform the conclusion into the stronger and simpler, "we accept the null hypothesis." Thus, two similar experiments—one in which the null hypothesis is rejected and one in which the null hypothesis is not rejected—can and often do lead to seemingly contradictory conclusions—"the null hypothesis is true" versus "the null hypothesis is false." The inevitable head scratching and subsequent flood of "critical experiments" that are generated by such "failures to replicate" may well constitute the single largest source of wasted time in the practice of psychology.

The Counternull.   Rosenthal and DiMatteo (Chap. 10, this volume) have suggested a simple score, called the counternull, that serves to underscore the difficulty in accepting H_0. The counternull revolves around an increasingly common measure called "effect size," which, essentially, is the mean magnitude of some effect (e.g., the mean difference between two conditions) divided by the standard deviation (generally pooled over the conditions). Obviously, all else equal, the smaller the effect size, the less inclined one is to reject H_0. Suppose, to illustrate, that in some experiment one found an effect size of 0.20, which was insufficiently large to reject H_0. As noted earlier, the temptation is often overwhelming to accept H_0 in such a situation because the world seems so much clearer that way. It is therefore useful to report Rosenthal and DiMatteo's counternull, which is simply twice the effect size, or 0.40 in this example. It is sobering to realize that the data permit a reality corresponding to the counternull (0.40) just as much as they permit a reality corresponding to H_0 (an effect size of zero). The use of the counternull also subtly underscores a fact that is almost invisible in an NHST framework, specifically that the best estimate of some population parameter is the corresponding statistic that is measured in the experiment. Thus, in this example the best estimate of the population effect size is exactly what was measured (0.20) rather than the zero value toward which the investigator is drawn in an hypothesis-testing framework.

The p (data | H_0) versus p (H_0 | data) Confusion. In the previous section I discussed the critical consequences of having a data set that produces $p = .050$ versus one that produces $p = .051$. To what, exactly, do these p values refer?

To address this question I again set aside the awkward fact of the null hypothesis's usual impossibility and suppose that the null hypothesis actually has a reasonable possibility of being true. It is taught in every statistics class that a p value less than .05 means that

$$p = p(\text{data} \mid H_0) < .05. \quad (5)$$

So what does one do with a sufficiently small p value? Reject the null hypothesis. What does it mean to reject the null hypothesis? In everyday language, to reject the null hypothesis in light of the data means pretty unequivocally that given the data, the probability of the null hypothesis is so low that it should be rejected, that is,

$$p(H_0 \mid \text{data}) \text{ is small.} \quad (6)$$

Thus, it should come as no surprise that the

sacred .05 is often incorrectly associated with the conditional probability of Equation (6) rather than correctly associated with the opposite conditional probability of Equation (5).

Now indeed, if $p(\text{data} \mid H_0) < .05$, then it is likely that $p(H_0 \mid \text{data})$ is also smallish: After all, because

$$p(H_0 \mid \text{data}) = \frac{p(H_0 \cap \text{data})}{p(\text{data})}$$

and

$$p(\text{data} \mid H_0) = \frac{p(H_0 \cap \text{data})}{p(H_0)}$$

the two conditional probabilities share the same numerator and are therefore somewhat related to one another. However, the probability that the investigator is primarily interested in—$p(H_0 \mid \text{data})$—is not known to any degree of precision. It is therefore breathtakingly silly to place such vast emphasis on the exact value of $p(\text{data} \mid H_0)$ when this probability is only indirectly interesting to begin with.

SUGGESTED DATA-ANALYSIS TECHNIQUES

I now turn to a description of six data-analysis techniques that are considerably more useful than is strict adherence to NHST in their ability to illuminate a data set's meaning and to answer whatever question originally prompted the experiment. The first two of these—the use of pictorial representations and the use of confidence intervals—are not novel; they are just not widely used, or at least are not widely used to the best advantage. The third and fourth techniques—use of planned comparisons and other means of accounting for different sources of variance—are also not novel, but are hardly ever used. The fifth—use of mathematical process models—has an honorable tradition in the area of mathematical psychology, but is still not pervasive. The final set of techniques, which I have termed

Table 9.2   Data (proportion correct) for an Experiment in Which Stimuli Are Presented at One of Six Durations and One of Three Contrast Levels

Duration (ms)	Contrast		
	0.05	0.10	0.20
10	0.069	0.134	0.250
20	0.081	0.267	0.375
40	0.230	0.466	0.741
80	0.324	0.610	0.872
160	0.481	0.768	0.898
320	0.574	0.799	0.900

equivalence techniques, are standard in vision science but are almost never used in other areas of psychology.

Pictorial Representations

If the results of an experiment consist of more than two numbers, then providing some form of pictorial representation of them is enormously useful in providing a reader with an overall, gestalt image of what the data are all about. (This seems so obvious that it is hardly worth saying, but the obviousness of the concept does not always translate into the concomitantly obvious behavior.)

To illustrate, Table 9.2 and Figure 9.2 show the same data set (response probabili-

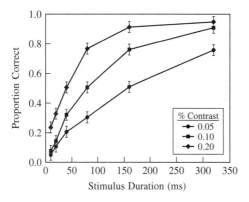

Figure 9.2   Hypothetical data from a 5 (stimulus exposure duration) × 3 (stimulus contrast level) experiment.
NOTE: The dependent variable is proportion correct recall. Error bars represent standard errors.

ties from a hypothetical experiment in which digit strings are presented for varying durations and contrasts) as a table and as a figure. It is obvious that the table can only be understood (and not very well understood at that) via a lengthy serial inspection of the numbers within it. In contrast, a mere glance at the corresponding figure renders entirely clear what is going on.

Graphs versus Tables

Despite the obvious and dominating expositional advantage of figures over tables, data continue to be presented as tables at least as often as figures, or possibly more often. For most of psychology's history, the reason for this curious practice appeared to be founded in a prosaic matter of convenience: Although it was relatively easy to construct a table of numbers on a typewriter, constructing a decent figure was a laborious undertaking. You drew a draft of the figure on graph paper, took the draft to an artist who invariably seemed to reside on the other side of the campus, following which you waited a week for the artist to produce a semi-finished version. Then you made whatever changes in the artist's rendering seemed appropriate. Then, you repeatedly iterated through this dreary process until the figure was eventually satisfactory. Finally, adding insult to injury, you had to take the finished drawing somewhere else to have its picture taken before the publisher would take it. Who needed that kind of hassle?

Today, obviously, things are much different, as electronic means of producing figures abound. To obtain information about popular graphing techniques, I conducted an informal survey in which I e-mailed to all researchers in my e-mail address book a request that they tell me what graphing techniques they use. The 161 respondents used a total of 229 techniques, and the summarized results are provided in Table 9.3.

Table 9.3 Techniques for Plotting Data, as Revealed by an Informal Survey

Application Name	Frequency
Microsoft Excel	55
CricketGraph	27
SigmaPlot	22
KaleidaGraph	17
SPSS	16
MATLAB	15
PowerPoint	10
DeltaGraph	9
S-plus	7
Mathematica	5
Microsoft Office	5
Systat	5
Igor/Igor Pro	4
Statistica	4
Gnuplot	3
Canvas	2
Hand plotting	2
StatView	3
ABC Graphics	1
Autocad	1
Axum	1
c graph-pac	1
ClarisDraw	1
Grapher	1
Graphpad	1
Illustrator	1
JMP	1
MacDraw	1
Maple 2D	1
Origin	1
PsiPlot	1
Quattro Pro	1
R	1
SciPlot	1
Smartdraw	1
TK solver	1

The results of this survey can be summarized as follows. Fewer than 25% of the application programs mentioned were statistical packages, perhaps because the most commonly used packages do not provide very flexible graphing options. Over a third of the applications were specialized drawing programs (CricketGraph, SigmaPlot, and KaleidaGraph were the most popular, but many others were mentioned). About 10% of the applications were general-purpose presentation programs (PowerPoint was the most popular) and the final one third was general-purpose analysis programs, with Microsoft Excel accounting for the majority of these instances. Excel was by far the single leading application used for graphing. Seven respondents reported never graphing data, and 13 reported assigning the task to someone else. Two people reported still drawing graphs by hand. The remaining 139 respondents used some form of electronic graphing techniques.

At the present time, a brief description of graphing programs is supplied by Denis Pelli (personal communication) and can be found at http://vision.nyu.edu/Tips/RecSoftware.html.

Graph-Making Transgressions

I have tried to present a fairly bright picture of the ease of creating high-quality graphs. There is, however, a dark side of this process: A graph creator has the capability of going wild with graphical features, thereby producing a graph that is difficult or impossible to interpret. For example David Krantz (personal communication on September 8, 2000) has noted that, for example, graph makers often attempt to pack too much information into a graph, that they produce graphs that are difficult to interpret without intense serial processing, that they produce unintended and distracting emergent perceptual features, or that they simply omit key information either in the graph itself or in the graph's legend. There are, of course, many other such transgressions, treatments of which are found in the references provided in the next section. (My own personal bête noire is the three-dimensional bar graph.)

Other Graphical Representations

A discussion of graphs is limited in the sense that there are myriad means of visually presenting the results of a data set. It is beyond the scope of this chapter to describe all of them.

For initial pointers to a set of sophisticated and elegant graphical procedures, the reader is directed to excellent discussions and examples in Tufte (1983, 1990), Tukey (1977), and Wainer and Thissen (1993). The main point I want to make is that pictorial representations almost always excel over their verbal counterparts as an efficient way of conveying the meaning of a data set.

The Use of Confidence Intervals

Earlier, I described the LM as the standard model for linking a data set to the answer to the scientific question at hand. Somewhere in a LM equation (e.g., Equation [1]) are always one or more error terms that represent the uncertainty in the world.

Using the LM to answer scientific questions is a two-stage process. The first stage is to determine knowledge of relevant population parameters given measured sample statistics along with the inevitable statistical noise. The second stage is to use whatever knowledge emerges about population parameters to answer the question at hand as best as possible.

It seems almost self evident that the second stage—deciding the implications of the pattern of population parameters for the answer to the question at hand—should be the investigator's fundamental goal. In contrast, the typical routine of statistical analysis—carrying out some procedure designed to cope with the noise-limited relation between the sample statistics and the corresponding population parameters—should be viewed as a necessary but boring nuisance. If the real world suddenly transformed into an ideal world in which experiments produced no statistical noise, there would be cause for rejoicing among investigators, as a major barrier to data interpretation would be absent.

Two basic procedures help to cope with statistical noise in the quest of determining the relations between a set of sample statistics and their population counterparts. The first procedure entails attempting to determine what the pattern of population parameters *is not*— that is, trying to reject a null hypothesis of some specific, usually uninteresting, pattern of population parameters, via NHST. The second procedure entails attempting to determine what the pattern of population parameters *is,* using the pattern of sample statistics as an estimate of the corresponding pattern of population parameters, along with error bars to represent the degree of conclusion-obscuring statistical noise. It is my (strong) opinion that trying to determine what something is generally more illuminating than trying to determine what it is not.

The use of error bars (e.g., in the form of 95% confidence intervals) around plotted sample statistics (usually sample means) is an ideal way of presenting data in such a way that the results of both these two data-analysis and data-interpretation stages are represented and that their relative importance is depicted. Consider a plot such as that shown in Figure 9.2. The pattern of sample means represents the best estimate of the corresponding pattern of population means. This pattern is fundamental to understanding how perception is influenced by contrast and duration, and this pattern is most obvious and fundamental in the graph. Furthermore, the confidence intervals provide a quantitative visual representation of the faith that should be placed in the pattern of sample means as an estimate of the corresponding pattern of population means. Smaller confidence intervals, of course, mean a better estimate: In the extreme, if the confidence intervals were of zero length, it would be clear that error was irrelevant and that the investigator could spend all of his or her energy on the fundamental task of figuring out the implications of the pattern of population means for answering the questions at hand.

The Interpretation of a Confidence Interval

The technically correct interpretation of a confidence interval is this: Suppose that many random samples of size n are drawn from some population. The sample mean, M, is computed for each sample, and a confidence interval—suppose, for simplicity of exposition, a 95% confidence interval—is drawn around each mean. Approximately 95% of these confidence intervals will include μ, the population mean.

Returning now to planet Earth, what does this logic imply in the typical case in which a single mean is computed from a single sample, and a single confidence interval is plotted around that sample mean? If the confidence interval were the only information available to the investigator, then the investigator would conclude that, with 95% probability, this confidence interval is one of the 95% of all possible confidence intervals that include μ; that is, the investigator can draw the simple conclusion that with 95% probability the confidence interval includes μ.

However, the caveat must be issued that sometimes an investigator *does* have additional information available (such information is, for instance, the basis for doing a one-tailed rather than a two-tailed test). In this case, the investigator's subjective probability that the confidence interval contains a population parameter may be influenced by this additional information as well as by the confidence interval itself. For instance, an investigator examining a 95% confidence interval constructed around a particular sample mean may, based on such other information, doubt that it does in fact contain μ. Whether an investigator chooses to quantify such beliefs using probabilities, it is sometimes misleading to state unequivocally, after examining the data, that the particular interval has a 95% probability of including μ.

Despite this caveat, however, construal of an x% confidence interval as including the population parameter with x% probability is generally a reasonable rule of thumb (as distinguished from something like, "since $p < .05$, H_0 is likewise true with a probability of less than about .05," which is definitely *not* a reasonable rule of thumb).

Confidence Intervals around Linear Combinations of Variables

For many of the examples to follow, the reader must keep in mind the relation between a confidence interval around a single mean and a confidence interval around a linear combination of means. In particular, suppose an experiment results in a series of means, $M_1, M_2, \ldots, M_J$. If the confidence interval around any of the M_js has a length of X, then the confidence interval around any linear combination of the means, $k_1 M_1 + k_2 M_2, \ldots, + k_J M_J$, has a length of

$$X \sqrt{k_1^2 + k_2^2 + \cdots + k_J^2}. \qquad (7)$$

The most frequent use of the property described by Equation (7) is when a confidence interval around a difference score, $(M_1 - M_2)$ is desired. In this situation, $k_1 = 1, k_2 = -1$, and the difference-score confidence interval is therefore the individual-mean confidence interval multiplied by $\sqrt{2}$. Some additional implications of this fact will be provided later in this chapter.

Confidence Intervals and Statistical Power

Within the context of NHST, the definition of power is simple: As indicated earlier, it is the probability of correctly rejecting the null hypothesis given that the null hypothesis is false. However (despite frequent requests on the part of journal editors) explicit power analyses rarely make their way into journal pages. The reasons for this deficit appear to be twofold. First, to compute an exact value of power requires a quantitative alternative hypothesis which is almost never available. Second, the concept of power, while seemingly straightforward is, as anyone who has tried to teach it well knows, almost impossible to get across to anyone who hasn't somehow figured it out already. Many educators and authors give up on the topic; for instance, in his widely read *Fundamental Statistics in Psychology and Education,* Guilford (1942) declared power to be "too complicated to discuss."

As has been frequently noted, the issue of power is particularly important if a scientific conclusion entails the acceptance of some null hypothesis. In such a situation, it is incumbent on the investigator to convince his or her audience that the power of the relevant statistical test is high. How should this be done?

Because there is indeed a profound dearth of quantitative alternative hypotheses in the social sciences, a single value of power typically cannot be computed. Therefore, some more general representation of power must be concocted for a particular experiment. One such representation that is occasionally suggested involves the use of power curves (e.g., Hays, 1973; p. 359) whereby power is plotted as a function of the value of the alternative hypothesis.

Another way of representing power is via the magnitude of confidence intervals. The rule here is simple: The greater the statistical power, the smaller are the confidence intervals. To illustrate, imagine a hypothetical experiment in which a clinical researcher is investigating the relative effectiveness of two methods, Method A and Method B, of reducing anxiety. Two groups of high-anxiety subjects participate in the experiment, one receiving Method A and the other receiving Method B. Following their treatment, subjects rate their anxiety on a 7-point scale. Suppose that the experiment results in a small, not statistically significant difference between the two methods. In what follows, I will demon-

strate two techniques of presenting the results for two hypothetical cases: a low-power case involving n subjects, and a high-power case involving $100n$ subjects.

The first analysis technique incorporates standard NHST, along with a formal power analysis. Figure 9.3 shows the graphical results of this kind of analysis for the low-power case (left panels) and the high-power case (right panels). The top panels show bar graphs depicting the main experimental results, and the bottom panels show power curves that depict power as a function of the difference between two population means according to a continuous succession of alternative hypotheses. Power is represented by the slope of the power curves. As illustrated by the arrows, the low-power curve achieves a power of 0.90 when the alternative hypothesis is that the population means differ by about 3.0, and the high-power curve achieves 0.90 when the alternative hypothesis is that the population means differ by about 0.3.

Figure 9.4 shows a different way of representing this power information for the same low-power case (left panel) and high-power case (right panel). Figure 9.4 again shows the bar graph, but here the bars are accompanied by 95% confidence intervals around the means that they depict. The free-floating error bars show the magnitude of the 95% confidence interval around the population mean differences in each of the panels. Here, power is represented quite simply by the size of the confidence intervals, which are large in the left (low-power) graph, but small in the right (high-power) graph.

In short, Figures 9.3 and 9.4 show the same information. However, Figure 9.4 presents the information in a much simpler and more intuitive manner than does Figure 9.3. Figure 9.4 makes it immediately and visually clear how seriously the sample means and the sample mean differences are to be taken as estimates of the corresponding population means; this, in turn, provides critical infor-

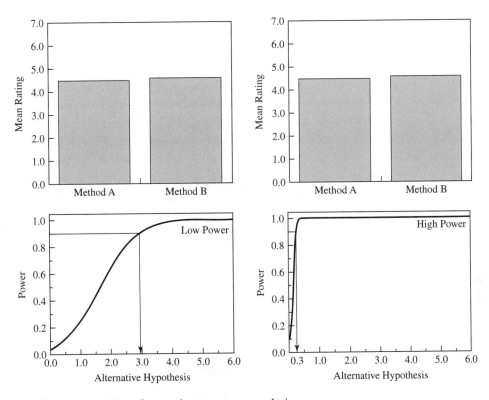

Figure 9.3 One technique for carrying out a power analysis.
NOTE: A low-power situation is in the left panels, and a high-power situation is in the right panels. The top panels show the data, and the bottom panels show power curves.

mation about how "nonsignificance" should be treated. The left panel of Figure 9.4 leaves no doubt that failure to reject the null hypothesis is a nonconclusion—that there is not sufficient statistical power to make any conclu-

sions at all about the relative magnitudes of the two population means. The right panel, in contrast, makes it evident that something very close to the null hypothesis is actually true—that the true difference between the population

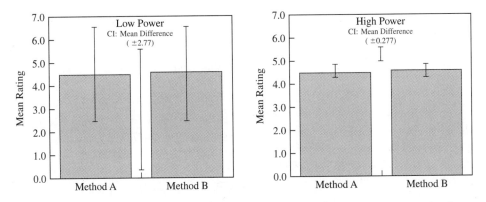

Figure 9.4 A second technique for carrying out a power analysis in the anxiety treatment method experiment.
NOTE: Smaller confidence intervals reflect greater power.

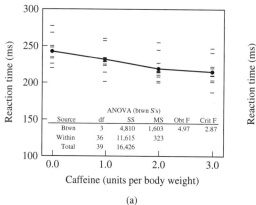
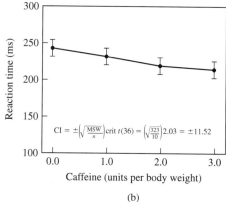

Figure 9.5   Data from a hypothetical experiment in which reaction time is measured as a function of caffeine consumption in a between-subjects design.
NOTE: The right panel shows the mean data with each mean surrounded by individual-subject data points. The right panel shows 95% confidence intervals around the sample means.

means is, with 95% confidence, restricted to a range of 0.277, which is very small in the grand scheme of things.

Confidence Intervals or Standard Errors?

Thus far I have been using 95% confidence intervals in my examples. This is one of the two standard configurations for error bars, the other being a standard error, which is approximately a 67% confidence interval.[8] In the interests of standardization, one of these configurations or the other should be used unless there is some compelling reason for some other configuration.

I suggest, in particular, being visually conservative, which means deliberately stacking the deck against concluding whatever one wishes to conclude. This means that one should use 95% confidence intervals, which have a greater effect of suggesting no difference, when the interest is in rejecting some null hypothesis. Conversely, one should use standard errors, which have a greater effect of suggesting a difference, when the interest is in confirming some null hypothesis (e.g., as

when comparing observed to predicted data points in a model fit).

Different Kinds of Confidence Intervals

The interpretation of a confidence interval is somewhat different depending on whether it is used in a between-subjects or in a single-factor within-subjects (i.e., repeated-measures) design, a multifactor within-subjects design, or a mixed design (some factors between, other factors within). These differences are discussed in detail by Loftus and Masson (1994). The general idea is as follows.

Between-Subjects Designs. A confidence interval is designed to isolate a population parameter, most typically a population mean, to within a particular range. A between-subjects design constitutes the usual venue in which a confidence interval has been used in psychology, to the extent that confidence intervals have been used at all. Consider as an example a simple one-way ANOVA experiment in which the investigator is interested in the effects of caffeine on reaction time (RT). Four conditions are defined by four levels of caffeine: 0, 1, 2, or 3 caffeine units per unit body weight. Suppose that $n = 10$ subjects are ran-

---

[8]The exact coverage of a standard error depends, of course, on the number of degrees of freedom going into the error term.

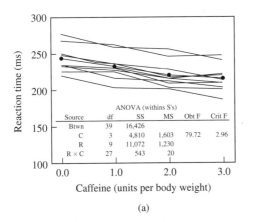
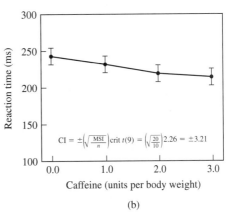

(a)   (b)

Figure 9.6   Data from a hypothetical experiment in which reaction time is measured as a function of caffeine consumption in a within-subjects design.
NOTE: All 40 data points are the same as those shown in Figure 9.5. The left panel shows the mean data (heavy line) along with individual-subject data points (light lines). The right panel shows 95% "within-subject" confidence intervals around the sample means that are based on the subject × interaction variance.

domly assigned to, and participate in, each of the four conditions. The outcome of the experiment is as represented in Figure 9.5a, which shows the mean data (solid line) along with dashes surrounding each mean that represent the 10 individual data points within each condition. The results of an ANOVA are shown at the bottom left of the panel and are straightforward. Note that the total sum of squares, which, of course, reflects the total variability of all 40 scores in the experiment is 16,426, and the 39 total degrees of freedom are divided into 3 (between, i.e., caffeine) and 36 (error, i.e., within). (These factoids will become relevant in the next section.)

Computing a confidence interval in such a design is entirely straightforward and is obtained by the equation at the bottom of Figure 9.5b:

$$CI = \pm \left(\sqrt{\frac{MS(Within)}{n}} \right) crit\, t\,(dfW)\quad (8)$$

using the MS (Within) from the ANOVA table in Figure 9.5a. The error term going into the confidence interval is the same as in the ANOVA—MS (Within)—and the criterion t

is based on dfW, which is 36 in this example. The resulting 95% confidence interval is ±11.52.

Single-Factor within Subjects Designs. I now treat the exact same data that I just described as having come from a within-subjects design. That is, I treat the data assuming that each of a total of $n = 10$ subjects had participated, at one time or another, in each of the 4 conditions. It is now possible to draw a curve relating RT to caffeine for each of the 10 subjects. These curves, along with the same mean curve from Figure 9.5, are shown in Figure 9.6a. At the bottom of Figure 9.6a is the within-subjects ANOVA. Note that the 16,426 total sum of squares (now referred to as "between cells") is divided into caffeine conditions (as with the between-subjects design, equal to 4,810, and based on 3 degrees of freedom), subjects (based on 9 degrees of freedom) and the subject × caffeine interaction (based on 27 degrees of freedom). The relative consistency of the caffeine effect across the different subjects is represented graphically by the relative parallelness of the individual subject curves and is represented within the

ANOVA by the relatively small interaction (i.e., error) term of MS (Interaction) = 20. The F ratio of 79.72 is considerably greater in this design than it was in the between-subjects design (where $F = 4.97$). The reason for this is that a large portion of the error variance—the between-subjects variability reflected by SS (Subjects) = 11,072—is irrelevant in this within-subjects design, whereas this very same variability formed part of the error term—was part of SS (Within)—in the between-subjects design.

How should a confidence interval be constructed in this kind of within-subjects design? Technically, as described earlier, a confidence interval is designed to isolate a population mean with some degree of probability. In this within-subjects design, the uncertainty of any condition population mean is based on exactly the same uncertainty as it was in the between-subjects design. More specifically, in the between-subjects design this uncertainty was referred to as "within-condition variance," and in that example it was SS (Within), based on 36 degrees of freedom. In this within-subjects design, the location of a condition mean is uncertain because of both variability due to subjects, SS (Subjects) = 11,072 based on 9 degrees of freedom, and variability due to the subject by condition interaction, SS (Interaction) = 543, based on the remaining 27 degrees of freedom. The combined error variance SS (Subjects plus Interaction) is therefore 11,615, based on 36 degrees of freedom, just as it was in the between-subjects design, and the confidence interval of 11.52 is therefore identical also.

Intuitively this seems wrong. Just as the within-subjects design includes a great deal more sensitivity, as reflected in the substantially greater F ratio in the ANOVA, so it seems that the greater sensitivity should also be reflected in a smaller confidence interval. What is going on?

To answer this question, it is necessary to consider not what a confidence interval is

technically used to accomplish, but what a confidence interval is actually used to accomplish. An investigator is usually interested not in absolute values of population means, but in *patterns* of population means. So, for instance, in the data in Figures 9.5 and 9.6, the mean RT declines from approximately 240 ms to 215 ms across the caffeine conditions. However, it is not the exact means that are important for determining caffeine's effect on RT; rather, it is the decrease, or perhaps the form of mathematical function describing the decrease, that is of interest.[9]

This observation has an important implication for the interpretation of confidence intervals: Confidence intervals are rarely used in their "official" role of isolating population means. Instead, they are generally used as a visual aid to judge the reliability of a *pattern* of sample means as an estimate of the corresponding pattern of population means. In the between-subjects data in Figure 9.5, for instance, the confidence intervals indicate that a hypothesis of monotonically decreasing population-mean RTs with increased caffeine is reasonable.

How does this logic relate to within-subjects designs? The answer, detailed by Loftus and Masson (1994), is that a confidence interval based on the interaction variance is appropriate for the goal of judging the reliability of a pattern of sample means as an estimate of the corresponding pattern of population means; thus, the within-subjects confidence interval equation is

$$CI = \pm \left(\sqrt{\frac{MS(Interaction)}{n}} \right) crit\, t\, (dfI)$$

(9)

where n again represents the number of observations on which each mean is based ($n = 10$

[9]I should note that this is not always true. Sometimes an investigator *is* interested in isolating some population mean. An obvious example would be when the investigator wishes to determine whether performance in some condition is at a chance value.

in this example). Using Equation (9) (see Figure 9.6b), the confidence intervals in Figure 9.6a were computed using the MS (Interaction) shown in the ANOVA table within Figure 9.6a. The resulting confidence interval is ± 3.21. This value is, of course, considerably smaller than the between-subjects counterpart of 11.52 shown in Figure 9.5. It bears emphasis, however, that this apparent increase in power occurs because information is lost: In particular, the confidence intervals no longer isolate absolute values of population means; rather, they are appropriate only for assessing the reliability of the pattern of sample means as an estimate of the underlying pattern of population means. That is, they serve the same function as they do in the between-subjects ANOVA.

Multifactor Within-Subjects Designs. In a pure between-subjects design, there is only one error term, MS (Within), regardless of the number of factors in the design. Therefore, assuming homogeneity of variance, a single confidence interval, computed by Equation (8) or Equation (9), is always appropriate.

In a multifactor within-subjects design, the situation is more complicated in that there are multiple error terms, corresponding to multiple subject-by-something interactions. For instance, in a two-factor within-subjects design, there are three error terms: one corresponding to Factor A, one corresponding to Factor B, and one corresponding to the (A × B) interaction. These error terms are summarized in Table 9.4 for a standard two-factor, within-subjects design.[10] This raises the problem of how to compute confidence intervals, as it

Table 9.4   ANOVA Table for a Two-Factor, Within-Subjects Design

Source	Degrees of Freedom	Error Term
Factor A(A)	df(A)	MS(A × S)
Factor B(B)	df(B)	MS(B × S)
Inter. (A × B)	df(A × B)	MS(A × B × S)
Subjects (S)	df(S)	
A × S	df(A) × df(S)	
B × S	df(B) × df(S)	
(A × B) × S	df(A) × df(B) × df(S)	

would appear that there are as many possible confidence intervals as there are error terms. Which confidence intervals are appropriate to display?

Often, the answer to this question is simple, because in many such two-factor designs—and in many multifactor within-subjects designs in general—the error terms are all roughly equal (i.e., they differ by no more than a factor of around 2:1). In such instances, it is reasonable simply to pool error terms, that is, to compute an overall error term by dividing the sum of the sum of squares (error) by the total degrees of freedom (error) to arrive at a single "subject × condition" interaction, where a "condition" is construed as single combination of the various factors (e.g., a 5 × 3 subjects design would have 15 separate conditions). This single error term can then be entered into Equation (9) to compute a single interaction. Here, dfI refers to degrees of freedom in the total interaction between subjects and conditions. So, for instance, in a 5 (Factor A) × 3 (Factor B) × 20 (subjects) design, dfI would be $(15 - 1) \times (20 - 1) = 266$. As before, n in Equation (9) refers to the number of observations on which each mean is based: 20 in this example.

Of course, nature is not always this kind, and the investigator sometimes finds that the various error terms have widely varying values. In this situation, the investigator is in a position of having to provide a more complex representation of confidence intervals, and the situation becomes akin to that described in the next section, where a mixed design is used.

---

[10]With more than two factors, the same general arguments hold, but they are simply more complex because there are yet more error terms. For example in a three-factor, within-subjects design, there are three main-effect error terms, three two-way interaction error terms, and one three-way interaction error term, or seven error terms in all.

Mixed Designs. A mixed design is one in which some of the factors are between subjects and other factors are within subjects. For simplicity, I describe the simplest such design: a two-factor design with one between-subjects factor and one within-subjects factor (see also Loftus & Masson, 1994, pp. 484–486).

Imagine the caffeine experiment described earlier except that two different subject populations are investigated: young adults (in their 20s) and older adults (in their 70s). Thus, there are two variables, one of which (caffeine) is within-subjects and the other of which (age) is between subjects. Again, there are $n = 10$ subjects in each of the two age groups. Suppose that the data are as depicted in Figure 9.7a (note that again the relevant ANOVA table is provided at the bottom of the figure).

As described in many standard statistics textbooks, there are two error terms in this design. The error term for the age effect is MS (Subjects within age groups) $= 1,656$, and the error term for caffeine and for the caffeine × age interaction is the MS (Caffeine × Subjects) $= 99$. Correspondingly, two separate confidence intervals can be computed. The first, computed by Equation (9), is the kind of within-subjects confidence interval that was described in the previous section. This confidence interval, which, as indicated at the bottom of Figure 9.7b, is computed to be ±6.3, is appropriate for assessing the observed effects of caffeine and of the age × caffeine interaction as estimates of the corresponding population effects. This confidence interval is plotted around each of the cell means in Figure 9.7b. Note that this confidence interval is not appropriate for describing the absolute age effect. The easiest way to conceptualize what this means is to think of an extreme situation in which the within-subjects confidence interval were zero; thus, one could be entirely confident of the nature of the caffeine effect and of the interaction (i.e., one could be entirely confident of the shape of each of the two curves in Figure 9.7). However, the vertical relations of the two age curves to one another would still be uncertain.

How uncertain? This would be determined by the size of the other, between-subjects confidence interval, based on MS (Subjects). As shown at the bottom of Figure 9.7b, the equation for computing this confidence

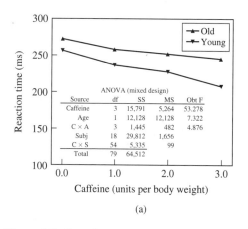

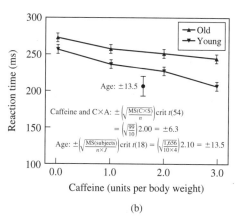

(a)   (b)

Figure 9.7 Data from a hypothetical experiment in which reaction time is measured as a function of caffeine consumption.

NOTE: Caffeine consumption is varied within subjects, and two different age groups are included. The right panel shows 95% "within-subject" confidence intervals around the sample means that are based on the subject × interaction variance, along with a free-floating confidence interval that is appropriate for comparing the two age curves.

interval is

$$\text{CI} = \sqrt{\frac{\text{MS(Subjects)}}{n \times J}} \, \text{crit } t \, (\text{dfS})$$

or 13.5. The value of this confidence interval, along with a pictorial representation of it, is shown in the middle of Figure 9.7b. Because there are only two age levels, an alternative way of depicting the age effect would be in terms of the age difference: The confidence interval around a difference score is always equal to the confidence interval around the individual component times $\sqrt{2}$. In this example, the observed mean difference is 25 ms, so the confidence interval around this mean difference score would be $25 \pm (13.5 \times \sqrt{2}) = 25 \pm 19.1$.

Why is the denominator of Equation (9) $n \times J \, (= 4 \times 10 = 40$ in this example) rather than the usual $n \, (= 10$ in this example), as would be the case if this were a pure between-subjects design? The reason for this further illustrates the different conclusions that can be made from a within-subjects design compared to a between-subjects design. In a purely between-subjects design, the confidence interval applies to a single condition mean. However, in this kind of mixed design, the confidence interval for the between-subjects factor—age—applies to the entire age curves rather than to just a single mean. For this reason, the confidence interval is actually around an entire curve mean that is based on $n \times J$, or, in this case, 40 observations. Again, this issue is most easily conceptualized by imagining the situation in which the within-subjects confidence interval is zero and the only uncertainty in the experiment is of age. The age uncertainty applies to an entire curve, not an individual mean; that is, once a given mean within a particular curve is known, the remaining three means in the curve are similarly known.

Confidence Intervals Around Interaction Effects.   Often the nature of an interaction is a key factor underlying the con-

Table 9.5   Hypothetical Data from a 2 × 2 Factorial Design

		Factor 1	
		Level 1	Level 2
Factor 2	Level 1	$M_{11} = 5$	$M_{21} = 8$
	Level 2	$M_{12} = 7$	$M_{22} = 12$

clusions that are made from some data set. Interactions with more than a single degree of freedom are the topic of a later section on contrasts. In this section, I briefly describe how a one-degree-of-freedom interaction may be assessed as a single value plus a confidence interval rather than within the usual hypothesis-testing context.

Table 9.5 shows a hypothetical example of a 2 × 2 design. The magnitude of the interaction may be computed as

$$I = (M_{21} - M_{22}) - (M_{11} - M_{12})$$

which in this case is $I = 2.0$. Suppose that the confidence interval around the individual mean is computed to be X (e.g., suppose $X = 0.4$ in this example). Thus, by Equation (7), the confidence interval around this interaction magnitude is

$$I \pm x \sqrt{1^2 + 1^2 + 1^2 + 1^2} = I \pm 2X$$

which would be 2.0 ± 0.8 in this example.

Asymmetrical   Confidence   Intervals.
Thus far in the chapter I have been describing confidence intervals that are symmetrical around the obtained sample statistics (generally the sample mean). However, some circumstances demand asymmetrical confidence intervals. In this section, I describe how to compute asymmetrical confidence intervals around three common statistics: variances, Pearson rs, and binomial proportions. In general, asymmetry reflects the bounded nature of the variable: variances are bounded at zero; Pearson rs are bounded at ± 1).

As described by Hays (1973, pp. 441–445) the confidence interval for a sample variance based on n observations $(X_i s)$ with mean M is

$$\text{CI} = \begin{cases} \text{(Upper limit): } \dfrac{(n-1)\text{est}\,\sigma^2}{\chi^2(n-1;\, p(\text{upper limit}))} \\[2em] \text{(Lower limit): } \dfrac{(n-1)\text{est}\,\sigma^2}{\chi^2(n-1;\, p(\text{lower limit}))}. \end{cases}$$

Here, est σ^2 (or s^2 in Hays' notation) is the best estimate of the population variance computed by

$$\text{est}\,\sigma^2 = \frac{\sum\limits_{i=1}^{n}(X_{ij}-M)^2}{n-1} = \frac{\sum\limits_{i-1}^{n}X_i^2 - nM^2}{n-1}$$

and $p(\text{upper limit})$ and $p(\text{lower limit})$ are the probability boundaries for the upper and lower limits of the confidence interval (e.g., 0.975 and 0.025 for a 95% confidence interval).

Suppose, to illustrate, that a sample of $n = 100$ scores produced a sample variance, est $\sigma^2 = 20$. The upper limit of a 95% confidence interval would be

$$\frac{(100-1)(20)}{\chi^2(9, 0.975)} = \frac{99 \times 20}{73.36} = 26.99$$

and the lower limit would be

$$\frac{(100-1)(20)}{\chi^2(9, 0.025)} = \frac{99 \times 20}{128.42} = 15.42.$$

The confidence interval around a Pearson r is based on Fisher's r-to-z transformation. In particular, suppose that a sample of n X-Y pairs produces some value of Pearson r. Given the transformation,

$$z = 0.5 \ln\left(\frac{1+r}{1-r}\right) \qquad (10)$$

z is approximately normally distributed, with an expectation equal to

$$0.5 \ln\left(\frac{1+\rho}{1-\rho}\right)$$

where ρ is the population correlation of which r is an estimate, and a standard deviation of

$$\sigma = \sqrt{1/(n-3)}.$$

Therefore, having computed an obtained z from the obtained r via Equation (10), a confidence interval can be constructed easily in z-space as

$$z \pm \text{criterion } z$$

where the criterion z corresponds to the desired confidence level (e.g., 1.96 in the case of a 95% confidence interval). The upper and lower z limits of this confidence interval can then be transformed back to upper and lower r limits.

Suppose, for instance, that a sample of $n = 25$ X-Y pairs produces a Pearson r of 0.90 and that a 95% confidence interval is desired. The obtained z is thus

$$z = 0.5 \times \ln[(1+.90)/(1-.90)] = 1.472$$

which is distributed with a standard deviation of

$$\sqrt{1/(25-3)} = 0.213.$$

The upper and lower confidence interval limits in z-space are therefore

$$1.472 + (.213)(1.96) = 1.890$$

and

$$1.472 - (.213)(1.96) = 1.054.$$

To translate from z-space back to r-space, it is necessary to invert Equation (10). It is easily shown that such an inversion produces

$$r = \frac{e^{2z} - 1}{e^{2z} + 1}. \qquad (11)$$

The upper and lower confidence interval limits may then be computed from Equation (11):

$$\text{upper limit: } r = \frac{e^{2 \times 1.890} - 1}{e^{2 \times 1.890} + 1} = 0.955$$

and

$$\text{lower limit: } r = \frac{e^{2 \times 1.054} - 1}{e^{2 \times 1.054} + 1} = 0.783.$$

Thus, the 95% confidence interval around the original obtained r of 0.90 ranges from 0.783 to 0.955.

To compute confidence intervals around binomial proportions, note first that the equation for the standard deviation of a proportion is

$$\sigma = \sqrt{\frac{pq}{n}}$$

where p is the proportion, q is $(1 - p)$, and n is the number of observations.

Suppose now that one wishes to compute the upper limit of a $X\%$ confidence interval. Call the corresponding criterion z, z_X (e.g., $z_X = 1.64$ for a 90% confidence interval, $z_X = 1.96$ for a 95% confidence interval, and so on). It follows then that the upper limit, U, for an $X\%$ confidence interval around some obtained proportion, p, can be written as,

$$U = p + \frac{1}{2n} + z_x \sigma$$
$$= p + \frac{1}{2n} + z_x \sqrt{\frac{U(1 - U)}{n}} \quad (12)$$

where the factor $(1/2n)$ corrects for continuity, as the normal approximation to the binomial is most easily used in these computations. The equation for the lower limit, L, is the same except that the second plus sign in Equation (12) is replaced with a minus sign, that is,

$$L = p + \frac{1}{2n} - z_x \sigma = p + \frac{1}{2n} - z_x \sqrt{\frac{L(1 - L)}{n}}.$$

These equations for both U or L, can, after suitable algebraic manipulation, be written as standard quadratics of the form,

$$aU^2 + bU + c = 0$$

and

$$aL^2 + bL + c = 0$$

where for both U and L, the values of a, b, and c can be computed as,

$$a = 1 + \frac{z_x^2}{n} \quad (13)$$

and

$$b = -2p - \frac{z_x^2}{n} - \frac{1}{n} \quad (14)$$

and

$$c = p^2 + \frac{p}{n} + \frac{1}{4n^2}. \quad (15)$$

The seemingly odd fact that the values of a, b, and c are the same for *both* U and L comes about because when one squares the far-right term in Equation (12) as part of the aforementioned algebraic manipulation, the minus sign in the equation for L disappears, and hence the equations for U and L become identical. Nevertheless, distinct values for both U and L emerge from the following quadratic solution.

A quadratic equation of the form

$$aX^2 + bX + c = 0$$

has two solutions, which are computed as follows:

$$X = \frac{-b \pm \sqrt{b^2 - 4ac}}{2a}. \quad (16)$$

When the values of a, b, and c obtained by Equations (13), (14), and (15) are plugged into Equation (16), the two resulting solutions correspond to the U and L, the upper and lower limits of the confidence interval.

As an example, suppose that an obtained proportion of $p = .96$ is obtained based on $n = 5$ observations, and suppose that one wishes to compute a 99% confidence interval around this obtained value of $p = .96$. The criterion z for a 99% confidence interval is $z_X = 2.576$. This information is sufficient to compute the values of the quadratic-equation coefficients, a, b, and c via Equations (13), (14), and (15). They are $a = 2.327$, $b = -3.447$, and $c = 1.124$. Plugging these three values, in turn, into Equation (16) leads to solutions—upper and lower limits—of $U = 0.997$ and $L = 0.484$.

Homogeneity of Variance

Let us return to the standard, one-way, between-subjects ANOVA design, as presented in the example of RT as a function of caffeine (see Figure 9.5). There is only a single MS (Error) in this design, in this case MS (Within) = 323. Computation of this single MS (Within) rests on the *homogeneity of variance assumption,* which is this: Although the treatment in some experiment (caffeine variation in this example) may affect the population means, it does not affect population variances. Accordingly, a single population variance, σ^2, is assumed to characterize the populations corresponding to all levels of the independent variable. Although not apparent in the usual formulas, the MS (Within) is the weighted average of separate estimates of σ^2 obtained from each level of the independent variable.[11]

Although almost invariably false, the homogeneity of variance assumption is necessary for carrying out an ANOVA. The consequences of violating the homogeneity of variance assumption to a mild degree are not severe (see, e.g., Hays, 1973, pp. 481–483). The homogeneity of variance assumption is not necessary at all, however, for computing confidence intervals. In the following sections, I touch on computation of confidence intervals in the absence of the homogeneity of variance assumption in several representative designs and, in the process, demonstrate the value of confidence intervals in illuminating the effects of the independent variable on condition variance as well as on condition mean.

Single-Factor Between-Subjects Designs.

In a single-factor between-subjects design such as the one illustrated in Figure 9.5, the

relevant LM equation is

$$Y_{ij} = \mu + \alpha_j + e_{ij} \qquad (17)$$

where Y_{ij} is the score for subject i in condition j, μ is the grand population mean, α_j is the effect of treatment (condition) j, and e_{ij} is an error associated with subject i in condition j. Homogeneity of variance is reflected by the assumption that the e_{ij}s are distributed normally with a mean of zero and a variance, σ^2, that is independent of j.

If the investigator is willing to forego an ANOVA, the homogeneity of variance assumption may be dropped in favor of the more general and realistic assumption that the independent variable affects condition variance as well as condition mean, that is, that the variance of the e_{ij}s in Equation (17) is σ_j^2 for condition j. To illustrate, I return to the single-factor caffeine experiment whose results are depicted in Figure 9.5. Suppose that the data from this experiment had turned out as depicted in Figure 9.8a. Making the standard homogeneity of variance assumption, a single confidence interval can be computed based on MS (Within) and displayed as shown.

Suppose that the homogeneity of variance assumption necessary for the ANOVA were dropped and that separate confidence intervals were computed for each condition by

$$CI_j = \left(\sqrt{\frac{\text{est}\,\sigma_j^2}{n_j}} \right) \text{crit}\, t(n_j - 1)$$

where j indexes condition. Here, est σ_j^2 is the estimate of condition j's population variance, computed by

$$\text{est}\,\sigma_j^2 = \frac{\sum\limits_{i=1}^{n_j}(x_{ij} - M_j)^2}{n_j - 1}$$

$$= \frac{\sum\limits_{i=1}^{n_j} x_{ij}^2 - T_j^2/n_j}{n_j - 1}$$

---

[11] The weighting is by degrees of freedom. In the example at hand, there are equal ns and hence equal degrees of freedom in each condition.

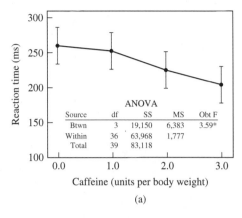
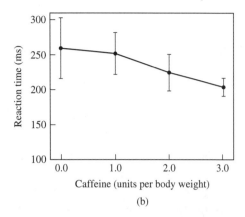

Figure 9.8   Caffeine data from a hypothetical between-subjects design similar to that of Figure 9.6. NOTE: Homogeneity of variance is assumed (as usual) in the left panel, in which an ANOVA is possible, and equal-sized 95% confidence intervals are shown. Homogeneity of variance is not assumed in the right panel. An ANOVA cannot be carried out; however, the different-sized 95% confidence intervals represent the differently estimated variances in the different conditions.

where T_j, M_j and n_j are, respectively, the total of, mean of, and number of subjects in the jth condition ($n_j = 10$ for all conditions in this example). Note that when assuming homogeneity of variance as in Figure 9.8a, the criterion t for the confidence interval is based on degrees of freedom within (36 in this example). When not assuming homogeneity of variance, the criterion t for the condition j confidence interval is based on ($n_j - 1$) degrees of freedom, the number of degrees of freedom in condition j.

These new confidence intervals— computed without assuming homogeneity of variance—are plotted in Figure 9.8b, which provides important intuitive pictorial information about the effect of caffeine on variance that is not available in the ANOVA of Figure 9.8a. In particular, it suggests that caffeine's effect on the variance should be construed as at least as important as caffeine's effect on the mean.

Multi-Factor Between-Subjects Designs. Considerations involving homogeneity of variance become more complex when more than a single factor is included in the design,

as there are many configurations of variance homogeneity that could be assumed. For a two-factor, $J \times K$ design, the most coherent possibilities are as follows (for simplicity, I assume equal ns in all conditions):

1. Complete homogeneity of variance is assumed. In this case, a single confidence interval can be computed, appropriate for each of the $J \times K$ conditions, based on ($J \times K$) $\times$ ($n - 1$) degrees of freedom within.

2. No homogeneity of variance is assumed at all. In this case, a confidence interval can be computed independently for the each of the $J \times K$ conditions. The confidence interval for the JKth condition is based on ($n - 1$) degrees of freedom.

3. Homogeneity of variance can be assumed across the J levels of Factor 1 but not across the K levels of Factor 2. In this case, K confidence intervals are computed, one for each level of Factor 2, each based on $J \times$ ($n - 1$) degrees of freedom. The confidence interval for Level k of Factor 2 is appropriate for all J Factor-1 levels within Level k of Factor 2.

4. Conversely, homogeneity of variance can be assumed across the K levels of Factor 2 but not across the J levels of Factor 1. In this case, J confidence intervals are computed, one for each level of Factor 1, each based on $K \times (n - 1)$ degrees of freedom. The confidence interval for Level j of Factor 1 is appropriate for all K Factor-2 levels within Level j of Factor 1.

Single-Factor Within-Subjects Designs. In a single-factor within-subjects design illustrated in Figure 9.6, the issue of homogeneity of variance is somewhat complicated. The relevant LM equation is

$$Y_{ij} = \mu + \beta_i + \alpha_j + \gamma_{ij}$$

where Y_{ij} and α_j are as in Equation (17), β_i is an effect of subject i, and γ_{ij} is an interaction term unique to the subject $i \times$ condition j combination. Homogeneity of variance in this design is the assumption that the γ_{ij} terms are all distributed normally with a variance of σ^2. Dropping the homogeneity of variance assumption would allow the variance of the γ_{ij} terms to have different variances σ_j^2 for the different conditions, j.

Estimation of the separate σ_j^2s is described by Loftus and Masson (1994, p. 484 and in their Appendix B). Unlike the corresponding between-subjects situation described in the previous section, such separate estimation is sufficiently involved that I do not redescribe it here. Moreover, the procedure entails potential estimation problems described by Loftus and Masson (which are exacerbated by small sample sizes). For this reason, I do not recommended that this procedure be used unless there is very good reason to do so.

Multifactor Within-Subjects Designs. Many of the considerations that apply to multi-factor between-subjects designs apply similarly to multifactor within-subjects designs. Consider for example a J (Factor 1) $\times$ K

(Factor 2) $\times$ n (subjects) design. Although, as just noted, it is somewhat tedious to estimate different variances, σ_j^2, of the γs corresponding to the J different levels within a given factor, it is simple to estimate values of γ if they are presumed different for different levels of Factor 2 but, within each level of Factor 2, the same for all levels of Factor 1: One need only apply Equation (9) separately and independently for each level of Factor 2. (Of course, the same logic applies when reversing Factors 1 and 2).

To illustrate, suppose that the effect of caffeine on RT is again under consideration. In this hypothetical example, Factor A is amount of caffeine (which again can be one of four levels), while Factor B is amount of sleep deprivation, which is either 1 or 24 hours. Suppose that $n = 10$ subjects participate in each of the 8 caffeine $\times$ deprivation conditions. Assume for the sake of argument that the three error terms—the interactions of subject $\times$ caffeine, subject $\times$ deprivation, and subject $\times$ caffeine $\times$ deprivation—are approximately the same. Using the logic described earlier, the investigator could compute a single confidence interval using the combined error term, which would be based on 9 (degrees of freedom for subjects) $\times$ 7 (degrees of freedom for the 8 conditions) = 63 degrees of freedom (or alternatively, $9 \times 3 + 9 \times 1 + 9 \times 3 \times 1 = 63$ degrees of freedom if one prefers to think in terms of adding the degrees of freedom from the three separate error terms).

Suppose, alternatively, that the investigator suspected that the effect of caffeine was less consistent over subjects with 24 hours of sleep deprivation than over subjects with 1 hour of sleep deprivation. Again, foregoing a standard ANOVA, the investigator could essentially view the design as comprising two separate experiments—one involving the effect of caffeine on RT following one hour of sleep deprivation and the other involving the effect of caffeine on RT following 24 hours of sleep deprivation. Two confidence intervals could then be computed, each based on of these two separate experiments—that is, each based on the subject × caffeine interaction within one of the sleep-deprivation levels—and each based on $9 \times 3 = 27$ degrees of freedom.

Planned Comparisons (Contrasts)

Psychological research, along with the analysis of psychological data, varies widely in the degree of quantitative sophistication that is used. At or near one end of this continuum is the use of mathematical process models to generate quantitative predictions for the summary statistics obtained in an experiment (and, in some cases, distributions of the raw data as well; see, e.g., Chap. 11, this volume). At or near the other end of the continuum is NHST, used to evaluate verbally presented hypotheses in which the only mathematical model is some form of the standard linear model. The use of planned comparisons falls somewhere in the middle. Planned comparisons provide an organized and systematic means of accounting for variability between conditions in an experiment.

The formal logic and details of the use of planned comparisons are presented in Hays (1973, pp. 584–593). The basic logic of a planned comparison is as follows

Some hypothesis about what the pattern of population means looks like is used to generate a set of numbers called weights—one weight corresponding to each condition in the experiment. The general idea is that the pattern of weights over conditions corresponds to the pattern of population means that is predicted by the hypothesis. It is important to realize that unlike a mathematical model designed to generate an exact quantitative prediction for each condition, each individual weight of a planned comparison need not bear any particular relation to its correspond-

ing sample mean. Rather, it is the *pattern* of weights that should correspond to the predicted pattern of means. In most applications of planned comparisons, the weights must sum to zero, in which case the comparison is conventionally referred to as a *contrast*.

The correlation (Pearson r^2) between the hypothesis weights and the sample means is computed. This Pearson r^2, like any Pearson r^2, is interpreted as the percent of variance between conditions, that is, the percent of SS (Between) that is accounted for by the hypothesis.

Accordingly, the product of the Pearson r^2 and SS (Between) is interpretable as a sum of squares. This sum of squares is based on one degree of freedom.

Within the context of NHST, two null hypotheses can be tested. The first, which I label a *uselessness null hypothesis,* is that the correlation between the hypothesis weights and the condition population means is 0.0 (informally, that the hypothesis is useless as a descriptor of reality). The second, which I label a *sufficiency null hypothesis,* is that the correlation between the hypothesis weights and the condition population means is 1.0 (informally, that the hypothesis is sufficient as a descriptor of reality).

An Example of the Use of Planned Comparisons

Suppose that an investigator is studying factors that influence attitude change. The general paradigm is this. Subjects listen to a speaker who describes the benefit of a somewhat controversial issue, specifically clearcutting in national forests. Following the speech, the subjects rate the degree to which they favor the speaker's position on a scale from 1 ("don't agree at all") to 7 ("agree fully"). In an initial experiment, the effect of speaker affiliation is investigated. In $J = 5$ conditions, subjects are provided either (a) no information or information that the speaker

Table 9.6　Data from a Hypothetical Experiment in Which Attitude Change (rating) Is Measured as a Function of the Perceived Affiliation of the Speaker

A. Means (Ms) and Construction of Weights (W_js)			
Speaker Information	M_j	$W_j(1)$	$W_j(2)$
None	2.25	0	−1.20
Sierra Club	6.05	2	0.80
Audubon Society	5.50	2	0.80
Timber industry	3.70	1	−0.20
Paper industry	2.90	1	−0.20

B. ANOVA					
Source	df	SS	MS	F	%var = r^2
Between	4	215.7			
Hypothesis	1	194.6	194.6	19.86	0.902
Residual	3	21.1	7.0	0.72	0.098
Within	95	931.0	9.8		

NOTE: Panel A provides original data plus two successively constructed sets of weights: The $W(2)$s are deviation scores obtained from the $W(1)$s. Panel B shows the ANOVA results for the contrast and for the residual.

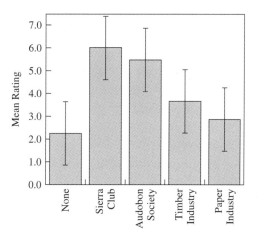

Figure 9.9　Data from a hypothetical experiment in which attitude change (rating) is measured as a function of the perceived affiliation of the speaker. NOTE: The error bars are 95% confidence intervals.

is a member of (b) the Sierra Club, (c) the Audubon Society, (d) the timber industry, or (e) the paper industry. The conditions are summarized in Table 9.6, Panel A.

Suppose that the investigator wishes to test a hypothesis that is the conjunction of the following two assumptions. First, knowing something about the speaker leads to more attitude change than does knowing nothing at all. Second, attitude change is greater for speakers whose affiliated organization is perceived to oppose the expressed opinion (i.e., the Sierra Club and the Audubon Society are perceived to oppose clear-cutting) than for speakers whose affiliated organization is perceived to support the expressed opinion (i.e., the timber and paper industries are perceived to support clear-cutting).

To assess the viability of this hypothesis, the sample means are plotted in Figure 9.9 along with the confidence intervals. The pattern of observed sample means appears roughly to bear out the hypothesis: The "None" condition produces the lowest mean

persuasion value; the values for the Sierra Club and Audubon Society are highest; and the timber and paper industry conditions are intermediate.

To acquire a quantitative handle on this apparent confirmation of the hypothesis, the investigator carries out a planned comparison. The investigator's first job is to create a set of weights that reflects the hypothesis just described. The first step is to create weights, ignoring for the moment the constraint that the weights must sum to zero. The simplest such weights would assign zero to the "None" condition, 2s to the Sierra Club and Audubon Society conditions, and 1s to the timber industry and paper industry conditions. These weights are provided in the column labeled "$W_j(1)$" in Table 9.6, Panel A. The next step is to preserve the pattern produced by this set of weights but to make the weights add to zero. This is easily accomplished by computing the mean of the $W_j(1)$s, which is 1.2, and subtracting that mean from the $W_j(1)$s to generate a set of *deviation scores* that, while preserving the pattern of the $W_j(1)$s, are, of course, guaranteed to add to zero. The resulting final weights are provided in the column labeled

"$W_j(2)$". (It is worth pointing out that this any-numbers-then-make-deviation-scores trick is quite useful for generating weights in *any* situation.)

Percent of Between-Condition Variance Accounted for by the Hypothesis.

As noted, a basic goal is to compute the Pearson r^2 between the sample means and the weights corresponding to the hypothesis. Although this could easily be done using the standard Pearson r^2 equation, it is more instructive, within the context of planned comparisons, to do the computation via a somewhat different route. In particular, a sum of squares due to the hypothesis may be computed using the equation

$$\text{SS (Hypothesis)} = \frac{n\left(\sum_{j=1}^{J} M_j W_j\right)^2}{\sum_{j=1}^{J} W_j^2} \quad (18)$$

where n is the number of subjects in each condition ($n = 20$ in this example). Applying Equation (18) to the present data produces SS (Hypothesis) = 194.6, shown in Panel B of Table 9.6. The ratio of SS (Hypothesis) to SS (Between) is $194.6/215.7 = 0.902$, which is the sought-after Pearson r^2 between the W_js and the M_js.

This sum of squares representing a single pattern of variation across the five conditions is based on one degree of freedom. By subtraction one can compute the portion of SS (Between) that is not accounted for by the hypothesis: $215.7 - 194.6 = 21.1$, a value that is referred to as SS (Residual). SS (Residual) represents all forms of variability other than that engendered in the original hypothesis, and it is based on 3 degrees of freedom $= 4$ [df (Between)] $- 1$[df (Hypothesis)].

Mean squares can be computed in the normal fashion based on sums of squares and degrees of freedoms due to the hypothesis and the residual; these mean squares are in the column labeled "MS" in Table 9.6, Panel B.

If one is inclined to work within the NHST framework, then these mean squares are used to test two null hypotheses.[12]

A Uselessness Null Hypothesis. The Pearson r^2 of 0.902 shown in the column labeled "%var $= r^2$" in Panel B of Table 9.6 is the r^2 between the sample means (M_js) and the weights (W_js). As in any situation involving unknown population parameters, it would be of more interest to address the Pearson r^2 between the W_js and the population means (i.e., the μ_js). Two null hypotheses are relevant to this issue. The first is the null hypothesis that the Pearson r^2 between the W_js and the μ_js is zero—that is, that the hypothesis is useless as an account of SS (Between). If this were true, then the MS (Hypothesis) as shown in Table 9.6 is an estimate of MS (Within), and a standard F test can be carried out wherein F (dfH, dfW) = MS (Hypothesis)/MS (Within). As indicated in Table 9.6, this F, which is 19.86, is statistically significant, thereby allowing rejection of this uselessness null hypothesis.

A Sufficiency Null Hypothesis. The second null hypothesis is that the Pearson r^2 between the W_js and the μ_js is 1.0—that is, that the hypothesis is sufficient to account for SS (Between). Testing this null hypothesis entails an F ratio of MS (Residual) against MS (Within). In Table 9.6 it can be seen that the resulting $F(3, 95)$ is 0.72, which is, of course, nonsignificant.

Reminder of Problems with NHST.

It is necessary to bear in mind that these uses of NHST carry with them all of the problems with NHST described earlier. In particular,

---

[12]Some terminology glitches arise here. I want to emphasize that the term *hypothesis,* when used alone, refers to a form of an alternative hypothesis. The term *null hypothesis* refers to the two specific quantitative hypotheses that will be described.

an outcome such as the one portrayed in Table 9.6—that the hypothesis is significant, but the residual is not—should be accompanied by a number of caveats, the most important of which is that failure to reject the sufficiency null hypothesis does not mean that the sufficiency null hypothesis is correct. Indeed, in the present example it should set off alarm bells that only 90% of the between-condition variance is accounted for by the hypothesis. These are the same alarm bells that should be set off by the relatively large confidence intervals that are depicted in Figure 9.9.

Planned Comparisons of Linearity

Investigators frequently use planned comparisons to test a hypothesis of *linearity*. To illustrate, suppose that an investigator is studying the effect of audience size on the degree of stage fright suffered by a public speaker (e.g., Jackson & Latané, 1981). In a hypothetical experiment, subjects give prepared speeches to audiences whose sizes are, in different conditions, 3, 6, 12, 20, or 29 people. Following, the speech, a subject indicates the degree of stage fright that he or she has experienced on a scale ranging from 0 ("not frightened at all") to 7 ("terrified"). A between-subjects design is used with $n = 15$ subjects participating in each of the $J = 5$ audience-size conditions. The data from this experiment, shown in Figure 9.10, are provided in Table 9.7, which is organized like Table 9.6.

Suppose the investigator wishes to test the hypothesis that stage fright, as measured by the rating, increases linearly with audience size; thus, the best linear fit is provided in Figure 9.10 along with the data points. It appears that a linearity hypothesis is roughly confirmed.

The first task in carrying out the planned comparison of linearity is to generate weights that are linearly related to audience size. This enterprise is complicated slightly because the audience-size levels (3, 6, 12, 20, 29) are not evenly spaced. The simplest way of coping

Table 9.7   Data from a Hypothetical Experiment in Which Stage Fright (rating) Is Measured as a Function of Audience Size

A. Means (Ms) and Construction of Weights (W_js)

Audience Size	M_j	$W_j(1)$	$W_j(2)$	$W_j(3)$
3	1.100	3	−11	−0.0244
6	0.833	6	−8	−0.0178
12	4.033	12	−2	−0.0044
20	4.167	20	6	0.0133
29	6.500	29	15	0.0333

B. ANOVA

Source	df	SS	MS	F	%var $= r^2$
Between	4	336.7			
Hypothesis	1	305.1	305.1	64.0**	0.906
Residual	3	31.6	10.6	2.11 ns	0.094
Within	70	514.5	7.3		

NOTE: Panel A provides original data plus three successively constructed sets of weights: The $W(1)$s are deviation scores obtained from the $W(1)$s, and the $W(3)$s are scaled $W(2)$s (scaling designed to render the contrast in "natural units" as described in the text). Panel B shows the ANOVA results for the contrast and for the residual.

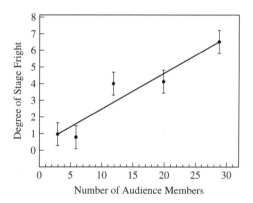

Figure 9.10   Data from a hypothetical experiment in which stage fright (rating) is measured as a function of audience size.
NOTE: The error bars are standard errors.

with this complication is to use the trick described earlier and to begin by selecting appropriate weights—in this case, weights that are linear with audience size—without concern about whether they add to zero. A simple and suitable candidate for such weights are the audience sizes themselves, as indicated in the column labeled "$W_j(1)$" in Table 9.7, Panel A. As in the previous example, this pattern of weights can be made to add to zero by transforming the $W_j(1)$s to deviation scores. The resulting weights are provided in the column labeled "$W_j(2)$". (The "$W_j[3]$" column is described in the next section). The remainder of the process is exactly as it was in the previous example: The $W_j(2)$s are plugged into Equation (18) to find the SS (Hypothesis); SS (Residual) is found by subtraction; the percentages of the SS (Between) accounted for by the Hypothesis and Residual are computed; and the uselessness and sufficiency null hypothesis tests are carried out. These results are shown in Panel B of Table 9.7.

A Contrast as a Dependent Variable: Scaling the W_js

The heart of Equation (18) is in the term that constitutes the actual contrast:

$$\text{Contrast} = C = \sum_{j=1}^{J} M_j W_j. \quad (19)$$

The larger C is, the "better" the hypothesis may be assumed to be. Often it is useful to view C as a dependent variable in the experiment. This strategy is particularly advantageous if the contrast has easily interpretable or "natural" units. A very simple example of such use occurs when the weights are all zero except for a "1" and a "−1," in which case the contrast is interpretable as a *difference score*.

However, more sophisticated uses of contrasts as a natural dependent variable can be engineered. Before providing an example of how this might be done, it is critical to point out the *scalability property* of the W_js. To understand this property, note that the denominator of Equation (18) serves to eliminate any effect of *scaling* the weights. Suppose that an investigator has chosen some suitable set of weights, $W = (W_1, W_2, \ldots, W_J)$, and that a SS (Hypothesis) were computed via Equation (18). Now suppose that an alternative set, $W' = kW = (kW_1, kW_2, \ldots, kW_J)$, were used where k is some nonzero constant. Applying Equation (18) to W' would yield a factor of k^2 in both the numerator and the denominator compared to using the original W. Therefore, the k^2s would cancel, and the same SS (Hypothesis) and r^2 would emerge. In short, once one has chosen a suitable set of weights, any other scaled set is equally suitable.

An investigator can use this fact to his or her advantage to scale weights in such a way that the contrast is expressed in some form of natural units. An obvious example of this sort of procedure is when a linear hypothesis is under investigation, as in the stage-fright example depicted in Figure 9.10 and Table 9.7. In particular, a natural unit for the contrast would be the *slope* of the function relating the stage-fright rating to audience size. How might the weights in Table 9.7 be scaled to accomplish this?

The $W_j(2)$ weights from Table 9.7 are already scaled in units of audience size; they are just shifted in order to constitute deviation scores. Thus, the slope of the audience-size function may be computed using the standard regression equation

$$\text{slope} = \frac{5\sum_{j=1}^{5} M_j W_j - \left(\sum_{j=1}^{5} M_j\right)\left(\sum_{j=1}^{5} W_j\right)}{\sum_{j=1}^{5} W_j^2 - \left(\sum_{j=1}^{5} W_j\right)^2}$$

or, because the W_js must sum to zero,

$$\text{slope} = \frac{\sum_{j=1}^{5} M_j W_j}{\sum_{j=1}^{5} W_j^2}.$$

This in turn means that if the original weights (i.e., the $W_j[2]$ weights from Table 9.7) are scaled by a factor of $1/\sum W_j^2 = 1/450$, then a set of weights will emerge that will produce as a contrast the slope of the function. It is these scaled weights that are labeled $W_j(3)$ in Table 9.7. Applying Equation (19) to the M_js and the $W_j(3)$s from Table 9.7 yields $C = 0.213$, which is the slope of the audience-size function.

Confidence Intervals around Contrasts

One can also compute a confidence interval around the observed value of C. Such computation is straightforward. As is well known, and as is indicated in Equation (7), any linear combination of means, as in Equation (19), has a variance of

$$\sigma_C^2 = \sigma_M^2 \left(W_1^2 + W_2^2 + \cdots + W_J^2 \right)$$

where σ_M^2 is the standard error of the mean (it is necessary, of course, to assume homogeneity of variance here). Because σ_M^2 is estimated by [MS (Within)]$/n$, the standard error of C may be computed as

$$\text{SE} = \pm \sqrt{\left[\frac{\text{MSW}}{n} \right] \left(W_1^2 + W_2^2 + \cdots + W_J^2 \right)}$$

$$(20)$$

and any desired-size confidence interval may be computed by multiplying Equation (20) by the appropriate criterion $t(\text{dfW})$.

Recall that the contrast from the $W_j(3)$s in Table 9.7 was C = slope = 0.213. Applying Equation (18) to the MS (Within) and the $W_j(3)$s yields a 95% confidence interval of 0.066. In short, one may summarize the stage-fright data by stating that the slope of the audience-size function is 0.213 with a 95% confidence interval of 0.066.

Using Planned Comparisons in Within-Subjects Designs

Planned comparisons can be used in within-subjects designs much in the same way that they can be used in between-subjects designs.

Example: Visual Search and "Popout."

As an example, consider a visual search task in which the subject's task is to determine whether some target stimulus is present in some set of distractors. Suppose that two conditions are constructed: a "search" condition in which it is predicted that the subject will have to search serially to make the decision and a "popout" condition in which it is predicted that the subject will be able to process all members of the stimulus array in parallel. The size of the search set is also varied and consists of 1, 2, 4, or 9 items. The design is entirely within-subjects, and the 8 conditions defined by 2 (search/popout) × 4 (set size) are presented randomly to each of $n = 9$ subjects over a long series of trials.

The data from this hypothetical experiment (means plus confidence intervals) are shown in Figure 9.11. It is clear that RT increases with set size in the search condition, whereas RT is relatively low and flat in the popout condition. These means are reproduced numerically in Table 9.8, Panel A. Panel B of Table 9.8 shows a standard ANOVA table for these data. F ratios have been computed for the standard three factors—effects of set size, search/popout, and the interaction. As one would surmise from Figure 9.11, all three of these effects are highly significant.

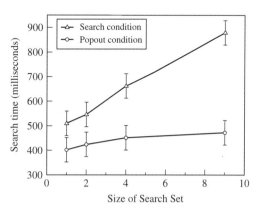

Figure 9.11 Data from a hypothetical experiment in which search time (reaction time) is measured as functions of set size and whether search is required.

NOTE: The error bars are 95% confidence intervals.

Testing the Hypothesis with Planned Comparisons.   Testing the prediction of the hypothesis that RT should increase linearly with set size in the search condition but should be flat (and presumably low) in the popout condition is of primary interest. I now describe two planned comparisons that are suitable for doing this. I should note that the overall ANOVA shown in Panel B of Table 9.8 was provided for expositional purposes only: When the investigator carries out planned comparisons, the overall ANOVA is generally not necessary.

The first planned comparison is shown in Table 9.8, Panel C. As with the previous examples, I use a two-part process to generate the appropriate W_{jk}s. The $W_{jk}(1)$s are constructed without regard to making the W_{jk}s add to zero, whereas the $W_{jk}(2)$s are the $W_{jk}(1)$ deviation scores.

This procedure illustrates an important point: When carrying out this kind of a planned comparison using a two-factor design (whether it be within-subjects, as in the present example, or between-subjects) the row × column design structure becomes relevant only as a mnemonic aid. From the perspective of the planned comparison, the experiment is simply viewed as containing $J \times K$ different conditions, and the W_{jk}s must add to zero across all $J \times K$ conditions. There are, for the moment, no other constraints on the W_{jk}s.

The statistical results of this procedure are shown at the bottom of Panel C, labeled "Contrast ANOVA." The top source of variance is from between conditions (i.e., the component in Panel B labeled "Conditions") and is based on seven degrees of freedom. The SS (Hypothesis), computed via Equation (18), is the next variance component; and finally, as in previous examples, SS (Residual) is computed by subtraction. Note from the rightmost column that the SS (Hypothesis) accounts for only 94% of the between-conditions variance. Both

Table 9.8   Hypothetical Data

A. Original Data (in ms)

	Number of Items in the Search Set			
	1	2	4	9
Search	509	544	662	882
Popout	400	422	449	472

B. Overall ANOVA

Source	df	SS	MS	F
Subjects (S)	7	219,325		
Conditions (C)	7	1,432,963		
Set Size (Z)	3	471,767	157,256	38.68
Search/Popout (P)	1	729,957	729,957	136.18
Z × P	3	231,239	77,080	13.80
S × Z	21	85,386	4,066	
S × P	7	37,522	5,360	
S × Z × P	21	117,336	5,587	
S × C	49	240,244	4,903	
TOTAL	63	1,892,532		

C. Contrast from Total SS (Between Cells)

	1	2	4	9
$W_{jk}(1)$	1	1	1	1
$W_{jk}(2)$	−1.5	−0.5	1.5	6.5
	−1.5	−1.5	−1.5	−1.5

		Contrast ANOVA			
Source	df	SS	MS	F	%var = r^2
Conditions	7	1,432,963			
Hypothesis	1	1,350,749	1,350,749	275.5	94.3
Residual	6	82,214	13,702	2.8	5.7

D. Contrast from Interaction SS Only

	5	6	8	13
$W_{jk}(1)$	11	10	8	3
$W_{jk}(2)$	−3	−2	0	5
	3	2	0	−5

		Contrast ANOVA			
Source	df	SS	MS	F	%var = r^2
Interaction	3	231,239			
Hypothesis	1	229,907	229,907	46.89	99.4
Residual	2	1,333	666	0.14	0.6

NOTE: Panel A: Original search-time data. Panel B: ANOVA results. Panels C and D: Contrasts described in the text.

the hypothesis and the residual are highly significant.

The planned comparison just described had a certain degree of arbitrariness about it. Essentially, the main prediction under investigation was that there should be a particular type of interaction between set size and search/popout; the main effects of the two variables were of secondary importance. For example, the large percentage of between-condition variance not accounted for by the hypothesis comes about because, as is evident in Figure 9.11, the search condition RT is greater than the popout condition RT even in the set size $= 1$ conditions; the arbitrary choice in the contrast in Panel C was to assume these two conditions to be equal.

Accordingly, it would be useful to carry out a planned comparison that investigated the role of the particular expected interaction. The resulting contrast is constructed in Table 9.8, Panel D. The goal here is to maintain the hypothesized interaction pattern in the eventual contrast, but to eliminate main effects. The resulting contrast shown in Panel D accomplishes this; note that each row and column of the final contrast (i.e., $W_{jk}[2]$) sums to zero, so only interaction variance is reflected. The interaction variance remains specifically that RT is positively linear with set size for search and negatively linear with set size for popout.[13]

The ANOVA relevant to this contrast is shown at the bottom of Panel D. The top source of variance is from the interaction (i.e., the component labeled "Z $\times$ P" in Panel B) and is based on three degrees of freedom. The interaction-only contrast accounts for over

99% of this interaction variance, and the small residual is not statistically significant.

Using a Contrast as a Dependent Variable. It is instructive to illustrate once again how a contrast may be translated into natural units via suitable scaling of the weights. In the present example, a useful natural unit for the contrast would be the difference between the search slope and the popout slope. To do this, I work from the weights in Panel B of Table 9.8, where only the interaction variance is at issue. Again, the $W_{jk}(2)$ weights are already scaled to set size. Using much the same logic entailed in scaling the weights in the stage-fright example, and noting the constraints on the $W_{jk}(2)$ weight pattern, it can be shown that the appropriate scaling factor is $2/ \sum W_{jk}^2$, where the sum is over all eight conditions. The resulting weights, $W_{jk}(3)$, are shown in Table 9.9, Panel B. (Note that Panel A, along with part of Panel B, presents relevant information from Table 9.8 again.) Panel C of Table 9.9 shows the contrasts (C_ks) that result for each subject, k. Thus, the contrast value for each subject, which has been designed to be the difference between the two slopes for that subject, can be treated as a standard dependent variable. The mean and 95% confidence interval shown at the bottom of Panel C of Table 9.9 are computed directly from the C_ks.

Multiple Planned Comparisons

Multiple planned comparisons may be carried out on the same data set by generating multiple sets of weights, presumably from multiple hypotheses, and iterating through the steps described at the beginning of this section. Any two contrasts (along with the hypotheses that generated them) are independent of one another if and only if the Pearson r^2 between the two sets of weights is equal to zero. In practice, because any set of weights sums to zero, the Pearson r^2 between the two sets of

---

[13]That the hypothesis includes "negatively linear for popout" may elicit some confusion because the original hypothesis predicted no set-size effect for popout. One must remember, however, that this contrast applies to the interaction variance only, which implies no main effect for set size, and which in turn implies canceling set-size effects for search and popout.

Table 9.9   Additional Information for the Visual-Search Data

A. Original Data (in ms)
Number of Items in the Search Set

	1	2	4	9
Search	509	544	662	882
Popout	400	422	449	472

B. Contrast from Interaction SS Only

$W_{jk}(1)$	5	6	8	13
	11	10	8	3
$W_{jk}(2)$	−3	−2	0	5
	3	2	0	−5
$W_{jk}(3)$	−0.070	−0.053	0.000	0.132
	0.079	0.053	0.000	−0.132

C. Contrast Values for Individual Subjects

Subject (k)	C_k
1	5.4
2	49.9
3	29.2
4	44.4
5	57.6
6	40.5
7	23.4
8	60.7

Mean	Confidence Interval
38.89	15.61

NOTE: Panels A and B show the original data along with $W_{jk}(1)$ and $W_{jk}(2)$ from Table 9.7. The $W_{jk}(3)$s are scaled $W_{jk}(2)$s (scaling designed to render the contrast in "natural units," as described in the text). Panel C: Values of the contrast for 8 subjects along with the mean and 95% confidence interval of the 8 contrast values.

weights is equal to zero if and only if the sum of the cross products of the two sets of weights is equal to zero.

Percent Total Variance Accounted For (ω^2)

In correlational studies the primary dependent variable is a Pearson r^2. Every psychologist realizes that a Pearson r^2 represents the percent of variance in some predicted variable, Y, accounted for by variation in some predictor variable, X.

Given the overwhelming prevalence of measures of percent accounted for, such as Pearson r^2 in correlational research, it is puzzling that there is little use of the equivalent measures in experimental research. These measures, termed ω^2, are generally applicable to any ANOVA-type design and are, essentially, the percentage of total variance in the experiment accounted for by variation in the independent variable. Computation of ω^2 is particularly useful in practical situations in which the emphasis is on the effect's real-world significance (as opposed to its statistical significance). Hays (1973, pp. 417–424, 484–491, & 512–514) provides formal analyses of ω^2 for several experimental designs. I briefly illustrate its use in a between-subjects, one-way ANOVA situation.

Vitamin C and Colds

Suppose that an investigator is interested in determining whether variations in dosages of vitamin C affect the amount of time a person is afflicted with colds. In a hypothetical experiment, subjects in three different double-blind conditions are provided 2 g, 3 g, or 4 g, respectively, of vitamin C per day for five years, and the number of days on which each subject considers him- or herself to have a cold is recorded. A very large sample size is used: $n = 10,000$ subjects per condition. The data are provided in Panel A of Table 9.10 and in Figure 9.12, both of which make it clear that there is a highly significant, decreasing effect of vitamin C on number of days with colds.

A closer inspection of the data, however, raises serious doubts about vitamin C's efficacy: The absolute decrease in cold days is miniscule, falling from about 9.8 days to about 9.6 days as vitamin C dosage is doubled from 2 to 4 g. The reason that such a small effect is so highly significant is, of course, that the $n = 10,000$ subjects per condition confers an enormous amount of statistical power, and therefore even a tiny effect of the independent variable will be detected.

Table 9.10   Data from a Hypothetical Experiment in Which the Effect of Dosages of Vitamin C on Cold Durations is Examined

A. Original Data (*n* = 10,000/Condition)

Amount of Vitamin C (g)	Mean Days with Colds
2	9.79
3	9.72
4	9.56

B. ANOVA

Source	df	SS	MS	F	Crit F
Between	2	290	145	16.12	3.00
Within	29,997	89,991	9		
Total	29,999	90,281			

NOTE: Panel A: Original data (10,000 subjects). Panel B: ANOVA results.

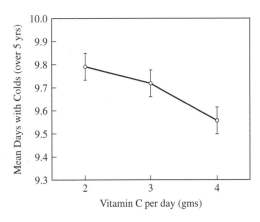

Figure 9.12   Data from a hypothetical experiment in which the effect of dosages of vitamin C on cold durations is examined.
NOTE: Note the limited range of the ordinate. The error bars are 95% confidence intervals.

How Much Vitamin C Should One Take?

There are 30,000 data points in this experiment. As indicated in Panel B of Table 9.10, the total variance is SS (Total) = 90,281, of which only SS (Between) = 290 is from between conditions. Thus, essentially only 290/90,281 or about 0.32% of the total variance is attributable to variation in vitamin C.

More precisely, because part of SS (Between) is attributable to random error, the appropriate computation is somewhat more complex. The reader is referred to the Hays (1973) references provided earlier for the formal logic. The end result is that to estimate the percent of total variance attributable to variation in the independent variable, one uses the equation.

$$\text{est } \omega^2 = \frac{\text{SS(Between)} - (J - 1) \times \text{MS(Within)}}{\text{SS(Between)} + \text{SS(Within)} + \text{MS(Within)}}$$

which in the present example is 0.30%. The inescapable implication is that vitamin C accounts for only a tiny percentage of total variability in days of having colds. The practical conclusion is that if one wishes to cut down on colds, there are probably many other more important variables to which one should pay attention than the amount of vitamin C one takes.

This ω^2 computation places the large statistical significance found in this experiment in a somewhat harsher light, and it serves to underscore the important difference between determining that an effect exists on the one hand (i.e., the high statistical significance implied by $F > 16$) and evaluating the effect's importance on the other hand (i.e., the minute practical significance implied by $\omega^2 < 1\%$).

A Caveat

In the example I have just provided, the consumer of the research is presumably most interested in very practical considerations: Specifically, in deciding whether to go through the hassle and expense of taking large doses of vitamin C, it is useful to understand the magnitude of the expected reward in terms of cold relief. However, one might be interested in a separate question altogether, namely, investigating the relation between vitamin C and colds strictly from the perspective of addressing some biological question. In such an instance, the relation between vitamin C and cold reduction, no matter how small, could potentially be of intense interest.

Model Fitting

Myung and Pitt (Chap. 11, this volume) describe the use of mathematical models in some detail. It is not my intent to reiterate what they have already said. Rather, in the spirit of the content of the present chapter, I provide suggestions for understanding and presenting some data/model combinations.

Finding and Presenting Optimal Parameter Values

A simple and familiar example of fitting a mathematical model is in the context of linear regression, in which some variable Y is assumed to be linearly related to some other variable X. Typically, some number of XY pairs constitute the data. Here, two parameters must be estimated: the slope and the intercept of the assumed linear function relating Y to X. The standard equations for determining the best-fitting slope and intercept are based on the proposition that "best" means the slope and intercept values that produce the smallest total squared error between the observed and predicted Y values.

Like regression models, typical mathematical models have parameters. The main difference between fitting a simple regression model and a typical mathematical model is that the former has an analytical solution,[14] whereas the latter usually do not. Even a model that is closely related to a linear model—an exponential growth to an asymptote model, expressed by the equation

$$Y = A(1 - e^{cX})$$

with two parameters c, the exponential decay rate, and A, the asymptote—does not have an analytical solution. To find the best-fitting parameter values, some sort of search procedure is needed whereby candidate parameter sets are systematically evaluated and the approximate best-fitting set is determined.

When carrying out such a search, it is necessary to decide what is meant by "best." Typically, one of three criteria is used to find the parameter set that (a) minimizes total squared error between observed and predicted data points, (b) minimizes the χ^2 between the observed and predicted frequencies, or (c) maximizes the probability of the data values given a particular parameter set (i.e., maximum likelihood techniques).

Fit Quality Expressed in Intuitive Units. My concern here is not with which technique is used—discussions of this issue may be found in many mathematical methods texts (e.g., Atkinson, Bower, & Crothers, 1965, Chapter 9)—but with how the results of the search are presented. In particular, I recommend that however the best-fitting parameter set is *found,* the quality of the fit should be presented as root-mean-square-error (RMSE), which is obtained by

$$\text{RMSE} = \sqrt{\frac{\sum_j (M_j - P_j)^2}{\text{degrees of freedom}}}$$

where the sum is over j experimental conditions, M_j and P_j are observed and predicted results in condition j, and degrees of freedom is degrees of freedom, which is approximately and most easily computed as the number of fitted data points minus the number of estimated parameters. The reason for this recommendation is that RMSE, being in units of the original dependent variable, is most straightforward and allows a reader to grasp and evaluate intuitively.

---

[14]This mean that equations for the best-fitting parameter values can be generated; for example, for a linear-regression model, slope $= (n \Sigma XY - \Sigma X \Sigma X)/ [n \Sigma X^2 - (\Sigma X)^2]$.

Parameters Expressed in Intuitive Units. In the same spirit, the results of applying a mathematical model are best understood if the parameters themselves are expressed in natural and well-defined units. Parameter units—such as probability correct raised to the 1.6 power, for instance—are not intuitively appealing, whereas parameter units such as time (e.g., ms) are much more intuitively appealing. When parameters are defined in natural units, results of experiments can be conveyed in terms of the effects of independent variables on parameter values, which is considerably simpler than trying to describe the data in terms of, say, a set of complex interactions. A simple example of such a model is Sternberg's (e.g., 1967) short-term scanning model, in which two parameters—the scanning time per item and a "time for everything else" parameter—are both defined in units of time (ms). Given the validity of the model, the results of any given experimental Sternberg-task condition can be described by one number: the slope of the search function, which is an estimate of the scanning time per item. Different conditions (e.g., degraded versus undegraded target-item conditions) can then be described simply in terms of the degree to which scanning time differs over the different conditions.

Model Fitting and Hypothesis Testing. Thus far, I have treated model fitting and hypothesis testing as separate enterprises. At their core, however, they are the same thing. In both instances, a model is proposed, and the data are treated in such a way as to evaluate the plausibility of the data given that the model is correct.

The difference between model fitting and hypothesis testing is one of tradition, not of substance. In a hypothesis-testing procedure, the null hypothesis is almost invariably that population means in some set are all equal to one another. However, such a characterization of the null hypothesis is not necessary; as suggested in the earlier section on planned comparisons, *any* single-degree-of-freedom hypothesis is a valid null hypothesis. Thus, the best-fitting set of parameter values issuing from the fit of a mathematical model to a data set can be characterized as a null hypothesis and can be tested with the standard hypothesis-testing machinery. Note that two other departures from tradition are involved in this process. First, the investigator's goal is typically to *accept* the null hypothesis (i.e., to confirm the model) rather than to reject the null hypothesis; second, reliance on the linear model is deemphasized considerably (the mathematical model being tested could be linear, but it often is not).

Display of Data Fits

My final comments about mathematical models revolve around displays of data fits. As just indicated, many experimental results can most parsimoniously be expressed as effects of independent variables on parameter values. This technique works best when the model under consideration is well-tested and accepted as an accurate description of the experimental paradigm under investigation. With this kind of mature model, the validity of the model is not under consideration; rather the model is being used as a tool to investigate something else (e.g., in the example from Sternberg, 1967, to investigate the effect of stimulus degradation on search slope, where "slope" is preaccepted as a meaningful entity within the context of the Sternberg, 1967, model).

With less developed models, however, a central issue is often whether (or the degree to which) the model is adequately fit by the data to begin with. In this case, the main result to be presented is the model fit itself. As noted, the most straightforward way of doing this is with a single number, the RMSE. However, a graphical display of the model fit is also critical in order that systematic failures of the model can be highlighted. How this is done depends on the relation between what the model predicts and the dependent variable measured in the experiment.

Quantitative Predictions. When the model is sufficiently precise that it predicts a specific value of the dependent variable for each experimental condition, the fit can be presented as a standard graph of the observed data plus predicted data. As an example, consider data from my laboratory generated by an experiment in which four-digit strings were presented at varying durations for immediate recall. The strings were either spatially filtered in order to leave only low spatial frequencies, or only high spatial frequencies, or were presented normally (i.e., including all spatial frequencies). A mathematical model described by Olds and Engel (1998), which predicted an exact value of the dependent variable (proportion recalled) for each condition, was fit to the data. The data and model fit are shown in Figure 9.13. I wish to emphasize several aspects of the data presentation.

First, the data are presented as symbols only (diamonds and triangles), whereas the model fits are presented as lines without symbols.

Second, the model predictions are "complete." By this I mean that the theoretical lines include predicted fits not just for the discrete durations selected for the experiment, but continuously over the selected range. This means that the predicted curves are smooth, and the predictions of the theory are clearer than they would be if only the predictions corresponding to the experimental durations were shown.

Finally, at the risk of sounding overly compulsive, it is mnemonically wise, as well as aesthetically elegant, to select, if possible, data symbols that are somehow naturally associated with the conditions. In the case of Figure 9.13, for example, downward-pointing triangles represent low spatial frequencies; upward-pointing triangles represent high spatial frequencies; and diamonds (i.e., the superimposition of downward- and upward-pointing triangles) represent all spatial frequencies.

Monotonic Predictions. Sometimes a mathematical model predicts a quantity that

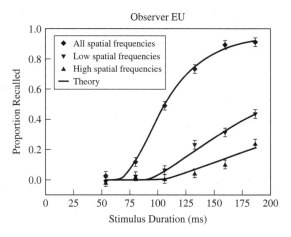

Figure 9.13 Unpublished data from Harley and Loftus showing digit recall performance as a function of stimulus duration and the nature of spatial filtering.

NOTE: Smooth lines through the data points represent theoretical predictions based on the best-fitting parameter values. The error bars are standard errors.

may be assumed to be only monotonically related to the dependent variable measured in the experiment. For example, Loftus and Irwin (1998) developed a theory of missing-dot, temporal-integration performance (e.g., Di Lollo, 1980). In this paradigm, 24 dots are briefly presented to a subject as a 5×5 dot array with one dot missing. The subject's task is to identify the position of the missing dot, and missing-dot detection probability is the dependent variable. The dots are presented in two temporal halves: During half 1, a random 12 of the 24 dots are presented, and the remaining 12 dots are presented during half 2. This means that in order to perform the missing-dot detection task, the subject must integrate the spatial information corresponding to the two dot-array halves over time. For purposes of the present discussion, the duration of half 2 was short (20 ms), and the duration of half 1 varied from 20 to 100 ms in 20-ms steps; the duration of the interstimulus interval (ISI) separating the end of half 1 from the start of half 2 varied from 20 ms to 60 ms in 20-ms steps.

Central to Loftus and Irwin's theory was the proposition that a visual stimulus triggers an internal *sensory-response function* that rises over time beginning at stimulus onset and falls, eventually back to zero, following stimulus offset (see also Busey & Loftus, 1994; Loftus & McLean, 1999). In the missing-dot paradigm, each stimulus half produces one such sensory-response function, and performance is determined by (i.e., is a monotonic function of) the correlation over time between the two sensory-response functions (as suggested by Dixon & Di Lollo, 1994). The theory can specify the magnitude of this correlation for any stimulus condition, but it does not specify the nature of the monotonic function that relates missing-dot detection probability to correlation magnitude.

In this kind of situation, it is not possible to fit the theory using the techniques listed earlier

because they require the theory to predict the actual dependent variable, not just something presumed to be monotonically related to the dependent variable. A straightforward alternative is to use as a fit criterion the rank-order correlation (Spearman ρ) over conditions between the data and the theory. The fit may then be represented as the data-theory scatter plot, which would be monotonic if the data fit the theory perfectly.

Figure 9.14 provides an example using the paradigm and theory that I have just described. The predicted data points are generated by the parameter values corresponding to the highest data $\times$ theory that Spearman ρ ($\rho = 0.987$) found by the search procedure. The scatter plot shows data (mean proportion of correctly detected missing-dot positions) plotted against theory (predicted correlation) across the 25 half-1 duration $\times$ ISI conditions. Within the scatter plot, different half-1 durations are represented by different curve symbols, whereas within each half-1 duration, increasing predicted and observed values correspond to decreasing ISIs.

Presenting the fit as a scatter plot confers at least two benefits. First, the shape of the scatter plot (which is ogival in this example) constitutes an empirical estimate of the actual monotonic function relating the dependent variable to the theoretical construct, thereby providing clues about the mechanism that relates the dependent variable to the theoretical construct. Second, the scatter plot underscores systematic discrepancies in the data fit. In this example, it appears that performance in the long half-1 duration conditions (e.g., the 100-ms half-1 duration conditions, represented by the open squares) are observed to be systematically higher than they are predicted to be compared to short half-1 duration conditions (e.g., the 20-ms half-1 duration conditions represented by the solid circles), thereby pinpointing a specific deficit in the theory.

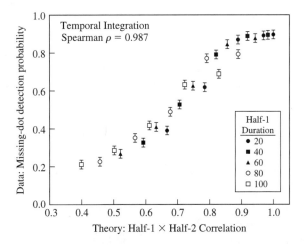

Figure 9.14 Obtained data as a function of a predicted theoretical construct for a missing-dot, temporal-integration experiment.
NOTE: The different curve symbols correspond to different values of half-1 duration. The 5 data points within each half-1 duration correspond to different ISI values (data from Loftus & Irwin, 1998). The error bars are standard errors.

Equivalence Techniques for Investigating Interactions

In the large majority of psychological experiments, an investigator sets the levels of some independent variable and measures the resulting values of the dependent variable. Of interest, then, is how changes in the independent variable lead to changes in the dependent variable. Moreover, a sizeable number of experiments are primarily concerned not with main effects, but with how one or more independent variables *interact* in their effects on the dependent variable.

As numerous writers have pointed out (e.g., Bogartz, 1976; Loftus, 1978), many conclusions resting on interactions have strong limitations, the most severe of which is that nonordinal (i.e., noncrossover) interactions lack generality both with respect to other performance measures that are nonlinearly related to one that is actually measured (e.g., an interaction in a memory experiment observed in terms of probability correct cannot necessarily be generalized to d') and

also with respect to underlying theoretical constructs that are nonlinearly related to the performance measure (e.g., an interaction observed in terms of probability correct cannot necessarily be generalized to some generically defined "memory strength").

To circumvent these difficulties, one can turn to *equivalence techniques,* which are a set of theoretical/methodological procedures for determining the rules under which different combinations of independent variables lead to equivalent states of some inferred internal psychological state. Equivalence techniques have roots in classical statistics (e.g., Hays, 1973) and in conjoint measurement (e.g., Krantz, Luce, Suppes, & Tversky, 1971; Krantz & Tversky, 1971; Tversky & Russo, 1969).

Equivalence techniques are common in vision science. Perhaps the best illustration of how such techniques are used to understand the workings of the visual system is the classic *color-matching experiment,* wherein an observer adjusts some additive combination of primary colors such that it matches a monochromatic test color (e.g., Wright, 1929, 1946). The resulting two stimuli—the combination of primaries and the monochrome stimulus—constitute *color metamers,* which, though entirely different physically, are equivalent psychologically in a fundamental way: They entail equal quantum catches in the three classes of cone photoreceptors. The original success of the color-matching experiment constituted the empirical foundation of the trichromacy theory of color vision, and versions of the color-matching experiment have been used more recently to refine and modify the theory (e.g., Wandell, 1982).

As is discussed in the next two subsections, equivalence techniques can be used in two ways virtually any area of psychology. First, relatively weak hypotheses about effects of certain variables can be studied using *state-trace analysis.* Second, stronger hypotheses make specific, unique, and testable predictions about the specific quantitative rules by which multiple independent variables combine to produce equivalent values of the dependent variable.

State-Trace Analysis

State-trace analysis was introduced by Bamber (1979) as a means of investigating relations among independent variables, dependent variables, and hypothesized internal dimensions. In particular, state-trace analysis can be used to answer two related questions. First, is the assumption of a single internal dimension sufficient to account for observed relations among multiple independent variables and multiple dependent variables? Second, if more than one dimension is necessary, what are the characteristics of the multiple dimensions; that is, how are they affected by the independent variables, and how do they influence the dependent variables?[15]

To illustrate the use of state-trace analysis, consider a face-recognition investigation described by Busey, Tunnicliff, Loftus, and Loftus (2000). The experimental paradigm entailed an initial study phase in which a series of face pictures was sequentially presented, followed by a yes-no recognition test phase in which two dependent variables—accuracy (hit probability) and confidence (on a four-point scale)—were measured. Of principal interest was whether accuracy and confidence were simply two measures of the same internal state that, for mnemonic convenience, might be termed "strength." The experiment entailed two independent variables that were manipulated during the study phase. First, exposure duration was varied, and second, each studied face was followed by a 15-s period during which visual rehearsal of the just-seen face was either required or prohibited. The main results were, not surprisingly, that both accuracy and confidence increased with increasing exposure duration and with rehearsal compared to no rehearsal. That is, qualitatively, both accuracy and confidence were affected in the same way by the two independent variables, thereby suggesting, in the tradition of dissociation techniques, that they were simply two measures of the same internal state.

However, the use of state-trace analysis allowed a much more precise answer to the question. More specifically, the proposition that any two dependent variables—accuracy and confidence in this instance—are measures of the same internal state can be couched in the form of a hypothesis called the *single-*

---

[15]Examples of state-trace analysis are rare in most of psychology. In addition to examples provided by Bamber

(1979) and Busey et al. (2000), see Loftus and Irwin (1998), who used such analyses to address the question, "Are visible persistence and iconic memory just two names for the same internal process?" Palmer (e.g., 1986a, 1986b) has used related (and formally identical) equivalence techniques to examine numerous issues in attention and perception.

dimension model: There exists a single internal dimension (call it "strength") whose value is jointly determined by duration and rehearsal, and that, in turn, determines the values of both confidence and accuracy. The form of this model is shown at the top of Figure 9.15. Pitted against this single-dimensional model is some form of multidimensional model, according to which the two dependent variables are determined at least in part by different internal dimensions. Although a single-dimensional model (akin to a standard null hypothesis) is unique, there are an infinite number of possible multidimensional models (as there are an infinite number of alternative hypotheses). One reasonable multidimensional model is shown at the bottom of Figure 9.15. Here, a second dimension, termed "certainty," is affected by rehearsal but not by duration, and it affects confidence but not accuracy.

The key prediction of the single-dimensional hypothesis rests on the logic that any two conditions—a long-duration, no-rehearsal condition, and a shorter-duration, rehearsal condition—that produce equal accuracy must have done so because they produced the same strength values. Thus—and

here is the key prediction—because confidence is also determined by strength, these same two conditions must also produce equal confidence values.

To evaluate this prediction, one constructs *state-trace plots,* which are scatter plots of one dependent variable plotted against the other (accuracy plotted as a function of confidence, in this instance) over the experimental conditions defined by the combination of the two independent variables—in this case, conditions defined by the duration × rehearsal combinations. The prediction then translates to the following: The curve traced out by the rehearsal conditions must overlie the curve traced out by the no-rehearsal conditions.

It should be noted, incidentally, that the success of state-trace analysis does not require that one be lucky enough to find pairs of duration × rehearsal conditions that happen to produce identical performance. The formal rationale for this assertion is described in Bamber (1979).

Essentially, one assumes that the measured points are samples from an underlying continuous function whose form can be estimated by "connecting the dots" in the state-trace plot.

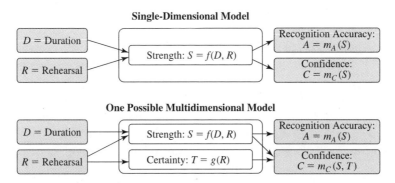

Figure 9.15 Two models on the relations between two independent variables and two dependent variables in a face-recognition experiment (reported by Busey et al., 2000).
Note: The shaded round rectangles on the left represent independent variables, whereas the shaded round rectangles on the right represent dependent variables. The unshaded round rectangles in the middle represent unidimensional theoretical constructs.

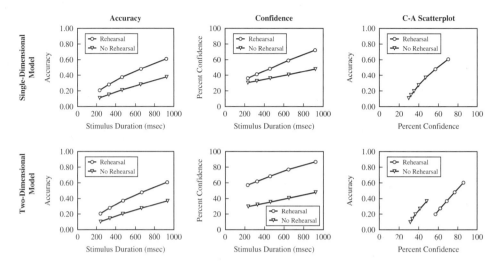

Figure 9.16   Theoretical predictions from the models shown in Figure 9.15.
NOTE: The left and middle panels show "standard" data presentation: the dependent variable plotted as functions of the independent variables. The right panels show state-trace plots that are scatter plots of one dependent variable plotted against the other. With the state-trace plots, the distinct predictions of the two models are considerably more apparent than they are in the standard plots.

Figure 9.16 shows predictions from the single-dimensional model (top panels) and from the multi-dimensional model (bottom panels) of Figure 9.15. In each panel, circles correspond to the rehearsal conditions while triangles correspond to the no-rehearsal conditions. The five instances of each curve symbol correspond to five exposure durations. For each of the two models, the two left-hand panels ("Accuracy" and "Confidence") present the data in the manner in which such data are normally presented: The dependent variable is plotted as a function of the independent variables (duration along the abscissa and rehearsal as the curve parameter in this example). Based on these standard data, there is nothing very obvious that distinguishes the predictions of the two models.

However, the state-trace plots shown as the rightmost panels ("C-A Scatterplot") distinguish strongly between the two models. As described above, the single-dimensional model predicts that the two scatterplots corre-

sponding to the two rehearsal levels fall atop one another. However, the multi-dimensional model predicts that the two scatterplots are distinguishable in some manner that depends on the exact construction of the multi-dimensional model. In the multi-dimensional model of Figure 9.15, a second internal dimension, "certainty" is increased by rehearsal but not duration, and increased certainty increases confidence but not accuracy. Therefore, according to this particular multi-dimensional model, two conditions that produce the same accuracy values must have done so because they produced the same strength value. However, comparing two conditions that produce the same strength values, the rehearsal condition will produce greater confidence than the no-rehearsal condition, because certainty is greater in the rehearsal condition than in the no-rehearsal condition. Therefore, as is evident in the prediction (Figure 9.16, bottom-right panel) this particular multidimensional model predicts the rehearsal curve to be displaced to the right of the no-rehearsal curve.

In sum, state-trace analysis has two virtues. First, it allows one to test any form of single-dimensional model, which is generally a strong test of the common question in psychology: "Are two dependent variables, Y and Y′ simply two measures of the same internal state?" Second, given that one rejects a single-dimensional model, the resulting form of the state-trace plots provides strong clues as to the nature of the implied multidimensional model. To briefly illustrate, Busey et al. (1990) actually investigated two kinds of confidence: prospective confidence, given at the time of study, and retrospective confidence, given at the time of test. They determined that a single-dimensional model was appropriate to describe retrospective confidence, but a multidimensional model of the sort depicted at the bottom of Figure 9.15 was necessary to describe prospective confidence.

Additive and Multiplicative Effects

As just described, state-trace analysis deals with the qualitative question: Do multiple independent variables affect the same internal memory dimension which then determines performance in the relevant memory tasks? An investigator can also use equivalence techniques to unveil stronger quantitative rules by which independent variables combine to produce a value on the internal dimension. To illustrate such rules, I will use two examples in which memory is measured as a function of the exposure duration of the to-be-remembered stimulus (as in the Busey et al., 2000 experiment described in the last section). In this kind of experimental paradigm, define a *performance curve* as a curve that relates memory performance to exposure duration (as, for example, in Figure 9.16, four left panels.) Define a *focal variable* as some variable under consideration that is factorially combined with exposure duration (e.g.,

rehearsal in the Busey et al. experiment). The equation relating performance curves for two levels of the focal variable is:

$$p[i, d] = p[j, f(d)] \qquad (21)$$

where $p[i, d]$ and $p[j, f(d)]$ denote performance for levels i and j of the focal variable, d and $f(d)$ are durations, and f is a monotonic function. Again in the spirit of equivalence, it is important to realize that Equation (21) describes duration relations that produce equal performance for different focal-variable levels.

Of theoretical interest in a given situation is the nature of the function $f(d)$ on the right side of Equation (21). Different $f(d)$s are implied by different hypotheses about the focal variable's effect. I illustrate this with two common hypotheses. The first is that the focal variable's effect is *additive*—that is, that $f(d) = d + k$—which means that

$$p(i, d) = p(j, d + k) \qquad (22)$$

Here, k is a constant in units of time. The interpretation of an additive effect is that being in level i of the focal variable is equivalent to having an additional k ms of stimulus duration compared to being in level j. As shown in Panel A of Figure 9.17, stimulus masked/not masked exemplifies an additive focal variable with $k = 100$ ms—which is the basis for the claim made by Loftus, Johnson, and Shimamura (1985) that an icon is worth 100 ms.

The second hypothesis is that the focal variable's effect is *multiplicative*—that $f(d) = cd$, which means that

$$p(i, d) = p(j, cd) \qquad (23)$$

Here, c is a dimensionless constant. The interpretation of a multiplicative effect is that being in level j of the focal variable slows down processing by a factor of c, compared to being in level i. As shown in Panel B of Figure 9.17, stimulus luminance exemplifies

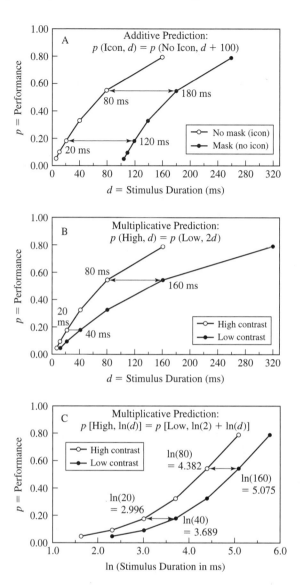

Figure 9.17   Additive and Multiplicative Predictions

NOTE: Panel A: Performance as a function of stimulus duration and stimulus masked/not masked. The horizontally parallel curves (after Loftus et al., 1992) reflect an additive effect of masking: The iconic image eliminated by the mask is worth 100 ms of additional physical exposure duration. Panel B: Stimulus contrast (high, low) replaces stimulus masked/not masked. Here a multiplicative result occurs: The exposure duration required to achieve a constant performance level is greater (by a factor of 2) for the low-contrast compared to the high-contrast condition (after Loftus, 1985c). Panel C: The multiplicative relation from Panel B plotted on a log-duration axis produces easy-to-test horizontally parallel curves rather than the difficult-to-test, constant-ratio diverging curves of Panel B.

a multiplicative focal variable with $c = 2$ (see Loftus, 1985c; Sperling, 1986; as shown by Loftus & Ruthruff, 1994, the same is true when contrast is the focal variable).

Figure 9.17 illustrates three important facets of using equivalence techniques. First, testing various hypotheses (e.g., that the effect of some focal variable is additive or multiplicative) involves *horizontally comparing* performance curves because, as indicated in Equations (16) through (18), the critical comparisons are of the durations d and $f(d)$ required to achieve equal performance for different focal-variable levels, i and j. Second, an additive hypothesis predicts that performance curves will be *horizontally parallel* as in Panel A of Figure 9.17, whereas a multiplicative hypothesis predicts that performance curves will be *constant-ratio diverging* as in Panel B of Figure 9.17. Third, Panel C of Figure 9.17 demonstrates that a multiplicative hypothesis can be conveniently tested by plotting performance on a log-duration scale instead of on a linear-duration scale. When d is on a log scale, Equation (23) becomes

$$p[i, \ln(d)] = p[j, \ln(c) + \ln(d)]$$

and performance curves are again horizontally parallel, separated by a constant of $\ln(c)$, which then, of course, can be exponentiated to recover c.

As I asserted earlier, equivalence techniques represent scale-independent means of identifying the fundamental nature of interactions among variables. Equivalence techniques allow conclusions that are more generalizable and robust than are conclusions based on most traditional statistical interactions. Because performance curves are compared horizontally, any conclusion issuing from the comparison (e.g., that the curves are or are not horizontally parallel on a linear or on a log-duration scale) is invariant over all monotonic transforms of the performance measure because any points that are equal in one scale must also be equal in any monotonically related scale. Therefore, conclusions issuing from equivalence techniques apply not only to the particular dependent variable being measured (e.g., proportion correct) but also to any theoretical construct that is assumed to be monotonically related to the dependent variable (e.g., "memory strength"). Such con-

clusions also apply, *mutatis mutandis,* to any dependent variable that is monotonically related to the dependent variable being measured (e.g., to d' if the measured variable is proportion correct).

CONCLUSIONS

It is worth concluding by briefly reiterating the sentiments expressed at the outset of this chapter. Lurking within a typical data set is often a wealth of fascinating information that can be summoned forth if sufficiently clever detective techniques are used. As has been argued in many places (see particularly, Loftus, 1996; Schmidt, 1996), there are, at present, many standard data-analysis techniques that not only are ill-crafted for eliciting such information, but also actively bias the investigator against finding anything interesting or nonobvious from the data. It is my hope that some of the less common techniques described in this chapter—and other related techniques that readers are left to devise on their own—will provide some assistance in coping with the vast sea of psychological data that our present technology currently produces for us.

REFERENCES

Abelson, R. P. (1995). *Statistics as principled argument.* Hillsdale, NJ: Erlbaum.

Atkinson, R. C., Bower, G. H., & Crothers, E. J. (1965). *An Introduction to Mathematical Learning Theory.* New York: Wiley.

Bakan, D. (1966). The test of significance in psychological research. *Psychological Bulletin, 66,* 423–437.

Bamber, D. (1979). State trace analysis: A method of testing simple theories of causation. *Journal of Mathematical Psychology, 19,* 137–181.

Berger, J. O. & Berry, D. A. (1988). Statistical analysis and the illusion of objectivity. *American Scientist, 76,* 159–165.

Bogartz, R. S. (1976). On the meaning of statistical interactions. *Journal of Experimental Child Psychology, 22,* 178–183.

Busey, T. A., & Loftus, G. R. (1994). Sensory and cognitive components of visual information acquisition. *Psychological Review, 101,* 446–469.

Busey, T. A., Tunnicliff, J., Loftus, G. R., & Loftus, E. F. (2000). Accounts of the confidence-accuracy relation in recognition memory. *Psychonomic Bulletin & Review, 7,* 26–48.

Carver, R. P. (1978). The case against statistical significance testing. *Harvard Educational Review, 48,* 378–399.

Carver, R. P. (1993). The case against statistical significance testing, revisited. *Journal of Experimental Education, 61,* 287–292.

Cohen, J. (1990). Things I have learned (so far). *American Psychologist, 45,* 1304–1312.

Cohen, J. (1994). The earth is round ($p < .05$). *American Psychologist, 49,* 997–1003.

Di Lollo, V. (1980). Temporal integration in visual memory. *Journal of Experimental Psychology: General, 109,* 75–97.

Dixon, P., & Di Lollo, V. (1994). Beyond visible persistence: An alternative account of temporal integration and segregation in visual processing. *Cognitive Psychology, 26,* 33–66.

Frick, R. W. (1995). Accepting the null hypothesis. *Memory & Cognition, 23,* 132–138.

Gigerenzer, G., Swijtink, Z., Porter, T., Daston, L., Beatty, J., & Kruger, L. (1989). *The empire of chance: How probability changed science and everyday life.* Cambridge: Cambridge University Press.

Grant, D. A. (1962). Testing the null hypothesis and the strategy and tactics of investigating theoretical models. *Psychological Review, 69,* 54–61.

Greenwald, A. G. (1975). Consequences of prejudice against the null hypothesis. *Psychological Bulletin, 83,* 1–20.

Greenwald, A. G., Gonzalez, R., Harris, R. J., & Guthrie, D. (1996). Effect Sizes and p values: What should be reported and what should be replicated? *Psychophysiology, 33,* 175–183.

Guilford, J. P. (1942). *Fundamental statistics in psychology and education.* New York: McGraw-Hill.

Harlow, L. L., Mulaik, S. A., & Steiger, J. H. (Eds.). (1997). *What if there were no significance tests?* Mahwah, NJ: Erlbaum.

Hays, W. (1973). *Statistics for the social sciences* (2nd ed.). New York: Holt.

Hunter, J. E., & Schmidt, F. (1990). *Methods of meta analysis: Correcting error and bias in research findings.* Newbury Park, CA: Sage.

Jackson, J. M., & Latané, B. (1981). All alone in front of all those people: Stage fright as a function of number and type of co-performers and audience. *Journal of Personality and Social Psychology, 40,* 73–85.

Jones, L. V. (1955). Statistics and research design. *Annual Review of Psychology, 6,* 405–430. Stanford, CA: Annual Reviews.

Krantz, D. H. (1999). The null hypothesis testing controversy in psychology. *Journal of the American Statistical Association, 44,* 1372–1381.

Krantz, D. H., Luce, R. D., Suppes, P., & Tversky, A. (1971). *Foundations of measurement.* New York: Academic Press.

Krantz, D. H., & Tversky, A. (1971). Conjoint measurement analysis of composition rules in psychology. *Psychological Review, 78,* 151–169.

Loftus, G. R. (1978). On interpretation of interactions. *Memory and Cognition, 6,* 312–319.

Loftus, G. R. (1985a). Consistency and confoundings: Reply to Slamecka. *Journal of Experimental Psychology: Learning, Memory and Cognition, 11,* 817–820.

Loftus, G. R. (1985b). Evaluating forgetting curves. *Journal of Experimental Psychology: Learning, Memory and Cognition, 11,* 396–405.

Loftus, G. R. (1985c). Picture perception: Effects of luminance level on available information and information-extraction rate. *Journal of Experimental Psychology: General, 114,* 342–356.

Loftus, G. R. (1991). On the tyranny of hypothesis testing in the social sciences. *Contemporary Psychology, 36,* 102–105.

Loftus, G. R. (1993a). Editorial Comment. *Memory & Cognition, 21,* 1–3.

Loftus, G. R. (1993b). A picture is worth a thousand *p*-values: On the irrelevance of hypothesis testing in the computer age. *Behavior Research Methods, Instrumentation and Computers, 25,* 250–256.

Loftus, G. R. (1995). Data analysis as insight. *Behavior Research Methods, Instrumentation and Computers, 27,* 57–59.

Loftus, G. R. (1996). Psychology will be a much better science when we change the way we analyze data. *Current Directions in Psychological Science, 5,* 161–171.

Loftus, G. R., & Bamber, D. (1990). Weak models, strong models, unidimensional models, and psychological time. *Journal of Experimental Psychology: Learning, Memory, and Cognition, 16,* 916–926.

Loftus, G. R., & Irwin, D. E. (1998). On the relations among different measures of visible and informational persistence. *Cognitive Psychology, 35,* 135–199.

Loftus, G. R., Johnson, C. A., & Shimamura, A. P. (1985). How much is an icon worth? *Journal of Experimental Psychology: Human Perception and Performance, 11,* 1–13.

Loftus, G. R., Kaufman, L., Nishimoto, T., & Ruthruff, E. (1992). Why it's annoying to look at slides with the room lights still on: Effects of visual degradation on perceptual processing and long-term visual memory. In K. Rayner (Ed.), *Eye Movements and Visual Cognition: Scene Perception and Reading.* New York: Springer-Verlag (pp. 203–226).

Loftus, G. R., & Masson, M. E. J. (1994). Using confidence intervals in within-subjects designs. *Psychonomic Bulletin & Review, 1,* 476–490.

Loftus, G. R., & McLean, J. E. (1999). A front end to a theory of picture recognition. *Psychonomic Bulletin & Review, 6,* 394–411.

Loftus, G. R., & Ruthruff, E. R. (1994). A theory of visual information acquisition and visual memory with special application to intensity-duration tradeoffs. *Journal of Experimental Psychology: Human Perception and Performance, 20,* 33–50.

Lykken, D. T. (1968). Statistical significance in psychological research. *Psychological Bulletin, 70,* 131–139.

Maltz, M. D. (1994). Deviating from the mean: The declining significance of significance. *Journal of Research in Crime and Delinquency, 31,* 434–463.

Meehl, P. E. (1967). Theory testing in psychology and physics: A methodological paradox. *Philosophy of Science, 34,* 103–115.

Meehl, P. E. (1978). Theoretical risks and tabular asterisks: Sir Karl, Sir Ronald and the slow process of soft psychology. *Journal of Consulting and Clinical Psychology, 46,* 806–834.

Meehl, P. E. (1990). Why summaries of research on psychological theories are often uninterpretable. *Psychological Reports, 66,* 195–244.

Melton, A. W. (1962). Editorial. *Journal of Experimental Psychology, 64,* 553–557.

Nunnally, J. (1960). The place of statistics in psychology. *Educational and Psychological Measurement, 20,* 641–650.

Olds, E. S., & Engel, S. A. (1998). Linearity across spatial frequency in object recognition. *Vision Research, 38,* 2109–2118.

Palmer, J. C. (1986a). Mechanisms of displacement discrimination with and without perceived movement. *Journal of Experimental Psychology: Human Perception and Performance, 12,* 411–421.

Palmer, J. C. (1986b). Mechanisms of displacement discrimination with a visual reference. *Vision Research, 26,* 1939–1947.

Rosnow, R. L., & Rosenthal, R. (1989). Statistical procedures and the justification of knowledge in psychological science. *American Psychologist, 44,* 1276–1284.

Rozeboom, W. W. (1960). The fallacy of the null hypothesis significance test. *Psychological Bulletin, 57,* 416–428.

Schmidt, F. (1996). Statistical significance testing and cumulative knowledge in psychology: Implications for training of researchers. *Psychological Methods, 1,* 115–129.

Schmidt, F., & Hunter, J. (1997). Eight false objections to the discontinuation of significance testing in the analysis of research data. In L. Harlow & S. Mulaik (Eds.), *What if there were no significance testing?* Hillsdale, NJ: Erlbaum.

Slamecka, N. J., (1985). On comparing rates of forgetting. *Journal of Experimental Psychology: Learning, Memory & Cognition, 11,* 812–816.

Slamecka, N. J., & McElree, B. (1983). Normal forgetting of verbal lists as a function of their degree of learning. *Journal of Experimental Psychology: Learning, Memory, and Cognition, 9,* 384–397.

Smith, A. F., & Prentis, D. A. (1993). Graphical data analysis. In G. Kerens and C. Lewis (Eds.), *A handbook for data analysis in the behavioral sciences: Statistical issues.* Hillsdale, NJ: Erlbaum.

Sperling, G. (1986). A signal to noise theory of the effects of luminance on picture memory: Commentary on Loftus. *Journal of Experimental Psychology: General, 115,* 189–192.

Sternberg, S. (1967). Two operations in character recognition: Some evidence from reaction time measurements. *Perception and Psychophysics, 2,* 43–53.

Tufte, E. R. (1983). *The visual display of quantitative information.* Cheshire, CT: Graphics Press.

Tufte, E. R. (1990). *Envisioning information.* Cheshire, CT: Graphics Press.

Tukey, J. W. (1977). *Exploratory data analysis.* Reading, MA: Addison Wesley.

Tversky, A., & Russo, J. E. (1969). Substitutibility and similarity in binary choices. *Journal of Mathematical Psychology, 6,* 112.

Tyler, R. W. (1935). What is statistical significance? *Educational Research Bulletin, 10,* 115–118, 142.

Wainer, H., & Thissen, D. (1993). Graphical data analysis. In G. Kerens and C. Lewis (Eds.), *A handbook for data analysis in the behavioral sciences: statistical issues.* Hillsdale, NJ: Erlbaum. pp. 391–458.

Wandell, B. A. (1982). Measurements of small color differences. *Psychological Review, 89,* 281–302.

Wright, W. D. (1929). A re-determination of the trichromatic coefficients of the spectral colors. *Transactions of the Optical Society of America, 30,* 141–164.

Wright, W. D. (1946). Researches on normal and defective colour vision. London: Kimpton.

CHAPTER 10

Meta-Analysis

ROBERT ROSENTHAL AND M. ROBIN DIMATTEO

CUMULATING SCIENTIFIC EVIDENCE

The fundamental goal of meta-analytic procedures is the cumulation of evidence. There has long been underlying pessimism in the younger social, behavioral, and biomedical sciences that our progress has been exceedingly slow and less orderly than we would like, at least when compared to the progress of older, more programmatic sciences such as physics and chemistry. In other words, the more recent work in physics and chemistry seems to build directly on the older work of those sciences, whereas the more recent work of the social, behavioral, and biomedical sciences seems often to be starting from scratch. Those who have looked closely at the issue of cumulation in the physical sciences have pointed out that these disciplines have ample problems of their own (Collins, 1985; Hedges, 1987; Mann, 1990; Pool, 1988). Nonetheless, in the matter of cumulating evidence, the social and biomedical sciences have much to be modest about.

Limited success in the process of cumulation does not seem to be caused by a lack of replication, or by the failure to recognize the need for replication. Indeed, there are many areas of the social, behavioral, and biomedical sciences for which the results of many studies, all addressing essentially the same question, are available. Our summaries of the results of these sets of studies, however, have not been nearly as informative as they might have been, either with respect to summarized significance levels or with respect to summarized effect sizes. Even the best reviews of research by the most sophisticated scholars have been primarily qualitative narratives and have rarely told us much more about each study than the direction of the relationship between the variables investigated and whether a given significance level was attained.

This state of affairs is beginning to change, however. More and more reviews of the literature are moving from the traditional literary approach to quantitative approaches to research synthesis described in an increasing number of textbooks of meta-analysis (Cooper, 1989; Cooper & Hedges, 1994a; Glass, McGaw, & Smith, 1981; Hedges & Olkin, 1985; Hunter & Schmidt, 1990; Light & Pillemer, 1984; R. Rosenthal, 1991a). The goals of these quantitative approaches of meta-analysis are to help us discover what we have learned from the results of the studies

In this chapter the authors have drawn on the work of many authors and especially on some of their earlier writings in this area, including R. Rosenthal (1991a, 1994b, 1995b, 1998, 2000); R. Rosenthal and DiMatteo (2001); R. Rosenthal and Rosnow (1991); and R. Rosenthal, Rosnow, and Rubin (2000).

conducted, and to help us discover what we have not yet learned.

DEFINING RESEARCH RESULTS

Before we can consider various issues and procedures in the cumulation of research results, we must become quite explicit about the meaning of the concept *results of a study*. It is easiest to begin with what we do not mean. We do not mean the prose *conclusion* drawn by the investigator and reported in the abstract, the results, or the discussion section of the research report. We also do not mean the results of an omnibus F test with $df > 1$ in the numerator or an omnibus chi-square test with $df > 1$.

What we do mean is the answer to the question, What is the relationship between any variable X and any variable Y? The variables X and Y are chosen with only the constraint that their relationship be of interest to us. The answer to this question should normally come in two parts: (a) the estimate of the magnitude of the relationship (the effect size), and (b) an indication of the accuracy or reliability of the estimated effect size (e.g., as indexed by a confidence interval placed around the effect size estimate). An alternative to the second part of the answer is one not intrinsically more useful, but rather one more consistent with the existing practices of researchers: the significance level of the difference between the obtained effect size and the effect size expected under the null hypothesis (usually an effect size of zero).

Because a complete reporting of the results of a study requires the report of both the effect size and level of statistical significance, it is useful to make explicit the relationship between these quantities. The general relationship is given by

Significance Test = Effect Size × Study Size.

In other words, the larger the study in terms of the number of sampling units, the more significant the results will be. This is true unless the size of the effect is truly zero, in which case a larger study will not produce a result that is any more significant than a smaller study. Effect sizes of exactly zero, however, are rarely encountered.

META-ANALYSIS: A BRIEF HISTORICAL NOTE

We are inclined to think of meta-analysis as a recent development, but it is older than the t test, which dates back to 1908 (Gosset, 1908)!

Let us simultaneously describe the early history of meta-analysis and provide a classic illustration of the meta-analytic enterprise. In 1904 Pearson (1904) collected six correlation coefficients: .58, .58, .60, .63, .66, and .77. The weighted mean of these six correlation coefficients was .64, the unweighted mean was .63, and the median was .61. Pearson was collecting correlation coefficients because he wanted to know the degree to which inoculation against smallpox saved lives. His own rough-and-ready summary of his meta-analysis of six studies was that there was a .6 correlation between inoculation and survival—a truly huge effect.

When Pearson quantitatively summarized six studies of the effects of smallpox inoculation, a meta-analysis was an unusual thing to do. Recently, however, there has been an explosion of meta-analytic research syntheses, such that a rapidly increasing proportion of all reviews of the literature are in the form of quantitative reviews (i.e., meta-analyses). Despite its increasing frequency in the literature, however, meta-analysis is not without controversy and criticism, which we examine later.

Before we do that, it will be useful to consider the concept of replication.

Meta-analysis, after all, involves summarizing or synthesizing studies that are broadly thought of as replications. It is important to note that studies typically included in meta-analyses are not replications in a narrow sense. Rather, they examine the same underlying relationships even if their independent and dependent variables are operationally defined in different ways.

HOW SHALL WE THINK OF SUCCESSFUL REPLICATION?

There is a long tradition in psychology of urging replication of each other's research. Although we have been very good at calling for such replications, we have not been very good at deciding when a replication has been successful. The issue we now address is, When shall a study be deemed successfully replicated?

Ordinarily, this is taken to mean that in a new study at time 2, a null hypothesis that has been rejected at time 1 is rejected again, and with the same direction of outcome. We have a "failure to replicate" when one study was significant and the other was not, but such "failures" may be quite misleading. Let us consider an example.

Pseudo-Failures to Replicate

The Saga of Smith and Jones

Smith has published the results of an experiment in which a certain treatment procedure was predicted to improve performance. She reported results significant at $p < .05$ in the predicted direction. Jones published a rebuttal to Smith, claiming a failure to replicate. Both had an effect size r of .24 and a d of .50. But Smith had 80 subjects and Jones had only 20. In this type of situation, it is often the case that although the p value associated with

Smith's results is smaller than that of Jones's, the studies were in quite good agreement on their estimated sizes of effect as defined either by Cohen's d [$(Mean_1 - Mean_2)/\sigma$] or by r, the point biserial correlation between group membership (coded 0 or 1) and performance score (a more continuous score; Cohen, 1988; R. Rosenthal, 1991a). Thus, studies labeled as failure to replicate may turn out to provide strong evidence for the replicability of the claimed effect.

On the Odds against Replicating Significant Results

A related error often found in the behavioral and social sciences is the implicit assumption that if an effect is real, we should expect it to be found significant again upon replication. Nothing could be farther from the truth.

Suppose there is, in nature, a real effect with a true magnitude of $d = .50$ (i.e., [$Mean_1 - Mean_2]\sigma = .50\sigma$ units), or, equivalently, $r = .24$, a difference in success rate of 62% versus 38%, as shown in the binomial effect size display in which r is the difference between the success rates of the two conditions. The success rates are given as $.50 + r/2$ and $.50 - r/2$ hence for this example, $.62 - .38 = .24$, the value of r. For further details see R. Rosenthal and Rubin (1982b). Further suppose that an investigator studies this effect with an N of 64 subjects or so, giving the researcher a level of statistical power of .50, a very common level of power for behavioral researchers in the last 35 years (Cohen, 1962; Sedlmeier & Gigerenzer, 1989). Even though a d of .50 or an r of .24 can reflect a very important effect, there is only one chance in four ($p = .25$) that both the original investigator and a replicator will get results significant at the .05 level; i.e., the probability (power) for the first study ($p = .50$) is multiplied by the probability for the second study ($p = .50$) to yield $.50 \times .50 = .25$. If there were two replications of the original study, there would be only one chance in eight ($p = .125$) that all three studies would be significant (i.e., $p = .5 \times .5 \times .5 = .125$), even though we know that the effect in nature is very real and very important.

Contrasting Views of Replication

The traditional, less useful view of replication has two primary characteristics: It (a) focuses on significance level as the relevant summary statistic of a study and (b) makes its evaluation of whether replication has been successful in a dichotomous fashion. For example, replications are successful if both or neither $p < .05$, and they are unsuccessful if one $p < .05$ and the other $p > .05$. Psychologists' reliance on a dichotomous decision procedure has been well documented (Nelson, Rosenthal, & Rosnow, 1986; R. Rosenthal & Gaito, 1963, 1964). In this dichotomous procedure, differences between p levels are all regarded as trivial except the difference between a $p \leq .05$ and a $p > .05$, or some other critical level of significance at which we have decided to "reject the null hypothesis." This dichotomous approach to significance testing has been increasingly criticized, for example, by the American Psychological Association's Task Force on Statistical Inference (Wilkinson & the Task Force on Statistical Inference, 1999).

The newer, more useful views of replication success have two primary characteristics: (a) a focus on effect size as the more important summary statistic of a study, with a relatively more minor interest in the statistical significance level, and (b) an evaluation of whether replication has been successful, made in a continuous fashion. For example, two studies are not said to be successful or unsuccessful replicates of each other; rather, the degree of failure to replicate is indexed by the magnitude of difference between the effect sizes obtained in the two studies.

CRITICISMS OF META-ANALYSIS

Does the enormous increase in the number of meta-analytic reviews of the literature represent a giant stride forward in the development of the behavioral and social sciences generally, or does it signal a lemming-like flight to disaster? Judging from reactions to past meta-analytic enterprises, there are at least some who take the more pessimistic view. Some three dozen scholars were invited to respond to a meta-analysis of studies of interpersonal expectancy effects (R. Rosenthal & Rubin, 1978a). Although much of the commentary dealt with the substantive topic of interpersonal expectancy effects, a good deal of it dealt with methodological aspects of meta-analytic procedures and products. Some of the criticisms offered were accurately anticipated by Glass (1978) who had earlier received commentary on his meta-analytic work (Glass, 1976) and that of his colleagues (Glass et al., 1981; Smith & Glass, 1977). Because these criticisms have been addressed elsewhere in detail (R. Rosenthal, 1991a; R. Rosenthal & Rubin, 1978b), we organize them into half a dozen conceptual categories and summarize them briefly.

Sampling Bias and the File Drawer Problem

This criticism holds that there is a retrievability bias such that studies retrieved do not reflect the population of studies conducted. One version of this criticism is that the probability of publication is increased by the statistical significance of the results, so that published studies may not be representative of the studies conducted. This is a well-taken criticism, though it applies equally to more traditional narrative reviews of the literature. Later in this chapter, we describe procedures that can be employed to address this problem in our discussion of the interpretive data of the results section of a meta-analytic review. More detailed discussions are available elsewhere (R. Rosenthal, 1979, 1991a; R. Rosenthal & Rubin, 1988).

Loss of Information

One criticism has been that summarizing a research domain by a single value, such as a mean effect size, loses valuable information. However, comparing studies, which means trying to understand differences between their results, is as much a part of meta-analytic procedures as is summarizing the overall results of the set of studies. We should also note that even *within* a single study psychologists have historically found it quite helpful to compute the mean of the experimental and control groups, despite the fact that computing a mean always involves a loss of information.

Heterogeneity of Method and Quality

Meta-analysts summarize studies with different operationalizations of independent and dependent variables as well as with different types of sampling units. Well-done meta-analyses take these differences into account by treating them as moderator variables. Meta-analyses are also criticized for throwing together good and bad studies. Aside from some difficulties in defining bad studies (e.g., the studies of my "enemies," as Glass et al., 1981, have put it), we can deal with this problem quite simply by weighting studies by their quality. Such weighting includes a weight of zero for the truly terrible study (R. Rosenthal, 1991a, 1991b).

Problems of Independence

Sometimes the same subjects generate multiple effect sizes within the same study, often creating a problem for significance testing in particular. Technical procedures are available for adjusting for nonindependence (R. Rosenthal, 1991a; R. Rosenthal & Rubin, 1986). More subtle problems of possible nonindependence arise because different studies conducted in one laboratory may yield results that are more correlated with each other than with different studies conducted in another laboratory. In other words, there may be laboratory effects (Jung, 1978; R. Rosenthal, 1966, 1969, 1976). These can be handled by treating laboratory effects as moderator variables and by analyzing research domains by laboratory as well as by study (R. Rosenthal, 1969, 1991a).

Exaggeration of Significance Levels

Perhaps the only criticism of meta-analysis that is based entirely on a misunderstanding of the fundamental equation of data analysis (i.e., $SignificanceTest = Effect\ Size \times Study\ Size$) is the criticism that as more and more studies are added to a meta-analysis, the results are more and more significant. That is certainly true, but it is difficult to perceive as a negative feature or as anything other than a mathematical fact.

Small Effects

The final criticism is that the results of socially important meta-analyses show only small effects because the r^2s obtained are small. This criticism has been addressed in detail elsewhere, where it has been shown that r^2s of nearly zero can save 34 lives per 1,000 (e.g., in the physicians' aspirin study; R. Rosenthal, 1995a; R. Rosenthal & Rubin, 1979a, 1982b; Steering Committee of the Physicians Health Study Research Group, 1988).

BENEFITS OF META-ANALYSIS

There are several fairly obvious benefits of meta-analysis. Quantitative summaries of research domains using meta-analytic procedures are likely to be more complete, more explicit, and more powerful (in the sense of decreasing type II errors), than are qualitative reviews, and, for all these reasons, are helpful to the process of cumulation. Moderator variables are more easily spotted and evaluated in the context of a quantitative research summary, thereby aiding theory development and increasing empirical richness. There are also some less obvious benefits.

Decreased Overemphasis on Single Studies

One less obvious benefit that will accrue to psychological science is the gradual decrease in the overemphasis on the results of a single study. There are good sociological grounds for our preoccupation with the results of a single study. Those grounds have to do with the reward system of science by which recognition, promotion, reputation, and the like depend on the results of the single study, the smallest unit of academic currency. The study is "good," "valuable," and above all, "publishable" when $p \leq .05$ and not when $p > .05$. Our discipline would be further ahead if we adopted a more cumulative view of psychology. With such a view, the impact of any one study would be evaluated less on the basis of p levels and more on the basis of its own effect size. In addition, such a view would lead us to evaluate the revised effect size and combined probability that resulted from the addition of the new study to any earlier studies investigating the same or a similar intervention or other relationship.

Decreased Differentiation Drive

Related to the problem of overemphasis on single studies is the problem of "differentiation drive," a motivational state (and possibly even a trait) sometimes found among scientists in all fields. This is the drive to be more different, more ahead, more correct, and more unique than others. "Priority strife" is one reflection of the differentiation drive. Another reflection is the occurrence of "renomination," the mechanism by which a well-known process is given a new name in hopes of effecting "concept capture"—the mechanism by which ownership of a concept is claimed by virtue of the renaming of the concept. Differentiation drive keeps us from viewing the world meta-analytically, or in a more Bayesian way, by keeping us from seeing the similarity of our work to the work of others. Skinner (1983, p. 39) has spoken eloquently, if indirectly, on this matter:

> In my own thinking, I try to avoid the kind of fraudulent significance which comes with grandiose terms or profound "principles." But some psychologists seem to need to feel that every experiment they do demands a sweeping reorganization of psychology as a whole. It's not worth publishing unless it has some such significance. But research has its own values, and you don't need to cook up spurious reasons why it's important.

The New Intimacy

This new intimacy is between the reviewer and the data. We cannot do a meta-analysis by reading abstracts and discussion sections. We are forced to look at the numbers and, very often, compute the correct ones ourselves. Meta-analysis requires us to cumulate *data,* not *conclusions. Reading* a paper is quite a different matter when we need to compute an effect size and a fairly precise significance level—often from a results section that does not include effect sizes or precise significance levels (and was not prepared following the *Publication Manual of the American Psychological Association*)!

The Demise of the Dichotomous Significance Testing Decision

Far more than is good for us, social and behavioral scientists operate under a dichotomous null hypothesis decision procedure in which the evidence is interpreted as antinull if $p \leq .05$ and pronull if $p > .05$. If our dissertation p is $< .05$, it means joy, a doctorate, and a tenure-track position at a major university. If our $p > .05$, it means ruin, despair, and our advisor suddenly thinking of a new control condition that should be run. That attitude is not helpful. God loves the .06 nearly as much as the .05. Indeed, there is good information that God views the strength of evidence for or against the null as a fairly continuous function of the magnitude of p. As a matter of fact, two .06 results are much stronger evidence against the null than one .05 result, and 10 ps of .10 are stronger evidence against the null than 5 ps of .05.

Exactly how two results of $p = .06$ constitute stronger evidence against the null hypothesis than one result of .05 is not at all intuitively obvious. Indeed, when asked to combine two probabilities of .06 and .06, almost all researchers would suggest multiplying the two values and calling their product the new combined level of significance. Mosteller and Bush (1954, p. 329) have pointed out, however, that the product of two p values will lead to $p \leq .05$ not 5% of the time but 20% of the time when the null hypothesis is true. That is due to the many different ways in which it is possible to achieve a product of two p values that is less than or equal to .05. A good many procedures for combining independent p values have been summarized over the years (e.g., Becker, 1994; Hedges & Olkin, 1985; Mosteller & Bush, 1954; R. Rosenthal, 1978). Three of the best known methods are the Fisher, Stouffer, and Edgington methods which yield combined p values (for two ps of .06) of .024, .014, and .0072, respectively (R. Rosenthal, 1991a).

The Overthrow of the Omnibus Test

It is common to find specific questions addressed by F tests with $df > 1$ in the numerator or by χ^2 tests with $df > 1$. For example, suppose that the specific question is whether increased frequency of meeting improves the effectiveness of therapy groups. We employ four levels of frequency so that our omnibus F test would have 3 df in the numerator, or our omnibus χ^2 would be on at least 3 df. Common as these tests are, they reflect poorly on our teaching of data-analytic procedures. The diffuse hypothesis tested by these omnibus tests usually tells us nothing of importance about our research question. The rule of thumb is unambiguous: Whenever we have tested a fixed effect with $df > 1$ for χ^2 or for the numerator of F, we have tested a question that almost surely does not really interest us.

The situation is even worse when there are several dependent variables as well as multiple df for the independent variable. The paradigm case here is canonical correlation, and special cases are MANOVA, MANCOVA, multiple discriminant function, multiple path analysis, and complex multiple partial correlation. Although all of these procedures have useful exploratory data-analytic applications, they are commonly used to test null hypotheses that are, scientifically, almost always of doubtful value. The effect size estimates they yield (e.g., the canonical correlation) are also almost always of doubtful value.

The Increased Recognition of Contrast Analysis

Meta-analytic questions are basically contrast questions. F tests with $df > 1$ in the numerator or χ^2s with $df > 1$ are useless in meta-analytic work. That leads to the following additional scientific benefit: Meta-analytic questions require precise formulation of questions, and contrasts are procedures for obtaining answers to such questions, often in the context of analysis of variance or table analysis. Although most statistics textbooks describe the logic and the machinery of contrast analyses, one still sees contrasts employed all too rarely. That is a real pity given the precision of thought and theory they encourage, and (especially relevant to these times of publication pressure) given the boost in power conferred with the resulting increase in .05 asterisks (R. Rosenthal & Rosnow, 1985, 1991; R. Rosenthal, Rosnow, & Rubin, 2000).

Meta-Analytic Procedures Are Applicable beyond Meta-Analyses

Many of the techniques of contrast analyses among effect sizes, for example, can be used within a single study (R. Rosenthal & Rosnow, 1985). Computing a single effect size from correlated dependent variables as well as comparing treatment effects on two or more dependent variables serve as illustrations (R. Rosenthal & Rubin, 1986).

The Decrease in the Splendid Detachment of the Full Professor

Meta-analytic work requires careful reading of research and moderate data-analytic skills. We cannot send an undergraduate research assistant to the computer or the library with a stack of 5×8 cards to bring us back "the results." That seems often to have been done with narrative reviews. With meta-analysis, the reviewer must get involved with the actual data, and that is all to the good of science.

EFFECT SIZE AND SIGNIFICANCE TESTS

When behavioral and biomedical researchers speak of "the results" of research, they are still referring most often to the statistical significance (p values) of the results, somewhat less often to the effect size estimates associated with those p values, and still less often to both the p value and the effect size. To make explicit the relationship between these two kinds of results, we can write the prose equation we presented earlier (Cohen, 1965; R. Rosenthal & Rosnow, 1991):

Significance Test = Effect Size × Study Size.

Any particular test of significance can be obtained by one or more definitions of effect size multiplied by one or more definitions of study size. For example, if we are interested in $\chi^2_{(1)}$ as a test of significance, we can write

$$\chi^2_{(1)} = \phi^2 \times N \qquad (1)$$

where $\chi^2_{(1)}$ is a χ^2 on 1 df (e.g., from a 2×2 table of counts), ϕ^2 is the squared Pearson product moment correlation (the effect size) between membership in the row category (scored 1 or 0) and membership in the column category (scored 1 or 0), and N (the study size) is the total number of sampling units, for example, found in the cells of the 2×2 table.

If we are interested in t as a test of significance, we have a choice of many equations (R. Rosenthal, 1991a, 1994b), including the following:

$$t = \frac{r}{\sqrt{1 - r^2}} \times \sqrt{df} \qquad (2)$$

$$t = d \times \sqrt{df}/2 \qquad (3)$$

where r is the point biserial Pearson r between group membership (scored 1 or 0) and obtained score, d is the difference between means divided by the pooled standard deviation (σ), and df is the degrees of freedom, usually $N - 2$.

TWO IMPORTANT FAMILIES OF EFFECT SIZES

Two of the most important families of effect sizes are the r family and the d family.

The r Family

The r family includes the Pearson product moment correlation in any of its popular incarnations with labels:

r when both variables are continuous

ϕ when both variables are dichotomous

r_{pb} when one variable is continuous and one variable is dichotomous

ρ when both variables are in ranked form

The r family also includes Z_r, the Fisher transformation of r, and the various squared indexes of r and r-like quantities, including r^2, ω^2 (omega-squared), ξ^2 (epsilon-squared), and η^2. Because squared indexes of effect size lose their directionality (is the treatment helping or hurting, is the correlation positive or negative?) they are of little use in scientific work for which information on directionality is essential. Another reason to avoid the use of the squared indexes of effect size is that the practical magnitude of these indexes is likely to be seriously misinterpreted as much less important than it really is; we illustrate this further in the section about the physicians' aspirin study (R. Rosenthal, 1990a; R. Rosenthal & Rosnow, 1991; R. Rosenthal & Rubin, 1979a, 1982b).

The d Family

The three central members of the d family are Cohen's d, Hedges's g, and Glass's Δ; all three employ the same numerator, the difference between the means of the groups being compared (i.e., $M_1 - M_2$). The denominators

of these three indexes differ, however:

$$\text{Cohen's } d = \frac{M_1 - M_2}{\sigma} \qquad (4)$$

$$\text{Hedges's } g = \frac{M_1 - M_2}{S} \qquad (5)$$

$$\text{Glass's } \Delta = \frac{M_1 - M_2}{S_{control}} \qquad (6)$$

where σ is the square root of the pooled variance computed from the two groups (i.e., $\sigma = \sqrt{\Sigma(X - M)^2/n}$), S is the square root of the pooled unbiased estimate of the variance $S = \sqrt{\Sigma(X - M)^2/(n - 1)}$, and $S_{control}$ is like the S in the denominator of Hedges's g but is computed only for the control group. Computing S based only on the control group is a useful procedure when we know or suspect that the treatment may affect not only the mean but also the variance of the scores in the treatment condition.

The d family of effect sizes also includes such other indexes of differences as the raw difference in proportions d^1 (Fleiss, 1994) and the difference between two proportions after each has been transformed to radians (Cohen's h, Case 1; Cohen, 1988, p. 200), probits, or logits (Glass, McGaw, & Smith, 1981). Readers employing categorical outcome variables should consult the references just cited.

EFFECT SIZES FOR THE ONE-SAMPLE CASE

The effect size estimates discussed so far have applied to situations in which we wanted to index the magnitude of a linear relationship between two variables by means of a correlation or by means of a comparison between the means of two conditions (e.g., by d, Δ, or g). In some situations, however, there is only a single sample in our experiment, perhaps with each sampling unit exposed to two different experimental conditions. Examples might include teachers' favorableness of nonverbal behavior toward children for whom they hold more versus less favorable expectations, or the health outcomes to the same patients of a new drug versus a placebo taken at different points in time. One test of significance of this effect of teachers' expectations on their non-verbal behavior, or of patients' reactions to the two different medications, could be the t for correlated observations. Two equations illustrating our basic relationship between significance tests and effect sizes for this one-sample case are (R. Rosenthal, 1994b)

$$t = \frac{r}{\sqrt{1 - r^2}} \times \sqrt{df} \qquad (7)$$

$$t = d \times \sqrt{df}. \qquad (8)$$

The first equation shows that an r index can be used in the one-sample case, and the second equation shows that a d index can be used in the one-sample case. It should be noted, however, that the r index is identical in the one-sample and two-sample cases, whereas the d index is quite different in the one-sample and two-sample cases (Cohen, 1988; R. Rosenthal, 1994b). This practical advantage of r over d is discussed shortly.

Dichotomous Data

When the data are dichotomous rather than continuous, a number of d family indexes are available, including Cohen's g and h (case 2) as well as a newer index, Π. Cohen's g is simply the difference between an observed proportion and .50. For example, the magnitude of an electoral victory is given directly by g. If .60 of the electorate voted for the winner, then $g = .60 - .50 = .10$. Such an effect size might be regarded as enormous in the case of an election result but as far less noteworthy as the result of a true-false test in a high school history class! Cohen's h (case 2) is the difference between an observed proportion and a theoretically expected proportion after each of these proportions has been transformed to

radians (an arcsin transformation). For example, in a multiple-choice history test in which one of four alternatives is correct and the position of the correct alternative has been assigned at random, guessing alone should yield an accuracy rate of .25. If the actual performance on this examination were found to be .75, we would compute h by transforming the actual (.75) and the expected (.25) proportions by means of 2 arcsin $\sqrt{P}$ yielding

$$h = 2 \arcsin \sqrt{.75} - 2 \arcsin \sqrt{.25}$$
$$= 2.09 - 1.05 = 1.04.$$

The reason for employing the arcsin transformation is to make the hs comparable. Differences between raw proportions are not all comparable, for example, with respect to statistical power. Thus a difference between proportions of .95 and .90 yields an h of .19, whereas a difference between proportions of .55 and .50 yields an h of only .10 (Cohen, 1988).

The one-sample effect size index, Π, is expressed as the proportion of correct guesses if there had been only two choices from which to choose. When there are more than two choices, Π converts the proportion of hits to the proportion of hits made if there had been only two equally likely choices:

$$\Pi = \frac{P(k - 1)}{P(k - 2) + 1} \qquad (9)$$

when P is the raw proportion of hits and k is the number of alternative choices available. The standard error of Π is

$$SE_{(\Pi)} = \frac{1}{\sqrt{N}} \left(\frac{\Pi(1 - \Pi)}{\sqrt{P(1 - P)}} \right) \qquad (10)$$

This index would be especially valuable in evaluating performance on a multiple-choice type of examination in which the number of alternatives varies from item to item. The index Π allows us to summarize the overall performance so that we could compare performances on tests made up of varying numbers of alternatives per item. Further details can be found in R. Rosenthal and Rubin (1989, 1991) and in Schaffer (1991).

In this section we have described some effect size estimates, obtained from just a single sample of research participants, that we may want to employ in our meta-analysis. In the next section we describe effect sizes employed when we want to compare two effect sizes in our meta-analysis.

EFFECT SIZES FOR COMPARING EFFECT SIZES

The Two-Sample Case

Sometimes the basic research question concerns the difference between two effect sizes. For example, a developmental psychologist may hypothesize that two cognitive performance measures will be more highly correlated in preschool children than in fifth graders. The degree to which the hypothesis is supported will depend on the difference between the correlations obtained from preschoolers and fifth graders, $r_1 - r_2$. Cohen's q is just such an index—one in which each r is transformed to Fisher's Z_r before the difference is computed, so that

$$\text{Cohen's } q = Z_{r1} - Z_{r2}. \quad (11)$$

The One-Sample Case

Cohen's q can also be employed when an obtained effect size is to be compared to a theoretical value of r. In this case we simply take the difference between the Z_r associated with our observed sample and the Z_r associated with our theoretical value of r (Cohen, 1988).

COMPARING THE *r* AND *d* FAMILIES

It seems natural to employ r-type effect size estimators when the original effect size estimates are reported in r-type indexes such as in meta-analyses of validity coefficients for test instruments (e.g., Hunter & Schmidt, 1990). Similarly, it seems natural to employ d-type effect size estimates when the original studies have compared two groups so that the difference between their means and their within-group Ss or σs are available. In meta-analytic work, however, it is often the case that the effect size estimates will be a mixture of r-type and d-type indexes.

Because r-type and d-type estimates can readily be converted into one another, obtaining both types of estimates will cause no hardship. However, it will be necessary to make a decision in meta-analytic work to convert all effect size estimates to just one particular index, usually to r or Z_r for the r family, or to Hedges's g (or Cohen's d) for the d family. Although any of these effect size estimates can be employed, there are some reasons for viewing r as the more generally useful effect size estimate.

Generality of Interpretation

If our data came to us as rs, it would not make much sense to convert rs to ds because the concept of a mean difference index makes little sense in describing a linear relationship over a great many values of the independent variable. On the other hand, given a d-type effect size estimate, r makes perfectly good sense in its point biserial form (i.e., just two levels of the independent variable).

Suppose that our theory calls for us to employ five levels of our independent variable, and that we predict a quadratic trend in the relationship between the level of arousal and the subsequent performance. The magnitude of the effect associated with our quadratic trend contrast is quite naturally indexed by r but not so naturally indexed by d-type indexes. The contrast weights for our quadratic trend would be $-2, +1, +2, +1, -2$, or better performance in the middle levels of arousal than in the more extreme levels of arousal, with the very best performance in the midmost condition. The effect size r would index the degree to which the contrast weights accurately predicted the actual obtained performance.

Consistency of Meaning in the One-Sample Case

The r-type index requires no computational adjustment in moving from the two-sample or multisample case to the one-sample case. As noted earlier, r is identically related to t for both the two-sample and the one-sample case. That is not the case for the d-type indexes, however. For example, the definition of the size of the study changes by a factor of 2 in going from a t test for two samples to a t test for one sample.

Simplicity of Interpretation

Finally, r is more simply interpreted in terms of practical importance than are the usual d-type indexes such as Hedges's g or Cohen's d. We give details in the following section.

THE INTERPRETATION OF EFFECT SIZES

Despite the growing awareness of the importance of estimating effect sizes, there is a problem in evaluating various effect size estimators from the point of view of practical usefulness (Cooper, 1981). R. Rosenthal and Rubin (1979a, 1982b) found that neither experienced behavioral researchers nor experienced statisticians had a good intuitive feel

for the practical meaning of common effect size estimators and that this was particularly true for such squared indexes as $r^2, \omega^2, \varepsilon^2$, and similar estimates.

The Physicians' Aspirin Study

At a special meeting held on December 19, 1987, the Steering Committee of the Physicians Health Study Research Group (1988) decided to end, prematurely, a randomized double-blind experiment on the effects of aspirin on reducing heart attacks. The reason behind this unusual termination was that it had become so clear that aspirin prevented heart attacks (and deaths from heart attacks) that it would be unethical to continue to give half of the research participants a placebo. And what was this magnitude of the experimental effect that was so dramatic as to call for the termination of this research? Was r^2 .80 or .60, so that the corresponding rs would have been .89 or .77? Was r^2 .40 or .20, so that the corresponding rs would have been .63 or .45? No, none of these. Actually, r^2 was .00—or, to four decimal places, .0011, with a corresponding r of .034. The decision to end the aspirin experiment was an ethical necessity; it saved lives. Most social and behavioral scientists are surprised that life-saving interventions can be associated with effect sizes as small as rs of .034 and r^2s of .0011.

The Binomial Effect Size Display

Table 10.1 shows the results of the aspirin study in terms of raw counts and percentages and as a binomial effect size display (BESD). This display is a way of showing the practical importance of any effect indexed by a correlation coefficient. The correlation is shown to be a simple difference in outcome rates between the experimental and the control groups in this standard table, which always adds up to column totals of 100 and row

Table 10.1   Effects of Aspirin on Heart Attacks among 22,071 Physicians

	Heart Attack	No Heart Attack	Total
I. Raw Counts in Four Conditions			
Aspirin	104	10,933	11,037
Placebo	189	10,845	11,034
Total	293	21,778	22,071
II. Percentages of Patients			
Aspirin	0.94	99.06	100
Placebo	1.71	98.29	100
Total	1.33	98.67	100
III. Binomial Effect Size Display			
Aspirin	48.3	51.7	100
Placebo	51.7	48.3	100
Total	100	100	200

totals of 100 (R. Rosenthal & Rubin, 1982b). We obtain the BESD from any obtained effect size r by computing the treatment condition success rate as .50 plus $r/2$ and the control condition success rate as .50 minus $r/2$. Thus an r of .20 yields a treatment success rate of $.50 + .20/2 = .60$ and a control success rate of $.50 - .20/2 = .40$, or a BESD of

	Success	Failure	Σ
Treatment	60	40	100
Control	40	60	100
Σ	100	100	200

Had we been given the BESD to examine before knowing r, we could have easily calculated it mentally for ourselves; r is simply the difference between the success rates of the experimental versus the control group $(.60 - .40 = .20)$.

The type of result seen in the physicians' aspirin study is not at all unusual in biomedical research. Some years earlier, on October 29, 1981, the National Heart, Lung, and Blood Institute discontinued its placebo-controlled study of propranolol because results were so favorable to the treatment that it would be unethical to continue withholding the life-saving drug from the control patients. Once again the effect size r was .04, and the leading digits of the r^2 were .00! As behavioral researchers, we are not used to thinking of rs of .04 as reflecting effect sizes of practical importance. But when we think of an r of .04 as reflecting a 4% decrease in heart attacks—the interpretation given r in a BESD—the r does not appear to be quite so small.

Additional Results

Table 10.2 gives three further examples of BESDs. In a study of 4,462 army veterans of the Vietnam War era (1965–1971), the correlation between having served in Vietnam (rather than elsewhere) and having suffered from alcohol abuse or dependence was .07 (Centers for Disease Control Vietnam Experience Study, 1988). The top display of Table 10.2 shows that the difference between the problem rates of 53.5 and 46.5 per 100 is equal to the correlation coefficient of .07.

Table 10.2   Other Examples of Binomial Effect Size Displays

Vietnam Service and Alcohol Problems ($r = .07$)			
	Problem	No Problem	Total
Vietnam Veteran	53.5	46.5	100
Non-Vietnam Veteran	46.5	53.5	100
Total	100	100	200
AZT in the Treatment of AIDS ($r = .23$)			
	Death	Survival	Total
AZT	38.5	61.5	100
Placebo	61.5	38.5	100
Total	100	100	200
Benefits of Psychotherapy ($r = .39$)[a]			
	Less Benefit	Greater Benefit	Total
Psychotherapy	30.5	69.5	100
Control	69.5	30.5	100
Total	100	100	200

[a]The analogous r for 464 studies of interpersonal expectancy effects was .30 (R. Rosenthal, 1994a).

Table 10.3 **Effect Sizes of Various Independent Variables**

Independent Variable	Dependent Variable	r	r^2
Aspirin[a]	Heart attacks	.03	.00
Beta Carotene[b]	Death	.03	.00
Streptokinase[c]	Death	.03	.00
Propranolol[d]	Death	.04	.00
Magnesium[e]	Convulsions	.07	.00
Vietnam veteran status[f]	Alcohol problems	.07	.00
Garlic[g]	Death	.09	.01
Indinavir[h]	Serious AIDS events	.09	.01
Testosterone[i]	Adult delinquency	.12	.01
Compulsory hospitalization versus treatment choice[j]	Alcohol problems	.13	.02
Cyclosporine[k]	Death	.15	.02
Ganzfeld perception[l]	Accuracy	.16	.03
Cisplatin & Vinblastine[m]	Death	.18	.03
AZT for neonates[n]	HIV infection	.21	.04
Cholesterol-lowering regimen[o]	Coronary status	.22	.05
AZT[p]	Death	.23	.05
Treatment choice vs. AA[q]	Alcohol problems	.27	.07
Psychotherapy[r]	Improvement	.39	.15
Compulsory hospitalization versus AA[s]	Alcohol problems	.40	.16
Progesterone[t]	SIV infection	.65	.42

[a] Steering Committee of the Physicians Health Study Research Group, 1988; [b] Alpha-Tocopherol, Beta Carotene Cancer Prevention Study Group, 1994; [c] GISSI, 1986; [d] Kolata, 1981; [e] Foreman, 1995; [f] Centers for Disease Control Vietnam Experience Study, 1988; [g] Goldfinger, 1991; [h] Knox, 1997; [i] Dabbs & Morris, 1990; [j] Cromie, 1991; [k] Canadian Multicentre Transplant Study Group, 1983; [l] Chandler, 1993; [m] Cromie, 1990, [n] Altman, 1994; [o] Roberts, 1987; [p] Barnes, 1986; [q] Cromie, 1991; [r] Smith, Glass, & Miller, 1980; [s] Cromie, 1991; [t] Contraceptive trials set for a link to AIDS risk, 1996.

The center display of Table 10.2 shows the results of a study of the effects of AZT on the survival of 282 patients suffering from AIDS or AIDS-related complex (ARC) (Barnes, 1986). This correlation of .23 between survival and receiving AZT (an r^2 of .054) was so dramatic that the clinical trial was prematurely terminated on the ethical grounds that it would be improper to continue to give placebos to the patients in the control group.

The bottom display of Table 10.2 shows the results of a famous meta-analysis of psychotherapy outcome studies reported by Smith, Glass, and Miller (1980). Of particular interest to behavioral researchers, the magnitude of the effect of psychotherapy was substantially greater than the effects of a good many breakthrough medical interventions. Table 10.3 shows the effect sizes obtained in a convenience sample of 20 different studies; eight of the studies, employing dependent variables of convulsions, AIDS events, alcohol problems, heart attacks, and death, were associated with effect size rs of less than .10. One desirable result of our consideration of these biomedical effect size estimates is to make those of us working in the social and behavioral sciences less pessimistic about the magnitude and importance of our research results (R. Rosenthal, 1990a, 1995a).

The examples of the BESDs shown in Tables 10.1 and 10.2 and of the effect sizes shown in Table 10.3 were all health related. However, the BESD can be applied appropriately in *any* domain of the behavioral, biomedical, brain, cognitive, and social sciences. Because it is always appropriate to compute a Pearson product moment correlation between *any* independent and *any* dependent variable, it is also always appropriate to employ a BESD.

For example, suppose investigators found support for their theory that condition A fostered improved memory more than did condition B. Further suppose that they employed Cohen's *d* to index the magnitude of their effect, finding it to be about .4. To display the magnitude of the effect as a BESD, they convert *d* to *r* by means of the equation

$$r = \sqrt{\frac{d^2}{d^2 + 4}} = \sqrt{\frac{(.4)^2}{(.4)^2 + 4}} = .20,$$

where *r* is readily displayed as a BESD as follows:

	Memory		
	Poorer	Better	Total
Condition A	40	60	100
Condition B	60	40	100
Total	100	100	200

OTHER EFFECT SIZE ESTIMATES FOR 2 × 2 TABLES OF COUNTS: THE BIOMEDICAL CONTEXT

The effect size index, *r*, can be readily applied to any 2 × 2 table of counts. Three other indexes of effect size have been found useful in biomedical contexts: relative risk, odds ratio, and risk difference. All three are illustrated for several hypothetical outcomes in Table 10.4. Each study compared a control condition to a treatment condition with two possible outcomes: not surviving or surviving.

Relative Risk

Relative risk is defined as the ratio of the proportion of the control patients at risk (not surviving) divided by the proportion of the treated patients at risk. With the cells of the 2 × 2 table of counts labeled A, B, C, and D from upper left to lower right (as shown in Table 10.4) relative risk (RR) is defined as:

$$RR = \left(\frac{A}{A+B} \middle/ \frac{C}{C+D} \right).$$

A limitation of this effect size estimate can be seen in Table 10.4. We examine the three

Table 10.4   Three Examples of Four Effect Size Estimates

	Die	Live	Relative Risk	Odds Ratio	Risk Difference	*r*
Control	A	B	$\left(\dfrac{A}{A+B} \middle/ \dfrac{C}{C+D} \right)$	$\left(\dfrac{A}{B} \middle/ \dfrac{C}{D} \right)$	$\left(\dfrac{A}{A+B} - \dfrac{C}{C+D} \right)$	
Treatment	C	D				
Study 1						
Control	10	990	10.00	10.09	.01	.06
Treatment	1	999				
Study 2						
Control	10	10	10.00	19.00	.45	.50
Treatment	1	19				
Study 3						
Control	10	0	10.00	∞	.90	.90
Treatment	1	9				

study outcomes closely and ask ourselves the following: If we had to be in the control condition, would it matter to us whether we were in Study 1, Study 2, or Study 3? We think most people would rather have been in Study 1 than Study 2, and we think that virtually no one would have preferred to be a member of the control group in Study 3. Despite the very important phenomenological differences among these three studies, however, Table 10.4 shows that all three relative risks are identical: 10.00. That feature may be a serious limitation to the value and informativeness of the relative risk index.

Odds Ratio

The odds ratio is defined as the ratio of the not-surviving control patients to the surviving control patients divided by the ratio of the not-surviving treated patients to the surviving treated patients. In Table 10.4 the odds ratio (OR) is defined as:

$$OR = \left(\frac{A}{B} \Big/ \frac{C}{D} \right).$$

In Table 10.4 the odds ratio behaves more as expected than does the relative risk in that the odds ratio increases with our phenomenological discomfort as we go from the results of Study 1 to Study 2 to Study 3. However, the high odds ratio for Study 1 seems alarmist. Indeed, if the data showed

	Die	Live	Total
Control	10	999,990	10^6
Treated	1	999,999	10^6
Total	11	1,999,989	$2(10^6)$

so that an even smaller proportion of patients were at risk, the odds ratio would remain at 10.00, an even more alarmist result.

The odds ratio for Study 3 is also unattractive. Because all the controls die, we could

perhaps forgive the infinite odds ratio. However, very different phenomenological results yield an identical odds ratio. If the data showed

	Die	Live	Total
Control	1,000,000	0	10^6
Treated	999,999	1	10^6
Total	1,999,999	1	$2(10^6)$

we would again have an infinite odds ratio—definitely an alarmist result. In this case even the problematic relative risk index would yield a phenomenologically more realistic result of 1.00.

Risk Difference

The risk difference is defined as the difference between the proportion of the control patients at risk and the proportion of the treated patients at risk. In Table 10.4 the risk difference (RD) is defined as

$$RD = \left(\frac{A}{A + B} - \frac{C}{C + D} \right).$$

The last column of Table 10.4 shows the Pearson product moment correlation (r) between the independent variable of treatment (scored 0, 1) and the dependent variable of outcome (scored 0, 1). Comparison of the risk differences with r in Table 10.4 (and elsewhere) shows that the risk difference index is never unreasonably far from the value of r. For that reason the risk difference index may be least likely to be quite misleading under special circumstances, so we prefer it as our all-purpose index if we have to use one of the three indexes under discussion. But even here we feel we can do better.

Standardizing the Three Risk Measures

We propose a simple adjustment that standardizes our measures of relative risk, odds

Table 10.5   Standardized Outcomes of Table 10.4

	Die	Live	Standardized Relative Risk	Standardized Odds Ratio	Standardized Risk Difference (r)
Control	A	C			
Treatment	C	A	(A/C)	(A/C)^2	(A − C)/100
Study 1					
Control	53	47	1.13	1.27	.06
Treatment	47	53			
Study 2					
Control	75	25	3.00	9.00	.50
Treatment	25	75			
Study 3					
Control	95	5	19.00	361.00	.90
Treatment	5	95			

ratio, and risk difference (R. Rosenthal & Rubin, 1998). We simply compute the correlation r between the treatment and outcome and display r in a BESD, as described above.

Table 10.5 shows the BESD for the three studies of Table 10.4. Although the tables of counts of Table 10.4 varied from Ns of 2,000 to 40 to 20, the corresponding BESDs of Table 10.5 all show the standard margins of 100, which is a design feature of the BESD. The computation of our new effect size indexes is straightforward. We simply compute relative risks, odds ratios, and risk differences on our standardized tables (BESDs) to obtain standardized relative risks, standardized odds ratios, and standardized risk differences. The computation of these three indexes is simplified because the A and D cells of a BESD always have the same value (as do the B and C cells). Thus, the computational equations simplify to A/C for standardized relative risk (SRR), to (A/C)^2 for standardized odds ratio (SOR), and to (A-C)/100 for standardized risk difference (SRD).

Table 10.5 shows the standardized relative risks increasing as they should in going from Study 1 to Study 3. The standardized odds ratios also increase as they go from Study 1 to Study 3 but without the alarmist value for Study 1 and the infinite value for Study 3.

(A standardized odds ratio could go to infinity only if r were exactly 1.00, an unlikely event in behavioral or biomedical research.) The standardized risk difference is shown in Table 10.5 to be identical to r, which is an attractive feature emphasizing the interpretability of r as displayed in a BESD.

MINIMIZING ERRORS IN THINKING ABOUT EFFECT SIZES: THE COUNTERNULL VALUE OF AN EFFECT SIZE

The counternull value of an effect size was recently introduced as a new statistic (R. Rosenthal & Rubin, 1994). It is useful in virtually eliminating two common errors: (a) equating failure to reject the null with the estimation of the effect size as equal to zero and (b) equating rejection of a null hypothesis on the basis of a significance test with having demonstrated a scientifically important effect. In most applications the value of the counternull is simply twice the magnitude of the obtained effect size (e.g., d, g, Δ, Z_r). Thus with $r = .10$ found to be nonsignificant, the counternull value of $r = .20$ is exactly as likely as the null value of $r = .00$. For any effect size with a symmetric reference distribution such as the normal or any t distribution, the counternull value of an effect size can always be found by doubling the obtained effect size and subtracting the effect size expected under the null hypothesis (usually zero). Thus, if we found that a test of significance did not reach the chosen level (e.g., .05), the use of the counternull would prevent us from concluding that the mean effect size was, therefore, probably zero. The counternull value of $2d$ or $2Z_r$ would be just as tenable a conclusion as concluding $d = 0$ or $Z_r = 0$.

The counternull is a kind of confidence interval conceptually related to the more traditional (e.g., 95%) confidence interval. As Cohen (1990, 1994) pointed out with his customary wisdom, the behavioral and medical sciences would be more advanced had we always routinely reported not only p values but also effect size estimates with confidence intervals.

DIFFERENTIATING FOUR CORRELATIONS

So far in our discussion of r as our preferred effect size, we have not mentioned that we can actually employ four rs usefully as effect size estimates. That is the case both in meta-analytic work and in the analysis of the data of a single study. The r to which we have been referring is only one of those rs, specifically, $r_{contrast}$. Ideally, both in meta-analytic work and in the analysis of the data of individual studies, we would report all four correlations, because each addresses a different question (R. Rosenthal et al., 2000).

The $r_{contrast}$ Correlation

This r is a partial correlation between the scores on the dependent variable of individual sampling units and the predicted mean score

(contrast weight) of the group to which they belong—with other between-group variation partialed out. This is the most frequently used correlation in meta-analytic work because it is often the only correlation we can calculate from other people's data. We can find $r_{contrast}$ from tests of significance by any of the following equations:

$$r_{contrast} = \sqrt{\frac{F_{contrast}}{F_{contrast} + df_{within}}}, \quad (15)$$

$$r_{contrast} = \sqrt{\frac{t^2_{contrast}}{t^2_{contrast} + df_{within}}}, \quad (16)$$

$$r_{contrast} = \sqrt{\frac{\chi^2_{(1)}}{N}}, \quad (17)$$

$$r_{contrast} = \frac{Z}{\sqrt{N}}, \quad (18)$$

and we can compute $r_{contrast}$ from the effect size estimate d using the following:

$$r_{contrast} = \sqrt{\frac{d^2}{d^2 + 4}}. \quad (19)$$

For further details on other equivalences among effect size estimates, see R. Rosenthal (1991a, 1994b) and R. Rosenthal and Rosnow (1991).

In the simplest case, where two groups are being compared, $r_{contrast}$ is the point biserial correlation between membership in one of the two groups (coded, e.g., 0 and 1) and the score on the dependent variable. In this simple two-group case we report only the value of $r_{contrast}$ and not the values of the other three correlations.

When three or more groups are being studied, however, each of the four correlations tells us something different about the relationship between the independent and dependent variables. For example, $r_{alerting}$, the correlation between the predicted and obtained mean scores per condition, often alerts us to an otherwise overlooked relationship. For example, we may read a report that there is no relationship between age level (e.g., ages 8, 9, 10, 11, 12) and cognitive performance with $F_{(4,95)} = 1.00$, $p = .41$. However, looking at the five means of this report may show a perfect correlation ($r_{alerting}$) between age level and mean performance, clearly contradicting the conclusion of the report that there was no relationship between age and performance. That claim had been based on an inappropriate omnibus F test with $4\,df$ in the numerator. A properly computed $F_{contrast}$ would have yielded $F_{(1,95)} = 4.00$, $p = .048$, $r_{contrast} = .20$, ($r_{alerting} = 1.00$, t very large, p very small). Other uses of $r_{alerting}$ include its role in the computation of contrasts in other people's data (R. Rosenthal & Rosnow, 1985; Rosnow & Rosenthal, 1996).

The $r_{effect\ size}$ Correlation

This is the correlation between the scores on the dependent variable of individual sampling units and the predicted mean score (contrast weight) of the group to which they belong without any partialing. Because it involves no partialing of other between-group effects out of the error term, $r_{effect\ size}$ is never larger than $r_{contrast}$ and is usually smaller than $r_{contrast}$— sometimes dramatically so. The $r_{effect\ size}$ correlation can be computed from

$$r_{effect\ size} = \sqrt{\frac{F_{contrast}}{F_{contrast} + F_{noncontrast}(df_{noncontrast}) + df_{within}}}. \quad (20)$$

The $r_{alerting}$ Correlation

This is the correlation between the condition means and the predicted mean scores (contrast weights). The $r_{alerting}$ correlation can

be computed from

$$r_{alerting} = \sqrt{\frac{F_{contrast}}{F_{contrast} + F_{noncontrast}(df_{noncontrast})}}. \quad (21)$$

The r_{BESD} Correlation

This is a usually more conservative effect size correlation that permits generalization not only to other sampling units in the same conditions but also to other levels of the same independent variable. The r_{BESD} correlation can be computed from

$$r_{BESD} = \sqrt{\frac{F_{contrast}}{F_{contrast} + F_{noncontrast}(df_{noncontrast} + df_{within})}}. \quad (22)$$

In Equation (22), when $F_{noncontrast}$ is less than 1.00, it is entered as equal to 1.00. $F_{noncontrast}$ is computed as

$$\frac{F_{between}(df_{between}) - F_{contrast}}{df_{between} - 1}. \quad (23)$$

The restriction that $F_{noncontrast}$ in Equation (22) cannot drop below 1.00 formalizes the assumption that the noncontrast variation is noise and forces r_{BESD} to be less than, or at most equal to, $r_{effect\ size}$. Detailed discussions of these four correlations are provided in R. Rosenthal et al. (2000).

PREPARING META-ANALYTIC REVIEWS

The purpose of the remainder of this chapter is to provide some guidelines for the preparation of meta-analytic reviews of the literature. Meta-analytic reviews are quantitative summaries of research domains that describe the typical strength of the effects or phenomena being described, their variability, their statistical significance, and the nature of the moderator variables from which one can predict their relative strength (Cooper, 1989; Glass et al., 1981; Hedges & Olkin, 1985; Hunter & Schmidt, 1990; Light & Pillemer, 1984; R. Rosenthal, 1991a).

Our goal is not to enumerate the many quantitative procedures employed in meta-analytic reviews, because these are described in detail in the textbooks just listed, as well as in a handbook edited by Cooper and Hedges (1994a).

As is the case in the analysis of the data of any individual study, the analysis of data from a set of studies can vary greatly in complexity. For example, the six texts just listed can be roughly divided into two levels of complexity and completeness. The books by Glass et al. (1981), Hedges and Olkin (1985), and Hunter and Schmidt (1990) are more detailed and quantitatively more demanding than those by Cooper (1989), Light and Pillemer (1984), and R. Rosenthal (1991a). There are theoretical differences among these six texts as well, and the remainder of this chapter should be useful to meta-analysts working within any of these frameworks. Thus, although some of the more complex procedures described by Hedges and Olkin and by Hunter and Schmidt are not specifically mentioned, those working within their frameworks can easily add those analyses to the "basics" here. Regardless of how complex the meta-analytic procedures will become in a given review of the literature, reporting the basics makes for a meta-analysis that the typical reader can follow more easily and understand at a deeper level. Reporting the basics also makes it easier for a reader to check the tenability of conclusions drawn by the meta-analyst.

The heart of what follows will be a discussion of what should be considered for inclusion in a meta-analytic report. Not all of the suggestions of what to report will apply equally well to all meta-analytic undertakings, but on average, researchers who seriously consider the suggestions mentioned here will likely minimize important omissions.

Who should be thinking of preparing meta-analytic reviews? Anyone considering a review of an entire literature, or of a specifiable subset of a literature, may as well do it quantitatively as nonquantitatively, because all of the virtues of narrative reviews can be preserved in a meta-analysis, which merely adds the quantitative features as a bonus. The level of quantitative skill and training required to employ basic meta-analytic procedures is so modest that any researchers capable of analyzing the results of their own research will be capable of learning the small number of calculations required to answer standard meta-analytic questions (e.g., what is the mean and standard deviation of this list of correlation coefficients or other effect size estimates?).

Keeping the basic meta-analytic procedures very descriptive, very simple, and very clear is a positive virtue. In many years of reviewing meta-analytic literature syntheses, we have never seen a meta-analysis that was too simple; however, we have often seen meta-analyses that were very fancy and very much in error.

The most important part of a meta-analysis is the descriptive section that displays the effect sizes (e.g., correlation coefficients) and summarizes their distribution and central tendency. Good meta-analytic practice, like good data-analytic practice in general, adopts an exploratory orientation toward these displays and summaries (Tukey, 1977), and little "high-tech statistication" is required for this valuable enterprise. Indeed, the computations required for the most basic meta-analytic work are so trivial that in much of our own meta-analytic work over the past many years we have never felt the need to use a software package that "does meta-analysis."

Good software for meta-analytic procedures can, of course, be a great time saver. However, a drawback to the development of sophisticated software that does meta-analytic (or any other data-analytic) computations is that some researchers (who feel less expert than they might like) believe that the software itself will do the analysis. Alas, that is not the case. The software will do a variety of computations, and it will do them fast, but for any given application, the computations may be either wise or foolish. Staying simple, keeping close to the data, and emphasizing description will prevent most serious errors. It is better to consult with a more experienced colleague who knows exactly what is being computed by the software than to trust the software to do the analysis. That advice applies to all data-analytic undertakings, of course, not merely to meta-analytic procedures. It is wise always to verify computer-based results by guesstimations or rough calculations; if that is not possible, they should be checked against the output of another program (Wilkinson & the Task Force on Statistical Inference, 1999).

Without any implication that all good meta-analyses will look alike and will incorporate all the suggestions to follow, the rest of this chapter discusses what might be reported in most meta-analyses and what should at least be considered for almost all meta-analyses. Some additional reporting checklist items for observational studies in epidemiology have also recently become available (Meta-analysis of Observational Studies in Epidemiology Group, 2000).

THE INTRODUCTION TO A META-ANALYTIC REVIEW

The introduction to a meta-analysis does not differ strategically from the introduction to any scientific paper. It tells readers why they should want to read the paper, what makes it important, and how it will achieve what has not been achieved before. The issue under study should be placed into a theoretical context.

If the literature is made up of several types of studies, it is helpful to describe a study typical of each of the several types. If the results of the research differ widely (e.g., some results strongly favor the treatment condition, some results strongly favor the control condition), it will be useful to give examples of studies showing this wide variation in results. This preliminary overview helps readers to understand better the need for the meta-analysis and its major function of examining moderator variables.

THE METHODS SECTION OF A META-ANALYTIC REVIEW

Literature Searches

Here, readers are told how the studies to be summarized were located, what databases were searched, what journals were painstakingly gone through, what research registers were consulted, and what steps were taken to retrieve the fugitive literature (i.e., the unpublished or otherwise difficult-to-retrieve research reports). For those of us not trained as information scientists, the *Handbook of Research Synthesis* edited by Cooper and Hedges (1994a) brings considerable help and enlightenment. Most of what any meta-analyst needs to know (and even more) about retrieving the data for a meta-analysis is contained in some 50 pages of the four chapters prepared by White (1994), Reed and Baxter (1994), Dickersin (1994), and M. C. Rosenthal (1994).

The reason for trying to locate all the research on the topic of our meta-analysis is primarily to avoid the biased retrieval of searching only the major journals, which may selectively publish only the results characterized by lower p values and larger effect sizes. If the domain being searched is one with a great many studies—more than we have the resources to analyze—it is better to sample the exhaustive listing of results than to select only the more readily retrievable results.

Criteria for Inclusion

Information Available

Not all the reports retrieved will be appropriate for inclusion in the meta-analysis. Some will turn out to have no data of any kind, and some will report on the data so poorly that they will be unusable. Some will be borderline cases in which we are given enough data that good detective work will allow us to obtain at least an approximate effect size estimate and significance level. Many studies, for example, simply say "there was no effect of X on Y" or "the effect was not significant." Meta-analysis involves the summarization of data, not of authors' conclusions, so the above statements are of little help to the meta-analyst. However, if the relevant means and standard deviations are given, we can compute effect sizes ourselves. If sample sizes are given as well, we can also compute accurate p values.

For studies claiming "no effects" or "no significant effects," we may well want to assign an effect size estimate of 0.00 and a one-tailed p of .50 ($Z = 0.00$). Experience suggests that this procedure is conservative and leads to effect size estimates that are too small. The alternative of not using those studies, however, is likely to lead to effect size estimates that are too large, and almost surely to p values that are too small (i.e., too significant). Confronted with this choice of procedures, we should "do it both ways" in order to

learn just how much difference it will really make to our overall view of the data. Considerations of alternative approaches to the data are part of the process of "sensitivity analysis" described by Greenhouse and Iyengar (1994).

Study Quality

Of the studies we retrieve, some will be methodologically exemplary, and others will be stunningly bad. Shall we include them all or only the good ones? The question of quality criteria for inclusion is really a question of weighting by quality (R. Rosenthal, 1991b). Including good studies and excluding bad ones is simply a 1, 0 weighting system and one that is often suspect on grounds of weighter-bias. We are too likely to think of our own studies, as well as those of our students, of our friends, and of those who successfully replicate our work as good studies. In addition, we are too likely to think of the studies of our enemies and of those who fail to replicate our work as bad studies. As protection against our biases, we do better to evaluate the retrieved studies for quality by some procedure that allows disinterested coders or raters to make the required judgments. Indeed, some workers feel that coders or raters should be "blind" to the results of the study.

Coding of studies for their quality usually requires only simple judgments of the presence or absence of desirable design features such as whether the experiment is randomized, whether the experimenter is blind to the hypothesis, and whether the demand characteristics are controlled. Quality points can then be assigned on the basis of the number of desirable features present. Rating of studies usually requires a more global, overall assessment of the methodological quality of a study, using, for example, a seven-point rating scale. Reliability of coding or rating should be reported. The quality weightings obtained for each study can then be employed as an adjustment mechanism in computing average effect size or as a moderator variable to see whether quality is, in fact, related to obtained effect size. Further detail on quality assessment, weighting, and reliability are available in Hall, R. Rosenthal, Tickle-Degnen, and Mosteller (1994); R. Rosenthal (1991a); and Wortman (1994).

Independence

For a database of any size, the meta-analyst will soon discover that some studies are not independent of one another; that is, the same subjects have been employed in two or more studies. Sometimes, slightly different dependent variables are reported in multiple reports on the same subjects. For example, if the subjects' responses had been recorded in video, audio, or transcript form, new ideas for dependent variables can be evaluated years later. Although such multiple uses of the subjects' data archives can be scientifically useful, they present a problem for the unwary meta-analyst. Most computational procedures dealing with significance testing require that the studies summarized be independent. Treating nonindependent studies as independent leads to significance tests that are in error. These errors can be avoided by treating the several nonindependent studies as a single study with multiple dependent variables (R. Rosenthal, 1991a; R. Rosenthal & Rubin, 1986). For a more technical treatment of problems of nonindependence, see Gleser and Olkin (1994).

Minimum Number of Studies

What if our meta-analytic efforts result in the retrieval of only a few studies? What number of studies is too few for a meta-analysis? Meta-analytic procedures can be applied to as few as two studies, but the meta-analytic results will be relatively unstable when there are very few studies. In such cases, it would be more economical of journal space and editors' and reviewers' time to incorporate the meta-analysis as an extension of the results section of the last in the series of a few studies. Thus, if our study finds a correlation r between the two variables of interest, we might end our results section by combining and comparing our r and p values with those obtained earlier by other investigators.

What Was Recorded?

Study Characteristics

Readers should be told what information was recorded for each study. For example, the subjects' number, age, sex, education, and volunteer status (R. Rosenthal & Rosnow, 1991) might be recorded for each study regardless of whether subjects themselves were the sampling unit or whether classrooms, therapists, groups, wards, clinics, or other organizations served as the unit of analysis (e.g., the basis for computing degrees of freedom for the analysis). Was the study conducted in a laboratory or in the field? Was it an observational study or a randomized experiment? What was the year of publication and the form of publication (book; article; chapter; convention report; bachelors, masters, or doctoral thesis; technical report; unpublished)? These particular study characteristics are often included, but each meta-anaysis should also include all the variables that the meta-analyst's knowledge of and intuition into the literature suggest may be important correlates of the magnitudes of the effect sizes obtained. More detailed discussions of the selection, coding, and evaluation of study characteristics have recently become available (Lipsey, 1994; Lipsey & Wilson, 2001; Orwin, 1994; Stock, 1994). All of the foregoing study characteristics will be used in two ways: as descriptions of the study set retrieved, and as potential moderator variables.

Summarizing Study Characteristics

An overview of various study characteristics is often valuable. These include the range and median of ages employed in the assembled studies, the range and median of dates of published and unpublished studies, the proportions found in various types of publication formats, the range and median of proportions of samples that were female or male, the proportion of studies found that were laboratory or field studies, and the proportion of studies that were randomized experiments rather than observational studies. These readily summarized statistics will be useful to readers.

Other Moderator Variables

All of the study characteristics recorded for each study and summarized for the set of studies can be employed as moderator variables, that is, variables correlated with the magnitude of effect size obtained for the different studies. In addition to these fairly standard potential moderators, however, specific moderator variables have particular meaning for the specific area of research being summarized.

For example, in a meta-analysis of thin slices of expressive behavior, short periods (under 5 min) of observation of expressive behavior were surprisingly predictive of various objective outcomes (Ambady & Rosenthal, 1992). One of the moderator variables examined was the presence or absence of verbal content accompanying the nonverbal behavior. It was found that studies including verbal content did not yield a higher average effect size of predictive accuracy. Another example of a moderator variable analysis grew out of a meta-analysis of studies of the effects of teachers' expectations on pupils' IQ gains (Raudenbush, 1994). Raudenbush employed the moderator variable of how long teachers had known their pupils before the teachers were given randomly assigned favorable expectations for pupils' IQs. He found that the

longer teachers had known their pupils before the experiment began, the smaller were the effects of experimentally induced teacher expectations.

Effect Size Estimates

Effect size estimates are the meta-analytic coin of the realm. Whatever else may be recorded, the estimated effect size must be recorded for each study entered into the meta-analysis.

As discussed earlier, the two main families of effect sizes are the r family and the d family. The most important members of the former are Pearson product moment correlations (r) and Z_r, the Fisher transformation of r. The most important members of the d family are Cohen's d, Hedges's g, and Glass's Δ, all characterized as differences between means divided by some standard deviation. Detailed explanations of these and other effect size estimates are given elsewhere (R. Rosenthal, 1991a, 1994; R. Rosenthal et al., 2000; and for categorical data, see also Fleiss, 1994).

Significance Levels

Though far less important than effect size estimates, significance levels should be recorded for each study unless the meta-analyst is certain that questions of the statistical significance of the overall results of the meta-analysis will not arise. All such levels should be computed as accurately as possible and recorded as the one-tailed standard normal deviates associated with the p level. Thus ps of .10, .01, .001, and .000001 are reported as Zs of 1.28, 2.33, 3.09, and 4.75, respectively. Results that are significant in the unpredicted or uncharacteristic direction are reported as negative Zs (e.g., if $p = .01$ one-tailed, but in the wrong direction—that is, the unpredicted direction—it is recorded as -2.33).

THE RESULTS SECTION OF A META-ANALYTIC REVIEW

Descriptive Data

The heart of a meta-analytic report is a description of the effect sizes obtained. Unless the number of studies is very small, it is often valuable to provide a visual display of the effect sizes obtained as well as various indexes of central tendency and variability. The value of visual displays in the analysis of psychological data in general has been emphasized by Wilkinson and the Task Force on Statistical Inference (1999).

Visual Display

Different visual displays may be useful under different conditions, and many of these are described by Cooper (1989); Glass et al. (1981); Greenhouse and Iyengar (1994); Hedges and Olkin (1985); Light and Pillemer (1984); Light, Singer, and Willett (1994); R. Rosenthal and Rosnow (1991); and Tukey (1977). Sometimes a specially prepared graphic would be most useful—one not found in any of these references. It would be instructive in that case to consult some of the excellent general texts on visual displays, for example, those by Cleveland (1985, 1995), Kosslyn (1994), and Tufte (1983). There is not space here to describe the many visual displays that may be instructive (e.g., box plots, funnel plots, stem-and-leaf displays), but as a single example of an often-useful visual display we describe Tukey's stem-and-leaf display. This is a versatile picture of the data that perfectly describes the distribution of results while retaining each of the recorded effect sizes (Tukey, 1977). Table 10.6 is a stem-and-leaf display from a recent meta-analysis of 38 studies of the predictive value of thin slices of nonverbal and verbal behavior. Each of the 38 effect sizes (rs) is recorded with the first digit found in the column labeled "Stem"

Table 10.6   Stem and Leaf Display of 38 Effect Size rs

Stem	Leaf
.9	
.8	7
.7	3, 4
.6	3, 8
.5	0, 2, 2, 3, 4, 4
.4	0, 0, 0, 1, 7
.3	1, 3, 5
.2	1, 1, 1, 2, 3, 3, 4, 5, 6, 6, 7, 8, 9
.1	0, 0, 4, 5, 6, 6
.0	

NOTE: rs include relationships between two continuous variables (r), two dichotomous variables (*phi*), and one dichotomous and one continuous variable (point biserial r).

SOURCE: Based on Ambady & R. Rosenthal (1992).

and the second digit found in the column labeled "Leaf." The top three entries of Table 10.6, therefore, are read as three rs of .87, .73, and .74.

Central Tendency

Several indexes of central tendency should be reported, and differences among these indexes should be discussed and reconciled. These include the unweighted mean effect size, the weighted mean effect size, the unweighted median, the weighted median, and (more optionally) the proportion of studies showing effect sizes in the predicted direction (Hiller, R. Rosenthal, Bornstein, Berry, & Brunell-Neuleib, 1999; R. Rosenthal, Hiller, Bornstein, Berry, & Brunell-Neuleib, in press). The number of independent effect sizes on which these indexes are based should be reported along with (again, more optionally) the total number of subjects on which the weighted mean is based, and the median number of subjects per obtained effect size. The weighted mean effect size here refers to weighting by size of study (e.g., the *df*), but other weightings can be used as well. For example, weighting may also be done by the quality of the study or by any other study characteristic that is likely to be of substantive or methodological interest. In larger meta-analyses, subsets of studies that can be meaningfully grouped together on the basis of study characteristics can be examined separately, subset by subset, with respect to their central tendencies and other descriptive features.

Variability

The most important index of variability of effect sizes is simply their standard deviation. It is also helpful to give the maximum and minimum effect sizes and the effect sizes found at the 75th percentile (Q_3) and the 25th percentile (Q_1). For normally distributed effect sizes the standard deviation is estimated by .75 $(Q_3 - Q_1)$. Table 10.7 provides a checklist of descriptive data that should often, if not always, be reported.

Examining the distance (e.g., in units of S) of the maximum and minimum effect sizes from the mean, median, Q_1, and Q_3 of the full distribution of effect sizes is a useful start in the analysis of the data for outliers. Valuable discussions of the problem of outliers are found in Barnett and Lewis (1978), Hedges and Olkin (1985), Hunter and Schmidt (1990), and Light and Pillemer (1984). If extreme outliers are found, they can be set aside by using equitable trimming. That is, if the very highest value is seen to be an outlier to be set aside, then the very lowest value should also be set aside so that there will be no effect on the median.

Several meta-analysts discuss separating the variability among effect sizes into components that are due to ordinary sampling error and components that are due to other sources (Hedges & Olkin; 1985, Hunter & Schmidt, 1990; Light & Pillemer, 1984). This can be especially valuable in alerting us to "nonsampling error" variability that must then be

Table 10.7   Checklist of Descriptive Data for the Results Section

Visual Displays of Effect Sizes (Often Useful)
stem-and-leaf plots (as in Table 10.6)
box plots (if many are to be compared)
funnel plots (e.g., to investigate publication bias)
other plots (as needed)

Central Tendency
unweighted mean
weighted mean[a]
unweighted median (repeated for convenience as Q_2 below)
weighted median[b]
proportion of positive effects
k (the number of independent studies)
N (the number of independent participants)
n (median number of participants per study)

Variability
S (the standard deviation)[c]
maximum effect size[d]
Q_3 (75th percentile effect size)
Q_2 (50th percentile effect size)
Q_1 (25th percentile effect size)
minimum effect size[d]
normal-based $S = .75 (Q_3 - Q_1)$

---

[a] Weighting usually by *df*; means weighted by study quality or by other weightings should also be reported, if computed.
[b] The weighted median correlation is the effect size for the study that includes the midmost participant. To obtain the weighted median we list studies in order of magnitude of their effect size and the associated cumulative frequency of their sample sizes. Thus, if there were 6,000 participants in a meta-analysis of 40 studies, we go from the smallest to the largest effect size until we have found the midmost (3,000.5th) participant. The effect size of the study in which we find the midmost participant is the weighted median.
[c] It is also often valuable to report separately the variability "corrected" for sampling variation.
[d] Useful in a preliminary check for outliers.

investigated in order to identify potential moderator variables. However, a conclusion that all of the effect size variability is due to "ordinary sampling error" does *not* mean that we cannot or should not investigate the variability by considering moderator variables. Indeed, scientific progress can be defined in terms of our continually reducing the magnitude of sampling error by increasing our understanding of moderator variables.

Inferential Data

Significance Testing

Many procedures are available for testing the significance of an estimate of the typical effect size found in a particular meta-analysis. Mosteller and Bush (1954) described three procedures; R. Rosenthal (1991a) described nine procedures; and Becker (1994) listed 18. One of the most generally useful of these methods is the Stouffer method, in which we simply compute the standard normal deviate (Z) associated with each p value in our meta-analysis. Then we add all these Zs (one per study) and divide this sum by $\sqrt{k}$, where k is the number of *independent* studies, to find the new Z that tests the overall statistical significance of the result of the meta-analysis.

A related procedure for significance testing has been described in detail by Hedges, Cooper, and Bushman (1992). This procedure, called the lower confidence limit (LCL) method, also yields a standard normal deviate, Z. The LCL Z and the Stouffer Z agree most (nearly 99%) of the time; but when they do disagree, the LCL method may be more powerful (unless the smaller studies summarized in the meta-analysis are associated with the larger effect sizes—a fairly likely situation). The LCL method tends to reject the null hypothesis when it is true (Type I error) more often than does the Stouffer method; but because the null hypothesis may essentially never be true, that is not a serious problem (Cohen, 1994).

In both the Stouffer and LCL methods, Z depends for its magnitude on both the effect sizes obtained and the sizes of the studies and is interpreted as a fixed effect. That is, generalization of the results is to other subjects of the type found in the specific k studies of the meta-analysis. Generalization to other studies is ordinarily not justified.

Because of this limitation of the generalizability of fixed effect analyses, it is desirable also to employ a random effects test of significance. Such tests permit generalization to other studies from the same population from which the retrieved studies were sampled. A simple one-sample t test on the mean effect size serves this purpose (Mosteller & Bush, 1954). For example, if we were working with Fisher Z-transformed rs, t would equal the mean Z_r divided by the square root of the quantity S^2/k where S is the standard deviation of Z_rs and k is the number of independent Z_rs. This t (with $df = k - 1$) tends to be more conservative than Stouffer's Z but should nevertheless also be employed because of its greater value in generalizing to other studies.

Another random effects approach to significance testing that is likely to be even more conservative than the one-sample t test is the one-sample $\chi^2(1)$ test. This test assesses the null hypothesis that there is no difference in the proportion of studies showing positive effect sizes rather than negative effect sizes. When there are fewer than 10 effect sizes, the binomial test will tend to give more accurate p values than will $\chi^2(1)$ (Siegel, 1956).

We should emphasize the difference between the fixed effect and the random effect view of the results obtained in our meta-analysis. When we adopt a fixed effect view of the results, the significance testing is based on the total number of sampling units (e.g., subjects, patients, organisms), but our generalization is restricted to other sampling units that might have been assigned only to the very same studies of our meta-analysis. The fixed effect good news, therefore, is greater statistical power; the bad news is more limited generalizability. When we adopt a random effect view of the results, the significance testing is based not on the total number of sampling units but on the total number of studies included. However, the generalization can go beyond the specific studies we have retrieved to others that belong to the same population from which we obtained our studies. The random effect good news, therefore, is increased generalizability; the bad news is decreased statistical power. We should not try to be overly precise in our application of "random effects," however, because there is precious little random sampling of studies in meta-analytic work. Indeed, even in the fixed effect model, when we generalize to other sampling units within studies, we assume that the new sampling units will be randomly sampled within the study from the same population from which we sampled the original sampling units. In behavioral or biomedical research, it is very seldom indeed that we sample our subjects or patients randomly. Hence "random" should be thought of as "quasi-random" at best.

Tables 10.8 and 10.9 give an intuitive feel for the fixed versus random effect issue. Table 10.8 shows a simple meta-analytic model in which 10 studies have been retrieved, each with a treatment and a control condition with 20 subjects in each of the $2 \times 10 = 20$ cells. Table 10.9 shows the expected mean squares

Table 10.8   Meta-Analytic Model Illustrating Fixed versus Random View of Studies Summarized

Study	Condition	
	Treatment	Control
1		
2		
3		
4		
5		
6		
7		
8		
9		
10		

NOTE: Assume $n = 20$ for each of the $2 \times 10 = 20$ cells.

and F tests when studies are regarded as fixed versus random (Snedecor & Cochran, 1989). With treatment always regarded as a fixed effect, the F tests for studies and for the treatment $\times$ studies interaction are the same whether studies are regarded as fixed or random. However, the treatment effect is tested against different error terms when studies are viewed as fixed versus random, and the degrees of freedom for the F test are also different. In the example of Tables 10.8 and 10.9, when studies are viewed as fixed, the error term is the one expected to be smallest (subject variation within cells) and the df for error $= 380$. When studies are viewed as random, the error term will often be larger than when viewed as fixed to the extent that there are nonzero treatment $\times$ study interaction effects. In addition, the df will be smaller (9 instead of 380 in this example). More recent and more detailed discussions of the fixed versus random effect issue can be found in Hedges (1994b), Raudenbush (1994), and Shadish and Haddock (1994).

Confidence Intervals

Confidence intervals should be computed around the mean effect size, preferably using a simple random effects approach. That is, the standard error of the mean effect size estimate (e.g., $\overline{Z}_r$) should be computed as $S/\sqrt{k}$, with k being the number of independent effect sizes. At least the 95% confidence interval should be recorded; sometimes it is useful to give the 90%, the 99%, and other intervals as well.

An example will be helpful. Suppose we have $k = 25$ independent studies available with an unweighted mean d of .50 and a standard deviation (S) of these 25 ds of 1.00. Then the standard error (SE) of the 25 ds will be given by $S/\sqrt{k} = 1.00/\sqrt{25} = .20$. The 95% confidence interval is then given by the rough and ready mean $d(\overline{d}) \pm 2(SE)$ or $.50 \pm 2(.20) =$ an interval from .10 to .90. A

Table 10.9   Expected Mean Squares and F Tests When Studies Are Viewed as Fixed versus Random

Source	df	Studies Fixed[a] EMS	F	Studies Random[b] EMS	F
(T) Treatment					
(Fixed Effect)	1	$\sigma^2 + 200K_T{}^2$	T/U	$\sigma^2 + 20\sigma_{TS}{}^2 + 200K_T{}^2$	T/TS
(S) Studies	9	$\sigma^2 + 40K_S{}^2$	S/U	$\sigma^2 + 40\sigma_S{}^2$	S/U
(TS) Treatment × Studies	9	$\sigma^2 + 20K_{TS}{}^2$	TS/U	$\sigma^2 + 20\sigma_{TS}{}^2$	TS/U
(U) Participants (Units)					
in cells	380	σ^2		σ^2	

[a]Recognizes these 10 studies as the entire population of studies that are of interest.
[b]Regards these 10 studies as a "random" sample from some larger population of studies to which the meta-analyst would like to generalize.

more accurate interval is obtained by replacing the 2 by the critical .025 one-tailed value of t for the appropriate df (i.e., $k - 1$). That critical value of t for $k = 25$, ($df = 24$) is 2.064. Therefore, in this example the confidence interval is .50 ± (2.064)(.20), an interval running from .09 to .91 (R. Rosenthal & Rubin, 1978a). Our interpretation of this confidence interval is that if we claim that the effect size for the population (from which our 25 studies must be viewable as a random sample) falls within the 95% confidence interval, our claim will be correct 95% of the time.

The example given is based on the conservative random effects procedure in which studies—not individual subjects within studies—are employed as the sampling units. It is often useful also to compute confidence intervals in which subjects rather than studies are employed as the sampling units. However, the confidence intervals obtained by such procedures can appear dramatically more optimistic (i.e., narrower) than those based on the random effects procedures just illustrated. Computational procedures for confidence intervals based on subjects as sampling units are described in varying degrees of detail by Hedges (1994b), Hedges and Olkin (1985), Hunter and Schmidt (1990), and Shadish and Haddock (1994).

Heterogeneity Tests

Statistical tests of the heterogeneity of significance levels (R. Rosenthal & Rubin, 1979b) and of effect size estimates (Hedges, 1982; R. Rosenthal & Rubin, 1982b) are readily available. By heterogeneity of significance levels we mean the degree of variability of p levels among the studies of our meta-analysis. By heterogeneity of effect sizes we mean the degree of variability of effect sizes among the studies of our meta-analysis. Statistical tests of heterogeneity (typically chi-square tests) provide p values associated with the degree of variability of the obtained significance levels or effect sizes. Usually we are more interested in the heterogeneity of effect sizes than of significance levels, and it is usually helpful to present the results of such an analysis. Two common problems in the use of these tests must be pointed out, however.

The first of these problems is a widespread belief that a test of heterogeneity must be found to be significant before contrasts can be computed among the obtained effect sizes. That is not the case. Contrasts, and particularly planned contrasts, can and should be computed among the obtained effect sizes whether the overall test of heterogeneity is significant or not. The situation is identical to that in a one-way analysis of variance in which many investigators believe it is improper to compute contrasts unless the overall F is significant. Actually, planned contrasts should be computed without reference to the overall F, and even unplanned contrasts can be computed with appropriate adjustments of their levels of significance (R. Rosenthal & Rosnow, 1985, 1991). If overall tests of heterogeneity are not to serve as licenses to pursue contrast analyses, why compute them at all? They do provide some useful information. If very significant, they alert us to the likelihood that all our effect sizes are not cut from the same cloth and that we should try to find the moderator variables accounting for the significant heterogeneity of our effect sizes. Thus, a very significant χ^2 for heterogeneity "morally" obligates us to search for moderators, whereas a nonsignificant χ^2 does not preclude our search.

The second common problem in the use of heterogeneity tests occurs when we treat them as though they were estimates of the *magnitude* of heterogeneity. They are not; they are tests of significance, and like all tests of significance they are a function of the magnitudes of the effect and the sample sizes. Thus, the widely varying ($S = .40$) effect sizes (r) .80, .40, and .00 may be found not to differ significantly if they are based on small sample sizes (e.g., $n = 10$), whereas the homogeneous ($S = .05$) rs of .45, .40, .35 may be found to differ significantly if they are based on large sample sizes (e.g., $n = 800$). The magnitude of the effect size heterogeneity is given by the indexes of variability described earlier, in particular by S, the standard deviation of the effect sizes.

Some meta-analysts like to present separately one or both of the ingredients of the standard deviation (S) of the effect size. We can illustrate these two ingredients by examining in Table 10.9 the expected mean squares for the treatment-by-studies interaction when studies are viewed as random. The two components of variance are σ^2 and σ_{TS}^2. We obtain the estimate of σ^2 directly from the mean square for subjects nested in conditions; we obtain the estimate of σ_{TS}^2 in two steps:

$$MS_{TS} - MS_U$$
$$= (\sigma^2 + 20\sigma_{TS}^2) - (\sigma^2) = 20\sigma_{TS}^2 \quad (1)$$
$$\sigma_{TS}^2 = \frac{20\sigma_{TS}^2}{20}, \quad (2)$$

where 20 was the number of subjects in each cell. The estimate of σ^2 gives us the basic "noise level" of the dependent variable, and the estimate of σ_{TS}^2 gives us the variation of the study outcomes over and above that basic noise level.

Contrasts

The statistical significance of the relationship between a moderator variable and the effect sizes obtained is given by the computation of a contrast test (R. Rosenthal, 1991a; R. Rosenthal & Rubin, 1982b) or by more complex procedures of fitting models to effect size data in the spirit of multiple regression (Hedges & Olkin, 1985). As was the case for tests of heterogeneity, however, the tests of significance of contrasts do not give a direct indication of the magnitude of the moderator variable's relationship to the effect sizes obtained. Such an indication is readily available, however, simply by correlating the effect sizes obtained with their corresponding score on the moderating variable. Such a correlation, in which the sample size is the number of independent studies, reflects a random effects view of the data with generalizability to other potential results drawn from the same population that yielded the obtained results. When the number of studies retrieved is quite small, such correlations of effect sizes with their moderators are not very stable, and we may be forced to take a less generalizable, fixed effect view of the data (Raudenbush, 1994). In such cases we can get a serviceable

Table 10.10   Checklist of Inferential Data for the Results Section

Significance Testing
  combined (Stouffer) Z (and/or other such tests as needed)
  t test (one-sample)
  test of proportion positive (Z)

Confidence Intervals
          From   To
  90%   (optionally)
  95%   (almost always desirable)
  99%   (optionally)
  99.9% (optionally)
  standard error ($S/\sqrt{k}$)

Heterogeneity Tests
  $\chi^2(k-1)$
  p of χ^2
  S (magnitude of heterogeneity; or other indexes of magnitude not dependent on sample size)

Contrasts
  For each contrast or predictor variable give:
  test of significance
  effect size for contrast

indicator of the magnitude of the moderator effect by dividing the obtained test of the significance of the contrast, Z, by the square root of the sum of the sample sizes contributing to the computation of the Z. This "fixed effect" type of r tends to be smaller than the random effects r but tends to be associated with a more significant test statistic. Table 10.10 provides a checklist of inferential data that should often, if not always, be reported.

Interpretive Data

In this section we summarize a number of procedures and statistics that are often useful in understanding and interpreting the descriptive and inferential data of the meta-analysis. They are described here more as a reminder of their availability and utility than as a standard requirement of all meta-analyses.

The Binomial Effect Size Display

The BESD is a display procedure that shows the practical importance of an effect size (R. Rosenthal & Rubin, 1982a). As described

earlier in this chapter, the input to the BESD is a specific effect size estimate, the Pearson r. Because any other effect size estimate can be converted to an r, the BESD can be used to display the mean or median effect size estimate of any meta-analysis.

The Coefficient of Robustness

The standard error of the mean effect size along with confidence intervals placed around the mean effect size are of great value (R. Rosenthal & Rubin, 1978a). Employing a statistic that does not increase simply as a function of the increasing number of replications may also be useful. Thus, if we want to compare two research areas for their robustness, adjusting for the difference in the number of replications in each research area, we may prefer the robustness coefficient. This is simply the mean effect size divided by the S of the effect sizes. This metric is the reciprocal of the coefficient of variation (R. Rosenthal, 1990b, 1993). The coefficient of robustness (CR) can also be viewed in terms of the one-sample t test on the mean of the set of k effect sizes, when each is given equal weight. Thus, CR is given by $t/\sqrt{k}$, or t adjusted for the number of studies.

The utility of this coefficient is based on two ideas. First, robustness (or replication success, or clarity) depends on the homogeneity of the obtained effect sizes. Second, robustness depends on the unambiguity or clarity of the directionality of the result. Thus, a set of replications grows in robustness when the variability (S) of the effect sizes (the denominator of the coefficient) decreases and when the mean effect size (the numerator of the coefficient) increases. Incidentally, the mean may be weighted, unweighted, or trimmed (Tukey, 1977). Indeed, it need not be the mean at all, but any measure of location or central tendency (e.g., the unweighted or weighted median).

The coefficient of robustness can be seen as a kind of second-order effect size. An illustration will be helpful. Imagine that three meta-analyses of three treatments have been conducted with mean effect size ds of .8, .6, and .4. If the variability (S) of the three meta-analyses were quite similar to one another, the analysis showing the .8 mean d would, of course, be declared the most robust. However, suppose that the Ss for the three analyses were 1.00, 0.60, and 0.20. Then the three coefficients of robustness would be $.8/1.00 =$ .8, $.6/.60 = 1.0$, and $.4/.20 = 2.0$. Assuming reasonable and comparable sample sizes and numbers of studies collected for the three analyses, the treatment with the smallest effect size (i.e., .4) would be declared most robust with the implication that its effect is the most consistently positive.

The Counternull

A new statistic was recently introduced to aid our understanding and presentation of research results: the counternull value of the obtained effect size (R. Rosenthal & Rubin, 1994). As described earlier in this chapter, in most meta-analytic applications the value of the counternull is simply twice the magnitude of the obtained effect size (e.g., d, g, Δ, Z_r) and indicates the value of the effect size that has exactly the same probability as the null value.

The File Drawer Analysis

The file drawer problem refers to the well-supported suspicion that the studies retrievable in a meta-analysis are not likely to be a random sample of all studies conducted (R. Rosenthal, 1979, 1991a). The suspicion has been that published studies are more likely to have achieved statistical significance than are studies that remain squirreled away in file drawers (Sterling, 1959). No definitive solution to this problem is available, but we can establish reasonable boundaries and can esti-

mate the degree of damage that could be done by the file drawer problem. The fundamental idea in coping with the file drawer problem is simply to calculate the number of studies averaging null results that must be in the file drawers before the overall probability of a Type I error can be brought to any precisely specified level of significance, for example, $p = .05$. This number of filed studies, or the *tolerance for future null results,* is then evaluated for whether such a tolerance level is small enough to threaten the reviewer's overall conclusion. If the overall level of significance of the research review will be brought down to the level of barely significant by the addition of just a few more null results, the finding is not resistant to the file drawer threat.

Details of the calculations and rationale are given elsewhere (R. Rosenthal, 1991a); briefly, however, we can find the number (X) of new, filed, or unretrieved studies averaging null results that is required to bring the new overall p to .05 from the following:

$$X = [(\Sigma Z)^2/2.706] - k \qquad (24)$$

where ΣZ is the sum of the standard normal deviates associated with the one-tailed ps of all the k studies we have retrieved.

It should be noted that the file drawer analysis addresses only the effects on publication bias of the results of significance testing. Very sophisticated graphic (Light & Pillemer, 1984), and other valuable procedures are available for the estimation and correction of publication bias (e.g., Begg, 1994; Hedges & Olkin, 1985; Hunter & Schmidt, 1990).

Power Analysis

In large meta-analyses it is usually the case that the null hypothesis is found to be unlikely at a very low p value. In smaller meta-analyses, however, the overall results may not be found to be significant. Before concluding that the population value of the effect size is

Table 10.11   Checklist of Interpretive Data for the Results Section

	Binomial Effect Size Display Dependent Variable		Σ
	High	Low	
Independent Variable			
High			100
Low			100
	100	100	

Coefficient of Robustness
   Mean/S^a

Counternull
   (Especially if overall results not significant)

File Drawer Analysis
   (Tolerance for future null results)

Power Analysis
   (If overall results not significant)

---

[a]Several may be reported employing weighted or unweighted mean or median effect size for the numerator and weighted or unweighted S for the denominator.

zero, it will be helpful to perform a power analysis along with computing the counternull value of the overall effect size obtained. In this application we assume a population effect size equivalent to the overall effect size actually obtained and simply enter Cohen's (1977, 1988) tables to find the power at which we have been testing the null hypothesis. If that power level is low, the evidence for the null hypothesis is weak and should be reported as such. Table 10.11 provides a checklist of interpretive data that should often be considered and reported when appropriate.

THE DISCUSSION SECTION OF A META-ANALYTIC REVIEW

The discussion may begin with a summary of the meta-analytic results followed by tentative explanations of these results. These explanations may be in terms of the theories of the area in which the meta-analysis was done, or they may require new theory (Hall, Rosenthal, Tickle-Degnen, & Mosteller, 1994). The im-

plications for theory (old or new), for practice (if relevant), and for further primary-level research may be discussed. Limitations of the meta-analysis should be pointed out, including possible sampling biases, the size of the sample of studies included (if quite modest), and the level of quality of the studies included (if that level seemed especially questionable).

The overall goal of the discussion may be seen as the answer to the question, Where are we now that this meta-analysis has been conducted? The meta-analysis is placed in the context of the field, and the field, very often, is placed into the context of the meta-analysis.

APPENDIXES TO A META-ANALYTIC REVIEW

One appendix should provide a full reference to each of the studies included in the meta-analysis.

An additional appendix should be in the form of a table that gives for each of the included studies the overall effect size, the sample size, the Z corresponding to an accurate p level, and the coded or rated score for each study of the primary study characteristics and moderator variables employed in the meta-analysis. The journal editor and reviewers will then have important information to guide them in their evaluation of the meta-analysis. If the printing of this appendix table would make the paper too long, the author note should offer a copy of this table to interested readers.

CONCLUSION

Most reviews of the literature should be quantitative, just as most primary research studies should be quantitative. The statistical procedures employed in meta-analyses range from the basic to the very complex, just as those of primary research studies do. There is no one way to do a meta-analysis or to report a meta-analysis any more than there is just one way to do or to report the data analysis of a primary research study. Therefore, the goal of this chapter has not been prescriptive in the sense that every meta-analysis should include everything suggested here. The goal instead has been to provide some conceptual and historical background and some general guidelines that may be useful to meta-analysts who want to follow the standard procedures of the various authors of meta-analytic textbooks. Our own bias has been to keep the analyses simple, basic, and intuitive, as well as to recommend simplicity and clarity of reporting even when complex analyses are required. When we write our meta-analytic reviews, after all, they are intended for a far larger audience than the other authors of texts and papers on meta-analytic methodology. That larger audience of content experts was advised by Fisher (1935) to remember that it was they, the experimenters, and not the statisticians, who knew best the working content and the working methods of their discipline (p. 49).

REFERENCES

Alpha-Tocopherol, Beta Carotene Cancer Prevention Study Group. (1994). The effect of vitamin E and beta carotene on the incidence of lung cancer and other cancers in male smokers. *New England Journal of Medicine, 330,* 1029–1035.

Altman, L. K. (1994, February 21). In major finding, drug limits H.I.V. infection in newborns. *New York Times,* pp. A1, A13.

Ambady, N., & Rosenthal, R. (1992). Thin slices of expressive behavior as predictors of interpersonal consequences: A meta-analysis. *Psychological Bulletin, 111,* 256–274.

Barnes, D. M. (1986). Promising results halt trial of anti-AIDS drug. *Science, 234,* 15–16.

Barnett, V., & Lewis, T. (1978). *Outliers in statistical data.* New York: Wiley.

Becker, B. J. (1994). Combining significance levels. In H. Cooper & L. V. Hedges (Eds.), *Handbook of research synthesis* (pp. 215–230). New York: Sage.

Begg, C. B. (1994). Publication bias. In H. Cooper & L. V. Hedges (Eds.), *Handbook of research synthesis* (pp. 399–409). New York: Sage.

Canadian Multicentre Transplant Study Group. (1983). A randomized clinical trial of cyclosporine in cadaveric renal transplantation. *New England Journal of Medicine, 309,* 809–815.

Centers for Disease Control Vietnam Experience Study. (1988). Health status of Vietnam veterans: 1. Psychosocial characteristics. *Journal of the American Medical Association, 259,* 2701–2707.

Chandler, D. L. (1993, February 15). Study finds evidence of ESP phenomenon. *Boston Globe,* pp. 1, 8.

Cleveland, W. S. (1985). *The elements of graphing data.* Monterey, CA: Wadsworth.

Cleveland, W. S. (1995). *Visualizing data.* Summit, NJ: Hobart Press.

Cohen, J. (1962). The statistical power of abnormal-social psychological research: A review. *Journal of Abnormal and Social Psychology, 65,* 145–153.

Cohen, J. (1965). Some statistical issues in psychological research. In B. B. Wolman (Ed.), *Handbook of clinical psychology* (95–121). New York: McGraw Hill.

Cohen, J. (1977). *Statistical power analysis for the behavioral sciences* (Rev. ed.). New York: Academic Press.

Cohen, J. (1988). *Statistical power analysis for the behavioral sciences* (2nd ed.). Hillsdale, NJ: Erlbaum.

Cohen, J. (1990). Things I have learned (so far). *American Psychologist, 45,* 1304–1312.

Cohen, J. (1994). The earth is round ($p < .05$). *American Psychologist, 49,* 997–1003.

Collins, H. M. (1985). *Changing order: Replication and induction in scientific practice.* Beverly Hills, CA: Sage.

Contraceptive trials set for a link to AIDS research. (1996, May 7). *Boston Globe,* p. B1.

Cooper, H. M. (1981). On the significance of effects and the effects of significance. *Journal of Personality and Social Psychology, 41,* 1013–1018.

Cooper, H. M. (1989). *Integrating research: A guide for literature reviews* (2nd ed.). Newbury Park, CA: Sage.

Cooper, H., & Hedges, L. V. (Eds.). (1994a). *Handbook of research synthesis.* New York: Sage.

Cooper, H., & Hedges, L. V. (1994b). Potentials and limitations of research synthesis. In H. Cooper & L. V. Hedges (Eds.), *Handbook of research synthesis* (pp. 521–529). New York: Sage.

Cooper, H., & Hedges, L. V. (1994c). Research synthesis as a scientific enterprise. In H. Cooper & L. V. Hedges (Eds.), *Handbook of research synthesis* (pp. 3–14). New York: Sage.

Cromie, W. J. (1990, October 5). Report: Drugs affect lung cancer survival. *Harvard Gazette,* pp. 1,10.

Cromie, W. J. (1991, September 13). Study: Hospitalization recommended for problem drinkers. *Harvard Gazette,* pp. 3–4.

Dabbs, J. M., Jr., & Morris, R. (1990). Testosterone, social class, and antisocial behavior in a sample of 4,462 men. *Psychological Science, 1,* 209–211.

Dickersin, K. (1994). Research registers. In H. Cooper & L. V. Hedges (Eds.), *Handbook of research synthesis* (pp. 71–83). New York: Sage.

Fisher, R. A. (1935). *The design of experiments.* Edinburgh, Scotland: Oliver & Boyd.

Fleiss, J. L. (1994). Measures of effect size for categorical data. In H. Cooper & L. V. Hedges (Eds.), *Handbook of research synthesis* (pp. 245–260). New York: Sage.

Foreman, J. (1995, July 27). Medical notebook: A new confirmation for a pregnancy drug. *Boston Globe.*

GISSI: Gruppo Italiano per lo Studio della Streptochinasi Nell'Infarto Miocardico. (1986, February 22). *Lancet,* 397–402.

Glass, G. V. (1976). Primary, secondary, and meta-analysis of research. *Educational Researcher, 5,* 3–8.

Glass, G. V. (1978). In defense of generalization. *The Behavioral and Brain Sciences, 3,* 394–395.

Glass, G. V., McGaw, B., & Smith, M. L. (1981). *Meta-analysis in social research.* Beverly Hills, CA: Sage.

Gleser, L. J., & Olkin, I. (1994). Stochastically dependent effect sizes. In H. Cooper & L. V. Hedges (Eds.), *Handbook of research synthesis* (pp. 339–355). New York: Sage.

Goldfinger, S. E. (1991, August). Garlic: Good for what ails you. *Harvard Health Letter, 16*(2), 1–2.

Gosset, W. S. (Student). (1908). The probable error of a mean. *Biometrika, 6,* 1–25.

Greenhouse, J. B., & Iyengar, S. (1994). Sensitivity analysis and diagnostics. (1994). In H. Cooper & L. V. Hedges (Eds.), *Handbook of research synthesis* (pp. 383–398). New York: Sage.

Hall, J. A., Rosenthal, R., Tickle-Degnen, L., & Mosteller, F. (1994). Hypotheses and problems in research synthesis. In H. Cooper & L. V. Hedges (Eds.), *Handbook of research synthesis* (pp. 17–28). New York: Sage.

Hedges, L. V. (1982). Estimation of effect size from a series of independent experiments. *Psychological Bulletin, 92,* 490–499.

Hedges, L. V. (1987). How hard is hard science, how soft is soft science? *American Psychologist, 42,* 443–455.

Hedges, L. V. (1994a). Statistical considerations. In H. Cooper & L. V. Hedges (Eds.), *Handbook of research synthesis* (pp. 29–38). New York: Sage.

Hedges, L. V. (1994b). Fixed effects models. In H. Cooper & L. V. Hedges (Eds.), *Handbook of research synthesis* (pp. 285–299). New York: Sage.

Hedges, L. V., Cooper, H., & Bushman, B. J. (1992). Testing the null hypothesis in meta-analysis: A comparison of combined probability and confidence interval procedures. *Psychological Bulletin, 111,* 188–194.

Hedges, L. V., & Olkin, I. (1985). *Statistical methods for meta-analysis.* New York: Academic Press.

Hiller, J. B., Rosenthal, R., Bornstein, R. F., Berry, D. T. R., & Brunell-Neuleib, S. (1999). A comparative meta-analysis of Rorschach and MMPI validity. *Psychological Assessment, 11,* 278–296.

Hunter, J. E., & Schmidt, F. L. (1990). *Methods of meta-analysis: Correcting error and bias in research findings.* Newbury Park, CA: Sage.

Jung, J. (1978). Self-negating functions of self-fulfilling prophecies. *The Behavioral and Brain Sciences, 3,* 397–398.

Knox, R. A. (1997, February 25). AIDS trial terminated: 3-drug therapy hailed. *Boston Globe,* pp. A1, A16.

Kolata, G. B. (1981). Drug found to help heart attack survivors. *Science, 214,* 774–775.

Kosslyn, S. M. (1994). *Elements of graph design.* New York: Freeman.

Light, R. J., & Pillemer, D. B. (1984). *Summing up: The science of reviewing research.* Cambridge: Harvard University Press.

Light, R. J., Singer, J. D., & Willett, J. B. (1994). The visual presentation and interpretation of meta-analyses. In H. Cooper & L. V. Hedges (Eds.), *Handbook of research synthesis* (pp. 439–453). New York: Sage.

Lipsey, M. W. (1994). Identifying potentially interesting variables and analysis opportunities. In H. Cooper & L. V. Hedges (Eds.), *Handbook of research synthesis* (pp. 111–123). New York: Sage.

Lipsey, M. W., & Wilson, D. B. (2001). *Practical meta-analysis.* Thousand Oaks, CA: Sage Publications.

Mann, C. (1990). Meta-analysis in the breech. *Science, 249,* 476–480.

Meta-analysis of Observational Studies in Epidemiology Group. (2000). *The Journal of the American Medical Association, 283,* 2008–2012.

Mosteller, F. M., & Bush, R. R. (1954). Selected quantitative techniques. In G. Lindzey (Ed.), *Handbook of social psychology: Vol. 1. Theory and method* (pp. 289–334). Cambridge, MA: Addison-Wesley.

Nelson, N., Rosenthal, R., & Rosnow, R. L. (1986). Interpretation of significance levels and effect sizes by psychological researchers. *American Psychologist, 41,* 1299–1301.

Orwin, R. G. (1994). Evaluating coding decisions. In H. Cooper & L. V. Hedges (Eds.), *Handbook of research synthesis* (pp. 139–162). New York: Sage.

Pearson, K. (1904). Report on certain enteric fever inoculation statistics. *British Medical Journal* (November 5), 1243–1246.

Pool, R. (1988). Similar experiments, dissimilar results. *Science, 242,* 192–193.

Raudenbush, S. W. (1994). Random effects models. In H. Cooper & L. V. Hedges (Eds.), *Handbook of research synthesis* (pp. 301–321). New York: Sage.

Reed, J. G., & Baxter, P. M. (1994). Using reference databases. In H. Cooper & L. V. Hedges (Eds.), *Handbook of research synthesis* (pp. 57–70). New York: Sage.

Roberts, L. (1987). Study bolsters case against cholesterol. *Science, 237,* 28–29.

Rosenthal, M. C. (1994). The fugitive literature. In H. Cooper & L. V. Hedges (Eds.), *Handbook of research synthesis* (pp. 85–94). New York: Sage.

Rosenthal, R. (1966). *Experimenter effects in behavioral research.* New York: Appleton Century Crofts.

Rosenthal, R. (1969). Interpersonal expectations. In R. Rosenthal & R. L. Rosnow (Eds.), *Artifact in behavioral research* (pp. 181–277). New York: Academic Press.

Rosenthal, R. (1976). *Experimenter effects in behavioral research* (Enlarged ed.). New York: Halsted Press.

Rosenthal, R. (1978). Combining results of independent studies. *Psychological Bulletin, 85,* 185–193.

Rosenthal, R. (1979). The "file drawer problem" and tolerance for null results. *Psychological Bulletin, 86,* 638–641.

Rosenthal, R. (1990a). How are we doing in soft psychology? *American Psychologist, 45,* 775–777.

Rosenthal, R. (1990b). Replication in behavioral research. *Journal of Social Behavior and Personality, 5,* 1–30.

Rosenthal, R. (1991a). *Meta-analytic procedures for social research* (Rev. ed.). Newbury Park, CA: Sage.

Rosenthal, R. (1991b). Quality-weighting of studies in meta-analytic research. *Psychotherapy Research, 1,* 25–28.

Rosenthal, R. (1993). Cumulating evidence. In G. Keren & C. Lewis (Eds.), *A handbook for data analysis in the behavioral sciences: Methodological issues* (pp. 519–559). Hillsdale, NJ: Erlbaum.

Rosenthal, R. (1994a). Interpersonal expectancy effects: A 30-year perspective. *Current Directions in Psychological Science, 3,* 176–179.

Rosenthal, R. (1994b). Parametric measures of effect size. In H. Cooper & L. V. Hedges (Eds.), *Handbook of research synthesis* (231–244). New York: Sage.

Rosenthal, R. (1995a). Progress in clinical psychology: Is there any? *Clinical Psychology: Science and Practice, 2,* 133–150.

Rosenthal, R. (1995b). Writing meta-analytic reviews. *Psychological Bulletin, 118,* 183–192.

Rosenthal, R. (1998). Meta-Analysis: Concepts, corollaries, and controversies. In J. Adair, D. Bélanger, & K. L. Dion (Eds.), *Advances in psychological science: Volume 1. Social, personal, and cultural aspects* (pp. 371–384). Hove, England: Psychology Press.

Rosenthal, R. (2000). Effect sizes in behavioral and biomedical research: Estimation and interpretation. In L. Bickman (Ed.), *Validity and social experimentation: Donald Campbell's legacy* (Vol. 1, pp. 121–139). Newbury Park, CA: Sage.

Rosenthal, R., & DiMatteo, M. R. (2001). Meta-analysis: Recent developments in quantitative methods for literature reviews. *Annual Review of Psychology, 52,* 59–82.

Rosenthal, R., & Gaito, J. (1963). The interpretation of levels of significance by psychological researchers. *Journal of Psychology, 55,* 33–38.

Rosenthal, R., & Gaito, J. (1964). Further evidence for the cliff effect in the interpretation of levels of significance. *Psychological Reports, 15,* 570.

Rosenthal, R., Hiller, J. B., Bornstein, R. F., Berry, D.T.R., & Brunell-Neuleib, S. (in press). Meta-analytic methods, the Rorschach, and the MMPI. *Psychological Assessment.*

Rosenthal, R., & Rosnow, R. L. (1985). *Contrast analysis: Focused comparisons in the analysis of variance.* New York: Cambridge University Press.

Rosenthal, R., & Rosnow, R. L. (1991). *Essentials of behavioral research* (2nd ed.). New York: McGraw-Hill.

Rosenthal, R., Rosnow, R. L., & Rubin, D. B. (2000). *Contrasts and effect sizes in behavioral research: A correlational approach.* New York: Cambridge University Press.

Rosenthal, R., & Rubin, D. B. (1978a). Interpersonal expectancy effects: The first 345 studies. *The Behavioral and Brain Sciences, 3,* 377–386.

Rosenthal, R., & Rubin, D. B. (1978b). Issues in summarizing the first 345 studies of interpersonal expectancy effects. *The Behavioral and Brain Sciences, 3,* 410–415.

Rosenthal, R., & Rubin, D. B. (1979a). A note on percent variance explained as a measure of the importance of effects. *Journal of Applied Social Psychology, 9,* 395–396.

Rosenthal, R., & Rubin, D. B. (1979b). Comparing significance levels of independent studies. *Psychological Bulletin, 86,* 1165–1168.

Rosenthal, R., & Rubin, D. B. (1982a). Further meta-analytic procedures in assessing cognitive gender differences. *Journal of Educational Psychology, 74,* 708–712.

Rosenthal, R., & Rubin, D. B. (1982b). A simple, general purpose display of magnitude of experimental effect. *Journal of Educational Psychology, 74,* 166–169.

Rosenthal, R., & Rubin, D. B. (1982c). Comparing effect sizes of independent studies. *Psychological Bulletin, 92,* 500–504.

Rosenthal, R., & Rubin, D. B. (1986). Meta-analytic procedures for combining studies with multiple effect sizes. *Psychological Bulletin, 99,* 400–406.

Rosenthal, R., & Rubin, D. B. (1988). Comment: Assumptions and procedures in the file drawer problem. *Statistical Science, 3,* 120–125.

Rosenthal, R., & Rubin, D. B. (1989). Effect size estimation for one-sample multiple-choice-type data: Design, analysis, and meta-analysis. *Psychological Bulletin, 106,* 332–337.

Rosenthal, R., & Rubin, D. B. (1991). Further issues in effect size estimation for one-sample multiple-choice-type data. *Psychological Bulletin, 109,* 351–352.

Rosenthal, R., & Rubin, D. B. (1994). The counternull value of an effect size: A new statistic. *Psychological Science, 5,* 329–334.

Rosnow, R. L., & Rosenthal, R. (1996). Computing contrasts, effect sizes, and counternulls on other people's published data: General procedures for research consumers. *Psychological Methods, 1,* 331–340.

Schaffer, J. P. (1991). Comment on "Effect size estimation for one-sample multiple-choice-type data: Design, analysis, and meta-analysis" by Rosenthal and Rubin (1989). *Psychological Bulletin, 109,* 348–350.

Sedlmeier, P., & Gigerenzer, G. (1989). Do studies of statistical power have an effect on the power of studies? *Psychological Bulletin, 105,* 309–316.

Shadish, W. R., & Haddock, C. K. (1994). Combining estimates of effect size. In H. Cooper & L. V. Hedges (Eds.), *Handbook of research synthesis* (pp. 261–281). New York: Sage.

Siegel, S. (1956). *Nonparametric statistics.* New York: McGraw-Hill.

Skinner, B. F. (1983, August). On the value of research. *APA Monitor,* 39.

Smith, M. L., & Glass, G. V. (1977). Meta-analysis of psychotherapy outcome studies. *American Psychologist, 32,* 752–760.

Smith, M. L., Glass, G. V., & Miller, T. I. (1980). *The benefits of psychotherapy.* Baltimore: Johns Hopkins University Press.

Snedecor, G. W., & Cochran, W. G. (1989). *Statistical methods* (8th ed.). Ames: Iowa State University Press.

Steering Committee of the Physicians Health Study Research Group. (1988). Preliminary report: Findings from the aspirin component of the ongoing physicians' health study. *New England Journal of Medicine, 318,* 262–264.

Sterling, T. D. (1959). Publication decisions and their possible effects on inferences drawn from tests of significance—or vice versa. *Journal of the American Statistical Association, 54,* 30–34.

Stock, W. A. (1994). Systematic coding for research synthesis. In H. Cooper & L. V. Hedges (Eds.), *Handbook of research synthesis* (pp. 125–138). New York: Sage.

Tufte, E. R. (1983). *The visual display of quantitative information.* Cheshire, CT: Graphics Press.

Tukey, J. W. (1977). *Exploratory data analysis.* Reading, MA: Addison-Wesley.

White, H. D. (1994). Scientific communication and literature retrieval. In H. Cooper & L. V. Hedges (Eds.), *Handbook of research synthesis* (pp. 41–55). New York: Sage.

Wilkinson, L., & the Task Force on Statistical Inference, APA Board of Scientific Affairs. (1999). Statistical methods in psychology journals: Guidelines and explanations. *American Psychologist, 54,* 594–604.

Wortman, P. M. (1994). Judging research quality. In H. Cooper & L. V. Hedges (Eds.), *Handbook of research synthesis* (pp. 97–109). New York: Sage.

CHAPTER 11

Mathematical Modeling

IN JAE MYUNG AND MARK A. PITT

INTRODUCTION

Why Do Mathematical Modeling?

As psychologists, we seek to identify lawful patterns of behavior, infer mental structures and processes underlying these patterns, and develop theories that provide a succinct explanation of the behavior. Within psychology today, most theories exist in a verbal form only. That is, they are a set of statements formulated from observations (i.e., data) about behavior. Verbal modeling is popular in current psychological research for a number of good reasons. First, a verbal model, stated in everyday language, helps readers to grasp the essence of an idea, thereby providing a good conceptual understanding of the phenomenon of interest. Second, verbal modeling is a somewhat conservative approach to knowledge acquisition because specification of the inner workings of the theory does not stretch too far beyond what is, in principle, observable in the data. Such a strategy makes sense when data are scarce or a clear understanding of the phenomenon is lacking, especially in the early stages of research. It is prudent to avoid assuming too much about the

phenomenon for fear of leading the research enterprise astray. Third, considerable mileage can be made with verbal modeling. In conjunction with hypothesis-driven experimentation, a verbal model can be used to identify key variables that affect the phenomenon of interest, such as the influence of word frequency in word recognition and the influence of serial position in memory retrieval.

At its best, a verbal model furnishes testable predictions about the relationship between variables and levels of a variable, while making as few assumptions as possible about the details of the underlying mental process. Verbal modeling can thus lead to good qualitative descriptions of the data, yielding many useful insights into the underlying process.

Although researchers have made many important advances in science and psychology through the use of verbal modeling, a case of diminishing returns can be reached unless the theory is specified in more detail. The lack of precision is a serious shortcoming of verbal modeling (Lewandowsky, 1993; Ratcliff, 1998). Because it is expressed verbally or graphically without making use of explicit mathematical formulations, a verbal model does not provide sufficient information about structural or functional characteristics of the phenomenon being studied. For instance, computational mechanisms may be vaguely specified or sometimes left

The authors thank Barbara Mellers for valuable comments on an earlier version of this chapter. The authors were supported by NIMH Grant MH57472.

undefined, making it unclear which predictions follow from the model and which do not (Forster, 1994). Moreover, the lack of precision in verbal modeling opens up the possibility of multiple interpretations of how a model functions, each with distinct predictions, possibly making the model too powerful to test or virtually unfalsifiable (Jacobs & Grainger, 1994). If two competing theories exhibit this property, a form of gridlock can arise, making scientific advancement difficult. Furthermore, although they furnish ordinal information about the effect of interest, most verbal models are silent about its magnitude. That is, verbal models do not specify how exactly the magnitude of an effect may be influenced by other relevant variables. For example, a model of the word frequency effect states that response time in a lexical decision task is a monotonically decreasing function of word frequency: the more frequent a word, the faster the response time. The model, however, is mute on the specific characteristic of the functional relationship between response time and word frequency, such as whether it is linear or nonlinear. From the standpoint of the theory of measurement, variables of verbal models can be specified only on ordinal scales of measurement, not on more precise interval and ratio scales. Consequently, many potentially important questions formulated in terms of magnitude relationships are left untestable.

Mathematical modeling represents an alternative approach that overcomes these limitations (Luce, 1995, 1997; Ratcliff, 1998). Mathematical models, which seek quantitative descriptions of data, attempt to characterize patterns of behavior by directly asking about the form of the underlying mechanism that gives rise to the behavior of interest. These include questions about how stimulus information is represented, what computations are performed on the input, what circuits are involved in information processing, and so on. In mathematical modeling,

researchers formulate hypotheses about the underlying mechanisms using closed-form expressions, algorithms, or other simulation procedures, thereby imposing precision and clarity on what is meant. As a result, mathematical modeling enables, even requires, precise predictions be made from the underlying assumptions, which improves the ability to discriminate among models and hypotheses. The virtue of the approach is particularly evident when the predictions and outcomes are not obvious.

As Luce (1995) put it, mathematical modeling is the "opened black box" approach to psychological inquiry, as opposed to the "unopened black box" characteristic of verbal modeling. Because the goal of mathematical modeling is to specify the details in the black box, it may not be the best strategy to use in the early, exploratory stage of research, when a phenomenon is first being investigated. Rather, it is probably most fruitful in the more advanced stage of research, when considerable knowledge has been acquired about the behavior through verbal modeling. Otherwise, one's quantitative formulation of the process is difficult to justify and most likely will be a poor approximation of the true form of the mental process. The following recent example from the literature demonstrates how research can benefit from mathematical modeling.

A Reinterpretation of Brinley Plots

A Brinley plot (Brinley, 1965) is a plot of mean response time by older adults against mean response time by younger adults on some cognitive task (e.g., mental rotation, memory scanning). A typical observation is that the mean response time for the older adults is slower than that for younger adults. The relationship between these two groups has proven to be very consistent, so much so that the data of older adults can be estimated from the data of younger adults by a straight-forward linear transformation:

$$RT_{old} = \alpha RT_{young} - \beta \quad (\alpha > 1, \beta > 0) \quad (1)$$

where β, the y intercept, is frequently positive, and α, the slope, often hovers around 1.5. Researchers have sought to explain the cause of this linear relationship, whereby the data of older subjects can be predicted from that of younger subjects through a constant factor (i.e., the slope). For example, for $\alpha = 1.5$ and $\beta = 200$, $RT_{old} = 700$ ms and $RT_{young} = 600$ ms would be observed in one cognitive task with a slowing effect of 100 ms. The consistency of this finding has been interpreted as an across-the-board, general slowing of cognitive processes in the elderly.

Although this cognitive-slowing interpretation of the Brinley plot seems clear-cut and convincing, Ratcliff, Spieler, and McKoon (2000) showed that the strong linear association might be an artifact of the analysis technique itself. Using simulations as well as analytic methods, they identified a set of statistical conditions under which the Brinley pattern can be observed. Most enlightening was their quantile-quantile (Q-Q) analysis, which revealed that (a) a Brinley plot is linear because the distributions of responses times for the older adults have about the same shape as that for the younger group, (b) the slope is greater than 1 because the standard deviation of the older group's response times is greater than that of the younger group's, and (c) the intercept is negative because the motor response time is more or less the same for both the older and younger groups. The linearity in Brinley plots derives from a constant difference in the variability in response time between the two groups (point b) and is not unambiguous evidence of a static (cognitive-slowing) relationship between the performances of older and younger adults.

Ratcliff et al. (2000) made this point even more strongly by showing that extant models of aging effects, such as Cerella's (1985) linear model, Meyerson, Hale, Wagstaff, Poon, and Smith's (1990) information loss model, and even Ratcliff's (1978) random walk model, can be reinterpreted as being consistent with the Q-Q analysis, making each model capable of accounting for the Brinley pattern of results, though with differing assumptions about the underlying cognitive process. Particularly disturbing is Ratcliff et al.'s (2000) demonstration through simulations that the diffusion model can reproduce the Brinley pattern of results by simply manipulating two parameters (the boundary-position and drift-rate parameters) independently or in combination, even when they were varied in a counterintuitive manner with respect to the effects of aging.

In short, the Brinley pattern can appear on first encounter to provide compelling evidence that performance differences as a function of age are related in a straightforward, linear fashion. Ratcliff et al.'s (2000) investigation shows the pattern can be observed under a variety of modeling assumptions and thus provides only very weak constraints on modeling. Such insights become evident only through quantitative analysis of the data and competing models.

Critical tests of cognitive slowing will require analysis of aspects of the data besides plots of means. Examples of such data are the shape of the response time distributions, the joint relationship between response time and accuracy, and the relative speeds of correct and error responses. Along with these data, researchers need a modeling approach that makes explicit assumptions about the underlying process, generates clearly falsifiable predictions about the shape of the data, and thus provides a means of discriminating among specific hypotheses about the mental process. Mathematical modeling is necessary to address such issues, and the random walk model is one example. For instance, by varying the appropriate parameters, one can test whether older adults respond slowly because the quality of the information that they use to make decisions is relatively poor or because they set more conservative decision criteria. Comparing the simulated data with the observed data in each case will answer this question. Much more information can be extracted from the data when evaluating quantitative models, allowing the researcher to test many pointed hypotheses, a feat that is not possible in verbal modeling.

Three lessons can be drawn from the above Brinley plot example. First, a reliance on verbal models, while useful initially, can lead to serious misinterpretations of observed patterns of results, because the evidence may be far less constraining than was imagined. Second, a formal mathematical analysis of the problem in question can provide a clearer picture of the theoretical constraints, revealing previously unsuspected insufficiencies in the model and in data interpretation. Third, mathematical modeling avoids the pitfalls of verbal modeling by formally expressing the details of the model and then squeezing as much information from the data as possible to test its accuracy, not just its mean performance. The end product is both a deeper understanding of the mental process of interest and the adequacy of one's approximation to it (Lewandowsky, 1993).

Overview

The aim of this chapter is to serve as an introduction to the field of mathematical modeling, first covering the different types of models and then discussing how to create (i.e., define) a model, how to test it, and how to compare it with competitors. Examples are provided along the way to illustrate points and serve as brief tutorials. The focus throughout most of the chapter is on statistical models, because these are in widespread use and their popular-

ity is growing. For in-depth, technically rigorous treatments of mathematical modeling in psychology, the reader may consult books on specialized topics and conference proceedings (see, e.g., Ashby, 1992; Brown & Keith-Smith, 1991; Dowling, Roberts, & Theuns, 1998; Estes, 1991; Healy, Kosslyn, & Shiffrin, 1992; Luce, 1986; Marley, 1997; McFall & Townsend, 1998; Townsend & Ashby, 1983; Wickens, 1982).

The chapter was written for graduate students who have completed a year of statistics courses. Some readers may be challenged by the technical details in a few sections, but a thorough understanding of the mathematics is not necessary to follow the discussion.

TYPES OF MODELS

Model Building via Regularity Constraints

In this approach, a model is created by constraining it to be subject to certain regularity conditions at the level of behavior. Functional equation models and axiomatic models are of this type.

Functional Equation Models

Rather than making specific assumptions about the form of functions in a mathematical model, this method (Aczel, 1966) makes certain equality restrictions involving an unknown function. The restrictions themselves, however, are so severe that they yield a particular solution as the only possible form for the function. To illustrate this approach, consider models of psychophysics, which aim to capture the relationship between physical scale (e.g., intensity of a tone) and psychological scale (e.g., perceived loudness). Fechner's logarithmic law and Stevens's power law are two well-known, well-studied models of psychophysics. Fechner's law can be derived using the functional equation method. That is, suppose that the following equation holds for all values x and y of physical stimulation strength,

$$\psi(xy) = \psi(x) + \psi(y)$$

for some unknown function Ψ. For instance, according to the above constraint, we must observe $\Psi(50) = \Psi(5) + \Psi(10) = \Psi(2) + \Psi(25)$, and so on, for various pairs of stimulation strengths. It is then shown (F. S. Roberts, 1979, p. 162) that the function that satisfies the above equation must be logarithmic in the form $\Psi(x) = k\ln(x)$ for a constant k, which is just Fechner's law. Note here that the model is derived entirely in terms of overt behavior, with no explicit assumption of any intervening variables or mental processes. Instead of the additive form of the functional equation, if a multiplicative constraint, $\Psi(xy) = \Psi(x)\Psi(y)$, is imposed, this gives rise to Stevens's power law of psychophysics, $\Psi(x) = x^k$.

In the above discussion, the set of objects or things under study on which the model equation is defined is continuous. If the set is discrete (e.g., set of people or cities), similar constraints may be used to derive the model equation. As an example, consider a system in which an individual is required to select between a pair of choices, say a and b. For instance, participants might be asked to decide whether they prefer choice a to choice b in a decision making experiment, to classify an ambiguous visual stimulus into category a or b in a categorization experiment, or to judge whether stimulus a is brighter than stimulus b in a psychophysical task. Let P_{ab} denote the probability of choosing stimulus a over b. By definition we should have $P_{ab} + P_{ba} = 1$ for all a and b. Suppes and Zinnes (1963) showed that the product rule

$$P_{ab}P_{bc}P_{ca} = P_{ba}P_{cb}P_{ac} \quad \text{for all } a, b, c$$

uniquely derives the following model of choice probability:

$$P_{ab} = \frac{f(a)}{f(a) + f(b)}$$

for some real-valued function $f(a)$. It is important to note that the product rule and the about model are logically equivalent, meaning that one implies the other and vice versa. The $f(a)$ in the previous equation is interpreted as a measure of response strength and defines a ratio scale (F. S. Roberts, 1979, pp. 281–283). Many models in cognitive psychology are of this form or of its extension, for example, Luce's (1959) choice model, context models of categorization (Medin & Schaffer, 1978; Nosofsky, 1986), and connectionist models of category learning (Gluck & Bower, 1988).

Axiomatic Models

In an axiomatic model, regularity conditions that are imposed upon observed variables are in the form of *ordinal* relations called axioms, rather than *equality* relations as in functional equation models. A set of such ordinal relations often sufficiently constrains the possible solution to be uniquely identified. The class of axiomatic models in judgment and decision making (Fishburn, 1982; Luce, 1996; Luce & Fishburn, 1991) is of this type. For example, the expected utility (EU) model of decision making under uncertainty (Von Neumann & Morgenstern, 1944) assumes that individuals select among a set of alternative choices the one that maximizes expected utility, which is defined as

$$\text{EU}(A) = \sum_i p(A_i)u(A_i)$$

where the sum is over probabilistic events of choice A, $p(A_i)$ is the probability of event A_i, and $u(A_i)$ is the utility of the event. For instance, the expected utility of a gamble in which one receives \$100 with probability 0.2 or \$0 with probability 0.8 is calculated as the sum $(0.2)u(\$100) + (0.8)u(\$0)$ for some nondecreasing function $u(x)$. A set of axioms on choice behavior that guarantees the existence of a utility function $u(x)$ defined on choice alternatives such that the expected utility model holds includes the following:

1. *Transitivity* (if choice A is preferred to choice B, which in turn is preferred to C, then choice A is preferred to choice C)
2. *Independence* (addition or subtraction of the same event to all choices does not change preference rankings)
3. *Dominance* (if choice A is preferred to choice B, then choice A is preferred to any probabilistic combination of choices A and B)
4. *Solvability* (no choice is infinitely better than any other choices)

For further detail on these and other axioms, see Fishburn (1982).

Model Building via Processing Assumptions

In the preceding approach, the model is derived from a set of regularity conditions imposed at the level of behavior. The models described in this section are created by making a set of assumptions about (unobservable) internal processes, which are presumed to be involved in generating an observed response given an input stimulus in an experimental task. These assumptions eventually give rise to a model equation that specifies observed response as a function of some internal variables (i.e., parameters). They are classified into four categories: differential-process, algorithmic, connectionist, and algebraic models.

Differential-Process Models

For this class a model is obtained by making assumptions about internal mental processes of interest in terms of *changes* in behavior. From these assumptions the model is derived

by integrating the constraining equations. As an example of this approach, consider again Fechner's logarithmic law of psychophysics. Fechner derived his law by assuming that every change (i.e., increase or decrease) in the strength of a physical stimulus does not necessarily result in a constant change in perception but, instead, that the change in perception is proportional to the relative change in stimulation, which is known as Weber's law:

$$\Delta \psi = k \frac{\Delta x}{x} \quad \textbf{(Weber's law)}$$

where Ψ is the psychological scale, x is the physical scale, and k is a positive scaling constant. Note that the internal process assumed to be responsible for this transformation is not directly observable. Rather, the observed response must be derived from such assumptions. This is carried out by integrating both sides of the above equation, resulting in the following logarithmic form:

$$\psi(x) = k \ln(x) \quad \textbf{(Fechner's Law)}.$$

Instead of Weber's law, if it is assumed that a *relative* increase in sensation occurs in proportion to the relative change in stimulation, this assumption then leads to the derivation of Stevens's power law of psychophysics:

$$\frac{\Delta \psi}{\psi} = k \frac{\Delta x}{x} \Rightarrow \psi(x) = x^k \quad \textbf{(Stevens' Law)}.$$

As another example, consider a model of forgetting that assumes that the rate of memory loss, rather than being constant across time, depends on the current memory load. Specifically, the rate of forgetting is proportional to the load: the more items stored in memory, the larger the mean number of items lost during each time interval after storage. This assumption leads to the exponential model of forgetting (Wickelgren, 1970):

$$\frac{\Delta y}{\Delta t} = -cy \Rightarrow y(t) = y(0)e^{-ct}$$

$$\textbf{(Exponential Model)}$$

where y denotes memory load at time t and c is a positive constant.

Algorithmic Models

For this class a model is defined in terms of a simulation procedure (Jacobs & Grainger, 1992). The procedure specifies in detail how specific internal processes interact with one another to yield output behavior as a final result. Often, the processes involved are too complicated to be expressed in closed form; consequently, to derive predictions from the model, the entire process must often be simulated on computer with help of random number generators (see the Appendix to this chapter). A sample of cognitive processes that algorithmic models have been employed to model includes discrimination (Link & Heath, 1975; Smith, 1995), memory retrieval (Ratcliff, 1978), recognition memory (Hintzman, 1988; Shiffrin & Steyvers, 1997), and decision making (Busemeyer & Townsend, 1993; Diederich, 1997). The random walk model of memory retrieval (Ratcliff, 1978) is described in detail to illustrate the idea.

The random walk model makes the assumption that memory retrieval is a search process. Specifically, given a probe item on a recognition memory test, the decision whether the probe is new or old is made by comparing it to each item in the memory search set simultaneously and in parallel. Each individual comparison proceeds by the gradual accumulation of evidence over time via a random walk process. On each trial of the random walk, the probe evokes either a sympathetic or a nonsympathetic "vibration" in a memory-set item, each determined with a fixed probability. The value of this probability is obtained as a random sample drawn from a normal distribution, the mean of which is assumed to be equal to the relatedness value between the probe and the memory-set item. If a sympathetic vibration occurs, then the walk moves upward by one unit, and downward otherwise.

Over a series of trials, the random walk of each comparison process moves up and down on the scale until it eventually hits an upper boundary (match) or a lower boundary (nonmatch).

The decision process is made by combining outcomes of such individual comparison processes; a positive "yes" response is made if any one of the parallel comparisons terminates with a match, and a negative "no" response is made if all comparisons terminate with a nonmatch. The distribution of reaction times for each positive or negative response and also the probability of the response are obtained by simulating the random walk process on computer. By using different parameter values for different experimental conditions, the model can generate simulated data sets for the entire experiment that are compared against observed data to determine the model's viability.

The algorithmic modeling approach provides an attractive environment in which to design models. Scientists can easily construct many variants of a model and quickly test a hypothesis to observe the model's behavior. The model can be made as sophisticated as one likes without having to worry about ensuring that there is a closed-form solution. Accordingly, the approach allows the scientist to work with ideas that cannot yet be expressed in precise mathematical form (Estes, 1975). All these features may explain its popularity.

The approach, however, is not without disadvantages. The main disadvantage is the lack of transparency between the parts of the model and their corresponding mental process. A typical algorithmic model makes a host of assumptions about the mental processes involved, which are difficult to verify empirically because they are not directly observable. This is problematic because the adequacy of the model can be evaluated only by relying upon its predictions of output responses, even if the model provides an excellent description of the data. Consequently, it can be difficult to determine which assumptions of the model are critical for explaining human performance and which assumptions serve no purpose but to provide a good redescription of the data. Furthermore, the ease with which algorithmic models can be constructed may make it tempting to add more assumptions (i.e., parts) to improve the model's ability to mimic human data. This exacerbates the problem and can lead to the creation of supermodels, which may do a good job of fitting the data but possess meaningless and poorly justified properties. In contrast, for models in the functional equation and axiomatic modeling approaches, their assumptions are usually theoretically well-grounded. To minimize the transparency problem, algorithmic models should be designed with a minimally sufficient number of assumptions, each of which is well justified and psychologically plausible.

Connectionist Models

Connectionist models (Grossberg, 1987; Kruschke, 1992; McClelland & Elman, 1986; Rumelhart & McClelland, 1986; Seidenberg & McClelland, 1989) are essentially of the algorithmic type, so all the advantages and disadvantages discussed in the preceding section apply also to this class of models, especially to localist connectionist models. On the other hand, connectionist models—in particular artificial neural networks—possess a few unique features that set them apart from other algorithmic models. First, these connectionist models make few explicit assumptions about the underlying processes in advance, but instead learn the regularities underlying the data through training (e.g., back-propagation rule). Because of this, the parameters (i.e., connection weights and architectural characteristics) of connectionist

models have no predefined meaning and can be difficult to interpret. Second, connectionist models might not be entirely falsifiable, enabling them to fit almost any pattern of data, including idiosyncratic noise. Mathematicians (Hecht-Nielsen, 1989; Hornik, Stinchcomb, & White, 1989, 1990) proved this unlimited flexibility for three-layer feedforward networks with hidden units. Specifically, their results showed that the three-layer network with back-propagation learning and a sufficient number of hidden units can approximate any continuous nonlinear input-output function to any desired degree of accuracy. If used blindly the power of such models can also be their downfall. Care must be taken to ensure that a connectionist model learns only the regularities underlying the data and not the whole data set, in which case it degenerates into a redescription of the data, which provides little useful insight into the phenomenon of interest, if any.

Algebraic Models

In an algebraic model the operation of the underlying cognitive process being modeled in the data is explicitly specified in its parameters and in the model equation. For example, the parameters may specify the relevant psychological or stimulus dimensions to which the underlying process is sensitive. The model equation may describe exactly how these parameters and the input stimulus are combined to produce an output response. This specificity creates a tight link between descriptive (verbal) theory and its computational instantiation because the relationships among the input, output, and parameters are clearly identifiable in the model equation. Accordingly, algebraic models can be easy to understand, and their assumptions can usually be well justified, often axiomatically or through functional equations. Further, quantitative as well as qualitative predictions can oftentimes be derived analytically. Examples of the algebraic modeling approach include the fuzzy logical model of perception (FLMP; Oden & Massaro, 1978), context models of categorization (Medin & Schaffer, 1978; Nosofsky, 1986), the signal detection theory of perceptual identification (Green & Swets, 1966), the processing tree models of memory (Batchelder & Riefer, 1990), and information processing models of cognitive slowing (Cerella, 1985; Meyerson et al., 1990). Cerella's (1985) linear model of cognitive slowing is described to illustrate the idea.

The model assumes that response time (RT) in a cognitive task is equal to the sum of the durations of two subprocesses:

$$RT = C + M$$

where C represents the amount of time required for central cognitive processing and thus reflects task difficulty. M represents sensory-motor processing time. The model explains age-related slowing by assuming that for the elderly, each of these processing times is increased by a constant proportion; that is, $C_{old} = aC_{young}$ and $M_{old} = bM_{young}$ $(a, b > 1)$. With this assumption and after simple algebraic manipulations, one can write response time for older adults in terms of response time for younger adults in the following form:

$$RT_{old} = aRT_{young} + (b - a)M_{young}. \quad (2)$$

Thus the model predicts that response time for old adults is a linear function of response time for young adults with a slope greater than 1 and an intercept that may be negative or positive depending upon the sign of $(b - a)$. As discussed earlier, these predictions were generally confirmed across many individual studies in a variety of experimental settings. According to the model, this outcome is due to a general slowing of cognitive and sensory-motor processing. In particular, the typical observation of a negative intercept in the linear

functional relationship in response time between older and younger adults may suggest that the slowing of central cognitive processes is more severe than that of sensory-motor processes (i.e., $a > b$).

To summarize, there are a number of approaches to modeling behavior. Each has pros and cons, and the modeler must be aware of these when choosing and using the approach. For example, if one is interested in developing the most accurate redescription of the data without reference to the underlying process (i.e., mapping the input-output relationship as in psychophysical modeling), then the functional equation approach might be most suitable. On the other hand, if the goal is to model the processes underlying this input-output relationship, then one of the other approaches should be used.

MODEL CONSTRUCTION AND TESTING

The goal of modeling in psychology is to infer the regularity present in given data while at the same time assessing the veridicality of the hypothesized model. From a statistical standpoint, the data $y = (y_1, \ldots, y_m)$ with m observations is a random sample generated from a true but unknown probability distribution, which represents the regularity underlying the data. Formally, a model is defined as a family of probability distributions, $\{f(y \mid \theta), \theta \in \Gamma\}$ where Γ is the parameter space. The probability distribution function $f(y \mid \theta)$ specifies the probability of observing data y given the parameter θ of the model. The same probability curve $f(y \mid \theta)$ when expressed as a function of the parameter θ given a particular value of data y, is called the likelihood function. The parameter $\theta = (\theta_1, \ldots, \theta_k)$ may be a vector as an element of a multidimensional parameter space. By varying values of the parameter, different shapes of probability distribution are generated. In formal terms, a model consists of the collection of all such probability distributions indexed by its parameter vector.

In some circumstances, the data y can be written as a sum of a deterministic component plus random error:

$$y_i = g(\theta, x_i) + e_i \quad (i = 1, \ldots, m) \quad (3)$$

where x_i is the value of an independent variable, $g(\theta, x_i)$ is the mean of y_i, and e_i is a random noise with zero mean.

As an illustrated example, consider again Cerella's (1985) linear model of cognitive slowing in Equation (2). The model relates response times for younger adults (x_i) to response times for older adult (y_i) across tasks (i) by a linear function,

$$y_i = \theta_1 x_i + \theta_2 + e_i$$

(Cerella's linear model) (4)

where $i = 1, \ldots, m$. According to this equation, the model assumes two parameters, $\theta = (\theta_1, \theta_2)$, and the mean function in the form of $g(\theta, x_i) = \theta_1 x_i + \theta_2$. Note that the two parameters a and $(b - a)M_{\text{young}}$ in Equation (2) now correspond to θ_1 and θ_2 in the Equation (4), respectively. As such, the slope parameter θ_1 is interpreted as a ratio of the cognitive processing time for older adults over younger adults, whereas the intercept parameter θ_2 is proportional to the difference in the age-related slowing ratio between sensory-motor and cognitive processing. The model may further assume that the error e_i is normally distributed with variance σ^2. This implies that for given values of θ_1, θ_2, and x_i, the data value y_i is normally distributed with mean $(\theta_1 x_i + \theta_2)$ and variance σ^2. The linear model therefore defines a family of normal probability distributions, $N(\theta_1 x_i + \theta_2, \sigma^2)$, created by varying the values of the two parameters θ_1 and θ_2 for a fixed value of x_i. The probability density function of y_i given all parameter values then takes the following form:

$$f(y_i | \theta) = \frac{1}{\sqrt{2\pi}\sigma} \exp\left(-\frac{(y_i - \theta_1 x_i - \theta_2)^2}{2\sigma^2}\right)$$

$$(i = 1, \ldots, m) \quad (5)$$

where $\exp(x)$ stands for the exponential function, that is, $\exp(x) = e^x$. Quite often, the equation $g(\theta, x_i)$ itself is taken to define a mathematical model and the underlying probability distribution is kept implicit. Assuming independent observations, the probability distribution function of the entire data set, $y = (y_1, \ldots, y_m)$, can be written as the multiplication of m individual density functions as follows:

$$f(y | \theta) = \prod_{i=1}^{m} f(y_i | \theta). \quad (6)$$

The model-testing approach presented later requires that a model be specified by its parametric family of probability distributions, $\{f(y | \theta), \theta \in \Gamma\}$, or at least by its mean function $g(\theta, x_i)$. Most of the models discussed in the preceding section, including algebraic models and connectionist models, satisfy this requirement. Exceptions are some axiomatic models, in which the specification of the probability distributions and the mean function is not possible. In this case, testing of such "nonstatistical" models requires an alternative approach, which is described briefly at the end of this section.

Before discussing model testing, a word about what one can reasonably hope to achieve in modeling behavior is in order. Psychological phenomena have the potential to be very complex and may involve many subsystems interacting with one another in a highly nonlinear fashion. It could easily be the case that a mathematical model with at least a dozen parameters is necessary to capture the phenomenon accurately. In the early stages of modeling, all models will most certainly be wrong in many details. Because of this, they are also likely to be misspecified, meaning that they do not include as a special case the "true" model that generated the observed data. It may also be impossible to build a model that captures the underlying mental process in every detail. Thus, it is probably most accurate and instructive to think of mathematical models as best approximations to the truth. Practically speaking, the goal of mathematical modeling is to find the best approximation to the truth, with the hope that the winning model is correctly specified (i.e., includes the true model as a special case). It is useful to keep this in mind to avoid placing undue faith in these models.

Model Falsifiability and Identifiability

Once a model is defined along with the family of probability distributions indexed by the model's parameters, two important issues must be checked before the model is fitted to observed data to assess its validity. They are falsifiability and identifiability.

Falsifiability (Popper, 1959), also called testability, refers to whether there exist potential observations that are inconsistent with the model (i.e., data that it does not predict). This is a necessary precondition for testing a model; unless a model is falsifiable, there is no point in *testing* the model. An unfalsifiable model is one that can describe all possible patterns of data that can arise in a given experiment. For example, one may wish to test a two-parameter linear model, $y = \theta_1 + \theta_2 x$, against data that consist of just two observations, (x_1, y_1) and (x_2, y_2). In this case the model is unfalsifiable because it can provide a perfect fit to the data for any (x_i, y_i) pairs ($i = 1, 2$). On the other hand, if one additional point (x_3, y_3) is added to the data, then the two-parameter model becomes falsifiable. In other words, whether a model is falsifiability or not depends upon the size of the data set.

A rule of thumb for assessing falsifiability is that a model is falsifiable if the number of free parameters is less than the number of observations in the data. Bamber and van Santen (1985) showed, however, that this "counting rule" can be misleading, especially for nonlinear models, and provided counterexamples as evidence. Consider Luce's (1959) choice model. The model assumes that the probability of choosing choice alternative i over alternative j is determined by their respective utility values in the following form:

$$P_{i>j} = \frac{u_i}{u_i + u_j} \quad (u_i > 0; i, j = 1, \ldots, s)$$

where u_i is the utility parameter to be estimated from the data. Note that the number of parameters in the model is equal to the number of choice alternatives (s), whereas the number of independent observations is equal to $s(s-1)/2$. Hence, for $s = 3$, both the number of parameters and the number of observations are equal. However, it is easy to show that the model is falsifiable in this case. In another, more dramatic example, Bamber and van Santen (1985, p. 453) showed that the number of parameters (7) in a model exceeded the number of data observations (6), yet the model was still falsifiable!

Rectifying the apparent limitations of the counting rule of falsifiability, Bamber and van Santen (1985) provided a formal definition of falsifiability and also a criterion for assessing falsifiability, which includes the counting rule as a special case. Specifically, the criterion states that a model is falsifiable if the rank of what is called the Jacobian matrix, defined as

$$J_{ij}(\theta) = [\partial E(y_j)/\partial \theta_i], \\ (i = 1, \ldots, k; j = 1, \ldots, m),$$

is less than the number of independent observations (m) in the data for all θ values.

Model identifiability refers to whether the parameters of a model are unique given observed data. As with falsifiability, a model is identifiable or unidentifiable with respect to data size. When a model is unidentifiable, the problem of equivalent models arises in which there exist multiple sets of parameter values that provide exactly the same fit to the data. When this happens, one cannot meaningfully interpret the parameter values of the model. To illustrate, consider a three-parameter model of $y = \theta_1 + \theta_2 x + \theta_3 x^2$ and suppose that two data points are obtained, say $(x_1, y_1) = (1, 1)$ and $(x_2, y_2) = (2, 5)$. The model is unidentifiable given these data because there exist multiple sets of the model's parameter values $(\theta_1, \theta_2, \theta_3)$ that fit the data perfectly, for example, $(\theta_1, \theta_2, \theta_3) = (-1, 1, 1)$ and $(\theta_1, \theta_2, \theta_3) = (-5, 7, -1)$. There are, in fact, an infinite number of such parameter values of the model that can provide a perfect description of the data. In order for this model to be identifiable, three or more data points are needed.

A rule of thumb for assessing identifiability is that a model is identifiable if the number of free parameters is less than or equal to the number of independent observations. Again, Bamber and van Santen (1985) provide a formal definition of identifiability and show that this rule is also imperfect.

Although it might appear that falsifiability and identifiability should be related to each other, there exists only one consistent relationship between the two: The counting rule of falsifiability is valid if the model is identifiable. If a model is not identifiable, the counting rule for assessing falsifiability may be inapplicable (Bamber & van Santen, 1985).

The lack of a tight relationship between these properties of a model means that a model can be falsifiable but not identifiable. A case in point is FLMP (Oden & Massaro, 1978). To demonstrate this situation, consider a letter recognition experiment in which participants have to classify the stimulus as belonging to one of two categories, A and B. Assume that the probability of classifying a stimulus as a member of category A is a function of the extent to which the two feature dimensions of the stimulus (i and j) support the category response (Massaro & Friedman, 1990). Specifically, FLMP assumes that the response probability P_{ij} is a function of two parameters, θ_i and λ_j, each of which represents the degree of support for a category A response given the specific i and j feature dimensions of an input stimulus:

$$P_{ij} = g(\theta_i, \lambda_j) = \frac{\theta_i \lambda_j}{\theta_i \lambda_j + (1 - \theta_i)(1 - \lambda_j)}$$

where $0 < \theta_i, \lambda_j < 1, 1 \le i \le s, 1 \le j \le v$. s and v represent the number of stimulus levels on the two feature dimensions, i and j, respectively, and together constitute the design of the experiment.

FLMP is falsifiable, which can be shown using the falsifiability rule mentioned earlier (Bamber and van Santen, 1985; see also Batchelder, 1997). For example, one can easily come up with a set of P_{ij}s that do not fit into the model equation, such as $P_{ij} = (a_i + b_j)/2$ for $0 < a_i, b_j < 1$ (N. H. Anderson, 1981).

Regarding the identifiability of FLMP, for the $s \times v$ experimental design, the number of independent observations is sv, and the number of parameters of FLMP is $(s + v)$. For example, for $s = v = 8$, the number of observations is 64, which far exceeds the number of parameters in the model (16). Surprisingly, however, Crowther, Batchelder, and Hu (1995) have shown that FLMP is not identifiable for all values of s and v. According to their analysis, for any given set of parameter values (θ_i, λ_j) that satisfy the above model equation, another set of parameter values $(\theta_i^*, \lambda_j^*)$ that also satisfy the same equation can always be obtained:

$$\theta_i^* = \frac{\theta_i}{1 + c(1 - \theta_i)}; \quad \lambda_j^* = \frac{\lambda_j}{1 + c(1 - \lambda_j)}$$

for any constant $c > -1$. One can easily verify the equivalence by plugging the parameters $(\theta_i^*, \lambda_j^*)$ into the model equation. Because there are an infinite number of possible c values, there will be an equal number of parameter sets, each of which provides exactly the same fit to the observed data, meaning that FLMP is not identifiable.

Can FLMP be made identifiable? The answer to this equation is yes. For example, one of its parameters can be fixed to a preset constant (e.g., $\theta_i = 0.15$, for some i). Alternatively, the model equation can be modified to accommodate four response categories instead of two. For further details, consult Crowther et al. (1995).

Parameter Estimation

Once data have been collected and the model is shown to be falsifiable as well as identifiable, one is in a position to assess the model's goodness of fit to the experimental data. Goodness of fit refers to how well the model fits the observed data. Given that the model contains many (theoretically infinite) probability distributions, each associated with a distinct set of parameter values, the objective is to find a set of parameter values that best fits the observed data in some defined sense. This process is called parameter estimation.

Two generally accepted methods of parameter estimation are least square estimation (LSE) and maximum likelihood estimation (MLE). In LSE the parameter values that minimize the mean squared error (MSE) between predictions and observations are sought:

$$\text{MSE} = \sqrt{\frac{1}{m} \sum_{i=1}^{m} (y_i - g(\theta, x_i))^2} \quad (7)$$

where $\Sigma (y_i - g(\theta, x_i))^2$ is the sum of squares error (SSE).

On the other hand, in MLE the likelihood of the data, $f(y \mid \theta)$, is maximized with respect

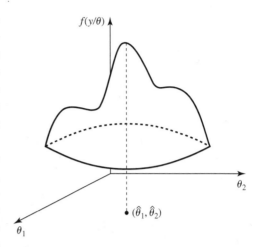

Figure 11.1 Schematic plot of the likelihood function $f(y \mid \theta)$ as a function of the two parameters.

NOTE: The best-fitting parameter vector that maximizes the likelihood function is indicated by $\hat{\theta} = (\hat{\theta}_1, \hat{\theta}_2)$.

to the model's parameter values, as illustrated schematically in Figure 11.1. Assuming independent observations and normal error with a constant variance σ^2, we can write the logarithm of the likelihood, called the log likelihood, as

$$\ln f(y \mid \theta) = -\frac{1}{2\sigma^2} \sum_{i=1}^{m} (y_i - g(\theta, x_i))^2$$
$$- m \ln(\sqrt{2\pi}\sigma) = \alpha \text{MSE}^2 + \beta \quad (8)$$

where $\alpha = -m/(2\sigma^2)$, $\beta = -m \ln(\sqrt{2\pi}\sigma)$. Note that α and β do not depend upon the parameter θ. Therefore, if y_is are normally distributed with equal variances, maximizing the likelihood is equivalent to minimizing MSE, and therefore the same parameter values are obtained under either method. Otherwise, the two solutions tend to differ. In general, MLE is a preferred method of estimation, especially when the equal variance assumption is violated (e.g., binomial probability distributions). Throughout this chapter the best-fitting

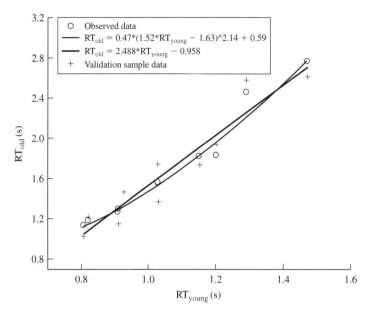

Figure 11.2   Modeling cognitive aging data.
NOTE: Open circles represent the data in Cerella et al. (1981). The thick and thin curves are best fits by the two-parameter linear model and the five-parameter nonlinear model, respectively. Plus signs represent artificial data points in a validation data set.

parameter vector obtained in MLE or LSE is denoted by $\hat{\theta}$.

Finding the parameter values that maximize MLE or minimize MSE usually requires use of nonlinear estimation techniques unless the solution can be found in analytic form. For example, suppose that the model is a linear regression model, $Y = X\theta + E$, where Y and E are $m \times 1$ dependent and error vectors respectively, X is a $m \times k$ design matrix and θ is a $k \times 1$ parameter vector. In this case, the solution that minimizes MSE can be obtained in analytic form. For nonlinear models, however, it is generally impossible to obtain such analytic form solutions; consequently, a solution must be sought numerically using optimization algorithms (Thisted, 1988).

To illustrate parameter estimation, consider again Cerella's (1985) linear model of cognitive slowing, which has two free parameters, θ_1 (slope) and θ_2 (intercept). We fitted

the model to a data set reported in Cerella, Poon, and Fozard (1981). The observed data consist of ten pairs of response times for old and young adults collected under the normal-parity condition in a letter rotation task, and are shown as open circles in Figure 11.2. The values of the parameters that minimized MSE were $\theta_1 = 2.488$ and $\theta_2 = -0.958$, with MSE minimization equal to 0.109. The model accounted for 95.7% of the total variance in the data. The thicker solid line in Figure 11.2 depicts this best-fitting linear model. What do the parameter values mean? According to the model, the slope parameter (θ_1) is interpreted as the proportion of slowing in central cognitive processing for older adults relative to younger adults, whereas the sign of the intercept parameter (θ_2) indicates whether slowing in sensory-motor processing is more (+) or less (−) severe than slowing in central cognitive processing. The results indicate that in the letter rotation task, the slowing of central cognitive processing is more severe than is slowing of sensory-motor processing.

Goodness-of-Fit Testing

Although parameter estimation yields a measure of how well the model fits the observed data, a goodness-of-fit measure, by itself, is not particularly meaningful. How good is an MSE of 0.109? To answer this question, one must conduct a goodness-of-fit test. One method of doing so is via hypothesis testing, in which the null hypothesis that the model is correct (i.e., viable) is tested against the alternative hypothesis that it is not correct.

Null Hypothesis Testing for Discrete Random Variables

In this test the model's goodness of fit is assessed by comparing the *expected* counts under the null hypothesis against the actually *observed* counts, y_is. The two most popular, general-purpose methods used to test the null hypothesis are the Pearson chi-square (χ^2) test and the log likelihood ratio (G^2) test:

$$\chi^2 = \sum_{i=1}^{m} \frac{(y_i - nf(y_i \mid \hat{\theta}))^2}{nf(y_i \mid \hat{\theta})};$$

$$G^2 = -2 \sum_{i=1}^{m} y_i \ln \frac{nf(y_i \mid \hat{\theta})}{y_i}. \tag{9}$$

In the equation, $\hat{\theta}$ is the MLE parameter estimate or any other reasonable estimate such as LSE, and n is the sample size, which is the number of repeated random samples (i.e., observations) collected to obtain count y_i. Note that when there is perfect agreement between the null hypothesis and the observed data, that is, $y_i = nf(y_i \mid \hat{\theta})(i = 1, \ldots, m)$, both statistics become zero, $\chi^2 = G^2 = 0$, and otherwise they take on positive values. The greater the discrepancies, the larger the value of the statistic. Under the null hypothesis, both statistics are distributed as a chi-square distribution with $(m - k - 1)$ degrees of freedom where k is the number of free parameters. Therefore, the null hypothesis may be retained or rejected by comparing the observed value of χ^2 or G^2 statistic to the critical χ^2 value obtained for an appropriate alpha level. If the model is rejected, one may look for some alternative model that is more consistent with the data. Although both statistics, χ^2 or G^2, are equivalent for large n under the assumption that the model is correct, we recommend the latter because it is more robust and requires fewer assumptions. Nevertheless, in practice, the difference between the two statistics is rarely large enough to lead to differing conclusions. When the model is not correct, however, the two statistics can yield very different results even with large sample sizes. A more comprehensive treatment of goodness-of-fit tests for discrete random variables, including the χ^2 and G^2 tests, can be found in Read and Cressie (1988).

Null Hypothesis Testing for Continuous Random Variables

Testing the goodness of fit of a model with the dependent variable y measured on a continuous scale is a bit complicated. No general-purpose method of testing the validity of a single model exists unless probability distributions are restricted to a few known families, such as exponential and normal families (D'Agostino & Stephens, 1986). On the other hand, the relative ability of two *nested* models to account for observed data can be tested via the generalized likelihood ratio test (Wilks, 1938). Two models are nested if one model can be reduced to a special case of the other. For example, a two-parameter linear model of the form $y = \theta_1 + \theta_2 x + \text{error}$ and a three-parameter quadratic model of the form $y = \theta_1 + \theta_2 x + \theta_3 x^2 + \text{error}$ with the same probability distribution of the error are nested.

This is because the former is obtained from the latter as its special case by setting $\theta_3 = 0$. On the other hand, an exponential model of the form $y = \theta_1 + \theta_2 \exp(-\theta_3 x) + \text{error}$ and $y = \theta_1 + \theta_2 x + \theta_3 x^2 + \text{error}$ are nonnested.

The basic idea of the generalized likelihood ratio test is to create two models, M_1 (restricted model) and M_2 (full model), in such a way that M_1 is nested within M_2. For example, M_1 might be created by holding constant values of one or several parameters of M_2, rather than treating them as free parameters. Each of the two models is then fitted to the data, and its best-fitting parameter values are obtained via MLE. Let L_1 and L_2 denote the maximized likelihood value of M_1 and M_2, respectively. The generalized likelihood ratio test is based on the G^2 statistic defined as

$$G^2 = 2(\ln L_2 - \ln L_1) \qquad (10)$$

which takes on nonnegative values. Under the null hypothesis that M_1 is correct, this statistic is distributed as a chi-square distribution with degrees of freedom equal to the difference in the number of free parameters between the two models. The standard hypothesis testing procedure is then applied to decide whether to retain or reject the null hypothesis. If the null hypothesis is retained, one concludes that the reduced model M_1 offers a sufficiently good description of the data, and thus the extra free parameters of the full model M_2 appear to provide no real improvement in fit and therefore may be unjustified. On the other hand, if the null hypothesis is rejected, one concludes that the extra parameters may be necessary to account for the observed pattern of data. This generalized likelihood test based on G^2 can also be applied to discrete random variables. It is worth noting that no comparable test based on χ^2 for the same purpose exists.

As an illustrated example of the above generalized likelihood test, suppose that one is interested in testing the adequacy of Cerella's

(1985) linear model of age-related deficits. In order to apply the method, we created the following nonlinear model that yields the linear model as a special case (i.e., $\theta_2 = \theta_4 = 1$ and $\theta_3 = 0$):

$$y_i = \theta_1 (\theta_2 x_i + \theta_3)^{\theta_4} + \theta_5 + e_i$$
$$(i = 1, \ldots, m).$$

This model is motivated from and is a generalized version of Meyerson et al.'s (1990) information loss model of cognitive aging. The latter model assumes that a constant proportion of information is lost in each successive step of cognitive processing and, further, that the proportion is greater for older adults than for younger adults. Specifically, the parameter θ_4 represents the ratio of information loss between older and younger adults; similarly, other parameters of the model can be related to information loss (see Meyerson et al., 1990, for details). Best-fit parameter values of the model for the same data set from Cerella et al. (1981) were obtained as $\theta_1 = 0.467, \theta_2 = 1.512, \theta_3 = -0.162, \theta_4 = 2.143, \theta_5 = 0.588$, with the minimized MSE equal to 0.089. The thinner solid line in Figure 11.2 represents the best-fitting nonlinear model. This five-parameter model fit the data almost perfectly, accounting for 97.1% of the variance, which is an increase of 1.4% over Cerella et al.'s (1981) two-parameter linear model. The generalized likelihood test can then be performed to determine whether the mere 1.4% increase represents meaningful improvement in fit. To obtain the required G^2 statistic, the MSE values must be converted to the corresponding maximized log likelihood values. This was done using Equation (10), and the resulting log likelihood values were equal to 7.99 and 10.0 for the restricted and full models, respectively. G^2 was then calculated and found to be equal to 4.02, which is smaller than 7.81, the critical value of $\chi^2 (df = 3, \alpha = 0.05)$. Therefore, the null hypothesis that the linear model is a correct description of the data should be retained. The three extra parameters (θ_2, θ_3, θ_4) do not seem necessary to account for the observed data.

Although null hypothesis testing is easy to use and provides a reasonable and informative assessment of the validity of a model in its own way, the usefulness of the method is somewhat over-sold, especially in the behavioral sciences. The reader should be aware of the limitations and criticisms of the method (Chap. 10; Berger & Berry, 1988; Cohen, 1994; but see Hagan, 1997) and is cautioned against possible misinterpretations of hypothesis testing results. For example, retaining the null hypothesis (i.e., failing to reject the null hypothesis) does not necessarily imply that the hypothesis is more likely to hold than is the alternative hypothesis, let alone that it is confirmed to be the correct (i.e., true) model. Jumping to such conclusions is still commonplace in the psychological literature, so it is particularly important to guard against making such errors in reasoning.

As mentioned earlier, the generalized likelihood ratio test requires that the two models be nested. If they are not, if both have the same number of parameters but differ in their model equation (e.g., $y = \theta x$ vs. $y = x^\theta$), or if more than two models are being compared, the generalized likelihood test is not appropriate. In such cases, another method of statistical inference must be used. This and related issues are discussed in the section titled "Model Selection."

Testing Nonstatistical Models

So far we have dealt with statistical models only. A statistical model specifies the probability of observing data—that is, $f(y \mid \theta)$—given the model's parameter values. This allows a probabilistic formulation for testing the validity of the model using null hypothesis testing. On the other hand, there are classes of nonstatistical models for which the probability distribution is not specified. Some axiomatic models that are formulated in the form of ordinal predictions fall into this category. For such qualitative models, it is not entirely clear how to construct a probabilistic formulation for model testing. To illustrate, suppose that an axiomatic model assumes transitivity and that when the axiom was tested against observed data sets, it was found that it held up pretty well, with violations observed in only 3% of the data. Should this be considered sufficient evidence for retaining the model? If this question were answered by performing a statistical test, one would need to calculate the probability of observing violations of the axiom in 3% or more of the data under the assumption that the model, or an appropriately chosen null model, holds. Because the model specifies no error theory for its axioms, it is not possible to calculate this probability.

Monte Carlo methodology may present a possible remedy for testing nonstatistical models. For example, Nygren (1983) proposed a Monte Carlo approach by which the likelihood of violating an axiom by chance is estimated through numerical simulations. Specifically, to assess the fit of an axiomatic model to observed data, we first generate artificial data sets under a random response model with no particularly meaningful structure. An axiom of interest is then tested individually in these random data sets, and the proportion of violations that would be expected under the random model is obtained. This baseline violation rate is then used as a benchmark against the empirically observed proportion. An appropriate statistical test, such as the t test using the binomial distribution, may be performed to examine whether the observed data represent a significantly better fit than would be expected under the null hypothesis of the random response model. The procedure may be repeated for each of the axioms of the model to assess an overall fit of the model.

Interpreting Good Fits

What does it mean when a model fits the data well? It is important not to jump to the conclusion that one has identified the form of the underlying process and therefore discovered the true model. As S. Roberts and Pashler (2000) noted, a good fit is only one of many conditions that must be satisfied before such a conclusion should even be contemplated. At first blush, a good fit would seem to be sufficient to claim that the model is accurate. After all, by fitting the data well, the model has demonstrated its ability to mimic the phenomenon of interest. However, a good fit merely qualifies the model as a true model, placing it in the set of models that could be true. As the example on interpreting the linearity of Brinley plots shows, this information is not terribly informative by itself, for there are without a doubt many models in this set.

Simply put, verification of a model's predictions (i.e., data fitting) can never amount to a sufficiency test of the model. What constitutes a sufficiency test? Given that a model is defined as a set of assumptions about the underlying mental processes of interest, the model is sufficient only when all of its assumptions are tested and validated independently, which could be a challenging task. The model itself must be well understood before such a claim can be made. For starters, we need to be able to answer the question, "Why does the model fit the data well?" The answer should be "because it is a good approximation of the mental process." As discussed in the next section, good fits can be achieved for reasons that have nothing to do with the model's exactness. For this reason we recommend that the more appropriate measure of a model's adequacy is a test of its generalizability, not its goodness of fit.

MODEL SELECTION

The preceding discussion should make it clear that the objective in model testing is to test the viability of a model, not to take the additional step and conclude that it is the correct model. To do so is unwarranted because one's model has not been demonstrated to be superior to others. Model selection, on the other hand, involves a set of competing models, all of which have passed goodness-of-fit tests and have been found to provide a "good" description of the data. The objective in model selection is to decide which one is the best model in the sense that it most closely approximates the underlying mental process. A more detailed and technically rigorous discussion of some of the issues presented here can be found in the book *Model Selection* (Linhart & Zucchini, 1986) and in a special issue on model selection of the *Journal of Mathematical Psychology* (Myung, Forster, & Browne, 2000).

There are a number of criteria for choosing among mathematical models (Jacobs & Grainger, 1994): (a) explanatory adequacy (is the theoretical explanation of the model reasonable and consistent with established findings?); (b) plausibility (are the assumptions of the model biologically and psychologically plausible?); (c) interpretability (do the parameters of the model make sense and have meaningful interpretations?); (d) goodness of fit or descriptive adequacy (does the model provide a good description of the observed data?); (e) generalizability (does the model predict well the statistics of new, as yet unseen, data?); and (f) complexity or simplicity (does the model capture the phenomenon in the simplest possible manner?). Although each of these criteria is important to consider in model selection, the last three (goodness of fit, generalizability, and complexity) are particularly pertinent to choosing among mathematical models, and quantitative methods have been developed with this purpose in mind. We begin by defining these criteria in more detail and then demonstrating their interrelationships in an illustrated example.

Model Selection Criteria

Goodness of Fit

Goodness of fit, such as MSE and maximized likelihood (ML), is a necessary component of model selection. Because data are our only link to the cognitive process under investigation, a model must be able to describe well the output from this process if a model is to be considered seriously. Failure to do so invalidates the model. As stated earlier, goodness of fit is not a sufficient condition for model selection. This is because model selection based solely on goodness of fit *will* result in the choice of a model that overfits the data. Why? Because the model will capture variability present in the particular data set that comes from sources other than the underlying process of interest.

Statistically speaking, the observed data are a sample generated from a population and therefore will contain at least three types of variation: variation due to sampling error because the sample is only an estimate of the population, variation due to individual differences, and variation due to the cognitive process of interest. Most of the time it is only the third of these that one is interested in modeling, yet goodness-of-fit measures do not distinguish between any of them. Measures such as MSE treat all variation identically. They are blind to its source and try to absorb as much of it as possible (this is demonstrated later). What is needed is a means of filtering out these unwanted sources of noise. Generalizability achieves this.

Generalizability

Generalizability refers to a model's ability to fit not only the observed data in hand but also future, unseen data sets generated from the same underlying process. To illustrate, suppose that the model is fitted to the initial set of data and that its best-fitting parameter values are obtained. With these parameter values held constant, if the model also provides a good fit to additional data samples collected from replications of that same experiment (i.e., the same underlying probability distribution or regularity), then the model generalizes well. Only under such circumstances can one be sure that a model is accurately capturing the underlying process, and not the idiosyncrasies of a particular sample.

The superiority of this criterion becomes readily apparent in the following illustration. In Figure 11.3 the solid circles represent observed data points, and the curves represent

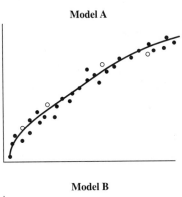

Model A

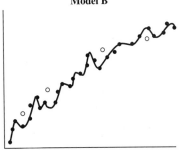

Model B

Figure 11.3 Illustration of the trade-off between goodness of fit and generalizability.
NOTE: Two models (curves) are fitted to the same data set (solid circles). New observations are shown by the open circle.

best-fits by two hypothetical models. Model A not only captures the general trend in the current data but also does a good job of capturing new observations (open circles). On the other hand, Model B provides a much better fit than model A, but it does so by fitting the random fluctuations of each data point as well as the general trend, and consequently suffers in fit when new observations are introduced into the sample. As the example shows, generalizability is a very reliable way to overcome the problem of noise and extract the regularity present in the data. Further examples later will demonstrate why generalizability should be adopted as the primary quantitative criterion on which the adequacy of a model is evaluated.

Complexity

Intuitively, model complexity refers to the flexibility inherent in a model that enables it to fit diverse patterns of data. For the moment, think of it as a continuum, with simple models at one end and complex models at the other. A simple model assumes that a relatively narrow range of more of less similar patterns will be present in the data. When the data exhibit one of these few patterns, the model fits the data very well; otherwise, its fit will be rather poor. All other things being equal, simple models are attractive because they are sufficiently constrained to make them easily falsifiable, requiring a small number of data points to disprove the model. In contrast, a complex model, usually one with many parameters that are combined in a highly nonlinear fashion, do not assume a single structure in the data. Rather, like a chameleon, the model is capable of assuming multiple structures by finely adjusting its parameter values. This enables the model to fit a wide range of data patterns.

There are at least two independent dimensions of model complexity: the number of free parameters in a model and its functional form, which refers to the way in which the parame-

ters are combined in the model equation. For example, $y = \theta x$ and $y = x^\theta$ have the same number of parameters (1) but differ in functional form. The two dimensions of model complexity, and their interplay, can improve a model's fit to the data but—strange though it may seem—not improve generalizability. This is illustrated next.

As shown in Table 11.1, four models were compared on their ability to fit two data samples generated by the two-parameter linear model (P_2), which by definition is the true model. Goodness of fit was assessed by finding parameter values for each model that gave the best fit to the first sample. With these parameters fixed, generalizability was assessed by fitting the models to the second sample. In the first row of Table 11.1 are each model's mean fit to data drawn from P_2. As can be seen, P_2 fitted better than P_1, which is an incorrect model having one fewer parameter than the true model. The results for P_3 and P_4 are more interesting. These two models have two more parameters than P_2 and contain the true model as a special case. Note that they both provided a better fit to the data than P_2 itself. Given that the data were generated by P_2, one would have expected P_2 to fit its own data best at least some of the time. But this *never* happened. Instead, P_3 and P_4 *always* fitted better. The improvement in fit of P_3 and P_4 over P_2 represents the degree to which the data were overfitted. The two extra parameters in the two models enabled them to absorb nonsystematic variation (i.e., random error) in the data, thus improving fit beyond what is needed to capture the underlying regularity. Note also that P_4 provided a better fit than P_3 (0.79 vs. 0.91), and did so much more often (99% vs. 1%). This difference in fit must be due to functional form because these two models differ only in how the parameters and data are combined in the model equation.

The results in the second row of Table 11.1 demonstrate that overfitting a specific sample

Table 11.1 Goodness of Fit and Generalizability of Models Differing in Complexity

Model	P_1	P_2 (true)	P_3	P_4
Goodness of fit	1.32 (0%)	0.89 (0%)	0.91 (1%)	0.79 (99%)
Generalizability	1.39 (6%)	1.06 (52%)	1.14 (21%)	1.13 (21%)

NOTE: Mean squared error of the fit of each model to the data and the percentage of samples in which the particular model fitted the data best (in parenthesis). The four models are as follows: $P_1 : y = \theta_1 x + e$; $P_2 : y = \theta_1 x + \theta_2 + e$; $P_3 : y = \theta_1(\theta_2 x + 1)^{\theta_3} + \theta_4 + e$; $P_4 : y = \theta_1 x + \theta_2 x^2 + \theta_3 x^3 + \theta_4 + e$. The error e was normally distributed with a mean of zero and a standard deviation of 1. A thousand pairs of samples were generated from M_2 (true model) using $\theta_1 = 4$ and $\theta_2 = -2.5$ on the same 12 points for x, which ranged from 3 to 14 in increments of 1.

of data results in a loss of generalizability. MSEs are now greater for P_3 and P_4 than for P_2; also, the two overly complex models yielded the best fit to the second sample much less often than the true model, P_2.

This example demonstrates that the best-fitting model does not necessarily generalize the best and that model complexity can significantly affect generalizability and goodness of fit. Because of its extra flexibility, a complex model can fit a single data set better than a simple model. The cost of the superior fit shows up in a loss of generalizability when fitted to new data sets, precisely because it overfitted the first data set by absorbing random error. Figure 11.4 illustrates the intricate relationship among goodness of fit, generalizability, and model complexity. Fit index such as percent variance accounted for is represented along the vertical axis, and model complex-

ity is represented along the horizontal axis. Goodness of fit increases as complexity increases. Generalizability also increases positively with complexity but only up to the point where the model is sufficiently complex to capture the regularities underlying in the data. Additional complexity beyond this point will cause a drop in generalizability as the model begins to capture random noise, thereby overfitting the data.

In conclusion, a model must not be chosen solely on the basis of its goodness of fit. To do so risks selecting an overly complex model that generalizes poorly to other data generated from the same underlying process. If the goal is to develop a model that resembles the underlying process, then the model must be able to fit all current *and* future data reasonably well. Only generalizability can measure this property of the model, and thus it should be used in model selection. The next section introduces techniques for measuring generalizability and demonstrates their application.

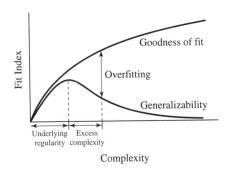

Figure 11.4 Illustration of the relationship among goodness of fit, generalizability, and model complexity.

Measures of Generalizability

The trade-off between goodness of fit and complexity illustrated in the preceding example is what makes model selection so difficult. The model must be complex enough to describe the variation in any data sample that is due to the underlying process, yet not overfit the data by absorbing noise and thus lose generalizability. Conversely, the model must not be too simple to capture the under-lying process and thereby underfit the data, which will also lower generalizability. The goal of model selection methods is to esti-mate a model's generalizability by weighting fit against complexity. This goal is realized by defining a selection criterion that makes an appropriate adjustment to its goodness of fit by taking into account the contribution of complexity. Five representative methods that are currently in use are the Akaike informa-tion criterion (AIC; Akaike, 1973; Bozdogan, 2000), the Bayesian information criterion (BIC; Schwarz, 1978), cross-validation (CV; Browne, 2000; Stone, 1974), Bayesian model selection (BMS; Kass & Raftery, 1995; Myung & Pitt, 1997; Wasserman, 2000), and minimum description length (MDL; Grunwald, 2000; Rissanen, 1983, 1996). The first two of these (AIC, BIC) are limited in their application because they take into ac-count only the number of parameters in their complexity measure. The other three (CV, BMS, MDL) consider the functional form di-mension of model complexity as well, either implicitly (CV, BMS) or explicitly (MDL).

The first two methods are defined as follows:

$$AIC = -2\ln f(y\,|\,\hat{\theta}) + 2k$$
$$BIC = -2\ln f(y\,|\,\hat{\theta}) + k\ln n$$

where $\ln f(y\,|\,\hat{\theta})$ is the natural logarithm of a model's maximized likelihood, k is the number of free parameters in the model, and n is the sample size. When errors are normally distributed, the first term of AIC and BIC, $-2\ln f(y\,|\,\hat{\theta})$, can be replaced by $(n\cdot\ln(SSE) + \text{constant})$. These selection methods prescribe that the model minimizing a given criterion should be chosen.

Note that each of these two criteria con-sists of two terms: The first represents lack of fit, and the second term is naturally inter-preted as model complexity (i.e., $2k$ for AIC

and $k\cdot\ln(n)$ for BIC). Model selection is car-ried out by trading lack of fit for complexity. A complex model with many parameters, hav-ing a large value in the complexity term, will not be chosen unless its fit justifies the extra complexity.

AIC and BIC are simple and easy to com-pute and are by far the most commonly used criteria. The only difference between the two is that BIC includes an extra complex-ity penalty term for sample size. The BIC is derived as a large sample approximation of BMS, described later.

The number of parameters is the only di-mension of complexity that is considered by these two methods. As discussed earlier, func-tional form can also significantly affect model fit and therefore needs to be taken into account in model selection. The selection methods de-scribed next are sensitive to functional form as well as the number of parameters.

The CV, BMS, and MDL methods are de-fined as follows:

$$CV = -\ln f(y_{val.}\,|\,\hat{\theta}_{cal.})$$
$$BMS = -\ln \int f(y|\theta)\pi(\theta)\,d\theta$$
$$MDL = -\ln f(y\,|\,\hat{\theta}) + \frac{k}{2}\ln\left(\frac{n}{2\pi}\right)$$
$$+ \ln \int \sqrt{\det I(\theta)}\,d\theta.$$

In the equation, $\pi(\theta)$ is the prior density of the model parameter, and $\det I(\theta)$ is the determi-nant of the Fisher information matrix defined as

$$I_{ij}(\theta) = -\frac{1}{n}E\left(\frac{\partial^2 \ln f(y|\theta)}{\partial\theta_i\partial\theta_j}\right)$$

for $i, j = 1, \ldots, k$ where the expectation E is taken over y (e.g., see Robert, 1994, p. 114). These methods prescribe that the model min-imizing a given criterion should be selected.

CV estimates a model's generalizability without explicitly considering model com-plexity. In this method, one first randomly

Table 11.2   Cross Validation Example

X	Y_{cal}	Y_{prd}	Y_{val}	$(Y_{cal} - Y_{prd})^2$	$(Y_{val} - Y_{prd})^2$
0.806	1.132	1.048	1.026	0.007	0.000
0.820	1.182	1.082	1.217	0.010	0.018
0.910	1.268	1.306	1.433	0.001	0.016
0.911	1.293	1.309	1.150	0.000	0.025
1.030	1.553	1.605	1.745	0.003	0.020
1.030	1.564	1.605	1.369	0.002	0.056
1.155	1.819	1.916	1.736	0.009	0.032
1.205	1.836	2.040	1.940	0.042	0.010
1.295	2.465	2.264	2.583	0.040	0.102
1.475	2.775	2.712	2.619	0.004	0.009

NOTE: In this example, the observed data sample was divided into two sub-samples of equal size, calibration (Y_{cal}) and validation (Y_{val}). Then a two-parameter linear model, $y = \theta_1 x + \theta_2 +$ error, was fitted to the calibration sample, and least square estimates of the parameter values were obtained as $\theta_1 = 2.448$ and $\theta_2 = -0.958$. These parameter estimates define the model's prediction (Y_{prd}) as $y_{prd} = 2.448x - 0.958$. From this, mean squared error (MSE) for the calibration sample is obtained as MSE $= \sqrt{SSE/m} = \sqrt{0.119/10} = 0.109$, where SSE stands for the sum of squares error, $\Sigma (Y_{cal} - Y_{prd})^2$, as shown on the fifth column of the table. This MSE is translated into 95.7% of the total variance accounted for (i.e., $1 - SSE/SST = 1 - 0.119/2.756 = 0.957$). Similarly, from the SSE, $\Sigma (Y_{val} - Y_{prd})^2$, shown on the last column of the table, MSE for the validation sample is obtained as MSE $= \sqrt{0.288/10} = 0.170$, or equivalently, 89.9% variance accounted for (i.e., $1 - SSE/SST = 1 - 0.288/2.853 = 0.89.9$).

divides the observed data into two subsamples, calibration and validation. One then uses the former to estimate the best-fitting parameter values of the model. These values, denoted by $\hat{\theta}_{Cal}$, are then fixed and used by the model to fit the validation sample, denoted by $y_{val.}$, yielding the model's CV index, which represents an estimate for the model's generalizability. This index may be expressed using an appropriate fit measure such as the negative log likelihood, the MSE, or the percent variance accounted for. Note that the value of the CV index is dependent on how the calibration and validation samples are selected. This unwelcome dependency can be removed or at least minimized by repeatedly performing cross validation for each combination of the calibration and validation samples and then calculating the average CV index.

The CV method somehow takes into account the effects of functional form, but how it does this is not clear. Complexity, therefore, cannot be independently measured in CV. Nevertheless, its ease of use and versatility (being applicable for comparing algebraic, algorithmic, and differential-process models) make it an extremely attractive method. Therefore, we recommend its use in model testing, especially when comparing nonnested models. A detailed example of how to use the procedure is provided here and in Table 11.2. Let us again consider Cerella's (1985) linear model of age-related deficits. Suppose that one wishes to calculate the CV index of this model given the data of Cerella et al. (1981), and further imagine that one divided the original data into two subsamples (calibration and validation), each consisting of ten (x, y) pairs. The open circles and plus signs in Figure 11.2 represent the calibration and validation samples, respectively. Application of CV requires that we first fit the model to the calibration sample and obtain its best-fitting parameter values. This part has already been completed, as described in the section titled "Parameter Estimation." The best-fitting parameter values were $\theta_1 = 2.448$ and $\theta_2 = -0.958$ with MSE $= 0.109$, or, equivalently, 95.7% variance accounted for. Now, using these parameter values, predictions from the model were generated, that is, $y_{\mathrm{prd},i} = 2.448x_i - 0.958, i = 1, \ldots, 10$. The predictions, as represented by the thicker solid line in Figure 11.2, were then fitted to the validation sample (plus signs), with no further parameter tuning. When this was done, the resulting MSE was 0.170, with 89.9% variance accounted for, yielding a poorer fit. The latter value represents an estimated generalizability measure of the model in the sense that it is expected, on average, that the linear model will account for about 89.9% of the variance when fitted to all potential data samples generated from the same underlying process. Consequently, the 5.8% ($= 95.7 - 89.9$) difference between the calibration and validation samples is the amount by which the calibration sample was overfitted—the amount of random error in the data that was absorbed by Cerella's 1981 model (Cerella, 1985). Finally, the value of the CV index defined earlier is obtained by converting the MSE value of the validation sample into the minus log likelihood value using Equation (8), in which the population standard deviation σ is replaced by the MSE value (0.170), its sample estimate. The resulting value is -3.55.

In BMS the goal is to select the one model among the set of models that maximizes the posterior probability of the model given the data in hand. Under the assumption of equal model priors, the inference leads to maximization of what is called the marginal likelihood, which is the average probability of the data given the model, weighted by the parameter prior density function, $\pi(\theta)$. BMS itself is defined as the minus logarithm of the marginal likelihood. Under the assumptions of normality and large sample, BMS can be written as

$$\mathrm{BMS} \approx -\ln f(y \mid \hat{\theta}) + (1/2) \ln \det(H(\theta)).$$

In the above equation, $H(\theta)$ denotes the observed Hessian matrix, whose elements consist of the second derivatives of the minus log

likelihood, $-\ln f(y \mid \theta)$, differentiated with respect to the parameter vector θ. The second term of the above expression can be interpreted as a Bayesian complexity measure. Note that the value of the Hessian matrix depends on the functional form of the model's likelihood function as well as on the number of parameters in the model, as does the Bayesian complexity measure. When the sample size is sufficiently large, BMS is simply reduced to one half of the BIC.

Finally, MDL was developed within the domain of algorithmic coding theory in computer science, where the goal of model selection is to choose the model that permits the greatest compression of data in its description. The assumption underlying the approach is that regularities or patterns in data imply redundancy. The more the data can be compressed by extracting this redundancy, the more we learn about the underlying regularities governing the cognitive process of interest. As with the other selection methods, the first term of MDL is the lack of fit measure. The second and third together constitute the intrinsic complexity of the model. The model that minimizes MDL uncovers the greatest amount of regularity in the data and thus should be preferred.

BMS and MDL are theoretically related to each other (Vitanyi & Li, 2000) and often perform similarly in practice. One drawback in the application of these methods is that they can be computationally intensive, as both require evaluation of numerical integration (see, e.g., Gilks, Richardson, & Spiegelhalter, 1996; Thisted, 1988).

Given the variety of selection methods, it is reasonable to wonder when each is appropriate to use. We end this section by offering a few guidelines. In the ideal situation in which (a) the models being compared are all nested within one another, (b) one of them is correctly specified, and (c) the sample size is sufficiently large (e.g., 200), all five criteria should perform equivalently and pick the true model most often. When models being compared are nonnested, functional form has the potential to play a significant role in model performance. In this situation, the first two methods (AIC, BIC) will in general perform worse than the other three (CV, BMS, MDL), which are sensitive to this dimension of model complexity. As a rule of thumb, the latter three may be the safest to use, though there is no guarantee that they will always perform the best. Relative performance of these selection methods can vary considerably depending on the specific set of models being compared, such as nested versus nonnested and correctly specified versus misspecified, and on the sample size, level of random noise, and other characteristics of the data.

Computational considerations will also influence the choice of method. The most general-purpose methods are likely to be MDL and BMS, which perform most accurately across a range of conditions. Unfortunately, they are difficult to implement and require substantial mathematical sophistication to use. The other methods are easier to implement and are likely to perform satisfactorily under restricted conditions. For example, when models have the same number of parameters but differ in functional form, CV is recommended because it, unlike AIC or BIC, is sensitive to this dimension of complexity. If models differ only in number of parameters, then AIC and BIC should do a good job.

OTHER ISSUES IN MATHEMATICAL MODELING

Because of space limitations, we cannot fully discuss a number of other issues of which the modeler should be aware, but we briefly touch on a few of these in this section. For a more in-depth treatment of each, the reader should consult the references provided herein.

Individual Differences

Individual differences are an important, though often neglected, topic in mathematical modeling (Luce, 1997). They arise when participants' data can be fit by the same model but with different values of the model's parameters. For example, suppose that in a forgetting study one participant's performance measured by proportion recall decreases according to a power curve with a forgetting rate of 0.25, $y_{t,\text{sub.1}} = t^{-0.25}$, as a function of the retention interval t. Another participant's performance may follow the same power curve but with a different value of the forgetting parameter, for example, $y_{t,\text{sub.2}} = t^{-0.40}$. Whenever individual differences are suspected, averaging across individuals' data should be done with extreme care; otherwise it can yield a distorted view of the underlying psychological structure, especially for nonlinear models (see, e.g., R. B. Anderson & Tweney, 1997; Ashby, Maddox, & Lee, 1994; Estes, 1956; Hintzman, 1980; Melton, 1936; Myung, Kim, & Pitt, 2000; Siegler, 1987; Singh, 1996). Perhaps a better solution is to analyze the data using a method that takes into account individual differences, such as the hierarchical modeling approach (Bryk & Raudenbush, 1992).

Random Error in Nonlinear Models

Random error in a nonlinear model can create the illusion of a statistically reliable and reproducible effect, which in actuality is an artifact. An implicit assumption behind the standard notation of a model, $y = g(\theta, x) + e$, is that the random error e is additive to the observed dependent variable y. It may be instructive to examine the integration of other types of random error. For instance, random error could arise *inside* the mean function $g(\theta, x)$, instead of outside:

$$y = g(\theta, x_i, e_i) \quad (i = 1, \ldots, m).$$

For example, a model may assume that the data are generated according to the following model equation: $y_i = \theta_1(x_i + e_i)^2 + \theta_2$ $(i = 1, \ldots, m)$. In this equation, x_i might represent the strength/magnitude of a variable representing an internal mental process (e.g., perceived loudness of a stimulus tone, subjective likelihood of an uncertain event), and because of the way it is coded internally in the brain (e.g., frequency of neuronal spikes), x_i itself is a random variable with an associated probability distribution. Or, simply, it may not be possible to obtain the exact value of the independent variable x_i, and instead, it is measured with error included. In either case, misspecification of the error for a nonlinear form of the mean function $g(\theta, x)$ can create an artifactual effect that has no relation to the underlying process that is being modeled. See Erev, Wallsten, and Budescu (1994) for an example. In short, to avoid such pitfalls, one must develop a proper error theory when modeling cognition and take it into account when analyzing data (Busemeyer, 1980; Busemeyer & Jones, 1983; Luce, 1995).

Equivalent Models

We often distinguish one model from another by the model's equation. For instance, the power model, $y = x^\theta + e$, is clearly different from the exponential model, $y = e^{\theta x} + e$. The look of the model equation can be deceiving, however, because models with distinct equations can often be the same model. For example, the exponential model is equivalent to the model $y = \alpha^x + e$, as the former can be obtained from the latter through a parameter transformation $\alpha = e^\theta$. When one model is transformed into another through such a reparameterization, both become equivalent models in the sense that they will fit any given data set with identical precision. Consequently, they are indistinguishable from one another. A similar problem of equivalent mod-

els, though in a different sense, arises in covariance structure modeling (see MacCallum, Wegener, Uchino, & Fabrigar, 1993).

As another example of reparameterization-equivalent models, consider the FLMP model (Oden & Massaro, 1978) and the Rasch (1960) model of aptitude defined as follows:

$$\text{FLMP} : g(\theta_i, \lambda_j) = \frac{\theta_i \lambda_j}{\theta_i \lambda_j + (1 - \theta_i)(1 - \lambda_j)}$$
$$(0 < \theta_i, \lambda_j < 1)$$

$$\text{Rasch} : g(\alpha_i, \beta_j) = \frac{1}{1 + \exp(\alpha_i + \beta_j)}$$
$$(0 < \alpha_i, \beta_j < \infty).$$

FLMP the two parameters θ_i and λ_j represent dimensions of input stimuli (e.g., auditory and visual) and are combined multiplicatively, which is represented by the mean function $g(\theta_i, \lambda_j)$. On the other hand, in the Rasch model the parameters α_i and β_j are combined in an additive fashion. Despite this difference, however, they are equivalent models under the following parameter transformation (Batchelder, 1997):

$$\alpha_i = \ln((1 - \theta_i)/\theta_i); \beta_j = \ln((1 - \lambda_j)/\lambda_j).$$

Thus one can perfectly mimic the other. Therefore, the question of whether the sensory dimensions are combined multiplicatively or additively cannot be answered using statistical tests alone. Answering the question will require use of some nonstatistical means such as an experimental manipulation. In short, for a model with at least one reparameterization-equivalent model, the specific form of the model's equation may not be identifiable.

CONCLUSION

The purpose of mathematical modeling is to add precision and clarity to the study of behavior. It forces the scientist to be explicit about the architectural characteristics of the processing system, specifying its structure in detail that almost always goes beyond what is known about the process from experimental data. Once specified, the model can be scrutinized in tests of internal consistency (e.g., identifiability) and rigorously evaluated by comparing model performance with human data and then with other competing models. Such tests are only meaningful when we understand what the tests actually measure and—just as importantly—what they do not measure. Another purpose of this chapter has been to alert the reader to the tough problems that must be tackled in order to do modeling. The widespread availability of modeling software bodes well for the future of the discipline. Consider this chapter a companion piece intended to guide would-be modelers and assist them in making informed decisions.

APPENDIX: RANDOM NUMBER GENERATORS

In this appendix we list random number generators for five selected probability distributions that are often assumed in modeling mental processes. For random number generators for other distributions not listed here, see Appendix B of Robert (1994), upon which the present appendix is based. The book by Bratley, Fox, and Schrage (1983) is also a useful reference. We assume that the user has an access to a routine that generates random numbers, U_i's, on the uniform probability distribution on $[0, 1]$.

Normal Distribution.   The normal probability distribution of mean μ and variance σ^2 is given by

$$f(y \mid \mu, \sigma^2) = \frac{1}{\sqrt{2\pi}\sigma} \exp\left(-\frac{(y - \mu)^2}{2\sigma^2}\right)$$

where $\exp(x)$ stands for the exponential function (that is, $\exp(x) = e^x$ and $-\infty < y < \infty$.

The following algorithm generates random numbers, ys, that are normally distributed with mean μ and variance σ^2:

Step 1. Generate U_1, U_2.

Step 2. Take $x = \sqrt{-2\ln(U_1)} \cos(2\pi U_2)$.

Step 3. Take $y = \mu + \sigma x$.

Note in the above algorithm that the function $\ln(x)$ denotes the natural logarithm of base e, not the logarithm of base 10.

Exponential Distribution.   The exponential probability distribution of mean α and variance α^2 is given by

$$f(y \mid \alpha) = \frac{1}{\alpha} \exp(-y/\alpha)$$

where $0 < y < \infty$ and $\alpha > 0$. The algorithm for exponential random numbers is as follows:

Step 1. Generate U.

Step 2. Take $y = -\ln(U)/\alpha$.

Beta Distribution.   The beta probability distribution of mean $\alpha/(\alpha + \beta)$ and variance $\alpha\beta/((\alpha + \beta)^2(\alpha + \beta + 1))$ is defined as

$$f(y \mid \alpha, \beta) = \frac{\Gamma(\alpha + \beta)}{\Gamma(\alpha)\Gamma(\beta)} y^{\alpha-1}(1 - y)^{\beta-1}$$

where $0 \leq y \leq 1$ and $\alpha, \beta > 0$. In the equation, $\Gamma(x)$ denotes the gamma function whose value is equal to $(x-1)(x-2) \cdot \cdots \cdot 2 \cdot 1$ for a positive integer x but otherwise must be evaluated numerically using a recursion formula. Note that the uniform distribution is obtained as a special case of the beta distribution for $\alpha = \beta = 1$.

The following algorithm generates beta random numbers:

Step 1. Generate G_α, G_β (see following)

Step 2. Take $y = G_\alpha/(G_\alpha + G_\beta)$.

The required random number, G_x $(x > 0)$, in the above algorithm is generated from one of the following routines depending upon the value of x:

Case 1: $x > 1$

Step 1. Define $a = x - 1, b = (x - (1/6x))/a, c = 2/a, d = 1 + c$, and $e = 1/\sqrt{x}$

Step 2. Generate U_1, U_2.

If $x \leq 2.5$, then proceed to Step 4. Otherwise, take $U_1 = U_2 + e(1 - 1.86 U_1)$.

Step 3. If $U_1 \leq 0$ or $U_1 \geq 1$, then go to Step 2.

Step 4. If $(cU_1 + bU_2/U_1 + U_1/(bU_2)) \leq d$ or $(c \ln(U_1) - \ln(bU_2/U_1) + bU_2/U_1) \leq 1$, then take $G_x = abU_2/U_1$. Otherwise, go to Step 2.

Case 2: $x = 1$ In this case, generate the desired random number, $G_{x=1}$, from the exponential distribution with $\alpha = 1$.

Case 3: $x < 1$

Step 1. Generate U.

Step 2. Generate $z = G_{x+1}$ using the above routine for $(x + 1) > 1$.

Step 3. Take $G_x = zU^{1/x}$.

Binomial Distribution. The binomial probability distribution of mean np and variance $np(1 - p)$ is given by

$$f(y \mid p) = \frac{n!}{y!(n - y)!} p^y (1 - p)^{n-y}$$

where $y = 0, 1, 2, \ldots, n, 0 \leq p \leq 1$. The following algorithm generates binomial random numbers:

Step 1. Generate $U_1, U_2, \ldots, U_n$.

Step 2. Define $x_i = 1$ if $U_i < p$, and $x_i = 0$ otherwise, for $i = 1, \ldots, n$.

Step 3. Take $y = x_1 + x_2 + \cdots + x_n$.

In essence, this algorithm counts the number of n uniform random numbers whose values are less than p.

Poisson Distribution.   The Poisson probability distribution of mean α and variance α is given by

$$f(y \mid \alpha) = \frac{e^{-\alpha}\alpha^y}{y!}$$

where $y = 0, 1, 2, \ldots, \infty, \alpha > 0$. The following algorithm generates Poisson random numbers:

Step 1. Initialize $a = 1, b = 0$.

Step 2. Generate U
Let $a = aU, b = b + 1$
If $a \geq e^{-\alpha}$, then go to Step 2. Otherwise, go to Step 3.

Step 3. $y = b$

REFERENCES

Aczel, J. (1966). *Lectures on functional equations and their applications*. New York: Academic Press.

Akaike, H. (1973). Information theory and an extension of the maximum likelihood principle. In B. N. Petrox & F. Caski (Eds.), *Second international symposium on information theory* (pp. 267–281). Budapest: Akademiai Kiado.

Anderson, N. H. (1981). *Foundations of information integration theory*. Academic Press.

Anderson, R. B., & Tweney, R. D. (1997). Artifactual power curves in forgetting. *Memory & Cognition, 25,* 724–730.

Ashby, F. G. (1992). *Multidimensional models of perception and cognition*. Hillsdale, NJ: Erlbaum.

Ashby, F. G., Maddox, W. T., & Lee, W. W. (1994). On the dangers of averaging across subjects when using multidimensional scaling or the similarity-choice model. *Psychological Science, 5,* 144–151.

Bamber, D., & van Santen, J. P. H. (1985). How many parameters can a model have and still be testable? *Journal of Mathematical Psychology, 29,* 443–473.

Batchelder, W. H. (1997). Mathematical models and measurement theory [Unpublished handout]. Mathematical Psychology Workshop, Institute of Mathematical Behavioral Sciences, University of California, Irvine.

Batchelder, W. H., & Riefer, D. M. (1990). Multinomial processing models of source monitoring. *Psychological Review, 97,* 548–564.

Berger, J. O., & Berry, D. A. (1988). Statistical analysis and the illusion of objectivity. *American Scientist, 76,* 159–165.

Bozdogan, H. (2000). Akaike information criterion and recent developments in information complexity. *Journal of Mathematical Psychology, 44,* 62–91.

Bratley, P., Fox, B. L., & Schrage, L. E. (1983). *A guide to simulation.* New York: Springer.

Brinley, J. F. (1965). Cognitive sets, speed and accuracy of performance in the elderly. In A. T. Welford & J. E. Birren (Eds.), *Behavior, aging and the nervous system* (pp. 114–149). Springfiled, IL: Thomas.

Brown, M. W. (2000). Cross-validation methods. *Journal of Mathematical Psychology, 44,* 108–132.

Browne, D. R., & Keith-Smith, J. E. (1991). *Frontiers of mathematical psychology: Essays in honor of Clyde Coombs.* New York: Springer.

Bryk, A. S., & Raudenbush, S. W. (1992). *Hierarchical linear models: Applications and data analysis methods.* Newbury Park, CA: Sage.

Busemeyer, J. R. (1980). The importance of measurement theory, error theory, and experimental design for testing the significance of interactions. *Psychological Bulletin, 88,* 237–244.

Busemeyer, J. R., & Jones, L. E. (1983). Analysis of multiplicative combination rules when the casual variables are measured with error. *Psychological Bulletin, 93,* 549–562.

Busemeyer, J. R., & Townsend, J. T. (1993). Decision field theory: A dynamic-cognitive approach to decision making in an uncertain environment. *Psychological Review, 100,* 432–459.

Cerella, J. (1985). Information processing rates in the elderly. *Psychological Bulletin, 98,* 67–83.

Cerella, J., Poon, L. W., & Fozard, J. L. (1981). Mental rotation and age reconsidered. *Journal of Gerontology, 36,* 620–624.

Cohen, J. (1994). The earth is round ($p < 0.05$). *American Psychologist, 49,* 997–1003.

Crowther, C. S., Batchelder, W. H., & Hu, X. (1995). A measurement-theoretic analysis of the fuzzy logical model of perception. *Psychological Review, 102,* 396–408.

D'Agostino, R. B., & Stephens, M. A. (1986). *Goodness of fit techniques.* New York: Marcel.

Diederich, A. (1997). Dynamic stochastic models for decision making under time constraints. *Journal of Mathematical Psychology, 41,* 260–274.

Dowling, C. E., Roberts, F. S., & Theuns, P. (1998). *Recent progress in mathematical psychology: Psychophysics, knowledge, representation, cognition, and measurement.* Mahwah, NJ: Erlbaum.

Erev, I., Wallsten, T. S., & Budescu, D. V. (1994). Simultaneous over- and underconfidence: The role of error in judgment processes. *Psychological Review, 101,* 519–527.

Estes, W. K. (1956). The problem of inference from curves based on group data. *Psychological Review, 53,* 134–140.

Estes, W. K. (1975). Some targets for mathematical psychology. *Journal of Mathematical Psychology, 12,* 263–282.

Estes, W. K. (1991). *Statistical models in behavioral research.* Hillsdale, NJ: Erlbaum.

Fishburn, P. C. (1982). *The foundations of expected utility.* Dordrecht, Netherlands: Reidel.

Forster, K. I. (1994). Computational modeling and elementary process analysis in visual word recognition. *Journal of Experimental Psychology: Human Perception and Performance, 20,* 1292–1310.

Gilks, W. R., Richardson, S., & Spiegelhalter, D. J. (1996). *Markov chain Monte Carlo in practice.* New York: Chapman & Hall.

Gluck, M. A., & Bower, G. H. (1988). From conditioning to category learning: An adaptive network model. *Journal of Experimental Psychology: General, 117,* 227–247.

Green, D. M., & Swets, J. A. (1966). *Signal detection theory and psychophysics.* New York: Wiley.

Grossberg, S. (1987). Competitive learning: From interactive activation and adaptive resonance. *Cognitive Science, 11,* 23–63.

Grunwald, P. (2000). The minimum description length principle. *Journal of Mathematical Psychology, 44,* 133–152.

Hagan, R. L. (1997). In praise of the null hypothesis statistical test. *American Psychologist, 52,* 15–24.

Healy, A. F., Kosslyn, S. M., & Shiffrin, R. M. (1992). *From learning processes to cognitive processes: Essays in honor of William K. Estes.* Hillsdale, NJ: Erlbaum.

Hecht-Nielsen, R. (1989). Theory of the backpropagation network. In *Proceedings of the 1989 international joint conference on neural networks* (Vol. 1; pp. 593–606). New York: IEEE Press.

Hintzman, D. L. (1980). Simpson's paradox and the analysis of memory retrieval. *Psychological Review, 87,* 398–410.

Hintzman, D. L. (1988). Judgment of frequency and recognition memory in a multiple-trace memory model. *Psychological Review, 95,* 528–551.

Hornik, K., Stinchcombe, M., & White, H. (1989). Multilayer feedforward networks are universal approximators. *Neural Networks, 2,* 359–368.

Hornik, K., Stinchcombe, M., & White, H. (1990). Universal approximation of an unknown mapping and its derivatives using multilayer feedforward networks. *Neural Networks, 3,* 551–560.

Jacobs, A. M., & Grainger, J. (1992). Testing a semistochastic variant of the interactive activation model in different word recognition experiments. *Journal of Experimental Psychology: Human Perception and Performance, 18,* 1174–1188.

Jacobs, A. M., & Grainger, J. (1994). Models of visual word recognition: Sampling the state of

the art. *Journal of Experimental Psychology: Human Perception and Performance, 29,* 1311–1334.

Kass, R. E., & Raftery, A. E. (1995). Bayes factors. *Journal of the American Statistical Association, 90,* 773–795.

Kruschke, J. K. (1992). ALCOVE: An exemplar-based connectionist model of category learning. *Psychological Review, 99,* 22–44.

Lewandowsky, S. (1993). The rewards and hazards of computer simulation. *Psychological Science, 4,* 236–243.

Linhart, H., & Zucchini, W. (1986). *Model selection.* New York: Wiley.

Link, S. W., & Heath, R. A. (1975). A sequential theory of psychological discrimination. *Psychometrika, 40,* 77–105.

Luce, R. D. (1959). *Individual choice behavior.* New York: Wiley.

Luce, R. D. (1986). *Response times: Their role in inferring elementary mental organization.* New York: Oxford University Press.

Luce, R. D. (1995). Four tensions concerning mathematical modeling in psychology. *Annual Review of Psychology, 46,* 1–25.

Luce, R. D. (1996). When four distinct ways to measure utility are the same. *Journal of Mathematical Psychology, 40,* 297–317.

Luce, R. D. (1997). Several unresolved conceptual problems of mathematical psychology. *Journal of Mathematical Psychology, 41,* 79–87.

Luce, R. D., & Fishburn, P. C. (1991). Rank- and sign-dependent utility using additive joint receipts. *Journal of Risk and Uncertainty, 4,* 29–59.

MacCallum, R. C., Wegener, D. T., Uchino, B. N., & Fabrigar, L. R. (1993). The problem of equivalent models in applications of covariance structure analysis. *Psychological Bulletin, 114,* 185–199.

Marley, A. A. J. (1997). *Choice, decision and measurement: Essays in honor of R. D. Luce.* Mahwah, NJ: Erlbaum.

Massaro, D. W., & Friedman, D. (1990). Models of integration given multiple sources of information. *Psychological Review, 97,* 225–252.

McClelland, J. L., & Elman, J. L. (1986). The TRACE model of speech perception. *Cognitive Psychology, 1,* 18.

McFall, R. M., & Townsend, J. T. (1998). Foundations of psychological assessment: Implications for cognitive assessment in clinical science. *Psychological Assessment, 10*(4), 316–330.

Medin, D. L., & Schaffer, M. M. (1978). Context theory of classification learning. *Psychological Review, 85,* 207–238.

Melton, A. W. (1936). The end-spurt in memorization curves as an artifact of the averaging of individual curves. *Psychological Monographs, 47*(2, Whole No. 202).

Meyerson, J., Hale, S., Wagstaff, D., Poon, L. W., & Smith, G. A. (1990). The information-loss model: A mathematical theory of age-related cognitive slowing. *Psychological Review, 97,* 475–487.

Myung, I. J., Forster, M., & Browne, M. W. (2000). Special issue on model selection. *Journal of Mathematical Psychology, 44*(1), 1–2.

Myung, I. J., Kim, C., & Pitt, M. A. (2000). Toward an explanation of the power-law artifact: Insights from response surface analysis. *Memory & Cognition, 28,* 832–840.

Myung, I. J., & Pitt, M. A. (1997). Applying Occam's razor in modeling cognition. A Bayesian approach. *Psychonomic Bulletin & Review, 4,* 79–95.

Nosofsky, R. M. (1986). Attention, similarity and the identification-categorization relationship. *Journal of Experimental Psychology: General, 115,* 39–57.

Nygren, T. E. (1983). An examination of conditional violations of axioms for additive conjoint measurement. *Applied Psychological Measurement, 9,* 249–264.

Oden, G. C., & Massaro, D. W. (1978). Integration of featural information in speech perception. *Psychological Review, 85,* 172–191.

Popper, K. R. (1959). *The logic of scientific discovery.* New York: Basic Books.

Rasch, G. (1960). *Probabilistic models for some intelligence and attainment tests.* Copenhagen: Denmarks Paedagogiske Institute.

Ratcliff, R. (1978). A theory of memory retrieval. *Psychological Review, 85,* 59–108.

Ratcliff, R. (1998). The role of mathematical psychology in experimental psychology. *Australian Journal of Psychology, 50,* 1–2.

Ratcliff, R., Spieler, D., & McKoon, G. (2000). Explicitly modeling the effects of aging on response time. *Psychonomic Bulletin & Review, 7,* 1–25.

Read, T. R. C., & Cressie, N. A. C. (1988). *Goodness of fit statistics for discrete multivariate data.* New York: Springer.

Rissanen, J. (1983). A universal prior for integers and estimation by minimum description length. *Annals of Statistics, 11,* 416–431.

Rissanen, J. (1996). Fisher information and stochastic complexity. *IEEE Transaction on Information Theory, 42,* 40–47.

Robert, C. P. (1994). *The Bayesian choice: A decision-theoretic motivation.* New York: Springer.

Roberts, F. S. (1979). *Measurement theory with applications to decision making, utility, and the social sciences.* Reading, MA: Addison-Wesley.

Roberts, S., & Pashler, H. (2000). How persuasive is a good fit? A comment on theory testing in psychology. *Psychological Review, 107,* 358–367.

Rumelhart, D. E., & McClelland, J. L. (1986). *Parallel distributed processing* (Vols. 1–2). Cambridge: MIT Press.

Schwarz, G. (1978). Estimating the dimension of a model. *Annals of Statistics, 6,* 461–464.

Seidenberg, M. S., & McClelland, J. L. (1989). A distributed, developmental model of word recognition and naming. *Psychological Review, 96,* 523–568.

Shiffrin, R. M., & Steyvers, M. (1997). A model for recognition memory: REM—retrieving effectively from memory. *Psychonomic Bulletin & Review, 4,* 145–166.

Siegler, R. S. (1987). The perils of averaging data over strategies: An example from children's addition. *Journal of Experimental Psychology: General, 116,* 250–264.

Singh, R. (1996). Subtractive versus ratio model of "fair" allocation: Can the group level analyses be misleading? *Organizational Behavior and Human Decision Processes, 68,* 123–144.

Smith, P. L. (1995). Psychophysically principled models of visual simple reaction time. *Psychological Review, 102,* 567–593.

Stone, M. (1974). Cross-validatory choice and assessment of statistical predictions [with discussion]. *Journal of Royal Statistical Society, Series B, 36,* 111–147.

Suppes, P., & Zinnes, J. (1963). Basic measurement theory. In R. D. Luce, R. R. Bush, & E. Galanter (Eds.), *Handbook of mathematical psychology* (Vol. 1, pp. 1–76). New York: Wiley.

Thisted, R. A. (1988). *Elements of statistical computing: Numerical computation.* New York: Chapman & Hall.

Townsend, J. T., & Ashby, F. G. (1983). *Stochastic modeling of elementary psychological processes.* Cambridge: Cambridge University Press.

Vitanyi, P., & Li, M. (2000). Minimum description length, Bayesianism and Kolmogorov complexity. *IEEE Transactions on Information Theory, 46,* 446–464.

Von Neumann, J., & Morgenstern, O. (1944). *The theory of games and economic behavior.* Princeton, New Jersey: Princeton University Press.

Wasserman, L. (2000). Bayesian model selection and model averaging. *Journal of Mathematical Psychology, 44,* 92–107.

Wickelgren, W. A. (1970). Trace resistance and decay of long-term memory. *Journal of Mathematical Psychology, 9,* 418–455.

Wickens, T. D. (1982). *Models of behavior: Stochastic processes in psychology.* San Francisco, CA: Freeman.

Wilks, S. S. (1938). The large sample distribution of the likelihood ratio for testing composite hypotheses. *Annals of Mathematical Statistics, 9,* 60–62.

CHAPTER 12

Analysis of Response Time Distributions

TRISHA VAN ZANDT

Response time (RT) is ubiquitous in experimental psychology. It is perhaps the most important measure used to investigate hypotheses about mental processing. Fifteen of the 24 studies published in the February 2000 issue of the *Journal of Experimental Psychology: Human Perception and Performance* used some form of RT analysis. Not restricted to cognitive psychology, RTs are collected routinely in empirical investigations in biological, social, developmental, and clinical psychology as well. RTs are collected from both human and animal subjects. Over 27,000 abstracts in the PsychInfo database spanning from 1887 to the end of April 2000 make reference to reaction, RT, or latency.

One reason that RTs are so important in experimental psychology is because they—like other physical measurements such as length, weight, or force—are defined on a *ratio* scale (Townsend, 1992). This means that one can bring all possible mathematical machinery to bear on the analysis of RT. One can devise precise mathematical models

of cognitive processing and make predictions about process durations as a function of physical (numerical) variables in the experimental context and about how those processes change with changes in these variables. Since Kinnebrook's brief tenure in Maskelyne's observatory in 1796 (Mollon & Perkins, 1996), variations in RT have seemed to be a clean and easy way to get at how mental processing unfolds over time.

Although the use of RTs in cognitive research has been established for over a century, basic issues of analysis still arise. Techniques such as Neyman-Pearson null hypothesis testing are routinely applied to RTs, even though the basic assumptions required for such analyses, such as normality and independence, are known to be violated.[1] RT distributions are not normally distributed; rather, they are positively skewed. Individual RTs are not typically independent of one another; some trial-by-trial sequential effects persist even in the most carefully controlled experiments. For these and other reasons, RT analysis is not always as straightforward as it appears.

While writing this chapter the author was very fortunate to have advice and criticisms from several prominent developers of tools for response time analysis, and she is extraordinarily grateful to them: Hans Colonius, Ehtibar Dzhafarov, Richard Schweickert, and James T. Townsend. Thanks are also due Tjeerd Dijkstra, who verified the accuracy of the MATLAB code. This chapter was also made possible by NSF grant SBR-9702291.

[1] These violations are particularly obvious in the analysis of single-subject data, where raw RTs are subjected to Neyman-Pearson methods. However, even in the more common group analysis, where the mean RTs from individual subjects are used to compute the test statistics, the critical assumption of identically distributed observations is violated, even though the individual means can safely be assumed to be normal.

For the most part, RT analyses occur at the level of the means. That is, hypotheses are formulated with regard to predicted average increases or decreases in RT, as opposed to effects on less obvious parameters of the RT distribution, such as skew. Of the 15 studies in the issue of the journal just cited, 12 reported only mean RTs. The remaining three studies investigated the RT distributions in greater depth. This disparity actually reflects a recent trend: It is becoming more and more important to consider the overall distribution, as many significant and interesting findings are typically hidden when observations are collapsed into averages. Some of my colleagues have seen changes in patterns of RTs in their data across conditions but faced the frustration that ANOVAs on the mean RTs failed to show significant main effects. They then performed the same ANOVAs on the RT medians, or on some trimmed or otherwise modified averages, in an attempt to demonstrate for some measure of central tendency what was obvious at the level of the distribution.

The purpose of this chapter is to provide an outline of RT analyses, particularly at the distributional level. Space constrains me from writing a complete primer or handbook of such analyses, but appropriate references will be provided along the way. There are many statistical and mathematical packages that can help those who are less skilled at programming to perform these analyses, and pointers to these packages will also be provided. In particular, I have provided in the appendix to this chapter some MATLAB routines that can perform some of the analyses I will examine. I begin by discussing RTs as random variables and the ways that random variables can be characterized. I present problems of estimation, not only of central tendency but also of the parameters of a given theoretical distribution. I also discuss estimation of the functional forms of the distribution. In the second half of the paper, I give some

thought to how distributional estimates can be used to test theories about the structure of processing.

CHARACTERIZATION OF RANDOM VARIABLES

RTs are random variables. A sample of RTs, such as might be collected in an experiment (under fixed conditions), is drawn at random from the entire population or distribution of possible RTs. The observations in the sample are assumed to be independent and identically distributed, or *iid*. That is, each observation was taken from exactly the same distribution as each other observation (there are no changes in the distributional parameters or in the form of the distribution across trials), and the observations are statistically independent from each other (so the probability of the ith observation is unaffected by the value of the jth observation). The *iid* assumption is important for a number of reasons, not the least of which is the desire that the many trials within identical experimental conditions all have exactly the same effect on the human observer. Note, however, that the independence assumption is likely to be violated by sequential effects and parameter drift (Burbeck & Luce, 1982). Unfortunately, researchers do not have the tools to deal with this problem and must assume that the covariances between observations are small enough that they can be neglected.

A random variable can be characterized in a number of ways. One way is to specify parameters of the distribution from which the variable is sampled, such as its mean or variance. Another way is to specify the functional form of the distribution itself. There are several useful functional forms, including the density, distribution, and survivor and hazard functions. Each of these different functions describes a different aspect of the behavior of the random variable, but the relationship between the functions is unique. That is, once a particular density function has been specified, for example, the distribution, survivor and hazard functions are then determined. Random variables from different distributions cannot have the same functional form, regardless of which kind of function is examined. Therefore, only one of these functions needs to be specified to characterize completely the behavior of the random variable.

I now discuss each functional form and the relationships between them. For additional information, the reader might consult Luce (Luce, 1986), Townsend and Ashby (1983), or any good textbook on probability theory (e.g., Hoel, Port, & Stone, 1971).

Density Function

The density functions $f(t)$ for an ex-Gaussian (the sum of a normal and an exponential random variable) and a Wald random variable are shown in Figure 12.1, top panel. The x-axis is time, or potential values of RT, and the y-axis is the height of the density function $f(t)$. If RT were a discrete random variable, the height of the function at a point t would give the probability of observing an RT equal to t. However, RT is generally considered to be a continuous random variable, and therefore the value of the density function does not represent probability. Instead, it is the area under the density function that gives measures of probability.

For example, suppose that we want to know the probability of observing an RT between values a and b. This probability is measured by integrating the density function between the values a and b:

$$P(a \leq \mathrm{RT} \leq b) = \int_a^b f(t)\, dt.$$

More generally, any positive function f that has total area of 1 when integrated from negative to positive infinity is a density function.

For RT data, the shapes of the empirical (estimated) density functions are typically unimodal and positively skewed, like those shown in Figure 12.1. The majority of the observations is generally fast, but a large proportion of the observations is slower, pulling the positive tail of the density function to the right. There are a number of distributions that have density functions of this form, including the gamma, Wald, and Weibull distributions, but by far the most popular characterization of RT densities is that of the ex-Gaussian (e.g., Balota & Spieler, 1999; Heathcote, Popiel, & Mewhort, 1991; Ratcliff & Murdock, 1976). The ex-Gaussian density can capture a very large number of shapes from almost symmetric (like the normal density) to very asymmetric (like the exponential density, which is shown in Figure 12.2).

The density function is a useful way of characterizing RTs because it is an intuitive way to think about how likely different RTs are to be observed. The shape of the density function can be useful in discriminating between some classes of random variables, but it should be noted that many unimodal, positively skewed distributions exist, and many are flexible enough that they can look very similar to each other. This is demonstrated by the close correspondence between the ex-Gaussian and Wald densities in the figure. I talk again about similarities between distributions at the close of this chapter.

Distribution Function

The cumulative distribution functions (CDFs) $F(t)$ of the same ex-Gaussian and Wald random variables are shown in Figure 12.1, center panel. The x-axis gives the possible values of RT, and the y-axis gives the values of the CDF $F(t)$. For a particular point t along the x-axis, the value of $F(t)$ gives the probability of observing an RT less than the value t:

$$F(t) = P(\mathrm{RT} < t).$$

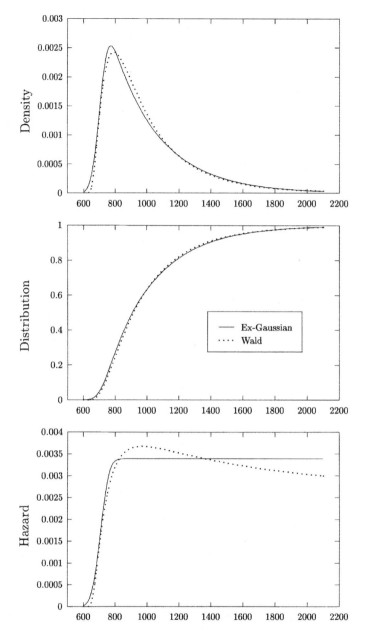

Figure 12.1   Density functions (top panel), CDFs (center panel), and hazard functions (bottom panel) for an ex-Gaussian (solid curves) and Wald (dotted curves) random variable.

The CDF is found from the density function by integration from $-\infty$ to the point t:

$$F(t) = \int_{-\infty}^{t} f(u)\,du.$$

Any positive function $F(t)$ that is non-decreasing and has the properties that $\lim_{t \to -\infty} F(t) = 0$ and $\lim_{t \to \infty} F(t) = 1$ is a CDF.

The CDF gives the percentile ranks of each possible value of RT. In Figure 12.1,

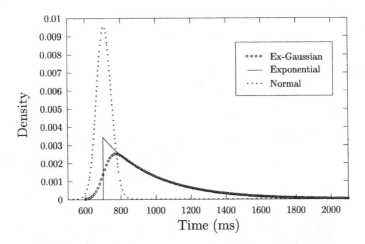

Figure 12.2 The ex-Gaussian density (open circles) plotted with its normal (dotted line) and exponential (solid line) components.

for example, the median RT can be found by drawing a horizontal line from the .50 point on the y-axis and dropping a vertical line to the x-axis at the point of intersection with the desired curve $F(t)$. This relationship between the CDF and the quantiles of the distribution is particularly useful for simulating different random variables. To simulate a random variable RT with a known CDF $F(t)$, select a point u on the y-axis at random (using a uniform [0, 1] generator), and then compute the corresponding quantile RT $= F^{-1}(u)$. Inverting F may require numerical methods but is typically straightforward.

Unlike the density function, the CDF is not as useful in distinguishing between different kinds of random variables. Most CDFs are S-shaped; all distributions increase from 0 to 1. Therefore, all CDFs tend to look similar regardless of the random variables that they describe. For example, in Figure 12.1 the Wald and ex-Gaussian CDFs are practically identical.

Survivor and Hazard Functions

The survivor and hazard functions are two alternative functions that characterize a random variable. These functions arise frequently in reliability and survival analysis (when machines break or people die), hence the choice of vocabulary.

The survivor function $\overline{F}(t)$ is the probability that the "lifetime" of an object is at least t, that is, the probability that failure occurs after t. In terms of RT,

$$\overline{F}(t) = P(\text{RT} > t) = 1 - F(t):$$

The survivor function is simply one minus the CDF.

The hazard function $h(t)$ gives the likelihood that an event will occur in the next small interval dt in time, given that it has not occurred before that point in time. From the definition of a conditional probability,

$$h(t) = \lim_{dt \to 0} P(t \le \text{RT} \le t + dt \mid \text{RT} \ge t)/dt$$
$$= \frac{f(t)}{\overline{F}(t)}.$$

The hazard function for the ex-Gaussian and Wald distributions are shown in Figure 12.1, bottom panel.

When $F(t)$ is differentiable, the hazard function can be expressed as a function of the survivor function:

$$h(t) = -\frac{d}{dt} \ln \overline{F}(t),$$

where ln indicates the natural logarithm. The function $-\ln \overline{F}(t)$ is called the log survivor function or integrated hazard function, and it can be useful for distinguishing between different distributions. I make use of it later to answer questions about certain properties of cognitive processes. The density function can also be expressed in terms of the hazard function:

$$f(t) = h(t) \exp \left[-\int_{-\infty}^{t} h(u)\,du \right].$$

Some attention has been paid to the analysis of hazard functions in RT work, because the hazard function can frequently be very useful in discriminating between different random variables (Ashby, Tein, & Balakrishnan, 1993; Bloxom, 1984; Colonius, 1988; Luce, 1986; Maddox, Ashby, & Gottlob, 1998; Thomas, 1971). Although it is very difficult to discriminate between the ex-Gaussian and Wald densities shown in the top panel of Figure 12.1, the differences between the two variables become clear by examining the hazard functions in the bottom panel. Whereas the ex-Gaussian hazard function increases to an asymptote, the Wald hazard function is nonmonotonic, increasing and then decreasing. It has been suggested, therefore, that estimation of hazard functions may provide a way to identify RT distributions, and hence the process underlying the execution of an RT task (Burbeck & Luce, 1982).

If one can determine how RTs are distributed, then one has gone a long way toward isolating the process responsible for generating the RTs. In practice, then, a researcher might try to estimate one or more of these functions in an attempt to identify or rule out various distributional forms for consideration. In the next section I talk about problems associated with estimating these functions. The problem of estimation is not a trivial one, however, and I must begin by discussing estimation in general. I then talk about estimation of parameters, and then about estimation of functional forms.

ESTIMATION

The goal of estimation is to determine from RT data the properties of the distribution from which the data were sampled. One may wish to know only gross properties, such as the mean or skewness, or one may hope to determine the exact functional form of the distribution. The most common sort of statistical analysis involves inferences about the mean and variance of the population distribution. Given a particular sample of size n, one can attempt to estimate the central tendency and dispersion of the population, perhaps using the sample mean $\overline{X}$ and variance s^2. Or, one might try to estimate the shape of the distribution itself, perhaps by constructing a histogram indicating the relative frequency of each observation in the sample. Both of these estimation problems are commonly encountered, and they are not necessarily separate problems. I discuss each in this section.

It is important to remember that any estimate, whether of a parameter or of a function, is a random variable. Associated with it is some degree of variation and some (often unknown) distributional form. The goal of estimation, therefore, is not just estimating values of parameters, but estimating those parameters in such a way that the distributions of those estimates have desirable properties. For example, the sample mean $\overline{X}$ is an estimate of a parameter, μ, the population mean. The estimate $\overline{X}$ is a random variable because its value will change for different samples, even when those samples are taken from the same population. There is a distribution associated with $\overline{X}$ that by the Central Limit Theorem is known to be approximately normal. The mean of this distribution is μ, the mean of the population from which the sample was drawn. Something is known also about the variance of the distribution of $\overline{X}$. As long as the sample is *iid*, the variance of the distribution is σ^2/n, the variance of the population from which the sample is drawn divided by the size of the sample n.

I begin by discussing problems of parameter estimation, including the mean and variance of the RT distribution, and also the more explicit problem of estimating the parameters of a theoretical RT distribution. I then discuss the problem of distribution estimation, including the estimation of the density, distribution, and hazard functions.

Throughout the rest of this chapter, I will refer to the data presented in Table 12.1 to motivate and illustrate the discussion. These data were collected in a simple detection experiment, roughly designed after an experiment presented by Townsend and Nozawa (1995), in which one, two, or no dots appeared in two locations on a computer screen. The observer's task was to press one key as soon as a dot was detected, and the other key if no dots were detected. Each dot could be either large or small. Only the target (dot) present data are provided in the table, and error RTs are not included. This experiment is an example of what Townsend and Nozawa have called the double factorial paradigm, which has proved to be very important in examining hypotheses about processing information from multiple sources of information, as discussed later.

Properties of Estimators

Consider an *iid* sample $\{X_1, X_2, \ldots, X_n\}$ of size n from a population with mean μ and variance σ^2. The sample mean $\overline{X} = \sum_{i=1}^{n} X_i/n$ is an estimate of the parameter μ. The sample mean has a number of desirable properties as an estimate of μ: it is (a) *unbiased*, (b) *consis-*

tent, (c) *efficient*, and, if the variable X is normally distributed, (d) a *maximum likelihood estimate*.

If an estimator is unbiased, then its expected value (mean) is equal to the parameter being estimated. For the sample mean, the expected value of $\overline{X}$ is equal to μ, the parameter that $\overline{X}$ estimates. In other words, on average the sample mean will equal the population mean. More generally, suppose that one wishes to estimate a parameter α with the estimator $\hat{\alpha}$. The estimator $\hat{\alpha}$ is unbiased if

$$E(\hat{\alpha}) = \mu_{\hat{\alpha}} = \alpha,$$

where E is the expected value operator, defined as

$$E(X) = \int_{-\infty}^{\infty} x f(x)\,dx.$$

If an estimator is also consistent, then as the sample size n grows, the probability that it differs from the estimated parameter shrinks to zero. We sometimes call this property *convergence in probability*. For the sample mean $\overline{X}$, this property takes the form of the *Law of Large Numbers*. As n grows very large, the probability that $\overline{X}$ differs from μ shrinks to zero. More generally, for a consistent estimator $\hat{\alpha}$,

$$\lim_{n \to \infty} P(|\hat{\alpha} - \alpha| \geq \epsilon) = 0,$$

for any $\epsilon > 0$, no matter how small. For practical purposes, this means that the accuracy of the estimator $\hat{\alpha}$ can be improved by increasing sample size n. Consistency is therefore a very important property. One might wish to sacrifice unbiasedness for consistency, as long as the variance of the estimator decreases fairly rapidly with n.

A property closely related to consistency is that of *asymptotic unbiasedness*, meaning that as n grows, the expected value of the

Table 12.1   Response Times from a Simple Detection Experiment

	Both								Left Only				Right Only			
	ss		sl		ls		ll		s		l		s		l	
i	RT_i	f_i	RT_i	f_i	RT_i	f_i	RT_i	f_i	RT_i	f_i	RT_i	f_i	RT_i	f_i	RT_i	f_i
1	374	1	340	1	353	1	350	2	350	1	361	1	334	1	374	1
2	381	1	354	1	354	1	365	1	365	1	378	1	430	1	377	1
3	398	1	357	1	374	2	369	1	375	1	379	1	453	1	381	1
4	400	1	377	1	377	1	376	1	409	1	389	1	456	1	398	1
5	401	1	378	2	382	1	377	1	422	3	398	1	461	1	401	1
6	406	1	380	1	384	1	382	1	423	1	402	1	470	1	405	1
7	408	1	385	1	385	1	408	1	426	1	405	1	473	1	409	1
8	412	1	388	1	398	1	422	4	428	1	413	1	477	1	425	1
9	425	1	398	1	405	2	425	1	429	1	418	1	480	1	426	1
10	426	1	401	1	422	2	426	1	449	1	422	1	481	1	429	1
11	428	1	404	1	425	1	428	1	450	3	426	2	485	1	446	1
12	429	1	405	1	428	1	429	1	454	1	429	1	494	1	448	1
13	432	1	412	1	429	2	430	1	457	2	433	2	497	1	450	2
14	446	3	421	1	436	1	432	1	465	1	436	1	498	1	457	1
15	452	1	422	1	444	1	441	1	470	1	446	2	501	1	465	1
16	457	1	424	1	446	1	445	1	476	1	450	1	505	1	466	1
17	469	1	425	1	448	1	446	1	480	1	452	2	509	2	470	4
18	470	1	432	2	457	1	453	3	485	1	453	2	518	2	473	1
19	476	1	433	3	461	2	456	1	498	1	457	1	524	1	474	1
20	484	1	445	1	465	1	460	1	505	1	458	1	525	1	478	1
21	485	1	446	1	470	1	464	1	512	1	473	1	526	1	480	1
22	489	1	452	1	473	1	470	3	525	1	474	1	542	2	481	1
23	494	1	453	2	477	1	474	1	532	1	477	1	544	1	485	3
24	502	1	457	1	478	1	476	2	537	1	481	2	552	1	497	2
25	505	1	460	1	494	1	493	1	542	1	498	1	553	1	500	1
26	517	1	473	2	498	1	497	1	545	1	501	1	557	1	504	1
27	522	1	477	2	500	1	498	1	589	1	513	1	565	1	516	1
28	524	1	480	1	501	1	500	1	590	1	518	1	566	1	518	1
29	526	1	485	1	504	1	504	1	618	2	524	2	580	1	525	2
30	528	1	493	1	518	1	505	1	633	1	525	2	596	2	545	1
31	529	1	494	1	541	2	512	1	665	1	533	1	613	1	565	1
32	548	2	496	1	544	1	517	1	740	1	535	1	614	1	566	1
33	562	1	501	1	546	1	518	1	765	1	538	1	640	1	569	2
34	613	1	504	1	550	1	522	1	809	1	541	1	689	1	577	1
35	628	1	506	1	613	1	536	1	811	1	549	1	694	1	594	1
36	637	1	522	1	614	1	541	1	829	1	566	1	700	1	618	1
37	665	1	524	1	618	1	586	1	927	1	593	1	733	1	645	1
38	713	1	525	1	628	1	593	1	944	1	617	1	734	1	661	1
39	720	1	545	1	641	1	604	1	1029	1	618	2	881	1	670	1
40	757	1	572	1	644	1	628	1			641	1	1188	1	716	1
41	788	1	593	1	661	1	748	1			785	1			848	1
42	931	1	661	1	688	1										
43	935	1	891	1	757	1										
44					787	1										

NOTE: Small (s) and large (l) circles were presented at left and right locations on a computer monitor (after Townsend and Nozawa, 1995).

estimator approaches the value of the estimated parameter. Although this may seem to be the same as consistency, it is not. It is a stronger property, meaning that the conditions under which it holds are more stringent than those for consistency. Therefore, an estimator may be consistent but asymptotically biased.

The third property, efficiency, refers to the variance of the estimator. Because the estimate of a parameter is a random variable, one would like for the variance of that variable to be relatively small. So, if the estimator is unbiased, it is not likely to vary too much from the true value of the parameter. The sample mean is efficient, which means that it has a smaller variance relative to any other estimate of μ that we might choose, such as the median or the mode.

The fourth property, maximum likelihood, has to do with the probability of the observed sample. That is, there is some probability associated with having sampled exactly the observations that we obtained: an n-fold joint probability distribution. To use a simplistic perspective, if one observes a particular sample, then it must have been highly probable, so one should choose the estimates of the population parameters that make this probability as large as possible. If X is normally distributed, then the sample mean is a maximum likelihood estimator of μ. Note that maximum likelihood estimators are not guaranteed to be unique or to exist at all. I discuss maximum likelihood estimation in some detail later.

Although I have been talking about properties of estimators of a single population parameter, it is important to remember that these properties also hold for estimators of functions, such as densities or CDFs. For example, suppose that a density function were to be estimated by a relative frequency histogram of a sample. The height of the histogram at every point is a random variable, and the shape of the histogram will change with every new sample. Therefore, one can characterize estimators of the density, distribution, and survivor and hazard functions as unbiased, consistent, efficient, and so forth.

Parameter Estimation

Mean and Variance

By far the most common parameters estimated in an RT analysis are the mean and variance (μ and σ^2) of the RT distribution. However, because of the asymmetric shape of the RT distribution, it is important to recognize that these parameters are not necessarily (perhaps not even frequently) the best parameters to characterize the RT distribution. Because of the RT distribution's skewness (see Figure 12.1), the mean does not represent the most typical or likely RT. It is pulled upward, in the direction of the skew. A similar problem exists with the variance σ^2. The large upper tail in the RT distribution has the effect of creating "outliers," values in the sample that are much longer than the majority of the observations. Outliers are a problem in all areas of statistical analysis, but the unusual aspect of outliers in RT data is that they potentially derive from the process of interest. That is, they are not necessarily outliers in the sense of contaminations of the data. Because the sample variance is greatly increased by such outliers, the power of the statistical tests to be performed on the data is greatly reduced.

As an example, consider the RTs shown in the condition labeled Left Only (s) in Table 12.1. These are the detection RTs for when a single small dot appeared in the left position. These data are positively skewed: Although most of the observations fall between 300 ms and 600 ms, a small proportion of the sample extends as high as 1,029 ms. The sample mean is $\overline{X} = 550.60$ ms, and the sample standard deviation $s = 164.58$ ms. If the value of the slowest RT, 1,029 ms, is changed to 2,060 ms—a value that might typically be observed in such an experiment—one finds now that the sample mean $\overline{X} = 573.50$ ms and the sample standard deviation $s = 270.42$ ms. As a result of changing a single observation, the sample mean increased by 23 ms (almost a detectable effect, in some RT experiments), and the sample standard deviation increased by over 60%.

One says that neither the mean μ nor the variance σ^2 is a *robust* parameter, meaning that very small changes in the shape of the distribution, such as the change of a single observation, can produce very large changes in the values of these parameters. In a practical sense, this means that confidence intervals constructed for these parameters are likely to be too large and placed incorrectly, reducing the power of hypothesis tests involving the mean RT (Wilcox, 1998). This is particularly a concern for RT data in which not only large degrees of skew but also a good number of outliers (either extremely long or short RTs) are to be expected. An alternative is to estimate parameters that are not as sensitive to outliers or skew, such as the median or interquartile range. Using the same example as in the previous paragraph, the original sample has median $Md = 485$ ms and interquartile range $IQR = 169$ ms. After doubling the slowest RT to 2,060 ms, these estimates are unchanged.

Unfortunately, the standard errors of $\overline{X}$ and s^2 are typically considerably smaller than the standard errors of Md and IQR (Stuart & Ord, 1999). For example, although the standard error of $\overline{X}$ is $\sigma/\sqrt{n}$, if the sample is taken from a normal population, the standard error of Md is approximately $1.25\sigma/\sqrt{n}$. Although the sampling distributions of $\overline{X}$, s^2, Md, and IQR are asymptotically normal, the sample sizes required to approximate normality are much larger for Md and IQR than for $\overline{X}$ and s^2. Furthermore, whereas the sample mean $\overline{X}$

is an unbiased estimator of μ, the sample median Md is a biased estimator of the population median when the population is skewed (J. Miller, 1988).[2] These factors have prevented widespread use of the statistics Md and IQR, despite the fact that they are probably better for characterizing central tendency and dispersion for RT data than are $\overline{X}$ and s^2.

Using Monte Carlo simulations, Ratcliff (1993) investigated a number of RT data treatments that reduce or eliminate the effects of outliers on the mean and variance. These included cutoff values, above and below which RTs are eliminated from the sample, and transformations such as the inverse and logarithm. For each of these strategies, he computed power and the probability of Type I errors for analyses of variance, with and without outliers mixed into the data. Although no method had strong effects on the number of Type I errors, the method chosen had strong effects on power.

Using Md as a measure of central tendency generally resulted in lower power than did using cutoffs or transformations, probably because of the greater variance and bias of Md. Fixed cutoffs (e.g., 2,000 or 2,500 ms) maintained the highest power. The use of fixed cutoffs, however, is highly dependent on the range of the data in different experimental conditions; a 2,000 ms cutoff in one experiment might eliminate half the observations in another experiment. Thus there is no hard and fast rule that could be used to establish cutoffs. Because of this problem, it is common to find examples in which cutoffs are based on the sample standard deviation. For example, one might eliminate all observations greater than 3 standard deviations above the mean.

---

[2]For even very skewed distributions, median bias is generally less than 10 ms for samples of size 25 or higher. When one or more groups has sample size less than 25, the median should not be used, as the bias difference between the groups could introduce an artifactual effect. See J. Miller (1988) for more details.

Unfortunately, Ratcliff (1993) found that basing cutoffs on the standard deviation could have disastrous effects on power, depending on whether the experimental factors had their effects on the fast or slow RTs. Ratcliff instead recommended exploring a range of potential cutoff values for different experimental conditions.

However, Ulrich and Miller (1994) have noted that using cutoffs can introduce asymmetric biases into statistics such as the sample mean, median, and standard deviation, and they cautioned strongly against the use of cutoffs without consideration of these effects. Van Selst and Jolicoeur (1994) presented a procedure that produces a uniform bias across sample sizes, thus minimizing the potential for artifactual differences between conditions. Unfortunately, even Van Selst and Jolicoeur's method produces a highly biased estimate (as great as 30 ms too small for the distributions they examined), and this could also result in significant artifacts, especially in the presence of floor or ceiling effects.

The next most powerful approach to minimizing the effects of outliers was the inverse transformation, which Ratcliff (1993) recommended as a way of verifying the appropriateness of the selected cutoffs if cutoffs were used. Transforming RTs to speed, 1/RT, reduces the effect of slow outliers and maintains good power. In the example taken from Table 12.1, the mean transformed RT is $\overline{X} = 1.947 \times 10^{-3}$/ms with standard deviation $s = 0.466 \times 10^{-3}$/ms. If the slowest RT is doubled, the mean transformed RT is $\overline{X} = 1.936 \times 10^{-3}$/ms with standard deviation $s = 0.494 \times 10^{-3}$/ms; there is some effect of the long outlier, but it is greatly reduced relative to the effect on the mean RT.

To see how outliers reduce power, consider the two conditions in Table 12.1 denoted Both (ss) and Right Only (s). The

nature of the experiment was such that one might have expected that RTs in the Right Only (s) conditions would be slower than RTs in the Both (ss) condition. This is because, essentially, twice the amount of information was available to the observer in the Both (ss) condition, resulting in a faster accumulation of evidence that targets were present. As predicted, the mean RT for Both (ss) responses is 524.61 ms, and the mean RT for Right Only (s) responses is 563.70 ms. Unfortunately, this difference (39 ms) does not reach statistical significance: $t(88) = 1.3734$, $p > .08$. If one considers instead the response rates—1.85×10^{-3}/ms and 2.00×10^{-3}/ms for Both (ss) and Right Only (s), respectively—then the rate difference ($-.15 \times 10^{-3}$/ms) is significant: $t(88) = 1.94$, $p < .05$.[3]

A large statistical literature has developed over the past few decades addressing robust statistics and how to reduce the effects of outliers or skewed distributions (Barnett & Lewis, 1994). Few psychology researchers are considering these alternative techniques for their data. Wilcox (1997, 1998) has made a special effort to bring robust analyses to the attention of experimental psychologists, and it is hoped that as more and more statistical packages incorporate robust techniques, the field will see more interest in these alternatives in the years to come. In the meantime, however, the best approach to dealing with outliers in RT data is probably the inverse transformation, which gives the greatest power. Cutoffs should be avoided unless one is willing to undertake either Ulrich and Miller's (1994) or Van Selst and Jolicoeur's (1994) procedures.

---

[3]Note that it is also possible to *eliminate* significant effects by transformation. Also note that transformed RTs will not necessarily be useful for testing some kinds of model predictions (e.g., serial stage models in which durations are summed). I am only advocating the use of transformed RTs for null hypothesis testing, not for verifying model predictions.

As with any procedures that involve removing data from a sample, when attempting to employ cutoffs to reduce the effects of outliers, statistical results should be presented for both the complete and trimmed data sets so that readers are aware of potential artifactual results.

The Ex-Gaussian Parameters

Because outliers are not only bothersome but also potentially interesting in the context of RTs, some have argued that the ex-Gaussian distribution could be used as a parametric (although atheoretical) estimate of RT distributions (Heathcote, Popiel, & Mewhort, 1991; Ratcliff, 1979; Ratcliff & Murdock, 1976) without excluding any data that are suspiciously slow or fast. The ex-Gaussian distribution—the distribution of the sum of a normal and an exponentially distributed variable—has three parameters. The normal component has parameters μ and σ^2, the normal mean and variance. The exponential component has parameter τ, the exponential mean. Figure 12.2 shows the ex-Gaussian density presented in the top panel of Figure 12.1, together with its component normal and exponential densities. (The exponential has been shifted from its minimum, 0, to demonstrate the relation between the tails of the exponential and ex-Gaussian densities.) The normal distribution determines the leading edge of the ex-Gaussian density, and the exponential distribution determines skewness, or the height of the positive tail. The mean of the ex-Gaussian is $\mu + \tau$, and its variance is $\sigma^2 + \tau^2$.

Rather than discussing RT means and variances, estimates of the parameters μ, σ^2, and τ could be used to characterize RT data and isolate the effects of experimental variables either in the slow or fast RTs (Heathcote et al., 1991; Hockley, 1984). I estimated these parameters for the data from the Both (ss) and Right Only (s) condition using maximum likelihood. For Both (ss), $\hat{\mu} = 390.47$ ms, $\hat{\sigma} = 16.60$ ms, and $\hat{\tau} = 134.09$ ms. For Right Only (s), $\hat{\mu} = 458.64$ ms, $\hat{\sigma} = 47.54$ ms, and $\hat{\tau} = 105.06$ ms. Several routines are publicly available to assist in performing these computations (Cousineau & Larochelle, 1997; Dawson, 1988; Heathcote, 1996), and MATLAB routines are provided in the Appendix.

Given the estimated ex-Gaussian parameters, one might want to infer that the presence of two dots decreased μ and σ and increased τ. However, because the distributions of the estimates of these parameters are unknown, inferential statistical procedures are difficult. One approach is to estimate the standard errors of the estimates by "bootstrapping" the samples (Efron, 1979). This is a simple procedure in which bootstrapped samples of size n are obtained from the original sample by selecting n observations from the sample *with replacement.* The ex-Gaussian parameters are then estimated from each bootstrapped sample, and the standard deviation of those estimates is a fairly good estimate of the standard error. I simulated 100 bootstrapped samples for each condition and computed the standard errors of $\hat{\mu}$, $\hat{\sigma}$, and $\hat{\tau}$ to be 14.80 ms, 13.09 ms, and 22.37 ms, respectively, for the Both (ss) condition, and 25.00 ms, 23.02 ms, and 31.79 ms, respectively, for the Right Only (s) condition. Given these standard errors, one can argue that μ is greater for the Right Only (s) than for the Both (ss) condition. However, one cannot conclude that any differences exist between σ or τ for the two conditions because the variance of the estimates is too large. This finding is consistent with earlier work showing the variance of the estimates in σ and τ to be quite large for smaller samples (Van Zandt, 2000).

In sum, the ex-Gaussian characterization of RTs could potentially be quite useful in skirting problems of skewness and outliers. Unfortunately, the sampling distributions of

$\hat{\mu}, \hat{\sigma}$, and $\hat{\tau}$ cannot be determined explicitly, and their distributions also depend on the underlying (and unknown) RT distribution. It may not be possible, therefore, to argue conclusively about the effects that experimental manipulations have on these parameters. An additional problem arises when one considers that despite the utility of the ex-Gaussian distribution, RTs are not generally distributed as ex-Gaussians (Burbeck & Luce, 1982; Luce, 1986; Van Zandt, 2001). Because the ex-Gaussian is an atheoretical model of the RT distribution, it is difficult, if not impossible, to attribute psychological meaning to changes in the different parameters. As Ratcliff (1993) argues, using the ex-Gaussian parameters to characterize RT distributions might not be very useful in the absence of a model explaining the processes that generated the RTs in the first place.

Nonparametric Function Estimation

Some estimation procedures, such as least-squares minimization and maximum likelihood estimation, ensure that estimates are unbiased, consistent, efficient, and so forth, given certain constraints on the sample. Unfortunately, these constraints are rarely satisfied when dealing with RT distributions. Furthermore, when estimating density functions, the extent of bias depends on the true form of the underlying population distribution, which is unknown. Therefore, when estimating RT densities, the extent of error is also unknown.

A number of issues bear on the estimation procedure. The issue of primary importance is whether the analysis is model-driven. That is, has a process been specified that states how RTs should be distributed and explains the relationship between the physical parameters of the experiment and the theoretical parameters of the RT distribution? If a model of this degree of precision has been specified, then a parametric procedure will be used to recover the theoretical parameters of the RT distribution. If not, then nonparametric procedures will probably be more appropriate.

Quantiles and the Cumulative Distribution Function

The CDF is the easiest of the functional forms to estimate because an unbiased, consistent, maximum likelihood estimate for the CDF exists in the form of the cumulative relative frequency distribution, empirical distribution function (EDF). That is,

$$\hat{F}(t) = [\text{number of observations less than or equal to } t]/n. \quad (1)$$

The EDF is an estimator of the percentile ranks of the possible RTs that might be observed and is asymptotically normal at every point. This means that at every point t, $\hat{F}(t)$ will be normally distributed around the value of the true CDF $F(t)$. Because the EDF $\hat{F}(t)$ is an unbiased estimate of the CDF, it should be noted that $1 - \hat{F}(t)$ is therefore an unbiased estimate of the survivor function. The survivor function estimate is used later in this chapter.

It is often useful to compute the estimates $\hat{F}^{-1}(p)$ of the quantiles of an RT distribution (e.g., Logan, 1992; Van Zandt, 2000; Van Zandt, Colonius, & Proctor, 2000). The CDF $F(t)$ can then be estimated by plotting p for a number of estimates $t_p = \hat{F}^{-1}(p)$. To estimate the pth quantile t_p, where $P(\text{RT} \leq t_p) = p$, the RTs are ordered from smallest to largest. The simplest way to estimate the pth quantile is to find the npth observation in the sample, if np is an integer. If np is not an integer, then an average of the $[np\text{th}]$ and $[np] + 1$th observation is computed, where $[np]$ indicates the integer part of np. Typically, the midpoint of $[np]$ and $[np] + 1$ is used, but other weighting schemes can be used as well (Davis & Steinberg, 1983).

As an example, consider the data in conditions Left Only (s) in Table 12.1. The median, the $p = .50$ quantile, is estimated. There are $n = 45$ observations in this sample, so $np = 22.5$. The $[np]$th observation is (counting frequencies from the smallest observed RT) $RT_{17} = 480$ ms, and the $[np] + 1$th observation is $RT_{18} = 485$ ms. The average of these two observations is 482.5 ms; therefore $\hat{F}^{-1}(.5) = Md = 482.5$ ms. Like the EDF, quantile estimates are asymptotically normal and unbiased. These characteristics of the EDF and quantile estimates make inferential statistical analyses easy to perform because the sampling distributions of quantiles and percentile ranks are known exactly (Stuart & Ord, 1999).

A widely used method for estimating quantiles of RT distributions is called "Vincentizing" (Ratcliff, 1979). To describe this procedure, suppose that q quantiles are to be

tile estimation procedure described above. These estimates would correspond to the 10th, 20th, ..., percentiles. Now suppose that 10 vincentiles were computed. We would assume that these vincentiles were located at approximately the 5th, 15th, 25th, ..., percentiles—the midpoints of the decile ranges. Thus, the vincentiles separate the sample into $q + 1$ groups; the relative frequencies of the middle groups are $1/q$, and the relative frequencies of the slowest and fastest groups are $1/2q$.

Consider the RTs for condition Left Only (s) shown in Table 12.1. There are $n = 45$ observations in this condition, and $q = 5$ vincentiles are to be estimated. To do this, one first makes q copies of each observation. Then, starting from the smallest RTs, one begins averaging the duplicated order statistics in groups of n. The first vincentile for this sample is therefore

$$V_1 = \frac{(5)(350\,\text{ms})+(5)(365\,\text{ms})+(5)(375\,\text{ms})+(5)(409\,\text{ms})+(15)(422\,\text{ms})+(5)(423\,\text{ms})+(5)(426\,\text{ms})}{45}$$
$$= 401.56\,\text{ms}.$$

estimated from a sample of n observations. I call the estimated quantiles "vincentiles"

The second vincentile is the average of the next $n = 45$ observations:

$$V_2 = \frac{(5)(428\,\text{ms})+(5)(429\,\text{ms})+(5)(449\,\text{ms})+(15)(450\,\text{ms})+(5)(454\,\text{ms})+(10)(457\,\text{ms})}{45}$$
$$= 447.11\,\text{ms}.$$

(Heathcote, Brown, & Mewhort, in press) to distinguish them from the quantiles estimated by the procedure described earlier. It is typically assumed (Ratcliff, 1979) that the vincentiles are evenly spaced across the data. Note, however, that the vincentiles are quantile midpoints, so that $q + 1$ bins are obtained through Vincentizing. For instance, suppose that 10 deciles were computed by the standard quan-

The averaging procedure is continued throughout the remaining observations in the duplicated sample, yielding $V_3 = 490.67$ ms, $V_4 = 578.22$ ms, and $V_5 = 835.44$ ms.

The vincentiles V_1, V_2, and so on should estimate the 10th, 30th, 50th, 70th, and 90th quantiles. It is informative to compare the values of the vincentiles to the estimates of the quantiles found using the standard quantile estimation procedure. For $p = .10$, $[np] = 4$ and $[np] + 1 = 5$. The average of the 4th and 5th order statistics (409 and 422 ms) is $\hat{t}_{.1} = 415.5$ ms. For $p = .30$, $[np] = 13$ and $[np] + 1 = 14$. The average of the 13th and 14th order statistics (450 and 450 ms) is $\hat{t}_{.3} = 450$ ms. Continuing in this way, $\hat{t}_{.5} = 482.50$ ms, $\hat{t}_{.7} = 567.00$ ms, and $\hat{t}_{.9} = 810$ ms. Although $\hat{t}_{.3} = 450$ ms is close to the value $V_2 = 447.11$ ms, none of the other vincentiles are as close to the estimated quantiles. Nor do the vincentiles divide the sample into equally frequent groups. It turns out that the only time that vincentiles are estimates of the quantiles to which they are supposed to correspond is when the sample is drawn from a symmetric distribution (Heathcote et al., 2000). Simulations show that the vincentiles do not correspond to known quantiles for nonsymmetric distributions, and therefore they are not useful for estimating RT CDFs (Van Zandt, 2000).

The major attraction of the Vincentizing procedure is that it allows for averaging of RT distributions across subjects in an experiment (Ratcliff, 1979). This is useful when small sample sizes prevent accurate estimates of RT distributions for individual subjects (although CDFs and quantiles can be accurately estimated with as few as 50 observations; see Van Zandt, 2000). To average RT distributions across subjects, the vincentiles are computed for each subject's data and then averaged. Because each vincentile corresponds (presumably) to a particular percentile rank, the resulting averages can be used to construct the EDF. However, because the vincentiles do not typically correspond to known percentiles, averaging should be performed using standard quantiles rather than the vincentiles. There seems to be no particular benefit to using vincentiles instead of quantiles, and using vincentiles may introduce error, depending on the goals of the analysis.

The Density Function

Probably the most popular and easiest method for density estimation is the simple histogram. Observations are binned, and the relative frequency of the number of observations within each bin is used as a density estimate. Unfortunately, there is no best estimator for the density function as there was for the CDF. A large area in statistics is devoted to density function estimation, only a little of which may be touched on in this chapter. See Silverman (1986) for a basic and accessible treatment of this problem.

The issue of unbiased and consistent estimators for density functions is a tricky one. To illustrate why, consider a rather large class of density function estimators called *general weight function estimators*. The simple histogram is one member of this class. Associated with each of the estimators in this class is a parameter h_n—sometimes called a smoothing or bandwidth parameter—that depends on the sample size n. In the case of a simple histogram, h_n would be the width of the bins. In general, the larger n is, the smaller h_n needs to be. Under some fairly general constraints, to be sure that the estimate is asymptotically unbiased, it must be that $\lim_{n \to \infty} h_n = 0$. But even if this holds, to ensure that the estimator is consistent, it must also be that $\lim_{n \to \infty} nh_n = \infty$. Thus, h_n must go to zero as n gets large, but it cannot go to zero too quickly. For any particular density estimator, bias will be a function of the sample size n and the true underlying density, which in practice is always unknown. Furthermore, RT densities have a special problem in their skew, which makes some potential estimators unsuitable. It is important to realize that a density estimate is probably biased, that the degree of bias will be unobservable, and that the bias will not necessarily get smaller with increases in sample size.

For this chapter, I present two types of density estimators. The simple and very popular histogram estimators are easy to compute but can be inaccurate. Kernel estimators are more accurate, but they are a little more difficult to understand and require more computation. These two types of estimators barely begin to cover the statistical literature on nonparametric density estimators. There are more accurate estimators than the ones presented here. However, it is especially important to remember that density estimation is an exercise in descriptive statistics only. Under no circumstances should parameter estimation (i.e., model fitting) depend in some way on a density estimate. Appropriate parameter estimation methods will be discussed shortly. For graphical purposes, the kernel estimator described later should suffice.

Histogram Estimators

Histogram estimators are perhaps the most well-known density estimators. Construction of the histogram estimate is fairly simple and involves selecting r bins with bin boundaries $\{t_0, t_1, t_2, \ldots, t_r\}$ along the time axis. The estimate is a function of the number of observations falling in each bin:

$$\hat{f}(t) = \frac{\text{number of observations in bin } i}{n h_i},$$
$$t_{i-1} \leq t < t_i,$$

where $h_i = t_i - t_{i-1}$ is the width of the ith bin. The bins can be of fixed width or can vary according to the density of the observations along the time axis.

For fixed-width estimators, an origin t_0 and a bandwidth h_n are selected, and the bin boundaries are computed as $\{t_0, t_0 + h_n, t_0 + 2h_n, \ldots\}$. The histogram estimate for the Left Only (s) data is shown in Figure 12.3, using $t_0 = 200$ ms and $h_n = 50$ ms. Unfortunately, there is no automatic way to select t_0 or h_n and no systematic way to adjust h_n with sam-

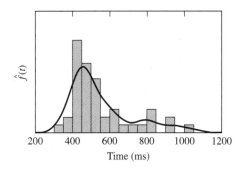

Figure 12.3 The histogram density estimate (bars) and Gaussian kernel estimate (solid curve) for the RTs from the Left Only (s) condition.

ple size to ensure asymptotic unbiasedness or consistency of the estimator. An appropriate t_0 and h_n must be selected after inspecting the sample for which the density is to be estimated.

For this reason, variable-width histograms that specify the frequency of observations within each bin are frequently used in RT analysis. One such estimator is based on the vincentiles (Ratcliff, 1979). For this estimator, the vincentiles are assumed to divide the sample into equally probable intervals (with the exception of the fastest and slowest bins), as described earlier. The height of the estimate for each bin is then computed so that the area of the interval is equal to $1/q$ (the number of vincentiles).

I previously investigated the accuracy of histogram estimators, both fixed and variable widths, for a number of different RT models (Van Zandt, 2000). Unfortunately, variable-width estimators based on quantiles and vincentiles were highly inaccurate and quite variable even for very large sample sizes. As I demonstrated earlier, the vincentiles do not divide the sample into groups of equal frequency, so the heights of the density estimate computed under this assumption are incorrect. The fixed-width histogram performed better than density estimates based on quantiles, but

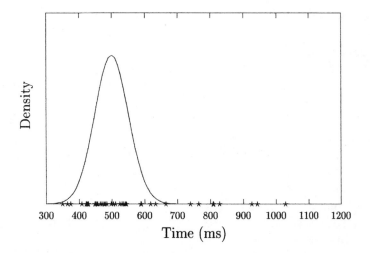

Figure 12.4   The method of Gaussian kernel estimation.
NOTE: The kernel is the normal density shown as a solid curve, and the sample observations are shown as points along the time axis.

because of the lack of an algorithm to adjust h_n with increasing sample size, accuracy did not improve with increases in sample size. Therefore, the histogram estimates should not be relied upon for any serious RT distributional analysis.

Kernel Estimators

The kernel estimator is also a member of the class of weight function estimators. A kernel is simply a function $K(x)$ that is integrated or, in the discrete case, summed, over x. To estimate the density at a particular point t, the kernel is summed over all of the observations T_i in the sample. Another way of looking at the kernel estimate is that every point on the estimate is a weighted average of all the observations in the sample.

The general form of the kernel estimate is

$$\hat{f}(t) = \frac{1}{nh_n} \sum_{i=1}^{n} K\left(\frac{t - T_i}{h_n}\right). \quad (2)$$

Notice the presence of the bandwidth parameter h_n in the denominator of the kernel variable. The larger h_n is, the smoother the esti-

mate will be: Large values of h_n will tend to minimize the deviations in the sample from the point t. The kernel $K(x)$ is itself a density function, a positive function that integrates to 1 over all x, and is typically symmetric. The kernel estimate of the density at the point t, then, is found by centering the kernel over the point t. Each observation is then weighted by the height of the kernel at its value, and the average height across the entire sample is the estimate of the density at time t. This is illustrated in Figure 12.4, which shows the observations from the sample Left Only (s) as points along the time axis, and a Gaussian kernel centered at 500 ms. The estimate of $f(500)$ is the average of the heights of the kernel at each of the observed points along the axis. Hence, the higher the density of the points around the center of the kernel (500 ms), the higher the estimated density function will be at that point.

The Gaussian kernel estimator is generally a good estimator of RT densities, especially for larger samples ($n > 500$; Van Zandt, 2000). It also gives reasonably accurate estimates for moderate samples ($100 \leq n \leq$

500), although accuracy will depend somewhat on the form of the distribution. For the Gaussian kernel, the kernel function $K(x)$ is the standard normal density function:

$$K(x) = \frac{1}{\sqrt{2\pi}} e^{-x^2/2}.$$

Note from Equation (2) that in the case of the Gaussian kernel, the bandwidth h_n serves as the standard deviation of the normal density. Alternative kernels may give more efficient estimates of the RT density (Silverman, 1986). Adaptive kernel techniques, in which the value of h_n varies with the local density of the sample, may also be worth considering. The adaptive techniques have the benefit of improving the estimate where few observations are obtained, a problem that is likely to be of concern with the long-tailed RT density. However, in my experience the simple Gaussian kernel gives acceptable density estimates with moderate ($n \geq 100$) sample sizes. Even with smaller sample sizes, the differences between the Gaussian kernel estimator and other, more complex estimators are quite small.

To illustrate how the Gaussian kernel estimate is computed, consider again the RT data from condition Left Only (s) given in Table 12.1. First, an appropriate bandwidth h_n needs to be determined. Using Silverman's (1986) method,

$$h_n = \frac{0.9}{n^{.2}} \min\left(s, \frac{IQR}{1.349}\right),$$

where s is the sample standard deviation and IQR is the interquartile range. This formula maintains the mean integrated squared error (the continuous version of the sum of squared error) between the estimated and true density at a small value. The value 0.9 can be adjusted, as long as it remains fairly small (less than 1), but not too small. Silverman recommends starting with 0.9 and then making adjustments

according to one's expectations about the density's appearance. The minimum statistic in this formula is a measure of the spread of the data and is selected to prevent problems of oversmoothing, in which critical details of an empirical density, such as bimodality or skewness, could be masked by selecting too large a value for h_n.

For the Left Only (s) data, $s = 164.58$ ms and $IQR = 165$ ms. Using Silverman's (1986) formula,

$$h_n = \frac{0.9}{45^{.2}} \min(164.58, 165/1.349) = 51.42.$$

One can now begin to estimate the density function. Consider the point $t = 500$, around which the kernel is centered in Figure 12.4. The height of this centered kernel at each of the observed sample points must be computed. Beginning with the smallest observation, $T_1 = 350$ ms, and using Equation (2),

$$K\left(\frac{t - T_1}{h_n}\right) \bigg/ h_n$$

$$= \frac{1}{\sqrt{2\pi}} \exp\left(-\frac{1}{2}\left(\frac{500 - 350}{51.42}\right)^2\right) \bigg/ 51.42$$

$$= .0050.$$

Similarly, for the next observation, $T_2 = 365$ ms,

$$K\left(\frac{t - T_2}{h_n}\right) \bigg/ h_n$$

$$= \frac{1}{\sqrt{2\pi}} \exp\left(-\frac{1}{2}\left(\frac{500 - 365}{51.42}\right)^2\right) \bigg/ 51.42$$

$$= .0111.$$

One continues in this way through all of the observations in the sample and averages the results to obtain

$$\hat{f}(500) = \frac{1}{45}(.0050 + .0111 + \cdots) = .0033.$$

This procedure is repeated for all points t at which an estimate of $f(t)$ is desired. Although it seems tedious, it is in fact quite simple, and the entire estimate can be computed using a single MATLAB command (see Appendix).

Notice that if the kernel is continuous in t, then the estimate $\hat{f}(t)$ is also continuous in t. This means that one can compute the estimate as finely or as sparsely as one needs. I computed the estimate for the Left Only (s) data at 10 ms intervals beginning from 200 ms. The result is shown as the curve in Figure 12.3. The sample size on which the estimate is based is quite small, so we might expect that the estimate is not a very accurate picture of the true density. In practice, one should obtain at least 100 observations for density estimation purposes and always remember that even with much larger samples, the Gaussian kernel estimate might be biased (Van Zandt, 2000).

The Hazard Function

Recall that the hazard function for a random variable X is defined as $h(t) = f(t)/\overline{F}(t)$: the variable's density function divided by its survivor function. A likely candidate for the estimate of $h(t)$ is therefore $\hat{h}(t) = \hat{f}(t)/(1 - \hat{F}(t))$. Although one can estimate $F(t)$ well, and one can estimate $f(t)$ reasonably well, problems arise in computing $\hat{h}(t)$ because the denominator goes to zero, inflating errors in the estimate $\hat{f}(t)$. The sparseness of data from the tail of the distribution in the sample generally makes the hazard function difficult to observe just at the point where the hazard function is most diagnostic (see Figure 12.1, bottom panel). This error inflation often results in large oscillations in the tail of the estimate, just before the estimate goes to infinity (because the denominator becomes $1 - 1 = 0$ for all $t > T_{(n)}$, where $T_{(n)}$ is the nth order statistic of the sample, or the largest observed RT).

A number of estimation methods try to work around this problem in the tail, including random smoothing (D. R. Miller & Singpurwalla, 1977), splines (Bloxom, 1985; Senthilselvan, 1997), and various types of kernel estimators (Tanner & Wong, 1983; Watson & Leadbetter, 1964). Unfortunately, those estimators that prevent oscillations in the tail of the hazard function often show artificial decreases in the tail, as well as severe biases in the early portion of the curve. Spline estimators have the additional difficulty in that in order to prevent the estimate from becoming negative, the shape of the hazard function (e.g., monotonic increasing) must be guessed in advance and appropriate constraints must be placed on the estimate (Bloxom, 1985). This renders the spline estimates less useful for examining questions such as whether a hazard function is monotonic increasing or increasing then decreasing. Note that more complicated spline estimators exist that do not have this problem, however (Senthilselvan, 1997).

In sum, hazard function estimation is very difficult, and conclusions based on such estimations should be backed up by independent evidence. The estimator that I have had the most success with is based on a kernel method, and it appears to be less biased and to preserve more accurate tail information than the other estimators presented.

The Epanechnikov Kernel Estimator

The basic idea of a kernel estimate was presented earlier in the context of density estimation. A function is centered over the point at which an estimate is desired, and the value of the estimate is a weighted sum of the value of the function at each observed point. The smoothing parameter of the kernel estimate h_n is a function of the spread of the data, as computed from the standard deviation and the interquartile range. The estimate used here is

$$\hat{h}(t) = \frac{\hat{f}(t)}{1 - \hat{F}(t)}, \tag{3}$$

where f will be estimated by $\hat{f}$ using an Epanechnikov kernel and $\hat{F}(t) = \int_0^t \hat{f}(t)$. Therefore,

$$\hat{f}(t) = \frac{1}{nh_n} \sum_{i=1}^{n} K\left(\frac{t - T_i}{h_n}\right),$$

and

$$\hat{F}(t) = \frac{1}{n} \sum_{i=1}^{n} \tilde{K}\left(\frac{t - T_i}{h_n}\right),$$

where $\tilde{K}(t)$ is the integral of $K(t)$ from $-\infty$ to t (see Silverman, 1986).

Unpredictable behavior in the tail of the hazard function estimate occurs because the decrease in $1 - \hat{F}(t)$ inflates errors in the estimate $\hat{f}(t)$, which are particularly pronounced in the tail where data is sparse. By estimating F with a kernel estimate, $\hat{F}(t)$ is continuous in t. That is, there is no discontinuity at the point $t = T_{(n)}$, which results in $1 - \hat{F}(t) = 0$. Eventually, however, $1 - \hat{F}(t)$ will be very close to zero, and the hazard function estimate will show a tremendous acceleration toward positive infinity. In my experience, however, this hazard estimate is to be preferred over many others because it gives the most accurate estimate for the greatest range, and the acceleration toward infinity is very sharp. Therefore, it is easy to see where the estimate is inaccurate. This is not true of other estimators, such as the variable kernel estimator (Tanner, 1983; Tanner & Wong, 1983), which, despite otherwise nice properties, always shows a slow decay in the tail of the estimate toward zero regardless of the true shape of the hazard function. This makes determining where the hazard estimate becomes inaccurate very difficult.

The Epanechnikov kernel (Silverman, 1986) is given by

$$K(x) = \begin{cases} \frac{3}{4\sqrt{5}}\left(1 - \frac{x^2}{5}\right) & \text{if } |x| < \sqrt{5} \\ 0 & \text{else} \end{cases}$$

This is a simple function that is similar to the Gaussian density, being symmetric and unimodal and integrating to 1. However, the domain of the Epanechnikov kernel is bounded between $-\sqrt{5}$ and $\sqrt{5}$. For density estimates this kernel is actually more efficient than the Gaussian kernel (although, in my experience, there is very little difference between them, but see Silverman, 1986). The integral of the kernel, necessary for computing $\hat{F}(t)$, is

$$\int_{-\sqrt{5}}^{x} K(u)\, du = \frac{3}{4\sqrt{5}}(x - x^3/15) + \frac{1}{2}.$$

To illustrate how the estimate $\hat{h}(t)$ is computed, consider again the Left Only (s) data from Table 12.1. One first must determine the appropriate bandwidth h_n, and to do this I again rely on Silverman's method, described above. However, I reduce the multiplying constant from .9 to .3, because the hazard functions I computed with the constant .9 were oversmoothed, resulting in significant bias for most points on the hazard estimate. I talk shortly about how one might objectively evaluate whether the bandwidth has been well-chosen. For this sample,

$$h_n = \frac{0.3}{45^{.2}} \min(164.58, 165/1.349) = 17.14$$

Next, the estimate for $f(t)$ is computed. For $t = 500$, the first term is

$$K\left(\frac{t - T_1}{h_n}\right) = K\left(\frac{500 - 350}{17.14}\right)$$
$$= K(8.75) = 0.$$

This first term is zero because the kernel K is zero outside the domain $[-\sqrt{5}, \sqrt{5}]$. Similarly, the next 12 terms ($i = 2, \dots, 13$)

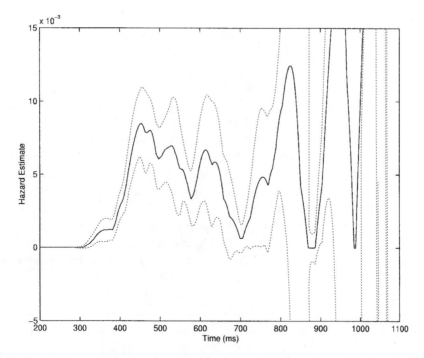

Figure 12.5   The Epanechnikov kernel estimate of the hazard function for the RTs from the Left Only (s) condition.
NOTE: The dotted lines show ± 1 estimated standard deviation of the estimate.

are zero. However, for $i = 14$,

$$K\left(\frac{t - T_{14}}{h_n}\right) = K\left(\frac{500 - 465}{17.14}\right)$$
$$= K(2.04) = .06.$$

Continuing throughout the sample,

$$\hat{f}(500) = (.06 + .13 + .20 + .24 + \cdots)/$$
$$[(45)(17.14)] = .0029.$$

Now $\hat{F}(500)$ must be computed. Proceeding in the same way, the first term in the expression for $\hat{F}(500)$ is

$$\tilde{K}\left(\frac{t - T_1}{h_n}\right) = \tilde{K}\left(\frac{500 - 350}{17.14}\right)$$
$$= \tilde{K}(8.75) = 1.00.$$

Continuing throughout the sample,

$$\hat{F}(500) = (1.00 + 1.00 + 1.00 + 1.00 + \cdots)/$$
$$45 = .5283.$$

The estimate of $h(t)$ for $t = 500$ is therefore

$$\hat{h}(500) = \frac{\hat{f}(500)}{1 - \hat{F}(500)} = \frac{.0029}{1 - .5283} = .0061.$$

The estimate of $h(t)$ for values of t from 200 to 1,100 ms is shown in Figure 12.5. The estimate increases and then decreases until 550 ms. It then increases and decreases over the range 550 ms to 700 ms. After 700 ms, the estimate oscillates, and the standard error of the estimate (estimated by bootstrapping[4]) is extraordinarily large, indicating that the oscillation is a result of error.

From this figure, one can see that the points estimated beyond around 700 ms are highly

---

[4]The standard errors estimated by bootstrapping were very close to the estimated asymptotic standard error of the hazard function estimate,

$$\frac{1}{n h_n} \frac{\hat{h}(t)^2}{\hat{f}(t)} \int K(u)^2 \, du.$$

suspect and can be ignored. The fact that the initial increase and decrease of the estimate to 700 ms appears to be real can be used to rule out candidate RT distributions that predict monotonic increasing hazard functions. (However, these results cannot be used to rule out *models* that predict increasing hazard functions, because parameter variability can produce nonmonotonic hazard functions; see Van Zandt & Ratcliff, 1995). Note that the sample size, $n = 45$, for this example is very small, and that a serious hazard function analysis would use samples of at least a few hundred observations.

To determine the value of the multiplicative constant in the bandwidth h_n, and also to evaluate the accuracy of the Epanechnikov kernel estimate, I simulated samples of RTs from known distributions and compared the estimated hazard functions to the real hazard functions. I simulated 1,000 samples of size $n = 45$ from an ex-Gaussian and a gamma distribution. The parameters of these distributions were the best-fitting (maximum likelihood) parameters derived from fitting the ex-Gaussian and gamma to the Left Only (s) data. The hazard function for each sample was estimated using the kernel method, and then the mean and standard deviations at each point were computed at each time point across the 1,000 estimates. The results are shown in Figure 12.6 together with the true hazard functions.

The true hazard functions, shown as dashed lines, rise monotonically to their asymptotes. Similarly, the average estimates, shown as solid lines, rise monotonically and closely to the true hazard function. For the ex-Gaussian,

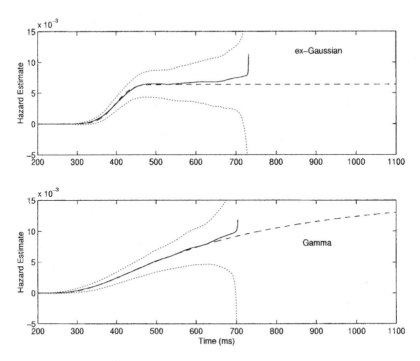

Figure 12.6 Mean Epanechnikov kernel estimates of ex-Gaussian (top panel) and gamma (bottom panel) hazard functions.

NOTE: The estimates are shown as solid lines, and the true hazard functions as dashed lines. The dotted lines show ±1 estimated standard deviation of the estimate.

the estimate rises to approximately the asymptote and remains there until about 700 ms, where the estimate becomes unstable. For the gamma, which asymptotes much later than the ex-Gaussian, the estimate also hugs the true hazard function quite closely until the estimate becomes unstable. If I use the constant .9 in the computation of h_n, there is a pronounced bias in both curves that results (for the ex-Gaussian) in an estimated asymptote much less than that of the true hazard function. By comparing the mean estimate to the true hazard function for a range of values of h_n, one can determine when the estimate is oversmoothed or undersmoothed. For different samples or different random variables, different smoothing parameters may be required.

There are two reasons why I like the Epanechnikov kernel estimator for hazard functions. One, mentioned earlier, is that it is clear when the estimates become unstable and when the behavior of the estimate can be disregarded. In Figures 12.5 and 12.6, this point occurred around 700 ms. The evaluation of instability is made by reference to the standard error of the estimate, which can be computed using bootstrapping or by computing the asymptotic standard error directly (see n. 4). The second reason is shown in Figure 12.6: Even with a very small sample size, the Epanechnikov kernel is surprisingly accurate for a function that is very difficult to estimate well. It bears repeating, however, that serious hazard function analyses will require samples much larger than the one used here. Also, the extent of bias will depend on the true distribution, which is in practice unknown.

Model Fitting

A common goal of any RT analysis is to evaluate hypotheses related to a proposed model of the cognitive task of study. Many models predict explicitly the distribution of RTs that should be observed. A natural point of investigation is therefore to fit the model to the data to determine whether the RTs are distributed as predicted. Such fits require an estimate of the distributional parameters. Often goodness-of-fit statistics, such as χ^2, are computed. Furthermore, changes of the estimated parameters under different experimental conditions can be evaluated according to whether the changes make sense in terms of the psychological interpretation placed on those parameters.

There are two good ways to estimate the parameters of a model. The first is maximum likelihood, and the second involves least-squares fits to the EDF. Whereas methods of maximum likelihood require numerical computation of the density function, least-squares fits to the EDF require numerical computation of the CDF. Therefore, when computation of the density is expensive or unwieldy, the CDF may be fit, or when the CDF is intractable, the density may be used in maximum likelihood.

Maximum Likelihood

The goal of maximum likelihood is to obtain estimates of the model parameters that make the probability of the observed sample as large as possible. Intuitively, the probability of having observed a particular sample should not be too small. Because the observations in the sample $\mathbf{T} = \{T_1, T_2, \ldots, T_n\}$ are *iid*, the probability of the sample can be written as

$$P(\mathbf{T}) = P(T_1 \cap T_2 \cap \cdots \cap T_n)$$
$$= \prod_{i=1}^{n} P(T_i).$$

Replacing the probability notation in this equation with the density function of T, the likelihood is defined as

$$L(\hat{\theta}) = \prod_{i=1}^{n} f_T(T_i; \hat{\theta}),$$

where $\hat{\theta}$ is a vector of parameters to be estimated (such as $\hat{\theta} = \{\hat{\mu}, \hat{\sigma}, \hat{\tau}\}$ for the ex-Gaussian distribution), and f_T is the theoretical (to-be-fit) density function. It is usually computationally simpler to work with the log likelihood function

$$\ln L(\hat{\theta}) = \sum_{i=1}^{n} \ln f_T(T_i; \hat{\theta}).$$

Because the relationship between L and $\ln L$ is monotonic, maximizing $\ln L$ also maximizes L.

The process of maximizing (or minimizing) any function requires a search algorithm. Given a set of starting values $\hat{\theta}_0$ for the parameters, the algorithm will adjust the values of the parameters until the function cannot be made any larger or smaller. There are many algorithms that one might use, including Gauss-Newton (Hartley, 1961) and the simplex algorithm (Nelder & Mead, 1965) among others. I do not discuss the selection of a search algorithm in this chapter, except to mention that I typically use a simplex algorithm (Van Zandt, 2000; Van Zandt et al., 2000). There are benefits and drawbacks to each method, and the choice must be determined by the analyses at hand. Prepackaged model-fitting applications, such as RTSYS (Heathcote, 1996) or those found in larger applications such as SAS, SPSS or MATLAB will typically explain the search algorithm that will be used if they do not provide a choice.

To illustrate parameter estimation using maximum likelihood, I step through how the ex-Gaussian distribution was fit to the Left Only (s) data in Table 12.1. The Gaussian kernel estimate of the density for this sample is shown in Figure 12.3. The expression for the ex-Gaussian density function is

$$f_T(t; \theta) = \frac{1}{\tau} e^{-\frac{t}{\tau} + \frac{\mu}{\tau} + \frac{\sigma^2}{2\tau^2}} \Phi\left(\frac{t - \mu - \sigma^2/\tau}{\sigma}\right),$$

where Φ is the standard normal CDF. Using the starting values $\hat{\theta}_0 = \{200, 15, 100\}$

for $\theta = \{\mu, \sigma, \tau\}$, the value of the density for the first observed RT is $f(T_1; \hat{\theta}_0) = f(350; \{200, 15, 100\}) = .0023$. For the second observed RT, it is $f(T_2; \hat{\theta}_0) = f(365; \{200, 15, 100\}) = .0019$. Continuing in this way, the values of the density function for all T_i in the sample are obtained. To compute the log likelihood, the log transform of all of the density values is summed:

$$\begin{aligned} \ln L(\hat{\theta}_0) &= \sum_{i=1}^{n} \ln f_T(T_i; \hat{\theta}_0) \\ &= \ln 0.0023 + \ln 0.0019 + \cdots \\ &= -364.4964. \end{aligned}$$

Now the values of the parameters must be changed to determine if the log likelihood ratio can be made larger. If $\hat{\mu}$ is changed to 300, the value of $\ln L(\hat{\theta})$ increases to

$$\begin{aligned} \ln L(\hat{\theta}) &= \sum_{i=1}^{n} \ln f_T(T_i; \{300, 15, 100\}) \\ &= \ln 0.0061 + \ln 0.0053 + \cdots \\ &= -319.4972. \end{aligned}$$

It would be nearly impossible, even with only three parameters, to adjust the values of $\hat{\theta}$ by hand to search thoroughly for a global maximum of the function $\ln L(\hat{\theta})$. This is why a good search algorithm is necessary. The surface of the function $\ln L(\hat{\theta})$ is shown in Figure 12.7 (the parameter σ is held constant in the figure). This function is smooth and well-behaved for the region plotted, meaning that there are no discontinuities and only one maximum. It is important to realize that this need not be the case in fitting RT distributions. Often, the function to be minimized or maximized is characterized by many local extrema and abrupt changes of contours, which complicates the search for global extrema. In this case, the maximum is quickly found to be $\hat{\theta} = \{\mu = 393.78, \sigma = 32.58, \tau = 156.58\}$. This point is marked on the figure.

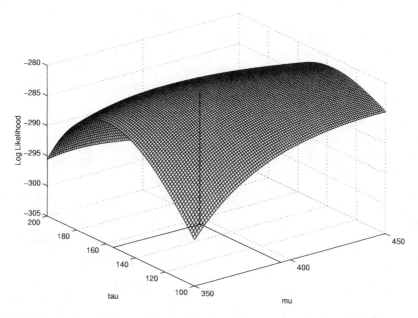

Figure 12.7   The surface of the ex-Gaussian likelihood function for the RTs from the Left Only (s) condition. The estimate $\hat{\sigma}$ is held constant, and likelihood is plotted as a function of $\hat{\mu}$ and $\hat{\tau}$.

Distributional Fits

An alternative to maximum likelihood estimation is least-squares fits of theoretical quantiles or CDFs. I have previously shown that this technique is of approximately equivalent accuracy as maximum likelihood when recovering parameters for a number of common RT models (Van Zandt, 2000). In this technique, a number of time points are selected in the range of the data, and the squared deviations between the percentile rank of the scores and the predicted percentile rank (as given by the CDF) are minimized. So, percentiles are computed for a set of times $\{t_1, t_2, \ldots, t_r\}$ according to the EDF $\hat{F}$ defined earlier. Then a set of estimated parameters $\hat{\theta}$ is selected, and the predicted percentile ranks $\{F_T(t_1; \hat{\theta}), F_T(t_2; \hat{\theta}), \ldots, F_T(t_r; \hat{\theta})\}$ are computed. The parameters $\hat{\theta}$ are adjusted to minimize

$$SSE(\hat{\theta}) = \sum_{i=1}^{r} [\hat{F}(t_i) - F_T(t_i; \hat{\theta})]^2.$$

A nearly equivalent procedure is to select the points $\{t_1, t_2, \ldots, t_r\}$ according to the proportion of observations falling between each (or according to the predicted proportions given by the model), and select parameters to minimize the χ^2 statistic

$$\chi^2 = n \sum_{i=0}^{r} (O_i - E_i)^2 / E_i$$

(Smith & Vickers, 1988; Van Zandt et al., 2000). In this expression, O_i and E_i are the observed and expected proportions of RTs between t_i and t_{i+1} ($t_0 = 0$ and $t_{r+1} = \infty$). One nice aspect of minimizing χ^2 is that the value of χ^2 after minimization gives an indication of how well the model is fit. However, such judgments must be made cautiously. If χ^2 is sufficiently small, the model fits well. But large values of χ^2 do not necessarily indicate an incorrect or misspecified model. The χ^2 statistic is very sensitive to sample size and frequently can be "significantly" large even when the model is correct (Van Zandt, 2000).

An important observation is that least-squares fits of the CDF result in parameter estimates that are of comparable accuracy to maximum likelihood estimate (MLE) parameters. Occasionally, the density function may be intractable or result in ill-behaved likelihood functions that make parameter searches difficult. Fitting the CDF can, in these circumstances, be considerably easier (Van Zandt et al., 2000). To illustrate the technique, I fit the ex-Gaussian CDF to the Left Only (s) data from Table 12.1. The ex-Gaussian CDF is given by

$$F(t) = \Phi\left(\frac{t-\mu}{\sigma}\right)$$
$$- e^{-\frac{t}{\tau}+\frac{\mu}{\tau}+\frac{\sigma^2}{2\tau^2}} \Phi\left(\frac{t-\mu-\sigma^2/\tau}{\sigma}\right).$$
$$(4)$$

I begin by selecting the same starting values as for the MLE procedure: $\hat{\theta} = \{200, 15, 100\}$ for $\theta = \{\mu, \sigma, \tau\}$. The EDF for the Left Only (s) data is computed as above for the time points between 200 and 1,400 ms. For each time point, the value of the ex-Gaussian GDF is then computed using Equation (4). For example, for $t = 200$ ms, $F(200) = .0546$. The EDF at time $t = 200$ ms is $\hat{F}(200) = .0000$. The first term in the sum of squared errors is therefore

$$(F(200) - \hat{F}(200))^2 = (.0546 - .0000)^2$$
$$= .0030.$$

For $t = 201$ ms, the process is repeated, obtaining

$$(F(201) - \hat{F}(201))^2 = (.0592 - .0000)^2$$
$$= .0035.$$

Continuing in this way through all values of t,

$$SSE(\hat{\theta}) = .0030 + .0035 + \cdots = 127.1986.$$

Now the parameter vector $\hat{\theta}$ must be changed to try to make $SSE(\hat{\theta})$ smaller. Changing μ from 200 ms to 350 ms, $SSE(\hat{\theta}) = 20.6001$ is obtained, a tremendous improvement. Continuing to adjust parameters and moving along the SSE surface shown in Figure 12.8, one reaches the minimum, $\hat{\theta} = \{\mu = 383.69, \sigma = 19.88, \tau = 166.94\}$, which is marked on the curve.

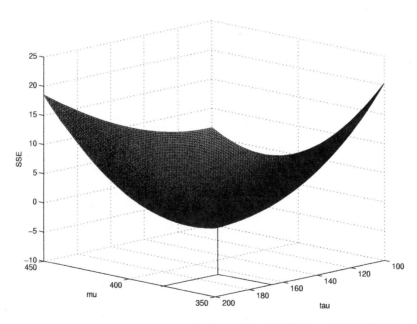

Figure 12.8   The surface of the ex-Gaussian sums of squares for the RTs from the Left Only (s) condition. The estimate $\hat{\sigma}$ is held constant, and sum of squared error (SSE) is plotted as a function of $\hat{\mu}$ and $\hat{\tau}$.

Notice that these parameter values are similar but not exactly equal to those obtained by maximum likelihood. I have shown elsewhere (Van Zandt, 2000) that, on average, the parameters recovered by least-squares fits are of the same accuracy as those recovered by maximum likelihood, at least for several popular RT models. This fact is convenient when the surface to be minimized or maximized is poorly behaved (i.e., has lots of local extrema and abrupt transitions).

Summary

In this first section, I discussed how RT distributions are described and how characteristics of the RT distribution may be estimated. These characteristics included not only the mean and variance of the distribution, but the functions that describe the distribution, that is, the density, CDF, and survivor and hazard functions. A vast statistical literature deals with these estimation problems, and the interested reader is encouraged to consult Silverman (1986) for background and further reading on density estimation, Wilcox (1997) for robust estimation procedures, and Wickens (1982) for discussion of estimation problems in a psychological context.

In the remainder of the chapter, I present a number of applications of RT distributional analysis that allow for testing of specific hypotheses concerning the nature and arrangement of mental processes measured by RT. I illustrate how these techniques are used by way of the data set presented in Table 12.1. However, the reader should be cautioned that these samples are much smaller than the samples that should be considered in a serious distributional analysis.

MODEL AND HYPOTHESIS TESTING

Over the past several years, a surprising wealth of theoretical tools has been developed that is indispensable for discriminating between different kinds of cognitive architectures. As explained earlier, the main idea is that the RT distribution can, when identified, provide information about the process that gave rise to it. If RTs from several conditions are examined simultaneously, it becomes possible not only to speculate about the forms of the RT distributions recovered, but also to use information derived from the relationships between the different RT distributions to make more general statements about processing architecture, even when the forms of the RT distributions are unknown. In this section I provide a review of some of these tools. I will not give any mathematical derivations of the tools examined; the reader should refer to the original references instead. My goal is to demonstrate how these tools can be applied to real data.

I start first by discussing the possible relationships between RT distributions in different experimental conditions that might be of interest. In this context, I present a number of important inequalities, relationships that hold or fail to hold between RT distributions under certain structural hypotheses. I also examine a number of ways that RTs can be decomposed into putative processing time components.

Orderings of Distributions

Hierarchical Inference

It is common to formulate hypotheses about the effects of certain experimental variables on RT. Masking a stimulus, making it surprising or emotionally disturbing, or increasing the number of possible responses could slow responses, whereas increasing its intensity or expectation could speed responses. But how exactly should an increase or decrease in processing time be measured? As I discussed in the opening paragraphs of this chapter, such changes are typically measured by mean RT. However, it may be possible that an experimental manipulation affects only slow responses, and that another affects only fast responses. It is not hard to imagine situations in which the mean RT is constant across conditions but the experimental factors have effects on other aspects of the RT distribution.

Townsend (1990) tackled this problem by considering all the ways that an experimental manipulation might affect RT and derived the implications of such effects not only on the mean RT, but also on the medians, CDF, densities, hazard functions, and likelihood ratio. For example, suppose that a manipulation slows mean RT by some amount, but the actual effect of the manipulation is to add some constant amount to the overall processing time. This means that the mean will increase by that constant amount, but it also means that the RT density is shifted by that constant amount. This in turn implies that the RT CDFs must be ordered, so that the CDF for the faster process is everywhere greater than the CDF for the slower process. This, then, implies not only that the mean RT is increased, but the median RT also, and that the probability of observing an RT from the fast condition that is faster than an RT from the slow condition is greater than 0.5 (see Townsend, 1990, Figure 12.1).

It makes sense, therefore, to examine changes in RT not just at the level of the means, but at the strongest level of Townsend's (1990) hierarchy, because all other weaker properties are then implied. If, for instance, I can show that the hazard functions for two experimental conditions are ordered, then it must follow that the CDFs, means, and medians are ordered as well. If I can show that the likelihood ratio (defined as the density of the faster process divided by the density of the slower process) is monotonic decreasing, then it follows that the hazard functions must be ordered and hence the CDFs, means, and medians are also ordered. If the density functions cross only once, then the CDFs must be ordered and the means and medians as well.

It is difficult, however, when dealing with estimates of functions, to determine whether significant violations of orderings exist. For the hazard function, for example, if the Epanechnikov kernel estimate is used, the variance of this estimate can be computed exactly only if the true hazard function is known. This is never going to be the case in practice, which leaves researchers at something of a loss. Not only the variance of $\hat{h}_{slow}(t)$ but also the variance of $\hat{h}_{slow}(t) - \hat{h}_{fast}(t)$ is unknown, so one cannot say with any certainty if the difference between the estimated hazard functions in the slow and fast conditions is greater than or less than zero. The only option is to estimate the variability in the hazard functions by bootstrapping, as described earlier.

For purposes of illustration, consider the data in Table 12.1 for conditions Both (ss) and Both (ll). Using Townsend's (1990) system of hierarchical inference, I attempt to determine the relationships between the distributions in these two conditions. The estimated density and hazard functions, EDFs, and likelihood ratio for these two samples are shown in Figure 12.9. The mean RT for condition Both (ll) is 469 ms, and for condition Both (ss) is 525 ms. In terms of the means, one can say that reducing the size of the circles in the detection task slowed responding. However, using Townsend's hierarchy, much more can be said. Examining the densities (top left panel), one can see that they cross exactly once. Also, the Both (ss) hazard function tends to dominate the Both (ll) hazard function (bottom left panel). These two characteristics of the samples show that the CDFs and therefore also the means and medians must be ordered. The relationship between the CDFs is verified in the figure: The EDF for the Both (ll) condition is everywhere larger than the EDF for the Both (ss) condition. The medians are 458 ms and 487 ms for the Both (ll) and Both (ss) conditions, respectively, as implied by the ordering of the EDFs.

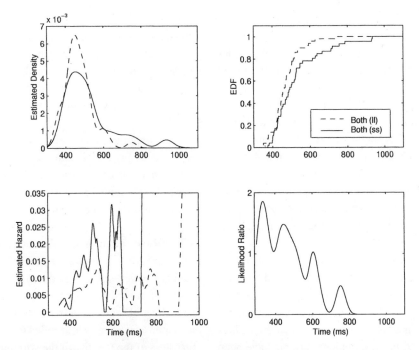

Figure 12.9 Estimated density functions (top-left panel), empirical distribution functions (EDF, top-right panel), estimated hazard functions (bottom-left panel), and likelihood ratio (bottom-right panel) for the Both (ss) (solid lines) and Both (ll) (dashed lines) conditions.

The strongest condition that we can examine for RTs under Townsend's (1990) hierarchy is the shape of the likelihood ratio. To estimate the likelihood ratio, I divided the Gaussian kernel density estimate of the Both (ll) condition by the Gaussian kernel density estimate of the Both (ss) condition. The result is shown in Figure 12.9 (bottom right panel). The estimate of the likelihood ratio decreases, but it wiggles along the way. Are these nonmonotonicities due to error in the density estimates, or are they real? To answer this question, I computed the standard error of the estimated likelihood at each time point using 1,000 bootstrapped samples. The results are shown in Figure 12.10 as error bars around the original estimate shown in Figure 12.9. Clearly, the variance of the estimate is very large at some points, especially for very fast and very slow RTs.

It appears from Figure 12.10 that the estimated likelihood ratio is not monotonic decreasing. The extent of the variance surrounding some of the nonmonotonicities

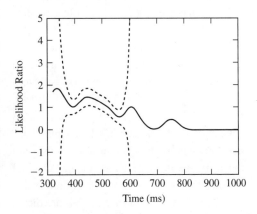

Figure 12.10 Likelihood ratio (solid curve) from Figure 12.9 (bottom right) plotted with estimated ± 1 standard deviation (dashed curves).

suggests that they are due to error in the density estimates, especially the very first non-monotonicity around 325 ms and all wiggles after 600 ms. However, the nonmonotonicity between 400 and 500 ms cannot be so easily dismissed. One might suspect that the method of dividing the two Gaussian kernel estimators is not the best way to estimate nonparametrically the likelihood ratio. Alternative methods are given by Dykstra, Kochar, & Robertson (1995), including a procedure for testing the hypothesis that the likelihood ratio is nondecreasing. I do not review these procedures here.

In sum, the hierarchical orders investigated by Townsend (1990) provide a broad basis for characterizing the effects of an experimental variable on RT. It should also be noted that these insights between the functional characterizations of a random variable have been very useful in the development of additional theoretical tools, some of which are presented next.

Parallel Channel Models and Self-Terminating Processes

Parallel channel models are a broad class of models that assume that information flows through more than one pathway toward the execution of a response. Some examples of these models are sequential sampling models (Grice, Canham, & Boroughs, 1984; Marley & Colonius, 1992; McGill, 1963; Pike, 1973; Vickers, 1979), and other examples make no mechanistic assumptions about how information flows (Mordkoff & Yantis, 1991; Egeth, Folk, & Mullin, 1989). These models are often conceptualized as a race in which each channel corresponds to a potential response and the response is made based on the channel that accumulates the requisite amount of information first. RTs for race models are therefore distributed as the minimum of the processing times for all of the channels. Such race models are often called self-terminating

because processing ends before all the channels are finished. Other models require that all channels complete processing before a response is made, and RTs are distributed as the maximum of the processing times for all of the channels. These models are often called exhaustive.

Many hypotheses have been proposed and tested about parallel channel models using RTs. A number of empirical tests based on the RT distributions have been designed, and I discuss several of them here.

The Race Inequality.   The race inequality (frequently referred to as the Miller inequality; Miller, 1982) was developed in the context of the redundant targets paradigm. In this task an observer is asked to make a simple response as soon as a stimulus is detected, regardless of the identity of the stimulus. The channels through which information flows depend on the properties of the stimulus. For instance, there could be visual and auditory channels for stimuli that can be either visual or auditory. There could be separate spatial channels for stimuli that appear in different locations. There could be channels defined by the nominal identities of the stimuli (e.g., animal versus vegetable). In the redundant targets paradigm, one or more stimuli might be presented simultaneously. It is assumed that the detection response can be made as soon as any channel signals the presence of a stimulus.

If stimuli are presented simultaneously to more than one channel, detection RT typically decreases relative to the detection RT for a single stimulus presented to one channel only. Because the RT in the redundant target case is assumed to arise from a race, some decrease in overall RT would be expected statistically. This is called the *statistical advantage:* The minimum of two random variables will have a smaller mean than the means of either of the two random variables alone. However, if there is any interaction between the two channels, one might expect to see a greater decrease in the redundant target mean RT than would be expected from a simple race, or one might expect to see not quite enough of a decrease if the two channels interfere with each other.

The race inequality is an empirical relationship between the RT distribution functions for the redundant and single target conditions that must hold if a parallel race model is responsible for the detection RTs. If the two channels (stimuli) are L and R, and F_{LR} is the RT CDF for the redundant condition and $F_{\overline{L}R}$ and $F_{L\overline{R}}$ are the RT CDFs for the R-only and L-only conditions, respectively, the race inequality [5] states that

$$F_{LR}(t) \le F_{\overline{L}R}(t) + F_{L\overline{R}}(t).$$

If this inequality is violated, then the parallel channel model is falsified. (It does not follow, however, that if the inequality holds, then the parallel channel model must be true.) The inequality can be tested empirically by estimating the RT CDFs in each condition $(LR, \overline{L}R,$ and $L\overline{R})$, and examining $\hat{F}_{LR}(t)$ versus $\hat{F}_{\overline{L}R}(t) + \hat{F}_{L\overline{R}}(t)$ for all values of t. Clearly, it is the faster RTs for which the inequality will be diagnostic. For longer RTs, the right-hand side of the inequality approaches 2, whereas the left-hand side approaches 1, so the inequality will always hold for long RTs.

This analysis can be applied to the data in Table 12.1. Consider the RTs collected in conditions Both (ii) (LR), Left Only (i) $(L\overline{R})$, and Right Only (i) $(\overline{L}R)$, where i is either s or l. The channels that are proposed to be operating in this task are spatial in nature, so that Both (ii) is the redundant condition—targets are present in both channels. Left Only (i) and Right Only (i) are the single target conditions. For each condition, the EDF must be computed as defined in Equation (1). Three sequences of cumulative proportions are obtained for each time point t between 300 ms and 1,200 ms for each sample of RTs: $\hat{F}_{L\overline{R}}(t)$, $\hat{F}_{\overline{L}R}(t)$, and $\hat{F}_{LR}(t)$. Then the sequence $\hat{F}_{L\overline{R}}(t) + \hat{F}_{\overline{L}R}(t)$ is examined and compared to $\hat{F}_{LR}(t)$ at each time point t. The results for both $i = s$ and $i = l$ are shown in Figure 12.11 in terms of the difference $\hat{F}_{LR}(t) - [\hat{F}_{L\overline{R}}(t) + \hat{F}_{\overline{L}R}(t)]$.

Violations of the race inequality occur whenever $\hat{F}_{LR}(t)$ is greater than $\hat{F}_{L\overline{R}}(t) + \hat{F}_{\overline{L}R}(t)$, or when the differences shown in Figure 12.11 are positive. The small target differences are shown in the top panel, and the large target differences are shown in the bottom panel. Both conditions show small positive excursions of the difference for very fast RTs. Are these excursions significant violations of the race inequality? The answer to that question seems to be no, based on the estimated standard deviations of the difference computed (again) by bootstrapping the sample. The error bars plotted around each difference as a dotted line show no positive excursions that are significantly different from zero. One therefore cannot conclude that the race inequality is violated in these data and must retain the hypothesis that the left and right channels operate in parallel. Of course, the sample sizes under consideration are quite small, and any serious effort to use the race inequality should use as many observations as possible.

Some efforts to test the race inequality have used sequential z-tests for each estimated point of the inequality. Because the numbers of observations falling below a point on the CDFs are binomial random variables, it is straightforward to construct the appropriate

---

[5]Note that this relationship between the CDFs is a special case of Boole's inequality: $P(L \cup R) \le P(L) + P(R)$, for events L and R, and Boole's inequality holds regardless of the degree of dependence between L and R. Note also that to apply this inequality, one must make the nontrivial assumption that the marginal CDFs for the left and right channel finishing times in the redundant condition are equal to the L-only and R-only CDFs, respectively. This assumption is called *context independence* (Colonius, 1990).

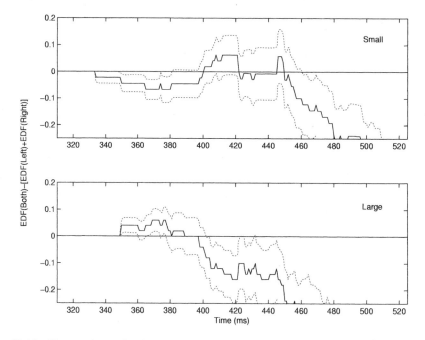

Figure 12.11 The race inequality for the small (top panel) and large (bottom panel) in the redundant targets conditions.

NOTE: The inequality is plotted as the difference between the redundant target empirical distribution function [EDF(Both)] and the sum of the single target empirical distribution functions [EDF(Left) − EDF(Right)].

z statistics for every time point and examine their p values. However, this procedure fails to consider that the points on each curve are not independent from each other. This dependence between the points artificially inflates the likelihood that significant differences will be found. That is, if one point along the inequality is spuriously significant, the points immediately surrounding it are likely to be as well. Bootstrapping to estimate the standard errors avoids this problem.

The Grice Inequality. An inequality closely related to the race inequality is the so-called Grice inequality (Grice, Canham, & Gwynne, 1984; Townsend & Nozawa, 1995). As for the race inequality, the Grice inequality relates the finishing time distributions for two processing channels in the conditions of the redundant targets paradigm. Colonius (1990)

has shown that the race and Grice inequalities correspond to maximal negative and positive dependence (respectively) between the parallel channels. Where the race inequality provides the upper (negative dependence) bound, the Grice inequality provides the lower (positive dependence) bound. The redundant targets RT distribution must satisfy (see n. 5)

$$\max\{F_{\overline{L}R}(t), F_{L\overline{R}}(t)\} \leq F_{LR}(t)$$

if a parallel channel race model is the appropriate processing architecture.

The data were analyzed with respect to the Grice inequality as for the race inequality. The maxima of the EDFs for the Left Only (i) and Right Only (i) conditions were computed at all time points and compared to the EDF for the Both (i) condition. The difference between the maximum and the Both (i) EDF is shown in Figure 12.12 together with error

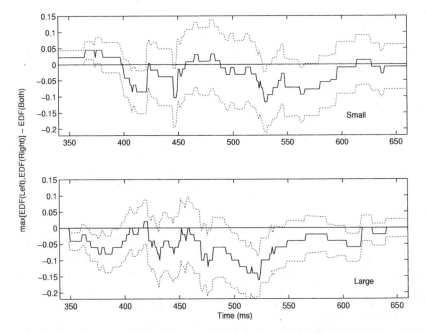

Figure 12.12   The Grice inequality for the small (top panel) and large (bottom panel) in the redundant targets conditions.

NOTE: The inequality is plotted as the difference between the maximum of the single target empirical distribution functions max[EDF(Left),EDF(Right)] and the redundant target empirical distribution function [EDF(Both)].

bars (dotted lines) of plus and minus 1 standard error computed via bootstrapping 1,000 samples. Positive differences are violations of the Grice inequality. Again, for both the small and large circle conditions, not one of the violations is significantly different from zero. Therefore one cannot conclude that these data are not generated by a parallel channel model.

The Survivor Function Interaction Contrast and Processing Capacity.   Townsend and Nozawa (1995) investigated the Miller and Grice inequalities in a more general context. They noted that the redundant target paradigm is a specific case of the more general double factorial design, in which two experimental factors are assumed to influence two separate processing channels (see the section titled "Selective Influence"). In the running example, the two factors are the size of the

circles (small or large) and the visual field in which they are presented (left or right). The size of the circle in one visual field is assumed to influence the processing time associated with only the channel in that visual field. That is, the size of the circles *selectively influences* the processing times in the left and right channels. The goal is to determine the relationship between the two (or more) channels. Must processing on both channels finish (an exhaustive strategy), or can a response be made as soon as one channel finishes (a self-terminating strategy)? Can processing take place in both channels at the same time (a parallel architecture), or must processing in the second channel wait until processing in the first channel is finished (a serial architecture)?

Letting l and s represent the conditions in which a large and small circle was presented, respectively, and letting $\overline{F}_{ij}(t)$ be the survivor function when stimulus i is presented in the left channel and stimulus j is presented in the right channel, the Grice and race inequalities can be recast in terms of the survivor functions:

$$\overline{F}_{sl}(t) + \overline{F}_{ls}(t) - 1 \leq \overline{F}_{ll}(t)$$
$$\leq \min\{\overline{F}_{sl}(t), \overline{F}_{ls}(t)\}.$$

Notice that this expression assumes that targets of different strength are presented in both the left and right channels. The redundant targets paradigm, to which the race and Grice inequalities are typically applied, is the special case in which the "low" level of the stimulus is actually a zero intensity level. As Townsend and Nozawa (1995) noted, the race and Grice inequalities are really statements about the *capacity* of the process. If both the race and Grice inequalities hold, the process is unlimited in capacity, meaning that the channels neither speed up nor slow down when both channels are processing. Increasing the amount of information to be processed does not harm the efficiency of the channels. If the Grice inequality is violated, the process is very limited in capacity: Processing that occurs in both channels slows the system down. If the race inequality is violated, the process is supercapacity: Processing that occurs in both channels improves system performance. Miller (1982) called such channels *coactive,* meaning that information passes between them in such a way that responses can be executed more quickly if both channels are occupied.

Townsend and Nozawa (1995) used the survivor functions to examine processing architectures not only in terms of the channels through which information flows but also in terms of their capacities. Of particular importance is the *survivor function interaction contrast,* given by

$$IC(t) = \overline{F}_{ss}(t) - \overline{F}_{sl}(t) - \overline{F}_{ls}(t) + \overline{F}_{ll}(t). \quad (5)$$

Capacity of the system can be examined using the *capacity coefficient:*

$$C(t) = \frac{-\ln \overline{F}_{LR}(t)}{-\ln \overline{F}_{L\overline{R}}(t) - \ln \overline{F}_{\overline{L}R}(t)}. \quad (6)$$

Note the difference between these two expressions. In the case of $IC(t)$, the important predictions are made with different levels of stimuli in both channels. In the case of $C(t)$, stimuli are present in only one or both of the channels—the redundant targets paradigm. The log survivor functions used in the capacity coefficient have to do with the relationship between the survivor function and the hazard function and with the fact that the hazard function reflects the processing capacity of the channels. See Townsend and Nozawa for more details on this measure.

Townsend and Nozawa (1995) derived the predicted form of the interaction contrast for different processing architectures. These predictions are shown in Table 12.2. For the capacity coefficient, if $C(t) > 1$ for all or some times t, processing is supercapacity (improves with additional stimuli to be processed) for those times t. If $C(t) < 1$ for all or some times t, processing is limited in capacity for those times t. If processing is unlimited in capacity, $C(t) = 1$. Townsend and Nozawa also investigated the implications of supercapacity processing with regard to violations of the Miller inequality. The relationships between these properties are discussed in their paper.

Table 12.2 Survivor Function Interaction Contrast Predictions for Different Cognitive Architectures (After Townsend & Nozawa, 1995.)

Serial self-terminating	$IC(t) = 0$ for all t
Serial exhaustive	$IC(t) < 0$ for $t < t^*$ and $IC(t) > 0$ for $t > t^*$
Parallel self-terminating	$IC(t) > 0$ for all t
Parallel exhaustive	$IC(t) < 0$ for all t
Coactivation	$IC(t) < 0$ for $t < t^*$ and $IC(t) > 0$ for $t > t^*$

Using the functions *IC(t)* and *C(t)*, Townsend and Nozawa (1995) showed that processing in the redundant targets paradigm seemed to occur over parallel channels, and that the response is likely to be based on a coactivation mechanism, although a race mechanism may still be plausible. One can perform the same sort of analysis of the data in Table 12.1. First, examine the capacity function. For the redundant targets conditions— Both (*ii*), Left Only (*i*), and Right Only (*i*), $i = s$ or l—the EDFs are constructed as before. Then, the EDFs are subtracted from 1 at each time point to arrive at estimates of the survivor functions. These values are then plugged into Equation (6) to estimate the function $C(t)$ over t. The results for the small and large circle conditions are shown in Figure 12.13, together with the bootstrapped estimates of the standard deviation of $\hat{C}(t)$. Any values of $\hat{C}(t)$ greater than 1 suggest supercapacity processing, such as might be found in

coactive processing channels, and any values of $\hat{C}(t)$ less than 1 suggest limited capacity processing.

Although portions of the early curves shown in Figure 12.13 suggest supercapacity processing, these portions do not seem to be significantly greater than 1 given the estimated standard deviations of the curves. It is clear, however, that the capacity coefficients are significantly less than one for much of the slower parts of the curves, indicating limited capacity processing for both small and large circles. One could do more at this point to determine, for example, whether the degree of limited capacity is above the limitation imposed by the Grice inequality, but I forgo that analysis here. Interested readers should consult Townsend and Nozawa (1995) for more details.

Next, the interaction contrast $IC(t)$ is examined. To compute this contrast, one needs the conditions corresponding to the factorial

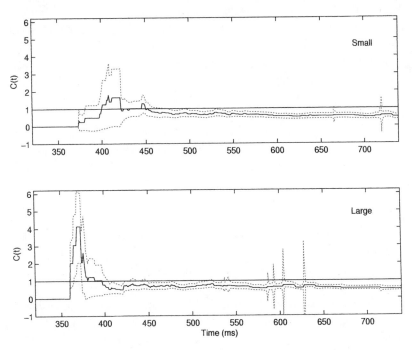

Figure 12.13   The capacity coefficient $C(t)$ for the small (top panel) and large (bottom panel) redundant targets conditions.

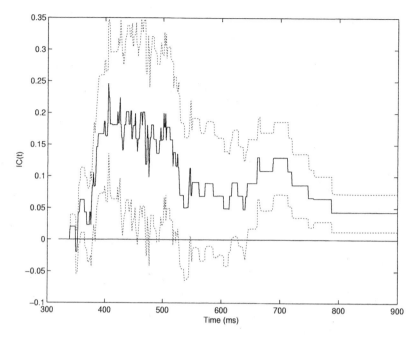

Figure 12.14 The interaction contrast $IC(t)$ for the redundant targets conditions.

combination of stimulus intensity with channel: Both (ll), Both (sl), Both (ls), and Both (ss). As before, the EDFs for the RTs in these conditions are computed. The EDFs are subtracted from 1 at all times t to estimate the survivor functions, and the results are plugged into Equation (5). The estimate of $IC(t)$ is shown in Figure 12.14 together with the bootstrapped estimate of its standard deviation. The estimate is positive for all values of t except for a single negative excursion around 350 ms. This excursion is not significantly less than zero. Although the estimate appears to be significantly greater than zero only at a limited number of points, all but a single point on the estimate are positive. From Table 12.2, one can determine that these data are consistent with parallel self-terminating processing of the channels or, if one wants to take seriously the estimated standard deviation of the estimate $\widehat{IC}(t)$, with serial self-terminating processing.

Again, it should be noted that the number of observations in these simple examples is probably not sufficient to draw strong conclusions about processing architecture in the detection task. Although the variance of the EDF is quite small even for samples around $n = 50$, functions of the EDF such as $C(t)$ and $IC(t)$ will have much greater variance. No one has yet performed simulation studies to determine the extent of variance in the estimates of these functions for standard models, so I have no concrete recommendations about sample size. Several hundred observations per condition, however, will probably provide sufficient power. (Townsend and Nozawa's 1995 experiment used approximately 100 observations per condition per subject.)

I conclude this discussion of distributional inequalities by noting that I have only touched on a few of the possible procedures that one might use to examine processing architecture. Many other techniques are discussed, for example, by Townsend and Ashby (1983) and Colonius and Vorberg (1994). Although these procedures are important in their own rights, they become even more powerful when used in the context of an explicit model of information processing. This is because the distributional inequalities predicted by certain models are necessary but not always sufficient conditions for the existence of those models. That is, the properties examined here are consistent with the models from which they were derived, but in many cases (e.g., the Miller inequality) they could also be consistent with other very different models, some with architectures that have not yet been considered (Townsend & Nozawa, 1997). However, when used to test characteristics of a model considered a priori, for which independent empirical evidence has been collected, these techniques can be very powerful indeed.

Reaction Time Decomposition

The goal of RT decomposition is twofold. First, one might wish to determine how two or more postulated stages of processing are arranged (e.g., in series or in parallel). Second, given that two or more stages of processing are serially arranged, the duration of one or more stages might be isolated from the overall processing time. In this section, I present the tools used to perform these analyses, beginning with a general theory of selective influence and an application, and followed by two techniques by which processing times might be isolated.

Selective Influence

One common aim of RT analysis is to infer the arrangement of individual processing components by examining the effects of experimental factors on RT. *Selective influence* of the factors is typically assumed (Dzhafarov & Cortese, 1996; Dzhafarov & Schweickert, 1995; Roberts & Sternberg, 1992). This means that a particular factor α will affect processing A in the processing chain but will not affect any other process B. Another factor β will affect process B but not process A.

The meaning of selective influence is obvious when the selectively influenced processes are stochastically independent, but the notion can be extended to dependent processes as well (Dzhafarov, 1999, in press; Townsend, 1984).

Tests of different processing stage compositions (e.g., serial versus parallel processing) often rely on the selective influence assumption, as in the previous section. Practically speaking, it is not an unrealistic assumption for a wide range of experimental paradigms. One example of presumed selective influence can be found in signal detection theory, in which it is proposed that a stimulus effect such as signal strength will affect discriminability but not bias; payoffs will affect bias but not discriminability. Given selective influence, one can perform a battery of tests to rule out different cognitive architectures.

Probably the most well-known RT tests are those related to Sternberg's additive factors method (Sternberg, 1969). Under selective influence, the changes in mean RT across experimental conditions in which different levels of α and β are manipulated are measured. If processing stages A and B are arranged serially, then one would expect to see an additive effect of α and β on mean RT (under certain general conditions). That is, the effect when manipulating α and β simultaneously will be equal to the sum of the effects when each are manipulated alone. If one were to plot mean RT as a function of α for each level of β, a series of parallel lines would result. Later work has concentrated on the predictions made by nonserial architectures, both at the level of mean RT (Schweickert, 1978) and at the level of the distribution (Townsend & Nozawa, 1995).

These issues have been tackled from a very general level that allows for testing not only of serial processing but also of a broad class of general decomposition rules. I present first Dzhafarov and Schweickert's

(1995) approach, followed by an application of their results to our data.

The General Theory. Dzhafarov and Schweickert (1995) provided a more general theory of RT decomposition under the selective influence assumption. This theory encompasses not just the additive effects predicted by the independent serial stage model but a wide range of composition rules connecting selectively influenced RT components. These components are assumed to be stochastically independent (like the independent serial stage model) or dependent in a special way (perfect positive dependence, described later). The range of composition rules covered by the theory includes all operations that are associative, commutative, and continuous. The authors call such rules *simple.* This broad class of operations includes simple addition ($a + b$), the maximum ($\max(a, b)$) and minimum ($\min(a, b)$) as special cases. These are the cases that this chapter concentrates on, although the theory applies equally to such unconventional composition rules as $a \times b$, $(a^p + b^p)^{(1/p)}$, and infinitely many others.

Suppose that, for an experimental task, there are two critical processing components A and B. Abusing notation for simplicity, let $A(\alpha)$ and $B(\beta)$ also represent the processing durations of the two components under levels α and β of two experimental conditions (say, the location of a light and its intensity). Assume that there are two levels of α, low and high, represented by $\alpha = 1$ and $\alpha = 2$, respectively, and that there are two levels of β, low and high, represented by $\beta = 1$ and $\beta = 2$, respectively. The durations $A(1)$, $A(2)$, $B(1)$, and $B(2)$ cannot be observed directly. What one observes in an experiment in which the levels of α and β are factorially combined is $T_{\alpha\beta}$ for each condition: T_{11}, T_{12}, T_{21}, and T_{22}.

One is interested in the way that $A(\alpha)$ and $B(\beta)$ combine to form $T_{\alpha\beta}$. For instance, if A and B are serial independent processes, then

$T_{\alpha\beta} \overset{d}{=} A(\alpha) + B(\beta)$.[6] If A and B are parallel independent processes, and a response can be executed as soon as either process is completed, then $T_{\alpha\beta} \overset{d}{=} \min[A(\alpha), B(\beta)]$. More generally, let any simple composition rule be denoted by the operator $\oplus$, so that $T_{\alpha\beta} \overset{d}{=} A(\alpha) \oplus B(\beta)$. Noting that

$$T_{11} \overset{d}{=} A(1) \oplus B(1),$$
$$T_{12} \overset{d}{=} A(1) \oplus B(2),$$
$$T_{21} \overset{d}{=} A(2) \oplus B(1), \quad \text{and}$$
$$T_{22} \overset{d}{=} A(2) \oplus B(2),$$

because $\oplus$ is associative and commutative, then

$$T_{11} \oplus T_{22} \overset{d}{=} [A(1) \oplus B(1)] \oplus [A(2) \oplus B(2)]$$
$$\overset{d}{=} [A(1) \oplus B(2)] \oplus [A(2) \oplus B(1)]$$
$$\overset{d}{=} T_{12} \oplus T_{21}.$$

Thus, one can examine the relationship between the observable random variables $T_{11} \oplus T_{22}$ and $T_{12} \oplus T_{21}$ to investigate candidate composition operators $\oplus$. Dzhafarov and Schweickert (1995) showed that if the above relationship holds, it must do so uniquely. Equality between the variables $T_{11} \oplus T_{22}$ and $T_{12} \oplus T_{21}$ cannot be satisfied by more than one operator $\oplus$ except in certain very artificial and stringent conditions.

We now need to be concerned about the relationship between A and B. Are A and B completely independent from each other, or are they dependent? A strong form of dependence is called perfect positive dependence (PPD), meaning that both A and B are increasing functions of the same random variable; when A increases by some amount, B must

---

[6]The relationship $\overset{d}{=}$ means "equal in distribution." When two variables are equal in distribution, it means that the values that each take on at a particular time might be different, but their probability distributions are the same. For instance, if we know that both X and Y are normally distributed with mean μ and variance σ^2, then it is not necessarily the case that $X = Y$, but it is true that $X \overset{d}{=} Y$.

also increase, and the amount of that increase will be perfectly predictable from the value of A. The distributional equality of $T_{11} \oplus T_{22}$ and $T_{12} \oplus T_{21}$ holds for both independent and PPD A and B as long as the T_{ij}s are all related by the same kind of dependence. However, the conclusions that we can draw from a positive or negative test of $T_{11} \oplus T_{22} \overset{d}{=} T_{12} \oplus T_{21}$ depends on whether A and B are independent or PPD. If A and B are PPD, then only one $\oplus$ can successfully decompose the RTs. That is, if $T_{11} \oplus T_{22} \overset{d}{=} T_{12} \oplus T_{21}$, then it must be the case that $\oplus$ is the correct decomposition. However, if A and B are independent, a successful test might be performed when in fact no decomposition is possible. In both situations, however, only one operation will result in a successful test.

In the special case where $\oplus$ represents addition and A and B are independent, Ashby and Townsend (1980) proposed the *summation test,* which was later applied to experimental data by Roberts and Sternberg (1992). Dzhafarov and Schweickert (1995) generalized this procedure to all simple operations $\oplus$, and Dzhafarov and Cortese formulated a statistical test of the null hypothesis $F_{T_{11} \oplus T_{22}} = F_{T_{12} \oplus T_{21}}$ (Cortese & Dzhafarov, 1996; Dzhafarov & Cortese, 1996). The next section demonstrates how this test is performed, using the data from the "Both" conditions in Table 12.1.

Application of the Theory. Let α represent the size of the dot presented in the left visual field and let β represent the size of the dot presented in the right visual field. The RTs in the Both (ss) condition will be represented by T_{11}, and the RTs in the Both (ll) condition will be represented by T_{22}. The RTs in the Both (sl) conditions will be represented by T_{12} and the RTs in the Both (ls) condition will be represented by T_{21}. For the case where independence is assumed, the test proceeds by constructing samples from

the distributions of $T_{11} \oplus T_{22}$ and $T_{12} \oplus T_{21}$. Denote the observed RTs in each condition as $\{T_{11}^1, T_{11}^2, \ldots, T_{11}^{n_{11}}\}$, $\{T_{12}^1, T_{12}^2, \ldots, T_{12}^{n_{12}}\}$, $\{T_{21}^1, T_{21}^2, \ldots, T_{21}^{n_{21}}\}$, and $\{T_{22}^1, T_{22}^2, \ldots, T_{22}^{n_{22}}\}$, where n_{11}, n_{12}, n_{21}, and n_{22} are the sample sizes in each condition. The notation T_{ij}^r indicates the RT observed on the rth trial, so it is important that the samples be *unordered*. We can then construct the samples $\{T_{11}^1 \oplus T_{22}^1, T_{11}^2 \oplus T_{22}^2, \ldots, T_{11}^{m_1} \oplus T_{22}^{m_1}\}$ and $\{T_{12}^1 \oplus T_{21}^1, T_{12}^2 \oplus T_{21}^2, \ldots, T_{12}^{m_2} \oplus T_{21}^{m_2}\}$, where $m_1 = \min\{n_{11}, n_{22}\}$ and $m_2 = \min\{n_{12}, n_{21}\}$.

For example, the unordered samples for T_{11} and T_{22} for the data shown in Table 12.1 are $T_{11} = \{484, 720, 485, \ldots\}$ and $T_{22} = \{536, 369, 430, \ldots\}$. If I wish to test the "minimum" decomposition, that is, that the RTs are of the form $T_{ij} = \min[A(i), B(j)]$, then I need to construct a sample of $\min(T_{11}, T_{22})$:

$$\{\min(484, 536), \min(720, 369),$$
$$\min(485, 430), \ldots\}$$
$$= \{484, 369, 430, \ldots\}.$$

I also need to do the same for the samples T_{12} and T_{21}. The observations in the two constructed samples are then ordered, and the EDFs are computed for both. For the "min" decomposition rule, the resulting EDFs are shown in Figure 12.15. The statistic that we need in order to test whether the min decomposition rule is appropriate—that is, whether the two EDFs shown in Figure 12.15 are statistically different from each other— is the maximum absolute value of the difference between the two EDFs across all time points: the Kolmogorov-Smirnov statistic, or the Smirnov distance. For the EDFs shown in Figure 12.15, this distance is $d = .1415$.

Dzhafarov and Cortese (1996) computed the asymptotic p values for this statistic under the assumption of independence and PPD. They showed that for large n, the p value of the Smirnov distance can be approximated by $1 - B(\sqrt{\frac{n}{2}}d)$, where $B(z)$ can be

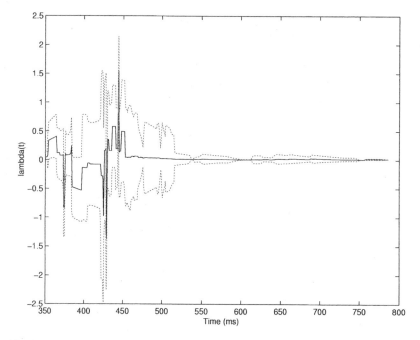

Figure 12.15   The rate function lambda (t) to test for the presence of an exponentially inserted stage of processing.

expressed as

$$B(z) = 1 - 2\sum_{j=1}^{\infty}(-1)^{j-1}\exp\{-2(jz)^2\}.$$

Note that this approximation holds only under the assumption of independence, or when the decomposition operator is min or max. For PPD, this approximation is actually the upper bound of a region containing the true p value, the lower bound of which is $1 - B(\sqrt{n}d)$.

The function B is easy to compute because it is something called a *theta function*. Mathematica and Maple, for example, both have built-in theta functions. I wrote a theta function for MATLAB, and it is included in the Appendix. Given that the observed Smirnov distance is $d = .1415$, and letting $n = 46.91$, the harmonic mean of the sample sizes $m_1 = 45$ and $m_2 = 49$, the p value of this statistic is approximately 1, indicating that the null hypothesis of equality in distribution must be retained. (A MATLAB routine to calculate the

upper and lower p values for any decomposition rule and dependence state is given in the Appendix.) Unfortunately, the small sample size ($n = 46.91$) means that there is very little power to reject the null hypothesis. Dzhafarov and Cortese (1996) showed that sample sizes of at least several hundred were necessary to obtain reasonable power—sample sizes easily obtained in most experiments but considerably larger than ours.

Under the PPD assumption, the test proceeds in almost exactly the same way, except that the samples are now formed by $\{T_{11}^{(1)} \oplus T_{22}^{(1)}, T_{11}^{(2)} \oplus T_{22}^{(2)}, \ldots, T_{11}^{(m_1)} \oplus T_{22}^{(m_1)}\}$ and $\{T_{12}^{(1)} \oplus T_{21}^{(1)}, T_{12}^{(2)} \oplus T_{21}^{(2)}, \ldots, T_{12}^{(m_2)} \oplus T_{21}^{(m_2)}\}$, where m_1 and m_2 are as before, but $T_{11}^{(1)} \oplus T_{22}^{(1)}$ (for example) is computed from the ordered samples as given in Table 12.1. For example, $\min(T_{11}, T_{22}) = \{\min(T_{11}^{(1)}, T_{22}^{(1)}), \min(T_{11}^{(2)}, T_{22}^{(2)}), \ldots\} = \{\min(374, 350), \min(381, 350), \ldots\} = \{350, 350, \ldots\}$. The samples for the two random variables are thus constructed;

the EDFs for each sample are computed; and the Smirnov distance is subjected to the decomposition test.

Although the decomposition test cannot tell us much about the process that produced the data in Table 12.1, this is because the sample sizes are too small to provide any power. The decomposition test is a very important method for testing hypotheses about mental architecture—far more powerful than traditional additive factors logic as applied to mean RT data—and should be considered whenever issues of processing stage arrangement are of concern. As with all of the tests presented here, the decomposition test should be used as one source of converging evidence to support a theory. If the assumption of selective influence is incorrect, then the outcome of the test will not be terribly meaningful.

Exponentially Inserted Stages

Ashby and Townsend (1980) explored RT decomposition under the assumption that an experimental variable resulted in the insertion of a stage of processing into a task's processing stream. This assumption was particularly important given the effort then being devoted to serial and parallel models of memory and visual search. Under the assumption of serial processing of some number of visual stimuli, a stimulus added to a display should require an additional stage of processing.

Ashby and Townsend (1980) explored a number of different hypotheses about the nature of the inserted stage of processing. For this chapter, I concentrate only on the case where the inserted stage has a processing time duration that is exponentially distributed. The reader should consult the original article for more information. Ashby and Townsend showed that a necessary and sufficient condition for an inserted stage to have exponential duration is that

$$\lambda = \frac{f_k(t)}{F_{k-1}(t) - F_k(t)},$$

where $k - 1$ represents the task before the experimental manipulation is made, and k represents the task with the experimental manipulation. The functions f_k, F_k, and F_{k-1} are the density and CDFs for conditions k and $k - 1$. It is assumed that the manipulation slows processing. For example, adding an item to a display of $k - 1$ elements to be searched will increase RT.

The condition above states that, for all times t, the ratio of the density function in the slowed condition (k) to the difference between the CDFs in the two conditions must be a constant λ, where λ turns out to be the rate of the exponentially inserted stage. To test whether this condition holds, Ashby and Townsend (1980) proposed estimating $f_k(t)$, $F_{k-1}(t)$, and $F_k(t)$ and using these estimates to compute the right-hand side of the previous equation. This will result in a series of values $\lambda(t)$. This series can then be subjected to a regression analysis to determine whether the slope of a least-squares regression line through the points $\lambda(t)$ is significantly different from zero. Ashby and Townsend proposed that the condition "holds" if the slope of the regression line is less than $1/10,000$.

As an example, consider the data from the Both (ll) and Both (ls) condition from Table 12.1. By making the right circle small—in the Both (ls) condition—RT is slowed by 31 ms. Is this slowing the result of inserting an additional, exponentially distributed stage of processing? I computed the Gaussian kernel estimate of $f_{LS}(t)$, and the EDFs $\hat{F}_{LL}(t)$ and $\hat{F}_{LS}(t)$. For every time point t, I then computed $\lambda(t) = \hat{f}_{LS}(t)/[\hat{F}_{LL}(t) - \hat{F}_{LS}(t)]$, giving the solid line shown in Figure 12.15. (The dotted lines are the standard error of the ratio at each point as computed from 1,000 bootstrapped samples.) The earliest sections of the curve vacillate around a constant value, and the later sections of the curve are constant around the value $\lambda = .02$. Regressing $\lambda(t)$ on t gives values of the slope and intercept of

$\lambda(t)$ of 0.000 (less than 1/10,000) and 0.016, neither of which is significantly different from zero.

Thus, the data from the Both (ll) and Both (ls) condition are consistent with the hypothesis of a serially inserted stage of processing. However, as in our previous examples, our sample sizes are very small, so power may be an issue. Ashby and Townsend (1980) showed that the constant λ could be recovered accurately with as few as 25 observations in the two conditions k and $k - 1$ when an exponential stage was present, but they did not examine power. Van Zandt and Ratcliff (1995) showed that a constant $\lambda(t)$ could be obtained from a model in which an exponential stage was not inserted, even though the constant $\lambda(t)$ is a necessary and sufficient condition for the presence of such a stage. That is, even though a constant $\lambda(t)$ implies that a serial exponential stage must have been inserted, other models can predict $\lambda(t)$ functions that are so close to being constant that they cannot be discriminated from the exponential models. This again underscores the importance of using techniques such as Ashby and Townsend's exponential RT decomposition in the context of an explicit model of processing that can be tested empirically, and as one piece of converging evidence among many.

Estimating a Processing Time

Suppose that RT can be modeled as the sum of two components, $T = R + D$. Often, R is a residual time, the unmodeled processing stages, and D is the decision time, the process for which a model exists and that can be tested. Now suppose that the distribution of R can be empirically estimated. As an example, consider Donders's (1868/1969) original method of subtraction, where the decision time in a go/no-go task is estimated by subtracting the time for simple RT (R) from the go/no-go RT ($R + D$). If enough observations of R are collected, then one can perhaps isolate the pro-

cessing time distribution of D and determine whether it is the same as that predicted by our model. To do this, we are going to make use of a convenient feature of Fourier transforms.

If the two variables R and D are independent and have density functions $f_R(t)$ and $f_D(t)$, respectively, then the density function $f_T(t)$ of RT is given by the *convolution* of the densities f_R and f_D:

$$f_T(t) = \int_{-\infty}^{\infty} f_R(u) f_D(t - u) \, du. \qquad (7)$$

Now, convolutions are either (at best) tricky to compute or (at worst) impossible to compute. However, something interesting happens if we examine the Fourier transform of $f_T(t)$. When applied to density functions, the Fourier transform is a special kind of expected value. It is the expected value of the function $\exp\{-2\pi i \theta X\}$, where i is the imaginary number $\sqrt{-1}$ and X is the random variable whose density is being transformed:

$$g(\theta) = \int_{-\infty}^{\infty} f(t) \exp\{-2\pi i \theta t\} \, dt.$$

The Fourier transform takes the variable X (or RT), which is a measure of time, and transforms it to the variable θ, which is a measure of frequency. The reader may recall that Fourier analysis allows one to write any function $f(t)$ as an infinite weighted sum of sine and cosine functions that vary in frequency. The Fourier transform function $g(\theta)$ provides the weights for each of those sines and cosines as a function of their frequencies θ.

Transforming both sides of Equation (7) into the frequency domain, one obtains

$$g_T(\theta) = g_R(\theta) g_D(\theta).$$

The messy convolution becomes simple multiplication after transformation. Further, if one has an estimate of $f_R(t)$ from one experimental condition and an estimate of $f_T(t)$ from another experimental condition, then one should be able to isolate $f_D(t)$ by transforming f_R

and f_T to g_R and g_T, estimating

$$g_D(\theta) = \frac{g_T(\theta)}{g_R(\theta)},$$

and then taking the inverse Fourier transform to the result, that is,

$$\hat{f}_D(t) = IFT\left[\frac{FT(\hat{f}_T(t))}{FT(\hat{f}_R(t))}\right],$$

where FT and IFT indicate the Fourier transform and inverse Fourier transform operators, respectively.

This technique has been used by Burbeck and Luce (1982), Green and Luce (1971), and Smith (1990), among others, with mixed results. Given the variance typically observed in RT data, it is often more difficult than the previous equations suggest to isolate uniquely a stage of processing. Before proceeding all the way through the steps just outlined, the data must be filtered. The process of filtering is identical to the kernel estimation problems already discussed: The data are smoothed, averaged, or truncated in some systematic way to make them less noisy. Smith examined a number of options for filtering noise from the data and showed how filtering the data after computing the Fourier transform is mathematically equivalent to using a kernel estimator of the density functions. Unfortunately, Smith also showed that recovery of reasonably accurate deconvolved density estimates requires several thousand data points per density, at least, which prevents me from demonstrating the procedure with the data from Table 12.1. Even with theoretically exact density functions, Smith demonstrated that a number of problems can arise if, for example, too few significant digits are used in the transform computation or if inappropriately designed filters are used.

Several tricks are required to perform a Fourier deconvolution successfully that I do not elaborate on here. Interested readers should consult Smith (1990) or a good numerical reference for details, such as Press, Teukolsky, Vetterling, & Flannery (1992). Although MATLAB has Fourier transform routines that are easy to use, the reader should not expect simply to step through the previous equations and obtain nice deconvolved density estimates. The reader should also be cautioned that even after the successful recovery of a candidate density for D, the decomposition obtained is not necessarily unique. That is, if there is error in the estimation of f_R or f_T, a density for D can be recovered, but it will not be the right one (Sheu & Ratcliff, 1995). This problem is particularly severe for densities that are sharply peaked, such as the exponential.

As Sheu and Ratcliff (1995) pointed out, once a density has been deconvolved from the data, there are no warnings that indicate when something might have gone wrong. The deconvolution technique does not care about the process that actually produced the RT data: Given a data set and a candidate estimate for the density of R, deconvolution will produce an estimated density for D even when the decomposition $RT = R + D$ is completely inappropriate. Again I must emphasize, as I have with all the techniques presented in this section, the importance of converging evidence in such a decomposition, that is, additional sources of evidence that suggest that the recovered f_D is in fact the correct one. Deconvolution should not be attempted without some a priori expectation of the form of the density that should result.

Dependence of Decision and Base Times

An approach related to both decision time deconvolution and selective influence of stages was suggested by Dzhafarov (1992; Dzhafarov & Rouder, 1996). Dzhafarov's techniques are useful primarily in psychophysical tasks, in which a stimulus can take on a fairly large range of values from weak to very strong. Typically, the time to detect the presence of a stimulus decreases with stimulus strength: for example, observers respond quite rapidly to the onset of a loud tone and more slowly to the onset of a soft tone. Dzhafarov (1992) used the finding that the decomposition RT $= R + D$ reflects mostly R for strong stimuli; that is, the decision time decreases to some small value as stimuli increase in strength (see also, e.g., Kohfeld, Santee, & Wallace, 1981). Therefore, the most direct way to estimate the distribution of R (required for the Fourier decomposition technique) is to take as R the RTs at the very highest stimulus strengths.

The quantiles of RT will decrease as a (not necessarily linear) function of stimulus strength. Under general assumptions about R and D, the quantiles of R at fixed percentiles can be estimated from the intercepts of regression lines computed for fixed percentiles of RT as a function of a "linearized" function of stimulus strength. Furthermore, whether the slopes of the regression lines for each quantile remain constant or vary will be determined by the dependent relationship between R and D.

The application of Dzhafarov's (1992) techniques is straightforward. The most difficult step is determining the function that linearizes the relationship between RT quantiles and stimulus strength. Once this function ($s[A]$, strength of the stimulus at amplitude A) has been found (by nonlinear regression), RT can be plotted as a function of $s(A)$, and slopes and intercepts can be determined by simple regression. Unfortunately, the present data set is inappropriate to demonstrate this technique, having only two stimulus strengths. Briefly, if R and D are independent, then the slopes of the regression lines should be equal for all percentiles. If R and D are PPD (see earlier), the slopes should increase as percentile increases. Dzhafarov's results suggested that the two components are positively correlated, because the slopes of the regression functions changed systematically with RT quantile. Dzhafarov

and Rouder (1996) gave further guidelines on the sample sizes required to distinguish accurately between types of dependence.

Mixture Distributions

It is usually hoped that the RTs collected in a condition in an experiment are sampled from a single distribution. This was the identically distributed assumption discussed earlier, and it is the critical assumption that allows us to attempt to estimate functions and perform inferential statistics. However, all RT researchers know that this assumption is probably false. The treatment of outliers was discussed earlier in this chapter. Outliers are RTs that are not distributed as the others in the sample. Often, the problem of fast guesses arises, in which RTs are collected from trials in which the stimulus was not processed. More generally, one might expect that the parameters of the process measured by RTs drift over time, perhaps from fatigue or from learning (Burbeck & Luce, 1982; Van Zandt & Ratcliff, 1995). RTs collected at the onset of a testing session might be sampled from a distribution with mean μ_1, but those collected at the close of that same session might be sampled from a distribution with mean μ_2. The parameters of the process may themselves be random variables that depend on particular aspects of the task. In this case, one must be prepared to deal with RTs collected from a very large number of populations, all with the same form (e.g., ex-Gaussian), but with different parameter values.

When a sample is assumed to arise from more than one population, the distribution of the random variable represented in the sample is a mixture. In psychology the binary mixture has received the most attention in the analysis of RTs. RTs are assumed to be sampled from one of two fixed distributions—for example, a guessing time distribution, in which the response is prepared before the stimulus is presented or processed, and a processing time distribution, in which the response is based on information obtained from the stimulus. Experimental conditions are designed to provoke changes in the guessing rate, such as emphasizing speed over accuracy. Although one might expect that the density function of the RTs obtained from a binary mixture would be multimodal, one mode reflecting the (usually fast) guesses and the other mode reflecting the slower process-based responses, binary mixtures result in multimodal densities only under fairly restrictive conditions. The presence or absence of bimodality, therefore, is not diagnostic of the presence or absence of a binary mixture.

Perhaps the most well-known diagnostic of a binary mixture is the *fixed-point property*, first discussed by Falmagne (1968). The fixed-point property states that the RT densities estimated for different experimental conditions should intersect at one and only one point. Taking into account the variability of the density estimates, the fixed-point property generally does not hold (Falmagne, 1968). Furthermore, even if it did, there would be no way to isolate the processing times from the guessing times without knowing the exact probability of guessing and the shape of the guessing time distribution.

It will not be possible to review the applications and results of mixture analyses as they have appeared in the cognitive psychology literature. Yantis, Meyer, and Smith (1991) provided a thorough review of the findings with respect to both mean RTs and RT distributions, and the reader is encouraged to consult this paper for more detail. It is important to note, however, that there are methods for isolating mixture components under more general conditions. A large statistical literature is devoted to just this problem. In psychology, Yantis et al. have proposed a multinomial maximum likelihood method that makes relatively few assumptions. They assume that RTs

are collected in a number of conditions, and that some number of those conditions represent the "basis" distributions. Basis distributions are those distributions that are not composed of mixtures, but of which mixtures are composed in the remaining conditions. The distinction between basis and mixture distributions is theoretically based and depends on the tasks for which RTs are measured. They then outline a simple technique that allows for recovery of the mixture probabilities in the "mixed" conditions. The technique also performs a goodness-of-fit analysis so that the hypotheses concerning the basis and mixture distributions and the mixing probabilities can be evaluated.

Determining the number of components in a finite mixture is the sticking point in mixture analyses. Priebe and colleagues (James, Priebe, & Marchette, 2000; Priebe & Marchette, in press) have investigated *semiparametric* methods for estimating the number of components of a mixture and the mixing probabilities. Unlike Yantis et al.'s (1991) approach of designating some conditions as the basis distributions and the other conditions as the mixtures of those, semiparametric methods require only a single sample and a parametric form for the densities composing the mixture. It is typically assumed that the basis densities are normal. Semiparametric methods compare the best-fitting parametric mixture of m distributions to a nonparametric (e.g., Gaussian kernel) estimate of the density. The number of components in the mixture is incremented, and the nonparametric density estimate is modified, until the difference between them is as small as possible. Under the assumption of normal basis distributions, James et al. presented conditions ensuring that the number of estimated components converges (almost surely) to the true number of components.

The utility of the semiparametric methods in RT analysis is limited at this point, primarily because of the normality assumption. (It should be noted, however, that the popular ex-Gaussian, discussed above, can be viewed as a mixture of normals with exponentially distributed means.) The best approach may be to model the mixing process directly, using empirical procedures to influence the mixing probabilities, and then to use these techniques to support or disconfirm the efficiency of the empirical procedures. Mixture analysis is difficult and without an explicit model of the process under study may be of limited utility.

CONCLUDING REMARKS

I began this chapter by emphasizing the importance of distributional analysis in the investigation of RT data. I defined the ways that RT distributions can be characterized, both at the level of means and variances and at the level of the functional descriptors of the RT distribution: the density, CDF, and survivor and hazard functions. I demonstrated how each function can be estimated from RT data and discussed briefly how theoretical parameters can be estimated from RT data. I then presented a number of powerful theoretical tools that can be used to test hypotheses about the properties of mental processes, including distributional ordering techniques, methods of RT decomposition, and a brief discussion of mixture analysis.

RT data is a very rich source of information about mental processing. However, the myriad components that enter into a single RT are surely far more complex than those considered by the models presented here. It is therefore very important that RT analyses be conducted in the context of one or more explicit mechanistic and quantitative explanations of the process under study. RT analysis without such explanations will not, in the long run, be very useful. RT analysis should also take place over several experimental conditions so

that the arguments for a particular model do not rest on goodness-of-fit statistics for limited samples (Roberts & Pashler, 2000).

The reason for this is that even with explicitly defined models in hand, RTs will not always be diagnostic. That is, the behavior of the RT distribution under different conditions will not necessarily be able to rule out alternative models. This means that no matter how sophisticated the RT analysis, the results of that analysis could possibly have been predicted by two or more very different kinds of mental processing. These kind of results have been called "mimicking," and mimicking between models can occur either through mathematical equivalence of two models (Townsend, 1972) or through the statistical properties of the models (Van Zandt & Ratcliff, 1995). Mathematical equivalence is a stronger property than is statistical equivalence. In the case of mathematical equivalence, two or more models predict exactly the same distribution of RTs. In the case of statistical equivalence, the models may predict different distributional forms, but parameters of those models may be chosen in such a way that the two forms are so similar that they cannot be discriminated by statistical tests. The densities shown in Figure 12.1 are examples of two distributional forms that statistically mimic each other.

Given that very different kinds of models can produce very similar distributions, knowing that, say, an ex-Gaussian distribution can be well-fit to a particular sample of data does not allow one to say much about the process that might have produced the data. The ex-Gaussian is typically conceived as the sum of an exponential and a normal random variable. Hohle (1965) proposed that decision times were exponentially distributed and that the sum of the many other stages of processing occurring between a stimulus and a response would be normally distributed by the Central Limit Theorem. If RTs are truly distributed as ex-Gaussians for some task, one might, using Hohle's model, start wondering about the exponentially distributed decision time. However, the ex-Gaussian could also arise from a process that produces normally distributed RTs, in which the mean of the process is itself a random variable that is distributed exponentially. Clearly, a model that predicts exponentially distributed decision times is not the same as a model that predicts normally distributed decision times, but one could not distinguish between them on the basis of the RT distribution.

Consider also theoretical results by Dzhafarov (1993, 1997), Townsend (1976), and Marley and Colonius (1992). Dzhafarov examined the Grice model of information accumulation (Grice, 1968). In this model, information accumulates at the response selection stage of processing according to some deterministic (nonrandom) function of time, say, a straight line increase in the level of information from the time a stimulus is presented. As soon as the level of information reaches a threshold level, which in Grice's model is a random variable (e.g., normally distributed), a response can be made. The variability in the threshold produces variability in the RTs. Dzhafarov showed that with the appropriate accumulation function and the appropriate threshold distribution, *any* simple RT distribution can be mathematically mimicked. He also showed that this result extends to N-choice RT by choosing N Grice accumulators and modeling RT as the fastest of these processes to reach threshold. These results imply that one can always find some form of Grice's model that will fit any observed RT distribution (see also Dzhafarov, 1997).[7]

Townsend (1976) and Marley and Colonius (1992) examined mathematical

equivalence in similar contexts. When RT is determined by a minimum process, such as the race of Grice accumulators just described, Townsend showed that there exists an equivalent RT representation in terms of a sum of independent (serial) subprocesses. Therefore, one can always find a serial process mimic to a parallel race model. Marley and Colonius's results can be applied to two different kinds of response mechanisms, one a random walk, in which information accumulates in both positive and negative directions toward two response thresholds (Laming, 1968; Link, 1975; Link & Heath, 1975; Ratcliff, 1978), and the other a race, in which information accumulates in two or more independent channels. Marley and Colonius showed that any race between arbitrarily correlated channels (of which the random walk is an asympototic case, being perfectly correlated) can be represented as a race between independent channels. Thus, these two very different kinds of models, the race and the random walk, can be mathematically equivalent to each other under certain circumstances.

In sum, even if the RT distribution is known exactly, researchers still have some way to go before being able to use that information in support of any particular model of cognitive processing. This is why it is so important to perform all RT analyses within the confines of a prespecified model. The model will make predictions about RT distributions that can be confirmed or disconfirmed. Furthermore, the model will suggest experiments that can be performed that should have predictable influences on the parameters of the RT distribution: what Townsend and Ashby (1983) have called the principle of correspondent change (Van Zandt et al., 2000). The model will also determine which of several of the methods presented (e.g., distributional ordering or RT decomposition) might provide good sources of converging evidence to evaluate the model.

[7]Note, however, that it is not trivial to find a Grice representation that will mimic the family of RT distributions produced by different types of stimuli; see Townsend and Ashby (1983) and Van Zandt et al. (2000) regarding the principle of correspondent change.

APPENDIX

I present here some MATLAB code to perform the analyses described in the text.

1. *Bootstrapping a sample.* If *y* is a column vector containing the ordered RTs, one bootstrapped sample may be taken as

```
yboot = y([fix(rand(length(y),1)*length(y)) + 1]);
```

The resulting column vector *yboot* contains the same number of observations as *y*, sampled with replacement from *y*. This line can be embedded in a *for* loop to obtain sufficient bootstrapped samples to compute standard deviations. For example, to compute the standard error of a hazard function estimate based on *n_samples* bootstrapped samples, execute the following commands:

```
for i=1:n_samples,
    yboot = y([fix(rand(length(y),1)*length(y)) + 1]);
    h_hat(:,i) = hazard(t,yboot);
end
```

The columns in the matrix *h_hat* will contain the estimated hazard functions for each bootstrapped sample. (See the hazard function presented later.)

The Statistics toolbox also has a bootstrap subroutine that computes desired statistics given the data vector *y*, but it cannot compute error estimates for a function, only for statistics that return a scalar-valued statistic from each sample (e.g., the mean).

2. *Computing the empirical distribution function.* The following function takes as an argument an ordered column vector of RTs *y* and a column vector of points *t* for which the EDF is desired. It returns a column vector equal in length to the vector *t* containing the points of the EDF.

```
function F=EDF(t,y)
% EDF The empirical distribution function
% Syntax F=EDF(t,y), where y is the ordered data vector and t is an
% ordered vector of points at which an estimate is desired.
F=ones(length(t),1);
for i=1:length(t)
    F(i) = sum(y<=t (i))/length(y);
end
```

3. *The Gaussian kernel estimator.* Given a column vector *y* containing the ordered RTs, a column vector *t* containing the time points at which the estimate is desired, and a smoothing parameter *h*, the Gaussian kernel estimator is computed with the function *Gausskernel*.

```
function fhat=Gausskernel(t,y,a)
% GAUSSKERNEL The Gaussian kernel density estimate.
% Syntax k=Gausskernel(t,y,a), where t are the time points, y is the
% sorted data, and a is an optional multiplicative constant for the
% bandwidth parameter h.
if (nargin==2)
    c=.9;
```

```
elseif (nargin==3)
   c=a;
end
h = c*min(std(y),iqr(y)/1.349)/length(y)^.2;
fhat = mean(normpdf( (ones(length(t),1) * y' - t * ones(1,length(y)))',0,h))';
```

The functions *normpdf* and *iqr* are in the Statistics toolbox.

Note that the argument to *normpdf* could be a rather large matrix. On smaller computers, the size of this matrix could cause memory errors. If this occurs, the routine can be modified by putting the computation in a loop, as follows:

```
for i=1:length(t)
     fhat(i,1) = mean(normpdf( (t(i) - y) ,0,h));
end
```

4. *The ex-Gaussian density and cumulative distribution function.* The following two functions, *exgauss* and *Iexgauss* give the density function and CDF, respectively, for the ex-Gaussian distribution. The arguments to both functions are t, a column vector of times for which the density or CDF is to be computed, and *theta,* a vector of three elements, μ, σ, and τ (in that order). Both functions return column vectors of the same length as t. The *normcdf* function is in the Statistics toolbox.

```
function f=exgauss(t,theta)
% EXGAUSS The ex-Gaussian pdf
% Syntax f=exgauss(t,theta), where t is a vector of times for which the
% density is to be computed, and theta is the vector of exgaussian
% parameters (mu,sigma,tau).
mu=theta(1); sigma=theta(2); tau=theta(3);
part1=exp(-t./tau + mu./tau + sigma.^2./2./tau.^2);
part2=normcdf((t-mu-sigma.^2./tau)./sigma)./tau;
f=part1.*part2;


function F=Iexgauss(t,theta)
% IEXGAUSS The ex-Gaussian CDF (Integrated ex-Gaussian)
% Syntax F=Iexgauss(t,theta), where t is a vector of times for which the
% CDF is to be computed, and theta is the vector of exgaussian
% parameters (mu,sigma,tau).
mu=theta(1); sigma=theta(2); tau=theta(3);
part1=-exp(-t./tau + mu./tau + sigma.^2./2./tau.^2);
part2=normcdf((t-mu-sigma.^2./tau)./sigma);
part3=normcdf((t-mu)/sigma);
F=part1.*part2 + part3;
```

5. *The Epanechnikov kernel estimate of the hazard function.* There are three parts to this routine: the functions *epanech* and *Iepanech*, the Epanechnikov kernel and its integral, and the function *hazard,* which returns the hazard function estimate. The function *hazard* takes two arguments, t and y. The argument t is the vector of points at which the estimate is desired. The argument y is the ordered vector of observed RTs.

```
function k=epanech(t)
% EPANECH The Epanechnikov kernel takes arguments between -sqrt(5) and sqrt(5).
% All other values return 0.
% Syntax k=epanech(t)
k=(abs(t)<sqrt(5)).*(.75.*(1.-0.2.*t.^2)/sqrt(5));


function k=Iepanech(t)
```

```
% IEPANECH The integrated Epanechnikov kernel.
% Syntax k=Iepanech(t)
k2=(t>=sqrt(5)).*ones(size(t));
k1=(abs(t)<=sqrt(5)).*(.75.*(t/sqrt(5) - t.^3/5/sqrt(5)/3) + .5);
k=k1+k2;

function [k,s]=hazard(t,y,a)
% HAZARD The Epanechnikov hazard function estimator.
% Syntax [k,s]=hazard(t,y,a)
% The column vector t is the points for which the hazard function
% is to be estimated. The column vector y is the ordered data.
% The optional constant a determines the degree of smoothing. If output
% argument s is specified, an estimated standard error of the
% hazard estimate k (Silverman, 1986) will be returned.
if (nargin==2)
   c=.3;
elseif (nargin==3)
   c=a;
end
n=length(y);
h = c*min(std(y),iqr(y)/1.349)/n^.2;
fhat = mean( epanech( ((ones(length(t),1)*y')-(t*ones(1,n)))'/h ))'/h;
Fhat = mean(Iepanech( (t*ones(1,n)-ones(length(t),1)*y')/h ))';
k=fhat./(1-Fhat);
if (nargout==2)
   s=sqrt(.2683281571*k.^2./fhat/n/h);
end
```

Note that as in the Gaussian kernel estimator, the arguments to *epanech* and *Iepanech* could be quite large matrices. If this causes memory errors, replace the expressions for *fhat* and *Fhat* with the following loop:

```
for i=1:length(t)
    fhat(i,1) = mean( epanech( (t(i) -y)/h ))/h;
    Fhat(i,1) = mean(Iepanech( (t(i) - y)/h ));
end
```

6. *Some routines for performing maximum likelihood and least-squares parameter estimation.* These routines use the *fminsearch* routine provided in the Optimization toolbox. The Optimization toolbox also has other routines that perform maximum likelihood and nonlinear least squares regression, but I found them difficult to use. There are two routines provided here, *MLE* and *SSE*. The reader may need to program his or her own density or CDF to be fit using these routines.

The function *MLE* takes three arguments: *p* is a vector of starting values for the parameters to be estimated; *func* is a character variable specifying the theoretical density function (e.g., *'exgauss'*) that may need to be programmed if a suitable density function is not already available in the Statistics toolbox, and *y*, the vector of observed RTs.

```
function F=MLE(p,func,y)
% MLE Objective function for maximizing likelihood
% Syntax F=MLE(p,func,y)
% Call as, e.g., X=fminsearch('MLE',p,[],func,y)
F=-sum(log(feval(func,y,p)));
```

The function *SSE* takes four arguments: *p* and *func* are as in the function *MLE*, but *tp* is the EDF computed for the sample, and *t* is the vector of times at which the EDF is computed.

```
function F=SSE(p,func,t,tp)
% SSE Objective function for minimizing SSE
% Syntax F=SSE(p,func,t,tp)
% Call as, e.g., X=fminsearch('SSE',p,[],func,t,tp)
F=norm(feval(func,t,p)-tp)^2;
```

As an example, to fit the ex-Gaussian distribution using maximum likelihood to a sample of observations *y*, the command

```
X=fminsearch('MLE',[200,7,150],[],'exgauss',y)
```

could be executed. The starting values of $\hat{\mu}$, $\hat{\sigma}$, and $\hat{\tau}$ are given by the vector [200, 7, 150], and the best-fitting parameter values will be returned in the vector *X*.

7. *The decomposition test.* The following two functions, *theta4* and *decomptest* together provide upper and lower *p* values for Dzhafarov and Cortese's (1996) sample-level decomposition test. The function *theta4* is the fourth theta function, which takes two arguments, *v* and *z*. The parameter *v* determines the periodicity of the function (which here is 0) and *z* is a (possibly vector-valued) variable proportional to the Smirnov distance *d*.

```
function theta=theta4(v,z)
% THETA4 The fourth theta function
% Syntax theta=theta4(v,z), where v is the periodicity of the function
% (possibly 0) and z is a (possibly vector-valued) argument.
tiny = 1E-10;
sum_terms = ceil(sqrt(-log(tiny)/2)/min(z));
j=[1:sum_terms]';
summed=((-1).^j)'* ...
       (exp(-2.*(j.^2)*(z.^2)') .* (cos(2.*j.*v.*pi)*ones(1,length(z))) );
theta = 1 + 2*summed';
```

The next function, *decomptest* is the decomposition test itself. It takes as arguments four *unordered* vectors t_{11}, t_{12}, t_{21}, and t_{22} containing the RTs from the four experimental conditions, a character variable rule, which specifies the addition-like operation to be tested (e.g., *'plus'* for addition, *'min'* for minimum, and *'max'* for maximum, or any other user-defined function), and the binary variable *dep*, which equals 0 for independence and 1 for perfect positive interdependence. It returns a vector of length 2 containing the upper and lower *p*-value limits, both of which may not be necessary for a particular hypothesis (see Dzhafarov and Cortese, 1996). The Smirnov distance is computed within the function. The routine uses the function *harmmean,* which is in the Statistics toolbox.

```
function [plo,phi]=decomptest(t11,t12,t21,t22,rule,dep)
% DECOMPTEST Test for decomposition rule "rule" given unordered
% RTs from four conditions (T11,T12,T21,T22) and presumed dependency
% "dep" (0=s.-independence or 1=p.p.s.-interdependence) between the
% components of Tij.  The function returns the lowest (plo) and highest
% (phi) p-values of the Smirnov statistic D under the hypothesis that
% the decomposition rule is "rule."  Rule can be anything, including
% "plus" (for addition), "min" (for minimum) or "max" (for maximum).
```

```
% Syntax [plo,phi]=decomptest(t11,t12,t21,t22,rule,dep)
%
% Note that plo and phi both are not required. For dep=0, only plo is
% needed.
%
% This routine makes use of the function THETA4, the fourth theta
% function, which provides the p-values. It also uses EDF, which
% computes the empirical distribution function.
if dep==1
    t11 = sort(t11);
    t12 = sort(t12);
    t21 = sort(t21);
    t22 = sort(t22);
end
%
% Compute the sample sizes:
n=harmmean([min(length(t11),length(t22)),min(length(t12),length(t21))]);
%
% Form the samples according to the desired rule:
t1122 = feval(rule,t11(1:n1),t22(1:n1));
t1221 = feval(rule,t12(1:n2),t21(1:n2));
%
% Determine the range over which the EDFs are to be computed:
low = min(min(t1122),min(t1221));
high =  max(max(t1122),max(t1221));
t = [low:high]';
t1122 = sort(t1122);
t1221 = sort(t1221);
F1 = EDF(t,t1122);
F2 = EDF(t,t1221);
%
% Compute the Smirnov distance:
d = max(abs(F1-F2));
%
% Compute the upper and lower p-values:
z = sqrt(2)*d/pi;
plo = 1-theta4(0,sqrt(n)*z);
phi = 1-theta4(0,sqrt(n/2)*z);
```

REFERENCES

Ashby, F. G., Tein, J.-Y., & Balakrishnan, J. D. (1993). Response time distributions in memory scanning. *Journal of Mathematical Psychology, 37,* 526–555.

Ashby, F. G., & Townsend, J. T. (1980). Decomposing the reaction time distribution: Pure insertion and selective influence revisited. *Journal of Mathematical Psychology, 21,* 93–123.

Balota, D. A., & Spieler, D. H. (1999). Word frequency, repetition, and lexicality effects in word recognition tasks: Beyond measures of central tendency. *Journal of Experimental Psychology: General, 128,* 32–55.

Barnett, V., & Lewis, T. (1994). *Outliers in statistical data* (3rd ed.). New York: Wiley.

Bloxom, B. (1984). Estimating response time hazard functions: An exposition and extension. *Journal of Mathematical Psychology, 28,* 401–420.

Bloxom, B. (1985). A constrained spline estimator of a hazard function. *Psychometrika, 50,* 301–321.

Burbeck, S. L., & Luce, R. D. (1982). Evidence from auditory simple reaction times for both change and level detectors. *Perception and Psychophysics, 32,* 117–132.

Colonius, H. (1988). Modeling the redundant signals effect by specifying the hazard function. *Perception and Psychophysics, 43,* 604–606.

Colonius, H. (1990). Possibly dependent probability summation of reaction time. *Journal of Mathematical Psychology, 34,* 253–275.

Colonius, H., & Vorberg, D. (1994). Distribution inequalities for parallel models with unlimited capacity. *Journal of Mathematical Psychology, 38,* 35–58.

Cortese, J. M., & Dzhafarov, E. N. (1996). Epirical recovery of response time decomposition rules: II. Discriminability of serial and parallel architectures. *Journal of Mathematical Psychology, 40,* 203–218.

Cousineau, D., & Larochelle, S. (1997). PASTIS: A program for curve and distribution analyses. *Behavioral Research Methods, Instruments, & Computers, 29,* 542–548.

Davis, C. E., & Steinberg, S. M. (1983). Quantile estimation. In S. Kotz & N. L. Johnson (Eds.), *Encyclopedia of statistical sciences: Vol. 7* (pp. 408–412). New York: Wiley.

Dawson, M. R. (1988). Fitting the ex-Gaussian equation to reaction time distributions. *Behavioral Research Methods, Instruments, & Computers, 20,* 54–57.

Donders, F. C. (1969). On the speed of mental processes (W. G. Koster, trans.). *Acta Psychologica, 30,* 412–431. (Original work published 1868)

Dykstra, R., Kochar, S., & Robertson, T. (1995). Inference for likelihood ratio ordering in the two-sample problem. *Journal of the American Statistical Association, 90,* 1034–1040.

Dzhafarov, E. N. (1992). The structure of simple reaction time to step-function signals. *Journal of Mathematical Psychology, 36,* 235–268.

Dzhafarov, E. N. (1993). Grice-representability of response time distribution families. *Psychometrika, 58,* 281–314.

Dzhafarov, E. N. (1997). Process representations and decompositions of response times. In A. A. J. Marley (Ed.), *Choice, Decision and Measurement: Essays in Honor of R. Duncan Luce* (pp. 255–278). Mahwah, NJ: Erlbaum.

Dzhafarov, E. N. (1999). Conditionally selective dependence of random variables on external factors. *Journal of Mathematical Psychology, 43,* 123–157.

Dzhafarov, E. N. (in press). Unconditionally selective dependence of random variables on external factors. *Journal of Mathematical Psychology.*

Dzhafarov, E. N., & Cortese, J. M. (1996). Empirical recovery of response time decomposition rules: I. Sample-level decomposition tests. *Journal of Mathematical Psychology, 40,* 185–202.

Dzhafarov, E. N., & Rouder, J. N. (1996). Empirical discriminability of two models for stochastic relationship between additive components of response time. *Journal of Mathematical Psychology, 40,* 48–63.

Dzhafarov, E. N., & Schweickert, R. (1995). Decompositions of response times: An almost general theory. *Journal of Mathematical Psychology, 39,* 285–314.

Efron, B. (1979). Computers and the theory of statistics: Thinking the unthinkable. *SIAM Review, 21,* 460–480.

Egeth, H. E., Folk, C. L., & Mullin, P. A. (1989). Spatial parallelism in the processing of lines, letters, and lexicality. In B. E. Shepp & S. Ballesteros (Eds.), *Object perception: Structure and process* (pp. 19–52). Hillsdale, NJ: Erlbaum.

Falmagne, J. C. (1968). Note on a simple fixed-point property of binary mixtures. *British Journal of Mathematical and Statistical Psychology, 21,* 131–132.

Green, D. M., & Luce, R. D. (1971). Detection of auditory signals presented at random times: III. *Perception and Psychophysics, 9,* 257–268.

Grice, G. R. (1968). Stimulus intensity and response evocation. *Psychological Review, 75,* 359–373.

Grice, G. R., Canham, L., & Boroughs, J. M. (1984). Combination rule for redundant information in reaction time tasks with divided attention. *Perception and Psychophysics, 35,* 451–463.

Grice, G. R., Canham, L., & Gwynne, J. W. (1984). Absence of a redundant-signals effect in a reaction time task with divided attention. *Perception and Psychophysics, 36,* 565–570.

Hartley, H. O. (1961). The modified Gauss-Newton method for the fitting of nonlinear regression functions by least squares. *Technometrics, 3,* 269–280.

Heathcote, A. (1996). Rtsys: A DOS application for the analysis of reaction time data. *Behavioral Research Methods, Instruments, & Computers, 28,* 427–445.

Heathcote, A., Brown, S., & Mewhort, D. J. (in press). Quantile based estimation of response time parameters. *Psychonomic Bulletin and Review.*

Heathcote, A., Popiel, S. J., & Mewhort, D. J. (1991). Analysis of response time distributions: An example using the stroop task. *Psychological Bulletin, 109,* 340–347.

Hockley, W. E. (1984). Analysis of response time distributions in the study of cognitive processes. *Journal of Experimental Psychology: Learning, Memory, and Cognition, 10,* 598–615.

Hoel, P. G., Port, S. C., & Stone, C. J. (1971). *Introduction to Probability Theory.* Boston: Houghton Mifflin.

Hohle, R. H. (1965). Inferred components of reaction times as a function of foreperiod duration. *Journal of Experimental Psychology, 69,* 382–386.

James, L., Priebe, C., & Marchette, D. (2000). Consistent estimation of mixture complexity. Manuscript submitted for publication.

Kohfeld, D., Santee, J. L., & Wallace, N. D. (1981). Loudness and reaction time: II. Identification of detection components at different intensities and frequencies. *Perception and Psychophysics, 29,* 550–562.

Laming, D. R. (1968). *Information theory of choice reaction time.* New York: Wiley.

Link, S. W. (1975). The relative judgment theory of two choice response time. *Journal of Mathematical Psychology, 12,* 114–135.

Link, S. W., & Heath, R. A. (1975). A sequential theory of psychological discrimination. *Psychometrika, 40,* 77–105.

Logan, G. D. (1992). Shapes of reaction-time distributions and shapes of learning curves: A test of the instance theory of automaticity. *Journal of Experimental Psychology: Learning, Memory, and Cognition, 18,* 883–914.

Luce, R. D. (1986). *Response times: Their role in inferring elementary mental organization.* New York: Oxford University Press.

Maddox, W. T., Ashby, F. G., & Gottlob, L. R. (1998). Response time distributions in multidimensional perceptual categorization. *Perception and Psychophysics, 60,* 620–637.

Marley, A. A. J., & Colonius, H. (1992). The "horse race" random utility model for choice probabilities and reaction times, and its competing risks interpretation. *Journal of Mathematical Psychology, 36,* 1–20.

McGill, W. J. (1963). Stochastic latency mechanisms. In R. D. Luce & R. R. Bush (Eds.), *Handbook of mathematical psychology: Vol. 1* (pp. 309–360). New York: Wiley.

Miller, D. R., & Singpurwalla, N. D. (1977). Failure rate estimation using random smoothing. Technical Report 67, Department of Statistics, University of Missouri-Columbia.

Miller, J. (1982). Divided attention: Evidence for coactivation with redundant signals. *Cognitive Psychology, 14,* 247–279.

Miller, J. (1988). Discrete and continuous models of information processing: Theoretical distinctions and empirical results. *Acta Psychologica, 67,* 191–257.

Mollon, J., & Perkins, A. (1996). Errors of judgment and Greenwich in 1796. *Nature, 380,* 101–102.

Mordkoff, J. T., & Yantis, S. (1991). An interactive race model of divided attention. *Journal of Experimental Psychology: Human Perception and Performance, 17,* 520–538.

Nelder, J. A., & Mead, R. (1965). A simplex method for function minimization. *Computer Journal, 7,* 308–313.

Pike, R. (1973). Response latency models for signal detection. *Psychological Review, 80,* 53–68.

Press, W. H., Teukolsky, S. A., Vetterling, W. T., & Flannery, B. P. (1992). *Numerical recipes in FORTRAN: The art of scientific computing* (2nd ed.). New York: Cambridge University Press.

Priebe, C., & Marchette, D. (in press). Alternating kernel and mixture estimates. *Computational Statistics and Data Analysis.*

Ratcliff, R. (1978). A theory of memory retrieval. *Psychological Review, 85,* 59–108.

Ratcliff, R. (1979). Group reaction time distributions and an analysis of distribution statistics. *Psychological Bulletin, 86,* 446–461.

Ratcliff, R. (1993). Methods for dealing with reaction time outliers. *Psychological Bulletin, 114,* 510–532.

Ratcliff, R., & Murdock, B. B., Jr. (1976). Retrieval processes in recognition memory. *Psychological Review, 83,* 190–214.

Roberts, S., & Pashler, H. (2000). How persuasive is a good fit? *Psychological Review, 107,* 358–367.

Roberts, S., & Sternberg, S. (1992). The meaning of additive reaction-time effects: Tests of three alternatives. In D. E. Meyer & S. Kornblum (Eds.), *Attention and Performance: Vol. 14* (pp. 611–654). Cambridge: MIT Press.

Schweickert, R. (1978). A critical path generalization of the additive factor methods analysis of a Stroop task. *Journal of Mathematical Psychology, 18,* 105–139.

Senthilselvan, A. (1997). Penalized likelihood estimation of hazard and intensity functions. *Journal of the Royal Statistical Society B, 49,* 170–174.

Sheu, C.-F., & Ratcliff, R. (1995). The application of Fourier deconvolution to reaction time data: A cautionary note. *Psychological Bulletin, 118,* 285–299.

Silverman, B. W. (1986). *Density estimation for statistics and data analysis.* London: Chapman & Hall.

Smith, P. L. (1990). Obtaining meaningful results from Fourier deconvolution of reaction time data. *Psychological Bulletin, 108,* 533–550.

Smith, P. L., & Vickers, D. (1988). The accumulator model of two-choice discrimination. *Journal of Mathematical Psychology, 32,* 135–168.

Sternberg, S. (1969). The discovery of processing stages: Extensions of donder's method. In W. G. Koster (Ed.), *Attention and performance: Vol. 2* (pp. 276–315). Amsterdam: North-Holland.

Stuart, A., & Ord, J. K. (1999). *Kendall's advanced theory of statistics* (6th ed.): *Vol. 1.* London: Arnold.

Tanner, M. A. (1983). A note on the variable kernel estimator of the hazard function from randomly censored data. *The Annals of Statistics, 3,* 994–998.

Tanner, M. A., & Wong, W. H. (1983). The estimation of the hazard function from randomly censored data by the kernel method. *The Annals of Statistics, 11,* 989–993.

Thomas, E. A. (1971). Sufficient conditions for monotone hazard rate: An application to latency-probability curves. *Journal of Mathematical Psychology, 8,* 303–332.

Townsend, J. T. (1972). Some results concerning the identifiability of parallel and serial processes. *British Journal of Mathematical and Statistical Psychology, 25,* 168–199.

Townsend, J. T. (1976). Serial and within-stage independent parallel model equivalence on the minimum completion time. *Journal of Mathematical Psychology, 14,* 219–238.

Townsend, J. T. (1984). Uncovering mental processes with factorial experiments. *Journal of Mathematical Psychology, 28,* 363–400.

Townsend, J. T. (1990). Truth and consequences of ordinal differences in statistical distributions: Toward a theory of hierarchical inference. *Psychological Bulletin, 108,* 551–567.

Townsend, J. T. (1992). On the proper scales for reaction time. In H.-G. Geissler, S. W. Link, & J. T. Townsend (Eds.), *Cognition, information processing, and psychophysics: Basic issues* (pp. 105–120). Hillsdale, NJ: Erlbaum.

Townsend, J. T., & Ashby, F. G. (1983). *Stochastic modeling of elementary psychological processes.* New York: Cambridge University Press.

Townsend, J. T., & Nozawa, G. (1995). Spatio-temporal properties of elementary perception: An investigation of parallel, serial, and coactive theories. *Journal of Mathematical Psychology, 39,* 321–359.

Townsend, J. T., & Nozawa, G. (1997). Serial exhaustive models can violate the race model inequality: Implications for architecture and capacity. *Psychological Review, 104,* 595–602.

Ulrich, R., & Miller, J. (1994). Effects of truncation on reaction time analysis. *Journal of Experimental Psychology: General, 123,* 34–80.

Van Selst, M., & Jolicoeur, P. (1994). A solution to the effect of sample size on outlier elimination. *Quarterly Journal of Experimental Psychology, 47,* 631–650.

Van Zandt, T. (2000). How to fit a response time distribution. *Psychonomic Bulletin and Review, 7,* 424–465.

Van Zandt, T. (2001). Response times are not distributed as ex-Gaussians. Manuscript in preparation.

Van Zandt, T., Colonius, H., & Proctor, R. W. (2000). A comparison of two response time models applied to perceptual matching. *Psychonomic Bulletin and Review, 7,* 208–256.

Van Zandt, T., & Ratcliff, R. (1995). Statistical mimicking of reaction time distributions: Mixtures and parameter variability. *Psychonomic Bulletin and Review, 2,* 20–54.

Vickers, D. (1979). *Decision processes in visual perception.* New York: Academic Press.

Watson, G. S., & Leadbetter, M. R. (1964). Hazard analysis II. *Sankhyā Series A, 26,* 101–116.

Wickens, T. D. (1982). *Models for behavior: Stochastic processes in psychology.* San Francisco: Freeman.

Wilcox, R. R. (1997). *Introduction to robust estimation and hypothesis testing.* San Diego: Academic Press.

Wilcox, R. R. (1998). How many discoveries have been lost by ignoring modern statistical methods? *American Psychologist, 53,* 300–314.

Yantis, S., Meyer, D. E., & Smith, J. E. K. (1991). Analyses of multinomial mixture distributions: New tests for stochastic models of cognition and action. *Psychological Bulletin, 110,* 350–374.

CHAPTER 13

Testing and Measurement
Advances in Item Response Theory
and Selected Testing Practices

RONALD K. HAMBLETON AND MARY J. PITONIAK

The assessment of an individual's status and change on constructs of interest is often carried out with educational and psychological tests. It has been noted that "the psychological test stands as the most important invention that psychological science has bequeathed to society" (Lubinski & Dawis, 1995, p. xxi). Although many would debate the validity of such a strong assertion, it seems likely that psychological tests, as well as the theory and practice of educational and psychological measurement, would be judged as very important to the success and progress of researchers and practitioners in the fields of psychology and education. Many of the changes that are occurring today in the field of educational and psychological measurement are addressed in this chapter.

Tests come in many forms. Anastasi (1988) noted that distinctions may be made among intelligence tests, ability/aptitude/ achievement tests, and personality tests. Tests may also be distinguished by the primary area in which they are used, leading to the specification of terms such as educational testing and psychological testing. Following the example set by the recently revised *Standards for Educational and Psychological*

Testing (*Standards*), produced by the American Educational Research Association (AERA), American Psychological Association (APA), and National Council on Measurement in Education (NCME; AERA, APA, & NCME, 1999), the term *educational testing* will be used for tests of ability (into which both aptitude and achievement tests fall), whereas the term *psychological testing* will be used for tests of general cognitive functioning (into which intelligence tests fall), personality, and vocational interests. These distinctions are made, however, with an awareness that, in practice, any given test may be given in a number of different settings.

Basic psychometric concepts such as reliability and validity—as well as standardization of administration in producing test scores that will measure up on both of these criteria— underlie both educational and psychological tests. However, there are often differences in the ways in which both types of tests are administered. For example, tests used for admission to college and postgraduate institutions are typically large-scale assessments administered several times a year in group settings. In contrast, a test of cognitive functioning is often administered one-on-one in a clinical setting.

Educational tests—both ability tests used for admissions purposes and achievement tests used to measure progress in kindergarten through grade 12—are perhaps the most visible tests. These tests are administered to millions of students annually, and in recent years they have become even more widespread. Educational reforms and accompanying emphases on student, school, district, and state accountability have led many states to implement statewide testing programs. Recent federal legislation would add more testing by denying federal funding for education unless states assess all students in grades 3 through 8 in the areas of reading and mathematics. Because these state and national tests are becoming increasingly important to students, to their parents, and to teachers and administrators, these tests are undergoing even greater scrutiny. The resulting examination of testing practices may cause discomfort for some, but it will undoubtedly lead to gains in knowledge about testing and improvements in testing practices as psychometricians conduct research to ensure that test scores are reliable and valid.

In the past several decades we have seen major advances in test theory and testing practices. Test theory itself has been reshaped since the classical works of Gulliksen (1950) and Lord and Novick (1968). Over the past 30 years modern test theory and practices have been replacing classical test theory and practices; paper and pencil tests are being replaced by computer-based tests; criterion-referenced tests have become a useful and well-developed alternative to norm-referenced tests for purposes such as assessing examinees' levels of accomplishment; new item types are emerging to assess high-level cognitive skills; cognitive models are being merged with psychometric models to generate new types of tests; the analysis of tests for ev-

idence of item bias is as common today as carrying out item analyses; and testing alternatives and accommodations are becoming common for students who need them. AERA, APA, and NCME revised the test standards in 1954, 1966, 1974, 1985, and 1999 to reflect these and many more changes in psychometric theory and practices.

Perhaps the biggest change in psychometric methods has been the gradual shift from classical test theory to modern test theory, better known as item response theory (IRT). IRT dates back at least to the 1940s, but it was the introduction of IRT in the widely read test theory text by Lord and Novick (1968) and in the text by Rasch (1960) that marked the beginning of the transition from classical to modern test theory and related models. Modern test theory is characterized by modeling test data at the item level and making strong but testable assumptions about the interactions between examinees and the test items that they are administered. This transition has occurred because IRT models permit more flexibility in the processes of test development and data analysis, because IRT models have many useful properties that classical test models do not (e.g., item statistics that are less dependent on examinee samples), and because IRT models allow psychometricians to model more effectively the test data with which they work. With emerging item types and new demands on testing (e.g., more flexibility in test administrations and shorter tests), this added flexibility is especially important.

Today, IRT models are used or have been used in many well-known testing programs, including the *National Education Longitudinal Study* (NELS; a national longitudinal study of achievement growth of high school students), the *National Assessment of Educational Progress* (NAEP; a national assessment of major subject areas given every two years to students in grades 4, 8, and 12), the *Third International Mathematics and Science*

Study (TIMSS in 1995 and TIMSS-Repeat in 1999; used to evaluate the quality of science and mathematics achievement in over 40 countries), the Organization for Economic Cooperation and Development's *Program for International Student Assessment* (PISA; an assessment of reading, mathematics, and science in 15-year-olds from over 30 countries initiated in 2000 and given every three years), nearly all of the national standardized achievement tests used in the United States (e.g., *California Achievement Tests, Comprehensive Tests of Basic Skills, Metropolitan Achievement Tests,* and *Stanford Achievement Tests*), major college and post-graduate admissions tests (e.g., the *Scholastic Assessment Test, Graduate Management Admissions Test, Law School Admissions Test,* and the *Graduate Record Exam*), the *Test of English as a Foreign Language* (a computer-based test used widely by universities and colleges to assess the English skills of foreign applicants), the *Armed Services Vocational Aptitude Battery* (used in the selection of recruits for the military service and to assign military recruits to occupational specialties), and major psychological test batteries such as the *Woodcock-Johnson Psychoeducational Battery*. Many of the test developers are using IRT models today in designing and constructing tests, in equating test scores, in identifying potentially biased test items, in administering computer-based tests, and in reporting scores. The list of applications today is very long. For an international perspective on IRT use, see the paper by Hambleton and Slater (1997).

The purposes of this chapter are (a) to introduce the main IRT concepts and to describe several widely used IRT models and their applications to the development of tests and computer-adaptive testing, and (b) to describe a number of other prominent changes that are taking place in the testing field and that have methodological implications for the practice of measurement (e.g., new item types,

cognitive-based models for assessment, setting standards on tests, new conceptions of validity, and testing of individuals with disabilities).

ITEM RESPONSE THEORY AND APPLICATIONS

Shortcomings of Classical Test Models

Theories and models are very useful in educational and psychological testing: They can describe anticipated relations among important variables such as examinee ability and errors of measurement, and these relations may provide the basis for a deeper understanding of the relationships among educational and psychological variables. These theories and models may be helpful also in predicting and explaining observable outcomes such as test score distributions and correlations between variables; often they are useful in understanding the role of errors and how errors might be controlled in the testing situation.

Classical test theory is concerned with the estimation and control of error in the testing process. Recent advances in generalizability theory, an extension of classical test theory, have furthered the study of error and components of error in a variety of test designs such as those involving multiple raters, multiple tasks, and multiple test occasions, as well as their interactions (Brennan, 1992; Shavelson & Webb, 1991).

The classical test model begins with a specification of a linear relationship among three constructs: test score (X), true score (T), and error (E). The model is well known: $X = T + E$. In the model, error is assumed to be randomly distributed with a mean of 0 across the population of examinees for whom the test is intended and to be uncorrelated with true scores and with error scores on parallel test administrations. No distributional assumptions need to be made about X, T, or E for producing the main results of the classical test theory. In some true score models, however, errors are assumed to be normally distributed, and this allows for hypothesis testing and the setting up of confidence bands around test scores with known probabilities.

From this simple linear model, true score theory has been advanced to produce numerous results that have been used to guide test development, test evaluations, and test score interpretations (see, e.g., Gulliksen, 1950; Lord & Novick, 1968; Crocker & Algina, 1986). These important results include (a) the estimation of the measurement error associated with a test (i.e., the standard error of measurement), (b) the estimation of reliability (e.g., test-retest, parallel-form, corrected split-half, internal consistency), (c) formulas showing the impact of test length on test score reliability and validity (e.g., the generalized Spearman-Brown formula and the test length–test validity formula), (d) a formula for adjusting the observed correlation between two variables for measurement error to estimate the correlation between true scores on the two variables, and (e) a formula for adjusting correlations for the restriction of range in one or both variables. Clearly, classical test theory has been valuable in the generation and evaluation of tests for nearly a century.

Unfortunately, classical test theory is associated also with a number of shortcomings. One important flaw is that standard item statistics (item difficulty and item discrimination) and test reliability estimates used in test development work are sample-dependent. The statistics themselves have descriptive value, and test developers can spot nonfunctioning items, tests that may be too easy, and so on. At the same time, these item and test statistics may be less useful when they are used to build a test for an examinee population for which the statistics are not representative. But obtaining representative samples of examinees for field-tests is not always possible. Sample-dependent item and test statistics are not without value, but constructing tests to meet detailed statistical specifications becomes problematic under these conditions.

A second shortcoming is that test scores are highly dependent on the particular choice of test items. Examinee scores rise and fall with the difficulty of test items that they are administered. The same examinee might score high on an easy mathematics test and low on a difficult mathematics test even though the that examinee's ability level remains the same on both test administrations. Critics of classical test theory would prefer to estimate ability rather than true score, which varies with test difficulty. Ability is considered to be a more fundamental construct because it is a characteristic of the examinee and is therefore invariant over tests measuring that ability. When all examinees see the same items, or when designs exist for effectively equating tests of different difficulty, then no problems arise. Because examiners currently wish to allow more flexibility in test administration times, to construct multiple forms, and to match test difficulty to examinee ability, the fact that test scores (and true scores) depend on the particular set of administered items is a major shortcoming.

A third shortcoming is that the classical test model assumes that the size of the error is the same for all examinees. This seems implausible: It should be obvious that errors of measurement for low-performing examinees will be higher than errors of measurement for high-performing examinees (see, e.g., Lord, 1984). Although this assumption may not seriously threaten the usefulness of the classical model, models that do not make this restrictive assumption would be preferable. Strong true-score models (Kolen & Brennan, 1995; Lord & Novick, 1968) represent one solution for obtaining error estimates that are conditional on test score or true score within the framework of classical test theory, but such a solution does not address the other shortcomings of the classical test model.

A fourth shortcoming is that classical test modeling of the test data is not done at the item level. There is no attempt, for example, to try and model the interaction between an examinee at a particular ability level and the examinee's performance on the item. It is precisely this level of modeling that is needed to accommodate some of the innovations in testing practices, such as computer-adaptive testing. This level of modeling is needed to choose test items in an optimal fashion.

Introduction to Models of Item Response Theory

Classical test theory and related models have been valuable to test developers for over 80 years, and nearly all important tests in this country—up until the last 20 years or so—have been constructed and evaluated with these models. However, these models lack four valuable features: (a) item statistics that are independent of the examinee group, (b) ability estimates for an examinee, apart from measurement error, that are statistically equivalent even though the tests from which the scores came may not be parallel, (c) models that are free of implausible or difficult assumptions, and (d) models that provide a basis for matching test items to ability levels.

These desirable properties or features can be obtained, in principle, within the framework of IRT (Hambleton & Swaminathan, 1985; Lord, 1952, 1980; Wright & Stone, 1979). IRT refers to a group of statistical procedures for modeling the relations between examinee ability and item and test performance. Here, the term *ability* is used to describe the construct measured by the test, which could be an aptitude, achievement, personality, or psychomotor variable. Perhaps the term *latent trait* would be more suitable for

psychologists, but the convention among IRT researchers has been to call the construct measured by the test *ability* regardless of the nature of the construct being measured. Only a few psychologists have resisted the convention (see, e.g., Embretson & Reise, 2000; Samejima, 1974). IRT models are based on strong assumptions about examinees and the test data, but the assumptions can be checked; when the assumptions are met, at least to a reasonable extent, estimates of examinee ability and item parameter have the desirable features just mentioned.

Over 100 IRT models have been developed to date, and many of these have been used to analyze real data (see van der Linden & Hambleton, 1997). Some current models can handle literally all types of educational and psychological data: discrete or continuous item responses that are dichotomously or polytomously scored; ordered or unordered item-score categories; and homogeneous (i.e., one ability) or heterogeneous (i.e., multiple) abilities.

IRT models are based on two strong assumptions. The first concerns the dimensional structure of the test—typically, unidimensionality is assumed (i.e., the test measures a single trait)—and the second concerns the mathematical relationship between examinee responses to items and the construct measured by the test. This is known as the item characteristic function (or item characteristic curve), and it may take many mathematical forms corresponding to different IRT models. Both are strong assumptions about the test data. Fortunately, unlike with classical test models, there are statistical approaches for assessing the viability of the assumptions.

Item Characteristic Functions or Curves

The upper part of Figure 13.1 shows the general form of item characteristic functions (ICFs; often called item characteristic curves, or ICCs) applied to dichotomous data. This

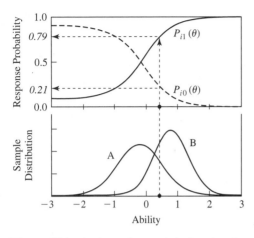

Figure 13.1   An item characteristic function for a dichotomously scored item and ability distributions for groups A and B.

model assumes that the ability measured by the test to which the model is applied is unidimensional, and the data are scored 0 or 1. (The lower part of Figure 1, labeled Sample Distribution, shows how two samples of examinees with different distributions of ability performed on the item; the relationship between the information presented in the two parts of the Figure will be discussed later, in the IRT Model Properties Section of this chapter.)

ICFs can be generated from, for example, the three-parameter logistic model by the expression

$$P_i(\theta) = c_i + (1 - c_i)\frac{e^{Da_i(\theta - b_i)}}{1 + e^{Da_i(\theta - b_i)}}$$
$$i = 1, 2, \ldots, n.$$

This expression links examinee (observable) performance on an item scored 0-1 to the underlying (unobservable) ability measured by the test. $P_{i1}(\theta)$ gives the probability of a correct response to item i as a function of ability (denoted θ)—a monotonically increasing function of ability. Of course, probabilities range from 0.00 to 1.00. The c parameter (i.e., pseudo-guessing parameter) in the model is

the height of the lower asymptote of the ICF. This parameter is introduced into the model to account for the performance of low-ability examinees on multiple-choice test items. This parameter is not needed in the model when fitting, for example, free-response data or any data for which the guessing probability is very low. The b parameter (i.e., item difficulty parameter) is the point on the ability scale at which an examinee has a $(1 + c)/2$ probability of a correct answer. Hard items are shifted to the higher end of the ability continuum, and easier items are shifted to the lower end. The a parameter (i.e., the item discrimination parameter) is proportional to the slope of the ICF at the point b on the ability scale. The higher the a parameter, the steeper the slope, and the more discriminating the item is said to be. The D in the model is simply a scaling factor that was introduced many years ago (see Lord & Novick, 1968, Chap. 17) to bring the interpretation of logistic and normal-ogive model parameters in agreement with one another. This is accomplished with D set to a value of 1.7. The symbol n refers to the number of items in the test.

It should be noted that choosing logistic or normal ogive functions to represent the monotonic relationships between item and ability parameters provides no information about the shape or placement of the ability distribution. The logistic and normal ogive functions are simply a convenient way to represent the relationships. The fact that they are cumulative distribution functions for the logistic and normal density functions is of no importance for ability estimation. In fact, one of the strengths of IRT is that no distributional assumptions need to be made about ability.

$P_{i0}(\theta)$ gives the probability of an incorrect response to item i as a function of ability, and this curve is also shown in Figure 13.1. It is not common to do so because $P_{i0}(\theta)$ is simply the complement of $P_{i1}(\theta)$. At the same time, drawing this second expression reminds people who use these models that there are two responses to this item and that each has an associated item-score category function. Considering an examinee with $\theta = 0.5$ (it is customary to scale ability scores to a mean of 0 and a standard deviation of 1) in Figure 13.1, the probability of a correct response is .79, and the probability of an incorrect response is .21. If this item were from a dichotomously scored personality scale, we might say that the examinee has a .79 chance of endorsing the item, and a .21 chance of not.

Many S-shaped ICFs can be generated to fit actual examinee item-response data by changing the item parameter values in the model. Figure 13.2 shows the ICFs for a set of six test items with the following item statistics:

Item	a	b	c
1	0.66	0.06	0.07
2	1.30	1.80	0.20
3	1.50	1.03	0.02
4	1.08	−1.08	0.20
5	1.40	−0.18	0.17
6	1.56	−2.19	0.14

These are typical item statistics for the three-parameter logistic model. Item difficulty parameters tend to range from −2.0 to +2.0; item discrimination parameters tend to range from 0.0 to 2.0; and the item pseudo-guessing parameters tend to take on values of 0.00 to 0.25. These are typical values when ability scores have been scaled to a mean of 0.0 and a standard deviation of 1.0. The ability scale itself is defined only up to a linear transformation. For score reporting it is common to transform the ability scores to a more convenient scale (i.e., a scale in which scores do not have decimals and are nonnegative). Figure 13.2 reveals that test items 2 and 3 are the most difficult and that test items 4 and 6 are the easiest. Test items 3 and 6 are the most discriminating (although this is not obvious from Figure 13.2 because test items 2 and 5 are only slightly less discriminating), and test item 1 is the least discriminating. Test items 2 and 4 have the highest lower asymptotes, and test item 3 has the lowest asymptote. Note too that the ICFs extend to plus and minus infinity. Only the portions of the ICFs between ability scores of −3.0 and +3.0 are shown in this and other figures in the chapter.

All the ICFs in Figure 13.2 were generated from the three-parameter logistic test model. Simpler logistic IRT models can be obtained either by setting $c_i = 0$ (to obtain the two-parameter logistic model) or by setting $c_i = 0$ and $a_i = 1$ (to obtain the one-parameter logistic model). The one-parameter logistic model is better known as the Rasch model after its original developer, Georg Rasch (1960). This model has become very popular among some testing specialists because it is simpler to work with than are other models, because the software available for it is user-friendly, and because it has been found to fit many sets of test data adequately. Also, with this model the number right score is a sufficient statistic for estimating ability, and some of the complexities of ability estimation with IRT models with more item parameters are avoided. At the same time, other researchers feel that model fit should be a main criterion in choosing IRT models, and they thus prefer to use more general models with the presence of additional

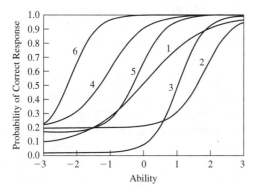

Figure 13.2 A set of six item characteristic functions.

parameters for fitting test data (for discussion of the issues of a priori choosing of models vs. choosing the best-fitting models, see Hambleton, 1989; Wright & Stone, 1979).

While researchers were conducting important technical studies and application analyses with the unidimensional, one-, two-, and three-parameter, normal and logistic IRT models, the late 1960s saw the advent of other model-building initiatives by Samejima (1969). By the early 1980s the increasing interest in polytomously scored tasks in student tests and credentialing exams (e.g., essays and extended problem-solving tasks) had steered many more researchers toward the earlier work of Samejima. Samejima (1969) introduced the useful graded response model to analyze data from Likert attitude scales and other polytomously scored performance data. Her model and extensions of it were the first of many models developed by psychometricians to handle polytomously scored data (for an extensive review of models for analyzing polytomously scored data, see van der Linden & Hambleton, 1997).

With Samejima's graded response model, the probability that an examinee with ability level θ will obtain a particular score, k, or a higher score up to the highest score m_i on item i, is assumed to be given by a two-parameter logistic model:

$$P_{ik}^*(\theta) = \frac{e^{Da_i(\theta - b_{ik})}}{1 + e^{Da_i(\theta - b_{ik})}} \quad \begin{aligned} & i = 1, 2, \ldots, n; \\ & k = 0, 1, \ldots, m_i. \end{aligned}$$

This expression, called the cumulative score category response function (CSCRF), gives the probability that the examinee will obtain a score of k or higher on item i. Figure 13.3 contains the CSCRFs for a task score 0 to 3.

In addition, the probabilities of obtaining scores of 0 or greater, $m_i + 1$ or greater, and

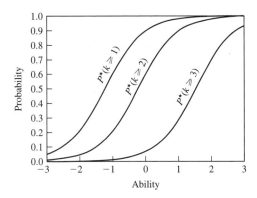

Figure 13.3 Cumulative score category response functions for the graded response model for a four-score category item.

k on item i need to be defined:

$$P_{i0}^*(\theta) = 1.0$$

$$P_{i(m_i+1)}^*(\theta) = 0.0$$

Then,

$$P_{ik}(\theta) = P_{ik}^*(\theta) - P_{i(k+1)}^*(\theta)$$

is the probability that the examinee will obtain a score of k on item i. It is assumed that each response category or item-score category has its own "score category response function," which provides the probability that examinees at each ability level will make that choice or obtain that particular score. At each ability level, then, the sum of probabilities associated with the available responses or possible score points is 1. High-ability examinees would have higher probabilities associated with the highest possible scores and lower probabilities associated with the lower possible scores, whereas low-ability examinees would have higher probabilities associated with the lowest possible scores and lower probabilities associated with the higher possible scores. This is easily seen in Figure 13.4. Examinees with higher abilities are more likely to obtain scores of 2 and 3 than scores of 0 and 1. In practice, of course, the CSCRFs are known (from the estima-

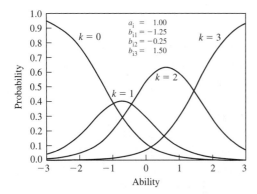

Figure 13.4 Score category response functions for the graded response model for a four-score category item.

tion process), and the abilities are not. The ability estimation task places examinees on the ability scale in a way that is most consistent with their responses to the items or tasks in the test. If the assessment were an attitude scale, then the scores 0 to 3 would correspond to ordered categories such as "strongly disagree," "disagree," "agree," and "strongly agree," and the goal would be to place examinees on the attitude scale in a position that is consistent with their responses. An examinee generally answering "strongly agree" to the statements in the instrument would tend to be positioned toward the higher end of the attitude scale; an examinee providing a mixed set of ratings would be positioned near the middle of the attitude scale; and an examinee tending to disagree with the majority of the statements in the instrument would be positioned toward the lower end of the attitude scale continuum.

Samejima's (1969) two-parameter graded response model also includes an item difficulty threshold for each score from 1 to m_i. It is denoted b_{ik} and is at the point on the ability scale at which the examinee has a 50% probability of obtaining a score of k or higher. In addition, the model includes an item discrimination parameter that reflects the fact that some

items are more discriminating than are others. Samejima's model (and variations of it) provides considerable flexibility in attempting to fit a model to a dataset.

Figure 13.3 highlights the cumulative score category response functions, $P^*_{ik}(\theta)$, for an item with four response categories; from these functions the item difficulty thresholds can be discerned. Equations for this model—as well as related IRT models for handling polytomously scored data such as the partial credit model and the generalized partial credit model—are found in van der Linden and Hambleton (1997). The discriminating power of the item depicted in Figures 13.3 and 13.4 is 1.00. The item thresholds, denoted b_{i1} (i.e., −1.25), b_{i2} (−0.25), and b_{i3} (1.50), are the points on the ability scale at which the item-score category response functions designate a 50% probability of that an examinee will obtaining scores of 1 or higher, 2 or higher, or 3, respectively. For example, at $\theta = -0.25$, an examinee has a 50% probability of obtaining a score of 2 or 3 (and, by extrapolation, a 50% chance of obtaining a score of 0 or 1). For all higher abilities the probability of obtaining a score of 2 or 3 is greater than 50%, and for all lower abilities the probability of obtaining a score of 2 or 3 is less than 50%.

The generalized partial credit model (Muraki, 1992) is another popular IRT model for analyzing ordered, polytomously scored data. The probability of receiving a score of k on item i is obtained directly from the model:

$$P_{ik}(\theta) = \frac{e^{\sum_{j=0}^{k} Da_i(\theta - b_{ij})}}{\sum_{h=0}^{m_i} e^{\sum_{j=0}^{h} Da_i(\theta - b_{ij})}}.$$

The modeling of the response process used by examinees differs from the graded response model but produces similar results (see, e.g., Fitzpatrick et al., 1996). A special case of Muraki's model is the partial credit model (Masters, 1982; Masters & Wright, 1997), in which all the polytomously scored items are assumed to have equal discriminating powers.

Even though it is still limited to unidimensional data, Bock's nominal response model is more general than Samejima's (1969) model or Muraki's (1992) model (see, e.g., Bock, 1972, 1997) because no ordering of the response categories that are available for each item or task is assumed (i.e., nominal response data can be fit by this model). This model then becomes useful for analyzing qualitative data such as might arise in survey research.

Multidimensional IRT models were introduced by Lord and Novick (1968), Samejima (1974), Embretson (1984, 1997), Fischer and Seliger (1997), McDonald (1989), and Reckase (1997a, 1997b). All of these models can fit data that are multidimensional in their underlying structure. Several of these models can handle only 0-1 data, and others can handle both binary and polytomously scored data. Multidimensional IRT models offer the prospect of better fitting certain types of test data (e.g., test items that require both verbal and quantitative skills to answer successfully) because they consider the interrelations among the items and can provide multidimensional representations of both items and examinee abilities. In the typical multidimensional IRT model, a vector of ability scores is produced for each examinee—one for each trait or dimension included in the model. In addition, vectors of item difficulties and item discrimination indexes can be estimated. Multidimensional IRT models are in their infancy, and software is limited (e.g., see Fraser & McDonald, 1988), but research is continuing and improvements in software, estimation algorithms, and model-fit procedures can be expected in the near future.

IRT Model Properties

When the assumptions of an item response model can be met by test data, at least to a reasonable degree, model item and ability parameters have two desirable properties. First, examinee ability is defined in relation to the pool of items from which the test items are drawn and does *not* depend on the particular sample of items selected for the test. (This property is not present for true scores in classical test theory. Examinee true scores are test-dependent.) Statistical characteristics of the particular test items administered to an examinee are taken into account during the process of ability estimation. Therefore, examinees can be compared to each other or to benchmarks on the ability scale even though they may not have taken identical or parallel sets of test items. Second, item parameters do not depend on the particular sample of examinees that is used to estimate them. Adjustments for the nonequivalence of the examinee sample characteristics are taken into account in the process of item parameter estimation. Thus it is said that IRT ability parameters are invariant or independent of the particular choice of test items, and IRT item parameters are invariant or independent of the particular choice of examinees.

The property of item parameter invariance can be observed in Figure 13.1. Notice that the ICF in the upper part of the figure applies equally well to examinees in the distributions for groups A and B that are shown in the bottom part of the figure. For examinees at a given ability level, $\theta = 0.5$, the probability of a correct response or answer to this dichotomously scored item is the same (i.e., 0.79 in this example) regardless of the number of examinees at this ability level in each distribution. For each ability level, there is one and only one probability of a correct response or answer. That probability does not depend on the number of examinees in each ability group at that ability level. In that sense, the ICF applies equally well to both groups, and the item parameters are said to be "invariant" across examinee groups. In contrast, classical item parameters such as item difficulty (i.e., the proportion of examinees answering an item correctly) are not invariant across examinee groups. In the example in Figure 13.1, the test item would be substantially more difficult in group A than in group B. This follows because examinees in Group A would be attempting the test item with relatively lower probabilities of success than would examinees in Group B, and therefore the classical item difficulty estimate (the proportion of examinees answering an item correctly) would be lower in Group A than in Group B. This property of item parameter invariance is present in all IRT models.

IRT models provide items and ability scores on the same scale, and this means, for example, that items can be selected to provide optimal measurement (minimum errors) at ability levels of interest. IRT models also allow the concept of parallel test forms—which is central to reliability estimation in the most popular and commonly used form of the classical test model—to be replaced by a statistical method that allows for estimation of measurement error at each ability level.

IRT models link examinee item responses to ability, and they provide item statistics on the same scale as ability, thus yielding information about where an item provides its best measurement on the ability scale, and about the exact relation between item performance and ability. All of these properties are valuable in designing tests and understanding examinee performance on a test.

Test Characteristic Function

The test characteristic function (TCF; sometimes called the test characteristic curve, or TCC) is the sum of the ICFs that make up a test. Using the following equation, the TCF or TCC can be used to predict scores of examinees at given ability levels:

$$TCF(\theta) = \sum_{i=1}^{n} Pi(\theta).$$

If a test consists of test items that are relatively more difficult than those in a typical test, the TCF is shifted to the right on the ability scale, and examinees tend to have lower expected scores on the test than if easier test items are included. Thus, the TCF is helpful in understanding how—apart from measurement error—examinees can perform differently on two tests. According to the TCF, examinees with a fixed ability level can be predicted to score lower on hard tests and higher on easier tests. Examinees have one ability level at a given point in time, but they will have a unique true score on each sample of test items that is selected.

IRT and classical test theory are related in that an examinee's expected test score at a given ability level, determined by the TCF, is by definition the examinee's true score on that set of test items. The TCF is a mathematical expression that links true score on a particular set of test items to the underlying ability measured by the test. The TCF is also valuable in predicting test score distributions for both known and hypothetical ability distributions and for considering the effects of test design changes on test score distributions. For example, for a given set of ability scores, the expected test score distributions can be compared for two or more samples of test items. A test developer may want to know how substituting 10 easy questions for 10 hard questions in a test will affect the test score distribution (or expected test score distribution). This can be studied with TCFs.

IRT Parameter Estimation, Available Software, and Model Fit

Many methods for estimating IRT model parameters are described in the measurement literature (see, e.g., Bock & Aitkin, 1981; Hambleton & Swaminathan, 1985; Hambleton, Swaminathan, & Rogers, 1991; Lord, 1980; Swaminathan, 1997). Variations on maximum likelihood estimation (MLE)—for example, joint MLE (JMLE), conditional MLE (CMLE), and marginal MLE (MMLE)—have been the most popular and appear in standard IRT software packages such as BILOG (Mislevy & Bock, 1986), MULTILOG (Thissen, 1983), and PARSCALE (Muraki & Bock, 1993).

These estimation procedures commonly assume that the principle of local independence applies. This is equivalent to assuming that a test measures a single trait. By the assumption of local independence, the joint probability of observing the response pattern $(U_1, U_2, \ldots, U_n)$ where (U_i) is either 1 (a correct response) or 0 (an incorrect response) (in the case of the common IRT models for handling dichotomously scored data) is

$$
\begin{aligned}
P(U_1, U_2, &\ldots, U_n \mid \theta) \\
&= P(U_1 \mid \theta) P(U_2 \mid \theta) \cdots P(U_n \mid \theta) \\
&= \prod_{i=1}^{n} P(U_i \mid \theta).
\end{aligned}
$$

This principle means that examinee responses to test items are independent of one another and depend only on examinee ability. The extension to polytomously scored models is accomplished easily by substituting the appropriate form of the mathematical model in the previous expression.

When the response pattern is observed, $U_i = u_i$, the expression for the joint probability is called the likelihood and is denoted

$$
L(u_1, u_2, \ldots, u_n \mid \theta) = \prod_{i=1}^{n} P_i^{u_i} Q_i^{1-u_i}
$$

where $P_i = P(u_i = 1 \mid \theta)$ and $Q_i = 1 - P(u_i = 0 \mid \theta)$. With MLE, the task is to find model parameters that maximize L or some monotonic function of L. L can be differentiated with respect to the ability parameter to produce an equation. If item parameters are known or assumed to be known, the differential equation can be set equal to zero

and solved for the unknown ability parameter. There is one equation for each examinee. Solving the equation for the ability parameter is carried out using the Newton-Raphson procedure. Item parameters are not known, but available estimates can be used instead to obtain the MLE of examinee ability. The same process is repeated for each examinee, substituting his or her response pattern into the equation in order to obtain the corresponding estimate of examinee ability. The basic goal with MLE is to find the value of the unknown ability parameter that maximizes the probability of the data for the examinee who was observed.

A similar procedure can be used to obtain item parameter estimates. The likelihood expression (formed for all examinees and items, assuming their independence) is differentiated with respect to the unknown parameters for an item; ability estimates are assumed to be known; and the resulting differential equations can be solved using the available examinee responses to the item for model item parameter estimates. The procedure is repeated for each item. Additional details of this procedure can be found in books by Hambleton and Swaminathan (1985) and Lord (1980).

In current IRT estimation, MMLE is preferred and is incorporated into software programs such as BILOG (Mislevy & Bock, 1986), MULTILOG (Thissen, 1983), and PARSCALE (Muraki & Bock, 1993). The main advantage is that the ability parameter is removed from the likelihood equation, which permits more satisfactory item parameter estimates to be obtained.

Table 13.1 contains basic information about six currently popular software packages: BILOG-W, LOGIST, LPCM-WIN 1.0, MULTILOG, NOHARM, and PARSCALE.

The usefulness of IRT modeling of test data depends on the extent to which model assumptions are met as well as the extent to which the

Table 13.1   Commonly Used IRT Software

	Models	Estimation Procedures	Fit Indexes	Input Data and Features	Output Documents
BILOG-W (Windows version 3.11) and **BILOG-MG** (DOS Extender)	Unidimensional, 1P, 2P, or 3P logistic models.	Single and multigroup marginal maximum-likelihood item calibration procedures. Scoring using maximum likelihood or Bayesian MAP/EAP estimation.	Test-level likelihood ratio statistic. Test- and item-level chi-square statistics. Raw and standardized item-level residuals conditional on ability.	Dichotomous scoring of response data, up to 1,000 items and unlimited number of examinees. Equating, DIF, and drift analyses can be performed with the multigroup version.	Classical item statistics; IRT item calibration and fit statistics; examinee parameter estimates (scoring); high-quality graphics including test information and measurement error, item response and item information functions, and item fit. Reviewed by Kim (1997).
LOGIST (DOS version)	Unidimensional, 1P, 2P, 3P logistic models.	Joint maximum-likelihood estimation.	N/A	Dichotomous response data. Flexible in holding some parameters fixed at specified values while estimating the others.	Disk file with final parameter estimates; summary of estimation procedure, final parameter estimates, standard error for each item parameter. Reviewed by Wingersky (1983), author of the software, in Hambleton (1983).
LPCM-WIN 1.0 (Windows version 1.0)	Rasch modeling with linear logistic test model, linear logistic model with relaxed assumptions, the rating scale model, the linear rating scale model, and the partial credit model; models for the measurement of change.	Conditional maximum likelihood estimation.	Conditional likelihood ratio statistic.	Dichotomous and multiple category data, unlimited number of examinees; number of items vary depending on the number of parameters estimated.	Input Information; log-likelihood function; parameter estimates; goodness-of-fit statistics; person parameter estimates (optional in RM, RSM and PCM); modifiability parameter estimates (optional in the LLTM for change); Matin–Lof test statistic (optional in RM).

(continued)

529

Table 13.1 Commonly Used IRT Software (*Continued*)

	Models	Estimation Procedures	Fit Indexes	Input Data and Features	Output Documents
MULTILOG (DOS version 6.0)	Unidimensional, 1P, 2P, 3P models, graded and nominal IRT models.	Marginal maximum likelihood estimation in parameter estimation and maximum likelihood and Bayesian estimation in scoring.	Likelihood ratio chi-square goodness-of-fit statistic. Observed and expected frequencies. Standardized residuals. Expected a posteriori.	Multiple category data, multiple group, no strict limitation on the number of items or on the number of examinees.	Internal control codes and the key, data format, and first observation; item summary: item parameters and information, and the observed and expected frequencies for each response alternative; population distribution, test information, and measurement error; summary of the goodness-of-fit.
NOHARM (DOS version)	Multidimensional IRT modeling.			Dichotomous data	
PARSCALE (DOS version 3.3)	Unidimensional 1P, 2P, 3P models, graded response and partial-credit models.	Marginal maximum likelihood estimation.	Likelihood ratio chi-square goodness-of-fit statistic.	Multiple category data, maximum test length and sample size depend on the extended memory.	

chosen IRT model fits the test data. Local independence of examinee responses to items or, equivalently, unidimensionality of the test and nonspeededness of the test are among the assumptions of most of the currently used IRT models (Hambleton & Swaminathan, 1985). Hambleton and Swaminathan classified the types of evidence that are needed to address the adequacy of model fit: (a) investigations of the violation of model assumptions, such as unidimensionality; (b) examinations of the presence of the expected advantages of item and ability invariance; and (c) assessments of the IRT model's performance in predicting item and test results. In addressing fit, researchers most frequently pursue categories (a) and (c).

IRT models are based on strong assumptions, some of which are difficult to attain in real testing situations. Researchers have developed various procedures for investigating violations of each assumption. One widely used method of evaluating test dimensionality is to calculate the tetrachoric correlations among the items, to submit the correlation matrix to a principal components or common factors analysis, and to examine the eigenvalues of the correlation matrix. Two general criteria have been used for interpreting eigenvalues: (a) The first factor should account for at least 20% of the variability, and (b) the first eigenvalue should be several times larger than the second largest eigenvalue (see, e.g., Reckase, 1979). This analysis provides a good approximation for the assessment of the dimensional structure of test data. More up-to-date procedures are identified in van der Linden and Hambleton (1997).

Other assumptions of some IRT models, such as nonspeededness, minimal guessing (with the one- and two-parameter models), and equal discrimination (for the one-parameter model), can be addressed by methods described in Hambleton, Swaminathan, and Rogers (1991).

Researchers have recommended many methods for assessing the extent to which an IRT model fits a dataset (for a review of these methods, see Hambleton, 1989). Examination of the residuals and standardized residuals for a study of model-data fit, investigations of model robustness when all assumptions are not fully met, and statistical tests of fit (e.g., chi-square) are but a few of the many methods used in investigations of model-data fit.

Figure 13.5 displays the ICFs and residuals for two dichotomously scored test items. To obtain these residuals, the ability scale is divided into ability score intervals (a range of 12 to 15 intervals is common). In each ability interval, the actual item performance of the examinees in that ability interval on the test item is plotted (often called the conditional item proportion-correct value). The residual is essentially the difference between actual item-level performance and expected item-level performance as given by the ICF. For the item that was fit by the one-parameter model, performance in Figure 13.5 tends to be lower than expected in the lower ability intervals. Performance tends to be higher than expected in the higher ability intervals. This pattern of performance suggests that the model misfit is due to constraints in the one-parameter model. If a more general model with a discrimination

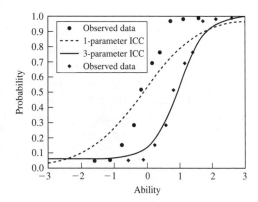

Figure 13.5   Residuals for two item characteristic functions.

parameter were fit to the data, a much better fit of the item data would be possible. (If the *a* parameter were increased, the slope of the curve would increase, and the ICF's fit to the data from the lower- and higher-performing examinees would be better.) For the second item in Figure 13.5, which is fit by a three-parameter logistic model (the curve shown by a solid line), the residuals are small and randomly distributed about the ICF. This characterizes an ICF that fits the available data. Some of the available software (e.g., BILOG) routinely provides residual plots like those in Figure 13.5. The concept of residuals (and of standardized residuals) easily extends to polytomously scored and multidimensional IRT models.

Additional Special Features of IRT Models

Another feature of IRT models is the item information function (IIF). In the case of simple logistic models, IIFs show the contribution of particular items to the assessment of ability. The following equation defines the IIF for logistic models applied to 0-1 data:

$$I_i(\theta) = \frac{[P_i'(\theta)]^2}{P_i(\theta)[1 - P_i(\theta)]}.$$

All variables in the equation were previously defined except $P_i'(\theta)$, which is the expression for the slope of the ICF calculated at each θ on the ability continuum. Items with greater discriminating power contribute more to measurement precision than do items with lower discriminating power. The location of the place on the ability scale at which information is a maximum for an item is

$$\theta_{i_{\max}} = b_i + \frac{1}{Da_i} \ln\left[0.5\left(1 + \sqrt{1 + 8c_i}\right)\right].$$

With the three-parameter model, items provide their maximum information at a point

slightly higher than their difficulty (i.e., because of the influence of guessing, as reflected in the *c* parameter). The one- and two-parameter logistic models for analyzing dichotomous response data assume that guessing does not influence performance on the item (i.e., $c_i = 0.0$), so the right-hand side of the equation reduces to b_i, indicating that items make their greatest contributions to measurement precision near their *b* value on the ability scale. Similar IIFs can be calculated for other IRT models.

Figure 13.6 shows the IIFs for the same six items shown in Figure 13.2. These items show highly variable information functions. Items such as 3, 5, and 6 are the most informative. Item 3 would be especially useful for estimating abilities of higher-performing examinees. In fact, item 2 would be more useful than item 5 or item 6 for estimating the abilities of higher-performing examinees even though item 2 has a lower discrimination level. Items 5 and 6 would be more suitable for estimating the abilities of lower-performing candidates. Item 1, which has the lowest discrimination level among the six items, provides relatively little information at any place on the ability scale but may still be useful when content constraints for a test must be met. From the perspective of measurement precision, however, item 1 is of limited value compared to

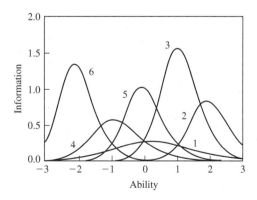

Figure 13.6 A set of six item information functions.

the others. Generally, the c parameter tends to influence the amount of information that an item provides. Because the c parameter is associated with guessing, the higher it is, the less information an item provides.

Another special feature of item response models is the test information function, which is the sum of IIFs in a test:

$$I(\theta) = \sum_{i=1}^{n} I_i(\theta).$$

The test information function provides estimates of the errors associated with (maximum likelihood) ability estimation, specifically,

$$SE(\theta) = \frac{1}{\sqrt{I(\theta)}}.$$

The more information that is provided by a test at a particular ability level, the smaller the errors associated with ability estimation. Figure 13.7 provides an example of both a test information function and the corresponding standard error of ability estimation at each ability level. (The test information function comes from one of the many state proficiency tests being constructed today.) Information from item and test information functions allows applied researchers to design tests that will yield desired levels of measurement precision at selected points along the ability continuum. Test information functions are also

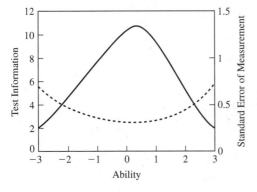

Figure 13.7   Test information function and corresponding standard errors.

important after test administration as a basis for interpreting test scores and setting up confidence bands for ability scores.

Two Applications

Item response theory models are receiving increasing use in test design, test-item selection, and computer-administered adaptive testing. Brief descriptions of these applications follow, and interested readers may consult the measurement literature for further details (for test development, see Hambleton, Swaminathan, & Rogers, 1991; for test score equating, see Lord, 1980; for detection of potentially biased test items, see Holland & Wainer, 1993; and for computer-based testing, see Wainer, 2000a).

Test Development

In test development within a classical framework, items are field-tested to obtain item statistics, item banks are established, and then items are selected from the banks whenever a test is needed. The test developer must consider the content that each item measures as well as the items' features (e.g., format) and statistics.

Test construction methods in an IRT framework are more flexible (Green, Yen, & Burket, 1989; Yen, 1983). IIFs and test information functions are used in place of item statistics and test reliability. IIFs inform the test developer about (a) the locations on the ability scale where items provide the most information, and (b) the relative amounts of information provided by the test items. A test information function informs test developers about the precision of measurement provided by a test at points along the ability scale. Basically, the more information that a test provides at an ability level, the more precisely ability scores can be estimated.

Unlike classical item statistics and reliability, IIFs are independent of the other test items, so the investigator can determine the independent contribution of each item to the measurement precision of the test. The item parameters (especially the discrimination parameter) determine the information offered by each item at each ability level. An item's difficulty controls the location of the highest slope of the ICC and hence the location where the item provides the highest information. The explanation of the functioning of polytomously scored items is more complex, but polytomously scored items are often two or three times more informative than are dichotomously scored items, and they often enhance the precision of measurement at the extremes of the ability continuum.

The precision of ability estimates is a function of the amount of information provided by a test at an ability level. For example, if a test developer wants to set a passing score at $\theta = -1.0$, then the developer should choose items that provide information in the region of -1.0. That would increase measurement precision around $\theta = -1.0$ and reduce the number of examinees that are misclassified (most of whom would have abilities near $\theta = -1.0$). IRT models allow test developers to determine the measurement precision that they want at each ability level and, in so doing, to specify the desired test information function. Test items can then be selected to produce the desired test.

An important feature of the IIF is its additive property: The test information function is obtained by summing up the IIFs (Lord, 1977; Hambleton & Swaminathan, 1985). The test developer selects items that can contribute to the target test information at a prespecified point or range along the ability scale. Those items reduce errors in ability estimation at desired ability levels and contribute to the test's content validity.

A common starting point in test development is to specify the standard error of estimation that is desired at a particular ability range or level. For example, the test developer might wish to produce a test resulting in standard errors of 0.33 in the interval -2.0 to $+2.0$, and 0.50 outside that interval. In addition, the information function of a previous administration of the test, for example, could be used to specify the target test information function. Items that contribute to the test information function at a particular ability level of interest are selected from a pool. When test developers select test items, they often determine their target test information function, compute the information that each item in the pool provides at different points along the ability scale, and choose those items that they believe will contribute the most information in constructing the desired test. When statistical as well as content and format considerations are taken into account, the process can be time-consuming and practically exhausting, even though the basic approach is conceptually satisfying.

Automated item selection methods that use IRT models are beginning to receive attention among testing practitioners (van der Linden & Boekkooi-Timminga, 1989). The development of powerful computers played a role in the inception of automated test development procedures, and many test publishers are using or considering the use of these approaches in the future (Green, Yen & Burket, 1989; Stocking, Swanson & Pearlman, 1990). In automated test development, mathematical optimization algorithms are used to select the items that contribute most to desirable test features, such as measurement precision, content balance, item-format balance, and the length of the test.

Computer-Based Test Designs

Computer-based testing (CBT) is playing an increasingly important role in assessment, and many believe that it will revolutionize testing practices (e.g., Bennett, 1998). The use of computers offers several practical benefits, such as allowing examinees to schedule their own time to take the test and providing unofficial score report information immediately upon test completion. However, using the computer to administer a standard paper and pencil test—in other words, using the computer as an electronic page turner (Bennett, 1998)—does not capitalize on the computer's potential features for improving testing practices. However, combining computer technology with IRT models allows the power of the computer to be more fully exploited leading to one of the most significant practical applications of IRT—computerized adaptive testing (CAT). In fact, many believe that CAT is the most important application of IRT, and it was Frederic Lord's interest in CAT in the 1960s that led to his pioneering IRT research in the following decades until his retirement in 1984 (Lord, 1980).

With CAT, decreased testing time and increased measurement precision result from the fact that the difficulty of the items is tailored or matched to each examinee's ability level. In CAT the examinee is generally first presented with a middle-difficulty item. If the examinee answers the first item correctly, he or she receives a more difficult item next. If the examinee answers the first item incorrectly, he or she receives an easier item next. This adaptation occurs throughout the test administration so that the next item presented is the one that provides the most information about the examinee's level of ability— subject to various constraints that are placed on the test, such as those related to content and item exposure. Figure 13.8 provides a display of the basic item selection procedure for a CAT design. Because of the efficiency of a test that targets items to the examinee's ability level, a CAT session is generally about 50% shorter than one in which a paper-and-pencil test is administered (Wainer, 2000b). Testing time is not wasted by administering items that provide little or no information about a given

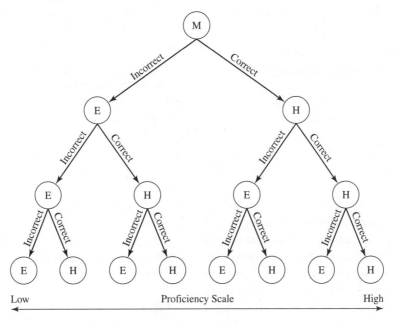

Figure 13.8 Sample item selection procedure for a CAT design.
NOTE: Difficulty of items is represented as follows: "E" for easy, "M" for medium, and "H" for hard.

examinee's ability level. Because the items are targeted toward the individual taking the test, the odds that the examinee will answer them correctly are about 50 percent, and this is the key to CAT's efficiency and increased measurement precision. These targeted items contribute the most to the estimation of examinee ability because they are the items for which examinee performance is the least certain.

Two technical problems presented by this testing design are (a) selecting items to target the examinee's ability level and (b) estimating ability levels for a group of examinees so that individuals can be compared to each other or to performance standards, if examinees are taking different test items at varying difficulty levels (Hambleton, Robin, & Xing, 2000). Solutions to these two technical problems are provided by four features of IRT (Hambleton & Jones, 1993, p. 44):

1. IRT items statistics are independent of the groups from which they were estimated.
2. Scores describing examinee proficiency are not dependent on test difficulty.
3. IRT models provide a basis for matching test items to ability levels.
4. IRT models do not require strict parallel tests for assessing reliability.

These features of IRT are the key to adaptive testing. The invariance of item and examinee parameters provides a means for comparing performances of examinees who do not see the same test items. It is thus possible to obtain ability estimates that are independent of the set of test items that the examinee receives. Also critical to the use of IRT in CAT is the fact that items and ability scores are reported on the same scale, which makes optimal item selection possible. That candidate ability can be estimated independently of the particular difficulty of the test items is especially important because in principle the difficulty level of items administered to candidates

will vary. IRT models provide an easy statistical adjustment for making ability scores comparable. As Wainer (2000b) noted, IRT is "the glue that holds all of the different tests together" (p. 12). In addition, the usefulness of any particular item for a given ability level can be determined (via a consideration of the information function for the item), which aids in item selection during administration of the CAT (Hambleton, Zaal, & Pieters, 1991).

Computer-Based Test Designs and Models

CAT is but one of three major CBT designs that are available; therefore, it is useful to recognize the differences among them. Two basic dimensions along which these test designs differ are unit of administration (item, testlet, or test) and flexibility of administration (adaptive or linear).

The basic unit of administration and analysis may be a single test item, a testlet, or a test. An item is a single test question, with stimulus, stem, and response choices. A testlet is a minitest, or "bundle" of items (Wainer & Kiely, 1987). A test is a collection of items or of testlets that has been prepared in advance and that will be administered in a predetermined order.

When a test proceeds adaptively, the selection of the subsequent unit, whether it is an item or a testlet, depends on the examinee's performance on the previous unit. The test therefore *adapts* to the examinee's proficiency level. When the test proceeds linearly, the selection of the next unit (i.e., item or testlet) has been predetermined; it has no relation to the examinee's performance on the previous unit.

Next we describe three CBT designs and briefly mention the advantages and disadvantages of each.

Linear-on-the-Fly Testing. Linear on-the-fly testing (LOFT) has a linear test design. Therefore, although it is a computer-based test, it is not adaptive. As described by Folk and Smith (1998), in LOFT a unique test form is produced before the examinee begins testing; thus, the unit of administration is the test. The test forms can be generated randomly, producing a unique test form for each examinee that is subject to content and statistical constraints, or a number of fixed test forms can be assembled well in advance and then assigned on a random basis to candidates; the latter approach offers advantages in terms of allowing for prior review of test forms by content experts. The benefits of LOFT include controlling in advance the exposure of items, thus addressing security concerns, and, in the case of fixed test forms, allowing for a preadministration review of content ordering, if desired. The disadvantages of LOFT stem from its linear nature; the design provides neither a reduction in testing time nor an increase in measurement precision compared to paper-and-pencil linear tests. Although IRT can certainly be used in the preparation of the linear tests utilized in LOFT, and although it is very convenient for statistically equating the multiple forms of the test, it is not as critical to its implementation as with the two designs discussed next.

Computerized Adaptive Testing. A CAT can generally be viewed as consisting of the following basic steps (Mills & Stocking, 1996). First, an initial test item is administered. Depending on whether the item is answered correctly or incorrectly, the next item is either harder or easier, respectively. Once there is at least one correct and one incorrect response (which are needed to obtain an ability estimate), the examinee's proficiency is estimated. After that time, items are selected in accordance with the current estimated proficiency level until the stopping rule (e.g., completion of some minimum number of items or achievement of a prespecified level of measurement precision) is satisfied. A diagram of the item selection process for CAT is presented in Figure 13.8.

The unit of administration in CAT is thus the item, and CATs are fully adaptive. Being fully adaptive at the item level obviously results in greater flexibility, but it may also require greater analysis of the effects of "random" item presentation. For example, CATs have been criticized for their failure to take into account context effects. Wainer and Kiely (1987) noted that in paper-and-pencil tests, the test form is previewed for potential context effects (e.g., whether clue from an earlier item could assist an examinee in answering a later item). In a CAT, the test is conducted in real time: Items are presented in any order, so context effects may occur. This is one of the reasons that researchers have investigated alternatives to the CAT approach (such as the multistage testing design, considered in the next section). Some context effects can be controlled via constraints placed on the selection of test items, but it would be next to impossible to control all of them in practice because so many combinations of test items are possible.

CAT presents additional practical challenges. The selection of items is more complex than is represented in Figure 13.8. Concerns regarding psychometrics, content coverage, and item exposure all influence the determination of which item is to be administered next. Psychometric considerations relate to the estimation of the examinee's ability, which is critical to subsequent item selection. Available estimation methods include MLE as well as Bayesian approaches such as expected a posteriori (EAP) and maximum a posteriori (MAP). Further information about ability estimation procedures can be found in Hambleton and Swaminathan (1985), Lord (1980), van der Linden and Pashley (2000), and Wainer and Mislevy (2000).

In addition to achieving a specified level of measurement precision (or, when scores are used to make decisions, achieving a specified level of decision accuracy), testing programs are nearly always concerned about content considerations in the selection of items administered to examinees. Therefore, there is often a tension between psychometric and content considerations in item selection. The weighted deviations model (WDM; Stocking & Swanson, 1993; Swanson & Stocking, 1993) sets target constraints consisting of both psychometric properties and the matching of content specifications. An alternative to the WDM is optimal constrained adaptive testing (van der Linden & Reese, 1998; van der Linden, 2000). Rather than selecting only a single item at each point in the test, a shadow test is constructed via the CAT software in which all remaining items are selected from the item pool for the current ability estimate. The shadow test meets all of the content and statistical constraints required for the total test and modifies them to reflect the items that have already been administered to the candidate. Then, the most optimal item is selected for administration. This process is repeated following each administration of a test item, and it has the advantage that at each point when an item is selected, it is selected from a collection of items that represents an optimal test for the examinee. Selecting items sequentially, as is done in the typical CAT administration, may not produce an optimal test for the examinee.

Even after psychometric and content considerations are addressed, however, the problem remains that any given item may be administered so often that it is overexposed, which could compromise test security. Items that show the highest level of validity but are overexposed to examinees will show less and less validity over time. An example of this problem occurred when a test preparation company sent examinees to take the CAT version of the *Graduate Record Examination* in order to memorize items. Because many

of the examinees were similar in ability, they saw some of the same items. As a result, they were able to corroborate each other's memories and provide the company with a fairly accurate representation of many items that examinees of similar ability levels could expect to encounter (Davey & Nering, 1998). Because of security concerns and their impact on validity, several approaches to controlling item exposure have been developed. These approaches include selecting less than optimal items (e.g., not always selecting the most discriminating item to administer to examinees) and placing restrictive limits on the proportion of examinees who will be administered particular items over prespecified intervals of time. For further information on procedures for controlling item exposure, see Davey and Nering (1998), Folk and Smith (1998), and Stocking and Lewis (2000).

Item pools for CAT should be large enough to support all the item selection considerations just described. High-quality items must exist for all levels of proficiency present in the population of examinees, and enough items must be available for any given difficulty level so that the same items are not repeatedly administered to examinees. This places a new demand on item writers: namely, to write items to specific levels of item difficulty. It is also important to have as many highly discriminating items as possible, because they play a role in maximizing the efficiency and precision of CATs. Similarly, because of the shorter length of a CAT, flawed items have an even greater consequence and thus should be located and eliminated in order to maintain the integrity of the item pool for a test (Hambleton, Zaal, & Pieters, 1991). Discussion of the challenges posed by CAT in terms of item pools, as well as some approaches that may be used to design optimal pools, may be found in Flaugher (2000), Mills and Steffen (2000), and van der Linden and Veldkamp (2000).

Even when item pools are sufficient to support optimal selection and administration of items, there may be difficulties in estimating the candidate's ability. An aberrant response pattern for an examinee, which may cause problems in ability estimation, may stem from several factors. Examinees may be responding randomly in an attempt merely to familiarize themselves with the test, or they may have advance knowledge of some items on the test, causing them to answer those items correctly regardless of the items' difficulty for their ability level (van Krimpen-Stoop & Meijer, 2000). Such aberrant response patterns may make the estimation of ability unstable. For that reason, person-fit measures such as those described by van Krimpen-Stoop and Meijer have been developed. Research into this area is an important avenue for CAT.

Other practical issues involved in the development and administration of a CAT include the choice of an IRT model and calibration of items (Wainer & Mislevy, 2000), item review by examinees (Mills, 1999; Wainer, 1993), and selection of a stopping rule (Thissen & Mislevy, 2000). Overviews of these issues, as well as others relevant to CAT, are included in Drasgow and Olson-Buchanan (1999), van der Linden and Glas (2000), and Wainer (2000a).

Multistage Testing. In the basic multistage testing (MST) design, the selectable entity is the testlet or block of items, in contrast to a full-adaptive CAT, in which the selectable entity is the item (Lord, 1980). Thus, MST can be seen as a partially adaptive design. The minimum number of testlets is two, and there are often more. The first testlet is a routing testlet for determining the examinee's general ability level. The testlets then branch, so that examinees who have received a relatively high ability-level estimate will get a testlet that differs from that given to examinees who have received a relatively low ability-level estimate. Items may also branch within a testlet: The subsequent item would be easier for an examinee who got the first item incorrect and more difficult for an examinee who got the first item correct. An example of a three-stage MST, without item branching within the testlets, is presented in Figure 13.9.

As outlined by Folk and Smith (1998), the MST design has several advantages, one being that the testlets can be assembled in advance. As a result, the test developer can balance content within and across the testlets, which is more difficult with a fully adaptive CAT. Within a testlet, items can be ordered in terms of difficulty, if desired. In addition, because the order of items is fixed, each examinee encounters the items in the same context,

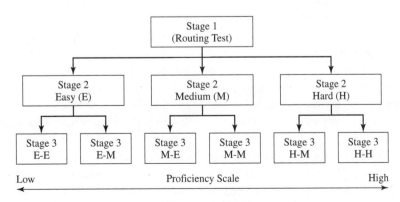

Figure 13.9 Sample testlet selection procedure for MST design.

thus decreasing any possible context effects and accommodating set-based items in which conditional independence cannot be assumed. MSTs can also assist in reducing item exposure, because they allow investigators to create in advance test forms that vary the items that are presented to examinees of a given ability level (Patsula & Hambleton, 1999).

Testlets also allow item review at least on a limited basis (i.e., within the testlet, prior to moving to the next testlet); this option is appealing to examinees and is a solution to two of the most frequent criticisms of CAT: Examinees must answer an item before moving forward in a test (i.e., they cannot skip an item and return to it later), and examinees may not review items once they have keyed in their answers. However, a disadvantage of testlets is that they are not as psychometrically efficient as CATs (Kingsbury & Zara, 1991). MSTs have received increased attention as fully adaptive CATs have shown their shortcomings and practical challenges; technical advances in MST include the development of testlet response theory (Wainer, Bradlow, & Du, 2000).

Automated Test Assembly

The process of constructing test forms from item banks can benefit tremendously from the use of computers. Automated test assembly (ATA) refers to the procedures used to automate test construction through the use of computer algorithms (Luecht, 1998). Utilizing the computer to meet numerous requirements of test form design allows the task to proceed more quickly. The computer is able to consider simultaneously test assembly goals more quickly and accurately than a test developer or test development committee can, although test developers may make minor adjustments to the resulting form to reflect concern with "fuzzy" criteria that are harder to specify (Luecht, 1998). Because classical test theory lacks meaningful item parameters that are additive in the test items, IRT is generally the measurement model of choice for ATA (van der Linden, 1998a, 1998b). Tests in all three CBT designs can be constructed with ATA.

Applications of CBT

One of the first large-scale assessments for which a CAT was implemented was the ASVAB, one of the largest testing programs in the world (Sands, Waters, & McBride, 1997). In addition to the ASVAB, other large-scale assessments currently administered via computer include the *Graduate Record Examination* (GRE), the *Computerized Placement Test,* the *Graduate Management Admissions Test* (GMAT), the *Test of English as a Foreign Language* (TOEFL), and licensure and certification tests administered by the National Council of State Boards of Nursing, the National Board of Medical Examiners, the National Council of Architectural Registration Boards, Microsoft, Novell, and many more. CBT is thus becoming a major force in educational and credentialing testing.

As Embretson and Reise (2000) noted, applications of CBT have been slower to come to psychological testing, in part because of the lack of software to facilitate the transition. However, two examples of areas in which some progress has been made are personality assessment and attitude measurement. In the former area, Waller and Reise (1989) found that the computerization of a personality scale resulted in a 50% reduction in the amount of items that needed to be administered, with minimal loss of information. Although there may be some resistance to the shortening of traditionally long personality assessments, as Reise (1999) noted attention should be directed to the possibility that shorter CATs will allow for the use of more varied item formats that better represent a given personality construct (Embretson & Reise, 2000). In the area of attitude measurement, researchers have found similar reductions in the length of scales needed for a given level of measurement precision. Also, the use of IRT-based CATs—in which different item formats may be used on the same test to estimate easily the examinee's point on a latent-trait continuum—is a logical choice for increasing the construct validity of scales that measure attitudes. Further information about CAT applications in the area of attitude measurement can be found in Koch, Dodd, and Fitzpatrick (1990) and Dodd, De Ayala, and Koch (1995). Finally, it should be noted that automated approaches to test construction such as ATA may play an important role also in the future construction of psychological assessments. The flexibility of automatization and the ability to handle content and statistical criteria in item selection will be valuable to psychologists assembling new versions of tests.

CHANGES IN TESTING PRACTICES

There have been many technical advances in educational and psychological measurement over the past several decades. IRT, a major focus of this chapter, has been one of the most important developments because of its practical applications in CBT, differential item functioning analyses, test development, and other topics described previously. Sometimes additional advances have also taken place because of a partnership with IRT. These include expanding new item formats to target more fully the construct of interest, for which IRT is critical in its capability of placing scores for examinee ability on a common reporting scale despite the use of several different item formats in one test or the administration of different items to each examinee. Efforts toward educational reform and mandates for accountability in high-stakes educational assessments have also focused intense interest in the technical adequacy of tests.

Although the validity of inferences made from test scores has always been an important issue, the increased use of high-stakes assessments (e.g., those required in some states for graduation) has intensified the scrutiny under which tests have come. This section highlights some of the major areas in which testing practices have evolved as a result of technical advances and the increased focus on test use.

New Item Types

The most commonly recognized item format is that of the multiple-choice question. Although some have criticized the multiple-choice question for relying too heavily on the recall of isolated facts at the expense of assessing higher-order cognitive skills, others counter that "items can be written to tap complex thinking processes, reasoning, evaluation of arguments, and the application of knowledge to new situations" (Anastasi & Urbina, 1997, p. x). In addition, multiple-choice questions are popular in part because they can be scored easily and relatively inexpensively and because they permit greater content coverage in that examinees can answer them more quickly than they can answer constructed-response items.

Regardless of the validity of criticisms of the multiple-choice item format, they have served as an impetus for the development and implementation of more varied item types. As a result, constructed-response questions—in which the examinee constructs or provides an answer (in contrast to selecting it from provided options)—have become very popular recently. In addition, increasing use of computers in test administration has greatly widened the types of item formats that are available. In its infancy, CBT was utilized mainly for its convenience in adapting tests and providing immediate score reports. Currently, researchers are increasingly taking advantage of the unique capabilities of

Table 13.2   Dimensions for Item Types

Dimension	Examples
Item format	Selected-response items: multiple-choice, passage editing (Davey et al., 1997); constructed-response items: text revision (Breland, 1998), essays (Educational Testing Service, 2000; College Board, 2000).
Response action	Bubble in oval on paper answer sheet; use mouse or touch screen to indicate answer on computer; use mouse to click and drag items to different positions, to use graphics tools, or to move among screens (National Council of Architect Registration Boards, 2000); joysticks, trackballs, microphones, voice recognition software.
Media inclusion	Graphics; animation; video (Drasgow et al., 1999); audio for tests of language proficiency and music knowledge, as well as a supplement to visually presented stimuli on other assessments.
Interactivity	Conflict resolution video assessment (Drasgow et al., 1999); patient care simulations (Federation of State Medical Boards of the United States, Inc., & National Board of Medical Examiners, 1999).

NOTE: Dimensions are those used by Parshall et al. (2000).

computers to aid in assessment. Parshall, Davey, and Pashley (2000) provided an overview of several dimensions along which innovative item types may be described: item format, response action, media inclusion, and level of interactivity. Brief descriptions of these dimensions are summarized in Table 13.2. As noted by Parshall et al., these dimensions are not independent and may interact with each other in the format of any given assessment.

Item Format

Items can be classified into two general formats: selected-response and constructed-response. The multiple-choice item is one example of a selected-response format, but there are many others. For example, Davey, Godwin, and Mittelholtz (1997) described a computer-based test of writing skills that uses an innovative selected-response format. Examinees are required to edit a passage presented on the computer. When the cursor is moved to a given place on the screen, alternatives for rewriting that section are presented. Examinees can choose revised versions of as many parts of the passage as they choose. Furthermore, examinees can either fix errors or leave them alone, and they can introduce errors into text that has none.

In a constructed-response item, an examinee does not choose among responses, but instead constructs them. In contrast to the writing assessment just described, Breland (1998) outlined an item format in which examinees constructed their own revisions to the text sections containing errors. Other examples of constructed-response formats include the essay question, which requires the examinee to construct a written response. Essay questions may assess writing skills (e.g., GRE Writing Assessment; Educational Testing Service, 2000) or content knowledge (e.g., Advanced Placement Test in Psychology; College Board, 2000).

The new focus on constructed-response items in educational assessment in the mid-1980s required measurement specialists to extend the earlier work of Samejima, Bock, and others in order to develop IRT models that could handle polytomous response data. This led to the development of new IRT models, new approaches to model parameter estimation and assessment of model fit, new IRT software such as MULTILOG and PARSCALE, and so on.

Response Action

The second dimension outlined by Parshall et al. (2000) is that of response action, or how the examinee physically responds to an item stimulus. The most commonly recognized response action may be bubbling in an oval on an answer sheet, as with multiple-choice items given as part of a paper-and-pencil test. Other paper-and-pencil response modes include writing an essay or filling in short answers. With the introduction of CBT, the range of available response actions becomes much greater. At the simplest level, examinees can now use a mouse or touch a screen to indicate their answers to multiple-choice questions. Similarly, essays can now be typed into the computer using a keyboard. However, the computer's capabilities allow for the development of much more innovative response modes, such as using the mouse to click and drag items into different positions and to move from screen to screen to access different sources of information. One example of the use of these innovative response modes is the *Architect Registration Examination* (National Council of Architect Registration Boards, 2000). In this exam, several vignettes are presented that require examinees to demonstrate specific skills and abilities. Examinees design their solutions on the screen using graphics tools that are provided; in addition, they move among information screens containing, for example, design requirements, building codes, and illustrations. Turning from the mouse to other response actions, Parshall et al. noted that other input devices may provide for better measurement of different skills, such as joysticks or trackballs for movement skills, and microphones and voice recognition software for speaking skills.

Media Inclusion

Using computers also expands the range of media that may be part of an assessment.

As described by Parshall et al. (2000), these media include graphics, audio, video, and animation. Graphics can be presented more realistically on a computer screen than on paper-and-pencil tests; for example, full-color images can be shown on a fine arts or medical examination, and these images can be enlarged or rotated as needed by the examinee. The use of audio is a fairly obvious choice for tests of language proficiency and music knowledge, where this medium has previously been used as a part of paper-and-pencil tests. Students with limited English proficiencies and those with reading-related special education plans may also benefit from this form of assessment.

Turning to the use of video in assessment, Drasgow, Olson-Buchanan, and Moberg (1999) described the development of a computerized interactive video assessment in which full-motion video and accompanying audio are presented to examinees. This assessment focuses on conflict resolution skills, and the authors noted that interactive video is a good choice for the assessment of social skills because the medium more closely reflects the context in which social interactions actually take place. They suggested that a high-quality video and audio presentation may effectively model real-world situations, leading to a visceral response from an examinee that might influence his or her response. Thus, the results may be more generalizable to an actual social setting than those obtained from a written test. Animation, another medium that may be employed in test items, may be viewed as a simpler form of video and may be more appropriate when the examinee's task is to focus on several critical details instead of a larger, more complex stimulus.

Level of Interactivity

Items may also differ along the dimension of interactivity, which Parshall et al. (2000)

described as the degree to which the context of the item changes as the examinee proceeds through it. Some items are not interactive at all, and once the examinee selects or constructs a response, the item is complete. In contrast, some assessments include problems that are very complex and have a high degree of interactivity. One example is the conflict resolution assessment just described (Drasgow et al., 1999). Another is Step 3 of the United States Medical Licensing Examination (Federation of State Medical Boards of the United States, Inc., and the National Board of Medical Examiners, 1999). In the simulations that comprise this test, examinees are presented with a clinical situation that they must manage by determining what diagnostic information to obtain and how to treat the patient. Based on the examinee's actions, the computer presents information on how the patient's condition changes over time, which can influence subsequent steps taken by the examinee. These simulations thus attempt to reflect the features of situations that physicians will encounter in the real world of patient care.

Cognitively Based Test Models

Over the past two decades, researchers have recognized the potential benefits of combining cognitive psychology principles and psychometrics in test development (e.g., see Glaser, 1981). Although the earliest psychological tests did reflect ties to cognitive science, this connection became weaker as psychometric developments evolved along less theoretically based lines (Snow & Lohman, 1989). In recent years, however, increasing attention has been paid to the ways in which information that is gained from research in cognitive psychology can inform measurement.

Several authors have noted that most early measurement models were focused on the measurement of one dominant trait underlying performance on a test, in the interest of making accurate predictions for selection purposes (Everson, 1999; Mislevy, 1993; Snow & Lohman, 1989). Validation efforts were similarly tied to gathering predictive validity evidence. Increasingly, however, psychometric models and cognitive information-processing models have been combined in an attempt to broaden the usefulness of test scores. Gains made in the conceptualization of previously broadly viewed constructs such as intelligence have informed these developments (Sternberg, 1985). As Mislevy observed, "learners increase their competence not by simply accumulating new facts and skills, but by reconfiguring their knowledge structures, by automating procedures and chunking information to reduce memory loads, and by developing strategies and models that tell them when and how facts and skills are relevant. The types of observations and the patterns in data that reflect the ways that students think, perform, and learn cannot be accommodated by traditional models and methods" (pp. 19–20).

There are several new types of approaches to model-based measurement. They share the objective of providing greater information about an individual's capabilities than could one test score that is presumed to reflect one underlying ability on which those tested can be ranked. Everson (1999) has classified these new models into three general types: IRT-based models, statistical pattern recognition methods, and Bayesian inference networks.

Within the first class, that of IRT-based models, the details of the approaches differ, but in general they aim to reveal a complex picture of an individual's competence in a given domain. Examples of this type of approach are the multidimensional IRT models developed by Embretson (1984, 1985, 2000), in which examinees' success depends on multiple traits. An example may best serve to illustrate the features of these models. Maris

(1995) utilized Embretson's multicomponent latent trait model (MLTM) (Embretson & Reise, 2000; Whitely, 1980) in a study of synonym items; specifically, he investigated the role that two components—generation and evaluation—played in solving the items. With MLTM, which uses a mathematical model of response processes in conjunction with an IRT model, the assumption is made that success on an item depends on more than one trait. Maris's results supported the presence of the two components, although the relative contribution of the generation component was judged to be generally greater than that of the evaluation component. Ability estimates were produced for each examinee on both components, thus providing information that could be used for diagnostic purposes. In addition, the degree to which each component contributed to the difficulty of any given item was estimated. This example shows that this type of model-based measurement has the potential to inform validation efforts, assist with diagnosis and remediation, and facilitate more efficient construction of test items (Embretson, 2000).

The second class of new test models summarized by Everson (1999) is that of statistical pattern recognition methods. One example of this type of model is the rule-space approach that was developed and applied by Tatsuoka (1983, 1990, 1993). Following a thorough task analysis of the domain under consideration (e.g., mathematics), classification spaces are created that relate to different states of knowledge and from which typical mistakes can be inferred. Bayesian decision rules are used to classify test takers into the different classification spaces, and diagnostic determinations can be made on the basis of these assignments. For example, review of responses made to subtraction items can reveal persistent patterns of errors, such as consistently subtracting the smaller absolute value from the larger absolute value and giving the answer the sign of the larger number (Tatsuoka, 1983). This pattern recognition approach clearly provides more fruitful information for diagnosis and remediation than does simply obtaining right or wrong scores for each test item. Currently, researchers are trying to use some of Tatsuoka's ideas to enhance the reporting of SAT scores in order to provide students with useful diagnostic information for improving their skills and performance on the test at a future time.

The third type of test model described by Everson (1999) is those using Bayesian inference networks. These models build on the statistical pattern recognition approaches just described but extend their use to larger and more complex assessments. As with the first two approaches, this model must be used within the context of a theory that governs individuals' responses to items with given characteristics. Everson notes that "thus, in theory, inference networks are able to build upon cognitive task analyses and statistical pattern recognition methods, extend them to draw inferences about the probabilistic structure of the student's knowledge state, and then update those 'beliefs' as the examinee moves through a set of assessment tasks" (p. 122). Further information about these Bayesian networks and their practical application can be found in Mislevy (1995).

The foregoing brief descriptions of new test models provide a glimpse at intriguing advances that are resulting from the merging of cognitive science and psychometrics. Glaser (1981) suggested that these cooperative efforts will be necessary as test developers seek to (a) expand the potential for assessments to help students achieve in the educational system as opposed to merely measuring their abilities, (b) develop the complex competencies that will be needed as technological advances continue, and (c) improve individuals' potential to learn from future experiences. These are noteworthy challenges, and steps toward meeting them are facilitated by the new test models just described.

Setting Performance Standards

Tests are often used to categorize individuals. When tests are used in this way, performance standards (also called cut points, cut scores, passing scores, and achievement levels) must be established along the score range. The *Standards for Educational and Psychological Testing* (AERA et al., 1999) provide three examples of how the establishment of performance standards depends on the setting in which the test is used, as well as its intended purpose. For example, in an employment setting standards may be set at the location that allows for the selection of enough candidates to meet a predetermined quota. In contrast, within an educational setting in which students are assigned to different types of instruction based on their test scores, performance standards may be selected by conducting research that establishes the type of instruction that was most beneficial to certain types of students. For example, a performance standard would be placed at the point on the test score scale at which neither type of instruction was clearly indicated as superior for the group on either side of that score. More common in educational testing is the establishment of performance standards on achievement tests that sort examinees into levels of accomplishment in a subject areas. The levels might be labeled "Below Basic," "Basic," "Proficient," and "Advanced."

In a third type of setting, that of certification and licensure, the *Standards for Educational and Psychological Testing* (AERA et al., 1999) note that a performance standard is set to distinguish between candidates who have achieved a desired level of knowledge and skills to practice the profession and those who have not. In this type of environment, as well as within other criterion-referenced testing contexts, such as high-stakes educational testing, judgmental procedures are used mainly to set performance standards. Scrutiny of such standard-setting procedures and the development of new approaches have been stimulated in part by three trends that have characterized large-scale testing—specifically educational testing—in the past decade. The first general trend is the overall increase in the use of high-stakes tests for accountability purposes in education, which has highlighted the importance of sound standard-setting procedures (Cizek, 2001). Two additional specific trends are the increased use of constructed-response items and the establishment of multiple cut scores (Berk, 1986). As a result, the more traditional standard-setting procedures have been expanded for these two uses, and additional procedures have also been developed.

Next we describe important methodological issues that need to be kept in mind for all procedures as well as and criteria that should be evaluated to judge the validity of a given procedure. For a comprehensive historical overview of specific standard-setting procedures used over the years, see Berk (1986), Hambleton (1980), and Livingston and Zieky (1982). For in-depth descriptions of more recent procedures, see Cizek (2001), Hambleton (1998), and Jaeger, Mullis, Bourque, and Shakrani (1996) for educational assessment and Mills (1995) and Plake (1998) for credentialing examinations.

A distinction has commonly been made between standard-setting procedures that are test-centered and those that are examinee-centered (Cizek, 1996a, 1996b; Jaeger, 1989; Kane, 1994). However, as assessments have become more diverse, due in part to the inclusion of more varied item types, additional dimensions have been formulated to describe more fully the differences among the emerging standard-setting procedures. Hambleton, Jaeger, Plake, and Mills (in press) outlined the following six dimensions that may be used to differentiate standard-setting procedures.

Dimension 1: Focus of Panelists' Judgments. The panelists may be instructed to focus on one of four types of stimuli in order to make their judgments. The first type is tasks or items on the assessment, including scoring rubrics, if applicable. The second type is the examinees themselves. The third type is examinees' responses to the tasks or items on the assessment. The fourth type of stimulus is candidates' scores on those tasks or items.

Dimension 2: Panelists' Judgmental Task. The second dimension is linked to the first. Given the focus of the panelists' judgments, what is their task? First, if panelists are focused on items, they may be asked to estimate the performance of borderline examinees on those tasks. In the second case, in which the focus is on examinees, panelists may be asked to sort those examinees into performance categories. Third, if examinee responses are the focus, panelists may be required to classify those responses into categories or determine which are characteristic of borderline examinees. Fourth, when panelists focus on scored performances, they may be asked to identify the performance categories into which those scored work samples should be sorted.

Dimension 3: Judgmental Process. The judgmental process may be characterized in several ways. Judgments may be made individually or in a group setting. As discussed earlier, the types of feedback that are given may vary, and there may be a second round of ratings after the initial round of ratings that consists of sharing of empirical information such as item statistics and discussion among panel members.

Dimension 4: Composition and Size of Panel. Panels may be composed of different types of members, including experts or stakeholders. The panels may be homogenous or heterogeneous, and their sizes may vary as well.

Dimension 5: Validation of Resulting Passing Standards. The validity of the resulting performance standards must be supported by different types of evidence.

Dimension 6: Nature of the Assessment. An assessment may be characterized by several features. For example, the types of items comprising the assessment may include selected response or constructed response. In addition, the assessment may be unidimensional or multidimensional. Scoring may be compensatory or conjunctive.

These six dimensions proposed by Hambleton et al. (in press) provide a flavor of the many ways in which standard-setting processes may vary. Several examples may serve to illustrate how several of these dimensions may play out within a given procedure. One of the most frequently used procedures for setting standards on educational tests is the Angoff (1971) procedure. The focus of the panelists' judgments (Dimension 1) is test items, which are first reviewed individually and then in a group (Dimension 3) in order to rate how likely panel members think a minimally competent candidate is to answer the item correctly (Dimension 2). Ratings for each panelist are summed across items, and these sums are averaged across panelists to calculate the cut score.

A different type of panelist task can be found in the contrasting groups procedure. In this approach, the panelists' focus is on examinees (Dimension 1). Their charge is to identify one group of examinees whose members are clearly above a particular standard and another group whose members are clearly below the standard (Dimension 2). The test is administered to these groups, and the test score distributions of the groups are then contrasted to select the cut score. Figure 13.10 depicts

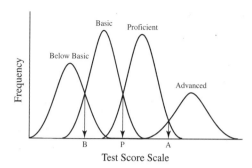

Figure 13.10   Contrasting group standard-setting method.

NOTE: The labeled points on the horizontal axis indicate the intersections of adjacent score distributions; initial cut scores are set at these points (B for basic, P for proficient, and A for advanced).

score distributions for students with four different levels of proficiency. Initial cut-scores are set at the three intersections of adjacent scores.

Perhaps one of the most critical dimensions listed by Hambleton et al. (in press) is Dimension 5, which relates to the validation of resulting cut scores. Regardless of how much time and effort is put into constructing, field-testing, and administering an assessment, the utility of resulting scores will be questionable if the standard set is not valid for a given use of the test. Numerous authors have outlined criteria on which standard-setting procedures may be evaluated. Table 13.3 presents some of

Table 13.3   Summary of Criteria for Evaluating a Standard-Setting Study

Evaluation Criterion	Description	Sources
Procedural		
"Explicitness"	The degree to which the standard-setting process was clearly and explicitly defined *before* implementation.	van der Linden (1995)
Documentation	The extent to which features of the standard-setting study are reviewed and documented.	Cizek (1996b); Hambleton (1998)
Practicality	The degree to which the standard-setting task can be visualized as being feasible (i.e., not too cognitively challenging) for judges.	Kane (1994); Cizek (1996b)
Internal		
Intrajudge consistency	Determine the degree to which judges are able to provide ratings that are consistent with the empirical item or task difficulties.	van der Linden (1982); Cizek (1996b); Berk (1986)
Caution indexes	Identify judges whose ratings are inconsistent with the majority.	Jaeger (1988, 1991)
Interjudge consistency	Evaluate consistency of item ratings and cut scores across judges.	Jaeger (1991); Cizek, (1996b); Berk (1986)
Other measures	Evaluate consistency of cut scores across item types, content areas, and cognitive processes.	Kane (1995)
External		
Intersession consistency	Evaluate consistency of cut scores across independent replications (e.g., consistency over two independent panels of judges using the same standard-setting procedure).	Cizek (1996b); van der Linden (1995)
Comparisons to other sources of information	Investigate the relationship between decisions made using the test to other criteria (e.g., grades, performance on a similar test, job performance, etc.).	Berk (1986); Giraud, Impara, & Buckendahl (2000); Shepard, Glaser, Linn, & Bohrnstedt (1993)
Reasonableness of standards	Evaluate the extent to which the resulting cut scores are feasible or realistic.	van der Linden (1995); Kane (1998)

NOTE: From Sireci, Pitoniak, Meara, & Hambleton, (2000). Adapted with permission.

these criteria, and the listed sources are useful for further information.

Changing Conceptions of Validity

For interpretations of test scores to be meaningful, evidence must be gathered to support their validity. The recently revised *Standards for Educational and Psychological Testing* (AERA et al., 1999) note that validity is therefore the most fundamental issue during test development and evaluation. The *Standards* characterize validity as "the degree to which evidence and theory support the interpretations of test scores entailed by proposed uses of tests" (p. 9).

Although the validity of test scores has always been an important consideration, recent trends in educational and psychological measurement have increased the attention that researchers are giving this critical concept. For example, high-stakes tests are becoming more prevalent, and with the increased visibility and impact of these assessments comes increased scrutiny of the validity of resulting test scores. Many of these assessments contain relatively new item types that are designed to assess more fully the construct under consideration, and exploration of the validity of these new item formats and associated scoring rubrics is warranted. Other tests are being administered via a computer with IRT model-based scoring. Clearly, with the many innovations in testing practices, and with heightened interest and use of the scores in hiring, graduating, selecting, diagnosing, and so on, validity questions have become very important.

In the 1999 *Standards for Educational and Psychological Testing,* evidence supporting the validity of test sources is seen to come from five sources (see Table 13.4): test content, response processes, internal structure, relations to other variables, and consequences of testing. This organizational structure reflects a unitary conceptualization of validity

in which the construct under investigation has assumed ultimate prominence. Over the past few decades, this formulation has gained increased support; its nature can perhaps best be illustrated by briefly describing past concepts of validity and contrasting them with current notions (for informative reviews of the history, see Messick, 1988, and Shepard, 1993).

The *Standards for Educational and Psychological Testing,* originally published in 1954 (by AERA et al.) and 1955 (by AERA, Committee on Test Standards) as two separate documents, were subsequently revised and published jointly by the APA, AERA, and NCME in 1966, 1974, 1985, and 1999. Review of early versions of the *Standards* reveals that validation efforts were then viewed as closely tied to the use of the test. In the 1954 document, four uses of testing are described, and four different types of validity are given, one for each type of use: (a) content validity, applicable to achievement tests, in which the test is assumed to sample performance from a larger domain of situations or subject matter; (b) predictive validity, relevant to tests used to predict an individual's performance on a future measure; (c) concurrent validity, for those tests used to estimate the individual's current status on a variable; and (d) construct validity, for tests used to infer the extent to which the individual can be characterized by the trait (construct) thought to underlie test performance. In later years, predictive validity and concurrent validity were collapsed into one type of validity, labeled criterion-related validity. This resulted in the common recognition of three separate types of validity, also termed the *trinitarian doctrine* (Guion, 1980).

In contrast, AERA et al.'s 1999 *Standards for Educational and Psychological Testing* note that "evolving conceptualizations of validity no longer speak of different types of validity but speak instead of different lines of validity evidence, all in service of providing information relevant to a specific intended

Table 13.4   Sources of Validity Evidence

Source	Description	Examples
Test content	The relationship between the content of the test and the construct that the test is intended to measure is examined.	(a) Conduct a job analysis to link test content specifications to knowledge, skills, and abilities required of practitioners to perform in the profession or occupation. (b) Obtain expert judgments of the degree to which test items represent the content domain.
Response processes	Individual responses to test items are analyzed.	(a) Gather information from examinees about their strategies for answering specific items. (b) Observe other facets of performance, such as response times and eye movements.
Internal structure	The extent to which the relationships among test items are consistent with the construct is reviewed.	(a) Examine the dimensionality of the test. (b) Conduct differential item functioning (DIF) analyses to examine group differences and possible test bias.
Relations to other variables	The relationship of test scores to variables that are external to the test is examined.	(a) Obtain convergent evidence (how test scores relate to other measures of similar constructs), and divergent evidence (how test scores relate to other measures of different constructs). (b) Examine how well test scores predict performance on an external criterion.
Consequences of testing	Evidence related to intended and unintended consequences of test use is reviewed.	(a) Examine sources of invalidity, such as construct underrepresentation or construct-irrelevant variance, for their possible contribution to group differences in test scores. (b) Examine whether benefits of the test score uses, whatever they are, are realized.

NOTE: Sources of validity evidence and some examples were taken from the Standards for Educational and Psychological Testing (AERA et al., 1999).

interpretation of test scores. Thus, many lines of evidence can contribute to an understanding of the construct meaning of test scores" (p. 5). The *Standards* now define construct as "the concept or characteristic that a test is designed to measure" (p. 5), for example, (a) achievement in a given subject, (b) skill in a particular job, or (c) psychological variables such as depression or self-esteem (p. 9). This broadening of the term *construct* contrasts with past uses, when it indicated unobservable traits inferred from observations, as implied by the 1954 limited use of the term.

AERA et al.'s 1999 *Standards for Educational and Psychological Testing* thus stress that the validity of all, not just some, test scores should be evaluated and that the construct or concepts that are intended to be measured by a test must be considered. A conceptual framework must be formulated for the test in order to delineate the features of the construct and how it relates to other constructs and variables. All of the different lines of validity evidence mentioned earlier (test content, response processes, internal structure, relations to other variables, and consequences of testing) are evaluated in the context of the construct and of the proposed use of the test. In essence, a validity argument is built in which evidence is collected, rival hypotheses are considered, and all information is carefully weighed and evaluated (see Kane, 1992, for an explication of the features of validity arguments).

In addition to a reformulation of validity as a unitary concept, emphasis has increasingly been given to the role of the test user in ensuring the appropriate uses of tests. This change in emphasis reflects a growing awareness that tests can have a great impact on those who take them and on society as a whole. For example, AERA et al.'s 1974 *Standards for Educational and Psychological Testing* took note of increased concern that tests invade people's privacy or discriminate against certain groups (p. 1). As a result, it was the first version to include a separate section related to the use of tests. Similarly, although previous versions of the *Standards* referred to validity as being the property of a *test,* the 1974 *Standards* emphasized that validity is tied to inferences made from test *scores*. Far from being only a semantic difference, this change in terminology reflected a growing recognition that validity is not a property attached to a test because it leaves the test developer's office; instead, validity must be evaluated by the test user in the context of the given inferences to be made from the test scores.

Awareness of the consequences of test use continued to grow, and AERA et al.'s 1985 *Standards for Educational and Psychological Testing* included the statement that "test users should be alert to probable unintended consequence of test use and should attempt to avoid actions that have unintended negative consequences" (p. 42). Consideration of value implications and social consequences, introduced by Messick (1980, 1989), has received increased focus in the testing literature, and debates have arisen about its proper role within psychometrics (see, e.g., Shepard, 1997; Popham, 1997; Linn, 1997; Mehrens, 1997). AERA et al.'s 1999 *Standards* reflected this increased attention to both the intended and unintended consequences of test use by including it as one of the five main sources of validity evidence, but care must be taken to distinguish between a lack of validity that may arise from construct-irrelevant components and a lack of validity that may stem from valid difference in examinee performance.

Despite the changing conceptualizations of validity, one idea has remained constant—that tests and test scores, used properly, can be of immense benefit both to individuals and to the societies in which they live and work. Inferences drawn from test scores can only become more useful as validity arguments, as well as the validation activities that they engender, draw from ever greater sources of information.

Testing Accommodations

The issue of testing accommodations for test takers with disabilities has become the focus of increased interest in recent years. Both governmental and educational initiatives have strengthened the need to give individuals with disabilities the same testing opportunities, and thus access to the same life experiences in education and employment, as individuals without disabilities have. Three major pieces of legislation have provided the impetus to provide disabled individuals with accommodations during testing: the Rehabilitation Act of 1973 (Section 504, 1973), the Americans with Disabilities Act (1990), and the Individuals with Disabilities Educational Act (IDEA; 1991, 1997). The Rehabilitation Act and ADA prohibit discrimination against individuals with disabilities that affect major life activities such as walking, seeing, hearing, speaking, learning, and working; the Rehabilitation Act applies to programs or activities that receive federal financial assistance, and ADA extends these protections to the private sector. IDEA requires that students with disabilities be provided with the same access to public education as students without disabilities have. Because of the integral role they play in the educational system, tests are among the services covered by IDEA;

specifically, the act requires that in order to qualify for funding, agencies must include students with disabilities in general state and district-wide assessments. A thorough review of legislation related to the provision of testing accommodations to individuals with disabilities is provided by Phillips (1994).

Generally, the laws just described require that the measurement of the abilities, skills, aptitudes, or achievements of persons with disabilities be conducted in such a manner as to eliminate the disability's interference with the construct being assessed (Geisinger, 1994). The laws seek to ensure that otherwise qualified persons with disabilities are given the opportunity to demonstrate their true strengths and that such individuals are not discriminated against through the lack of reasonable and appropriate testing accommodations.

These regulations also acknowledge, however, that the test accommodations must not interfere with the measurement of the factors that are being assessed. Therein lies the challenge. The recently revised *Standards for Educational and Psychological Testing* (AERA et al., 1999) note that a balance must be struck between tailoring accommodations to the individual test taker, taking into account his or her particular disability, past experiences, and characteristics, and ensuring that "the test score inferences accurately reflect the intended construct rather than any disabilities and their associated characteristics extraneous to the intent of the measurement" (p. 106).

Accommodations provided to test takers depend, of course, on the disability involved. The composition of the pool of examinees with disabilities has changed over the years. Many of the earliest testing accommodations were provided to examinees with physical impairments, hearing impairments, or visual impairments. For example, examinees with visual impairments might be given a test in

Braille; examinees with hearing impairments may receive a written copy of administration directions that are usually read aloud; and examinees with physical impairments might use the services of an amanuensis (scribe) to record answers.

In recent years, however, greater attention has been paid to accommodations provided for examinees with cognitive disabilities such as learning disabilities and to how these accommodations affect the validity of test results (Phillips, 1994). In fact, learning disabilities now account for the largest percentage of those examinees provided with accommodations (Camara, 1998). The accommodations often approved for students with learning disabilities in large-scale assessments are extra time, readers, scribes, and the use of word processors. The provision of extra time is intended to compensate for the information-processing deficits of students with learning disabilities, as is the use of a reader. Scribes and word processors are aimed at compensating for the deficits that most students with learning disabilities have in writing skills (MacArthur, 1996; Raskind & Higgins, 1998).

Researchers have studied the issue of how well large-scale testing programs are able to strike this balance. One examination of the impact of providing accommodations is contained in a comprehensive series of studies conducted by Educational Testing Service, the College Board, and the Graduate Record Examinations Board, which was published in Willingham et al. (1988). These studies revealed that in many cases, the provision of testing accommodations does not appear to change the meaning of the test score; that is, the construct targeted for assessment appears to be unchanged by the testing accommodation. However, the research did raise questions about the results obtained for individuals with learning disabilities, in that their later academic success was slightly overpredicted by their test scores. Other research has supported these same concerns (e.g., Camara, 1998), and it appears that the common practice of providing individuals with learning disabilities with extra testing time may be one of the causes of this problem. Because learning disabilities are the most frequent condition for which accommodations are provided in large-scale testing programs, it is also in this area that several legal cases have addressed the characteristics and needs of this population. However, the judgments rendered have not been consistent, and they raise even more questions about the role that testing accommodations should play in the assessment of individuals with learning disabilities. The area of testing accommodations is a complex one. For a more complete overview of the issues involved, of research findings, and of relevant court cases, see Pitoniak and Royer (in press).

Further research into the use of testing accommodations is certainly warranted. However, this research is complicated by the presence of two factors. First, given the heterogeneous nature of disabilities, particularly learning disabilities, the results of any given research study may not be generalizable to other examinees. Second, the sample sizes of examinees with disabilities are typically too small to allow definitive conclusions.

These difficulties in conducting adequate research poses an additional dilemma for testing organizations: Test takers' rights to confidentiality must be balanced with an acknowledgment that enough research may not have been conducted to ensure that the test score obtained by that person means the same thing as one obtained without accommodations. As a result, the test scores may have to be flagged as having been obtained under nonstandard conditions. Standard 10.11 (see AERA et al., 1999) acknowledges the conflict between indicating when interpretation of test scores should be made with caution and when an

examinee's privacy must be maintained in order to prohibit discrimination: "when there is credible evidence of score comparability across regular and modified administrations, no flag should be attached to a score. When such evidence is lacking, specific information about the nature of the modification should be provided, if permitted by law, to assist test users properly to interpret and act on test scores" (p. 108). The provision of testing accommodations, and the decision of whether to flag these scores, is clearly an issue that will continue to receive attention.

The increased use of computers in testing may also provide for new and different ways to offer examinees with disabilities appropriate accommodations while ensuring that the construct being assessed is not changed by the modifications provided. However, this avenue is not without challenges (see Bennett, 1999). The provision of testing accommodations for examinees with disabling conditions will certainly continue to be an important issue for consideration by measurement specialists, psychologists, educators, and the legal system in the years ahead.

CONCLUSIONS

Over the 30 years since the publication of Lord and Novick's (1968) classic text on test theory, the measurement field has changed substantially. Multiple-choice items are being supplemented with, if not replaced by, performance-based assessments. With this change, more polytomous response data are available for analyzing and providing additional information about examinees; computers are being used in place of paper-and-pencil administrations; new test designs are becoming available; and assessing for competence is more often the focus of testing than is assessing to determine relative standing. In addition, methodological advances are making it possible to identify potentially biased test items routinely (see Holland & Wainer, 1993) and to move to more cognitively based test design (see, e.g., Embretson & Reise, 2000; Sheehan & Mislevy, 1990). In this chapter we have attempted to describe some of the important technical advances as well as how they are being addressed with new theories of testing and measurement practices. At the same time, hard choices had to be made about the material to include in this chapter. Missing are all of the major developments in generalizability theory and applications of it (see, e.g., Brennan, 1992), and major areas of item response theory have been omitted (see, e.g., van der Linden & Hambleton, 1997). Also missing are details of specific IRT technical problems such as parameter estimation. IRT software and goodness-of-fit have only been touched upon (see, for example, Embretson & Reise, 2000; Hambleton et al., 1991), and major advances in merging cognitive psychology and psychometrics have been only briefly mentioned. At the same time, we hope that the material that has been included in the chapter will provide readers with a good overview of recent advances and that the references will facilitate follow-up study.

REFERENCES

American Educational Research Association, American Psychological Association, & National Council on Measurement in Education. (1954). *Technical recommendations for psychological tests and diagnostic techniques.* Washington, DC: American Psychological Association.

American Educational Research Association, American Psychological Association, & National Council on Measurement in Education. (1966). *Standards for educational and psychological tests and manuals.* Washington, DC: American Psychological Association.

American Educational Research Association, American Psychological Association, & National Council on Measurement in Education. (1974). *Standards for educational and psychological tests.* Washington, DC: American Psychological Association.

American Educational Research Association, American Psychological Association, & National Council on Measurement in Education. (1985). *Standards for educational and psychological testing.* Washington, DC: American Psychological Association.

American Educational Research Association, American Psychological Association, & National Council on Measurement in Education. (1999). *Standards for educational and psychological testing.* Washington, DC: American Educational Research Association.

American Educational Research Association, Committee on Test Standards. (1955). *Technical recommendations for achievement tests.* Washington, DC: American Educational Research Association.

Americans with Disabilities Act of 1990. (1990). 42 U.S.C. §12101 et seq.

Anastasi, A. (1988). *Psychological testing* (6th ed.). New York: Macmillan.

Anastasi, A., & Urbina, S. (1997). *Psychological testing* (7th ed.). Upper Saddle River, NJ: Prentice-Hall.

Angoff, W. H. (1971). Scales, norms, and equivalent scores. In R. L. Thorndike (Ed.), *Educational measurement* (2nd ed., pp. 508–597). Washington, DC: American Council on Education.

Bennett, R. E. (1998). *Reinventing assessment: Speculations on the future of large-scale educational testing.* Princeton, NJ: Educational Testing Service.

Bennett, R. E. (1999). Computer-based testing for examinees with disabilities: On the road to generalized accommodations. In S. J. Messick (Ed.), *Assessment in higher education: Issues of access, quality, student development, and public policy* (pp. 181–191). Hillsdale, NJ: Erlbaum.

Berk, R. A. (1986). A consumer's guide to setting performance standards on criterion-referenced tests. *Review of Educational Research, 56,* 137–172.

Bock, R. D. (1972). Estimating item parameters and latent ability when responses are scored in two or more nominal categories. *Psychometrika, 37,* 29–51.

Bock, R. D. (1997). The nominal categories model. In W. J. van der Linden & R. K. Hambleton (Eds.), *Handbook of modern item response theory* (pp. 33–49). New York: Springer.

Bock, R. D., & Aitkin, M. (1981). Marginal maximum likelihood estimation of item parameters: Application of an EM algorithm. *Psychometrika, 46,* 443–459.

Breland, H. M. (1998, April). *Writing assessment through automated editing.* Paper presented at the meeting of the National Council on Measurement in Education, San Diego, CA.

Brennan, R. L. (1992). *Elements of generalizability theory.* Iowa City, IA: ACT.

Camara, W. F. (1998). *Effects of extended time on score growth for students with learning disabilities.* New York: College Board.

Cizek, G. J. (1996a). Setting passing scores. *Educational Measurement: Issues and Practice, 15*(2), 20–31.

Cizek, G. J. (1996b). Standard setting guidelines. *Educational Measurement: Issues and Practice, 15*(1), 12, 13–21.

Cizek, G. J. (2001). Conjectures on the rise and call of standard setting: An introduction to context and practice. In G. J. Cizek (Ed.), *Setting performance standards: Concepts, methods, and perspectives* (pp. 3–17). Hillsdale, NJ: Erlbaum.

College Board. (2000). *2000 Advanced Placement Program free-response questions.* New York: Author.

Crocker, L., & Algina, J. (1986). *Introduction to classical and modern test theory.* New York: Holt, Rinehart, & Winston.

Davey, T., Godwin, J., & Mittelholtz, D. (1997). Developing and scoring an innovative computerized writing assessment. *Journal of Educational Measurement, 34,* 21–41.

Davey, T., & Nering, M. (1998, September). *Controlling item exposure and maintaining item security.* Paper presented at the Conference on Computer-Based Testing: Building the Foundation for Future Assessments, Philadelphia, PA.

Dodd, B. G., De Ayala, R. J., & Koch, W. R. (1995). Computerized adaptive testing with polytomous items. *Applied Psychological Measurement, 19,* 5–22.

Drasgow, F., & Olson-Buchanan, J. B. (Eds.) (1999). *Innovations in computerized assessment.* Hillsdale, NJ: Erlbaum.

Drasgow, F., Olson-Buchanan, J. B., & Moberg, P. J. (1999). Development of an interactive video assessment: Trials and tribulations. In F. Drasgow & J. B. Olson-Buchanan (Eds.), *Innovations in computerized assessment* (pp. 177–196). Hillsdale, NJ: Erlbaum.

Educational Testing Service. (2000). *Graduate Record Examinations information and registration bulletin.* Princeton, NJ: Author.

Embretson, S. E. (1984). A general multicomponent latent trait model for response processes. *Psychometrika, 49,* 175–186.

Embretson, S. E. (1985). Multicomponent latent trait models for test design. In S. E. Embretson (Ed.), *Test design: Developments in psychology and psychometrics* (pp. 195–218). Orlando, FL: Academic Press.

Embretson, S. E. (1997). Multicomponent response models. In W. J. van der Linden & R. K. Hambleton (Eds.), *Handbook of modern item response theory* (pp. 305–322). New York: Springer.

Embretson, S. E. (2000). Psychometric approaches to understanding and measuring intelligence. In R. J. Sternberg (Ed.), *Handbook of intelligence* (pp. 423–444). Cambridge, England: Cambridge University Press.

Embretson, S. E., & Reise, S. P. (Eds.). (2000). *Item response theory for psychologists.* Hillsdale, NJ: Erlbaum.

Everson, H. T. (1999). A theory-based framework for future college admissions tests. In S. J. Messick (Ed.), *Assessment in higher education: Issues of access, quality, student development, and public policy* (pp. 113–131). Hillsdale, NJ: Erlbaum.

Federation of State Medical Boards of the United States, Inc., & National Board of Medical Examiners. (1999). *USMLE bulletin of information 2000.* Philadelphia, PA: Authors.

Fischer, G. H., & Seliger, E. (1997). Multidimensional linear logistic models for change. In W. J. van der Linden & R. K. Hambleton (Eds.), *Handbook of modern item response theory* (pp. 323–346). New York: Springer.

Fitzpatrick, A. R., Link, V. B., Yen, W. M., Burket, G. R., Ito, K., & Sykes, R. C. (1996). Scaling performance assessments: A comparison of one-parameter and two-parameter partial credit models. *Journal of Educational Measurement, 33*(3), 291–314.

Flaugher, R. (2000). Item pools. In H. Wainer (Ed.), *Computerized adaptive testing: A primer* (pp. 37–58). Hillsdale, NJ: Erlbaum.

Folk, V. G., & Smith, R. L. (1998, September). *Models for delivery of computer-based tests.* Paper presented at the Conference on Computer-Based Testing: Building the Foundation for Future Assessments, Philadelphia, PA.

Fraser, C., & McDonald, R. P. (1988). NOHARM: Least squares item factor analysis. *Multivariate Behavioral Research, 23,* 267–269.

Geisinger, K. F. (1994). Psychometric issues in testing students with disabilities. *Applied Measurement in Education, 7,* 121–140.

Giraud, G., Impara, J. C., & Buckendahl, D. (2000). Making the cut in school districts: Alternative methods for setting cut-scores. *Educational Assessment, 6,* 291–304.

Glaser, R. (1981). The future of testing: A research agenda for cognitive psychology and psychometrics. *American Psychologist, 36,* 923–936.

Green, R., Yen, W., & Burket, G. (1989). Experiences in the application of item response theory in test construction. *Applied Measurement in Education, 2,* 297–312.

Guion, R. M. (1980). On trinitarian doctrines of validity. *Professional Psychology, 11,* 385–398.

Gulliksen, H. (1950). *Theory of mental tests.* New York: Wiley.

Hambleton, R. K. (1980). Test score validity and standard setting methods. In R. A. Berk (Ed.), *Criterion-referenced measurement: State of the art* (pp. 80–123). Baltimore, MD: Johns Hopkins University Press.

Hambleton, R. K. (1989). Principles and selected applications of item response theory. In R. L. Linn (Ed.), *Educational measurement* (3rd ed., pp. 147–200). New York: Macmillan.

Hambleton, R. K. (1998). Setting performance standards on achievement tests: Meeting the requirements of Title I. In L. Hansche (Ed.), *Handbook for the development of performance standards: Meeting the requirements of Title I* (pp. 87–114). Washington, DC: Council of Chief State School Officers.

Hambleton, R. K., Jaeger, R. M., Plake, B. S., & Mills, C. N. (in press). *Handbook for setting performance standards.* Washington, DC: Council of Chief State School Officers.

Hambleton, R. K., & Jones, R. W. (1993). Comparison of classical test theory and item response theory and their applications to test development. *Educational Measurement: Issues and Practice, 12*(3), 38–47.

Hambleton, R. K., Robin, F., & Xing, D. (2000). Item response models for the analysis of educational and psychological data. In H. E. A. Tinsley & S. D. Brown (Eds.), *Handbook of applied multivariate statistics and mathematical modeling* (pp. 553–581). San Diego: Academic Press.

Hambleton, R. K., & Slater, C. S. (1997). Item response theory models and testing practices: Current international status and future directions. *European Journal of Psychological Assessment, 13*(1), 21–28.

Hambleton, R. K., & Swaminathan, H. (1985). *Item response theory: Principles and applications.* Boston: Kluwer Academic.

Hambleton, R. K., Swaminathan, H., & Rogers, H. J. (1991). *Fundamentals of item response theory.* Newbury Park, CA: Sage.

Hambleton, R. K., Zaal, J. N., & Pieters, P. (1991). Computerized adaptive testing: Theory, applications, and standards. In R. K. Hambleton & J. N. Zaal (Eds.), *Advances in educational and psychological testing* (pp. 341–366). Norwell, MA: Kluwer Academic.

Holland, P. W., & Wainer, H. (Eds.). (1993). *Differential item functioning*. Hillsdale, NJ: Erlbaum.

Individuals with Disabilities Educational Act. (1991). Authority: 20 U.S.C. §1400 et seq.

Individuals with Disabilities Education Act. (1997). Authority: 20 U.S.C. 1412(a) (17)(A).

Jaeger, R. M. (1988). Use and effect of caution indices in detecting aberrant patterns of standard-setting judgments. *Applied Measurement in Education, 1,* 17–31.

Jaeger, R. M. (1989). Certification of student competence. In R. L. Linn (Ed.), *Educational measurement* (3rd ed., pp. 485–514). Washington, DC: American Council on Education.

Jaeger, R. M. (1991). Selection of judges for standard-setting. *Educational Measurement, Issues and Practices, 10*(2), 3–6, 10, 14.

Jaeger, R. M., Mullis, I. V. S., Bourque, M. L., & Shakrani, S. (1996). Setting performance standards for performance assessments: Some fundamental issues, current practice, and technical dilemmas. In G. W. Phillips (Ed.), *Technical issues in large-scale performance assessment* (pp. 79–115). Washington, DC: National Center for Education Statistics.

Kane, M. T. (1992). An argument-based approach to validity. *Psychological Bulletin, 112,* 527–535.

Kane, M. (1994). Validating the performance standards associated with passing scores. *Review of Educational Research, 64,* 425–461.

Kane, M. (1995). Examinee-centered vs. task-centered standard setting. In *Proceedings of the Joint Conference on Standard Setting for Large Scale Assessments of the National Assessment Governing Board (NAGB) and the National Center for Educational Statistics (NCES): Volume 2* (pp. 119–141). Washington, DC: U. S. Government Printing Office.

Kane, M. (1998). Choosing between examinee-centered and test-centered standard-setting methods. *Educational Assessment, 5,* 129–145.

Kim, S. H. (1997). BILOG 3 for Windows: Item analysis and test scoring for binary logistic models. *Applied Psychological Measurement, 21*(4), 371–376.

Kingsbury, G. G., & Zara, A. R. (1991). A comparison of procedures for content-sensitive item selection in computerized adaptive tests. *Applied Measurement in Education, 4,* 241–261.

Koch, W. R., Dodd, B. G., & Fitzpatrick, S. J. (1990). Computerized adaptive measurement of attitudes. *Measurement and Evaluation in Counseling and Development, 7,* 15–32.

Kolen, M. J., & Brennan, R. L. (1995). *Test equating: Methods and practices*. New York: Springer.

Linn, R. L. (1997). Evaluating the validity of assessments: The consequences of use. *Educational Measurement: Issues and Practice, 16*(2), 14–16.

Livingston, S. A., & Zieky, M. J. (1982). *Passing scores: A manual for setting standards of performance on educational and occupational tests*. Princeton, NJ: Educational Testing Service.

Lord, F. M. (1952). *A theory of test scores* [Psychometric Monograph No. 7]. Iowa City, IA: Psychometric Society.

Lord, F. M. (1977). Practical applications of item characteristic curve theory. *Journal of Educational Measurement, 14,* 117–138.

Lord, F. M. (1980). *Applications of item response theory to practical testing problems*. Hillsdale, NJ: Erlbaum.

Lord, F. M. (1984). Standard errors of measurement at different ability levels. *Journal of Educational Measurement, 21,* 239–243.

Lord, F. M., & Novick, M. R. (1968). *Statistical theories of mental test scores*. Reading, MA: Addison-Wesley.

Lubinski, D., & Dawis, R. V. (Eds.). (1995). *Assessing individual differences in human behavior*. Palo Alto, CA: Davies-Black.

Luecht, R. M. (1998). Automated test assembly (ATA) in the era of computerized testing. *CLEAR Exam Review, 9*(2), 19–22.

MacArthur, C. A. (1996). Using technology to enhance the writing processes of students with learning disabilities. *Journal of Learning Disabilities, 29,* 344–354.

Maris, E. M. (1995). Psychometric latent response models. *Psychometrika, 60,* 523–547.

Masters, G. N. (1982). A Rasch model for partial credit scoring. *Psychometrika, 47,* 149–174.

Masters, G. N., & Wright, B. D. (1997). Partial credit model. In W. J. van der Linden & R. K. Hambleton (Eds.), *Handbook of modern item response theory* (pp. 101–121). New York: Springer.

McDonald, R. P. (1989). Future directions for item response theory. *International Journal of Educational Research, 13*(2), 205–220.

Mehrens, W. A. (1997). The consequences of consequential validity. *Educational Measurement: Issues and Practice, 16*(2), 16–18.

Messick, S. (1980). Test validity and the ethics of assessment. *American Psychologist, 35,* 1012–1027.

Messick, S. (1988). The once and future issues of validity: Assessing the meaning and consequences of measurement. In H. Wainer & H. I. Braun (Eds.), *Test validity* (pp. 33–45). Hillsdale, NJ: Erlbaum.

Messick, S. (1989). Validity. In R. Linn (Ed.), *Educational measurement* (3rd ed., pp. 13–103). New York: Macmillan.

Mills, C. N. (1995). Establishing passing standards. In J. C. Impara (Ed.), *Licensure testing: Purposes, procedures, and practices* (pp. 219–252). Lincoln, NE: Buros Institute of Mental Measurements.

Mills, C. N. (1999). Development and introduction of a computer adaptive Graduate Record Examinations General Test. In F. Drasgow & J. B. Olson-Buchanan (Eds.), *Innovations in computerized assessment* (pp. 117–135). Hillsdale, NJ: Erlbaum.

Mills, C. N., & Steffen, M. (2000). The GRE computer adaptive test: Operational issues. In W. J. van der Linden & C. A. W. Glas (Eds.), *Computer adaptive testing: Theory and practice* (pp. 75–99). Norwell, MA: Kluwer Academic.

Mills, C. N., & Stocking, M. L. (1996). Practical issues in large-scale computerized adaptive testing. *Applied Measurement in Education, 9,* 287–304.

Mislevy, R. J. (1993). Foundations of a new test theory. In N. Frederiksen, R. J. Mislevy, &

I. I. Bejar (Eds.), *Test theory for a new generation of tests* (pp. 19–39). Hillsdale, NJ: Erlbaum.

Mislevy, R. J. (1995). Probability-based inference in cognitive diagnosis. In P. Nichols, S. Chipman, & R. Brennan (Eds.), *Cognitively diagnostic assessment* (pp. 43–71). Hillsdale, NJ: Erlbaum.

Mislevy, R., & Bock, R. D. (1986). *BILOG: Maximum likelihood item analysis and test scoring with logistic models.* Mooresville, IN: Scientific Software.

Muraki, E. (1992). A generalized partial credit model: Application of an EM algorithm. *Applied Psychological Measurement, 16,* 159–176.

Muraki, E., & Bock, R. D. (1993). *PARSCALE: IRT based test scoring and analysis.* Chicago, IL: Scientific Software International.

National Council of Architect Registration Boards. (2000). *ARE guidelines.* Washington, DC: Author.

Parshall, C. G., Davey, T., & Pashley, P. J. (2000). Innovative item types for computerized testing. In W. J. van der Linden & C. A. W. Glas (Eds.), *Computerized adaptive testing: Theory and practice* (pp. 128–148). Norwell, MA: Kluwer Academic.

Patsula, L. N., & Hambleton, R. K. (1999, April). *A comparative study of ability estimates obtained from computer-adaptive and multi-stage testing.* Paper presented at the meeting of the National Council on Measurement in Education, Montreal, Quebec.

Phillips, S. E. (1994). High-stakes testing accommodations: Validity versus disabled rights. *Applied Measurement in Education, 7,* 93–120.

Pitoniak, M. J., & Royer, J. M. (in press). Testing accommodations for examinees with disabilities: A review of psychometric, legal, and social policy issues. *Review of Educational Research.*

Plake, B. S. (1998). Setting performance standards for professional licensure and certification. *Applied Measurement in Education, 5,* 63–72.

Popham, W. J. (1997). Consequential validity: Right concern, wrong concept. *Educational Measurement: Issues and Practice, 16*(2), 9–13.

Rasch, G. (1960). *Probabilistic models for some intelligence and attainment tests*. Copenhagen: Denmarks Paedagogiske Institut.

Raskind, M. H., & Higgins, E. L. (1998). Assistive technology for postsecondary students with learning disabilities: An overview. *Journal of Learning Disabilities, 31,* 27–40.

Reckase, M. (1979). Unifactor latent trait models applied to multifactor tests: results and implications. *Journal of Educational Statistics, 4,* 207–230.

Reckase, M. (1997a). A linear logistic multidimensional model for dichotomous item response data. In W. J. van der Linden & R. K. Hambleton (Eds.), *Handbook of modern item response theory* (pp. 271–286). New York: Springer.

Reckase, M. (1997b). The past and future of multidimensional item response theory. *Applied Psychological Measurement, 21,* 25–36.

Reise, S. P. (1999). Personality measurement issues viewed through the eyes of IRT. In S. E. Embretson & S. L. Hershberger (Eds.), *The new rules of measurement: What every psychologist and educator should know* (pp. 219–241). Hillsdale, NJ: Erlbaum.

Samejima, F. (1969). *Estimation of latent ability using a response pattern of graded scores* [Psychometric Monograph No. 17]. Iowa City, IA: Psychometric Society.

Samejima, F. (1974). Normal ogive model on the continuous response level in the multidimensional latent space. *Psychometrika, 39,* 111–121.

Sands, W. A., Waters, B. K., & McBride, J. R. (Eds.). (1997). *Computerized adaptive testing: From inquiry to operation.* Washington, DC: American Psychological Association.

Section 504, Rehabilitation Act of 1973. (1973). 29 U.S.C. 701 § et seq.

Shavelson, R. J., & Webb, N. M. (1991). *Generalizability theory: A primer.* Newbury Park, CA: Sage.

Sheehan, K., & Mislevy, R. J. (1990). Integrating cognitive and psychometric models to measure document literacy. *Journal of Educational Measurement, 27*(3), 255–272.

Shepard, L. A. (1993). Evaluating test validity. *Review of Research in Education, 19,* 405–450.

Shepard, L. A. (1997). The centrality of test use and consequences for test validity. *Educational Measurement: Issues and Practice, 16*(2), 5–8, 13, 24.

Shepard, L., Glaser, R., Linn, R., & Bohrnstedt, G. (1993). *Setting performance standards for student achievement.* Stanford, CA: National Academy of Education.

Sireci, S. G., Pitoniak, M. J., Meara, K. C., & Hambleton, R. K. (2000). *A review of standard setting methods applicable to the Advanced Placement examination program* [Laboratory of Psychometric and Evaluative Research Report No. 375]. Amherst: University of Massachusetts, School of Education.

Snow, R. E., & Lohman, D. F. (1989). Implications of cognitive psychology for educational measurement. In R. L. Linn (Ed.), *Educational measurement* (3rd ed., pp. 263–331). New York: Macmillan.

Sternberg, R. J. (1985). *Beyond IQ: A triarchic theory of intelligence.* Cambridge: Cambridge University Press.

Stocking, M. L., & Lewis, C. (2000). Methods of controlling the exposure of items in CAT. In W. J. van der Linden & C. A. W. Glas (Eds.), *Computer adaptive testing: Theory and practice* (pp. 163–182). Norwell, MA: Kluwer Academic.

Stocking, M. L., & Swanson, L. (1993). A method for severely constrained item selection in adaptive testing. *Applied Psychological Measurement, 17,* 277–292.

Stocking, M. L., Swanson, L., & Pearlman, M. (1990, April). *Automated item selection using item response theory.* Paper presented at the meeting of the National Council on Measurement in Education, Boston.

Swaminathan, H. (1997, August). *Bayesian estimation in item response models.* Paper presented at the meeting of the American Statistical Association, Anaheim, CA.

Swanson, L. & Stocking, M. L. (1993). A model and heuristic for solving very large item selection problems. *Applied Psychological Measurement, 17,* 151–166.

Tatsuoka, K. K. (1983). Rule space: An approach for dealing with misconceptions based on item response theory. *Journal of Educational Measurement, 20,* 345–354.

Tatsuoka, K. K. (1990). Toward an integration of item-response theory and cognitive error diagnoses. In N. Frederiksen, R. L. Glaser, A. M. Lesgold, & M. G. Shafto (Eds.), *Diagnostic monitoring of skill and knowledge acquisition* (pp. 453–488). Hillsdale, NJ: Erlbaum.

Tatsuoka, K. K. (1993). Item construction and psychometric models appropriate for constructed responses. In R. E. Bennett & W. C. Ward (Eds.), *Construction versus choice in cognitive measurement: Issues in constructed response, performance testing, and portfolio assessment* (pp. 107–134). Hillsdale, NJ: Erlbaum.

Thissen, D. (1983). *MULTILOG: Item analysis and scoring with multiple category response models* [Computer software]. Chicago: International Educational Services.

Thissen, D., & Mislevy, R. J. (2000). Testing algorithms. In H. Wainer (Ed.), *Computerized adaptive testing: A primer* (2nd ed., pp. 101–132). Hillsdale, NJ: Erlbaum.

van der Linden, W. J. (1982). A latent trait method for determining intrajudge consistency in the Angoff and Nedelsky techniques of standard setting. *Journal of Educational Measurement, 19,* 295–308.

van der Linden, W. J. (1995). A conceptual analysis of standard setting in large-scale assessments. In *Proceedings of the Joint Conference on Standard Setting for Large Scale Assessments of the National Assessment Governing Board and the National Center for Educational Statistics: Volume 2* (pp. 97–117). Washington, DC: U. S. Government Printing Office.

van der Linden, W. J. (1998a). Optimal assembly of psychological and educational tests. *Applied Psychological Measurement, 22,* 195–211.

van der Linden, W. J. (Ed.). (1998b). Optimal test assembly [Special issue]. *Applied Psychological Measurement, 22*(3).

van der Linden, W. J. (2000). Constrained adaptive testing with shadow tests. In W. J. van der Linden & C. A. W. Glas (Eds.), *Computer adaptive testing: Theory and practice* (pp. 27–52). Norwell, MA: Kluwer Academic.

van der Linden, W. J., & Boekkooi-Timminga, E. (1989). A maximum model for test design with practical constraints. *Psychometrika, 54,* 237–247.

van der Linden, W. J., & Glas, C. A. W. (Eds.). (2000). *Computer adaptive testing: Theory and practice.* Norwell, MA: Kluwer Academic.

van der Linden, W. J., & Hambleton, R. K. (Eds.). (1997). *Handbook of modern item response theory.* New York: Springer.

van der Linden, W. J., & Pashley, P. J. (2000). Item selection and ability estimation in adaptive testing. In W. J. van der Linden & C. A. W. Glas (Eds.), *Computer adaptive testing: Theory and practice* (pp. 1–25). Norwell, MA: Kluwer Academic.

van der Linden, W. J., & Reese, L. M. (1998). A model for optimal constrained adaptive testing. *Applied Psychological Measurement, 22*(3), 259–270.

van der Linden, W. J., & Veldkamp, B. P. (2000). An integer programming approach to item bank design. *Applied Psychological Measurement, 24,* 139–150.

van Krimpen-Stoop, E. M. L. A., & Meijer, R. R. (2000). Detecting person misfit in adaptive testing using statistical process control techniques. In W. J. van der Linden & C. A. W. Glas (Eds.), *Computer adaptive testing: Theory and practice* (pp. 201–219). Norwell, MA: Kluwer Academic.

Wainer, H. (1993). Some practical considerations when converting a linearly administered test to an adaptive format. *Educational Measurement: Issues and Practice, 12*(1), 15–20.

Wainer, H. (Ed.). (2000a). *Computerized adaptive testing: A primer* (2nd ed.). Hillsdale, NJ: Erlbaum.

Wainer, H. (2000b). Introduction and history. In H. Wainer (Ed.), *Computerized adaptive testing: A primer* (2nd ed., pp. 1–20). Hillsdale, NJ: Erlbaum.

Wainer, H., Bradlow, E. T., & Du, Z. (2000). Testlet response theory: An analog for the 3PL model useful in testlet-based adaptive testing. In W. J. van der Linden & C. A. W. Glas (Eds.), *Computer adaptive testing: Theory and practice* (pp. 245–269). Norwell, MA: Kluwer.

Wainer, H., & Kiely, G. L. (1987). Item clusters and computerized adaptive testing: A case for testlets. *Journal of Educational Measurement, 24,* 185–201.

Wainer, H., & Mislevy, R. J. (2000). Item response theory, item calibration, and proficiency estimation. In H. Wainer (Ed.), *Computerized adaptive testing: A primer* (2nd ed., pp. 61–99). Hillsdale, NJ: Erlbaum.

Waller, N. G., & Reise, S. P. (1989). Computerized adaptive personality assessment: An illustration with the absorption scale. *Journal of Personality and Social Psychology, 57,* 1051–1058.

Whitely, S. E. (1980). Multicomponent latent trait models for ability tests. *Psychometrika, 45,* 479–494.

Willingham, W. W., Ragosta, M., Bennett, R. E., Braun, H., Rock, D. A., & Powers, D. E. (1988). *Testing handicapped people.* Boston: Allyn and Bacon.

Wingersky, M. S. (1983). LOGIST: A program for computing maximum likelihood procedures for logistic test models. In R. K. Hambleton (Ed.), *Applications of item response theory* (pp. 45–70). Vancouver, BC: Educational Research Institute of British Columbia.

Wright, B. D., & Stone, M. H. (1979). *Best test design.* Chicago, IL: MESA.

Yen, W. (1983). Use of the three-parameter model in the development of a standardized achievement test. In R. K. Hambleton (Ed.), *Applications of modern item response theory* (pp. 121–141). Vancouver, BC: Educational Research Institute of British Columbia.

CHAPTER 14

Personality and Individual Differences

STEPHEN A. PETRILL AND NATHAN BRODY

Experimental psychologists create variability by manipulating the environment. Individual difference psychologists study variability that occurs naturally. A measure of a variable may contain several independent sources of variance. The experimental psychologist seeks to eliminate the influences of confounded variables that may be present in the natural environment by experimental manipulations. The individual difference psychologist uses statistical methodologies to partition sources of variance in a measure and to analyze the contributions of several sources of variance to relationships among measures.

Our chapter deals with five broad topics: (a) the analysis of relationships among one or more measures of the same or related constructs; (b) continuity and change in constructs over time; (c) relationships among constructs and the use of exploratory and confirmatory methods of analysis to construct taxonomies and to infer causal relationships among constructs; (d) cases in which constructs are structurally invariant within groups and structurally variant between groups; and (e) cross-domain relationships in which we consider methodologies that are appropriate for relating constructs derived from different domains. We consider relationships between individual difference constructs and constructs derived from biological, genetic, and cognitive experimental

psychology. At several places we indicate the way in which theoretical assumptions structure methodological approaches.

FROM MEASURES TO CONSTRUCTS

In this section we consider relationships between measures and individual differences constructs. We begin with the simplest case in which constructs are inferred by the relationships among similar items. Then we consider the more complex case in which different kinds of measures are used to infer the values of constructs. Here, we consider the case in which aggregates are formed across measures to infer the value of the same construct. We also consider cases in which the differences among measures are informative. Our discussion of inferences based on different measures is structured by a consideration of the extent to which personality traits exhibit cross-situational consistency.

Repeated Measures of the Same Construct

A single item or measure of a construct is likely to contain at least two sources of variance—construct-relevant variance and error variance. Assume that a psychologist wishes to measure an individual's tendency to experience positive or negative mood states.

563

It is possible to ask a person if he or she feels happy. Such a single measure of behavior may provide insight into a person's state at the moment when it is being reported, but it may not provide a particularly accurate index of the individual's overall propensity to experience positive mood states. Many sources of variance may contribute to single scores. Some of these are not germane to the construct of a disposition to report positive mood states. The person answering the question may have misinterpreted what is being asked. The response to the question may be influenced by transitory mood states that are not characteristic of the usual way in which a person responds to such questions. In order to obtain a measure that is a more accurate index of the construct, it is necessary to study the covariance between a single measure and other related measures. For example, it would be possible to obtain measures of mood on a second occasion. Epstein (1977) obtained self-report measures of positive and negative moods repeatedly from the same subjects. He found that these measures were positively related to each other—the correlations between single measures were close to .2. Epstein also found that an aggregate index based on several independent reports of mood states correlated with a second aggregate index of reports of mood states close to .8. The study indicates that single measures of behavior are unlikely to be accurate indexes of the construct that they assess.

The increased accuracy of measurement obtained by aggregating single measures occurs when all of the individual measures are positively correlated with each other. As long as this condition is met, an aggregate index of several measures will provide an increasingly accurate index of that which is common to all of the individual measures as the number of positively correlated individual items increases. The degree to which the final aggregated index is an accurate index (i.e., is saturated with true-score variance

resulting from the commonalities among its constituents) is a function of the number of independent indexes that enter into the aggregate and of the average correlation of the indexes. The Spearman-Brown prophecy formula may be used to estimate the value of the hypothetical correlation between the common element present in all of the items as a function of the number of items and the average correlation among the items. Cronbach's (1951) coefficient alpha may be used to derive an index of the reliability of items based on the average correlation among the items.

It is possible to derive methodological injunctions from the formal relationships defined by indexes of internal consistency reliability. Relationships among independent measures of the same construct should be examined in order to ascertain if all of the individual items are positively correlated with each other. Applied to the construction of personality tests, this procedure is an essential aspect of item analysis and permits one to decide whether to retain or eliminate an item in the test. Each item retained in a test should have a positive correlation with the aggregate score obtained from the combination of all of the remaining items. It is not necessary for the item to have a statistically significant positive correlation with the aggregate.

This analysis also underscores the importance of the number of individual measures that form an aggregate. It is desirable to increase the number of items and the number of individual measures in order to obtain more accurate measures of a construct.

In recent years, another approach, called Item Response Theory (IRT; see Embretson, 1995), has been used to examine the links between individual items, item difficulty, and aggregate scores. In contrast to classical test theory, which assumes that all items are a function of "true score" variance and error, IRT posits that the probability of obtaining a score on a given item is also dependent on the difficulty of the item. IRT models allow for more precise models of missing data, discrimination, and guessing and lead to the construction of shorter tests and multiple forms of the same test. These models have begun to be used more widely in intelligence and personality research (see Embretson & Hershberger, 1999) and offer enormous potential for the development of more precise measurement models of these constructs.

Correlations among Aggregated Indexes of the Same Construct

An aggregated index of positively correlated items assumed to be a measure of a construct provides little or no evidence of validity. An analysis of the internal consistency of items may provide information about the extent to which the items measure something in common. Such information is not indicative of whether the aggregated index is an adequate index of a construct. In order to ascertain whether an aggregated index is valid (i.e., whether it is an index of the construct that it is assumed to measure), it is usually necessary to examine relationships that exist among diverse indexes.

We will illustrate the way in which diverse indexes that are related to each other may be used to derive measures of personality traits. Personality constructs are often construed as latent traits. They are hypothetical properties of persons that consist of dispositions to respond in particular ways. Appropriate eliciting conditions are required for their manifestation. In this respect they are analogous to such physical properties as solubility—a property of a substance that is not invariably manifested by the substance. Substances may or may not be in a dissolved state; they enter into the state if they are placed in a suitable medium (e.g., water). Likewise, the disposition to behave in an extraverted manner may or may not be manifested by a person in a particular situation. Although the appropriate

eliciting circumstances for latent dispositions may not be completely specified, it is assumed that there exists a set of circumstances (situations) that serve as appropriate eliciting conditions for a personality disposition. In order to establish the validity of a particular measure of a latent trait, one must examine relationships among a diverse set of manifestations of the trait. An important issue in personality research is the extent to which behavioral tendencies are consistent across different situations. Such traits as Conscientiousness or Extraversion are expressed in various situations, implying that there are positive correlations in behavioral tendencies that exhibit cross-situational generality.

In 1968 Mischel argued that there was relatively little evidence for the cross-situational consistency of traits. He noted that correlations between measures of individual differences in behavior in one situation rarely correlated in excess of .3 with measures of trait-related behavior in other situations. He argued that trait variance rarely accounts for more than 9% of the variance in behavior. The ubiquitous tendency to describe individuals in terms of generalized trait dispositions may be viewed as a linguistically derived error. Mischel noted that individuals were likely to behave in similar ways in the same situations but were unlikely to behave in similar ways in different situations. There are appropriate methodologies available to investigate the generality of cross-situational consistencies in behavior. The use of self-report ratings and peer ratings of personality dispositions is not, in and of itself, an appropriate methodology for addressing this issue. It is necessary to obtain appropriate behavioral indexes in several different situations in order to investigate this problem. There is a tendency to behave in a consistent manner in the same situation—an assumption that is accepted by virtually all personality researchers. If this is correct, it should be possible to aggregate several observations of behavior in the same situation to obtain an index that more closely corresponds to the true-score value of a person's behavioral tendency in a particular situation. Composite indexes for each of several behavioral observations, as well as the correlations among the indexes, may be obtained. Cross-situational generalities of dispositions would be demonstrated if the correlations are all positive.

Moscowitz (1982) studied the cross-situational generality of the trait of dominance. She observed 56 children in a nursery school for eight weeks using a time-sampling procedure that allowed her to note whether a child exhibited any one of five behaviors that were indicative of dominance. That is, she developed a theoretical analysis of dominance as a construct that implied that any one of five different behaviors might be indicative of a tendency to be dominant. These behaviors were assessed in a free play situation or in a situation in which the activity was constrained by a teacher's directive. She also noted whether the person with whom the child interacted was a male or female, an adult or another child. Moscowitz obtained aggregate indexes of each child's dominance behaviors in each of these settings. She found that the five different indexes of dominance were related to each other: An optimal combination of any set of four could be used to predict the excluded fifth with an average correlation of .66. She also found that tendencies to exhibit dominant behavior in one setting were predictive of tendencies to exhibit dominance behavior in other settings: The average correlation across targets of interaction was .62. Thus, children who were dominant toward same-sex peers tended to be dominant toward opposite-sex peers and toward male and female adults. Dominance exhibited cross-situational consistency. Moscowitz and Schwarz (1982) also found that the correlation between teachers' ratings of dominant behaviors and behavioral indexes of dominance was .59.

Moscowitz's (1982) study illustrates the importance of assessing constructs using multiple behavioral indexes. Dominance behavior in a particular setting was based on a composite index of repeated observations of five different behavioral manifestations of dominance. The use of a composite index in each setting contributed to the demonstration of cross-situational consistency of behavior.

The Moscowitz (1982) study demonstrates that it is possible to obtain behavioral indexes of individual differences in a particular setting that are predictive of individual differences in behavioral tendencies in other settings. It should be noted that the extent of cross-situational consistency demonstrated in this study is limited by the use of one behavioral setting. Children were not observed in their home or in settings outside of the context of the nursery school. The methodology employed in this investigation is subject to practical limitations. It is difficult to obtain behavioral indexes relevant to personality in a wide variety of natural settings. Research in personality may be contrasted with research in intelligence that employs a similar methodology. It is relatively easy to assess a person's intellectual skills in a particular domain. For example, it is possible to obtain a measure of a person's vocabulary using a test that contains a relatively small number of items. Similarly, there are tests of an individual's ability to perform a variety of cognitive tasks, including tests of memory, spatial reasoning, and numerical skills, among others. Many studies in the literature involve the administration of a diverse battery of intellectual tasks to individuals. As long as the tests are administered to individuals who do not exhibit extreme restriction in range of talent for intellectual abilities, the correlations among all of the different tasks are invariably positive. Individuals who excel in one type of intellectual task are likely to excel in another type of task even if the tasks, on the surface, appear to be relatively diverse with respect to the contents and processes required for solution. The cross-situational consistency of intellectual behaviors has been replicated in thousands of investigations. There is only a handful of studies indicating cross-situational consistencies of personality dispositions. The difference is attributable in part to differences in the difficulty of obtaining reliable indexes of intellectual performance and personality dispositions. The difficulty is practical rather than theoretical. Individual differences in diverse intellectual abilities may be examined in a single test session. The assessment of the cross-situational consistency of personality dispositions requires the observation of behavior in diverse natural settings. Such observations are time-consuming. The use of peer ratings and self-reports circumvents the practical difficulty of arranging observations in several natural settings. Of course, such measures are not informative about the actual level of cross-situational consistency that is present.

Systematic Analysis of Noncorrelated Indexes

The use of cross-situational aggregates is appropriate when examining cross-situational consistency. Some personality researchers assume that understanding an individual's profile of behavioral responses across situations may provide a meaningful level of analysis. Mischel and his colleagues developed appropriate methodologies. Shoda, Mischel, and Wright (1994; see also Mischel & Shoda, 1994) obtained measures of aggressive behavior for children attending a summer camp. They obtained behavioral indexes of the tendency to express verbal or physical aggressive behavior in five interpersonal situations: a peer initiating positive contact; a peer teasing, provoking, or threatening the child; an adult praising the child; an adult warning the child; and an adult punishing the child. They obtained test-retest correlations for children's aggressive tendencies in these various situations. Some children behaved consistently, but some did not. Figure 14.1 presents

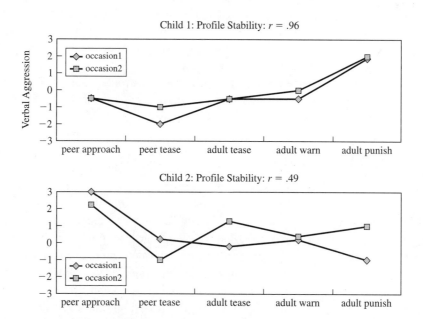

Figure 14.1   Individual profiles of verbal aggression across five types of psychological situations based on two measurement occasions.
Source: Based on Shoda, Michel, and Wright (1994).

examples of profile similarities for different children with respect to the expression of verbal aggression in different eliciting situations. Note that children differ with respect to their tendencies to exhibit consistent profiles of responses and differ with respect to the eliciting situations that trigger verbal aggression. Child 1, for example, quite consistently exhibits verbal aggression in response to adult punishment but rarely responds with verbal aggression to peers. Child 2, in contrast, consistently exhibits verbal aggression to peers who approach.

The Shoda et al. (1994) study indicates that certain characteristic individual patterns of response to particular situations may be overlooked in studies that focus on the generality of behavior in different situations.

The kinds of data collected by Moscowitz (1982) and Shoda et al. (1994) are comparable. The differences in the analyses arise from different theoretical assumptions about personality. Moscowitz is committed to a trait theory in which consistency across situations is used to infer general personality dispositions. In contrast, Shoda et al. believe that personality is best understood by examining the ways in which a person expresses a disposition in a particular situation. Thus, the methodologies used to analyze the data are defined by different theoretical assumptions about personality dispositions.

Theoretically Derived Interactions

The Shoda et al. (1994) study attempts to discover individual differences in behavioral consistencies by using an exploratory procedure. It is also possible to design studies that use general psychological laws to derive predictions of interactions between personality and situations. Feather (1961) used a general theory of goal-setting behavior developed by Atkinson (1957) to derive predictions about individual differences in tendencies to per-

sist in tasks at which individuals encountered repeated failures. Atkinson's theory assumes that goal-setting behavior is determined by two motivational tendencies: the positive approach motivation that leads individuals to try to succeed at a task that involves competition against a standard of excellence (e.g., an athletic competition) and the aversive avoidance motivation that leads individuals to avoid failure at the same task. The theory implies that individuals who tend to seek success will be most highly motivated when the difficulty of the task is intermediate. In contrast, individuals who are primarily motivated by an avoidance of failure will tend to seek either very easy or very difficult tasks.

Feather (1961) used this theory to derive predictions about persistence following failure at a task. Individuals who seek success and repeatedly fail at a task that they believed would be easy will find the task to be of increasing interest and will tend to persist on this task. By contrast, individuals who seek to avoid failure will find the task increasingly aversive and will fail to persist. Individuals who seek success and repeatedly fail at a task that they believed would be difficult will find the task to be of decreasing interest and will be less likely to persist. Individuals who are motivated to avoid failure will find such a task decreasingly aversive and will, therefore, tend to persist.

Feather (1961) assumed that individuals who scored high on a projective measure of need achievement and low on a paper-and-pencil measure of test anxiety were higher in success motivation than in failure motivation. Individuals who demonstrated the opposite pattern were higher in failure motivation than in success motivation. Therefore, he predicted that the former individuals would persist on a task initially thought to be easy and would fail to persist on a task that they thought to be difficult following repeated failure on the task. The latter individuals would show the opposite pattern of results. Feather obtained results consistent with these predictions. This experiment illustrates how researchers can use a theory to derive predictions about the ways in which individuals with different personality dispositions will respond in different situations.

Both the Feather (1961) and Shoda et al. (1994) studies deal with the ways in which personality dispositions are expressed in different situations. They differ in that the Shoda et al. study employs an exploratory approach whereas Feather uses a hypothetical model to derive predictions about the ways in which different classes of individuals will respond to different situations.

Cross-Method Analyses

We have examined the issue of cross-situational generality of constructs. Constructs may also exhibit consistency across different methods of measurement. Any single method of measuring a construct is imperfect. A common methodological assumption of personality research has been that all methods of measuring personality have specific method variance. For example, self-reports about personality might be influenced by a tendency to describe oneself in a socially desirable way. Therefore, it is often necessary to measure the same construct of personality using different methods (e.g., self-report, peer report, behavioral observation) in order to obtain a measure of the construct that is not unduly influenced by method-specific variance. The method-specific variance associated with any one method of measuring a trait is unlikely to be correlated with method-specific sources of variance associated with alternative methods of measuring the trait. An aggregate index based on different methods of measuring a trait is likely to contain more true-score trait variance than is a measure derived from any single method.

The multitrait-multimethod matrix (Campbell & Fiske, 1959) can be used to assess construct validity. Its use can be illustrated by the analysis of the relationship of personality traits assessed by the methods of peer ratings and self-report. It is possible to measure five personality traits (Extraversion, Agreeableness, Conscientiousness, Neuroticism, and Openness to Experience) using these two methods. A correlation matrix is formed in which the row variables constitute the five traits assessed by self-reports and the column variables constitute the five traits assessed by peer ratings. Validity is demonstrated when different methods of measuring the same construct are positively correlated and when different constructs assessed by the same method are not correlated. McCrae and Costa (1990) indicated that self-reports and peer ratings of the same personality trait tend to be positively correlated (r around .5). On the other hand, different constructs measured by the same method have near-zero correlations.

CONTINUITY AND CHANGE IN CONSTRUCTS OVER TIME

In this section we consider the continuity and change of personality. One way to study development is to examine the stability of individual difference measures across time. Again, we begin with the simplest case in which one examines a single measure of personality at different times. We also describe analyses of change. Finally, we consider cohort effects.

Relationships among Single Measures Obtained at Different Times

The simplest methodology available for ascertaining the consistency of a personality construct over time is to obtain test-retest correlations for a particular measure. McCrae and

Costa (1990) obtained test-retest correlations using a longitudinal design for self-report measures of five different personality traits: Extraversion, Conscientiousness, Agreeableness, Neuroticism, and Openness to Experience. They obtained test-retest correlations for different time intervals and found that the test-retest correlations for 6-year time intervals were comparable to the test-retest correlations for 12-year intervals. The correlations were close to .8. They also obtained measures of short-term test-retest correlations that may be used to estimate the reliability of the test. In order to evaluate test-retest consistency over long periods of time, it is necessary to relate long-term consistency to short-term consistency. Short-term variation in measurement is treated as error variance. This error variance then sets the upper bound of long-term correlations. The correlations for age differences of 6 and 12 years may be disattenuated (corrected for unreliability) by dividing the correlation by the square root of the product of the reliabilities of the variables that are being correlated. The disattenuated correlations provide estimates of the true-score test-retest consistency of the self-report trait measures. The disattenuated correlations are above .90. The disattenuated correlation for Extraversion was .97, implying that self-report measures for this trait are invariant over relatively long periods of the adult life span. The methodological implication of this analysis is widely applicable. Disattenuated correlations may be more accurate indexes of the true relationship between constructs than are obtained correlations. Low correlations between measures may occur because the constructs that they putatively measure are not strongly related or because the measures are imperfect indexes of the constructs that they are assumed to measure. Most theoretical investigations benefit from the use of disattenuated correlations.

In another example, Funder, Block, and Block (1983) observed the behavior of 4-year-old children in two situations. In one situation children were presented with an attractive toy and were told that they could have it at the end of the experimental session. The toy was in plain sight while the children were asked to perform another task. Funder et al. obtained measures of the extent to which children were distracted by the presence of the toy. In another situation, children were shown an attractive toy and were told that they should not play with it. The experimenter left the room and observed the child's behavior, and the child's tendency to play with the toy was noted. Funder et al. formed a composite behavioral index of "*ego control,*" or the tendency to be distracted by a toy or to play with a toy in violation of the experimenter's instructions based on aggregating scores in the two situations that they investigated. They related this index to ratings of ego control based on interviews of their subjects that psychologists conducted at different ages in a longitudinal study. They obtained a correlation of .31 between ratings for males obtained at age 4 years and the composite behavioral index obtained at the same age. Funder et al. obtained a correlation between ratings of ego control for males at age 11 years and the composite behavioral index obtained at age 4 of .43. A comparison of the correlation from measures obtained at the same age with the time-lagged correlation provides an index of the degree of stability of the underlying personality dimension assessed by these different measures. Because the time-lagged correlation is equivalent to the contemporaneous correlation, it is possible to infer that the underlying personality characteristic assessed by these different measures is invariant between age 4 and age 11. This inference is based on the assumption that the contemporaneous correlation based on data obtained when the children were age 4 is a measure of the extent to which the behavioral measure and the psychologist's ratings are indexes of a common latent personality trait. The common trait may be considered a latent trait or a hypothetical construct that accounts for the correlation for these methodologically distinct ways of measuring the same construct (e.g., behavioral responses at age 4 and psychologist's ratings based on interviews with the subjects). Because the contemporaneous and time-lagged correlations are comparable, it is possible to argue that the latent trait assessed at age 4 is comparable to the latent trait assessed at age 11.

Methodologically distinct measures of the same construct are especially useful in attempts to relate behavior in early childhood or infancy to characteristics exhibited in older children or adults. The indexes that are appropriate to assess common dimensions of personality vary with age: Aggression in children aged 2 years is not assessed in the same way as is aggression in adults. Columbo (1993) summarized a series of studies relating measures of infant information processing to childhood measures of intelligence. Standard IQ tests such as the Wechsler Preschool and Primary Scale of Intelligence (see Kaufman, 2000) test or the Stanford Binet Intelligence Scale IV (Thorndike, Hagen, & Sattler, 1986) cannot be administered to preverbal children. Attempts to study the continuity of intelligence starting with the first year of life can only be performed using measures of intellectual ability that are different in content and form from those used to assess intelligence in older individuals. Columbo summarized studies relating measures of infant novelty preference and fixation times in a habituation paradigm in which individuals were repeatedly presented with the same stimulus to performance on tests of intelligence administered to children between 2 and 7 years of age. The infant measures were administered prior to age 1 as early as the neonatal period and often during the

first 6 months of life. Fixation times in habituation had a mean correlation with childhood IQ of .46. These results indicate that there is some degree of consistency in intelligence from the neonatal period through early childhood. These results also indicate that certain methodologies are available for studying continuities in behavior from childhood to adulthood even when the adult behavior has no obvious childhood counterpart. What may be continuous over the life span is a disposition to respond to the world in common ways, though manifested in different ways at different points in a person's life. The methodology for such investigations is contingent on the development of appropriate theoretical insights. That is, one must develop a theoretical analysis that explains why a construct may manifest itself in very different ways. Thus, although the discovery of this relationship between infant and child cognition was serendipitous, subsequent research requires one to construct a theory that predicts the ways in which a latent trait may be manifested in different ways at different times in a person's life.

The analysis of relationships between indexes of a construct obtained at different ages can be quantitatively assessed by a consideration of disattenuated correlations that correct for unreliability of measurement. The disattenuated correlation between infant measures and childhood IQ is .76. This correlation is an estimate of the true relationship between the variables after accounting for unreliability of measurement.

The magnitude of the difference between obtained and disattenuated correlations is a function of the reliability of the measures. If measures are unreliable, then disattenuated correlations will be substantially higher than obtained correlations. Whether one should focus on observed or disattenuated correlations depends on the way in which correlations are used. For example, if one wishes to predict childhood IQ from measures of infant habituation, the accuracy of prediction would best be judged by using an observed correlation. On the other hand, if one wishes to address a theoretical question about the continuity of intelligence from infancy to early childhood, one would be interested in the disattenuated correlations.

Systematic Sources of Variance in Change Scores

In the typical longitudinal investigation, test-retest correlations between various indexes of personality are used to assess the continuity of personality characteristics. It is also possible to study systematic change in personality characteristics over time. Block and Robins (1993) studied change in self-esteem between ages 14 and 23. At age 14 Block and Robins obtained measures of self-esteem from their subjects. In addition, each of the subjects in their study was assigned personality ratings by psychologists as a result of a comprehensive personality assessment. Self-esteem measures were obtained from the same subjects at age 23. Block and Robins obtained a measure of change in self-esteem. They correlated change scores with personality ratings. For both male and female subjects they found that change scores were inversely correlated with personality ratings that were indicative of Neuroticism or poor adjustment. These results suggest that self-report measures of self-esteem changed to reflect personality characteristics that were present at age 14. The psychologists who assessed the personalities of the subjects in this investigation were able to ascertain characteristics of these subjects that may very well not have been understood by the subjects themselves. Self-esteem measures and measures of Neuroticism are highly correlated (see McCrae & Costa, 1990). The subjects may not have developed a clear sense of their neurotic tendencies at age 14. Over the next 9 years they may have had additional opportunities to understand their personality. Subjects who were well adjusted at age 14 experienced increases in self-esteem; those who were poorly adjusted experienced declines in self-esteem. Thus, the change in self-reports may be viewed as being determined by personality characteristics present at an earlier age. In this instance, individuals may have changed in a way that increased the relationship between their self-reports and their actual personality characteristics.

Caspi and Herbener (1990) studied personality change in married couples in an 11-year longitudinal study. They obtained personality ratings for the couples at both time periods. They assigned the couples to one of three groups depending on their degree of similarity in initial personality ratings. They found that change in personality was inversely related to the degree of similarity of the couples' initial personality ratings. The test-retest correlations for personality were positively related to the similarity of spouses' personalities. The direction of change in personality was not predictable from knowledge of a spouse's ratings—only the absolute magnitude of change. The studies by Block and Robins (1993) and Caspi and Herbener both point to the importance of investigating change as well as continuity in personality. Just as it is inappropriate to assume that lack of correlation across situations is merely error, so too it is inappropriate to assume that the differences in personality characteristics across time are not systematic.

Cohort Effects

It is possible to study changes over the life span using cross-sectional designs in which individuals of different ages are tested at the same time. Conducting longitudinal studies encompassing large periods of the life span is difficult. Cross-sectional analyses of age differences are confounded with cohort effects. Individuals of different ages tested at the same time will of necessity differ in time of birth. It is difficult to separate age and cohort effects.

Cohort effects may be studied by administering the same test to representative samples of individuals who are assessed at the same age at different times. Three fundamental methodological requirements must be met in any study of cohort effects. First, the samples or populations studied must be comparable. For example, an analysis of cohort changes in the Scholastic Aptitude Test (SAT) is complicated by changes in the composition of the sample of individuals who take the test; for example, there has been an increase in the number of individuals who take the test over time. It is possible that more individuals who are likely to score low on the test have been taking the test in recent years. Changes in test scores may be attributable to cohort effects on the sample of test takers. Second, the test that is administered should remain constant over time. If easy items are excluded and difficult items are added, changes in test scores over time may reflect changes in the composition of the test rather than cohort changes in the construct measured by the test. In the case of cohort changes in intelligence, data series exist in which the identical test is administered in the same way to comparable samples. Third, the relationship between a measure and the construct that is assessed by that measure must remain invariant. Consider a hypothetical example. There may be cohort effects in the tendency to admit that one is depressed. Measures of depression may demonstrate increases not because of a change in the construct assessed by various self-reports of depression but in the relationship between the

self-report and the underlying construct that is assessed by the measure. More recent cohorts of individuals may be more inclined to admit to being depressed than cohorts of individuals born in an earlier period. Cohort changes on a particular index of a construct may be indeterminate with respect to whether the cohort changes constitute changes in the construct that is putatively assessed by the index. In order to address this issue, it is necessary to examine the network of laws and relations that provide evidence for the validity of the index as a measure of the construct. Consider a hypothetical example. Assume that there is a biological theory of depression. If the theory is correct and if a particular self-report measure is a valid measure of depression, then there should be a relationship between the self-report measure and one or more biological indexes of depression specified by the theory. Assume that evidence exists that supports this prediction for several different cohorts. This evidence would provide evidence in support of the assumption that the index of depression has equivalent construct validity for different cohorts. The construct validity of the index can be ascertained by examining the hypothetical set of all the laws and relationships that are related to the theory of the construct. This network of laws and relationships is sometimes called the *nomological network*. The demonstration of cohort effects based on changes in one or more indexes of a construct requires one to demonstrate that the indexes for different cohorts exhibit comparable construct validity—that is, that they exhibit cohort invariance with respect to their nomological networks. Research on cohort effects cannot be interpreted without attention to theoretical assumptions about the meaning of the constructs.

The clearest evidence of cohort effects in the study of individual differences is contained in a series of investigations of changes in intelligence reported by Flynn (1998; see also Neisser, 1998). The most convincing data derive from studies of European countries that require universal assessment of potential military recruits. These studies provide data for the entire male population of testable individuals who are administered the same tests at the same age each year. These data as well as other data obtained from other sources in other countries indicate that scores on tests of intelligence have been increasing in most technologically advanced countries for several decades. Cross-sectional studies of performance on tests of intelligence reported dramatic declines in intelligence for individuals of different ages taking the same test at the same time (see Schaie & Strother, 1968, for an early analysis of this issue). Some of these declines were attributable to cohort effects.

RELATIONS AMONG CONSTRUCTS

We have discussed methodologies that may be used to study the relationship between different indexes of the same construct. We have not considered studies of the relationships that exist among constructs. Researchers have examined the analysis of relationships among constructs as a basis for the construction of taxonomies. There are many investigations in which a battery of measures is given to a group of subjects. One goal of such investigations is to determine whether the measures are related to each other. Many personality measures assumed to measure the same construct are uncorrelated. Measures with different names may be substantially correlated with each other. John (1990) described the existence of a large set of measures with different or related names as constituting a Tower of Babel. One goal of studying relationships among measures is to discover which

measures are highly related and which are independent.

Exploratory Factor Analysis

Exploratory factor analysis may be used to study relationships among measures of different constructs. The method begins by obtaining a correlation matrix in which each measure is correlated with every other measure. The goal of the analysis involves determining the minimal number of hypothetical factors that account for the covariance in the matrix.

Although the emergence of windows-based statistical programs has made it quite simple to run exploratory factor analyses, several important issues are often overlooked (see Bollen, 1989, for a more thorough discussion). Most importantly, a factor analysis is only as good as the measures that go into the analysis. Individual measures with skewed or kurtotic variance will reduce the values of correlations, possibly resulting in unclear factor solutions. Low covariance among measures will also lead to unclear factor analytic results.

Beyond the quality of the data, it is important to decide on the following before conducting one's factor analysis:

1. *Definition of the factor solution.* Factors can be determined through a number of methods. One way is to conduct an analysis in which the factor solution is not rotated. In this analysis the goal is to derive the smallest set of factors necessary to account for the largest amount of variance in the measures. Although these factors account for much of the total variance in the individual measures, the individual measures themselves may correlate moderately with the factor. Higher factor loadings may be obtained through the use of factor solutions based on orthogonal rotations (the factors are hypothesized to

be uncorrelated) or oblique rotations (the factors may be correlated).

2. *Determining the number of factors.* Exploratory factor analysis does not provide inferential tests of significance. Thus, it is important to decide beforehand what criteria will be used to determine whether a factor is meaningful. Although there are many criteria (e.g., eigenvalue, scree plot, etc.), they have a common goal: to determine whether factors retained in the solution account for significant sources of variance in the matrix.

3. *Examination of factor loadings.* It is necessary to decide the minimal factor loading that is required for a measure to load meaningfully on a factor. Factor loadings are hypothetical correlations. They are estimates of the degree to which a variable covaries with the factor. In interpreting the meaning of a factor, one should be aware of the magnitude of the loadings of variables that collectively define the factor. A loading of .7 indicates that 49% of the variance in the variable loads on the factor, whereas a loading of .3 indicates that 9% of the variance in the variable is shared with the factor. Although both variables may meet a criterion of minimal loading on a factor, the interpretation of the factor should consider differences in the magnitude of the loadings of individual variables on the factor. Additionally, in a multifactorial solution, individual measures should not load on all factors. Instead, individual measures should load on certain theoretically meaningful factors.

The end result of the factor analysis is a factor matrix in which the loading of each test in the battery is noted. Tests may load on more than one factor, suggesting that variance on the test is determined by more than one factor. A factor analysis permits a decomposition of the covariance between a test and all other tests in a battery by separate components of variance associated with each of the factors. An individual's performance on the test battery may be described in terms of scores on the factors that account for the covariance among the tests in the battery.

Factor structures may be replicated by comparing the similarity of factor loadings obtained in different investigations of comparable test batteries. The attempt to ascertain whether two factors obtained in different investigations are related can be based on an informal examination of the pattern of loadings of variables on the factors. There are also more formal methods of testing the similarity between factors derived from separate investigations (see Stevens, 1986). These methods are usually preferable to informal methods because they lead to quantitative indexes that may be used to gauge the degree of identity of factors.

Application to Personality

Factor analytic investigations have led to progress in the construction of taxonomies in personality and intelligence. Considerable evidence exists for five factors in the domain of personality: Extraversion, Agreeableness, Conscientiousness, Neuroticism, and Openness to Experience (John, 1990). Analyses of both self-report ratings and peer ratings of personality dimensions have quite typically led to a five-factor solution of the correlation matrix. The solution exhibits some degree of cross-cultural and cross-linguistic replicability. Analyses of ratings in several different languages obtained in several different countries have led to comparable factor structures in which each of the "Big Five" is defined by traits that have comparable factor loadings. Some trait characteristics have significant loadings on a single factor; for example, talkativeness is a trait that has high ratings on Extraversion and may be considered a marker variable for that factor. A marker variable for a factor is a variable that has a high loading on the factor, which implies that scores on the variable may be used to estimate scores on the factor. In one review of 15 factor analyses of trait ratings based on both self-report and peer ratings obtained from German- and English-speaking subjects, talkativeness had an average loading on Extraversion of .76 and no loading in excess of .03 on any other factor. Affectionate versus Reserved had a mean loading of .61 on Extraversion and a mean loading of .44 on Agreeableness (Johnson & Ostendorf, 1993). These loadings imply that affectionate ratings are determined, to different degrees, by both Extraversion and Agreeableness. The Big Five factors are usually uncorrelated, which implies that a person's scores on the tests that define any one of these factors tend to be unrelated to scores on tests that define other factors.

The Big Five has come to be a measure of criterion validity for new measures of personality. If a measure is substantially correlated with the Big Five, it does not provide substantially new variance to the study of personality. On the other hand, a measure that does not relate to the Big Five may contribute new variance to the study of personality.

Application to Intelligence

Although the appropriate taxonomy of intellectual abilities has been a vexed topic in the history of intelligence (Brody, 2000), considerable progress in the resolution of different views about the structure of intellect has been attained as a result of the contributions of Carroll (1993). Carroll reanalyzed over 400 correlation matrices of relationships among different measures of cognitive ability. The analyses included the total set of usable matrices available at the time of the analysis.

Carroll's integration of the corpus of factor analytic investigations led to the development of a three-stratum hierarchical model. The third and most general stratum contains a single general factor: Spearman's g. This factor usually accounts for approximately 50% of the covariance in the matrix. The second stratum contains eight second-order factors arrayed in terms of their relationship to g. The two factors with the highest g loadings at this stratum are Gf (fluid ability, a factor related to abstract reasoning) and Gc (crystallized ability, a factor related to verbal ability). Each of the second-stratum abilities is related to several first-stratum factors.

Carroll's analyses are based on Schmid and Leiman (1957) orthogonalizations of the factor structure. In a traditional multilevel factorial solution, measures load only on the first-order factors. In a Schmid-Leiman analysis, the individual measures load on both first- and all higher-order factors. This permits the decomposition of the variance on a particular ability measure by a consideration of the contributions of separate factors at each stratum of the taxonomy. It is also possible to describe the abilities of an individual by his or her score on each of the factors at each of the strata of the taxonomy. Figure 14.2 presents Carroll's three-stratum taxonomy.

The existence of taxonomies permits one to decompose the variance in a particular measure into orthogonal components. A correlation between a measure of intelligence and another variable may be attributable to any one of several components of variance that are present in the measure of intelligence. For example, it is known that measures of intelligence are correlated with performance on a number of relatively simple experimental tasks, such as two-choice reaction time (the correlation is negative). The correlation between a measure of intelligence and performance on a measure of reaction time may be attributable to any of the orthogonal

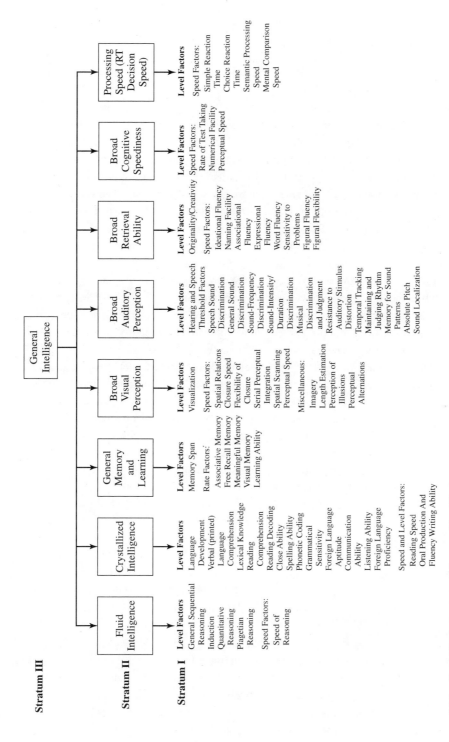

Figure 14.2 Carroll's three-stratum theory of intelligence.
SOURCE: Based on Carroll (1993).

components of variance that are assumed to contribute to the variance of scores on a test of intelligence. A similar ambiguity in the interpretation of correlations between measures exists in the area of personality. Blended variables load on more than one personality dimension in the Big Five taxonomy. The correlation between a blended variable and some other measure may be attributable in different degrees to the independent sources of variance that contribute to scores on the measure of a blended trait. For example, the correlation between the blended scale "affectionate" and some other variable may be due to Extraversion and/or Agreeableness. These observations lead to a number of critical methodological injunctions that derive from the use of individual-difference taxonomies. It is useful to decompose the variance in any particular individual-difference measure and to discover its location in the taxonomic structure to which it may belong. Such a procedure enables the researcher to discover the extent to which the covariance between measures is attributable to the contributions of several independent sources of variance present in the measures. It is problematic to assume that a particular measure is uncorrelated with sources of variance present in standard taxonomies. Each measure may be a measure of many different things. Such individuals will be inclined to ascertain the extent to which sources of variance contained within a measure are related to well-defined, taxonomically structured variables.

From Exploratory to Confirmatory Analysis of Relationships

In order to decompose the sources of variance, researchers can conduct analyses of relationships among variables using confirmatory rather than exploratory procedures. These procedures enable the researcher to test various models of the relationships that exist

among variables and to select from among classes of models those that provide an optimal fit to the obtained data.

Confirmatory analyses test competing theoretical models. The development of confirmatory models creates an unusually strong relationship between theory and method. These methods stress that good methodology requires good theory (see Bollen, 1989, for an introduction to confirmatory analysis). Competing models are composed of a set of equations that are used to estimate the covariance among a set of variables. The estimated covariances are then compared to the actual measured covariance. The model that best estimates the measured covariance is deemed the best-fitting model.

Several important issues must be dealt with before initiating a confirmatory analysis. The availability of powerful statistical programs that conduct confirmatory analysis may be a seductive influence on researchers. Insufficient exploration of alternative methods of analysis within a confirmatory model and insufficient comparison with other statistical methods may yield results that are not optimal. When initiating a confirmatory analysis, the researcher should pay particular attention to the following:

1. *Deriving theoretically meaningful models.* The principal advantage of confirmatory methods is that they allow for the explicit testing of competing models. Thus, it is important to derive a set of theoretically meaningful models so that the best-fitting model emerges out of a set of plausible alternatives.

2. *Deriving identifiable models.* In addition to deriving models that are theoretically possible, it is also important to derive models that are analyzable. In a confirmatory analysis the researcher uses a set of equations to estimate the covariance among a set of variables. These equations are

composed of parameter estimates that are analogous (although not identical) to regression weights or factor loadings in an exploratory analysis. In certain circumstances (e.g., too many parameters given the number of variables in the analysis) some models cannot be identified. The equations do not result in unique parameter estimates.

3. *Determining which data to use.* Confirmatory analysis can be conducted on correlations, covariances, and raw data. Most analyses have employed covariances. Recent analyses have examined raw data. This procedure leads to a more systematic analysis of missing data. Confirmatory analysis of correlations is not recommended.

4. *Determining starting values and the fit procedure.* In confirmatory analysis starting values for each parameter are subjected to a goodness-of-fit procedure to derive a set of final parameter estimates that yield an estimated covariance matrix that is as similar as possible to the actual covariance matrix. It is desirable to explore different initial starting values. It is possible that different final solutions will emerge from different starting values. Additionally, alternative minimization procedures should be employed (e.g., least squares, maximum likelihood, etc.) because they may affect the final solution as well.

5. *Determining goodness of fit.* Once a set of identifiable models has been derived, it is then necessary to describe the manner in which the best-fitting model will be determined. Chi-square tests are often used, but other fit indexes are also frequently used (see Bollen, 1989).

6. *Testing competing models.* Once the fit of each model has been determined, a chi-square difference test can be used to test the comparative fit of the various compet-

ing models. The model with the smallest number of parameters with the best fit is determined to be the best-fitting and most parsimonious model.

7. *Testing parameter estimates.* Competing models can be used also to test the significance of particular parameter estimates. Two confirmatory solutions are compared, one with a parameter and one without the parameter. If the model without the parameter fits significantly worse, then that parameter is judged to be significant. Another way to test parameter estimates is by calculating confidence intervals for each parameter (see Neale, 2000).

The controversy surrounding Carroll's (1993) taxonomy provides an excellent example of how confirmatory factor analysis has been used to test competing theories. Carroll's exploratory analyses indicate that cognitive abilities include a higher-order general intelligence factor. Gustafsson (1999) proposed a criticism of the third-stratum g factor in Carroll's taxonomy. He noted that Carroll's analyses were based on exploratory factor analyses with rotations of models to various criteria of best fit.

Gustafsson (1999) performed a confirmatory factor analysis on a comprehensive battery of tests of ability. He attempted to test whether a battery of cognitive abilities is best fit by a model that hypothesizes a general factor. In order to test the importance of g, he formed competing models that postulated the existence or absence of g. He found that he was able to fit a model in which the second-order fluid ability factor was perfectly correlated with the general factor. He concluded, therefore, that there was no need to postulate a higher-order g factor to explain the relationships among cognitive abilities.

Both Gustafsson (1999) and Horn (1985) accept the distinction between Gf and Gc as fundamental. They are inclined to accept the

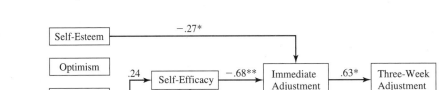

Figure 14.3   Control, self-efficacy, and adjustment following abortion.
SOURCE: Based on Cozzarelli (1993).

validity of additional second-stratum factors as well. They both object to the notion that there is a separate *g* factor that is independent of *Gf* and *Gc*.

In response, Carroll (1997) reported a set of additional analyses using confirmatory factor analyses. After testing alternative models, the best-fitting model was one that included a third-order general factor. Carroll then examined the loadings in this best-fitting model and found that all variables loaded on *g*. In addition, there were variables that had substantial loadings on *g* that had near-zero loadings on the fluid ability factor. Thus, the confirmatory analysis indicated that *g* and *Gf* were not identical. For further details of Carroll's analyses demonstrating the way in which confirmatory analyses may be used to test competing models, see Carroll (1997).

Correlation and Causality

It is possible to study relationships among measures to construct models indicating the way in which several different variables combine to influence outcome variables. Path models are used for this purpose. For example, Cozzarelli (1993) studied the influence of personality characteristics (Self-esteem, Optimism, Perceived control, and Depression) and self-efficacy beliefs about the ability to cope with an abortion on adjustment to the experience of having an abortion immediately

following the abortion and three weeks after the abortion. She performed a path analysis of the influence of these related variables. Figure 14.3 presents her final path model. The figure indicates that two of the personality variables, Control and Depression, are related to self-efficacy beliefs. Self-efficacy beliefs are strongly related to the immediate adjustment to the experience of abortion. Furthermore, immediate adjustment is the strongest influence on adjustment three weeks after the abortion. Her path model indicates that personality characteristics do not have a direct influence on the adjustment to the experience of an abortion three weeks after its occurrence. Personality variables influence adjustment indirectly, and primarily in terms of their influence on self-efficacy. This study illustrates how researchers can use a path model to construct a causal analysis of the way in which variables combine to influence a dependent variable.

Cozzarelli's (1993) model illustrates how researchers can use path models to infer causal relationships. Because the measures are arrayed in time, the final measure in the analysis (3-week adjustment) cannot possibly influence the other variables. Thus, it must be a dependent variable. The variables on the left of the diagram (e.g., control and depression) are assumed to be enduring personal characteristics. Self-efficacy is assumed to be a variable that is based on a belief that is itself variable. Enduring personal characteristics may influence self-efficacy, but self-efficacy is unlikely to influence an enduring personal characteristic. Thus, the model examines the influence of enduring personal characteristics on self-efficacy but does not examine the influence of self-efficacy on enduring personal characteristics. These theoretical assumptions provide a way of examining causal relationships among the variables that are considered by partitioning the covariance between variables into a direct unmediated influence and an indirect influence. The analysis provides evidence for a causal influence of self-efficacy on adjustment to abortion that is independent of the other variables considered in the analysis.

Like confirmatory analysis, path models require the use of explicit theories that define appropriate sequences of relationships among variables. They require an explicit integration of theory and method.

GROUP DIFFERENCES

Individual difference psychologists are often interested in differences among various groups of individuals. There are many contemporary analyses of gender and ethnic differences, but there are many other potential ways in which groups may be formed. For example, researchers may compare individuals who do or do not share some common experience, such as the death of a parent prior to adolescence. Group comparisons may account for systematic variance in psychological characteristics. It is possible to distinguish three ways in which groups may differ in psychological characteristics.

Mean Differences

Groups may differ in their mean score on a measure. Meta-analysis (see Chap. 10, this volume) is used to examine group differences

on a particular characteristic. Meta-analyses involve the calculation of an effect-size measure usually defined as a mean difference divided by the standard deviation of the measure. Systematic searches of the literature are accomplished by entering appropriate key words relevant to a comparison of two groups on some measure. An effect-size measure is calculated for each sample, and the mean effect size over samples is obtained. The mean effect size provides an estimate of the magnitude of group differences on some variable. It is possible to perform additional analyses on effect-size data. Systematic variance in effect sizes may be examined as a function of variables of interest to the investigator. The choice of independent variables in meta-analyses can be quite varied and can include consideration of indexes of the methodological adequacy of different investigations, additional individual difference variables that may affect effect sizes, and the type of publication from which the effect-size measures were derived. Meta-analyses provide a comprehensive method for systematically ascertaining the outcomes of all of the literature relevant to the determination of the magnitude of mean differences on a measure.

Many meta-analyses of gender differences in psychological characteristics have been conducted (see Hoyenga & Hoyenga, 1993). For example, Eagly (1987) performed a meta-analysis comparing male and female performance on ability to judge the meaning of nonverbal behaviors. She found that the mean effect size for female-to-male performance on this ability was .43.

Variance Differences

Group differences may occur on any parameter of the distribution of scores on some variable. Differences may exist in skew, variance, or means of distributions as well as in the overall shape of a distribution. Hedges and

Newell (1995) performed a meta-analysis of gender differences in scores on tests of intelligence. They found very little evidence of mean gender differences in performance on composite measures of intelligence, but they did obtain evidence of a variance difference: Males are marginally more variable on tests than are females. Variance differences lead to differences in the frequency of occurrence of extreme scores in a distribution. Males are more likely than females to have very high (and very low) scores on various measures of ability. The Johns Hopkins talent search for adolescents with unusually high scores on mathematical ability uses the SAT quantitative aptitude test. The test is administered to 7th-grade students. Benbow (1988) found that males were approximately 13 times more likely than females to have scores above 700 on this test. Note that at this age there is little or no mean difference in scores on measures of mathematical knowledge and ability. The large male-to-female ratio of adolescents attaining this relatively high cutoff score is primarily attributable to differences in variance.

Correlational Differences

Group differences in means and variances are not usually informative with respect to the construct equivalence of different individual difference measures. Groups may differ with respect to the relationships that exist among different measures. Differences in covariance matrices may be informative with respect to the invariance of psychological laws for members of different groups.

Group Equivalence

Rowe, Vazsonyi, and Flannery (1994) analyzed several covariance matrices reporting relationships among variables related to academic achievement and juvenile delinquency for large samples of African-American and White subjects. For each study they obtained covariance matrices separately for their two

racial groupings and obtained a measure of similarity of the matrices. They then divided their samples into two randomly selected within-race groups. They found that differences in the covariance matrices within randomly selected groups of individuals belonging to the same racial group were of the same order of magnitude as were differences between covariance matrices obtained from different racial groups. Thus, the between-race group differences in these investigations may be attributable to random error. The analyses imply that one may reasonably assume that the outcomes investigated were determined by influences that were cross-racially invariant. Rowe et al. noted that investigators of racial differences often assume that the processes that determine the outcomes being investigated are likely to be different for members of different racial groups. They believe that researchers should begin with the parsimonious assumption that the processes that they study are racially invariant. Researchers should proceed to the more complex assumption that the processes are racially distinct only after an examination of the covariance matrices indicates that they are racially distinct.

The method used to study racial differences in covariance matrices may be used to study any group difference. It is useful to form two randomly chosen subsets of a group to study random variations in the total set of relationships that are obtained within a group. These differences may be compared with between-group differences to ascertain whether group invariance of relationships is present.

Group Nonequivalence

Covariance matrices may vary systematically as a function of one or more parameters. Using the Wechsler Adult Intelligence Scale–Revised (WAIS-R) and the Wechsler Intelligence Scale for Children–Revised (WISC-R), Detterman and Daniel (1989) obtained mean correlations for subtests for individuals who

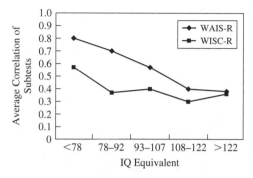

Figure 14.4   Average correlation of WAIS-R and WISC-R subtests by ability level.
SOURCE: Based on Detterman and Daniel (1989).

differed in their scores on the Vocabulary subtest. They used the large standardization sample for the Wechsler to divide their subjects into five groups based on their performance on the Vocabulary subtest. They then calculated the mean correlation for the correlations among the remaining subtests on the Wechsler for each of the five groups of subjects. Figure 14.4 presents their data. The results summarized in the figure indicate that the mean correlation obtained for these groups tends to be a monotonically decreasing function of performance on the Vocabulary subtest. These results are compatible with the assumption that the g variance in tests of intelligence is inversely related to the mean level of intelligence.

The Detterman and Daniel (1989) study provides evidence of a relationship between scores and changes in a single property of a covariance matrix. Hoyenga and Hoyenga (1993) summarized studies of depression in male and female subjects. Table 14.1 presents a summary of some of the principal differences in characteristics of depression in male and female subjects. The table indicates that depression is expressed in quite different ways in males and females. The pattern of results is complex and does not lend itself readily to a simple and compelling theoretical explanation. Nevertheless, the results do lead to a compelling methodologically relevant con-

clusion. The meaning of a particular construct may be different for individuals belonging to different groups. Psychological laws and relationships are not necessarily invariant for members of different groups. Results such as these complicate the attempt to integrate individual difference psychology with the search for laws that are invariant for all humans (or even all mammalian species), which is often taken as the ultimate goal of experimental psychology.

Group differences can extend to the level of item analyses, and various techniques are available for examining item characteristics. Item analyses are used in the construction of tests. In tests of ability, items are analyzed with respect to their difficulty level in order to ascertain the relationship between performance on a particular item and performance on a test overall. Freedle and Kostin (1997) analyzed 20 analogy items on the SAT Verbal Ability test. They contrasted the performance of individuals belonging to either the Black or White group of test takers on these items in an effort to ascertain whether the items functioned in a comparable manner for individuals belonging to these two groups. They obtained an index of differential item functioning (DIF score) for each item by contrasting the performance of the Black and White individuals on each of these items. A positive DIF score indicated that the item was more difficult for White subjects than for Black subjects with the same total score on the test. They also assigned an overall difficulty score to each item by noting the percentage of individuals who obtained the correct response on an item. The correlation between the DIF score and the difficulty score for the items was .49, indicating that difficult items were more difficult for White subjects than for Black subjects with the same overall score on the test. Black subjects tended to perform better on difficult items and worse on easy items. Individuals belonging to different groups may respond in different ways to the same items.

Table 14.1   Sex Differences in the Structure of Depressive Syndrome in Females and Males

The sexes differ not only in overall frequency but also in symptom patterns displayed within the various depressive syndromes:

1. Clinically depressed females more often report excessive eating and weight gain as a symptom (loss of appetite and weight loss are the most common eating symptoms in both sexes).

2. In nonselected populations, females are more likely to report that they eat when they become depressed; women also are more likely to report crying, becoming irritable, and confronting their feelings; males are more likely to report becoming aggressive and engaging in sexual activity.

3. Factor structure of depression scales is different for males and females, both in nonselected populations and among depressed subjects.

4. Working females are more likely to go to health services, and males are more likely simply to miss work when depressed.

5. The personality factors that differentiate depressed males from depressed females are the same as those that differentiate nondepressed males from nondepressed females.

6. Psychomotor agitation (nervous activity) seems to be more common in female depressives; retardation (inactivity) may be relatively more common in males.

7. Among depressed college students (rating-scale measures), males are more socially withdrawn, express more motivational and cognitive problems, use drugs, and have somatic symptoms (e.g., aches and pains); women have greater lack of confidence, lack of concern over what happens to them, more self blame, more crying spells, and irritability, and are more hurt by criticism.

8. Depression is associated with decreased instrumentality (as measured by sex-role scales), but this may be an effect rather than a precursor of depression.

9. When under stress, college student females report feeling more depressed and anxious than males do, and females say that they are more likely to express their feelings; males become more active in response to stress; stress from school or from intimate relationships depressed personal self-esteem only in females.

10. Age of onset of bipolar and unipolar syndromes is the same for both sexes, although female/male ratios for bipolar onset may be greatest from ages 30 to 75.

11. Incidence of depression before puberty is the same in both sexes; female incidence of depressive episodes increases at puberty.

12. Males are more likely to commit suicide; females are more likely to make nonfatal suicide attempts.

SOURCE: Adapted from Hoyenga and Hoyenga (1993).

Individual differences in response to a common task may be understood by assuming that individuals have different parametric values on a model that is assumed to apply to all individuals. Alternatively, it may be necessary to assume that the theories or models required to explain behavior in a particular situation are not invariant for different individuals. Sternberg and Weil (1980) contrasted two different models that could be used for the solution of deductive logic problems, one based on linguistic analyses and the other based on spatial reasoning. By examining the pattern of solution latencies for problems that were assumed to vary in difficulty as a function of whether an individual used a spatial or a lin-

guistic method of solution, they were able to classify their subjects by the type of solution pattern that they used. They correlated solution latencies with individual differences in verbal and spatial ability measures for these two types of subjects. For subjects who relied on a linguistic model of solution, verbal and spatial ability scores correlated with solution latencies $-.76$ and $-.29$, respectively. The comparable correlations for subjects who were assumed to use spatial solutions for the problems were $-.08$ and $-.60$. These results indicate that the relationship between an ability measure and performance on this task is dependent on the nature of the methods that are used to solve the task. This experiment also indicates that in order to understand the way in which individual differences influence performance on a task, it may be necessary to understand the nature of the processes elicited by the task. These processes may not be invariant for different individuals. Appropriate methodology for this type of investigation requires the use of a theory that explains behavior in a particular situation. Sternberg and Weil relied on two competing theories of the solution of deductive logic problems.

CROSS-DOMAIN RELATIONSHIPS

Often, scientific progress is made when researchers study the relationships between methods and theories that develop in what are initially disparate areas of investigation. For example, it is common in scientific research to attempt to relate constructs derived from one scientific domain to constructs that are derived from another domain that is assumed to be more elementary. Thus, chemical concepts may be related to physical concepts in the study of physical chemistry; biological concepts may be related to chemical concepts in the study of biochemistry; and psychological concepts may be related to biological concepts in the study of biological psychology. Individual difference psychologists have tried to relate their constructs to constructs that derive from experimental psychology and from biological psychology. We briefly consider cross-domain relationships among individual difference parameters and constructs derived from biology, genetics, and cognitive-experimental psychology.

Psychometric Intelligence and Cognitive-Experimental Psychology

Psychologists who investigate intelligence using psychometric methods assume that they are studying individual differences in cognitive functioning. Given this assumption, it would seem reasonable to attempt to relate the constructs derived from such investigations to those developed by cognitive-experimental psychologists. It is possible to distinguish two methodologies with somewhat different emphases that are used in the attempt to relate tests of intelligence to laboratory-based measures of cognitive processes.

Theoretical Parameters

Hunt, Lunneborg, and Lewis (1975) related individual differences in verbal ability to measures derived from a task used by Posner, Bois, Eichelman, and Taylor (1969). Posner et al. obtained reaction times to same and different judgments for letter pairs that were physically identical (AA) or semantically identical (Aa). The time taken to perform the latter judgment exceeded the time taken to perform the former judgment. The difference in reaction times in these two tasks may be taken as an index of the speed with which an individual is able to access semantic information. These difference scores are inversely related to measures of verbal ability. The Hunt et al. investigation attempts to integrate cognitive-experimental psychology with individual difference analyses of abilities by relating individual differences to measures derived from the experimental analysis of cognition. This approach has encountered one major difficulty. The parameters of greatest interest to the experimental psychologist are often not those that are most highly related to individual differences. For example, McGue and Bouchard (1989) obtained a correlation between differences in semantic and physical judgment reaction times and scores on a verbal ability factor of $-.27$. The correlation between the sum of the reaction times for these two tasks and scores on the verbal ability factor was $-.49$. The sum of the reaction times for both tasks, a parameter of little interest to the cognitive-experimental psychologist, accounts for almost three times as much variance in verbal ability than the theoretically meaningful parameter related to the speed of access to semantic information. Investigators of the relationship between parameters derived from the experimental investigation of behavior and individual difference characteristics should be alert to the possibility that theoretically meaningful parameters may not have the strongest relationship with the individual difference measure. Cross-domain integration is difficult and in some instances may require theoretical modifications in each of the domains being related.

Cognitive Composites

A second methodology attempts to discover one or more core information-processing abilities that have a substantial relationship to general intelligence. Deary (1999) used three different measures of discrimination. One measure was a visual inspection time task (see Deary & Stough, 1996). Subjects are presented with two parallel vertical lines that clearly differ in length. This stimulus is followed by a stimulus of two heavy lines of the same length that occlude the initial stimulus and serve as backward masks for the initial stimuli. The duration of the presentation of the initial stimulus prior to the onset of the masking stimulus is manipulated, and a threshold of the minimal inspection time required to attain some predetermined accuracy of judgment of the stimulus is obtained. A substantial body of research indicates that inspection time is inversely related to measures of nonverbal intellectual ability (see Deary and Stough, 1996). Deary (1999) obtained visual inspection times and measures of performance in two other tasks requiring subjects to make judgments of stimuli that were briefly presented. In these additional tasks, subjects were presented with

an array of 49 rectangular black stimuli on a white background. In one version of this task a single stimulus was moved. In another version a new stimulus was added to the array. The inspection time for the original array was varied, and thresholds were obtained for the minimal amount of time required for inspection in order to enable participants to indicate accurately which stimulus had been added to the array or which stimulus had changed locations in the array. Although all three tasks involve the ability to rapidly notice distinctions among visually presented stimuli, the attentional processes that are required to perform the initial inspection time task involving line lengths appear to be different from those required to perform the tasks involving arrays of rectangular stimuli. The former task requires focused attention, and the latter tasks require diffuse attentional processes. Deary (1999) related performance on these tasks to performance on psychometric measures of nonverbal reasoning ability. Confirmatory analyses indicated that the covariances between each of the cognitive tasks and his composite nonverbal intelligence measure were completely overlapping. This analysis implies that each of the cognitive tasks measures a latent trait—perhaps a trait related to the speed of visual information processing—that is related to measures of nonverbal intelligence. The correlation between the latent trait based on the composite of the three visual tasks and the composite index of nonverbal intelligence was .66.

Deary's (1999) analysis illustrates one method of validating latent traits. The evidence for a latent trait derives from three desiderata: (a) The indexes that combine to form the trait are positively correlated; (b) the covariance between each of them and an external criterion is overlapping; and (c) the composite index correlates with the external criterion more substantially than with its constituents.

Personality to Neurophysiology

There have also been attempts to relate measures of personality to neurophysiological measures. Kagan and Snidman (1999) argued that about 20% of all healthy infants are born with a behavioral tendency to show aversion to novel social situations as measured by videotaped observation. One third of these children are likely to show signs of intense social anxiety by early adulthood. These children are also likely to display a number of physiological characteristics associated with increased arousal, such as increased sympathetic cardiovascular response and increases in brain activity in the right frontal area and limbic area (Kagan, Reznick, & Snidman, 1999). The research of Kagan and his colleagues is instructive because it uses observational and physiological measurements to bring together multiple measurements of the same underlying construct across time. The broad scope of this research not only increases the validity of Kagan's construct of behavioral inhibition but also begins to unravel the physiological pathways by which behavioral tendencies are expressed in more general personality characteristics. The search for cross-domain relationships is guided by the development of explicit theories. Kagan's theory integrates constructs derived from behavioral observations of individual differences with constructs derived from theoretical analyses of brain functioning.

Behavioral Genetics

Another particularly active area of contemporary cross-domain investigation involves the attempt to integrate the study of individual differences with concepts derived from genetics. Behavioral genetic techniques permit one to study genetic and environmental influences on psychological characteristics (called phenotypes when the characteristics are treated as dependent variables in a behavioral genetic investigation) as well as genetic and environmental influences on relationships among phenotypes. In addition, new developments in molecular genetics have led to a search for specific DNA markers related to individual difference characteristics.

Asserting that individual differences must result from genetic or environmental influences, or both, is a truism. Behavioral genetic methodologies may be used to ascertain the contributions of several distinct genetic and environmental components of variance to the phenotype. The integration of behavioral genetic concepts with the study of individual difference measures provides a particularly apt demonstration of the usefulness of cross-domain integration.

Twin and adoption studies may be used to study genetic and environmental influences on phenotypic measures. In contemporary quantitative genetic methods, genetic and environmental influences are estimated through confirmatory models. One can test a model in which identical twins and fraternal twins possess the same correlation. If this model is rejected relative to a model that posits greater monozygotic (MZ) resemblance, then it is appropriate to infer that there are genetic influences on that trait. It is also possible to test for the effects of common rearing (called the shared environment). If adoptive siblings reared in the same family are correlated on some phenotypic measure, then shared environmental influences are implicated. Thus, by examining differences in correlations among family members who vary in their genetic and environmental similarity, it is possible to estimate the importance of genetic and environmental influences on a particular characteristic.

Petrill, Thompson, and Detterman (1995) provides an illustrative example. The study examined the genetic and environmental influences found in six elementary cognitive tasks hypothesized to relate to general intelligence. We describe one such task, Stimulus Discrimination. The covariance among identical and fraternal twins was compared using several competing models.

1. Nonshared Environment Only (E) = no correlation among twins on Stimulus Discrimination.

2. Nonshared Environment + Shared Environment (EC) = identical twins were hypothesized to be no more similar in Stimulus Discrimination than fraternal twins because of shared environmental influences. Nonshared environment is also hypothesized because twins' correlations are below 1.0.

3. Nonshared Environment + Additive Genetic (EH) = identical twins are hypothesized to be twice as similar to each other than are fraternal twins on Stimulus Discrimination.

4. Nonshared Environment + Shared Environment + Additive Genetic (ECH) = identical twins are hypothesized to be more similar than fraternal twins, but less than twice as similar to each other, presumably due to the influence of the shared environment.

5. Nonshared Environment + Additive Genetic + Nonadditive Genetic (EDH) = identical twins are more than twice as similar to each other than are fraternal twins, presumably due to the influence of nonadditive (e.g., dominance) genetic factors.

The covariances for Stimulus Discrimination for identical and fraternal twins were then examined using the ECH model. This model fit the data (chi-square = 2.53, $df = 3$, $p = .47$). This model also yielded estimates of heritability = .50, shared environment = .12, and nonshared environment = .38. To test the statistical significance of these estimates, the other four submodels were then tested against the ECH model. If the submodel fit the data significantly worse than did the ECH model, then it was assumed that the parameter dropped in the submodel was necessary. The E and EC models fit the data significantly worse than did the ECH model, suggesting that additive genetic influences are important. Conversely, the EH and EDH models did not result in a significant decrease in fit, suggesting that the shared environment and nonadditive genetics were not important to model fit. As stated earlier, the statistical significance of h^2, c^2, and e^2 can also be tested using confidence intervals (Neale, 2000).

The substantive results derived from behavioral genetic analyses of various personality measures have led to a number of methodological innovations in the study of individual differences. Twin studies of personality phenotypes usually obtain MZ correlations close to .5 and dizygotic (DZ) correlations that are equal to or less than half the value of MZ correlations (Loehlin, 1992). These results lead to three substantive conclusions: First, personality traits are heritable; MZ correlations are larger than DZ correlations. Second, nonshared environmental influences that lead individuals reared in the same family to differ from one another contribute to individual differences in phenotypic measures of personality. MZ twins reared in the same family who are genetically identical differ in personality phenotypes. These differences imply that personality phenotypes are influenced by nonshared environmental events. Third, shared family influences on personality phenotypes are close to zero. Phenotypic variability attributable to genetic influences and to nonshared environmental influences accounts for most of the variance in personality phenotypes. If shared environmental influences were important determinants of personality characteristics, DZ twin correlations would be larger than half the size of MZ correlations, but they are not. Family studies provide additional evidence for the absence of strong, shared environmental influences on personality. Siblings are not similar in personality, and children are not similar to their parents on various measures of personality (Ahern, Johnson, Wilson, McClearn, & Vandenburg, 1982).

Nonshared environmental influences cannot be studied using the traditional designs in which children reared in different families are compared to one another. In order to study nonshared environmental influences, it is necessary to study two or more children reared in the same family. Studies of MZ twin differences are a useful methodology for studying nonshared environmental influences. Variables that are shown to predict differences in characteristics of MZ twin pairs reared together provide direct evidence for nonshared environmental influences that are totally independent of genotypes. Evidence for the existence of nonshared environmental influences is obtained by noting relationships between sibling differences and differences in environmental experiences. Dunn and Plomin (1990) developed a measure designed to survey differences in the environmental experiences of siblings reared in the same family.

In addition to signaling the importance of studying the nonshared environment, behavioral genetic findings have methodological implications for studies attempting to understand environmental influences on personality. Many "environmental" measures may be heritable; consider, for example, divorce and television watching. McGue and Lykken (1992) studied the heritability of divorce. They found that MZ twins were more likely to be concordant for divorce than were DZ twins. Plomin et al. (1990) obtained a measure of the amount of time spent watching television for a sample of adopted children. They found that television watching was predicted by the television-watching habits of both the adopted and biological parents of the children. Studies of the influence of television

watching or the influence of divorce on children are difficult to interpret because the independent variables (divorce, television watching) combine both environmental and genetic influences. The effects of these variables on a dependent variable may be attributable to either genetic or environmental influences or to some mixture of these two kinds of influences. They cannot, in the standard design that is not genetically informative, be construed as a direct influence of an environmental variable.

Similar problems occur in various studies of socialization experiences. Consider a study of the amount of time that parents read to children. The amount of time that a parent reads to a child may be influenced by genetic characteristics of the parent; it may be attributable to a direct genetic link between parent and child and may have little or nothing to do with the experience of being read to. It is also possible that genetic characteristics of children may influence the amount of time that parents read to them. The experience of being read to in this case may not be a significant influence on the outcome variable; it is merely a variable that is confounded with the genetic influences that are causally related to the outcome variable.

There are several appropriate methodologies available that enable the investigator to separate the influences of genetic and environmental events on the covariance between independent and dependent variables. The appropriate designs are genetically informative and may include some variant of adoption and twin designs. For example, it is possible to study genetic contributions to the covariance between variables in a twin study by correlating the score of a twin on one variable with the score of his or her cotwin on the second variable. Comparisons of the correlations across twin pairs for MZ and DZ twins may be used to ascertain whether genetic and environmental components of variance contribute to the covariance between the variables. For example, Plomin and Bergeman (1991) reported an analysis of the family experiences of adult twins on the Moos Family Environmental Scale, and they related this measure to measures of Extraversion and Neuroticism. They found that self-report indexes of the family environment were heritable. The correlation for MZ twins was higher than that for DZ twins. The correlation between self-reports of family environments and personality characteristics was primarily attributable to common genetic influences on both the family environment measure and the personality measures. In a recent comprehensive study of children reared in the same family who differed in their degree of genetic resemblance, Reiss et al. (1995) found that it was difficult to obtain evidence for the influence of either shared or nonshared environmental events on personality. Individuals reared in the same family reported both experiences that were similar to those of their siblings and experiences that were different from those of their siblings. Genetic covariance analyses indicated that the experiences that influenced personality were often heritable and that the covariances between the measures of environmental events and of personality were often mediated by common genetic influences. Without the use of genetically informed designs, it is difficult to know whether the influence of an event is an environmental influence or a genetic influence.

Behavioral genetic research contributes to an understanding of issues addressed by individual difference psychologists. It is also the case that methodological issues that are addressed in individual difference research contribute to the development of methodologically sophisticated research designs in behavioral genetics.

We have indicated that measures of personality constructs derived from different methods of measurement may be more valid than those based on a single method of measure-

ment. Most of the behavioral genetic studies of adult personality have relied on self-report measures of personality. Behavioral genetic studies that use different methods of measurement to obtain composite indexes of personality (heteromethod measures) should provide better estimates of the magnitude of genetic and environmental influences on personality dispositions than could studies based solely on self-report phenotypes. Several studies of heteromethod composites obtain substantially higher heritability than comparable studies of the heritability of self-report measures of personality dispositions. (Heritability is a statistical concept defined as the proportion of variance in a phenotype in a particular population that is attributable to genetic variation present in the members of that population.) For example, Heath, Neale, Kessler, Eaves, and Kendler (1992) obtained self-report measures of Neuroticism and Extraversion from twins and ratings of these characteristics by cotwins. Composite indexes based on both sources of information about these traits had heritabilities of .73 and .63 for Extraversion and Neuroticism, respectively. These values were approximately 50% higher than those obtained from analyses based solely on self-report data. Kendler, Neale, Kessler, Heath, and Eaves (1993) obtained self-report measures of depression and psychiatric ratings of depression one year later from a large sample of female twins. The heritability of depression based on either of their single methods of measurement was close to .4. The heritability of their combined index of depression was .70. An important methodological implication may be derived from these results. Personality dispositions are hypothetical constructs that are not equivalent to any single method used to measure the construct. Heteromethod, hetero-occasion indexes that attempt to assess dispositions comprehensively provide better estimates of the true-score value of the disposition. The heritability of a phenotypic measure of a construct is not equivalent to the heritability of the construct.

Longitudinal Behavioral Genetics

Behavioral genetic analyses using longitudinal data can provide information about continuity and change in individual difference characteristics. Longitudinal consistency and change in individual difference characteristics may be attributable either to genetic or environmental influences. Plomin, Fulker, Corley, and DeFries (1997) repeatedly administered tests of intelligence from age 1 to age 16 to adopted children participating in the Colorado Adoption Project. They obtained correlations between the intelligence test scores of the adopted children's biological parents and of their children adopted shortly after birth. These correlations may be contrasted with the correlations between the adopted children's intelligence and the intelligence of their adopted parents. Plomin et al. also used a control group of parents rearing their biological children who were from the same community and whose social class background was comparable to that of the adoptive and biological parents in the study. Figure 14.5 presents the correlations in intelligence between parent and child from age 1 to age 16. An examination of the figure indicates that the correlations between biological parents and their adopted children increases as the children become older even though the parents have no contact with the children. Correlations between the intelligence test scores of adopted parents and their adopted children do not increase and remain close to zero. Plomin et al. also found that the relationships between the intelligence scores of biological parents and their children were quite similar for parents who reared their biological children and for biological parents who did not. Their results indicate that relationships between the intelligence of parents and children are primarily determined by the genes that they share rather than by the influence of a shared environment. In addition, the correlations between biological parents and their children tend to be a monotonically increasing function of age. These data imply that the heritability of intelligence tends to increase from early childhood through late adolescence. These data also imply that the determinants of the phenotypic measure of intelligence are not invariant over the early life span of an individual. Furthermore, these data imply that changes in phenotypic measures of intelligence over this period are those that are likely to increase the congruence between phenotype and genotype. Thus, these data are informative with respect to the ways in which genetic and environmental influences contribute to change and continuity in intelligence. Genetic influences are not invariant over the life span. Longitudinal studies are needed to ascertain changing influences of genotypes on phenotypes over time.

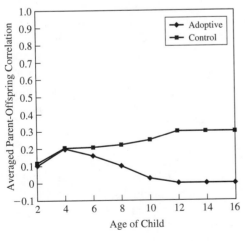

Figure 14.5 Parent-offspring correlations between parents' IQ scores and children's IQ scores. SOURCE: Based on Plomin et al. (1997).

Behavioral Genetic Analyses of Taxonomic Relationships

Several methods may be used to assess genetic and environmental influences on the relationship between measures. Twin data may be used for this purpose. A correlation may be obtained between the score of a twin on one measure and the score of his or her cotwin on a second measure. If the correlation between measures is higher for MZ twins than for DZ twins, it is possible to infer that the relationship between the measures is genetically influenced. These methods may be used to analyze individual difference taxonomies. McCrae, Jang, Livesley, Riemann, and Angleitner (in press) used a large sample of German and Canadian twins to study genetic covariances among the scales that are used to measure the Big Five. They also derived measures of shared environmental covariances among the scales and measures of nonshared environmental covariances. They conducted a factor analysis of these covariance matrices and found that the factor structures of genetic covariance matrices were highly congruent with the factor structures derived from conventional factor analyses of these scales. By contrast, the factor analyses of shared environmental covariances and nonshared environmental covariances did not obtain factors that were congruent with the conventional phenotypic factor analyses of these scales. The use of this methodology permits an understanding of the origins of the taxonomic structure of personality. Items that load on the same factor may do so because they share a common genetic origin.

Petrill (in press) reviewed studies of the genetic and environmental covariances among different measures of intellectual ability. His analyses indicate that genetic influences account for most of the phenotypic covariance between different measures of intellectual ability. These analyses provide an explanation of the origins of the g factor in the domain of intelligence. Various measures of intellectual ability correlate positively because they are subject to common genetic influences.

The studies just reviewed indicate that genetically informed designs can provide information about the foundations of taxonomic structures of personality and intelligence. The use of genetic covariance matrices derived from genetically informed designs provides a general methodology for studying cross-domain relationships. It should be apparent that analyzing taxonomic relationships using genetically informed designs is not directed solely toward the attempt to uncover the genetic foundations of taxonomic relationships. It is rather a general methodology that is designed to test the contributions of different environmental and genetic components of variance to the structure of relationships among different variables.

Genetic and Environmental Interactions

Behavioral genetic analyses may be used to provide information about interactions between genetic and environmental influences. Adoption studies may be used for this purpose. Relationships between biological parents and their children who were adopted provide evidence of additive genetic influences (i.e., those that contribute to phenotypic similarity for individuals who are genetically similar). Relationships between adoptive parents and their children provide evidence of the influence of shared family environments on phenotypes. Capron and Duyme (1989) studied the influence of social class background on intelligence. They studied adopted children whose biological parents exhibited large differences in social class who were subsequently adopted by parents who differed in social class. Their results suggest that the adopted child's IQ is related both to the biological parents' social class and to the adopted parents' social class. There are two main effects in this study. The effects combine additively, and there is no evidence of an interaction.

Rowe, Jacobson, and Van den Oord (1999) used sibling and twin data to obtain information about the influence of parents' educational backgrounds on their children's IQ. They obtained correlations for full siblings and half siblings reared in the same family. They also obtained twin data for their sample. The twin and sibling correlations were used to derive measures of the heritability of scores on a measure of intelligence for children whose parents differed in the amount of education that they had received. They found that the heritability of intelligence was relatively invariant for individuals whose parents had received moderate to high levels of education. The heritability of intelligence of children whose parents had little or no formal education (i.e., they had not completed elementary school) exhibited near-zero heritability. These data provide evidence for a genetic X environmental interaction in the determinants of intelligence. These data also provide additional evidence that the determinants of individual differences are not necessarily invariant for individuals belonging to different groups. Genetic and environmental influences may differ for individuals in different social settings. Generalizations about genetic and environmental influences derived from samples occupying a particular social position may not be valid for individuals whose environmental exposures differ because of different social positions. Both the Rowe et al. study and the Capron and Duyme study provide data that permits a test of the presence of genetic X environmental interaction. The studies reach opposite conclusions and provide evidence for an issue considered in the discussion of group differences. Studies of individual differences may or may not obtain results that are invariant for different groups of individuals. Invariance (or its absence) is not a useful general assumption in the study of individual differences. It should be empirically investigated.

Molecular Genetics

Using molecular genetic approaches to identify DNA markers associated with personality is another example of cross-domain integration. Initially, the search for genetic effects on complex behavior assumed a major gene model in which the presence of a single gene was both necessary and sufficient to produce a disorder. More recently, researchers have hypothesized that quantitative traits such as Sociability, or Neuroticism, or intelligence are influenced by a number of genes. Each gene may account for a small proportion of phenotypic variance (Plomin & Caspi, 1999; Plomin, Owen, & McGuffin, 1994).

The majority of the molecular genetic studies examining personality have employed an allelic association methodology. First, the personality traits of unrelated individuals are measured, and DNA is extracted. Differences in personality are then correlated with allelic differences in DNA markers. If this covariance is significant, then an association between a DNA marker and personality is present. This covariance is often called a quantitative trait locus (QTL). Differences in the allelic frequency at a particular locus on the genome have an impact on the quantitatively distributed trait being studied.

Molecular genetic studies of personality routinely examine hundreds if not thousands of markers. As the number of markers increases, the number of markers that are likely to be discovered increases. Some of these "discoveries" may be attributable to type I statistical errors. Molecular genetic studies are heavily dependent on replication, both within and across research sites. Chorney et al. (1998) examined allelic frequency between 37 DNA markers located on the short arm of Chromosome 6 and general intelligence. From this analysis, one marker—insulin-like growth factor 2 (IGF2R)—was found to be associated with high versus average intelligence groups. Chorney et al. were able to replicate these results in an independent sample. More recently, markers on chromosome 4 have been shown to be associated with general cognitive ability in the same sample (Fisher et al., 1999).

An association between Novelty Seeking and Dopamine Receptor D4 (DRD4) was reported in two separate studies (Cloninger, Adolfsson, & Svrakic, 1996). In the first study, Ebstein et al. (1996) found that DRD4 accounted for 6% of the variance in Novelty Seeking. In an independent study, Benjamin et al. (1996) reported a significant association between DRD4 and a measure of novelty seeking. These results have since been replicated and extended (e.g., Okuyama et al., 1999; Tomitaka et al., 1999). Additionally, DRD4 has been associated with other outcomes associated with novelty seeking, such as heroin use (Kotler et al., 1997; Li et al., 1997). These positive results are offset by studies that have failed to replicate the association between DRD4 and novelty seeking. Some of these studies have shown effects in the expected direction (e.g., Jönsson et al., 1997); others show no trends (e.g., Gebhardt et al., 1997; Gelernter et al., 1997; Pogue-Geil, Ferrell, Deka, Debski, & Manuck, 1998; Vandenbergh, Zonderman, Wang, Uhl, & Costa, 1997).

Although the profusion of mixed results makes interpretation of these data difficult, it is important to remember that the search for DNA markers involves making thousands of statistical analyses on very small effects. Differences in sampling and measurement have an important impact on the replication of molecular genetic results. Individual genetic influences are likely to have very small effects and to function in a nonlinear interactive manner.

The number of molecular genetic studies on complex human behavior is rapidly increasing. In the not-too-distant future many researchers will routinely use DNA markers as a tool in their research. This is already happening in the study of Alzheimer's disease. Corder et al. (1993) found an association between apolipoprotein E (APOE-4), a gene on Chromosome 19, and late-onset Alzheimer's disease. Since that time, many new studies of Alzheimer's disease that routinely use APOE-4 have been published.

How will this impact the personality researcher (see Plomin & Caspi, 1999, for a discussion of this issue)? We can only speculate. We assume that at some point in the future a number of markers will be discovered that will be related to personality and intelligence. One obvious consequence of this discovery will be the attempt to understand the way in which genes influence phenotypes. At one level, this analysis will lead to the development of hypotheses about the biological basis of personality. Indeed, biological hypotheses may be used to direct the search process for individual genes that are related to psychological phenotypes. We can imagine the development of an interdisciplinary study of personality that will combine traditional studies of personality, molecular genetics, and biological psychology.

Although the integration of psychological and biological concepts appears to be an obvious consequence of the discovery of the molecular genetic foundations of individual differences, it may not be the only important consequence of this discovery. The study of behavioral genetics has led to a new understanding of the environment. The central role of nonshared environmental influences and the study of differences in the experiences of siblings reared together are methodological consequences of research in behavioral genetics. Developments in molecular genetics may enable the individual difference psychologist to study the environment in new ways. We have no generally valid way of studying discrepancies between phenotypes and genotypes because we can only infer the value of the latter characteristic by observations of the former. If it were possible to ascertain independently the value of a genotype without examining a phenotype, it would then become possible to study discrepancies between phenotypes and genotypes. If a person has a genotype that predisposes him or her to the development of a particular phenotype and if the person does not manifest that phenotype, it should be possible to examine the specific environmental events that may have contributed to the difference between the phenotype and a genotype.

At present only one methodology permits researchers to study differences between genotypes and phenotypes: the study of differences in MZ twin pairs. It has been difficult to ascertain the specific environmental events that contribute to such differences among individuals who are genetically identical. For example, we know that the concordance rate for schizophrenia in MZ twins is .46, and we know that MZ twins who are discordant for schizophrenia are at equal risk of having children who are schizophrenic (Gottesman & Bertelsen, 1989). These results imply that genotypes that predispose individuals to the development of schizophrenia may not lead to a phenotypic outcome of schizophrenia. The precise environmental events that contribute to the discordance between genotypes that predispose an individual to schizophrenia and to the development of the characteristic are unknown. Advances in molecular genetics may enable researchers to investigate the environmental events that contribute to discrepancies between phenotype and genotype in new ways.

The anticipation of discoveries in molecular genetics has led to one current methodology. Many behavioral geneticists who are not conducting molecular genetic investigations obtain blood samples or buckle smears from their subjects. These samples are stored for future use. If and when more is known about the molecular genetics of individual differences, these samples may be analyzed in order to relate previous findings to more recent molecular genetic discoveries. This methodology should be widely applicable. Many individual difference researchers may want to obtain buckle smears for future analysis in order to relate contemporary findings to future developments in molecular genetics. The procedure is neither costly nor invasive. The data obtained in this way are easily stored. The use of this methodology enables researchers to relate their ongoing investigations to future developments in the study of individual differences.

A CONCLUDING COMMENT

Spearman (1904) was the first psychologist to examine a matrix of correlations and to attempt to ascertain the latent traits that might contribute to the covariances among several measures. In a companion paper to his empirical study of the relationship between experimental indexes related to intelligence that was published in the same issue of the *American Journal of Psychology,* Spearman noted that observed correlations may provide inadequate indexes of the true relationships between measures. He introduced the correction for attenuation as a way of modifying the obtained correlation to provide a more accurate index of the relationship between latent traits. Spearman's insights defined the central issue in the diverse methodologies used in the study of individual differences. The measures we use presumably reflect some more general dispositional tendency of persons. These dispositional tendencies or latent traits are always imperfectly indexed by any particular measure. The various methodologies that are used are designed to permit the researcher to make inferences about hypothetical constructs that are never identical with the measures that are used to infer their values.

Spearman (1904) relied on a theoretical insight to interpret the structure of relationships he observed. If all of his correlations were positive, diverse indexes of intelligence must measure something that is common to all possible measures of intelligence. Contemporary research also requires a clear integration of theory and observations in order to reach appropriate conclusions about individual differences. Cross-domain integration is based on using theoretical constructs in both domains. For example, behavioral genetic analyses of personality constructs are based on theoretical assumptions about differences in the genetic similarities of MZ and DZ twins. The use of different indexes of the same construct to form composite measures of latent traits is based on a theoretical understanding of the meaning of a construct. Path analyses and confirmatory analyses create an unprecedented integration of theory and methodology. Although methodologies may on occasion influence theories, we believe that the more fundamental and enduring influence is from theory to methodology. Good methodology requires good theory.

REFERENCES

Ahern, F. M., Johnson, R. C., Wilson, J. R., McClearn, G. C., & Vandenberg, S. G. (1982). Family resemblances in personality. *Behavior Genetics, 18,* 261–280.

Atkinson, J. W. (1957). Motivational determinants of risk-taking behavior. *Psychological Review, 64,* 359–372.

Benbow, C. P. (1988). Sex differences in mathematical reasoning ability in intellectually talented preadolescents: Their nature, effects, and possible causes. *Behavioral and Brain Sciences, 11,* 169–232.

Benjamin, J., Li., L., Patterson, C., Greenburg, B. D., Murphy, D. L., & Hammer, D. W. (1996). Population and familial association between the D4 dopamine receptor gene and measures of novelty seeking. *Nature Genetics, 12,* 81–84.

Block, J., & Robins, R. W. (1993). A longitudinal study of consistency and change in self-esteem from early adolescence to early adulthood. *Child Development, 64,* 909–923.

Bollen, K. A. (1989). *Structural equations with latent variables.* New York: Wiley.

Brody, N. (2000). History of theories and measurements of intelligence. In R. J. Sternberg (Ed.), *Handbook of intelligence* (pp. 16–33). New York: Cambridge.

Campbell, D. T., & Fiske, D. W. (1959). Convergent and discriminant validation by the multitrait-multimethod matrix. *Psychological Bulletin, 56,* 81–105.

Capron, C., & Duyme, M. (1989). Assessment of effects of socio-economic status on IQ in a full cross-fostering study. *Nature, 340,* 552–554.

Carroll, J. B. (1993). *Human cognitive abilities.* New York: Cambridge.

Carroll, J. B. (1997). Theoretical and technical issues in identifying a factor of *general* intelligence. In B. Devlin, S. E. Fienberg, D. P. Resnick, & K. Roeder (Eds.), *Intelligence, genes, and success: Scientists respond to the bell curve* (pp. 125–156). New York: Springer.

Caspi, A., & Herbener, E. S. (1990). Continuity and change: Assortative marriage and the consistency of personality in adulthood. *Journal of Personality and Social Psychology, 58,* 250–258.

Chorney, M. J., Chorney, K., Seese, N., Owen, M. J., Daniels, J., McGuffin, P., Thompson, L. A., Detterman, D. K., Benbow, C., Lubinski, D., Eley, T., & Plomin, R. (1998). A quantitative trait locus associated with cognitive ability in children. *Psychological Science, 9*(3), 159–166.

Cloninger, C. R., Adolfsson, R., & Svrakic, D. M. (1996). Mapping genes for human personality. *Nature Genetics, 12,* 3–4.

Columbo, J. (1993). *Infant cognition: Predicting later intellectual functioning.* Newbury Park, CA: Sage.

Corder, E. H., Saunders, A. M., Strittmatter, W. J., Schmechel, D. E., Gaskell, P. C., Small, G. W., Roses, A. D., Haines, J. L., & Pericak-Vance, M. A. (1993). Gene dose of apolipoprotein E type 4 allele and the risk of Alzheimer's disease in late onset families. *Science, 261,* 921–923.

Cozzarelli, C. (1993). Personality and self-efficacy as predictors of coping with abortion. *Journal of Personality & Social Psychology, 65*(6), 1224–1236.

Cronbach, L. J. (1951). Coefficient alpha and the internal structure of tests. *Psychometrika, 17,* 297–334.

Deary, I. J. (1999). Intelligence and visual and auditory information processing. In P. L. Ackerman, P. C. Kyllonen, & R. D. Roberts (Eds.), *Learning and individual differences: Process, trait, and content determinants* (pp. 111–133). Washington, DC: American Psychological Association.

Deary, I. J., & Stough, C. (1996). Intelligence and inspection time: Achievements, prospects, and problems. *American Psychologist, 51*(6), 599–608.

Detterman, D. K., & Daniel, M. H. (1989). Correlations of mental tests with each other and with cognitive variables are highest for low IQ groups. *Intelligence, 13*(4), 349–359.

Dunn, J., & Plomin, R. (1990). *Separate lives: Why siblings are so different.* New York: Basic Books.

Eagly, A. H. (1987). Reporting sex differences. *American Psychologist, 42,* 756–757.

Ebstein, R. P., Novicck, O., Umansky, R., Priel, B., Osher, Y., Blaine, D., Bennett, E. R., Nemanov, L., Katz, M. S., & Belmaker, R. W. (1996). Dopamine D4 receptor (D4DR) exon III polymorphism associated with the human trait of novelty seeking. *Nature Genetics, 12,* 78–80.

Embretson, S. E. (1995). The new rules of measurement. *Psychological Assessment, 8,* 341–349.

Embretson, S. E., & Hershberger, S. L. (1999). *The new rules of measurement: What every psychologist and educator should know.* Mahwah, NJ: Erlbaum.

Epstein, S. (1977). Traits are alive and well. In D. Magnusson & N. S. Endler (Eds.), *Person-ality at the crossroads: Current issues in interactional psychology* (pp. 25–46). Hillsdale, NJ: Erlbaum.

Feather, N. T. (1961). The relationship between persistence at a task to expectation of success and achievement related motives. *Journal of Abnormal and Social Psychology, 63,* 552–561.

Fisher, P. J., Turic, D., Williams, N. M., Mc-Guffin, P., Asherson, P., Ball, D., Craig, I., Eley, T., Hill, L., Chorney, K., Chorney, M. J., Benbow, C. P., Lubinski, D., Plomin, R., & Owen, M. J. (1999). DNA pooling identifies QTLs on chromosome 4 for general cognitive ability in children. *Human Molecular Genetics, 8*(5), 915–922.

Flynn, J. R. (1998). IQ gains over time: Toward finding the causes. In U. Neisser (Ed.), *The rising curve* (pp. 25–66). Washington, DC: American Psychological Association.

Freedle, R., & Kostin, I. (1997). Predicting Black and White differential item functioning in verbal analogy performance. *Intelligence, 24*(2), 417–444.

Funder, D. C., Block, J. H., & Block, J. (1983). Delay of gratification: Some long-term correlates. *Journal of Personality and Social Psychology, 44,* 1198–1213.

Gebhardt, C., Füreder, T., Fuchs, K., Urmann, A., Gerhard, E., Heiden, A., Stompe, T., Fathi, N., Meszaros, K., Hornik, K., Sieghart, W., Kasper, S., & Aschauer, H. N. (1997, October 19–23). No evidence for normal personality traits related to dopamine 4 receptor gene polymorphism. Paper presented at the 1997 World Congress on Psychiatric Genetics, Santa Fe, NM.

Gelernter, J., Kranzler, H. Coccaro, E., Seiver, L., New, A., & Mulgrew, C. L. (1997). D4 dopamine receptor (DRD4) allele and novelty seeking in substance-dependent, personality disorder, and control subjects. *American Journal of Human Genetics, 61,* 114–1152.

Gottesman, I. I., & Bertelsen, A. (1989). Confirming unexpressed genotypes for schizophrenia: Risks in the offspring of Fischer's Danish identical and fraternal discordant twins. *Archives of General Psychiatry, 46*(10), 867–872.

Gustafsson, J.-E. (1999). Measuring and understanding G: Experimental and correlational approaches. In P. L. Ackerman, P. C. Kyllonen, & R. D. Roberts (Eds.), *Learning and individual differences: Process, trait, and content determinants* (pp. 275–291). Washington, DC: American Psychological Association.

Heath, A. C., Neale, M. C., Kessler, R. C., Eaves, L. J., & Kendler, K. S. (1992). Evidence for genetic influence on personality from self-reports and informant ratings. *Journal of Personality and Social Psychology, 63,* 85–96.

Hedges, L. V., & Newell, A. (1995). Sex differences in mental test scores, variability, and numbers of high-scoring individuals, *Science, 269,* 41–45.

Horn, J. L. (1985). Remodeling old models of intelligence. In B. B. Wolman (Ed.), *Handbook of intelligence: Theories, measurements and applications* (pp. 267–300). New York: Wiley.

Hoyenga, K. B., & Hoyenga, K. T. (1993). Gender-related differences: Origins & outcomes. Boston: Allyn & Bacon.

Hunt, E., Lunneborg, C., & Lewis, J. (1975). What does it mean to be high verbal? *Cognitive Psychology, 7*(2), 194–227.

John, O. P. (1990). The "big five" taxonomy: Dimensions of personality in the natural language and in questionnaires. In L. A. Pervin (Ed.), *Handbook of personality: Theory and research* (pp. 66–100). New York: Guildford.

Johnson, J. A., & Ostendorf, F. (1993). Clarification of the five-factor model with the abridged big five dimensional circumplex. *Journal of Personality and Social Psychology, 65,* 563–576.

Jönsson, E., Nöthen, M. M., Gustavsson, J. P., Neidt, H., Brené, S., Tylec, A., Propping, P., & Sedvall, G. C. (1997). Lack of evidence for allelic association between personality traits and the dopamine D4 receptor gene polymorphism. *American Journal of Psychiatry, 154,* 697–699.

Kagan, J., Reznick, J. S., & Snidman, N. (1999). Biological basis of childhood shyness. In A. Slater & D. Muir (Eds.), *The Blackwell reader in development psychology* (pp. 65–78). Malden, MA: Blackwell.

Kagan, J., & Snidman, N. (1999). Early childhood predictors of adult anxiety disorders. *Biological Psychiatry, 46*(11), 1536–1541.

Kaufman, A. S. (2000). *Essentials of wise III & WPPSI-R assessment.* New York: Wiley.

Kendler, K. S., Neale, M. C., Kessler, R. C., Heath, A. C., & Eaves, L. J. (1993). A longitudinal twin study of 1-year prevalence of major depression in women. *Archives of General Psychiatry, 50,* 843–852.

Kotler, M., Cohen, H., Serman, R., Gritsenko, L., Nemanov, L., Lerer, B., Kramer, I., Zer-Zion, M., Kletz, I., & Ebstein, R. P. (1997). Excess dopamine D4 receptor (D4DR) exon III seven repeat allele in opiod-dependent subjects. *Molecular Psychiatry, 2,* 251–254.

Li, T., Xu, K., Deng, H., Cai, G., Liu, J., Liu, X., Wang, R., Xiang, X., Zhao, J., Murray, R. M., Sham, P. C., & Collier, D. A. (1997). Association analysis of the dopamine D4 gene exon III VNTR and heroin abuse in Chinese subjects. *Molecular Psychiatry, 2,* 413–416.

Loehlin, J. C. (1992). *Genes and environment in personality development.* Newbury Park, CA: Sage.

McCrae, R. R., & Costa, P. T. (1990). *Personality in adulthood.* New York: Guildford.

McCrae, R. R., Jang, K. L., Livesley, W. J., Riemann, R., & Angleitner, A. (in press). Sources of structure: Genetic, environmental, and artifactual influences on the covariance of personality traits. *Journal of Personality.*

McGue, M., & Bouchard, T. J., Jr. (1989). Genetic and environmental determinants of information processing and special mental abilities: A twin analysis. In R. J. Sternberg (Ed.), *Advances in the psychology of human intelligence* (Vol. 5, pp. 7–45). Hillsdale, NJ: Erlbaum.

McGue, M., & Lykken, D. T. (1992). Genetic influences on risk of divorce. *Psychological Science, 3,* 368–373.

Mischel, W. (1968). *Personality and assessment.* New York: Wiley.

Mischel, W., & Shoda, Y. (1994). Personality psychology has two goals: Must it be two fields? *Psychological Inquiry, 5,* 156–158.

Moos, R. H. (1975). *Evaluating correctional and community settings.* New York: Wiley-Interscience.

Moscowitz, D. S. (1982). Coherence and cross-situational generality in personality: A new analysis of old problems. *Journal of Personality and Social Psychology, 47,* 754–768.

Moscowitz, D. S., & Schwarz, J. D. (1982). Validity comparison of behavior counts and ratings by knowledgeable informants. *Journal of Personality and Social Psychology, 42,* 518–528.

Neale, M. C. (2000). Individual fit, heterogeneity, and missing data in multigroup structural equation modeling. In T. D. Little, K. U. Schnabel, & J. Baumert (Eds.), *Modeling longitudinal and multilevel data: Practical issues, applied approaches, and specific examples* (pp. 249–267, 269–281). Mahwah, NJ: Erlbaum.

Neisser, U. (Ed.). (1998). *The rising curve.* Washington, DC: American Psychological Association.

Okuyama, Y., Ishiguro, H., Nankai, M., Shibuya, H., Watanabe, A., & Arinami, T. (1999). Identification of a polymorphism in the promoter region of DRD4 associated with the human novelty seeking personality trait. *Molecular Psychiatry, 5*(1), 64–69.

Petrill, S. A. (in press). The case for general intelligence: A behavioral genetic perspective. In R. Sternberg & E. Grigorenko (Eds.), *The general factor of intelligence: How general is it?* Hillsdale, NJ: Erlbaum.

Petrill, S. A., Thompson, L. A., & Detterman, D. K. (1995). The genetic and environmental variance underlying elementary cogntive tasks. *Behavior Genetics, 25*(3), 199–209.

Plomin, R., & Bergeman, C. S. (1991). The nature of nurture: Genetic influence on "environmental" measures. *Behavioral and Brain Sciences, 14,* 373–427.

Plomin, R., & Caspi, A. (1999). Behavioral genetics and personality. In L. A. Pervin & O. P. John (Eds.), *Handbook of personality: Theory and research* (pp. 251–276). New York: Guildford.

Plomin, R., Corley, R., DeFries, J. C., & Fulker, D. W. (1990). Individual differences in television viewing in early childhood: Nature as well as nurture. *Psychological Science, 1*(6), 371–377.

Plomin, R., Fulker, D. W., Corley, R., & DeFries, J. C. (1997). Nature, nurture, and cognitive development from 1 to 16 years: A parent-offspring adoption study. *Psychological Science, 8*(6), 442–447.

Plomin, R., Owen, M. J., & McGuffin, P. (1994). The genetic basis of complex human behaviors, *Science, 264*(5166), 1733–1739.

Pogue-Geil, M., Ferrell, R., Deka, R., Debski, T., & Manuck, S. (1998). Human novelty seeking personality traits and dopamine D4 receptor polymorphisms: A twin and genetic association study. *Neuropsychiatric Genetics, 81,* 44–48.

Posner, M. I., Boies, S. J., Eichelman, W. H., & Taylor, R. L. (1969). Retention of visual and name order of single letters. *Journal of Experimental Psychology, 79,* 1–16.

Reiss, D., Hetherington, E. M., Plomin, R., Howe, G. W., Simmens, S. J., Henderson, S. H., O'Connor, T. J., Bussel, D. A., Anderson, E. R., & Law, T. (1995). Genetic questions for environmental studies: Differential parenting and psychopathology in adolescence. *Archives of General Psychiatry, 52,* 925–936.

Rowe, D. C., Jacobson, K. C., & Van den Oord, E. J. C. G. (1999). Genetic and environmental influences on vocabulary IQ: Parental education level as moderator. *Child Development, 70*(5), 1151–1162.

Rowe, D. C., Vazsonyi, A. T., & Flannery, D. J. (1994). No more than skin deep: Ethnic and racial similarity in developmental process. *Psychological Review, 101,* 396–413.

Schaie, K. W., & Strother, C. R. (1968). A cross-sequential study of age changes in cognitive behaviors. *Psychological Bulletin, 70,* 671–680.

Schmid, J., & Leiman, J. (1957). The development of hierarchical factor solutions. *Psychometrika, 22,* 53–61.

Shoda, Y., Mischel, W., & Wright, J. C. (1994). Intraindividual stability in the organization and patterning of behavior: Incorporating psychological situations into the idiographic analysis of personality. *Journal of Personality and Social Psychology, 76,* 674–687.

Spearman, C. (1904). "General intelligence" objectively determined and measured. *American Journal of Psychology, 15,* 201–293.

Sternberg, R. J., & Weil, E. M. (1980). An aptitude-strategy interaction in linear syllogistic reasoning. *Journal of Educational Psychology, 72,* 226–234.

Stevens, J. (1986). *Applied multivariate statistics for the social sciences.* Hillsdale, NJ: Lawrence Erlbaum.

Tomitaka, M., Tomitaka, S., Otuka, Y., Kim, K., Matuki, H., Sakamoto, K., & Tanaka, A. (1999). Association between novelty seeking and dopamine receptor D4 (DRD4) exon III polymorphism in Japanese subjects. *American Journal of Medical Genetics, 88*(5), 469–471.

Thorndike, R. L., Hagen, E. P., & Sattler, J. M. (1986). *Guide for administering and scoring the fourth edition: Stanford Binet Intelligence Scale.* Chicago: Riverside.

Vandenbergh, D. J., Zonderman, A. B., Wang, J., Uhl, G. R., & Costa, P. T. (1997). No association between Novelty Seeking and dopamine D4 receptor (D4DR) exon III seven repeat alleles in Baltimore Longitudinal Study of Aging participants. *Molecular Psychiatry, 2,* 417–419.

CHAPTER 15

Electrophysiology of Attention

RISTO NÄÄTÄNEN, KIMMO ALHO, AND ERICH SCHRÖGER

INTRODUCTION: PSYCHOLOGICAL THEORIES OF ATTENTION AND THEIR TESTING BY USING EVENT-RELATED POTENTIALS

Kahneman and Treisman (1984), in their excellent review on the behavioral-attention research, divide this research into two main categories: studies of selective attention and divided attention. According to the authors, selective-attention research was directed mainly to issues involving resistance to distraction and to determining the locus in the processing chain beyond which relevant and irrelevant stimuli are differently treated, whereas divided-attention research sought the limits of performance and the extent to which different tasks can be combined without loss. A further important difference was that selective-attention studies dealt almost exclusively with perceptual performance, whereas perceptual-motor tasks were often employed in studies of divided attention (Näätänen 1988). The early studies on selective attention exposed their subjects to high perceptual load, and usually a large difference in performance was established between selective- and divided-attention instructions. These results, mainly obtained in the dichotic-listening paradigm introduced by Cherry (1953), gave rise to the *early-selection theories* of selective attention (Broadbent, 1958, 1970, 1971).

Physically different (e.g., in the locus of origin or in pitch) types of concurrent stimulus streams were described as arriving via separate "channels," of which any one could be chosen for attention. Further, according to these theories, stimuli arriving via the attended channel were accepted for further processing, whereas the processing of the other stimuli was terminated at an early stage; thus they received no, or only very little, semantic processing.

It was soon noticed, however, that there was in fact more unattended-channel processing than was previously thought. For instance, subjects often became aware of their own names occurring in the to-be-ignored message in selective-dichotic listening (Moray, 1959). Such findings, referred to as the "breakthrough of the unattended," gave rise to the *late-selection theories of attention* (Deutsch & Deutsch, 1963; Norman, 1968), which proposed that even unattended stimuli are fully processed and reach long-term memory (LTM) and that the role of attention only was to control for *access to response*. Thus the late-selection theories assumed much more automaticity of information processing than did the early-selection theories.

In the 1970s a shift in the predominant paradigm occurred in attention research, and the selective-set paradigm became the leader (Kahneman & Treisman, 1984). Its two most popular versions were studies of search (Schneider & Shiffrin, 1977; Shiffrin & Schneider, 1977) and of the costs and benefits of attention or expectations (Posner, 1978). Both types of studies tended to view the human subject to a large extent as an automatic processor, but this might, according to Kahneman and Treisman, result from the fact that performances investigated under the selective-set paradigm are considerably easier than those of the previously predominant filtering paradigm. This may explain why results from the selective-set paradigm naturally favor views proposing much automaticity and late selection in information processing. Indeed, after reviewing a large number of studies, Kahneman and Treisman concluded that there is, in fact, no compelling evidence for completely automatic perceptual processing: "All these results are surprising within a framework that describes information processing in terms of automatic access to nodes in LTM. Processing that might be expected to be automatic was . . . shown to depend on attention" (Kahneman & Treisman, p. 54).

Consequently, it is evident that the issue of the degree of automaticity is central in the field, as the greater the extent to which information processing is automatic, the less there is to be explained by attention. Kahneman and Treisman (1984) distinguished three levels of automaticity:

1. *Strong automaticity.* An act of perceptual processing is neither facilitated by focusing attention to a stimulus, nor impaired by diverting attention from it.
2. *Partial automaticity.* An act is normally completed even when attention is diverted from the stimulus, but can be facilitated by attention.
3. *Occasional automaticity.* An act generally requires attention but can sometimes be completed without it.

The extent and quality of automatic processing is very hard to determine reliably with behavioral means, for such measurements necessarily are indirect and "off-line," and therefore usually quite inaccurate. Furthermore, these measurements tend to call the subject's attention to stimuli whose automatic processing should be the object of the study, which of course contaminates the measurement results. In contrast, neurophysiological activity underlying stimulus processing occurring in the absence of attention (i.e., automatically) can be studied without this contamination by recording event-related potentials (ERPs) of the brain that are elicited by the to-be-ignored stimuli. Therefore, ERPs may provide a data basis for making inferences with regard to the extent and quality of automatic processing. Moreover, when ERPs to accepted and rejected stimuli are compared with one another, they may also elucidate the mechanisms of attentional stimulus selection and rejection. Such comparisons can, for example, provide the earliest moment in time at which the neurophysiological processes elicited by attended and unattended stimuli start to depart from each other. Such data naturally are of prime importance particularly in deciding between the early- and late-selection theories.

In this chapter, we first examine ERP work on auditory attention, starting with studies aimed at determining the extent and quality of the processing that occurs in the absence of attention, in order to provide a baseline against which the effects of attention can be evaluated.

ATTENTION IN THE AUDITORY MODALITY

Auditory Processing in the Absence of Attention

When a sound is presented, it elicits in the human auditory system an afferent activation pattern that carries specific stimulus information toward higher mechanisms. This pattern travels through the ascending auditory pathway, rapidly changing in time as new afferent neurons are activated while previously activated ones return to their preactivated state. Before the sound-initiated afferent activation pattern reaches the primary auditory cortex, a complex set of subcortical processes is activated, carrying information on sensory features of the sound, such as its frequency (see, e.g., Greenberg, Marsh, Brown, & Smith, 1987; Horst, Javel, & Farley, 1986) and spatial locus of origin (Masterton, 1992).

In the subcortical part of the ascending auditory pathway, the excitability of the neurons fully recovers almost immediately after the afferent volley passes through, making these neurons ready for the next stimulus. This is indicated by the rate-of-presentation effects on the sound-induced electric potentials originating from the neuronal populations of the ascending auditory pathway. These ERPs are products of the synchronous activation of large neuronal populations time-locked to the eliciting stimulus event. Because the amplitude of ERPs is typically much smaller than that of the other ongoing electric activity of the brain, very many responses usually have to be averaged to delineate an ERP from the rest of the electroencephalogram (EEG). The averaging procedure is illustrated in Figure 15.1.

Brainstem auditory evoked potentials[1] (BAEPs; Jewett, 1970) are a sequence of responses originating from the brainstem to a discrete acoustic stimulus, typically recorded as the electric potential difference between an electrode placed on the vertex and another attached to the earlobe or the mastoid. BAEPs are generated in structures ranging from the

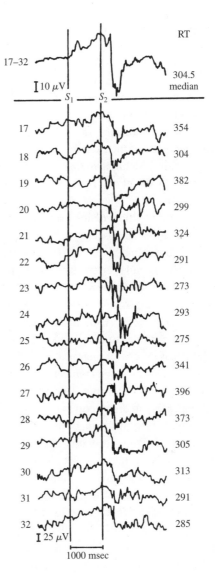

Figure 15.1   The averaging procedure.

NOTE: Top trace: Vertex (Cz electrode) potential of one subject averaged over trials 17–32 in a visual choice-reaction time (choice-RT) task in which S_1 denotes a warning stimulus and S_2 an imperative stimulus, either an *H* requiring a left-hand press or an *X* requiring a right-hand press. The S_1-S_2 interval was 1 s. Lower traces: Single vertex records resulting in the averaged potential presented by the upper trace. Negativity at the vertex relative to a reference electrode at the left ear is represented by an upward deflection.

SOURCE: From Gaillard and Näätänen (1973). Copyright © 1973 by the North-Holland Publishing Company. Reprinted with permission.

---

[1]Traditionally, obligatory short-latency electric responses evoked by sensory stimulation are labeled EPs, whereas later components usually associated with complex psychological processes are termed ERPs.

auditory (8th) nerve to the thalamus within the first 10 ms from stimulus onset (for a review, see Legatt, Arezzo, & Vaughan, 1988). They show no significant peak-latency changes as a function of the stimulus rate with rates below 10 Hz (Picton, Stapells, & Campbell, 1981), which indicates an almost instantaneous recovery of the excitability of the neuronal circuits generating these responses. Furthermore, Picton et al. (1981) found that the peak amplitude of wave V, the predominant aspect of the BAEP, remains relatively stable when the stimulus-onset asynchrony (SOA) exceeds 30 ms. In addition, BAEPs appear to manifest no overall decrement over time; their amplitudes are not reduced during stimulus sequences lasting as long as even 1 hr (Salamy & McKean, 1977). Also, BAEPs recorded in sleep are similar to those obtained during wakefulness except for their prolonged latencies due to decreased body temperature during sleep (Marshall & Donchin, 1981).

The primary auditory cortex is reached by the afferent volley in about 10 ms from stimulus onset, judging from the elicitation of the earliest sound-initiated electric response, a small surface-negative potential wave, in the human auditory cortex. This initial cortical potential deflection is followed by two more prominent waves, a positivity at 15 ms and a further negativity at 19 ms (Vaughan & Arezzo, 1988). These waves—recorded with intracranial electrodes near Heschl's gyrus, and thus the primary auditory cortex, by Celesia and Puletti (1971) and Celesia (1976)—correspond in their timing to the scalp-recorded deflections No, Po, and Na, the earliest potential deflections belonging to the wave complex called the auditory middle-latency response (MLR; Picton et al., 1974). The MLR refers to the sequence of fast cortical electric responses measurable from the scalp within approximately 10 ms to 40 ms from stimulus onset, the ensuing slower potentials being termed the long-latency responses (LLRs). The individual deflections are denoted by their polarity (N and P for negative and positive, respectively, and usually measured at the vertex) and a unique letter (MLRs) or number (LLRs). Figure 15.2 illustrates the auditory ERP in three different time scales.

The first LLRs are a positive reponse P1 peaking at about 50 ms and a major negative response N1 peaking at about 100 ms from stimulus onset; the latter has played a particularly important role in electrophysiological studies of selective attention, to be reviewed later. The N1 wave represents no unitary stimulus-evoked process originating from a localized set of neuronal elements but rather is a product of several simultaneously active neuronal generators. Besides the auditory cortical source (the supratemporal component peaking at about 100 ms from stimulus onset; Vaughan & Ritter, 1970; for a further distinction between the N1 subcomponents generated in the supratemporal plane, see Loveless, Levänen, Jousmäki, Sams, & Hari, 1996; Lü, Williamson, & Kaufman, 1992; Sams, Hari, Rif, & Knuutila, 1993), the N1 wave receives contributions from the lateral temporal lobe and perhaps also from the frontal lobe (for a review, see Näätänen & Picton, 1987; see also Alcaini, Giard, Thevenet, & Pernier, 1994; Giard et al., 1994b; Halgren et al., 1995a, 1995b; Richer, Alain, Achim, Bouvier, & Saint-Hilaire, 1989; Scherg, Vajsar, & Picton, 1989).

The building blocks of the ERP are called components. An ERP component is defined as "the contribution to the recorded waveform of a particular generator process" (Näätänen & Picton, 1987, p. 376). Because of the overlap of the N1 subcomponents (the components summed in the observed N1 wave), it is not easy to measure separately the one originating from the supratemporal plane. However, by measuring the N1 from the mastoid region, one gets an undistorted estimate of the

HUMAN AUDITORY
EVOKED POTENTIALS

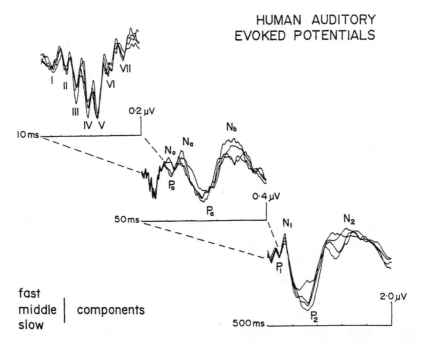

Figure 15.2   The brainstem (top), middle-latency (middle), and long-latency (bottom) deflections of the auditory ERP (recorded between the vertex and the right mastoid) to a 60-dB sensation level (SL) click stimulus presented to the right ear at a rate of 1 per s.
NOTE: Relative negativity at the vertex is represented by an upward deflection. Note the different time scales and amplitude calibrations. Each tracing represents the average of 1,024 individual responses.
SOURCE: From Picton (1980). Copyright © 1980 by Wiley. Reprinted with permission.

supratemporal subcomponents because only this N1 subcomponent reverses its polarity (i.e., appears as a positive deflection) at the mastoids when the common reference electrode is attached to the nose. (Electric brain potentials are measured as the voltage between two scalp locations. The term *common reference* denotes the electrode relative to which the potentials picked up by other electrodes are measured.) This polarity reversal of the supratemporal N1 subcomponent is due to the fact that the pyramidal neurons, the major cortical source of ERPs, are oriented approximately vertically in the supratemporal plane and therefore generate electric fields with opposite polarities at recording sites above the supratemporal plane (e.g., at the central midline areas of the scalp) and below the supratemporal plane (e.g., at the mastoids),

whereas the voltage is approximately $0 \mu V$ at the level of the supratemporal plane (e.g., at the nose).

Another means of obtaining a reliable estimate of the supratemporal N1 component is to measure the magnetoencephalographic (MEG; the measurement of magnetic field changes resulting from electric brain activity) equivalent of the supratemporal N1 component, the N1m. Because of the physical properties of the magnetic fields and the orientation of the pyramidal cells in the human supratemporal auditory cortex generating them, MEG recordings from sensors placed over the scalp covering the supratemporal area of the brain reveal the electromagnetic activity of the auditory cortex with only a minimal amount of contribution from other areas (for reviews, see Hari, 1990; Näätänen,

Ilmoniemi, & Alho, 1994). However, magnetic measurements do not pick up the radial component of the electric brain activity (i.e., electric changes with a direction perpendicular to the surface of the scalp). Therefore, a part of the supratemporal N1 component is absent from MEG recordings, as all supratemporal pyramidal neurons are not oriented exactly tangentially to the skull (cf. Scherg et al., 1989).

There is evidence for the presence of stimulus-specific sensory information in the neuronal circuits generating the supratemporal N1. For example, the N1m shows a tonotopic organization in the human auditory cortex such that when sound frequency is increased, the estimated locus of origin of the N1m moves deeper, indicating that at least partially different neuronal elements of the N1m respond to tones of different frequencies (Hari & Mäkelä, 1986; Pantev et al., 1988; Romani, Williamson, & Kaufman, 1982). These data therefore suggest that some of the neuronal populations generating the supratemporal N1 (N1m) have narrow receptive fields with regard to stimulus frequency, thus being capable of precise stimulus encoding.

Electric data, too, implicate the involvement of stimulus-specific neuronal circuits in N1 generation. For example, consistent with the MEG data just reviewed, the N1 scalp topography varies with stimulus frequency; the topography for higher tones is anterior to that for lower tones (Bertrand, Perrin, Echallier, & Pernier, 1988; Näätänen, Teder, Alho, & Lavikainen, 1992; Woods, Alho, & Algazi, 1991).

However, a good deal of the neuronal elements underlying the supratemporal N1 have a wide receptive field (i.e., respond to a large variety of different sounds), therefore being incapable of encoding stimulus features to an accuracy strictly preserving the individuality of a stimulus (Näätänen, 1990; Näätänen & Picton, 1987). Consistent with this, Hari

et al. (1987) have shown that very different sounds elicit an N1m originating from the same or approximately the same cerebral locus. Furthermore, the supratemporal-N1 refractoriness (lasting at least 10 s for the N1m, according to Hari et al., 1987; see, however, Lü et al., 1992) is widely generalized; that is, even the responses to stimuli that are very different from the repeated stimulus are strongly attenuated (Butler, 1968; Näätänen et al., 1988). These and other converging results (for a review, see Näätänen & Picton, 1987) suggest that the major part of the supratemporal N1 neuronal elements is involved in transient detection, which provides information about stimulus onsets and, for stimuli of longer durations, also about offsets (see Näätänen 1992; Näätänen & Picton, 1987; Parasuraman & Beatty, 1980), rather than about specific stimulus features. Thus, the activation of these neurons is probably associated with attention switch to the outcome of the preceding preattentive (i.e., subjectively unnoticed) processing of the same stimulus (Näätänen, 1986, 1990, 1992). More recently, however, Giard et al. (1994b) described a frontal N1 subcomponent that, according to them, might be a better candidate than the auditory-cortex-generated N1 subcomponent for this attention-switching function.

All the ERP components just discussed are called exogenous or obligatory components because they are elicited even in the absence of attention (although, as discussed later, some of these components might be modulated by attention). Therefore, one might ask whether these ERPs permit some conclusions regarding the quantity and quality of the unattended-channel processing. Unfortunately, the answer is negative: Even though many of the exogenous components are not at all affected—or only to a quite modest extent—by attention, this does not imply that the sensory processing of unattended stimuli would not be affected by the withdrawal of attention from them. This is because the relationship of all these ERP components to sensory information extracted by the auditory system from the stimulus is unclear; these components usually serve only as an index of stimulus detection, not as an index of the accuracy of processing and discrimination of different auditory stimulus features (Näätänen & Winkler, 1999).

Fortunately, there is one component in the ERP that is highly informative about the actual processing of unattended input. This component is the *mismatch negativity* (MMN), isolated from the so-called N2 wave or the N2-P3a wave complex (Ford, Roth, & Kopell, 1976; Snyder & Hillyard, 1976; Squires, Squires, & Hillyard, 1975) by Näätänen, Gaillard, and Mäntysalo (1978). The MMN data suggest, as is reviewed later, that physical sound features of even unattended stimuli might be fully processed at least under most attention conditions.

The MMN, elicited when some regularity in auditory stimulation is violated by a change (deviant stimulus), can be best observed when the subject's attention is directed away from this stimulus sequence. Otherwise, deviant stimuli elicit, besides the MMN, another negative component partially overlapping the MMN, the N2b (Fitzgerald & Picton, 1983, Näätänen, Simpson, & Loveless, 1982; Sams, Alho, & Näätänen, 1984; Sams, Paavilainen, Alho, & Näätänen, 1985b; for a review, see Näätänen & Gaillard, 1983). The MMN can be best evaluated from the difference wave obtained by subtracting the ERP of the standard (repetitive) stimulus from that of the deviant stimulus. Figure 15.3 illustrates an MMN elicited by small frequency changes. A problem, of course, is posed by the possible effects of stimulus change (activating new afferent elements) on the generator processes of the exogenous N1 and P2 components. Fortunately, these effects are usually quite small when stimulus change is not large. Furthermore, they occur at the same latency as the

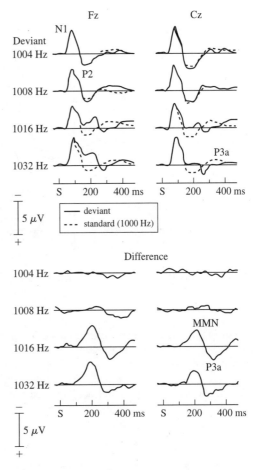

Figure 15.3 The mismatch negativity (MMN). NOTE: Top: Grand-average ERPs to standard stimuli of 1000 Hz (thin line) and deviant stimuli (thick line) of 1004, 1008, 1016, and 1032 Hz. In each block, 80% of stimuli were standard stimuli and 20% were deviant stimuli in a random order (one type in a block). Bottom: The corresponding difference waveforms obtained by subtracting the standard-stimulus ERP from the deviant-stimulus ERP.
SOURCE: From Sams, Paavilainen, Alho, and Näätänen (1985b). Copyright © 1985 by Elsevier Science Publishers, Ireland. Reprinted with permission.

respective components in response to the standard stimulus (Näätänen & Picton, 1987). For further issues and details of MMN measurement, see Schröger (1998).

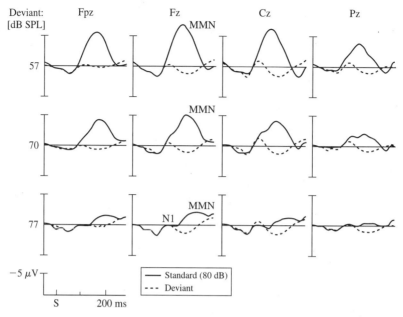

Figure 15.4 Grand-average ERP from 4 different electrodes along the midline to standard stimuli of 80 dB SPL (thin lines) and to deviant stimuli of lower intensities (thick lines) as indicated on the left.
NOTE: Weaker-intensity deviants elicit larger and earlier mismatch negativities (MMN).
SOURCE: From Näätänen, Paavilainen, Alho, Reinikainen, and Sams (1989). Copyright © 1989 by Elsevier Science Publishers, Ireland. Reprinted with permission.

That a stimulus change is essential in MMN elicitation is illustrated in Figure 15.4. In this experiment (Näätänen, Paavilainen, Alho, Reinikainen, & Sams, 1989), the standard stimulus was of an intensity of 80 dB SPL, and in different blocks the deviant stimulus ($p = 0.1$) was of an intensity of 57, 70, 77 (intensity decrements), and 83, 90, or 95 (intensity increments) dB SPL. The subject was instructed to read a book and ignore the sequence of auditory stimuli presented at short constant intervals. The response to the 77-dB stimulus shows two consecutive negative waves, of which the earlier may be interpreted as the (supratemporal) N1 component and the later as the MMN. When the intensity of the deviant stimulus is further reduced, the MMN becomes larger and earlier, overlapping the N1.

The increase of the response amplitude when stimulus energy is decreased can be attributed only to the increased difference between the deviant and standard stimuli; that is, the MMN is a response to the *relation* (difference) between the present stimulus and the previous stimuli rather than to the present stimulus per se. If we deliver deviant stimuli in their temporal positions but omit the intervening standards, then no MMN is elicited (Figure 15.5). This means that, unlike for N1, which responds mainly to stimulus onsets and offsets, MMN elicitation requires stimulus change; that is, the MMN can be used as a probe in studying the properties of the neural sensory-memory traces formed by sound stimuli.

The MMN can be elicited also by other types of changes in auditory stimulation; in

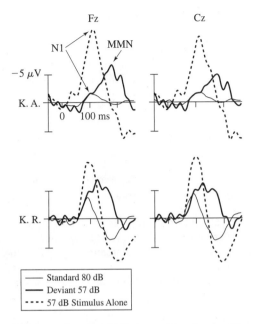

Fz   Cz

N1   MMN

−5 μV

K. A.

0   100 ms

K. R.

——— Standard 80 dB
——— Deviant 57 dB
- - - - 57 dB Stimulus Alone

Figure 15.5   Frontal (Fz electrode) and vertex (Cz electrode) ERPs of two subjects to 80-dB standard stimuli (thin lines), 57-dB deviant stimuli (thick lines), and to identical 57-dB stimuli (dashed lines) when presented with no standards (without changing the ISIs between the 57-dB stimuli).
SOURCE: From Näätänen, Paavilainen, Alho, Reinikainen, and Sams (1989). Copyright © 1989 by Elsevier Science Publishers, Ireland. Reprinted with permission.

fact, it can be elicited by any discriminable change in acoustic input. Furthermore, numerous studies (e.g., Lang et al., 1990; for a review, see Näätänen, 2001) established that the MMN provides an index of the perceptual discrimination accuracy such that if an MMN is elicited when one stimulus is used as the standard and the other as the deviant, then the two stimuli can be behaviorally discriminated (Kraus et al., 1996; Amenedo & Escera, 2000). Consequently, the MMN can serve as an objective measure of perceptual discrimination and thus of the accuracy of the processing of the different features of auditory stimulation.

Therefore, several studies have used the MMN in evaluating the accuracy of sensory processing in the unattended channel. For example, Sams et al. (1985b) showed that an MMN is elicited by occasional frequency changes in a repetitive train of auditory stimuli even when the subject is attending to visual stimuli (Figure 15.3). Furthermore, Alho, Woods, Algazi, and Näätänen (1992) found that the MMN to slightly higher-pitched deviant tones in an auditory stimulus sequence was of very similar amplitude during easy and difficult visual discrimination tasks that demanded very different amounts of attention. However, this MMN was larger in amplitude when subjects attended to auditory stimuli than when they attended to visual stimuli (see also Woods, Alho, & Algazi, 1992). In addition, Trejo et al. (1995) found that the MMN amplitude for a frequency change in a binaurally presented repetitive tone was considerably larger when subjects attended to this tone sequence than when they attended to a concurrent narrative. However, a number of dichotic studies with an instruction to attend to stimuli in a designated ear found MMNs of very similar amplitudes to occasional frequency changes in both the attended and unattended ears (Alho, Sams, Paavilainen, Reinikainen, & Näätänen, 1989; Näätänen, Paavilainen, Tiitinen, Jiang, & Alho, 1993; Paavilainen, Tiitinen, Alho, & Näätänen, 1993; see Figure 15.6).

In contrast, in the dichotic studies of Woldorff, Hackley, and Hillyard (1991) and Näätänen et al. (1993), the MMN elicited by occasional decrements in the intensity of unattended sounds was considerably attenuated in amplitude (but was not totally abolished) relative to that for attended sounds. Moreover, more recently, Woldorff, Hillyard, Gallen, Hampson, and Bloom (1998) demonstrated the attenuation of the intensity-reduction MMNm (the magnetic equivalent of the supratemporal component of the MMN) by the withdrawal of attention from this stimulus channel under dichotic-listening conditions.

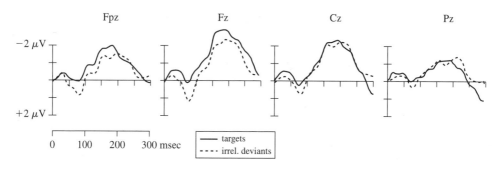

Figure 15.6   Grand-average difference waves from 4 different electrodes along the midline showing the MMN to the target (continuous lines) and nontarget (broken lines) infrequent stimuli in selective dichotic listening.

NOTE: Frequent (80%) 75-dB (SPL) and infrequent (20%) 60-dB (SPL) tones were presented in random order to the left and right ears. The subject's task was to count silently the number of infrequent tones (targets) delivered to the designated ear. The difference waves were obtained by subtracting the ERP to the standard tones from that to the infrequent tones delivered to the same ear.

SOURCE: From Alho, Sams, Paavilainen, Reinikainen, and Näätänen (1989). Copyright © 1989 by the Society for Psychophysiological Research, Inc. Reprinted with permission.

Nevertheless, not one of the studies conducted to date casts any doubt on MMN elicitation even by a slight sound change in the absence of attention. Perhaps the strongest evidence for the automaticity of the MMN was, however, provided by an MMN recorded in comatose patients to changes in frequency (Kane, Curry, Butler, & Gummins, 1993; Kane et al., 1996) and duration (Fischer et al., 1999; Morlet, Bouchet, & Fischer, 2000).

Woldorff et al. (1991, 1998), however, interpreted their MMNm amplitude reduction for the unattended channel in terms of attenuated sensory processing in the absence of attention. Questioning this interpretation, Näätänen (1991) suggested that it would be important to determine whether attention affects only the MMN amplitude or also the threshold of the MMN-generator activation. If this threshold is not affected (as is the case if MMN is not abolished by the withdrawal of attention, even for slight stimulus changes), then an attentional reduction of the MMN amplitude cannot be taken, according to him, as suggesting that the processing of sensory information is deteriorated

in the unattended channel, because even a very weak MMN-generator process implicates differential antecedent processing (and encoding to sensory memory) of the standard and deviant stimuli (i.e., apparently the full sensory processing in the unattended channel).

In conclusion, ERPs have opened an unprecedented view to auditory sensory processing in the absence of attention, suggesting that the accuracy of sensory processing is not decreased by the withdrawal of attention, at least under most attention conditions. These data further show that not even consciousness is needed for sensory discrimination (at least of sounds widely differing from each other), judging from MMNs recorded from comatose patients.

Involuntary Attention to Auditory Stimuli

The Mismatch Negativity and Involuntary Attention Switching

As already reviewed, the MMN is elicited by deviant auditory stimuli or events occurring among regularly repeating stimuli or events even when the listener's attention is directed elsewhere (Näätänen, Gaillard, & Mäntysalo, 1978; for recent reviews, see Näätänen & Alho, 1997; Näätänen & Winkler, 1999; Schröger, 1997). It appears that this generator process has a central initiating role in the orienting response to changes in the acoustic environment (Sokolov, 1975; Sokolov, Spinks, Lyytinen, & Näätänen, in press). This is supported by results showing that responses of the autonomic nervous system (ANS) associated with involuntary orienting of attention (heart-rate deceleration and the skin-conductance response) tend to be elicited by MMN-eliciting stimulus changes (Lyytinen et al., 1992). Furthermore, MMNs, and especially those to wider stimulus changes, are often accompanied by a positive P3a component (Figure 15.3; for a combined ERP and MEG study, see Alho et al., 1998) that was proposed by Squires et al. (1975) as being an ERP sign of the involuntary orienting of attention.

In addition to changes in ongoing auditory stimulation, sound onsets, and especially those after a relatively long silent period, may involuntarily capture our attention. As shown in Figure 15.5, such sounds do not elicit an MMN but evoke an N1 deflection, which is considerably larger in amplitude than that elicited by sounds appearing at faster rates (see also Hari et al., 1982; Näätänen & Picton, 1987; Korzyukov et al., 1999; Kropotov et al., 2000). Moreover, the N1 is also markedly enhanced in response to MMN-eliciting, widely deviant sounds, for instance, by tones deviating by an octave from the repeating tones (Scherg et al., 1989) or by complex novel sounds (e.g., Alho et al., 1998; Escera et al., 1998; see Figure 15.7) occurring in a sequence of repetitive tones. The N1 enhancement to such widely deviant sounds is probably explained by the fact that these sounds activate frequency-specific, auditory-cortex neu-

ron populations that are in a nonrefractory state because they were not activated by the preceding sounds (Butler, 1968). The large N1 to sounds occurring after a longer silent period is enhanced partly for the same reason (Korzyukov et al., 1999), although this N1 also appears to get contributions from modality-nonspecific generators outside the auditory cortex (Alcaini et al., 1994; Hari et al., 1982; Näätänen & Picton, 1987). Because of the feature-specific (e.g., frequency-specific) refractoriness of the N1—as well as the dependence of the N1 amplitude on the time from the previous stimulus onset, stimulus energy and rise time, and, to some extent, on some other stimulus features (e.g., frequency and location) it is highly important that the researcher does not assume that a negative ERP response to a deviant sound is caused solely by the MMN unless contributions from the N1 generators can be ruled out. In his model of auditory attention, Näätänen (1990) proposed that the auditory N1 reflects involuntary attention to the onsets of any events, especially new ones, in the acoustic environment. This proposal is supported by findings that novel sounds that elicit a large N1 also elicit a large P3a (Figure 15.7), indicating their attention-catching nature (see, e.g., Alho et al., 1998; Escera et al., 1998; Woods, 1990). An experimental technique for disentangling the refractoriness effects (N1) from the memory-comparison effects (the genuine MMN) has been proposed by Schröger and Wolff (1996) for the location MMN and by Jacobsen and Schröger (2001) for the frequency MMN. The basic idea is that the state of refractoriness is controlled in a separate control block that must be conducted in addition to the oddball block consisting of frequent standard stimuli and infrequent deviant stimuli. The probability of each stimulus in the control block equals the probability of the deviant stimulus in the oddball block. If p for the deviant stimulus is 0.10 in the oddball block,

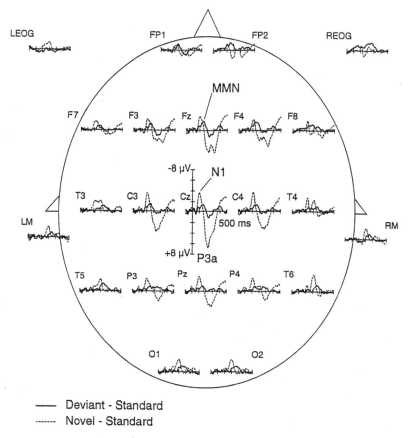

— Deviant - Standard
------ Novel - Standard

Figure 15.7 Grand-average (10 subjects) ERP difference waves at different scalp locations obtained by subtracting the ERP to repeating standard tones from those to slightly higher, deviant tones and to complex, novel sounds that infrequently replaced the standard tone.

NOTE: The auditory stimuli were presented to subjects concentrating on watching a silent movie. The difference waves for deviant tones show a mismatch negativity (MMN) that is largest over the frontal scalp, followed by a small positive P3a response, whereas the difference waves for novel sounds show a negative response, caused by the MMN and the enhanced N1 to these sounds, followed by a large positive P3a response.

SOURCE: From Escera et al. (1998). © 1998 by the Massachusetts Institute of Technology.

then 10 different stimuli are presented (each with $p = 0.10$) in the control block. Furthermore, two of these stimuli are identical to the deviant and standard stimuli of the oddball block, whereas the others should be physically more distant from the deviant stimulus than are the standard and deviant stimuli of the oddball block from each other. With this protocol, the state of refractoriness cannot be higher for the control stimulus (which is physically identical to the deviant stimulus of the oddball block) than that for the deviant stimulus in the oddball block. Then the deviant-control difference wave yields the minimum genuine MMN effect (cf. Näätänen & Alho, 1997).

Measurements of Event-Related Brain Potentials and Behavior in the Attention-Switching-to-Stimulus-Change Paradigm

A number of recent studies have been aimed at determining the role of the MMN in the initiation of involuntary attention switching apparently indexed by the P3a. In a paradigm recently developed by Escera et al. (1998), subjects are instructed to discriminate between visually presented odd and even numbers, or between numbers and letters, and to press the corresponding response button as fast and accurately as possible. Further, a task-irrelevant auditory stimulus is delivered shortly before each visual stimulus (e.g., 300 ms from onset to onset). In most cases, this auditory stimulus is a repetitive standard tone that is, however, infrequently replaced by a slightly higher deviant tone or by a widely deviant novel sound (e.g., telephone ringing, thunder, or the starting of a car engine). In such conditions, the reaction time (RT) to the visual stimuli following deviant tones and novel sounds was prolonged by about 5 ms and 20 ms, respectively, relative to the RT to the visual stimuli preceded by a standard tone (Alho et al., 1997; Escera et al., 1998; Jääskeläinen et al., 1996). The hit rate (HR), in turn, was similar after both the standard tones and the novel sounds but decreased by about 2% after the occurrence of a deviant tone. This decrease resulted from an increased number of wrong button presses in the visual choice RT task. The ERPs recorded by Escera et al. (1998) showed an MMN to the deviant tones followed by a small P3a. Novel sounds, in turn, elicited an MMN and a large P3a in addition to an enhanced N1. The authors interpreted their results as supporting the proposed roles of N1 and MMN generators in initiating involuntary attention switching.

However, the distracting effects of the deviant tones and novel sounds on the visual task performance reported by Escera et al. (1998) and Jääskeläinen et al. (1996) might not indicate truly involuntary attention switching from the visual task to auditory stimuli; perhaps subjects covertly attended to the task-irrelevant auditory stimuli, which may then have served as warning cues for the subsequent task-relevant visual stimulus (although the type of visual stimulus could not be predicted from the type of auditory stimulus). This was indicated by the shorter RT in the main experimental condition of Escera et al. (1998) compared with the RT in their control condition, in which the task-relevant visual stimuli were presented alone (i.e., without the preceding auditory stimuli).

In another related study (Alho et al., 1997), attempts were made to withdraw attention from the task-irrelevant auditory stimuli (either a standard tone or a deviant tone; no novel sounds were presented) by presenting simultaneously with each tone a visual warning stimulus that informed the subject of whether this trial would be a "go" trial (i.e., a visual task stimulus requiring discrimination and responding will follow) or a "no-go" trial (i.e., no visual task stimulus will follow). Thus, in this experiment the auditory stimulus did not predict the occurrence of a subsequent task-relevant visual stimulus, whereas the coinciding visual warning stimulus did. Therefore, it is unlikely that subjects covertly attended to the auditory stimuli that gave no support for the visual task. The deviant tones nevertheless elicited an MMN and had distracting effects on the visual task similar to those found by Escera et al. (1998) and Jääskeläinen et al. (1996). Moreover, the deviant tones were followed by the attenuation of the occipital N1 deflection in response to the succeeding visual task stimuli, presumably indicating that less attention was paid to these visual stimuli than when they were preceded by standard tones (cf. Mangun and Hillyard, 1991). These results support the involuntary nature of the engagement of attention by the deviant and novel sounds also in the related studies of Escera et al. (1998) and Jääskeläinen et al. (1996).

Distraction effects caused by MMN-eliciting sound changes were also found in dichotic selective-attention tasks. The discrimination of the target sounds in the to-be-attended ear (channel) tended to be deteriorated when they were preceded by deviant or novel sounds in this or in the opposite ear (Schröger, 1996; Woods, 1992; Woods et al., 1993b).

Performance in an auditory discrimination task may also be distracted by task-irrelevant changes in the target sound itself. Schröger and Wolff (1998a, 1998b) instructed their subjects to discriminate the duration of tones that equiprobably was either short (200 ms) or long (400 ms). The tones were either of the standard frequency (600 Hz) or, with a low probability, of a slightly higher frequency (650 Hz), the tone frequency having no task relevance. It was found that the duration-discrimination RT was longer to the deviant- than to the standard-frequency tones. In addition, the deviant-frequency tones elicited an MMN followed by a P3a. Schröger and Wolff (1998b) and Schröger, Giard, & Wolff (2000) observed that the ERP responses to frequency changes in this stimulus paradigm differentially depended on the allocation of attention. In one condition in which the tones were not at all to be attended, the relatively small frequency changes elicited an MMN but no P3a, whereas in another condition, the MMN to similar, task-irrelevant frequency changes that occurred in tones whose duration was to be discriminated (and thus the tones were to be attended) by the listeners was followed by a prominent P3a.

In the studies of Schröger and his colleagues just reviewed, the P3a to frequency changes was followed by a fronto-centrally distributed negativity at 400 ms to 600 ms from deviant-tone onset. This negativity was observed when subjects performed a tone-duration discrimination task, but not when frequency deviations were task-relevant or when the tones were to be ignored. Therefore, this negativity, named the *reorienting negativity* (RON), was proposed to reflect the reorienting of attention toward the task-relevant aspects of stimulation after a distracting event (Schröger & Wolff, 1998b).

The Cerebral Network of Involuntary Attention to Sounds

As the research reviewed in the previous section indicates, the neural generators of the MMN are involved in initiating ("calling for"; Öhman, 1979, 1992) an attention switch to sound change, and those of the P3a in the actual resulting involuntary switching of attention to sounds. Therefore, studies clarifying the MMN and P3a generator sources might help to determine the neural network of involuntary attention to auditory stimuli. The primary generators of the MMN have been located in the auditory cortex by the source modeling of the MMN (Giard et al., 1995; Scherg et al., 1989) and by recording the MEG counterpart of the MMN, that is, the MMNm (Figure 15.8; see also Alho et al., 1998; Hari et al., 1984; Levänen et al., 1996; Sams et al., 1985a; Tiitinen et al., 1993a; for a review, see Alho, 1995). However, the MMN also receives a contribution from the frontal-lobe activity, as indicated by the scalp current density (SCD) mapping of the MMN scalp distribution (Figure 15.9; see also Deouell et al., 1998; Levänen et al., 1996; Rinne et al., 2000). This supports the MMN generator process's assumed role in involuntary attention switching, for one of the important frontal-lobe functions is to control the direction of attention (e.g., Fuster, 1989; Knight, 1991; Stuss & Benson, 1986). Furthermore, evidence for the involvement of the frontal cortex in the MMN generation is provided by results showing that

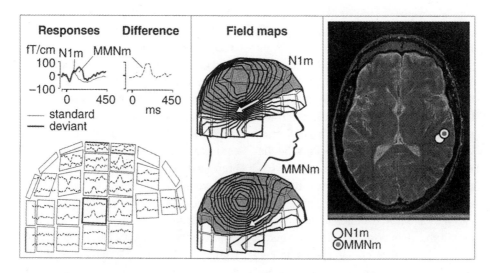

Figure 15.8   The MMNm.
Left panel, top left: MEG responses over the right hemisphere of one subject to repeating standard tones and to slightly higher infrequent deviant tones delivered to the left ear while the subject was concentrating on a reading task. The responses shown were recorded by one sensor within the thick square below. Left panel, top right: the magnetic counterpart of the mismatch negativity (MMNm) to deviant tones is indicated by the difference wave obtained by subtracting the response to standard tones from that to deviant tones. Left panel, bottom: The corresponding difference waves from different recording sites over the right hemisphere. Each square shows signals from two orthogonal planar gradiometers that record the largest signal above the cortical generator source. Middle panel: Magnetic field maps for the N1m (the MEG counterpart of the N1 ERP response) to the standard tones and for the MMNm to the deviant tones. The arrows indicate the N1m and MMNm sources modeled with equivalent current dipoles (ECDs). The gray area indicates magnetic flux into the head and the white area the flux out of the head. Right panel: Locations of the estimated N1m and MMNm sources in the right auditory cortex.
SOURCE: Adapted from Huotilainen et al. (1993).

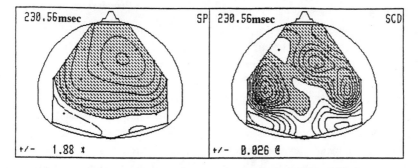

Figure 15.9   Isopotential (SP) map showing the scalp distribution of the mismatch negativity (MMN) to small frequency changes in unattended tones delivered to the right ear during attention to the left-ear tones (left), and the corresponding scalp-current density (SCD) map (right).
NOTE: The SP map (negative polarity indicated by shading) shows that the MMN is maximal over the right frontal scalp. The SCD map shows a pattern of sources (white area) and sinks (shaded area) indicating MMN generators in the left and right auditory cortices. In addition, the SCD map suggests a frontal MMN generator predominantly in the right hemisphere.
SOURCE: Adapted from Giard et al. (1990).

lesions of dorsolateral prefrontal cortex atten-
uate the MMN amplitude (Alain et al. 1998;
Alho et al., 1994c).

The fronto-central scalp distribution of the
P3a distinguishes it from the parietally maximal P3b (Ford et al., 1976; Squires et al., 1975;
Knight & Scabini, 1998; Woods, 1990), the
later component of the P3 (P300) deflection
typically elicited by target stimuli to be discriminated by the subject (Sutton et al., 1965).
Alho et al. (1998) located the source of the
MEG counterpart of the P3a response to deviant tones and novel sounds in the auditory
cortex in the vicinity of the MMNm source.
This accords with the intracranial recordings
of the P3a activity in the superior temporal
cortex (Halgren et al., 1995a; Kropotov et al.,
1995). Furthermore, Escera et al. (1998) observed that the early portion of the P3a elicited
by novel sounds reaches its maximal amplitude over the central midline areas and in-
verts its polarity at the mastoid electrode sites
below the auditory cortex (with nose reference), whereas the later P3a portion has a
more frontal scalp distribution and does not
invert polarity (Figure 15.9). Judging from its
latency, the earlier, centrally distributed part
of the P3a, that reversing its polarity below the
auditory cortex (consistent with a generator
there), might be explained by the supratemporal P3a subcomponent observed by Alho et
al. (1998) in their MEG recordings. The
later and more frontally distributed portion of
the P3a, in turn, might originate from the prefrontal cortex (see also Friedman & Simpson,
1994; Friedman et al., 1993; Mecklinger &
Ullsperger, 1995). This interpretation is supported by results showing attenuated P3a responses to novel sounds in patients with dorsolateral prefrontal lesions (Knight, 1984) and
by direct recordings from the prefrontal cortices of epileptic patients (Baudena, Halgren,
Heit, & Clarke, 1995).

In conclusion, the source localizations of
the MMN and P3a indicate that both the auditory and frontal cortices are involved in initiating involuntary attention to auditory stimulus
changes and in the consequent switching of
attention. However, the lesion and intracranial P3a data suggest that several additional
areas are also involved in the actual attention
switching; because according to these data,
the P3a is generated by a network of brain areas including—in addition to the auditory and
prefrontal cortices—the parietal cortex, the
temporo-parietal junction, the parahippocam-
pal gyrus, the anterior cingulate gyrus, and
the hippocampus (Alain et al., 1989; Baudena
et al., 1995; Halgren et al., 1995a, 1995b;
Knight et al., 1989; Kropotov et al., 1995;
Knight, 1996).

As just reviewed, in some studies the P3a
was followed by the RON response, suggested as reflecting the reorienting of attention back to the current task after a distracting
event (Schröger and Wolff, 1998b). The SCD
maps for the RON suggest bilateral frontal
generators and thus the involvement of the
frontal lobes also in the reorienting of attention (Schröger et al., 2000).

Selective Attention to Auditory Stimuli

N1 Effect or Processing Negativity

Hillyard, Hink, Schwent, & Picton (1973)
were the first to demonstrate a reliable effect
of selective attention on the amplitude of the
N1 deflection of the ERP elicited by auditory
stimuli. They presented tone pips with very
short, random (100–800 ms) interstimulus intervals (ISIs) in a random order to the left and
right ears. Subjects were instructed to attend to
either left- or right-ear tones and to discriminate slightly higher ones among the repetitive, standard tones delivered to the attended
ear. The effect of attention was measured as
a difference between the ERPs to the same
standard stimuli when they were attended (but
required no overt response) and when they

were not attended. Therefore, the attention effect on the standard-tone ERPs could not be explained by physical stimulus differences or by differences in response-related brain activity between the attended and unattended stimuli. Moreover, because of the random stimulus order, the effect of attention on the N1 amplitude could not be explained by differences in the arousal level at the time of the delivery of the attended and unattended stimuli. Previous results interpreted as showing selective-attention effects on ERPs failed to do this reliably because the non-random stimulus sequences applied gave subjects a possibility to predict, at least above the chance level, the occurrence of the to-be-attended stimulus, leading to an increased cortical excitability at the time of the delivery of these stimuli (Näätänen, 1970a, 1970b; for a review, see Näätänen, 1975). Importantly, the "attend right ear" and "attend left ear" tasks used by Hillyard et al. (1973) were similarly difficult, guaranteeing that the differences in the ERPs between these two conditions were not caused by differences in the subjects' general arousal levels during the tasks.

Hillyard et al. (1973) interpreted the larger N1 amplitude to attended tones than to the same tones when unattended in terms of the selective tonic facilitation of the input to the attended ear. They further proposed that this selective facilitation, appearing as early as 60 ms to 70 ms from stimulus onset, might underlie the early stimulus-set mode of selective attention proposed by Broadbent (1958, 1970). Näätänen and his collegues (Näätänen, 1975; Näätänen et al., 1978; Näätänen & Michie, 1979), however, suggested that despite its early latency, this effect was not due to an attentional modulation of any exogenous or obligatory N1 component but rather to an endogenous attention-related negative ERP component whose early portion overlapped with the N1 components. Consistent with this, Näätänen et al.'s (1978) ERP effect of selective attention obtained in the Hillyard et al. (1973) type of dichotic paradigm, but with a constant, 800-ms ISI, appeared as a slow, endogenous negative ERP component, continuing for several hundreds of milliseconds, which they termed the processing negativity (PN; Figure 15.10). Rather than being a modulation of any exogenous ERP component, the PN, recorded over the vertex and both the left and right temporal cortices, was a new component that emerged only when the stimulus was

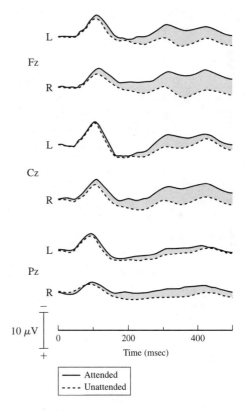

Figure 15.10 Grand-average ERPs at frontal (Fz), central (Cz), and parietal (Pz) midline scalp sites to left-ear (L) and right-ear (R) tones when attended and when the tones in the opposite ear were attended. The ERPs to attended tones are negatively displaced relative to the ERPs to unattended tones as the result of the processing negativity (hatched area) elicited by the attended tones.
SOURCE: Adapted from Näätänen and Michie (1979).

attended. This displacement was observed especially after 150 ms and therefore did not significantly affect the measured N1 amplitudes.

Hillyard and Näätänen, with their respective colleagues, interpreted the attention effect on the auditory ERP at the N1 latency differently, with very different implications for the nature of the brain processes underlying selective attention. If selective attention to auditory stimuli enhances an exogenous ERP response such as the N1, as suggested by Hillyard et al. (1973), then attention would be manifested by a tonic facilitation of the whole input channel rather than by an active discrimination and recognition of each individual stimulus, and could be explained by an amplification of the afferent neural activity caused by the attended stimuli. Such theories were termed *gain theories* by Näätänen (1986). However, if attended stimuli do not elicit enhanced exogenous ERP components but, as proposed by Näätänen et al. (1978), elicit instead a separate attention-specific endogenous PN that overlaps with the exogenous components, including the N1, then this would suggest that attentional stimulus selection is based on the comparison of each sensory input against some memory representation ("template") of the stimulus to be attended, with the PN being generated by this comparison process (Näätänen, 1982, 1990, 1992). Unlike the gain theories, such as that of Hillyard et al. (1973), this stimulus-comparison theory permits unattended-stimulus representations that are not attenuated by the absence of attention (cf. the MMN studies discussed earlier in this chapter).

The two different explanations for why the N1 deflection is larger to the attended sounds than to the unattended sounds, given by Hillyard and colleagues and by Näätänen and colleagues and leading to very different implications on the mechanisms of auditory selective attention, illustrate the importance of carefully studying the component structure

of any ERP effect before making any theoretical conclusions from it. Because of the importance of this issue, several subsequent studies have aimed at determining whether all attention effects at the N1 latency range are in fact due to an overlap by an endogenous PN, or whether some exogenous N1 component, at least under certain conditions, is enhanced by selective attention. These studies typically used dichotic paradigms with a very fast stimulus rate (e.g., 3 stimuli per s) and difficult target discrimination in order to force subjects to focus maximally their attention on the to-be-attended stimuli, as suggested by Hillyard et al. (1973). In such conditions, the timing of the attention effect on the ERP, revealed by the ERP difference wave obtained by subtracting the ERP to unattended stimuli from the ERP to the same stimuli when attended, is very similar to the timing of the N1 elicited by unattended stimuli (Figure 15.11; see also Woldorff & Hillyard, 1991; Teder, Alho, Reinikainen, & Näätänen, 1993a; Alho et al., 1994a). The scalp distribution of this attention effect, however, was anterior to, and more symmetrical than, that of the N1, which typically shows larger amplitudes over the hemisphere contralateral to the stimulated ear than over the hemisphere ipsilateral to the stimulated ear (Alho et al., 1994a; Woods & Clayworth, 1987). This does not, however, rule out the possibility that attention enhances some subcomponent of the N1 (Hackley, 1993; Woldorff & Hillyard, 1991).

Näätänen et al. (1992) compared the topographies of the N1 and the attention effect at the N1 latency for high-pitched (6000 Hz) and low-pitched (300 Hz) tones. Whereas unattended high tones elicited an N1 with its amplitude maximum clearly anterior to that for the low tones (reflecting the tonotopic organization of the auditory cortex; see also Romani et al., 1982; Tiitinen et al., 1993a; Woods, Alho, & Algazi, 1993a), no topographic difference was observed between the attention

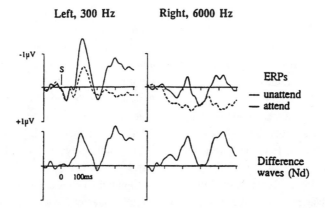

Figure 15.11   Grand-average ERPs at the central midline scalp site (Cz) to attended (solid line) and unattended (dashed line) tones delivered to the left (300 Hz) and right ear (6000 Hz) in a selective dichotic-listening study. Note the negative N1 deflection peaking at about 120 ms from stimulus onset. Bottom: Difference waves obtained by subtracting the ERPs to unattended tones from those to attended tones. These difference waves show an early effect of attention peaking at about 120 ms and a later effect peaking after 300 ms.
SOURCE: Adapted from Näätänen et al. (1992).

effects for the high and low tones, suggesting a dissociation between the N1 and the attention effect. In contrast, Alcaini, Giard, & Perrin (1995), using SCD analysis, found that a part of the attention effect followed the N1 topography (see also Woods et al., 1993a). Alho et al. (1994a) made a similar observation but found also that, unlike the N1, the tonotopically distributed attention effect was not larger over the hemisphere contralateral to the stimulated ear. Therefore, this tonotopic attention effect might not emerge from the tonotopically organized N1 generator structure but rather from some tonotopically organized part of the PN generator. Hence, in this case the auditory cortex would contain, in addition to the tonotopically organized generators of the exogenous responses, a tonotopically organized selective-attention system (cf. Näätänen, 1982).

Näätänen et al. (1992) observed also that the N1 to unattended 300-Hz tones was much larger in amplitude than was the N1 to unattended 6000-Hz tones (see also Alho et al.,

1994a). In contrast, the attention effects at the N1 latency were of very similar sizes for the two tones, further dissociating the attention effect from the enhancement of the exogenous N1 (Figure 15.11). However, no difference between the locations of the supratemporal generators of the MEG counterparts of the attention effect and of the exogenous N1 was observed in several studies with fast stimulus rates (Kaufman & Williamson, 1987; Rif, Hari, Hämäläinen, & Sams, 1991; Woldorff et al., 1993). This in turn supports the view that selective attention enhances the supratemporal N1 generator process, although even a perfect overlap of two generators, as estimated on the basis of MEG recordings, does not necessarily mean that they are identical.

Thus, at least a major portion of the selective-attention effect at the N1 latency appears to be caused by an overlapping PN, which may begin surprisingly early with very high stimulus rate, apparently indexing very rapid stimulus selection (Näätänen & Michie, 1979). However, the possibility that the supratemporal N1, or some of its subcomponents, is modulated by selective attention in some highly focused (fast-rate) conditions cannot be excluded. It should be noted, however, that although studies using very fast stimulation rates and large physical differences between the attended and unattended sounds have reported that the auditory N1 is enhanced by attention (e.g., Hillyard et al., 1973; Woldorff & Hillyard, 1991; Woldorff et al., 1993), the PN is also observed in conditions with considerably slower stimulation rates (e.g., Näätänen et al., 1978; Näätänen et al. 1981) and very small physical separations between the attended and unattended sounds (Alho et al., 1987a; Alho, Paavilainen, Reinikainen, & Näätänen, 1986; Alho, Töttölä, Reinikainen, Sams, & Näätänen, 1987b). The PN therefore appears to be a general index of auditory stimulus selection in a large variety of selective-listening conditions (see also Alho, 1992).

The existence of two selective-attention mechanisms, one causing the enhancement of the N1 and the other generating the PN, was proposed by Hansen and Hillyard (1980), who varied the magnitude of the pitch difference between the attended and unattended sounds. Their ERP attention effect, which they called the Nd, referring to the negative difference between ERPs to attended and unattended sounds, appeared to be composed of two components (see also Figure 15.11): (a) an early, centrally distributed Nd component peaking at about 100 ms from sound onset and caused, according to the authors, by an enhancement of the exogenous N1, and (b) a later Nd that was somewhat more frontally distributed than the early Nd and appeared as a slower, PN type of component.

Very Early Attention Effects

A number of studies have aimed at demonstrating that selective attention could affect auditory processing even before the sensory

input arrives at the auditory cortex. Some of these results were interpreted as suggesting effects of attention on the BAEPs, but because of failures to replicate these findings (Woldorff and Hillyard, 1991) and of several methodological problems (see Connolly, Aubry, McGillivary, & Scott, 1989; Näätänen, 1990, 1992), one must conclude that there is no convincing evidence for such effects. Attention directed to stimuli delivered to a designated ear has even been reported to enhance evoked otoacoustic emissions (EOAEs) to these stimuli (Giard et al., 1994a), suggesting effects of spatial attention on auditory processing as early as at the level of the cochlear receptors. However, despite their several attempts, Michie, LePage, Solowij, Haller, and Terry (1996) could not replicate this finding.

A very early attention effect, one preceding the N1, was also found by Woldorff, Hansen, and Hillyard (1987; see also Woldorff & Hillyard, 1991). In their selective dichotic-listening study with a very fast stimulus rate, this effect appeared at 20 ms to 50 ms after stimulus onset as a positive displacement of the ERP to attended stimuli in relation to the same stimuli when unattended. A subsequent MEG study suggested that this *P20-50 effect* is generated in the supratemporal cortex (Woldorff et al., 1993).

In contrast, in their spatial-attention study with stimuli delivered from different loudspeakers, McCallum, Curry, Cooper, Pocock, & Papakostopoulous (1983) found at the same latency range a negative displacement of the ERP to sounds from the attended direction in relation to those from the unattended direction. This very early attention effect in the auditory free-field situation might be caused by a very early onset of the PN under such conditions. This is supported by the PN onset at about 40 ms from stimulus onset observed by Teder et al. (1993b), who recorded ERPs to words (starting with /k/) occurring in attended and unattended speech passages delivered through loudspeakers located on opposite sides of the subject.

However, when concurrent attended and unattended auditory inputs consist of speech, then a very early PN-like attention effect may be observed even when the attended and unattended messages are delivered through headphones to the opposite ears, as shown by Woods, Hillyard, & Hansen (1984). They reported a PN-like attention effect starting as early as at the latency of 50 ms in ERPs to probe words "a" and "but" embedded into the attended message in relation to the ERPs to the same words occurring in the unattended message. Moreover, Tiitinen et al. (1993b) observed that the 40-Hz (gamma-band) transient oscillatory response lasting for 100 ms to 150 ms evoked by stimulus onsets in the attended ear is enhanced relative to that in the opposite ear. Thus, there might be several different kinds of ERP attention effects preceding the N1 deflection, of which at least some—especially those observed during selective attention to speech—appear to be caused by an early onset of attention-related endogenous brain activity and therefore can be identified as PNs.

Multidimensional Selection of Auditory Stimuli

In an ERP study on multidimensional stimulus selection during selective listening, Hansen and Hillyard (1983) defined their relevant sounds on two physical dimensions: The to-be-attended tones had a certain location and pitch, whereas the to-be ignored tones differed from them in location, pitch, or both (see also Alho, Sams, Paavilainen, Reinikainen, & Näätänen, 1989; Michie et al., 1993; Woods, Alho, & Algazi, 1994). The difficulty of discrimination was varied from "Easy" to "Hard" on each dimension by varying the physical separation between the at-

tended and unattended tones along this dimension. Comparison of the ERPs to the attended tones with the ERPs to the ignored tones differing from the attended ones on the "Easy" dimension showed a large Nd with an early onset, whereas the comparison of the ERPs to the to-be-attended tones satisfying both the "Easy" and the "Hard" dimensions with the ERPs to the to-be-ignored tones satisfying the "Easy" but not the "Hard" dimension revealed a low-amplitude, late-onset (at 150–200 ms) Nd, suggesting that rejection of the to-be-ignored tones on the "Hard" dimension took longer than rejection of them on the "Easy" dimension (regardless of which dimension was "Hard" and which was "Easy"). In contrast, if the to-be-ignored tone failed to satisfy the "Easy" dimension, then the processing of the "Hard" dimension was also terminated early or did not occur at all, as suggested by the lack of any Nd between the ERPs to tones satisfying the "Hard" dimension and to those not satisfying this dimension when both tones failed to satisfy the "Easy" dimension.

In quite similar two-dimensional selective-listening conditions, Woods et al. (1994) observed a difference in scalp distribution between the location- and pitch-specific Nd effects derived by subtracting the ERP to unattended tones differing from the attended tones both in pitch and location from the ERPs to unattended tones sharing either pitch or location with the attended tones. The pitch-specific Nd was more frontally distributed than was the location-specific Nd, suggesting that the pitch and location selections are carried out by different neuronal mechanisms, each of them generating a feature-specific PN. Moreover, the subtraction of the sum of these pitch- and location-specific Nd effects from the Nd obtained for the to-be-attended tones (both pitch and location relevant) suggested that a part of the Nd to the to-be-attended tones is related to conjoining the relevant stimulus features during the selection of these stimuli on the pitch and location dimensions.

The Attentional-Trace Theory

Näätänen (1982, 1990, 1992) proposed that the PN is generated by the selection of attended stimuli for further processing in a gradual matching process to which each sound is subjected during selective listening. In this matching process, each sound would be compared with an *attentional trace,* an actively maintained representation of the physical features of the attended stimuli (e.g., their pitch, location, or both; see also Alho et al., 1989). Sounds matching with the trace would be processed further, whereas the others would be rejected. Furthermore, the timing of this rejection would depend on how widely the stimulus differs from the attended stimulus on the critical dimensions; more different, and therefore more discriminable, stimuli would be rejected earlier, and thus the PN generated by them would terminate earlier.

Importantly, the attentional-trace model implies that the Nd wave (Hansen & Hillyard, 1980)—obtained by subtracting the ERP to unattended stimuli from the ERP to attended stimuli (Figure 15.11)—does not reveal the total PN elicited by the selection of the attended stimuli. This is because, as already mentioned, the unattended stimuli also elicit some PN that is larger in amplitude and longer in duration for smaller differences between the to-be-ignored and the to-be-attended stimuli, as shown by a number of studies (Alho et al., 1986, 1987a, 1987b; Hari et al., 1989; Michie et al., 1993). This is schematically illustrated in Figure 15.12.

Some results, however, suggest that the later phase of the difference wave between the ERPs to the same stimuli when attended and when unattended might be caused partly by an endogenous positive ERP component elicited by unattended stimuli rather than solely by PN that is larger to the attended than to the

unattended stimuli (Alho et al., 1987b, 1994b; Michie et al., 1993). This *rejection positivity* was proposed as possibly being related to the active suppression of unattended stimuli after they were found not to correspond to the stimulus represented by the attentional trace, that is, after the termination of the PN to these sounds (Alho et al., 1987b). However, when the effects of attention on brain activity are interpreted as being caused either by the more extensive processing of attended stimuli or by the suppressed processing of unattended stimuli, a problem arises with regard to the proper baseline condition. For example, in their control condition, Alho et al. (1994b) recorded ERPs to to-be-ignored auditory stimuli presented while their subjects concentrated on a visual task. These auditory ERPs were then used as the baseline for estimating the amount of the PN elicited in another condition by attended sounds delivered to one ear and the amount of the rejection positivity in response to unattended sounds delivered to the opposite ear. However, it is possible that the amount of the assumed rejection positivity to the unattended-ear sounds was overestimated, for subjects might have covertly attended to sounds even during the visual task, which would, presumably, have resulted in some PN to the to-be-ignored sounds even during the visual task.

The attentional trace is, according to Näätänen's (1982, 1990, 1992) theory, formed by rehearsing the sensory-memory representation of the attended stimulus and would therefore depend both on the sensory reinforcement provided by the attended sounds and on the active rehearsal of the trace. The attentional trace's dependence on sensory input was shown by results indicating that no PN is elicited by the first two to three stimuli in the very beginning of the selective-listening task (Hansen and Hillyard, 1988) or when the to-be-attended sounds are delivered with very long intervals (Alho et al., 1990).

Pitch Separation

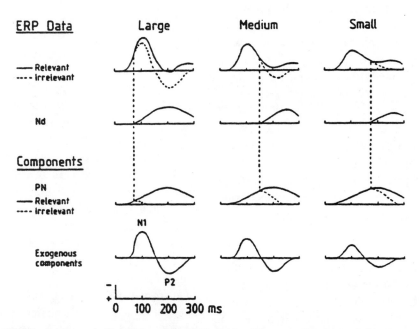

Figure 15.12   A schematic illustration of the ERP and its different components elicited in a condition in which the listener's task is to attend selectively to one of two frequently occurring tones differing in pitch, the pitch difference being either large, medium, or small.

NOTE: Top row: ERPs to the relevant (solid lines) and irrelevant (dashed lines) tones. Second row: The corresponding negative difference (Nd) waves obtained by subtracting the ERP to irrelevant, to-be-ignored tones from that to relevant, to-be-attended tones. The latency of the Nd onset increases and the Nd amplitude decreases with diminishing pitch separation. Third row: These effects on the Nd are due to the prolongation and increase of the processing negativity (PN) to irrelevant tones (dashed lines) with diminishing pitch difference, whereas the PN to relevant stimuli (solid lines) is similar in all conditions. Bottom row: Attenuation of the exogenous N1 and P2 components (identical for the relevant and irrelevant tones) with a diminishing pitch difference between the two tones, due to the increasing overlap of frequency-specific auditory-cortex neuron populations activated by them. The ERPs shown in the top row are composed of the summation of these exogenous components with the corresponding PNs shown on the third row.

SOURCE: From Alho et al. (1987b). © 1987. Reproduced with permission from Elsevier Science.

As already discussed, and as shown in Figure 15.11, the early attention effect commencing at the latency of the N1, or sometimes even earlier, is typically followed by a later negative component (usually peaking at 300–400 ms from stimulus onset). This later PN, having a frontally dominant scalp distribution (e.g., Alho et al., 1994a; Giard, Perrin, Pernier, & Peronnet, 1988; Hansen & Hillyard, 1980; Näätänen et al., 1992; Näätänen & Michie, 1979; Teder et al., 1993a; Woods & Clayworth, 1987), might be related either to the further processing of attended sounds after their initial selection or to the rehearsal and maintenance of the attentional trace (Näätänen, 1982, 1990, 1992).

The Cerebral Network of Selective Listening

As reviewed earlier, perhaps the strongest evidence that the N1 component is genuinely enhanced by selective attention was provided by the MEG studies indicating that the same, or at least largely overlapping, source in the auditory cortex on the superior temporal plane generates the N1 and the attention effect at the N1 latency (Kaufman & Williamson, 1987; Rif et al., 1991; Woldorff et al., 1993). However, other MEG studies (Arthur, Lewis, Medvick, & Flynn, 1991; Hari et al., 1989) showed that even slower, PN-like attention-related responses are generated in the superior temporal cortex. In accordance with the MEG results of Kaufman and Williamson (1987), Rif et al. (1991), and Woldorff et al. (1993), the SCD analyses of the scalp-potential maps suggested that the auditory cortices' contribution to the attention effects at the N1 latency range could not be separated from the N1 source by these analyses (Giard et al., 1988; Alcaini et al., 1995). These SCD analyses further suggested that the later PN component is generated in the frontal lobes.

The importance of the role of the frontal-lobe functions in attention is indicated by attentional deficits typically accompanying frontal lesions (Stuss & Benson, 1986). For example, in their selective dichotic-listening study, Knight, Hillyard, Woods, and Neville (1981; see also Woods & Knight, 1986) observed an attenuated PN, relative to that in healthy control subjects, in patients with unilateral lesions of the dorsolateral prefrontal cortex. This effect involved both the early and late phases of the PN. Moreover, the unilateral lesions attenuated the PN components over both the affected and intact hemispheres. Therefore, the lesions probably involved no PN generator directly, but rather caused the PN attenuation indirectly, presumably by affecting the prefrontal areas modulating the activity of the PN generators located elsewhere.

Even the temporal and parietal areas appear to be involved in the neural circuitry underlying the later PN component. Woods, Knight, and Scabini (1993b), recording the ERPs of patients with unilateral lesions of the parietal or temporo-parietal cortices in a selective dichotic-listening condition, found that both patient groups had attenuated amplitudes of the later portion (at latencies longer than 150 ms) of the PN compared with those of healthy controls. In contrast, these lesions did not affect the early attention effect (at 50–100 ms), although attenuated exogenous N1 components were observed in patients with temporo-parietal lesions. The unaffected early attention effect in these patients supports the view that this early effect is generated by a source separable from the exogeneous N1 generators.

Other methods of functional brain research, such as positron-emission tomography (PET) and functional magnetic resonance imaging (fMRI), both of which measure hemodynamic brain activity, may give important converging evidence for locating the brain mechanisms of auditory selective attention by means of ERP and MEG recordings. Although it should be borne in mind that the relationship between electrophysiological and hemodynamic brain responses is not yet exactly understood, the hemodynamic and electrophysiological measures of attentional brain activity may be made more comparable by using similar experimental paradigms in these studies.

In their recent PET study, Alho et al. (1999) used dichotic tone stimulation and selective-attention tasks similar to those administered in ERP studies. As in the ERP study of Alho et al. (1994b; see above), Alho et al. (1999) instructed their subjects to attend to the tone sequence delivered to a designated ear in order to discriminate slightly higher ones among these tones, whereas in the control condition they were instructed to ignore both tone sequences and to attend to visual stimuli (presented in each condition). The stimulus rate in each of the three sequences was very high: on average 6 stimuli per second in order to facilitate selective attention (Hillyard et al. 1973). It was found that selective listening increased brain activity, measured as changes in the regional cerebral blood flow (rCBF), bilaterally in the auditory cortices (see also O'Leary et al. 1996, 1997; Tzourio et al., 1997; Zatorre, Mondor, & Evans, 1999). Furthermore, this attention effect was more pronounced in the auditory cortex of the hemisphere contralateral to the ear to which the attended tones were delivered, which was interpreted as indicating the selective tuning of the auditory cortices during selective listening. In addition, selective listening enhanced the rCBF in the prefrontal cortex bilaterally and in the right parietal cortex, as also found in other PET studies (Tzourio et al., 1997; Zatorre et al., 1999). The right parietal cortex's importance in directing auditory attention is also indicated by the neglect of sounds in the left hemispace by patients with right parietal lesions (Heilman & Valenstein, 1972). Consequently, Alho et al.'s (1999) PET results are in accordance with the electrophysiological results in healthy subjects and in patients with local brain lesions, reviewed earlier, in that they show the involvement of the temporal, parietal, and prefrontal cortical areas in auditory selective attention.

ATTENTION IN THE VISUAL MODALITY

As in the auditory modality, a great diversity of processing also takes place in the visual modality in the absence of attention. Presenting a stimulus in the visual field evokes a series of neural processes in the brain that can partly be recorded by the EEG and MEG techniques and that depend on the physical characteristics of the stimulus, such as its location, color, or spatial frequency (Regan, 1989). The different features of the stimulus are registered independently and in parallel across the visual field. Attention is needed in order to select some of this information for further processing (James, 1890), but it is also assumed that attention is required for accurately "gluing" these features into unitary perceptual objects (Treisman & Gelade, 1980).

Electrophysiological measures have been used to investigate the neural substrates of the perception of various types of visual stimulation, such as visual motion (e.g., Ahlfors et al., 1999; Probst, Plendl, Paulus, Wist, & Scherg, 1993) or faces (e.g., Halgren, Raij, Marinkovic, Jousmäki, & Hari, 2000; Linkenkaer-Hansen et al., 1998). For example, there is electrophysiological evidence for category-specific face, letter-string, and number "modules" with different neural generators (Allison, McCarthy, Nobre, Puce, & Belger, 1994; Allison, Puce, Spencer, & McCarthy, 1999). One fundamental question is how attention modulates the processing in these modules and elsewhere along the visual pathway. It was shown, for example, that some of the face-specific ERP deflections are prone to top-down influences, whereas others are not (Puce, Allison, & McCarthy, 1999).

Before discussing the electrophysiological effects of attention in vision, one might ask whether there exists a visual analogue of the auditory MMN described earlier. Negative deflections in the ERPs elicited by infrequent ("deviant") stimuli relative to those elicited by frequent ("standard") stimuli have been reported in the visual modality as well (Alho et al., 1992; Berti & Schröger, 2001; Czigler & Csibra, 1990; Heslenfeld, 1998; Nordby, Brønnick, & Hugdahl, 1996; Nyman et al., 1990; Tales, Newton, Troscianko, & Butler, 1999; Woods et al., 1992). The deviance-related negative deflections obtained in these studies reveal a posterior or occipital distribution, suggesting that they are generated in visual areas. For example, Tales et al. (1999) recorded ERPs elicited by target stimuli in the center of the visual field, and by frequent standard and infrequent deviant stimuli presented outside the focus of attention, in the peripheral field. Deviant stimuli evoked a larger negative potential than did standard stimuli, and this potential was distributed over the supplementary visual areas of the occipital and posterior temporal cortex at 250 ms to 400 ms from stimulus onset. Unlike in the auditory modality, however, it is still debated whether these effects are really based on memory comparison and whether they reveal the same degree of automaticity as does the auditory MMN (cf. Kenemans & Verbaten, 2000).

The electrophysiology of selective attention in vision has been studied in different types of conditions using different techniques. An issue of central importance involves the earliest stages of visual information processing that can be influenced by attention. For example, it has been asked whether processing as early as at the level of striate cortex may be prone to attentional effects. Another issue involves the comparison of the effects of selective attention between different criteria used in information selection. Researchers have, for example, studied whether attentional selection based on different stimulus dimensions such as spatial location, color, spatial frequency, orientation, form, or the direction of movement yields spatiotemporal ERP effects that differ from one another. Moreover, attention can be voluntarily oriented, via the subject's intention, to a particular subset of information impinging on his or her visual system, but it may also be involuntarily captured by particular features in the stimulation. Some researchers have, for example, asked whether the voluntary and reflexive (involuntary) forms of attention share the same neural locus.

In addition, attention can be focused for a longer period on a particular stimulus feature (sustained attention), but it can also be quickly shifted to different features between the successive trials (transient attention). Several studies have investigated the effects of sustained versus transient attention.

Other important issues involve the influence of the task demands on attentional effects and the nature of the selection mechanism producing measurable effects. As for the latter, the question of whether attentional selection is based more on the suppression of irrelevant information or on the facilitation of relevant information has been asked.

Furthermore, the effects of the orienting of attention were distinguished from those of attention on the processing of stimuli occurring in the focus of attention. For example, electrophysiological measures have been used to study the orienting of attention after a cue indicated the to-be-attended stimulus feature but before the next target stimulus was presented. In the next section we review some of the most important ERP studies on visual attention.

Visuo-Spatial Attention

Sustained Attention

Due mainly to the spatiotopic organization of the visual system, selection according to spatial location may be regarded as the primary form of selection in vision (e.g., Treisman & Gelade, 1980; van der Heijden, 1993). This notion is also supported by the fact that the electrophysiological effects of visuospatial attention have a shorter latency than do those for the other features such as color or form. However, these studies have not yet settled whether there is attentional modulation of subcortical visual processing in humans or whether the first electrophysiological effects of selective attention start at the cortical level. Some findings (Oakley & Eason, 1990; Eason,

Oakley, & Flowers, 1983) suggest that when subjects are instructed to attend to a specified location in a given visual field and to ignore stimuli presented in the opposite field, the amplitudes of the visually evoked responses falling within the range of 40 ms to 70 ms depend on whether the location of the evoking stimulus was being attended or not. However, a further study (Mangun, Hansen & Hillyard, 1986) failed to confirm these results, and even at the level of the primary visual cortex, no reliable ERP effects of spatial attention were found. Furthermore, in Clark and Hillyard's (1996) study, the initial afferent response evoked by visual stimuli in V1 (i.e., the C1), with an onset latency of about 50 ms to 55 ms (Clark, Fan, & Hillyard, 1995), did not vary as a function of spatial attention. These authors flashed circular checkerboards in a random order to left and right locations in the visual field while subjects maintained the central fixation and attended to one visual field.

As with the electrophysiological studies of auditory attention discussed earlier in this chapter, it is important to compare the results of electrophysiological visual-attention studies with those obtained with other brain-research methods. Using a novel optical-imaging technique, Gratton (1997) confirmed the absence of attentional modulation in the striate cortex suggested by the visual ERP studies. The event-related optical signal (EROS) is based on localized changes in the optical properties—probably changes in the scattering of near-infrared photons—that accompany neural activity. Presented with frequent squares and infrequent rectangles 2° from the left and right of fixation, subjects had to attend to the left or right hemifield and press a button for infrequent rectangles on the attended side. Although the EROS was sensitive at the striate cortex (Brodmann area 17) to whether a stimulus was frequent or infrequent, its strength did not depend on whether

the stimulus was presented to the attended or unattended side.

The absence of ERP or EROS effects in the primary visual cortex, however, does not imply that V1 is not involved in visuospatial attention. This was shown by a recent combined ERP and fMRI study (Martínez et al., 1999). Again, the absence of the effect of visuospatial attention on the initial sensory processing in V1 was confirmed by the ERPs, but the fMRI data revealed increased neural activity in the striate cortex with spatial attention. The authors attempted to resolve this conflict by suggesting that the attention effect on the fMRI in the striate cortex reflects a delayed re-entrant feedback from higher visual areas back into V1 or a sustained top-down biasing of neurons during attention, which does not modulate stimulus-evoked responses, at least not to the extent that such effects could be detected with ERPs.

The first exogenous ERP component to be established firmly as being modulated by visuospatial attention is the P1 starting at about 70 ms to 90 ms from stimulus onset (e.g., Clark & Hillyard, 1996; Eason, 1981; Hillyard & Münte, 1984; Johannes, Münte, Heinze, & Mangun. 1995; Mangun & Hillyard, 1990a, 1990b; Wijers, Lange, Mulder, & Mulder, 1997; for a review, see Hillyard, Vogel, & Luck, 1998). A typical paradigm with the corresponding ERP effects is illustrated in Figure 15.13.

The SCD analyses and dipole-source modeling of ERPs, together with fMRI or PET measures, suggest that this attentional modulation of the P1 is generated in the ventrolateral and dorsal extrastriate cortex (Clark & Hillyard, 1996; Gomez, Clark, Fan, Luck, & Hillyard, 1994; Heinze et al., 1994; Johannes et al., 1995; Mangun, Hillyard, & Luck, 1993; Martínez et al., 1999; Woldorff et al., 1997). These attention effects on the dorsal extrastriate cortex (area V3 and the anterior regions of the middle occipital gyrus) start at 70 ms

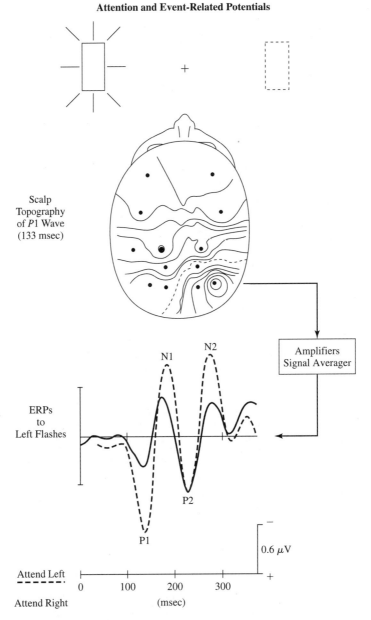

Figure 15.13   Selective-attention effects on the visual ERP in a typical spatial-attention task.
NOTE: Stimuli (illustrated on top) were bars flashed on a video screen in random order to locations 5 degrees to the left or right of fixation (+) with short, irregular ISIs. The subject was instructed to attend to the bars at one location and to press a button upon detection of an occasional, slightly shorter bar (target) at this location. In the middle, the scalp topography of the P1 is shown. In the bottom, ERPs to left flashes when attended (dot-dash lines) and ignored (attend right; solid lines) are shown.
Source: From Mangun and Hillyard (1990a).

to 75 ms poststimulus. Because these early P1 generator effects are confined to stimuli presented to the lower visual field, it seems likely that they occur in the retinotopically organized extrastriate cortex. The generators of the later, ventrolateral P1 attention effect, occurring between 100 ms and 140 ms post-stimulus, are located at areas V4v and posterior fusiform gyrus (Brodmann area 19).

Eimer (1997b) developed a slightly different visuospatial attention paradigm to determine the locus of the attention effect. Most stimuli appeared in a regular clockwise or counterclockwise order in one of the four visual quadrants, but some were separated from the expected location by one or both visual meridians. Subjects had to respond to occasional target stimuli regardless of whether they were presented in this quadrant. As indicated by the RT benefits to targets presented in the to-be-expected visual quadrant relative to targets presented in an unexpected quadrant, subjects moved their focus of attention according to the expected location of the forthcoming stimulus. The ERPs elicited by stimuli from the lower visual field in the range of 70 ms to 80 ms were of the opposite polarity (positive) to those elicited by stimuli in the upper visual field. This effect is due to the fact that the visual cortex is folded within the calcarine fissure so that stimuli from the lower and upper visual fields are projected to the oppositely oriented cortical areas within the upper and lower banks of the calcarine fissure. Interestingly, this component, called NP80, was not affected by attention, whereas the P1 and N1 showed the typical attention effects.

The control of eye movements is of special importance in such studies. In addition to a conservative cutoff value of ± 25 μV for the horizontal electrooculogram (EOG), Eimer (1997b) included in the final analysis only those subjects in whom the averaged EOG did not exceed 2 μV in the direction of the next expected stimulus position.

Johannes et al. (1995) and Wijers et al. (1997) were able to show that manipulations of the luminance of stimuli that affect the latency and amplitude of the P1 did affect the parameters of the P1 attention effect correspondingly. This supports the hypothesis that these attention effects indeed involve the exogenous components and thus reflect enhanced sensory input from a stimulus appearing in the attended location of the visual field (Mangun & Hillyard, 1990a, 1990b). On the other hand, Clark and Hillyard (1996) found that the SCD topographies of the P1 were shifted by attention, suggesting that additional, attention-dependent neurons were also activated (Figure 15.14).

The subsequent ERP effects of spatial attention consist of enhanced negativities in the N1 and N2 ranges (Figures 15.13 and 15.14). The locus of the attention effect on these later components is less clear because their generator structures are more complicated. For example, the N1 consists of several subcomponents arising from spatially distinct generators, including sources in occipito-parietal, occipital, and frontal areas (Gomez et al., 1994; Johannes et al., 1995). However, attempts at localizing the N1 attention effect gave rise to the assumption that attention modulates different N1 generators (Clark & Hillyard, 1996). The ventral pathway connecting V1 and V2 with V3 and V4 and with the posterior and anterior areas of the inferotemporal cortex (IT) is engaged with the identification and discrimination of visual objects, whereas the dorsal pathway connecting V1 and V2 with the posterior parietal cortex is concerned with the spatial aspects of object perception (Ungerleider & Mishkin, 1982). Several authors suggest that the P1 attention effect is caused mainly by a modulation of the sensory flow in the ventral visual processing stream, whereas the N1 attention effect primarily reflects attentional control over the dorsal projection to the

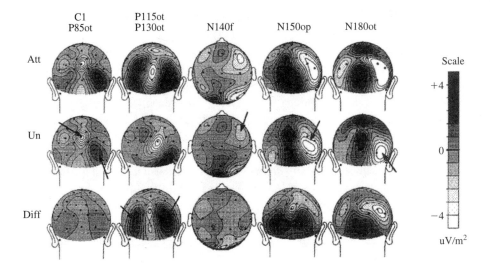

Figure 15.14 SCD maps of visual-evoked potential maps in different latency ranges: C1 (60–85 ms), P1, P115ot (100–120 ms), N140f (140–170 ms), N180ot (170–190 ms).
NOTE: Maps are collapsed across ERPs to left- and right-field stimuli and averaged such that the right side of each head icon represents the scalp sites contralateral to the visual field and the left side the ipsilateral sites. Arrows indicate foci associated with the labeled components. Columns represent distributions of components in the Attend (At) and Unattend (Un) conditions and of the Difference waves (Diff). Topographical SCD maps show where the current flows in and out of the scalp, helping one in estimating the number of generators and their orientation.
Source: From Clarke and Hillyard (1996).

parietal lobe (Harter & Aine, 1984; Mangun, 1995).

Transient Attention

In most visuospatial-attention studies, attention had to be focused on one location for a longer period while stimuli were randomly presented at this location and at to-be-ignored locations. However, visuospatial attention may often be characterized as an active, dynamic process in which attention is transiently shifted between different locations (Posner, 1980). Therefore, electrophysiological research of spatial attention has recently started to investigate also transient attention in which different locations are cued on a trial-by-trial basis (Anllo-Vento, 1995; Eimer, 1993, 1994a, 1994b, 1995, 1996a, 1997b, 1999; Harter, Miller, Price, LaLonde, &

Keyes, 1989; Mangun & Hillyard, 1991). In these studies, the to-be-attended location was indicated by a symbolic cue, an arrow pointing to the right or left, or by a direct cue (a lateralized stimulus occurring at the to-be-attended location). Mangun and Hillyard (1991) recorded ERPs to lateralized flashes delivered to visual-field locations correctly or falsely precued by a central arrow. In simple-RT and choice-RT tasks, valid stimuli caused amplitude enhancement of the early, sensory-evoked P1 (90–130 ms poststimulus); the subsequent N1 (150–200 ms) was enhanced for validly cued stimuli in the choice-RT task condition only. Because these ERP effects were accompanied by RT advantages to validly cued stimuli, Mangun and Hillyard proposed that they reflected information that underlay perceptual judgments. However, Eimer

(1993) showed that such RT cuing effects can be obtained even without the corresponding P1 and N1 modulations, suggesting that these RT attention effects may also reflect later processing stages.

The occurrence of the P1 and N1 effects also depends on the type of trial-by-trial cuing paradigm that is used. Eimer (1994b) varied the response relevance of stimuli at uncued locations. A central arrow cue pointing to the left or right was presented for 200 ms; 700 ms after the offset of the cue, the stimulus (the letter "W" or "M"), lateralized by ±6°, was presented for 100 ms. Subjects had to make a choice reaction to this stimulus (stimulus-response mapping being counterbalanced). In 75% of the trials the stimulus was presented at the cued location, and in 25% of the trials the stimulus was presented contralaterally to the cued location. In one condition, subjects had to respond to all stimuli regardless of whether they occurred at a cued location. Although there were RT benefits in validly cued trials, no statistically significant P1 and N1 effects occurred. In the other condition, subjects had to respond to validly cued stimuli only, and then the P1 and N1 amplitudes were enhanced by cue validity (apparently because attention could be focused on one location, with the other location being completely task-irrelevant).

In the trial-by-trial cuing paradigms, Eimer (1993, 1994a, 1994b, 1995, 1996a, 1997b) reported additional ERP effects of visuospatial attention consisting of a negative enhancement of the ERPs elicited by the stimuli at the attended location relative to those elicited by the stimuli at the unattended location, with a parietally distributed first peak at around 160 ms poststimulus (Nd1) and a second, more broadly distributed peak between 200 ms and 400 ms (Nd2). These effects were obtained both in the classical Posner-type cuing tasks, in which invalidly cued stimuli may also require a response, and in modified cuing

paradigms, in which only validly cued stimuli are to be responded, the amplitudes being larger in the latter case. These effects can also be obtained with lateralized cues and even in conditions in which the cue is not spatially informative with respect to the location of the forthcoming target stimulus (Eimer, 1994a).

Interestingly, very similar Nd1 and Nd2 effects were obtained in the auditory modality when a visual arrow cue indicated the location of a forthcoming auditory target (e.g., Schröger, 1993; Schröger & Eimer, 1993, 1997; cf. Figure 15.15). Like the visual Nd effects, the auditory Nd effects can also be obtained with lateralized auditory cues even when they are not informative with respect to the location of the forthcoming target (Schröger & Eimer, 1996). Eimer (1998) suggested that the visual and auditory Nd1 reflect spatially selective activity within the posterior parietal cortex and, further, that they may reveal the presence of an attentional gradient centered around the cued location (cf. LaBerge, 1995). In turn, the Nd2 can be assumed, according to Eimer, to reflect an attentional influence on the later stages of processing, such as the differential processing of attended and unattended information within inferotemporal cortex or response selection occurring after stimulus identification.

Costs and Benefits in Attentional Effects

As with the attentional effects on the auditory ERPs (discussed earlier), one might ask whether in the visuospatial-attention studies, the electrophysiological effects revealed by the attend-minus-unattend ERP difference waves are due to impoverished processing of stimuli at unattended locations or to facilitated processing of stimuli at attended locations. Several studies have aimed at clarifying this issue. In their sustained-attention experiment, Mangun and Buck (1998) presented flash stimuli equiprobably to the left and right visual hemifields. In three blocked,

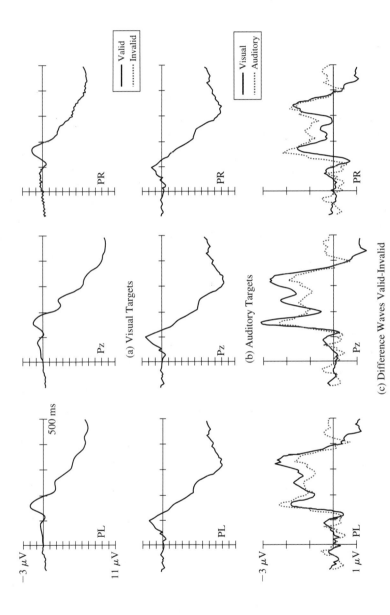

Valid
Invalid

Visual
Auditory

500 ms

−3 µV

11 µV

−3 µV

1 µV

PL   Pz   PR

(a) Visual Targets

PL   Pz   PR

(b) Auditory Targets

PL   Pz   PR

(c) Difference Waves Valid-Invalid

Figure 15.15 ERPs at left-parietal (PL), midline-parietal (Pz), and right-parietal (PR) electrode sites elicited by stimuli occurring at invalidly and validly cued locations and the corresponding valid-minus-invalid difference waves obtained in separate trial-by-trial visual and auditory experiments.

NOTE: Although the ERPs per se are highly modality-specific, the ERP effects of spatial cuing that can be seen in the difference waves are strikingly similar, suggesting the same neural substrate for the visual and the auditory Nd1 and Nd2.

SOURCE: Eimer (1998, Fig. 5, p. 274). © 1998, Psychology Press Limited. Reprinted by permission.

632

covert-attention conditions, subjects were instructed to divide their attention equally between the left and right hemifield locations, to bias their attention toward the left location, or to bias it toward the right location. The RT was significantly faster for targets occurring where more attention was allocated (benefits) and slower to targets occurring where less attention was allocated (costs), relative to the divided-attention condition. The P1 (100–140 ms) over the lateral occipital scalp regions showed attentional benefits, whereas there was no amplitude modulation of the occipital N1 (125–180 ms) with attention. Between 200 ms and 500 ms in latency, a later positive deflection showed both attentional costs and benefits. The authors proposed that the RT benefits of spatial attention might arise as the result of modulations of visual information processing in the extrastriate visual cortex. Hence, these results suggest that sustained attention may cause both the suppression and the facilitation of visual processing.

This issue was also investigated in transient-attention conditions. Luck et al. (1994) presented an arrow cue followed by a luminance-increment target that in turn was followed by a pattern mask. The arrow cue indicated the location of the target-mask complex correctly (valid trials) in most of the trials but incorrectly (invalid trials) in some of the trials. Further, in some trials all possible target locations were cued, and the target-mask complex occurred equiprobably at each of those locations (neutral trials). The P1 was reduced in invalid trials relative to neutral and valid trials, whereas the N1 was enhanced in valid trials relative to neutral and invalid trials. This dissociation of suppression and enhancement suggests that they arise from independent attentional mechanisms.

In another transient-attention experiment, Eimer (1996a) used single arrow cues that validly or invalidly indicated the location of forthcoming target stimuli as well as double arrows that were spatially uninformative, neutral cues. There was no P1 attention effect but rather a small N1 attention effect that was dominant over the hemisphere ipsilateral to the attended location and consisted of increased N1 amplitudes in valid trials as compared with neutral and invalid trials (i.e., of benefits in the processing of stimuli at attended locations). Eimer also investigated costs and benefits in the subsequent Nd effects and found that the Nd1 effect consisted mainly of costs in invalid trials relative to neutral and valid trials and that the Nd2 consisted of both costs and benefits (with costs being larger than benefits), suggesting that different mechanisms are involved in attentional selection.

Covert Orienting

Most visuospatial-attention studies have investigated the effects of attention that was already oriented in space rather than the process of orienting attention itself. Only some ERP studies on attentional effects in the cue-target interval have been interested in the orienting of attention per se (Harter et al., 1989; Hopf & Mangun, 2000; Nobre, Sebestyen, & Miniussi, 2000; Yamaguchi, Tsuchiya, & Kobayashi, 1994, 1995, 1998). In one of these studies, Harter et al.'s (1989) arrow cues indicated to their subjects (children of 6–9 years) the location at which targets had to be detected. Right-cue versus left-cue ERP comparisons revealed a negative deflection over the hemisphere contralateral to the attention-directing cue between 200 ms and 400 ms relative to cue onset, termed the *early directing-attention negativity* (EDAN). A second effect, one between 500 ms and 700 ms after cue onset, consisted of a positivity over the hemisphere contralateral to the attention-directing cue (the late directing-attention positivity, or LDAP).

Yamaguchi et al. (1994) used arrow cues that predicted the location of the target after a variable cue-target interval with a validity of 80%, the remaining 20% being invalidly cued trials. They found enhanced negativities in the range of 240 ms to 380 ms relative to cue onset over the lateral posterior leads contralateral to the attention-directing cue. In addition, there were also later effects (380–440 ms) that again consisted of enhanced negative deflections contralateral to the direction of the attentional shift.

Hopf and Mangun (2000), in turn, presented central arrow cues instructing their subjects to attend covertly to either a left-field or right-field location in order to compare two simultaneously presented target stimuli with one another. On half of the trials targets were presented to the cued location, whereas in the other half they occurred at the opposite visual-field location. An initial component over the occipito-parietal electrode sites, occurring at 200–400 ms after cue onset and resembling EDAN, was consistent with an early involvement of the posterior-parietal cortex in directing attention. A second negative component over the lateral-prefrontal cortex in the range of 300 ms to 500 ms was consistent with the presumed function of prefrontal cortex in the voluntary control and maintenance of attention. A subsequent late positive deflection in the range of 400 ms to 850 ms, narrowly focused over the occipito-temporal electrode sites, was most plausibly related to the activation of parts of the ventral extrastriate cortex. The authors suggested that voluntarily orienting visual attention in space leads to top-down modulations in the cortical excitability of ventral extrastriate regions, initiated by posterior-parietal cortical structures and mediated by lateral-prefrontal cortical structures.

Nobre et al. (2000) used foveal symbolic cues with physical appearance that could be decoupled from the cuing properties (unlike the studies employing arrow cues). Again, the earliest effects, starting at 160 ms after cue onset, consisted of enhanced negative potentials over the posterior scalp contralateral to the cued location. Later effects occurred over the right anterior scalp sites, where activity associated with shifts of attention to the right visual field elicited enlarged positive potentials. This posterior-anterior progression of the ERP effects suggests contributions from several brain areas and processes in directing spatial attention.

Overt Orienting

The electrophysiology of visuospatial attention has not been engaged only with the so-called covert orienting (Posner, 1978) occurring without eye movements. There exists a close coupling between the focusing of attention and the saccadic eye movements (e.g., Chelazzi et al., 1995; Deubel & Schneider, 1996). Wauschkuhn et al. (1998) investigated the relation between shifting visual attention and saccade preparation. Their subjects had to make saccades to either a saliently colored or a gray circle, simultaneously presented in the opposite visual hemifields. In one condition a saccade had to be made to the location of the relevant circle, whereas in another condition it had to be made to a predefined location depending on the color of the circle but not on its location. ERP measurements were targeted on the lateralized activity contralateral to either the side of the relevant stimulus or the direction of the saccade. Three components of lateralization were found: (a) activity contralateral to the relevant stimulus regardless of the saccade direction, peaking at 250 ms after stimulus onset and being largest above the lateral parietal sites; (b) activity contralateral to the relevant stimulus if the stimulus was also the target of the saccade, largest in amplitude at 330 ms to 480 ms after stimulus onset, widespread over the scalp but with a focus again above the lateral parietal sites; and (c) activity contralateral to the saccade direction, beginning at about 100 ms before the saccade, largest above mesial parietal sites, with some task-dependent fronto-central contribution. The authors interpreted the first component as reflecting the shifting of attention to the relevant stimulus, the second component as reflecting the enhancement of the attentional shift if the relevant stimulus was also the saccade target, and the third component as reflecting the triggering signal for the saccade execution.

Recently, Verleger, Vollmer, Waushkuhn, van der Lubbe, and Wascher (2000) studied event-related lateralizations following an arrow that in turn was followed by a stimulus to which subjects had to perform a manual response or a saccade. Due to the distribution of the lateralizations and to their similar amplitudes in both conditions, the authors suggested that the event-related lateralizations reflect the activity of the lateral premotor cortex encoding the spatial properties of arrows for action.

The Time Course of Attentional Facilitation

The repetitive flickering of a visual stimulus at a rate of 8 Hz to 30 Hz evokes the steady-state visual evoked potential (SSVEP; cf. Morgan, Hansen, & Hillyard, 1996). This oscillatory response has the same fundamental frequency as the driving stimulus and has a focal origin in the contralateral cortex (Müller et al., 1998a). It has been used to investigate the temporal dynamics of attentional switching. Müller, Teder-Sälejärvi, and Hillyard's (1998b) subjects were presented with flickering LED displays in the left and right visual fields with different flicker frequencies for the left and right sides (Figure 15.16). At 1.3 s after flicker onset, a central cue indicated the to-be-attended side on which the subject was to report unpredictable color changes. The variations of the SSVEP amplitude over time revealed enhanced neural activity in the visual cortex during the latency range of 600 ms to 800 ms after the attention-directing cue. The combined recording of the SSVEP and

the transient ERP revealed significant correlations between the N1, N2, and the SSVEP attention effects but not between the P1, P3, and the SSVEP attention effects, suggesting that the SSVEP and the ERP reflect partially overlapping attentional mechanisms that facilitate the discriminative processing of stimuli at attended locations (Müller & Hillyard, 2000).

Eimer (2000) studied differences in the time course of attentional orienting triggered by salient peripheral events (exogenous orienting, involuntary attention switch) and by central symbolic precues (endogenous orienting, voluntary attention switch). He recorded ERPs in response to letter stimuli following spatially informative central symbolic stimuli that served as a cue for a voluntary attention switch or to peripheral direct precues that caused an involuntary attention switch after a cue-target interval of either 200 ms or 700 ms. Stimuli at cued (attended) locations elicited an enhanced negativity relative to stimuli at uncued locations. With short intervals, these effects started at around 150 ms from stimulus onset for the peripheral cues but were delayed by about 100 ms for the central cues. This latency difference is assumed to reflect fast exogenous orienting elicited by peripheral, but not by central, cues. Beyond 200 ms poststimulus, attentional negativities were larger with long intervals than with short ones for both cue types, which was probably related to the gradual buildup of the endogenous orienting triggered by spatially predictive events.

Voluntary versus Reflexive Orienting

Eimer's (2000) finding that the ERP effects of voluntary, endogenous attentional orienting (directed via symbolic cues) and those of involuntary, exogenous attentional orienting (triggered via lateralized direct cues) were very similar suggested that similar processes may underlie voluntary and reflexive

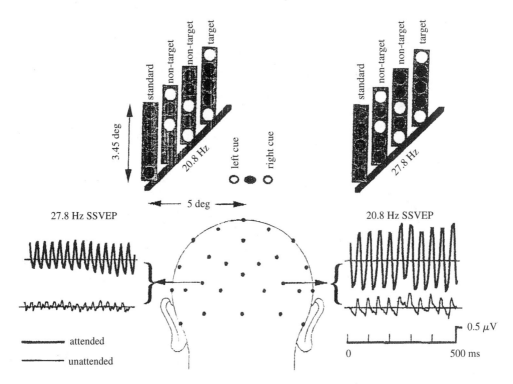

Figure 15.16 Schematic diagram of stimulus array and steady-state visual evoked potentials (SSVEP) from one subject shown for the attended (bold line) and unattended (thin line) conditions recorded from the contralateral occipito-temporal sites TO2 and TO1.
NOTE: The flicker rates were 20.8 Hz for the left stimulus array and 27.8 Hz for the right one. The 4 possible color configurations are shown for each row, with all 5 LEDs being red in the standard configuration. Target and non-target color changes (two LEDs changed to green) occurred in a random order on both sides with stimulus-onset asynchrony of 400–700 ms. The oval in the middle represents the fixation point. Attention increased the amplitude of the SSVEPs showing the frequency of the driving stimulus 600–800 ms after the attention-directing cue.
SOURCE: From Müller et al. (1998b), Nature Neuroscience. © 1998, Nature Publishing Group.

orienting. This hypothesis was tested by Hopfinger and Mangun (1998), whose targets were preceded by a flash (cue) that was un-informative with regard to the target location and thus did not cause voluntary spatial ori-enting. Targets at both the cued and uncued lo-cations elicited the P1, but it had an enhanced amplitude for cued locations, though with a scalp distribution similar to that of the P1 for uncued locations, suggesting that involun-tary orienting causes attentional modulations of the P1 that are similar to those caused by voluntary orienting.

Attentional Selection According to Other Stimulus Attributes

Feature Processing

As already mentioned, spatial attention does not enhance exogenous components in all cir-cumstances but may rather result in the emer-gence of a slow, PN type of negativity (e.g., Harter, Aine, & Schroeder, 1982; Hillyard & Münte, 1984; Wijers, Lamain, Slopsema, Mulder, & Mulder, 1989). This appears to be the case when the spatial separation between the loci of origin of relevant and irrelevant stimuli is not large (Hillyard & Münte, 1984). ERP studies of visual selective attention based on differences between relevant and irrelevant stimuli other than those in the spatial locus of origin, such as color (Wijers et al., 1989), orientation (Kenemans, Kok, & Smulders, 1993; Rugg, Milner, Lines, & Phalp, 1987), shape (Harter et al., 1982), or spatial frequency (Harter & Previc, 1978; Heslenfeld, Kenemans, Kok, & Molenaar, 1997), usually revealed attentional effects in the range of 150 ms to 300 ms, including "selection negativities" and "selection positivities" (cf. Harter & Aine, 1984, Michie et al., 1999). For example, Harter and Previc (1978) presented checkerboards of varying sizes while subjects had to respond to a particular check size only. The attention effect on the SSVEP started at around 160 ms from stimulus onset. In another study, Kenemans et al. (1993) asked their subjects to push a button in response to a given conjunction of spatial frequency and orientation (target) and to ignore the conjunctions sharing with the target only frequency (frequency-relevant), only orientation (orientation-relevant), or neither (irrelevant). The differences between ERPs to frequency-relevant and frequency-irrelevant stimuli were identified as the frontal selection positivity (Fz; 150–200 ms), the occipital selection negativity (Oz; 200 ms), and the vertex N2b (200–250 ms). For the orientation-relevant stimuli, the selection negativity and the N2b were also found, but the frontal selection positivity was elicited only when the spatial frequency was relevant as well. There was no support for the hypothesis that the attentional modulation of ERPs reflects the differential enhancement of the activity in stimulus-specific pathways.

Interestingly, in a recent study by Anllo-Vento, Luck, and Hillyard (1998), an ERP effect of color attention consisting of an enhanced positivity started as early as 100 ms from stimulus onset and peaked at 130 ms

(PD130). They presented randomized sequences of checkerboards consisting of isoluminant red or blue checks superimposed on a gray background. Subjects were required to attend to the red or blue checks in separate blocks of trials and to press a button each time they detected a dimmer stimulus of the attended color. The C1, with an onset latency of 50 ms, was sensitive to stimulus color but was unaffected by the attentional manipulation. The inverse dipole modeling of the PD130 effect suggested a source in the region of the dorsal extrastriate area 18 (Figure 15.17). The authors could not settle whether this PD130 color-attention effect reflects the same selection processes as does the visuospatial attention P1 effect. The subsequent selection negativity with an onset at 160 ms had a source in inferior occipito-temporal cortex (Brodmann area 19), consistent with the results of a previous study (Buchner, Weyen, Frackowiak, Romaya, & Zeki, 1994) suggesting effects of color attention on V4.

Hierarchical Processing

Several studies investigated the timing of the sequential, parallel, and contingent stages of visual processing. For example, Anllo-Vento and Hillyard's (1996) results supported the early-selection theories of attention that stipulate attentional control over the initial processing of stimulus features (gain theories; Näätänen, 1986). The authors presented pairs of adjacent colored squares that were sequentially flashed to produce an illusory perception of movement. Subjects' tasks consisted of attending selectively to stimuli in one visual field and detecting slower moving targets that contained the critical value of the attended feature, be it color or movement direction.

As expected, attention to location was reflected by the modulation of the early P1 and N1, whereas the selection of the relevant stimulus feature was associated with a later

Standard Stimuli Color Attention Effect

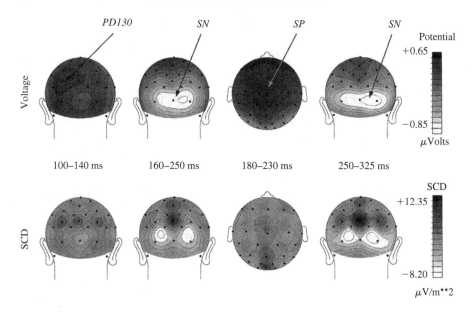

Figure 15.17   Topographical voltage and SCD maps for different color-attention effects.
NOTE: Effects of selection according to color start at around 100 ms after stimulus onset.
SOURCE: From Anllo-Vento et al. (1998).

selection or processing negativity. The ERP indexes of feature selection, elicited only by stimuli at the attended location, had distinctive scalp distributions for features mediated by ventral (color) and dorsal (motion) cortical areas. The ERP indexes of target selection were also contingent on the prior selection of location but initially did not depend on the selection of the relevant feature.

Smid, Jakob, and Heinze (1999) investigated attention to one conjunction of color, global shape, and local shape while the other conjunctions of these attributes had to be ignored. Attending to color and shape produced a frontal selection positivity (FSP), a central negativity (N2b), and a posterior selection negativity. These results suggested that the processes underlying the selection negativity and the N2b perform independent within-dimension selections, whereas the process underlying the FSP carries out hierarchical between-dimension selections. At poste-

rior leads, the manipulation of discriminability changed the ERPs to the relevant stimuli but not those to the irrelevant stimuli, suggesting that the selection negativity does not involve the selection process itself but rather a cognitive process initiated after the selection is finished.

Visual Search

Electrophysiological research of visual attention has also involved visual search tasks. For example, Luck and Hillyard (1994) presented stimulus arrays containing eight identical items (homogeneous arrays) or seven identical items and one deviant item (pop-out arrays). In different experiments, different classes of stimulus arrays were designated as targets, and the remaining stimulus arrays were designated as nontargets. Target pop-outs elicited enlarged anterior P2, posterior N2, occipital P3, and parietal P3 waves. The enlarged posterior N2 contained a contralateral subcomponent (N2pc) that exhibited a focus over the occipital cortex in the SCD maps. These results are consistent with the guided-search models in which preattentive stimulus information is used to guide attention to task-relevant stimuli. The N2pc is believed to reflect an attentional filter that suppresses the processing of interfering distractors during object identification (Girelli & Luck, 1997; Luck & Hillyard, 1994). However, Eimer (1996b) showed that this component is also elicited when targets are presented together with just one nontarget item, suggesting that it may reflect the attentional selection of task-relevant stimuli in multielement displays.

Texture Segmentation

A phenomenon related to visual search is visual texture segmentation, which characterizes the ability to detect a deviation or discontinuity in an otherwise homogeneous field. In texture-segmentation tasks, large displays are presented that either consist of the same texture elements only (e.g., lines with a certain orientation) or contain a small region of different texture elements (e.g., lines with a different orientation) embedded within the larger, homogeneous region. Subjects in texture-segmentation tasks are usually asked to discriminate between these two cases, that is, between homogeneous textures and inhomogeneous textures containing a target. Under some circumstances, the detection of an embedded irregularity occurs effortlessly and preattentively; the discontinuity seems to pop out from the homogeneous background. Some studies investigated texture segmentation with electrophysiological measures. Bach and Meigen (1992), for example, found a segmentation-specific negativity in the VEP between 161 and 225 ms after stimulus onset. Saarinen, Vanni, and Hari (1998), using MEG techniques, found activity in the right occipito-temporal area during a pop-out

task that was also present (though reduced) in a passive viewing condition. Very recently, Schubö, Meinecke, and Schröger (2001) investigated the role of attention in texture segmentation by varying the task relevance of the texture stimuli. Subjects had to either discriminate homogeneous or inhomogeneous textures or perform a different primary task of varying complexity. Two components were found to be sensitive to texture segmentation, a posterior N2 and a positivity within the P3 time interval. Both components were observed also when texture segmentation was task-irrelevant. However, although the posterior N2 was not affected by the complexity of the primary task and thus showed some degree of automaticity, the P3 depended on the attentional resources left over by the primary task (cf. also Schlaghecken, Meinecke, & Schröger, 2001).

Binding

As stated earlier, attention may function not only in the selection of stimulus information but also in the integration of the processing in different brain areas involved in building a coherent percept (Treisman & Gelade, 1980). It has been assumed that the rhythmic synchronization of neural discharges in the gamma band (around 40 Hz) may provide the necessary spatial and temporal links for this binding process (e.g., Abeles, 1982). Several authors proposed that one particular type of gamma activity—the so-called induced gamma activity reflecting oscillations that are not time-locked to the stimulus—may underlie the construction of object representations that are driven by sensory input or internal, top-down processes in humans (for reviews, see Müller, Elliott, Herrmann, & Mecklinger, in press; Tallon-Baudry & Bertrand, 1999). It has, for example, been demonstrated that directing attention modulates the gamma-band power (Gruber, Müller, Keil, & Elbert, 1999).

Electrophysiology of visual attention has revealed a diversity of effects of attentional selection located at different levels in terms of the time scale, of the brain regions involved, and of the underlying mechanisms. The research reviewed in this chapter suggests that there is no uniform causal mechanism of visual-attentional selection (cf. Allport, 1993) but rather a complex network of different processes, depending on the type of stimulation, the task demands, and the state of the subject.

REFERENCES

Abeles, M. (1982). *Local cortical circuits.* Berlin: Springer.

Ahlfors, S. P., Simpson, G. V., Dale, A. M., Belliveau, J. W., Liu, A. K., Korvenoja, A., Virtanen, J., Huotilainen, M., Tootell, R. B., Aronen, H. J., & Ilmoniemi, R. J. (1999). Spatiotemporal activity of a cortical network for processing visual motion revealed by MEG and fMRI. *Journal of Neurophysiology, 82,* 2545–55.

Alain, C., Richer, F., Achim, A., & Saint-Hilaire, J. M. (1989). Human intracerebral potentials associated with target, novel and omitted auditory stimuli. *Brain Topography, 1,* 237–245.

Alain, C., Woods, D. L., & Knight, R. T. (1998). A distributed cortical network for auditory sensory memory in human. *Brain Research, 812,* 23–37.

Alcaini, M., Giard, M.-H., & Perrin, F. (1995). Selective auditory attention modulates effects in tonotopically organized cortical areas: A topographic ERP study. *Human Brain Mapping, 2,* 159–169.

Alcaini, M., Giard, M.-H., Thevenet, M., & Pernier, J. (1994). Two separate frontal components in the N1 wave of the human auditory evoked response. *Psychophysiology, 31,* 611–615.

Alho, K. (1992). Selective attention in auditory processing as reflected by event-related brain potentials. *Psychophysiology, 29,* 247–263.

Alho K. (1995). Cerebral generators of mismatch negativity (MMN) and its magnetic counterpart (MMNm) elicited by sound changes. *Ear and Hearing, 16,* 38–51.

Alho, K., Donauer, N., Paavilainen, P., Reinikainen, K., Sams, M., & Näätänen, R. (1987a). Stimulus selection during auditory spatial attention as expressed by event-related potentials. *Biological Psychology, 24,* 153–162.

Alho, K., Escera, C., Díaz, R., Yago, E., & Serra, J. M. (1997). Effects of involuntary auditory attention on visual task performance and brain activity. *Neuroreport, 8,* 3233–3237.

Alho, K., Lavikainen, J., Reinikainen, K., Sams, M., & Näätänen, R. (1990). Event-related brain potentials in selective listening to frequent and rare stimuli. *Psychophysiology, 27,* 73–86.

Alho, K., Medvedev, S. V., Pakhomov, S. V., Roudas, M. S., Zeffiro, T., Tervaniemi, M., Reinikainen, K., & Näätänen, R. (1999). Selective tuning of the left and right auditory cortices during spatially directed attention. *Cognitive Brain Research, 7,* 335–342.

Alho, K., Paavilainen, P., Reinikainen, K., & Näätänen, R. (1986). Small pitch separation and the selective-attention effect on the ERP. *Psychophysiology, 23,* 189–197.

Alho, K., Sams, M., Paavilainen, P., Reinikainen, K., & Näätänen, R. (1989). Event-related brain potentials reflecting processing of relevant and irrelevant stimuli during selective listening. *Psychophysiology, 26,* 514–528.

Alho, K., Teder, W., Lavikainen, J., & Näätänen, R. (1994a). Strongly focused attention and auditory event-related potentials. *Biological Psychology, 38,* 73–90.

Alho, K., Töttölä, K., Reinikainen, K., Sams, M., & Näätänen, R. (1987b). Brain mechanisms of selective listening reflected by event-related potentials. *Electroencephalography and Clinical Neurophysiology, 68,* 458–470.

Alho, K., Winkler, I., Escera, C., Huotilainen, M., Virtanen, J., Jääskeläinen, I. P., Pekkonen, E., & Ilmoniemi, R. J. (1998). Processing of novel sounds and frequency changes in the human auditory cortex: Magnetoencephalographic recordings. *Psychophysiology, 35,* 211–224.

Alho, K., Woods, D. L., & Algazi, A. (1994b). Processing of auditory stimuli during auditory and visual attention as revealed by event-related potentials. *Psychophysiology, 31,* 469–479.

Alho, K., Woods, D. L., Algazi, A., Knight, R. T., & Näätänen, R. (1994c). Lesions of frontal cortex diminish the auditory mismatch negativity. *Electroencephalography and Clinical Neurophysiology, 91,* 353–362.

Alho, K., Woods, D. L., Algazi, A., & Näätänen, R. (1992). Intermodal selective attention: II. Effects of attentional load on processing of auditory and visual stimuli in central space. *Electroencephalography and clinical Neurophysiology, 82,* 356–368.

Allison, T., McCarthy, G., Nobre, A., Puce, A., & Belger, A. (1994). Human extrastriate visual cortex and the perception of faces, words, numbers, and colors. *Cerebral Cortex, 4,* 544–554.

Allison, T., Puce, A., Spencer, D. D., & McCarthy, G. (1999). Electrophysiological studies of human face perception: I. Potentials generated in occipitotemporal cortex by face and non-face stimuli. *Cerebral Cortex, 9,* 415–430.

Allport, A. (1993). Attention and control: Have we been asking the wrong questions? A critical review of twenty-five years. In D. E. Meyer & S. Kornblum (Eds.), *Attention and performance: Vol. 14. Synergies in experimental psychology, artificial intelligence, and cognitive neuroscience* (pp. 183–218). Cambridge, MA: MIT Press.

Amenedo, E., & Escera, C. (2000). The accuracy of sound duration representation in the human brain determines the accuracy of behavioural perception. *European Journal of Neuroscience, 12,* 2570–2574.

Anllo-Vento, L. (1995). Shifting attention in visual space: The effects of peripheral cueing on brain cortical potentials. *International Journal of Neuroscience, 80,* 353–70.

Anllo-Vento, L., & Hillyard, S. A. (1996). Selective attention to the color and direction of moving stimuli: Electrophysiological correlates of hierarchical feature selection. *Perception and Psychophysics, 58,* 191–206.

Anllo-Vento L., Luck S. J., & Hillyard, S. A. (1998). Spatio-temporal dynamics of attention to color: Evidence from human electrophysiology. *Human Brain Mapping, 6,* 216–38.

Arthur, D. L., Lewis, P. S., Medvick, P. A., & Flynn, E. R. (1991). A neuromagnetic study of selective auditory attention. *Electroencephalography and Clinical Neurophysiology, 78,* 348–360.

Bach, M., & Meigen, T. (1992). Electrophysiological correlates of texture segregation in the human visual evoked potential, *Vision Research, 32,* 417–424.

Baudena, P., Halgren, E., Heit, G., & Clarke, J. M. (1995). Intracerebral potentials to rare target and distractor auditory and visual stimuli: III. Frontal cortex. *Electroencephalography and Clinical Neurophysiology, 94,* 251–264.

Berti, S., & Schröger, E. (2001). A comparison of auditory and visual distraction effects: Behavioral and event-related indices. *Cognitive Brain Research, 11,* 265–273.

Bertrand, O., Perrin, F., Echallier, J., & Pernier, J. (1988). Topography and model analysis of auditory evoked potentials: Tonotopic aspects. In G. Pfurtscheller & F. H. Lopes da Silva (Eds.), *Functional brain imaging* (pp. 75–80). Toronto, Ontario: Huber.

Broadbent, D. E. (1958). *Perception and communication.* New York: Pergamon.

Broadbent, D. E. (1970). Stimulus set and response set: Two kinds of selective attention. In D. I. Mostofsky (Ed.), *Attention: Contemporary theory and analysis* (pp. 51–60). New York: Appleton-Century-Crofts.

Broadbent, D. E. (1971). *Decision and stress.* New York: Academic Press.

Buchner, H., Weyen, U., Frackowiak, R. S., Romaya, J., & Zeki, S. (1994). The timing of visual evoked potential activity in human area V4. *Proceedings of the Royal Society, London B. Biological Sciences, 257,* 99–104.

Butler, R. A. (1968). Effect of changes in stimulus frequency and intensity on habituation of the human vertex potential. *Journal of the Acoustical Society of America, 44,* 945–950.

Celesia, G. G. (1976). Organization of auditory cortical areas in man. *Brain, 99,* 403–417.

Celesia, G. G., & Puletti, F. (1971). Auditory input to the human cortex during states of drowsiness and surgical anaesthesia. *Electroencephalography and Clinical Neurophysiology, 31,* 603–609.

Chelazzi, L., Biscaldi, M., Corbetta, M., Peru, A., Tassinari, G., & Berlucchi G. (1995). Oculomotor activity and visual spatial attention. *Behavioral Brain Research, 71,* 81–88.

Cherry, E. C. (1953). Some experiments on the recognition of speech with one and with two ears. *Journal of Acoustical Society of America, 25,* 975–979.

Clark, V. P., Fan, S., & Hillyard, S. A. (1995). Identification of early visual evoked potential generators by retinotopic and topographic analyses. *Human Brain Mapping, 2,* 170–187.

Clark, V. P., & Hillyard, S. A. (1996). Spatial selective attention affects early extrastriate but not striate components of the visual evoked potential. *Journal of Cognitive Neuroscience, 8,* 387–402.

Connolly, J. F., Aubry, K., McGillivary, N., & Scott, D. W. (1989). Human brainstem auditory evoked potentials fail to provide evidence of efferent modulation of auditory input during attentional tasks. *Psychophysiology, 26,* 292–303.

Czigler, I., & Csibra, G. (1990). Event-related potentials in a visual discrimination task: negative waves related to detection and attention. *Psychophysiology, 27,* 669–676.

Deouell, L., Bentin, S., & Giard, M.-H. (1998). Mismatch negativity in dichotic listening: evidence for interhemispheric differences and multiple generators. *Psychophysiology, 35,* 355–365.

Deubel, H., & Schneider, W. X. (1996). Saccade target selection and object recognition: Evidence for a common attentional mechanism. *Vision Research, 36,* 1827–1837.

Deutsch, J. A., & Deutsch, D. (1963). Attention: Some theoretical considerations. *Psychological Review, 70,* 80–90.

Eason, R. G. (1981). Visual evoked potential correlates of early neural filtering during selective attention. *Bulletin of the Psychonomic Societey, 18,* 203–206.

Eason, R. G., Oakley, M., & Flowers, L. (1983). Central and neural influences on the human retina during selective attention. *Physiological Psychology, 11,* 18–28.

Eimer, M. (1993). Spatial cueing, sensory gating and selective response preparation: An ERP study on visuo-spatial orienting. *Electroencephalography and Clinical Neurophysiology, 88,* 408–420.

Eimer, M. (1994a). An ERP study on visual-spatial priming with peripheral onsets. *Psychophysiology, 31,* 154–163.

Eimer, M. (1994b). "Sensory gating" as a mechanism for visuo-spatial orienting: Electrophysiological evidence from trial-by-trial cueing experiments. *Perception & Psychophysics, 55,* 667–675.

Eimer, M. (1995). ERP correlates of transient attention shifts to color and location. *Biological Psychology, 41,* 167–182.

Eimer, M. (1996a). ERP modulations indicate the selective processing of visual stimuli as a result of transient and sustained spatial attention. *Psychophysiology, 33,* 13–21.

Eimer, M. (1996b). The N2pc component as an indicator of attentional selectivity. *Electroencephalograpy and Clinical Neurophysiology, 99,* 225–234.

Eimer, M. (1997a). An event-related potential (ERP) study of transient and sustained visual attention to color and form. *Biological Psychology, 44,* 143–160.

Eimer, M. (1997b). Attentional selection and attentional gradients: An alternative method for studying transient visual-spatial attention. *Psychophysiology, 34,* 365–376.

Eimer, M. (1998). Mechanisms of visual-spatial attention: Evidence from event-related brain potential studies. *Visual Cognition, 5,* 257–286.

Eimer, M. (1999). Attending to quadrants and ring-shaped regions: ERP effects of visual attention in different spatial selection tasks. *Psychophysiology, 36,* 491–503.

Eimer, M. (2000). The time course of spatial orienting elicited by central and peripheral cues: evidence from event-related brain potentials. *Biological Psychology, 53,* 253–258.

Escera, C., Alho, K., Winkler, I., & Näätänen, R. (1998). Neural mechanisms of involuntary attention switching to novelty and change in the acoustic environment. *Journal of Cognitive Neuroscience, 10,* 590–604.

Fischer, C., Morlet, D., Bouchet, P., Luauté, J., Jourdan, C., & Salord, G. (1999). Mismatch negativity (MMN) and late auditory evoked potentials in comatose patients. *Clinical Neurophysiology, 110,* 1601–1610.

Fitzgerald, P. G., & Picton, T. W. (1983). Event-related potentials recorded during the discrimination of improbable stimuli. *Biological Psychology, 17,* 241–276.

Ford, J. M., Roth, W. T., & Kopell, B. S. (1976). Auditory evoked potentials to unpredictable shifts in pitch. *Psychophysiology, 13,* 32–39.

Friedman, D., & Simpson, G. (1994). ERP amplitude and scalp distribution to target and novel events: effects of temporal order in young, middle-aged and other adults. *Cognitive Brain Research, 2,* 49–63.

Friedman, D., Simpson, G., & Hamberger, M. (1993). Age-related changes in scalp topography to novel and target stimuli. *Psychophysiology, 30,* 383–396.

Fuster, J. (1989). *The perfrontal cortex: Anatomy, physiology, and neuropsychology of the frontal lobe.* New York: Raven.

Gaillard, A. W. K., & Näätänen, R. Slow-potential changes and choice reaction time as a function of interstimulus interval. *Acta Psychologica, 1973, 37,* 173–186.

Giard, M.-H., Collet, L., Bouchet, P., & Pernier, J. (1994a). Auditory selective attention in the human cochlea. *Brain Research, 633,* 353–356.

Giard, M.-H., Lavikainen, J., Reinikainen, K., Perrin, F., Bertrand, O., Thévenet, M., Pernier, J., & Näätänen, R. (1995). Separate representation of stimulus frequency, intensity, and duration in auditory sensory memory. *Journal of Cognitive Neuroscience, 7,* 133–1143.

Giard, M.-H., Perrin, D., Echallier, J. F., Thevenet, M., Froment, J. C., & Pernier, J. (1994b). Dissociation of temporal and frontal components in the human auditory N1 wave: A scalp current density and dipole model analysis. *Electroencephalography and Clinical Neurophysiology, 92,* 238–252.

Giard, M.-H., Perrin, F., Pernier, J., & Bouchet, P. (1990). Brain generators implicated in processing of auditory stimulus deviance: A topographic event-related potential study. *Psychophysiology, 27,* 627–640.

Giard, M.-H., Perrin, F., Pernier, J., & Peronnet, F. (1988). Several attention-related waveforms in auditory areas: A topographic study. *Electroencephalography and Clinical Neurophysiology, 69,* 371–384.

Girelli, M., & Luck, S. J. (1997). Are the same attentional mechanisms used to detect visual search targets defined by color, orientation, and motion? *Journal of Cognitive Neuroscience, 9,* 238–253.

Gomez, C. M., Clark, V. P., Fan, S., Luck, S. J., & Hillyard, S. A. (1994). Sources of attention sensitive visual event-related potentials. *Brain Topography, 7,* 41–51.

Gratton, G. (1997). Attention and probability effects in the human occipital cortex: An optical imaging study. *Neuroreport, 8,* 1749–1753.

Greenberg, S., Marsh, J. T., Brown, W. S., & Smith, J. C. (1987). Neural temporal coding of low pitch: I. Human frequency-following responses to complex tones. *Hearing Research, 25,* 91–114.

Gruber, T., Müller, M. M., Keil, A., & Elbert, T. (1999). Selective visual-spatial attention alters induced gamma band responses in the human EEG. *Clinical Neurophysiology, 110,* 2074–2085.

Hackley, S. A. (1993). An evaluation of the automaticity of sensory processing using event-related potentials and brain-stem reflex. *Psychophysiology, 30,* 415–428.

Halgren, E., Baudena, P., Clarke, J. M., Heit, G., Liégeois, C., Chauvel, P., & Musolino, A. (1995a). Intracerebral potentials to rare target and distractor auditory and visual stimuli: I. Superior temporal plane and parietal lobe. *Electroencephalography and Clinical Neurophysiology, 94,* 191–220.

Halgren, E., Baudena, P., Clarke, J. M., Heit, G., Marinkovic, K., Devaux, B., Vignal, J. P., & Biraben, A. (1995b). Intracerebral potentials to rare target and distractor auditory and visual stimuli. II. Medial, lateral, and posterior temporal lobe. *Electroencephalography and Clinical Neurophysiology, 94,* 229–250.

Halgren, E., Raij, T., Marinkovic, K., Jousmäki, V., & Hari, R. (2000). Cognitive response profile of the human fusiform face area as determined by MEG. *Cerebal Cortex, 10,* 69–81.

Hansen, J. C., & Hillyard, S. A. (1980). Endogenous brain potentials associated with selective auditory attention. *Electroencephalography and Clinical Neurophysiology, 49,* 277–290.

Hansen, J. C., & Hillyard, S. A. (1983). Selective attention to multidimensional auditory stimuli. *Journal of Experimental Psychology: Human Perception and Performance, 9,* 1–19.

Hansen, J. C., & Hillyard, S. A. (1988). Temporal dynamics of human auditory selective attention. *Psychophysiology, 25,* 316–329.

Hari, R. (1990). The neuromagnetic method in the study of the human auditory cortex. In F. Grandori, M. Hoke & G. L. Romani (Eds.), *Auditory evoked magnetic fields and electric potentials* (pp. 222–282). Basel, Switzerland: Karger.

Hari, R., Hämäläinen, M., Ilmoniemi, R., Kaukoranta, E., Reinikainen, K., Salminen, J., Alho, K., Näätänen, R., & Sams, M. (1984). Responses of the primary auditory cortex to pitch changes in a sequence of tone pips: Neuromagnetic recordings in man. *Neuroscience Letters, 50,* 127–1132.

Hari, R., Hämäläinen, M., Kaukoranta, E., Mäkelä, J., Joutsiniemi, S.-L., & Tiihonen, J. (1989). Selective listening modifies activity of the human auditory cortex. *Experimental Brain Research, 74,* 463–470.

Hari, R., Kaila, K., Katila, T., Tuomisto, T., & Varpula, T. (1982). Interstimulus interval dependence of the auditory vertex response and its magnetic counterpart: Implications for their neural generation. *Electroencephalography and Clinical Neurophysiology, 54,* 561–569.

Hari, R., & Mäkelä, J. P. (1986). Neuromagnetic responses to frequency modulation of a continuous tone. *Acta Otolaryngologica, 432*(Suppl.), 26–32.

Hari, R., Pelizzone, M., Mäkelä, J. P., Hällström, J., Leinonen, L., & Lounasmaa, O. V. (1987). Neuromagnetic responses of the human auditory cortex to on- and offsets of noise bursts. *Audiology, 26,* 31–43.

Harter, M. R., & Aine, C. J. (1984). Brain mechanisms of visual selective attention. In R. Parasuraman & R. Davies (Eds.), *Varieties of attention* (pp. 293–321). London: Academic Press.

Harter, M. R., Aine, C. J., & Schroeder, C. (1982). Hemispheric differences in the neural processing of stimulus location and type: Effects of selective attention on visual evoked potentials. *Neuropsychologia, 20,* 421–436.

Harter, M. R., Millter, S. L., Price, N. J., LaLonde, M. E., & Keyes, A. L. (1989). Neural processes involved in directing attention. *Journal of Cognitive Neuroscience, 1,* 223–237.

Harter, M. R., & Previc, F. H. (1978). Size-specific information channels and selective attention: Visual evoked potential and behavioral measures. *Electroencephalography and Clinical Neurophysiology, 45,* 628–640.

Heilman, K. M., & Valenstein, E. (1972). Auditory neglect in man. *Archives of Neurology, 26,* 32–35.

Heinze, H. J., Mangun, G. R., Burchert, W., Hinrichs, H., Scholz, M., Münte, T. F., Gos, A., Scherg, M., Johannes, S., & Hundeshagen, H. (1994). Combined spatial and temporal imaging of brain activity during visual selective attention in humans. *Nature, 372,* 543–546.

Heslenfeld, D. J. (1998). *Features and attention in vision: an analysis of electromagnetic brain responses.* Unpublished doctoral dissertation, University of Amsterdam.

Heslenfeld, D. J., Kenemans, J. L., Kok, A., & Molenaar, P. C. (1997). Feature processing and attention in the human visual system: An overview. *Biological Psychology, 45,* 183–215.

Hillyard, S. A., Hink, R. F., Schwent, V. L., & Picton, T. W. (1973). Electrical signs of selective attention in the human brain. *Science, 182,* 177–180.

Hillyard, S. A., & Münte, T. F. (1984). Selective attention to color and location: An analysis with event-related brain potentials. *Perception and Psychophysics, 36,* 185–198.

Hillyard, S. A., Vogel, E. K., & Luck, S. J. (1998). Sensory gain control (amplification) as a mechanism of selective attention: Electrophysiological and neuroimaging evidence. *Philosophical Transactions of Royal Society, London, B. Biological Sciences, 353,* 1257–1270.

Hopf, J., & Mangun, G. R. (2000). Shifting visual attention in space: An electrophysiological analysis using high spatial resolution mapping. *Clinical Neurophysiology, 111,* 1241–1257.

Hopfinger, J. B., & Mangun, G. R. (1998). Reflexive attention modulates processing of visual stimuli in human extrastriate cortex. *Psychological Science, 9,* 441–447.

Horst, J. W., Javel, E., & Farley, G. R. (1986). Coding of spectral fine structure in the auditory nerve: I. Fourier analysis of period and interspike interval histograms. *Journal of the Acoustical Society of America, 79,* 398–416.

Huotilainen, M, Ilmoniemi, R. J., Lavikainen, J., Tiitinen, H., Alho, K., Sinkkonen, J., Knuutila, J., & Näätänen, R. (1993). Interaction between representations of different features of auditory sensory memory. *Neuroreport, 4,* 1279–1281.

Jääskeläinen, I. P., Alho, K., Escera, C., Winkler, I., Sillanaukee, P., & Näätänen, R. (1996). Effects of ethanol and auditory distraction on forced choice reaction time. *Alcohol, 13,* 153–156.

Jacobsen, T., & Schröger, E. (2001). Is there pre-attentive memory-based comparison of pitch? *Psychophysiology, 38,* 723–727.

James, W. (1890). *The principles of psychology.* New York: Holt.

Jewett, D. L. (1970). Volume-conducted potentials in response to auditory stimuli as detected by averaging in the cat. *Electroencephalography and Clinical Neurophysiology, 28,* 609–618.

Johannes, S., Münte, T. F., Heinze, H. J., & Mangun, G. R. (1995). Luminance and spatial attention effects on early visual processing. *Brain Research, Cognitive Brain Research, 2,* 189–205.

Kane, N. M., Curry, S. H., Butler, S. R., & Gummins, B. H. (1993). Electrophysiological indicator of avakening from coma. *The Lancet, 341,* 688.

Kane, N. M., Curry, S. H., Rowlands, C. A., Manara, A. R., Lewis, T., Moss, T., Cummings, B. H., & Butler, S. R. (1996). Event-related potentials: Neurophysiological tools for predicting emergence and early outcome from traumatic coma. *Intensive Care Medicine, 22,* 39–46.

Kahneman, D., & Treisman, A. (1984). Changing views of attention and automaticity. In R. Parasuraman & D. R. Davies (Eds.), *Varieties of attention* (pp. 29–61). London: Academic Press.

Kaufman, L., & Williamson, S. J. (1987). Recent developments in neuromagnetism. In C. Barber & T. Blum (Eds.), *Evoked potentials* (Vol. 3, pp. 100–113). Boston: Butterworths.

Kenemans, J. L, Kok, A., & Smulders, F. T. (1993). Event-related potentials to conjunctions of spatial frequency and orientation as a function of stimulus parameters and response requirements. *Electroencephalography and Clinical Neurophysiology, 88,* 51–63.

Kenemans, J. L., & Verbaten, M. N. (2000, May). *Attentive and pre-attentive visual processing.* Paper presented at the European Conference of the Federation of European Psychophysiology Societies, Amsterdam.

Knight, R. T. (1984). Decreased response to novel stimuli after prefrontal lesion in man. *Electroencephalography and Clinical Neurophysiology, 59,* 9–20.

Knight, R. T. (1991). Evoked potential studies of attention capacity in human frontal lobe lesions. In H. Levin, H. Eisenberg, & F. Benton (Eds.), *Frontal lobe function and dysfunction* (pp. 139–153). Oxford: Oxford University Press.

Knight, R. T. (1996). Contribution of human hippocampal region to novelty detection. *Nature, 383,* 256–259.

Knight, R. T., Hillyard, S. A., Woods, D. L., & Neville, H. J. (1981). The effects of frontal cortex lesions on event-related potentials during auditory selective attention. *Electroencephalography and Clinical Neurophysiology, 52,* 571–582.

Knight, R. T., & Scabini, D. (1998). Anatomic bases of event-related potentials and their relationship to novelty detection in humans. *Journal of Clinical Neurophysiology, 15,* 3–13.

Knight, R. T., Scabini, D., Woods, D. L., & Clayworth, C. (1989). Contributions of temporal-parietal junction to the human auditory P3. *Brain Research, 502,* 109–116.

Korzyukov, O., Alho, K., Kujala, A., Gumenyuk, V., Ilmoniemi, R. J., Virtanen, J., Kropotov, J., & Näätänen, R. (1999). Electromagnetic responses of the human auditory cortex generated by sensory-memory based processing of tone frequency changes. *Neuroscience Letters, 276,* 169–172.

Kraus, N., McGee, T., Carrell, T. D., Zecker, S. G., Nicol, T. G., & Koch, D. B. (1996). Auditory neurophysiologic responses and discrimination deficits in children with learning problems. *Science,* 273, 971–973.

Kropotov, J. D., Alho, K., Näätänen, R., Ponomarev, V. A., Kropotova, O. V., Anichkov, A. D., & Nechaev, V. B. (2000). Human auditory-cortex mechanisms of preattentive sound discrimination. *Neuroscience Letters, 280,* 87–90.

Kropotov, J. D., Näätänen, R., Sevostianov, A. V., Alho, K., Reinikainen, K., & Kropotova, O. V. (1995). Mismatch negativity to auditory stimulus change recorded directly from the human temporal cortex. *Psychophysiology, 32,* 418–422.

LaBerge, D. (1995). *Attentional processing: The brain's art of mindfulness.* Cambridge: Harvard University Press.

Lang, H., Nyrke, T., Ek, M., Aaltonen, O., Raimo, I., & Näätänen, R. (1990). Pitch discrimination performance and auditory event-related potentials. In C. H. M. Brunia, A. W. K. Gaillard, A. Kok, G. Mulder, & M. N.Verbaten (Eds.), *Psychophysiological brain research* (pp. 294–298). Tilburg, Netherlands: Tilburg University Press.

Levänen, S., Ahonen, A., Hari, R., McEvoy, L., & Sams, M. (1996). Deviant auditory stimuli activate human left and right auditory cortex differently. *Cerebral Cortex, 6,* 288–296.

Linkenkaer-Hansen, K., Palva, J. M., Sams, M., Hietanen, J. K., Aronen, H. J., & Ilmoniemi, R. J.

(1998). Face-selective processing in human extrastriate cortex around 120 ms after stimulus onset revealed by magneto- and electroencephalography. *Neuroscience Letters, 253,* 147–150.

Legatt, A. D., Arezzo, J. C., & Vaughan, H. G., Jr. (1988). The anatomic and physiologic bases of brain stem auditory evoked potentials. *Neurology Clinics, 6,* 681–704.

Loveless, N., Levänen, S., Jousmäki, V., Sams, M., & Hari, R. (1996). Temporal integration in auditory sensory memory: Neuromagnetic evidence. *Electroencephalography and Clinical Neurophysiology, 100,* 220–228.

Lü, S. T., Williamson, S. J., & Kaufman, L. (1992). Human auditory primary and association cortex have differing lifetimes for activation traces. *Brain Research, 572,* 236–241.

Luck, S. J., & Hillyard, S. A. (1994). Electrophysiological correlates of feature analysis during visual search. *Psychophysiology, 31,* 291–308.

Luck, S. J., Hillyard, S. A., Mouloua, M., Woldorff, M. G., Clark, V. P., & Hawkins, H. L. (1994). Effects of spatial cuing on luminance detectability: Psychophysical and electrophysiological evidence for early selection. *Journal of Experimental Psychology: Human Perception and Performance, 20,* 887–904.

Lyytinen, H., Blomberg, A.-P., & Näätänen, R. (1992). Event-related potentials and autonomic responses to a change in unattended auditory stimuli. *Psychophysiology, 29,* 523–534.

Mangun, G. R. (1995). Neural mechanisms of visual selective attention. *Psychophysiology, 32,* 4–18.

Mangun, G. R., & Buck, L. A. (1998). Sustained visual-spatial attention produces costs and benefits in response time and evoked neural activity. *Neuropsychologia, 36,* 189–200.

Mangun, G. R., Hansen, J. C., & Hillyard, S. A. (1986). Electroretinograms reveal no evidence for centrifugal modulation of retinal input during selective attention in man. *Psychophysiology, 23,* 156–165.

Mangun, G. R., & Hillyard, S. A. (1990a). Electrophysiological studies of visual selective attention in humans. In A. Scheibel & A. Wechsler (Eds.), *The neurobiological foundations of higher cognitive function* (pp. 271–294). New York: Guilford.

Mangun, G. R., & Hillyard, S. A. (1990b). Allocation of visual attention to spatial locations: Tradeoff functions for event-related brain potentials and detection performance. *Perception and Psychophysics, 47,* 532–550.

Mangun, G. R., & Hillyard, S. A. (1991). Modulations of sensory-evoked brain potentials indicate changes in perceptual processing during visual-spatial priming. *Journal of Experimental Psychology: Human Perception and Performance, 17,* 1057–1074.

Mangun, G. R., Hillyard, S. A., & Luck, S. J. (1993). Electrocortical substrates of visual selective attention. In D. E. Meyer & S. Kornblum (Eds.), *Attention and performance: Vol. 14. Synergies in experimental psychology, artificial intelligence, and cognitive neuroscience* (pp. 219–243). Cambridge: MIT Press.

Marshall, N. K., & Donchin, E. (1981). Circadian variation in the latency of brainstem responses and its relation to body temperature. *Science, 212,* 356–358.

Martínez, A., Anllo-Vento, L., Sereno, M. I., Frank, L. R., Buxton, R. B., Dubowitz, D. J., Wong, E. C., Hinrichs, H., Heinze, H. J., & Hillyard, S. A. (1999). Involvement of striate and extrastriate visual cortical areas in spatial attention. *Nature-Neuroscience, 2,* 364–369.

Masterton, R. B. (1992). Role of the central auditory system in hearing: The new direction. *Trends in Neurosciences, 15,* 280–285.

McCallum, W. C., Curry, S. H., Cooper, R., Pocock, P. V., & Papakostopoulos, D. (1983). Brain event-related potentials as indicators of early selective processes in auditory target localization. *Psychophysiology, 20,* 1–17.

Mecklinger, A., & Ullsperger, P. (1995). The P300 to novel and target events: a spatiotemporal dipole model analysis. *Neuroreport, 7,* 241–245.

Michie, P. T., Karayanidis, F., Smith, G. L., Barrett, N. A., Large, M. M., O'Sullivan, B. T., & Kavanagh, D. J. (1999). An exploration of varieties of visual attention: ERP findings. *Cognitive Brain Research, 7,* 419–450.

Michie, P. T., LePage, E. L., Solowij, N., Haller, M., & Terry, L. (1996). Evoked otoacoutic emissions and auditory selective attention. *Hearing Research, 98,* 54–67.

Michie, P. T., Solowij, N., Crawford, J. M., & Glue, L. C. (1993). The effects of between-source discriminability on attended and unattended auditory ERPs. *Psychophysiology, 30,* 205–220.

Moray, N. (1959). Attention in dichotic listening: Affective cues and the influence of instructions. *Quarterly Journal of Experimental Psychology, 9,* 56–60.

Morgan, S. T., Hansen, J. C., & Hillyard, S. A. (1996). Selective attention to stimulus location modulates the steady-state visual evoked potential. *Proceeding of National Academy of Science USA, 93,* 4770–4774.

Morlet, D., Bouchet, P., & Fischer, C. (2000). Mismatch negativity and N100 monitoring: Potential clinical value and methodological advances. *Audiology & Neuro-Otology, 5,* 198–206.

Müller, H. J., Elliott, M., Herrmann, C., & Mecklinger, A. (Eds.). (in press). Gamma-band and neural binding in space and time [Special issue]. *Visual Cognition.*

Müller, M. M., & Hillyard, S. (2000). Concurrent recording of steady-state and transient event-related potentials as indices of visual-spatial selective attention. *Clinical Neurophysiology, 111,* 1544–1552.

Müller, M. M., Picton, T. W., Valdes-Sosa, P., Riera, J., Teder-Sälejärvi, W. A., & Hillyard, S. A. (1998a). Effects of spatial selective attention on the steady-state visual evoked potential in the 20–28 Hz range. *Brain Research: Cognitive Brain Research, 6,* 249–261.

Müller, M. M., Teder-Sälejärvi, W. A., & Hillyard, S. A. (1998b). The time course of cortical facilitation during cued shifts of spatial attention. *Nature Neuroscience, 1,* 631–634.

Näätänen, R. (1970a). EEG, slow potential and evoked potential correlates of selective attention. *Acta Psychologica, 33,* 178–192.

Näätänen, R. (1970b). The diminishing time-uncertainty with the lapse of time after the warning signal in reaction-time experiments with varying foreperiods. *Acta Psychologica, 34,* 399–419.

Näätänen, R. (1975). Selective attention and evoked potentials in humans: A critical review. *Biological Psychology, 2,* 237–307.

Näätänen, R. (1982). Processing negativity: An evoked-potential reflection of selective attention. *Psychological Bulletin, 92,* 605–640.

Näätänen, R. (1986). The neural-specificity theory of visual selective attention evaluated: A commentary on Harter and Aine. *Biological Psychology, 23,* 281–295.

Näätänen, R. (1988). Implications of ERP data for psychological theories of attention. *Biological Psychology, 26* (suppl.), 117–163.

Näätänen, R. (1990). The role of attention in auditory information processing as revealed by event-related potentials and other brain measures of cognitive function. *Behavioral and Brain Sciences, 13,* 201–288.

Näätänen, R. (1991). Mismatch negativity (MMN) outside strong attentional focus: A commentary on Woldorff et al. *Psychophysiology, 28,* 478–484.

Näätänen, R. (1992). *Attention and brain function.* Hillsdale, NJ: Erlbaum.

Näätänen, R. (2001). The perception of speech sounds by the human brain as reflected by the mismatch negativity (MMN) and its magnetic equivalent MMNm [Presidential Address]. *Psychophysiology, 38,* 1–21.

Näätänen, R., & Alho, K. (1997). Higher-order processes in auditory change detection. *Trends in Cognitive Sciences, 2,* 44–45.

Näätänen, R., & Gaillard, A. W. K. (1983). The orienting reflex and the N2 deflection of the event-related potential (ERP). In A. W. K. Gaillard & W. Ritter (Eds.), *Tutorials in event-related potential research: Endogenous components* (pp. 119–141). Amsterdam: North-Holland.

Näätänen, R., Gaillard, A. W. K., & Mäntysalo, S. (1978). Early selective-attention effect on evoked potential reinterpreted. *Acta Psychologica, 42,* 313–329.

Näätänen, R., Gaillard, A. W. K., & Varey, C. A. (1981). Early attention effect on evoked potential as a function of interstimulus interval. *Biological Psychology, 13,* 173–187.

Näätänen, R., Ilmoniemi, R. J., & Alho, K. (1994). Magnetoencephalography in studies of human cognitive brain function. *Trends in Neuroscience, 17,* 389–395.

Näätänen, R., & Michie, P. T. (1979). Early selective attention effects on the evoked potential: A critical review and reinterpretation. *Biological Psychology, 8,* 81–136.

Näätänen, R., Paavilainen, P., Alho, K., Reinikainen, K., & Sams, M. (1989). Do event-related potentials reveal the mechanism of the auditory sensory memory in the human brain? *Neuroscience Letters, 98,* 217–221.

Näätänen, R., Paavilainen, P., Tiitinen, H., Jiang, D., & Alho, K. (1993). Attention and mismatch negativity. *Psychophysiology, 30,* 436–450.

Näätänen, R., & Picton, T. (1987). The N1 wave of the human electric and magnetic response to sound: A review and an analysis of component structure. *Psychophysiology, 24,* 375–425.

Näätänen, R., Sams, M., Alho, K., Paavilainen, P., Reinikainen, K., & Sokolov, E. N. (1988). Frequency and location specificity of the human vertex N1 wave. *Electroencephalography and Clinical Neurophysiology, 69,* 523–531.

Näätänen, R., Simpson, M., & Loveless, N. E. (1982). Stimulus deviance and evoked potentials. *Biological Psychology, 14,* 53–98.

Näätänen, R., Teder, W., Alho, K., & Lavikainen, J. (1992). Auditory attention and selective input modulation: A topographical ERP study. *NeuroReport, 3,* 493–496.

Näätänen, R., & Winkler, I. (1999). The concept of auditory stimulus representation in cognitive neuroscience. *Psychological Bulletin, 6,* 826–859.

Nobre, A. C., Sebestyen, G. N., & Miniussi, C. (2000). The dynamics of shifting visuospatial attention revealed by event-related potentials. *Neuropsychologia, 38,* 964–974.

Nordby, H., Brønnick, K. S., & Hugdahl, K. (1996). Processing of deviant visual events reflected by event-related potentials. In C. Ogura, Y. Koga,

& M. Shimokochi (Eds.), *Recent advances in event-related brain potentials research* (pp. 99–104). Amsterdam: Elsevier.

Norman, D. A. (1968). Toward a theory of memory and attention. *Psychological Review, 75,* 522–536.

Nyman, G., Alho, K., Laurinen, P., Paavilainen, P., Radil, T., Reinikainen, K., Sams, M., & Näätänen, R. (1990). Mismatch negativity (MMN) for sequences of auditory and visual stimuli: Evidence for a mechanism specific to the auditory modality. *Electroencephalography and Clinical Neurophysiology, 77,* 436–444.

Oakley, M. T., & Eason, R. G. (1990). Subcortical gating in the human visual system during spatial selective attention. *International Journal of Psychophysiology, 9,* 105–120.

Öhman, A. (1979). The orienting response, attention and learning: An information-processing perspective. In H. D. Kimmel, E. H. van Olst, & J. F. Orlebeke (Eds.), *The orienting reflex in humans* (pp. 443–471). Hillsdale, NJ: Erlbaum.

Öhman, A. (1992). Orienting and attention: Preferred preattentive processing of potentially phobic stimuli. In B. A. Campbell, R. Richardson, & H. Hayne (Eds.), *Attention and information processing in infants and adults: Perspectives from human and animal research* (pp. 263–295). Hillsdale, NJ: Erlbaum.

O'Leary, D. D., Andreasen, N. C., Hurtig, R. R., Hichwa, R. D., Watkins, L., Ponto, L. L. B., Rogers, M., & Kirchner, P. T. (1996). A positron emission tomography study of binaurally and dichotically presented stimuli: Effects of level of language and directed attention. *Brain and Language, 53,* 20–39.

O'Leary, D. D., Andreasen, N. C., Hurtig, R. R., Torres, I. J., Flashman, L. A., Kesler, M. L., Arndt, S. V., Cizadio, T. J., Poles L. L. B., Watkins, L., & Hichwa, R. D. (1997). Auditory and visual attention assessed with PET. *Human Brain Mapping, 5,* 422–436.

Paavilainen, P., Tiitinen, H., Alho, K., & Näätänen, R. (1993). Mismatch negativity to slight pitch changes outside strong attentional focus. *Biological Psychology, 37,* 23–41.

Pantev, C., Hoke, M., Lehnertz, K., Lütkenhöner, B., Anogianakis, G., & Wittkowski, W. (1988). Tonotopic organization of the human auditory cortex revealed by transient auditory evoked magnetic fields. *Electroencephalography and Clinical Neurophysiology, 69,* 160–170.

Parasuraman, R., & Beatty, J. (1980). Brain events underlying detection and recognition of weak sensory signals. *Science, 210,* 80–83.

Picton, T. W. (1980). The use of human event-related potentials in psychology. In I. Martin & P. H. Venables (Eds.), *Techniques in psychophysiology* (pp. 357–395). New York: Wiley.

Picton, T. W., Hillyard, S. A., Krautz, H. J., & Galambos, R. (1974). Human auditory evoked potentials I: Evaluation of components. *Electroencephalography and Clinical Neurophysiology, 36,* 179–190.

Picton, T. W., Stapells, D. R., & Campbell, K. B. (1981). Auditory evoked potentials from the human cochlea and brainstem. *Journal of Otolaryngology, 10,* 1–41.

Posner, M. I. (1978). *Chronometric explorations of mind.* New York: Erlbaum.

Posner, M. I. (1980). Orienting of attention. *Quarterly Journal of Experimental Psychology, 32,* 3–25.

Probst, T., Plendl, H., Paulus, W., Wist, E. R., & Scherg, M. (1993). Identification of the visual motion area (area V5) in the human brain by dipole source analysis. *Experimental Brain Research, 93,* 345–351.

Puce, A., Allison, T., & McCarthy, G. (1999). Electrophysiological studies of human face perception: III. Effects of top-down processing on face-specific potentials. *Cerebral Cortex, 9,* 445–458.

Regan, D. (1989). *Human brain electrophysiology: Evoked potentials and evoked magnetic fields in science and medicine.* New York: Elsevier.

Richer, F., Alain, C., Achim, A., Bouvier, G., & Saint-Hilaire, J. M. (1989). Intracerebral amplitude distributions of the auditory evoked potential. *Electroencephalography and Clinical Neurophysiology, 74,* 202–208.

Rif, J., Hari, R., Hämäläinen, M. S., & Sams, M. (1991). Auditory attention affects two different areas in the human supratemporal cortex. *Electroencephalography and Clinical Neurophysiology, 79,* 464–472.

Rinne, T., Alho, K., Ilmoniemi, R. J., Virtanen, J., & Näätänen, R. (2000). Separate time behaviors of the temporal and frontal mismatch negativity sources. *Neuroimage, 12,* 14–19.

Romani, G. L., Williamson, S. J., & Kaufman, L. (1982). Tonotopic organization of the human auditory cortex. *Science, 216,* 1339–1340.

Rugg, M. D., Milner, A. D., Lines, C. R., & Phalp, R. (1987). Modulation of visual event-related potentials by spatial and non-spatial visual selective attention. *Neuropsychologia, 25,* 85–96.

Saarinen, J., Vanni, S., & Hari, R. (1998). Human cortical-evoked fields during detection, localisation, and identification of "pop-out" targets. *Perception, 27,* 215–224.

Salamy, A., & McKean, C. M. (1977). Habituation and dishabituation of cortical and brainstem evoked potentials. *International Journal of Neuroscience, 7,* 175–182.

Sams, M., Alho, K., & Näätänen, R. (1984). Short-term habituation and dishabituation of the mismatch negativity of the ERP. *Psychophysiology, 21,* 434–441.

Sams, M., Hämäläinen, M., Antervo, A., Kaukoranta, E., Reinikainen, K., & Hari, R. (1985a). Cerebral neuromagnetic responses evoked by short auditory stimuli. *Electroencephalography and Clinical Neurophysiology, 61,* 254–266.

Sams, M., Hari, R., Rif, J., & Knuutila, J. (1993). The human auditory sensory memory trace persists about 10 msec: Neuromagnetic evidence. *Journal of Cognitive Neuroscience, 5,* 363–370.

Sams, M., Paavilainen, P., Alho, K., & Näätänen, R. (1985b). Auditory frequency discrimination and event-related potentials. *Electroencephalography and Clinical Neurophysiology, 62,* 437–448.

Scherg, M., Vajsar, J., & Picton, T. W. (1989). A source analysis of the late human auditory evoked potentials. *Journal of Cognitive Neuroscience, 1,* 336–355.

Schlaghecken, F., Meinecke, C., & Schröger, E. (2001). Processing spatial and temporal discontinuities: Electrophysiological indicators. *Journal of Psychophysiology, 15,* 80–94.

Schneider, W., & Shiffrin, R. M. (1977). Controlled and automatic human information processing: I. Detection, search, and attention. *Psychological Review, 84,* 1–166.

Schröger, E. (1993). Event-related potentials to auditory stimuli succeeding transient shifts of spatial attention in a go/no-go task. *Biological Psychology, 36,* 183–207.

Schröger, E. (1996). A neural mechanism for involuntary attention shifts to changes in auditory stimulation. *Journal of Cognitive Neuroscience, 8,* 527–539.

Schröger, E. (1997). On the detection of auditory deviations: A pre-attentive activation model. *Psychophysiology, 34,* 245–257.

Schröger, E. (1998). Measurement and interpretation of mismatch negativity. *Behavioral Research Methods Instrumentation and Computing, 30,* 131–145.

Schröger, E., & Eimer, M. (1993). Effects of transient spatial attention on auditory event-related potentials. *NeuroReport, 4,* 588–590.

Schröger, E., & Eimer, M. (1996). Effects of lateralized cues on the processing of lateralized auditory stimuli. *Biological Psychology, 43,* 203–226.

Schröger, E., & Eimer, M. (1997). Covert spatial orienting in audition: "Cost-Benefit" analyses of reaction times and event-related potentials. *The Quarterly Journal of Experimental Psychology, 50A,* 457–474.

Schröger, E., Giard, M.-H., & Wolff, C. (2000). Auditory distraction: Event-related potential and behavioral indices. *Clinical Neurophysiology, 111,* 1450–1460.

Schröger, E., & Wolff, C. (1996). Mismatch response of the human brain to changes in sound location. *Neuroreport, 7,* 3005–3008.

Schröger, E., & Wolff, C. (1998a). Behavioral and electrophysiological effects of task-irrelevant sound change: a new distraction paradigm. *Cognitive Brain Research, 7,* 71–87.

Schröger, E., & Wolff, C. (1998b). Attentional orienting and reorienting is indicated by human event-related brain potentials. *NeuroReport, 9,* 3355–3358.

Schubö, A., Meinecke, C., & Schröger, E. (2001). Automaticity and attention: Investigating automatic processing in texture segmentation with event-related brain potentials. *Cognitive Brain Research, 11,* 341–361.

Shiffrin, R. M., & Schneider, W. (1977). Controlled and automatic information processing: II. Perceptual learning, automatic attending, and a general theory. *Psychological Review, 84,* 127–189.

Smid, H. G., Jakob, A., & Heinze, H. J. (1999). An event-related brain potential study of visual selective attention to conjunctions of color and shape. *Psychophysiology, 36,* 264–79.

Snyder, E., & Hillyard, S. A. (1976). Long-latency evoked potentials to irrelevant deviant stimuli. *Behavioural Biology, 16,* 319–331.

Sokolov, E. N. (1975). The neuronal mechanisms of the orienting reflex. In E. N. Sokolov, & O. S. Vinogradova (Eds.), *Neuronal mechanisms of the orienting reflex* (pp. 217–338). New York: Wiley.

Sokolov, E. N., Spinks, J. A., Lyytinen, H., & Näätänen, R. (in press). The orienting response in information processing. Hillsdale, N.J.: Erlbaum.

Squires, N. K., Squires, K. C., & Hillyard, S. A. (1975). Two varieties of long-latency positive waves evoked by unpredictable auditory stimuli in man. *Electroencephalography and Clinical Neurophysiology, 38,* 387–401.

Stuss, D. T., & Benson, D. F. (1986). *The frontal lobes.* New York: Raven Press.

Sutton, S., Braren, M., Zubin, J., & John, E. P. (1965). Evoked-potential correlates of stimulus uncertainty. *Science, 150,* 1187–1188.

Tales, A., Newton, P., Troscianko, T., & Butler, S. (1999). Mismatch negativity in the visual modality. *Neuroreport, 10,* 3363–3367.

Tallon-Baudry, C., & Bertrand, O. (1999). Oscillatory gamma activity in humans and its role in object representation. *Trends in Cognitive Science, 3,* 151–162.

Teder, W., Alho, K., Reinikainen, K., & Näätänen, R. (1993a). Interstimulus interval and the selective attention effect on auditory ERPs: "N1 enhancement" vs. processing negativity. *Psychophysiology, 30,* 71–81.

Teder, W., Kujala, T., & Näätänen, R. (1993b). Selection of speech messages in free-field listening: First measurements of brain responses to real speech. *NeuroReport, 5,* 307–309.

Tiitinen, H., Alho, K., Huotilainen, M., Ilmoniemi, R. J., Simola, J., & Näätänen, R. (1993a). Tonotopic auditory cortex and the magnetoencephalographic (MEG) equivalent of the mismatch negativity. *Psychophysiology, 30,* 537–540.

Tiitinen, H., Sinkkonen, J., Reinikainen, K., Alho, K., Lavikainen, J., & Näätänen, R. (1993b). Selective attention enhances the auditory 40-Hz transient response in humans. *Nature, 364,* 59–60.

Treisman, A. M., & Gelade, G. (1980). A feature-integration theory of attention. *Cognitive Psychology, 12,* 97–136.

Trejo, L. J., Ryan-Jones, D. L., & Kramer, A. F. (1995). Attentional modulation of the mismatch negativity elicited by frequency differences between binaurally presented tone bursts. *Psychophysiology, 32,* 319–328.

Tzourio, N., El Massioui, F., Crivello, F., Joliot, M., Renault, B., & Mazoyer, B. (1997). Functional anatomy of auditory attention studied with PET. *NeuroImage, 5,* 63–77.

Ungerleider, L. G., & Mishkin, M. (1982). Two cortical visual systems. In D. J. Ingle, M. A. Goodale, & R. W. Mansfield (Eds.), *Analysis of visual behavior* (pp. 549–986). Cambridge: MIT Press.

van der Heijden, A.H.C. (1993). The role of position in object selection in vision. *Psychological Research, 56,* 44–58.

Vaughan, H. G., Jr., & Arezzo, J. C. (1988). The neural basis of event-related potentials. In T. W. Picton (Ed.), *Human event-related potentials* (pp. 45–96). Amsterdam: Elsevier.

Vaughan, H. G., Jr., & Ritter, W. (1970). The sources of auditory evoked responses recorded from the human scalp. *Electroencephalography and Clinical Neurophysiology, 28,* 360–367.

Verleger, R., Vollmer, C., Wauschkuhn, B., van der Lubbe, R. H., & Wascher, E. (2000). Dimensional overlap between arrows as cueing stimuli and responses? Evidence from contra-ipsilateral differences in EEG potentials. *Brain Research: Cognitive Brain Research, 10,* 99–109.

Wauschkuhn, B., Verleger, R., Wascher, E., Klostermann, W., Burk, M., Heide, W., & Kompf, D. (1998). Lateralized human cortical activity for shifting visuospatial attention and initiating saccades. *Journal of Neurophysiology, 80,* 2900–2910.

Wijers, A. A., Lamain, W., Slopsema, S., Mulder, G., & Mulder, L. J. M. (1989). An electrophysiological investigation of the spatial distribution of attention to colored stimuli in focused and divided attention conditions. *Biological Psychology, 29,* 213–245.

Wijers, A. A., Lange, J. J., Mulder, G., & Mulder, L. J. (1997). An ERP study of visual spatial attention and letter target detection for isoluminant and nonisoluminant stimuli. *Psychophysiology, 34,* 553–565.

Woldorff, M. G., Fox, P. T., Matzke, M., Lancaster, J. L., Veeraswamy, S., Zamarripa, F., Seabolt, M., Glass, T., Gao, J. H., Martin, C. C., & Jerabek, P. (1997). Retinotopic organization of early visual spatial attention effects as revealed by PET and ERPs. *Human Brain Mapping, 5,* 280–286.

Woldorff, M. G., Gallen, C. G., Hampson, S. A., Hillyard, S. A., Pantev, C., Sobel, D., & Bloom, F. E. (1993). Modulation of early sensory processing in human auditory cortex during auditory selective attention. *Proceedings of the National Academy of Sciences, 90,* 8722–8726.

Woldorff, M. G., Hackley, S. A., & Hillyard, S. A. (1991). The effects of channel-selective attention on the mismatch negativity wave elicited by deviant tones. *Psychophysiology, 28,* 30–42.

Woldorff, M. G., Hansen, J. C., & Hillyard, S. A. (1987). Evidence for effects of selective attention in the mid-latency range of the human auditory event-related brain potential. In R. Johnson Jr., J. W. Rohrbaugh, & R. Parasuraman (Eds.), *Currrent trends in event-related brain potential research* (Suppl. 40 to *Electroencephalography*

and Clinical Neurophysiology; pp. 146–154). Amsterdam: Elsevier.

Woldorff, M. G., & Hillyard, S. A. (1991). Modulation of early auditory processing during selective listening to rapidly presented tones. *Electroencehalography and Clinical Neurophysiology, 79,* 170–191.

Woldorff, M. G., Hillyard, S. A., Gallen, C. C., Hampson, S. R., & Bloom, F. E. (1998). Magnetoencephalographic recordings demonstrate attentional modulation of mismatch-related neural activity in human auditory cortex. *Psychophysiology, 35,* 283–292.

Woods, D. L. (1990). The physiological basis of selective attention: Implications of event-related potential studies. In J. W. Rohrbaugh, R. Parasuraman, & R. Johnson, Jr. (Eds.), *Event-related potentials: Basic issues and applications* (pp. 178–209). New York: Oxford University Press.

Woods, D. L. (1992). Auditory attention in middle-aged and elderly subjects: An event-related brain potential study. *Electroencephalography and Clinical Neurophysiology, 84,* 456–468.

Woods, D. L., Alho, K., & Algazi, A. (1991). Event-related brain potential signs of feature processing during auditory selective attention. *NeuroReport, 2,* 189–192.

Woods, D. L., Alho, K., & Algazi, A. (1992). Intermodal selective attention: I. Effects of event-related potentials to lateralized auditory and visual stimuli. *Electroencephalography and Clinical Neurophysiology, 82,* 341–355.

Woods, D. L., Alho, K., & Algazi, A. (1993a). Intermodal selective attention: Evidence for processing in tonotopic auditory fields. *Psychophysiology, 30,* 287–295.

Woods, D. L., Alho, K. & Algazi, A. (1994). Stages of auditory feature conjunction: An event-related brain potential study. *Journal of Experimental Psychology: Human Perception and Performance, 20,* 81–94.

Woods, D. L., & Clayworth, C. C. (1987). Scalp topographies dissociate N1 and Nd components during auditory selective attention. In R. Johnson Jr., J. W. Rohrbaugh, & R. Parasuraman (Eds.), *Current trends in event-related brain potential research* (Suppl. 40 to *Electroencephalography and Clinical Neurophysiology;* pp. 155–160). Amsterdam: Elsevier.

Woods, D. L., Hillyard, S. A., & Hansen, J. C. (1984). Event-related brain potentials reveal similar mechanisms during selective listening and shadowing. *Journal of Experimental Psychology: Human Perception and Performance, 10,* 761–777.

Woods, D. L., & Knight, R. T. (1986). Electrophysiologic evidence of increased distractability after dorsolateral prefrontal lesions. *Neurology, 36,* 212–216.

Woods, D. L., Knight, R. T., & Scabini, D. (1993b). Anatomical substrates of auditory selective attention: Behavioral and electrophysiological effects of posterior association cortex lesions. *Cognitive Brain Research, 1,* 227–240.

Zatorre, R. J., Mondor, T. A., & Evans, A. C. (1999). Auditory attention to space and frequency activates similar cerebral systems. *NeuroImage, 10,* 544–554.

Yamaguchi, S., Tsuchiya, H., & Kobayashi, S. (1994). Electroencephalographic activity associated with shifts of visuospatial attention. *Brain, 117,* 553–562.

Yamaguchi, S., Tsuchiya, H., & Kobayashi, S. (1995). Electrophysiologic correlates of age effects on visuospatial attention shift. *Brain Research: Cognitive Brain Research, 3,* 41–49.

Yamaguchi, S., Tsuchiya, H., & Kobayashi, S. (1998). Visuospatial attention shift and motor responses in cerebellar disorders. *Journal of Cognitive Neuroscience, 10,* 95–107.

CHAPTER 16

Single versus Multiple Systems of Learning and Memory

F. GREGORY ASHBY AND SHAWN W. ELL

One of the most hotly debated current issues in psychology and neuroscience is whether human learning and memory are mediated by a single processing system or by multiple qualitatively distinct systems. Although it is now generally accepted that there are multiple memory systems (Cohen & Squire, 1980; Corkin, 1965; Gaffan, 1974; Hirsh, 1974; Klein, Cosmides, Tooby, & Chance, in press; Mishkin, Malamut, & Bachevalier, 1984; O'Keefe & Nadel, 1978; Schacter, 1987; Squire, 1992; Zola-Morgan, Squire, & Mishkin, 1982), this issue is far from resolved in the case of learning and other cognitive processes. Even so, arguments for multiple systems have been made in such diverse fields as reasoning (Sloman, 1996), motor learning (Willingham, Nissen, & Bullemer, 1989), discrimination learning (Kendler & Kendler, 1962), function learning (Hayes & Broadbent, 1988), and category learning (Ashby, Alfonso-Reese, Turken, & Waldron, 1998; Brooks, 1978; Erickson & Kruschke, 1998). Interestingly, many of these papers have hypothesized at least two similar systems: (a) an explicit, rule-based system that is tied to language function and conscious awareness, and (b) an implicit system that may not have access to conscious awareness. In many cases, there has been resistance to these

proposals, and a number of researchers have responded with papers arguing that single-system models can account for many of the phenomena that have been used to support the notion of multiple systems (Nosofsky & Johansen, 2000; Nosofsky & Zaki, 1998; Poldrack, Selco, Field, & Cohen, 1999).

This chapter explores the debate between single and multiple systems. The focus is on the methodologies that have been proposed for testing between these two positions. Thus, rather than attempting to resolve the debate by arguing for one position or another, our goals are to answer the following questions: (a) What constitutes a separate system? (b) What is the appropriate way to resolve this debate empirically? (c) What are the best empirical methodologies for testing between single and multiple systems? Many of the different areas currently engaged in the debate over single versus multiple systems use similar methodologies to test between these two opposing arguments, and as just mentioned, they have all postulated similar explicit and implicit systems. For this reason, a detailed study of the debate in one area will most likely benefit the other areas as well. Thus, in the last major section, as a model of this debate, we focus on the question of whether human category learning is mediated by single or multiple systems.

WHAT IS A SYSTEM?

Before one can examine methods for testing between single and multiple systems, one must first decide what is meant by a separate system. This question turns out to be as difficult as any that we examine in this chapter. This is because all tasks in which we are interested are performed somewhere in the brain, and at one level the brain is part of a single system (e.g., the central nervous system). At the other extreme, a strong argument can be made that each single cell, or even each single ion channel, forms its own system. So there is a continuum of levels, from macroscopic to microscopic, at which a system could be defined. It seems clear, however, that the level chosen should match the task in question. Thus, a more macroscopic system is required to learn a new category of automobiles than to detect a sine-wave grating of a certain orientation. In the latter case, one could reasonably ask whether a column of cells in visual cortex defines the system, whereas in the former case this is clearly too reductionistic.

Given that an appropriate level and task are selected, what criteria should we use to decide whether some model postulates one or more systems? Suppose we have a model with two modules S_1 and S_2. The question is whether S_1 and S_2 define separate systems, or whether they should be viewed as two components of a single system. We believe that no single criterion can be used to answer this question. Instead, we propose a hierarchy of criteria— from the mathematical to the psychological to the neurobiological. Two modules that meet all these criteria are clearly separate systems. Modules that meet none of the criteria clearly do not constitute separate systems, and modules that meet some but not all of the criteria

are in some ambiguous gray region along the single system–multiple system continuum.

Suppose that the model for S_1 is characterized by a set of parameters denoted by the vector θ_1 and that the model for S_2 is characterized by the parameters θ_2. For any specific set of numerical values of θ_1 and θ_2, the models of S_1 and S_2, respectively, each predict a certain probability distribution of the relevant dependent variable, whatever that might be. Denote these probability distributions by $f_1(x \mid \theta_1)$ and $f_2(x \mid \theta_2)$, respectively. As the numerical values of θ_1 and θ_2 change, these predicted probability distributions also change. Therefore, let $\{f_1(x \mid \theta_1)\}$ and $\{f_2(x \mid \theta_2)\}$ denote the set of all possible probability density functions that can be generated from the S_1 and S_2 models, respectively (i.e., any numerical change in θ_1 or θ_2 creates a new member of these sets). Then a mathematical criterion for S_1 and S_2 to be separate systems is that $\{f_1(x \mid \theta_1)\}$ and $\{f_2(x \mid \theta_2)\}$ are not identical, and that neither is a subset of the other. In other words, the models of S_1 and S_2 are not mathematically equivalent, and one is not a special case of the other—that is, they each make at least some unique predictions. If the models were completely mathematically equivalent, so that no experiment could ever be run that could produce data that might differentiate the two, then it is difficult to see how they could qualify as separate systems.

Note that an implicit assumption of this definition is that S_1 and S_2 each make predictions about observable behavior (because they each predict some probability distribution on the relevant dependent variable). This itself is a stringent requirement that eliminates many possible models. For example, signal detection theory postulates separate sensory and decision processes, each described by its own parameter (d' and X_C, respectively). But either process, by itself, is incapable of making predictions about behavior. Instead, the two subsystems are assumed always to work together to produce a behavioral response. As such, standard signal detection theory is a single-system theory, even though it postulates functionally separate sensory and decisional subsystems.

At the psychological level, to qualify as separate systems, S_1 and S_2 should postulate that different psychological processes are required to complete the task in question successfully. For example, a multiple-systems account of category learning might postulate separate prototype abstraction and rule-based systems, but a model that proposed two different prototype abstraction processes might be better described as a single-system model. This criterion would also apply the single system label to a theory that postulated two separate signal detection systems, one, for example, with a more efficient sensory process and the other with a more efficient decision process. This is because both systems would postulate similar (but not identical) sensory and decision processes that are active on all trials.

At the neurobiological level, separate systems should be mediated by separate neural structures or pathways. In most cases, there will be widespread agreement within the field of neurobiology about whether a pair of structures is part of the same or different systems, so this criterion should usually be straightforward to test. Within cognitive psychology this should be the gold standard for establishing the existence of separate systems. It is highly likely that if the neurobiological condition is met, then the psychological and mathematical conditions will also be met. However, it is very easy to find examples in which the reverse implication fails. For example, one could easily construct two different exemplar-based category-learning models that are mathematically identifiable (i.e., the mathematical condition is met) but postulate the same process of accessing category exemplars and computing their similarity to the presented stimulus, and therefore are also mediated by the same neural structures and pathways.

Just as the theoretical criteria for the existence of separate systems can be formulated at several different levels of analysis, so too is it vitally important to appeal to converging operations when testing empirically between single and multiple systems of learning and memory. It is extremely unlikely that any single experiment will yield data that definitively decide the question of whether there are single or multiple systems in any specific area of learning or memory. For any single set of data that purportedly supports the existence of multiple systems, for example, it is highly likely that a clever researcher will be able to construct a single-system model that can account for those data. Thus, it is vital when evaluating any new model, whether it postulate single or multiple systems, that data are considered from many different experimental paradigms. Ideally, such data would come from several different levels of analysis, including behavioral neuroscience and traditional cognitive psychology, as well as cognitive neuroscience and neuropsychology.

SPECIFIC METHODOLOGICAL TESTS OF SINGLE VERSUS MULTIPLE SYSTEMS

A formal investigation of the efficacy of various methods for testing between single and multiple systems of learning and memory requires more structure than our previous discussions. Consider an experiment with several different conditions in which the dependent variable on condition i is denoted by the random variable X_i. Denote the probability density function (PDF) of X_i in condition i by $g_i(x)$. As concrete examples, X_1 and X_2 might be the response times (RTs) from an experiment with two different conditions that load on different putative memory systems, or they might be the number of trials required to reach some criterion accuracy level in this same experiment. In the former case, $g_i(x)$ might be the RT distribution produced by a single subject in condition i, but in the latter case $g_i(x)$ would be the trials-to-criterion distribution across a group of subjects who all participated in condition i (i.e., because each subject produces many RTs but only one value for trials-to-criterion in each condition).

Next consider an organism with two separate memory systems, either of which might be sufficient to complete the experimental task by itself. Let $\mathbf{X}_{Ai}$ and $\mathbf{X}_{Bi}$ denote the value of the dependent variable on trials when condition i is completed by systems A and B, respectively, and let $f_A(x \mid i)$ and $f_B(x \mid i)$ denote their respective PDFs. The PDF $g_i(x)$ is the distribution of observable data values, so it can always be estimated directly. As we will see, however, whether the PDFs $f_A(x \mid i)$ and $f_B(x \mid i)$ can be estimated directly depends on the model that we assume.

In this section, we consider three different types of multiple systems models. In the *strong model,* the observer uses only system A in experimental condition 1, and only system B in experimental condition 2. Thus,

$$g_1(x) = f_A(x \mid 1) \quad \text{and} \quad g_2(x) = f_B(x \mid 2). \tag{1}$$

The assumption that different systems are used in the two tasks has been called *selective influence* in the literature on single versus multiple systems (Dunn & Kirsner, 1988), after a similar assumption in the RT literature that was identified by Sternberg (1969). Almost all of the formal analysis of methodologies that purport to test between single and multiple systems (e.g., double dissociations) are based on this strong model.

In practice, however, it seems possible that both systems may contribute to performance in both conditions, with the relative contributions of systems A and B varying from condition 1 to condition 2. For example, explicit memory systems may contribute to performance on putative implicit memory tasks (and vice versa). There are two obvious models of how this division of labor might proceed. In the *mixture model,* the observable response is determined by a single system on each trial, but memory system A determines the response on some trials and memory system B determines the response on the remaining trials. Let p_i denote the probability that memory system A determines the response in condition i. Then the mixture model predicts that the observable PDF is a probability mixture of the two component PDFs; that is,

$$g_i(x) = p_i f_A(x \mid i) + (1 - p_i) f_B(x \mid i). \tag{2}$$

The third possibility that we consider is that both systems contribute to the observable response on every trial. In fact, in the *averaging model* the observable dependent variable is a weighted average of the outputs of the two component systems. In particular,

$$\mathbf{X}_i = r_i \mathbf{X}_{Ai} + (1 - r_i)\mathbf{X}_{Bi}, \tag{3}$$

where $0 \leq r_i \leq 1$ is the weight given memory system A in condition i. The observable PDF is found from a generalization of the so-called convolution integral:

$$g_i(x)$$
$$= \frac{1}{r_i(1 - r_i)} \int_{-\infty}^{\infty} f\left(\frac{x - w}{r_i}, \frac{w}{1 - r_i} \,\middle|\, i\right) dw, \tag{4}$$

where $f(x_A, x_B \mid i)$ is the joint PDF of $\mathbf{X}_{Ai}$ and $\mathbf{X}_{Bi}$.

Equations (2) and (3) are in a similar form, but mathematically their behavior is very different. For example, suppose systems A and B can both complete task i, but that system A is much better adapted to performing this task than is system B. Then $f_A(x \mid i)$ and $f_B(x \mid i)$ will have very different means. In the mixture model, this will be obvious because on trials when the observer uses system A, RT will be short, whereas RT will be long on trials when the observer uses system B. In fact, if the A and B means are far enough apart, then the observable PDF, $g_i(x)$, will be bimodal. However, in the averaging model the observer does the same thing on every trial, and as a result RT will always be of intermediate value, and $g_i(x)$ will therefore be unimodal. For these reasons, mixture models will generally be easier to discriminate from single-system models than will averaging models, which like single-system models assume that observers do the same thing on all trials.

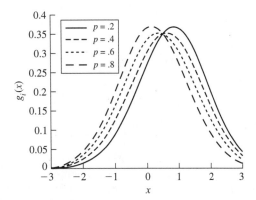

Figure 16.1 Examples of probability density functions that satisfy the fixed-point property.

The Fixed-Point Property of Binary Mixtures

An obvious signature of a mixture model would be a bimodal PDF (in the case of binary mixtures). Unfortunately, mixture models will produce unimodal PDFs unless the component distributions are far apart. Thus, it is important to find some other less obvious signature left by mixture models. A solution to this problem was discovered more than 30 years ago.

The issue of whether choice RT was mediated by a mixture model or by a single-system model achieved intense scrutiny during the 1960s and 1970s (e.g., Falmagne, 1968; Falmagne & Theios, 1969; Lupker & Theios, 1977; Townsend & Ashby, 1983; Yellott, 1969, 1971). The interest was generated by Yellott's (1969) proposal that some proportion of responses in speeded-choice tasks were simple guesses, and thus the observable RTs were a mixture of fast guesses and slower times from trials when complete processing occurred. In response Falmagne proposed a clever test of mixture models that he called the *fixed-point property*. Consider a special case of Equation (2) in which the mixture probability p_i varies across the experimental conditions (i.e., varies with i), but

the component system PDFs do not; that is,

$$f_A(x \mid i) = f_A(x) \quad \text{and}$$
$$f_B(x \mid i) = f_B(x), \quad \text{for all values of } i.$$

In each experimental condition, all that we can estimate, of course, is the observable PDF, $g_i(x)$. The fixed-point property of binary mixtures states that all such mixtures must intersect at the same time point, if they intersect at all (Falmagne, 1968).

Figure 16.1 shows examples of $g_i(x)$ when the component PDFs, $f_A(x)$ and $f_B(x)$, are each normal distributions with equal variance, and the mixture probability p_i varies across conditions from 0.2 to 0.8. Note that the resulting PDFs (which are not themselves normal) all intersect at the point $x = 0.5$. Although it is mathematically possible that a single-system model could coincidentally mimic this result, such a possibility seems highly unlikely, so a set of empirical PDFs that satisfy the fixed-point property should be taken as strong evidence of multiple systems. On the other hand, the converse result is much weaker. There are many reasons why the mixture model might fail to display the fixed-point property, so data in which the fixed-point property fails do not constitute strong evidence against the mixture model. For example, it might

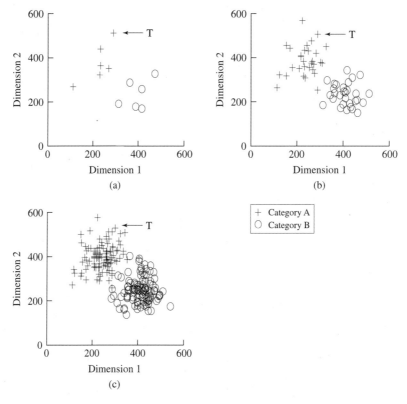

Figure 16.2 Example of category structures to which the fixed-point property might be applied. NOTE: a) A memorization strategy may be employed to learn this structure with few exemplars. However, as the numbers of exemplars increases (in b and c), it seems more likely that an abstract rule may be applied.

be the case that the component PDFs change across conditions, in addition to the mixture probability p_i.

The fixed-point property has not been used to test for single versus multiple systems of learning or memory, but there is no reason, in principle, why it could not. For example, consider the category structures shown in Figure 16.2. Suppose a researcher believes that learning of these structures will depend heavily on memorization when there are only a few exemplars per category, but that as the number of exemplars is increased, observers begin learning and applying a more abstract rule. This dual-system hypothesis could be tested via the fixed-point property. For example, consider the stimulus labeled T in

Figure 16.2. Note that this stimulus appears in every condition. Suppose that the conditions are ordered so that the smallest categories are learned first and more exemplars are successively added (so that the order is Figure 16.2a, 16.2b, 16.2c). In each condition, enough data are collected to estimate the RT distribution for stimulus T. If the theory is right, then in Figure 16.2a the RT distribution for stimulus T will be determined primarily by a memorization strategy, and in Figure 16.2c by applying an abstract rule. If during the transition the observer intermixes trials in which the response to stimulus T is generated by these two systems, then the stimulus-T RT distributions across conditions should satisfy the fixed-point property.

In this case, dual systems are supported if the observable RT PDFs all intersect at the same point. Unfortunately, however, it is difficult to draw any strong conclusions if they do not satisfy the fixed-point property. Recall that a condition necessary for the fixed-point property to hold is that $f_A(x \mid i) = f_A(x)$ and $f_B(x \mid i) = f_B(x)$—in other words, the component system PDFs for the time to categorize stimulus T are the same in all three conditions shown in Figure 16.2. This is a strong assumption that could fail for a variety of reasons. For example, the rule-based system might use a slightly different rule in the three conditions. There is much evidence that categorization RT is strongly affected by the distance from the stimulus to the category boundary (Ashby, Boynton, & Lee, 1994; Maddox, Ashby, & Gottlob, 1998), so if the boundary (i.e., rule) changes, then the distance between T and the boundary will change, and so will the time it takes the rule-based system to categorize stimulus T. Similarly, it may be that the memorization system slows down when the number of exemplars that must be memorized increases. This would cause the PDF from the memorization system to change (i.e., move to the right) as more stimuli are added from one condition to the next.

Double Dissociations

The most widely used current method for establishing that there are multiple systems of learning or memory is to find a double dissociation between two tasks that load differently on the two systems. Many such examples exist. To name one, several studies have found that rats with lesions of the tail of the caudate nucleus are impaired in visual discrimination learning but not in spatial learning, whereas rats with lesions to the fornix (the output structure of the hippocampus) show the opposite pattern—namely, they are impaired in spatial learning but are normal in visual discrimi-

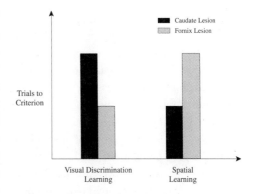

Figure 16.3   Hypothetical results showing a double dissociation between visual discrimination learning and spatial learning for two different types of lesions (tail of the caudate nucleus or fornix).

nation learning (McDonald & White, 1994; Packard, Hirsch, & White, 1989; Packard & McGaugh, 1992). An example of the pattern of results one would expect in such a situation is given in Figure 16.3. Note that the dependent variable is trials-to-criterion.

Several properties of the Figure 16.3 results are necessary for them to qualify as a double dissociation (a term first coined by Teuber, 1955). First, the interaction must be of the cross-over type. A noncrossover interaction does not qualify as a double dissociation, no matter what its level of statistical significance. This is because it is relatively easy for single-system models to account for noncrossover interactions (this is demonstrated later). Second, the cross-over interaction must come from measuring the same dependent variable in two different tasks. Thus, a cross-over interaction by itself is not sufficient to qualify as a double dissociation. Again, this is because it is straightforward for single-system models to account for cross-over interactions in 2 × 2 designs when only one task is used and different dependent variables are measured (more detail on this is provided later in this section).

A third condition, which is not strictly necessary but greatly strengthens the argument that a double dissociation supports multiple systems, is that the two groups in the experiment each are representative of some homogeneous population. In the Figure 16.3 example, the same results would be assumed to hold for any group of rats that received these same lesions. McCloskey (1993), in particular, has forcefully argued this point. Of the phrase "homogeneous population," both words are important. For example, McCloskey showed that spurious conclusions are possible (or perhaps likely) if each group contains a mixture of observers with different types of lesions. This requirement of homogencity makes the interpretation of a double dissociation especially problematic if each group comprises humans who have suffered some particular type of lesion. Because human lesions are generally the result of accident or stroke, no two are alike. For example, they are often unilateral and do not respect the neuroanatomical boundaries established by Broadman (1909) and others. From this perspective, neurodegenerative disease groups (e.g., Parkinson's disease) are probably better candidates for double dissociation studies, but even in Parkinson's disease there is widespread individual difference in the neuroanatomical locus and extent of damage (e.g., van Domburg & ten Donkelaar, 1991). For this reason, it is important that, whenever possible, any double dissociations reported in humans are replicated in nonhuman animals under more controlled conditions.

The term "population" in the phrase "homogeneous population" is equally important. For example, suppose one of our groups is normal, healthy, adult humans, and that a single neuropsychological patient is discovered who, when defined as the second group, produces data that satisfy a double dissociation. Several researchers have emphasized the dangers in attempting to make inferences from such data (e.g., Shallice, 1988; Van Orden, Pennington, & Stone, 2001). For example,

because we have no data from this particular patient before his or her neurological trauma, we do not know whether the patient would have produced these idiosyncratic data before the trauma, and thus, whether the peculiar data are the result of the neurological damage. When one samples from any variable population, eventually an extreme outlier is encountered that might not be representative of any existing population.

Another popular argument against the logic of double dissociation is that it leads to the conclusion that there are too many functionally separate systems (e.g., Van Orden et al., 2001). For example, consider two tasks: Both are yes/no detection tasks in which the signal is a sine wave grating and the noise is a uniform field. In the first task, however, the frequency of the signal grating is f_1 degrees, and in the second task the signal has frequency f_2 degrees. Our two groups are animals with lesions to specific spatial frequency columns in primary visual cortex. Group 1 has a lesion to columns sensitive to spatial frequencies centered at f_1 degrees, and Group 2 has a lesion to columns sensitive to frequencies centered at f_2 degrees. This experiment should produce a double dissociation, so the standard conclusion would be that there are separate systems for the detection of gratings of f_1 and f_2 degrees. Furthermore, if we repeat this experiment with other frequencies, we will have to conclude that a number of other such systems also exist. In a sense, our logic is correct because visual psychophysiologists often treat different cortical columns (or hypercolumns) as separate (mini) systems. On the other hand, from the perspective of cognitive psychology this conclusion seems too reductionistic. Cognitive psychologists might be satisfied to learn, for example, only that there are separate systems for spatial frequency and orientation perception. At this point, any more detail would just overwhelm theory development.

From a practical perspective, the problems arise in our hypothetical detection experiment because the two tasks are so similar.[1] According to standard signal detection theory, they require the same sensory and decision processes. Therefore, a practical solution to the problem is to use current theory regarding the function of the postulated systems to aid in selecting the tasks to be used in the double-dissociation experiment. In particular, two tasks should be used only if there is current theoretical debate over whether they are mediated by one or more separate systems.

In the remainder of this section, we formally examine the validity of claims that a double dissociation is strong evidence for multiple systems. We assume throughout this discussion that the double dissociation was produced in an experiment that satisfies all of the guidelines just described above (and avoids the pitfalls).

To begin, consider the strong multiple-systems model described in Equation (1). Suppose that system A is based in the hippocampus (e.g., the fornix) and specializes in spatial memory tasks and that system B is based in the caudate nucleus and specializes in visual discrimination tasks. Denote the PDF of system A in the spatial memory task when the fornix is lesioned by $f'_A(x \mid S)$, and the PDF of system B in the visual discrimination task when the caudate is lesioned by $f'_B(x \mid V)$. Such lesions will impair the two systems. We can document this by assuming that lesions affect the entire PDFs. Specifically, we assume that the performance of system A in the normal and lesioned groups is related via

$$P(\mathbf{X}_A \le x) \ge P(\mathbf{X}'_A \le x), \text{ for all values of } x. \tag{5}$$

---

[1] In fact, one might easily argue that they are so similar that they should be considered the same task, a conclusion that would violate our earlier condition that two different tasks are needed to test for a double dissociation.

These two functions are called the cumulative probability distribution functions, denoted by $F_A(x)$ and $F'_A(x)$, respectively, so Equation (5) is equivalent to

$$F_A(x) \ge F'_A(x), \quad \text{for all } x. \tag{6}$$

Similarly, we assume

$$F_B(x) \ge F'_B(x), \quad \text{for all } x. \tag{7}$$

Note that the orderings specified by Equations (6) and (7) guarantee that the means will also be ordered (although in the reverse direction; i.e., lesions will increase mean trials-to-criterion). Figure 16.4a presents hypothetical cumulative distribution functions (left) and the relative ordering of the means (right) predicted by Equations (6) and (7).

Let $G_{IJ}(x)$ denote the cumulative distribution function of trials-to-criterion for group J ($J = F$ or C for fornix or caudate lesions) in task I ($I = S$ or V for spatial memory or visual discrimination). We assume that this function provides a complete description of the dependent variable of interest (e.g., trials-to-criterion).

In the strong multiple-systems model, the observable cumulative distribution functions in the four conditions are the following:

Spatial Memory Task

Fornix Lesion	$G_{SF}(x) = F'_A(x \mid S)$
Caudate Lesion	$G_{SC}(x) = F_A(x \mid S)$

Visual DiscriminationTask

Fornix Lesion	$G_{VF}(x) = F_B(x \mid V)$
Caudate Lesion	$G_{VC}(x) = F'_B(x \mid V)$

Equations (6) and (7) guarantee that this model produces the cross-over double dissociation. Figure 16.4b presents a graphical example of these orderings.

Next, consider what a single-system model predicts in this experiment. Even if the same

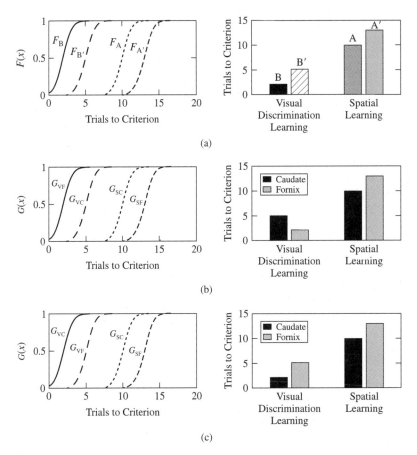

Figure 16.4 Cumulative distribution functions (left) and means (right) in four conditions of a hypothetical experiment.
NOTE: a) Orderings induced by Equations (6) and (7). b) Predictions of the strong multiple-systems model. c) Predictions for a single-system model that satisfies Equation (8); that is, fornix lesions are more detrimental than are caudate lesions.

system is used on every trial of all conditions, that system might not be equally suited to the two types of tasks, and the two types of lesions might not inflict the same amount of damage to the system. With these caveats in mind, single system models predict the following:

Spatial Memory Task

Fornix Lesion	$G_{SF}(x) = F'_F(x \mid S)$
Caudate Lesion	$G_{SC}(x) = F'_C(x \mid S)$

Visual DiscriminationTask

Fornix Lesion	$G_{VF}(x) = F'_F(x \mid V)$
Caudate Lesion	$G_{VC}(x) = F'_C(x \mid V)$

where the subscripts F and C refer to the fornix and caudate, respectively. Now, if the fornix lesion causes more damage to the system than does the caudate lesion, then we assume that the ability of the system to perform in any task is poorer with fornix lesions than with caudate lesions. Thus,

$$F'_C(x \mid S) \geq F'_F(x \mid S) \quad \text{and}$$
$$F'_C(x \mid V) \geq F'_F(x \mid V), \quad \text{for all } x. \quad (8)$$

Similarly, if the caudate lesion causes more damage, then

$$F'_F(x \mid S) \geq F'_C(x \mid S) \quad \text{and}$$
$$F'_F(x \mid V) \geq F'_C(x \mid V), \quad \text{for all } x. \quad (9)$$

In either case, there is no crossover interaction and, therefore, no double dissociation (see Figure 16.4c for an example of the Equation [8] predictions).

There are several points worth noting here. First, even if Equation (8) or (9) holds, an interaction is possible in the single system model—only a cross-over interaction is precluded. Additive effects (i.e., no interaction) would occur only if the deleterious effect of the more damaging lesion was exactly the same in both tasks. This might occur, but there is no reason to expect it.

Second, this analysis makes it clear that a single system model can predict a double dissociation if Equations (8) and (9) both fail—that is, if the deficit is more severe with the first lesion in one task and with the second lesion in the other task. For example, single system models predict a double dissociation if

$$F'_C(x \mid S) \geq F'_F(x \mid S) \quad \text{and}$$
$$F'_F(x \mid V) \geq F'_C(x \mid V), \quad \text{for all } x. \quad (10)$$

This point was noted by Dunn and Kirsner (1988), who called Equation (10) a negative relation between the tasks. With lesion data it is difficult to imagine how this might occur in a true single-system model. One possibility, though, is that the single system is composed of several subsystems, one of which is knocked out by fornix lesions and another by caudate lesions. A double dissociation could result if the subsystem damaged by the fornix lesion were more important in the spatial memory task and if the subsystem damaged by the caudate lesion were more important in the visual discrimination task. There are several problems with this scenario, however. First, if the subsystems are arranged in series, with the output of one serving as the input for the other, then it is not clear whether a double dissociation would result. Damage to the upstream subsystem would cause poor performance on both tasks because the input to the downstream, undamaged subsystem would be corrupted. On the other hand, damage to the downstream subsystem would affect performance only on one task, because the input and processing in the upstream subsystem would be unaffected by such a lesion. Thus, the only way that the double dissociation is guaranteed is if the two subsystems operate in parallel. Such a parallel system, however, shares many properties with multiple systems, so it is unclear whether its existence should be taken as support for a single system.

If different dependent variables are used for the two groups, then it becomes easy for single-system models to predict crossover double dissociations. For example, consider the hypothetical categorization RT data shown in Figure 16.5a. In this experiment, subjects must decide whether each presented stimulus is a member of category A. Figure 16.5a shows mean RT for "A" and "not A" responses as a function of the similarity between the stimulus and the category A prototype. These data are easily predicted by a single-system model that assumes subjects compute the similarity of the stimulus to the category A prototype and then compare this similarity to a criterion. Similarities above the criterion elicit an "A" response, and similarities below the criterion elicit a "not A" response. Such a model predicts the Figure 16.5a data if the time to determine whether the similarity is above or below criterion decreases with the magnitude

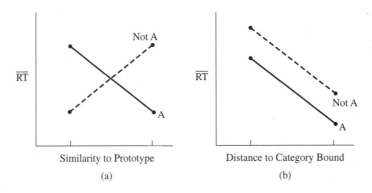

Figure 16.5   Hypothetical categorization RT data.

NOTE: a) Mean RT plotted as a function of similarity to prototype in an A-not-A task. b) Data from the same experiment plotted as a function of distance to category bound.

of the difference between the similarity and the criterion. Clearly, in such a case it would be a mistake to infer from Figure 16.5a that there are separate systems on "A" and "not A" trials.

From the perspective of double dissociation logic, there are several problems with the Figure 16.5a example. First, there are neither two groups nor two tasks. Instead, the Figure 16.5a data are from one group of subjects in one task. Second, data from two different types of response are plotted in Figure 16.5: RT for "A" responses and RT for "not A" responses. Note that this contrasts with the double dissociation shown in Figure 16.3, in which the response is the same in all conditions. In Figure 16.5a, data from one experimental condition are divided into two categories (according to the response given). Then a variable is constructed (similarity-to-prototype) that subdivides these two categories in such a way that a cross-over interaction occurs. It is important to note, however, that other variables could be defined that subdivide the categories differently, and for which the interaction might disappear. For example, the same data are replotted in Figure 16.5b against the variable "psychological distance to category bound."

If performance in some task is mediated by a single system, then it is natural that there may exist negative relations between different kinds of responses or between different dependent variables (e.g., speed vs. accuracy). Clearly, it would be a mistake to apply double-dissociation logic to a cross-over interaction in such a case.

These analyses provide a rigorous justification for the practice of inferring multiple systems when double dissociations are found, but only under a fairly limited set of circumstances (e.g., different tasks, same response, separate homogeneous populations). On the other hand, the only multiple-systems model that we have considered so far is the strong model that assumes selective influence—that is, that the observer uses separate systems in the two tasks under study. Perhaps a more plausible multiple-systems alternative is that the observer uses both systems in both conditions, but that the two tasks load differently on the two systems and the observable response is determined either by only one of the systems on any given trial or by a weighted average of the two system outputs. In other words, it is of interest to consider the conditions under which the mixture and averaging models predict a double dissociation. To our knowledge, this question has not previously been investigated.

We begin with the mixture model. Let p_S and p_V denote the probability that the hippocampal-based system is used on any given trial of the spatial memory task and the visual discrimination task, respectively. We assume that observers are more likely to use the hippocampal system in the spatial memory task and the caudate system in the visual discrimination task. This means that $p_S > 1/2 > p_V$. As before, we assume that the effect of the lesions is as described in Equations (6) and (7). Under these assumptions, the cumulative distribution functions in each condition are given by the following:

Spatial Memory Task

Fornix Lesion

$$G_{SF}(x) = p_S F'_A(x \mid S) + (1 - p_S) F_B(x \mid S)$$

Caudate Lesion

$$G_{SC}(x) = p_S F_A(x \mid S) + (1 - p_S) F'_B(x \mid S)$$

Visual Discrimination Task

Fornix Lesion

$$G_{VF}(x) = p_V F'_A(x \mid V) + (1 - p_V) F_B(x \mid V)$$

Caudate Lesion

$$G_{VC}(x) = p_V F_A(x \mid V) + (1 - p_V) F'_B(x \mid V)$$

It is not difficult to show[2] that this mixture model predicts a (crossover) double dissociation if and only if for all values of x,

$$\frac{p_S}{1 - p_S} > \frac{F_B(x \mid S) - F'_B(x \mid S)}{F_A(x \mid S) - F'_A(x \mid S)}, \quad (11)$$

and

$$\frac{1 - p_V}{p_V} > \frac{F_A(x \mid V) - F'_A(x \mid V)}{F_B(x \mid V) - F'_B(x \mid V)}. \quad (12)$$

---

[2]If the caudate group performs better than the fornix group in the spatial memory task, then $p_S F_A(x \mid S) + (1 - p_S) F'_B(x \mid S) > p_S F'_A(x \mid S) + (1 - p_S) F_B(x \mid S)$, for all x, which implies that $p_S[F_A(x \mid S) - F'_A(x \mid S)] > (1 - p_S)[F_B(x \mid S) - F'_B(x \mid S)]$, for all x. Equation (11) follows readily from this result. Equation (12) follows in a similar fashion from the result that a double dissociation requires the fornix group to perform better than the caudate group in the visual discrimination task.

Because $p_S > 1/2 > p_V$, the left side is greater than 1 in both equations. By Equations (6) and (7), the numerator and denominator of the right-hand side are positive in both equations. Thus, the mixture model predicts a double dissociation any time the effects of the lesions are the same on the two systems. If they are not (e.g., if the caudate lesion more effectively impairs the caudate-based system than the fornix lesion impairs the hippocampal-based system), then whether the mixture model predicts a double dissociation depends on the mixture probabilities p_S and p_V. If the experimenter is effective at finding two tasks that each load heavily on different systems, then p_S will be near 1 and p_V will be near 0, and the left side of Equations (11) and (12) will both be large. In this case, a double dissociation will occur even if there are large differences in the efficacy of the various lesions. Thus, with the mixture model of multiple systems, a double dissociation is not guaranteed, but it should generally be possible to find tasks and conditions (e.g., lesions) that produce one.

The predictions of the averaging model are qualitatively similar to those of the mixture model if we shift our focus from the cumulative distribution functions, $F_A(x)$ and $F_B(x)$, to the means $E(\mathbf{X}_{Ai})$ and $E(\mathbf{X}_{Bi})$ (e.g., this allows us to avoid dealing with the convolution integral of Equation (4)). Let r_S and r_V denote the weights given the hippocampal-based system on any given trial of the spatial memory task and the visual discrimination task, respectively. We assume that observers weight the hippocampal system more heavily in the spatial memory task and the caudate system more heavily in the visual discrimination task. Thus $r_S > 1/2 > r_V$. As before, we assume that the lesions impair performance; that is, because the dependent variable is trials-to-criterion, this means that $E'_A(\mathbf{X}) > E_A(\mathbf{X})$ and $E'_B(\mathbf{X}) > E_B(\mathbf{X})$. Under these assumptions, the observable means in each condition are given by the following:

Spatial Memory Task

Fornix Lesion

$$E_{SF}(\mathbf{X}) = r_S E'_A(\mathbf{X} \mid S) + (1 - r_S) E_B(\mathbf{X} \mid S)$$

Caudate Lesion

$$E_{SC}(\mathbf{X}) = r_S E_A(\mathbf{X} \mid S) + (1 - r_S) E'_B(\mathbf{X} \mid S)$$

Visual Discrimination Task

Fornix Lesion

$$E_{VF}(\mathbf{X}) = r_V E'_A(\mathbf{X} \mid V) + (1 - r_V) E_B(\mathbf{X} \mid V)$$

Caudate Lesion

$$E_{VC}(\mathbf{X}) = r_V E_A(\mathbf{X} \mid V) + (1 - r_V) E'_B(\mathbf{X} \mid V).$$

Note the similarity to the structure of the cumulative distribution functions in the mixture model. As a result, the averaging model predicts a double dissociation if

$$\frac{r_S}{1 - r_S} > \frac{E'_B(\mathbf{X} \mid S) - E_B(\mathbf{X} \mid S)}{E'_A(\mathbf{X} \mid S) - E_A(\mathbf{X} \mid S)}, \quad (13)$$

and

$$\frac{1 - r_V}{r_V} > \frac{E'_A(\mathbf{X} \mid V) - E_A(\mathbf{X} \mid V)}{E'_B(\mathbf{X} \mid V) - E_B(\mathbf{X} \mid V)}. \quad (14)$$

The conclusions are therefore similar to those in the case of the mixture model. The averaging model predicts a double dissociation if the effects of the two lesions are approximately equal. If one lesion is more severe than the other, then a double dissociation can still be predicted if the two tasks load heavily on different systems.

We believe that this analysis provides strong theoretical justification for the current practice of interpreting a double dissociation as evidence of multiple systems. However, we have also noted some important and severe limitations on this methodology. For example, it is essential that the observed interaction be of the cross-over type—not just any interaction that achieves statistical significance. Also, the same dependent variable should be measured in two different tasks that sample from separate populations of homogeneous subjects. It is also important to note that there is an asymmetry in interpreting double-dissociation results. Whereas the existence of a double dissociation (under the appropriate experimental conditions) is strong evidence for multiple systems, the failure to find a double dissociation must be interpreted more cautiously, because there are several reasonably plausible ways in which multiple-systems models could produce this null result (e.g., see our discussion of the mixture model).

Single Dissociations

Although other definitions are possible, we operationally define a single dissociation as an interaction of the type described in the last section for which there is no crossover. As already mentioned, in the absence of extenuating circumstances, it is difficult or impossible to draw strong conclusions about whether such data were produced by single or multiple systems. As we have seen, in many cases it is straightforward for single-system models to predict single dissociations. Even so, there are certain special circumstances in which single dissociation data have been used to argue for multiple systems.

Perhaps the most common argument that a single dissociation signals multiple systems has been in cases in which two groups perform equally on one task but one of these groups is impaired on a second task relative to the other group. For example, amnesic patients perform poorly on explicit memory tests but often are relatively normal on a variety of tests of implicit memory (e.g., Warrington & Weiskrantz, 1970). It is dangerous, however, to infer simply from this result that there are separate explicit and implicit memory systems. For example, there have been several formal demonstrations that certain single-system models can account for such data (e.g., Nosofsky, 1988; Nosofsky & Zaki, 1998). In addition, recently it has been argued that even garden-variety single-system models can account for single dissociations of this type if the explicit memory tests are more reliable than are the implicit tests (Buchner & Wippich, 2000; Meier & Perrig, 2000).

These arguments generally assume no a priori knowledge about the nature of the tasks that are used. When such knowledge is considered, stronger tests are sometimes possible. One such attempt employs what has been called the *logic of opposition* to test for unconscious learning (Higham, Vokey, & Pritchard, 2000; Jacoby, 1991). Consider a categorization task with two categories, denoted A and B. To begin, subjects are trained to identify members of these two categories. There are two different test conditions. In the control condition, subjects are shown a series of stimuli and are asked to respond "Yes" to each stimulus that belongs to Category A *or* B and to respond "No" to stimuli that are in neither category. In the opposition condition, subjects respond "Yes" only if the stimulus belongs to Category A. If it belongs to Category B or to neither category, then the correct response is "No." The key test is to compare the accuracy rates in the opposition condition for these two kinds of stimuli (i.e., those in Category B and those in neither category). The idea is that if responding is based solely on conscious learning, then the accuracy rates to these two kinds of stimuli should be equal, but unconscious learning could cause Category B exemplars to become associated with the notion that these stimuli are valid category members, thereby causing more "Yes" responses to Category B exemplars than to stimuli in neither category. This logic, which is not without controversy (Redington, 2000), takes advantage of our knowledge that subjects were trained on Category B exemplars but not on the stimuli in neither category.

Another possible use of a priori knowledge is to focus on the relative difficulty of the two tasks. For example, consider the two tasks de-

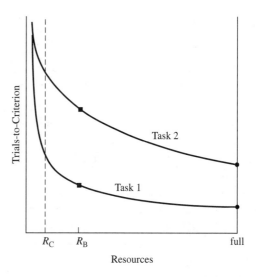

Figure 16.6   Performance operating characteristics of two tasks.

scribed by the performance operating curves shown in Figure 16.6. When full resources are available, Task 1 is easier to learn than is Task 2 (i.e., criterion performance is achieved in fewer trials for Task 1 than for Task 2). As resources are withdrawn, performance naturally declines in both tasks, although at different rates. A small to moderate decline in the available resources is more deleterious to the more difficult Task 2 (e.g., when R_b resources are available for both tasks). However, as performance on Task 2 nears floor (i.e., worst possible performance), Task 1 performance begins to narrow the gap until eventually performance on both tasks is equally bad. The point marked R_C in Figure 16.6 denotes the critical level of resources in which the rate of decline on Task 1 first exceeds the rate of decline on Task 2.

Now, suppose Tasks 1 and 2 are both learned by the same system, and consider an experiment with two conditions. In one, observers learn the two tasks with full resources available. This condition produces data points denoted by the closed circles in Figure 16.6. In the second condition, observers learn the tasks with reduced resources. This could be accomplished either by requiring observers to perform a simultaneous dual task, or perhaps through instruction (e.g., by forcing a quick response). As long as the observer has available R_C or more resources in this latter condition, single-system models predict that the reduced-resources condition will cause more problems in the more difficult Task 2. For example, with resources equal to R_B, the reduced-resources condition produces data points denoted by the closed squares in Figure 16.6. The only potential problem with this prediction is if the observer had available less than R_C resources for the learning task in the reduced-resources condition. This possibility should be easy to avoid, however, by ensuring that performance on Task 2 is well below ceiling.

Next, consider predictions in this experiment if the observer uses different systems to learn Tasks 1 and 2, and for some reason the experimental intervention to reduce resources works more effectively on the system that learns Task 1. In this case, the greater interference will be with Task 1—a result that is problematic for single system models.

This was the strategy of a recent experiment reported by Waldron and Ashby (2001). Participants in this study learned simple and complex category structures under typical single-task conditions and when performing a simultaneous numerical Stroop task. In the simple categorization tasks, each set of contrasting categories was separated by a unidimensional, explicit rule that was easy to describe verbally. An example is shown in Figure 16.7 for the rule "respond A if the background color is blue, and respond B if the background color is yellow." On the other hand, the complex tasks required integrating information from three stimulus dimensions and resulted in implicit rules that were difficult to verbalize. An example is shown in Figure 16.8. Ashby et al. (1998) hypothesized

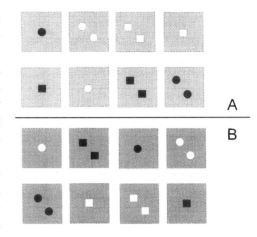

Figure 16.7 Category structure of a rule-based category-learning task.

NOTE: The optimal explicit rule is the following: Respond A if the background color is blue (depicted as light gray), and respond B if the background color is yellow (depicted as dark gray).

that learning in such tasks will be dominated by different systems—in particular, that the simple categories would be learned by an explicit, rule-based system that depends heavily on frontal cortical structures, whereas the complex categories would be learned primarily by an implicit, procedural learning system

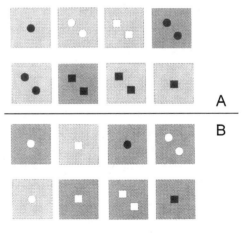

Figure 16.8 Category structure of an information-integration category-learning task with only a few exemplars in each category.

that depends heavily on subcortical structures. Stroop tasks are known to activate frontal cortex (Bench et al., 1993), so it was hypothesized that the concurrent Stroop task would interfere with the explicit system more strongly than with the implicit system. In support of this prediction, the concurrent Stroop task dramatically impaired learning of the simple explicit rules but did not significantly delay learning of the complex implicit rules. These results support the hypothesis that category learning is mediated by multiple learning systems.

Mapping Hypothesized Systems onto Known Neural Structures

Testing between single and multiple systems of learning and memory will always be more difficult when the putative systems are hypothetical constructs with no known neural basis. For example, the Waldron and Ashby (2001) dual-task study was more effective because it had earlier been hypothesized that the putative explicit system relied on frontal cortical structures much more strongly than did the implicit system. Given this and the neuroimaging evidence that Stroop tasks activate frontal cortex (Bench et al., 1993), it becomes much easier to argue that if there are multiple systems, then the concurrent Stroop task should interfere more strongly with the learning of the simpler, rule-based category structures.

In general, the memory literature has enthusiastically adopted this constraint. Most of the memory systems that have been proposed have become associated with a distinct neural basis. For example, cognitive neuroscience models of working memory focus on prefrontal cortex (e.g., Fuster, 1989; Goldman-Rakic, 1987, 1995); declarative memory models focus on the hippocampus and other medial temporal lobe structures (e.g., Gloor, 1997; Gluck & Myers, 1997; McClelland, McNaughton, & O'Reilly, 1995; Polster,

Nadel, & Schacter, 1991; Squire & Alvarez, 1995); procedural memory models focus on the basal ganglia (e.g., Jahanshahi, Brown, & Marsden, 1992; Mishkin et al., 1984; Saint-Cyr, Taylor, & Lang, 1988; Willingham et al., 1989); and models of the perceptual representation system focus on visual cortex (Curran & Schacter, 1996; Schacter, 1994; Tulving & Schacter, 1990).

CATEGORY LEARNING AS A MODEL OF THE SINGLE VERSUS MULTIPLE SYSTEMS DEBATE

Category learning is a good example of an area in which the debate over single versus multiple systems is currently being waged. The issues that have arisen in the category-learning literature are similar to issues discussed in other areas that are wrestling with this same debate. This is partly because similar methodologies are used in the different areas to test between single and multiple systems, and partly because the different subdisciplines engaged in this debate—motor learning, discrimination learning, function learning, category learning, and reasoning—have all postulated similar explicit and implicit systems. Thus, there is a very real possibility that if there are multiple systems of category learning, then these same (or highly similar) systems might also mediate other types of learning. For this reason, this section examines the debate over whether there are single or multiple systems of category learning.

Within the field of categorization, the debate over whether there is one or more than one learning system is just beginning. There have been no attempts to test the fixed-point property, and empirical demonstrations of double dissociations are rare. Nevertheless, there have been some encouraging attempts to map category-learning systems onto distinct neural structures and pathways, and as mentioned earlier, there has been at least one attempt to test for multiple systems by exploiting a known a priori ordering of task difficulty. Even so, in the case of category learning the debate over single versus multiple systems is far from resolved. Not only is there insufficient empirical evidence to decide this issue, but there is still strong theoretical disagreement as well. Although there have been a number of recent articles arguing for multiple category-learning systems (Ashby et al., 1998; Erickson & Kruschke, 1998; Pickering, 1997; Waldron & Ashby, 2001), there have also been recent papers arguing for a single system (e.g., Nosofsky & Johansen, 2000; Nosofsky & Zaki, 1998).

Category-Learning Theories

As one might expect, the early theories of category learning all assumed a single system. There were a number of such theories, but four of these have been especially important. *Rule-based theories* assume that people categorize by applying a series of explicit logical rules (e.g., Bruner, Goodnow, & Austin, 1956; Murphy & Medin, 1985; Smith & Medin, 1981). Various researchers have described this as a systematic process of hypothesis testing (e.g., Bruner et al., 1956) or theory construction and testing (e.g., Murphy & Medin, 1985). Rule-based theories are derived from the so-called classical theory of categorization, which dates back to Aristotle, although in psychology it was popularized by Hull (1920). The classical theory assumes that categorization is a process of testing whether each stimulus possesses the necessary and sufficient features for category membership (Bruner et al., 1956). Much of the work on rule-based theories has been conducted in psycholinguistics (Fodor, Bever, & Garrett, 1974; Miller & Johnson-Laird, 1976) and in psychological studies of concept formation (e.g., Bourne, 1966; Bruner et al., 1956).

Prototype theory assumes that the category representation is dominated by the prototype, or most typical member, and that categorization is a process of comparing the similarity of the stimulus to the prototype of each relevant category (Homa, Sterling, & Trepel, 1981; Posner & Keele, 1968, 1970; Reed, 1972; Rosch, 1973, 1977; Smith & Minda, 2000). In its most extreme form, the prototype *is* the category representation, but in its weaker forms the category representation includes information about other exemplars (Busemeyer, Dewey, & Medin, 1984; Homa, Dunbar, & Nohre, 1991; Shin & Nosofsky, 1992).

Exemplar theory assumes that people compute the similarity of the stimulus to the memory representation of every exemplar of all relevant categories and select a response on the basis of these similarity computations (Brooks, 1978; Estes, 1986a; Hintzman, 1986; Medin & Schaffer, 1978; Nosofsky, 1986). The assumption that the similarity computations include *every* exemplar of the relevant categories is often regarded as intuitively unreasonable. For example, Myung (1994) argued that "it is hard to imagine that a 70-year-old fisherman would remember every instance of fish that he has seen when attempting to categorize an object as a fish" (p. 348). Even if the exemplar representations are not consciously retrieved, a massive amount of activation is assumed by exemplar theory. Nevertheless, exemplar models have been used to account for asymptotic categorization performance from tasks in which the categories (a) were linearly or nonlinearly separable (Medin & Schwanenflugel, 1981; Nosofsky, 1986, 1987, 1989), (b) differed in base rate (Medin & Edelson, 1988), (c) contained correlated or uncorrelated features (Medin, Alton, Edelson, & Freko, 1982), (d) could be distinguished using a simple verbal rule (or a conjunction of simple rules; Nosofsky, Clark, & Shin, 1989), and (e) contained differing exemplar frequencies (Nosofsky, 1988).

Finally, *decision bound theory* (also called general recognition theory) assumes that there is trial-by-trial variability in the perceptual information associated with each stimulus, so the perceptual effects of a stimulus are most appropriately represented by a multivariate probability distribution (usually a multivariate normal distribution). During categorization, the observer is assumed to learn to assign responses to different regions of the perceptual space. When presented with a stimulus, the observer determines which region the perceptual effect is in and emits the associated response. The decision bound is the partition between competing response regions (Ashby, 1992; Ashby & Gott, 1988; Ashby & Lee, 1991, 1992; Ashby & Maddox, 1990, 1992, 1993; Ashby & Townsend, 1986; Maddox & Ashby, 1993). Thus, decision bound theory assumes that although exemplar information may be available, it is not used to make a categorization response. Instead, only a response label is retrieved.

Three Different Category-Learning Tasks

Each of these theories has intuitive appeal, especially in some types of categorization tasks. For example, rule-based theories seem especially compelling when the rule that best separates the contrasting categories (i.e., the optimal rule) is easy to describe verbally (Ashby et al., 1998), and an exemplar-based memorization strategy seems ideal when the contrasting categories have only a few highly distinct exemplars. Not surprisingly, proponents of the various theories have frequently collected data in exactly those tasks for which their pet theories seem best suited. If there is only one category learning system, then this strategy is fine. However, if there are multiple systems, then the different tasks that have been used might load differently on the different systems. In this case, two researchers arguing that their data best support their own theory might both be correct. As we will see later, neuropsychological and neuroimaging evidence supports this prediction. Therefore, before we examine the debate over single versus multiple systems within the categorization literature, we take some time to describe three different types of categorization tasks that each seem ideally suited to the specific psychological processes hypothesized by the different theories.

As mentioned, rule-based theories seem most compelling in tasks in which the rule that best separates the contrasting categories (i.e., the optimal rule) is easy to describe verbally (Ashby et al., 1998). As a result, observers can learn the category structures via an explicit process of hypothesis testing (Bruner et al., 1956) or theory construction and testing (Murphy & Medin, 1985). Figure 16.7 shows the stimuli and category structure of a recent rule-based task that used eight exemplars per category (Waldron & Ashby, 2001). The categorization stimuli were colored geometric figures presented on a colored background. The stimuli varied on four binary-valued dimensions: background color (blue or yellow; depicted as light or dark gray, respectively), embedded symbol color (red or green; depicted as black or white, respectively), symbol numerosity (1 or 2), and symbol shape (square or circle). This yielded a total of 16 possible stimuli. To create rule-based category structures, one dimension is selected arbitrarily to be relevant. The two values on that dimension are then assigned to the two contrasting categories. At the end of training, observers are able to describe the rule they used in rule-based tasks quite accurately. Most categorization tasks used in studies that have argued for rule-based learning have been designed in a similar fashion (e.g., Bruner et al., 1956; Salatas & Bourne, 1974), as are virtually all categorization tasks used in neuropsychological assessment, including the well-known Wisconsin Card Sorting Test (WCST; e.g., Grant & Berg, 1948; Kolb & Whishaw, 1990).

Information-integration tasks are those in which accuracy is maximized only if information from two or more stimulus components (or dimensions) must be integrated at some predecisional stage (Ashby & Gott, 1988; Shaw, 1982). A conjunction rule (e.g., respond A if the stimulus is small on dimension x and small on dimension y) is a rule-based task rather than an information-integration task because separate decisions are first made about each dimension (e.g., small or large) and then the outcome of these decisions is combined (integration is not predecisional). In many cases, the optimal rule in information-integration tasks is difficult or impossible to describe verbally (Ashby et al., 1998). That people readily learn such category structures seems problematic for rule-based theories, but not for prototype, exemplar, or decision bound theories. The neuropsychological data reviewed later suggest that performance in such tasks is qualitatively different depending on the size of the categories; in particular, when a category contains only a few highly distinct exemplars, memorization is feasible. However, when the relevant categories contain many exemplars (e.g., hundreds), memorization is less efficient. An exemplar strategy seems especially plausible when the categories contain only a few highly distinct exemplars. Not surprisingly, most articles arguing for exemplar-based category learning have used such designs (e.g., Estes, 1994; Medin & Schaffer, 1978; Nosofsky, 1986; Smith & Minda, 2000).

Figure 16.8 shows the stimuli and category structure of a recent information-integration task that used only eight exemplars per category (Waldron & Ashby, 2001). The categorization stimuli were the same as those in Figure 16.7. To create these category structures,

one dimension was arbitrarily selected to be irrelevant. For example, in Figure 16.8 the irrelevant dimension is symbol shape. Next, one level on each relevant dimension was arbitrarily assigned a value of $+1$, and the other level was assigned a value of 0. In Figure 16.8 a background color of blue (depicted as light gray), a symbol color of green (depicted as white), and a symbol number of 2 were all assigned a value of $+1$. Finally, the category assignments were determined by the following rule:

The stimulus belongs to Category A if the sum of values on the relevant dimensions > 1.5;

Otherwise it belongs to Category B.

This rule is readily learned by healthy young adults, but even after achieving perfect performance, they can virtually never accurately describe the rule they used.

When there are many exemplars in each category, memorization strategies, which are necessarily exemplar-based, become more difficult to implement. In these situations, it seems especially plausible that observers learn to associate category labels with regions of perceptual space (as predicted by decision bound theory). Figure 16.9 shows the category structure of an information-integration categorization task in which there are hundreds of exemplars in each category (developed by Ashby & Gott, 1988). In this experiment, each stimulus is a line that varies across trials in length and orientation. Each cross in Figure 16.9 denotes the length and orientation of an exemplar in Category A, and each dot denotes the length and orientation of an exemplar in Category B. The categories overlap, so perfect accuracy is impossible in this example. Even so, the quadratic curve is the boundary that maximizes response accuracy. This curve is difficult to describe verbally, so this is an information-integration task. Many of

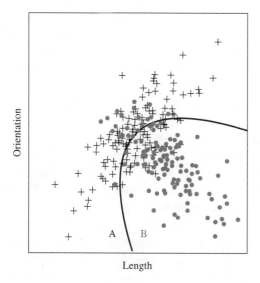

Figure 16.9 Category structure of an information-integration category-learning task with many exemplars per category.

NOTE: Each stimulus is a line that varies across trials in length and orientation. Every black plus sign depicts the length and orientation of a line in Category A, and every gray dot depicts the length and orientation of a line in Category B. The quadratic curve is the boundary that maximizes accuracy.

the studies supporting decision bound theory have used this randomization design (Ashby & Gott, 1988; Ashby & Maddox, 1990, 1992; Maddox & Ashby, 1993).

A prototype abstraction process does not work well in the Figure 16.9 experiment because prototype theory always predicts linear decision bounds (Ashby & Gott, 1988), and there is much data showing that quadratic bounds give a much better account of the resulting data than do linear bounds (Ashby & Maddox, 1992). A prototype abstraction process seems most plausible in prototype distortion tasks in which each category is created by first defining a category prototype and then creating the category members by randomly distorting these prototypes. In the most popular version of prototype distortion tasks, the category exemplars are random dot patterns

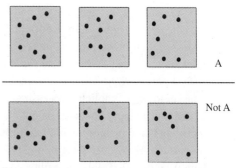

Figure 16.10 Some exemplars from a prototype distortion category-learning task with random dot patterns.

(Posner & Keele, 1968, 1970). An example of the random dot pattern task is shown in Figure 16.10. To begin, many stimuli are created by randomly placing a number of dots on the display. One of these stimuli is then chosen as the prototype for Category A. The others become stimuli not belonging to Category A. The other Category A exemplars are then created by randomly perturbing the position of each dot in the Category A prototype. Categories created from these random dot patterns have been especially popular with prototype theorists (e.g., Homa, Cross, Cornell, Goldman, & Schwartz, 1973; Homa & Cultice, 1984; Homa et al., 1981; Posner & Keele, 1968, 1970).

Explicit versus Implicit Category Learning

As mentioned previously, many of the current theories that postulate multiple category-learning systems propose separate explicit and implicit subsystems. The literature on multiple memory systems also frequently uses the terms explicit and implicit, but usually in a slightly different fashion. Therefore, before proceeding further, we briefly discuss the existing criteria that are used to determine whether category learning is explicit or implicit.

There is widespread agreement, within both the category-learning and memory literatures, that explicit processing requires conscious awareness (e.g., Ashby et al., 1998; Cohen & Squire, 1980). The disagreements relate more to how implicit processing is defined. Many memory theorists adopt the strong criteria that a memory is implicit only if there is no conscious awareness of its details *and* there is no knowledge that a memory has even been stored (e.g., Schacter, 1987). In a typical categorization task (e.g., any of those described in the last section) these criteria are impossible to meet when trial-by-trial feedback is provided (as it usually is). When an observer receives feedback that a response is correct, this alone makes it obvious that learning has occurred, even if there is no internal access to the system that is mediating this learning. Thus, in category learning, a weaker criterion for implicit learning is typically used in which the observer is required only to have no conscious access to the nature of the learning, even though he or she would be expected to know that some learning had occurred.

The stronger criteria for implicit processing that have been adopted in much of the memory literature could be applied in unsupervised category-learning tasks, in which no trial-by-trial feedback of any kind is provided. In the typical unsupervised task, observers are told the number of contrasting categories and are asked to assign stimuli to these categories but are never told whether a particular response is correct or incorrect. Free sorting is a similar but more unstructured task in which participants are not told the number of contrasting categories (e.g., Ashby & Maddox, 1998). Although unsupervised and free-sorting tasks are ideal for using the stricter criteria to test for implicit learning, so far the only learning that has been demonstrated in such tasks is explicit (Ashby, Queller, & Berretty, 1999; Medin, Wattenmaker, & Hampson, 1997).

One danger with equating explicit processing with conscious awareness is that this shifts the debate from how to define "explicit" to how to define "conscious awareness." Ashby et al. (1998) suggested that one pragmatic solution to this problem is to define operationally a categorization rule as explicit if it is easy to describe verbally. By this criterion, the rule that separates the categories in Figure 16.7 is explicit, whereas the rules best separating the categories in Figures 16.8 and 16.9 are implicit. This definition works well in most cases, but it seems unlikely that verbalizability should be a requirement for explicit reasoning. For example, the insight displayed by Köhler's (1925) famous apes seems an obvious example of explicit reasoning in the absence of language. Ultimately, then, a theoretically motivated criterion for conscious awareness is needed.

One way to develop a theory of conscious awareness is by exploiting the relationship between awareness and working memory. For example, the contents of working memory are clearly accessible to conscious awareness. In fact, because of its close association to executive attention, a strong argument can be made that the contents of working memory *define* our conscious awareness. When we say that we are consciously aware of some object or event, we mean that our executive attention has been directed to that stimulus. Its representation in our working memory gives it a moment-to-moment permanence. Working memory makes it possible to link events in the immediate past with those in the present, and it allows us to anticipate events in the near future. All of these are defining properties of conscious awareness.

The association between working memory and the prefrontal cortex makes it possible to formulate cognitive neuroscience models of consciousness. The most influential such model was developed by Francis Crick and Christof Koch (Crick & Koch, 1990, 1995,

1998). The Crick-Koch hypothesis states that one can have conscious awareness only of activity in brain areas that project directly to the prefrontal cortex.[3] Primary visual cortex (area V1) does not project directly to the prefrontal cortex, so the Crick-Koch hypothesis asserts that we cannot be consciously aware of activity in V1. Crick and Koch (1995, 1998) described evidence in support of this prediction. Of course, many other brain regions also do not project directly to the prefrontal cortex. For example, the basal ganglia do not project directly to the prefrontal cortex (i.e., they first project through the thalamus), so the Crick-Koch hypothesis predicts that we are not aware of activity within the basal ganglia. Memory theorists believe that the basal ganglia mediate procedural memories (Jahanshahi et al., 1992; Mishkin et al., 1984; Saint-Cyr et al., 1988; Willingham et al., 1989), so the Crick-Koch hypothesis provides an explanation of why we do not seem to be aware of procedural (e.g., motor) learning.

Category Learning and Memory

The notion that there may be multiple category learning systems goes back at least to 1978, when Brooks hypothesized that category learning is mediated by separate "deliberate, verbal, analytic control processes and implicit, intuitive, nonanalytic processes" (p. 207). Nevertheless, most quantitative accounts of category learning have assumed the existence of a single system (e.g., Estes, 1986a; Hintzman, 1986; Kruschke, 1992; Medin & Schaffer, 1978; Nosofsky, 1986). Recently, however, quantitative models that assume multiple category learning systems

have been developed (e.g., Ashby et al., 1998; Erickson & Kruschke, 1998). For example, Ashby et al. (1998) proposed a formal neuropsychological theory of multiple category learning systems called COVIS (competition between verbal and implicit systems), which assumes separate explicit (rule-based) and implicit (procedural learning-based) systems. In response to these multiple-systems proposals, Nosofsky and Zaki (1998) and Nosofsky and Johansen (2000) argued that single-system (exemplar) models can account for many of the phenomena that have been used to support the notion of multiple systems.

Another way to study category learning systems is to emphasize the relationship between category learning and memory. Of course, every category-learning system requires memory. In fact, one could characterize category learning as the process of establishing some durable record (i.e., a memory) of the structure of the relevant categories, or possibly of a rule for correctly assigning new stimuli to one of the categories. Because much is now known about the neurobiology of memory, this might be a way to learn quickly about the neurobiology of category learning.

Each of the multiple memory systems that have been proposed is thought to have a distinct neural basis. Cognitive neuroscience models of working memory focus on prefrontal cortex (e.g., Fuster, 1989; Goldman-Rakic, 1987, 1995); declarative memory models focus on the hippocampus and other medial temporal lobe structures (e.g., Gloor, 1997; Gluck & Myers, 1997; McClelland et al., 1995; Polster et al., 1991; Squire & Alvarez, 1995); procedural memory models focus on the basal ganglia (Jahanshahi et al., 1992; Mishkin et al., 1984; Saint-Cyr et al., 1988; Willingham et al., 1989); and models of the perceptual representation system focus on visual cortex (e.g., Curran & Schacter, 1997; Schacter, 1994).

---

[3]Crick and Koch (1998) did not take the strong position that working memory is necessary for conscious awareness. Even so, they did argue that some short-term memory store is required. However, they left open the possibility that an extremely transient iconic memory might be sufficient.

In addition, each of the category-learning theories just described maps in a natural way onto a different one of these memory systems. To learn and apply explicit rules, one must construct and maintain them in working memory. Executive attention is also required to select and switch among alternative rules. Thus, rule-based theories depend on working memory. Exemplar theory assumes that people store and access detailed representations of specific exemplars that they have seen. The declarative memory system seems tailor made for this type of memory encoding and storage. Indeed, it has specifically been proposed that medial temporal lobe structures (i.e., the hippocampus) mediate the encoding and consolidation of exemplar memories (Pickering, 1997). On the other hand, declarative memory retrieval is typically thought to occur with conscious awareness (e.g., Cohen & Squire, 1980), whereas exemplar theorists are careful to assume that activation of the exemplar memories does *not* require awareness (e.g., Nosofsky, 1986; Nosofsky & Alfonso-Reese, 1999; Nosofsky & Zaki, 1998).

Decision bound theory assumes that people learn to associate abstract response programs (e.g., response labels) with groups of similar stimuli (Ashby & Waldron, 1999). Thus, the stored memories are of stimulus-response associations, rather than of rules or previously seen exemplars. This is a form of procedural memory (Ashby et al., 1998).

The prototype abstraction process assumed by prototype theory is perhaps the most difficult to map onto existing accounts of memory. The memory of a prototype is durable, so working memory by itself is insufficient. Prototype theorists also have been clear that the prototype might not correspond exactly to any previously seen exemplar, which rules out simple declarative memory. Finally, prototypes are not tied to responses in any direct way, so procedural memory can also be ruled out. Although it is not clear that such a result is necessary, we present evidence later that prototype abstraction depends, at least sometimes, on perceptual learning and, as a result, on the perceptual representation memory system.

It is important to point out that even if multiple memory systems participate in category learning, this does not necessarily imply that there are multiple category-learning systems. For example, it is logically possible that a single category-learning system accesses different memory systems in different category-learning tasks. Such a model could predict double or triple dissociations across tasks. As mentioned in the last major section, however, such a model also shares many properties with a multiple-systems perspective. As such, it would probably lie somewhere in the middle of the continuum between pure single-system and pure multiple-system models. In our view, it would be counterproductive to place a sharp boundary on this continuum in an attempt to produce a criterion that classifies every model as postulating either single or multiple systems. Instead, the goal in all areas of learning and memory should be to understand how humans perform this vitally important skill. In the case of category learning, understanding what memory systems are involved is an important first step in this process.

A good example of this blurring between single and multiple systems can be seen with prototype abstraction. If this process is mediated by a perceptual representation system that depends on perceptual learning in visual cortex, then it is not clear that prototype abstraction would meet our criteria as a separate system. When the stimuli are visual in nature, then any category-learning system must receive input from the visual system. If some category-learning system X depends on input from the brain region mediating prototype abstraction, then system X and the

Table 16.1   Performance of Various Neuropsychological Populations on Four Types of Category-Learning Tasks

Neuropsychological Group	Task			
		Information-Integration		Prototype Distortion
	Rule-Based	Many Exemplars	Few Exemplars	
Frontal Lobe Lesions	Impaired	?	Normal	?
Parkinson's Disease	Impaired	Impaired	Impaired	Normal
Huntington's Disease	Impaired	Impaired	Impaired	Normal
Medial Temporal Lobe Amnesia	Normal	Normal	Late Training Deficit	Normal

prototype abstraction system would not be mediated by separate neural pathways—a criterion that we earlier decided was a necessary condition for separate systems. For example, under this scenario a double dissociation between system X and the prototype system should be impossible. Damage to the neural structures downstream from visual cortex that mediate system X should induce deficits in category-learning tasks mediated by system X, but not in prototype abstraction tasks. On the other hand, damage to visual cortex should impair all types of visual category learning. Thus, if prototype abstraction is mediated within visual cortex, then any group impaired in prototype abstraction should also be impaired on all other category-learning tasks. In addition, it should be extremely difficult, or impossible, to find neuropsychological patient groups that are impaired in prototype abstraction, but not in other types of category learning. As we will see shortly, this latter prediction is supported by current neuropsychological category-learning data.

Under the assumption that the category-learning tasks just described differentially load on different memory systems, then theoretically it should be possible to find neuropsychological populations that establish at least a triple dissociation across the tasks. Ashby and Ell (2001) reviewed the current neuropsychological category-learning data to test this prediction. Presently, there is exten-

sive category learning data on only a few neuropsychological populations. The best data come from four different groups: (a) patients with frontal lobe lesions, (b) patients with medial temporal lobe amnesia, and two types of patients suffering from a disease of the basal ganglia: either (c) Parkinson's or (d) Huntington's disease. Table 16.1 summarizes the performance of these groups on the three different types of category learning tasks.

Note first that Table 16.1 does not establish a triple dissociation. At best, one could argue from the table only for a double dissociation—between frontal lobe patients and medial temporal lobe amnesiacs on rule-based tasks and information-integration tasks with few exemplars per category. Specifically, frontal patients are impaired on rule-based tasks (e.g., the WCST; Kolb & Whishaw, 1990) but medial temporal lobe amnesiacs are normal (e.g., Janowsky, Kritchevsky, & Squire, 1989; Leng & Parkin, 1988). At the same time, the available data on information-integration tasks with few exemplars per category indicates that frontal patients are normal (Knowlton, Mangels, & Squire, 1996) but medial temporal lobe amnesiacs are impaired (i.e., they show a late-training deficit; that is, they learn normally during the first 50 trials or so, but thereafter show impaired learning relative to age-matched controls; Knowlton, Squire, & Gluck, 1994). Therefore, the neuropsychological data support the hypothesis that at least two memory systems participate in category learning. Of course, until more data are collected on the information-integration tasks, this conclusion must be considered tentative.

Note also that Table 16.1 supports the prediction that it should be difficult to find patient groups that are impaired in the prototype distortion task but not in the other types of tasks. We know of no data on the performance of frontal lobe patients in prototype distortion tasks, but if learning in these tasks is mediated within visual cortex, then frontal patients should not be impaired in prototype distortion tasks.

If three or more memory systems participate in category learning, then why does Table 16.1 not document a triple dissociation? There are several reasons why a triple dissociation might not be observed even if multiple memory systems are involved. First, Table 16.1 is incomplete. There are several cells with no known data. For example, we know of no data on the performance of frontal patients in information-integration tasks with many exemplars per category. Conclusions in some other cells are based on very little data. As mentioned earlier, this is the case for the late-training deficit reported for medial temporal lobe amnesiacs in information-integration tasks with few exemplars per category. Second, even with unlimited data in each cell, there is no guarantee that these four patient groups are appropriate for establishing a triple dissociation. The groups included in Table 16.1 were selected because they are the groups for which there is the most current data, rather than for some theoretical purpose. For example, the ideal groups might each have focal damage to a different memory system. This condition is surely not met for the Table 16.1 groups. For example, Parkinson's and Huntington's diseases affect similar structures (i.e., the basal ganglia). Of course, to select groups that satisfy this condition requires specific hypotheses about the neural structures and pathways that mediate the putatively separate systems. There are two ways to generate such hypotheses. One is to use Table 16.1 and recent neuroimaging results to make such inferences, and another is to examine current neuropsychological theories of multiple systems in category learning. We follow these two approaches in the next section.

The Neurobiological Bases of Category Learning

Patients with frontal or basal ganglia dysfunction are impaired in rule-based tasks (e.g., Brown & Marsden, 1988; Cools, van den Bercken, Horstink, van Spaendonck, & Berger, 1984; Kolb & Whishaw, 1990; Robinson, Heaton, Lehman, & Stilson, 1980), but patients with medial temporal lobe damage are normal in this type of category-learning task (e.g., Janowsky et al., 1989; Leng & Parkin, 1988). Thus, an obvious first hypothesis is that the prefrontal cortex and the basal ganglia participate in this type of learning but the medial temporal lobes do not. Converging evidence for the hypothesis that these are important structures in rule-based category learning comes from several sources. First, a functional magnetic resonance imaging (fMRI) study of a rule-based task similar to the Wisconsin Card Sorting Test showed activation (among other regions) in the right dorsal-lateral prefrontal cortex, the anterior cingulate, and the right caudate nucleus (i.e., head; Rao et al., 1997). Second, many studies have implicated these structures as key components of executive attention (Posner & Petersen, 1990) and working memory (e.g., Fuster, 1989; Goldman-Rakic, 1987), both of which are likely to be critically important to the explicit processes of rule formation and testing that are assumed to mediate rule-based category learning. Third, a recent neuroimaging study identified the (dorsal) anterior cingulate as the site of hypothesis generation in a rule-based category-learning task (Elliott & Dolan, 1998). Fourth, lesion studies in rats implicate the dorsal caudate nucleus in rule switching (Winocur & Eskes, 1998).

Next, note that in information integration tasks with large categories, only patients with basal ganglia dysfunction are known to be impaired (Filoteo, Maddox, & Davis, 2001a; Maddox & Filoteo, 2001). In particular, medial temporal lobe patients are normal (Filoteo, Maddox, & Davis, 2001b). Therefore, a first hypothesis should be that the basal ganglia are critical in this task but that the medial temporal lobes are not. If the number of exemplars per category is reduced in this task to a small number (e.g., 4 to 8), then medial temporal lobe amnesiacs show late training deficits; that is, they learn normally during the first 50 trials or so but thereafter show impaired learning relative to age-matched controls (Knowlton et al., 1994). An obvious possibility, in this case, is that normal observers begin memorizing responses to at least a few of the more distinctive stimuli—a strategy that is not available to the medial temporal lobe amnesiacs, and which is either not helpful or impossible when the categories contain many exemplars. Because patients with basal ganglia dysfunction are also impaired with small categories requiring information integration (Knowlton, Mangels, et al., 1996; Knowlton, Squire, et al., 1996), a first hypothesis should be that learning in such tasks depends on the basal ganglia and on medial temporal lobe structures. The hypothesis that the basal ganglia are active in information-integration tasks was supported by Poldrack, Prabhakaran, et al. (1999), who used fMRI to measure neural activation at four different time points of learning in a probabilistic version of the information-integration task with few exemplars per category. They re-ported learning related changes within prefrontal cortex and in the tail of the right caudate nucleus. Interestingly, they also reported a simultaneous suppression of activity within the medial temporal lobes. Thus, the available neuroimaging data predict that the deficits of basal ganglia disease patients in information-integration tasks may arise from dysfunction in the tail of the caudate nucleus.

Finally, not one of these four patient groups is impaired on the prototype distortion tasks, which suggests that learning on these tasks does not depend on an intact medial temporal lobe or basal ganglia (Knowlton, Ramus, & Squire, 1992; Knowlton, Squire, et al., 1996; Kolodny, 1994; Meulemans, Peigneux, & Van der Linden, 1998). As mentioned earlier, it has been suggested that learning might depend instead on the perceptual representation memory system—through a perceptual learning process (Knowlton, Squire, et al., 1996). In the random dot pattern experiments, this makes sense because all category A exemplars are created by randomly perturbing the positions of the dots that form the category A prototype (see Figure 16.9). Thus, if there are cells in visual cortex that respond strongly to the category A prototype, they are also likely to respond to the other category A exemplars, and perceptual learning will increase their response. If this occurs, the observer could perform well in this task by responding "yes" to any stimulus that elicits a strong feeling of visual familiarity. Recent fMRI studies of subjects in prototype distortion tasks show learning related changes in visual cortex (Reber, Stark, & Squire, 1998), and are thus consistent with this hypothesis.

Table 16.2 summarizes the neural implications of the current neuropsychological and neuroimaging data. Note that the table is consistent with current theories about the neurobiological bases of memory—in particular, that the basal ganglia are important in procedural memory and that the medial temporal

Table 16.2   Brain Regions that Current Neuropsychological Data Implicate in the Various Category Learning Tasks

Brain Region	Rule-Based	Information-Integration		Prototype Distortion
		Many Exemplars	Few Exemplars	
Prefrontal Cortex	X			
Visual Cortex				X
Basal Ganglia	X	X	X	
Medial Temporal Lobe			X	

lobes are critical for declarative memory. Despite the arguments and evidence in support of the Table 16.2 conclusions, however, much more work is needed before the table can be considered more than speculative.

The Explicit System

Several recent neurospsychological theories agree with some of the same conclusions drawn in Table 16.2. For example, Figure 16.11 describes a recent neurobiological model of the explicit system (Ashby et al., 1998, Ashby, Isen, & Turken, 1999). The key structures are the anterior cingulate, the prefrontal cortex, and the head of the caudate nucleus. Figure 16.11 shows the model during a trial of the rule-based category learning task illustrated in Figure 16.7. Various salient explicit rules reverberate in working memory loops between prefrontal cortex (PFC) and thalamus (Alexander, DeLong, & Strick, 1986). In Figure 16.11, one such loop maintains the representation of a rule focusing on the shape of the symbols, and one loop maintains a rule focusing on symbol number. An excitatory projection from the PFC to the head of the caudate nucleus prevents the globus pallidus from interrupting these loops. The anterior cingulate selects new explicit rules to load into working memory, and the head of the caudate nucleus mediates the switch from one active loop to another (facilitated by dopamine projections from the ventral tegmental area and the substantia nigra).

The Figure 16.11 model is consistent with the neuroimaging data described in the previous section, and it accounts for the rule-based category-learning deficits described in

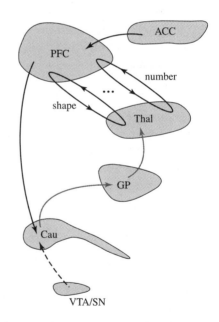

Figure 16.11 A model of the explicit category-learning system.
NOTE: Black projections are excitatory; gray projections are inhibitory; and dashed projections are dopaminergic. PFC = prefrontal cortex; ACC = anterior cingulate cortex; Thal = thalamus; GP = globus pallidus; Cau = caudate nucleus; VTA = ventral tegmental area; SN = substantia nigra.

Table 16.1. First, of course, it is obvious that the model predicts that patients with lesions of the prefrontal cortex will be impaired on rule-based category learning tasks. It also predicts that the deficits seen in Parkinson's disease are due to dysfunction in the head of the caudate nucleus. Postmortem autopsy reveals that damage to the head of the caudate is especially severe in Parkinson's disease (van Domburg & ten Donkelaar, 1991), so the model predicts that this group should show widespread and profound deficits on rule-based categorization tasks. The neuropsychological evidence strongly supports this prediction (e.g., on the WCST; Brown & Marsden, 1988; Cools et al., 1984). In fact, the model described in Figure 16.11 predicts that because of its reciprocal connection to the prefrontal cortex, many of the well documented "frontal-like" symptoms of Parkinson's disease might actually be due to damage in the head of the caudate nucleus.

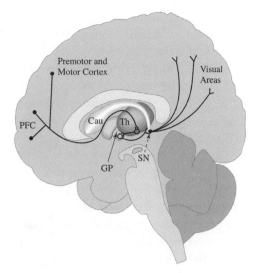

Figure 16.12 A procedural-memory-based category-learning system.
NOTE: Excitatory projections end in solid circles; inhibitory projections end in open circles; and dopaminergic projections are dashed. PFC = prefrontal cortex; Cau = caudate nucleus; GP = globus pallidus; Th = thalamus.

The Procedural Learning System

Figure 16.12 shows the circuit of a putative procedural memory-based category-learning system (proposed by Ashby et al., 1998; Ashby & Waldron, 1999). The key structure in this model is the caudate nucleus, a major input structure within the basal ganglia. In primates, all of extrastriate visual cortex projects directly to the tail of the caudate nucleus, with about 10,000 visual cortical cells converging on each caudate cell (Wilson, 1995). Cells in the tail of the caudate (i.e., medium spiny cells) then project to prefrontal and premotor cortex (via the globus pallidus and thalamus; e.g., Alexander et al., 1986). The model assumes that through a procedural learning process, each caudate unit learns to associate a category label, or perhaps an abstract motor program, with a large group of visual cortical cells (i.e., all that project to it). This learning is thought to be facilitated by a reward-mediated dopamine signal

from the substantia nigra (pars compacta; e.g., Wickens, 1993).

Lesions of the tail of the caudate, in both rats and monkeys, impair the animal's ability to associate one motor response with one visual stimulus and a different response with some other stimulus (e.g., vertical vs. horizontal lines; McDonald & White, 1993, 1994; Packard et al., 1989; Packard & McGaugh, 1992). For example, in one study, rats with lesions in the tail of the caudate could not learn to discriminate between safe and unsafe platforms in the Morris water maze when the safe platform was marked with horizontal lines and the unsafe platform was marked with vertical lines (Packard & McGaugh, 1992). The same animals learned normally, however, when the cues signaling which platform was safe were spatial. Because the tail of the caudate nucleus is not a classic visual area, it is unlikely that these animals have an impaired ability to perceive the stimuli. Rather, it seems more likely that their deficit is in learning the appropriate stimulus-response associations. The Figure 16.12 model predicts that this same type of stimulus-response association learning mediates performance in the information-integration category learning tasks described in Figures 16.8 and 16.9.

The Figure 16.12 model accounts for the category learning deficits of patients with Parkinson's and Huntington's disease in information-integration tasks because both of these populations suffer from caudate dysfunction. It also explains why frontal patients and medial temporal lobe amnesiacs are relatively normal in these tasks—that is, because neither prefrontal cortex nor medial temporal lobe structures play a prominent role in the Figure 16.12 model.

The model shown in Figure 16.12 is strictly a model of *visual* category learning. However, it is feasible that a similar system exists in the other modalities because almost all of them also project directly to the basal ganglia, and then indirectly to frontal cortical areas (again via the globus pallidus and the thalamus; e.g., Chudler, Sugiyama, & Dong, 1995). The main difference is in where within the basal ganglia they initially project. For example, auditory cortex projects directly to the body of the caudate (i.e., rather than to the tail; Arnalud, Jeantet, Arsaut, & Demotes-Mainard, 1996).

The Perceptual Representation and Medial Temporal Lobe Category-Learning Systems

No one has yet proposed a detailed category-learning model that is based on the perceptual representation memory system. However, as noted earlier, based on work in the memory literature, it seems likely that such a category learning system would be based in sensory cortex (Curran & Schacter, 1996; Schacter, 1994).

In cognitive psychology, one of the most popular and influential theories of category learning is exemplar theory (Brooks, 1978; Estes, 1986b; Medin & Schaffer, 1978; Nosofsky, 1986), which assumes that categorization decisions are made by accessing memory representations of previously seen exemplars. Although most exemplar theorists have not taken a strong stand about the neural basis by which these memory representations are encoded, those who have assume that the medial temporal lobes are heavily involved (e.g., Pickering, 1997). Despite the popularity of exemplar theory within cognitive psychology, however, the most convincing direct neuropsychological evidence in support of a key role of the medial temporal lobes in category learning remains the late-training deficit identified in Table 16.1 (Knowlton et al., 1994). Even so, this finding is not without controversy, as a recent neuroimaging study found suppression of medial temporal lobe activity in this same task (Poldrack, Prabhakaran, et al., 1999). Although many neurobiological models of hippocampal function have been proposed, there have been only a few attempts to apply these models to category learning (Gluck, Oliver, & Myers, 1996; Pickering, 1997).

Summary

Although hotly debated, the question of whether human category learning is mediated by one or several category-learning systems is currently unresolved. Recent neuropsychological and neuroimaging data support the hypothesis that different memory systems may participate in different types of category-learning tasks, but current data do not allow stronger conclusions to be drawn.

CONCLUSIONS

The debate over whether learning and memory are mediated by one or several distinct systems is being waged in many areas of cognitive psychology. Although the setting of these debates differs—from memory to function learning to discrimination learning to category learning—a number of common themes tie all these debates together. First, the methodologies that are most appropriate for testing between single and multiple systems are the same no matter what the domain. For example, the fixed-point property and double dissociations are powerful tools that can (and should) be used in any area trying to resolve this issue. Second, regardless of the field, it is unrealistic to expect any single study to resolve the debate over single versus multiple system. Instead, it is imperative that all available evidence be evaluated simultaneously. For example, given three data sets that all seemingly point toward multiple systems, it is not valuable to show that there exists three different single-system models that are each consistent with one set of data. The important question is really whether the single model that best accounts for all three data sets simultaneously postulates one or multiple systems of learning and memory. Third, all fields engaged in the debate over single versus multiple systems should look seriously toward cognitive neuroscience as a way to add more constraints to the existing models, and as a mechanism for building bridges to other related areas of cognitive psychology.

In our view, however the debate is resolved, it is likely to prove a valuable experience for whatever field engages it. The benefit of asking whether there are single or multiple systems of learning and memory is that this question organizes new research efforts, encourages collecting data of a qualitatively different nature than has been collected in the past, and also immediately ties the field in question to the memory literature and a variety of other seemingly disparate literatures. The one danger that must be resisted consists of engaging in endless debate about what con-stitutes a system. One's definition of system will obviously affect how the question of single versus multiple systems is answered, but the process of asking—and all its associated benefits—is far more important than the answer itself.

REFERENCES

Alexander, G. E., DeLong, M. R., & Strick, P. L. (1986). Parallel organization of functionally segregated circuits linking basal ganglia and cortex. *Annual Review of Neuroscience, 9,* 357–381.

Arnalud, E., Jeantet, Y., Arsaut, J., & Demotes-Mainard, J. (1996). Involvement of the caudal striatum in auditory processing: C-fos response to cortical application of picrotoxin and to auditory stimulation. *Brain Research: Molecular Brain Research, 41,* 27–35.

Ashby, F. G. (1992). Multidimensional models of categorization. In F. G. Ashby (Ed.), *Multidimensional models of perception and cognition.* Hillsdale, NJ: Erlbaum.

Ashby, F. G., Alfonso-Reese, L. A., Turken, A. U., & Waldron, E. M. (1998). A neuropsychological theory of multiple systems in category learning. *Psychological Review, 105,* 442–481.

Ashby, F. G., Boynton, G., & Lee, W. W. (1994). Categorization response time with multidimensional stimuli. *Perception & Psychophysics, 55,* 11–27.

Ashby, F. G., & Ell, S. W. (2001). *The neurobiology of human category learning. Trends in Cognitive Sciences, 5,* 204–210.

Ashby, F. G., & Gott, R. E. (1988). Decision rules in the perception and categorization of multidimensional stimuli. *Journal of Experimental Psychology: Learning, Memory, and Cognition, 14,* 33–53.

Ashby, F. G., Isen, A. M., & Turken, A. U. (1999). A neuropsychological theory of positive affect and its influence on cognition. *Psychological Review, 106,* 529–550.

Ashby, F. G., & Lee, W. W. (1991). Predicting similarity and categorization from identification. *Journal of Experimental Psychology: General, 120,* 150–172.

Ashby, F. G., & Lee, W. W. (1992). On the relationship between identification, similarity, and categorization: Reply to Nosofsky and Smith (1992). *Journal of Experimental Psychology: General, 121,* 385–393.

Ashby, F. G., & Maddox, W. T. (1990). Integrating information from separable psychological dimensions. *Journal of Experimental Psychology: Human Perception & Performance, 16,* 598–612.

Ashby, F. G., & Maddox, W. T. (1992). Complex decision rules in categorization: Contrasting novice and experienced performance. *Journal of Experimental Psychology: Human Perception & Performance, 18,* 50–71.

Ashby, F. G., & Maddox, W. T. (1993). Relations between prototype, exemplar, and decision bound models of categorization. *Journal of Mathematical Psychology, 37,* 372–400.

Ashby, F. G., & Maddox, W. T. (1998). Stimulus categorization. In M. H. Birnbaum (Ed.), *Handbook of perception and cognition: Judgment, decision making, and measurement* (Vol. 3). New York: Academic Press.

Ashby, F. G., Queller, S., & Berretty, P. T. (1999). On the dominance of unidimensional rules in unsupervised categorization. *Perception & Psychophysics, 61,* 1178–1199.

Ashby, F. G., & Townsend, J. T. (1986). Varieties of perceptual independence. *Psychological Review, 93,* 154–179.

Ashby, F. G., & Waldron, E. M. (1999). The nature of implicit categorization. *Psychonomic Bulletin & Review, 6,* 363–378.

Bench, C. J., Frith, C. D., Grasby, P. M., Friston, K. J., Paulesu, E., Frackowiak, R. S. J., & Dolan, R. J. (1993). Investigations of the functional anatomy of attention using the Stroop test. *Neuropsychologia, 33,* 907–922.

Bourne, L. E. (1966). *Human conceptual behavior.* Boston: Allyn & Bacon.

Broadman, K. (1909). Vergleichende Lokalisationslehre der Grosshimrinde in ihren Prinzipien dargestellt auf Grund des Zellenbaues. Leipzig: Barth.

Brooks, L. (1978). Nonanalytic concept formation and memory for instances. In E. Rosch & B. B. Lloyd (Eds.), *Cognition and categorization* (pp. 169–211). Hillsdale, NJ: Erlbaum.

Brown, R. G., & Marsden, C. D. (1988). Internal versus external cues and the control of attention in Parkinson's disease. *Brain, 111,* 323–345.

Bruner, J. S., Goodnow, J., & Austin, G. (1956). *A study of thinking.* New York: Wiley.

Buchner, A., & Wippich, W. (2000). On the reliability of implicit and explicit memory measures. *Cognitive Psychology, 40,* 227–259.

Busemeyer, J. R., Dewey, G. I., & Medin, D. L. (1984). Evaluation of exemplar-based generalization and the abstraction of categorical information. *Journal of Experimental Psychology: Learning, Memory, and Cognition, 10,* 638–648.

Chudler, E. H., Sugiyama, K., & Dong, W. K. (1995). Multisensory convergence and integration in the neostriatum and globus pallidus of the rat. *Brain Research, 674,* 33–45.

Cohen, N. J., & Squire, L. R. (1980). Preserved learning and retention of pattern analyzing skill in amnesics: Dissociation of knowing how and knowing that. *Science, 210,* 207–210.

Cools, A. R., van den Bercken, J. H. L., Horstink, M. W. I., van Spaendonck, K. P. M., & Berger, H. J. C. (1984). Cognitive and motor shifting aptitude disorder in Parkinson's disease. *Journal of Neurology, Neurosurgery and Psychiatry, 47,* 443–453.

Corkin, S. (1965). Tactually-guided maze learning in man: Effect of unilateral cortical excision and bilateral hippocampal lesions. *Neuropsychologia, 3,* 339–351.

Crick, F., & Koch, C. (1990). Towards a neurobiological theory of consciousness. *Seminars in the Neurosciences, 2,* 2263–275.

Crick, F., & Koch, C. (1995). Are we aware of neural activity in primary visual cortex? *Nature, 375,* 121–123.

Crick, F., & Koch, C. (1998). Consciousness and neuroscience. *Cerebral Cortex, 8,* 97–107.

Curran, T., & Schacter, D. L. (1996). Memory: Cognitive neuropsychological aspects. In T. E. Feinberg & M. J. Farah (Eds.), *Behavioral neurology and neuropsychology* (pp. 463–471). New York: McGraw-Hill.

Curran, T., & Schacter, D. L. (1997). Implicit memory: What must theories of amnesia explain? *Memory, 5,* 37–48.

Dunn, J. C., & Kirsner, K. (1988). Discovering functionally independent mental processes: The principle of reversed association. *Psychological Review, 95,* 91–101.

Elliott, R., & Dolan, R. J. (1998). Activation of different anterior cingulate foci in association with hypothesis testing and response selection. *Neuroimage, 8,* 17–29.

Erickson, M. A., & Kruschke, J. K. (1998). Rules and exemplars in category learning. *Journal of Experimental Psychology: General, 127,* 107–140.

Estes, W. K. (1986a). Array models for category learning. *Cognitive Psychology, 18,* 500–549.

Estes, W. K. (1986b). Memory storage and retrieval processes in category learning. *Journal of Experimental Psychology: General, 115,* 155–174.

Estes, W. K. (1994). *Classification and cognition.* Oxford: Oxford University Press.

Falmagne, J. C. (1968). Note on a simple fixed-point property of binary mixtures. *British Journal of Mathematical & Statistical Psychology, 21,* 131–132.

Falmagne, J. C., & Theios, J. (1969). On attention and memory in reaction time experiments. *Acta Psychologia, 30,* 319–323.

Filoteo, J. V., Maddox, W. T., & Davis, J. D. (2001a). A possible role of the striatum in linear and nonlinear category learning: Evidence from patients with Huntington's disease. *Behavioral Neuroscience, 115,* 786–798.

Filoteo, J. V., Maddox, W. T., & Davis, J. D. (2001b). Quantitative modeling of category learning in amnesic patients. *Journal of the International Neuropsychological Society, 7,* 1–19.

Fodor, J. A., Bever, T. G., & Garrett, M. F. (1974). *The psychology of language: An introduction to psycholinguistics and generative grammar.* New York: McGraw-Hill.

Fuster, J. M. (1989). *The prefrontal cortex* (2nd ed). New York: Raven Press.

Gaffan, D. (1974). Recognition impaired and association intact in the memory of monkeys after transsection of the fornix. *Journal of Comparative and Physiological Psychology, 86,* 1110–1109.

Gloor, P. (1997). *The temporal lobe and limbic system.* New York: Oxford University Press.

Gluck, M. A., & Myers, C. E. (1997). Psychobiological models of hippocampal function in learning and memory. *Annual Review of Neuroscience, 48,* 481–514.

Gluck, M. A., Oliver, L. M., & Myers, C. E. (1996). Late-training amnesic deficits in probabilistic category learning: A neurocomputational analysis. *Learning and Memory, 3,* 326–340.

Goldman-Rakic, P. S. (1987). Circuitry of the prefrontal cortex and the regulation of behavior by representational knowledge. In F. Plum & V. Mountcastle (Eds.), *Handbook of physiology* (pp. 373–417). Bethesda, MD: American Physiological Society.

Goldman-Rakic, P. S. (1995). Cellular basis of working memory. *Neuron, 14,* 477–485.

Grant, D. A., & Berg, E. A. (1948). Behavioral analysis of degree of reinforcement and ease of shifting to new responses in a Weigl-type card-sorting problem. *Journal of Experimental Psychology, 38,* 404–411.

Hayes, N. A., & Broadbent, D. (1988). Two modes of learning for interactive tasks. *Cognition, 28,* 249–276.

Higham, P. A., Vokey, J. R., & Pritchard, J. L. (2000). Beyond dissociation logic: Evidence for controlled and automatic influences in artificial grammar learning. *Journal of Experimental Psychology: General, 129,* 457–470.

Hintzman, D. L. (1986). Schema abstraction: In a multiple-trace memory model. *Psychological Review, 93*, 411–428.

Hirsh, R. (1974). The hippocampus and contextual retrieval of information from memory: A theory. *Behavioral Biology, 12*, 421–442.

Homa, D., Cross, J., Cornell, D., Goldman, D., & Schwartz, S. (1973). Prototype abstraction and classification of new instances as a function of number of instances defining the prototype. *Journal of Experimental Psychology, 101*, 116–122.

Homa, D., & Cultice, J. (1984). Role of feedback, category size, and stimulus distortion on the acquisition and utilization of ill-defined categories. *Journal of Experimental Psychology: Learning, Memory, and Cognition, 10*, 83–94.

Homa, D., Dunbar, S., & Nohre, L. (1991). Instance frequency, categorization, and the modulating effect of experience. *Journal of Experimental Psychology: Learning, Memory, and Cognition, 17*, 444–458.

Homa, D., Sterling, S., & Trepel, L. (1981). Limitations of exemplar-based generalization and the abstraction of categorical information. *Journal of Experimental Psychology: Human Learning and Memory, 7*, 418–439.

Hull, C. L. (1920). Quantitative aspects of the evolution of concepts. *Psychological Monographs, 28*, 1–86.

Jacoby, L. L. (1991). A process dissociation framework: Separating automatic from intentional uses of memory. *Journal of Memory and Language, 30*, 513–541.

Jahanshahi, M., Brown, R. G., & Marsden, C. (1992). The effect of withdrawal of dopaminergic medication on simple and choice reaction time and the use of advance information in Parkinson's disease. *Journal of Neurology, Neurosurgery, and Psychiatry, 55*, 1168–1176.

Janowsky, J. S., Kritchevsky, A. P., & Squire, L. R. (1989). Cognitive impairment following frontal lobe damage and its relevance to human amnesia. *Behavioral Neuroscience, 103*, 548–560.

Kendler, T. S., & Kendler, H. H. (1962). Inferential behavior in children as a function of age

and subgoal constancy. *Journal of Experimental Psychology, 64*, 460–466.

Klein, S. B., Cosmides, L., Tooby, J., & Chance, S. (in press). Decision making and the evolution of memory: Multiple systems, multiple functions. *Psychological Review.*

Knowlton, B. J., Mangels, J. A., & Squire, L. R. (1996). A neostriatal habit learning system in humans. *Science, 273*, 1399–1402.

Knowlton, B. J., Ramus, S. J., & Squire, L. R. (1992). Intact artificial grammar learning in amnesia: Dissociation of classification learning and explicit memory for specific instances. *Psychological Science, 3*, 172–179.

Knowlton, B. J., Squire, L. R., & Gluck, M. A. (1994). Probabilistic classification learning in amnesia. *Learning and Memory, 1*, 106–120.

Knowlton, B. J., Squire, L. R., Paulsen, J. S., Swerdlow, N. R., Swenson, M., & Butters, N. (1996). Dissociations within nondeclarative memory in Huntington's disease. *Neuropsychology, 10*, 538–548.

Köhler, W. (1925). *The mentality of apes.* New York: Harcourt, Brace.

Kolb, B., & Whishaw, I. Q. (1990). *Fundamentals of human neuropsychology* (3rd ed.). New York: Freeman.

Kolodny, J. A. (1994). Memory processes in classification learning: An investigation of amnesic performance in categorization of dot patterns and artistic styles. *Psychological Science, 5*, 164–169.

Kruschke, J. K. (1992). ALCOVE: An exemplar-based connectionist model of category learning. *Psychological Review, 99*, 22–44.

Leng, N. R., & Parkin, A. J. (1988). Double dissociation of frontal dysfunction in organic amnesia. *British Journal of Clinical Psychology, 27*, 359–362.

Lupker, S. J., & Theios, J. (1977). Further tests of a two-state model for choice reaction times. *Journal of Experimental Psychology: Human Perception & Performance, 3*, 496–504.

Maddox, W. T., & Ashby, F. G. (1993). Comparing decision bound and exemplar models of categorization. *Perception and Psychophysics, 53,* 49–70.

Maddox, W. T., Ashby, F. G., & Gottlob, L. R. (1998). Response time distributions in multi-dimensional categorization. *Perception & Psychophysics, 60,* 620–637.

Maddox, W. T., & Filoteo, J. V. (2001). Striatal contribution to category learning: Quantitative modeling of simple linear and complex non-linear rule learning in patients with Parkinson's disease. *Journal of the International Neuropsychological Society, 7,* 710–727.

McClelland, J. L., McNaughton, B. L., & O'Reilly, R. C. (1995). Why there are complementary learning systems in the hippocampus and neocortex: Insights from the successes and failures of connectionist models of learning and memory. *Psychological Review, 102,* 419–457.

McCloskey, M. (1993). Theory and evidence in cognitive neuropsychology: A "radical" response to Robertson, Knight, Rafal, and Shimamura (1993). *Journal of Experimental Psychology: Learning, Memory, and Cognition, 19,* 718–734.

McDonald, R. J., & White, N. M. (1993). A triple dissociation of memory systems: Hippocampus, amygdala, and dorsal striatum. *Behavioral Neuroscience, 107,* 3–22.

McDonald, R. J., & White, N. M. (1994). Parallel information processing in the water maze: evidence for independent memory systems involving dorsal striatum and hippocampus. *Behavioral and Neural Biology, 61,* 260–270.

Medin, D. L., Alton, M. W., Edelson, S. M., & Freko, D. (1982). Correlated symptoms and simulated medical classification. *Journal of Experimental Psychology: Learning, Memory, and Cognition, 8,* 37–50.

Medin, D. L., & Edelson, S. M. (1988). Problem structure and the use of base-rate information from experience. *Journal of Experimental Psychology: General, 117,* 68–85.

Medin, D. L., & Schaffer, M. M. (1978). Context theory of classification learning. *Psychological Review, 85,* 207–238.

Medin, D. L., & Schwanenflugel, P. J. (1981). Linear separability in classification learning. *Journal of Experimental Psychology: Human Learning and Memory, 1,* 335–368.

Medin, D. L., Wattenmaker, W. D., & Hampson, S. E. (1997). Family resemblance, conceptual cohesiveness, and category construction. *Cognitive Psychology, 19,* 242–279.

Meier, B., & Perrig, W. J. (2000). Low reliability of perceptual priming: Consequences for the interpretation of functional dissociations between explicit and implicit memory. *The Quarterly Journal of Experimental Psychology, 53A,* 211–233.

Meulemans, T., Peigneux, P., & Van der Linden, M. (1998). Preserved artificial grammar learning in Parkinson's disease. *Brain & Cognition, 37,* 109–112.

Miller, G. A., & Johnson-Laird, P. N. (1976). *Language and perception.* Cambridge: Harvard University Press.

Mishkin, M., Malamut, B., & Bachevalier, J. (1984). Memories and habits: Two neural systems. In G. Lynch, J. L. McGaugh, & N. M. Weinberger (Eds.), *Neurobiology of human learning and memory* (pp. 65–77). New York: Guilford.

Murphy, G. L., & Medin, D. L. (1985). The role of theories in conceptual coherence. *Psychological Review, 92,* 289–316.

Myung, I. J. (1994). Maximum entropy interpretation of decision bound and context models of categorization. *Journal of Mathematical Psychology, 38,* 335–365.

Nosofsky, R. M. (1986). Attention, similarity, and the identification-categorization relationship. *Journal of Experimental Psychology: General, 115,* 39–57.

Nosofsky, R. M. (1987). Attention and learning processes in the identification and categorization of integral stimuli. *Journal of Experimental Psychology: Learning, Memory, and Cognition, 13,* 87–108.

Nosofsky, R. M. (1988). Exemplar-based accounts of relations between classification, recognition, and typicality. *Journal of Experimental Psychology: Learning, Memory, and Cognition, 14,* 700–708.

Nosofsky, R. M. (1989). Further tests of an exemplar-similarity approach to relating identification and categorization. *Perception and Psychophysics, 45,* 279–290.

Nosofsky, R. M., & Alfonso-Reese, L. A. (1999). Effects of similarity and practice on speeded classification response times and accuracies: Further tests of an exemplar-retrieval model. *Memory & Cognition, 27,* 78–93.

Nosofsky, R. M., Clark, S. E., & Shin, H. J. (1989). Rules and exemplars in categorization, identification, and recognition. *Journal of Experimental Psychology: Learning, Memory, and Cognition, 15,* 282–304.

Nosofsky, R. M., & Johansen, M. K. (2000). Exemplar-based accounts of "multiple-system" phenomena in perceptual categorization. *Psychonomic Bulletin & Review, 7,* 375–402.

Nosofsky, R. M., & Zaki, S. R. (1998). Dissociations between categorization and recognition in amnesic and normal individuals: An exemplar-based interpretation. *Psychological Science, 9,* 247–255.

O'Keefe, J., & Nadel, L. (1978). *The hippocampus as a cognitive map.* New York: Oxford University Press.

Packard, M. G., Hirsh, R., & White, N. M. (1989). Differential effects of fornix and caudate nucleus lesions on two radial maze tasks: Evidence for multiple memory systems. *Journal of Neuroscience, 9,* 1465–1472.

Packard, M. G., & McGaugh, J. L. (1992). Double dissociation of fornix and caudate nucleus lesions on acquisition of two water maze tasks: Further evidence for multiple memory systems. *Behavioral Neuroscience, 106,* 439–446.

Pickering, A. D. (1997). New approaches to the study of amnesic patients: What can a neurofunctional philosophy and neural network methods offer? *Memory, 5,* 255–300.

Poldrack, R. A., Prabhakaran, V., Seger, C. A., & Gabrieli, J. D. E. (1999). Striatal activation during acquisition of a cognitive skill. *Neuropsychology, 13,* 564–574.

Poldrack, R. A., Selco, S. L., Field, J. E., & Cohen, N. J. (1999). The relationship between skill learning and repetition priming: Experimental and computational analyses. *Journal of Experimental Psychology: Learning, Memory, & Cognition, 25,* 208–235.

Polster, M. R., Nadel, L., & Schacter, D. L. (1991). Cognitive neuroscience analyses of memory: A historical perspective. *Journal of Cognitive Neuroscience, 3,* 95–116.

Posner, M. I., & Keele, S. W. (1968). On the genesis of abstract ideas. *Journal of Experimental Psychology, 77,* 353–363.

Posner, M. I., & Keele, S. W. (1970). Retention of abstract ideas. *Journal of Experimental Psychology, 83,* 304–308.

Posner, M. I., & Petersen, S. E. (1990). Attention systems in the human brain. *Annual Review of Neuroscience, 13,* 25–42.

Rao, S. M., Bobholz, J. A., Hammeke, T. A., Rosen, A. C., Woodley, S. J., Cunningham, J. M., Cox, R. W., Stein, E. A., & Binder, J. R. (1997). Functional MRI evidence for subcortical participation in conceptual reasoning skills. *Neuroreport, 8,* 1987–1993.

Reber, P. J., Stark, C. E. L., and Squire, L. R. (1998). Contrasting cortical activity associated with category memory and recognition memory. *Learning & Memory, 5,* 420–428.

Redington, M. (2000). Not evidence for separable controlled and automatic influences in artificial grammar learning: Comment on Higham, Vokey, and Pritchard (2000). *Journal of Experimental Psychology: General, 129,* 471–475.

Reed, S. K. (1972). Pattern recognition and categorization. *Cognitive Psychology, 3,* 189–221.

Robinson, A. L., Heaton, R. K., Lehman, R. A. W., & Stilson, D. W. (1980). The utility of the Wisconsin Card Sorting Test in detecting and localizing frontal lobe lesions. *Journal of Consulting and Clinical Psychology, 48,* 605–614.

Rosch, E. (1973). Natural categories. *Cognitive Psychology, 4,* 328–350.

Rosch, E. (1977). Human categorization. In N. Warren (Ed.), *Studies in cross-cultural psychology,* Vol. 1 (pp. 3–47). London: Academic Press.

Saint-Cyr, J. A., Taylor, A. E., & Lang, A. E. (1988). Procedural learning and neostriatal dysfunction in man. *Brain, 111,* 941–959.

Salatas, H., & Bourne, L. E. (1974). Learning conceptual rules: III. Processes contributing to rule difficulty. *Memory and Cognition, 2,* 549–553.

Schacter, D. L. (1987). Implicit memory: History and current status. *Journal of Experimental Psychology: Learning, Memory, and Cognition, 13,* 501–518.

Schacter, D. L. (1994). Priming and multiple memory systems: Perceptual mechanisms of implicit memory. In D. L. Schacter & E. Tulving (Eds.), *Memory systems 1994* (pp. 233–268). Cambridge: MIT Press.

Shallice, T. (1988). *From neuropsychology to mental structure.* New York: Plenum Press.

Shaw, M. L. (1982). Attending to multiple sources of information: I. The integration of information in decision making. *Cognitive Psychology, 14,* 353–409.

Shin, H. J., & Nosofsky, R. M. (1992). Similarity-scaling studies of "dot-pattern" classification and recognition. *Journal of Experimental Psychology: General, 121,* 278–304.

Sloman, S. A. (1996). The empirical case for two systems of reasoning. *Psychological Bulletin, 119,* 3–22.

Smith, D. J., & Minda, J. P. (2000). Thirty categorization results in search of a model. *Journal of Experimental Psychology: Learning, Memory, and Cognition, 26,* 3–27.

Smith, E. E., & Medin, D. L. (1981). *Categories and concepts.* Cambridge: Harvard University Press.

Squire, L. R. (1992). Memory and the hippocampus: A synthesis from findings with rats, monkeys, and humans. *Psychological Review, 99,* 143–145.

Squire, L. R., & Alvarez, P. (1995). Retrograde amnesia and memory consolidation: A neurobiological perspective. *Current Opinion in Neurobiology, 5,* 169–177.

Sternberg, S. (1969). The discovery of processing stages: Extensions of Donders' method. *Acta Psychologica, 30,* 276–315.

Teuber, H. L. (1955). Physiological psychology. *Annual Review of Psychology, 6,* 267–296.

Townsend, J. T., & Ashby, F. G. (1983). *Stochastic modeling of elementary psychological processes.* New York: Cambridge University Press.

Tulving, E., & Schacter, D. L. (1990). Priming and human memory systems. *Science, 247,* 302–306.

van Domburg, P. H. M. F., & ten Donkelaar, H. J. (1991). *The human substantia nigra and ventral tegmental area.* Berlin: Springer.

Van Orden, G. C., Pennington, B. F., & Stone, G. O. (2001). What do double dissociations prove? *Cognitive Science, 25,* 111–172.

Waldron, E. M., & Ashby, F. G. (2001). The effects of concurrent task interference on category learning. *Psychonomic Bulletin & Review, 8,* 168–176.

Warrington, E. K., & Weiskrantz, L. (1970). Amnesic syndrome: Consolidation or retrieval? *Nature, 228,* 628–630.

Wickens, J. (1993). *A theory of the striatum.* New York: Pergamon.

Willingham, D. B., Nissen, M. J., & Bullemer, P. (1989). On the development of procedural knowledge. *Journal of Experimental Psychology: Learning, Memory, and Cognition, 15,* 1047–1060.

Wilson, C. J. (1995). The contribution of cortical neurons to the firing pattern of striatal spiny neurons. In J. C. Houk, J. L. Davis, & D. G. Beiser (Eds.), *Models of information processing in the basal ganglia* (pp. 29–50). Cambridge: Bradford.

Winocur, G., & Eskes, G. (1998). Prefrontal cortex and caudate nucleus in conditional associative learning: Dissociated effects of selective brain lesions in rats. *Behavioral Neuroscience, 112,* 89–101.

Yellott, J. I. (1969). Probability learning with non-contingent success. *Journal of Mathematical Psychology, 6,* 541–575.

Yellott, J. I. (1971). Correction for fast guessing and the speed-accuracy tradeoff in choice reaction time. *Journal of Mathematical Psychology, 8,* 159–199.

Zola-Morgan, S., Squire, L. R., & Mishkin, M. (1982). The neuroanatomy of amnesia: Amygdala-hippocampus versus temporal stem. *Science, 218,* 1337–1339.

CHAPTER 17

Infant Cognition

CAROLYN ROVEE-COLLIER AND RACHEL BARR

Infancy covers the period from birth through 2 years of life. The beginnings of research on infant cognition can be traced to the publication of a baby diary by Preyer in 1882. Subsequently, detailed diaries that systematically documented their own children's behavior stimulated Morgan (1900), Baldwin (1894/1915), Guillaume (1926/1971), Piaget (1927/1962), and Valentine (1930) to publish independent, theoretical accounts of early cognitive development (for review of the diary method, see Wallace, Franklin, & Keegan, 1994). Even Darwin (1877) recorded observations of his own infant in a diary—observations that formed the basis of his argument for developmental continuities between species.

Subsequent knowledge about infant cognition can be traced to a series of methodological advances that enabled researchers to ask new questions. Today, researchers no longer ask whether infants can selectively learn or remember but ask what variables influence these processes and what mechanisms under-

lie them. As in the past, the answers are limited only by the ingenuity of the investigator.

GENERAL CONSIDERATIONS IN RESEARCH WITH INFANTS

Because infants are defined as a risk population by institutional review boards and funding agencies, the research that is proposed to study them must meet stringent criteria. The following factors must be considered in the design and conduct of all studies with infants.

Recruitment and Sample Characteristics

The availability of newborns for research is related to the amount of time they spend in the lying-in hospital after birth. Infants were typically hospitalized for 2 weeks in the 1940s and for 4 days in the 1960s, but for only 1 to 2 days currently. Not surprisingly, studies of early risk factors using infants in intensive care units, whose hospitalization is longer, have correspondingly increased. Such studies, however, must not interfere with hospital procedures or jeopardize the well being of infants. Researchers examining the cognitive impact of early risk factors must also be alerted to the problem of *comorbidity*, a term referring to the fact that variables often appear in clusters, or *covary*. Mothers who abuse drugs, for example, often smoke and

Preparation of this chapter was supported by grant nos. MH32307 and K05-MH00902 from the National Institute of Mental Health to the first author. We thank Ramesh S. Bhatt, Edward H. Cornell, Alan Leslie, Amy Needham, Peter Gerhardstein, Mark S. Strauss, and Barbara A. Younger-Rossman, and Karen Wynn for providing figures of apparatus and stimuli and Teresa Wilcox for granting permission to reprint.

drink; have poor prenatal care and nutrition, fewer financial resources, and less family and community support; are less educated; and so forth, and measures of these associated factors must also be obtained. Accurate and complete information is difficult to come by later if it was not originally recorded. Not only is it retrospective or anecdotal and heavily influenced by social demands, but also it can rarely be cross-validated. Intervening events that influence cognitive outcomes typically go unmeasured as well.

Once infants have left the hospital, their availability for study is limited by factors such as the type of study, sample age, whether they can be tested at home, and whether they can be tested on evenings or weekends (which may be necessary if both parents work). Infants are commonly recruited from published birth announcements via letters that describe the study, its significance, and the precise participation request (avoiding the term "test"). Follow-up telephone calls can also be made. Infants are also obtained via birth records filed with state departments of health or vital statistics, commercial mailing lists, public notices in apartment complexes, newspaper releases, La Leche leagues, hospital prenatal or parenting classes, pediatricians, day-care centers for infants or siblings, preschools, orphanages, and local play or parent groups.

Researchers cannot use convenience samples. Samples must be heterogeneous; journals and granting agencies require reporting of sex, racioethnic membership (census categories), and socioeconomic status (SES). General descriptors (e.g., "middle-class") are meaningless; researchers must report the traditional components of SES: parents' educational statuses (highest levels attained), occupations (converted to ranks via such instruments as the *1989 Socioeconomic Index of Occupations;* Nakao & Treas, 1992), and annual incomes. If necessary, the last can be inferred from the other components.

Racioethnic, educational, and occupational information can be obtained when the requisite consent form is signed. The identity of individual infants is confidential. Parents must receive a final report of the study's findings, and infants usually receive a signed certificate of participation. Parents should be reimbursed for taxi fares and parking fees but not for their infant's participation.

Attrition

Infant research is characterized by high attrition, and multiple sessions increase the opportunity for attrition even more. Before each study, experimenters must specify criteria for excluding infants from the final sample; later, they must report how many were excluded and why. Exclusion criteria often include failure to meet a training criterion or a state criterion (e.g., crying for a specified duration in any session), inattention for a specified duration, failure to maintain the requisite posture, failure to interact with the stimulus, caregiver or sibling interference, illness, equipment failure, a scheduling conflict, or baselines either too low or too high. Visiting infants in their own homes at times of day when caregivers think their infants are likely to be alert and playful and maintaining a flexible schedule will optimize experimental conditions and minimize attrition.

Sensory Systems

An infant's experience is defined by what he or she is able to detect. Because different modalities become functionally mature at different rates, the cognitive impact of early sensory experience will necessarily reflect these differences. The determination of ages at which different modalities become important has a long and controversial history (Brackbill & Koltsova, 1967; Peiper, 1963). On the basis of electrophysiological, anatomical, and behavioral data, Gottlieb (1971) concluded that the vestibular system becomes functional first, followed by the tactile, auditory, and visual systems—an order that is invariant across mammalian species, irrespective of the timing of birth. Subsequently, Alberts (1984) concluded that thermal sensitivity, olfaction, and taste precede the onset of audition.

After a sensory system has initially become functional, its "psychophysical operating characteristics" continue to change, decreasing further in absolute and difference thresholds; only when these characteristics stabilize is the system considered functionally mature (Alberts, 1984). The adaptive significance of stimuli in different sensory systems also changes ontogenetically. These factors complicate interpretations of age-related changes in learning and cognition. The fact that a particular stimulus *can* be detected or even discriminated with some specificity, however, does not guarantee that it *will* be selectively attended or that it will participate in the learning process. Experimenters must therefore select stimuli sufficiently intense to be detected and sufficiently salient to be selectively attended but not so intense or salient as to interfere with or distract from the process that the experimenters seek to establish.

State of Arousal

An infant's state of arousal on a sleep-wake continuum determines not only what is detected but also how a response is expressed (for reviews, see Ashton, 1973; Brackbill & Fitzgerald, 1969; Graham & Jackson, 1970; Korner, 1972; Prechtl, 1965). The relative efficacy of stimulation in different modalities during waking changes differentially during sleep (Brackbill & Fitzgerald, 1969; Brown, 1964), as do the forms of many reflexes elicited by the same physical stimulus (Lenard, Von Bernuth, & Prechtl, 1968). This relation is not simple, however, because

stimulus detection is impaired when infants are highly aroused and crying, and their state characteristics vary widely both within and between individuals. Brown (1964), for example, recorded an average of 12 state changes per hr in newborns, but the transitional probabilities depended on the direction of the change (from sleeping to waking, or vice versa). In addition, the organization of behavioral states changes markedly during early development. Particularly striking are differences between infants born prematurely or at term (Aylward, 1981). Although sensory thresholds of full-term infants decline steadily over the first 4 postnatal days (Lipsitt & Levy, 1959), those of premature infants remain high; as a result, they often startle and cry when the intensity of stimulation is increased to a detectable level.

The infant's changing state presents a number of methodological problems. First, the subjective intensity of a stimulus will vary with infant state even though its physical intensity remains constant. Large individual differences in momentary state will inevitably produce subjectively different stimulus intensities for different subjects, and stimuli that are equally detectable may produce different responses in different infants in the same state, depending on their developmental statuses. In addition to affecting stimulus salience, changes in perceived stimulus intensity affect the rate of learning in procedures in which the degree of stimulus specificity is critical. The common finding that infants require more trials to criterion when they are younger, for example, may simply reflect the fact that arousal states are more labile in younger infants.

Second, the experimental procedure per se may induce state changes. Some state changes may accompany and result from the learning process, others may follow from difficulty in performing the experimental task, and yet others may be unlearned consequences of repeated stimulation. Three-month-olds in operant conditioning studies, for example, exhibit less fussing and heightened alertness during contingent than during noncontingent reinforcement (Rovee-Collier, Morrongiello, Aron, & Kupersmidt, 1978; Siqueland, 1969). Withdrawing reinforcement often increases fussing and inattentiveness (Allesandri, Sullivan, & Lewis, 1990; Blass, Ganchrow, & Steiner, 1984; Rovee-Collier & Capatides, 1979). Papousek (1967), however, reported that both newborns and older infants, when confronted with either problems they could not solve or an extinction phase, occasionally reverted to sleep-like inhibitory states reminiscent of "paradoxical sleep" (Pavlov, 1927). Increasing fussiness and inattention over trials also plagues habituation procedures. To ensure that their response measures do not simply reflect increases or decreases in arousal, experimenters must use appropriate state controls for the amount and pattern of stimulation, time in the experiment, and time in relation to other factors that influence state (e.g., feeding).

Heart-rate measures are particularly sensitive to infants' rapid state changes and can be used in association with other response measures (e.g., visual fixation) to assess the influence of arousal state on an infant's cognitive performance. Although newborns may be classified as alert and awake, for example, the pattern of heart-rate responses predicts how soon the infant will change state. Thus, only infants who maintain an alert state for 5 min after a series of habituation trials exhibit heart-rate deceleration, whereas infants who remain alert for less than 5 min or who are in a drowsy state exhibit heart-rate acceleration (Clifton & Nelson, 1976).

Response Repertoire

Because infants are preverbal, their cognitive processes must be inferred from changes in behavior. A large number of such responses, originally described by Dennis (1934), have now been studied with remarkable success, and citations of classic studies or methodological reviews are presented below. The particular responses that very young infants will readily perform, however, are constrained by the requirement that they channel as much energy as possible into growth. Sometime between 4 and 9 weeks of age, the physiological mechanisms for thermoregulation become functional; before then, infants thermoregulate behaviorally. During this earlier period, experimenters should avoid studies that require high-energy responses (e.g., foot kicking) that compete with behavioral thermoregulation because infants will not perform them (for discussion, see Rovee-Collier, 1996b).

The earliest experiments with infants involved changes in *specific reflexes*. Pavlov's research, for example, motivated studies of the *feeding reflexes* (swallowing: Krasnogorskii, 1907; mouthing: Mateer, 1918; sucking: Denisova & Figurin, 1929; rooting: Papousek, 1959) and associated digestive processes (leukocytosis: Krachkovskaia, 1959; gastric secretions: Bogen, 1907); the *defensive reflexes* (fear/escape: Watson & Rayner, 1920; foot withdrawal: Wickens & Wickens, 1940; eyeblink: DeLucia, 1968; pupillary dilation and constriction: Fitzgerald, Lintz, Brackbill, & Adams, 1967); and the *orienting reflex (OR)*, defined as directing the receptors toward a source of environmental variation. These include head-turning (Siqueland & Lipsitt, 1966), visual fixation (Fantz, 1956), and eye-opening (Siqueland, 1969).

Behaviors in a second class of responses, *general reactions*, are not elicited by stimulating a specific organ with a specific stimulus but may reflect stimulus intensity (Peiper, 1963). Irwin (1930), for example, observed cyclical changes in activity that seemed to be keyed to feeding periods, and activity change—often measured on a stabilimeter placed under a thin mattress in a specially outfitted experimental crib—was used as an index of learning either singly or in combination with other measures. (A sensitive stabilimeter, calibrated for infant weight, can detect deviations from baseline that are produced by movements as slight as a deep inspiration in the breathing cycle.) In a study designed to determine whether infants could learn a feeding schedule during the neonatal period, for example, Marquis (1941) found that infants' activity increased immediately before a scheduled feeding, but that their learning was most apparent when the feeding schedule was shifted. Infants lay in bassinets that were outfitted with stabilimeters from 6:00 a.m. to 6:00 p.m. daily except during actual feedings, which lasted about 45 min. Beginning at 2 days of age, one group was fed on a 4-hr schedule and another on a 3-hr schedule. Compared to the 4-hr group, the 3-hr group was less active and showed no increase in activity prior to a feeding. On day 9, the 3-hr group was shifted to the 4-hr schedule. At the time they had previously been fed, their activity increased abruptly, and 30 min before the 4-hr feeding, activity reached a level higher than had been seen in either group. In addition, their increase in activity was accompanied by fussing and crying—a behavior never seen in the original 4-hr feeding group. Marquis concluded that infants in the 3-hr group had learned to expect a feeding at the end of 3 hr, but that their expectation was not manifested until it was violated when the milk was withheld at the end of that time on day 9.

Other researchers have studied general reactions associated with increases or decreases in distress (crying: Watson & Rayner, 1920; calming: Gekoski, Rovee-Collier, & Carulli-Rabinowitz, 1983; Thoman, Korner, & Beason-Williams, 1977) as well as psychophysiological responses (heart rate [HR]: Bridger, 1961; respiration: Kasatkin & Levikova, 1935; galvanic skin response

[GSR]: Jones, 1930; cortical evoked potential [ERP]: Molfese & Wetzel, 1992; Nelson & Collins, 1991; Nelson & Nugent, 1990). Graham and Clifton (1966) hypothesized that cardiac deceleration and cardiac acceleration are physiological reflections of orienting (information processing) and defensive reactions (stimulus rejection), respectively. This interpretation of directional HR changes is widely accepted in research with both human and animal infants (Campbell & Ampuero, 1985).

Newborns were long thought to be incapable of HR deceleration. Because their sensory thresholds are higher, however, a stimulus sufficiently intense to be detected also makes them startle because of its sudden subjective onset, thereby eliciting HR acceleration. Experimenters now sidestep this problem by presenting the alert newborn with a moderately intense stimulus that has a slow rise time (e.g., a sound that is first presented at a low volume and gradually is increased in intensity to the target volume). If stimuli are presented in this fashion, they will elicit HR deceleration. Newborn HR patterns can also be examined during sleep: A slight pinch to the ear lobe, for example, elicits HR acceleration, whereas a stroke on the cheek (a rooting stimulus) elicits HR deceleration (Clifton & Nelson, 1976). Psychophysiological measures used with infants are reviewed elsewhere (Atkinson, 1984; Berg & Berg, 1987; deHaan & Nelson, 1997; Fox, 1989; Richards, 2000; Richards & Lansink, 1998).

A third class of responses includes relatively simple *motoric acts* such as foot-kicks (Rovee & Rovee, 1969), arm-pulls (Friedlander, 1961), nonnutritive sucks (Siqueland & DeLucia, 1969), high-amplitude sucks (Jusczyk, 1985), mouth movements (Blass et al., 1984), smiles (Brackbill, 1958), vocalizations (Rheingold, Gewirtz, & Ross, 1959), visual fixations (Watson, 1966), panel-presses (Simmons & Lipsitt, 1961), lever-presses (Hartshorn &

Rovee-Collier, 1997), pillow presses (Watson & Ramey, 1972), head-turns (Caron, 1967), facial and manual gestures (Meltzoff & Moore, 1977), and sphere touches (Rheingold, Stanley, & Cooley, 1962). Responses that are recursive are suitable for studies of operant conditioning.

Responses requiring a greater degree of coordination have been used in studies with older infants. These include selective reaching to either a discriminative stimulus (Fagen, 1977) or a location in the dark (Goubet & Clifton, 1998), serial touching of objects (Mandler, Fivush, & Reznick, 1987), displacing a cover over a hidden well (Diamond, 1990a, 1990b; Smith, Thelen, Titzer, & McLin, 1999), performing an action sequence on a series of objects (Bauer & Shore, 1987), and touching a target on a video monitor (Gerhardstein & Rovee-Collier, in press).

Any response that is not automatically recorded must be accompanied by a measure of interobserver reliability. Typically, this is accomplished by having a second trained observer, blind with respect to either the experimental procedure or an infant's group assignment, independently score the responses of a percentage of randomly selected subjects in each group over the course of the experiment. Some researchers report a mean or median percentage of agreement between independent observers as the index of interobserver reliability. Others use a Cohen's Kappa (κ), which also expresses the percent agreement but controls for chance agreements between the two observers. To calculate a kappa, the agreement expected by chance is subtracted from the observed percent agreement. The denominator of the equation is 1 minus chance agreement. A kappa value less than 0.70 is unacceptable. Still others compute a Pearson product-moment correlation coefficient between independent pairs of observations over trials or minutes of a session; here, coefficients less than 0.90 are considered unac-

ceptable. Although observers initially should be trained to a criterion (e.g., $r = 0.95$ between the trainee and the primary observer for three successive sessions), pretraining to an acceptable criterion does not substitute for an independent assessment of interobserver reliability during actual data collection. Both slippage in response criteria over the course of an experiment and experimenter bias will compromise results. One solution is to videotape sessions and have them scored blind by a second observer. The experimenter must report, however, how discrepancies between the observers' scores were resolved (e.g., by consensus, rescoring the tape, a third observer, etc.). Taping sessions requires both prior approval by the appropriate institutional review board and parental consent.

Developmental Comparisons

As illustrated in Figure 17.1, infants undergo radical physical and behavioral changes over the first 18–24 months of life. As a result, tasks that are suitable for older infants are rarely suitable for younger ones. A major challenge facing developmental researchers, therefore, is to develop tasks that are appropriate across a large age range (Barr, Dowden, & Hayne, 1996; Hartshorn et al., 1998b). If different tasks are used with younger and older infants, experimenters must ensure that they yield comparable performance at overlapping ages so that differences in performance will reflect true age differences rather than simply the paradigm shift. In general, a common pattern of cognitive competence emerges across age and task—a fact highlighted in the *Categorization* and *Memory* sections. More interesting than the *absolute age* at which a particular capacity emerges (which is task-dependent) is the *general pattern or order* in which different cognitive skills appear.

Figure 17.1   From left to right, infants are 2, 3, 6, 9, 12, 15, and 18 months of age; note the dramatic physical and behavioral differences between the youngest and oldest infant.

Researchers must also attempt to equate potential age differences in task demands, stimulus salience, motivation, and original learning. For this last item, age equivalence can be determined by calibrating task parameters across ages. Younger infants, for example, learn more slowly than older infants; therefore, the duration of training must be longer for younger infants to ensure that they learn the task. In addition, older infants process information more rapidly than younger infants, therefore, sessions must be shortened and/or the complexity of the visual display must be increased for older infants so that they remain interested in the task. Finally, experimenters must not use verbal prompts or instructions with infants of different ages or linguistic ability. Failure to observe any one of these precautions jeopardizes cross-age comparisons. Although longitudinal designs are more powerful than cross-sectional ones, they are contaminated by repeated measurements.

Social and Motivational Factors

The infancy period is also characterized by dramatic social changes. Between 9 and 12 months of age, for example, both social referencing and stranger anxiety appear (for reviews, see Ainsworth, Blehar, Waters, & Wall, 1978; Bretherton & Waters, 1985; Feinman, 1985). Factors related to the novelty of new faces and voices (e.g., the experimenters) and new settings (e.g., the laboratory) increasingly contribute to infants' unwillingness to engage in experimental tasks, even when the tasks are well within their capabilities. For many years, social factors were largely ignored in infant research (Uzgiris, 1981). Now that researchers have begun to appreciate the varied interactions that underlie infant sociocognitive development, they have turned to more complex and ecologically valid tasks (Deutsch, 1994; Kuhl et al., 1997; Meltzoff & Kuhl, 1989; Perner, Ruffman, & Leekam, 1994). Perner et al. (1994), for example, found that children with older siblings passed a false belief test earlier than children without siblings, and Kuhl et al. (1997) have examined the development of phonetic boundaries as a function of the infant's language environment.

Overview

In this chapter, we review various methods that have been used to assess the classic experimental problems in infant cognition, including habituation, classical and operant conditioning, detour learning, concept formation, categorization, and memory processing. We also highlight a few well-developed methods that have been used to address a number of different issues in infant cognition. In the learning section, for example, we describe the basic features of the habituation and conditioning procedures in some detail. In later sections of this chapter, we consider how these procedures have been used as tools to study a wide range of cognitive abilities, including categorization, memory, and serial learning. At the end of the chapter, we consider methods that have been used to address some new problems, including infants' understanding of number, objecthood, and causality. Although we did not include a separate section on perception, most of the experimental methods described here can also be applied to the study of infant perception.

Finally, throughout the chapter, we highlight experimental procedures that can lead to ambiguous results and erroneous conclusions. Researchers, for example, are warned not to overestimate the verbal competence of very young children when designing their studies.

INFANT LEARNING

Learning is traditionally defined as "a more or less permanent change in a behavior which occurs as a result of practice" (Kimble, 1961).

This definition excludes temporary changes due to arousal, fatigue, illness, medication, or biological rhythms and more permanent changes associated with aging, growth, or physiological intervention. Although this definition is not met in all instances (for example, learning can occur either in a single trial or vicariously), it holds for the greatest number of cases. The traditional categories of learning—habituation, classical and instrumental (operant) conditioning, imitation, and various kinds of concept learning—are considered in the following sections.

Habituation

Habituation is a form of nonassociative learning that occurs at all phyletic levels. It is defined as a stimulus-specific response decrement that results from repeated exposure to a stimulus that causes the individual to orient either toward or away from it (Wyers, Peeke, & Herz, 1973). The term *repeated* implies that a single stimulus presentation followed by a test is not an habituation procedure; at least two discrete stimulus presentations are required. In addition, the response must be an active one. If this condition is not met, as when an infant is swaddled, in bright illumination, or under a heat lamp, then the resulting response decrement is called *acclimatization*. Fatigue, sensory adaptation, circadian rhythms, and physiological processes produce other response decrements not attributable to habituation.

The essential characteristics of habituation (Thompson & Spencer, 1966) are summarized as follows:

1. The response decrement is a negative exponential function of the number of presentations that eventually reaches asymptote or zero response level.

2. Other things being equal, the more rapid the frequency of stimulation or the weaker

the stimulus, the more rapid and/or pronounced is habituation.

3. If the stimulus is withheld, responding tends to recover over time (*spontaneous recovery*). Over repeated series of habituation training and spontaneous recovery trials, habituation is progressively more rapid.

4. Habituation can proceed below the observable baseline (*sub-zero habituation*). This occurrence will subsequently be reflected in a lower level of spontaneous recovery.

5. Presentation of another (usually strong) stimulus results in recovery of the previous habituated response to the original habituating stimulus (*dishabituation*). Presumably, the strong distractor disrupts the active inhibitory process of habituation, with the result that the response is expressed at a higher level. By this account, habituation does not permanently eliminate a response but only temporarily suppresses it. The renewed responding also habituates if the distractor is repeatedly presented.

Terminology

Researchers should take special note of some terms that are used differently in the infancy literature than elsewhere. *Dishabituation* is the term that traditionally refers to the higher level of response to the *original* habituation stimulus after a strong, interpolated distractor (Pavlov, 1927; see item 5 in the preceding list), whereas *sensitization* is the term that traditionally refers to a higher level of response to a novel test stimulus after a series of habituation trials with the original stimulus. In the infancy literature, however, *dishabituation* is used to describe a higher level of responding to a novel test stimulus relative to one that was preexposed; no interpolated distractor is involved at all. Also, *familiarization,* a term that traditionally describes exposure learning or perceptual learning, is used interchange-

ably with the term *habituation,* despite operational differences between them. Habituation is a discrete-trials procedure in which responding decreases over repeated presentations of a particular stimulus, whereas familiarization requires neither repeated stimulus presentations nor a response decrement. In the infancy literature, *familiarization* refers to any procedure in which a stimulus is preexposed in any way prior to testing. Presumably, the preexposure affects test performance. Response decrements produced by familiarization are attributed to a change in the perception of the stimulus rather than to a change in response strength to a subjectively constant stimulus, as in habituation. In other words, during familiarization, the response always remains stimulus-appropriate; changes in responding reflect changes in the properties of the subjective stimulus that elicits it.

Experimental Procedures

Independent variables typically reflect some parameter of stimulation (intensity, rate, number of presentations, pattern, modality, quality, relative efficacy, salience, biological significance) and, in the infancy literature, frequently appear in conjunction with subject variables (e.g., age, sex, state of arousal, prior experience) or environmental variables (e.g., test setting). *Dependent variables* reflect the relative rapidity of habituation, its extent, or its relative permanence. These measures may include one or more of the following: number of trials to criterion, magnitude, duration or latency of response, percent of original (or control) response, habituation slope, duration of habituation (latency to a recovery criterion), magnitude of recovery, and savings during rehabituation. An important but often overlooked consideration involves the treatment of data when the initial level of responding to two different stimuli differs. Because of the lower limit of observable responding, stimuli that evoke an initially smaller response cannot produce an absolute response decrement as profound as stimuli that evoke an initially greater response. Transforming the data to reflect performance in terms of the percent of the original level of responding can actually reverse the relation between the two habituation curves. The effect of different parameters of stimulation on habituation and issues of measurement are discussed in detail elsewhere (Graham, 1973; Olson & Sherman, 1983).

The choice of parameters will depend on both the nature of the question being investigated and the age of the infant. Slater (1995) reviewed the specific methodological considerations for studies with newborns. Experimenters are cautioned to use more than a single stimulus from a given modality when comparing habituation across modalities, and more than a single stimulus intensity and intertrial interval when comparing across ages. The latter is particularly important to ensure that developmental differences do not result from the choice of a parameter that is optimal at one age but not at another. Because stimulus salience also changes with age, a variety of stimuli should be used to equate stimulus differences over age and to ensure that, at any given age, a particular outcome is not unique to a particular stimulus (for an extensive review of methodological considerations in habituation, see Clifton & Nelson, 1976; see also neonatal heart rate response to auditory stimuli in an earlier section, *Response Repertoire*).

Habituation Criterion-Setting

Researchers can present a stimulus either for a fixed number of trials or until responding meets a predetermined criterion. The habituation criterion is typically defined as mean responding (e.g., looking time, suck rate, magnitude of startle or heart-rate change) on three consecutive trials at a level that is 50% of the mean response level during the first three

habituation trials. The habituation criterion can also be specified in terms of some absolute level of responding (e.g., less than 4 s on each of two consecutive trials; 60 s of accumulated looking time) or in terms of some other aspect of the infant's behavior (e.g., crying or falling asleep). Each of these alternatives introduces a selective statistical bias into the analysis and interpretation of the data (for discussion, see Bogartz, 1965; Dannemiller, 1984). Because infants are likely to be looking at different extraneous stimuli at the beginning of each habituation trial, their looking times will also include their latency to detect the stimulus. To reduce variability and ensure that all infants are initially fixating the same stimulus at the outset of every trial, each stimulus presentation is typically signaled by a blinking light adjacent to where the target will appear (or by some other attention-getting stimulus), and the target stimulus is not presented until an infant is judged to be fixating the signal (Cohen, 1972, 1973). At that point, the signal is turned off, and the target stimulus is presented, initiating the next trial.

Once the stimulus is presented, the experimenter must decide when to terminate it. Most experimenters use trials of a fixed duration or an *infant-control procedure* (Horowitz, Paden, Bhana, & Self, 1972) in which stimulus duration is contingent on the infant's own looking behavior. In the latter case, the stimulus is typically terminated when the infant looks away for 2 s, although terminating the stimulus after 1 s yields the same outcome (Colombo & Horowitz, 1985). Because the infant-control procedure results in different effective stimulus durations per trial for each subject, some investigators present the visual stimulus until a specified amount of total looking time has been accumulated, irrespective of the number of trials required to do so.

Evidence that infants who fail to complete habituation procedures perform differently on the completed portions than infants who do

(Wachs & Smitherman, 1985) has raised concerns about the generality of findings from habituation studies. Researchers are cautioned to ensure that their final sample is unbiased.

A Prototypic Procedure: Visual Habituation

Looking is the most frequently measured infant behavior, probably because it requires little special instrumentation and because all waking infants look continuously at something. In a typical visual habituation experiment, the infant sits on the parent's lap or in an infant seat with the parent standing or sitting nearby. If the stimulus is projected on a front screen or presented on a lighted stage, then the test room is dimly lit to increase attention to the target, and potential distractors in the laboratory are draped with black cloth. When a three-dimensional object instead of a two-dimensional display is used, a metronome set at 1 s facilitates accurate timing of stimulus presentations according to a second-by-second script. In this case, experimenters practice the task until they have attained a reliable and accurate level of performance (see Baillargeon, 1995).

Looking behavior (direction, duration, frequency) is usually scored by one or two hidden experimenters looking through a one-way window or peephole centered in the apparatus. The observers are blind to an infant's experimental condition and cannot see the test display. They depress hand-held buttons that correspond to each measure and that are connected to a computer, which computes cumulative looking time and interobserver reliability. The computer also alerts the experimenter via headphones or an inconspicuous visual cue when the preprogrammed criterion for ending a trial has been met. Alternatively, looking behavior can be scored in an adjacent room from a monitor that receives a direct feed from a video camera, which records looking behavior through a peephole. When possible, scoring from a monitor is preferred

because videotapes can be saved for further analysis, which is not possible when behavior is scored through a peephole. When a three-dimensional display is used, the experimenter usually presents the object on a table or a stage in front of the infant (e.g., Mandler et al., 1987; Oakes, Madole, & Cohen, 1991; Ruff, 1986). If the object is presented on a stage, then curtains are used to shield it from the infants' view prior to the onset of the trial.

Special precautions are taken to avoid experimenter bias or caregiver interference: First, the parent or caregiver is either blindfolded or instructed to look away from the stimulus or close his/her eyes. When auditory stimuli are used, the adult is fitted with headphones to mask auditory input. Second, the adult is asked not to interact with or respond to the infant during the test.

Looking Measures: Advantages and Limitations

Gelman (1978) argued that looking measures minimize the procedural aspects of a task and allow the experimenter to focus on infants' conceptual capacities. Others argued that traditional visual attention paradigms underestimate the representational and conceptual abilities of young infants (Rovee-Collier & Hayne, 1987). Yet others have made intermediate claims; Spelke (1994), for example, argued that looking is not superior to other measures of navigation but may simply reflect a different underlying process, and Smith et al. (1999) argued that looking is not necessarily a better index of infants' spatial knowledge than reaching. A major problem with looking measures is that we have no way of quantifying whether looks of equal duration reflect equivalent depths of concentration. In addition, we assume that infants encode information about a target when they look at it, but we have no way of knowing exactly what they are encoding or how rapidly they are encoding it.

Individual differences in looking time are reliable and have been linked to information processing (Colombo, Mitchell, Coldren, & Freeseman, 1991; McCall & Kagan, 1970). Infants with shorter looking times, for example, habituate significantly faster than infants with longer looking times. This difference was strikingly illustrated in a study by Colombo et al. (1991), who classified 4-month-olds as short- or long-lookers on the basis of how long they took to reach a standard habituation criterion during an initial series of habituation trials with a single visual stimulus. On the pretest, the mean fixation time was 7 s for short-lookers and 38 s for long-lookers. During the main experiment, the researchers first exposed each infant to a visual stimulus for an accumulated looking time of 30 s, then immediately afterward gave each infant a paired-comparison test with two stimuli that were defined by either global or local features. The global stimuli were shapes constructed from identical dots that could be differentiated only on the basis of their overall shape; the feature stimuli were letters of the alphabet (C, G) that could be differentiated only by their specific features. The amount of time infants were allowed to view the test stimuli was systematically increased from 30 to 45 s in the feature task and systematically decreased from 30 to 15 s in the global task. In order to fixate the novel stimulus significantly longer than the familiar one, long-lookers required the longest looking times available in each task, and short-lookers required the briefest looking times available in each task. Given that most developmental studies are age-based, and that a variety of individual differences are particularly pervasive in the infancy period, the potential systematic contribution of individual differences must be considered in the design and analysis of experiments on infant cognition—especially of those measuring looking behavior.

Researchers should be aware that during the first few postnatal months, four looking phenomena are neurophysiologically constrained: obligatory attention, the externality effect, biased orienting to portions of the visual field, and object tracking. One-month-olds, for example, have difficulty disengaging attention from a stimulus and will fixate it for prolonged periods—the phenomenon called *obligatory attention,* but newborns can fixate new targets more readily. Hood (1995) attributed this paradox to a higher level of physiological arousal that promotes more saccadic eye movements in the newborn. He stressed the importance of controlling for infant state and behavioral arousal in studies of infant visual learning and attention. Johnson (1990) proposed that obligatory attention signals the onset of inhibitory control over the subcortical pathway. This phenomenon obviously limits an infant's ability to process competing visual stimuli or disengage attention from a central stimulus, particularly within a brief period (for reviews, see Hood, 1995; Johnson, 1990).

Infants younger than 2 months also exhibit the *externality effect* (Milewski, 1976)—a phenomenon in which infants scan until they reach a well-defined, external boundary of a stimulus and then they stop, failing to scan its internal portion. As a result, they fail to discriminate between two visual stimuli with identical borders that are differentiated only by their internal components. Adding movement to the internal components of a stimulus, however, facilitates scanning of them (Hood, 1995). Infants younger than 2 months also orient more to objects presented in the temporal visual field than to objects presented in the nasal visual field (Johnson, 1990). Finally, object tracking improves significantly over the first few postnatal months. Before 2 months of age, tracking is characterized by jerky saccadic movements in pursuit of the object; older infants' tracking is smooth and anticipatory (for review, see Aslin, 1981).

Adaptive Function of Habituation

From an adaptive perspective, habituation eliminates nonessential responses to irrelevant stimuli, freeing the organism to respond to others. Wyers et al. (1973), for example, argued that because in natural settings habituation occurs in the context of many stimuli, any decrement in responding to one of them must shift the weighting to other competing stimuli, thereby altering response dominance. In the laboratory, however, habituation studies typically allow only one response opportunity in a very simple setting. In addition, only one aspect of this response is typically measured. This practice precludes the opportunity to observe other behavioral changes that accompany habituation.

Visual habituation studies are particularly suited for revealing this shift in stimulus weighting because the infant's eyes are continuously open, and any decrease in looking at one stimulus or stimulus component must necessarily be accompanied by an increase in looking at something else. An early study by Fantz (1964) is notable in this regard. He presented 2- to 6-month-olds with pairs of complex visual stimuli for ten 60-s trials. One member of each pair remained the same from trial to trial, and one changed. As infants spent less time looking at the stimulus that remained constant over trials, they spent more time looking at the varying stimulus, so that total looking time was conserved. In studies of infant categorization, objects from the same category may be repeatedly paired with objects from a changing category. In this case, both stimuli change from trial to trial, but the category membership of one member of the stimulus pair remains constant, while the category membership of the other varies (e.g., Greco & Daehler, 1985). Infants tested in this procedure might treat objects from the varied category as novel, while habituating to objects from the same category.

The serial-habituation procedure also reveals shifts in visual attention over successive trials. This procedure is based on Jeffrey's (1968) hypothesis that infants process visual information about a compound stimulus hierarchically, habituating to the most salient element first, then habituating to the second most salient element, and then to the third, and so forth. Miller, Ryan, Sinnott, and Wilson (1976) tested this hypothesis by obtaining initial visual preference scores for the individual elements of a complex stimulus during a pretest and then repeatedly exposing infants to the compound for a fixed number of trials. They tracked the progress of habituation to individual elements by interspersing them throughout the habituation series. During posttests with the individual elements, infants spent the least time fixating those elements that they had most preferred during the pretest. These data were consistent with the hypothesis. Taken together, the findings of Fantz (1964) and Miller et al. (1976) reveal that habituation is more complex than suggested when researchers measure decreased responding over trials to only a single, relatively simple stimulus.

Classical Conditioning

Like habituation, classical conditioning involves the repetitious presentation of a stimulus. Unlike in habituation, however, the stimulus in classical conditioning becomes predictive, enabling the organism to respond in anticipation of an event instead of simply reacting to it. The habituation of the orienting reflex to the CS within the CS-UCS interval is a critical determinant of classical conditioning (Kimmel, 1973). Papousek (1967), for example, reported that habituation of orienting to the CS usually preceded the appearance of the first CR, and Little (1973) found that habituation of orienting to the *offset* of the CS in a trace conditioning procedure similarly facilitated acquisition. The two essential components for classical conditioning are the UCS (*unconditional stimulus*), which reliably elicits a reflex without any prior training (i.e., unconditionally), and the CS (*conditional stimulus*), which is within the organism's sensory range but is initially neutral with respect to the reflex elicited by the UCS. When they are repeatedly presented in close temporal contiguity, the CS and UCS become associated, so that one predicts the occurrence of the other. Originally, Pavlov (1927) thought that the CS and UCS must be contiguous, but Rescorla (1967) found that they need only be correlated. The correlation (contingency) can be either positive (the CS predicts that the UCS will occur) or negative (the CS predicts that the UCS will not occur). In traditional classical conditioning procedures, *excitatory learning* (the extent to which subjects respond above zero or baseline) can readily be measured, but *inhibitory learning* (the extent to which subjects respond below zero or baseline) cannot. Experimenters who wish to study inhibitory learning must first train subjects to perform an operant response. When the operant response rate is high and stable, then they can introduce the classical inhibitory procedure while the operant behavior is ongoing. This manipulation will allow the CS-UCS contingency to be manifested as a *decrease* in operant response rate (inhibitory learning) (Estes & Skinner, 1941; Little, 1973; Rescorla, 1966).

In the past, experimenters used a *backward conditioning group* to control for behavioral arousal. This group receives the same total number and intensity of CSs and UCSs as the experimental group, except that for this group, the UCS precedes the CS. Because this procedure can produce inhibitory conditioning, however, researchers are encouraged to use instead a *truly random control group*. For this group, the CSs and UCSs are programmed independently; thus, they occur randomly with respect to each other (zero correlation) but as frequently as for the experimental group. A learning interpretation requires a difference in responding between the experimental and the control groups. Because some researchers have obtained chance acquisition in the random control group, however, many experimenters use an *explicitly unpaired control group* for which the CS precedes the UCS at nonoptimal intervals.

Because classical conditioning research has traditionally focused on the feeding, defensive, and orienting reflexes, we will consider the procedures that have been used to condition an exemplar of each type—sucking, eye blinking, and head turning, respectively.

Conditioned Sucking

Because sucking on a nipple is obligatory and readily observed, it has long been the response of choice in learning studies with newborns and young infants. Although sucking declines over the first year of life, it can be reinstated by the contingent introduction of reinforcing consequences (Siqueland & DeLucia, 1969).

Lipsitt and Kaye (1964) were the first to demonstrate classically conditioned sucking in newborns under carefully controlled laboratory conditions. They tested two groups ($n = 10$ each) of 3- and 4-day-olds on a single occasion 3 hr after their last feeding and prior to their morning feeding. The experimental group received a 93-dB, 23-cps tone (CS) and, 1 s later, a nonnutritive nipple in the mouth (UCS); the paired stimuli co-terminated 14 s later. The explicitly unpaired control group received the CS and UCS for the same amount of time, but the CS was presented 30 s after the UCS was removed. Sessions consisted of 5 baseline trials (CS-alone), 20 training trials (CS-UCS) with five interspersed test trials (CS-alone every fifth trial), and 30 extinction trials (CS-alone)—fewer if an infant failed to respond to the CS on two consecutive trials.

During conditioning, the number of responses of both groups on the interpolated test trials increased, but the experimental group showed a moderate advantage. During extinction, however, sucks continued to increase in the control group but returned to baseline in the experimental group.

To ensure that increased sucking to the tone in the control group was not merely sensitization, Kaye (1967) repeated the preceding experiment with four sensitization control groups—a CS-alone group and three UCS-alone groups. In addition, he increased the duration of the CS and UCS by 5 s each and counted sucks throughout the session, both during and between CS presentations. The findings replicated those of the previous study and unequivocally confirmed that classical conditioning had occurred. This time, sucking in the experimental group increased sharply during training and decreased to the control level during extinction. Kaye attributed the greater conditioning effect in his study to the fact that his procedure increased by 33% the opportunity for the tone and sucking to be paired on each conditioning trial—an important factor to consider in future research designs.

Conditioned Eye-Blinking

The eye-blink CR is the most widely studied response in the classical conditioning literature, irrespective of age or species, and offers a particularly advantageous model for the study of early cognition. First, its neural circuitry has been thoroughly investigated in other species, and the effects of damage to the circuitry are well known, making this a useful cognitive neural model (Woodruff-Pak & Steinmetz, 2000a, 2000b). Second, conditioned eye blinking is a classic paradigm for the study of inhibitory development, associative learning, memory, and higher-order cognitive functions such as learned irrelevance. Third, because it entails neither a difficult motor response nor a verbal response, it can be used with very young and even preterm infants. Finally, as a form of aversive or fear conditioning (rather than appetitive conditioning), it can help researchers elucidate how traumatic events are processed early in life and how they impact later cognition. Such understanding also has obvious clinical implications.

When the UCS is a corneal air puff and the UCR is an eye-blink, a CR that immediately anticipates the UCS is a functional avoidance response. Many of the earlier failures to document conditioned eye-blinking in young infants undoubtedly resulted from use of a nonoptimal *interstimulus interval* (ISI) between the CS (tone) and UCS (air puff). In fact, the optimal ISI for eye-blink conditioning during the first month of life is three times longer than the 500-ms ISI that is optimal for adults (Little, 1970). By 5–6 months of age, infants can acquire a conditioned association with a 650-ms ISI (Ivkovich, Collins, Eckerman, Krasnegor, & Stanton, 1999, 2000), and by adulthood, the optimal ISI has fallen to 500 ms (Kimble, 1961).

Using the nonoptimal 500-ms ISI as the explicitly paired control condition and a 1,500-ms ISI as the experimental condition, Little, Lipsitt, and Rovee-Collier (1984) trained supine infants with a 1,000-cps, 70-dB tone (CS) and a 400-ms, 2.5-psi air puff (UCS). Because of the possibility that the efficacy of the 500-ms ISI might increase with age, they also introduced a truly random control group for each ISI condition for the groups first trained at 30 days of age. Their device for delivering the UCS and recording eye-blinks is pictured in Figure 17.2. The tone was presented from a speaker positioned 30.48 cm behind the infant's head and lasted 1,900 ms, overlapping and terminating with UCS termination (a delayed conditioning procedure). In addition, respiration was recorded by means

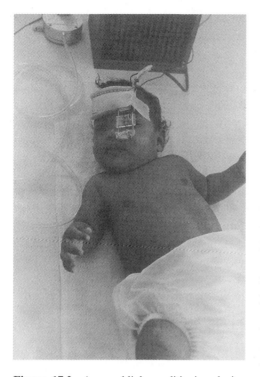

Figure 17.2 An eye-blink conditioning device for infants between 0 and 4 months of age (DeLucia, 1968). A stainless steel wire frame with a pair of Amperex germanium photocells mounted on two 16.76-mm pieces of Plexiglas. One photocell is focused on the sclera, and the other is focused on the lower lid. When the eye is open, ambient light reflects equally from both surfaces, producing no current flow. A blink reduces the light reflected from the sclera, producing a current flow proportional to the difference in light intensity on the two photocells. The output is fed into a polygraph adjusted to produce a full pen deflection when the eye is open. Secured in and projecting through the Plexiglas is a 7.94-mm (diam) nozzle through which a 2.5-psi air puff is delivered to the left corner of the infant's left eye from a distance of 2.54 cm. The device is taped to the infant's forehead, leaving the eyelid unrestricted and unencumbered.

of an infant pneumobelt connected to the polygraph.

Session 1 began with three CS-alone and three UCS-alone trials to ensure that infants blinked to the UCS but not to the CS. Next, infants received 50 paired CS-UCS presen-

tations and 20 CS-alone trials interspersed randomly among the CS-UCS trials, with the stipulation that 10 CS-alone trials would occur in each half of the session and that no more than 2 CS-alone trials would occur in succession. A truly random control group, first introduced at 30 days of age, received 70 CS (1,900 ms) and 50 UCS (400 ms) presentations in each session. Half of the UCSs were presented randomly during a CS presentation, and half were presented randomly in the absence of a CS, with the stipulation that their frequencies of occurrence were approximately equivalent in each half of each session. Each infant in the random control group received a different schedule of stimulus presentations.

Researchers should note the procedures that were included to control for infant state: (1) No trial began unless respiration was regular and eyes were open; (2) a minimum of 8 s elapsed between trials; (3) sessions began after an infant had awakened from a nap and consumed approximately half the ration of a regular feeding; (4) a pacifier was used to maintain alertness; and (5) sessions were conducted in a sound-attenuated room.

At all ages, the percentage of anticipatory CRs increased over blocks of trials, but only the 1,500-ms ISI groups learned the association—the 500-ms ISI groups did not. Although age was not a significant factor in acquisition, the conditioning performance of the oldest group was significantly higher than for the youngest group. Notably, a significantly greater percentage of CRs occurred on CS-alone trials than within the CS-UCS interval at all ages. Experimenters should note that interspersing UCS-omission trials among CS-UCS training trials is often the only way to reveal a conditioned response. Because CR latencies of infants who are immature or otherwise compromised can be quite long, such infants are often unable to respond within the prescribed CS-UCS interval. In fact, studies of heart-rate conditioning regularly use a *UCS-omission procedure* with newborns, premature infants, and decerebrate infants (e.g., Berntson, Tuber, Ronca, & Bachman, 1983; Clifton, 1974; Tuber, Berntson, Bachman, & Allen, 1980).

Conditioned Head-Turning

Ipsilateral head-turning is reliably elicited in newborns by stroking the cheek near the mouth. It is the initial member of an adaptive reflex chain that terminates in feeding. For this reason, one establishes and maintains conditioned head-turning in an infant by providing an opportunity for the infant to suck *at the end of the arc of rotation* after elicitation of a head-turn. This procedure is ineffective if the nipple is presented at midline. Thus, Papousek (1959, 1961) reinforced each head-turn with milk, and Siqueland and Lipsitt (1966) reinforced each head-turn with a 5% dextrose-water solution.

Following Papousek's (1959, 1961) work, Siqueland and Lipsitt (1966) sounded a buzzer (the CS) for 2 s and then stroked the infant's left cheek (the UCS) while the buzzer continued to sound for another 3 s. Each leftward head-turn was immediately followed by sucking from a bottle for 2 s. After ipsilateral head-turning to the UCS stabilized, Siqueland and Lipsitt initiated formal conditioning trials. The experimental group received 30 acquisition trials with 30-s intertrial intervals on which the buzzer and stroking were followed by dextrose, and then 12 to 30 extinction trials with the buzzer alone. The mean percentage of trials on which head-turning occurred to the buzzer increased during acquisition and decreased during extinction. A matched control group receiving dextrose 8–10 s after stroking showed no increase in head-turning over trials.

In a second experiment, Siqueland and Lipsitt established differential conditioning by pairing a tone (S+) and stroking of one cheek with dextrose and pairing a buzzer (S−) and stroking of the other cheek with no dextrose. Ipsilateral responding to the S+ increased during acquisition and decreased during extinction. Subsequently, they introduced a reversal procedure in which right turns following right-sided stimulation were initially reinforced with dextrose in the presence of S+ but not S−; after initial training, this contingency was reversed. Initially, infants responded increasingly to S+; when the contingency was reversed and became S−, they responded to it less, and by the end of reversal training, they responded more to the new S+. In the differential and reversal conditioning studies, the control group received the same total number of reinforcements as the experimental group 8–10 s after the S+. These are model experimental procedures that researchers can use with infants of any age.

Instrumental and Operant Conditioning

Instrumental conditioning and its variant, operant conditioning, differ from classical conditioning in that the conditioned response is not elicited by a stimulus that precedes it, but is emitted and followed by a stimulus that reinforces it. *Instrumental conditioning* is a discrete-trials procedure in which the experimenter initiates the trial by presenting a cue or problem situation, and the subject terminates the trial by responding. The experimenter also controls the interval between trials and the number and distribution of reinforcers. The typical measures of instrumental learning are the number or percent frequency of correct responses over trials, response latency, or response speed. In discrete-trials procedures, reinforcement that either is delayed longer than 3 s (Brody, 1981; Millar, 1990; Millar & Watson, 1979; Ramey & Ourth, 1971) or is spatially discontiguous with the locus of response (Millar & Schaffer, 1972, 1973) is usually ineffective between 6 and 8 months of age unless a cue that indicates the locus of reinforcement is provided (Millar, 1974).

The bulk of conditioning research with infants has used operant procedures. In *operant conditioning,* subjects control both the intertrial interval and the number of reinforcers by responding at whatever rate they choose— in effect, self-presenting their own "trials." Because there is no discrete stimulus event from which to time response latency, experimenters measure *response rate* (number of responses over time). Furthermore, in operant conditioning, the response or some component of it must be in the infant's repertoire prior to training. Because the measurement of learning requires a comparison of the rate of response before the introduction of reinforcement (i.e., the baseline rate, or *operant level*) with the rate of response afterward, researchers are cautioned that an accurate measure of operant level is critical. Accurate measures require a baseline period sufficiently long that infants can adapt to the experimental situation but not so long that they become restless or distressed. If an infant's operant level is too high, then a response ceiling for reinforcement effects will be reached rapidly. If their operant level is too low, then the lesser opportunity to reinforce it in the allotted time will reduce the probability that the infant will detect the correlation between the response and its outcome.

Many operant-conditioning studies involve brief sessions with only a couple of minutes each for baseline and extinction and only slightly longer for acquisition. Because younger infants require more time to learn some tasks, brief acquisition periods lessen their opportunities to learn. In fact, any of the preceding scenarios can lead to the erroneous conclusion that the reinforcer is ineffective, or that an infant cannot learn. Although conditioned responding can be measured during the initial portion of an extinction period, once infants have detected the

withdrawal of reinforcement, their arousal (fussing) may increase.

An *arousal control group* must be used to establish that the increase in responding during acquisition is due solely to the contingency and not to state changes elicited by the reinforcing stimulation or to other factors in the experimental situation that might increase arousal (a long session duration, satiation, hunger, etc.). Experimenters must also demonstrate *operant control,* that is, that increases in response rate are due to the contingency and not to the eliciting effects of the reinforcing stimulation. Both concerns are best satisfied by infants in a yoked-control group who receive the same number of reinforcements as the experimental group, but the reinforcement is not contingent on responding. Finally, in studies that use a differential reinforcement procedure, experimenters must be careful to selectively reinforce each infant's nonpreferred response or responding to the nonpreferred stimulus, as determined during a pretest or baseline period (see, e.g., Rovee-Collier & Capatides, 1979). Only in this way can subsequent differential responding be unequivocally attributed to the effect of differential reinforcement.

Reinforcers

Appetitive stimuli (positive reinforcers) have been used more frequently than *aversive stimuli* (negative reinforcers) to modify operant responding. Experimenters using nutritive reinforcers cannot manipulate deprivation level and usually have access to infants only between feedings; in addition, their manipulations are generally restricted to sugar water or milk in small amounts that will not influence the infant's subsequent intake. A few researchers have studied infants immediately prior to (Kron, 1966) or during (Papousek, 1959, 1961) a regularly scheduled feed, using the reinforcement as part of the daily ration. The use of nonnutritive reinforcers sidesteps many of these problems. These typically involve the presentation or termination of an auditory or visual stimulus (Butterfield & Siperstein, 1972; Lipsitt, Pederson, & DeLucia, 1966; Siqueland & DeLucia, 1969), although the opportunity to engage in non-nutritive sucking can be reinforcing too. Newborns, for example, suck most on a standard Davol nipple, next most on a blunt Davol nipple with the elongated portion cut off, and least on a piece of rubber tubing (Brown, 1972). If sucking on a standard nipple is made contingent upon tube sucking, the rate of sucking on a tube increases; although the same contingency does not increase the rate of blunt-nipple sucking, the latter decreases significantly if followed by tube sucking. These changes are effected through decreasing or increasing the interval of pausing between successive sucking bursts (Brassell & Kaye, 1974).

The reinforcer and the response it influences need not be biologically related. For example, an infant's rate of sucking will increase as readily when the sucks are followed by his or her mother's voice (DeCasper & Fifer, 1980; Mills & Melhuish, 1974), a computer-generated speech sound (Eimas, Siqueland, Jusczyk, & Vigorito, 1971), music (Butterfield & Siperstein, 1972), a movie (Kalnins & Bruner, 1973), colored slides of patterns or geometric shapes (Franks & Berg, 1975; Milewski & Siqueland, 1975), the movement of a crib mobile (Little, 1973), or termination of white noise (Butterfield & Siperstein, 1972) as when the infant's sucks are followed by a squirt of sugar water (Kobre & Lipsitt, 1972; Siqueland & Lipsitt, 1966) or milk (Sameroff, 1968; Siqueland, 1964). Likewise, head turning is readily reinforced by a visual pattern (Caron, 1967; Cornell & Heth, 1979; Levison & Levison, 1967), a novel toy (Koch, 1967, 1968), a human jack-in-the-box (Bower, 1966, 1967), visual access to the mother or a stranger (Koch, 1967, 1968), a nonnutritive nipple (Siqueland,

1968), or simply "being correct" (Papousek, 1967). These consequences are as effective as a squirt of milk (Papousek, 1961) or sugar water (Siqueland & Lipsitt, 1966). Vocalizations can be modified by both auditory (Hulsebus, 1973) and visual (Ramey & Watson, 1972) stimulation, as can visual behavior (Watson, 1969), foot-kicking (McKirdy & Rovee, 1978), and panel-pressing (Lipsitt et al., 1966; Simmons & Lipsitt, 1961). The commonality among these reinforcers is that infants can *control* them. The fact that infants continue to perform old responses or even acquire new ones while at the same time rejecting the nominal reinforcers (Papousek, 1969) reveals that they are ultimately reinforced by problem-solving.

Social reinforcers are particularly effective in establishing and maintaining infant behavior. The features that define a social stimulus change with age. Although newborns prefer to look at faces than at other visual stimuli (Hainline, 1978), the fact that their scanning patterns for static faces and other two-dimensional stimuli are identical (Maurer & Salapatek, 1976) suggests that this preference is not based on a social dimension. Nonetheless, infants discriminate among facial expressions at birth (Field, Woodson, Greenberg, & Cohen, 1982); display greater pupillary dilation to social than nonsocial stimuli at 1 and 4 months of age (Fitzgerald, 1968); display differential cardiac responses to mothers and strangers by 6 weeks (Banks & Wolfson, 1967) and differential pupillary responses to them by 12 weeks (Fitzgerald, 1968); and smile more frequently when social reinforcement is delivered by the mother than by a stranger (Hulsebus, 1973; Wahler, 1967). Contrast and movement, which are critical features of the human face, influence infants' scanning patterns (Girton, 1979; Salapatek & Kessen, 1966) and are effective nonsocial reinforcers during the first 2 months (Milewski & Siqueland, 1975). As a rule, both social and nonsocial reinforcers effectively modify nonsocial behaviors at all ages, but nonsocial reinforcers are less effective in doing so as infants get older. Not only are older infants more likely to discriminate social from nonsocial consequences, but they also have more experience that the natural environment does not provide such contingencies.

Over the first few postnatal months, social and nonsocial response-contingent reinforcers are functionally equivalent, but by the end of the fourth month, most infants treat social and nonsocial stimuli differently. Watson and Ramey (1972) suggested that 2-month-old infants perceive response-contingent mobiles as social stimuli; Caron, Caron, Caldwell, and Weiss (1973) reported that the eyes of others do not acquire special significance for the infant until the fourth month; and Dolgin and Azmitia (1985) concluded that, "before 4 months, faces do not have a special status (p. 332)." Watson (1972) proposed that the defining feature of a social stimulus for infants is that it responds contingently to the infant. He argued that people become important to infants during the first 3–4 months of life *because* they "play the game," that is, because they respond to the infant contingently.

The observation that infant social behaviors share many characteristics with nonsocial behaviors that are influenced by their reinforcing consequences led researchers to study the effect of contingent social stimulation (stimuli delivered by other humans) on the rate or frequency of infant social behaviors (behaviors directed toward other humans). Rheingold et al. (1959), for example, attempted to socially condition the nonfussy vocalizations of 12-week-olds. During a 2-day baseline phase prior to the conditioning phase, and again during a 2-day extinction phase afterward, vocalizations made while the experimenter leaned over the crib and stared impassively at the infant were tallied. Dur-

ing the 2-day conditioning phase, the experimenter maintained the original posture and expression except when administering a 1-s reinforcement immediately after each vocalization. Reinforcement consisted of a smile, three "tsk" sounds, and a light touch to the infant's abdomen. For the first 10 infants, the researchers gradually shifted reinforcement from a continuous to a fixed ratio-3 schedule. Because the intermittent schedule depressed response rates, however, the responses of the remaining 11 infants were continuously reinforced. Vocalizations increased reliably above baseline on the first conditioning day and increased even more on the second day. When reinforcement was withdrawn, vocalizing decreased and returned to baseline on the second extinction day. Despite the lack of a noncontingent-reinforcement control group, Rheingold et al. argued that the reliable increase in responding from the first to the second day of conditioning, and the continuing decline in responding from the first to the second day of extinction, were inconsistent with interpretations based on either arousal or the possibility that some aspect of the reinforcing stimulus was a "releaser" of social responses.

Weisberg (1963) repeated the Rheingold et al. (1959) study but added five control groups: (1) a group who received noncontingent social reinforcement (to control for *elicitation* effects of a social stimulus); (2) a group for whom the experimenter remained in view but expressionless throughout the study (to control for the effect of an *unresponsive adult* on vocalization rate/min); (3) a group with no experimenter at all (to provide a continuous baseline of nonstimulated vocalizations); (4) a group who received contingent nonsocial reinforcement from a door chime (delivered by an experimenter sitting in front of the infant); and (5) noncontingent nonsocial reinforcement. The latter two groups were included in the event that detectable environmental change might increase the rate of vocalization (group 4) and to control for the possibility of arousal induced by the door chime (group 5). The experimental group received the same reinforcement as in the Rheingold et al. study, but the reinforcement was timed to last for a total of 2 s.

Weisberg (1963) conducted two 10-min sessions per day for 8 consecutive days. On days 1 and 2, baseline rates in the absence of the experimenter were recorded for all infants; on days 3 and 4, all groups except group 3 were exposed to an unresponsive experimenter who was seated facing the infant; on days 5 and 6, the contingent- and noncontingent-reinforcement conditions were imposed; and on days 7 and 8, the two contingent-reinforcement groups were shifted to an extinction procedure, while the noncontingent-reinforcement groups continued to receive response-independent stimulation. Weisberg found that, from days 3 and 4 to days 5 and 6, the group who received contingent social reinforcement increased its rate of vocalization; on days 7 and 8, the groups did not differ. Ramey and Ourth (1971) replicated this study with 6- and 9-month-olds but reinforced vocalizations after delays of 0, 3, or 6 s. Only the 0-s delay groups increased vocalizations.

Subsequently, researchers questioned whether social reinforcers actually elicit social behaviors from infants (Bloom, 1984; Bloom & Esposito, 1975; Hulsebus, 1973; Sameroff & Cavanagh, 1979). Poulson (1983, 1984) settled the issue by demonstrating social reinforcement control over social responses in a within-subjects design. Today, researchers control for social elicitation by routinely including a noncontingent-stimulation control group in their designs or by reinforcing social responses after a delay. This precaution is necessitated by the fact that infants who expect social (and even nonsocial) stimuli to behave in particular ways often become distraught when those expectancies are violated, as when an adult's face remains still and expressionless during an extinction period (Brackbill, 1958; Rheingold et al., 1959).

A major constraint on session length is the rapidity with which infants satiate to the reinforcer. Siqueland (1968) found that slides to which infants had been preexposed for only 2 min were less effective than novel slides in reinforcing high-amplitude sucks. Similarly, 20-month-olds performed more responses when their responses were reinforced with a series of different pictures or brightnesses of light than if their responses produced the same consequence on each occasion (Weisberg & Fink, 1968). If a reinforcer is relatively novel (Berlyne, 1960), then sessions can be quite long. The lengthy and multiple sessions (15–45 min) used in mobile conjugate reinforcement studies, for example, are due partly to the relative novelty associated with the continuous rearrangements of the highly detailed mobile components. The reinforcing value of mobiles that offer a smaller range of variation declines more rapidly.

Given the difficulty in finding comparable tasks that are suitable for infants of different ages, we will focus on three tasks that have been successfully used to answer a variety of experimental questions across a wide age range—head-turning, foot-kicking, and lever-pressing.

Head-Turning

In classical conditioning studies, head-turns were elicited in neonates by a touch to the face and were reinforced with milk or dextrose (Papousek, 1959; Siqueland & Lipsitt, 1966). By 3 months of age, head-turning is elicited by the mother's voice or a novel sound (Levison & Levison, 1967) and is reinforced by visual access to the source of the sound. As before, reinforcement is most effective if presented at the end of the arc of rotation (not at midline) and is necessary to maintain head-turning. In a typical experimental procedure (Schneider & Trehub, 1985), the infant sits on the parent's lap in a sound-attenuating booth, and the experimenter sits in the opposite corner. Both the parent and the experimenter wear headphones to mask all auditory signals.

When the infant is quiet and looking straight ahead at a sticker or blinking light, a second experimenter presents a signal through one of two speakers that are located 45 deg to the left and right of midline. If the infant's head rotates 45 deg to either side, then the experimenter opposite the infant presses one of two buttons to indicate the direction of turn. Turns toward the signal are followed by a 4-s illumination and activation of a toy over the speaker; turns away from the signal are followed by silence for 4 s. The side position of the signal (or S+) is counterbalanced or randomized (to eliminate side biases) with the constraint that the signal cannot appear consecutively on one side more than three times. To ensure that infants are capable of performing the response, they must meet a criterion of four successive correct responses to signals from alternating sides. Typically, 95% of 6- to 18-month-olds meet criterion, and 85–90% complete 25–30 trials without fussing or crying. Infants can usually be tested for as many as 50–60 trials in a single visit. Moreover, interobserver reliability is usually excellent.

Foot-Kicking

Foot-kicking has been used in free-operant studies of mobile conjugate reinforcement. This procedure produces very rapid learning, possibly because two aspects of the reinforcer (frequency and intensity) vary and sustain attention for long periods both within and across sessions. Specifically in the mobile task, when the ribbon is attached to the mobile, foot-kicks move the mobile in a graded manner that is commensurate with their rate and vigor (*conjugate reinforcement*). Because each infant essentially "shops" for his or her own preferred momentary level of reinforcing stimulation by varying the rate and vigor of kicking, the conjugate reinforcement procedure eliminates problems associated with equating motivation across infants and ages. The mobile task and its upward extension, the train task (described in the next section), have been successfully used with infants between 2 and 24 months of age, can easily be adapted to study different problems of infant cognition and perception, and are portable and inexpensive. For these reasons, we will focus on these methodologies. Although hand-waving can be used instead of foot-kicking (Timmons, 1994), movement of the hand in front of the face induces younger infants to suck their fingers, which, like a pacifier, attenuates the very response the experimenter seeks to study.

At 2–3 months, L-shaped mobile stands are clamped to opposite rails of the infant's home crib so that both suspension bars protrude over the infant's upper abdomen. At 6 months, floor microphone stands with a horizontal mobile suspension bar welded to the top are placed on opposite sides of the playpen, where the infant is situated in a sling-seat. Although mobile suspension bars must offer some resistance, they still must also be flexible; for this reason, one-piece plastic mobile stands should not be used. A narrow, white satin or grosgrain ribbon is strung from one of the two suspension bars to the infant's ankle. During reinforcement periods, a ribbon connects one of the infant's ankles to the same hook as the mobile (see Figure 17.3a). It is important that the ribbon be neither too tight nor slack. During nonreinforcement periods, the ankle ribbon is connected to the second mobile hook (see Figure 17.3b). In this arrangement, the infant can see the mobile, but his or her kicks cannot move it. It is important that the experimenter move the ribbon rather than the mobile from one stand to the other because the ribbon acts to keep the mobile from bouncing off the stand when the infant kicks very hard or fast.

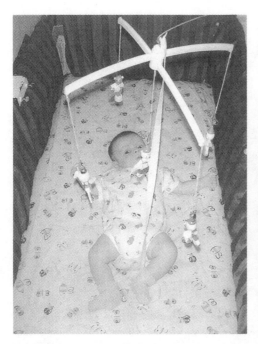 

Figure 17.3   The experimental arrangement used with 2- to 6-month-olds in the operant mobile task, shown here with a 3-month-old. (a) Acquisition: Kicks conjugately move the mobile via an ankle ribbon that is connected to the mobile hook. (b) Baseline, immediate retention test, long-term retention test: The ankle ribbon and mobile are connected to different hooks, and kicks do not move the mobile.

Whenever possible, training should take place in the infant's home. This practice minimizes attrition by allowing infants to be tested under optimal conditions—the only novel stimulus is what the experimenter provides, the infant's normal schedule is not disrupted, and the infant is most likely to be alert and playful. The best time to test younger infants is after a nap, diapering, and feeding. Although this time of day will vary across infants, it should be relatively constant across multiple sessions for a given infant. Allowing the caregiver to arouse the sleeping infant when the experimenter arrives for a scheduled session, or allowing the caregiver to hurry feeding, will only increase the chance of attrition. Infants who do not receive their typical ration prior to testing invariably become fussy. Finally, a pacifier must not be used to calm the infant; pacifiers actually prevent infants from learn-

ing by inhibiting activity. If the infant seems inconsolable at the outset, the best tactic is simply to reschedule the session.

Training sessions occur on 2 consecutive days unless the training regimen per se is the independent variable (Ohr, Fagen, Rovee-Collier, Hayne, & Vander Linde, 1989; Rovee-Collier, Evancio, & Earley, 1995). At all ages, each training session begins with a nonreinforcement period; in Session 1, this period serves as a *baseline phase,* when the infant's mean rate of unlearned activity (kicks/min or operant level) is determined. Next follows the *acquisition phase,* when kicks are conjugately reinforced (see Figure 17.3a). The acquisition phase is usually 2 to 3 times longer than the baseline period. Finally, each session ends with another nonreinforcement period; in Session 2, this period serves as the *immediate retention test,* when both

Figure 17.4 The experimental arrangement used with 6- to 18-month-olds in the operant train task, shown here with a 6-month-old. Each lever press moves the toy train for 1-2 s during acquisition; during baseline and all retention tests, the lever is deactivated, and presses do not move the train. Note the complex array of toys within the train box.

the final level of learning and retention after zero delay are measured. After a delay, the infant receives a third, procedurally identical session; here, the initial nonreinforcement period serves as a *long-term retention test* (see Figure 17.3b). Because the mobile is stationary during all tests, the infant will attempt to move it by kicking robustly; and because each nonreinforcement period is so brief, the infant's responding will not extinguish. After the long-term test, the reacquisition phase serves as a motivational control procedure to ensure that infants who responded poorly during the preceding test were not ill, fatigued, or otherwise unable or unmotivated to perform the response on that particular day. Infants who fail to respond appropriately when the contingency is reintroduced are excluded from the final sample.

Lever-Pressing

The parameters used in the train task are identical to those used in the mobile task except

that the reinforcement is not conjugate. Instead, each lever-press moves the miniature train around a circular track for only 1 s (2 s at 6 months of age) (see Figure 17.4). As in the mobile task, the baseline phase and all retention tests occur when the lever is deactivated, and infants' responses do not move the train. Infants between 6 and 18 months of age are trained with one of two miniature train sets, counterbalanced within groups. The features common to both sets are the frame of the train box (58 × 58 × 35 cm), the front Plexiglas window, a lever (30 × 12.5 cm) at the base of the window, a light bulb (60 W, 120 v) in the upper-right inside corner of the box that illuminates its interior, a circular track (47.5 cm diam), and an HO-scale train (an engine and three rail cars).

The wooden frames, patterns on the walls, and railroad cars in the two sets are different colors. Also, different toys and miniature figures are positioned about the track to make the display sufficiently "busy" that all ages will continue to find it interesting over multiple sessions. During nonreinforcement periods, the interior light remains on to give infants a clear view of the inside of the train set. During reinforcement periods, each lever press activates the train for 1 s (2 s at 6 months of age). Lever presses that occur while the train is in motion are registered by the computer but do not affect the train's movement. Infants must release the lever and press it again in order to activate the train again.

The train set is placed on a table in the infant's home, and the infant sits in front of it on the caregiver's lap or in a high chair. The context is defined as the particular room in the infant's home (kitchen, living room, bedroom) where training and testing take place. A laptop computer times all experimental phases, delivers the reinforcement, and registers all microswitch operations activated by lever presses in 10-s bins.

Despite the vast physical differences between 2- and 18-month-olds (see Figure 17.1), the range of unlearned responding to the mobile and the train (operant levels) is the same between 2 and 18 months, irrespective of task (Hartshorn et al., 1998b). Because both responses are very simple and well within the motoric competence of all ages, the relative level of learning achieved during original training is also the same at all ages whether infants are trained with mobiles or trains. In addition, infants of all ages reach the same learning criterion within just a few minutes of the first training session and take the same amount of time to do so. Although the rate of responding during acquisition is slightly lower at 2 and 3 months of age, the acquisition functions at these ages are otherwise quite comparable to those of older infants. Although 6-month-olds lever-press at half the rate of the older age groups, their duration of reinforcement is twice as long—2 s instead of 1 s. When adjusted for this factor, their acquisition function is the same as that of older infants.

Imitation

Simply put, imitation tasks involve a "monkey see, monkey do" procedure in which an experimenter models a behavior, then gives the infant the opportunity to reproduce it immediately afterward. Sometimes, the infant is given an opportunity to imitate the target actions both immediately and after a delay (see the section titled "Infant Memory"). In studies with infants, the definition of imitation has been translated methodologically into a strict focus on experimental control.

Facial Imitation

Piaget (1962) thought that "true" facial imitation did not emerge until 8–12 months of age and that facial imitation at younger ages was stimulus-bound and reflexive. The most carefully controlled studies of imitation from birth to 3 months were conducted by Meltzoff and Moore (1977, 1983, 1989, 1992, 1994). In their procedure, Meltzoff and Moore first exposed the infant to a passive face in a dimly lit room where the face (that of the experimenter) was the only thing illuminated. To prevent infants from developing idiosyncratic games with the experimenter, they did not interact with experimenter before the sessions. Each session began with a 90-s baseline phase, when the experimenter assumed an unresponsive or passive face, and infants' spontaneous production of the target facial gestures was assessed. This phase was followed by a 90-s modeling phase, when the experimenter demonstrated a burst of target actions (e.g., O-shaped mouth-openings) alternating with a neutral face (a pause) for 15 s each. The target actions were repeated four times per burst for a total of 12 demonstrations during the 90-s modeling phase. Each modeling phase was followed by a 150-s response period, when the experimenter resumed a passive face, and the infant could imitate the facial gesture. The experimenter then repeated the procedure, modeling another gesture. All gestures were modeled at the same distance from the infant and at the same temporal rate. To ensure that infants did not imitate during a modeling phase or that the experimenter's facial gestures were unaffected by the infant's responses to them, the experimenter gave each infant a pacifier before each modeling phase and withdrew it before each response period. Finally, observers who were blind to infants' experimental conditions scored all responses from videotapes.

In their original study with 12- to 21-day-olds, Meltzoff and Moore (1977) demonstrated four different gestures—tongue protrusion, an O-shaped mouth-opening gesture, lip protrusion, and sequential finger movement—using a repeated-measures design. They measured the frequency with which infants reproduced all of the target actions during the response period immediately after each particular gesture was demonstrated. Reasoning that if an infant were truly imitating the modeled gesture—mouth-opening, for example—then he or she should produce more mouth-openings after a demonstration of mouth-opening than after a demonstration of tongue protrusion, and so forth. An infant's differential responding to the demonstrated gesture was expressed as the rate of a given target response relative to the rate of other responses the infant produced during the same response period. This cross-target comparison measure controlled for changing levels of behavioral arousal throughout the session as well as for any arousing effects of the adult demonstration per se. The rate of the infant's target response immediately after the demonstration relative to its rate both during other response periods and during the baseline phase were also calculated. Meltzoff and

Moore found that significantly more infants responded with gestures that matched the four modeled behaviors than one would expect by chance.

Meltzoff and Moore (1983, 1989) subsequently found that even newborns could imitate tongue protrusion, mouth-opening, and head-turning, and that 1- and 3-month-olds could imitate mouth-opening and tongue protrusion (Meltzoff & Moore, 1992). They concluded that prior failures to eliminate young infants' social games and idiosyncratic routines had obscured evidence of early imitation. They also concluded that early imitation is neither stimulus-bound nor reflexive and does not disappear by 3 months of age.

Vocal Imitation

Meltzoff and Kuhl (1996) documented vocal imitation by 12-, 16-, and 20-week-old infants. In this kind of research, one must consider developmental changes in the anatomy of infants' vocal cords. Methodological considerations in this instance included use of a prerecorded audiovisual taped presentation so that adults could not respond to infants' vocalizations on-line, three different vowel types, and spectrographic analyses of infants' vocalizations. The latter provided a precise measure of developmental change.

Sensory Preconditioning

Because infants spend the better part of their first 6 months visually inspecting the world around them, it is likely that they learn many of the predictive relationships in their visual surroundings during this time. They cannot display what they have learned, however, until given a specific opportunity to do so. *Sensory preconditioning* is a preexposure phenomenon in which subjects later receive an opportunity to manifest their "silent learning" (Brogden, 1939). In this procedure, two discriminably different stimuli (S1, S2) are repeatedly exposed in close temporal or spatial contiguity. Subsequently, infants are trained to perform a distinctive response to one stimulus (S1) and are tested with the other stimulus (S2). If they perform the distinctive response to S2, then they are presumed to have learned an association between S1 and S2 when the two stimuli were initially exposed together. This inference requires three essential control groups—a *no-change control group* that is tested with S1 (to ensure that infants actually learned the distinctive response in the first place); a *no-preexposure control group* that is tested with S2 (to ensure that infants actually discriminate it and do not respond on the basis of simple generalization); and an *unpaired preexposure control group* that is preexposed to S1 and S2 for exactly the same amount of time at different times of day, is later trained with S1, and then is tested with S2 (to ensure that the two stimuli are equally familiar but that no association between them could be formed). For the researcher to conclude that an association had been formed between S1 and S2, the no-change control group would have to respond to S1 during the test, and the other two control groups would have to fail to respond to S2.

Sensory preconditioning has been reported in infants as young as 6 months in the operant mobile procedure and in the imitation procedure. Boller (1997) exploited the fact that at 6 months, infants' memories are highly context-specific. In most mobile studies, a highly distinctive context is created by draping a distinctively colored and patterned cloth over the sides of the playpen where infants are trained. One day after training, infants who learned to kick to move a particular mobile in one context do not recognize the mobile (i.e., do not kick above baseline) if the context is different; yet, they kick robustly if tested in the training context. Boller exposed 6-month-olds to two contexts hanging side-by-side anywhere in the home (e.g., over the back of the couch, in their crib) for a total of 60 min daily for 7 consecutive days. Beginning 1 day later, she trained infants for 2 days to kick to move a mobile in one of the preexposed contexts. When tested 1 day after training in the other preexposed context, infants kicked significantly above baseline, suggesting that they had formed an association between the two contexts when they had been preexposed together. Infants in an unpaired control group were successively exposed to the same two contexts for a total of 30 min each at two different times of day for 7 days, trained in one context, and then tested in the other. This group did not kick in the second context even though the test mobile was the same, and neither did a no-preexposure control group that was trained in one context and tested with the original training mobile in the other context. Boller found no evidence of latent inhibition—a preexposure effect characterized by retarded learning to a preexposed stimulus.

Barr, Marrott, and Rovee-Collier (2001) used a sensory preconditioning procedure to associate two hand-puppets that they subsequently used with 6-month-olds in an imitation task. Puppets A and B were placed side-by-side on two hat stands in the infant's home in full view for a total of 60 min per day for 1 week. One day later, the target actions were modeled six times on puppet A (or, for half of the infants, on puppet B) for a total of 60 s. Immediately afterward, infants were allowed to imitate the target actions three times. During a 24-hr retention test, groups of infants imitated the target actions if tested with either puppet A or B but not with a novel puppet—puppet C. The unpaired control group, which was successively exposed to puppets A and B for 30 min each in either the morning or in the afternoon, respectively, did not imitate the target actions on puppet B.

Concept Learning

Learning-Set Formation

Using a discrete-trials procedure, Ling (1941) conducted an elegant series of discrimination studies that yielded some of the earliest documentation of learning-set formation—a phenomenon not formally described until some years later (Harlow, 1949). Altogether, 50 infants were studied longitudinally between 6 and 15 months of age. Depending on the study, the stimuli were two to five different yellow forms (circle, oval, square, triangle, cross) that were presented on a tray. The S+ was covered with a saccharine solution (the reinforcement) and could be grasped and removed from the tray, but the S− was fastened down so that infants could not remove it. In the initial experiment, 18 infants received a simultaneous two-choice discrimination between S+ (the circle) and S− (the cross or oval) until they responded correctly on 8 of 10 consecutive trials. At this point, another form was introduced as the S−, and so forth, until infants had learned to select the circle over all of the other forms. The nine infants tested on the circle/cross discrimination reached criterion after an average of 124 trials, whereas the nine tested on the more difficult circle/oval discrimination reached criterion after an average of 147 trials. In succeeding experiments, the spatial orientation of S− was changed, the relative size of both stimuli was varied, and the number of stimuli used as S− was progressively increased from two to five. Finally, the circle became the S− and remained constant over trials, while the other four stimuli were used as the S+ and varied over trials.

Over the first three experiments, all infants responded to form per se, irrespective of relative position, size, spatial position, sequence, or pattern complexity, indicating that the ability to abstract the common features of the total configuration was present even at 6 months. Changes in spatial orientation and relative size influenced reaction time but not the number of trials to criterion. Similarly, infants in the final experiment responded differentially to a single contour in a changing array in which as many as five different geometric forms served as the S+ at one time or another. Most importantly, the number of trials to criterion on each successive combination of forms progressively decreased throughout the study, irrespective of whether the initial discrimination series was difficult (circle/oval) or easy (circle/cross). Even the relatively profound change associated with a discrimination reversal in the final experiment, when the circle became S− and the other forms became S+, did not disrupt infants' discriminative performance. These results suggested that their performance was based on some primitive kind of insight and led Ling to conclude, "some common *general* factor in the experience begins to operate very early and very permanently" (1941, p. 16). The rapidity with which infants solved the discrimination reversal—in fewer than 100 trials—was surprising. Ling attributed infants' rapid improvement on the conceptually difficult reversal problem to their learning to inhibit the formerly correct response.

Ling's (1941) finding that infants developed a set to discriminate among forms and recognized them over a series of transformations led Fagen (1977) to ask whether young infants could form concepts or rules. To answer this, he used an object-discrimination learning-set task with 10-month-olds. Learning-set formation is *between-problem learning* and is rule-based, whereas simple discrimination learning is *within-problem learning* and does not require that subjects acquire a general rule. In learning-set formation, the general rule or concept is usually that one of two objects will always be correct (reinforced), even though the particular object that is correct on any given problem (i.e., over successive trials with a particular S+

and S−) will change. Acquisition of this rule is reflected in a *win-stay, lose-shift response strategy*. The number of problems required to achieve correct Trial 2 performance is the dependent measure in learning-set studies, whereas the number of trials to reach criterion is the dependent measure in simple discrimination studies.

The general procedure followed in all learning-set studies is the same: The experimenter presents two unrelated, randomly selected, junk objects (randomly designated S+ and S−) for a limited number of trials (e.g., six) per problem, then uses another pair of unrelated junk objects as S+ and S− for a given number of trials on another problem, and so forth, until subjects respond correctly on Trial 2 irrespective of the particular stimuli that are presented on a given problem. Trial 1 performance is always expected to be at chance (50% correct). On Trial 2 and thereafter, however, subjects will pick the correct object if they have learned the rule. Likewise, subjects who chanced to pick the correct object on Trial 1 will continue to respond to it thereafter if they have acquired the rule. If mean correct responding jumps from 50% correct to 100% correct by Trial 2, instead of gradually improving over successive trials, then subjects have adopted a win-stay, lose-shift strategy, demonstrating that they learned the rule.

Fagen (1977) tested four infants in their own homes twice daily for 10 days (excluding weekends). Infants sat in a high-chair in front of a large wooden box with a large, central Plexiglas window on the front and a smaller Plexiglas window on either side of the central window. When the compartment behind the large central window was illuminated, the infant could view an electrically operated, brightly colored plastic circus train moving around a circular track, sounding a bell, and flashing a signal light (the reinforcement). On each trial, a single stimulus (S+, S−) was illu-minated behind each of the smaller side windows. Stimuli consisted of 240 different junk objects, randomly organized into 120 pairs, with one member of each pair serving as the S+ for a given problem (side position counterbalanced across trials of a given problem). When an infant pushed a door knob (chosen because it was too large for infants to clutch) that was affixed directly to the window in front of S+, the lights illuminating S+ and S− turned off, and the light in the central box and the reinforcement turned on for 8 s. Two s after the central light and reinforcement went off, the side lights went back on, illuminating the next pair of objects to begin the next trial.

Because children usually acquire a learning set more rapidly if they first solve one or two object discrimination problems to criterion, Fagen (1977) trained infants on two object discriminations first. In each of the first two sessions, infants received 42 simultaneous discrimination trials with a single stimulus pair—a procedure that facilitates subsequent learning-set formation in children. In Session 1, infants met criterion in a mean of 70 trials. At the outset of the second session, 4–5 hr after Session 1, infants displayed some forgetting but still responded reliably above chance. The 18 learning-set sessions began in Session 3. Each consisted of 7 six-trial problems, with a different pair of stimuli presented in each problem to make a total of 126 six-trial problems. Over successive learning-set sessions, discrimination performance within a problem progressively improved. The family of intraproblem learning curves, averaged over every 20 problems, assumed the classic learning-set appearance (Harlow, 1949). Performance over all six trials of the initial problems (1–63) was relatively flat. During problems 64–84, Trial 2 performance first exceeded chance, and during the final third of training (problems 85–126), Trial 2 performance stabilized at 75% correct, and the percent correct improved over succeeding trials.

In the last half of training, Trial 2 performance on Problem 1 was as good from session to session, in spite of the longer retention interval, as was problem-to-problem performance within a session.

Although response latencies were shorter on incorrect than on correct trials throughout all trials, infants tended to respond impulsively. This, in turn, was a major factor underlying their failure to achieve a 100%-correct final level of performance on Trial 2. An error-factor analysis revealed that *differential-cue errors* and *position preferences* also affected Trial 2 performance. *Stimulus-preservation* errors (continuing to respond to S−) influenced performance during only the first half of training, disappearing initially on long-latency response trials and disappearing by the end of training on short-latency response trials. *Response-shift errors* (tendencies to err more on later trials after a correct than an incorrect Trial 1 response) were negligible. A hypothesis-model analysis indicated that a win-stay, lose-shift strategy appeared by the end of training and was particularly prominent on trials with long-latency responses. These data unequivocally demonstrate that infants can acquire general response rules based on the abstraction of general relationships over successively encountered problems. As a result, later behavior is rule-guided rather than being based solely on within-problem, trial-and-error learning. The fact that infants demonstrated a reliable improvement in Trial 2 performance with completely novel stimuli after only nine learning-set sessions is evidence that infants had indeed learned a rule.

Categorization

Fundamentally, categorization is a problem of memory. Category information, when first encountered, must be retained long enough that when a subsequent category member is encountered, the new information can be inte-grated with the category information that was encountered first. Not surprisingly, therefore, the same factors that affect infants' memory performance also affect their ability to categorize. Habituation and operant mobile procedures have been used to study categorization with younger infants, whereas object manipulation and object touching have been used with older infants.

In *habituation studies* of categorization, infants view a series of slides of different objects from the same category, then are tested with two new slides: one of a novel object that is a category member and one that is not. Longer looking at the novel noncategory member is taken as evidence that an infant had formed a category based on information shared by the training objects; that is, the novel test object that is not in the training category is presumably more dissimilar to the training exemplars. These studies have found that infants respond categorically on the basis of redundant information encountered over the habituation series irrespective of whether they habituate. A study by Cornell (1974) is typical. He found that both 19- and 23-week-olds exhibited a decline in looking time when the same stimulus (a male or female face) was repeatedly presented for six 10-s trials. Only older infants, however, exhibited a decline in looking time when the same male or female face in a different perspective was presented on each trial. Neither age exhibited a decline in looking time when a different male or female face was presented. During category testing, all infants saw a frontal view of a novel face of the opposite gender. Older infants who repeatedly saw the same face during training (Set 3) looked longer at the novel test face, as did older infants who saw different views of the same face (Set 2) or different faces (Set 1). The fact that initial looking times to male and female faces in Set 3 were equal (as were looking times on the first trial of the other habituation conditions) excluded the possibility that the male frontal view was more salient than the female frontal view or vice versa. Unfortunately, whether infants exposed to Set 2 would have treated a frontal view of a different female face as more novel than a frontal view of a male face (or vice versa) was not assessed.

Cohen and Strauss (1979) questioned whether infants in Cornell's (1974) study might have responded to a common feature in the different photographs of the same person (e.g., the length or shape of hair) instead of to the person's gender. In addition, they worried that Cornell's subjects did not habituate, although others (e.g., Oakes et al., 1991; Younger, 1990; Younger & Cohen, 1983, 1986) have since found the same result as Cornell. To address these concerns, they habituated 18-, 24-, and 30-week-olds to color photographs of a female face in one of four side orientations (looking to the upper or lower right or left) and either smiling, frowning, or looking surprised. Group 1 saw the same photograph repeatedly; Group 2 saw the same female in different side orientations; and Group 3 saw different females in different side orientations. To ensure that infants actually habituated, they trained them to a 50% looking-time habituation criterion and then gave them three additional habituation trials prior to the test. All infants were tested on two successive trials with frontal views of a familiar female and a completely novel one (order counterbalanced) wearing a neutral expression. Times spent looking at a checkerboard pattern during pre- and posttests were compared to ensure that all infants had remained attentive throughout the session. As the measure of reliability, Cohen and Strauss reported that "two independent observers agreed to within 0.5 s of fixation times for over 98% of the trials."

All groups and ages habituated (i.e., looked less during the three posthabituation trials than during the first three habituation tri-

als) and did so at the same rate. During test trials with either the same face in a novel orientation or a different face in a different orientation, however, only the 30-week-olds generalized habituation (i.e., did not increase looking time). This finding suggested that during the habituation trials, they had abstracted both the invariant features of a particular face and of faces in general, respectively. In contrast, both 18- and 24-week-olds increased looking time (i.e., dishabituated) in all test conditions, suggesting that they had not abstracted the invariant features of the habituation stimuli over successive trials. These results led Cohen and Strauss (1979) to conclude that 7.5 months is the pivotal age for infant categorization: Before that age, infants presumably cannot form categories, whereas after that age, they can.

Even more sophisticated questions can be asked using the habituation procedure, such as whether infants abstract summary representations (prototypes) of category information (Sherman, 1985; Strauss, 1979; Younger, 1990; Younger & Gotlieb, 1988) or representations of individual category exemplars (Greco, Hayne, & Rovee-Collier, 1990; Medin & Schaffer, 1978). Strauss (1979), for example, asked whether 10-month-olds could abstract a prototypical representation of a category and, if so, whether the prototype would be modal (counted) or averaged (a mean). Based on studies with adults, he hypothesized that the larger the distinctions between the individual features, the higher the probability that infants would form a modal prototype. To quantify the category exemplars, he used schematic drawings of faces from a police Identikit, which contains sets of clear, plastic templates, each depicting a variation of a particular facial feature. When the templates of one value of each feature are superimposed, a complete face is formed. From the five values that defined each length of face, length of nose, width of nose, and amount of

Table 17.1   Values of Faces Constructed from the Police Identikit Used during Familiarization with Category Exemplars from the Wide Condition

Familiarization Faces	Facial Dimension Values			
	Eye Separation	Nose Width	Nose Length	Head Length
1	1	1	5	5
2	5	3	1	5
3	1	1	5	3
4	1	3	1	5
5	5	5	3	1
6	5	1	1	5
7	1	5	1	5
8	3	5	1	1
9	5	5	1	1
10	3	1	5	5
11	1	5	5	1
12	1	5	3	1
13	5	1	5	1
14	5	1	5	3

NOTE: Each face was formed from four continuous dimensions (length of face, length of nose, width of nose, amount of separation between eyes). Category exemplars for the wide condition had values of 1, 3, and 5; category exemplars for the narrow condition had values of 2, 3, and 4.
SOURCE: From M. S. Strauss (1979, Figure 1, p. 622). Reprinted with permission. Copyright 1979, American Psychological Association.

eye separation, he constructed a wide and a narrow category. Faces in the wide category were constructed from the extreme values (1 and 5) of each feature (see Table 17.1), and faces in the narrow category were constructed from values 2 and 4. During the 14 habituation trials, infants saw six faces from each category (12 trials) and a face constructed from the intermediate value 3 (2 trials). The average prototype for both the wide and narrow conditions was face 3-3-3-3; the modal prototypes for the wide condition were faces 1-1-1-1 and 5-5-5-5, and for the narrow condition were faces 2-2-2-2 and 4-4-4-4 (see Figure 17.5).

Looking times declined over trials whether faces were in the narrow category (where differences in the values of recurrent features were smaller) or the wide category (where differences in feature values were more discriminable). During testing, infants in both conditions (wide, narrow) looked longer at the modal face (1-1-1-1 or 5-5-5-5, 2-2-2-2 or 4-4-4-4) than at the average face (3-3-3-3), suggesting that they had formed an average prototype (i.e., the average face was more familiar).

Habituation procedures mirror only a small subset of real-world situations in which categorization occurs. Although some exemplars of real-world categories are encountered in close temporal succession (e.g., items on successive pages of a mail-order catalog or on a grocery store aisle; animals in the monkey house in a zoo), others are successively encountered over periods of hr, days, or even weeks. Moreover, infants who have seen a series of category exemplars rarely look longer at a category member—whether an individual exemplar or a prototype—after delays longer than a few minutes. A major benefit of categorizing for adults, however, is its retention advantage: Category information is remembered longer (Posner & Keele, 1970). Another experimental method that has been used to study infant categorization—the *operant mobile task*—exploits this benefit. Both 3- and 6-month-olds can remember this task for days or weeks. Also, whereas infants first form conceptual categories at 7.5 months of age when trained and tested in habituation procedures (Cohen & Strauss, 1979), they form conceptual categories by at least at 3 months of age when trained and tested in the mobile conjugate reinforcement paradigm (for review, see Hayne, 1996).

In a typical mobile study of 3-month-olds' ability to categorize shapes, for example, Hayne, Rovee-Collier, and Perris (1987) affixed the critical category cues (A or 2)

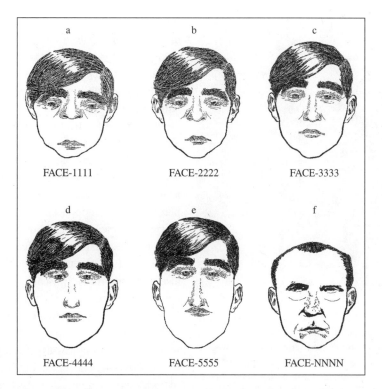

Figure 17.5   The sets of test faces, constructed from a police Identikit, that were used with 10-month-olds to study categorization and prototype formation (Strauss, 1979). During familiarization infants saw faces in one of two categories (wide, narrow) that varied along five values (1–5) on each of four dimensions (length of face, length of nose, width of nose, eye separation). Faces in the wide category had values of 1, 3, and 5; faces in the narrow category had values of 2, 3, and 4 (see Table 17.1).
SOURCE: M. Strauss, *Journal of Experimental Psychology: Human Learning and Memory, 5*. Abstraction of prototypical information by adults and 10-month-old infants. Figure 1, p. 623. Copyright 1979, American Psychological Association. Reprinted with permission.

directly to the side panels of a mobile composed of painted yellow blocks (see Figure 17.6). These shapes were selected because pigeon and human adult subjects scale them identically and as polar opposites (Blough, 1982), and because pigeons respond categorically to artificial classes constructed of these same characters (Morgan, Fitch, Holman, & Lea, 1975). In Experiment 1, Hayne et al. asked whether infants could actually discriminate the attributes that were used to differentiate between the categories (different shapes) and category exemplars (different colors). To answer this, they trained independent groups for three sessions with A's or 2's in the same color, then tested them 24 hr later with a mobile displaying the same shape in a different color, the novel shape in the same color, or the novel shape in a novel color. Although infants tested with the original training mobile responded robustly, the three groups tested with a novel mobile did not respond above baseline, indicating that 3-month-olds could discriminate if a single attribute (color, shape) on the training mobile was different after 24 hr. We note that infants' memory across the first year and a half is highly specific to the objects in the original task in both operant and imitation studies. This specificity contrasts sharply with their novelty preferences in

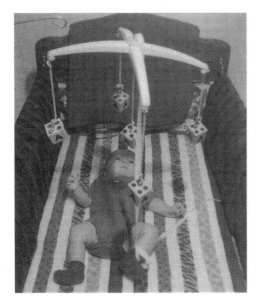

Figure 17.6 An exemplar of the A category (a mobile composed of yellow-blocks displaying A's in a particular color) used with infants between 3 and 6 months, shown here during category training with a 3-month-old. Exemplars of a second category display 2's of different colors. The crib rails are draped with a red-and-blue striped cloth to create a distinctive training context.

looking-behavior tasks. This specificity probably has a functional component: The fact that young infants will not respond to stimuli that are even slightly different and potentially lack predictive value compensates for their lack of inhibitory control. In contrast, the stimuli presented during a looking-behavior task have no predictive value in the first place. Looking at a novel stimulus, moreover, is less precarious than acting on it.

In a second experiment, Hayne et al. (1987) trained infants with a different category exemplar (e.g., blocks displaying A's in a particular color) each day for 3 days and tested them 24 hr later with a novel exemplar from either the training category (A) or a novel one (2). Infants trained with *black, green,* and *blue A's* on successive days, for example, were tested with either *red A's* (a novel member of the

training category) or *red 2's* (a member of the novel category). This time, infants tested with a novel category member responded to it, indicating that they recognized it, but infants tested with a mobile from the novel category still did not.

Instead of testing infants with experimenter-defined categories, Greco et al. (1990) asked how the infants themselves construct a category. They collected a number of different stimuli that might be perceived as a mobile and tested groups of infants with each of these 1 day after training with mobiles displaying differently colored A's or 2's (see Hayne et al., 1987). Adults also psychophysically scaled the physical similarity of each object to a training mobile. Greco et al. then selected the object to which infants did not respond and that adults had scaled as most physically dissimilar to a training mobile—a stained-glass-and-metal butterfly wind chime—and asked under what conditions might infants treat it like the prior category exemplars. To answer this, they provided new groups of infants with different kinds of information about the object's function. Its function was either shared by the category exemplars (e.g., it moved like the training mobiles) or was not shared (e.g., it rang, but the training exemplars did not). For 3 min immediately after training was over, experimental groups saw the wind chime moving as the training mobiles had moved, while a control group saw the stationary wind chime.

All groups were tested with the wind chime 1 day later. During the test, infants who had seen the wind chime moving the day before treated the wind chime as a category member and kicked above their baseline rate. Infants obviously did not respond on the basis of its net functional similarity to the training exemplars because it looked entirely different from the A and 2 training mobiles. Furthermore, because the wind chime remained stationary during the test, its functional information was not perceptible. This result means that infants must have classified the wind chime as a member of the mobile category during its 3-min moving exposure. Infants who viewed a stationary wind chime for 3 min after training, however, did not respond above baseline during the 24-hr test. That is, because it did not move, the stationary wind chime was not functionally similar to the A and 2 training mobiles; as a result, infants did not include it in the mobile category. Even infants who were first tested 1 week after exposure to the moving wind chime treated it as a category member. Researchers have found that infants remember category information longer in operant than in habituation paradigms because their successive category exemplars are more separated in time—not because their category training lasts longer (Merriman, Rovee-Collier, & Wilk, 1997).

Another sophisticated question that has been asked using both habituation and operant mobile procedures is whether infants can perceive and use correlated attributes to categorize novel stimuli. Correlated attributes (e.g., animals with wings usually have feathers) are vital to adult categorization because

novel stimuli that possess the same correlated features can be classified as members of the same category (e.g., bird). Younger and Cohen (1983) habituated 4-, 7-, and 10-month-olds to either one of two categories, each containing four schematic animals. Animals in each category were constructed from values 1 and 2 of each of five attributes—body (b: giraffe, cow, elephant); tail (t: feathered, fluffy, horse); feet (f: web, club, hoof), ears (e: antlers, round, human); and legs (l: two, four, six). The values of the first three attributes (b, t, f) were correlated (Group A: 1-1-1 or 2-2-2; Group B: 1-2-2 or 2-1-1), whereas the values of the remaining two attributes (e, l) occurred in all possible combinations (see Table 17.2).

During habituation trials, each of four slides per category was presented two times (order block-randomized) for a total of eight trials. Each trial began with a blinking light above a peephole in the center of the projection screen through which the infant's face was videotaped; when the light was fixated, it was terminated, and a slide was projected 40 cm to its right for 20 s. When the 20 s timed out, the slide was turned off, and the blinking light was turned on again, beginning the next trial. During testing, all infants saw

Table 17.2 Habituation and Test Stimuli for Experiment 1 Represented in Abstract Notation

	Group A					Group B				
	b	t	f	e	l	b	t	f	e	l
Habituation stimuli:										
1	1	1	1	1	2	1	2	2	1	2
2	1	1	1	2	1	1	2	2	2	1
3	2	2	2	1	1	2	1	1	1	1
4	2	2	2	2	2	2	1	1	2	2
Test stimuli:										
CORR	2	2	2	1	2	2	1	1	1	2
UNCORR	2	1	1	1	2	2	2	2	1	2
NOVEL	3	3	3	3	3	3	3	3	3	3

NOTE: The letters b, t, f, e, and l stand for body, tail, feet, ears, and legs, respectively. Values 1, 2, and 3, respectively, for each of the five attributes are as follows: giraffe, cow, and elephant body (b); feathered, fluffy, and horse tail (t); webbed, club, and hoofed feet (f); antlers, round ears, and human ears (e); two four, and six legs (l).
SOURCE: Younger & Cohen (1983, Table 2, p. 859). Reprinted with permission. Copyright 1983, Society for Research in Child Development.

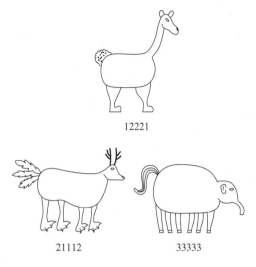

12221

21112   33333

Figure 17.7 Examples of stimuli used to study the role of correlated attributes in infant categorization. The stimulus figures vary on five attributes: body, tail, feet, ears, and legs. The abstract notation under each figure represents the value for each attribute. The notation 12221 represents a giraffe body, fluffy tail, club feet, round ears, and two legs; 21112 represents a cow body, feathered tail, webbed feet, antlers, and four legs; 33333 represents an elephant body, horse tail, hoofed feet, human ears, and six legs.
SOURCE: Younger & Cohen. *Child Development, 54.* Infant perception of correlations among attributes. Figure 1, p. 860. Reprinted with permission. Copyright 1983, Society for Research in Child Development.

the same three stimuli—one with features that preserved the correlation, one with the same features but uncorrelated, and one with features in a novel value (3; see Figure 17.7). The correlated test stimulus for Group A was the uncorrelated test stimulus for Group B and vice versa (see Table 17.2). The order of test stimuli was counterbalanced across infants. Looking times were scored from a video monitor in an adjacent room, and a second observer later scored one-third of the videotapes. The correlation coefficient between the two observers' total fixation times per infant was 0.98.

During testing, 10-month-olds remained habituated to the correlated stimulus but looked significantly longer at the novel and the uncorrelated stimuli. Because categorization requires that the exemplars be discriminably different, Younger and Cohen (1983) confirmed in a second experiment that 10-month-olds had indeed discriminated differences in the two uncorrelated features—the different kinds of ears and the different number of legs. In a third experiment, they examined the potential relationship between the ability to perceive correlations among attributes and the ability to categorize. Because infants in habituation studies first categorize at 7.5 months (Cohen & Strauss, 1979), Younger and Cohen tested younger infants (4- and 7-month-olds) with the stimuli and procedures used in Experiment 1, except that they added a pre- and a posttest to check for any decrease in attentiveness during the experiment. Unlike the 10-month-olds, both younger groups remained habituated to the correlated and uncorrelated test stimuli but looked significantly longer at the novel one. Because the correlated and uncorrelated attributes were equally familiar, younger infants apparently responded to the test stimuli on that basis, whereas the oldest infants had responded to the preserved correlation between the features. This study and a sequel led Younger and Cohen (1986) to conclude that infants are insensitive to the correlations between object features before 9 months of age and cannot use correlated features to categorize new objects before 10 months of age.

Using the mobile task to examine infants' sensitivity to correlated attributes, Bhatt and Rovee-Collier (1994) trained 3-month-olds with a mobile displaying *yellow A's on three red blocks* (Set A) and *black 2's on three green blocks* (Set B). They tested independent groups 24 hr later with a mobile on which a single attribute had been switched between sets—*figure color* (from yellow A's to black

A's and from black 2's to yellow 2's), *figure shape* (from A to 2 and vice versa, but the shape on the red block remained yellow, and the shape on the green block remained black), or *block color* (the block with the yellow A's became green, and the block with the black 2's became red). Thus, as in Younger and Cohen (1983), all three attributes on the test mobile were familiar, but the correlation between one attribute and the remaining two (which remained correlated) was broken.

During the 24-hr delayed recognition test, infants tested with a change in figure color, figure shape, or block color discriminated the feature recombination. These data revealed that even 3-month-olds can learn "what goes with what" and can detect when these feature correlations have been changed, even though all of the original, individual features are still present at the time of testing. In a subsequent study, Bhatt and Rovee-Collier (1996) found that infants forgot the correlations between different attributes at different rates. Three days after training, testing infants with a feature recombination that broke the original correlation between figure color and the other two attributes no longer disrupted infants' responding (i.e., they kicked significantly above baseline, generalizing to the feature recombination). That is, infants forgot the particular correlation in which figure color participated within 3 days. Four days after training, feature recombinations that broke the correlations between both block color and figure shape and the other two attributes also failed to disrupt test responding, indicating that the correlations involving those attributes had also been forgotten. Even though infants no longer discriminated any of the feature recombinations after 4 days, introducing a single novel attribute (block color, figure color, or figure shape) on the test mobile completely disrupted responding. In other words, although infants had forgotten what goes with what within 4 days, they still had not forgotten whether they had seen a particular test feature before. Subsequently, Bhatt, Wilk, and Rovee-Collier (2001), using the same type of stimuli, found that 6-month-olds—but not 3-month-olds—could use correlated attributes to categorize.

In categorization studies with older children, experimenters frequently use a *sorting task* in which subjects are asked to place items that belong together into groups. Comparable tasks that have been developed for preverbal infants are *sequential touching* and *object manipulation*. Like the operant mobile task, children performing both tasks interact actively with the items—a feature that distinguishes them from visual habituation tasks in which infants only look passively at items. In the sequential touching task, children are simultaneously presented with an array of objects or toys from two groups. They usually touch all of the items that belong to a single category before touching the others (Mandler & Bauer, 1988; Mandler et al., 1987; Starkey, 1981). The object manipulation task is like the sequential touching task except that the duration for which children differentially manipulate or examine items belonging to the same category is measured, and objects can be presented either successively or simultaneously (Ross, 1980; Ruff, 1984, 1986; Sugarman, 1982). Because infants look intensely at the objects they actively manipulate, looking measures are usually obtained as well. In general, the sequential touching task should not be used with infants younger than 12 months, who often touch objects on some basis other their category membership (e.g., salience). In contrast, the object manipulation task can be used with infants as young as 6 months.

In a typical study using the *sequential touching* procedure, Mandler et al. (1987) asked whether 14- and 20-month-olds could form categories of physically different objects on the basis of the common spatial and temporal relations in which the objects are typically encountered. To this end, they tested children with an array of four small kitchen items (pan, cup, spoon, plate) and bathroom items (toothbrush, soap, toothpaste, comb). They placed the eight objects randomly on a table in front of the infants and verbally encouraged them to manipulate the objects. Infants received a single trial without feedback. Every object that each infant contacted with his or her hand (or another object) and the order of contact was coded by the experimenter from videotapes. Two observers independently scored 25% of the sessions; interobserver agreement was 94% for both touches and order of touching. Both repeated touches (excluding two touches in succession) and only one touch per object were tallied, and the mean number of objects from the same category touched in succession (a "run") was compared to the mean run length that would be expected by chance (1.75) if infants touched objects randomly. The mean run length significantly exceeded chance at 20 months and did so marginally at 14 months. Furthermore, significantly more older than younger children categorized.

In a typical study using the *object manipulation* procedure, Oakes et al. (1991) familiarized 6- and 10-month-olds with four different small plastic toy trucks of different colors over sixteen 30-s trials (block randomized). They then tested them successively with a novel toy truck (fire truck, cement mixer) and one of two novel toy animals (dinosaur, pony) for one 30-s trial each. Each trial began when the experimenter put a toy on the table or high-chair tray in front of the infant and rolled it back and forth while calling the child's name and "Look at this." The experimenter then placed the toy within reach of the infant, who was allowed to manipulate it while the experimenter timed the trial with a stopwatch. Dropped toys were immediately replaced but did not affect the timing of a trial. When the 30 s timed out, the experimenter removed the toy and immediately initiated the

next trial. Two observers coded from videotape how long infants looked at and examined each object. Reliability coefficients computed between the two sets of scores for eight randomly chosen infants ranged from .94–.99 for looking time and .82–.99 for examining.

Neither examining time nor looking time decreased during the initial habituation phase, but infants of both ages looked longer at the novel toy animal and examined it longer than either the familiar toy truck on the last habituation trial or the novel toy truck on the test trial. These results were taken as evidence that both ages had formed a truck category. The finding that even 6-month-olds did so is inconsistent with Cohen and Strauss's (1979) conclusion that infants younger than 7.5 months cannot form conceptual categories, underscoring the main point of this chapter. Namely, different tasks yield different estimates of the earliest age at which a given cognitive capacity appears. More interesting than the *absolute age* at which a particular capacity emerges, which is task-dependent, is the *general pattern or order* in which different cognitive skills appear. This pattern should be the same across tasks.

Detour Learning and Barrier Problems

Detour and barrier tasks are closely related to object search tasks (see the next section). Once infants have learned where and when a particular object or activity is available, they may encounter obstacles in attempting to get it or get to it. Infants can overcome these impediments either indirectly, by getting someone else to intervene, or directly. If the obstacle is physical, for example, then the infant might either remove it or detour around it. The correct solution is particularly difficult when the alternative route requires that infants initially backtrack or move away from the goal, or when auditory or visual information specifying a direct route to the goal conflicts with tactile or other sensory information specifying the presence of a barrier. When a barrier is transparent instead of opaque, for example, younger infants will attempt to reach through it rather than around it (Diamond, 1981; Lockman, 1984). Infants correctly reach around a barrier before they correctly locomote around it, however, even when they are physically capable of both.

The procedure used by Lockman (1984) to study the development of detour learning is exemplary for its completeness. Beginning at 8–9 months of age, he tested infants in their own homes every 3–4 weeks on four detour problems in which the infants had to reach or locomote around an opaque or transparent barrier to retrieve an object. The order of reaching and locomotor problems was counterbalanced within and across infants. Each received three trials per problem, and testing was continued until a given infant had solved each problem on two of three trials for 2 consecutive weeks. During all trials, the caretaker remained out of view. Infants also received two Piagetian object-permanence tests (Stage 4, Stage 6), adapted from the Uzgiris-Hunt (1975) scales of infant development, after completing the four detour problems. The Stage 4 task is a standard object-search task in which an object is placed under a cloth, and the infant is required to search for and retrieve it (see the next section). The Stage 6 task requires the infant to find an object that has undergone a series of invisible displacements through several hiding places, ending up hidden under a cover quite removed from where the infant last saw it.

In the reaching problems, each infant sat at a table in a booster chair facing an upright board that was 14 cm high and 30.5 cm wide and constructed from wood (the opaque barrier) or Plexiglas (the transparent barrier). To begin a trial, the experimenter gave an infant a common object (e.g., pen, watch, keys). After the infant became interested in it, the experimenter took it away and drew it up, over, and behind the barrier. If the infant failed to retrieve the object within 1 min, then the experimenter returned it along the same path and gave it to the infant, beginning the next trial. The locomotor problems were procedurally identical except that infants sat on the floor facing the barrier. This time, the opaque barrier was Masonite; to prevent infants from climbing or looking over them, both barriers were 75 cm high and 106 cm wide.

The results were consistent within and across individuals. First, infants solved the Stage 4 object concept task several weeks (at least) before they solved any of the detour problems, revealing that their failure to solve the detour problems was not due to an inability to understand that the object continued to exist behind the barrier after they could no longer see it. Second, most solved the reaching/detour problems 4–5 weeks before they solved the corresponding locomotor ones. Again this was not due to infants' inability to locomote because all were adept crawlers even at the outset of the study, and in follow-up experiments, Lockman (1984) eliminated both the length of the barrier and the infants' positions relative to it as reasons for their superior performance on the reaching problems. Third, the infants solved opaque-barrier problems an average of 4 weeks before they solved transparent-barrier ones. By the end of the first year, when they finally solved the locomotor detour problems, almost half mastered the opaque- and transparent-barrier problems in the same session; even so, infants made significantly more errors when the barrier was transparent. Overall, infants succeeded on the opaque-barrier reaching detour problem first and on the transparent-barrier locomotor detour problem last. Fourth, infants solved all detour problems before they solved the Stage 6 invisible-displacement task. These data reveal that detour learning emerges gradually and systematically in different motor systems at different rates, despite the same spatial knowledge and understanding of object permanence and despite adeptness at both reaching and crawling. Moreover, this knowledge and skill alone, although necessary, are not sufficient to enable infants to plan and execute a detour.

A naturalistic approach to barrier problems was reported by Hendersen and Dias (1985), who observed infants' solutions when obstacles of different sorts impeded their ongoing activity in their home environments. Four infants, aged 2–12 months, were observed while engaging in their normal daily activities for sessions lasting 30–45 min each over a 5-month period. Narrative records were coded for ongoing activity, blocking condition (physical, social, or cognitive), the infant's response (physical, social, cognitive, or other), the effectiveness of the response in removing the obstacle, and how the response influenced the infant's subsequent behavior. Infants encountered a surprising number of obstacles—an average of one every 3 min. Most obstacles were social (50%) and physical (38%) rather than cognitive (4%), and infants tended to respond in kind, removing the obstacles 67% of the time. On almost 90% of these occasions, infants solved the problems directly. Paradoxically, however, infants who removed the obstacles resumed their prior activities only 25% of the time. It is interesting to note that obstacles were removed more often when a parent was present. These data suggest that problem-solving is a major component of the infant's daily behavior. Given the frequency with which infants encounter problems and solve them in complex natural settings, it is curious that there has been so little evidence of this in the laboratory. We encourage future researchers to increase both the complexity of the experimental context and the number of behavioral options available to the infant.

The solution to a physical barrier problem may require a circuitous detour around the barrier or that the infant temporarily move away from the goal. An analog of this problem is one in which the infant is prevented from moving his or her body toward an unreachable object and must obtain it by operating on some aspect of the environment, such as a string (Richardson, 1932) or a lever (Richardson, 1934) that brings an otherwise unattainable object into reach. In Richardson's 1934 study, for example, 15 infants were examined monthly from 7 to 12 months of age. Infants were tested in a crib, separated by a grill barrier from a toy mounted on the end of a lever screwed to a table top. To get the toy, the infant had to rotate the lever counterclockwise. This could be accomplished by either *pushing* the near end of the lever to the right, away from the infant and in a direction opposite that of the toy's movement, or *pulling* the distal portion of the lever to the left, toward the infant and in the same direction as the toy movement. The latter was the easier of the two responses, but both were made difficult because the path of the toy was an arc described by the lever rather than a straight line directly toward the infant. At age 7 months, 70% of the infants approached the lever, but less than half touched it. The number of infants who manipulated the lever, either effectively (rotating) or ineffectively (tugging, scratching, poking), increased over succeeding weeks, with the percent producing ineffective responses peaking at 9 months and declining thereafter. Between 10 and 12 months, almost half of the infants were obtaining the toy on two consecutive trials with no more than one erroneous move per trial; in every instance, infants were correct after Trial 1 if not on Trial 1. Richardson interpreted these data in terms of infants' insight into the use of tools.

Object Search

The very first experimental study of any kind with children was an object search problem (Hunter, 1913). Although Hunter framed the problem as a *delayed response task,* he focused on the cues that children used in responding to an object that was not immediately present at the time they performed the response. In this task, children saw a food reward hidden behind one of three doors. A light over the door signaled the hiding location and then was turned off. After a delay, children attempted to retrieve the reward. The maximum delay tolerated was 50 s (after 5–7 trials) at 30 months and 25 min (after 15–46 trials) at 6–8 years; interestingly, all children initially encountered difficulty at delays of 4–6 s.

In a subsequent study, Hunter's focus shifted to the kinds of strategies used to bridge the temporal delay between seeing the object disappear at a particular location and retrieving it (Hunter, 1917). He tested a preverbal infant longitudinally between 13 and 16 months of age. The infant watched the experimenter hide an object in one of three boxes; during the delay (timed from when the lid was shut), the infant was distracted. The infant tolerated a delay of 12 s at 13–15 months and 24 s at 16 months. Using only two locations, Brody (1981) operantly trained younger infants to touch one of two locations where a light had cued an auditory-visual reward. Here, the maximum delay tolerated was 0.25 s at 8 months and 9 s at 12 and 16 months.

Note that both Brody (1981) and Hunter (1913) used a symbol (the light) to cue the location of reward. The use of symbols in studies with infants and young children is a general problem that has surfaced in many experimental studies. Using a symbol to cue the reward, to accumulate and exchange for a reward (e.g., poker chips), or simply to indicate "correct" (e.g., a green light) dramatically increases task difficulty because children must learn that the symbol stands for the reward before they learn the reward's location. Errors that are attributed to poor spatial learning may actually reflect children's difficulty in learning the significance of the symbol.

Infants also may possess the cognitive ability that a task requires but be unable to express it because of the specific task demands. In the standard delayed nonmatching-to-sample (DNMS) task, for example, infants are shown an object, and a screen is lowered for a brief delay; it is then raised to reveal the original object (the sample) adjacent to a novel one. By displacing the novel object, the infant can retrieve a reward. Infants typically fail this task until they are 15–21 months of age, even with delays of only 5–10 s. Yet, when toys are used as the objects, and the reward is the opportunity to play with the novel toy instead of the displacement of it to find a hidden reward, infants can solve the DNMS task by 6 months of age (Diamond, Churchland, Cruess, & Kirkham, 1999)—the youngest age at which they reliably exhibit visually guided reaching. Under these conditions, infants can also perform significantly above chance after delays as long as 10 min. Infants' DNMS performance is also enhanced when the reward is verbal praise for a correct choice. Finally, the physical, temporal, and spatial relationships between the well and the reward are critical variables. If the reward is attached directly to the underside of the well lid, so that infants are able to associate the reward with the well lid both physically and temporally, then they can solve this task almost a year earlier than they otherwise can. If there is either a physical separation (the reward is under the well lid but is not attached to it) or a temporal separation (the reward is attached to the well lid by a piece of string), then infants' performance is impaired.

The A-Not-B Task

The delayed response task was subsequently renamed the *A-not-B task* by Piaget (1954). Piaget hid his watch under a cloth cover on the sofa (Place A), and his 9.5-month-old son (Laurent) retrieved it. When Piaget rehid the watch under the same cover, Laurent retrieved it again. Then, however, Piaget hid the watch under a similar-looking cover (Place B) while Laurent watched. Yet, Laurent looked in Place A, where he had found the watch before, instead of in Place B (the *A-not-B error*). From this, Piaget concluded that Laurent did not understand that objects continue to exist and are permanent, independent of his own actions on them.

In a typical object search study, infants sit on a parent's lap in front of a table containing two identical wells (A, B) where an object can be hidden. Typically, infants learn the hiding task during a pretraining period, when they are shown the toy outside Well A and are encouraged to reach for it immediately. The final hiding task is then successively approximated: First, the object is placed in the open well; then, a lid partially covers the well; and finally, the lid completely covers the well. Infants who reach to the empty well are shown the object in the other well but are not given the object. In other pretraining procedures, the object is hidden in a single, centrally positioned well with a uniquely colored lid on it, and infants are pretrained until they reach a criterion (e.g., responding correctly on two consecutive trials) for recovering the object. Once the infant has reached criterion, formal testing begins.

During the test trials, the experimenter shows the infant an object (usually an attractive toy), places it in Well A as the infant watches, and simultaneously covers both wells. After a delay ranging from 0 to 10 s, the infant is allowed to reach. The trial ends when either the infant retrieves the object or a defined interval (e.g., 15 s) elapses. On Trial 2, the experimenter again hides the object in Well A. On Trial 3, however, the experimenter hides the object in Well B. After the hiding well is reversed, infants often continue to search in Well A despite having seen the object hidden in Well B (the A-not-B error). On all trials, the first lid to which infants reach is recorded—a measure on which inter-

observer reliability is usually very high. In the Smith et al. (1999) procedure, observers also coded the parent's behaviors to ensure that they complied with instructions not to direct, encourage, or correct the infant's behavior.

If looking rather than reaching is the dependent variable, even younger infants can solve object search tasks successfully. Eight-month-olds who were tested in a violation-of-expectancy task, for example, remembered the location where an object had been hidden 15 s earlier; yet 15 s is the longest delay that 16-month-olds can tolerate and still perform the traditional object search task successfully (Baillargeon, DeVos, & Graber, 1989; Baillargeon & Graber, 1988). In the looking studies, infants saw an object on a stage at one of two locations, and then identical screens were placed in front of both locations, hiding the object. After 15 s, infants watched as a gloved hand retrieved the object from behind either the screen that had originally hidden it (the *possible event*) or the other one (the *impossible event*). Longer looking at the impossible event was taken as evidence that infants remembered the location where they had previously seen the object and were surprised when it was retrieved from the other location. These results suggest that young infants do not fail the traditional object search task because they cannot remember where an object was hidden.

Although the A-not-B error has been replicated numerous times (for reviews, see Diamond, 1990b; Smith et al., 1999; Wellman, Cross, & Bartsch, 1987), seemingly minor changes in task parameters can reduce or eliminate it. First, the error can be significantly reduced by using transparent lids (Butterworth, 1977), increasing the number of wells (Bjork & Cummings, 1984; Cummings & Bjork, 1983; Diamond, Cruttenden, & Niederman, 1989), or making the lids more distinctive (Butterworth, Jarrett, & Hicks, 1982; Wellman et al., 1987). First, when

Smith et al. (1999) used two red lids or a red lid and an orange lid, for example, infants' error rate was 80%; when they used a red lid and a yellow lid, the error rate dropped to 60%; and when they put distinctive stripes or faces on the lids, the error rate fell to 22%. Smith et al. argued that because infants rarely reach repeatedly in one direction and new objects are usually distinctive, the A-not-B error probably does not occur often in everyday life.

Second, the A-not-B error does not occur if the pretraining period is eliminated. Smith et al. (1999) compared a no-pretraining group, a group pretrained to reach to Well A, and a group pretrained to reach to a single center-line well. Only the group pretrained to reach to Well A exhibited the A-not-B error; the other groups did not. In fact, infants pretrained to reach to Well A exhibited the A-not-B error even when no object at all was hidden, if the experimenter had waved the lid of the well to call their attention to it. In addition, if infants made even one reach to Well B throughout the course of pretraining or training, then they were less likely to perseverate reaching to Well A. Because perseverative errors arise only after repeated responding to Well A, the error may be related to how infants are taught to respond (for discussion, see Smith et al., 1999).

Third, the A-not-B error does not occur if infants are tested immediately. The delay that infants can tolerate without error increases gradually and continuously with age at the rate of approximately 2 s per month, and infants tolerate slightly longer delays if they are tested longitudinally instead of cross-sectionally (Diamond, 1990b). Irrespective of the experimental design, however, decreasing the delay eventually eliminates the A-not-B error, and increasing it leads to random search.

Fourth, the A-not-B error is eliminated if either the infant's posture is changed from sitting to standing between test trials (Smith et al., 1999) or if a "cover of darkness" instead of a cloth cover is used to hide the object (Hood & Willatts, 1986). Hood and Willatts, for example, showed 5-month-olds an object at one of two locations, then turned the lights off and removed the object. When they turned the lights back on, infants reached more to the side where the object had been than to the other side. Goubet and Clifton (1998) also tested 6.5-month-olds in the dark. The sound of a noisy ball rolling down a tube to the left or right side of the infant's midline signaled where to retrieve the ball after a delay. Infants who had previously practiced reaching directionally in the light were able to reach correctly in the dark, but infants who had practiced reaching to midline were not. Notably, in the preceding studies, infants were not required to execute a coordinated motor sequence. These studies provide further evidence that infants' search errors do not reflect their inability to remember an object's prior location.

Finally, visual orientation to location also determines where infants reach. Smith et al. (1999) placed a blue rod beside either Well A or Well B, for example, and the experimenter tapped the rod before the initial trials. If the experimenter tapped the rod beside Well A, then infants reached to Well A on all test trials; if the experimenter tapped the rod beside Well B, then infants reached to Well B on all test trials. In both cases, infants disregarded the hiding location of the object. These data reveal that the A-not-B error also reflects the dynamics of the test situation.

As a rule of thumb, children perform better in more naturalistic and meaningful situations, especially when they are younger. This rule is well-illustrated in two highly innovative experiments. In both, the parent was present and participating. In the first study, Corter, Zucker, and Galligan (1980) exploited the fact that in everyday life, infants who can locomote usually follow their mothers when they leave the room (which occurs frequently) instead of crying. In a laboratory free-play setting, they observed the behavior of 9-month-olds after each watched the mother go out of the test room through one of two open doors. Mothers of infants in the experimental group departed through different doors on Trials 1 and 2. Mothers of infants in the control group departed though the same door on both trials. The control group then received a third trial on which the mothers now departed through the other door. On Trial 1, most infants in both groups successfully found their mothers by crawling to the doorways where she had departed. Subsequently, when the mothers departed though another door, most infants failed to find them, going instead to the doors where they had previously found her (the A-not-B error).

In the second study, DeLoache (1980) tested 18- to 36-month-olds in their homes in the context of a familiar object-search game—hide-and-seek. Each child was told that a small, stuffed animal (Big Bird®) was going to hide and that he or she should remember where it hid so that he or she could find it later. The child then watched the parent hide the toy (e.g., under a pillow, behind a door, in a cabinet). When a timer rang, the child attempted to retrieve the toy. After 3- and 5-min delays, younger children (18–24 months) averaged 69% errorless retrievals, and older children (25–30 months) averaged 84%. After delays of 30 min, 1 hr, and overnight, younger children averaged 80%, 69%, and 77% errorless retrievals, respectively.

The hide-and-seek task is structurally analogous to Hunter's (1913) original delayed response task: In both tasks, the location of a hidden object must be remembered for a specified period of time. To compare children's performances on the hide-and-seek and delayed response tasks, DeLoache (1980) tested 22- to 29-month-olds at home after 3–5 min. In the delayed response task, the experimenter hid a different small toy on each trial in one of four metal boxes arranged in a semicircle in the middle of the floor. Each box had a color photograph of a common object on its lid. To call their attention to the pictures, the children were asked to name them; if he or she could not name a picture, the experimenter supplied the name. After a toy was hidden, the experimenter started a timer and left that area of the room with the child; when the bell rang, they returned, and the child attempted to find the toy. If an incorrect box was selected, the child was allowed to search in the other boxes until the toy was found (a correction procedure). That is, the hide-and-seek task involved the use of familiar landmarks, such as a piece of furniture in the home, to find the object. In contrast, the delayed response task involved using pictures on boxes that the infant had never seen before, that were the same size and shape, and that were arranged arbitrarily in a circle. Most children performed the hide-and-seek task better than the delayed response task.

To determine whether landmarks had facilitated performance in the hide-and-seek task (see also the section titled "Spatial Learning"), DeLoache (1980) repeated the hide-and-seek and delayed response tasks but added a hybrid task in which each hiding box was placed next to a specific piece of furniture (the landmark + box task). This time, she tested children in the original age groups (younger, older) with each child performing all three tasks (order counterbalanced). Older children performed the hide-and-seek and landmark + box tasks equivalently but were worse on the delayed response task, whereas younger children performed the hide-and-seek task best and were worse on the landmark + box task, with their delayed response performance intermediate between these. DeLoache attributed the advantage of the hide-and-seek task to the fact that the hiding locations used in that task were more naturalistic—familiar parts of the natural environment versus unfamiliar boxes with picture cues—and suggested that older and younger children might use different cues or different strategies in the no-landmark task. These findings suggest that associative learning based on a new element—the spatial relationship between two objects—selectively benefited older infants. Spatial learning, therefore, is considered next.

Spatial Learning

Broadly speaking, *spatial learning* (also called *spatial cognition*) studies ask how infants know where things are as they move around in the environment. This question is actually a combination of the questions that were asked in studies of locomotor detour learning (Lockman, 1984) and in studies of object search (Diamond, 1990b). In typical spatial learning problems, infants orient, reach, or locomote to one of two spatial locations where a target disappeared or was hidden. Not surprisingly, the same factors that affect an infants' performance in delayed response, object search, and detour tasks also affect their performance in spatial learning tasks. As before, possessing the concept of object permanence, although necessary, is insufficient for solving spatial learning problems.

Experimenters have focused, therefore, on what kind of information infants use and at what age they effectively use it. This information includes *egocentric* and *allocentric cues* (response cues and place cues, respectively), location distinctiveness cues, proximal and distal landmarks, visual tracking, and geometric information in the spatial environment (Acredolo, 1978, 1990; Acredolo & Evans, 1980; Cornell & Heth, 1979; Corter et al., 1980; DeLoache, 1980; Hermer & Spelke, 1994; Hunter, 1913, 1917).

Cornell and Heth (1979) used a head-turning procedure to ask when infants first use place cues instead of response cues

to localize spatial events (Tolman, 1948; Tolman, Ritchie, & Kalish, 1946). Their basic paradigm resembled the object search task except that they moved the infant instead of the object. Infants sat on the mother's lap in the center of a standard laboratory room. A 1.0-m movie screen was centered 2.0 m in front of the infant, and another, 2.0 m behind the infant; a 0.5-m × 0.7-m rear projection screen was placed on either side. Responses were observed through louvers located on one side of each movie screen (see Figure 17.8). Each trial began with the projection of a moving, colored pattern on the screen in front of the infant. When the infant fixated the moving pattern, it was turned off, and a static (unmoving) pattern was simultaneously projected on each side screen for 10 s. Infants had to turn their heads 90 deg to view a pattern, and the first head-turn to the pattern defined a response.

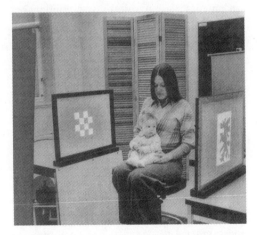

Figure 17.8   The experimental arrangement in the operant head-turning task. The experiment is shown here with a 4-month-old, who has turned toward the side where a novel pattern is projected; the pattern projected on the other side is the same on all trials. In studies of response learning versus place learning, the mother will rotate her chair 180° so that the novel pattern appears on the right, requiring the infant to turn in the opposite direction to view it. A hidden observer records head turns through the louvered panels.
SOURCE: Photo courtesy of Edward H. Cornell.

In their first experiment, infants aged 4–12 months were randomly assigned to either a constant or a variable group. On every training trial, the constant group saw slides of the same pattern on the same side screen (position counterbalanced) and of a novel pattern on the opposite side screen. The variable group saw the same pair of slides as the constant group, but the old/new patterns changed sides randomly over trials; this condition was included to assess whether infants might detect the novel (preferred) slide through peripheral vision without a head-turn. After 20 training trials, the mother rotated her chair 180 deg so that the infant now faced the opposite screen, the green moving pattern that infants fixated to begin a trial was projected, and the original procedure was repeated for 20 transfer trials. For the constant group, the absolute position of the old and new patterns was the same; thus, if the novel slides had appeared on an infant's left side during training before, they appeared on the right side after rotation. For the varied group, the repeated slide now appeared on the same side on all trials, and the novel slide appeared on the opposite side. Learning was expressed as the percentage of first head-turns to the novel pattern over blocks divided by the number of trials in a block.

If infants in the constant group used *place cues,* then they would turn toward the novel stimulus after the rotation, but if they used *response cues,* then they would turn toward the familiar one. At all ages, head-turns to the novel pattern increased over the initial training trials for the constant groups but remained at chance for the variable groups. After the rotation, 4-month-olds relied on response cues but slowly relearned to orient to the novel stimulus and were responding at the same level as older infants within 16–20 trials. In contrast, the two older groups (8 and 12 months) used both response and place cues. In a second experiment with 4- to 16-month-

olds, response and place cues were assessed independently. The results revealed that infants' use of *response cues* did not decline with age but remained stable; however, their use of *place cues* gradually increased with age. Cornell (1981) proposed that infants must learn to maintain orientation to external cues before they can use them to mark a particular location.

Acredolo (1978) used the same basic procedure to ask infants aged 6–18 months the same question, except that an entertaining adult appeared for 5 s in the same side window, and a buzzer sounded 5 s before the adult appeared. After the infant turned toward the window on three of four consecutive trials in anticipation of the event, the mother rotated the infant's chair 180 deg, and the infant received five test trials during which the buzzer sounded, but no adult appeared in the window. Six- to 11-month-olds and a third of the 16-month-olds relied solely on response cues, turning in the same direction (right or left) as they had turned before the reversal. Making the target location more distinctive by adding proximal cues (either a yellow star around the target window or a blinking light around the target window and orange stripes on that wall) overrode infants' reliance on response cues at all ages except 6 months. Adding the same cues to the opposite window and wall, however, was ineffective until infants were 11 months old, and even then their use of less salient landmarks was equivocal (Acredolo & Evans, 1980; for review, see Acredolo, 1990). Finally, Acredolo (1980) found that infants performed a spatial learning task better in the familiar setting of their own home than in the laboratory.

The preceding studies demonstrated that infants are able to use place cues (e.g., landmarks) to locate objects or events. Hermer and Spelke (1994) examined the cues that infants use to *reorient* themselves after their position and heading were disrupted. Eighteen- to

24-month-olds were tested inside a 6 × 4-ft room that was either all white with identical red corner panels or additionally had one blue wall. Parents hid a small toy in one corner and then disoriented children by covering their eyes, lifting them, spinning them at least four times, and releasing them to face a randomly predetermined corner. To find the toy, children had to reorient themselves. Reorientation could be accomplished in the white room by using the geometric information provided by its rectangular shape and, in the blue-walled room, by using the geometric information plus the landmark (the blue wall). Children completed 3–4 trials in each room, but the hiding place remained the same. All variables (hiding place, search order, the wall that was blue) were counterbalanced across subjects.

Children searched equally often in the correct corner and in the diagonally opposite corner more than in the other two corners. Moreover, their search performance was the same whether one wall was blue or not. Next, two triangular solid containers of the same size but in different patterns and colors were placed in the target (hiding) corner and the one diagonally opposite it for two trials. Despite the fact that the experimenter pointed out the landmarks, and the parent and child played with them, children's search performance was the same as before. Their failure to use the landmarks was attributed to their tendency to search at one of the two corners they saw immediately after being released. Finally, children were disoriented in one test condition but not in the other. In one condition, the distinctive landmarks were again placed in diagonally opposite corners, the toy was hidden in one, and children were disoriented. In the other, the objects were placed in the center of the room, the toy was hidden in one, and children closed their eyes but remained oriented while the objects were moved to diagonally opposite corners. In the first condition, children again searched equally at the two

corners specified by the shape of the room, unaffected by the landmarks. In the second condition, however, infants searched more in the correct corner that was specified by the landmark. The authors concluded that human infants, like adult rats but unlike adult humans, rely on *geometric cues* and not on landmarks for reorientation, even though they had successfully used the same landmarks in another search task. Learmonth (1998) subsequently found that infants did, in fact, use the blue wall as a landmark when they were tested in a room that was twice as large.

These studies reveal that infants' use of landmarks is task-specific. Infants tested in locomotor search problems are relatively impervious to distinctive landmark information about a target location until they are older, particularly if they must reorient to a spatial location in a relatively small space. On the other hand, distinctive landmarks facilitate infants' solutions of reaching and head-turning search problems at younger ages (Cornell, 1981; Smith et al., 1999). Recall that detour problems that required reaching were also solved by infants significantly before they were able to solve detour problems that required locomotion in space (Lockman, 1984).

Serial Learning

Given that infants as young as 3 months can learn the structure of a category over a succession of items, it is not surprising that they can also detect the serial structure of a list. Researchers have used a variety of experimental techniques to study serial-order effects. Using a visual expectancy paradigm, Smith and colleagues (Smith, 1984; Smith, Arehart, Haaf, & deSaint Victor, 1989) trained 5-month-olds to sequentially fixate four identical white doors arranged in a quadrant, and assessed their ability to visually anticipate the next stimulus in the sequence. On each training trial, a signal light blinked, and when infants fixated it, the first door opened, briefly revealing a visual stimulus, then shut; then the second door opened and shut, and so forth. During the test immediately after training, the signal light blinked, but the doors did not open. An infant's correct sequential eye movements to the doors constituted the index of learning. On the test trial immediately after training, a significant number of infants demonstrated sequential memory for three event locations. Infants trained on structured sequences exhibited greater response accuracy, indicative of chunking than infants trained on unstructured sequences (Smith, Jankowski, Brewster, & Loboschefski, 1990). Anticipatory responding was also facilitated by ordered visual information or "scripts" (Smith, Loboschefski, Davidson, & Dixon, 1997).

Using an eye-tracker to study infants' eye movements, Haith, Hazan, and Goodman (1988) exposed 3- to 4-month-olds to a series of slides that appeared in one of two locations (right or left) and either in an alternating sequence or randomly. When infants were exposed to the alternating sequence, their reaction times decreased, and they anticipatorily shifted their eyes in the direction of the location where the slide would appear next. (The apparatus and procedure are described in detail by Haith, Wentworth, and Canfield, 1993.) In a subsequent study, 3-month-olds who were exposed to a 2-1 (LLR, RRL) and 3-1 (LLLR, RRRL) pattern produced anticipatory eye movements, but 2-month-olds did not (Canfield & Haith, 1991). Furthermore, anticipatory responding decreased as a function of increasing sequence complexity. Haith et al. (1993) reported that when the picture in one location remained constant, 3-month-olds responded significantly faster and made significantly more anticipatory responses to that side.

Serial learning has also been studied using an imitation procedure in which an experimenter models a specific sequence of actions with a set of props and then allows children to imitate the sequence. Their correct sequence of imitation is the measure of serial-order learning. In general, infants' imitation of a sequence of actions that can be performed only in a specific order (i.e., *an enabling relation,* such as making a rattle by placing a ball in a container, putting a lid on it, and shaking it) is consistently superior to their imitation of a sequence of actions that can be performed in any order (i.e., an *arbitrary relation,* such as dressing a teddy bear by putting a ring on its finger, a scarf around its neck, and a cap on its head). This result is found regardless of whether or not the target actions and event goals are matched (Barr & Hayne, 1996; Bauer & Shore, 1987) and whether imitation is immediate or deferred (Barr & Hayne, 1996). With increasing age, infants correctly reproduce increasingly long, ordered sequences that contain enabling relations. Thus, they can correctly reproduce familiar and novel sequences of enabling actions that contain two steps at 11 months of age (Mandler & McDonough, 1995), three steps at 13.5 months (Bauer & Mandler, 1992), and eight steps at 30 months (Bauer & Fivush, 1992). There are at least two possible explanations for this finding. First, each action in the enabling chain may provide an effective retrieval cue for the next action in the same sequence (Bauer, 1992, 1995). Second, the structure of the sequence may influence the expression of the memory once it has been retrieved. That is, although the same amount of information is accessible at the time of the test, infants may recognize that enabling sequences demand a particular temporal order, whereas arbitrary sequences do not (Fivush, Kuebli, & Clubb, 1992). Given that the total number of actions that infants recall is exactly the same whether the event structure is enabling or arbitrary, we conclude that an event's structure, rather than the number of cues that are required for memory retrieval, influences how the to-be-remembered information is organized in memory.

The *serial-probe recognition task* has been used with animal and human adults (Wright, Santiago, Sands, Kendrick, & Cook, 1985) and preverbal infants (Cornell & Bergstrom, 1983) to study the memory processing of serial lists of arbitrary items. In this task, the subject views a list of items (slides, pictures, etc.) and then is tested with a mix of old items from different serial positions and new items. The subject's task is to indicate whether a test stimulus was on the original list. Human adults usually exhibit a recency effect after very short delays and a primacy effect after longer ones, as do adult monkeys and pigeons, but on a progressively shorter time scale, respectively (Wright et al., 1985).

Using a looking-time measure with 7-month-olds, Cornell and Bergstrom (1983) familiarized infants with a serial list and then tested them with an item from the familiarized list and with one that was novel after different delays. Longer looking at the new stimulus was taken as evidence that infants recognized the old one. They found that infants exhibited both primacy and recency effects after 5 s but only a primacy effect after 5 min.

The serial-probe recognition task has also been used in operant studies using the mobile paradigm. In the initial study, which was actually designed to assess the spacing of category exemplars (see the "Categorization" section), Merriman et al. (1997) had trained 3- and 6-month-old infants with three yellow-block mobiles, each displaying A's or 2's in a different color, in a fixed order each day for 3 days. In effect, the mobiles constituted a three-item list. On Day 4, infants were tested with one of the training mobiles or a novel mobile and indicated by kicking whether a particular mobile had been on the list (a serial-probe recognition test). Infants recognized only the mobile from Serial Position 1—a classic primacy effect. The slope of the serial-position

curve, however, was steeper at 6 months. This finding mirrors primacy effects that have been obtained with animals and adults after longer test delays.

Knowledge of serial order implies knowledge of a *relation* between two items (i.e., 1 comes before 2, 3 comes after 2), but testing with only a single mobile does not query the infant about its order relative to another stimulus (i.e., "Did the test stimulus come before or after?"). To query infants explicitly about their knowledge of serial order, Gulya, Rovee-Collier, Galluccio, and Wilk (1998) used a pretest cuing procedure that essentially asked the infant, "Did the test stimulus come after the precue or not?" This procedure was originally used by Clayton, Habibi, and Bendele (1995). In their study, undergraduates learned two successive 18-item word lists, each followed by a recognition test on which each test item was preceded either by the same item that had preceded it on the study list or by another one. Test items that were precued by the items that had immediately preceded them on the study list were recognized more quickly. Therefore, immediately before the 24-hr test, Gulya et al. (1998) precued each test mobile for 2 or 3 min (depending on infant age) with either a mobile from the immediately preceding serial position or another mobile. The experimenter moved the precue at the same rate that a given infant had moved it by kicking in the last training session.

Infants who were precued with the immediately preceding mobile on the list recognized the test mobile, but infants who were precued with another training mobile—even though it was equally familiar—did not. For example, infants recognized the test mobile from Serial Position 2 if they were precued with the mobile from Serial Position 1 but not if they were precued with the mobile from Serial Position 3. Interestingly, infants reliably recognized the mobile from Serial Position 3 if they were successively precued with the mobiles from both of the preceding serial positions (1 and 2). These results confirmed that 3- and 6-month-olds can learn the order of items on a serial list and can recognize all list members 24 hr later if provided with retrieval cues that provide valid order information.

As with adults, increasing list length from three to five mobiles impairs infants' memory for *serial order* after 24 hr but does not affect their memory for *item identity* (Gulya, Sweeney, & Rovee-Collier, 1999).

INFANT MEMORY

The procedures most commonly used to study infant memory are novelty preference (habituation, paired-comparison), long-term familiarization, visual expectancy, classical and operant conditioning, and deferred imitation. All of these were described previously (see "Infant Learning"); here, the question is what infants remember of what they have learned.

Novelty Preference

Novelty-preference procedures exploit the infant's propensity to look at a novel stimulus. Practically speaking, infants would not be able to perceive that a stimulus is novel unless they remembered what they had seen before. Otherwise, they would perceive a stimulus that they had seen before as subjectively novel. Theoretically, novelty-preference tests are based on Sokolov's (1963) model of habituation of the orienting reflex, which assumes that when a novel stimulus is encountered, an internal representation or engram of it is formed. The engram is not completed in a single trial but becomes progressively fleshed out over successive encounters. As that occurs, the subject attends to the external stimulus progressively less because there is progressively less new information to be gleaned from it. Once the representation is complete

(i.e., once the external stimulus and the internal representation exactly match), subjects no longer look at the stimulus at all. Over time, the representation decays (i.e., forgetting), and subjects will again look at the stimulus to the extent that it no longer matches the internal representation. Recognition of the previously encountered stimulus, therefore, is inferred from the extent to which infants direct attention elsewhere, looking at something they do not remember seeing before (i.e., a novelty preference).

Paired-Comparison Test

During a paired-comparison test, infants are simultaneously presented with two stimuli following a brief, single exposure to one of them. Typically, the test immediately follows the preexposure. The proportion of total looking time that is allocated to the novel member of the test pair (the *novelty-preference score*) is subjected to a directional one-sample t test against 0.50 (chance looking); retention of the preexposed stimulus is inferred if the novelty-preference score significantly exceeds 0.50. In theory, if the internal representation of the preexposed stimulus has completely dissipated, then infants will fixate the two test stimuli equally (i.e., they perceive the test stimuli as equally novel). In practice, experimenters determine the limit of retention by increasing the interval between preexposure and testing until this occurs. Olson (1976) has cautioned that the determinants of looking on a paired-comparison trial can include discriminability factors (interstimulus contrasts), preference factors (perceptual features and infant interpretation), and response biases (position habits, gaze-shifting criteria, state; see above) in addition to familiarity/novelty factors.

After single sessions, maximum retention in paired-comparison tests is on the order of 10 s at 4 months, 1 min at 6 months, and 10 min at 9 months (Diamond, 1990a). After multiple sessions, retention is much longer. Fagan

(1970), for example, tested infants with a set of three stimuli (e.g., A-B-C) on 3 successive days. On each day, the familiarization stimulus (e.g., A) was tested in both the right and left positions against each of the other novel stimuli (e.g., A-B, C-A). On succeeding days, another stimulus in the set was the familiarization stimulus, and the two remaining members served as the novel stimuli. Infants exhibited greater attention to novel test stimuli in Session 1 only. Using a similar design, Fagan (1971) exposed 4- to 7-month-olds to black-and-white patterns for approximately 1 min and found novelty preferences after 7 min. In later studies, he found that 5- to 6-month-olds looked longer at a novel black-and-white pattern after 48 hr and at a novel facial photograph after 2 weeks (Fagan, 1973).

An interpretative problem arises when infants either look longer at the familiar stimulus or look equally at both test stimuli. In the first instance, some researchers have discarded the Sokolov (1963) model and argued that proportionally longer looking at the pre-exposed stimulus also constitutes evidence of retention because it represents nonchance attention (Cohen & Gelber, 1975; Colombo & Bundy, 1983; Hunter & Ames, 1988). In fact, researchers should always report any significant deviation from chance, whether a novelty or a familiarity preference. In the second instance, some researchers have argued that proportionally equivalent looking at the novel and familiar stimuli should also be taken as evidence of retention instead of forgetting or a discrimination failure. The latter argument is based on evidence that infants older than 8 weeks exhibit a novelty preference after short delays, no preference (equal looking at both test stimuli) after longer delays, and then a familiarity preference after still longer delays that may extend to weeks or months, even though initial exposure times were a minute or less. Equal looking thereafter is taken as evidence of forgetting (Bahrick, Hernandez-

Reif, & Pickens, 1997; Bahrick & Pickens, 1995). Longer looking at a briefly exposed stimulus after a 3-month retention interval, however, is unlikely to represent recognition given that 3-month-olds who are trained for a total of 30 min over the course of 2 days do not remember after a delay longer than 5 days (Galluccio & Rovee-Collier, 2001; Hayne, 1990). More likely, infants' selective looking after long delays is mediated by an automatic or implicit memory function akin to that proposed by Hasher and Zacks (1979). Similarly, Stolz and Merikle (2000), using a within-subjects design, obtained evidence of a conscious influence on adults' memory performance (i.e., explicit memory) after a short delay (2 min), but this shifted to an unconscious influence (i.e., implicit memory) after a longer delay (2 weeks). Beyond this, the four-stage model is fundamentally flawed in two major respects. First, it accepts the null hypothesis as support for retention in one instance but not in another. Yet, the null hypothesis should only be rejected—never accepted. Second, any looking behavior during the test—whether a novelty preference, a familiarity preference, or no preference—is taken as evidence of retention. As a result, the model is unfalsifiable. What *is* unique to this account is the predicted pattern of looking, namely, that novelty preference may precede familiarity preference.

Habituation Test

After a series of habituation trials (see "Infant Learning" section), infants are shown a novel and the original stimulus (order counterbalanced) on successive test trials. Longer looking at the novel stimulus than at the original one indicates that infants' decrease in looking during the habituation phase was not due to fatigue and that the two stimuli are discriminable. (Testing with novel stimuli that share different elements with the habituation stimulus is a common means of determining what infants can and cannot discriminate; the extent to which infants generalize to the novel test stimulus defines the extent to which they perceive it as similar to the original one.) As the delay increases between the final habituation trial and testing, infants increasingly respond to the original stimulus. At some point, their responding returns to the level that was seen at the outset of the habituation trials. Significantly greater responding to the novel stimulus after a delay is taken as evidence that infants still remember the original one.

To obtain the upper limit of retention, the delay between the final habituation trial and the retention test is increased. Presumably, as infants forget, they will look increasingly longer at the original stimulus; when they look at the original stimulus as long as they looked at it on the first habituation trial, forgetting is said to be complete. At this time, they should also look at the original stimulus and the novel one equally. Because both comparisons predict no difference (i.e., the null hypothesis), responding to the original stimulus is also compared with their responding to it on the final habituation trial. Usually little or no retention is found after delays longer than 30–60 s over the first 10 months of life (e.g., Cohen & Gelber, 1975; but see Bomba & Siqueland, 1983).

Some researchers have followed the initial habituation trials with a paired-comparison test, directly pitting two stimuli against each other (Cornell, 1974; Pascalis, deHaan, Nelson, & deSchonen, 1998; Weizmann, Cohen, & Pratt, 1971). Because the two test stimuli are presented simultaneously instead of successively, a paired-comparison test is thought to incur a lesser memory load than a habituation test.

Long-Term Familiarization

Long-term familiarization procedurally resembles habituation except that infants are preexposed to a stimulus for at least 1 day before being tested for a novelty preference or the differential production of a target response. During familiarization, responding may not be measured, and no experimenter may be present. A visual stimulus, for example, may simply be left in the home where the infant can view it. Bushnell, McCutcheon, Sinclair, and Tweedlie (1984), for example, asked mothers to expose their infants (1–2 months old) to distinctive color and form stimuli for 15 min each day for 2 weeks. They gave infants a novelty-preference test with a sequence of familiar and novel stimuli 1 day after their last exposure. Although home-tested infants looked longer at all novel stimuli, laboratory-tested infants looked longer only at stimuli that were novel in both color and form. These data demonstrate that after long-term familiarization with specific visual stimuli, even very young infants can recognize them 1 day later. More importantly, the novelty of the test setting can impair recognition. This is a recurrent finding in many areas of infant research.

Using auditory instead of visual stimuli, Ungerer, Brody, and Zelazo (1978) asked mothers to repeat one of two words 60 times/day for 13 days beginning when infants were 14 days old. Recognition was tested intermittently between 22 and 29 days of age with a tape-recording of the mother saying a familiarized word and the novel one. Infants' facial expressions and eye/head movements differentiated the training word from the novel word by the third test. Recently, investigators using auditory stimuli have measured *event-related potentials* (ERPs)—electrophysiological correlates of retention. Molfese and Wetzel (1992), for example, familiarized 14-month-olds in their own homes for 2 days with one of two nonsense syllables. During laboratory testing 1 day and 1 week later, ERPs recorded from frontal electrodes differentiated familiar from novel syllables.

Visual Expectancy

This training procedure was also described earlier (see "Infant Learning" section). In this paradigm, infants are initially exposed to a recurring sequence of stimuli. Their memory for the sequence is tested by increasing the interval between the original exposure trials and testing and assessing whether infants can still anticipate the next stimulus in the sequence. After training 5-month-olds to sequentially fixate four identical doors arranged in a quadrant and that opened and closed successively, for example, Smith et al. (1989) cued infants by opening and closing the first door 1 min and 1 week later. They found that infants looked at the remaining three locations in the correct order after both delays.

Similarly, Arehart and Haith (1990) found that 3-month-olds retained an alternation rule for 4–7 days. After being exposed to either a random or a left-right alternating sequence of pictures, all infants were tested with a left-right alternating sequence. Infants who were tested with the same sequence that they saw during training anticipatorily shifted their eyes in the direction of where the picture would appear next more rapidly and more often than infants who were tested with a different sequence. This result was subsequently replicated with a more complex, left-left-right sequence (Canfield & Haith, 1991).

Classical Conditioning

Retention of classical conditioning is measured as *savings* (more rapid reacquisition than in Session 1) or cued recall (responding to the CS-alone or prior to the UCS). Newborns' anticipatory responses when their feeding schedules were shifted from 3 to 4 hr is an example of retention that was described earlier (Marquis, 1941). In a study explicitly designed to measure retention, Jones (1930) exposed a 7-month-old female to repeated pairings of a tapping sound (CS) and an electrotactual stimulus (UCS) over 5 consecutive days. The anticipatory CR (a galvanic skin reflex) was established midway through Day 1. The CR was still present 7 weeks later.

In a study described previously, Little et al. (1984) established an eye-blink CR in a single session with 10-, 20-, and 30-day-olds by pairing a tone (CS) with an air puff (UCS) using a 500- or 1,500-ms ISI. During a second conditioning session 10 days later, all 1,500-ms groups responded more in Session 2 than Session 1, but only groups that were first trained at 20 or 30 days of age performed above age-matched controls 10 days later.

Operant Conditioning

In operant studies, retention measures are based on the rationale that infants who lack a verbal response can perform a motoric response (foot-kick, lever-press) to indicate whether they recognize a stimulus. If they do, then they respond above baseline; otherwise, they do not. In most studies, retention is measured *prior to* reacquisition during a nonreinforcement phase (i.e., what infants bring into the session) rather than during reacquisition (savings). Because the test phase is procedurally identical to the baseline phase and the immediate retention test that follows training, each infant can contribute two retention measures—one indicates whether the infant recognizes the stimulus at all (i.e., whether the infant's rate of responding during the test exceeds the baseline rate before training) and the other indicates how much the infant remembers of what he or she had learned (i.e., how much the infant's responding declined since training was over). Each measure is calculated as a ratio for each infant, and the two ratios constitute the two units of analysis.

The use of individually-based measures of relative response is important because group means based on absolute levels of response before and after a retention interval are not sensitive to individual variability in the base rate of the target response, and group changes in absolute responding over the retention interval do not necessarily reflect individual changes. The use of individually-based ratios eliminates these problems. (For extended discussion of measurement problems, see Rovee-Collier, 1996a).

The *baseline ratio* is the primary retention measure and expresses each infant's kick rate during the long-term retention test (LRT) as a fraction of the same infant's baseline rate (BASE): LRT/BASE. The resulting value indexes the extent to which test performance exceeds baseline. A mean baseline ratio significantly greater than 1.00 indicates significant retention. The *retention ratio* measures the degree of retention, expressing the infant's response rate during the LRT as a fraction of that infant's posttraining response rate during the immediate retention test (IRT): LRT/IRT. A mean retention ratio of 1.00 indicates that performance has not decreased from the immediate to the long-term test; a mean retention ratio significantly less than 1.00 indicates that memory performance is significantly impaired. Responding is not predicted to fall significantly *below* baseline after an infant has forgotten, and forgetting implies that memory performance declines. For this reason, the baseline and retention ratios, respectively, are analyzed by directional (one-way), one-sample *t* tests in which the denominator is the predicted baseline or retention ratio of the population (1.00 in both cases). If the data are skewed (as baseline ratios are likely to be because they have no upper limit), then they should be transformed to natural logs ($M = 0$) prior to analysis. Also prior to all analyses, all group ratios should be subjected to a median outliers test (Tukey, 1977). If an outlier is found, it should be replaced with the next highest or lowest baseline or retention ratio in the group (Winsorized), and a degree

of freedom must be subtracted in subsequent analyses.

The assumption underlying the use of responding during the IRT as a measure of the final level of learning and immediate retention is that the infant has responded at the same rate as during the final minutes of acquisition. Because the IRT is a nonreinforcement phase, however, it cannot be so long that the response undergoes extinction, or so short that the frustrating effects of reinforcement withdrawal will dominate responding. In fact, in most operant studies, responding characteristically increases sharply, and then decreases following the withdrawal of reinforcement, producing a pattern called a *response elbow*. In order for the infant's mean response rate during the IRT to reflect veridically the mean response rate at the end of acquisition, the entire response elbow must be captured. If the IRT is appropriately timed, then this requirement will usually be met—but not always.

The pattern of responding during the IRT is also related to age: Two-month-olds may continue to increase responding for a longer period because they are slow to discriminate the withdrawal of reinforcement, whereas 6-month-olds may abruptly decrease responding because they discriminate it so rapidly. If the IRT rate is higher than at the end of acquisition, then in order to exhibit retention, an infant would have to respond during the delayed test at a rate higher than that at which the infant had responded by the end of training. Conversely, if an infant's response rate during the IRT drops to the baseline level, then responding at the baseline level during the long-term test would erroneously be credited as perfect retention, when the infant actually exhibited none. Under either of these conditions, responding during the final minutes of acquisition must be used as the alternative denominator of the retention ratio. This choice is less preferred because it means comparing responding during a period of reinforcement (acquisition) with responding during a period of nonreinforcement (the long-term test).

Most studies of infant long-term memory have used the mobile task with 2- to 6-month-olds and the train task with 6- to 18-month-olds. In the mobile task (described earlier), infants learn to move a particular mobile by kicking via a ribbon strung from one ankle to an overhead mobile suspension hook. The critical target information is displayed either directly on the mobile objects or on a distinctive cloth context draped around the crib or playpen. In the standardized procedure, infants are trained in their own homes for 15 min each day (10 min at 6 months) for 2 successive days. During baseline and all retention tests (3 min at 3 months, 2 min at 6 months), the ribbon and the mobile are attached to different hooks so that infants' kicks cannot move the mobile. The delayed recognition test usually follows 1 or more days later during a nonreinforcement phase with a mobile or context that is the same as or different from the one present during training. The train task, also described earlier, uses the same parameters of training and testing as the mobile task at 6 months of age except that reinforcement is discrete and lasts 2 s, and the context is defined by a particular room in the house. Not surprisingly, the retention data from the two tasks are identical. At older ages, each reinforcement lasts 1 s, and the training and test phases are only half as long. At all ages, the lever is simply deactivated during baseline and all retention tests.

In the initial study of long-term retention using the mobile task, 3-month-olds were trained for 3 consecutive days with the same mobile (Rovee & Fagen, 1976). Twenty-four hr later, some infants were tested for 3 min with the original mobile, and others were tested for 3 min with a different one. Infants tested with the original mobile kicked significantly above baseline, but infants tested with a different mobile did not. These data demonstrated that infants not only recognized their training mobiles after 24 hr, but also discriminated the test mobile from the training mobile even though they had not seen the training mobile for 24 hr.

The mobile and train tasks yield identical measures of retention from 6-month-olds. Not only are the forgetting functions identical, but so are infants' sensitivity to cue and context changes (Hartshorn & Rovee-Collier, 1997), latency of responding to a memory prime (Hildreth & Rovee-Collier, 1999), and rate of reforgetting after priming (Sweeney, Hildreth, & Rovee-Collier, 2000). These results established the validity of using the train task as an upward extension of the mobile task—thus overcoming the problem that had plagued studies of the ontogeny of learning and memory with infants, namely, the problem of finding a task or equivalent tasks that could be used over the entire infancy period.

Ontogeny of Memory

The younger infants are, the more rapidly they forget. The forgetting functions of 2- to 18-month-olds who were trained with standardized and age-calibrated parameters in the mobile and train tasks indicate that the maximum duration of retention improves monotonically over the first 1.5 years of life (Hartshorn et al., 1998b). These age differences in retention are not due to age differences in operant level or original learning—there are none (see "Infant Learning" section). The function in Figure 17.9 provides reference points for future investigators who use the same tasks and parameters with special populations, the same tasks with different parameters, or different tasks altogether. The maximum duration of retention in the deferred imitation task with a hand puppet is also plotted in Figure 17.9. Although different ages remember the operant and imitation tasks for different absolute durations—undoubtedly a reflection of

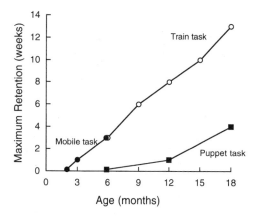

Figure 17.9   Standardized reference functions for the maximum duration of retention (in weeks) as a function of infant age.

NOTE: Data for each function were collected from independent groups of infants who were trained and tested in standardized procedures with age-calibrated parameters. The experimental paradigms were the operant mobile and train tasks and the deferred imitation (puppet) task. Differences in the slopes of the two functions are due solely to the use of different parameters.

different task parameters—the patterns of retention are the same.

The use of standardized parameters is critical in comparing data from infants of different ages. The slightest changes in the parameters of training can dramatically affect retention, and can do so differently at different ages. If 2-month-olds are trained for three 6-min sessions instead of two 9-min sessions, for example, they recognize the training mobile for 2 weeks—the same as 6-month-olds—instead of for only 1–2 days, even though total training time is the same in both instances (Vander Linde, Morrongiello, & Rovee-Collier, 1985). These data suggest that the number of times a memory is retrieved affects how long it will be remembered in the future—a factor whose effects also differ with age. Moreover, at all ages, future retention will be longer if more time has elapsed since the memory was retrieved last (Galluccio &

Rovee-Collier, 2001; Rovee-Collier, Greco-Vigorito, & Hayne, 1993; Schmidt & Bjork, 1992; see the "Special Problems in Infant Cognition: Time Windows" section). Therefore, infants should be tested only once unless the effect of repeated testing on retention is the specific research question. If infants must be tested repeatedly, then experimenters should consider progressively expanding the delay between successive tests in order to ensure that the difficulty of retrieval remains equivalent over successive tests (Hartshorn, Wilk, Muller, & Rovee-Collier, 1998c). Finally, to ensure that test performance reflects an infant's memory of the original experience and not new learning that has accrued over repeated tests, experimenters must include an age-matched control group that is tested repeatedly without having received the original experience (e.g., Rovee-Collier, Hartshorn, & DiRubbo, 1999).

Specificity of Memory

Because only cues that are similar to what was originally encoded can retrieve a memory, one way to ascertain the contents of infants' memories is to probe them with different retrieval cues and note which cues are effective and which are not (for discussion of this experimental approach, see Tulving, 1983, p. 251). If the memory is retrieved despite the fact that the retrieval cue differs in some way from when the memory was encoded, then this can be taken as evidence that the aspect of the cue that was changed was either not encoded or, depending on the timing of the retention test, was forgotten. The latter can be determined by testing after a shorter delay. For example, 3-month-olds discriminate L's from T's after 1 hr but not after 24 hr (Adler & Rovee-Collier, 1994), and a single + in the original training color pops out from differently colored, + distractors after 1 hr but not after 24 hr (Gerhardstein, Renner, & Rovee-Collier, 1999). Conversely, if the memory is not retrieved when some aspect of the retrieval cue is changed but is retrieved otherwise, then that aspect is represented in the memory.

At 2–6 months of age, infants do not kick above baseline during a 24-hr test if the test mobile is even slightly different from what was present during training (Hartshorn et al., 1998b). Three-month-olds, for example, will not recognize the original mobile 1 day later if more than a single object on it is different during the test (Fagen, Rovee, & Kaplan, 1976; Hayne, Greco, Earley, Griesler, & Rovee-Collier, 1986). Likewise, they will fail to recognize a test mobile if it displays "+" shapes that are only 25% (Adler & Rovee-Collier, 1994) or 33% (Gerhardstein, Adler & Rovee-Collier, 2000) smaller or larger than the "+" shapes displayed on the training mobile 1 day earlier.

In contrast, by at least 9 months of age, infants are unaffected by some cue changes *only after relatively short delays* (see left panel of Figure 17.10). At 9–12 months, infants in

conditioning studies generalize to a novel cue after test delays of 1–14 days but not longer (Hartshorn et al., 1998a). Similarly, in deferred imitation tests at 12–14 months, infants generalize to a cue that differs only in color after 10 min (Barnat, Klein, & Meltzoff, 1996; Hayne, MacDonald, & Barr, 1997) but not after 1 day (Hayne et al., 1997); at 18 months, they generalize to cue that differs in color after 1 day; and at 21 months, they generalize to a cue that differs in color and form after 1 day (Hayne et al., 1997). The fact that older infants generalize to novel test cues after short but not long delays reveals that they can discriminate differences between the cues but *actively* disregard them after short delays.

Even when infants are tested with the same distinctive cue with which they were trained, they may fail to recognize it in a different context. This conclusion is qualified by the test delay and the infant's age (Hartshorn et al., 1998a). Although 6-month-olds do not respond if the context is changed 24 hr after training, 3-, 9-, and 12-month-olds are

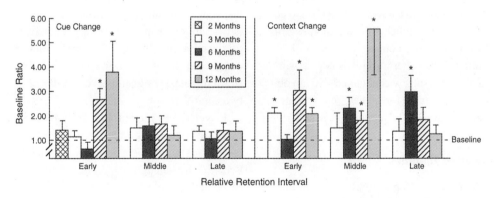

Figure 17.10 The effect of cue and context changes on the memory performance of 2- to 12-month-olds.
NOTE: Infants were tested in the operant mobile or train task after common relative retention intervals corresponding to the first (Early), middle (Middle), and last (Late) points on the forgetting function for each age. The Late test delay corresponds to the longest absolute delay at which infants of each age exhibited retention (see Figure 17.9). Left panel: Infants trained with a particular cue (mobile, train set) were tested with a different cue in the original context. Right panel: Infants trained in a particular context were tested in a different context with the original cue. Asterisks indicate significant retention. Vertical bars indicate ±1 *SE*.

affected by a context change *only after relatively long delays* (see right panel of Figure 17.10). Experimenters should be aware that because infants remember longer when they are older (i.e., their forgetting functions are increasingly protracted), the effect of different variables must be compared at equivalent points on the forgetting functions at different ages rather than after the same absolute delays at different ages. Conceivably, infants simply need more retrieval cues—here, provided by the context—when a memory is relatively difficult to retrieve. Alternatively, memory may have evolved to be conservative: When the memory is older, the likelihood that the retrieval context will differ from the encoding context is greater, and retrieving it only in a context that veridically matches the encoding context may be adaptive. Nonetheless, both cue and contextual specificity can be overridden by initially training infants with more than one cue (Hayne et al., 1987; Shields & Rovee-Collier, 1992), in more than one context (Amabile & Rovee-Collier, 1991; Rovee-Collier & DuFault, 1991), or by merely exposing infants to a novel mobile (Greco et al., 1990; Rovee-Collier, Borza, Adler, & Boller, 1993) or novel context (Boller & Rovee-Collier, 1992) after training is over. A similar pattern of results was obtained with an object segregation task (for review, see Needham & Baillargeon, 2000; Needham & Modi, 1999).

Deferred Imitation

When the first opportunity to reproduce a modeled behavior occurs after a delay, the behavior is called *deferred imitation*. Piaget (1962) first described deferred imitation in recounting that his daughter precisely imitated a temper tantrum that a peer had performed 24 hr earlier. In deferred-imitation experiments, target actions involving single or multiple steps are demonstrated by an adult experimenter with an unfamiliar object. During the demonstration, the infant is not allowed to touch the object on which the actions are performed, and the experimenter does not verbally label the object or describe the action. To maintain the infant's attention during the demonstration, however, the experimenter may either say "Look" or call the child by name. Two age-matched control groups establish the probability that infants will produce the target action spontaneously, in the absence of explicit modeling: The baseline control group encounters the test object for the first time during the test, and the no-demonstration control group or adult manipulation group receives equivalent exposure to the test stimuli and experimenter but does not see the target actions demonstrated.

The test procedure is identical for all groups. During the test, the experimenter positions the object(s) in front of the infant and videotapes the infant's behavior. Later, the behavior is scored from videotape by two independent observers, one of whom is blind to the infant's group assignment, for a fixed period from the time the infant first touches the test object. The imitation score for each infant is the sum of the number of target behaviors produced during the test. Deferred imitation occurred if the imitation score of the demonstration group significantly exceeds that of the two control groups.

Piaget's (1962) claim that deferred imitation does not emerge before 18–24 months of age was initially supported (e.g., McCall, Parke, & Kavanaugh, 1977), but most of the early studies lacked essential control groups and/or used tasks that infants younger than 18 months could not readily perform. Using appropriate control groups and multiple, one-step tasks, Meltzoff (1988a) demonstrated that 9-month-olds could defer imitation for 24 hr. In his study, the experimental group watched an adult demonstrate three novel actions (push a hinged panel to flatten it, push a hidden button on a black box to make a sound, and shake an egg to make a rattling noise) three times each. The demonstration for each action lasted 20 s. Three age-matched control groups—a baseline control group and two no-demonstration control groups—saw no demonstration. Twenty-four hr later, all infants were tested for production of the target actions during a 20-s response period. Deferred imitation was scored on a scale of 0–3 (1 point for each of the three actions). The experimental group had significantly more high-imitation scores (scores of 2–3) than did either control group.

Subsequently, Meltzoff (1995) reported that 14- and 16-month-olds can defer imitation for 4 months. In this study, infants watched an adult demonstrate a simple action on each of four objects (pull apart a dumbbell, touch his head on a panel to light it, push collapsible stacking cups to flatten them, and push a hidden button on a black box to make a sound). The adult modeled each target action three times, and infants saw three demonstrations altogether. The baseline control group came to the lab but saw no demonstration. All infants were tested twice with each object during a 20-s response period. Naive observers, blind to an infant's experimental condition, scored imitation from videotapes on a scale of 0–4 (1 point per target action imitated in either block of test trials). At both ages, the experimental group produced significantly more target actions than the baseline control group did 4 months later.

Using no-demonstration control groups, Barr et al. (1996) studied infants' ability to imitate a sequence of three actions on a hand-puppet (remove, shake, and replace a mitten) after a 24-hr delay. The experimenter demonstrated the actions either three or six times each for a total of 30 s or 60 s, respectively. Barr et al. found that the spontaneous production of target behaviors by a no-demonstration

control group was virtually zero between 6 and 24 months of age. This result is important because the reproduction of zero-probability behaviors after a delay is the hallmark of deferred imitation (Piaget, 1962). The developmental invariance in spontaneously produced target actions enabled the assessment of developmental differences in deferred imitation; otherwise, comparisons across such a wide age range would have been precluded.

Barr et al. (1996) also found that all demonstration groups between 6 and 24 months of age had significantly higher imitation scores than the corresponding no-demonstration control groups, and that older infants in the demonstration group produced significantly more target behaviors than younger infants. Significantly, even 6-month-olds could defer imitation for 24 hr when the series of actions was modeled on an attractive hand-puppet, when the response period lasted 120 s, and when the demonstration lasted 60 s. The finding that only older infants could defer imitation for 24 hr when the response period was 25% shorter (90 s) and the demonstration was 50% briefer (30 s) testifies to the critical importance of choosing optimal tasks, stimuli, and task parameters for studies with very young infants.

Meltzoff and Moore (1994) have demonstrated that even 6-week-olds can imitate the specific facial gestures an experimenter had modeled 1 day earlier. In their study, infants were randomly assigned either to a baseline control group, who always saw an adult model a passive face, or to one of three experimental groups who saw an adult demonstrate mouth opening, mid-tongue protrusion, or side-tongue protrusion. Infants received five sessions on consecutive days. In Sessions 1, 3, and 5, a 90-s modeling phase was followed by a 90-s immediate imitation period. In Sessions 2 and 4, infants' memory for the target gesture was assessed for 90 s while the experimenter presented a passive face in all conditions. Overall, infants in the experimental conditions imitated the appropriate gesture on Days 2 and 4. In particular, infants in the side-tongue protrusion condition imitated the side-tongue protrusion. Although infants may not have imitated this gesture precisely on their initial attempts, they gradually self-corrected their behaviors to match the unique gesture modeled by the experimenter 24 hr earlier.

Deferred imitation is particularly appealing to study because it is so commonplace in real-world settings. A particularly rich source of imitation is television. Infants' ability to imitate a televised demonstration lags well behind their ability to imitate a live demonstration. When the demonstration is live, 6-month-olds readily imitate an adult's actions after a 24-hr delay (Barr et al., 1996), but when the same demonstration is televised, infants cannot imitate the same actions 1 day later until they are 18 months old (Barr & Hayne, 1999). By 15 months of age, however, infants can imitate some televised actions after a 24-hr delay (Barr & Hayne, 1999; Meltzoff, 1988b). Troseth and DeLoache (1998) observed the same phenomenon in an object search task. Deferred-imitation procedures have also been used to investigate the effects of context and cues on memory performance. The results are extremely consistent with those obtained using operant procedures (Barnat et al., 1996; Hayne, Boniface, & Barr, 2000a; Hayne et al., 1987).

Experimenters designing imitation studies should take care to avoid introducing unsystematic variations that will preclude meaningful comparisons within and across laboratories. Examples of problematic variations include the following:

1. Allowing infants to control the duration of both the baseline and test phases (e.g., Bauer & Shore, 1987); this practice exposes different infants to the test object for different durations and can produce an underestimation of the spontaneous rate of target behaviors.

2. Remodeling sequences for some infants but not others; this practice produces unequal exposure to the sequences across subjects (Bauer & Hertsgaard, 1993; Bauer, Hertsgaard, & Wewerka, 1995; Bauer & Mandler, 1992), which, in turn, differentially affects their long-term retention of the sequences (Bauer, 1995; Bauer et al., 1995).

3. Narrating the target actions or providing verbal instructions and/or prompts (Bauer et al., 1995); this practice selectively facilitates the imitation performance of older and verbally competent infants, and attaching verbal labels to stimuli and target actions during demonstration and testing significantly enhances long-term retention and generalization (Herbert & Hayne, 2000).

In addition, the effects of immediate imitation on later retention are not fully understood (for review, see Barr & Hayne, 2000). Although imitating immediately appears to have no major effect on later retention in simple imitation tests (Abravanel, 1991; Barr & Hayne, 1996; Bauer, Hertsgaard, & Dow, 1994; Meltzoff, 1995), differences do emerge when test complexity is increased. Eighteen-month-olds who imitated target actions on the training puppet immediately, for example, also imitated the target actions on a novel puppet 24 hr later, but infants who did not imitate immediately also did not imitate later on a novel puppet (Barr & Hayne, 2000).

Reminder Procedures

The two reminder procedures, reinstatement and reactivation, were originally developed in studies with animal infants but have also been used with human infants to protract retention for significant periods. These reminder procedures are not paradigm-specific, but they are differentially effective depending on the state of the memory (active, inactive) at the time of reminding—particularly when infants are very young.

A *reinstatement* is a small amount of practice or a partial repetition of the original event that is given periodically throughout the retention interval (Campbell & Jaynes, 1966). Because reinstatements are given when the memory is active, they *forestall* forgetting—like throwing a log on a dying fire. *Reactivation* is a variant of reinstatement (Spear & Parsons, 1976) in which the subject is exposed to an isolated component of the original event after the memory has been forgotten (i.e., when it is no longer expressed in behavior) but in advance of the long-term test. The reminder—a memory prime—re-activates the latent or dormant memory and increases its subsequent accessibility to a retrieval cue. Whether the memory was indeed reactivated is assessed later during a delayed recognition test. If it was, then infants will respond to the test cue as they had responded to it immediately after training was over. In natural settings, the probability is higher that, as time goes by, infants will encounter only a fraction of a prior event rather than the event in its entirety, as in reinstatement. This factor may reflect a biological adaptation after longer delays. Because the reactivation stimulus is presented *before* the response is produced and at a time when the infant does not recognize it, reactivation is like priming procedures that are used with amnesic adults, who similarly cannot recognize a stimulus at the time of priming (see "Memory Dissociations").

For many years, the effects of reinstatement and reactivation reminders were thought to be equivalent (Spear & Parsons, 1976), and most developmental psychologists still do not distinguish between them (e.g., Howe, Courage, & Bryant-Brown, 1993; Hudson &

Sheffield, 1998; Mandler, 1998). Studies with human infants, however, have shown that the two reminders differ functionally as well as procedurally.

Reinstatement

Although reinstatement was introduced a decade before reactivation, fewer studies have been conducted with human infants using reinstatement than reactivation because visiting an infant once to give a single reactivation treatment at the end of the retention interval is more economical than visiting periodically throughout the retention interval to give multiple reinstatements. During reinstatement in the mobile task, the ankle ribbon is connected to the mobile hook, and infants' kicks can move the mobile for 2 min (6-month-olds) or 3 min (2- and 3-month-olds). During reinstatement in the train task, the lever is active, and the infant has 2 min in which to respond. In both of these tasks, the duration of the reinstatement period is timed from the first response (kick, lever-press).

Because each reinstatement entails additional training, it is considerably more effective in extending the memory than reactivation. A single reinstatement protracts the retention of 3-month-olds twice as long after training as a single reactivation treatment given after the same delay (Adler, Wilk, & Rovee-Collier, 2000), and three reinstatements protract retention longer than three reactivations given after the same delays (Galluccio & Rovee-Collier, 2000). In addition, a single reinstatement protracts the retention of 6-month-olds more than six times longer than a single reactivation given after the same delay (Sweeney et al., 2000).

The greater the separation between successive reinstatements, the more protracted retention is. This effect was demonstrated with infants who were trained in the standard mobile task (Galluccio & Rovee-Collier, 2001). Three-month-old infants, who forget the task after 5 days, were given a single 3-min reinstatement at the beginning, middle, or end of their forgetting function. A reinstatement given 1 day after training protracted retention for 1 additional day (6 days after training); a reinstatement given 3 days afterward protracted retention for 9 additional days (14 days after training); and a reinstatement given 5 days afterward protracted retention for 16 additional days (21 days after training).

Reactivation

Reactivation was originally adapted for use in the mobile task with 3-month-olds (Rovee-Collier, Sullivan, Enright, Lucas, & Fagen, 1980; Sullivan, 1982) and has since been used in this task as well as in other paradigms with older infants. Effective memory primes for infants include such diverse stimuli as the following:

- A previously familiarized photograph in a paired-comparison study with 5-month-olds (Cornell, 1979)
- The distinctive training context in mobile studies with 3-month-olds (Hayne & Findlay, 1995; Rovee-Collier, Griesler, & Earley, 1985)
- The original moving mobile or moving train in operant conditioning studies with 2–12-month-olds (Hildreth & Rovee-Collier, 1999; Rovee-Collier & Hayne, 1987)
- A partial (30-s) demonstration of the target actions on a hand-puppet in deferred imitation and sensory preconditioning studies with 6-month-olds (Barr et al., 2001; Vieira, Barr, & Rovee-Collier, 2000)
- The dancing hand-puppet in deferred imitation studies with 18-month-olds (Barr & Hayne, 2000)
- A demonstration of three of the six activities in which 14- and 18-month-olds had engaged (Sheffield & Hudson, 1994)

- A video of the six activities in which 24-month-olds had engaged (Agayoff, Sheffield, & Hudson, 1999)
- A small-scale model or photograph of a room where 24-month-olds had performed six activities (Agayoff et al., 1999)

As a rule, what is used as a reminder must veridically match what is in the original memory representation, or it will not alleviate forgetting; generalized reminders, for example, are ineffective. For this reason, and because the memory is forgotten at the time a reactivation reminder is presented, reactivation is thought to be an automatic, perceptual-identification process.

During reactivation in the mobile task, the infant sits in a sling-seat beneath the mobile (see Figure 17.11) in order to minimize random kicking that might be adventitiously reinforced, although it cannot be eliminated (Sullivan, 1982). During a reactivation treatment, the end of the ribbon is not connected to the ankle but is held by the experimenter. The experimenter, crouching out of view at the side of the crib, draws and releases the ribbon in a jerky, patterned manner, moving the mobile noncontingently at the rate that the same infant had kicked to move it during each of the final 2 min (6 months) or 3 min (2–3 months) of acquisition. In this way, the reactivation reminder will phenomenologically match what the infant saw during the final minutes of training. During reactivation in the train task, the lever is deactivated, and the computer moves the train noncontingently in the 2-min reactivation period exactly as the same infant had moved it by lever-pressing in the last 2 min of acquisition. The infant is free to press the lever during the reactivation period, just as the infant can kick randomly during the reactivation period in the mobile task.

Although the reactivation procedure was designed to alleviate forgetting, an individual can encounter fractional components of

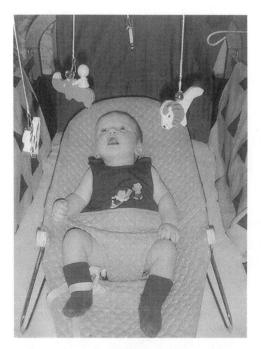

Figure 17.11 The experimental arrangement used with 2- to 6-month-olds during a reactivation treatment in the operant mobile task, shown here with a 3-month-old. The end of the ribbon that is attached to the mobile hook is held by the experimenter, who pulls it to move the mobile noncontingently. The infant seat minimizes random activity. The experimental arrangement during a reinstatement procedure is the same as it was during original training: The ribbon is strung from the infant's ankle to the mobile hook so that kicks move the mobile.

a prior event at any time—not only after the event is forgotten. Priming when the original memory is still active will boost retention, but not for as long as priming when it is inactive. In fact, exposure to the prime when the memory is active can actually impair retention by enabling new learning that either competes with or subtracts from what infants learned before (Adler et al., 2000; Gordon, 1981). The same result can occur if the prime is exposed for so long when the memory is inactive that the memory is reactivated while the prime continues to be exposed (Hayne, 1990).

Priming with a novel mobile for 3 min immediately after training, for example, when the memory is active, retroactively interferes with infants' recognition of the original mobile the next day (Rossi-George & Rovee-Collier, 1999), but this effect is temporary and disappears within 2 days. The interference phenomenon also occurs if infants are primed with a novel mobile 3 days after training and are tested the next day with the original mobile (Rovee-Collier, Adler, & Borza, 1994). As before, this phenomenon is temporary; infants again recognize the training mobile 4 days later.

Between 3 and 12 months of age, a single reactivation treatment essentially doubles the life of the original memory, so that the duration of the reactivated and original memories are the same (Hildreth, Wawrzyniak, Barr, & Rovee-Collier, 1999; Rovee-Collier et al., 1980). This equivalence is seen even though the duration of the original memory increases linearly over this period (Hartshorn et al., 1998b). The latency with which a reactivation reminder recovers the forgotten memory also decreases linearly over the first year of life (Hildreth & Rovee-Collier, 1999). At all ages, the reactivation treatment was given 1 week after infants of a given age had last remembered the task (note that the time since training when reactivation occurred increased linearly with age). At 3 months of age, the memory was recovered 24 hr after reminding; at 6 months, the memory was recovered 1 hr after reminding; at 9 months, it was recovered 1 min after reminding; and at 12 months, it was recovered instantaneously.

Even at 3 months of age, however, a reactivation treatment recovers a forgotten memory instantaneously if the prime is presented closer in time to training. This effect was demonstrated 24 hr after training in a serial-learning study in which a precuing procedure, which is procedurally identical to a reactivation treatment, was used to recover forgotten order information (Gulya et al., 1998; see *Infant Learning*). At 3 months, the latency of retrieval also decreases from 24 hr to only 4 hr if infants receive two reactivation treatments instead of one (Hayne, Gross, Hildreth, & Rovee-Collier, 2000b). Multiple reactivations also protract retention substantially longer than one reactivation as long as infants have forgotten the previously reactivated memory before a succeeding reactivation treatment is given (Hayne, 1990).

Memory Dissociations

A number of independent variables produce memory dissociations in adults, having a major effect on their performance on recognition tests and no effect on their performance on priming tests. These same variables have the same differential impact on the memory performance of infants on delayed recognition and reactivation (priming) tests. They include age, the retention interval, retroactive interference, the number of study trials, the amount of study time, the number of studied items, level of processing, trial and session spacing, affect, the serial position of list items, studied size, and the memory load (for review, see Rovee-Collier, 1997). In adults, memory dissociations are taken as evidence of dichotomous memory systems (implicit and explicit, or nondeclarative and declarative).

On the basis of evidence that implicit (nondeclarative) memory is spared by amnesia, but explicit (declarative) memory is impaired, these systems were assumed to emerge hierarchically during the infancy period, with implicit memory appearing at birth or shortly thereafter and explicit memory emerging at the end of the first year. Evidence that even 2-month-olds exhibit memory dissociations of the same form as those exhibited by adults, however, has shown that these memory systems develop simultaneously from very early in infancy (Rovee-Collier, Hayne, & Colombo, 2001).

SPECIAL PROBLEMS IN INFANT COGNITION

A number of experimental problems that came to center stage at the end of the 20th century have major significance for research on infant cognition but do not fall clearly into one of the preceding sections of this chapter. These problems are considered in the following sections. Researchers exploring these problems have exploited much of the methodology that was described earlier in the chapter, in particular, the habituation procedure. This research is current, and many of the procedures and findings discussed here are hotly contested.

Objecthood: Segmentation, Number, Individuation, and Causality

Researchers focusing on the nature of infants' object representations have been heavily influenced by work on adult attention and particularly by the idea that visual attention is structured by objects in space (Baillargeon, 1995; Spelke, 1994). The general method used in these studies is a *violation-of-expectancy procedure* in which the impact of information presented during an initial familiarization phase is assessed by measuring the duration of looking during the ensuing test (for review, see Baillargeon, 1995). Hauser (2000) described the violation-of-expectancy procedure as being analogous to a magic show: During a magic show, information that violates the laws of physics is presented and arrests the viewer's attention, which suggests that the viewer has some knowledge of the underlying principle. The same logic is applied to human infants. The information presented during the familiarization period presumably sets up an expectation of a particular outcome (the *possible outcome*), and infants appear to be surprised (i.e., they look longer) if the test event violates that expectancy (the *impossible outcome*).

The same methodological precautions that are taken in habituation studies (see *Infant Learning*) apply to studies using the violation-of-expectancy paradigm. A problem unique to this paradigm arises, however, if the experimenter uses more than a single test trial. In fact, the first test trial provides the only uncontaminated test of infants' expectations. Each additional test trial with the impossible event is an occasion for learning a new expectation or modifying the old one. By the same token, succeeding test trials with the possible event resemble an habituation series.

Baillargeon and colleagues, for example, used this paradigm to examine infants' physical reasoning, exploiting an arrested motion event called the *drawbridge event* (for review, see Baillargeon, 1995). During familiarization, a screen was rotated smoothly through a 180-deg arc from front to back for a fixed number of trials. During the test, a box was placed so that it obstructed the path of the rotating screen. In the impossible test event, the screen continued to rotate unimpeded through the same arc, whereas in the possible test event, the rotating screen was stopped by the box and came to a rest against it. Both groups received two test trials; the experimental group was tested with an impossible event on one trial and with a possible event on the other, and the control group was tested with a possible event on both trials. Developmental differences were investigated by determining whether infants could discriminate between the two events and then systematically decreasing the events' discriminability by increasing the difficulty of the impossible task. Initially, for example, the impossible task was an 80% violation in the arc of rotation. Reducing the degree of violation from 80% to 50% increased the difficulty of the

task. Conversely, the task was made easier by placing a second box to act as a reference (i.e., a memory prompt) for the height of the unseen box that was placed in the path of the rotating screen.

The amount of physical information that infants required to discriminate the two events decreased with age. Whereas 4.5- and 6.5-month-olds discriminated between the possible and impossible events when the violation was 80% with the reference cue, 6.5-month-olds discriminated an 80% violation (but not the more difficult 50% violation) without a reference cue, and 8.5-month-olds discriminated the 50% violation without a reference cue. When the drawbridge event was modified during the test to reveal the screen as it rotated through a 180-deg arc and retraced its path, infants as young as 4.5 months discriminated between the impossible and possible events without the reference cue (for discussion, see Baillargeon, 1995).

Segmentation

The question underlying segmentation studies is whether infants parse a stationary display into multiple objects or perceive it as a single object, perhaps with multiple parts. During an initial familiarization phase, infants view a stationary display consisting of two objects (e.g., a box and a cylinder) abutting each other. Familiarization ends when infants meet a looking criterion (e.g., looking away for 2 s after accumulating 10 s of looking time or looking continuously for 30 s; Needham, 1998). During the test phase, a gloved hand appears, grasps one of the objects, and pulls it to the left or the right (see top panel of Figure 17.12). Younger infants may receive up to six trials; older infants receive fewer (e.g., two). A test trial ends when the stage curtain is lowered after infants have again met a looking criterion (e.g., looking away for 2 s after looking continuously for 6–8 s or accumulating 60 s of looking time; Needham, 1998).

Support Condition

Move-together Event

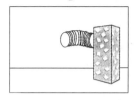 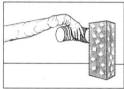 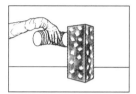

Move-apart Event

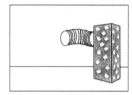 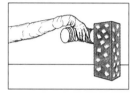 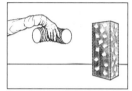

No-support Condition

Move-together Event

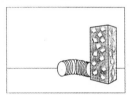 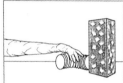 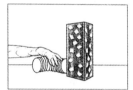

Move-apart Event

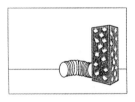 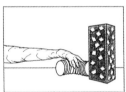 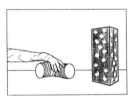

Figure 17.12 Top panel: The move-together and move-apart events in the cylinder up condition. (Needham & Baillargeon, 1997). In the move-apart event, the infant is familiarized with the cylinder and the box; during the test event, the hand grabs the cylinder, and the cylinder moves away from the box. In the move-together event, the hand grabs the cylinder, and the cylinder and box move together. The move-together event is expected. Bottom panel: The move-together and move-apart events in the cylinder down condition. The move-apart event is expected.
SOURCE: Figure courtesy of Amy Needham.

During testing, half of the infants see the object that is grasped by the gloved hand move away from the other object (*move-apart event*), and half see the two objects move together (*move-together event*). If infants perceive the stationary display as two separate objects, then they will expect the objects to be capable of moving independently and will look longer at the unexpected event (i.e., the objects moving together). That is, infants' attention will be prolonged if the motion of the objects is inconsistent with how they segmented the stationary display during the familiarization phase. Needham and Modi (1999) argued that a between-subjects design avoids cross-contamination of responses to the two events and is more realistic: In real life, two separate objects are not suddenly transformed into only one object or vice versa, which would be the case in a within-subjects design.

Needham (1998) displayed a blue box with white squares beside a yellow- and white-zigzagged cylinder to 6.5- and 7.5-month-old infants. The cylinder was curved and the corner of the box faced the infant (*complex cylinder-box display*). During the test trials, 7.5-month-olds looked significantly longer at the unexpected move-together event than at the expected move-apart event, but 6.5-month-olds looked equally at both. When the cylinder was straightened instead of curved, and the side of the box faced the infant (*simplified cylinder-box display*), both 4.5- and 6.5-month-olds looked significantly longer at the unexpected move-together event than at the expected move-apart event. To test whether discrimination during the test phase was actually produced during the familiarization phase, control groups received no familiarization phase. Because the control groups looked equally at both events, the author concluded that the experimental groups had segmented the cylinder and the box into two independent objects during the familiarization phase.

Needham and Baillargeon (1997) displayed the same complex cylinder-box display to 8-month-olds. In an additional experimental condition, the cylinder was suspended in the air (*cylinder up*) instead of lying flat on the stage (*cylinder down*) during the familiarization phase (see Figure 17.12). Because the cylinder could not be physically suspended in the air unless it were *attached* to the box, when the experimenter grasped and pulled the box, infants should expect the two objects to move together. During the test trials, 8-month-olds looked significantly longer at the unexpected move-apart event than at the expected move-together event.

To investigate whether infants' prior experience with a test object affects its segmentation, Needham and Baillargeon (1998) exposed 4.5-month-old infants to either the box or the cylinder during the familiarization phase and then tested them with the complex cylinder-box display in either the move-apart or move-together event. Infants were familiarized with the box for 5 s (accumulated looking time) and with the cylinder for a total of 5 s or 15 s. Infants looked significantly longer at the unexpected move-together event after either a 5-s exposure to the box or a 15-s exposure to the cylinder. The authors argued that infants required longer exposure to the cylinder because it was more complex. When 4.5-month-olds were familiarized with the complex cylinder-box display, however, they looked equally at the move-together and move-apart events. When infants were familiarized with the box for a total of 2 min in their homes 24 hr prior to testing in the laboratory, 4.5-month-olds looked significantly longer at the unexpected move-together event, but only in the second block of trials (Trials 3–6). These data suggest that infants were learning during the first three test trials (for discussion, see Rovee-Collier, 2001). After a 72-hr delay, infants looked equally at both displays (Needham & Baillargeon, 2000). Needham and Modi (1999) concluded that 4.5-month-olds use prior experience with an object to determine object boundaries when a new display contains the same previously encountered object. Finally, preexposing infants to objects that were similar to the box did not promote object segregation (see Needham &

Baillargeon, 2000; Needham & Modi, 1999; see also *Specificity of Memory* section). Similarly, this specificity was overridden by training infants with three different exemplars of the cue. These studies exemplify an important point: Seemingly mundane methodological modifications, such as changing the orientation of the one of the objects, often provide new insights and enable more sophisticated analyses than would otherwise be possible.

Number

Piaget (1954) argued that conservation of length and density preceded the concept of number. Piaget presented children with two rows of pebbles that were either spread out or close together and asked them which row contained more pebbles. At the outset, when the two rows contained the same number, 4-year-olds had difficulty answering the question. He then added or subtracted from a row and again asked children which row contained more pebbles. This time, they answered that the row in which the pebbles were more spread out contained more, regardless of whether pebbles had actually been added to that row. Because children aged 4 years were unsuccessful on this task, Piaget did not test younger infants. Mehler and Bever (1967) repeated the experiment but used M&M's candies instead of pebbles and provided children with a nonverbal response instead of a verbal one, telling children, "Pick the row you want, and you can eat all the M&M's in that row." Children as young as 2.3 years consistently chose the row containing more M&M's, irrespective of whether the candies were spread out. Hauser (2000) reported similar results from a foraging experiment with rhesus monkeys. These findings suggest that Piaget's task had required a level of verbal skills too high to allow young children to demonstrate their understanding of number. Experimenters are warned that this procedural error is not unique to studies of

number; it is one of the most common errors in studies with very young children.

Mehler and Bever's (1967) findings spawned studies using nonverbal measures with even younger infants. Wynn (1992) used a violation-of-expectancy procedure with 5-month-olds to investigate their understanding of addition and subtraction (see Figure 17.13). During a pretest, she placed either one or two Mickey Mouse dolls on a stage and measured infants' looking times to each display. Infants exhibited a baseline preference, looking significantly longer at two dolls than at one—a problem that arises frequently in this literature. To circumvent potential interpretative problems associated with a baseline preference, Wynn elected to test only infants who looked equally at the displays during the pretest. In the *addition condition,* the experimenter placed one doll on an empty stage, raised a screen to shield the stage from the infant's view, and then placed a second doll behind the screen as the infant watched. During the test, the screen was lowered, and independent groups saw either two dolls (the expected or possible event) or one doll (the unexpected or impossible event) on the stage. In the *subtraction condition,* the experimenter placed two dolls on the empty stage, raised the screen, and then removed one of the dolls as the infant watched. Infants in the subtraction condition received an identical test except that seeing one doll was the expected or possible event, and seeing two dolls was the unexpected or impossible event.

Infants in each condition looked significantly longer at the unexpected event. Wynn (1992) interpreted this result to mean that infants had counted the number of dolls on the stage and were surprised when their expectation of seeing that number was violated. Mehler (cited in Wynn, 1995) asked whether infants might have been responding to dolls' prior spatial locations instead of counting

Sequence of events: 1+1 = 1 or 2

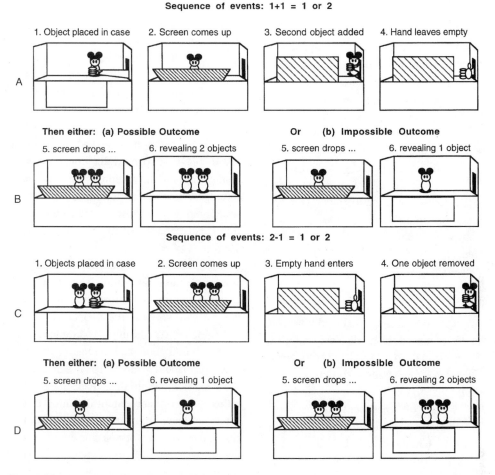

Figure 17.13 The addition and subtraction events used by Wynn (1992). Panel A: Familiarization for the 1+1 task. Panel B: Test conditions for the 1+1 event, possible outcome (left) and impossible outcome (right). Panel C: Familiarization for the 2-1 event. Panel D: Test conditions for the 2-1 event, possible outcome (left) and impossible outcome (right).
SOURCE: Reprinted with permission from *Nature, 358,* Wynn, K. (1992). Addition and subtraction by human infants. Figure 1, p. 749. Copyright (1992) Macmillan Magazines Limited.

them—that is, looking longer when the spatial field where a doll had previously been was now empty, or vice versa. To answer this, he repeated the addition and subtraction conditions but used a rotating stage so that the dolls did not occupy a fixed spatial location. The results were the same—longer looking at the unexpected event.

Another experimental means of asking whether infants can count is to see whether they can discriminate different numbers of ac-

tions. Using a procedure similar to the one described previously but this time using a hand puppet, Wynn (1996) habituated 6-month-olds to a two- or a three-jump sequence. Infants discriminated a change in the number of jumps, looking significantly longer when the number of jumps changed. By matching tempo and duration, Wynn was able to conclude that infants had responded on the basis of numerosity (see also Starkey, Spelke, & Gelman, 1983).

Object Individuation

Object individuation is a refined instance of the numerosity problem. It is defined as the representation of the *specific numerosity of objects* in a scene and is considered requisite for the representation of a distinct object (Leslie, Xu, Tremoulet, & Scholl, 1998). *Object identification* is defined as the reassignment of an already active object representation to the appropriate object if it was encountered before (Leslie et al., 1998). Spelke (1990) derived three spatiotemporal factors—cohesion, continuity, and contact—that constrain infants' object identification. Although infants rely on spatiotemporal information for object identification, they are commonly confronted with the problem of occlusion (i.e., one object moves behind another). How infants identify and track occluded objects and the experimental methods designed to answer these questions have been hotly debated (Needham & Baillargeon, 2000; Xu & Carey, 2000).

A number of experiments have suggested that infants use spatiotemporal information to identify and track occluded objects. Using a violation-of-expectancy procedure, Spelke and Kestenbaum (1986) showed 4-month-olds a cylinder continuously moving back and forth across a stage behind two occluders, briefly appearing in the gap between them. During the test, when the occluders were lowered so that infants' view of the whole object was no longer obstructed, infants saw either one cylinder (the expected event) or two cylinders (the unexpected event) moving back and forth across the stage. Infants looked significantly longer at the two-cylinder event. Other infants were also shown a cylinder continuously moving back and forth across the stage behind two occluders, but the cylinder never appeared in the gap between the two occluders. Presumably, these infants would expect to see two cylinders instead of only one when the screen was lowered. In fact, they looked significantly longer at the one-cylinder display (the unexpected event) during the test. Spelke and Kestenbaum concluded that infants perceived the display as containing one occluded object when the cylinder appeared in the gap and two occluded objects when it did not. When a single wide screen instead of two narrower screens was used, infants looked equally at the one- and two-cylinder test displays, supporting the conclusion that spatiotemporal information associated with the appearance or nonappearance of the object in the gap was the basis of their discrimination (Spelke, Kestenbaum, Simons, & Wein, 1995).

Baillargeon and colleagues extended this line of research by putting a window in either the top or bottom of the single, wide screen and varying the properties of the occluded object during the familiarization phase. Baillargeon and DeVos (1991) and Baillargeon and Graber (1987) familiarized 3.5- and 5.5-month-olds, respectively, with either a tall or short rabbit that moved continuously back and forth behind the occluding screen. During the test, a window was cut in the top of the screen so that the tall rabbit could be seen in the window, but the short rabbit could not. Infants in both familiarization groups observed a rabbit going behind the screen and appearing on the other side. Irrespective of its height, the rabbit did not appear in the top window. Infants in the tall-rabbit group (the unexpected or impossible event) looked significantly longer than infants in the short-rabbit group (the expected or possible event). If, however, two tall or two short rabbits were presented on both sides of the screen during familiarization, then infants looked equally at the short- and tall-rabbit events. The authors concluded that because infants knew there were two objects from the outset, they did not expect the tall rabbit to appear in the gap (for an alternative explanation, see Meltzoff & Moore, 1998).

The preceding studies suggest that infants use spatiotemporal information to decide how many objects are present behind an occluder. Performance on this task varies as a function of age (Baillargeon, 1995). Although 2.5-month-olds looked longer at a single test object if no object had appeared in a space between two occluders, they do not look longer if the object had appeared in the bottom window of a single occluder (a screen); 3-month-olds looked longer if no object had appeared in the bottom window but not if no objects had appeared in the top window. Not until infants are 3.5 months old does the height of the object affect test performance, with infants looking longer if the tall rabbit did not appear in the top window.

Xu and Carey (1996) modified Spelke and Kestenbaum's (1986) original procedure to examine whether infants use spatiotemporal or property/kind information to individuate the number of objects in a display. During the four baseline trials, 10- and 12-month-olds faced an empty stage, and a screen was lowered to reveal either one object or two different objects. Each baseline trial ended when the infant looked away for 2 s. Infants exhibited a baseline preference, looking significantly longer at two objects than at one. During the four familiarization trials (eight emergences and returns), an object moved out from behind the left screen and then moved back, and another object moved out from behind the right screen and then moved back. The objects used during the familiarization and test trials were a duck and a truck. Only one procedural difference differentiated the spatiotemporal and property/kind groups: At the beginning of each trial for the spatiotemporal group, the duck and the truck were simultaneously presented, one object on either side of the screen. Infants were initially tested with either the expected event (two objects) or the unexpected event (one object). The familiarization and test phases were then repeated,

but the number of familiarization trials was halved, and infants were tested with the other event. The whole procedure was then repeated with a different set of stimuli. Altogether, infants were tested with two expected and two unexpected events in a within-subjects design.

Although 10-month-olds in the spatiotemporal condition overcame their baseline preference and looked equally at the two displays, 10-month-olds in the property/kind condition continued to exhibit their baseline preference for two objects. In contrast, 12-month-olds in both the spatiotemporal and property/kind conditions overcame their baseline preference for two objects and looked equally at the one- and two-object displays during test. Unfortunately, infants were not tested with a two-duck or two-truck display, so whether they actually monitored property/kind information or only number information cannot be determined (Leslie et al., 1998). Furthermore, overcoming their baseline preference was not compelling evidence that infants had individuated objects on the basis of featural information.

To overcome the baseline preference problem, Leslie and colleagues used two objects during both familiarization and testing, and to avoid cross-contamination of results, they used a between-subjects design (for review, see Leslie et al., 1998). In a typical study, for example, infants were familiarized with a sequential presentation of one red and one green disk. During testing, infants saw either two red disks (the unexpected event) or one red disk and one green disk (the expected event). Because 12-month-olds looked equally at both the red/green and red/red disks, Leslie et al. concluded that they did not individuate objects on the basis of color (see Figure 17.14).

In another condition, infants were successively familiarized with one red disk and then with another red disk (the expected event was one red disk). When infants were again tested with either two red disks or one red and one

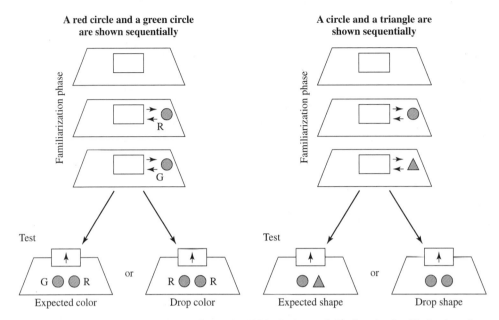

Figure 17.14   The events used by Leslie et al. (1998). Left panel: During the familiarization phase, the infant is shown a stage with a screen; a red circle is first removed from behind the screen and then is returned behind the screen. Then, a green circle is removed from behind the screen and is returned behind it. During the test, the screen is lowered to reveal either a red and a green circle (expected) or two red circles (unexpected). Right panel: The same experiment except that a triangle and a circle are shown during familiarization and, during the test, the screen is lowered to reveal either a triangle and a circle (expected) or two circles (unexpected).

Source: Reprinted from *Trends in Cognitive Sciences, 2,* Leslie, A., Xu, F., Tremoulet, P., & Scholl, B. Indexing and the object concept: developing "what" and "where" systems. Figures 4 & 5, p. 16, Copyright 1998 with permission from Elsevier Science.

green disk, they looked longer at both displays than had infants tested with the expected event in the previous condition. The authors concluded that infants who saw two red disks expected, conservatively, to see one disk and thus looked longer at two objects, regardless of their color. When groups were simultaneously presented with either a red disk and a green disk or two red disks and were tested with two red disks, their looking times did not differ. Taken together, these two conditions suggest that infants used color information to individuate objects but not to identify objects. Leslie et al. (1998) have also conducted this experiment using two different shapes (circle, triangle). Although 12-month-olds looked significantly longer if they were subsequently

tested with two circles, 6- and 9-month-olds did not.

Wilcox and Baillargeon (1998a) overcame the baseline preference problem by testing infants with only one object and changing the familiarization phase. The ball-box group saw a ball and a box emerge successively from opposite sides of the occluding screen during the familiarization phase and was tested with one ball (an unexpected or impossible event). The ball-ball group saw a ball emerge separately on each side of the screen and was also tested with one ball (an expected or possible event). Although 11.5-month-olds looked significantly longer at the unexpected event, 9.5-month-olds did not. When the familiarization event was simplified, 9.5-month-olds looked significantly longer at the impossible event as well. In the simplified version, the ball and box did not reverse trajectory; instead, the box initially appeared at the left side of the screen, then disappeared behind it, and finally the ball emerged on the right side of the screen. When the screen was lowered during the test, infants saw an empty stage behind the screen with the ball still on the right side of the stage (Wilcox & Baillargeon, 1998a).

Wilcox and Baillargeon (1998a, 1998b; Wilcox, 1999) argued that infants do not use featural information to individuate objects for a procedural reason, namely because the tasks described above require *mapping between two events:* the occlusion event seen during familiarization and the no-occlusion event seen during the test. This process necessitates retrieving the representation of the occlusion event, comparing it with the current representation of the no-occlusion event, and judging

whether these two representations are consistent (Wilcox & Baillargeon, 1998a). Although infants given unambiguous spatiotemporal information can discriminate objects on occlusion tasks at ages younger than 10 months, they cannot do so in its absence.

In contrast, during an *event-monitoring task,* infants monitor an ongoing occlusion event and discriminate inconsistencies *within that single event,* and the screen is not removed (see Figure 17.15). In the event-monitoring task, infants are familiarized with a ball and box emerging from behind a wide screen (ball-box) or a ball emerging from each side of the wide screen (ball-ball). The ball and box are then returned to their original locations behind the screen. During the test, the ball and box successively emerge from behind a wide or a narrow screen. In the wide-screen condition, both objects—either the ball and box or two balls—can fit behind the screen, but in the narrow-screen condition,

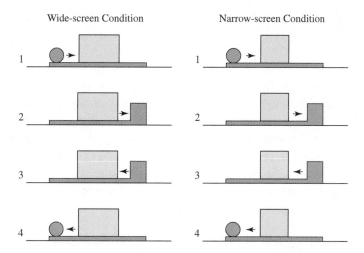

Figure 17.15   An event-monitoring task with narrow screen/wide screen conditions that was used in individuation studies with 4.5- to 9.5-month-old infants (Wilcox, 1999). Left panel: In the wide screen/different shape event, a ball is placed behind the right side of the screen; then, a box emerges from the left side and returns; finally, the ball emerges from the right side again. Right panel: The narrow screen/different shape event, which is identical except that the screen is narrow. The ball and the box cannot fit behind the screen at the same time and is the unexpected outcome.

SOURCE: Reprinted from *Cognition, 72,* Wilcox, T., Object individuation: Infants' use of shape, size, pattern, and color. Figure 5, p. 140, Copyright 1999 with permission from Elsevier Science.

they cannot. The only unexpected or impossible event is the *ball-box/narrow-screen* event. Because the two balls were identical in *the ball-ball/narrow-screen* event, infants should have expected to see only one ball (the possible event). Wilcox and Baillargeon found that infants as young as 4.5 months looked significantly longer at the unexpected ball-box/narrow-screen event than at any of the other three events (ball-ball/narrow-screen, ball-box/wide-screen, and ball-ball/wide-screen).

To control for the possibility that infants simply prefer to look at the narrow screen, Wilcox and Baillargeon (1998a) also used smaller objects that fit behind it. Both 7.5- and 9.5-month-old infants in the ball-box and ball-ball groups looked equally long when the ball and box were small enough to fit behind the narrow screen at the same time. Using the event-monitoring task, these same researchers also documented a developmental progression in the use of featural information to individuate objects (for review, see Wilcox, 1999). By systematically varying the features of the ball and box, they found that 4.5-month-olds discriminate on the basis of size and shape information, that 7.5-month-olds can also discriminate on the basis of pattern, and that, by 11.5 months, infants can use color to discriminate (see also Leslie et al., 1998). Needham (1998) observed the same developmental progression in object segregation tasks.

The preceding studies reveal some of the ways in which researchers have overcome the baseline preference problem and suggest that event-monitoring tasks are most suitable for studies of object individuation with younger infants.

Causality

Studies of causality ask when infants can first detect different forms of causality, and what conditions underlie causal perception at different ages. Three-month-olds who are tested in the operant mobile paradigm appear to be quite deliberate when making the mobile move, and seeminqly do so intentionally, and 6-month-olds who are tested in a deferred imitation paradigm likewise seem very deliberate in removing the mitten from the hand-puppet (Rovee-Collier & Hayne, 2000). Because young infants do not possess language, however, and because researchers cannot be certain that even older infants who are linguistically competent understand questions about what causes what, conclusions about infants' understanding of causality can only be inferred from their behavior. Attempts to answer these questions have used modifications of experimental procedures that were previously used with preschoolers to study causal understanding.

One such procedure assesses infants' response to a *direct-launching event* in which one object collides with another object and moves it, as when one pool ball hits another and sends it forward (Leslie, 1984; Leslie & Keeble, 1987; Oakes & Cohen, 1995). In this procedure, infants are familiarized with either a causal (direct-launching) event or with one of three noncausal events in which a temporal gap (delayed launch), a spatial gap (no collision), or both (delayed launch with no collision) separate the two parts of the event. Leslie (1984), for example, showed 7-month-old infants a filmed sequence of a causal event or one of the three types of a noncausal event. During the causal event, an animated block moved to the middle of the screen and collided there with a differently colored block, which then moved to the other side of the screen. In the noncausal delayed-launch event, a 500-ms delay intervened between when the first block collided with the second block and when the second block moved to the other side of the screen. In the noncausal no-collision event, the first block stopped 6 cm short of the second block, but the second block moved immediately after the first block stopped. The noncausal delayed-launch/no-collision event included both spatial and temporal delays. Using a between-subjects design, Leslie played the filmed sequences on a continuous loop during each familiarization trial until the infant looked away for 1 s, and trials continued until infants reached a 50% looking-time criterion (see "Habituation Criterion Setting").

Leslie (1984) found that the duration of infants' looking at the test events varied with the degree of spatial and temporal causality, with the direct-launch event at one polar extreme and the delayed-launch/no-collision event at the other. Subsequently, Leslie and Keeble (1987) familiarized infants with either the direct-launch or the delayed-launch sequence and tested them with a reversed film sequence. The direct-launching group exhibited a significant increase in looking time relative to the group's *final* looking time during familiarization, but the delayed-launch group did not. A no-change control group that saw the same film sequence in the same order during the test exhibited no increase in looking time. Because the looking time of the delayed-launch group significantly increased relative to that of the control group, however, Leslie and Keeble (1987) concluded that infants can discriminate the spatiotemporal properties of events and that causal events are more salient than noncausal ones. They also concluded that 6-month-olds are capable of causal perception.

Oakes and Cohen (1995) rejected the preceding conclusions, arguing that the pattern of results obtained by Leslie and Keeble might have represented a developmental transition in causality processing. Using videotaped presentations of real objects engaging in causal and noncausal events with 6- and 10-month-olds, they found no evidence of causality perception before 10 months. Ten-month-olds who were familiarized with a causal event looked significantly longer at the noncausal delayed-launch and no-collision test events

than at the causal test event. In contrast, infants who were familiarized with either of the noncausal events looked significantly longer at the causal event but not at the other two noncausal events. They took these results as evidence that 10-month-olds can discriminate causal from noncausal events over and above the spatial and temporal dimensions that Leslie and Keeble had previously documented. Oakes and Cohen attributed the negative results obtained from 6-month-olds to the complexity of the objects. Yet, Baillargeon (1995) had found evidence of causal perception at 4 months of age when she used three-dimensional objects. When Oakes and Cohen used simpler, ball-like, computer-generated objects during familiarization and testing, 7-month-olds exhibited the same pattern of results as 10-month-olds.

These studies underscore the fact that the choice of stimulus materials significantly influences the age at which a particular cognitive competence may be observed. Often experimenters race to document the earliest age at which a given competence is present. In doing so, however, they must not overlook important questions regarding the choice of paradigm, stimuli, and parameters.

Time Windows

Individual differences abound in the real world but are less obvious in controlled laboratory settings. Although considerable attention has focused on genetic contributions to differences between individuals, each individual's unique history of experiences also plays a role but until recently, defining this role in general terms had proven elusive. The *time window construct* attempts to do this by describing the conditions that permit the integration of a current event or experience with a prior one and the consequences of such integration for future cognition (Rovee-Collier, 1995).

A time window is a limited period, timed from the onset of an event, within which subsequent information will be integrated with the memory representation of that initial event. New information that is encountered before a time window has opened (i.e., before the event has occurred) or after a time window has closed will be treated as unique and will not be integrated with the initial event. Thus, for example, although distributed training is clearly superior to massed training for both infants (Vander Linde et al., 1985) and adults (Cohen, 1985), there is an upper limit to the time that can elapse between successive training sessions in order for their effects to accrue (Rovee-Collier et al., 1995).

The time window construct is based on the fundamental assumption that information is integrated in short-term or primary memory when some cue in a current event retrieves the memory of a previous event. In other words, representations that are coactive in short-term memory are, by definition, integrated. Because memory retrieval is prerequisite for a present event to be integrated with a previous one, the time window closes when the memory representation can no longer be retrieved (i.e., when the prior event is forgotten). Thus, factors that affect retention will also affect the width of a time window (see *Infant Memory*). Unlike a simple forgetting function, however, the width of a time window expands nonlinearly with successive retrievals of the memory. Because the successively retrieved memory takes progressively longer to be reforgotten, new information can be integrated with it after progressively longer delays. In addition, the quantitative effects of retrieving a memory at different points within a time window (i.e., at different points on the forgetting function) are nonuniform: Retrieving a memory at the end of the time window expands the future width of that time window more than retrieving it at the beginning or middle of the time window (Galluc-

cio & Rovee-Collier, 2001; Hartshorn et al., 1998c). The effects of retrieving a memory and integrating new information with it at different points in the time window may also differ qualitatively. New information that is encountered late in the time window, for example, may facilitate retention of that information at the expense of other components of the original memory (Rovee-Collier et al., 1993).

Implications for Research

Although time windows are not restricted to a particular age or stage of development, their consequences are particularly significant during infancy, when the knowledge base is just being formed. As a result, their implications should be considered in the design of studies on infant learning and memory. Because the width of a given time window depends on the number of previous retrievals (e.g., either direct or indirect), experimenters should determine the forgetting function for a particular event before introducing manipulations that might affect it—a particularly crucial factor in studies with younger infants, who forget more rapidly. Also, because different experimental manipulations affect performance differently after different delays (i.e., at the end of the time window), studies that introduce a manipulation after a single delay may obtain a large, moderate, or small effect, or none at all, depending on when within the time window that manipulation occurs.

Intelligence

Early attempts to predict later intellectual performance from infant performance were unsuccessful because they either focused on sensory and motor performance, which change radically during the infancy period, or used assessment and outcome tasks too simple to reveal the impact of early risk factors on later cognitive behavior. In studies using animal models of mental retardation, increasing task complexity improved prediction (Strupp & Levitsky, 1990). A promising avenue of research on individual differences in infant memory was initiated by Fagen and Ohr (1990) using operant tasks (mobile, train) with 3-, 7-, and 11-month-olds. They obtained correlations between 0.40 and 0.50 between infants' 1-week retention ratios and their performance on standard assessment tests at 2 and 3 years. These correlations would have probably been higher had they tested older infants nearer the end of their respective forgetting functions (see Hartshorn et al., 1998b), where the range of variation is greater.

A widely used, standardized intelligence test for infants, the Fagan Test of Infant Intelligence, is based on their selective attention to novelty during a paired-comparison test (Fagan, 1990). McCall and Carriger (1993) concluded that novelty preference scores obtained during the first year of life predict IQ scores between 1 and 8 years of age. Infants' percent novelty scores at 4 and 7 months of age, for example, predict their scores on the Peabody Picture Vocabulary Test at 3, 4, 5, and 7 years of age, with correlations between 0.37 and 0.57 (Fagan & Detterman, 1992; Fagan & McGrath, 1981; Fagan & Singer, 1983). Percent novelty scores at 5 and 7 months also correlate significantly with Bayley Scale Scores at 2 years and with Stanford-Binet scores at 3 years (Thompson, Fagan, & Fuller, 1991). Investigators have used the Fagan Test to study the effects of early exposure to toxins (e.g., PCBs, lead, mercury) and substances of abuse (e.g., alcohol, cocaine) as well the effects of infant nutrition, iron supplements, and specialized feeding formulas on later intellectual functioning. In addition, the Fagan Test has been used to assess the cognitive sequelae of maternal HIV infection, intraventricular hemorrhage, bronchopulmonary dysplasia, failure to thrive, intrauterine growth retardation, genetic anomalies, and various neurological abnormalities. Whereas measures of selective attention on paired-comparison tests following a brief familiarization period reflect how an infant's memory was implicitly biased by the prior exposure, operant measures reflect an infant's memory of a past experience that has been retrieved from a long-term store. Both of these measures reveal that if an infant's ability to attend selectively to a visual stimulus or to retrieve a memory of a past experience is compromised early in life, then it is likely to be compromised later on as well.

Preattentive Processing: The Pop-Out Effect

Adult visual processing is thought to involve two stages—a *preattentive stage,* in which visual information is decomposed into its constituent parts, and a *focused attention* stage, in which this information is reconstituted into an object percept. The object percept is then compared with the contents of long-term memory and if a match is struck, the object is identified or takes on meaning. The preattentive and focused attention stages process "what" and "where" information, respectively.

In *visual pop-out,* a unique critical feature (Treisman, 1988) or texton (Julesz, 1984) immediately and effortlessly captures attention and perceptually stand outs from the rest of an otherwise homogeneous display. Pop-out is attributed to a preattentive-processing mechanism that extracts unique primitive features involuntarily and in parallel across a visual field without requiring focused attention. Features that pop out for adults include line segments and crossings (Julesz, 1984), line orientation and length (Treisman, 1988), shape (Treisman, 1982), curvature (Wolfe, Yee, & Friedman-Hill, 1992), angles (Treisman & Sato, 1990), size (Sagi, 1988), luster (Wolfe, Franzel, & Cave, 1988), and color

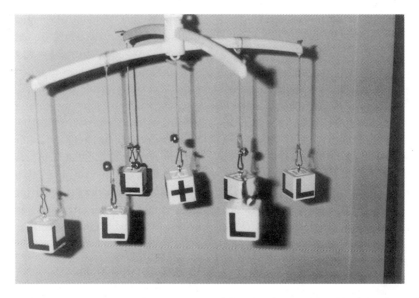

Figure 17.16   The long-term retention test: The mobile with six novel (L) blocks and one familiar pop-out stimulus (+).

(Nakayama & Silverman, 1986). The features known to pop out for infants are line crossings (Rovee-Collier, Hankins, & Bhatt, 1992), line segments (Adler, Inslicht, Rovee-Collier, & Gerhardstein, 1998; Colombo, Ryther, Frick, & Gifford, 1995; Gerhardstein, Liu, & Rovee-Collier, 1998), shape (Gerhardstein & Rovee-Collier, in press), color (Catherwood, Skoien, & Holt, 1996; Gerhardstein et al., 1999), and three-dimensional targets (Bhatt & Bertin, 2000). The experimental procedures used to study pop-out effects in infants are described below.

Operant Tasks

If 3-month-olds are trained to kick to move a mobile displaying stimuli composed of black horizontal and vertical bars that differ only in their spatial arrangement (T, L) or in the additional presence of a line crossing (+), then they discriminate L's and T's from +'s during a recognition test 24 hr later. When tested with a pop-out array after 24 hr, however, whether 3-month-olds recognize the test mobile is determined by the unique target that pops out from the surrounding distractors. If trained with seven +'s, for example, infants respond vigorously when tested with one + among six L's, despite the large number of novel L's surrounding it (Rovee-Collier et al., 1992; see Figure 17.16). Normally, infants cannot recognize a test mobile that contains more than a single novel object, but a single novel object on a test mobile does not disrupt 24-hr retention. Therefore, the single, familiar training item in the test display—despite being surrounded by novel items—must have popped out and captured infants' attention, and infants behaved as if the mobile were composed entirely of blocks like the target. Conversely, if trained with a mobile displaying L's and tested with one + among six L's, infants behaved as if the mobile were composed only of novel +'s and failed to recognize it, despite the fact that it is surrounded by a large number of familiar training L's. Therefore, it also must have popped out and captured infants' attention. As a result, they again behaved as if the test mobile were composed entirely of blocks like the target.

Rovee-Collier et al. (1992) used a reactivation procedure to provide convergent evidence of pop-out. Reactivation is a perceptual identification task in which the stimulus that is used as a memory prime must strike a fairly veridical perceptual match with what was originally encoded. If more than a single object on the prime is novel, then it will not reactivate the memory after it has been forgotten. For infants who were trained with a mobile containing seven +'s, a mobile containing a single familiar block (+) and six novel distractor blocks (L) was an effective prime, but the same prime did not reactivate the memory of infants trained with a mobile containing seven L's. For these infants, the pop-out target on the memory prime was novel. Thus, whether the pop-out target is familiar or novel completely controls whether a forgotten training memory is or is not reactivated, respectively. Paradoxically, *increasing* the number of familiar training blocks on the mobile prime from one to three eliminated the pop-out effect, despite the fact that the number of novel blocks was correspondingly *reduced* (Bhatt, Rovee-Collier, & Weiner, 1994).

The litmus test for parallel processing is the demonstration that perceptual pop-out is independent of the number of other elements (distractors) in the display. In studies with adults, the slope of reaction times across different numbers of distractors is flat (Treisman, 1988). The same result was obtained from independent groups of infants who were trained with a mobile displaying seven L blocks and who were reactivated with an L pop-out mobile containing 4–12 distractors (Rovee-Collier, Bhatt, & Chazin, 1996). If the single pop-out target was a novel +, however, then despite being embedded in as many as 11 or as few as 4 training distractors, infants would not respond to the test mobile. When the reactivation mobile contained 13 objects, however, the functions reversed— but for an uninteresting reason: With so many objects on the mobile, the single pop-out target was visually obscured by the remaining objects (the distractors) in the display. Under

these conditions, whether the large number of distractors was familiar or novel determined whether the memory was or was not reactivated, respectively.

Familiarization and Paired-Comparison Tests

This procedure has also been used to examine pop-out effects in infancy (for reviews, see Bhatt, 1997; Colombo et al., 1995; Sireteanu, 2000). Quinn and Bhatt (1998), for example, exposed 4-month-old infants to two homogeneous 5×5 arrays of L's, +'s, or T's during four successive 15-s trials, then tested the infants on two successive 10-s paired-comparison tests. The two test arrays were counterbalanced for position on each test trial. One test array contained a single novel character amidst familiar characters, and the other array contained a single familiar character amid novel characters. The characters + and either L or T were used in the pop-out condition, and L and T only were used in the non-pop-out condition (see Figure 17.17). If infants in the pop-out condition experienced a pop-out effect, then they should treat the complete array with the single novel character as novel even though 24 of the 25 stimuli were familiar, and vice versa. That is, despite the fact that infants of this age usually look proportionally longer at a novel stimulus, they were expected to look significantly longer at the array containing more familiar items if the novel item popped out. In the non-pop-out condition, however, infants should look significantly longer at the array containing more novel items than familiar ones. Both results were obtained with 3-month-old infants.

Sireteanu and colleagues (for review, see Sireteanu, 2000) used a texture-segmentation task in which a *patch* of features (e.g., a square patch of lines oriented obliquely to the left) was embedded in a field of distractors (e.g., lines oriented obliquely to the right). In this task, the space between the patch and its surround appears as a distinctive boundary

Familiar Stimuli

```
T ⊥ ⟨ ⅄ ⊦     T ⊥ ⟨ ⅄ ⊦
⟨ ⅄ ⊣ T ⊥     ⟨ ⅄ ⊣ T ⊥
T ⊦ ⅄ ⅃ ⟨     T ⊦ ⅄ ⅃ ⟨
⊣ ⋏ T T ⅃     ⊣ ⋏ T T ⅃
⊥ ⟨ ⊣ ⋏ ⊤     ⊥ ⟨ ⊣ ⋏ ⊤
```

Test Stimuli Pop-out condition

```
⋋ + + ⋋ ⋌     T ⊥ ⟨ ⅄ ⊦
+ ⟨ + + ⋋     ⟨ + ⊣ T ⊥
⋋ ⋌ ⋋ + ⋋     T ⊦ ⅄ ⅃ ⟨
⋋ + + ⋋ ⋌     ⊣ ⋏ T T ⅃
+ ⋌ ⋋ + ⋌     ⊥ ⟨ ⊣ ⋏ ⊤
```

Test Stimuli Nonpop-out condition

```
∨ ⌐ ⌒ ∨ ⌐     T ⊥ ⟨ ⅄ ⊦
⅃ ⅄ ⟨ ∧ ∨     ⟨ ⟨ ⊣ T ⊥
⌐ ⅃ ∨ L L     T ⊦ ⅄ ⅃ ⟨
⅃ L ∨ ⟨ ∧     ⊣ ⋏ T T ⅃
⌐ ∨ ⌐ ⅃ ∧     ⊥ ⟨ ⊣ ⋏ ⊤
```

Figure 17.17 Top panel: The homogeneous 5 × 5 array used during familiarization trials with T's. Middle panel: The two pop-out condition arrays shown during the paired-comparison test. On one side is a single familiar character (T) amid novel characters (+'s); on the other side is a single novel character (+) amidst familiar characters (T's). Bottom panel: The two non-pop-out condition test arrays. On one side is a single familiar character (T) amid novel characters (L's); on the other side is a single novel character (L) amidst familiar characters (T's).
SOURCE: Figure courtesy of Ramesh S. Bhatt.

that segregates the patch from the rest of the field. During paired-comparison tests, infants and children of different ages simultaneously viewed a pop-out display (either a single feature or a patch of features) and a homogeneous display. They found that a patch popped out earlier in development than single feature and that a single feature first popped out when

infants were older than they were in the mobile pop-out studies described above. Mirror-image oblique-line elements and texture differences, however, are much more difficult for young infants to discriminate than single horizontal versus vertical line segments. This discrepancy in the age at which stimuli first pop out highlights the importance of the type of stimulus materials that experimenters use in investigating infant cognition, particularly with younger infants.

Touch-Screen Procedure

This procedure was developed as a nonverbal task for studying visual search in toddlers. It allows experimenters to measure reaction times of infants as young as 12 months, substitutes a motoric response for a verbal one, and substitutes operant shaping for verbal instructions. Gerhardstein and Rovee-Collier (in press) trained 12- to 36-month-olds to locate and touch a target (a Barney-like cartoon character) on the screen (see Figure 17.18). The target was presented amid a regular pattern

Figure 17.18 An 18-month-old responding to the uniquely colored target during a feature-search test; the target is surrounded by distractors that differ only in color.
SOURCE: Photo courtesy of Peter Gerhardstein.

of distractors and jogged around the screen. When the toddler touched the moving target, a sound ("ta-da") was triggered, and four other animated cartoon characters danced around the target for 1 s. These conditions remained in effect for 17 trials (Trials 2–18), after which the target jogged in one spot for six trials (Trials 23–28) and then remained stationary for the final six trials. To proceed to the test phase, the toddler had to make three consecutive correct responses within 5 s of the appearance of the target during the final six trials. During the test phase, the single target appeared in either a feature-search or a conjunction-search display.

In the *feature-search display,* distractors that differed only in color surrounded the unique target. In the *conjunction-search display,* the unique target was a conjunction of a particular color and a particular shape and was surrounded by distractors that were either the same color but different in shape, or different in color but the same in shape. Toddlers received 32 test trials: eight trials each with 2, 4, 8, and 12 distractors presented in random order. Specially-designed software recorded toddlers' latency to touch the screen, their errors, and their correct responses. The 12-month-olds completed only the feature-search task; during the more difficult conjunction-search task, they eventually lost interest when their incorrect responses were not reinforced during the learning phase (a problem common to many infant learning studies); infants older than 12 months completed both tasks.

In the feature-search task, the slope of reaction time was flat over distractor number at all ages, but toddlers responded more rapidly with age. A flat reaction-time slope over distractor number in pop-out studies with adults is the defining characteristic of parallel search (Treisman, 1988). In the conjunction-search task, reaction time increased monotonically with distractor number, which is the defining characteristic of a serial (element-by-element)

search process (Treisman, 1988). The finding that infants and toddlers perform like adults on visual search tasks when the same measure is used and verbal competence is not a limiting factor reveals that the same attentional processes underlie visual search in infants and adults. This procedure can be adapted to study other experimental problems with preverbal toddlers and young children. Gulya (2000), for example, used it to study the development of serial-list learning from 3 to 20 years. A major advantage of this procedure is that it eliminates the age differences in verbal competence and motivation that often confound developmental studies of infant cognition.

CONCLUSIONS

Early research on infant cognition treated motor development, visual development, auditory processing, classical conditioning, and so forth as unrelated problems (for discussion, see Meltzoff & Kuhl, 1989). Since then, research has revealed that infant cognition is the product of many different modalities and processes acting together. Increasingly advanced technology will permit researchers to reexamine answers to old questions, to ask new ones, and to extend the study of cognition to the developing fetus.

Although the present chapter focused on learning and memory, experimenters who seek to pursue research on a particular problem should recognize that methodologies that were developed to study other problems can, depending on the ingenuity of the experimenter, usually be adapted to investigate it. Speaking more broadly, all of the topics covered here, along with their multiple and complex relationships with other topics such as neural, motor, perceptual, social, and language development that were not covered, will eventually have to be included in an integrative experimental analysis if we are ever to develop a complete science of infant cognition.

REFERENCES

Abravanel, E. (1991). Does immediate imitation influence long-term memory for observed actions? *Journal of Experimental Child Psychology, 51,* 235–244.

Acredolo, L. (1978). Development of spatial orientation in infancy. *Developmental Psychology, 14,* 224–234.

Acredolo, L. (1980). Laboratory versus home: The effect of environment on the nine-month-old infant's choice of a spatial reference system. *Developmental Psychology, 15,* 666–667.

Acredolo, L. (1990). Behavioral approaches to spatial orientation in infancy. In A. Diamond (Ed.), *Annals of the New York Academy of Sciences: Vol. 608. The development and neural bases of higher cognitive functions* (pp. 594–612). New York: New York Academy of Sciences.

Acredolo, L., & Evans, D. (1980). Developmental changes in the effects of landmarks on infant spatial behavior. *Developmental Psychology, 16,* 312–318.

Adler, S. A., Inslicht, S., Rovee-Collier, C., & Gerhardstein, P. (1998). Perceptual asymmetry and memory retrieval in three-month-old infants. *Infant Behavior and Development, 21,* 253–272.

Adler, S. A., & Rovee-Collier, C. (1994). The memorability and discriminability of primitive perceptual units in infancy. *Vision Research, 34,* 449–459.

Adler, S. A., Wilk, A., & Rovee-Collier, C. (2000). Effects of reinstatement and reactivation on active memory in infants. *Journal of Experimental Child Psychology, 75,* 93–115.

Agayoff, J. L., Sheffield, E. G., & Hudson, J. A. (1999, April). *Effects of video reminders on young children's long-term recall.* Paper presented at the meeting of the Society for Research in Child Development, Albuquerque, NM.

Ainsworth, M. S., Blehar, M. C., Waters, E., & Wall, S. (1978). *Patterns of attachment: A psychological study of the strange situation.* Hillsdale, NJ: Erlbaum.

Alberts, J. R. (1984). Sensory-perceptual development in the Norway rat: A view toward comparative studies. In R. Kail & N. E. Spear (Eds.), *Comparative perspectives on the development of memory* (pp. 65–101). Hillsdale, NJ: Erlbaum.

Allesandri, S. M., Sullivan, M. W., & Lewis, M. (1990). Violation of expectancy and frustration in early infancy. *Developmental Psychology, 26,* 738–744.

Amabile, T. A., & Rovee-Collier, C. (1991). Contextual variation and memory retrieval at six months. *Child Development, 62,* 1155–1166.

Arehart, D. M., & Haith, M. M. (1990, April). *Memory for space-time rules in the infant visual expectation paradigm.* Paper presented at the International Conference on Infant Studies, Montreal, Canada.

Ashton, R. (1973). The state variable in neonatal research. *Merrill-Palmer Quarterly, 19,* 3–20.

Aslin, R. H. (1981). Development of smooth pursuit in human infants. In D. F. Fisher, R. A. Monty, & J. W. Senders (Eds.), *Eye movements: Cognition and visual perception* (pp. 31–51). Hillsdale, NJ: Erlbaum.

Atkinson, J. (1984). Human visual development over the first six months of life: A review and a hypothesis. *Human Neurobiology, 3,* 61–74.

Aylward, G. P. (1981). The developmental course of behavioral state in preterm infants: A descriptive study. *Child Development, 52,* 564–568.

Bahrick, L. E., Hernandez-Reif, M., & Pickens, J. (1997). The effect of retrieval cues on visual preferences and memory in infancy: Evidence for a four-phase attention function. *Journal of Experimental Child Psychology, 67,* 1–20.

Bahrick, L. E., & Pickens, J. (1995). Infant memory for object motion across a period of three months: Implications for a four-phase attention function. *Journal of Experimental Child Psychology, 59,* 343–371.

Baillargeon, R. (1995). A model of physical reasoning in infancy. In C. Rovee-Collier & L. P. Lipsitt (Eds.), *Advances in infancy research* (Vol. 9, pp. 1–51). Norwood, NJ: Ablex.

Baillargeon, R., & DeVos, J. (1991). Object permanence in 3.5- and 4.5-month-old infants: Further evidence. *Child Development, 62,* 1227–1246.

Baillargeon, R., DeVos, J., & Graber, M. (1989). Location memory in 8-month-old infants in a non-search AB task: Further evidence. *Cognitive Development, 4,* 345–367.

Baillargeon, R., & Graber, M. (1987). Where's the rabbit? 5.5-month-old infants' representation of the height of hidden object. *Cognitive Development, 2,* 375–392.

Baillargeon, R., & Graber, M. (1988). Evidence of location memory in 8-month-old infants in a non-search AB task. *Developmental Psychology, 24,* 502–511.

Baldwin, J. M. (1915). *Mental development in the child and the race* (3rd ed.). New York: MacMillan. (Original work published 1894)

Banks, J. H., Jr., & Wolfson, J. H. (1967, April). *Differential cardiac response of infants to mother and stranger.* Paper presented at the meeting of the Eastern Psychological Association, Philadelphia, PA.

Barnat, S., Klein, P., & Meltzoff, A. N. (1996). Deferred imitation across changes in context and object: Memory and generalization. *Infant Behavior and Development, 19,* 241–252.

Barr, R., Dowden, A., & Hayne, H. (1996). Developmental changes in deferred imitation by 6- to 24-month-old infants. *Infant Behavior and Development, 19,* 159–170.

Barr, R., & Hayne, H. (1996). The effect of event structure on imitation in infancy: Practice makes perfect? *Infant Behavior and Development, 19,* 253–258.

Barr, R., & Hayne, H. (1999). Developmental changes in imitation from television during infancy. *Child Development, 70,* 1067–1081.

Barr, R., & Hayne, H. (2000). Age-related changes in imitation: Implications for memory development. In C. Rovee-Collier, L. P. Lipsitt, & H. Hayne (Eds.), *Progress in infancy research* (Vol. 1, pp. 21–67). Hillsdale, NJ: Erlbaum.

Barr, R., Marrott, H., & Rovee-Collier, C. (2001). Sensory preconditioning and deferred imitation by preverbal infants. Manuscript submitted for publication.

Bauer, P. J. (1992). Holding it all together: How enabling relations facilitate young children's event recall. *Cognitive Development, 7,* 1–28.

Bauer, P. J. (1995). Recalling past events: From infancy to early childhood. *Annals of Child Development, 11,* 25–71.

Bauer, P. J., & Fivush, R. (1992). Constructing event representations: Building on a foundation of variation and enabling relations. *Cognitive Development, 7,* 381–401.

Bauer, P. J., & Hertsgaard, L. A. (1993). Increasing steps in recall of events: Factors facilitating immediate and long-term memory in 13.5- and 16.5-month-old children. *Child Development, 64,* 1204–1223.

Bauer, P. J., Hertsgaard, L. A., & Dow, G. A. (1994). After 8 months have passed: Long-term recall of events by 1- to 2-year-old children. *Memory, 2,* 353–382.

Bauer, P. J., Hertsgaard, L. A., & Wewerka, S. S. (1995). Effects of experience on long-term recall in infancy: Remembering not to forget. *Journal of Experimental Child Psychology, 59,* 260–298.

Bauer, P. J., & Mandler, J. M. (1992). Putting the horse before the cart: The use of temporal order in recall of events by one-year-old children. *Developmental Psychology, 28,* 197–206.

Bauer, P. J., & Shore, C. M. (1987). Making a memorable event: Effects of familiarity and organization on young children's recall of action sequences. *Cognitive Development, 2,* 327–338.

Berg, W. K., & Berg, K. M. (1987). Psychophysiological development in infancy: State, startle, and attention. In J. D. Osofsky (Ed.), *Handbook of infant development* (2nd ed., pp. 238–317). New York: Wiley.

Berlyne, D. E. (1960). *Conflict, arousal, and curiosity.* New York: McGraw-Hill.

Berntson, C. G., Tuber, D. S., Ronca, A. E., & Bachman, D. S. (1983). The decerebrate human: Associative learning. *Experimental Neurology, 81,* 77–88.

Bhatt, R. S. (1997). The interface between perception and cognition: Feature detection, visual pop-out effects, feature integration, and long-term memory in infancy. In C. Rovee-Collier & L. P. Lipsitt (Eds.), *Advances in infancy research* (Vol. 11, pp. 143–191). Norwood, NJ: Ablex.

Bhatt, R. S., & Bertin, E. (2000, July). *Attentional engagement by three-dimensional cues in infancy*. Paper presented at the International Conference on Infant Studies, Brighton, UK.

Bhatt, R. S., & Rovee-Collier, C. (1994). Perception and 24-hour retention of feature relations in infancy. *Developmental Psychology, 30,* 142–150.

Bhatt, R. S., & Rovee-Collier, C. (1996). Infants' forgetting of correlated attributes and object recognition. *Child Development, 67,* 172–187.

Bhatt, R. S., Rovee-Collier, C., & Weiner, S. (1994). Developmental changes in the interface between perception and memory retrieval. *Developmental Psychology, 30,* 151–162.

Bhatt, R. S., & Waters, S. E. (1998). Perception of three-dimensional cues in early infancy. *Journal of Experimental Child Psychology, 70,* 227–224.

Bhatt, R. S., Wilk, A., & Rovee-Collier, C. (2001). Development of infant categorization based on feature relations. Manuscript submitted for publication.

Bjork, E. L., & Cummings, E. M. (1984). Infant search errors: Stage of concept development or stage of memory development. *Memory & Cognition. 12,* 1–19.

Blass, E. M., Ganchrow, J. R., & Steiner, J. E. (1984). Classical conditioning in newborn humans 2–48 hours of age. *Infant Behavior and Development, 7,* 223–235.

Bloom, K. (1984). Distinguishing between social reinforcement and social elicitation. *Journal of Experimental Child Psychology, 38,* 93–102.

Bloom, K., & Esposito, A. (1975). Social conditioning and its proper control procedures. *Journal of Experimental Child Psychology, 19,* 209–222.

Blough, D. S. (1982). Pigeon perception of letters of the alphabet. *Science, 218,* 397–398.

Bogartz, R. S. (1965). The criterion method: Some analyses and remarks. *Psychological Bulletin. 64,* 1–14.

Bogen, H. (1907). Experimentelle Untersuchungen uber psychische und assoziative Magensaftsekretion beim Menschen. *Jahrbuch fur Kinderheilkunde, 65,* 733–740.

Boller, K. (1997). Preexposure effects on infant learning and memory. *Developmental Psychobiology, 31,* 93–105.

Boller, K., & Rovee-Collier, C. (1992). Contextual coding and recoding of infant memory. *Journal of Experimental Child Psychology, 52,* 1–23.

Bomba, P. C., & Siqueland, E. R. (1983). The nature and structure of infant form categories. *Journal of Experimental Child Psychology, 35,* 294–328.

Bower, T. G. R. (1966). Slant perception and shape constancy in infants. *Science, 151,* 832–834.

Bower, T. G. R. (1967). Phenomenal identity and form perception in an infant. *Perception & Psychophysics, 2,* 74–76.

Brackbill, Y. (1958). Extinction of the smiling response in infants as a function of reinforcement schedule. *Child Development, 29,* 115–124.

Brackbill, Y., & Fitzgerald, H. E. (1969). Development of sensory analyzers during infancy. In L. P. Lipsitt & H. W. Reese (Eds.), *Advances in child development and behavior* (Vol. 4, pp. 174–208). New York: Academic Press.

Brackbill, Y., & Koltsova, M. M. (1967). Conditioning and learning. In Y. Brackbill (Ed.), *Infancy and early childhood* (pp. 207–286). New York: Free Press.

Brassell, W. R., & Kaye, H. (1974). Reinforcement from the sucking environment and subsequent modification of sucking behavior in the human neonate. *Journal of Experimental Psychology, 18,* 448–463.

Bretherton, I., & Waters, E. (Eds.). (1985). Growing points in attachment theory and research. *Monographs of the Society for Research in Child Development, 50* (Serial No. 209), 1–2.

Bridger, W. H. (1961). Sensory habituation and discrimination in the human neonate. *American Journal of Psychiatry, 117,* 991–996.

Brody, L. R. (1981). Visual short-term cued recall memory in infancy. *Child Development, 52,* 242–250.

Brogden, W. J. (1939). Sensory preconditioning. *Journal of Experimental Psychology, 25,* 323–332.

Brown, J. L. (1964). States in newborn infants. *Merrill-Palmer Quarterly, 10,* 313–327.

Brown, J. L. (1972). Instrumental control of the sucking response in human newborns. *Journal of Experimental Child Psychology, 14,* 66–80.

Bushnell, I. W. R., McCutcheon, E., Sinclair, J., & Tweedlie, M. E. (1984). Infants' delayed recognition memory for colour and form. *British Journal of Developmental Psychology, 2,* 11–17.

Butterfield, E. C., & Siperstein, G. N. (1972). Influence of contingent auditory stimulation upon non-nutritional suckle. In J. Bosma (Ed.), *Third symposium on oral sensation and perception: The mouth of the infant* (pp. 313–334). Springfield, IL: Thomas.

Butterworth, G. (1977). Object disappearance and error in infancy in Piaget's stage IV task. *Journal of Experimental Child Psychology, 23,* 391–401.

Butterworth, G., Jarrett, N., & Hicks, L. (1982). Spatiotemporal activity in infancy: Perceptual competence or conceptual deficit? *Developmental Psychology, 18,* 435–449.

Campbell, B. A., & Ampuero, M. X. (1985). Conditioned orienting and defensive responses in the developing rat. *Infant Behavior and Development, 8,* 425–434.

Campbell, B. A., & Jaynes, J. (1966). Reinstatement. *Psychological Review, 73,* 478–480.

Canfield, R. L., & Haith, M. M. (1991). Young infants' visual expectations for symmetric and asymmetric stimulus sequences. *Developmental Psychology, 27,* 198–208.

Caron, A. J., Caron, R. F., Caldwell, R. C., & Weiss, S. J. (1973). Infant perception of the structural properties of the face. *Developmental Psychology, 9,* 385–399.

Caron, R. F. (1967). Visual reinforcement of head-turning in young infants. *Journal of Experimental Child Psychology, 5,* 489–511.

Catherwood, D., Skoien, P., & Holt, C. (1996). Colour pop-out in infant response to visual arrays. *British Journal of Developmental Psychology, 14,* 315–326.

Clayton, K., Habibi, A., & Bendele, M. S. (1995). Recognition priming effects following serial learning: Implications for episodic priming effects. *American Journal of Psychology, 108,* 547–561.

Clifton, R. K. (1974). Heart rate conditioning in the newborn infant. *Journal of Experimental Child Psychology, 18,* 9–21.

Clifton, R. K., & Nelson, M. N. (1976). Developmental study of habituation in infants: The importance of paradigm, response system, and state. In T. J. Tighe & R. N. Leaton (Eds.), *Habituation* (pp. 159–205). Hillsdale, NJ: Erlbaum.

Cohen, L. B. (1972). Attention-getting and attention-holding processes of infant visual preferences. *Child Development, 43,* 869–879.

Cohen, L. B. (1973). A two-process model of infant visual attention. *Merrill-Palmer Quarterly, 19,* 157–180.

Cohen, L. B., & Gelber, E. R. (1975). Infant visual memory. In L. B. Cohen & P. Salapatek (Eds.), *Infant perception: From sensation to cognition* (Vol. 1, pp. 347–403). New York: Academic Press.

Cohen, L. B., & Strauss, M. S. (1979). Concept acquisition in the human infant. *Child Development, 50,* 419–424.

Cohen, R. L. (1985). On the generality of the laws of memory. In L.-G. Nilsson & T. Archer (Eds.), *Perspectives on learning and memory* (pp. 247–277). Hillsdale, NJ: Erlbaum.

Colombo, J., & Bundy, R. S. (1983). Infant response to auditory familiarity and novelty. *Infant Behavior and Development, 6,* 305–311.

Colombo, J., & Horowitz, F. D. (1985). A parametric study of the infant control procedure. *Infant Behavior and Development, 8,* 117–121.

Colombo, J., Mitchell, D. W., Coldren, J. T., & Freeseman, L. J. (1991). Individual differences in infant visual attention: Are short lookers faster processors or feature processors? *Child Development, 62,* 1247–1257.

Colombo, J., Ryther, J. S., Frick, J. E., & Gifford, J. J. (1995). Visual pop-out in infants: Evidence for preattentive search in 3- and

4-month-olds. *Psychonomic Bulletin and Review, 2,* 266–268.

Cornell, E. H. (1974). Infants' discrimination of photographs of faces following redundant presentations. *Journal of Experimental Child Psychology, 18,* 98–106.

Cornell, E. H. (1979). Infants' recognition memory, forgetting, and savings. *Journal of Experimental Child Psychology, 28,* 359–374.

Cornell, E. H. (1981). The effects cue distinctiveness on infants' manual search. *Journal of Experimental Child Psychology, 32,* 330–342.

Cornell, E. H., & Bergstrom, L. I. (1983). Serial-position effects in infants' recognition memory. *Memory & Cognition, 11,* 494–499.

Cornell, E. H., & Heth, C. D. (1979). Response versus place learning in human infants. *Journal of Experimental Psychology: Human Learning and Memory, 5,* 188–196.

Corter, C. M., Zucker, K. J., & Galligan, R. F. (1980). Patterns in the infant's search for mother during brief separation. *Developmental Psychology, 16,* 62–69.

Cummings, E. M., & Bjork, E. L. (1983). Perseveration and search on a five-choice visible displacement hiding task. *Journal of Genetic Psychology. 142,* 283–291.

Dannemiller, J. L. (1984). Infant habituation criteria: I. A Monte Carlo study of the 50% decrement criterion. *Infant Behavior and Development, 7,* 147–166.

Darwin, C. (1877). A biographical sketch of an infant. *Mind: Quarterly Review of Psychology and Philosophy, 2,* 285–294.

DeCasper, A. J., & Fifer, W. P. (1980). Of human bonding: Newborns prefer their mothers' voices. *Science, 208,* 1174–1176.

deHaan, M., & Nelson, C. (1997). Recognition of the mother's face by six-month-old infants: A neurobehavioral study. *Child Development, 68,* 187–210.

DeLoache, J. S. (1980). Naturalistic studies of memory for object location in very young children. *New Directions for Child Development, 10,* 17–32.

DeLucia, C. A. (1968). Apparatus for recording eyeblink. *Journal of Experimental Child Psychology, 6,* 427–430.

Denisova, M. P., & Figurin, N. L. (1929). The problem of the first associated food reflexes in infants. *Voprosy Geneticheskoy Reflexogii i Pedologii Miadenchestva, 1,* 81–88. [Cited in G. H. S. Razran, Conditioned responses in children: A behavioral and quantitative review of experimental studies. In R. S. Woodworth (Ed.), *Archives of Psychology* (Vol. 23, No. 148). New York: Columbia University Press, 1933.]

Dennis, W. A. (1934). A description and classification of the responses of the newborn infant. *Psychological Bulletin, 31,* 5–22.

Deutsch, W. (1994). Commentary. *Human Development, 37,* 30–35.

Diamond, A. (1981, April). *Retrieval of an object from an open box: The development of visual-tactile control of reaching in the first year of life.* Paper presented at the meeting of the Society for Research in Child Development, Boston.

Diamond, A. (1990a). Rate of maturation of the hippocampus and the developmental progression of children's performance on the delayed non-matching to sample and visual paired comparison tasks. In A. Diamond (Ed.), *Annals of the New York Academy of Sciences: Vol. 608. The development and neural bases of higher cognitive functions* (pp. 394–426). New York: New York Academy of Sciences.

Diamond, A. (1990b). The development and neural bases of memory functions as indexed by the AB and DR tasks in human infants and infant monkeys. In A. Diamond (Ed.), *Annals of the New York Academy of Sciences: Vol. 608. The development and neural bases of higher cognitive functions* (pp. 267–309). New York: New York Academy of Sciences.

Diamond, A., Churchland, A., Cruess, L., & Kirkham, N. Z. (1999). Early developments in the ability to understand the relation between stimulus and reward. *Developmental Psychology, 35,* 1507–1517.

Diamond, A., Cruttenden, L., & Niederman, D. (1989). Why have studies found better performance with multiple wells than with only two wells on AB? *Society for Research in Child Development Abstracts, 6,* 227.

Dolgin, K. G., & Azmitia, M. (1985). The development of the ability to interpret emotional signals: What is and is not known. In G. Zivin (Ed.), *The development of expressive behavior* (pp. 319–346). Orlando, FL: Academic Press.

Eimas, P., Siqueland, E. R., Jusczyk, P. W., & Vigorito, J. (1971). Speech perception in infants. *Science, 171,* 303–306.

Estes, W. K., & Skinner, B. F. (1941). Some quantitative properties of anxiety. *Journal of Experimental Psychology, 29,* 390–400.

Fagan, J. F., III. (1970). Memory in the infant. *Journal of Experimental Child Psychology, 9,* 217–226.

Fagan, J. F., III. (1971). Infants' recognition memory for a series of visual stimuli. *Journal of Experimental Child Psychology, 11,* 244–250.

Fagan, J. F., III. (1973). Infants' delayed recognition memory and forgetting. *Journal of Experimental Child Psychology, 16,* 424–450.

Fagan, J. F., III. (1990). The paired-comparison paradigm and infant intelligence. In A. Diamond (Ed.), *Annals of the New York Academy of Sciences: Vol. 608. The development and neural bases of higher cognitive functions* (pp. 337–364). New York: New York Academy of Sciences.

Fagan, J. F., III., & Detterman, D. K. (1992). The Fagan Test of Infant Intelligence: A technical summary. *Journal of Applied Developmental Psychology, 13,* 173–193.

Fagan, J. F., III., & McGrath, S. K. (1981). Infant recognition and later intelligence. *Intelligence, 5,* 121–130.

Fagan, J. F., III., & Singer, L. (1983). Infant recognition memory as a measure of intelligence. In L. P. Lipsitt (Ed.), *Advances in infancy research* (Vol. 2, pp. 31–78). Norwood, NJ: Ablex.

Fagen, J. W. (1977). Interproblem learning in ten-month-old infants. *Child Development, 48,* 786–796.

Fagen, J. W., & Ohr, P. S. (1990). Individual differences in infant conditioning and memory. In J. Colombo & J. W. Fagen (Eds.), *Individual differences in infancy: Reliability, stability, prediction* (pp. 167–191). Hillsdale, NJ: Erlbaum.

Fagen, J. W., Rovee, C. K., & Kaplan, M. G. (1976). Psychophysical scaling of stimulus similarity in 3-month-old infants and adults. *Journal of Experimental Child Psychology, 22,* 272–281.

Fantz, R. L. (1956). A method for studying early visual development. *Perceptual and Motor Skills, 6,* 13–15.

Fantz, R. L. (1964). Visual experience in infants: Decreased attention to familiar patterns relative to novel ones. *Science, 46,* 668–670.

Feinman, S. (1985). Emotional expression, social referencing, and preparedness for learning in early infancy: Mother knows best, but sometimes I know better. In G. Zivin (Ed.), *The development of expressive behavior* (pp. 291–318). Orlando, Fl: Academic Press.

Field, T. M., Woodson, R., Greenberg, R., & Cohen, D. (1982). Discrimination and imitation of facial expressions by neonates. *Science, 218,* 179–181.

Fitzgerald, H. E. (1968). Autonomic pupillary reflex activity during early infancy and its relation to social and nonsocial visual stimuli. *Journal of Experimental Child Psychology, 6,* 470–482.

Fitzgerald, H. E., Lintz, L. M., Brackbill, Y., & Adams, G. (1967). Time perception and conditioning of an autonomic response in human infants. *Perceptual & Motor Skills, 24,* 479–486.

Fivush, R., Kuebli, J., & Clubb, P. A. (1992). The structure of events and event representations: A developmental analysis. *Child Development, 63,* 188–201.

Fox, N. A. (1989). Psychophysiological correlates of emotional reactivity during the first year of life. *Developmental Psychology, 25,* 364–372.

Franks, A., & Berg, W. K. (1975). Effects of visual complexity and sex of infant in the conjugate reinforcement paradigm. *Developmental Psychology, 11,* 388–389.

Friedlander, B. Z. (1961). Automated measurement of differential operant performance. *American Psychologist, 16,* 350.

Galluccio, L., & Rovee-Collier, C. (2000). Reinstatement effects on retention at 3 months of age. *Learning and Motivation, 30,* 296–316.

Galluccio, L., & Rovee-Collier, C. (2001). Time window effects of reinstatement on infant long-term retention. Manuscript submitted for publication.

Gekoski, M. J., Rovee-Collier, C., & Carulli-Rabinowitz, V. (1983). A longitudinal analysis of inhibition of infant distress: The origins of social expectations? *Infant Behavior and Development, 6,* 339–351.

Gelman, R. (1978). Counting in the preschooler: What does and does not develop. In R. S. Siegler (Ed.), *Children's thinking: What develops?* (pp. 213–241). Hillsdale, NJ: Erlbaum.

Gerhardstein, P., Adler, S. A., & Rovee-Collier, C. (2000). A dissociation in infants' memory for stimulus size: Evidence for the early development of multiple memory systems. *Developmental Psychobiology, 36,* 123–135.

Gerhardstein, P., Liu, J., & Rovee-Collier, C. (1998). Perceptual constraints on infant memory. *Journal of Experimental Child Psychology, 69,* 109–131.

Gerhardstein, P., Renner, P., & Rovee-Collier, C. (1999). The role of conceptual and perceptual similarity in colour pop-out in infants. *British Journal of Developmental Psychology, 17,* 403–420.

Gerhardstein, P., & Rovee-Collier, C. (in press). The development of visual search in infants and very young children. *Journal of Experimental Child Psychology.*

Girton, M. (1979). Infants' attention to intrastimulus motion. *Journal of Experimental Child Psychology, 28,* 416–423.

Gordon, W. C. (1981). Mechanisms of cue-induced retention enhancement. In N. E. Spear & R. R. Miller (Eds.), *Information processing in animals: Memory mechanisms* (pp. 319–339). Hillsdale, NJ: Erlbaum.

Gottlieb, G. (1971). Ontogenesis of sensory function in birds and mammals. In E. Tobach, L. A. Aronson, & E. Shaw (Eds.), *The biopsychology of development* (pp. 67–128). New York: Academic Press.

Goubet, N., & Clifton, R. K. (1998). Object and event representation in 6½-month-old infants. *Developmental Psychology, 34,* 63–76.

Graham, F. K. (1973). Habituation and dishabituation of responses innervated by the autonomic nervous system. In H. V. S. Peeke and M. J. Herz (Eds.), *Habituation* (Vol. 1, pp. 163–218). New York: Academic Press.

Graham, F. K., & Clifton, R. K. (1966). Heart-rate change as a component of the orienting response. *Psychological Bulletin, 65,* 305–320.

Graham, F. K., & Jackson, J. C. (1970). Arousal systems and infant heart rate responses. In H. W. Reese & L. P. Lipsitt (Eds.), *Advances in child development and behavior* (Vol. 5, pp. 59–117). New York: Academic Press.

Greco, C., & Daehler, M. W. (1985). Immediate and long-term retention of basic-level categories in 24-month-olds. *Infant Behavior and Development, 8,* 459–474.

Greco, C., Hayne, H., & Rovee-Collier, C. (1990). The roles of function, reminding, and variability in categorization by 3-month-old infants. *Journal of Experimental Psychology: Learning, Memory, and Cognition, 16,* 617–633.

Guillaume, P. (1926/1971). *Imitation in children* (E. P. Halperin, Trans.). Chicago: University of Chicago Press.

Gulya, M. (2000, May). *The development of memory for serial order.* Unpublished doctoral dissertation, Rutgers University, New Brunswick, NJ.

Gulya, M., Rovee-Collier, C., Galluccio, L., & Wilk, A. (1998). Memory processing of a serial list by very young infants. *Psychological Science, 9,* 303–307.

Gulya, M., Sweeney, B., & Rovee-Collier, C. (1999). Memory processing of a serial list by infants: List length effects. *Journal of Experimental Child Psychology, 73,* 72–91.

Hainline, L. (1978). Developmental changes in visual scanning of faces and nonface patterns by infants. *Journal of Experimental Child Psychology, 25,* 90–115.

Haith, M. M., Hazan, C., & Goodman, G. S. (1988). Expectation and anticipation of dynamic visual events by 3.5-month-old infants. *Child Development, 59,* 467–479.

Haith, M. M., Wentworth, N., & Canfield, R. L. (1993). The formation of expectations in early infancy. In C. Rovee-Collier & L. P. Lipsitt (Eds.), *Advances in infancy research* (Vol. 8, pp. 251–297). Norwood, NJ: Ablex.

Harlow, H. F. (1949). The formation of learning sets. *Psychological Review, 56,* 51–65.

Hartshorn, K., & Rovee-Collier, C. (1997). Infant learning and long-term memory at 6 months: A confirming analysis. *Developmental Psychobiology, 30,* 71–85.

Hartshorn, K., Rovee-Collier, C., Gerhardstein, P., Bhatt, R. S., Klein, P. J., Aaron, F., Wondoloski, T. L., & Wurtzel, N. (1998a). Developmental changes in the specificity of memory over the first year of life. *Developmental Psychobiology, 33,* 61–78.

Hartshorn, K., Rovee-Collier, C., Gerhardstein, P., Bhatt, R. S., Wondoloski, T. L., Klein, P. J., Gilch, J., Wurtzel, N., & Campos-de-Carvalho, M. (1998b). The ontogeny of long-term memory over the first year-and-a-half of life. *Developmental Psychobiology, 32,* 1–31.

Hartshorn, K., Wilk, A., Muller, K., & Rovee-Collier, C. (1998c). An expanding training series protracts retention for 3-month-old infants. *Developmental Psychobiology, 33,* 271–282.

Hasher, L., & Zacks, R. T. (1979). Automatic and effortful processes in memory. *Journal of Experimental Psychology: General, 108,* 356–388.

Hauser, M. (2000). What do animals think about numbers? *American Scientist, 88,* 144–151.

Hayne, H. (1990). The effect of multiple reminders on long-term retention in human infants. *Developmental Psychobiology, 23,* 453–477.

Hayne, H. (1996). Categorization in infancy. In C. Rovee-Collier & L. P. Lipsitt (Eds.), *Advances in infancy research* (Vol. 10, pp. 79–120). Norwood, NJ: Ablex.

Hayne, H., Boniface, J., & Barr, R. (2000a). The development of declarative memory in human infants: Age-related changes in deferred imitation. *Behavioral Neuroscience, 114,* 77–83.

Hayne, H., & Findlay, N. (1995). Contextual control of memory retrieval in infancy: Evidence for associative priming. *Infant Behavior and Development, 18,* 195–207.

Hayne, H., Greco, C., Earley, L. A., Griesler, P. C., & Rovee-Collier, C. (1986). Ontogeny of early event memory: II. Encoding and retrieval by 2- and 3-month-olds. *Infant Behavior and Development, 9,* 441–460.

Hayne, H., Gross, J., Hildreth, K., & Rovee-Collier, C. (2000b). Repeated reminders increase the speed of memory retrieval in 3-month-old infants. *Developmental Science, 3,* 312–318.

Hayne, H., MacDonald, S., & Barr, R. (1997). Developmental changes in the specificity of memory over the second year of life. *Infant Behavior and Development, 20,* 233–245.

Hayne, H., Rovee-Collier, C., & Perris, E. E. (1987). Categorization and memory retrieval in 3-month-olds. *Child Development, 58,* 750–767.

Henderson, B. B., & Dias, L. (1985, April). *An exploratory study of infant problem solving in natural environments.* Paper presented at the meeting of the Society for Research in Child Development, Toronto, Canada.

Herbert, J., & Hayne, H. (2000). *Differences between deferred and elicited imitation procedures: Do they matter?* Paper presented at the International Conference on Infant Studies, Brighton, UK.

Hermer, L., & Spelke, E. S. (1994). A geometric process for spatial reorientation in young children. *Nature, 370,* 57–59.

Hildreth, K., & Rovee-Collier, C. (1999). Decreases in the response latency to priming over the first year of life. *Developmental Psychobiology, 35,* 276–290.

Hildreth, K., Wawrzyniak, K., Barr, R., & Rovee-Collier, C. (1999, April). *The reforgetting of reactivated memories between 6 and 12 months of age.* Paper presented at the meeting of the Eastern Psychological Association, Providence, RI.

Hood, B. M. (1995). Shifts in visual attention in the human infant: A neuroscientific approach. In C. Rovee-Collier & L. P. Lipsitt (Eds.), *Advances in infancy research* (Vol. 9, pp. 163–216). Norwood, NJ: Ablex.

Hood, B. M., & Willatts, P. (1986). Reaching in the dark to an object's remembered position: Evidence for object permanence in 5-month-old infants. *British Journal of Developmental Psychology, 4,* 57–65.

Horowitz, F. D., Paden, L., Bhana, K., & Self, P. (1972). An infant-control procedure for studying infant visual fixations. *Developmental Psychology, 7,* 90.

Howe, M. L., Courage, M. L., & Bryant-Brown, L. (1993). Reinstating preschoolers' memories. *Developmental Psychology, 29,* 854–869.

Hudson, J., & Sheffield, E. G. (1998). Deja vu all over again: Effects of reenactment on toddlers' event memory. *Child Development, 69,* 51–67.

Hulsebus, R. C. (1973). Operant conditioning of infant behavior: A review. In H. W. Reese (Ed.), *Advances in child development and behavior* (Vol. 8, pp. 111–158). New York: Academic Press.

Hunter, M. A., & Ames, E. W. (1988). A multifactor model of infant preferences for novel and familiar stimuli. In C. Rovee-Collier & L. P. Lipsitt (Eds.), *Advances in infancy research* (Vol. 5, pp. 69–95). Norwood, NJ: Ablex.

Hunter, W. S. (1913). The delayed reaction in animals and children. *Behavioral Monographs, 2,* 52–62.

Hunter, W. S. (1917). The delayed reaction in a child. *Psychological Review, 24,* 74–87.

Irwin, O. C. (1930). Amount and nature of activities of newborn infants under constant external stimulating conditions during the first ten days of life. *Genetic Psychology Monographs, 8,* 1–92.

Ivkovich, D., Collins, K., Eckerman, C. O., Krasnegor, N. A., & Stanton, M. E. (1999). Classical delay eyeblink conditioning in 4- and 5-month-old human infants. *Psychological Science, 10,* 4–8.

Ivkovich, D., Collins, K., Eckerman, C. O., Krasnegor, N. A., & Stanton, M. E. (2000). Using eyeblink conditioning to assess neurocognitive development in human infants. In D. S. Woodruff-Pak & J. E. Steinmetz (Eds.), *Eyeblink classical conditioning. Vol. 1: Applications in humans* (pp. 119–142). Boston: Kluwer Academic.

Jeffrey, W. E. (1968). The orienting reflex and attention in cognitive development. *Psychological Review, 75,* 323–334.

Johnson, M. H. (1990). Cortical maturation and the development of visual attention in early infancy. *Journal of Cognitive Neuroscience, 2,* 81–95.

Jones, H. E. (1930). The retention of conditioned emotional reactions in infancy. *Journal of Genetic Psychology, 37,* 485–498.

Julesz, B. (1984). A brief outline of the texton theory of human vision. *Trends in Neurosciences, 7,* 41–45.

Jusczyk, P. W. (1985). The high-amplitude sucking technique as a methodological tool in speech perception research. In G. Gottlieb & N. A. Krasnegor (Eds.), *Measurement of audition and vision during the first year of postnatal life: A methodological overview.* Norwood, NJ: Ablex.

Kalnins, I. V., & Bruner, J. S. (1973). The coordination of visual observation and instrumental behavior in early infancy. *Perception, 2,* 307–314.

Kasatkin, N. I., & Levikova, A. M. (1935). The formation of visual conditioned reflexes in infants during the first year of life. *Journal of General Psychology, 12,* 416–435.

Kaye, H. (1967). Infant sucking and its modification. In L. P. Lipsitt & H. W. Reese (Eds.), *Advances in child development and behavior* (Vol. 3, pp. 1–52). New York: Academic Press.

Kimble, G. (Ed.). (1961). *Hilgard and Marquis' conditioning and learning.* New York: Appleton-Century-Crofts.

Kimmel, H. D. (1973). Habituation, habituability, and conditioning. In H. V. S. Peeke & M. J. Herz (Eds.), *Habituation* (Vol. 1, pp. 219–238). New York: Academic Press.

Kobre, K. R., & Lipsitt, L. P. (1972). A negative contrast effect in newborns. *Journal of Experimental Child Psychology, 14,* 81–91.

Koch, J. (1967). Conditioned orienting reactions in two-month-old infants. *British Journal of Psychology, 58,* 105–110.

Koch, J. (1968). Conditioned orienting reactions to persons and things in 2–5 month old infants. *Human Development, 11,* 81–91.

Korner, A. F. (1972). State as variable, as obstacle, and as mediator of stimulation in infant research. *Merrill-Palmer Quarterly, 18,* 77–94.

Krachkovskaia, M. V. (1959). Conditioned leukocytosis in newborn infants. *Pavlov Journal of Higher Nervous Activity, 9,* 193–199. [Translated and reprinted in Y. Brackbill & G. G. Thompson (Eds.), *Behavior in infancy and early childhood.* New York: Free Press, 1967.]

Krasnogorskii, N. I. (1907). The formation of conditioned reflexes in the young child. [Translated and reprinted in Y. Brackbill & G. G. Thompson (Eds.), *Behavior in infancy and early childhood.* New York: Free Press, 1967.]

Kron, R. E. (1966). Instrumental conditioning of nutritive sucking behavior in the newborn. *Recent Advances in Biological Psychiatry, 9,* 295–300.

Kuhl, P., Andruski, J. E., Chistovich, I. A., Chistovich, L. A., Kozhevnikova, E., Ryskina, V. L., Stolyarova, E. I., Sundberg, U., & Lacerda, F. (1997). Cross-language analysis of phonetic units in language addressed to infants. *Science, 277,* 684–686.

Learmonth, A. E. (1998). *Disoriented toddlers can use both landmarks and geometry to reorient.* Unpublished doctoral dissertation, Temple University, Philadelphia, PA.

Lenard, H. G., von Bernuth, H., & Prechtl, H. F. R. (1968). Reflexes and their relationship to behavioral state in the newborn. *Acta Paediatrica Scandinavica, 57,* 177–185.

Leslie, A. (1984). Spatiotemporal continuity and the perception of causality in infants. *Perception, 13,* 287–305.

Leslie, A., & Keeble, S. (1987). Do six-month-old infants perceive causality? *Cognition, 25,* 265–288.

Leslie, A., Xu, F., Tremoulet, P., & Scholl, B. (1998). Indexing and the object concept: Developing "what" and "where" systems. *Trends in Cognitive Sciences, 2,* 10–18.

Levison, C. A., & Levison, P. K. (1967). Operant conditioning of head turning for visual reinforcement in three-month-old infants. *Psychonomic Science, 8,* 529–530.

Ling, B. C. (1941). Form discrimination as a learning cue in infants. *Comparative Psychology Monographs. 17,* No. 2, 1–66.

Lipsitt, L. P., & Kaye, H. (1964). Conditioned sucking in the human newborn. *Psychonomic Science, 1,* 29–30.

Lipsitt, L. P., & Levy, N. (1959). Electrotactual threshold in the neonate. *Child Development, 30,* 547–554.

Lipsitt, L. P., Pederson, L. J., & DeLucia, C. A. (1966). Conjugate reinforcement of operant responding in infants. *Psychonomic Science, 4,* 67–68.

Little, A. H. (1970). *Eyelid conditioning in the human infant as a function of the interstimulus interval.* Unpublished master's thesis, Brown University, Providence, RI.

Little, A. H. (1973). *A comparative study of trace and delay conditioning in the human infant.* Unpublished doctoral dissertation, Brown University, Providence, RI.

Little, A. H., Lipsitt, L. P., & Rovee-Collier, C. (1984). Classical conditioning and retention of the infant's eyelid response: Effects of age and interstimulus interval. *Journal of Experimental Child Psychology, 37,* 512–524.

Lockman, J. J. (1984). The development of detour ability during infancy. *Child Development, 55,* 482–491.

Mandler, J. M. (1998). Representation. In W. Damon (Ed.), *Handbook of child psychology: Cognition, perception, & language* (Vol. 2, pp. 255–307). New York: Wiley.

Mandler, J. M., & Bauer, P. J. (1988). The cradle of categorization: Is the basic level basic? *Cognitive Development, 3,* 247–264.

Mandler, J. M., Fivush, R., & Resnick, J. S. (1987). The development of contextual categories. *Cognitive Development, 2,* 339–354.

Mandler, J. M., & McDonough, L. (1995). Long-term recall of event sequences in infancy. *Journal of Experimental Child Psychology, 59,* 457–474.

Marquis, D. P. (1941). Learning in the neonate: The modification of behavior under three feeding schedules. *Journal of Experimental Psychology, 29,* 263–282.

Mateer, F. (1918). *A critical and experimental study of young children by the method of conditioned reflexes.* Boston: Gorham.

Maurer, D., & Salapatek, P. (1976). Developmental changes in the scanning of faces by young infants. *Child Development, 47,* 523–527.

McCall, R. B., & Carriger, M. S. (1993). A meta-analysis of infant habituation and recognition memory performance as predictors of later IQ. *Child Development, 64,* 57–79.

McCall, R. B., & Kagan, J. (1970). Individual differences in the infants' distribution of attention to stimulus discrepancy. *Developmental Psychology, 2,* 90–98.

McCall, R. B., Parke, R. D., & Kavanaugh, R. D. (1977). Imitation of live and televised models by children one to three years of age. *Monographs of the Society for Research on Child Development, 42*(5, Serial No. 173).

McKirdy, L. S., & Rovee, C. K. (1978). The efficacy of auditory and visual conjugate reinforcers in infant conditioning. *Journal of Experimental Child Psychology, 25,* 80–89.

Medin, D. L., & Schaffer, M. (1978). Context theory of classification learning. *Psychological Review, 85,* 207–238.

Mehler, J., & Bever, T. G. (1967). Cognitive capacity of very young children. *Science, 158,* 141–142.

Meltzoff, A. N. (1988a). Infant imitation and memory: Nine-month-olds in immediate and deferred tests. *Child Development, 59,* 217–225.

Meltzoff, A. N. (1988b). Imitation of televised models by infants. *Child Development, 59,* 1221–1229.

Meltzoff, A. N. (1995). What infant memory tells us about infantile amnesia: Long-term recall and deferred imitation. *Journal of Experimental Child Psychology, 59,* 497–515.

Meltzoff, A. N., & Kuhl, P. (1989). Infants' perception of faces and speech sounds: Challenges to developmental theory. In P. R. Zelazo & R. G. Barr (Eds.), *Challenges to developmental paradigms: Implications for theory, assessment, and treatment* (pp. 67–91). Hillsdale, NJ: Erlbaum.

Meltzoff, A. N., & Kuhl, P. (1996). Infant vocalizations in response to speech: Vocal imitation and developmental change. *Journal of Acoustical Society of America, 100,* 2425–2438.

Meltzoff, A. N., & Moore, M. K. (1977). Imitation of facial and manual gestures by human neonates. *Science, 198,* 75–78.

Meltzoff, A. N., & Moore, M. K. (1983). Newborn infants imitate adult facial gestures. *Child Development, 54,* 702–709.

Meltzoff, A. N., & Moore, M. K. (1989). Imitation in newborn infants: Exploring the range of gestures imitated and the underlying mechanisms. *Developmental Psychology, 25,* 954–962.

Meltzoff, A. N., & Moore, M. K. (1992). Early imitation within a functional framework: The importance of person identity, movement, and development. *Infant Behavior and Development, 15,* 479–505.

Meltzoff, A. N., & Moore, M. K. (1994). Imitation, memory, and the representation of persons. *Infant Behavior and Development, 17,* 83–99.

Meltzoff, A. N., & Moore, M. K. (1998). Object representation, identity, and the paradox of early permanence: Steps toward a new framework. *Infant Behavior and Development, 21,* 201–236.

Merriman, J., Rovee-Collier, C., & Wilk, A. (1997). Exemplar spacing and infants' memory for category information. *Infant Behavior and Development, 20,* 219–232.

Milewski, A. E. (1976). Infants' discrimination of internal and external pattern elements. *Journal of Experimental Child Psychology, 22,* 229–246.

Milewski, A. E., & Siqueland, E. R. (1975). Discrimination of color and pattern novelty in one-month human infants. *Journal of Experimental Child Psychology, 19,* 122–136.

Millar, W. S. (1974). The role of visual-holding cues and the simultanizing strategy in infant operant learning. *British Journal of Psychology, 65,* 505–518.

Millar, W. S. (1990). Span of integration for delayed-reward contingency learning in 6- to 8-month-old infants. In A. Diamond (Ed.), *Annals of the New York Academy of Sciences: Vol. 608. The development and neural bases* of higher cognitive functions (pp. 239–266). New York: New York Academy of Sciences.

Millar, W. S., & Schaffer, H. R. (1972). The influence of spatially displaced feedback on infant operant conditioning. *Journal of Experimental Child Psychology, 14,* 442–453.

Millar, W. S., & Schaffer, H. R. (1973). Visual-manipulative response strategies in infant operant conditioning with spatially displaced feedback. *British Journal of Psychology, 64,* 545–552.

Millar, W. S., & Watson, J. S. (1979). The effect of delayed feedback on infant learning reexamined. *Child Development, 50,* 747–751.

Miller, D. J., Ryan, E. B., Sinnott, J. P., & Wilson, M. A. (1976). Serial habituation in two-, three-, and four-month-old infants. *Child Development, 20,* 367–373.

Mills, M., & Melhuish, E. (1974). Recognition of mother's voice in early infancy. *Nature, 252,* 123–124.

Molfese, D. L., & Wetzel, W. F. (1992). Short- and long-term auditory recognition in 14-month-old human infants: Electrophysiological correlates. *Developmental Neuropsychology, 8,* 135–160.

Morgan, C. L. (1900). *Animal behaviour.* London: Arnold.

Morgan, M. J., Fitch, M. D., Holman, J. G., & Lea, S. E. G. (1975). Pigeons learn the concept of an "A." *Perception, 5,* 57–66.

Nakao, K., & Treas, J. (1992). *The 1989 Socioeconomic Index of Occupations: Construction from the 1989 Occupational Prestige Scores* (General Social Survey Methodological Reports No. 74). Chicago: NORC.

Nakayama, K., & Silverman, G. H. (1986). Serial and parallel processing of visual feature conjunctions. *Nature, 320,* 264–265.

Needham, A. (1998). Infants' use of featural information in the segregation of stationary objects. *Infant Behavior and Development, 21,* 47–76.

Needham, A., & Baillargeon, R. (1997). Object Segregation in 8-month-old infants. *Cognition, 62,* 121–149.

Needham, A., & Baillargeon, R. (1998). Effects of prior experience on 4.5-month-old infants'

object segregation. *Infant Behavior and Development, 21,* 1–24.

Needham, A., & Baillargeon, R. (2000). Infants' use of featural and experiential information in segregating and individuating objects: A reply to Xu, Carey, & Welch (2000). *Cognition, 74,* 255–284.

Needham, A., & Modi, A. (1999). Infants' use of prior experiences with objects in object segregation: Implications for object-recognition in infancy. In H. W. Reese (Ed.), *Advances in child development and behavior* (Vol. 27, pp. 99–133). San Diego: Academic Press.

Nelson, C. A., & Collins, P. A. (1991). Event-related potential and looking time analysis of infants' responses to familiar and novel events: Implications for visual recognition memory. *Developmental Psychology, 31,* 723–735.

Nelson, C. A., & Nugent, K. (1990). Recognition memory and resource allocation as revealed by children's event-related potential responses to happy and angry faces. *Developmental Psychology, 26,* 171–179.

Oakes, L. M., & Cohen, L. B. (1995). Infant causal perception. In C. Rovee-Collier & L. P. Lipsitt (Eds.), *Advances in infancy research* (Vol. 9, pp. 1–51). Norwood, NJ: Ablex.

Oakes, L. M., Madole, K. L., & Cohen, L. B. (1991). Infants' object examining: Habituation and categorization. *Cognitive Development, 6,* 377–392.

Ohr, P. S., Fagen, J. W., Rovee-Collier, C., Hayne, H., & Vander Linde, E. (1989). Amount of training and retention by infants. *Developmental Psychobiology, 22,* 69–80.

Olson, G. M. (1976). An information processing analysis of visual memory and habituation in infants. In T. J. Tighe & R. N. Leaton (Eds.), *Habituation* (pp. 239–277). Hillsdale, NJ: Erlbaum.

Olson, G. M., & Sherman, T. (1983). Attention, learning, and memory in infants. In P. H. Mussen (Series Ed.), M. M. Haith, & J. J. Campos (Vol. Eds.), *Handbook of child psychology: Vol. 2. Infancy and developmental psychobiology* (4th ed., pp. 1001–1080). New York: Wiley.

Papousek, H. (1959). A method of studying conditioned food reflexes in young children up to the age of six months. *Pavlov Journal of Higher Nervous Activity, 9,* 136–140.

Papousek, H. (1961). Conditioned head rotation reflexes in infants in the first months of life. *Acta Pediatrics, 50,* 565–576.

Papousek, H. (1967). Conditioning during early postnatal development. In Y. Brackbill & G. G. Thompson (Eds.), *Behavior in infancy and early childhood* (pp. 259–274). New York: Free Press.

Papousek, H. (1969). Individual variability in learned responses in human infants. In R. J. Robinson (Ed.), *Brain and early behaviour* (pp. 251–263). London: Academic Press.

Pascalis, O., deHaan, M., Nelson, C. A., & deSchonen, S. (1998). Long-term recognition memory for faces assessed by visual paired comparison in 3- and 6-month-old infants. *Journal of Experimental Psychology: Learning, Memory, and Cognition, 24,* 1–12.

Pavlov, I. P. (1927). *Conditioned reflexes* (G. V. Anrep, Trans.). London: Oxford University Press.

Peiper, A. (1963). *Cerebral function in infancy and childhood.* New York: Consultants Bureau.

Perner, J., Ruffman, T., & Leekam, S. R. (1994). Theory of mind is contagious: You catch it from your sibs. *Child Development, 65,* 1228–1238.

Piaget, J. (1954). *The construction of reality in the child.* New York: Basic Books.

Piaget, J. (1962). *Play, dreams, and imitation in children.* London: Routledge & Kegan Paul. (Original work published 1927)

Posner, M. I., & Keele, S. W. (1970). Retention of abstract ideas. *Journal of Experimental Psychology, 83,* 304–308.

Poulson, C. L. (1983). Differential reinforcement of other-than-vocalization as a control procedure in the conditioning of infant vocalization rate. *Journal of Experimental Child Psychology, 36,* 471–489.

Poulson, C. L. (1984). Operant theory and methodology in infant vocal conditioning. *Journal of Experimental Child Psychology, 38,* 103–113.

Prechtl, H. F. R. (1965). Problems of behavioral studies in the newborn infant. In D. S. Lehrman, R. A. Hinde, & E. Shaw (Eds.), *Advances in the study of behavior* (Vol. 1, pp. 75–98). New York: Academic Press.

Preyer, W. (1882/1888–1889). *Die Seele des Kindes.* Leipzig: Greiben. [Published in 1888–89 as *The mind of the child, Parts 1 & 2,* H. W. Brown, Trans.]. New York: Appleton.

Quinn, P. C., & Bhatt, R. S. (1998). Visual pop-out in young infants: Convergent evidence and an extension. *Infant Behavior and Development, 21,* 273–288.

Ramey, C. T., & Ourth, L. L. (1971). Delayed reinforcement and vocalization rates of infants. *Child Development, 42,* 291–297.

Ramey, C. T., & Watson, J. S. (1972). Nonsocial reinforcement of infants' vocalizations. *Developmental Psychology, 6,* 538.

Rescorla, R. A. (1966). Predictability and the number of pairings in Pavlovian fear conditioning. *Psychonomic Science, 4,* 383–384.

Rescorla, R. A. (1967). Pavlovian conditioning and its proper control procedures. *Psychological Review, 74,* 71–80.

Rheingold, H. L., Gewirtz, J. L., & Ross, H. W. (1959). Social conditioning of vocalizations. *Journal of Comparative and Physiological Psychology, 52,* 68–73.

Rheingold, H. L., Stanley, W. C., & Cooley, J. A. (1962). Method for studying exploratory behavior in infants. *Science, 136,* 1054–1055.

Richards, J. E. (2000). Localizing the development of covert attention in infants with scalp event-related potentials. *Developmental Psychology, 36,* 91–108.

Richards, J. E., & Lansink, J. M. (1998). Distractibility during visual fixation in young infants: The selectivity of attention. In C. Rovee-Collier, L. P. Lipsitt, & H. Hayne (Eds.), *Advances in infancy research* (Vol. 12, pp. 407–444). Norwood, NJ: Ablex.

Richardson, H. M. (1932). The growth of adaptive behavior in infants: An experimental study at seven age levels. *Genetic Psychology Monographs, 12,* 195–359.

Richardson, H. M. (1934). The adaptive behavior of infants in the utilization of the lever as a tool: A developmental and experimental study. *Pedagogical Seminary & Journal of Genetic Psychology, 44,* 352–377.

Ross, G. S. (1980). Categorization in 1- and 2-year-olds. *Developmental Psychology, 16,* 391–396.

Rossi-George, A., & Rovee-Collier, C. (1999). Retroactive interference in 3-month-old infants. *Developmental Psychobiology, 35,* 167–177.

Rovee, C. K., & Fagen, J. W. (1976). Extended conditioning and 24-hr retention in infants. *Journal of Experimental Child Psychology, 21,* 1–11.

Rovee, C. K., & Rovee, D. T. (1969). Conjugate reinforcement of infant exploratory behavior. *Journal of Experimental Child Psychology, 8,* 33–39.

Rovee-Collier, C. (1995). Time windows in cognitive development. *Developmental Psychology, 51,* 1–23.

Rovee-Collier, C. (1996a). Measuring infant memory: A critical commentary. *Developmental Review, 16,* 301–310.

Rovee-Collier, C. (1996b). Shifting the focus from What to Why. *Infant Behavior and Development, 19,* 385–401.

Rovee-Collier, C. (1997). Dissociations in infant memory: Rethinking the development of implicit and explicit memory. *Psychological Review, 104,* 467–498.

Rovee-Collier, C. (2001). Information pickup by infants: What is it, and how can we tell? *Journal of Experimental Child Psychology, 78,* 35–49.

Rovee-Collier, C., Adler, S. A., & Borza, M. A. (1994). Substituting new details for old? Effects of delaying postevent information on infant memory. *Memory & Cognition, 22,* 644–656.

Rovee-Collier, C., Bhatt, R. S., & Chazin, S. (1996). Set size, novelty, and visual pop-out in infancy. *Journal of Experimental Psychology: Human Perception and Performance, 22,* 1178–1187.

Rovee-Collier, C., Borza, M. A., Adler, S. A., & Boller, K. (1993). Infants' eyewitness testimony: Effects of postevent information on a prior memory representation. *Memory & Cognition, 21,* 267–279.

Rovee-Collier, C., & Capatides, J. B. (1979). Positive behavioral contrast in 3-month-old infants on multiple conjugate reinforcement schedules. *Journal of the Experimental Analysis of Behavior, 32,* 15–27.

Rovee-Collier, C., & DuFault, D. (1991). Multiple contexts and memory retrieval at 3 months. *Developmental Psychobiology, 24,* 39–49.

Rovee-Collier, C., Evancio, S., & Earley, L. A. (1995). The time window hypothesis: Spacing effects. *Infant Behavior and Development, 18,* 69–78.

Rovee-Collier, C., Greco-Vigorito, C., & Hayne, H. (1993). The time window hypothesis: Implications for categorization and memory modification. *Infant Behavior and Development, 16,* 149–176.

Rovee-Collier, C., Griesler, P. C., & Earley, L. A. (1985). Contextual determinants of infant retention. *Learning and Motivation, 16,* 139–157.

Rovee-Collier, C., Hankins, E., & Bhatt, R. S. (1992). Textons, visual pop-out effects, and object recognition in infancy. *Journal of Experimental Psychology: General, 121,* 436–444.

Rovee-Collier, C., Hartshorn, K., & DiRubbo, M. (1999). Long-term maintenance of infant memory. *Developmental Psychobiology, 35,* 91–102.

Rovee-Collier, C., & Hayne, H. (1987). Reactivation of infant memory: Implications for cognitive development. In H. W. Reese (Ed.), *Advances in child development and behavior* (Vol. 20, pp. 185–238). New York: Academic Press.

Rovee-Collier, C., & Hayne, H. (2000). Memory in infancy and early childhood. In E. Tulving & F.I.M. Craik (Eds.), *The Oxford handbook of memory* (pp. 267–282). New York: Oxford University Press.

Rovee-Collier, C., Hayne, H., & Colombo, M. (2001). *The development of implicit and explicit memory.* Amsterdam: John Benjamins.

Rovee-Collier, C., Morrongiello, B. A., Aron, M., & Kupersmidt, J. (1978). Topographical response differentiation and reversal in

3-month-old infants. *Infant Behavior and Development, 1,* 323–333.

Rovee-Collier, C., Sullivan, M. W., Enright, M. K., Lucas, D., & Fagen, J. W. (1980). Reactivation of infant memory. *Science, 208,* 1159–1161.

Ruff, H. A. (1984). Infants' manipulative exploration of objects: Effects of age and object characteristics. *Developmental Psychology, 20,* 9–20.

Ruff, H. A. (1986). Components of attention during infants' manipulative exploration. *Child Development, 57,* 105–114.

Sagi, D. (1988). The combination of spatial frequency and orientation is effortlessly perceived. *Perception & Psychophysics, 43,* 601–603.

Salapatek, P., & Kessen, W. (1966). Visual scanning of triangles by the human newborn. *Journal of Experimental Child Psychology, 3,* 155–167.

Sameroff, A. J. (1968). The components of sucking in the human newborn. *Journal of Experimental Child Psychology, 6,* 607–623.

Sameroff, A. J., & Cavanagh, P. J. (1979). Learning in infancy: A developmental perspective. In J. D. Osofsky (Ed.), *Handbook of infant development* (pp. 344–392). New York: Wiley.

Schmidt, R. A., & Bjork, R. A. (1992). New conceptualizations of practice: Common principles in three paradigms suggest new concepts for training. *Psychological Science, 3,* 207–217.

Schneider, B. A., & Trehub, S. E. (1985). Infant auditory psychophysics: An overview. In G. Gottlieb & N. A. Krasnegor (Eds.), *Measurement of audition and vision in the first year of postnatal life* (pp. 113–126). Norwood, NJ: Ablex.

Sheffield, E. G., & Hudson, J. A. (1994). Reactivation of toddlers' event memory. *Memory, 2,* 447–465.

Sherman, T. (1985). Categorization skills in infants. *Child Development, 56,* 1561–1573.

Shields, P. J., & Rovee-Collier, C. (1992). Long-term memory for context-specific category information at 6 months. *Child Development, 63,* 245–259.

Simmons, M. W., & Lipsitt, L. P. (1961). An operant-discrimination apparatus for infants.

Journal of the Experimental Analysis of Behavior, 4, 233–235.

Siqueland, E. R. (1964). Operant conditioning of headturning in four-month infants. *Psychonomic Science, 1,* 223–224.

Siqueland, E. R. (1968). Reinforcement patterns and extinction in human newborns. *Journal of Experimental Child Psychology, 6,* 431–432.

Siqueland E. R. (1969, July). *Further developments in infant learning.* Paper presented at the meeting of the 19th International Congress of Psychology, London.

Siqueland, E. R., & DeLucia, C. A. (1969). Visual reinforcement of nonnutritive sucking in human infants. *Science, 165,* 1144–1146.

Siqueland, E. R., & Lipsitt, L. P. (1966). Conditioned headturning in human newborns. *Journal of Experimental Child Psychology, 3,* 356–376.

Sireteanu, R. (2000). Texture segmentation, "popout," and feature binding in infants and children. In C. Rovee-Collier, L. P. Lipsitt, & H. Hayne (Eds.), *Progress in infancy research* (Vol. 1, pp. 183–249). Mahwah, NJ: Erlbaum.

Slater, A. (1995). Visual perception and memory at birth. In C. Rovee-Collier & L. P. Lipsitt (Eds.), *Advances in infancy research* (Vol. 9, pp. 107–162). Norwood, NJ: Ablex.

Smith, P. H. (1984). Five-month-old infants' recall of temporal order and utilization of temporal organization. *Journal of Experimental Child Psychology, 38,* 400–414.

Smith, P. H., Arehart, D. M., Haaf, R. A., & deSaint Victor, C. M. (1989). Expectancies and memory for spatiotemporal events in 5-month-old infants. *Journal of Experimental Child Psychology, 47,* 210–235.

Smith, P. H., Jankowski, J. J., Brewster, M., & Loboschefski, T. (1990). Preverbal infant response to spatiotemporal events: Evidence of differential chunking abilities. *Infant Behavior and Development, 13,* 129–146.

Smith, P. H., Loboschefski, T., Davidson, B. K., & Dixon, W. E., Jr. (1997). Scripts and checkerboards: The influence of ordered visual information on remembering locations in infancy. *Infant Behavior and Development, 20,* 549–552.

Smith, L. B., Thelen, E., Titzer, R., & McLin, D. (1999). Knowing in the context of acting: The task dynamics of the A-not-B error. *Psychological Review, 106,* 235–260.

Sokolov, E. N. (1963). Higher nervous functions: The orienting reflex. *Annual Review of Physiology, 25,* 545–580.

Spear, N. E., & Parsons, P. J. (1976). Analysis of a reactivation treatment: Ontogenetic determinants of alleviated forgetting. In D. L. Medin, W. A. Roberts, & R. T. Davis (Eds.), *Processes of animal memory* (pp. 135–165). Hillsdale, NJ: Erlbaum.

Spelke, E. (1990). Principles of object perception. *Cognitive Science, 14,* 29–56.

Spelke, E. (1994). Initial knowledge: Six suggestions. *Cognition, 50,* 431–445.

Spelke, E., & Kestenbaum, R. (1986). Les origines du concept d'object. *Psychologie Francaise, 31,* 67–72.

Spelke, E., Kestenbaum, R., Simons, D. J., & Wein, D. (1995). Spatiotemporal continuity, smoothness, of motion and object identity in infancy. *British Journal of Developmental Psychology, 13,* 113–143.

Starkey, D. (1981). The origins of concept formation: Object sorting and object preference in early infancy. *Child Development, 52,* 489–497.

Starkey, D., Spelke, E. S., & Gelman, R. (1983). Detection of intermodal numerical correspondences by human infants. *Science, 222,* 179–181.

Stolz, J. A., & Merikle, P. M. (2000). Conscious and unconscious influences of memory: Temporal dynamics. *Memory, 8,* 333–343.

Strauss, M. S. (1979). Abstraction of prototypical information by adults and 10-month-old infants. *Journal of Experimental Psychology: Human Learning and Memory, 5,* 618–632.

Strupp, B. J., & Levitsky, D. A. (1990). An animal model of retarded cognitive development. In C. Rovee-Collier & L. P. Lipsitt (Eds.), *Advances in infancy research* (Vol. 6, pp. 149-185). Norwood, NJ: Ablex.

Sugarman, S. (1982). Developmental change in early representational intelligence: Evidence from spatial classification strategies and related verbal expressions. *Cognitive Psychology, 14,* 410–449.

Sullivan, M. W. (1982). Reactivation: Priming forgotten memories in human infants. *Child Development, 57,* 100–104.

Sweeney, B., Hildreth, K., & Rovee-Collier, C. (2000, March). *Comparing reforgetting after reactivation and reinstatement at 6 months of age.* Paper presented at the meeting of the Eastern Psychological Association, Baltimore, MD.

Thoman, E. G., Korner, A. F., & Beason-Williams, L. (1977). Modification of responsiveness to maternal vocalization in the neonate. *Child Development, 48,* 563–569.

Thompson, L. A., Fagan, J. F., III., & Fuller, D. W. (1991). Longitudinal prediction of specific cognitive abilities from infant novelty preference. *Child Development, 62,* 530–538.

Thompson, R. F., & Spencer, W. A. (1966). A model phenomenon for the study of neuronal substrates of behavior. *Psychological Review, 73,* 16–43.

Timmons, C. T. (1994). Associative links between discrete memories in infancy. *Infant Behavior and Development, 17,* 431–445.

Tolman, E. C. (1948). Cognitive maps in rats and men. *Psychological Review, 55,* 189–208.

Tolman, E. C., Ritchie, B. F,, & Kalish, D. (1946). Studies in spatial learning: II. Place learning versus response learning. *Journal of Experimental Psychology, 36,* 221–229.

Treisman, A. M. (1982). Perceptual grouping and attention in visual search for features and for objects. *Journal of Experimental Psychology: Human Perception and Performance, 8,* 194–214.

Treisman, A. M. (1988). Features and objects: The Fourteenth Bartlett Memorial Lecture. *Quarterly Journal of Experimental Psychology, 40A,* 201–237.

Treisman, A. M., & Sato, S. (1990). Conjunction search revisited. *Journal of Experimental Psychology: Human Perception and Performance, 16,* 459–478.

Troseth, G. L., & DeLoache, J. S. (1998). The medium can obscure the message: Young children's understanding of video. *Child Development, 69,* 950–965.

Tuber, D. S., Berntson, G. G., Bachman, D. S., & Allen, J. N. (1980). Associative learning in premature hydraencephalic and normal twins. *Science, 210,* 1035–1037.

Tukey, J. W. (1977). *Exploratory data analysis.* Reading, MA: Addison-Wesley.

Tulving, E. (1983). *Elements of episodic memory.* Oxford, UK: Clarendon Press.

Ungerer, J. A., Brody, L. R., & Zelazo, P. R. (1978). Long-term memory for speech in 2- to 4-week-old infants. *Infant Behavior and Development, 1,* 177–186.

Uzgiris, I. C. (1981). Two functions of imitation during infancy. *International Journal of Behavioral Development, 4,* 1–12.

Uzgiris, I. C., & Hunt, J.McV. (1975). *Assessment in infancy.* Chicago: University of Illinois Press.

Valentine, C. W. (1930). The psychology of imitation with special reference to early childhood. *British Journal of Psychology, 21,* 105–132.

Vander Linde, E., Morrongiello, B. A., & Rovee-Collier, C. (1985). Determinants of retention in 8-week-old infants. *Developmental Psychology, 21,* 601–613.

Vieira, A., Barr, R., & Rovee-Collier, C. (2000, March). *Mediated recognition and priming at 6 months.* Paper presented at the meeting of the Eastern Psychological Association, Baltimore, MD.

Wachs, T. D., & Smitherman, C. H. (1985). Infant temperament and subject loss in a habituation procedure. *Child Development, 56,* 861–867.

Wahler, R. G. (1967). Infant social attachments: A reinforcement theory interpretation and investigation. *Child Development, 38,* 1079–1088.

Wallace, D. B., Franklin, M. B., & Keegan, R. T. (1994). The observing eye: A century of baby diaries. *Human Development, 37,* 1–29.

Watson, J. B., & Rayner, R. (1920). Conditioned emotional reactions. *Journal of Experimental Psychology, 3,* 1–14.

Watson, J. S. (1966). The development and generalization of "contingency awareness" in infancy:

Some hypotheses. *Merrill-Palmer Quarterly, 19,* 123–135.

Watson, J. S. (1969). Operant conditioning of visual fixation in infants under visual and auditory reinforcement. *Developmental Psychology, 1,* 508–516.

Watson, J. S. (1972). Smiling, cooing, and "the game." *Merrill-Palmer Quarterly, 18,* 323–329.

Watson, J. S., & Ramey, C. T. (1972). Reactions to response-contingent stimulation. *Merrill-Palmer Quarterly, 18,* 219–227.

Weisberg, P. (1963). Social and nonsocial conditioning of infant vocalizations. *Child Development, 34,* 377–388.

Weisberg, P., & Fink, E. (1968). Effect of varying and nonvarying stimulus consequences on visual persistence in twenty-month-old infants. *Perceptual & Motor Skills, 26,* 883–887.

Weizmann, F., Cohen, L. B., & Pratt, R. J. (1971). Novelty, familiarity, and the development of infant attention. *Developmental Psychology, 4,* 149–154.

Wellman, H. M., Cross, D., & Bartsch, K. (1987). Infant search and object permanence: A meta-analysis of the A-not-B error. *Monographs of the Society for Research in Child Development, 51,* 259–272.

Wickens, D. D., & Wickens, C. A. (1940). A study of conditioning in the neonate. *Journal of Experimental Psychology, 26,* 94–102.

Wilcox, T. (1999). Object individuation: Infants' use of shape, size, pattern, and color. *Cognition, 72,* 125–166.

Wilcox, T., & Baillargeon, R. (1998a). Object individuation in infancy: The use of featural information in reasoning about occlusion events. *Cognitive Psychology, 37,* 97–155.

Wilcox, T., & Baillargeon, R. (1998b). Object individuation in young infants: Further evidence with an event-monitoring paradigm. *Developmental Science, 1,* 127–142.

Wolfe, J. M., Franzel, S. L., & Cave, K. R. (1988). Parallel visual search for conjunctions of color and form. *Journal of the Optical Society of America, 4A,* 95.

Wolfe, J. M., Yee, A., & Friedman-Hill, S. R. (1992). Curvature is a basic feature for visual search tasks. *Perception, 21,* 465–480.

Woodruff-Pak, D. S., & Steinmetz, J. E. (Eds.). (2000a). *Eyeblink classical conditioning: Vol. 1. Applications in humans.* Boston: Kluwer Academic.

Woodruff-Pak, D. S., & Steinmetz, J. E. (Eds.). (2000b). *Eyeblink classical conditioning: Vol. 2. Applications in animals.* Boston: Kluwer Academic.

Wright, A. A., Santiago, H. C., Sands, S. F., Kendrick, D. F., & Cook, R. G. (1985). Memory processing of serial lists by pigeons, monkeys, and people. *Science, 22,* 287–289.

Wyers, E. J., Peeke, H. V. S., & Herz, M. J. (1973). Behavioral habituation in invertebrates. In H. V. S. Peeke & M. J. Herz (Eds.), *Habituation* (Vol. 1, pp. 1–57). New York: Academic Press.

Wynn, K. (1992). Addition and subtraction by human infants. *Nature, 358,* 749–750.

Wynn, K. (1995). Infants possess a system of numerical knowledge. *Current Directions in Psychological Science, 4,* 172–177.

Wynn, K. (1996). Individuals' individuation and enumeration of actions. *Psychological Science, 7,* 164–169.

Xu, F., & Carey, S. (1996). Infants' metaphysics: The case of numerical identity. *Cognitive Psychology, 30,* 111–153.

Xu, F., & Carey, S. (2000). The emergence of kind concepts: A rejoinder to Needham & Baillargeon (2000). *Cognition, 74,* 285–301.

Younger, B. A. (1990). Infant categorization: Memory for category-level and specific item information. *Journal of Experimental Child Psychology, 50,* 131–155.

Younger, B. A., & Cohen, L. B. (1983). Infant perception of correlations among attributes. *Child Development, 54,* 858–867.

Younger, B. A., & Cohen, L. B. (1986). Developmental change in infants' perceptions of correlations among attributes. *Child Development, 57,* 803–815.

Younger, B. A., & Gotlieb, S. (1988). Development of categorization skills: Changes in the nature or structure of infant form categories? *Developmental Psychology, 24,* 611–619.

CHAPTER 18

Aging and Cognition

PATRICK RABBITT

Demographic changes make the study of cognitive aging of urgent practical interest. It is also theoretically important because it highlights the inadequacy of current functional models in mainstream cognitive psychology. These, almost without exception, describe artificial single-steady-state systems that do not account for individual differences in cognitive competence, describe how peoples' abilities change as they grow up or grow old, or explain how older people lose skills that they once performed superbly well.

Individual differences in age may seem trivially simple to define and measure in comparison to more contentious dimensions of individual difference, such as intelligence (Howe, 1999). This is not so, because aging is not merely the passage of time but rather a complex of processes that proceed at different rates in different people and in different parts of the brain and central nervous systems of individual persons. This distinction between time and process has been acknowledged by a contrast between chronological aging, indexed in calendar time, and biological aging, indexed in terms of the progress of changes in physiological indices of aging, or in terms of residual life expectancy (e.g., Jalavisto & Nakkonen, 1963). The particular models for biological aging that we adopt are key to methodology in cognitive gerontology because they determine both the groups

of people that we study and the tasks on which we compare them.

It is therefore surprising that most studies in a voluminous literature have ignored both the theoretical necessity to relate cognitive changes to biological changes in the sense organs and central nervous system (CNS) and the opportunity to enrich mainstream cognitive psychology by developing better functional models for change and for individual differences. Most investigators have compared small groups of younger and older people whose biological and health status have been established by unelaborated self-report of adequacy, or not at all, on tasks that were originally designed to test details of hypothetical steady-state functional models for attention, memory, and decision in young adults. Biological changes are not the sole determinants of cognitive status in later life, but cognitive change in old age cannot be understood unless biology is taken into account. Models for biological or cognitive aging are also inadequate unless they also include demographic, social, and life-style factors. For example, prolonged education, lengthy marriage to an intelligent spouse, complexity of workplace environment, higher income, and personality factors have all been shown to affect maintenance of cognitive functioning in old age (e.g., Arbuckle, Gold, & Andres, 1986; Hayslip, 1988; Schaie, 1990b). Some useful frameworks have been proposed to account for these relationships (e.g., Schooler, 1984). However because the overwhelming majority of studies of behavioral changes in old age have been based on comparisons between very small groups of older and younger people, they have found it convenient to ignore these factors and so to promote a tacit assumption that cognitive aging follows an identical path in all individuals. This is unfortunate because the key finding that theories of cognitive gerontology must explain is not that the average levels of performance of small samples decline as they age but the striking individual differences in the trajectories of change that individuals experience (Rabbitt, Diggle, Holland, Smith, & McInnes, 2001). Methodology must be guided by recognition that because individual differences in trajectories of aging are determined by the separate and interactive effects of a very large number of different factors, the time course of changes at the levels of individuals are usually strikingly different from that of population averages.

MEASURING BIOLOGICAL AGING

The passage of time affects all physiological systems, and there is little agreement as to which of many changes are the best markers for processes that may be collectively termed biological aging. Because no single marker is adequate, investigators have used a range of different measures of physiological function to develop biological aging profiles for animals of different ages, or have sought relationships between physiological indices that can be included in factor analyses (e.g., Borkan & Norris, 1980; Clark, 1960) or discrimination analyses (e.g., Hofecker, Skalicky, Khment, & Niedermuller, 1980) to derive composite, or aggregated, indices of aging. The most common tool for modeling biological aging has

been the use of hierarchical linear regression analyses to assess the relative strengths of predictors of longevity (e.g., Dundikova, Silvon, & Dubina, 1978; Furkawa, Inoue, Kajiya & Abe, 1975; Voitenko, & Tokar, 1983). In applied studies of human aging, biological age has sometimes been equated to functional age with reference to externally determined criteria of capability for self-maintenance in the community, or the ability to keep up with the demands of particular industrial tasks (e.g., Dirken, 1972).

Many physiological indices are known to predict mortality and longevity, but no single master index, or composite factor derived from many different indices, has yet provided a satisfactory measure of biological age. An early summary by Shock (1985) still fairly represents the current situation:

> There is little evidence for the existence of a single factor that regulates the rate of aging in different functions in a specific individual. Because of the large range in the performance of most physiological variables among subjects of the same chronological age, it appears that age alone is a poor predictor of performance. Subjects who perform well on physiological tests when they are first tested, however, are more likely to be alive ten years later than subjects who perform poorly. (p. 723)

Because attempts to find composite indexes of biological aging have been unrewarding, a pragmatic solution has been to examine associations between particular indexes of physiological efficiency and particular indexes of current cognitive status. Physiological indexes are generally chosen for convenience of measurement or because they are practically important in the everyday lives of individuals. For example, Birren, Botwinnick, Weiss, and Morrison (1963); Birren, Butler, Greenhouse, et al. (1963) and Heron and Chown (1967) found modest but consistent relationships between easily measured indexes of grip strength and sensory acuity and performance on choice reaction time (CRT), memory, and problem-solving tasks.

Loss of leg muscle strength is one of the most thoroughly researched indexes of biological aging because it is one of the causes of falls, which are a particular hazard for older people. Dean (1988) reports benchmark data on relationships between muscle strength and calendar age in 4,767 women aged 65 years and older. Many other investigators such as Lord, Clark, and Webster (1991a) and Lord, McLean, and Stathers (1992) have replicated these findings and also found correlations between leg muscle strength and cognitive performance in later life. The variety of different, and mutually compatible, explanations for such relationships illustrates the complexity of causal inference. One explanation is that changes in muscle strength are due to muscle atrophy associated with loss of fibers and, to a lesser extent, to reduction in fiber size (Brooks & Faulkner, 1994; Tzankoff & Norris, 1977), and that these changes are due to a process of de-nervation and re-innervation of individual fibers caused by a continuous age-related loss of motor neurons in the spinal cord, which may reflect similar changes in the cortex (Lexell, Downham, & Sjostrom, 1986). Another is that age-related depletion of neurotransmitters and neurohistological changes in the motor cortex and higher motor areas of the brain reduce efficiency of innervation to muscles (e.g., Haarlkand, Temkin, Randahl, & Dikmen, 1994). Less directly, both muscle strength and the CNS may be affected by nutritional deficiencies or by cardiovascular or respiratory problems that are likely to impair brain blood supply and oxygenation (Rikli & Busch, 1986). Causal relationships are complicated to disentangle because many age related changes in muscle mimic those in disuse. In so far as loss of muscle strength is due to disuse, and disuse tends to be associated with reductions of cardiovascular and respiratory function, improvements brought about by exercise should also improve cognitive performance. This partially explains findings that older people who take regular exercise have faster reaction times than those who do not (e.g. Bayllor & Spirduso, 1988; Clarkson, 1978; Dustman, Ruhling, Russell, Shearer, Bonekay, Shigeoka, Wood, & Bradford, 1984; Kroll, & Clarkson, 1978; Sherwood & Selder, 1979). However these differences in reaction time do not only reflect muscle efficiency because age increases the lag between stimulus onset and initiation of muscle contraction (premotor time, PMT) much more than subsequent contraction time (CT) in the agonist muscle. Age slowing of reaction time must reflect central as well as peripheral changes (Spirduso, 1975, 1980; Spirduso & Clifford, 1978).

Longitudinal studies of correlated changes in cognitive function and in fitness are more persuasive than are cross-sectional comparisons between groups of more and less active elderly people. Clement (1974) found both cross-sectional and longitudinal associations between maintenance of grip strength and vocabulary and *Wechsler Adult Intelligence Scale* (WAIS) subtest coding performance in later life. Clarkson-Smith and Hartley (1990), Powell and Pohndorf (1971), and Stones and Kozma (1988) reported positive correlations between oxygen uptake, physical activity, and motor and cognitive performance that provide a sufficient explanation.

Correlations are also regularly found between simple measures of visual and auditory acuity and levels of cognitive performance in older samples (e.g., Birren, Botwinnick, et al., 1963; Heron & Chown 1967; Sklar & Edwards, 1962). Birren and Cunningham (1985) suggested that these associations are strong enough to make sensory acuity a useful marker of the amount of individual differences in age-related cognitive change. The issue of interpretation is highlighted by a neat comparison by Granick, Kleban, and Weiss (1976), who compared the strengths of relationships between calendar age, hearing threshold, and cognitive performance in 47 very healthy older men and in 38 older women with some pathologies. Within both groups hearing losses in the range of 125 to 8,000 cps correlated with performance on most of the WAIS subtests. Within the group of healthy men these were modest, appeared for only a few of the WAIS tests, and disappeared when variance associated with their calendar ages had been taken into consideration. Within the less healthy female group correlations were stronger, occurred for more WAIS subtests and persisted even when age-associated variance had been removed. This suggests that in healthy individuals "normal" hearing loss may reflect factors that are associated with the passage of time, such as progressive mechanical damage to the cochlear hair cells, rather than with changes in the CNS. In less healthy groups additional hearing loss is likely to be associated with pathologies that also affect global CNS integrity.

Recent studies confirm relationships between hearing acuity and cognitive status in old age (e.g., van Boxtel et al., 2000). Anstey, Stankov, and Lord (1996) and Anstey, Lord, and Williams (1997) found positive correlations between visual and hearing acuity and leg-muscle strength that were consistent with the idea that age-related changes in these indices reflect operation of a common physiological cause. Both sensory and strength measures separately and jointly predicted performance on choice reaction time and problem-solving tasks even after variance associated with education, mood, and self-reported general health status had been partialed out.

All these studies computed only simple regressions between biological indices, calendar age, and cognitive performance. These are invariably statistically significant but modest, falling in the range $R = .2$ to $.4$ and so accounting for no more than 16% of variance in cognitive function between individuals. However Lindenberger and Potter (1998) argued that it is more pertinent to ask what is the proportion of the *age-related* variance in cognitive function for which any marker can account. For example, if within a sample simple correlations between individuals' unadjusted intelligence test scores and their calendar ages are $r = .45$ accounting for 20.25% of variance, the point of interest is for what proportion of this 20.25% of age-related variance physiological markers can account. To do this, Lindenberger and Potter proposed a method of computing "shared over simple" effects in multivariate regression analysis. The logic can best be illustrated by the computational procedure as follows:

First we compute the R^2 value for the regression of age on the variable of interest (e.g., let us suppose that this is CRT, and that $R^2 = .346$). Next we compute the R^2 value for the predictor of interest; let us suppose that this is diabetes, and that the $R^2 = .121$. In a third step we compute the joint R^2 for age and diabetes as predictors of CRT, obtaining $R^2 = .346$. To obtain the unique effect of age, we subtract the R^2 for diabetes from the joint R^2 for age and diabetes (i.e., $.346 - .121 = .225$). We then compute the shared effects of age and diabetes by subtracting the unique effects of age (i.e., .225) from the simple effect of age (i.e., .346), giving .121. The proportion of the age effect that is accounted for by diabetes, the shared over simple effect, is then .121 (shared effect of age and diabetes)/.346 (simple effect of age), which gives us .349, or an estimate of 34.9 percent. We conclude that diabetes accounts for up to 34.9% of the observed age-related variance in CRT.

With this method Baltes and Lindenberger (1997), Lindenberger and Baltes (1994) and

Li, Jordanova, and Lindenberger (1998) obtained the striking result that simple measures of visual and auditory acuity and gait can account for up to 85% to 90% of age-related variance in scores on intelligence tests and verbal memory tasks. They proposed three explanations: that losses of sensory acuity experienced over long periods amount to sensory deprivation that gradually leads to cognitive decrements; that sensory decrements might have knock-on effects on cognitive function, and, most convincingly, as suggested by all earlier investigators of these relationships, that age-related changes in sensory acuity, gait, and cognitive function reflect an age-related physiological common cause.

Granick et al. (1976) neatly illustrated a problem of interpretation of these striking findings in their comparison of relationships between hearing acuity and cognitive performance in more and less healthy older people. Even causally unrelated processes may have strongly correlated temporal courses. For example, in an imaginary country where it is the pleasant custom to plant a tree on the natal day of each citizen, the growth of individuals' birth-trees would act as timekeepers, indexing their calendar ages and so, also the progress of all the time-dependent physiological and CNS changes that they experience, including those responsible for the changes in sensory and mental abilities that occur late in their lives. Within the population, birth-tree bulk will, therefore, not only be a strong predictor of both physiological and cognitive indexes in old age but also an even stronger predictor of age-related variance in these abilities.

Analogously to birth-trees, processes of anatomical change can act as clocks or calendars that account for substantial proportions of age-related or, more properly, time-related variance in other processes to which they are causally unrelated. For instance, progressive mechanical wear of joints impairs gait, and loss of basilar membrane hair cells due to cumulative mechanical damage from loud noise increasingly impairs hearing. These changes progress regularly over time and so can keep pace with causally quite unrelated changes in the CNS that affect cognition. Correlations between the time courses of different processes are not illuminating unless causal relationships are shown.

It follows that some of the shared variance between sensory and cognitive changes must be due to temporal concurrence rather than to common causes. Unfortunately, in any given case, it is not easy to estimate the relative contributions of these factors. Researchers may gain some impression of the amounts of error that occur—for example, by computing predictions of cognitive status from balance only after the effects of age-associated variables that affect balance, such as leg joint flexibility and muscle-strength, have also been taken into consideration. Researchers may also simultaneously examine predictions from several different biological markers on the assumption that overlap in prediction of cognitive status is more likely to reflect variance associated with a common cause that also affects the CNS than with temporal coincidence of changes experienced over a lifetime. However, in my opinion, satisfactory solutions have not yet been found.

The common-cause hypothesis implies that particular age-related physiological changes jointly affect vision, hearing, gait, and mental abilities but leaves open the question whether these reflect pathology (but note Granick et al., 1976). Until now, all of the evidence has come from examination of variance *between,* rather than *within,* individuals. The fact that variance between individuals in a population increases as they grow older means that they must change at different rates but does not tell us whether this is because even ideally healthy people "age" at different rates, or because inequalities in incidence of pathologies inevitably increase with sample age. If properly understood, this issue of the etiology of age-related changes must define our models for cognitive gerontology and so determine how we select groups of individuals for comparison.

In studying the cumulative effects of pathologies and negative biological life events (e.g., van Boxtel, Bentinck et al., 1998), peoples' ages, per se, may be irrelevant, and researchers may compare the cognitive status of healthy controls and patients suffering from particular pathologies, particularly those such as hypertension and late-onset diabetes, which become increasingly common in later life. There is excellent evidence that if older groups are rigorously screened for health, age differences in performance on some tasks are markedly reduced (Houx, 1991). If most variance in cognition in older samples can be attributed to pathology, cognitive gerontology loses much of its rationale as an independent intellectual discipline and becomes a branch of health psychology in which patients' ages are of interest only inasmuch as they affect the intensity of expression of the illnesses that they suffer. A contrary position is that the process of "natural" aging causes cognitive changes that are additional to, and functionally independent of, those due to a lifetime accumulation of pathologies and traumata. This distinction between processes of "primary," "normal," or "usual" aging and the "secondary" effects of pathologies and "biological life events" has powerfully, though tacitly, determined models for cognitive change and so for the methodology of group selection.

PRIMARY AND SECONDARY AGING

A distinction between processes of primary and secondary aging has been useful to biologists because changes such as telomerization (Kirkwood, 1999) are arguably primary in the sense that they occur in all members of a species independently of their life histories and may well have genetically determined courses. Evolutionary biologists find this distinction useful at the species level. For example, in the disposable soma theory (Kirkwood, 1999—in our view, *nomen est omen*), this has been interpreted as a distinction between endogenous inheritable characteristics that determine the course of evolution of a species and exogenous environmental factors that may affect the life spans of individual animals. Even here the distinction should be made cautiously. One might, for instance, take heritable differences in immune system efficiency to be a primary factor in determining longevity. However, this primary factor acts by protecting against the secondary effects of environmental exposure to diseases (Takata, Ishii, Suzuki, Sekiguchi, & Iri, 1987). The boundaries of causal linkages between primary and secondary factors are unclear, and it seems more useful to treat them as loose descriptors of sets of related factors in a system of complex interactive relationships than as either-or explanations or guides for investigations.

The importance of the distinction between normal or primary and secondary factors as determinants of rates of cognitive change was early recognized (e.g., by Busse, 1969). Nevertheless, the overwhelming bulk of investigations of cognitive change in old age is still based on cross-sectional comparisons between small groups of older and younger people and is tacitly assumed to explore primary age-related changes in the cognitive system, and thus in the brain and CNS. The distinction between groups suffering from primary and secondary changes works best if the aim is to study the cognitive effects of pathologies such as diabetes (e.g., Bent, Rabbitt, & Metcalf, 2000) or hypertension (e.g., Hertzog, Schaie, & Gribbin, 1978) or links between cardiovascular efficiency and cognitive performance in later life (e.g., Barrett & Watkins, 1986; Elias, Robbins, Schultz, & Pierce, 1990;

Siegler & Nowlin, 1985; Wilkie, Eisdorfer, & Nowlin, 1985). However, even such comparisons do not necessarily allow clear disassociations between primary and secondary processes because the cognitive effects of particular pathologies may well vary with the ages at which they are first contracted and thus with their durations. It is unsafe to assume that primary and secondary changes must necessarily be of qualitatively different kinds, that they affect different functional processes and so different cognitive abilities, or that their effects are entirely independent of each other.

Criteria for selecting groups to study the effects of primary aging are much less clear because they depend on exclusion rather than inclusion of potentially influential factors: "aging processes are always defined by default after effects of disease have been taken into consideration" (Fozard, Metter, & Brant, 1990). It is possible to recruit groups that are sufficiently large and diverse to be plausibly representative of the population at large, to further assume that we can obtain quantifiable indexes for their levels on all of the secondary factors that are likely to contribute to differences between them, and then to use post hoc statistics to identify all of the variance that is associated with these secondary factors in order to estimate the residual variance that may be considered, by default, to reflect pure processes of primary aging. This is probably the best option available, but it is important to bear in mind that it relies on the assumption that we have actually identified, and taken into consideration, *all* important secondary factors.

Authors of nearly all cross-sectional studies of differences in particular cognitive functions such as memory, decision speed, or problem solving between small groups of different ages take pains to state that their older groups are "healthy." Epidemiological statistics suggest that unverified assumptions of health in randomly or carelessly selected samples are unsafe. For example, U.K. National Health Service statistics show that 60% of individuals aged 65 years and older and more than 65% of individuals aged 75 years and older have been diagnosed as suffering from two or more pathologies, with a sizeable proportion having unrecognized conditions that will manifest themselves and begin to limit their lifestyles within two years. Symptom-free cardiovascular problems that may affect brain blood supply for many years before they are diagnosed are common, and marked neurophysiological changes may pass undetected. For example, Guttman et al. (1998, p. 977) reported a marked decrease with age in cortical white matter in a population that was selected as being "optimally healthy." Another statistic that is uncomfortable for group selection is that over 20% of a sample of 60 individuals aged from 60 to 82 years who had been selected on the basis of exceptionally well-maintained cognitive ability during a 17-year longitudinal study and had also been screened by detailed clinical physical examinations and by their self-reports of the Brodman, Erdman, and Wolff (1949) Cornell Medical Index (CMI) nevertheless showed marked and diverse neurophysiological abnormalities on brain imaging (Alan Jackson, personal communication, March 2001). Even when investigators have been as painstaking as possible in their selection of older participants, it seems likely that many or even all of them have been affected by covert pathologies.

These points can be met in two different ways: by showing that the screening methods used to eliminate pathology are, in fact, adequate or that differences in health do not matter because their effects are trivial in comparison with those of calendar age.

The Adequacy of Self-Reports and of Other Health-Screening Methods

Almost all small cross-sectional studies have depended on peoples' unelaborated self-reports that they are well, but the more painstaking have used well-validated instruments such as the CMI (Brodman et al., 1949). Unfortunately, interpretations of differences in self-report data from older and younger people are not straightforward. For example, it seems a very economical and fruitful procedure to study cognitive changes in old age simply by asking older people to report their experiences of difficulties that they may have begun to experience with their everyday lives. Many excellent instruments such as the Short Inventory of Mental Lapses (Reason, 1993), the Cognitive Failures Questionnaire (Broadbent, Cooper, et al., 1982), or the Memory Failures Questionnaire (Harris & Morris, 1984) have been shown to work well when eliciting younger adults' reports of their everyday competence. Unfortunately, these give paradoxical results when administered to older people. Reports of memory failures and absentmindedness in specified everyday situations do not increase (Rabbitt & Abson, 1990) and may even significantly fall with sample ages of between 49 and 96 years (Reason, 1993). This is unexpected because when very large elderly samples have been asked which aspects of old age they find most inconvenient, complaints of memory failures are second only to those of arthritis (Buchler, Pierce, Robinson, & Trier, 1967; Guttman, 1980). The validity of self-report memory questionnaires is questionable because individuals' self-ratings do not predict their scores on objective laboratory tasks (Hermann, 1982; Rabbitt & Abson, 1990). Similarly, when older people answer health questionnaires, although the numbers of different specific pathologies that they report increases markedly with their ages, their subjective ratings of their general health status do not alter accordingly (McInnes & Rabbitt, 1997).

The most general explanation for such findings is that individuals cannot make absolute judgments of their own abilities or health status but can only compare themselves against particular task demands or, as is more typical, against others (Herrmann, 1982; Rabbitt & Abson, 1990; Rabbitt, Maylor, McInnes, & Bent, 1995). As people age, their environments and the demands that their lives impose on them may change more rapidly than their abilities. Busy people in their 40s and 50s are daily made conscious of their lapses in contrast to able young colleagues, but elderly retired people live in lenient environments that do not challenge even their reduced cognitive resources. Thus, even objectively, memory failures may be more frequent and more disturbing for the busy young than for the sheltered old. Similarly, even clinically significant respiratory and cardiovascular changes may be underestimated where demands on physical effort are slight.

A related issue is that inventories of everyday lapses are effective only to the extent that they probe the particular scenarios that people frequently encounter and in which they have opportunities to make errors. The nature, as well as the frequency of occurrence of these difficult, error-generating scenarios changes with age and social role. To be useful, questionnaires must probe scenarios that older people often encounter in their daily lives. Thus, questionnaires developed for and standardized on young adults may be inappropriate for the elderly. (Harris & Morris, 1984; Rabbitt et al., 1995).

Other problems that cannot easily be avoided by better design of questionnaires or self-rating scales are that attention deficits may cause older people to monitor themselves less stringently and also, because their memories have become increasingly unreliable, they may forget mental lapses or episodes of poor health.

Because people can only assess their performance relative to some external standard, even if they realize that the demands that their lives make of them have changed, they can only adjust for this by comparing themselves against others in similar positions. Older people tend to compare themselves against their age peers rather than against the population at large. Especially when they are among the elite minority who are fit and motivated enough to volunteer for psychological studies, they may, quite accurately, assess themselves favorably against others of their ages. McInnes and Rabbitt (1998) found that people's assessments of their general states of health on a 5-point scale vary markedly with the standards of reference that they are asked to use. When people were asked to compare their health against that of their age peers, their self-assessments declined only marginally between the ages of 49 and 96 years. This was also the case when, as has been typical in most investigations, no particular standard of reference was given and they were simply asked to rate their health in general terms on a scale from "Very Good" to "Very Poor." In contrast, when they were asked to rate their current health in comparison to their health 5 years previously, self-ratings became significantly less positive with age. Unless questionnaires make clear precisely what standards of comparison are to be used, contrasts between older and younger people's self-evaluations will be misleading. There are useful discussions of best practice in administration of health questionnaires to the elderly, and when instruments are properly designed and used, they can sensitively reveal individual variations in health (e.g., McNair, 1979).

How Large Are the Effects of Health on Cognitive Performance?

It is clear that there are statistically robust differences in average levels of performance on cognitive tasks between groups of people who do and do not suffer from conditions such as hypertension and cardiovascular problems (Hertzog et al., 1978), diabetes (Bent et al., 2000), respiratory problems, and negative biological life events such as episodes of surgery and other age-related illnesses (see the review by Holland & Rabbitt, 1991). One way to assess the impact of pathologies is to use regression analyses to estimate the relative proportions of variance between individuals that are accounted for by presence or absence of particular pathologies and by calendar age. The effects of particular pathologies have rarely been analyzed in this way, but at least in one case presence or absence of late-onset diabetes accounted for no more than 2%, whereas calendar age accounted for more than 16% of variance in cognitive performance between individuals (Bent et al., 2000). Thus, specific comparisons between groups of patients and controls do confirm that illness reduces cognitive competence in later life but seem to suggest that the effects of primary aging, as indexed by calendar age, are far stronger.

In the clearest and best documented defense of this position, Salthouse (1991, chap. 4) lucidly reviews the general literature and a study of his own (Salthouse, Kausler, & Saults, 1990), concluding that the effects of individual differences in health have very slight or no effects on cognitive performance in older samples. This conclusion is important at three different levels. Theoretically, it suggests that the effects of primary aging are greater than, and independent of, secondary pathologies. Methodologically, it allows investigators to compare small groups without the inconvenience of rigorous health screening. Politically, it establishes a platform for the study of cognitive aging as a field of study independent of medical models of aging that interpret age differences as the outcome of accelerating accumulations of pathologies as age advances.

Lindenberger and Potter's (1998) focus on the age-related rather than the total variance associated with biological markers suggests that it is more informative to compute how much of the total variance in cognitive function that is associated with differences in individuals' ages may be explained by differences in their health. McInnes and Rabbitt (1998) used Lindenberger and Potter's (1998) method to compute the proportions of age-related variance in scores on the Heim (1970) AH4 (1) intelligence test that were predicted by various health indexes such as self-ratings, CMI scores, and inventories of prescribed medications. Estimates of age-related variance associated with these increased with respect to total variance, but only from 1.0% to 4.0% to about 11%. This does not compromise Salthouse's (1991) position.

However, a study by Perlmutter and Nyquist (1990) illustrates how these apparently weak relationships may be misleading. They found that reports of both physical ($r = .36$) and mental ($r = .32$) health problems increased with age from 20 to 90 years. A robust correlation between calendar age in this range and WAIS intelligence test scores ($r = -.78$) contrasted with much weaker correlations between health indexes and test scores that, nevertheless, accounted for a small but significant proportion of variance even after the effects of age had been taken into consideration. The key point was that correlations between CMI scores and fluid intelligence were $r = .112$ for people aged 20 to 50 years but increased to $r = .355$ for people aged 60 to 90 years. This was because incidence of pathologies was very low among younger adults but increased significantly among the middle-aged and elderly. This shows that the proportion of variance between individuals that is associated with pathologies strongly depends on the incidence of pathologies in the samples screened. The methodological limitations to self-reports imply that the incidence of pathological changes in the relatively small samples examined in other health surveys of the aged

may have been much higher than their authors supposed.

A related problem is that the cognitive effects of pathologies must increase with their severities of expression and their durations at time of assessment, and these factors will vary with calendar age. We do not know of any analyses that have been able to examine relationships between the severities of expression of pathologies and the ages at which they are suffered. The nearest approach to a solution of this problem has been to assume that at the time when individuals are cognitively assessed, their distances from death (survival durations) can serve as a proxy index for the combined effects and degrees of severity of their current pathologies. Thus, effects of distance from death can be compared with effects of distance of birth (calendar age) to allow comparisons of the relative effects of primary and secondary aging on cognitive function.

Relationships between Cognitive Function at Assessment and Subsequent Survival Duration: Effects of Terminal Drop

Predictions of cognitive function from survival duration, and vice versa, may seem methodologically straightforward but, as excellent reviews by Botwinick (1984), Cunningham (1987), Cunningham and Brookbank (1988), Palmore and Jefferies (1971), and Palmore and Cleveland (1976) show, there are many methodological problems.

Many studies, such as those by Berkowitz (1965), Kleemeier (1962), Lieberman (1965), and Brown, Chobor, and Zinn (1993), have examined only institutionalized patients. These have consistently found that individuals who died before a later census date had significantly lower mean cognitive test scores on initial assessment than did those who survived beyond it. None of these studies documented incidence of dementias, which cause rapid and marked cognitive decline and early death and are common in institutionalized samples. In contrast, studies of active, elderly community residents have found slight (Cunningham & Brookbank, 1988; Small & Backman, 1997; Steuer, La Rue, Blum, & Jarvik, 1981) or no (Blum, Clark, & Jarvik, 1973; White & Cunningham, 1988) relationships between current cognitive performance and subsequent survival duration. Because these studies have investigated small groups ($N = 20$ to 200 deceased plus survivors) over brief periods (6 months to 5 years), data have been insufficient to determine whether different terminal pathologies affect different mental abilities, or how the cognitive impacts of pathologies vary with the periods for which they have been experienced or the ages at which they first appeared.

The strengths of relationships between current ability and subsequent survival vary with the age ranges sampled. Palmore and Cleveland (1976) pointed out that because as a sample ages the brief survival of its members becomes increasingly probable, one must also enter calendar age into multivariate analyses made to predict probability of survival from current cognitive status. Those few studies that have done this find that the proportion in variance accounted for by survival duration is very much less than that predicted by calendar age (e.g., Rabbitt et al., 2000; Small & Backman, 1997).

A different issue is that the likelihood of detecting changes in mental abilities before death depends jointly on the relative difficulty of the tests used and on the average levels of ability of the populations studied. Very easy tests such as the Mini Mental State Examination (Folstein, Folstein, & McHugh, 1975) can detect individual differences in cognitive status among frail and confused institutionalized elderly but not among people who still competently manage independent lives. Even when tests are sufficiently demanding to avoid

ceiling effects, it is possible that because particular terminal pathologies may affect some mental abilities more than others, some tests may be correspondingly poor predictors of survival. As Siegler (1993) pointed out, the best evidence that calendar age and pathology have functionally different effects would be that they affect different mental abilities. Because investigators have been remarkable for their creative ingenuity in using very different test batteries, evidence remains inconclusive. Many studies have found that tests of verbal ability are sensitive predictors of mortality (e.g., Berg, 1987; Rabbitt et al., 2001; Siegler, McCarty, & Logue, 1982). Suedfeld and Piedrahita (1984) found progressive declines in the "integrative complexity" of letters written by famous authors up to 10 years before they died. However, some studies have not found that vocabulary is a sensitive predictor of mortality (e.g., Botwinick, West, & Storandt, 1978).

Verbal ability is a highly practiced crystallized skill that declines little, or may even improve until the ninth decade of life (Horn, 1982; Horn, Donaldson, & Engstrom, 1981; Rabbitt, 1993a). This robustness of verbal skills makes it paradoxical that they may be exceptionally sensitive markers for survival. A possible explanation is that verbal abilities may remain unaffected by age until pathologies become so severe that death is immanent.

It is important to distinguish evidence that declines in vocabulary may be a marker for immanent death from the quite different evidence that levels of verbal ability in youth may predict both life span and duration of the maintenance of cognitive skills in old age. A striking epidemiological study by Snowden et al. (1996) showed that the grammatical complexity and density of ideas of autobiographical notes written by 93 nuns as young novices predicted their longevity as well as their levels of cognitive function and their probability of contracting Alzheimer's disease in old age.

This conclusion may yet turn out to be correct, but the data are still insufficient. For example, recent studies show that birth weight, adequacy of infant nutrition, and childhood health all affect very markedly both mortality and maintenance of intellectual competence in later life (Leon, 1998; Sorensenson, 1997). Thriving in infancy and childhood is associated with higher adult levels of cognitive performance, possibly because healthy infants are more likely to belong to relatively affluent and better-educated families. Differences in birth weight and health in infancy may have determined the life histories of Snowden et al.'s (1996) nuns long before they wrote the autobiographical essays from which their young adult intellectual abilities were deduced. A different inference that may be drawn from Snowden et al.'s (1996) data is that continued practice at particular cognitive skills, such as language, may preserve general mental ability in later life. All right-minded people, especially those who subscribe to a robust work ethic, will find this a congenial hypothesis and will hope that it will eventually be validated. Unfortunately, at the moment researchers know only that people who were more able than their coevals when they were young remained so as they grew old.

Demographic factors such as socioeconomic advantage, education, and area of residence all markedly affect the prevalence of pathologies (Pincus, Callahan, & Burkhauser, 1987), mortality (Snowden, Ostwald, Kane, & Keenan, 1989), and the prevalence of dementias resulting in marked premortem cognitive decline (Roth, 1986). Unfortunately, samples have been too small and too homogenous to study interactions between these variables, and this limits our understanding of possible primary effects of age. For example, the effects of gender have been neglected in most investigations of terminal decline. Women live longer than men and also tend to perform better than men of the same age on tests of verbal memory and on some vocabulary tests (Rabbitt, Donlan, Watson, McInnes, & Bent, 1996). Unless overrepresentation of women in older samples is taken into account, we may mistakenly conclude that better verbal memory is a good marker for longer survival when, in fact, gender is the actual determinant.

Mental abilities are impaired not only by physical illness but also by affective states such as anxiety and depression. Brumback's (1985) hypothesis that all of the cognitive decline observed in terminally ill patients may be caused by their understandable depression is extreme. More recent studies show that major depression is not, in fact, a necessary concomitant of severe, or even of terminal, illness (e.g., Cohen-Cole & Kaufman, 1993). Current evidence is that the critical risk factor for major depression is functional impairment rather than disease per se (Zeiss, Lewinshohn, & Seeley, 1996). Large studies by La Rue, Swan, and Carmelli (1995) have found that clinically significant levels of depression reduce cognitive performance in old age, and Rabbitt et al. (1996) have also found that scores on depression inventories indicating mild to moderate unhappiness rather than clinical depression are associated with lower performance on cognitive tests. Understandable depression concomitant with illness and approaching death may contribute to apparent terminal drop in cognitive performance, and this must be taken into account by including depression inventories in assessment batteries.

A basic methodological problem when studies of terminal decline are used to distinguish the effects of primary and secondary aging is illustrated by counterintuitive evidence that the cognitive effects of impending death may be greater in younger than in older adults (Cunningham & Brookbank, 1988; Riegel & Riegel, 1972; Steuer, La Rue, Blum, & Jarvik,

1981). This counterintuitive finding can be explained by the fact that although nearly all members of young samples are in excellent health and will survive for many years after a future census date, most members of elderly samples suffer from one or more pathologies, and all are likely to survive only a few years after the census has closed. In elderly samples increased blurring of differences in health status between those who die before census dates and those who survive beyond census dates provides a sufficient explanation for paradoxical findings of stronger relationships between cognitive performance and survival in younger than in older adults and also for observations that individual pathologies, such as diabetes, have greater effects on the cognitive performance of younger than of older patients (Bent et al., 2000). Consistent with the idea that increasing likelihood of early death for all members blurs differences between survivors and nonsurvivors in older samples is that within a group of 464 people who died within 11 years of cognitive assessment, Rabbitt et al. (2001) found no significant relationship between initial cognitive status and subsequent survival durations between 36 and 4,018 days.

A corollary is that differences in cognitive performance between survivors and deceased in younger and older samples will also depend on the durations of the census periods over which deaths are logged. Because most young adults will live many years beyond any arbitrary census date, in young samples the cognitive status at initial assessment of those who survive a subsequent point will be little affected by the census duration sampled. In contrast, for elderly samples, the longer the census period, the larger the proportion of survivors who die soon after it closes and, consequently, the smaller the difference, at initial testing, between the average cognitive scores of those elderly who do, and those who do not, survive.

Thus, findings that older individuals' current calendar ages account for much larger proportions of variance in their cognitive performance than do their probabilities of subsequent survival can be misleading because they do not take into account the fact that individual differences in survival duration markedly reduce as sample age increases.

Assumptions about the Processes of Aging that Have Determined the Design of Small-Scale Cross-Sectional Studies

To compare "older" and "younger" groups researchers must decide on the age boundaries that separate them. Investigators typically do not discuss the assumptions underlying their choices. As Robertson-Tchabo has neatly put it, "one investigator's middle-aged group is another investigator's young or elderly group". Such uncertain and arbitrary categorizations ignore evidence that because detectable age-related physiological and cognitive changes occur by the age of 30 (Kirkwood, 1999), processes of aging are continuous throughout most of the life span. Sensible choices can only be made in terms of clearly defined assumptions about the form of the true trajectory of cognitive aging. Although it is generally assumed that declines in cognitive performance with age are negatively accelerated rather than linear, their precise forms are uncertain. Recent evidence from longitudinal studies shows that different mental abilities decline at different rates and that for some abilities these declines may be well-described by linear rather than accelerated functions (Rabbitt, Diggle, Holland, & McInnes, 2001). Figure 18.1 illustrates that assumptions about the time courses of age-related changes are important practical issues because the form of the true trajectory of change for any particular mental ability will affect the experimental outcomes resulting from different choices of age boundaries for the groups that are compared.

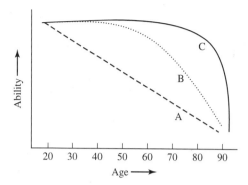

Figure 18.1 The selection of appropriate age-groups for comparisons depends on the "real" trajectory of change with Age. If this is best described by function A the linear decline would mean that the sizes of the difference observed would depend only on the number of years separating age groups and not on the particular ages of the groups selected. In the case of function B little or no difference would be observed if groups are younger than 50 years but, since the function thereafter accelerates, the size of the difference observed for a constant age-gap would increase with the ages of the groups compared. In the case of function C little difference would be observed between groups younger than 80 years.

Figure 18.1 shows that appropriate choices of group age boundaries for detecting age-related changes differ depending on whether researchers assume changes to be continuous and linear (Rabbitt, 1993a), continuous and accelerating (Rabbitt et al., in press), or, at least for some cognitive abilities, abruptly discontinuous (e.g., Arenberg, 1974).

It is not surprising that inconsistencies between studies often reflect differences in the age-ranges of the groups compared. Often, this becomes apparent only in the rare cases in which exceptionally conscientious investigators replicate their experiments using extended age ranges (e.g., Jacewicz & Hartley, 1979). The risk of assuming that only two data points (i.e., group mean ages) will be sufficient to detect an age trend is illustrated by well-conducted studies in which three or

more different age groups have been compared. A concrete example is a study of age changes in efficiency at inhibiting interference in the Stroop (1935) test by Spieler, Balota, and Faust (1996), who found no differences between a young-old and an old-old group, but found that both differed from a young-adult group. To make cross-sectional comparisons, it is desirable always to compare at least three different, and preferably quite widely separated, age groups. Moreover, since appropriate choices of group age boundaries will vary with anticipated trajectories of change, and because these latter may differ with task demands, the particular assumptions that have determined group selection must always be articulated and justified in terms of the particular comparisons to be made.

Even tasks that make logically identical demands may differ in difficulty and so may show different trajectories of age-related change. A relatively easy version of a task may not pick up small individual differences between young adults but will detect gross changes between older people. A difficult version of the same task may detect differences early but fail to do so late in the life span when all successive age groups perform at, or near, chance. Such ceiling and floor effects can readily be identified, although not all investigators have recognized them in their data. A less obvious consequence is that the appearance or absence of differences between small groups of people of different ages will depend on complex interactions between the true form of the trajectory of age-related change in the particular mental ability tested, in the number of data points (group mean scores) that can be obtained, in the particular choice of age boundaries made for each group, and in the average level of difficulty of the tasks on which participants are compared.

The sensitivity of experiments is also affected by the decision of how large the groups compared should be. On most cognitive tests, the degree of variability between individuals markedly increases with the average ages of the groups sampled (Morse, 1993; Rabbitt et al., in press). Neglect of age-related increases in within-sample variance has two different methodological implications. One is that the older the groups that are sampled, the larger they must be in order to maintain power of statistical comparisons. Appropriate choices of sample size must be guided by power analyses that take this increased variability into account. This increase in variance between individuals with group age is also theoretically interesting because it must reflect the fact that individuals age at different rates so that their trajectories of aging diverge over time (Rabbitt, 1982, 1993a). The older the groups compared, the greater will be the differences in the relative extents to which their members have been affected by the processes that we hope to study. Pressure for economy of experimental designs has blunted sensitivity to the methodological implications of increased variance in older samples so that there are serious doubts about the replicability of many small cross-sectional studies that show significant but weak effects and about the meaningfulness of demonstrations of very small differences in the effects of task demands between older and younger samples.

Methodological Precautions in Small-Scale Cross-Sectional Studies

Matching Groups for Levels of General Intellectual Ability

There have been many forceful pronouncements on the limitations of unadjusted intelligence test scores (ITSs) as meaningful indexes of intellectual differences between people (e.g., Howe, 1999). Accepting the points made, it remains the case that ITSs, pragmatically, are the best current predictors

of individual differences in performance on all of the laboratory tasks on which older and younger adults have been compared. Table 18.1 illustrates this with R values for predictions of scores on some laboratory tests from calendar ages and from unadjusted scores on the Heim (1970) AH4 (1) intelligence test and the Cattell and Cattell (1960) Culture Fair intelligence test obtained from 4,876 individuals aged 49 to 92 years.

Table 18.1   Associations between scores on laboratory tasks and calendar Age, and scores on a test of fluid intelligence, the Cattell and Cattell "Culture Fair" test. Note that variance between individuals associated with their ages becomes non-significant when variance associated with their intelligence test scores is taken into consideration.

Task	Correlation with Age	Correlation with age with variance associated with Cattell Culture Fair Test scores Removed
Visual Search Time	.34 ($p = .01$)	.09 (ns)
4 Choice RT	.46 ($p = .000$)	.11 ($p = .079$)
Cumulative Learning of 15 words	−.39 ($p = .000$)	−.06 (ns)
Free Recall of 30 Words	−.29 ($p = .01$)	−.10 (ns)
Delayed Free Recall of 30 words	−.33 ($p = .000$)	−.09 (ns)
Baddeley "Doors" Memory Test	−.31 ($p = .000$)	−.03 (ns)
Delayed Recognition of 20 Pictures	−.19 ($p = .05$)	−.05 (ns)
Embedded Figures Test	−.240 ($p = .000$)	.02 (ns)
Digit Span	−.18 ($p = .046$)	−.08 (ns)
"Stroop Test" Time for interference Condition.	.39 ($p = .000$)	.10 ($p = .081$)

Predictions from age after variance associated with differences in intelligence test scores has been taken into consideration are also shown.

As Table 18.1 illustrates, both individuals' ages and their ITSs predict modestly, but very consistently, their scores on most laboratory tasks. However, after ITSs are taken into consideration, individuals' ages make little or no additional prediction. This means that differences in performance on laboratory tasks between groups of younger and older people are likely to be more strongly determined by differences in their current levels of ITSs than by differences in their ages. In other terms, ITSs appear to pick up all, or most, of the age-related variance in many laboratory tasks. Thus, if groups of older and younger people are matched in terms of their current ITSs, differences between them will be absent or minimal. It might seem that an optimal solution is to match older and younger samples in terms of the levels of the ITSs that the older group achieved as younger adults, and from which they have declined as they have grown old. Fortunately, one does not need time travel to do this. When people are young, their scores on vocabulary tests correlate robustly with their scores on intelligence tests that measure fluid general intellectual abilities. As seen, ITSs decline but vocabulary test scores remain stable, or may even slightly increase into the late eighth or even the ninth decade of life (Horn, 1982, 1987; Horn et al., 1981; Rabbitt, 1993a). This means that older peoples' scores on vocabulary tests remain good proxy measures for their ITSs as young adults, so that when younger and older groups are matched in terms of their current vocabulary test scores, one may assume that the older participants' ITSs have declined from the same levels as those currently attained by their younger controls.

Many investigators have taken advantage of this relationship and have exactly matched their older and younger groups in terms of vocabulary test scores. Unfortunately, this procedure also raises problems because it guarantees that the current ITSs of the young group are higher than those of the older group. To the extent that all age-related changes in performance on many, if not most, cognitive tests can be picked up by changes in ITSs, this raises the question whether the differences that one finds between vocabulary-matched age groups add more to the knowledge of cognitive changes in old age than researchers already know from age changes in ITSs. Supposing, with some reason, that in many cases they do not, one might more conveniently study age effects by comparing readily available samples of undergraduates with higher and lower ITSs. If, on the contrary, one is interested only in age differences that are qualitatively different from, or quantitatively greater than, those that can be picked up by ITSs, simple comparisons between group means cannot make this point. To do this one must carry out multivariate analyses to obtain separate estimates of the effects of age and of ITSs on task performance.

It must be emphasized that intelligence tests are not uniquely informative indexes of individual differences in cognitive function. They are only pragmatic instruments that have been gradually evolved to make predictions as good as can be empirically attained of individual differences in competence over as wide a range of real-life tasks as possible. They succeed because the problems that they incorporate make demands across a very wide range of (putatively) different cognitive abilities such as working memory efficiency, attention, planning, and information processing speed. This breadth of demands makes it unsurprising that they also predict the performance of individuals of all ages across a wide range of different laboratory tasks. Thus, findings that ITSs may predict age differences in performance as well as, or better than, calendar age do not necessarily offer any useful theoretical leverage to understand the functional changes that occur as people grow older. In particular, as shown later, the idea that all cognitive changes in old age are driven by declines in a single master performance index derived from ITSs, such as Spearman's (1924) single factor g_f, is not a useful conclusion to draw from data such as those shown in Table 18.1.

The everyday utility of ITSs as practical measures of general intellectual competence raises other methodological difficulties for selection criteria for cross-sectional age comparisons. As has been seen, young adults who have higher levels of intellectual ability also tend to live longer and so to experience less cognitive change over time. That is to say, when individuals are young, their ITSs are likely to be correlated with the rates at which their cognitive performance changes as they age. This may be because ITSs are associated with protective factors associated with socioeconomic advantage or because they are associated with intrinsic differences in longevity and so with different rates of cognitive change, or possibly both. Therefore, irrespective of differences in task demands, the sizes of any age effects observed will vary with the average levels of ITSs of the older and younger groups compared.

Investigators sometimes, but not often, acknowledge the complexity of influences that may affect the course of aging by matching groups in terms of influential demographic variables such as years of education, lifetime occupation, and socioeconomic status. These precautions are desirable but tend to confound effects of age, time, and period. For example, in most developed countries duration of education was much more strongly related to socioeconomic status, parental education, and other demographic factors that are also known to affect rates of cognitive aging during the first than during the second half of the 20th century. The difficulty of disentangling complex relationships between the effects of aging, period, and cohort has generated a great deal of discussion but not, so far, a completely satisfactory solution.

Cohort Effects

The term *cohort* derives from a military unit in the Roman army, but its current usage is a group of people who are identified by some common characteristic. In cognitive gerontology it most commonly refers to a group of people of similar ages, but it can also refer to individuals of different ages who have undergone similar experiences, such as war, marriage, divorce, a particular illness, or a particular social environment.

Criteria for defining and matching age cohorts are obviously problematic. As many empirical studies have shown, people who volunteer for laboratory studies are not representative of national populations and tend to be socioeconomically more advantaged, better educated, healthier, and more highly motivated to perform well on the sometimes boring and arbitrary tasks that they are given in psychological laboratories, as well as to have higher levels of fluid general ability (g_f) than those who do not choose to participate (e.g., Lachman, Lachman, & Taylor 1982). This obviously limits the generality of the conclusions that we can draw, but much can be still be learned by documenting the individuals we compare as completely as possible so that we can make post hoc estimates of the effects of factors that we cannot completely control by selection. For example, although levels of health and education are certain to be both higher and less variable in groups of self-selected volunteers than in the population at large, provided that samples are thoroughly documented we can estimate from the range of observations that we have been able to make the sizes of the effects that might have occurred if we had access to a truly representative sample. Statistical techniques for replacing missing data so as to simulate a demographically normal sample such as those described by Diggle, Liang, and Zeger (1994) and Rubin (1976) also allow us to model virtually normal population samples from the actual sample that we have recruited.

Solutions have not been found for the more fundamental problems that arise because differences in the average ages of groups are neither the only nor necessarily the most important determinants of cognitive differences between them. Groups of different ages have been born in different historical periods and socioeconomic circumstances and have had very different life experiences. Cohort background and calendar age present special problems when they are used as defining characteristics for groups because they are not independent variables and cannot be manipulated by assigning volunteers to aging and nonaging conditions. For this reason investigators have been obliged to adopt quasi-experimental designs for the study of aging and developmental effects (see Schaie, 1977). Unfortunately, as Campbell and Stanley (1963) first pointed out, such designs always allow the possibility of alternative explanations. After nearly half a century of discussion these difficulties remain unresolved.

This chapter has discussed how outcomes of comparisons will depend on the precise forms of the trajectories of change to be expected on the various tests that researchers use. The problem deepens when age groups are viewed in a wider socio-historical context where it becomes a serious question whether people who are aged, say, between 40 and 49 are, actually, more similar to each other in some important way than are people who are aged between 50 and 59. As always, answers are only possible in terms of some clearly specified model of the processes that we hope to study. If we are concerned with social attitudes, it may well be a good working assumption, justified by external evidence, that calendar age is not the most meaningful way of identifying changes during the life span. Here it may be more sensible to classify people in terms of role-defined stages that are only

roughly associated with age, such as working life or retirement, or in terms of passages of time defined in terms of socio-historical periods—events or transitions such as pre- and postwar or pre- and postdepression. In choosing defining criteria for cohorts, it is essential to accept that the attempt to answer any particular question must prevent us from simultaneously asking others. Failure to come to terms with this can lead to nihilistic positions such as that taken by Gergen (1977), who argued that a chance model of change in adulthood is necessary because the knowledge of gerontologists at this point in the history of their science is so limited that they constrain their comparisons in entirely arbitrary ways in order to answer questions that currently seem relevant but that, from the point of view of future scientists, miss central issues. This curious idea that we must indefinitely defer explanation because it must currently, and perhaps always, be provisional and incomplete seems to reflect a radical misunderstanding of the ways in which scientific progress continues to be made.

Historical decades and generations may often have less relevance if we are concerned with biological processes, but assumptions about the rates at which biological changes occur will determine the fineness of the temporal grain necessary to track them. Divisions in terms of 5-year, 7-year or 20-year cycles are all defensible in terms of particular selections of research questions and assumptions about rates of change of different variables. Further, unless one assumes that rate of change is linear, there are good arguments for varying cohort boundaries to make comparisons across the life span, selecting wide agebands within those periods during which we assume that changes occur slowly and narrow bands over periods during which they are known to happen faster.

Obviously, researchers need not restrict themselves to comparing cohorts at a single

Table 18.2 Dummy data illustrating how information collected during a longitudinal study allows analysis of birth cohort effects, of Age trended between different birth cohorts and of Period effects.

Age when sampled	Sampled in 1960	Sampled in 1970	Sampled in 1980	Sampled in 1990	Sampled in 2000
20–29	35%	39%	39%	41%	42%
30–39	38%	38%	40%	42%	43%
40–49	52%	67%	67%	68%	70%
50–59	65%	68%	73%	75%	77%
60–69	58%	59%	59%	61%	63%
70–79	44%	45%	45%	46%	49%
80–89	38%	39%	41%	43%	43%

NOTE: This "Cohort Table" uses dummy data for percentages of individuals complaining of frequent memory in 7 successive age groups sampled at the beginning of 5 successive decades (sampling years). The cross-sectional effects of Age can be tracked down columns, the effects of Period of sampling along rows, and the longitudinal effects of Age (Age × Period effects) along diagonals. Note that the interactions between the Ages of individuals at successive samplings and the effects of the period, or social environment, during which they were interrogated, are not straightforward. We might, for example, wish to test the hypothesis that increased informational complexity of the environment between 1960 and 2000 has resulted in greater demands on memory for all groups, increasing complaints in some, vulnerable, groups more than in others. To do this we would have to bear in mind the problems of distinguishing the effects of Age, Period and Cohort described in the text.

time point but may make many successive measurements on the same cohorts. This allows cross-sequential comparisons that can add analytical power to the experimental design. Table 18.2 shows dummy data for the same age cohorts who were tested on five successive occasions, 10 years apart. In this table comparisons of birth cohorts (cohort effects) can be tracked by reading down the columns; age trends within individual cohorts over successive time points (age effects) can be tracked by reading down the diagonals, and trends at each age level, as age cohorts replace each other, (period effects) can be tracked by reading along the rows. Such data is sometimes referred to as panel data (Glenn, 1977), in which a range of cohorts is tested at regular intervals, and new cohorts may be recruited to replace groups as they move into older age bands. This is an example of the way in which the maximum analytic strength can be obtained from a longitudinal investigation. The term *longitudinal study* is generally reserved for less complicated undertakings in which the same age cohort is repeatedly as-

sessed at a number of successive time points. The difficulties that apply to longitudinal studies also apply to cross-sectional studies, but it is convenient to consider them in this simpler context.

Unfortunately, cross-sequential studies cannot answer all of the questions about age-related changes that researchers may wish to ask; nor can they exclude, or even identify by posthoc analyses, the effects of all factors that may possibly affect the conclusions that can be drawn. This is because there is no way to select or compare groups of people without confounding the effects of age with those of generational cohort and time of assessment. Consider cross-sectional comparisons in which groups of individuals of different ages are compared at the same time point. This means that they must have been born at different times and so have lived through different historical periods and are likely to have experienced very different socioeconomic conditions such as degree of affluence and access to education, knowledge of good health habits, and quality of medical treatment. In short, age differences will be confounded with generational differences. An alternative is to test one group when it reaches a particular age and then wait until a second, different group reaches the same age. Here, age group and time of measurement are separated, but both are confounded with cohort and generational differences, and the factors are identifiable as "aging cohort" and "time/cohort." Schaie (1965) argued that although any of these designs is ambiguous when used alone, it may be possible to distinguish age, period, and cohort effects if all are used and analyzed simultaneously. He suggested numerical decision rules based on F ratios that might be used to decide which effects were responsible for particular observed differences. Adam (1978) argued that these decision rules are unsound because it is always possible to explain an observed difference in more than one way. For example, a pure maturational effect that is linear over the life span should be seen in significant effects for cohort and time in the cross-sequential design and for age but not for time in the time-sequential design. However, an identical pattern of results may be obtained if linear effects for cohort and time of measurement are present in equal amounts but in opposite directions. Other possible sets of effects can also produce these results.

As Adam (1978) pointed out, in both cross-sequential and time-sequential designs there are possible confounds between age, period, and cohort effects. If age, period, and cohort are treated as continuous variables, then it will be impossible to estimate all parameters in a model of the form

$$D = a + S1A + S2P + S3C + e$$

where D is the dependent variable, S1A is the partial slopes associated with age, S2P is the slopes associated with period, S3C is the slopes associated with cohort, and e is a random error term. Because $C = P - A$, it is impossible to attribute unique effects to all

three variables. Under the assumptions that Schaie (1965) suggests, no mathematical manipulation of the data can disentangle these effects.

If one could experimentally vary age, period, and cohort, then one could estimate the effects of any one of them on the dependent variable by manipulating its value while holding the other two constant. This cannot be done, and in the quasi experiments that Schaie (1977) subsequently suggested, one can only compare the effects of age, cohort, and period by post hoc statistical analyses. Even so, it is impossible to hold constant the effects of any two of these factors, such as age and period, and then vary the third, such as cohort. As Adam (1978) pointed out, "Once we select a group of a particular age in a particular year there is only one birth cohort whose behaviour we can observe."

Although no good solution to these problems is yet known, the debate has provoked very useful discussions by Adam (1978); Baltes (1968); Baltes, Cornelius, and Nesselroade (1979); Costa and McCrae (1982); Glenn (1981); Maddox and Wiley (1976); Mason, Winsborough, Mason, and Poole (1973); Palmore, (1978); and Schaie and Baltes (1975).

Baltes and Nesselroade (1970) realized that Schaie's (1965) suggestions could not solve the problem and suggested that meaningful analyses are still possible when it is reasonable to suppose that one of these three variables has very small effects on the dependent variable and thus to ignore it in order to analyze the effects of the remaining two. Though very few investigators explicitly state and defend the assumptions on which they have based their decisions, this pragmatic solution has been tacitly adopted in all of the small-scale cross-sectional comparisons that make up the bulk of the literature. To ignore one of these three factors may often be the only choice available; however, for example, if the effects of age and cohort on the dependent variable are causally unrelated, then omission of either of them from an analysis risks serious misinterpretation. In this case, the only remedy is laborious replication of studies with new samples in order to check that any factor that is omitted actually does not affect the outcome. The lack of experimental replications to test assumptions (which, in any case, usually remain covert) is a basic weakness in the literature on cognitive gerontology.

No solution to these confounds has yet been found for cases in which empirical investigations show that none of these three factors can be safely ignored. Here researchers must have recourse to the usual props of scientific induction: replicability of experiments, consistency of trends across experiments, and parsimony of explanation. As Adam (1978, p. 238) put it, "If we impose certain restrictions on the system, and if we look beyond that system to other independent sources of evidence, we can begin to establish an interpretation of the data."

Further problems remain because discussions have as yet considered only a simplified model in which the effects of age, cohort, and period are all linear and do not interact. It is increasingly clear that age-related changes in cognitive performance are better described by accelerated functions than by linear functions (e.g., Rabbitt et al., 2001), and it is very likely that cohort effects, such as socioeconomic advantage, and period effects, such as availability of medical care, are markedly interactive, rather than simply additive to the effects of calendar age.

Models for the Time Course of Aging

The difficulties caused by failures to distinguish between descriptions of the process of aging at the individual and at the population level become clear when we consider how to differentiate between different models for

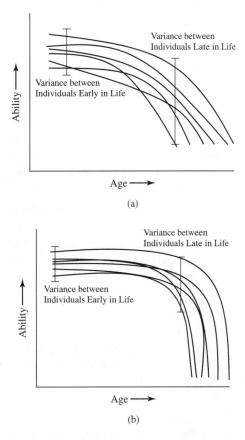

Figure 18.2   Illustration of how both continuous declines and abrupt "terminal drops" in performance of individuals in aging samples can result in very similar changes in average levels of performance and in increases in variance in performance between individuals as sample age increases.

the time course of aging. In terms of limiting cases, aging can be regarded as continuously progressive or as abrupt and catastrophic. Figure 18.2a illustrates aging as a continuous and accelerating process, which has the same form for all individuals, but at different rates for each. Here, the average trajectory of population aging is the central tendency of a sheaf of individual trajectories that show continuous declines at different rates. Because their aging trajectories decline at different rates, differences between individuals will increase with the age of the group sampled: the older the group, the greater will be the gap in performance between its most and least able members.

Figure 18.2b illustrates the alternative limiting case of a terminal drop model in which each person attains an early plateau of performance that is maintained until an abrupt decline that occurs soon before death. Here, individuals' trajectories of cognitive aging will show prolonged stability followed by rapid decline but, because their terminal drops occur at different ages, the form of the average of all trajectories will show continuous and accelerating change. Variance between individuals will also increase with sample age because the older the sample, the more people in it will be undergoing terminal declines, and the fewer will still maintain their performance plateaus. Thus, the models assume very different forms of trajectories of aging at the *individual level,* but they generate very similar predictions at the *population level.*

These are hypothetical limiting cases. In reality, the best-fitting description will depend on the particular life circumstances of the sample that is examined. In an underprivileged population in which rapid death by disease or accident sharply curtails life expectancy, individual trajectories of cognitive change will tend to follow a pattern of terminal drops rather than of continuous declines. In affluent societies in which life expectancy is much longer, and in which medical treatment postpones death from pathology, a continuous decline model will provide a better description. In any of these cases, single cross-sectional comparisons between different age groups will not distinguish whether continuous decline or terminal drop models are more appropriate. In a mixed population sample in which some individuals are underprivileged and others are affluent, both patterns of change will be present. To distinguish differences in forms of trajectories for individuals from differences in the forms of trajectories

for populations, researchers need data from longitudinal studies in which the same people are repeatedly assessed over many years. The relative advantages and limitations of cross-sectional and longitudinal studies have been one of the main topics of methodological discussion.

Advantages and Difficulties of Longitudinal Studies

Longitudinal studies avoid some of the problems with matching of control and experimental groups that beset cross-sectional investigations. Participants are their own controls in repeated-measures designs that may uncover interactions between the processes of aging and other factors such as demographics, health, and socioeconomic advantage (see Winer, 1971). Shock (1985), whose pioneer Baltimore Aging Study is one of the largest, longest, and best-designed yet, identified a serious practical difficulty: "Few investigators can afford to dedicate their careers to one longitudinal study, let alone a series of longitudinal studies, each building on the results of the previous one." Longitudinal studies also have other problems. As in cross-sectional and cross-sequential studies, the effects of age are always confounded with those of cohort and period. The problems of selective recruitment that affect cross-sectional comparisons are compounded by the much heavier commitments for participants that longitudinal studies demand. Problems that are not found in cross-sectional comparisons are the effects of progressive selective sample attrition and of practice. Although practice and attrition effects have long been recognized, nearly all studies to date have ignored or mishandled them and thus have underestimated their effects.

An underused advantage of longitudinal studies is that they allow researchers to compare average changes in performance at the population level and at the individual level by plotting regressions for individual participants (e.g., Shock et al., 1984). As Shock (1985) pointed out, the implications of the wide differences between curves for individuals have been entirely ignored:

> Relatively few individuals follow the pattern of age changes predicted from averages based on measurements made on different subjects. Aging is so highly individual that average curves give only a rough approximation of the pattern of aging followed by individuals. . . .
>
> Longitudinal observations have shown that the rates of change for some variables observed in individual subjects did not differ from the mean rates derived from analysis of cross-sectional observations. On the other hand, many individuals followed patterns of aging that could never have been identified from cross-sectional data alone. For example many subjects experienced periods of 5–10 years during which their kidney function showed no significant change, while the average curve was declining. In a few, kidney function actually improved over a ten year interval when average values were falling.

This chapter will repeatedly return to the fact that changes in group-average performance on cognitive tasks with age are often less informative than accompanying changes in variability of performance, both within and between individuals.

The general methodological framework for designing longitudinal studies, with useful discussion of calculations of statistical power and of frequency of measurement, have been thoroughly worked out by epidemiologists and insightfully discussed by Nesselrode and Baltes (1979); Schaie (1983); Schlesselman (1973a, 1973b); Schulsinger, Knopf, and Mednick (1981); and many others. Unfortunately, these guidelines do not provide ways of resolving the problems of bias from selective enrollment that are present in all cross-sectional studies but are exaggerated

in longitudinal studies that require volunteers to commit time not merely on a single occasion, but repeatedly over many years. Post hoc studies of empirical data have also shown that these selection effects are indeed substantial and that they markedly bias the demographics of studies toward a preponderance of unusually healthy, affluent, well-educated, and highly motivated participants. Longitudinal studies encounter the added problem that they also suffer from dropout, which is not random but selective. The frailest and least able participants drop out earliest, leaving an increasingly elite residue of the healthiest, most competent, and most highly motivated (Lachman et al., 1982).

In longitudinal studies of cognitive change, participants must repeatedly be given identical or very similar tests, and researchers must therefore expect that they will improve with practice. Schaie, Labouvie, and Barrett (1973) found that individuals in a group of volunteers aged from 21 to 75 years who returned for retesting were those who, on initial testing, had scored higher on all of the 10 cognitive variables measured. Schaie (1965), who was also among the first to recognize the possibility of practice effects, suggested that cross-sequential designs could identify and eliminate them because independent samples of individuals born in the same period are compared at different times of measurement. Because each given individual is assessed only once means that there is a way of separating practice effects from those of age and even of examining age × practice, and cohort × practice interactions. The next sections present the problems of selective dropout and practice in turn.

Dropout Effects

An obvious cause of selective dropout in longitudinal studies is that older people are more likely to die or become too frail to attend.

Death not only reduces selectively the numbers of older participants but also alters the demographics of studies in other ways because mortality markedly differs with socioeconomic advantage and because more and less prosperous individuals also tend to die from different causes. Thus, not only the incidence but also the duration and steepness of the slope of terminal declines probably varies with socioeconomic class (Nagi & Stockwell, 1973).

People drop out for a variety of other reasons than death. It is essential to document the reasons that participants give for dropping out because, as analyses by Rabbitt, Donlan, Watson, et al. (1993) have found, individuals who drop out because they become ill or frail have lower levels of ability than do those who leave because they have acquired new responsibilities or employment. Unless the causes, as well as the incidence, of dropout are taken into consideration, comparisons of rates of cognitive change in different population subgroups may be misleading.

Although dropout effects have been widely documented, very few analyses of longitudinal changes have taken them into consideration. Some investigators have tried to estimate the likely impacts of selective dropout by comparing the patterns of age trends observed in cross-sectional analyses of initial screenings of a volunteer population against the cross-sectional and longitudinal patterns of trends observed in later screens of the same sample. Such studies have often found that the age trends revealed by successive cross-sectional comparisons are similar and have concluded that although selective dropout occurs, it does not necessarily alter age trends in the data in any substantial way (e.g., Sliewinski & Bushke, 1999; Zelinski & Burnight, 1997; Zelinski & Stewart, 1998). Checking cross-sectional trends against longitudinal trends is a useful initial exploratory step in data analysis, but it is not a complete solution. The effects of demographic factors on selective dropout during longitudinal studies are usually simple exaggerations of patterns of initial self-selection among those volunteering for entry. Older, frailer, and less healthy individuals as well as the less able, the less socially advantaged, and males are all less likely to volunteer for longitudinal studies and are all more likely to drop out. It can be argued that selective dropout simply exaggerates biases that are already present at the first screening of a volunteer sample. However, although comparisons of cross-sectional against longitudinal trends may reassure us that average changes in ability with age have not been greatly misrepresented by selective dropout, they do not resolve the equally important issue that large increases in variability between members of an aging population may be obscured because the less-able participants drop out earlier. Where comparisons of cross-sectional and longitudinal trends have been used to check whether dropout affects the patterns of observed changes, the intervals over which longitudinal data have been collected have often been too short for the effects of selective dropout over time to become marked (e.g., in Zelinski, Gilewski, & Stewart, 1993).

Technically, it is important to distinguish three different scenarios (Rubin, 1976):

1. The dropout process is independent of the measurement process and thus does not bias results.

2. The dropout process is random: It is dependent on the observed measurements prior to dropout but is independent of the measurements that would have been observed had the subject not dropped out.

3. The dropout process is informative: It is dependent on the measurements that would have been observed had the subject not dropped out.

Not surprisingly, analyses made under the informative dropout assumption are fraught with difficulty. Their results typically depend on modeling assumptions that are difficult, or impossible, to check from the observed data. This is especially the case for the kind of unbalanced data that arise in observational studies in which even a firm dropout time may be very hard to identify. At the opposite extreme, analyses under the assumption of completely random dropout are generally straightforward because no distinction need be made between measurements that are unavailable because of dropout and those that are unavailable because they were never intended to be made. Put another way, completely random dropout implies that the incomplete data can simply be treated as if from an unbalanced experimental design, with no commonality to the times at which measurements are made on different subjects.

The simplicity of analysis under the completely random dropout assumption is bought at a price. If this assumption is invalid, then so may be the resulting inferences about the measurement process. However, if likelihood-based methods of inference are used, validity is retained under the weaker assumption of random dropout. This is important because longitudinal data are typically correlated over time. This means that even when the true dropout process is informative, the most recent observed measurements on a given subject are partially predictive of the missing measurements after dropout. Therefore, by allowing for the effects of these measurements on dropout (which is what the random dropout assumption implies), we can partly compensate for the missing information (see, e.g., Scharfstein, Rotnitzky, & Robins, 1999). To appreciate how likelihood-based methods automatically make this kind of compensation, a simple synthetic example may be useful. Figure 18.3, derived from Diggle et al. (1994, chap. 11) shows a simulated data set from a model in which the mean response is constant over time but the probability of dropout for

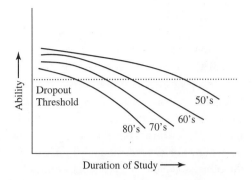

Figure 18.3 We may assume that volunteers in a longitudinal study drop out when they fall below a particular threshold of competency. As a study continues individuals in older groups cross this threshold earlier than those in younger groups. Among other effects this means that increased variance in competence between individual members of an ageing sample is disguised.

any given subject at any given time is a decreasing function of that subject's most recent measurement. The effect is progressively to cause the low-responding subjects to drop out, leading to an apparent rising trend in the mean response over time as the observed mean is calculated from the progressively more highly selected subpopulation of survivors. This rising trend is what would be estimated by a naive regression analysis of the data, which ignores both the dropout process and the longitudinal correlation within the data. In contrast, a likelihood-based analysis that takes account of the longitudinal correlation in the data correctly infers a constant mean response over time.

An important consequence is that for longitudinal data with dropout, there is no reason why a fitted mean response curve should track the observed mean response trajectory of the survivors. On the contrary, a model fitted by likelihood-based methods under the assumption of random dropouts estimates what the mean response would have been if it had been possible to follow up the entire study population, whereas the observed means estimate the mean response conditional on not dropping out before the time in question. The unconditional and conditional means coincide only if the data are uncorrelated in time, or if the dropout process is completely random. Rabbitt et al. (in press) provide a practical illustration of how random-effect models can be used to estimate the forms of functions describing age-related changes during a longitudinal study by, in effect, modeling what trends would have been if the substantial and selective dropout that was empirically observed had not occurred.

Practice Effects

The extent to which practice effects can mask true trends in data has recently been recognized in relatively brief investigations of the effects of surgery and anesthesia on the cognitive performance of older patients. Here the optimal methodology is to give patients the same cognitive tests immediately before and at short intervals after surgery. Many excellent studies failed to find changes from presurgical performance on retests later than 3 to 11 days following surgery—a period in which patients are still suffering from the immediate effects of their operations. It was only when the extent and persistence of practice effects were recognized and taken into account that it became clear that many older patients do suffer some cognitive loss that may persist as long as three months after surgery (Dijkstra, van Boxtel, Houx, & Jolles, 1998; Moller et al., 1998). Brief laboratory studies have also shown that practice effects can interact in complex ways with the levels of difficulty and with the qualitative demands of the tasks on which individuals are assessed. On some very easy tasks such as high-compatibility CRT tasks, practice effects are counterintuitively much greater for older and less able individuals than for younger and more able individuals (Rabbitt, 1993b). However, with more difficult tasks, such as

complex video games, more able individuals show much greater initial as well as longer-sustained gains (Rabbitt, Banerji, & Szemanski, 1989). Failure to recognize the extent of systematic individual differences in practice effects will lead to serious misinterpretations of longitudinal data. Tasks on which older individuals show greater practice gains will mask the true extent of age-related decline; tasks on which younger and more able individuals show greater practice gains will exaggerate age-related changes; and we may also, wrongly, conclude that more able individuals decline more slowly as they age. When batteries include both of these kinds of tasks, we may be misled into assuming that differences in apparent rates of age-related change between tasks reflect patterns of cognitive aging rather than differences in practice effects.

Perhaps practice effects have been neglected because investigators have made the plausible assumption that they must be absent or negligible when intervals between successive tests are as long as 1 to 10 years, and have also assumed that they can be avoided or minimized by retesting participants on logically similar but superficially different parallel forms of tasks. Unfortunately, work on training and transfer between versions of the letter-letter substitution task have shown significant and asymmetrical practice effects, with more able individuals being aided, and less able individuals being slowed on transfer from one to another vocabulary of code letters (Rabbitt, Stollery, Moore, & Han, submitted 2001). The assumption that practice effects are negligible when assessments are separated by many years has also been empirically disproved. Rabbitt et al. (in press) used random-effect models to identify practice effects and to estimate their relative sizes. Over test-retest intervals of 2 to 8 years, practice effects on the Heim (1970) AH4 intelligence tests were significantly greater for older and less able participants and on average across all participants aged from 49 to 92 years counteracted losses sustained over 4 years of aging.

It must again be stressed that methodological problems do not arise in the abstract but derive rather from the particular models from which arise the questions we ask. Ideally, experimental questions should arise from the necessity to choose between equally well-articulated models of the processes under scrutiny. In cognitive gerontology we have, as yet, only contrasts between loose working assumptions. The first of these is made by applied cognitive gerontologists who, because they are obliged to ask practical questions about what older people can and cannot do, are not so much concerned with the functional etiology as with the entire condition of human aging and practical implications of age-related changes. These practical interests oblige them to consider changes in competence at complex everyday activities rather than to design laboratory tasks that are supposed to be so simple and stripped down that they can measure the effects of single task demands that are putatively met by different functional processes such as those we label with terms uneasily borrowed from common language such as "attention," "memory," or "control." Applied cognitive gerontologists are more concerned to understand how changes in anatomical, physiological, and mental competencies interact to affect performance in everyday life than to work out functional etiologies. If pressed for theoretical explanations that transcend the demands of the particular systems and situations for which they undertake to give advice, applied cognitive gerontologists might suggest, as have very distinguished applied cognitive psychologists such as Broadbent (1971) and Sanders (1998), that investigations of the ways in which humans cope with complex task demands lead to better models and richer insights than does the increasingly finicky reductionism characteristic of much theoretical discussion.

In contrast, theoretical cognitive gerontologists have found no useful general principles and currently camp on either side of what is, in my view, a false dichotomy. Some espouse a global single-factor theory that seems to adopt parsimony of description as the overriding criterion for scientific explanation and so start with the premise that all age-related changes in cognitive abilities can be understood as consequences of changes in information processing speed (Salthouse, 1985, 1991, 1996a). As shown later, however, adoption of the psychometric construct g_f would be at least equally defensible but, in my view, this would impoverish research for the same reasons. The alternative position—which is much more widely, though tacitly, adopted, and perhaps for that reason less grimly defended—recognizes evidence that neurophysiological and neuroanatomical changes may not be uniform in extent and time course over the entire brain and CNS, so that it makes sense to ask whether age may affect changes in different mental abilities at different rates and by different amounts. This more open-minded attitude seems to open new lines of research rather than block them by premature proclamation of a final theoretical solution. Because it encourages investigations as to whether aging affects some cognitive skills earlier and more severely than it does others, it may be caricatured as a modular theory. The next section considers the successes and limitations of these three different approaches.

METHODOLOGICAL AND THEORETICAL CONTRIBUTIONS OF APPLIED COGNITIVE GERONTOLOGY TO UNDERSTANDING COGNITIVE AGING

To forecast demands for support in an aging population and to suggest how services, systems, and equipment can best be adapted for effective use, applied cognitive gerontologists need to investigate how the characteristics of populations change as they age. A useful example is a report by Melzer, McWilliams, Brayne, Johnson, and Bond (1999) on how increasing incidence of disabilities in a large community resident population entails corresponding demands for particular kinds of services and support. The emphasis on disabilities and the extent of social support can be misleading. For example, Melzer et al. estimate that 11% of men and 19% of women in the United Kingdom who are aged 65 years or older are disabled, that 38% of these are aged 85 years or older, and that a similar percentage is cognitively impaired. Although this is a clear warning for investigators who rely on random selection of small samples, it also implies the happy conclusion that 89% of men and 81% of women aged 65 years or older do *not* experience any severely life-restricting disabilities or marked cognitive impairments before they die. The equation of increasing age with increasing incidence of disability and the inevitable politicization of issues of resource distribution are illustrated by the protocols of successive European Union initiatives to develop Technological Innovations for the Disabled and Elderly (TIDE) initiatives, in which the elderly have been implicitly categorized as members of a group who suffer from "disabilities" that require marked changes in lifestyle and the provision of prostheses and special help.

Melzer et al. (1999) showed that this characterization is statistically invalid. Nevertheless, the political strategy of labeling age-related changes as disabilities forces informative contrasts between the kinds of disabilities suffered by younger and older adults. Among younger adults even markedly limiting conditions such as blindness, deafness, or loss of mobility affect only a small minority of individuals and, in most of them, disable particular competencies without af-

fecting others. In contrast, the disabilities inevitable in old age are mainly minor but are very widespread both at the population level where they affect everybody to a greater or lesser extent and at the individual level where they impair all sensory, motor, and cognitive systems to some degree. Thus, for applied cognitive psychologists, the condition of old age is defined in terms of the cumulative and interactive effects of many concurrent different and slight sensory, motor, and cognitive changes. For example, most partially sighted people are older, but older people are also much more likely than younger partially sighted people to be deaf, to have reduced accuracy of touch discrimination that makes it harder for them to read Braille and to handle and discriminate between small objects, to have problems of mobility, and, perhaps most importantly, to have impoverished cognitive backup to compensate for all these losses. Younger adults may compensate remarkably for blindness by maintaining and efficiently updating a complex memory map of where they and other objects are located in space. Older blind people, with increasingly inefficient working memories, find this much more difficult. Elderly partially sighted and deaf people are also more handicapped by their conditions because their reduced cognitive resources make it more difficult for them to make the most of the degraded sensory information available to them. That is to say, older people process sensory information more slowly (Birren, 1956 and 1959; Birren, Woods, & Williams, 1980), with less efficient attentional selectivity, and with less efficient backup from prospective memory and working memory (Craik, 1996; Craik & Jennings, 1992; Maylor 1996). Consequently, applied cognitive psychologists need theoretical models for the additive and multiplicatively interactive effects of these minor changes. It follows that they tend to find the speculation that all of these changes result from a global decline in a single factor, such as g_f or "mental speed," unhelpful.

Although this attitude may seem ploddingly pragmatic, it has uncovered phenomena that theoretically more focused research has missed. It is well known that age causes relatively mild degradations of information from all sensory systems (Corso, 1987). It is less appreciated that these mild impairments of sensory input have knock-on effects on higher cognitive functions. Able young adults who can correctly repeat aloud continuous speech, whether it is presented in clear or through noise, nevertheless better remember what has been said when it is presented it in clear (Rabbitt, 1968a). The size of this effect varies with individuals' general mental ability indexed by their unadjusted ITSs and thus, implicitly, with their relative speeds of information processing and working memory efficiency. For example, mild astigmatism induced by distorting lenses does not affect the speed with which young adults can read text but does reduce the ability of those with lower ITSs to remember what they have just faultlessly read aloud (Dickenson & Rabbitt, 1991). Even slight sensory degradation increases demands on central cognitive resources that are necessary to identify words and to read them aloud as well as to use context to understand and remember their content. Individuals with higher ITSs have correspondingly higher levels of resources that allow them both to overcome sensory degradation and to comprehend and remember better what they have read. Similarly, older people with hearing losses of 40 dB to 60 dB that do not impair their ability to repeat continuous speech correctly nevertheless find it more difficult to remember what has been said to them, and older individuals who have higher ITSs can tolerate their hearing losses better than those with lower ITSs (Rabbitt, 1991).

Applied cognitive gerontologists are also forced to recognize another point missed by theoreticians. Older people often perform much better in their familiar environments than might be predicted from their performance in the laboratory. Familiar everyday settings provide compensatory support systems for proficient performance that are absent in laboratory settings. Equally, loss of familiar environmental support can have catastrophic consequences. Failure to appreciate growing dependency on familiar context may prevent those who need it from seeking help, or from adapting easily to apparently very minor changes in life demands (e.g., Humphrey, Gilhome-Herbst, & Farqui, 1981).

A basic lesson from applied cognitive gerontology is that aging affects the whole organism, and that it may be difficult, and in practice pointless, to try to separate the etiology and practical consequences of primary and secondary age-related changes because they interact to limit performance in all but the most simplified laboratory tasks. This has at least three different methodological implications. Most obviously, older volunteers will always suffer some degree of sensory loss in contrast to their younger controls. Even when researchers are satisfied that they have selected people with apparently inconsequential sensory losses we must try to make sure that the stimuli used are as clearly visible and audible as possible. This can be hard to achieve. For example, during the pilot stages of a protracted longitudinal study of normal healthy people aged from 49 to 96 years (Rabbitt, Donlan, Bent, McInnes, & Abson, 1993), variations in the acoustic qualities of rooms used for presentations of tape-recorded lists of words for recall resulted in concomitant variations of 19% to 32% in the total numbers of errors made, and led to marked differences in estimates of declines in the numbers of memory efficiency with age. Until conditions were improved and standardized, age comparisons were grossly misleading.

A second implication is that even when both participants and stimulus materials have been selected with all possible care, researchers must be careful not to neglect the point that even slight peripheral losses can be markers of marked age-related central changes (see Baltes & Lindenberger, 1997; Lindenberger & Baltes, 1994). A third implication derives from the obligation of applied cognitive gerontologists to consider how the majority of elderly people cope with the complexities of their lives. To do this they must ensure that the samples that they study are as representative as possible of the population at large and, especially, that they include substantial proportions of individuals with minor disabilities. In contrast, theoretical cognitive gerontologists who hope to study the cognitive effects of primary aging deliberately exclude a substantial majority of elderly individuals who have experienced more than minimal sensory changes. This not only means that samples are not normative with respect to the population but also that deliberate selection of people with few or no sensory impairments will exclude those who have experienced more than minimal central changes, whether these result from primary or from secondary causes.

In theoretical cognitive gerontology, current models polarize into global models based on the idea that changes in all mental abilities and cognitive skills are driven by changes in a single functional characteristic of the cognitive system and into "modular" models that use evidence that biological aging differentially affects different brain areas and functions as a starting point for investigations into whether the different mental abilities that these systems support may also age at different rates.

MODELS THAT HAVE GUIDED THEORETICAL INVESTIGATIONS IN COGNITIVE GERONTOLOGY

Global Slowing and Single-Factor Models

Because age-related biological changes probably affect all brain systems, and therefore all cognitive abilities, researchers are always certain to find some commonality in the extent and time courses of changes in cognitive performance. For example, increasing cerebrovascular impairment is likely to affect most of the brain and thus cause weakly correlated changes in most cognitive abilities. As a result, correlations between scores on different tests increase with sample age and principal-components analyses of results from test batteries show reduced differentiation ("de-differentiation") of factor structures. This can be seen as a particular and easily explainable example of the so-called Detterman effect: that correlations between levels of performance on different tests are greater in samples with lower than in those of higher intellectual ability. It is important to emphasize that the claims of the global slowing model go beyond this inevitability of increasing associations between test scores by proposing that regardless of what the biological changes that drive cognitive changes may be, they functionally express themselves by slowing cognitive speed or information processing speed and that this general slowing is directly and causally responsible for, rather than merely contributory to, all age-related changes in all cognitive abilities, especially memory (Salthouse, 1985, 1991, 1996a).

The gap between speculations about the nature of the changes in brain function that may bring about general slowing and the empirical description of the behavioral changes that ensue is illustrated by empirical findings that the same evidence for uniform multiplicative scaling of mean CRTs across tasks with different demands and levels of difficulty (Cerella, 1985), on which the general slowing model of aging was originally based, are duplicated by slowing of CRTs by differences in adult intelligence (Brand & Deary, 1982; Rabbitt, 1996; Rabbitt & Maylor, 1991), by maturation during childhood (Anderson, 1988, 1992; Hale, 1990; Kail, 1988, 1991), by ingestion of alcohol (Rabbitt & Maylor, 1991), and by neurological damage consequent on multiple sclerosis (Kail, 1997). Although intoxication, brain trauma, diffuse neurological damage, maturation, general intelligence, and senescence affect patterns of performance across simple tasks in very similar ways, this does not allow us to assume that they all reflect an identical functional common cause. However, this generality of application does not affect the validity of global slowing as an explanatory framework for any of these conditions because it is possible that quite different biological changes may produce similar patterns of functional changes. Unfortunately, muddles occur when researchers lose sight of the necessary distinction between the levels of description of behavioral data and of functional process.

The ways in which we can compare how well different individuals can perform any tasks are surprisingly limited. Consequently, nearly all functional models for how humans perform tasks are based on comparisons of how quickly people can do different things and how many errors they make while doing them. Directly measurable indexes such as speed and accuracy may be called task performance indexes to distinguish them from hypothetical constructs in functional models of performance that cannot directly be measured, and that have meaning only within a framework of assumptions about processes in the CNS. Examples of these, which we may call hypothetical system performance characteristics, are Beta, d-prime, and trace decay rate, or, in connectionist models, unit activa-

tion threshold and system temperature, and, in somewhat dated information processing models, information processing rate (e.g., Garner, 1988; Hick, 1952).

All cognitive gerontologists hope that the functional models in terms of which these performance characteristics are defined will eventually be validated against convergent data from a third level of description; that of biological processes in the CNS. Some investigators propose that both measurable task performance indexes, such as CRTs, or system performance characteristics, such as information processing speed, may directly reflect particular functional characteristics of the CNS such as synaptic conductivity or neuronal conduction speed (see, e.g., Eysenck, 1986; Reed, 1993; Reed & Jensen, 1992). To emphasize their derivation from physiological measurements independently of any behavioral data, we may call this third class of constructs measurable neurophysiological system performance characteristics.

These three levels of constructs must be distinguished from a fourth that derives from psychometric theory. Spearman (1924) found that when large numbers of people were given two or more different intelligence tests, factor analyses of their scores generally showed that most of the variance between them could be well expressed in terms of a single factor, which he termed general fluid ability (g_f). We may call such entities statistically derived psychometric constructs. Constructs such as g_f can be considered theoretically neutral because they can be taken as descriptions of the extents and patterns of abstract statistical relationships between different empirically measured performance indexes without any functional implications. However, some researchers speculate that g_f can, in turn, be reified in terms of hypothetical system performance characteristics such as mental or cognitive speed (Eysenck, 1986; Jensen, 1980, 1982; Nettelbeck, 1987;

Vernon, 1985) or even in terms of measurable neurobiological system characteristics such as synaptic conduction or latency of the visual pathway (Reed & Jensen, 1992).

This taxonomy is cumbersome but may help to keep researchers aware that terms such as speed or slowing mean quite different things depending on which level of description is currently being used. At the level of task performance indexes, speed seems a transparent construct, and differences in speed between individuals can be measured directly by comparing their reaction times in identical tasks. As is shown later, this is not actually the case, and measured speed in reaction time experiments is not interchangeable with performance operating characteristics that might be used in models to account for differences in speed between more or less efficient systems. These latter may be entities such as operating threshold or degree of connectivity, or may also be higher-order mathematical or gross statistical properties such as system temperature. Although changes in these performance characteristics can determine the maximum externally measurable operating speed of a system—because none of them can be expressed in terms of units of speed or of time at this level of description—the term *global slowing model* loses meaning (for an extended discussion of these issues see Rabbitt, 1996).

Consistent with these arguments, reviews of the mainstream literature on models for CRTs shows that none of them incorporates speed per se as a performance characteristic of the functional processes that they specify (see Laming, 1968, 1985; Luce, 1986; Ratcliff, van Zandt, & McKoon, 1999; Townsend & Ashby, 1983). Descriptions of decision criteria can be framed in terms of different kinds of models and therefore can be quantified and compared in different ways, but temporal units are not sensible indexes for this purpose. In sum, although it is clear that most elderly people respond more slowly than do most younger adults in both simple and complex tasks, functional models for how these differences come about require much more detailed and better considered assumptions than simply that the functional processes by which fast decisions are made are unaltered by age in any way except in the sense that they all take longer to complete.

A brief historical review may help to explain how the global slowing model has persisted despite the obvious confusions that its use entails.

A Short History of Global Slowing

Perhaps the first broad generalization in cognitive gerontology was that age slows performance on all tasks (Birren, 1965; Fozard, Vercruyssen, Reynolds, Hancock, & Quilter, 1994; Schaie, 1989, 1990b; Siegler, 1983). A more interesting corollary was the discovery of age × task complexity interactions: As tasks become harder, differences between the average CRTs of older and younger groups markedly increase (Birren, 1979; Birren et al., 1980).

This simple insight has methodologically nontrivial consequences. A digression may be useful because the general understanding of age-related changes in memory has been weakened by the neglect of similar relationships in analyses of tasks in which performance is assessed in terms of accuracy rather than in terms of speed. Rabbitt, Coward, and Lowe (manuscript in preparation) plotted data from 30 studies of age differences in recall and recognition memory, published between 1970 and 1999, in older and younger groups that were compared on a baseline condition on which a particular theoretical model predicted little or no age-related change, and on an experimental condition on which the model predicted that older people would make more errors. Because, at least in these cases, these predictions were always fulfilled, the authors of the published studies concluded that the functional subsystems that met the particular task demands that distinguished the experimental from the baseline conditions must be especially vulnerable to aging. A simple linear regression with a slope of 1.4 fits the with $R^2 = .73$. The precise form of the function is not of interest because the points are only that in every study both the younger and the older groups made more errors on the experimental condition than on the baseline condition, that this increase in errors was invariably greater for the older groups, and that the proportional amount of this increase (the form of the age × task difficulty interaction) is quite similar across both baseline and experimental conditions and across a variety of different task demands.

If age has proportionately similar effects on all conditions of all these tasks, it is hard to argue that in any one of them the finding that old people show greater increases in errors between the control and the experimental conditions occurs because they are more sensitive to a particular qualitative task demand than simply to an increase in task difficulty. Even if age always had proportionately greater effects on experimental conditions than on baseline conditions, it would still be necessary to further check whether this happened only because baseline conditions were so easy that both younger and older participants showed floor effects. A more satisfactory demonstration would be that a particular task demand, A, markedly increases errors for both younger and older groups but that a different and theoretically critical demand, B, produces a smaller increase in errors for the older group than does demand A but nevertheless increases the difference in errors between the younger and the older group by a greater amount than does A. This hypothetical situation is illustrated in Figure 18.4.

Chapman and Chapman (1973) showed that it is methodologically crucial when studying individual differences not to confuse

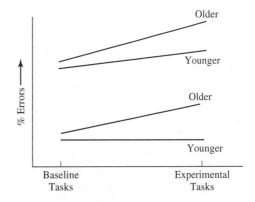

Figure 18.4 The conventional methodology in small scale studies of the effects of age on memory has been to compare older and younger groups on Baseline and experimental versions of particular tasks. When, as for the lower comparison, scores for the young group on the experimental task are the same as or better than their scores on the baseline task we can safely assume that the difference observed for the Older group is not brought about by a simple increase in task difficulty but is, rather, due to the particular nature of the demands of the experimental task. However when, as in the upper comparison, both the Younger and the Older group perform worse on the experimental than on the baseline task the effects of task demands are confounded with the effects of task difficulty.

global effects of task difficulty with specific effects of task demands. This view has recently been updated, with illustrations of the problems that can arise and with methods to circumvent them, by Miller, Chapman, Chapman, and Collins (1995).

The methodological implications of age × task difficulty interactions have been neglected in many memory experiments but were brilliantly realized in CRT studies by Cerella (1985), who used a methodology first described by Brinley (1965) of plotting mean CRTs obtained from older groups against corresponding mean CRTs obtained from younger groups in over 140 different published experiments. Cerella found that, across all conditions of all tasks, these Brinley plots were well fitted by linear functions with slopes averaging 1.4 or 1.5. Because all age × task complexity interactions seemed to be expressed by the same simple constant across qualitatively very different task demands and across all levels of task difficulty, Cerella (1985) concluded that he could find no evidence that older people are more sensitive to some task demands than to others.

Methodologically, this is a bleak conclusion because it means that CRT measurements cannot reveal whether age affects different cognitive subsystems to different extents. However, note that for applied cognitive gerontologists this is a very cheerful and useful discovery. Even if Cerella's (1985) analyses are only approximately correct and the data are better fitted by complex than simple linear functions, the knowledge that regular relationships exist allows researchers to estimate older individuals' decision times on any task for which we have already collected data from young adults.

Cerella's meta-analysis (1985) followed earlier attempts by Anders and Fozard (1973) and by Anders, Fozard, and Lilliquist (1972) to apply Sternberg's (1969, 1975) decomposition logic to discover whether age affects some subprocesses more than others. Sternberg (1969, 1975) made the strong assumption that individuals' mean CRTs represent the sum of the individual durations of a linear entrained sequence of mutually independent processing stages. He suggested that by varying task demands, it was possible to increase task loads on one of these stages without affecting others. In this way, the form of interactions between the effects of task loadings and of intersubject differences can reveal whether some stages are more affected than others by states such as alcohol ingestion or conditions such as learning difficulties (Sternberg, 1975).

Cerella's (1985) findings have been replicated in numerous studies that have further found similar apparently linear Brinley functions when quantiles of CRT distributions obtained from older individuals were plotted against those obtained from younger individuals (e.g., Rabbitt & Maylor, 1991) and also when mean reaction times were rank-ordered from fastest to slowest in an elderly group and in a younger group and plotted against each other (e.g., Maylor & Rabbitt, 1994). These ubiquitous regularities supported the idea that if all the hypothetical processing stages or subprocesses necessary to meet any task demands are equally slowed by age, then the effects of age are best described as global slowing of information processing rate across all cognitive systems. Cerella (1990) subsequently revised his interpretation of Brinley plots and suggested that they are best fitted by asymptotic rather than linear functions, but this does not alter the idea that they represent regularities in scaling that are common across all tasks and suggest that all processing stages are slowed to the same proportional extent. Note that it is a much more radical and logically unwarranted step to propose, as with Salthouse (1985), that information processing rate is a single master performance characteristic that underlies efficiency in all cognitive tasks, including especially memory tasks in which performance is measured in units of accuracy rather than in units of speed.

The variety of conditions and states that seem to bring about similar scaling effects of decision times has become somewhat embarrassing for a general slowing theory of aging. As noted, similar regularities are observed for differences between individuals who have and who have not ingested alcohol (Rabbitt & Maylor, 1991), between individuals with lower and higher scores on intelligence tests (Rabbitt, 1996; Rabbitt & Maylor, 1991), between children and adolescents of various ages (Kail, 1988; 1991), and between individuals who suffer from multiple sclerosis and their well controls (Kail, 1997). Zheng, Myerson, and Hale (2000) also neatly showed similar regularities when rank-ordered CRTs for the faster and slower members of a group of young adults are plotted against each other. Evidently, no one would wish to argue that the neurophysiological bases of all these conditions are identical. The best that can be done is to argue that very different kinds of changes at the neurophysiological level may bring about differences in some vaguely defined construct such as mental capacity (Salthouse, 1996a, 1996b) or, perhaps, may be mediated by some common hypothetical system performance characteristic such as random noise (Eysenck, 1986; Kail, 1997). Although taken out of context, perhaps the best summary statement is, again, by Zheng et al. (2000, p. 113): "It is not generally recognized how little examination of differences in mean CRTs of different age groups reveals about individuals."

Confidence in the use of Brinley functions as devices for analyzing individual differences in reaction times has been gradually eroded by so many different kinds of problems that it may be useful to discuss them in order.

First, as has been strongly argued by Fisk and Fisher (1994) Brinley functions do not, in fact, provide useful analyses of individual differences because even markedly nonlinear computer-simulated data can be excellently fitted by simple linear functions, as Anderson (1995) and Perfect (1994) have separately showed. Thus, the procedure of attempting to fit a large number of data points obtained from different studies with single functions guarantees artifactual regularities, even where the real functions may be not only nonlinear but also mutually quite discrepant. Note that the methodological implications of Cerella's (1985) findings do not depend on his conclusion that age scaling is linear and therefore are not affected by his later revised findings that age scaling may be better described by a power function or by a positively accel-

erating asymptotic function (Cerella, 1990). Whatever the true form of the age × complexity scaling function may prove to be, the key issue is whether it remains invariant across all differences in task demands and difficulty. Anderson's and Perfect's simulations make the different and much more general point that Brinley plots cannot provide adequate tests for comparisons between rival models.

Second, the slopes of Brinley plots derived by plotting mean CRTs for older people against those of younger people are not invariant over all kinds of task demands. Cerella and Fozard (1984) found that slopes differ between tasks involving verbal and nonverbal material, and Hale, Lima, and Myerson (1991); Hale, Myerson, and Wagstaff (1987); Lima, Hale, and Myerson (1991); and Myerson, Ferraro, Hale, and Lima (1992) confirmed and extended these results. It also seems that age changes in speed are minimal in other highly practiced skills such as mental arithmetic and, when they are present, that they relate to decrements in peripheral rather than central processes (e.g., Allen, Ashcraft, & Weber, 1992; Allen, Smith, Jerge, & Vires-Collins, 1997; Geary, Frensch, & Wiley, 1993; Geary & Wiley, 1991). This suggests that practice throughout a lifetime, and perhaps also more limited practice in laboratory situations, not only reduces the decision times of older participants more than those of younger participants but also reduces the slopes of age-scaling functions across the tasks on which they are compared. Attempts have been made to explain such findings by suggestions that lexical decision tasks or, by implication, other tasks involving very highly practiced material require fewer resources than do tasks that require unpracticed decisions with novel material (e.g., Salthouse, 1988). David Navon wittily caricatured this use of the term *resource* as "A Theoretical Soupstone" to add some illusion of substantive content to mere redescriptions of experimental results (Navon, 1984). It is more fruitful to break out of this circularity and to develop better models to describe the functional changes that practice brings about that make performance easier and more automatic in the sense that it is faster and more accurate and also less vulnerable to distraction from other concurrent activities (Shiffrin & Schneider, 1977; Schneider & Detweiler, 1988, 1998) or to the effects of age (see Fisk, Fisher, & Rogers, 1992). It seems likely that age has less effect on the speed and accuracy of decisions that have become automatic through extensive practice than on relatively unpracticed decisions that must be made in a controlled manner (Hasher & Zacks, 1979). Perhaps well-articulated models for the transition from controlled to automatic performance, such as those proposed by Schneider (1994) and Schneider and Detweiler (1988), may also help us to understand better the changes in functional processes that bring about age-related changes in the efficiency of fast decisions. A different question is whether Brinley functions for subsets of tasks that make qualitatively different demands do have reliably different slopes. An example is an excellent meta-analysis by Verhagen and De Meersman (1998), who compared slopes of Brinley functions obtained from published studies of age differences in the baseline and the conflict condition of the Stroop test (Stroop, 1935). Because slopes for baseline and conflict conditions did not differ, they concluded that there was no evidence that older people are relatively more sensitive to Stroop interference. However, as shown later, comparisons of slopes are inappropriate for this purpose.

A different way to test whether older people find particular kinds of tasks more difficult than others is to consider whether particular data points obtained from some tasks are consistent outliers from those plotted for other tasks. Rabbitt (1996) gave 15 different tasks, including the color/word Stroop test and a version of the trails test, to groups of older people with higher and lower scores on the Cattell and Cattell (1960) Culture Fair intelligence test (CCF). We might expect from the literature that the relationship between mean CRTs for low and high CCF scorers was excellently fitted by a simple linear function. However, each data point on this Brinley plot is, essentially, a ratio of mean low CCF scores over mean high CCF scores. Between tasks these ratios varied within the wide range 1.1 to 1.5. This might be attributed to random measurement error, but the rank orders of these Brinley ratios for individual tasks remained stable across replications with different groups of more and less able people. Despite the excellent linear fits obtained by least squares methods, ratios of low ability CRTs to high ability CRTs were consistently greater for some tasks than for others. A crucial methodological point is that a finding that these ratios were largest for the most difficult and therefore slowest tasks would be evidence only that the intelligence test-score scaling function (and, by implication, also the age scaling function because unadjusted intelligence test scores markedly drop with age) is nonlinear. For example, a positively accelerating function would always produce larger ratios for the most difficult and therefore slower tasks. In fact, the highest ratios were produced by the conflict condition of the color/word Stroop test and the trails test, for which mean CRTs were in the middle of the range of all the tasks compared. Even if scaling effects are better described by asymptotic rather than by linear functions, as Cerella (1990) suggested, reduced general ability affects performance on two tests that involve central executive function more than on other slower and thus inferentially more difficult tasks that do not.

Third, even in the very simple tasks on which global slowing models of cognitive aging have been based, people do not passively recognize signals and make responses to them but rather actively control their performance to optimize both speed and accuracy. Consequently, their mean CRTs are not simple indexes of the maximum transmission rate of a passive information channel but rather of the efficiency of complex and often conscious control processes. Schouten and Bekker (1967) first showed that in even the simplest possible CRT tasks, humans can deliberately and consciously trade off speed against accuracy. Differences in efficiency of task control are not evident from published comparisons because tasks have always deliberately been made so easy that older and younger participants make indistinguishably few errors and can only differ in terms of their decision speeds. Rabbitt and Vyas (1969) suggested that people actively modify their reaction times from trial to trial to maximize speed and minimize errors by first locating and then learning to control their performance in relation to the speed-error tradeoff function that defines the area in which increased speed costs accuracy, and that older people respond more slowly than do younger people partly because they are less efficient at exercising active control of their own performance. Exemplary analyses by Smith and Brewer (1995) showed that this is indeed the case and that even in a very easy CRT task, older and younger participants control the speed and accuracy of their performance in different ways. Recent work by Brand (personal communication, April 2000) also found that older people adjust to increasing task difficulty by exercising an increasingly cautious strategy, by slowing their responses more, and also, consequently, by making fewer errors than the more impulsive young.

To understand how age changes in efficiency at CRT tasks, researchers need to compare not only the maximum speeds with which people of different ages can make correct responses but also the ways in which they monitor and actively control their performance.

To trade off speed effectively against accuracy, they must somehow discover the point at which any increase in their speed begins sharply to reduce their accuracy; in other terms, they must locate their own personal speed-error tradeoff functions. They may do this in many functionally quite different ways. For example, they may only be able to discover that they have responded "too fast" by recognizing that they have just made an error (Rabbitt, 1968b) and then use this information to slow down on the immediately succeeding responses (Rabbitt, 1968b). Alternatively, they may be able to assess continuously even their correct responses for relative "riskiness." One way in which they might do this is by accurately judging how long correct and incorrect responses take and by slowing down or speeding up accordingly. Note in this case that although the efficiency with which they can do this will certainly determine their average speed, it will depend on the accuracy of their time estimation, a functional limitation that is quite different from their maximum information processing rate and may have no necessary relation to it. Another way in which people might control their accuracy would be to judge when they have accumulated sufficient perceptual evidence about an event to make a confident response to it. Again, although their fastest correct CRTs will be limited by the maximum rate with which they can accumulate evidence, they will also depend on whether the criterion set for adequacy of an information sample is lax or stringent. That is, they will be determined by a process of risk assessment that is not necessarily determined by, or usefully modeled, in terms of information processing speed. A similar issue occurs when we consider how people avoid making unnecessarily slow responses. As interesting results by Bunce, Warr and Cochrane (1993) show, older people tend to produce unnecessarily slow responses ("blocks" or "gaps") more often than the young do, suggesting that the precision with which they can control their response speed has deteriorated. Models for how people carry out even very simple CRT tasks must incorporate descriptions of complex processes such as self-monitoring of performance, capability of detection of errors, and efficiency of maintenance of control. The efficiency of such control processes must determine the average CRTs of older people, but speed is not necessarily a useful construct in our functional models for any of them.

Fourth, the most radical criticism of the use of the slopes of Brinley functions as measures of relative slowing is that it reflects a misunderstanding of the mathematical properties of a family of functions, quantile-quantile (Q-Q) plots, of which they are a subset. Ratcliff, Spieler, and McKoon (2000) argued that Brinley functions are special cases of plots in which quantiles of one distribution are plotted against those of another. The properties of Q-Q plots have been comprehensively discussed by Thomas and Ross (1980) and reviewed by Chambers, Cleveland, Kleiner, and Tukey (1983). As for all Q-Q functions, the slopes of Brinley plots are not determined by the mean CRTs of older and younger groups but rather by the ratio of the standard deviation of older groups' response times to the standard deviation of younger groups' response times. It follows that the intercepts, rather than the slopes, of Brinley plots are the appropriate indexes for relative slowing. The key questions that models for age differences in CRTs need to explain are why age increases the variance of response times within individuals, and, in the case where mean CRTs for members of an older group are rank ordered and then plotted against the corresponding means CRTs for rank-ordered members of a younger group, why age increases the variance between older individuals. Ratcliff et al. commented that an important conclusion from simulation studies is that Brinley plots provide only weak

constraints on theory, and that a variety of different models such as the diffusion model proposed by Ratcliff and Rouder (1998) and Ratcliff et al. (1999), or the accumulator model proposed by Smith and Vickers (1988), or a variety of other models first proposed by Laming (1968) and reviewed by Luce (1986), will produce Brinley plots with the characteristics that have been reported in empirical studies of individual differences related to depression, neurophysiological damage, ingestion of alcohol, differences in general intellectual ability, developmental maturation, and aging. Molenaar and van der Molen (1994) came to very similar conclusions and offered a framework for testing between the hypotheses that cognitive changes throughout the life span are mediated by global or local changes in information processing rate.

This drastic reinterpretation means that the slopes of Brinley plots reflect the relative forms and variances of the distributions of CRTs that older and younger groups produce and that they cannot be used to compare the relative effects on the mean CRTs of older and younger people of differences in task demands such as use of verbal stimuli against nonverbal stimuli (e.g., Hale et al., 1991; Hale et al., 1987; Lima et al., 1991; and Myerson et al., 1992) or the baseline condition against the interference condition of the Stroop test (Verhagen & De Meersman, 1998). However, it does not mean that it is inappropriate to compare the rank-orders of the ratios of the means of CRTs of older and younger groups between sets of tasks that make different kinds of demands (e.g., Rabbitt, 1996).

Fifth, Cerella's (1985) conclusion that age slows all subprocesses by the same proportion was based on Sternberg's (1969, 1975) assumption that variations in overall mean CRTs must reflect precisely corresponding proportional variations in the times taken by each of a series of linearly entrained subprocesses involved in the discriminations of signals and the choice and production of responses to them. Because overall mean CRTs were scaled up by the same constant across all task demands, he concluded that the times taken by the different subprocesses that met these demands must also be increased in the same proportion. Ratcliff et al. (2000) have shown that proportionally equivalent slowing cannot be assumed from comparisons of slopes of Brinley plots. Fisher and Glaser (1996) formally showed that Sternberg's (1969, 1975) assumptions are arbitrary because ratios of mean CRTs between consistently faster and consistently slower groups may remain constant across tasks, although times for linear serially entrained processes vary markedly. This is, of course, even more likely to be the case if processes are not, in fact, serially entrained but proceed partially or wholly in parallel. For this latter class of situations, Townsend and Ashby (1983) have formally shown that empirical data from mean CRTs often cannot choose between subclasses of models.

Fisher and Glaser (1996) pointed out that because one cannot use mean CRTs to infer whether component processes are equally affected by individual differences or by task demands, researchers risk making two kinds of errors: false positives if they assume that component processes do change in precise proportion to observed mean CRTs, and false negatives if they assume that they do not. In either case differences in mean CRTs are not analytic in the ways that Sternberg (1969, 1975) and Cerella (1985) had hoped and therefore cannot provide evidence for proportionately equal slowing of all subsystems involved in discriminations between signals and choices between responses.

These issues are later discussed where attempts to relate localized brain changes associated with aging to differential impairments of some, rather than all, cognitive skills are reviewed. First consider other kinds of evidence that have been offered as support for the idea that global slowing of the CNS drives age-related changes in all cognitive skills, including those, such as memory, in which performance is evaluated in terms of accuracy rather than in speed of responses.

Other Ways of Testing the General Slowing Hypothesis

The general slowing model was derived from the assumption that age affects the speed of all kinds of decisions in the same way, lagging them by the same simple multiplicative constant. As seen, this assumption is not obligatory or even tenable. However, the much stronger claim of the general slowing model is that slowing of information processing speed is the basic functional element that determines age-related changes in efficiency on all cognitive tasks, of whatever kind, but especially tests of working memory, recognition, and recall.

Note that this assertion need only be based on analyses that are logically equivalent to those from which Spearman (1924) concluded that individual differences in levels of performance across disparate tests of intelligence could best be described in terms of a single common factor that he termed general intellectual ability, or g_f. As an illustration, Miller and Vernon (1992) found that a factor analysis of scores produced by the same group of people on tests of short-term memory, intelligence, and reaction time yielded a dominant principal component in which all were represented. They take this as evidence that Spearman's measure of general fluid ability, g_f, can be reified in terms of information processing speed (see also Eysenck, 1986; Jensen, 1980, 1982; Vernon, 1985; Vernon & Jensen, 1994). Following a similar line of reasoning, Salthouse (1985) gave the same batteries of tests to groups of older and younger people and found that variance associated with age fell into a single dominant factor that also accounted for decision speed and memory efficiency. Salthouse took this as evidence that age-related changes in information processing speed are functionally responsible for age-related changes in all other cognitive skills, including memory.

A limitation of this methodology is that factor analyses are descriptive rather than confirmatory procedures and the best descriptions of shared variance that they yield markedly vary with the particular test scores, and individuals, to which they are applied. Rabbitt and Yang (1996) failed to replicate Salthouse's (1985) results with data from very similar batteries of tests given to large groups of older and younger people. Although scores on tcsts of decision speed were often represented in a dominant factor, variance in age was best represented in a second and statistically distinct factor that also included variance in memory test scores.

Nevertheless, Salthouse's (1985) conclusions are plausible because there are good, commonsense reasons why accuracy of recognition and recall should be affected by individual differences in information processing rate. For example, levels of performance on memory tests are strongly determined by the total time allowed to study material, or the rate at which items are presented for inspection. Obviously, the time available determines whether and how much rehearsal is possible. Furthermore, the depth to which material can be processed determines the accuracy with which it can subsequently be recognized or recalled (Craik & Lockhart, 1972). When inspection times are limited, the depth to which individuals can process material will vary with individual differences in information processing speed. There is direct evidence that age decrements in memory task performance are inversely proportional to the time that is available to inspect the material presented (see reviews in Kausler, 1990, and particularly Canestrari, 1963; Hulicka, Sterns, & Grossman, 1967; Monge & Hultsch, 1972;

Waugh & Barr, 1980; Witte, 1975). Within the range of presentation rates within which older people are inconvenienced, age differences in memory efficiency must relate to individual differences in information processing rates.

Models for one aspect of memory performance, so-called working memory, also relate efficiency of recall directly to information processing speed. The evidence for this is largely derived from experiments in which people are given dual tasks that either do or do not require similar kinds of decisions (see Baddeley, 1986). It is therefore very plausible that age changes in information processing speed should directly affect working memory capacity (see Salthouse, 1991). The issue is whether changes in information processing rate are entirely, or only partially, responsible for concomitant changes in working memory. Jenkins, Myerson, Hale, and Fry (1999) reported a direct test of these relationships by giving groups of children, young adults, and elderly people a variety of different tests of spatial working memory, with and without secondary tasks. Surprisingly, they found that there was little evidence of change in the effects of interference. Within samples of all ages, those who had larger memory spans were relatively more affected by the secondary tasks. They concluded that although there is good evidence that both memory span and information processing speed increase with developmental age and decline in old age, within age groups these performance indexes are nevertheless relatively independent of each other. The functional relationships between these indexes are, therefore, more complicated than a simple version of a general slowing theory can explain.

However, these results also raise an interesting methodological and logical problem, as indicated by Wickens (personal communication, May 2001). The issue of how to evaluate whether a secondary task has produced different or similar changes in span from individuals with larger and smaller working memory capacities rests on the kind of functional model that we use to interpret the data. If interference from a secondary task reduces the span of a less able individual from 2 to 1, and that of a more able individual from 10 to 8, then one might be tempted to conclude that the more able individual with the larger span has suffered more from interference. Relative to baseline performance, however, the less able individual has lost 50%, and the more able individual has lost 20%. On some functional models, especially one similar to that proposed by Baddeley (1986), the life spans of items in working memory are determined by the balance between the rate at which they decay and the rate at which they can be refreshed by being cycled around a loop system. In terms of such a model, a 50% loss would indicate a much more rapid decay rate, or a very much greater reduction in refreshment rate than would a 20% loss. Myerson, Jenkins, Hale, and Sliwinski (2000) have recently acknowledged these difficulties and conclude that the question of whether high span individuals lose relatively more items from working memory as a result of interference has not yet been worked out. This is a useful reminder that the decision whether relative or absolute differences between older and younger people are the more meaningful depends entirely on the functional model in terms of which one interprets the data. It also, incidentally, makes the point that functional models for individual differences in working memory efficiency require specification of two parameters, only one of which can sensibly be discussed in terms of speed or information processing rate. One must also discuss the possibility of individual differences in the rates at which traces decay, and for this reason simple assumptions of global changes in mental speed are inappropriate.

The general slowing model goes well beyond uncontroversial associations between information processing speed and memory efficiency such as those discussed by Canestrari (1963), Hulicka et al. (1967), Kausler (1990), Monge and Hultsch (1972), Waugh and Barr (1980), and Witte (1975) to the much stronger claim that *all* of the changes in the functional processes underlying memory efficiency that occur with age causally follow from general slowing of the entire cognitive system. This implies that one must choose between two possibilities. The first is that for people of any age, information processing speed must be the *sole* determinant of the efficiency of individual differences in all functional processes that underlie recognition and recall (a proposition that most memory theorists would find unacceptable). The second is that although information processing speed is not the *sole* determinant of memory efficiency in young people, it gradually becomes so as age advances. The challenging task of empirically testing these possibilities has not yet been attempted.

There is some evidence that slowing of information processing rate cannot be responsible for all of the functional changes in memory efficiency that are observed in all individuals as they age. Rabbitt (1993a) found that within a very large sample of people aged from 40 to 92 years, intelligence test scores modestly but significantly predicted performance on memory tasks, but that the incidence of persons who were outliers in the sense that their memory test scores fell markedly below the levels that would be predicted from their ITSs increased with the age of the group sampled. Nettelbeck, Rabbitt, Wilson and Batt (1996) compared a group of these memory-impaired outliers with controls who had been precisely matched for age and ITSs and whose ITSs still modestly predicted their scores on memory tests. Within both of these groups there were similar modest correlations between ITSs and measures of information processing speed (CRTs and inspection times). However, within the memory-impaired group, although the association between information processing speed and intelligence test scores remained normal, no association between decision speed and memory test scores was apparent.

A disassociation between performance on intelligence tests and on memory tests is one of the main diagnostic criteria for amnesia caused by focal brain damage. It is quite possible that increased incidence of memory-poor individuals in older groups reflects increased incidence of undiagnosed focal damage due to cerebrovascular accidents or to other causes. It is also possible that relatively marked decline in memory function reflects increasing tissue loss and tissue changes in prefrontal and temporal cortex, which have been observed on postmortem examinations of older brains and, more recently, with brain imaging (e.g., Albert, 1993; Haug & Eggers, 1991; Mittenberg et al., 1989; Scheibel & Scheibel, 1975; Whelihan & Lesher, 1985). The data do not choose between these possibilities, but they do strongly make the point that the neurophysiological changes responsible for these cases of age-related memory impairment do not impair memory simply because they reduce information processing speed. It is quite another question how far the average declines in scores on memory tests that are observed in aging populations reflect an increase in the incidence of individuals who show relatively greater decline in memory performance than in general fluid intellectual ability.

Salthouse (1985, 1991) also used statistical techniques other than factor analysis to demonstrate that all age-related changes in memory can be attributed to general slowing. He gave people of different ages a memory task and a number of different tests of information processing speed. Participants' ages and their scores on putatively pure measures of information processing speed were then successively entered into the regression

equation as predictors of their performance on memory tests. He found that as increasing numbers of scores from tests of "speed" were entered, the proportion of variance independently predicted by calendar age decreased and eventually disappeared entirely. He concluded that all age-related variance in memory efficiency could be accounted for if scores on sufficient, or on sufficiently good, measures of information processing speed have been entered.

The logical errors in the use of multiple regression analyses to support this particular argument have received such magisterial reproof (Pedhozur, 1997) that they need not be recapitulated here. A simpler and more pervasive logical difficulty follows from Weiskrantz's (1992) observation that "there is no such thing as a 'pure' test." It is noteworthy that in all reported studies this process of successively entering increasing numbers of speed test scores to predict memory test scores has only been successful when scores from some version of the WAIS coding tasks (e.g., letter-letter, letter-digit, or letter-symbol substitution test) is entered as a measure of information processing speed. This is important because individuals' scores on this particular test are known to be closely related to the efficiency with which they partially learn substitution codes that, as we might expect, declines with their ages (Piccinin and Rabbitt, 1999). Demonstrations that all age-related variance in memory test performance can eventually be eliminated by entry of scores from a test in which the speed of performance is largely supported by learning efficiency does not provide good support for the general slowing model as applied to memory function.

Does Age Alter Speed or, Rather, Variability of Performance?

As Ratcliff et al. (2000) have pointed out, the correct interpretation of all of the comparisons that have used the slopes of Brinley plots as evidence for age related slowing is that variability of performance increases with age both within and between individuals. Even when participants are practiced to a point at which they no longer improve, decline of general fluid intellectual ability is reflected by marked increase in trial-by-trial variance in CRTs (Rabbitt, Osman, Stollery, & Moore, in press). Furthermore, the degree of trial-to-trial variability in CRTs that individuals show during single experimental sessions correlates robustly with the variability of their mean CRTs between sessions or from day to day (Rabbitt, 1999; Rabbitt, Osman, et al., in press). This relationship can be explained as a statistical inevitability on the premise that every response that a person makes during any experimental session can be considered to be a random sample from a hypothetical latent distribution of all of the CRTs that he or she would produce if repeatedly tested over a long period of time. The form of this latent distribution of CRTs will, of course, reflect the form of the actual distributions of CRTs obtained during the experimental sessions whose sums it represents. Thus, an individual whose CRT distributions during individual experimental runs have large standard errors will also, necessarily, have a latent distribution with the same large standard error. Regardless what the particular functional mechanisms by which CRTs are produced may be, then, it follows as a mathematical rather than a functional necessity that the standard errors of the means of CRT distributions observed in independent experimental sessions will directly reflect the standard error of the latent distribution from which they have been drawn. Whatever factors may determine moment-to-moment variability in performance during individual experimental runs must, necessarily, also determine variability in average levels of performance from day to day and week to week.

It is important to note that this does not mean that moment-to-moment variability is the only factor that determines session-to-session and day-to-day variability. When participants are run on several different tasks during weekly experimental sessions, levels of performance on each of these tasks covary across sessions (Rabbitt, Osman, et al., in press). It seems that because of factors other than their intrinsic moment-to-moment variability, people experience relatively "good" or "bad" days or sessions during which they perform relatively well or poorly on all of the tasks that they carry out. The causes of this additional day-to-day variability, and the ways in which it may be affected by age, remain topics for further research.

These findings have strong consequences for the methodology of studying age differences. People who vary more with respect to themselves from day to day must, for that reason alone, also vary more with respect to each other when their performance is sampled on any single occasion. Because older people vary more from day to day, they will also vary more with respect to each other when they are compared at any time point. Therefore, as a population ages variability between its members will increase not only because of increasing divergences in their trajectories of cognitive aging but also because of age-related increases in within-individual variability. We have seen that increasing variability between individuals in an aging population is a neglected finding in longitudinal studies that raises central theoretical issues in cognitive gerontology. It is now apparent that in order to estimate reliably how much of this variance is due to increasing divergence in individual trajectories of aging, one must determine the extent to which intrinsic variability within individuals contributes to the observed variability between them at any point of comparison.

Another methodological crux is for estimates of circadian variability that persists and may even become more marked in old age, as recent work suggests (Li, Hasher, Jones,

Rahhal, & May, 1998). That individuals' levels of moment-to-moment and day-to-day variability are necessarily coupled means that estimates of the extent of circadian variability will be unreliable unless this intrinsic source of variability is computed and taken into consideration. In particular, because between-session variability increases with age, this will tend increasingly to disguise any additional effects of circadian variability on the performance of older groups.

One theoretical implication is that, at least as far as CRTs are concerned, variability of performance is a stable individual characteristic in that the degree of variability that individuals show on a particular task on a particular occasion will predict the extent of variability that they will show on the same task on other occasions. A corollary would be that the degree of variability that individuals show on a particular task on a particular occasion will predict their degree of variability on different tasks on different occasions. Rabbitt, Osman, et al. (in press) found that within-session variability and between-session variability were very strongly correlated across 6 very similar CRT tasks. It remains a further question whether the extent of variability that individuals show on one kind of tasks (e.g., CRT tasks) predicts the degree of variability that they show on very different kinds of tasks (e.g., tasks involving psychophysical judgments, memory, or maintenance of selective attention).

It may be useful to ask whether age increases variability on all cognitive tasks, not just those on which CRTs are the performance index measured. Wearden, Wearden, and Rabbitt (1997) found that individuals' ages and ITSs predicted their trial-to-trial variability on all of four different time-interval comparison, estimation, and production tasks. Thus, it is useful to ask whether individuals' levels of moment-to-moment and session-to-session variability on CRT tasks, in which

their performance is measured in units of time, also strongly and directly predicts their variability in time estimation and interval production tasks, memory tasks, and psychophysical judgments in which time measures are not used.

Testing Alternative Modular Models for Cognitive Aging

A disappointing feature of the global speed hypothesis, and of other single-factor models such as those based on g_f, is that they are based entirely on behavioral evidence and make little attempt to relate this evidence to the particular CNS changes that occur during aging. It is interesting to work in the opposite direction and to use the increasing body of evidence on the neurophysiology and neuroanatomy of brain aging to derive predictions about changes in behavior. There is accumulating evidence that age-related changes affect the frontal lobes earlier, and more severely, than they affect other parts of the brain. Postmortem and imaging studies suggest that age-related loss of cortical volume is greater in the frontal lobes than in other brain areas (Haug & Eggers, 1991; Mittenberg et al., 1989; Whelihan & Lesher, 1985) and that older adults show greater cell loss in the prefrontal than in other cortical regions (Albert, 1993; Scheibel & Scheibel, 1975). Reductions in cerebral blood flow after the age of 60 years have also been reported to be greater in prefrontal than in posterior regions (Gur, Gur, Orbist et al., 1987; Shaw et al., 1984). Goldman-Rakic and Brown (1981) have reported age-related region-specific declines in the concentration, synthesis, and number of receptor sites for some neurotransmitters. Age-related changes in dopamine receptors have also been found in monkeys (Arnsten, Cai, Murphy, & Goldman-Rakic, 1994). These findings encourage researchers to investigate age-related changes on cognitive tasks that are known from clinical experience to be sensitive to local damage to the cortex, especially the frontal cortex (West, 1996). Unfortunately, all such tasks involve comparison of decision times, so the design and interpretation of experiments must take scaling effects into account. The methodological implications of this have not fully been recognized.

The ability to inhibit irrelevant or distracting perceptual input or intrusive memories and to suppress incorrect responses has long been linked to frontal lobe integrity. It is natural to consider whether some cognitive changes in old age may be explained in terms of declining efficiency of inhibition (e.g., Connelly, Hasher, & Zacks, 1991; Hasher, Quig, & May, 1997; Hasher, Stoltzfus Zacks & Rypma, 1991; Hasher & Zacks, 1988). Among many findings consistent with this hypothesis are that older people are more distractible and disinhibited in verbal fluency tasks (Birren, 1959), that they produce more intrusions from external items in free recall (Cohen, 1988), that they find it harder to suppress previously generated but no longer relevant inferences in text recall (Hamm & Hasher, 1992), that they produce more false positives to semantic associates of actually presented words (Rankin & Kausler, 1979), and that they are less able to suppress irrelevant information held in memory (Hartman & Hasher, 1991). Note in this last case, however, that the suggestion that the ability to inhibit interfering input and memories is directly related to working memory capacity is inconsistent with Jenkins et al.'s (1999) intriguing finding that individuals with large memory spans are relatively more impaired by a secondary task than are those who have smaller memory spans. There are also suggestions that older people are less able to forget items on demand (Zacks, Radvansky, & Hasher, 1996), that they find it more difficult to inhibit both well-practiced and newly

learned response patterns in order to acquire new ones (Kausler & Hakami, 1982), and that they are more distracted by irrelevant items adjacent to targets in visual displays (Shaw, 1991). Unfortunately, as this extraordinarily wide range of quite disparate uses of the term *inhibition* illustrates, discussions of neuropsychological tests involve problems of the appropriate definition and validity of the hypothetical constructs that they are supposed ostensively to define.

PROBLEMS OF DEFINITIONS OF CONSTRUCTS IN DISCUSSIONS OF FRONTAL AND EXECUTIVE FUNCTION

Goel and Grafman (1995) point out that the construct of inhibition has been overextended to cover an implausibly wide range of functions from suppression of very simple and automatic responses such as saccades (Walker et al., 1998) to very complicated behaviors such as the ability to inhibit unacceptable or unwise social responses. The imprecision of the common usage of the word *inhibition* has encouraged misleading analogies between very disparate functional processes (Rabbitt, 1997). On one hand, there is general agreement that the term has been overextended to cover functionally unrelated activities; on the other hand, tasks that in research practice have been taken to make very different demands can all be supported by identical functional architectures. For example, Kimberg and Farah (1993) have formally shown that performance on four quite distinct tasks that have been widely regarded as measures of frontal function, including inhibition in the Stroop (1935) paradigm, can be successfully simulated by identical production systems that do not include any component process analogous to inhibition as understood in common discourse or in the neuropsychological literature.

A voluminous literature includes puzzlingly frequent inconsistencies in age effects on logically similar experimental paradigms and outright failures of replication of results from identical tasks. Some investigators have found age deficits in verbal fluency (e.g., Pendleton et al., 1982; Whelihan & Lesher, 1985), but others have not (e.g., Axelrod & Henry, 1992; Daigneault, Braun, & Whitaker, 1992). Some (Daigneault et al., 1992; Heaton, 1981; Loranger & Misiak, 1960) but not others (Boone et al., 1990; Nelson, 1976) have found that perseverative errors on the Wisconsin Card Sorting Test increase with age. In particular, some studies find that older people have particular difficulty suppressing irrelevant responses in the conflict condition of the Stroop (1935) paradigm (Connelly et al., 1991; Hasher and Zacks 1988; Hasher et al., 1997; Kane, Hasher, Stoltzfus, Zacks, & Connelly, 1994; Rabbitt, 1996), whereas others do not (Salthouse, 1998; Salthouse, Fristoe, & Rhee, 1998; Salthouse & Meinz, 1995). Many of these discrepancies are due to definition of constructs and to the likelihood that apparent differences between task demands do not reflect real differences between the functional systems that support them (Rabbitt, 1997). Other reasons for inconsistencies are problems of measurement, problems of task familiarity, problems of construct validity and, finally, and probably most basically, much-neglected problems of participant selection. As usual, these problems stem from the particular model for the nature and time course of cognitive aging that one adopts.

Problems of Measurement

A good example of problems of measurement is provided by experiments using the Stroop test in which the efficiency of inhibition of irrelevant signals and responses is indexed by computing the differences between individuals' mean CRTs for easier and faster baseline conditions and their mean CRTs for more difficult and slower interference conditions (Stroop, 1935). Increases in absolute differences between mean CRTs for interference and baseline conditions have been interpreted as losses in efficiency of inhibition of intrusive information. Unfortunately, as has been seen, pervasive age × task-difficulty interactions ensure that age increases CRTs for the harder and slower interference conditions more than it does for easier and faster baseline conditions, and so must also increase the absolute difference between them. An inhibitory deficit can only be claimed if increases in CRTs for an interference condition are disproportionately greater than for the corresponding baseline condition. Not all investigators have taken this point into account (e.g., Baumler, 1969; Cohn, Dustman, & Bradford, 1984; Comalli, Wapner, & Werner, 1962; Houx, Jolles, & Vreeling, 1993; Panek, Rush, & Slade, 1984). The methodological problem of adjusting for across-the-board age-scaling effects is not easy to resolve because recent analyses (Cerella, 1990) suggest that scaling effects are better described by accelerated exponential functions than by simple linear functions. If this is so, age will always lag CRTs for the slower interference conditions proportionally more than CRTs for the faster baseline conditions of the Stroop test. Until it is generally agreed that age-scaling functions for all tasks have the same form, and what this form may be, researchers cannot carry out post hoc statistical adjustments and can only claim differential effects by comparing the same groups of younger and older people both on some simple, and therefore fast, tasks that involve inhibition and on more difficult, and therefore much slower, tasks that do not involve inhibition. There is only evidence for inhibitory deficits if older groups show proportionately greater slowing of *faster* mean CRTs for tasks involving inhibition than of *slower* mean CRTs for tasks that do not involve inhibition. Neglect of this methodological point raises problems for all studies that have argued for age-related loss of inhibitory inefficiency only from single comparisons between baseline and conflict conditions of the same tasks.

It once seemed that an elegant way out of the methodological difficulties introduced by scaling effects might be to follow an excellent meta-analysis by Verhagen and De Meersman (1998), who plotted data from published studies of age differences on the Stroop test to compare the slopes of Brinley functions derived from their interference and from their baseline conditions. Finding no differences in slope, these authors concluded that they had no evidence that age differences on interference conditions are greater than a general slowing theory would predict. We must now accept that the slopes of Brinley functions are not appropriate measures of scaling effects for mean CRTs and, rather, that they reflect differences in the degrees of variability within and between older and younger individuals (Molenaar & van der Molen, 1994; Ratcliff et al., 2000). It seems that explorations of age differences in the effects of interference and baseline conditions of the Stroop test, as well as of other neuropsychological tests such as the trails test, require investigations of changes in the shapes of distributions between conditions, rather than simply comparisons between mean CRTs (Faust, Balota, Spieler, & Ferraro, 1999). There is also interesting recent evidence that innovative statistical analyses can reveal changes in component subdistributions of CRTs from Stroop interference conditions that appear to be especially sensitive to changes related to age and the onset of dementias (Spieler et al., 1996).

Problems with Task Reliability and Validity

Burgess (1997, pp. 81–116) wittily described his exasperation that, in clinical practice, frontal tasks can generally be used only once with any particular patient because their sensitivity depends on their novelty; therefore, a patient who fails on one frontal test may nevertheless succeed on "any number" (sic) of others. Thus, one must conclude that tests, patients, or both are inconsistent with respect to each other (Burgess, ibid, pp. 81–116). There may be several distinct reasons for this.

TASK NOVELTY AND AGE EFFECTS ON NEUROPSYCHOLOGICAL TESTS: PROBLEMS OF TEST RELIABILITY

Lowe and Rabbitt (1997) tested the same groups of older and younger individuals twice on the same series of 15 different tests described by Rabbitt (1996). When these tests were first administered, Brinley ratios for the Stroop and trails tests were larger than they were for any of the other tasks. However, when tests were readministered, Brinley ratios for the Stroop and trails test declined more than they did for any others, and no differences in proportional slowing between baseline and interference conditions were now evident. This is not just another illustration that the Stroop effect is abolished by practice in people of all ages. For both older and younger groups, mean CRTs for the interference condition of the Stroop test and for the switching condition of the trails test remained significantly greater than for the corresponding baseline conditions. The crucial point is that the disproportionate age-related increase in CRTs for the critical conditions of these tests disappears well before the main effects of interference are lost. This reduction of specific test sensitivity to age effects is consistent with Burgess's observation that frontal tests can identify patients with well-defined frontal lesions only when they are novel. It also raises problems of data interpretation because it suggests that, as practice continues, localized or modular age differences may gradually disappear and that residual differences between conditions can be increasingly well explained by proportional slowing. Thus, inconsistencies in the literature between findings of age-related changes on the Stroop test and on other neuropsychological tests may be explained, at least partly, by differences in the amounts of practice that different investigators have given their participants or, more generally, on uncontrollable differences in the extent to which participants may have become familiar with similar task demands during their daily lives. Whether age comparisons across a disparate set of tasks provide evidence for general slowing or for modular change may depend on duration of practice and on often unattainable control for task familiarity.

This raises the further problem that because older individuals' relative sensitivity to frontal tasks sharply reduces with practice, these tasks are likely to rank order groups of individuals in different ways on successive administrations. In psychometric terms, such tests are likely to have low test-retest reliability. Lowe and Rabbitt (1998) analyzed data from two batteries of neuropsychological and other tests: the excellent CANTAB (Sahakian & Owen, 1992) and the International Study for Post Operative Cognitive Decrement (ISPOCD) battery used in a large study of cognitive impairment following surgery and anesthesia (Moller et al., 1998). Test-retest correlations for the frontal and executive tests in these batteries were generally much below levels considered acceptable in psychometric practice and markedly lower than for other, equally difficult nonfrontal tasks. This does not mean that these particular frontal tests

are poorly designed or insensitive. It confirms Burgess's (1997) clinical observation that a defining characteristic of frontal tests is that they are sensitive only when they are novel. Unfortunately, this also means that longitudinal investigations using such tests may be compromised because repeated administration reduces their sensitivity.

TASK SPECIFICITY AND CONSTRUCT VALIDITY: ARE PARTICULAR TESTS SPECIFIC TO PARTICULAR FUNCTIONAL SYSTEMS?

Basic criteria for acceptability of a test as a measure of a hypothetical functional construct, such as intelligence, are that it must shown to be valid in at least four senses:

1. Scores on tests of a particular functional construct must correlate with performance in everyday situations that also provide ostensive definitions of that same construct.
2. Individuals' scores on parallel versions of the same test must correlate robustly.
3. Scores on different tests that are supposed to assess the same functional construct must correlate robustly.
4. Correlations between scores on different versions of the same test, or on different tests, should not be explainable in terms of individual differences in the efficiency of any functional process other than in the particular one that they are supposed to measure.

Frontal tests are assumed to be valid in the first of these senses because they have become recognized in clinical practice as reliable diagnostic markers of particular kinds of brain injury but not others. They may also be said to be valid in the third sense, inasmuch as some of them often successfully diagnose a frontal syndrome that includes other behavioral deficits that they do not directly assess. Unfortunately, for the most part the functional properties of frontal tests have been inferred from studies of patients who have sustained focal frontal damage or from studies of controlled lesions in primates. Costa (1988) points out that limitations to these studies may contribute to discrepancies between findings of patterns of associations between scores on particular frontal measures and particular lesion sites. The association of loss of a particular function to a particular locus of damage in the brain loses sight of the point that removal or injury of particular parts of the cortex may cause secondary changes in regions that send projections to or receive projections from the damaged area. Costa (1988, p. 5) commented that, as a result, "it is easy to find tests that are sensitive to frontal-lobe dysfunction and very difficult to find tests that are specific for it!"

Many so-called frontal tests do not meet the second and third criteria of validity. The problem stems partly from vagueness of conceptual boundaries. As Goldman-Rakic (1993, p. 13) remarked, "Such a bewildering array of behavioral deficits have been attributed to frontal lobe injury that a common functional denominator would appear elusive." A less recognized problem is that researchers still do not have empirical evidence that parallel or slightly different versions of the same test, or different tests that are held to assess integrity of the same functional system, are mutually valid in the sense that they rank order individuals in the same way. Rabbitt, Lowe, and Shilling (2001) found that correlations between scores on different measures of frontal function are always very modest and, in many cases, statistically unreliable and that they cannot be replicated with different groups of individuals. Finally, Duncan (1995) and Duncan, Burgess, and Emslie (1995) reported that the modest correlations observed between scores on some frontal tests may be explained entirely in terms of their mutual correlations with an extraneous functional construct that they are not designed to measure: in this case general intellectual ability (g_f), as indexed by unadjusted scores on the CCF. Shilling, Chetwynd, and Rabbitt (2001, *Neuropsychologia,* in press) tested the validity of the construct of inhibition as indexed by the Stroop test by examining correlations between participants' scores on different versions of the Stroop test. They found no evidence of consistency of sensitivity to inhibition (i.e., to interference conditions of these tasks) at the individual level, except when almost identical versions of the Stroop task were compared. They also found no evidence for consistency of sensitivity across age groups, but there was some evidence for consistency across groups with higher and lower CCF scores. In other words the amount of difficulty that individuals experienced in coping with the Stroop tasks was predicted by their g_f scores rather than by their ages. Similar claims have been made that correlations between individuals' scores on different tasks are mediated by differences in their speeds of processing. Neumann and DeSchepper (1992) found that faster participants showed greater levels of negative priming (indicating greater inhibitory efficiency) than did slower participants, and Salthouse and Meinz (1995) found that almost all of the age differences found in three measures of Stroop interference were related to individual differences in processing speed rather than to differences in calendar age. As Salthouse, Fristoe, and Rhee (1996) and Phillips (1998) have remarked, many previous studies have failed to take into account the point that age-related changes on frontal measures may, at least to some extent, be explained by global slowing (see the earlier discussion of scaling effects).

This highlights a methodological issue for all studies of frontal changes in old age.

Nearly all studies of age-related differences in frontal tasks have either matched older and younger groups on educational attainment or on vocabulary test scores. The rationale is that this provides the best possible assurance that when the older groups were younger their levels of general mental ability (g_f) were comparable to those of the young adults against whom they are currently compared. Because g_f scores markedly decline during the life span, this procedure also guarantees that the older groups will have much lower g_f scores than the younger groups. Thus, unfortunately, pending further work, many reported age-related differences on frontal tasks remain cryptic unless the inevitable differences in g_f associated with age are taken into consideration.

ARE DIFFERENT NEUROPSYCHOLOGICAL TESTS VALID IN THE SENSE THAT THEY ASSESS THE EFFICIENCY OF THE SAME FUNCTIONAL PROCESSES?

Reitan and Wolfson (1994) warn that many experimental studies have concluded that there are differences in frontal efficiency between younger and older children (e.g., Dempster, 1992; Harnishfinger & Bjorkland, 1993) or between younger and elderly adults without any independent evidence that the particular groups compared actually differed in frontal lobe integrity. Conclusions often rest entirely on the logically unsafe assumption that because the tasks used had previously been validated as identifying patients with frontal brain lesions, individuals who performed more poorly on them must, necessarily, be frontally impaired. This raises the possibility that the performance on frontal tasks of participants who do not suffer from focal deficits or damage will, as on most other tasks, be well predicted by global task performance indexes such as unadjusted intelligence test scores or measures of information processing speed.

Burgess (1997) suggested that this mutual dependency of efficiency of both frontal and nonfrontal tasks on measures of g_f means that within groups of individuals who do not have brain damage, correlations between scores on all tasks are equally determined by individual differences in levels of these indexes of global cognitive resources. By analogy it might equally be claimed that strengths of associations between frontal test scores are partly, or entirely, due to their mutual dependence on information processing speed. If scores on frontal tests are determined mainly by information processing speed then, within groups of normal intact adults or children, scores on frontal tasks may be found to correlate as strongly with scores on nonfrontal tasks as often and as strongly as they do with scores on other frontal tasks that are also predicted by g_f. Furthermore, associations between frontal tasks may be completely or mainly explained by their mutual loading on g_f. Burgess gave a battery of frontal tests to a clinically normal sample of older people and found that this was indeed the case. He administered the same battery to a group of patients with local frontal damage and found that, for them, associations between scores on frontal tests were markedly stronger and were not abolished when variance associated with CCF scores (g_f) was partialled out. Burgess argued that to the extent that frontal tests do pick out individuals who have focal frontal deficits, those individuals who perform poorly on one frontal task will also be likely to perform poorly on others. The strength of such associations between different tasks will be as much, or more, determined by the loci and extents of the brain damage that they have sustained than by their levels of general mental ability. Consequently, within brain-damaged groups measures of g_f will not be the main determinant of associations between scores on tests of focal damage but will, in contrast, continue to predict performance on all tasks that have not been compromised by damage.

This result raised the possibility that if old age increases the incidence, or the extent, of changes to the frontal cortex and associated systems, older volunteers should perform more like Burgess's patients than like his normal controls. That is, the strengths of correlations between frontal test scores should increase with the age of the population sampled, and the levels of these stronger correlations should be little reduced after variance due to individual differences in general ability has been taken into consideration. Rabbitt, Lowe, et al. (in press) tested this possibility by analyzing data from a large battery of putatively frontal tasks, including those used by Burgess in his study. These had been given twice to two groups of individuals aged from 61 to 86 years, in Manchester ($N = 93$), and from 63 to 87 years ($N = 99$), in Newcastle-upon Tyne, in 1994 (time point 1, TP1) and again in 1999 (time point 2, TP2; the age range given is at second time of testing). In both cities, samples were divided into old-old (more than 70 years) and young-old (less than 70 years) groups on the basis of their ages in 1994. At TP1, for both young-old and old-old groups in both centers, correlations between test scores were few, modest, and almost entirely explained by individual differences in scores on the CCF. At TP2 the young-old groups in both centers showed the same pattern of results, but within the Manchester sample of old-old volunteers correlations between scores on different frontal tests had become stronger and were now independent of CCF scores. This contrast resembles that between the data on patient and control groups described by Burgess (1997) and encourages the hypothesis that as the older subgroup aged still further, increasing numbers of them began to perform like Burgess's frontal patients. A discrepant, but usefully provocative, finding was that no such change in pattern of relationships between test scores occurred for individuals in the old-old group in the Newcastle sample, who, on the basis of 11 years of longitudinal assessment previous to 1994, had seemed identical to their Manchester age peers.

Because this was a longitudinal study, it allowed a check that could not be made in any of the cross-sectional studies described in the literature. Some 30% of the volunteers who had been tested at TP1 had dropped out of the study by TP2 because of death or increasing frailty. This allowed investigation into whether dropout of frail individuals affects not only the average levels of scores obtained but also the patterns of relationships observed between scores on different tasks. In both cities the TP1 scores of individuals who had dropped out by TP2 showed the same pattern of stronger correlations and robustness of associations to the removal of variance associated with CCF scores (g_f), as was observed for the Manchester old-old group at TP2.

These findings strongly suggest that as a group of people ages, increasing numbers of them begin to experience changes that affect frontal brain function. Until these changes occur, levels of scores—and therefore correlations between scores on most tasks, including tests of frontal function—are mainly determined by levels of general intellectual ability. If frontal tests have any validity, individuals who begin to perform poorly on one frontal test because they have begun to suffer from frontal changes will also tend to perform poorly on others. Consequently, as a sample ages, correlations between scores on different frontal tests will become stronger. Because exceptionally poor performance on frontal tests is increasingly likely to be due to damage to specific frontal systems rather than to changes or differences in general mental ability, correlations between scores on frontal tests will not greatly reduce when variance associated with intelligence test scores is partialled out. However, it is precisely those individuals who are beginning to experience frontal changes who are most likely to drop out from longitudinal studies or to decline to volunteer for cross-sectional laboratory comparisons. Unless researchers extend their samples beyond the "elite" survivors of older groups, they will not only underestimate average age changes in performance on all cognitive tests but also fail to observe age-related changes in patterns of relationships between measures that indicate differential and modular, rather than global and general, changes in performance with age.

CONCLUSIONS

An unacknowledged but pervasive issue underlying methodological problems in cognitive gerontology is how observations of behavioral and CNS changes should be interpreted at the population level and at the individual level. I would argue that it is essential at all times to make explicit which of four possible hypotheses about the ways in which age changes the brain we are using to interpret evidence. These hypotheses represent alternatives resulting from combinations of two pairs of alternative assumptions: whether one assumes that patterns of brain changes invariably follow the same or different patterns in all individuals and whether we assume that patterns of local changes occur in all individuals and proceed continuously, but at different rates in different individuals, or that local changes occur in some, but not all individuals, but that the incidence of individuals suffering local changes increases as a population ages.

These alternative scenarios can be further expanded: One may assume that the same characteristic patterns of brain changes invariably occur in all members of an aging population, but that the rates at which these changes proceed differs between individuals. This may be termed universal, progressive, single-pattern brain aging. One may, alternatively, assume that characteristic patterns of local brain changes occur and gradually progress in all individuals, but that different individuals may show different patterns, as well as different rates, of change. This may be termed, albeit rebarbatively, universal, progressive, multiple-pattern brain aging. Either of these possibilities may be modified by an additional plausible assumption that apart from local changes that may occur gradually or suddenly, and which may be detected by changing patterns of performance across specific neuropsychological tests, there are also continuous global changes that affect performance on all tests of any kind.

The permutations of possible outcomes from these various scenarios are dauntingly complex, but it has been naive to ignore them for so long. In particular, note that they bring into question the conveniently simplistic assumption that two empirically separable factors are responsible for cognitive changes in aging populations: the increasing and accelerating accumulation throughout a lifetime of pathologies, biological life events (see Houx et al., 1993), and other processes that are supposed to be distinct in their etiological provenance and, with less rationale, different even in their functional effects. These processes remain undefined both in terms of their biological nature and in their effects on the CNS, and are referred to by the blanket term *normal*, or *usual*, *aging*.

The contrast between normal and pathological processes in old age now seems a weak guide to further work. It implies that there exists a subset of "superhealthy" older people who, though their numbers sharply diminish with the age of the population sampled, remain unaffected by any pathology and thus experience only primary brain changes. Because processes of normal or usual aging of the CNS still lack any clear physiological description, it has been possible for them to be taken, without evidence, to be both continuous in their progress and global in their effects. In the absence of evidence, this has focused attention on a rare, and perhaps even mythical, cohort of "ideally healthy" older people and has reduced interest in the majority of people for whom age is accompanied by an increasing variety and intensity of pathologies, including cerebrovascular changes, that can produce localized, as well as global, changes in intellectual competence and in the ability to manage everyday life. The politics of an area of research in which there is public pressure for reassuring identification of an universally attainable condition of "ideal aging" has contributed to persistence of an unhelpful concentration on what is, at best, a minority of all of the people whose various conditions deserve the attention of researchers.

Perhaps it is also time to acknowledge that researchers cannot hope to base models for age-related cognitive change on behavioral evidence alone. Among the most common concomitants of aging in the CNS are the sequelae of cerebrovascular accidents or insufficiencies of cerebrovascular circulation. As Shaw et al. (1984) pointed out, these changes are likely to occur more often in the frontal lobes than in other areas of the brain. Some cerebrovascular problems will have relatively continuous and gradual effects; others will produce more abrupt changes; but the impacts of these conditions will, in general, occur over relatively short time spans compared to changes that have been attributed to the progress of "normal" aging. Furthermore, and perhaps most importantly, many aging individuals will show some general impairment from cerebrovascular changes but will die before they show any easily identified focal deficits. On these grounds the ef-

fect of age-related brain changes, particularly in the frontal lobes, is best considered as a question of the increasing incidence, and of the differential rates of progress, of patterns of local deficits. It remains an open question whether these deficits usually occur in a particular characteristic pattern or whether they may take different patterns in different individuals. On balance it does seem probable that they occur earlier and more often in the frontal cortex than in other brain areas, but comprehensive investigations of other areas have not yet been undertaken. In any case, it may be more fruitful to set out to investigate the relative incidence and severity of different patterns of age-related brain changes than to assume naively that small samples of "healthy" older people will include only individuals who have not, or only those who have, experienced either the same global changes or a particular focal change. A change of labels may, for once, be therapeutic. If, instead of discussing "cognitive gerontology" researchers begin to discuss "the epidemiology of age-related cognitive change," then we may open our minds to wider and more interesting theoretical perspectives of relationships between brain aging and behavior, and avail ourselves of more realistic models and more appropriate statistical and methodological tools with which to exploit them.

Admissions that brain aging can be modular as well as global and that it may be better described as a matter of increasing incidence of particular kinds of changes rather than as a continuous progression of uniform patterns of change may trespass on well-established vested interests in cognitive gerontology and will certainly make the design of further studies more complicated and expensive than the resources available to many investigators can support. Nevertheless, it is hard to see how progress can be made unless we study much larger and clinically better-investigated samples. Indeed, it is dubious whether it is still cost-effective to pursue research in cognitive gerontology without data from both structural and functional brain imaging. In recompense, acceptance of a more realistic point of view offers the advantage that it can resolve inconsistencies in what is, currently, a very untidy and tentative literature. It entails acceptance that without direct evidence for the extent and patterns of brain changes in old age, the contrasts that we have observed may depend more on how we selected our samples, or on how our samples have selected themselves, than on the models that we have adopted or the paradigms we developed to test them.

REFERENCES

Adam, J. (1978). Sequential strategies and the separation of age, cohort and time of measurement contributions to developmental data. *Psychological Bulletin, 85,* 1309–1316.

Albert, M. (1993). Neuropsychological and neurophysiological changes in healthy adult humans across the age range. *Neurobiology of Aging, 14,* 623.

Allen, P. A., Ashcraft, M. H., & Weber, T. A. (1992). On mental multiplication and age. *Psychology and Aging, 7,* 536–545.

Allen, P. A., Smith, A. F., Jerge, K. A., & Vires-Collins, K. (1997). Age differences in mental multiplication: Evidence for peripheral but not central decrements. *Journal of Gerontology, Psychological Sciences, 52,* P81–P90.

Anders, T. R., & Fozard, J. L. (1973). Effects of age upon retrieval from primary and secondary memory. *Developmental Psychology, 9,* 411–415.

Anders, T. R., Fozard, J. L., & Lillyquist, T. D. (1972). Effects of age upon retrieval from short-term memory. *Developmental Psychology, 6,* 214–217.

Anderson, M. (1988). Inspection time, information processing and the development of intelligence. *British Journal of Developmental Psychology, 6,* 43–57.

Anderson, M. (1992). *Intelligence and development: A cognitive theory.* Oxford. Blackwell.

Anderson, M. (1995). Evidence for a single global factor of developmental change: Too good to be true? *Australian Journal of Psychology, 47,* 18–24.

Anstey, K. J., Lord, S. R., & Williams, P. (1997). Strength in the lower limbs: Visual contrast sensitivity and simple reaction time predict cognition in older women. *Psychology and Aging, 12*(1), 137–144.

Anstey, K. J., Stankov, L., & Lord, S. R. (1996). Primary aging, secondary aging and intelligence. *Psychology and Aging, 8,* 562–570.

Arbuckle, T. Y., Gold, D., & Andres, D. (1986). Cognitive functioning of older people in relation to social and personality variables. *Psychology and Aging, 1,* 55–62.

Arenberg, D. (1974). A longitudinal study of problem-solving in adults. *Journal of Gerontology, 29,* 650–658.

Arnsten, A. F. T., Cai, J. X., Murphy, B. L., & Goldman-Rakic, P. S. (1994). Dopamine D1 receptor mechanisms in the cognitive functioning of young adult and aged monkeys. *Psychopharmacology, 116,* 143–151.

Axelrod, B. N., & Henry, R. R. (1992). Age-related performance on the Wisconsin card sorting, similarities and controlled oral word association tests. *The Clinical Neuropsychologist, 6,* 16–26.

Baddeley, A. D. (1986). *Working Memory.* Oxford: Oxford University Press.

Baltes, P. B. (1968). Longitudinal and cross-sectional sequences in the study of age and generation effects. *Human Development, 11,* 145–171.

Baltes, P. B., Cornelius, S. W., & Nesselroade, J. R. (1979). Cohort effects in developmental psychology. In J. R. Nesselrode & P. B. Baltes (Eds.), *Longitudinal research in the study of behaviour and development* (pp. 38–49). New York: Academic Press.

Baltes, P. B., & Lindenberger, U. (1997). Emergence of a powerful connection between sensory and cognitive functions across the lifespan: A new window to the study of cognitive aging? *Psychology and Aging, 12,* 12–21.

Baltes, P. B., & Nesselrode, J. (1970). Multivariate longitudinal and cross-sectional sequences for analysing ontogenetic and generational change: A methodological note. *Developmental Psychology, 2,* 163–168.

Barrett, T. R., & Watkins, S. K. (1986). Word familiarity and cardiovascular health as determinants of age-related recall differences. *Journal of Gerontology, 41,* 222–224.

Baumler, G. (1969). Decrease in achievement capacity as a result of age with particular reference to the Stroop-interference tendency. *Psychologische Beitrage, 11,* 34–68.

Bayllor, A. M., & Spirduso, W. W. (1988). Systematic aerobic exercise and components of reaction time in older women. *Journals of Gerontology, Psychological Sciences, 43,* P121–P126.

Bent, N., Rabbitt, P. M. A., & Metcalf, D. (2000). Diabetes mellitus and the rate of cognitive change. *British Journal of Clinical Psychology, 39,* 349–362.

Berg, S. (1987). Intelligence and terminal decline. In G. Maddox and E. W. Busse (Eds.), *Aging: The universal human experience* (pp. 234–259). New York: Springer.

Berkowitz, B. (1965). Changes in intellect with age: IV. changes in achievement and survival in older people. *Journal of Genetic Psychology, 107,* 3–14.

Birren, J. E. (1956). The significance of age-changes in speed of perception and psychomotor skills. In J. E. Anderson (Ed.), *Psychological aspects of aging* (pp. 97–104). Washington, DC: American Psychological Association.

Birren, J. E. (1959). Sensation, perception and the modification of behaviour in relation to aging. In J. E. Birren, H. A. Imus, & W. F. Windle (Eds.), *The process of aging in the central nervous system* (pp. 143–165). Springfield, IL: Thomas.

Birren, J. E. (1965). Age changes in the speed of behaviour: Its central nature and physiological correlates. In A. T. Welford & J. E. Birren (Eds.), *Behaviour, aging and the nervous system* (pp. 191–216). Springfield, IL: Thomas.

Birren, J. E. (1979). Tutorial review of changes in choice reaction time with advancing age. In H. Baumeister (Ed.), *Bayer symposium no. 6* (pp. 232–247). Bonn, Germany: Springer.

Birren, J. E., Botwinnick, J., Weiss, A. D., & Morrison, D. F. (1963). Interrelations of mental and perceptual tests given to healthy elderly men. In J. E. Birren, R. N. Butler, S. W. Greenhouse, L. Sokoloff, & M. R. Yarrow (Eds.), pp. 83–104 in *Human aging* (DHEW, PGS Publication No. HSM 71-9051). USGPO, Washington, DC: U.S. Government Printing Office.

Birren, J. E., Butler, R. N., Greenhouse, S. W., Sokoloff, L., & Yarrow, M. R. (1963). *Human aging* (Publication No. 986). Washington, DC: U.S. Government Printing Office.

Birren, J. E., & Cunningham, W. (1985). Research on the psychology of aging: Principles, concepts and theory. In J. E. Birren & K. W. Schaie (Eds.), *Handbook of the psychology of aging* (2nd ed., pp. 3–34). New York: Van Nostrand Reinhold.

Birren, J. E., Woods, A. M., & Williams, M. V. (1980). Behavioral slowing with age. In L. W. Poon (Ed.), *Aging in the 1980s: Psychological issues* (pp. 293–308). Washington, DC: American Psychological Association.

Blum, J. E., Clark, E. T., & Jarvik, L. F. (1973). The NYs Psychiatric Institute study of aging ruins. In L. F. Jarvik, C. Eisdorter, and J. E. Blum (Eds.), *Intellectual Function in Adults* (pp. 39–76). New York: Springer.

Bohannon, R. W. (1991). Interrelationships of trunk and extremity muscle strengths and body awareness following unilateral brain lesions. *Perceptual and Motor Skills, 73,* 1016–1018.

Boone, K. B., Miles, B. L., Lesser, I. M., Hill, E., & D'Elia, L. (1990). Performance on frontal lobe tests in healthy older individuals. *Developmental Neuropsychology, 6,* 215–223.

Borkan, G., & Norris, A. H. (1980). Biological age in adulthood: Comparison of active and inactive US males. *Human Biology, 52,* 787–802.

Botwinick, J. (1984). Aging and Behaviour (3rd ed.). New York: Springer.

Botwinick, J., West, R., & Storandt, M. (1978). Predicting death from behavioral test performance. *Journal of Gerontology, 33,* 755–776.

Brand, C. R., & Deary, I. J. (1982). Intelligence and inspection time. In H. J. Eysenck (Ed.), *A model for intelligence* (pp. 104–136). New York: Springer.

Brinley, J. F. (1965). Cognitive Sets, speed and accuracy of performance in the elderly. In A. T. Wellford & J. E. Birren (Eds.), *Behaviour, aging and the nervous system* (pp. 114–149). Springfield, IL: Thomas.

Broadbent, D. E. (1971). *Decision and stress.* New York: Academic Press.

Broadbent, D. E., Cooper, P. J., Fitzgerald, P. F., & Parkes, K. R. (1982). The Cognitive Failures Questionnaire (CFR) and its correlates. *British Journal of Clinical Psychology, 21,* 1–16.

Brodman, E., Erdman, A. J., Jr., & Wolff, H. G. (1949). *Manual for the Cornell Medical Index Health Questionnaire.* New York: Cornell University Medical School.

Brooks, S. V., & Faulkner, J. A. (1994). Skeletal muscle weakness in old age: Underlying mechanisms. *Medicine and Science in Sport and Exercise, 26,* 432–439.

Brown, J. W., Chobor, M. S., & Zinn, F. (1993). Dementia testing to the elderly. *Journal of Nervous and Mental Disease, 181,* 695–698.

Brumback, R. A. (1985). "Terminal drop" as a sign of depression in elderly patients: An hypothesis. *Psychological Reports, 57,* 84–86.

Buchler, R., Pierce, J. T., Robinson, P., & Trier, K. S. (1967). Epidemiological survey of older Canadians (Government of Canada Report). Ottawa: HMSO.

Bunce, D. J., Warr, P. B., & Cochrane, T. (1993). Blocks in choice responding as a function of age and physical fitness. *Psychology and Aging, 8,* 26–33.

Burgess, P. (1997). Theory and methodology in executive function research. In P. M. A. Rabbitt (Ed.), *Methodology of frontal and executive function* (pp. 81–116). Hove, England: Psychology Press.

Busse, E. W. (1969). Theories of aging. In E. W. Busse & E. Pfeifer (Eds.), *Behaviour and adaptation in later life* (pp. 11–32). Boston: Little, Brown.

Campbell, D. T., & Stanley, J. C. (1963). *Experimental and quasi-experimental designs for research.* Chicago: Rand McNally.

Canestrari, R. E., Jr. (1963). Paced and self-paced learning in young and elderly adults. *Journal of Gerontology, 18,* 165–168.

Cattell, R. B., & Cattell, A. K. S. (1960). Handbook for the individual or Group Culture Fair Intelligence Test. Champaign, IL: IPAT.

Cerella, J. (1985). Information processing rates in the elderly. *Psychological Bulletin, 98,* 67–83.

Cerella, J. (1990). Age and information processing rate. In J. E. Birren & K. W. Schaie (Eds.), *Handbook of the psychology of aging* (3rd ed., pp. 201–221). San Diego: Academic Press.

Cerella, J., & Fozard, J. L. (1984). Lexical access and age. *Developmental Psychology, 20,* 235–243.

Chambers, J. M., Cleveland, W. S., Kleiner, B., & Tukey, P. A. (1983). *Graphical methods for data analysis.* Boston: Duxbury.

Chapman, L. J., & Chapman, J. P. (1973). Problems in the measurement of cognitive deficits. *Psychological Bulletin, 79,* 380–385.

Clark, J. W. (1960). The aging dimension: A factorial analysis of individual differences with age on psychological and physiological measurement. *Journal of Gerontology, 15,* 183–187.

Clarkson, P. M. (1978). The effect of age and activity level on simple and choice fractionated response time. *European Journal of Applied Psychology, 40,* 17–25.

Clarkson-Smith, L., & Hartley, A. A. (1990). Structural equation models of relationships between exercise and cognitive abilities. *Psychology and Aging, 5,* 437–446.

Clement, F. J. (1974). Longitudinal and cross-sectional assessments of age changes in physical strength as related to sex, social class and mental ability. *Journal of Gerontology, 29,* 423–429.

Cohen, G. (1988). Age differences in memory for text: Production deficiency or processing limitations? In L. Light & D. Burke (Eds.), *Language, memory and aging* (pp. 171–190). Cambridge: Cambridge University Press.

Cohen-Cole, S. A., & Kaufman, K. G. (1993). Major depression in physical illness: Diagnosis, prevalence and anti-depression treatment: (a ten-year review, 1982–1992). *Depression, 1,* 181–204.

Cohn, N. B., Dustman, R. E., & Bradford, D. C. (1984). Age-related decrements in Stroop colour test performance. *Journal of Clinical Psychology, 40,* 1244–1250.

Comalli, P. E., Wapner, S., & Werner, H. (1962). Interference effects of Stroop colour-word test in children, adulthood and aging. *Journal of Genetic Psychology, 100,* 47–53.

Connelly, S. L., Hasher, L., & Zacks, R. T. (1991). Age and reading: The impact of distraction. *Psychology and Aging, 6,* 533–541.

Corso, J. F. (1987). Sensory-perceptual processes and aging. In K. W. Schaie (Ed.), *Annual review of gerontology and geriatrics* (pp. 29–55). New York: Springer.

Costa, L. (1988). Clinical neuropsychology: Prospects and problems. *The Clinical Neuropsychologist, 2,* 3–11.

Costa, P. T., & McCrae, R. R. (1982). An approach to the attribution of aging, period and cohort effects. *Psychological Bulletin, 92,* 238–250.

Craik, F. I. M. (1996). Commentary: Prospective memory—Aging and lapses of attention. In M. Brandimonte, G. O. Epstrein, & M. A. McDaniel (Eds.), *Prospective memory: Theory and applications* (pp. 227–238). Mahwah, NJ: Erlbaum.

Craik, F. I. M., & Jennings, J. M. (1992). Human memory. In F. I. M. Craik & T. Salthouse (Eds.), *The handbook of aging and cognition* (pp. 51–110). Hillsdale, NJ: Erlbaum.

Craik, F. I. M., & Lockhart, R. S. (1972). Levels of processing: A framework for memory research. *Journal of Verbal Learning and verbal Behaviour, 11,* 671–684.

Cunningham, W. R. (1987). Intellectual abilities and age. In K. W. Schaie, (Ed.), *Annual Review of Gerontology and Geriatrics, 7,* pp. 34–69. New York: Springer.

Cunningham, W. R., & Brookbank, J. W. (1988). *Gerontology.* New York: Harper and Row.

Daigneault, S., Braun, C. M. J., & Whitaker, H. A. (1992). Early effects of normal aging in perseverative and non-perseverative prefrontal measures. *Developmental Neuropsychology, 8,* 99–114.

Dean, W. (1988). *Biological aging measurement: Clinical applications.* Los Angeles: Center for Biogerontology.

Dempster, F. N. (1992). The rise and fall of the inhibitory mechanism: Towards a unified theory of cognitive development and aging. *Developmental Review, 12,* 45–75.

Dickenson, C. M., & Rabbitt, P. M. A. (1991). Simulated visual impairment: Effects on text comprehension and reading speed. *Clinical Vision Science, 6,* 301–308.

Diggle, P. J., Liang, K. Y. & Zeger, S. L. (1994). Analysis of longitudinal data. Oxford: Oxford University Press.

Dijkstra, J. B., van Boxtel, M. P. J., Houx, P. J., & Jolles, J. (1998). An operation under general anaesthetic is a risk factor for age-related cognitive decline: Results from a large cross-sectional population study. *Journal of the American Geriatrics Society, 46,* 1258–1265.

Dirken, J. M. (1972). *Functional age of industrial workers.* Groningen, Netherlands: Wolters-Noordhof.

Dundikova, V. A., Silvon, Z. K. & Dubina, T. L. (1978). Biological age and its estimation. *Experimental Gerontology, 16,* 13–24.

Duncan, J. (1995). Attention, intelligence and the frontal lobes. In M. S. Gazzaniga (Ed.), *The cognitive neurosciences* (pp. 721–733). Cambridge; M.A.: MIT Press.

Duncan, J., Burgess, P., & Emslie, H. (1995). Fluid intelligence after frontal lobe lesions. *Neuropsychologia, 33,* 261–268.

Dustman, R. E., Ruhling, R. O., Russell, E. M., Shearer, D. E., Bonekay, H. W., Shigeoka, J. W., Wood, J. S., & Bradford, C. (1984). Aerobic exercise training and improved neuropsychological function of older adults. *Neurobiology of Aging, 5,* 35–42.

Elias, M. F., Robbins, M. A., Schultz, N. R., & Pierce, T. W. (1990). Is blood pressure an important variable in research on aging and neuropsychological test performance? *Journal of Gerontology, 45,* 128–135.

Eysenck, H. J. (1986). The theory of intelligence and the psychophysiology of cognition. In R. J. Sternberg (Ed.), *Advances in the psychology of human intelligence* (Vol. 31, pp. 1–45). Hillsdale, NJ: Erlbaum.

Faust, M. E., Balota, D. A., Spieler, D. H., & Ferrara, F. R. (1999). Individual differences in interaction processing rate and amount: Implications for group differences in response latency. *Psychological Bulletin, 125,* 777–799.

Fisher, D. L., & Glaser, R. A. (1996). Molar and latent models of cognitive slowing: Implications for aging, dementia, depression, development and intelligence. *Psychonomic Bulletin and Review, 3,* 458–480.

Fisk, A. D., & Fisher, D. L. (1994). Brinley plots and theories of aging: The explicit, muddled and implicit debates. *Journal of Gerontology, Psychological Sciences, 49,* P81–P89.

Fisk, A. D., Fisher, D. L., & Rogers, W. A. (1992). General slowing alone cannot explain visual search effects: A reply to Cerella. *Journal of Experimental Psychology: General, 120,* 131–149.

Folstein, M. F., Folstein, S. E., & McHugh, P. R. (1975). The mini mental state, a practical method for grading the cognitive states of patient for the clinician. *Journal of Psychiatric Research, 12,* 189–198.

Fozard, J. L. (1990). Vision and hearing in aging. In J. E. Birren & K. W. Schaie (Eds.), *Handbook of the psychology of aging* (3rd ed.), pp. 303–349. San Diego: Academic Press.

Fozard, J. L., Metter, E. J., & Brant, L. J. (1990). Next steps in describing aging and disease in longitudinal studies. *Journal of Gerontology, 45,* 116–127.

Fozard, J. L., Vercruyssen, M., Reynolds, S. L., Hancock, P. A., & Quilter, R. E. (1994). Age differences and changes in reaction time: The Baltimore Longitudinal Study of Aging. *Journal of Gerontology, 49*(4), P179–P189.

Furkawa, T., Inoue, M., Kajiya, F., & Abe, H. (1975). Assessment of biological age by multiple regression analysis. *Journal of Gerontology, 30,* 422–434.

Garner, W. R. (1988). The contribution of information theory to psychology. In W. Hirst (Ed.), *The making of cognitive science: Essays in honor of George A. Miller* (pp. 19–35). New York: Cambridge University Press.

Geary, D. C., Frensch, P. A., & Wiley, J. G. (1993). Simple and complex mental substraction: Strategy choice and speed of processing differences in young and older adults. *Psychology and Aging, 8,* 242–256.

Geary, D. C., & Wiley, J. G. (1991). Cognitive addition: Strategy choice and speed of processing differences in young and elderly adults. *Psychology and Aging, 6,* 474–483.

Gergen, K. J. (1977). Stability, change and chance in understanding human development. In N. Datan & H. W. Reese (Eds.), *Life-span developmental psychology: Dialectical perspectives on experimental research* (pp. 31–56). New York: Academic Press.

Glenn, N. D. (1977). Cohort analysis. Beverley Hills: Sage University Press.

Glenn, N. D. (1981). Age, birth cohort and drinking: An illustration of inferring effects from cohort data. *Journal of Gerontology, 36,* 362–369.

Goel, V., & Graffman, J. (1995). Are the frontal lobes implicated in "planning" function? Interpreting data from the Towers of Hanoi. *Neuropsychologia, 33*(5), 623–642.

Goldman-Rakic, P. S. (1993). Specification of higher cortical functions. *Journal of Head Trauma Rehabilitation, 8,* 13–23.

Goldman-Rakic, P. S., & Brown, R. M. (1981). Regional changes of monoamines in cerebral cortex and subcortical structures of aging rhesus monkeys. *Neuroscience, 6,* 177–187.

Granick, S., Kleban, M. H., & Weiss, A. D. (1976). Relationships between hearing loss and cognition in normally hearing aged persons. *Journal of Gerontology, 31,* 434–440.

Gur, R. C., Gur, R. E., Orbist, W. D., Skolnick, B. E., & Reivich, M. (1987). Age and regional cerebral blood flow at rest and during cognitive activity. *Archives of General Psychiatry, 44,* 617–621.

Guttman, J. M. (1980). The elderly at home and in retirement housing: A comparative study of health problems, functional difficulties and support service needs. In V. W. Marshall (Ed.), *Aging in Canada: Social perspectives* (pp. 232–259). Don Mills, Ontario: Fitzhugh & Whiteside.

Guttman, C. R. G., Jolesz, F. A., Kikinis, R., Killiany, R. J., Moss, M. B., Sandor, T., & Albert,

M. S. (1998). White matter and gray matter differences with age. *Neurology, 50,* 972–978.

Haarlkand, K. Y., Temkin, N., Randahl, G., & Dikmen, S. (1994). Recovery of simple motor skills after head injury. *Journal of Clinical and Experimental Neuropsychology, 16,* 448–456.

Hale, S. (1990). A global developmental trend in cognitive processing speed. *Child Development, 61,* 653–663.

Hale, S., Lima, S. D., & Myerson, J. (1991). General cognitive slowing in the non-lexical domain: An experimental validation. *Psychology and Aging, 6,* 512–521.

Hale, S., Myerson, J., & Wagstaff, D. (1987). General slowing of non-verbal information processing: Evidence for a power law. *Journal of Gerontology, 42,* 131–136.

Hamm, V. P., & Hasher, L. (1992). Age and the availability of inferences. *Psychology and Aging, 7,* 56–64.

Harnishfinger, K. K., & Bjorkland, D. F. (1993). The ontogeny of inhibitory mechanisms: A renewal approach in cognitive development. In M. L. Howe and R. Pasnak (Eds.). *Emerging Themes in Cognitive Development* (pp. 28–49). New York: Springer.

Harris, J. E., & Morris, P. E. (1984). *Everyday memory, actions and absentmindedness.* New York: Academic Press.

Hartman, M., & Hasher, L. (1991). Aging and suppression: Memory for previously relevant information. *Psychology and Aging, 6,* 587–594.

Hasher, L., Quig, M. B., & May, C. P. (1997). Inhibitory control over no-longer-relevant information: Adult age differences. *Memory and Cognition, 25*(3), 286–295.

Hasher, L., Stoltzfus, E. R., Zacks, R. T., & Rypma, B. (1991). Age and inhibition. *Journal of Experimental Psychology: Learning, Memory and Cognition, 17,* 163–169.

Hasher, L., & Zacks, R. T. (1979). Automatic and effortful processes in memory. *Journal of Experimental Psychology: General, 108,* 356–388.

Hasher, L., & Zacks, R. T. (1988). Working memory: Comprehension and aging—A review and a new view. In G. K. Bower (Ed.), *The psychology of learning and motivation* (Vol. 22, pp. 193–225). San Diego: Academic Press.

Haug, H., & Eggers, R. (1991). Morphometry of the human cortex cerebri and cortex striatum during aging. *Neurobiology of Aging, 12,* 336–338.

Hayslip, B., Jr. (1988). Personality-ability relationships in aged adults. *Journal of Gerontology, 45,* 116–127.

Heaton, R. K. (1981). Wisconsin card-sorting test manual. Odessa, FL: Psychological Assessment Resources.

Heim, A. (1970). The AH4 test batteries. Slough, England: NFER-NELSON.

Heron, A., & Chown, S. (1967). *Age and function.* London: Churchill.

Hermann, D. J. (1982). Know thy memory: The use of questionnaires to assess and study memory. *Psychological Bulletin, 92,* 434–452.

Hertzog, C., Schaie, K. W., & Gribbin, K. (1978). Cardiovascular disease and changes in intellectual functioning from middle to old age. *Journal of Gerontology, 33*(6), 872–883.

Hick, W. G. (1952). On the rate of gain of information. *Quarterly Journal of Experimental Psychology, 4,* 11–26.

Hofecker, G., Skalicky, M., Khment, A., & Niedermuller, H. (1980). Models of biological aging in the rat: I. *Mechanisms of Aging and Development, 14,* 345–360.

Holland, C. M., & Rabbitt, P. M. A. (1991). The course and causes of cognitive change with advancing age. *Reviews in Clinical Gerontology, 1,* 81–96.

Horn, J. (1982). The theory of fluid and crystallized intelligence in relation to concepts of cognitive psychology and aging in adulthood. In F. I. M. Craik & S. Trehub (Eds.), *Aging and cognitive processes* (pp. 237–278). New York: Plenum Press.

Horn, J. L. (1987). A context for understanding information processing studies of human abilities. In P. A. Vernon (Ed.), *Speed of information processing and intelligence* (pp. 201–238). Norwood, NJ: Ablex.

Horn, J. L., Donaldson, G., & Engstrom, R. (1981). Application, memory and fluid intelligence decline in adulthood. *Research on Aging, 3,* 33–84.

Houx, P. J. (1991). Rigorous health screening reduces age effects on a memory scanning task. *Brain and Cognition, 15,* 246–260.

Houx, P. J., Jolles, J., & Vreeling, F. W. (1993). Stroop interference: Aging effects assessed with the Stroop colour-word test. *Experimental Aging Research, 19,* 209–224.

Howe, M. J. (1999). *The psychology of higher abilities.* New York: New York University Press.

Hulicka, I. M., Sterns, H., & Grossman, J. L. (1967). Age group comparisons of paired associate learning as a function of paced and self-paced association and response times. *Journal of Gerontology, 22,* 274–280.

Humphrey, C., Gilhome-Herbst, K., & Farqui, S. (1981). Some characteristics of the hearing impaired elderly who do not present themselves for rehabilitation. *British Journal of Audiology, 15,* 25–30.

Jacewicz, M. M., & Hartley, A. A. (1979). Rotation of mental images by young and old college students: The effects of familiarity. *Journal of Gerontology, 34,* 396–403.

Jalavisto, E., & Nakkonen, T. (1963). On the assessment of biological age. *Annales Academiae Scientiarum Finnicae, Series A*(v), 1–38.

Jenkins, L., Myerson, J., Hale, S., & Fry, A. F. (1999). Individual and developmental differences in working memory across the lifespan. *Psychonomic Bulletin and Review, 6,* 28–40.

Jensen, A. R. (1980). Chronometric analysis of mental ability. *Journal of Social and Biological Structures, 3,* 181–224.

Jensen, A. R. (1982). Reaction time and psychometric *g*. In H. J. Eysenck (Ed.), *A model for intelligence* (pp. 69–78). Berlin: Springer.

Kail, R. (1988). Developmental functions for speed of cognitive processes. *Journal of Experimental Child Psychology, 45,* 339–364.

Kail, R. (1991). Developmental change in speed of processing during childhood and adolescence. *Psychological Bulletin, 109,* 490–501.

Kail, R. (1997). The neural noise hypothesis: Evidence from processing speed in adults with multiple sclerosis. *Aging, Neuropsychology and Cognition, 4,* 157–165.

Kane, M. J., Hasher, L., Stoltzfus, E. R., Zacks, R. T., & Connelly, S. L. (1994). Inhibitory attentional mechanisms and aging. *Psychology and Aging, 9,* 103–112.

Kausler, D. H. (1990). *Experimental psychology, cognition and human aging.* New York: Springer.

Kausler, D. H., & Hakami, M. K. (1982). Frequency judgments by young and elderly adults for relevant stimuli with simultaneously presented irrelevant stimuli. *Journal of Gerontology, 37,* 438–442.

Kimberg, D. Y., & Farrah, M. J. (1993). A unified account of impairments following frontal lobe damage: The role of working memory in complex organised behaviour. *Journal of Experimental Psychology: General, 122,* 411–428.

Kirkwood, T. (1999). *The years of our lives.* Oxford, England: Oxford University Press.

Kleemeier, R. W. (1962). Intellectual changes in the senium. *Proceedings of the Social Statistics Section of the American Statistical Association, 23,* 290–295.

Kroll, W., & Clarkson, P. M. (1978). Age, isometric knee extension strength and fractionated resisted response time. *Experimental Aging Research, 4,* 389–409.

Lachman, R., Lachman, J. L., & Taylor, D. W. (1982). Reallocation of mental resources over the productive lifespan: Assumptions and task analyses. In F. I. M. Craik and S. Trehub, (Eds.), *Aging and the cognitive process* (pp. 237–252). New York: Plenum Press.

Laming, D. R. J. (1968). *Information theory of choice reaction time.* New York: Wiley.

Laming, D. R. J. (1985). *Sensory analysis.* London: Academic Press.

La Rue, A., Swan, G. E., & Carmelli, D. (1995). Cognition and depression in a cohort of aging men: Results from the Western Collaborative Study. *Psychology and Aging, 16,* 30–33.

Leon, D. A. (1998). Reduced foetal growth rate are increased risk of death from ischuemic heart disease: A cohort study of 15,000 Swedish men and women, 1915 to 29: *British Medical Journal, 317*(7153), 241–245.

Lexell, J., Downham, D., & Sjostrom, M. (1986). What is the cause of aging atrophy? Total number, size and proportion of different fibre types studied in whole vastus lateralis muscle from 15- to 83-year-old men. *Journal of the Neurological Sciences, 84,* 275–294.

Li, K. Z. H., Hasher, L., Jones, D., Rahhal, T. A., & May, C. P. (1998). Distractability, circadian arousal and aging: A boundary condition? *Psychology and Aging, 13,* 574–583.

Li, S. C., Jordanova, M., & Lindenberger, U. (1998). From good senses to good sense: A link between tactile information processing and intelligence. *Intelligence, 26,* 99–122.

Lieberman, M. A. (1965). Psychological correlates of impending death: Some preliminary observations. *Journal of Gerontology, 20,* 181–190.

Lima, S. D., Hale, S., & Myerson, J. (1991). How general is general slowing? Evidence from the lexical domain. *Psychology and Aging, 6,* 416–425.

Lindenberger, U., & Baltes, P. (1994). Sensory functioning and intelligence in old age: A strong connection. *Psychology and Aging, 9,* 339–355.

Lindenberger, U., & Potter, U. (1998). The complex nature of unique and shared effects in hierarchical linear regression: Implications for developmental psychology. *Psychological Methods, 3,* 218–230.

Loranger, A. W., Misiak, H. (1960). The performance of aged females on five nonlanguage tests of intellectual function. *Journal of Clinical Psychology, 16,* 189–191.

Lord, S. R., Clark, R. D., & Webster, I. W. (1991a). Physiological factors associated with falls in an elderly population. *Journal of the American Geriatrics Society, 39,* 1194–1200.

Lord, S. R., McLean, D., & Stathers, G. (1992). Physiological factors associated with injurious falls in older people living in the community. *Gerontology, 38,* 338–346.

Lowe, C., & Rabbitt, P. M. A. (1997). Cognitive models of aging and frontal lobe deficits. In P. M. A. Rabbitt (Ed.), *Methodology of frontal and executive function* (pp. 39–60). Hove, England: Psychology Press.

Lowe, C., & Rabbitt, P. M. A. (1998). Test-retest reliability of the CANTAB and ISPOCD neuropsychological batteries: Theoretical and practical issues. *Neuropsychologia, 36,* 915–923.

Luce, R. D. (1986). *Response times: Their role in inferring elementary mental organization.* Oxford: Oxford University Press.

Maddox, G. L., & Wiley, J. (1976). Scope, methods and constructs in the study of aging. In R. H. Binstock and A. E. Shanas (Eds.), (pp. 326–349). *Handbook of aging and the social sciences.* New York: Van Nostrand Reinhold.

Mason, K. O., Winsborough, H. H., Mason, W. W., & Poole, W. K. (1973). Some methodological issues in cohort analysis of archival data. *American Sociological Review, 38,* 242–258.

Maylor, E. A. (1996). Does prospective memory decline with age? In M. Brandimonte, G. O. Einstein, & M. A. McDaniel (Eds.), *Prospective memory: Theory and applications* (pp. 173–198). Mahwah, NJ: Erlbaum.

Maylor, E. A., & Rabbitt, P. M. A. (1994). Applying Brinley plots to individuals: Effect of aging on performance distributions in two speeded tasks. *Psychology and Aging, 9,* 224–230.

McCarty, S. M., Siegler, I. C., & Logue, P. E. (1982). Wechsler memory scale scores, selective attrition and distance from death. *Journal of Gerontology, 37,* 176–181.

McInnes, L., & Rabbitt, P. M. A. (1997). The relationship between functional ability and cognitive ability among elderly people. In *Facts and research in gerontology* (pp. 34–45). Paris: Serdi.

McInnes, L. & Rabbitt, P. M. A. (1998). *The relationship between functional ability and cognitive ability among elderly people: Research and practice in Alzheimer's disease.* New York: Springer.

McNair, D. M. (1979). Self-rating scales for assessing psychopathology in the elderly. In A. Raskin & L. Jarvik (Eds.), *Psychiatric symptoms and cognitive loss in the elderly* (pp. 157–168). Washington, DC: Hemisphere.

Melzer, D., McWilliams, B., Brayne, C., Johnson, T., & Bond, J. (1999). Profile of disability in elderly people: Estimates from a longitudinal population study. *British Medical Journal, 318,* 1108–11.

Miller, L. T., & Vernon, P. A. (1992). The general factor in short-term memory, intelligence and reaction time. *Intelligence, 16,* 5–29.

Miller, M. B., Chapman, J. P., Chapman, L. J., & Collins, J. (1995). Task difficulty and cognitive deficits in schizophrenia. *Journal of Abnormal Psychology, 104,* 251–258.

Mittenberg, W., Seidenberg, M., O'Leary, D. S., & Di Ginlio, D. V. (1989). Changes in cerebral functioning associated with normal aging. *Journal of Clinical and Experimental Neuropsychology, 11*(6), 918–932.

Molenaar, P. C. M., & van der Molen, M. W. (1994). On the discrimination between global and local trend hypotheses of life-span changes in processing speed. *Acta Psychologica, 86,* 273–293.

Moller, J. T., Cluitmans, P., Rasmussen, L. S., Houx, P., Canet, J., Rabbitt, P. M. A., Jolles, J., Larsen, K., Hanning, C. D., Langeron, O., Johnson, T., Lauven, P. M., Kristensen, P. A., Biedler, A., van Been, H., Fraidakis, O., Silverstein, J. H., Beneken, J. E. W., & Gravenstein, J. S. (1998). Long-term postoperative cognitive dysfunction in the elderly: ISPOCD1 study. *The Lancet, 351*(9186), 857–861.

Monge, R. H., & Hultsch, D. F. (1972). Paired associate learning as a function of adult age and the length of the anticipation and inspection intervals. *Journal of Gerontology, 26,* 157–162.

Morse, C. K. (1993). Does variability increase with age? An archival study of cognitive measures. *Psychology and Aging, 8,* 156–164.

Myerson, J., Ferraro, F. R., Hale, S., & Lima, S. D. (1992). General slowing in semantic priming and word recognition. *Psychology and Aging, 7,* 257–270.

Myerson, J., Jenkins, L., Hale, S., & Sliwinski, M. (2000). Individual and developmental differences in working memory across the lifespan: Reply. *Psychonomic Bulletin and Review, 7,* 734–740.

Nagi, M. H., & Stockwell, E. G. (1973). Socioeconomic differentials in mortality by cause of death. *Health Services Reports, 88,* 449–456.

Navon, D. (1984). Resources: A Theoretical Soupstone. *Psychological Review, 91,* 216–234.

Nelson, H. E. (1976). A modified card sorting test sensitive to frontal lobe defects. *Cortex, 12,* 313–324.

Nesselrode, J. R., & Baltes, P. B. (1979). *Longitudinal research in the study of behaviour and development.* New York: Academic Press.

Nettelbeck, T. (1987). Inspection time and intelligence. In P. A. Vernon (Ed.), *Speed of information processing and intelligence* (pp. 126–153). New York: Ablex.

Nettelbeck, T., Rabbitt, P. M. A., Wilson, C., & Batt, R. (1996). Uncoupling learning from initial recall: The relationship between speed and memory deficits in old age. *British Journal of Psychology, 87,* 593–597.

Neumann, E., & De Schepper, B. C. (1992). An inhibition-based of an effect: Evidence for an active suppression mechanism for selective attention. *Canadian Journal of Psychology, 46,* 1–40.

Palmore, E. (1978). When can age, period and cohort be separated? *Soc. Forces, 57,* 282–295.

Palmore, E., & Cleveland, W. (1976). Aging, terminal decline and terminal drop. *Journal of Gerontology, 31,* 76–81.

Palmore, E., & Jefferies, F. C. (Eds.), (1971). *Prediction of lifespan.* Lexington, MA: D.C. Health.

Panek, P. E., Rush, M. C., & Slade, L. A. (1984). Focus of the age-Stroop interference relationship. *Journal of Genetic Psychology, 145,* 209–216.

Pedhozur, E. L. (1997). *Multiple regression in behavioral research: Explanation and prediction* (3rd ed.). Fort Worth, TX: Harcourt Brace.

Pendleton, M. G., Heaton, R. K., Lehman, R. A., & Hulihan, D. (1982). Diagnostic utility of the Thurstone word frequency test in neuropsychological evaluation. *Journal of Clinical Neuropsychology, 4,* 307–317.

Perfect, T. (1994). What can Brinley plots tell us about cognitive aging? *Journal of Gerontology: Psychological Sciences, 49,* 60–64.

Perlmutter, M., & Nyquist, L. (1990). Relationships between self-reported physical and mental health and intelligence performance across adulthood [Special issue]. *Journal of Gerontology: Psychological Sciences, 45*(4), 145–155.

Phillips, L. H. (1998). Do "frontal tests" measure executive function? Issues of assessment and evidence from fluency tests. In P. M. A. Rabbitt (Ed.), *Methodology of frontal and executive function.* Hove, UK: Psychology Press.

Piccinin, A. M., & Rabbitt, P. M. A. (1999). Contribution of cognitive abilities to performance and improvement on a substitution coding task. *Psychology and Aging, 14,* 539–551.

Pincus, T., Callahan, L. F., & Burkhauser, R. V. (1987). Most chronic diseases are reported more frequently by individuals with fewer than 12 years formal education in the age 18–64. U.S. population. *J. Chronic Disorders, 40,* 865–874.

Powell, R. R., & Pohndorf, R. H. (1971). Comparison of adult exercisers and non-exercisers on fluid intelligence and selected physiological variables. *Research Quarterly, 42,* 70–77.

Rabbitt, P. M. A. (1968a). Channel-capacity, intelligibility, and immediate memory. *Quarterly Journal of Experimental Psychology, 20,* 241–240.

Rabbitt, P. M. A. (1968b). Three kinds of error-signalling responses in a serial choice task. *Quarterly Journal of Experimental Psychology, 20,* 241–248.

Rabbitt, P. M. A. (1982). Cognitive psychology needs models for old age. In A. D. Baddeley and J. Long (Eds.), *Attention and performance* (Vol. 9). Hove, England: Erlbaum.

Rabbitt, P. M. A. (1991). Mild hearing loss can cause apparent memory failures which increase with age and reduce with IQ. *Otolaryngologica, 476,* 167–176.

Rabbitt, P. M. A. (1993a). Does it all go together when it goes? *Quarterly Journal of Experimental Psychology, 46*(A), 385–433.

Rabbitt, P. M. A. (1993b). Crystal quest: An examination of the concepts of "fluid" and "crystallised" intelligence as explanations for cognitive changes in old age (pp. 197–231). In A. D. Baddeley and L. Weiskrantz (Eds.), *Attention, selection, awareness and control.* Oxford: Oxford University Press (144–169).

Rabbitt, P. M. A. (1996). Intelligence is not just mental speed. *Journal of Biosocial Science, 28,* 425–449.

Rabbitt, P. M. A. (1997). Methodologies and models in the study of executive function. In P. M. A. Rabbitt (Ed.), *Methodology of frontal and executive function* (pp. 1–38). Hove, England: Psychology Press.

Rabbitt, P. M. A. (1999). Measurement indexes, functional characteristics and psychometric constructs in cognitive aging. In T. J. Perfect and E. A. Maylor (Eds.), *Models of cognitive aging.* Oxford: Oxford University Press.

Rabbitt, P. M. A., & Abson, V. (1990). Lost and found: Some logical and methodological limitations of self-report questionnaires as tools to study cognitive aging. *British Journal of Psychology, 82,* 137–151.

Rabbitt, P. M. A., Banerji, N., & Szemanski, A. (1989). Space Fortress as an IQ test? Predictions of learning and of practised performance in a complex video game. *Acta Psychologica, 71,* 243–257.

Rabbitt, P., Diggle, P., Holland, F., & McInnes, L. (2001). Practice and dropout effects during a 17 year study of cognitive ageing. Submitted to *Journal of Gerontology, 2001.*

Rabbitt, P. M. A., Diggle, P. J., Holland, C. M., Smith, G. A., & McInnes, L. (2001). Identifying and separating the effects of practice and of cognitive aging during a large longitudinal study of elderly community residents. *Neuropsychologia, 39,* 532–543.

Rabbitt, P. M., Donlan, C., Bent, N., & McInnes, L. (1993). Subject attrition in a longitudinal study of cognitive performance in community-based elderly people. *Facts and Research in Gerontology* (pp. 203–207). Paris: Serdi.

Rabbitt, P. M. A., Donlan, C., Bent, N., McInnes, L., & Abson, V. (1993). The University of Manchester Age and Cognitive Performance Research Centre and North East Age Research longitudinal programmes 1982 to 1997. *Zeitschrift Gerontology, 26,* 176–183.

Rabbitt, P. M. A., Donlan, C., Watson, P., McInnes, L., & Bent, N. (1996). Unique and interactive effects of depression, age socio-economic advantage and gender on cognitive performance of normal healthy older people. *Psychology and Aging, 10,* 221–235.

Rabbitt, P. M. A., Lowe, C., & Shilling, V. (2001). Frontal tests and models for cognitive aging. *European Journal of Cognitive Psychology, 13,* 5–28.

Rabbitt, P. M. A., & Maylor, E. A. (1991). Investigating models of human performance. *British Journal of Psychology, 82,* 259–290.

Rabbitt, P. M. A., Maylor, E. M., McInnes, L., & Bent, N. (1995). What goods can self-assessment questionnaires deliver for cognitive gerontology? *Applied Cognitive Psychology, 9,* 127–152.

Rabbitt, P. M. A., Osman, P., Stollery, B., & Moore, B. (in press). Individual differences in performance variability. *Quarterly Journal of Experimental Psychology.*

Rabbitt, P. M. A., Stollery, B., Moore, B., & Han, X. (2001). Transfer effects in coding tasks vary with level of intelligence. In Preparation.

Rabbitt, P. M. A., & Vyas, S. M. (1969). An elementary preliminary taxonomy for some errors in laboratory choice RT tasks. *Acta Psychologica, 33,* 56–76.

Rabbitt, P. M. A., Watson, P., Donlan, C., Bent, L., & McInnes, L. (1994). Subject attrition in a longitudinal study of cognitive performance in community-based elderly people. In *Facts and research in gerontology* (pp. 203–207). Paris: Serdi.

Rabbitt, P. M. A., Watson, P., Donlan, C., Bent, N., McInnes, L., Horan, M., Pendleton, N., & Clague, J. (2000). Effects of death within 11 years on cognitive performance in old age. Manuscript submitted for publication.

Rabbitt, P. M. A., & Yang, Q. (1996). What are the functional bases of individual differences in memory ability? In D. Herrman, C. McEvoy, C. Hertzog, P. Hertel, & M. K. Johnson (Eds.), *Basic and applied memory research: Vol. 1. Theory in context* (pp. 127–159). Mahwah, NJ: Erlbaum.

Rankin, J. L., & Kausler, D. H. (1979). Adult age differences in false recognitions. *Journal of Gerontology, 34,* 58–65.

Ratcliff, R., & Rouder, J. F. (1998). Modeling response times for two choice decisions. *Psychological Science, 9,* 347–356.

Ratcliff, R., Spieler, D., & McKoon, G. (2000). Explicitly modeling the effects of age on reaction times. *Psychonomic Bulletin and Review, 7,* 1–25.

Ratcliff, R., van Zandt, T., & McKoon, G. (1999). Connectionist and diffusion models of reaction time. *Psychological Review, 106,* 261–300.

Reason, J. (1993) Self-report questionnaires in cognitive psychology: Have they delivered the goods? In A. D. Baddeley & L. S. Weiskrantz (Eds.), *Attention, selection, awareness and control* (pp. 406–439). Oxford: Oxford University Press.

Reed, T. E. (1993). Effects of enriched (complex) environment on nerve conduction velocity: New data and implications for the speed of information processing. *Intelligence, 17,* 461–474.

Reed, T. E., & Jensen, A. R. (1992). Conduction velocity in a brain-nerve pathway of normal adults correlates with intelligence level. *Intelligence, 16,* 259–272.

Reitan, R. M., & Wolfson, D. (1994). A selective and critical review of neuropsychological deficits and the frontal lobes. *Neuropsychology Review, 4,* 161–198.

Riegel, K. E., & Riegel, R. M. (1972). Development, drop and death. *Developmental Psychology, 6,* 308–316.

Rikli, R., & Busch, S. (1986). Motor performance of women as a function of age and physical activity level. *Journal of Gerontology, 41,* 645–649.

Roth, M. (1986). The association of clinical and neuropsychological findings and its bearing on the classification and etiology of Alzheimer's disease. *British Medical Bulletin, 42,* 42–50.

Rubin, D. B. (1976). Inference and missing data. *Biometrika, 63,* 581–92.

Sahakian, B. J., and Owen, A. M. (1992). Computerised assessment in neuropsychiatry using CANTAB. *Journal of the Royal Society of Medicine, 85,* 399–402.

Salthouse, T. A. (1985). *A cognitive theory of aging.* Berlin: Springer.

Salthouse, T. A. (1988). Resource reduction interpretations of cognitive aging. *Developmental Review, 8,* 238–272.

Salthouse, T. A. (1991). *Theoretical perspectives in cognitive aging.* Hillsdale, NJ: Erlbaum.

Salthouse, T. A. (1996a). The processing-speed theory of adult age-differences in cognition. *Psychological Review, 103,* 403–428.

Salthouse, T. A. (1996b). General and specific speed mediation of adult age differences in memory. *Journal of Gerontology: Psychological Sciences, 51B,* P30–P42.

Salthouse, T. A., Fristoe, N., & Rhee, S. H. (1996). How localized are age-related effects on neuropsychological measures? *Neuropsychology, 10*(2), 272–285.

Salthouse, T. A., Kausler, D. H., & Saults, J. S. (1990). Age, self-assessed health status and cognition. *Journal of Gerontology, 45,* P156–P160.

Salthouse, T. A. and Meinz, E. J. (1995). Aging, inhibition working memory and speed. *Journal of Gerontology: Psychological Sciences, 50B*(6), 297–306.

Sanders, A. F. (1998). *Elements of human psychology: Performance, reaction processes and attention in human skill.* Mahwah, NJ: Erlbaum.

Schaie, K. W. (1965). A general model for the study of developmental problems. *Psychological Bulletin, 64,* 92–107.

Schaie, K. W. (1977). Quasi-experimental research design in the psychology of aging. In J. E. Birren & K. W. Schaie (Eds.), *Handbook of the psychology of aging.* New York: Van Nostrand Reinhold.

Schaie, K. W. (1983). The Seattle Longitudinal Study: A 21-year exploration of psychometric intelligence in adulthood. In K. W. Schaie (Ed.), *Longitudinal studies of adult psychological development* (pp. 64–135). New York: Guilford Press.

Schaie, K. W. (1989). Perceptual speed in adulthood: Cross-sectional studies and longitudinal studies. *Psychology and Aging, 4,* 443–453.

Schaie, K. W. (1990a). Correction to Schaie (1989). *Psychology and Aging, 5,* 171.

Schaie, K.W. (1990b). Intellectual development in adulthood. In J. E. Birren & K. W. Schaie (Eds.), *Handbook of the psychology of aging* (3rd ed.). San Diego, CA: Academic Press.

Schaie, K. W., & Baltes, P. B. (1975). On sequential strategies in developmental research: Description or explanation? *Human Development, 18,* 384–390.

Schaie, K. W., Labouvie, G. V., & Barrett, T. J. (1973). Selective attrition effects in a fourteen-year study of adult intelligence. *Journal of Gerontology, 28,* 328–334.

Scharfstein, D. O., Rotnitzky, A., & Robins, J. M. (1999). Adjusting for non-ignorable dropout using semiparametric non-response models [with discussion]. *Journal of the American Statistical Association, 94,*1096–1120.

Scheibel, M. E., & Scheibel, A. B. (1975). *Structural changes in the aging brain.* In H. Brody, D. Harmon, & J. M. Ordy (Eds.), *Structural changes in the aging brain* (Vol. 1, pp. 11–37). New York: Raven Press.

Schlesselman, J. J. (1973a). Planning a longitudinal study: I. Sample size determination. *Journal of Chronic Diseases, 26,* 532–560.

Schlesselman, J. J. (1973b). Planning a longitudinal study: II. Frequency of measurement and study duration. *Journal of Chronic Diseases, 26,* 561–570.

Schneider, W. (1994). The neurobiology of attention and automaticity. *Current Opinion in Neurobiology, 4,* 177–182.

Schneider, W., & Detweiler, M. (1988). The role of practice in dual task performance: Towards workload modeling in a connectionist control architecture. *Human Factors, 30,* 539–566.

Schooler, C. (1984). Psychological effects of complex environments during the life span: A review and theory. *Intelligence, 8,* 258–281.

Schouten, J.F., & Bekker, J. A. M. (1967). Reaction time and accuracy. *Acta Psychologica, 27,* 143–153.

Schulsinger, F., Knopf, J., & Mednick, S. A. (1981). *Longitudinal research.* Hingham, MA: Kluwer-Nijhoff.

Shaw, R. J. (1991). Age-related increases in the effects of automatic semantic activation. *Psychology and Aging, 6,* 595–604.

Shaw, T. G., Mortel, K. F., Meyer, J. S., Rogers, R. L., Hardenberg, J., & Cutaia, M. M. (1984). Cerebral blood flow changes in benign aging and cerebrovascular disease. *Neurology, 34,* 855–862.

Sherwood, D. E., & Selder, D. J. (1979). Cardiovascular health, reaction time and aging. *Medicine and Science in Sports and Exercise, 71,* 186–189.

Shiffrin, R. M., & Schneider, W. (1977). Controlled and automatic information processing: II. Perceptual learning, automatic attending and a general theory. *Psychological Review, 84,* 127–190.

Shiffrin, R. M., & Schneider, W. (1984). Automatic and controlled processing revisited. *Psychological Review, 91,* 269–276.

Shilling, V., Chetwynd, A., & Rabbitt, P. M. A. (2001). The constant validity of inhibition: Individual inconsistency across four measures of Stroop interference. Accepted for publication by *Neuropsychologia.*

Shock, N. W. (1985). Longitudinal studies of aging in humans. In C. E., Finch & E. L. Schneider (Eds.), *The handbook of the psychology of aging,* 2nd ed. (pp. 721–743). New York: Van Nostrand Reinhold.

Shock, N. W., Greulich, R. C., Andres, R., Arenberg, D., Costa, P. T., Jr., Lakatta, E. G., & Tobin, J. D. (1984). Normal human aging: The Baltimore Longitudinal Study of Aging (NIH Publication No. 84-2450). Washington, DC: U.S. Government Printing Office.

Siegler, I. C. (1983). Psychological aspects of the Duke Longitudinal Studies. In K. W. Schaie (Ed.), *Longitudinal studies of adult psychological development* (pp. 136–190). New York: Guilford Press.

Siegler, I. C., & Butwinick, J. (1979). A long-term longitudinal study of intellectual ability of older adults: The matter of selective attrition. *Journal of Gerontology, 34,* 242–245.

Siegler, I. C., McCarty, S. M., & Logue, P. E. (1982). Wechsler memory scale scores, selective attrition and distance from death. *Journal of Geronotology, 37,* 176–181.

Siegler, I. C., & Nowlin, J. B. (1985). Cardiovascular disease, intellectual function and personality. In E. Palmore, J. B. Nowlin, G. L. Maddox, E. W. Busse, & C. Siegler (Eds.), *Normal aging* (Vol. 3, pp. 51–55). Durham, NC: Duke University Press.

Sklar, M., & Edwards, A. E. (1962). Presbyacusis: A factor analysis of hearing and psychological characteristics of men over 65 years old. *Journal of Auditory Research, 2,* 194–207.

Sliewinski, M., & Buschke, M. (1999). Cross-sectional and longitudinal relationships among age, cognition and information processing speed. *Psychology and Aging, 12,* 309–313.

Small, B. J., & Backman, L. (1997). Cognitive correlates of mortality: Evidence from a population based sample of very old adults. *Psychology and Aging, 12,* 309–313.

Smith, G. A., & Brewer, N. (1995). Slowness and age: Speed-accuracy mechanisms. *Psychology and Aging, 10*(2), 238–247.

Smith, P. L., & Vickers, D. (1988). The accumulator model of two-choice discrimination. *Journal of Mathematical Psychology, 32,* 135–168.

Snowden, D. A., Kemper, S. J., Mortimer, J. A., Greinier, L. H., Wekstein, D. R., & Markesbery, W. R. (1996). Linguistic ability in early life and cognitive function and Alzheimer's disease in later life: Findings from the nun study. *Journal of the American Medical Association, 21,* 528–532.

Snowden, D. A., Ostwald, S. K., Kane, R. E. L., & Keenan, N. L. (1989). Years of life with good and poor mental and physical functions in the elderly. *J. Clinical Epidemiology, 42,* 1055–1066.

Sorensenson, H. T. (1997). Birth weight are cognition: A historical cohort study. *British Medical Journal, 315*(7105), 401–403.

Spearman, C. (1924). *The abilities of man.* London: Methuen.

Spieler, D. H., Balota, D. A., & Faust, M. E. (1996). Stroop performance in healthy younger and older adults and in individuals with dementia of the Alzheimer's type. *Journal of Experimental Psychology: Human Perception and Performance, 22,* 461–479.

Spirduso, W. (1980). Physical fitness, aging and psychomotor speed: A review. *Journals of Gerontology: Psychological Sciences, 35,* P859–P865.

Spirduso, W. W. (1975). Reaction and movement time as a function of physical activity level. *Journal of Gerontology, 30,* 435–440.

Spirduso, W. W., & Clifford, P. (1978). Replication of age and physical activity effects on reaction time and movement time. *Journal of Gerontology, 33,* 26–30.

Sternberg, S. (1969). Memory scanning: Mental processes revealed by reaction time experiments. *American Scientist, 57,* 421–457.

Sternberg, S. (1975). Memory scanning: New findings and current controversies. *Quarterly Journal of Experimental Psychology, 17,* 1–27.

Steuer, J., La Rue, A., Blum, J., & Jarvik, L. (1981). Critical loss in the eighth and ninth decades. *Journal of Gerontology, 36,* 211–213.

Stones M. J., & Kozma, A. (1988). Physical activity, age and cognitive/motor performance. In M. L. Howe & C. J. Brainerd (Eds.), *Cognitive development in adulthood* (pp. 273–321). New York: Springer.

Stroop, J. R. (1935). Studies of interference in serial verbal reactions. *Journal of Experimental Psychology, 18,* 643–662.

Suedfeld, P., & Piedrahita, L. E. (1984). Intimations of mortality: Integrative simplification as a precursor of death. *Journal of Personality and Social Psychology, 47,* 848–852.

Takata, H., Ishii, T., Suzuki, M., Sekiguchi, S., & Iri, H. (1987). Influence of major histocompatibility complex region genes on human longevity among Okinawan-Japanese centenarians and monogenarians *Lancet, ii,* 824–826.

Thomas, E. A. C., & Ross, B. H. (1980). On appropriate procedures for combining probability distributions within the same family. *Journal of Mathematical Psychology, 21,* 136–152.

Townsend, J. T., & Ashby, F. G. (1983). Stochastic modelling of elementary psychological processes. Cambridge: Cambridge University Press.

Tzankoff, S. P., & Norris, A. H. (1977). Effect of muscle mass decrease on age-related BMR changes. *Journal of Applied Physiology, 43,* 1001–1006.

van Boxtel, M. P. J., Bentinck, F., Houx, P. J., Metsemakers, J. F. M., Knottmerus, A., & Jolles, J. (1998). The relation between morbidity and cognitive performance in a normal aging population. *Journals of Gerontology: Biological Sciences and Medical Sciences, 55*(A), M147–M154.

van Boxtel, M. P. J., van Beijsterveldt, C. E., Houx, P. J., Actewin, L. J. C., Metsemakers, J. F. M., & Jolles, J. (2000). Mild hearing impairment can reduce memory performance in a healthy adult population. *Journal of Experimental and Clinical Neuropsychology, 22,* 147–154.

Verhagen, P., & De Meersman, L. (1998). Aging and the Stroop effect: A meta-analysis. *Psychology and Aging, 13*(1), 120–126.

Vernon, P. A. (1985). Individual differences in general cognitive ability. In L. C. Hartledge & C. F. Telzner (Eds.). *The neuropsychology of individual differences: A developmental perspective.* New York: Plenum.

Vernon, P. A., & Jensen, A. R. (1994). Individual and group differences in intelligence and speed of information processing. *Personality and Individual Differences, 5,* 411–423.

Voitenko, V. P., & Tokar, A. V. (1983). The assessment of biological age and sex differences of human aging. *Experimental Aging Research, 9,* 239–244.

Waugh, N. C., & Barr, R. A. (1980). Memory and mental tempo. In L. W. Poon, J. L. Fozard, L. S. Cermak, D. Arenberg, & L. W. Thompson (Eds.), *New directions in memory and aging: Proceedings of the George A. Talland Memorial Conference.* Hillsdale, NJ: Erlbaum.

Walker, R., Husain, M., Hodgsen, T. L., Harrison, J., & Kennard, C. (1998). Saccadic eye-movements and working memory deficits following damage to human pre-frontal cortex. *Neuropsychologia, 36*(11), 1141–1159.

Wearden, J. H., Wearden, A. J., & Rabbitt, P. M. A. (1997). Age and IQ effects on stimulus and response timing. *Journal of Experimental Psychology: Human Perception and Performance, 23,* 423–438.

Weiskrantz, L. (1992). Introduction: Dissociated issues. In A. D. Miller & M. D. Rugg (Eds.),

The Neuropsychology of consciousness: Foundations of neuropsychology (pp. 1–10). London: Academic Press.

West, R. L. (1996). An application of prefrontal cortex function theory to cognitive aging. *Psychological Bulletin, 120,* 272–292.

Whelihan, W. M., & Lesher, E. L. (1985). Neuropsychological changes in frontal functions with aging. *Developmental Neuropsychology, 1,* 371–380.

White, N., & Cunninghan, W. R. (1998). Is terminal drop pervasive or specific? *Journal of Gerontology, Psychological Sciences, 43,* 141–144.

Wilkie, F. L., Eisdorfer, C., & Nowlin, J. B. (1985). Memory and blood pressure. In E. Palmore, J. B. Nowlin, G. W. Maddox, E. W. Busse, & C. Siegler (Eds.), *Normal aging* (pp. 206–214). Durham, NC: Duke University Press.

Winer, B. J. (1971). *Statistical principles in experimental design* (2nd ed.). New York: McGraw Hill.

Witte, K. L. (1975). Paired associate learning in young and elderly adults as related to presentation rate. *Psychological Bulletin, 82,* 975–985.

Zacks, R. T., Radvansky, G., & Hasher, L. (1996). Studies of directed forgetting in older adults. *Journal of Experimental Psychology: Learning, Memory and Cognition, 22* (1), 143–156.

Zeiss, A. M., Lewinsohm, P. M., & Seeley, J. R. (1996). Relationship of physical disease and functional impairment to depression in older people. *Psychology and Aging, 11,* 572–581.

Zelinski, E. M., & Burnight, K. P. (1997). Sixteen-year longitudinal and time-lag changes in memory and cognition in older adults. *Psychology and Aging, 12,* 503–513.

Zelinski, E. M., & Stewart, S. T. (1998). Individual differences in 16-year memory changes. *Psychology and Aging, 13,* 622–630.

Zheng, Y., Myerson, J., & Hale, S. (2000). Age and individual differences in visuospatial processing speed: Testing the magnification hypothesis. *Psychonomic Bulletin and Review, 7,* 113–120.

Author Index

Subject Index

Ability, 521
Abnormality:
  performance, 158
  system, 158
Abortion, 580–581
Absolute magnitude estimation
  (AME), 119–120, 129
Accuracy:
  classification compared to
    discrimination, 62–63
  observed success correct, 45
  proportion correct, 45
  SDT as framework for
    understanding, 43
Acquired Immune Deficiency
  Syndrome (AIDS), 403–404
Adaptive resonance, 224, 233
  Models:
    ART *1*, 243, 246, 252, 256
    ART 2, 256
    ART$_a$, 257–258
    ART$_b$, 257–258
    fuzzy ART, 256
Additive factors method, 275,
  285, 497
Advanced Placement Test in
  Psychology, 542
Afferent activation pattern,
  602–603
Aggression:
  cross-situational consistency in
    study of, 567–568
  in retarded children,
    317–318, 332
Aging and cognition:
  biological aging
    measurement, 798
  composite indexes, 794
  diabetes in, 796, 801
  hierarchical linear regression
    analysis, 794
  muscle strength loss, 795

sensory acuity, 795–797,
  821–822
cognitive gerontology role in
  understanding of, 819–821
  theoretical vs. applied, 822
constructs, difficulties with:
  inhibition, 837
  measurement, 838–839
  task reliability, 839
  validity, 839
elderly viewed as disabled, 820
functional brain imaging, 846
global slowing:
  alternative modular models,
    836–837
  choice reaction times
    (CRTs), 825–831, 835,
    838–839
  circadian variability, 835–836
  CNS processes, 823, 836–837
  control of performance,
    828–830
  day-to-day variability, 835
  general fluid ability, 823–824,
    831, 841–842
  history of, 824–831
  information processing speed,
    833–834
  memory, 833–834
  models for testing, 831–834
  performance variability,
    834–836
  practiced tasks, 827–828
  single-factor models and,
    822–824
  task performance
    measurement, 823, 825–826
  working memory, 832–833
hypotheses about, 844
ideal aging myth, 844–845
individual differences in,
  793–794

novelty and validity of tests,
  839–840
physiological indexes, 794–794
primary and secondary aging:
  aging process assumptions,
    805–807
  demographics and pathology
    prevalence, 804
  disposable soma theory, 798
  distinctions between,
    798–799
  dropout effects, 815–818
  health screening methods,
    adequacy of, 799–801
  health's effects on cognition,
    801–802
  longitudinal studies, 814–815
  practice effects, 818–819
  terminal drop, 802–805
  time course models for aging,
    813–814
  verbal ability as survival
    marker, 803–804, 808
small-scale cross-sectional
  studies:
  cohort effects, 809–813
  design, 805–807
  matching groups for
    intellectual ability, 807–809
tests for specific functional
  systems, 840–844
Aging effects:
  Brinley plot, 430–432, 825–827,
    830, 834–835, 839–840
  information loss model, 431
  linear model, 431, 437–438,
    442, 444
  nonlinear model, 442
  random walk model of, 431
Agnosia:
  mirror, 171
  visual, 149, 151–154, 159